Child Welfare Services

Fourth Edition

Alfred Kadushin, Ph.D.
Julia Lathrop Professor of Social Work
University of Wisconsin, Madison

Judith A. Martin, Ph.D.
Associate Professor of Social Work
University of Pittsburgh

Macmillan Publishing Company
NEW YORK

Collier Macmillan Publishers
LONDON

Macmillan Publishing Company

A Simon & Schuster Company
Needham Heights, MA 02194

LIBRARY OF CONGRESS CATALOGING-IN-PUBLICATION DATA

Kadushin, Alfred.
  Child welfare services.

  Includes bibliographical references and index.
  1. Child welfare—United States. I. Martin, Judith A.,
1945- . II. Title.
HV741.K26 1988   362.7′0973   87-18523
ISBN 0-02-362710-7

Printing: 6 7   Year: 1 2 3 4

Photo Credits
Page 1, © Magnum Photos, Inc.; page 35, © Magnum Photos, Inc.; page 83, © Magnum Photos,
Inc.; page 143, © National Action for Foster Children; page 173, © Eric Breitbart, Brooklyn, N.Y.;
page 218, © Dennis Stock, Magnum Photos, Inc.; page 344, © Bruce Davidson, Magnum Photos,
Inc.; page 462, © Bruce Davidson, Magnum Photos, Inc.; page 533, © W. Suschitzky, Longon; page
669, © Patricia Costa, Westwood, California; page 733, © Magnum Photos, Inc.

To Sylvia; to Goldie; to Raphael—with love
To J. G.—with much love;
To N. and all the hurting children and families
who need child welfare services

Preface

This book is a comprehensive study of the principal child welfare services. It begins by defining child welfare, placing it as a field of practice within social work, and presents a scheme for the categorization of child welfare problems in terms of role theory. It goes on to provide a historical perspective on how and why child welfare services developed and to describe the current socioeconomic context in which they operate. Separate chapters are devoted to each of the principal supportive, supplementary, and substitutive child welfare services: home-based and family services, protective services, day care, homemaker service, foster care, adoption, and institutional child care. Each chapter includes material on the historical development of the service, the situations for which the service is appropriate, scope of the service, process in offering the service, evaluation of the service, problems encountered by the service, and trends in offering the service.

A chapter on child welfare services in other countries provides an international perspective on the practice of child welfare in the United States.

A special effort has been made to include as much of the relevant research as possible and to supplement material from casework with material available from other practice methods.

The book is directed to the student of social work both at the undergraduate level and at the graduate level. Undergraduate students—whether they plan to work in a social agency after graduation or to go on to a graduate school of social work—will find the material in the text useful preparation. Graduate students enrolled in child welfare seminars or taking courses that are concerned, in part, with child welfare problems will find this a useful, systematic, and detailed review of child welfare services.

The text, then, can appropriately be used at both the undergraduate and the graduate levels. Previous editions have been widely used for courses at both levels.

The book is also directed to the child welfare worker currently employed in social agencies. The volume is designed to offer both fully trained professional workers and those with limited professional training a systematic review of the substantive knowledge available concerning child welfare services and to provide a synthesis of widely scattered material for the busy practitioner.

Finally, the book is designed to give the reader a broad knowledge of child welfare services rather than to develop skills for working directly with people who present child welfare problems. The primary purpose of the text is to teach about child welfare—the *what* and the *why*—rather than to teach the *how* of doing child welfare work. It is directed toward developing a knowledge about, concern for, and understanding of child welfare services rather than oriented toward developing technical, professional skills required in treating clients. It is important to note that "knowing" about a field of social work practice is a necessary prerequisite for effective "doing" and "treating." Charlotte Towle aptly notes:

> Students must have knowledge with which to think. Feeling as a professional person must come to feel is developed through, and in response to, knowledge. Understanding comes about through knowledge that has been integrated through emotional acceptance, which permits the faculties of knowing and thinking to function in the doing. The nature of doing will, therefore, reflect integration or lack of integration of knowledge.[1]

The presentation is primarily descriptive and expository, concerned with explicating current child welfare practices—how child welfare services actually operate rather than how they should operate. Admittedly, what *is* is a far cry from what *should be*. The detailed material on each of the particular services presented in the text makes it clear that American society has failed large numbers of its children and that child welfare services have relatively low priority in the allocation of national resources. Ours has not been, and is not likely to be, a filiocentric society. Although the needs and rights of children are a matter of great concern within the individual family unit, this concern has not been reflected in public policy.

The congressionally appointed Joint Commission on Mental Health of Children, making its report to the nation in 1970 after three years of study, categorically states that "this nation, the richest of all world powers, has no unified national commitment to its children and youth. The claim that we are a child-centered society . . . is a myth. Our words are made meaningless by our actions. . . ."[2]

The finding was repeated by a prestigious committee of the National Academy of Sciences that, in reviewing the situation, concluded, "existing government programs are not adequately meeting the needs of America's children and families."[3]

Essential data for planning child welfare services are not available at the national level and often not at the state level. Inequities are imposed on children by virtue of the accident of where they live. Some communities spend considerably more on child welfare services than do other communities. No determined effort to reduce such inequities, which has been made in education, is being attempted in child welfare.[4]

Through the detailed exposition on services, this book also makes clear that in many significant respects the field of child welfare social work has failed large numbers of America's children. In general the field is oriented toward crisis, rescue, and remedy rather than toward prevention and planning. It is reactive rather than proactive, responding primarily in an *ad hoc* manner to emergency

---

[1]Charlotte Towle, *The Learner in Education for the Professions* (Chicago: University of Chicago Press, 1954), p. 358.

[2]*Crisis in Mental Health: Challenge for the 1970's*, Report of the Joint Commission on the Mental Health of Children (New York: Harper and Row, Publishers, 1970), p. 2.

[3]National Academy of Sciences. *Toward a National Policy for Children and Families* (Washington, D.C.: The Academy, 1976).

[4]Michael Kirst, Walter Garms, and Theo Oppermann. *State Service for Children: An Exploration of Who Benefits, Who Governs* (Palo Alto, Calif.: Stanford University, 1978, mimeo).

situations rather than planning long-term policies. It serves only a limited percentage of America's children and is concerned with life at the margins of society rather than at the center. Services are offered to the few who have limited problems and considerable strengths rather than to the many who have multiple problems and few resources.

The tendency is for "different agencies to respond disconnectedly to a series of discrete crises," so that service to any one family is poorly coordinated. Much of the basic policy in child welfare is founded on intuition and tradition rather than on empirical research and precise information. There is little follow-up and disciplined evaluation of results.

But the text also attempts to make clear the factors that help to explain, although they do not excuse, the failures of society and of the agencies, and to point out the very real achievements of child welfare social work. As a consequence of the efforts of the individual child welfare worker and the agencies under whose auspices he or she practices, we have rescued for life a sizable number of children. We have found families, protection, care, and physical and emotional support for children who would otherwise have endured greater suffering and pain—if they had lived at all. This is the measure of the victory we have achieved, and it is a record of which we can justifiably be proud.

The First Edition of this book was published in 1967. The Second Edition in 1974. The Third in 1980.

What justifies a Fourth Edition of the text at this time? One traditional justification for another edition of any text is applicable here—and applicable with greater validity than in many other instances. The justification is that considerable research and expository material has become available in the past seven years that supplements, revises, and/or modifies much of the material in the previous edition. The pace of change and the production of additional information in child welfare services seems to be greater than is true for many other subjects. It's a fast-moving, fast-changing field of practice.

Since the publication of the previous edition, national as well as regional Child Welfare Training Centers have been established. Although funded for a limited period, the centers formulated, tested, and distributed a considerable amount of child welfare training materials. The availability of such materials further argues for the need for a Fourth Edition.

Legislative changes since the publication of the Third Edition has made for changes in child welfare services and practice. The enactment of the Adoption Assistance and Child Welfare Act–1980, which came into force after the Third Edition was written, is one example of such changes. In addition to the pace of change, the nature and direction of changes in the social services argue for the desirability of a revised edition.

With the election of President Reagan in 1980, the year the Third Edition of the text was published, significant fundamental changes were inaugurated in the national social welfare picture. The steady growth of the welfare state, of initiation, proliferation, and increased funding of federally supported social service programs—which had characterized Roosevelt's New Deal, Truman's Fair Deal, Kennedy's New Frontier, and Johnson's Great Society—was halted and reversed. The election of President Reagan represented the victory of a trend that had been gathering increasing strength and support during the 1960s and 1970s—the trend toward the dominant reemergence of a more conservative set of beliefs and attitudes about the nature and responsibility of government. This philosophy, in opposition to the welfare state orientation, has been present throughout our history, but during the half-century between President Roosevelt's election to his first term in office in 1932 and the election of President Reagan in 1980, this more conservative philosophy of government had been out of power. The dominant themes of this philosophy are: less government; state and local rather than federal control of programs; faith in the social problem-solving capacity of a free market economy; and greater emphasis on voluntarism, individual autonomy, self-reliance, self-discipline in opposition to governmental interventionism, and active communal responsibility in support of people in need.

Economic change made ideological change persuasive to a large segment of the voters. Between 1950 and 1970, real Gross National Product more than doubled. It was a period of the greatest sustained economic boom in American history. Increases in social service spending could be legislated without engendering a feeling of sacrifice on the part of any group. A growing pie permitted a growing slice for social programs.

This was and has been followed by a period of declining economic growth and escalation of welfare expenditures owing in part to a growing proportion of the aged in the population and a sustained period of relatively high inflation and unemployment. Although there is public commitment to the desirability of supporting many welfare state programs, as frequent opinion polls confirm,[5] there is currently more discomfort, personal sacrifice, and pain associated with implementing such support.

In signing the Omnibus Reconciliation Act of 1981, President Reagan hailed it as representing "a turn-around of almost half a century" of expansion of federal government responsibilities. He noted that passage of the act marked "an end to the excessive growth in government bureaucracy and government spending."

> A counter revolution is under way. After a half century of growing federal efforts to stabilize the economy, ensure individuals against misfortune, redistribute income and opportunity, and respond to other perceived national needs, the nucleus of this counter revolution is a philosophy of more limited government.[6]

The growing disillusion with, and distrust of, what expanding social welfare programs can accomplish has been employed by the political left as well to undermine confidence in the welfare state ideology. The left points to the fact that such programs at best achieve social security, not social equality, equality of opportunity rather than equality of results, and merely act to shore up the inherent instability of a capitalist economy by reducing social tensions while failing to redistribute the nation's wealth.

The Third Edition was written at a time when there were increasing demands for accountability of the effectiveness of social welfare programs but when the basic legitimacy of such programs was unquestioned. The Fourth Edition is written at a time when, in addition to the question of effectiveness of social work interventions, a more fundamental question is being asked, namely—whether such programs and services are the legitimate responsibility of government. The welfare state orientation, which led to the development of support of the network of social welfare programs is based on the idea that the community, the collectivity, has some responsibility for helping people with their social problems. Anti-

---

[5]Seymour M. Lipset, "The Elections, The Economy and Public Opinion, 1984" PS: *The Journal of the American Political Science Association,* 18.1 (Winter 1985), 28–38.

[6]John L. Palmer, Isabel V. Sawhill, *The Reagan Experiment* (Washington, D.C. Urban Institute Press), 1982, p. 1.

welfare state ideology claims that this is not an appropriate function of government and that support for such programs is not an appropriate expenditure of public funds. The view is that only minimal "last resort", "safety-net" help is a legitimate function of government.

Certain programs and certain population groups were disproportionately and adversely affected by cuts in funding. Social services were more heavily cut than health services, and children were more greatly affected than the aged.

Totaling the changes between 1981 and 1984 in federal outlays for social services and child care, health/nutrition, and other programs affecting children, Kimmich (1985)[7] estimated a reduction of 11 percent overall.

The Children's Defense Fund in its annual analysis of the federal budget estimated that over the 1980 decade, programs for low-income families and children would see a loss of $91 in per capita outlays—from $486.8 in 1980 to $395.8 in 1990, a reduction of 18.7 per cent (Children's Defense Fund, 1985, p. 2).[8]

More and more categorical child welfare programs were folded into a small number of comprehensive, consolidated block grants with greater discretion on spending given to states, and some child welfare programs lost protected funding status. The change is from categorical programs clearly targeted toward particular child welfare services to consolidated block grant funding and relatively less specific targeting. Furthermore, the total amount of block grant funding for programs was generally less than had been available previously if one added together the funding granted to each of the individual programs.

In response to the implementation of a philosophy of a more limited government responsibility during the 1980s, all social welfare programs experienced cuts in funding and diminished support for services. The Fourth Edition is written during a period characterized by reductions in staff, retrenchment in programming, and increasing limitations in resources available to agencies. Child welfare agencies are being asked to do more with less.

Agencies have adjusted to lower budgetary support by selectively increasing fees for service, reducing the quality of service, prioritizing service demands, and eliminating less serious, less emergent, situations for service, reducing staff and staff training, increasing work loads. Costly purchase of services is being more carefully scrutinized.

Scarce resources force implementation of a triage orientation, and computerized routinization and standardization of services. Such changes are likely to be with us for some time into the future. Declassification and reclassification of child welfare positions have eroded the level of professional expertise of many child welfare programs.

The very large federal government deficits incurred in the 1980s are likely to make very difficult, if not impossible, significant expansions of social service programs through the end of the century.

Federal government control of program funding and operations previously made for some minimum standardization and uniformity in child welfare programs. Decreased federal participation in regulation and evaluation of child welfare programs has increased the heterogeneity of such programs.

From a relatively elite program in both public and voluntary social work, child welfare is now perceived as having modest status. The most skilled and ambitious

---

[7]Madeleine H. Kimmich, *America's Children Who Cares: Growing Needs and Declining Assistance in the Reagan Era* (Washington, D.C.: Urban Institute Press, 1985).

[8]Children's Defense Fund, *A Children's Defense Budget: An Analysis of the President's Fiscal Year 1985 Budget and Children* (Washington, D.C.: Children's Defense Fund, 1985).

social workers currently do not as consistently gravitate toward child welfare as their career choice. Within the large public human service configuration, child welfare has lost its unique identity and clearly defined specialized visibility as child welfare units were divided, reorganized, reallocated, and merged into non-existence.

Some barely discernible trends for the period covered by the Third Edition became more strongly established after its publication. Such trends made for significant changes in the organization and delivery of child welfare services that now need to be addressed in a new edition. The distrust of agencies and professionals, leading to client consumerism and increased citizen participation in the work of agencies, increasing the number of "actors" in the child welfare decision making picture, and the shift of public welfare child welfare service workers from a direct service focus to a case manager focus are examples of such recent changes. There has been an increase in the entrepreneurization of some services and increasing emphasis on permanence and in-home care.

Rather than expanding or maintaining the system, "new" federal efforts have been aimed at removing children from the system—particularly through the search for adoptive parents for system children. Older, retarded, disturbed or otherwise handicapped children who previously remained in care for many years are now considered adoptable.

Since the publication of the Third Edition, certain social changes affecting child welfare service have become more visible and more clearly pronounced. These include the increase in children living in single parent families, the increasing percentage of mothers of young children in the work force, increases in the percentage of the population in poverty and changes in the population profile.

As a consequence of such trends, the demands on the child welfare system have increased in a variety of different ways since the publication of the Third Edition. There has been an increase in the numbers of children and families for which such agencies have responsibility. Child abuse and reporting laws have identified increasing number of families that might need service. Deinstitutionalization of status offenders and diversionary delinquency programs have shifted responsibility for many predelinquents and delinquents from the correctional system to the child welfare system. But demands for a change in what the agencies are expected to achieve are even more significant than an increase in numbers to be served. The agency is now asked to guarantee continuity and permanence in parent–child relationships whereas, earlier, protection and care were sufficient. The expectation is that we assure permanence and continuity not only for general run of deprived and dependent children, but also for children who present special problems for care.

Recent advances in medical technology have presented new, previously unencountered, problems which affect child welfare. The ability to rescue infants born with serious anomalies from death has raised questions regarding parental choice in agreeing to permit extraordinary measures to prolong the life of a child who will be severely handicapped. In vitro fertilization, mother surrogates, and advances in artificial insemination have had an impact on the adoption services.

Since the Third Edition there has been an increased sensitivity to, and concern with, the needs of minority group children. The period has also seen the emergence of a feminist orientation to child welfare problems and services.[9]

Keeping the text within reasonable limits required some deletions as more

[9]See *Child Welfare* 64.3 (1985) for a special issue on a feminist approach to child welfare.

current material was added. Previous editions of the book contained a chapter on "The Social Insurances and Income Maintenance Programs" and a chapter on the "Sociology of the Child Welfare Worker." Given the considerable continued increase in the volume of material related to the core child welfare services, regretably both these chapters had to be deleted from the current edition.

A word of explanation needs to be offered for what additionally is excluded from the book. Services to the delinquent child and to the physically handicapped and mentally retarded child have not been discussed. The material on these services is considered in more specialized texts and is so vast that even a condensed review would have made this book immoderately long and prohibitively expensive. Also, these services have a frame of reference different from that of the services discussed. As Jenkins pointed out:

> Services to the delinquent child must involve detailed consideration of the "legal structure and court apparatus." Services to the physically handicapped and mentally retarded have traditionally been of primary concern to the health and education professions respectively. The traditional child welfare agencies operate in these areas only tangentially.[10]

A more recent national study of social services to children specifically excluded "services to juvenile delinquents or handicapped children" from its definition of child welfare services.[11]

The Fourth Edition is a collaborative effort. Professor Judith Martin, after years of experience as a direct service child welfare worker, completed a Ph.D. in Social Welfare and went on to teach child welfare at the School of Social Work, University of Pittsburgh. Professor Alfred Kadushin has been teaching at the School of Social Work, University of Wisconsin–Madison since 1950. Both authors have collaborated on all chapters in the text and are jointly responsible for the total text.

A. K.

J. A. M.

[10]Shirley Jenkins, *Priorities in Social Services: A Guide for Philanthropic Funding.* Vol I: *Child Welfare in New York City* (New York: Praeger Publishers, Inc., 1971), p. 25.

[11]Ann W. Shyne and Anita G. Schroeder, *National Study of Social Services to Children and Their Families* (Rockville, Md.: Westat, Inc., 1978), p. 14.

Acknowledgments

The list of people to whom I am indebted is extremely long. It includes teachers and supervisors, students and clients, friends and adversaries, co-workers and colleagues in the United States, the Netherlands, and Israel. It includes the many teachers and students who, having used earlier editions of the text, gave me their very constructive suggestions for revision. And it includes the National Institute for Mental Health, the Children's Bureau, the University of Wisconsin Graduate School, and the Silberman Fund, from whom I have received research grants to support the studies that have increased my understanding of child welfare. To name one is to slight another, yet some must be named:

Professor David Fanshel, School of Social Work, Columbia University and Professor Joan F. Shireman, School of Social Work, University of Illinois; Professor Charles Zastrow, School of Social Work, University of Wisconsin, Whitewater; Professor Benson Jaffee, School of Social Work, University of Washington— who read and perceptively commented on portions of the manuscript; Dr. Abraham Lurie, Director of Social Services, Hillside Hospital, New York, a friend of many years with whom I have often discussed social work problems to my invariable enlightenment; and my wife, Sylvia, who has helped me, beyond calculable measure.

My sincerest thanks to Carol D. Betts who patiently, uncomplainingly, and very proficiently typed revised revisions of previously revised material.

A. K.

Sufficient space to thank all those from whom I have learned critical information about child welfare clients, problems and programs simply is not available. I am first and foremost indebted to the families and children with whom I have worked and collaborated for teaching about pain and need and the necessity to help them alleviate it with sensitivity and respect. Professor Edward Sites, School of Social Work, University of Pittsburgh offered both the questions and the answers with regard to the linkages between need and methods for meeting it, programming and broader policy. My students, as always, served as a most informative and critical audience. Without the editorial and secretarial support made available by Jean Anne Fitzpatrick, Tina Naylor-Riston and Mary Pat Campbell, this manuscript might have remained indefinitely in "rough draft" form.

J. A. M.

Contents

1

Child Welfare:

Orientation and Scope

Introduction

The term *child welfare* in a general sense has very broad connotations. If we include under the term every activity that either directly or indirectly promotes the welfare of children, we would end by including most of the significant activities engaged in by society.

The sanitary engineer working toward the organization of a physically healthier environment for children, the traffic engineer working toward the reduction of automobile accidents, the research scientist studying congenital anomalies, and the military specialist guarding the country from attack—all promote the welfare of children, and thus these activities may be subsumed under a general definition of *child welfare*. Carstens (1937) notes that "child welfare has in the course of time acquired a significance that is so broad and vague that it has come to be applied to almost every effort in social and community work that is likely to benefit children" (p. 64*).

Broadly defined, child welfare is concerned with the general well-being of all children. It encompasses any and all measures designed to protect and promote the bio-psycho-social development of children. The general welfare of children has been implemented in legislation regarding compulsory education, child labor laws, required immunizations, and other areas.

Social Work

A more specific and more meaningful definition of child welfare for a text such as this is based on the fact that society has granted to the profession of social work responsibility for helping to resolve many of the problem situations encountered by children. In its narrower sense, *child welfare* is regarded as a field of social work practice. Because it is of the genus *social work*, it shares the characteristics of the genus. To clarify the nature of child welfare, therefore, we must attempt to delineate the normative characteristics of social work. The following illustration may be of help.

*References are to be found at the end of each chapter.

Nine years ago Mrs. F., then unmarried, gave birth to a boy and placed him in the home of a childless married couple whom she knew well. She then left town. Her friends raised the boy as their own, although they never legally adopted him. When Mrs. F. married, she told her husband of her out-of-wedlock child, and he agreed to accept the boy into the family. Mrs. F. visited her friends to tell them of her marriage and of her husband's decision to have the child live with them. Her friends, who had become very much attached to the boy, were reluctant to give him up.

Mrs. F. consulted a lawyer, who agreed to help her establish her legal rights and privileges. However, he felt that aspects of the problem other than the legality of Mrs. F.'s claim to the boy needed to be considered. How would it affect him to be removed from the home in which he was loved and accepted and to be placed in another that was unfamiliar? How would her own marriage be affected? And how would her friends feel when they were suddenly deprived of a child whom they had for a long time regarded as their own? These were not questions with which the lawyer was, by training, competent to deal. These were questions involving social relationships, marital relationships, parent–child relationships, and the social institution of marriage and the family. To help Mrs. F. clarify, for herself, the possible social effects of a decision based on her legal rights alone, the lawyer referred her to a social worker.

The inclusion of the word *social* in the title of the profession reflects the social worker's primary concern with the relation of the individual, the group, or the community to the social environment. Early in the profession's history, Mary Richmond (1922) defined *social work* as "those processes which develop personality through adjustments consciously effected individual by individual between man and his social environment" (pp. 98–99). The United Nations Secretariat defines *social work* as an "activity designed to help towards a better mutual adjustment of the individual and his social environment" (Friedlander, 1961, p. 25).

The Model Statute Social Workers' License Act defines *social work* as the "professional activity of helping individuals, groups, or communities enhance or restore their capacity for social functioning and for creating societal conditions favorable to this goal" (*National Association of Social Workers' News,* May 1970, p. 7).

The National Asssociation of Social Workers sponsored two special conferences of social work theoreticians and practitioners in efforts to define the uniquely differentiating occupational functions of social work. The proceedings of these special conferences were reported in special issues of *Social Work* (vol. 22, no. 5, Sept. 1977; vol. 26, no. 1, 1981). Although there are variations in details presented by different participants regarding the functional specificity, the unique domain of social work, there is repeated emphasis on the distinctive concerns of social work with social functioning, social problems, social roles, social needs, social policy, social institutions, and social well-being.

Because social behavior is carried out primarily in the performance of social roles, there have been attempts to define *social work* in terms of social role performance. Thus Boehm (1959) defines *social work* as the profession that

> seeks to enhance the social functioning of individuals singly and in groups by activities focused upon their social relationships which constitute the interaction between man and his environment. The focus of activities is the professional intervention in

that aspect of man's functioning only which lies in the realms of social relationships or of social role performance [p. 54].

In another article, Boehm (1960) notes that

social work is concerned with enhancing of social functioning of those activities considered essential for the performance of the several social roles which each individual, by virtue of his membership in social groups, is called upon to carry out. . . . Social work intervenes as the interaction (between the individual and the social structure) manifests itself in problematic social relationships.

And in 1977 a National Conference on Social Welfare task force once again focused on social role as the unique and differentiating concern of social services in its definition of *social services* as "those activities purposely and critically used to assist, to develop, and to maintain the ability of individuals and families to cope with the social roles and requirements necessary for productive participation in society" (p. 24).

Physical disease results in the need for the application of specific remedial measures designed to alleviate or cure the disease. Similarly, disabilities in the enactment of social roles require the application of specific remedial measures designed to help people to enact social roles in a more effective manner. Such treatment is made available through the profession of social work.

If the doctor as medical technologist is concerned with physical well-being, and the psychiatrist and psychologist with mental well-being, the social worker is concerned with social well-being.

Other professional groups, notably sociologists, are also interested in the phenomenon of social functioning. However, social work is distinguished from sociology because it is a technology. As a technology, social work is concerned with, and responsible for, helping to "achieve controlled changes in natural relationships via relatively standardized procedures which are scientifically based" (Greenwood, 1955, p. 24).

Basic sciences study particular phenomena, and what is learned may be applied by technologists. For example, the doctor, as technologist, uses the findings of the biologist, the engineer uses the findings of the physicist, and the social worker uses the findings of the sociologist. The doctor repairs a tumorous brain, the engineer shapes the metal to support a bridge, and the social worker uses knowledge of family interaction to help a conflicted family become a harmonious family.

The sociologist, as a social scientist, seeks only to understand the world of the client. The social worker, as a technologist, seeks to change it.

In distinguishing between the social scientist and the social worker, Rothman (1980) notes that "the fundamental difference—is one of function. The social scientist has the primary function of *comprehending the world:* producing knowledge that permits him and others to understand it better. The practitioner has the *key function of changing the world* (italics in original) or more specifically, parts thereof" (p. 15).

For the sociologist, social problems are subject matters to be studied and explained; for the social worker, social problems. call for functions to be performed and situations that require change.

One might object, however, that, like the social worker, guidance counselors, marriage counselors, clinical psychologists, and psychiatrists are also technologists seeking to effect change in problem situations. Although this is true, there is a difference in responding to these problems that points to the distinction between social work and these other technologies.

Every situation that social workers, counselors, psychologists, and psychiatrists encounter is a psychosocial situation—the result of people's interactions with their social environment. However, the principal concerns of social work have been, and are, the social antecedents, concomitants, and consequences of the problem situation. The principal concerns of the counselor, the psychologist, the psychiatrist have been the psychological aspects. The social worker is primarily concerned with the psycho*SOCIAL* situation; the counselor, psychologist, and psychiatrist are traditionally more concerned with the *PSYCHO*social situation.

Admittedly the analysis is not neat and valid for the social worker offering "psychotherapy" in, let us say, a child guidance clinic. The activity of such a social worker is not clearly distinguishable from that of a clinical psychologist or psychiatrist. Here we have the beginnings of another profession that unites the "psychotherapists," however diverse their formal professional affiliation (Henry, 1971).

In seeking to help clients with seemingly similar psychosocial problems, these different professional groups give different emphases to the variety of therapeutic possibilities available. Since every difficulty is psychosocial, help can be directed either toward the person or toward the social situation. Thus one can make an effort to help the person cope with the situation, or one may work to change the situation so that it is easier to cope with; one can help to make the person more capable or the situation more "copeable."

All those interventions that focus on the client's adjustive and adaptive capacity and seek to effect changes in the client's functioning through the psychic interaction between client and professional are known as *psychotherapies*. All those interventions that focus on the social situation, the social context of the psychosocial problem, and seek to ameliorate or change the social situation in favor of the client or to remove the client from a stressful social environment are known as *sociotherapies*. In some measure, all approaches are based on some combination of psychotherapy and sociotherapy. However, social workers have greater access to, and more frequently employ, sociotherapeutic resources. This is particularly true in child welfare services. The child's almost total dependency on the environment makes sociotherapeutic resources—homemakers, day care, foster homes, adoptive homes, institutions, and so on—the therapeutic resource of choice.

When a particular kind of social problem, or a difficulty in social role performance, is sufficiently recurrent and widespread, a social agency is organized to help people who encounter this particular problem, and a specialized field of social work is thus institutionalized. For instance, physical illness requiring hospitalization is a recurrent problem that has more than physical consequences: it disrupts family relationships, requiring the reallocation of social roles and the introduction of social role substitutes within the family. If a mother is hospitalized, someone else must perform her activities in the home. In the hospital, the mother temporarily assumes a new social role—that of a patient. If she is to make optimum use of the hospital facilities, she has to relate effectively to the hospital, which is a medical institution with a social structure. Medical social workers have the responsibility of helping people to deal with the social concomitants of illness.

Similarly, psychiatric social workers have the responsibility of helping people adjust to the social antecedents, concomitants, and consequences of the recurrent problem of mental illness. School social workers help children who have difficulty in enacting the social role of pupil or in relating to a social institution—the school system. The social worker in corrections has the responsibility of helping the individual with the problems that arise from contact with the legal institutions of society. The social worker in public assistance has the responsibility of helping clients in their roles as wage earners and with the social antecedents, concomitants, and consequences of the family's relationship to the economic institutions of our society.

These occupational functions are organized for delivery and administered through a social agency and are implemented through specialized sets of activities termed social services. These social service activities are performed by a special cadre of people holding the occupational title of "social worker." The social worker is to the social services and the social agency what the doctor is to health services and the hospital and the teacher is to educational services and the school. Social workers have been recruited and trained so that they have the knowledge, skills, and competence to perform those activities for which the social services have responsibility and they have been granted the sanction by the community to perform these activities. Social workers are the sanctioned functionaries who are charged with performing the social services activities on behalf of social agency clients.

Services generally are defined as functions performed for others that are helpful and beneficial. Social services are the helping activity performed by social workers on behalf of their social agency clients in relation to the clients' social situations.

When the activities performed by those who hold an occupational title, such as "social worker," are theoretically based, esoteric in nature, and require prolonged training, those who hold the occupational title are termed professionals.

Technology is defined as a particular pattern of action performed to produce a particular change. Technologies that are concerned with effecting changes in people and in social situations are grouped under the rubric "human service professions."

Social work is a human service profession concerned with helping people in the enactment of significant social roles. This community-sanctioned responsibility is implemented by social workers performing these social services offered through a social agency.

Child Welfare as a Field of Social Work Practice

For a variety of historical and political reasons, social work, as a profession, is concerned with only a limited number of the great variety of existing social roles and related social problems. The social roles and social problems relating to child welfare are clearly designated as among those for which social work has responsibility. The authority and permission for social workers to act in relation to these problems has been sanctioned by the community, the client group served, and the profession, which has historically recognized social work in child welfare as a specialized field of practice.

Child welfare services are a more clearly defined domain than most other fields of social work practice. Child welfare is one of the few major "employment arenas in which social workers may be said to substantially lead, manage, guide and control the system for which they are responsible" (Morris, Anderson, 1975, p. 160). For instance, interviews with a random sample of 250 householders in four Western communities indicated that their image of social work was most clearly defined in terms of child welfare activities and functions. Asked to identify the practice setting in which they expected to find social workers employed, respondents mentioned foster care agencies, adoption agencies, and family counseling agencies among the first four agencies most frequently identified. The most frequent single function identified by respondents as being characteristic of social work related to "helping troubled children" (Condie et al., 1978).

In an analysis of the domain of social work, O'Connor and Waring (1981) describe child welfare as one of the few fields of social work service "in which social work has historically held a dominant and influential position," (p. 3).

In 1984 Carol Meyer in an Editorial in *Social Work* termed child welfare as "the centerfold of Social Services" and "as the only field in which social workers are in control of their own programs" (p. 499).

Child and family service programs continue to be among the leading employers of both MSW and BSW social workers. It must be acknowledged, however, that over the 1980 decade child welfare generally and public child welfare in particular have clearly lost status among the fields of social work practice. This was a matter of sufficient concern so as to prompt the National Association of Social Workers to call a special meeting in March 1986 to address the issue of the crisis in public child welfare (*NASW News* 31,5 (May 1986), p. 1).

Child welfare is a specialized field of social work practice, and like each of the other specialized fields of practice, it is concerned with a particular set of significant social roles and with their effective implementation. The recurrent problems with which child welfare is concerned are related to the specific relationships between parents and children. According to the Child Welfare League of America, child welfare involves providing social services to children and young people whose parents are unable to fulfill their child-rearing responsibilities or whose communities fail to provide the resources and protection that children and families require. Child welfare services are designed to reinforce, supplement, or substitute the functions that parents have difficulty in perfoming and to improve conditions for children and their families by modifying existing social institutions or organizing new ones. A child welfare service, like any social service, is an "organized formalized way of dealing with a social problem" (Turitz, 1967, p. 248), the social problem in this instance arising from difficulty in the parent–child relationship.

A special field of practice arises from the need for specialized knowledge and specialized methods of intervention to deal with clusters of related problems. In order to provide efficient and effective service, agencies and their staffs focus on special problem areas and thus come to constitute a specialized field of practice. The term *child welfare* as used here applies, then, to a particular set of social problems that become the responsibility of a group of professionals, the child welfare social workers, who attempt to help in the prevention or amelioration of problems in the social role functioning of the parent–child network.

Child welfare, broadly defined, has to do with the general well-being of all children and with any and all measures designed to promote the optimal development of the child's bio-psycho-social potential in harmony with the needs of the community. Child welfare services, as a field of social work practice, are more narrowly focused. Such services are concerned with particular groups of children and their families. They are "specific services, provided to specific populations by specific types of agencies" (Neel, 1971, p. 25). In defining child welfare service as a field of social work practice, the Child Welfare League of America notes that these "are specialized social welfare services which are primarily concerned with the child whose needs are unmet within the family and/or through other social institutions" (Council on Social Work Education, 1959, p. 5).

The family is regarded as the primary child welfare social service system for all children. Throughout history the family has been the first and most effective social service agency providing care, support, and maintenance for dependent, handicapped, deprived members. When this primary social service system has some problem in effectively performing its tasks in relation to the child, the formal child welfare service system is called upon. Recognizing the fact that children are embedded in families, which are the principal and foremost agencies providing care and nurturance for the child, helping children can best be accomplished by helping to strengthen, preserve, and restore families.

If a child is incorporated in a family system in which his or her needs are adequately met, there is no need for intervention of child welfare services. Only if there is some dysfunction in the parent–child network, for whatever reason, is service intervention called for. Child welfare services are thus alternatives to the normative familial arrangements for the care, protection, and nurturing of children. The child welfare network is mobilized either when a breakdown of the primary child care system has taken place or when there is danger that such a breakdown might take place. At this point, child welfare services have both the responsibility and the authority to intervene in such situations to effect change.

The social service system is a surrogate parent system that does for the disadvantaged child what the well-functioning family does for the advantaged child.

The approach suggesting that child welfare services are responsible primarily in those situations in which the usual normative social provisions are failing to meet the child's needs adequately is generally called a *residual* or *minimalist* orientation to social services. The *residual* conception of social welfare sees social services as appropriate when the normal institutional arrangements for meeting crucial social needs break down.

The contrasting *institutional* or *developmental* orientation suggests that child welfare services are social utilities, like public schools, libraries, and parks (Wilensky & Lebeaux, 1958). Such services, then, should be made available to all children in all families and should be appropriatley helpful to all. Child welfare services, rather than being only for the "poor, the troubled, the dependent, the deviant and the disturbed," should also be directed to "average people under ordinary circumstances" to meet "normal living needs" (Schorr, 1974; Kahn Kamerman, 1975; Kahn, 1976). Rather than defining the adequate family as the family that needs no help from the social services, the presumption is that every family might need such help, that in a complex world no family is entirely self-sufficient. A series of recent comprehensive formulations of suggested national policy programs regarding families and children unanimously urges adoption of such an orientation on the part of child welfare services (National Academy of Sciences, 1976; Moroney, 1976; Kenniston, 1977; Rice, 1977).

It is hoped that people will turn or will be referred to social work agencies, and to child welfare agencies in particular, to enhance social functioning. Just as the World Health Organization has defined *health* as the "state of complete physical, mental, and social well-being, not merely the absence of disease or infirmity," adequate social functioning might be defined as the state of optimum satisfaction in social relationships, rather than merely the absence of problems in social functioning.

A residual orientation to child welfare service has been justifiably criticized for its admitted deficiencies. A residual orientation encourages a two-tier dual system of meeting children's needs—one through the family and the marketplace and the other through the family and public and voluntary child welfare programs. The second system is bound to be inferior to the first. A residual orientation may leave the child without protection until much harm has been done since it is essentially crisis-oriented and reactive rather than proactive, remedial rather than preventative in approach. A residual approach also gives priority to parental autonomy to the detriment of child protection. It is frequently termed a "deficit model," in that it is focused on family breakdown.

We are struggling here with the differences between what actually is and what ought to be. However desirable it might be for child welfare services to be offered universally in response to the needs of all families, the fact is that only residual services are currently offered. Although the field is striving toward the "institutional" orientation of services that are available to all, because of limited resources the priority is given to meeting the needs of the deprived, the disadvantaged, the dependent, and the vulnerable. Aside possibly from day-care service, the clientele of child welfare service agencies is composed largely of social casualties.

The fact is that most individuals come to social agencies only when they are in trouble. Hence, realistically, we are justified in focusing on problems in social role implementation and performance; we are justified in focusing on the unmet, or inadequately met, needs of children. It might further be noted that federal legislation embodying definitions of child welfare service is primarily residual in orientation, identifying particular groups of children on whose behalf the legislation is enacted. Thus the Social Security Act of 1935 identified child welfare services as being for the "protection and care of homeless, dependent and neglected children and children in danger of becoming delinquent." Although the 1962 Amendment to the Social Security Act talks of "protecting and promoting the welfare of children," it defines child welfare services as "social services which supplement or substitute for parental care and supervision" so as to ensure protection and care for "homeless, dependent or neglected children" in order to "prevent or remedy" such problems as "abuse, exploitation or delinquency of children."

A recent detailed design of a *System of Social Services for Children and Families* (1978) prepared for the Federal Administration for Children, Youth and Families defined clients of child welfare agencies in residual terms. The design notes that such clients "are the children, youth and their families . . . for whom the traditional measures of the community—the school, churches, the extended family group—have been found to be unavailable, inappropriate or inadequate. Therefore, these children, youth and their families must turn to the children and family social service system for treatment to ameliorate or solve their problem" (U.S. Department of Health, Education, and Welfare, Children's Bureau, 1978, p. 3).

The most recent definition of child welfare as it appears in federal government legislation again identifies a residual group of children as the principal targets of the legislation's objectives. The Adoption Assistance and Child Welfare Act of 1980 (Public Law 96-272) identifies neglected, abused, exploited, dependent, handicapped, delinquent, and homeless children as targets of concern.

Antler (1985), in an analysis of child welfare policies as implemented in legislation, notes that they "tend to be residual, categorical and aimed primarily at poor or dysfunctional families" (p. 85).

Steiner (1976) says,

> The children's policy most feasible—and most desirable—is one targeted on poor children, handicapped children, and children without permanent homes; unlucky children whose parents cannot provide them a start equal to that provided to most children. Ultimately a far more complex, universal program may be warranted. . . . However, a children's policy will be successful enough if it concentrates on ways to compensate demonstrably unlucky children whose bodies or minds are sick or whose families are unstable or in poverty [p. 255].

The aim of this book is to describe the residually oriented activities that child welfare services actually do perform. The universally oriented programs that, in the best of all possible worlds, should be implemented must, unfortunately, be left for another text.

It might be argued that the orientation toward child welfare services presented here does violence to the reality of the child's living situation. Our attention, it is argued, should not be focused narrowly on the parent–child relationship but on the total family configuration. One might do better to be concerned with family welfare, of which child welfare is a specialized aspect. It is frequently noted that "good family welfare is the best child welfare."

The social system of the family may be seen as consisting of three principal, interrelated subsystems—the marital-pair system, the parent–child system, and the system of sibling relationships. Difficulty in any one of the three subsystems is very likely to produce problems in the related subsystems. But if a conflict between husband and wife is not reflected to any significant degree in the parent–child subsystem, then marital counseling might be more helpful than child welfare services. One might further argue that although children live within the family, they have special needs. Child welfare specialists have developed a particular understanding of these needs and the services required to meet them.

Social Roles

Because child welfare services focus on malfunctions in role enactment within the parent–child relationship, it might be helpful at this point to discuss the concept of *social role* and to clarify the specific role responsibilities inherent in the parent–child role network. A role is the prescribed behavior and attitudes that a person occupying a particular status is expected to assume. As Sarbin (1954) says, "A role is a pattern of attitudes and actions which a person takes in a social situation" (p. 224).

Kluckhohn notes (quoted in Parsons & Shils, 1954):

> The set of behaviors which ego is expected to perform by virtue of his position as father, mother, or child is called a social role. A man in his role as father is expected to behave in certain ways; a woman in her role as mother in certain other ways; and each child according to age, sex, and birth order in still other ways. A role is thus a series of appropriate and expected ways of behaving relative to certain objects by virtue of a given individual's status in a given social structure or institution [p. 350].

As Bernard (1957) puts it, "A role, figuratively speaking, is a job description" (p. 43). It is a job description to be followed by the person performing the "job" of parent or child, and it includes not only the statement of the expected behavior but also the statement of the expected accompanying emotion. It prescribes that the parent not only feed the child but also love him or her; it prescribes that the child not only obey the parent but also be respectful. Nevertheless society sanctions a variety of patterns of behavior as well as different levels of adequacy in role performance (Geismer & Ayers, 1959).

> An important feature of a large proportion of social roles is that the actions which make them up are not minutely prescribed and that a certain range of variability is regarded as legitimate. Sanctions are not invoked against deviants within certain limits [Parsons & Shils, 1954, p. 24].

Sanctioned alternatives, however, fall within prescribed limits. Generally, alternative modes of behavior will be sanctioned as long as the responsibility of the role is successfully discharged. For example, spanking and withdrawal of attention are both acceptable modes of disciplining a child, but physical brutality is not acceptable because it conflicts with one of the principal purposes of the role of parenthood: care and protection of the child. As Brim says (1957), "role prescriptions include the behavior believed in the society to be the instrumental means to the achievement of some desired result" (p. 346).

The role prescription, therefore, will change with changes in society's conception of the purpose of the role. A society that asks parents to prepare the child to live obediently under an authoritarian regime will require forms of behavior in discharging the responsibilities of parenthood different from those required by a society that asks parents to prepare the child to live as a participating member of a democracy. Different subcultural groups in a given society may have differing conceptions of parenthood, so that the role prescription of the black middle-class parent may be different from that of a lower-class white parent.

Unlike some other social roles, such as church member, for instance, the parental role, around which a good deal of one's life is organized, demands a high level of involvement and commitment. It can be given up only at considerable emotional, social, and legal cost. On the other hand, it is enacted under conditions of limited visibility. How the parent cares for the child, disciplines the child, or interacts with the child is not generally visible to the community.

Role enactment requires interaction with others; it involves a set of complementary expectations concerning the individual's own actions and those of others with whom he or she interacts—his or her counterparts. For the parent, the nature of his or her counterpart, the child, is always changing, so that the parental role prescription needs constantly to be revised. The parent of the young child is required to meet the child's dependency needs, but the same parent must change his or her behavior to meet the child's growing need for independence in adolescence. Recognizing that the role prescriptions for parent and child vary with time and with subcultural groups, and that each role description carries with it acceptable alternatives, let us attempt to delineate the normative aspects of role behavior for parent and child in our society.

The Parental Role

The acceptable behavior associated with the performance of a given role includes rights (the behavior expected by us from our reciprocals—the husband from the wife, the child from the parent) as well as obligations (the behavior that others expect us to perform toward them—the husband to the wife, the parents to the child). One person's rights in the role set are the other person's obligations.

What are the parents expected to do and feel in relation to their child in acceptably discharging the parental role?

1. They are expected to provide an income that will permit them to meet the needs of the child for food, clothing, shelter, education, health care, and social and recreational activities.
2. They are expected to provide for the emotional needs of the child—to provide love, security, affection, and the emotional support necessary for the healthy emotional development of the child.
3. They are expected to provide the necessary stimulation for normal intellectual, social, and spiritual development if the family believes this to be important. The parent should see that a school is available and that the child goes to school, that a peer group is available and that the child is encouraged to play, that religious training is available and that the child is encouraged to participate.
4. They must help to socialize the child. Socialization is the process of inducting "new recruits" into the social group and teaching them the behavior that is customary and acceptable to the group.
5. They must discipline the child and keep the child from developing patterns of behavior and attitudes disapproved of by the society.
6. They must protect the child from physical, emotional, or social harm.
7. They must present a model for the identification with ethnic, racial and sex-linked behavior.
8. They must help to maintain family interaction on a stable, satisfying basis so that an effort is made to meet the significant needs of all the members of the family. The parent must help to resolve discomforts, frictions, and dissatisfactions and must meet emotional needs with accepting, affectionate responses.
9. They must provide a fixed place of abode for the child and provide a clearly defined "place" for her in the community. Thus the child comes to know who she is and to whom she belongs and ultimately comes to achieve a stable self-identification.
10. The parent stands as an intermediary between the child and the outer world, defending the child's rights in the community and protecting the child from unjust demands by the community. Because the parental responsibility for socialization of the child is now shared with many community agencies, parents find that their role requires making "decisions concerning which agencies should do the job for them and which ones should be allowed to exercise influence. Parents are necessarily culture brokers for their children before the age of consent; they encourage and facilitate access to some parts of culture, censor others and unconsciously or ambivalently screen out still others in response to their own preferences and sensibilities (Benson, 1968, p. 53).

The parents are the principal emotional support system available to the child. They provide the child with comfort, praise, empathic understanding, sympathy, and affection. They are a source of unconditional positive regard for the child in sensitive response to his or her individualized needs.

Providing care, emotional support, direction, and guidance over the period of the child's dependency, the parent provides the child with the sense of permanence and associated stability and continuity in relationships needed for healthy development.

The listing of the components of the responsibilities associated with the parental role evolves an image that might be regarded as idealistically utopian. Admittedly, this is a prescription that is difficult to fill. But the listing actually includes nothing that has not been recognized by parents as essentials of the job and which most ordinarily devoted parents perform with reasonable levels of competence. Historical studies suggest, further, that these functions have been performed by parents throughout history (Pollock, 1983, pp. 111–112); Ozment, 1983; Borstelmann, 1983).

These functions of the parental role derive from the facts that the child is for a number of years totally dependent on adults for life supplies that include affection. These functions also derive from the biological fact that conception requires a male and a female adult and that most frequently the procreating adults take on the responsibility of caretaking. Biological kinship provides the ties that sustain long-term partisan commitment by parents to support and care of the child.

Furthermore, the caretaking adults and the dependent child system are once again embedded in a larger social group to which they need to relate. But within these parameters, which caretaking parent does what, what functions are emphasized and which are given less priority and which functions are shared between parents and the community and in what ways, are open to almost infinite variation. The Mexican-American family, the Native American family, the Black family and the White-Anglo family may allocate different caretaking functions in different ways. The bi-nuclear family, the single-parent family, and the extended family may allocate different caretaking function in different ways to different parents and parental surrogates in the family system.

The term *parent* is used in a broad sense to include not only biological parent but also step, adoptive, and foster parents and other parental surrogates who perform the functions of the role with some consistency.

Instead of the separate and distinct cultural expectations of behaviors, attitudes, and values associated with the mother's role and another set associated with the father's role, there is a movement toward an undifferentiated set of parental behaviors, attitudes, and values that is shared and implemented, without gender distinction, by both parents. Although for the largest percentage of the population the traditional allocation of the various aspects of the parental role still obtains, in a small but growing percentage of the population the father carries more of the traditional mother's responsibilities and the mother carries more of the traditional father's responsibilities (Nye, 1976). Previously crystallized normative role prescriptions are currently in transition. (Caplow et al., 1982).

The fact of the matter is, however, that by the late 1980s despite all the rhetoric and exhortation about shared parenting, the functions continue to be differentially allocated in accordance with gender. Within the nuclear family the burden of child care is still primarily allocated to the mother (Blumstein & Schwartz, 1983).

Parenthetically, this analysis seems to imply that the nuclear family of father, mother, and children is the only acceptable family structure. Actually, however, it merely identifies the role responsibilities that must be implemented if the child's needs are to be adequately met. The role responsibilities can be implemented by a woman in a single-parent family acting as both mother and father, by a father in a single-parent family acting as father and mother, or by different members in a communal family who each discharge different role functions, or by a couple in a "married" homosexual or lesbian relationship. The family need not necessarily be nuclear, or monogamous or heterosxual or continuous. It is conceivable that the child's needs can be adequately met in a variety of different family structures in which the necessary role tasks are implemented by a variety of allocations of task assignment. If, however, the role arrangements established to meet the child's needs fall short in any one of the variety of different family forms, child welfare service would be the appropriate source of help.

Over the life cycle of the parent(s)–child system the primary responsibility for the implementation of basic caretaking functions may shift between one parent and another as well as between the parents and the community. At different times in the life cycle of the parent(s)–child system, different functions have higher visibility and concern than others. Not only are the duties and privileges of the father and the mother undergoing change, with reassignment or greater sharing of responsibilities, but there is also a reformulation of the respective responsibilities between parents and the community, with the community assuming more responsibility for child care, for example, through day-care or early education programs.

The Child's Role

The child's role is inevitably somewhat more limited. As Sarbin (1954) notes, "assignment of tasks imposed by a particular role must be appropriate to the physical and intellectual capacity of the role participants." Totally or partially dependent, the child is limited in physical and mental capacity and possesses a limited repertoire of skills. Nevertheless, the status of child carries with it a set of obligations, and these are reciprocal to the parental roles:

1. If the parental role requires that the parent teach the child the appropriate attitudes and values of the society, the role of the child demands that he or she learn these attitudes and values and act in accordance with them and in accordance with age-and sex-appropriate prescriptions.
2. If the parent's role is to discipline the child who engages in inappropriate behavior, the child's role is to accept such discipline, to obey the parent, and to make the necessary changes in behavior. The child is required to display the behavior that is acceptable to the family, to the peer group, and to the community.
3. The child is expected to meet some of the emotional needs of his or her parents by responding affectionately to them, confiding in them, and respecting them. The child is expected to act in a manner that will reflect credit on her or his parents and elicit praise for them in the community.
4. The child must cooperate with the parent in the parent's protective efforts to meet his or her physical, emotional, and educational needs. The child is required to eat the food offered, to go to the school provided, and to refrain from activity that is likely to be physically, socially, or emotionally damaging.
5. The child has some responsibility for maintaining family unity and reducing family tensions by cooperating and sharing with other members of the family and by showing loyalty to members of the family group.
6. The child is required to perform whatever appropriate chores are asked of

him or her and to care for whatever clothes, toys, and furniture the parents have provided.

The older child also has some responsibility in performing three different, significant roles: as a child in the family unit, as a pupil in the school system, and as a friend in his or her peer group. The listing relates primarily to the role of the child in the family unit. However, problems in role performance as a pupil or persistent disturbance relationships with the peer group may create problems in parent-child relationships.

As O'Neill and Reddick (1979) point out, children have duties of facilitation and noninterference in cooperating with parental efforts to implement their parental functions (p. 120). Children have the duty to act in ways that facilitate parents' efforts to socialize them, care for them, keep them out of danger, and help them develop. The child, by not interfering with such parental efforts, and by being obedient to parents reduces the possibility that such efforts will be frustrated. Children's duties are thus the corollary of parental obligations and aid in the fulfillment of those functions.

The parent-child relationships involves reciprocity. When the child's capacity permits this, parents, not unreasonably, expect some developing reciprocal responses from children that provide affection, pleasure, and comfort to parents. Children who consistently refrain from, or are incapable of, responding with feeling toward parental displays of affection incur the danger of growing parental dissatisfaction in the relationship.

The Community's Role

Although less visible and apparent than either the parent or the child, the community is an authentic component of the parent–child network. The community, represented by the state, is a parent, beyond the biological parent, to all children. This is the meaning of the concept of *parens patriae*. As such, the community has some rights and obligations in implementing its role in the parent–child network. When the community fails to implement its role effectively, we have another group of situations requiring the intervention of child welfare services.

The community fulfills its "parental" obligations by exercising its regulatory and legislative powers in protecting children and providing the resources they need for proper biological and psychosocial development. The community protects children by licensing day-care centers and providing legal sanctions against child labor, neglect and abuse of children, truancy, and the sale of alcohol, tobacco, and pornography to minors. Through legislation establishing adequate programs for social insurance, income maintenance, health care, public welfare agencies, schools, and recreational facilities, the community provides resources that enable children to meet their needs. A community that fails to function adequately on behalf of its children becomes a legitimate focus of social action on the part of child welfare services.

Problems of Role Functioning: Parent–Child Network

Most children live in a reasonably well-established family group, in which both parents and children are effectively discharging their respective role requirements. As Le Masters and DeFrain (1983) note, "in a well-organized family, the major roles have been identified, assigned, and are performed with some degree of competence," having been understood and accepted (p. 67). However, the community must still provide school facilities, health facilities, clean water, a decent sewerage system, adequate police protection, and so on. These services, required by normal children in normal families, are not child welfare services as we have defined them here.

Child welfare services are those services that are required when parents or children are either incapable of implementing or unwilling to implement (or both) their respective role requirements, or when a serious discrepancy arises between the role expectations of the community and the individual's performance. We can now categorize recurrent problems of role implementation and fulfillment that might require the intervention of child welfare social work services. (Alternative categorizations are available in social work literature: Perlman 1953, Maas, 1957; Atherton, 1971a; Atherton, 1971b; Chescheir, 1979).

1. Parental role unoccupied.
2. Parental incapacity.
3. Parental role rejection.
4. Intrarole conflict.
5. Interrole conflict.
6. Role transitions
7. Child incapacity and/or handicap.
8. Deficiency of community resources.

Parental Role Unoccupied

The most obvious difficulty results when the position of parent is unoccupied. The role may never have been occupied, as is true of the paternal role in the truncated family system of the unmarried mother and the illegitimate child; death, separation, or divorce may leave the role of the father or the mother—or sometimes both—permanently unfilled; long hospitalizations, military service, or imprisonment may leave the role of the parent temporarily vacant. In all these cases, some essential requirements for the normal operation of the parent–child system remain unmet. As long as the role is unfilled, the child may not be incorporated in an adequately functioning family and is likely to be deprived. This, then, is an area of concern for child welfare services.

Role Unfilled—Death of Mother

Gregory C., thirty-seven, a factory clerk, is devoted to his motherless children— Pete, twelve; Violet, ten; Rose, nine; and Billy, seven—and is determined to keep them together.

Eight months ago Mr. C.'s wife died of cancer. He tried to carry on alone, asking a neighbor to care for the children after school until he returned from work. But the double burden of running the home and providing for his family became overwhelming. Relatives suggested that he divide the children among them, but the children, terrified, begged their father not to send them away.

Upset and confused as to how to proceed in caring for his children, Mr. C. came to an agency.

Role Unfilled—Death of Father

Mrs. Lillian C., thirty-seven, came to the agency for help with her two boys—Ben, sixteen, and Tommy, eleven. While their mother went to work, both boys were playing truant regularly from school. Tommy would idle about the house, awaiting her return. Ben loitered on street corners with a gang of boys and was becoming unmanageable.

During the past five years, Mrs. C. has had little time for the children. When her husband died ten years ago, she managed on their small savings supplemented by financial help from her brother. But this help stopped when her brother suffered business reverses, and Mrs. C. had to take a job as cashier to make ends meet. Constantly fatigued by the need to be both mother and father to her children, she became hopeless and bitter. She often told her sons that they were being "cheated by life."

Role Unfilled—Physical Illness

Ordinarily, Jack R., ten, and his brothers—William, seven, and Saul, five—are punctual pupils, neatly though poorly dressed, and attentive in class. But recently they began to be tardy and were frequently absent. Jack fell behind in his work; the younger boys were unruly; all three looked unkempt.

When teachers finally enlisted the agency's aid, the social worker found that the boy's mother, Mrs. Janet R., twenty-nine, had been hospitalized for several weeks with asthma, and the boys and their father, Henry R., thirty, were trying to carry on alone. Mr. R., who works long hours as a store clerk, spent nights and weekends doing heavy chores while Jack handled the light tasks and supervised his brothers. But the lunches Jack prepared were skimpy; he couldn't keep up with the dishwashing and the baths and the marketing.

The doctors say it may be several months before Mrs. R. can return home. Mr. R. and the boys would make any sacrifice to remain together, but they cannot manage alone any longer.

Role Unfilled—Imprisonment

Larry V. is ten and normally active and boisterous. He looks like his father. His mother's great fear is that he will follow in his father's footsteps. Mr. V. recently was sentenced to a prison term for mugging. Mrs. Dorothy V., thirty-five, is so ashamed of her husband's criminal record that she has cut herself off from friends and neighbors. She has also become unduly strict with Larry, disciplining him severely and setting inflexible rules about homework and bedtime. The result is that he has grown increasingly rebellious, which has been very upsetting to Mrs. V. The family has been receiving public assistance.

Role Unfilled—Mental Illness

Mrs. Sylvia P., thirty, was lost when she came to the agency several months ago. Last winter her husband Milton, thirty-three, a salesman, suddenly became quarrelsome and erratic. He was dismissed from his job and soon after was committed to a mental institution.

To support her children—George, nine, and Sue, five—Mrs. P. went to work as a file clerk. But she had to move into an overcrowded apartment with her sister and her ailing mother, both of whom complained endlessly about the children's noise. George became restless and disobedient. Both he and Sue were disturbed by their father's absence, and Mrs. P., ashamed, answered their questions evasively. The children became such a problem that Mrs. P. asked the agency for help.

Role Unfilled—Illegitimacy

A year ago, Betty N., twenty-four, was happy and secure. Now she faces the problem of caring for an illegitimate child.

Betty's fiancé, Stephen S., twenty-five, entered medical school two years ago. A year later, Betty was graduated from college and began to teach, saving for their wedding day. Last summer she became pregnant. Stephen offered financial help for an abortion, but he refused to marry her, saying it would hurt his career. Betty broke off with him.

Betty's parents have agreed to pay for her confinement but they have refused to provide for the baby and have urged her to give it up for adoption. Torn by indecision, Betty came to the agency.

Role Unfilled—Migration

Paul's father, after a long period of unemployment, recently decided to try his luck elsewhere. Because he was uncertain about the job possibilities in Chicago, he decided to go without the family. He left Appalachia six months ago and is still looking for steady work. Paul, ten, misses his father, with whom he used to hunt and fish frequently. He is becoming depressed and his schoolwork suffers as a result.

Parental absence may be for a limited period during which dependent children are inadequately supervised.

Two young children, a girl of four and a boy of two were fatally injured in a fire which broke out yesterday at 2 A.M. in a four-story tenement building in New York City. An exposed heater apparently started the fire. The children were left unattended by their mother who had left to go to a party from which she did not return until the next day.

Parental Incapacity

Inadequate role implementation sometimes results from incapacity. The role incumbent may be physically present and want to fulfill his or her role requirements but may be incapacitated by physical, mental, or emotional inadequacy or by lack of training or knowledge. A physically handicapped mother may find it difficult to meet the demands of an active, healthy youngster. A mentally deficient mother may be incapable of learning the essential routines of child care. A mother who is herself emotionally immature cannot meet the dependent needs of her infant child. Some parents, who were deprived in their own childhoods, may have come to parenthood without adequate education or marketable job skills and without having learned essential child-care skills from *their* parents. Sometimes addiction to drugs or alcohol may render parents incapable of providing adequate physical and emotional care for their children. In all of these cases, because the role of the parent is inadequately implemented and the child suffers, child welfare services are an appropriate remedial resources.

Role Incapacity—Illness

Frank F. and his wife Rose, both thirty-six, have been married for fifteen years. They have lived from crisis to crisis, but now it has become too much for them. Mr. F. is a laborer; his earnings have never adequately covered the family's needs. Mrs. F. is diabetic; the care of three children leaves her suffering chronic fatigue. She upbraids her husband for being a bad provider. He lashes out at her for being a poor manager. They quarrel bitterly and endlessly.

The continual tension is reflected in the children: Mark, fourteen, refuses to play with other children; Frances, eleven, often cannot eat; Therese, eight months old, cries constantly. Their pastor suggested that they seek the help of a social agency.

Role Incapacity—Physical Handicap

Mrs. Belle H., thirty-two, is crippled in body but not in spirit. A year ago Mrs. H. was striken with polio and had to be hospitalized. Her husband Victor, thirty-four, sent ten-year-old Shirley to live with relatives. Sylvia, four, was placed in a foster home.

Two months ago Mrs. H. was brought home in a wheelchair, with both legs useless and one arm partially paralyzed. Believing it would aid her rehabilitation, her doctors advised that the family be reunited, and the children are now home again.

Mrs. H. goes to a clinic for therapy several times a week and eventually will recover partial use of her limbs. Now, however, the handicap prevents Mrs. H. from fully caring for her children.

Role Incapacity—Ignorance

Peter's mother was making a small but constant error, out of ignorance, that had serious effects on his health. It was noticed at the well-baby clinic that he was not gaining any weight and that his color was poor. When, at the request of the authorities, the situation was investigated, it was found that Peter's mother had been using teaspoonfuls instead of tablespoonfuls in making up his formula.

Role Incapacity—Emotional Immaturity

Kathy is only eleven, but she bears a burden far beyond her years. Her mother, Mrs. Maureen L., forty, is an alcoholic. Her father, George, forty-one, works nights in a factory and takes little interest in his family, which includes, besides Kathy, George, Jr., eight; Louis, seven, and Peter, six. For the past two years Kathy more and more has had to do the housework and care for the children. When her mother disappears, as often happens, Kathy does the marketing and cooking. When her mother has fits of weeping, Kathy anxiously tries to "mother" her, too.

Recently Kathy began to show signs of the strain she is under. She daydreamed in school. She lied to her teacher. She took money from her mother's purse to spend on classmates. Mr. L., alarmed, came to the agency.

Role Incapacity—Mental Retardation

Tommy is four, a bright, sturdy, normal little boy with a quick smile. But he needs help, because his parents are mentally retarded.

Tommy's parents grew up in institutions; there they received enough training to be self-sufficient. His father, who is twenty-eight, works as a dishwasher and is able to support his family adequately. But his unpredictable attitudes confuse Tommy. When Tommy misbehaves, sometimes his father scolds him, sometimes he laughs at him. Tommy's mother is bewildered by her lively son and is unable to understand or anticipate his actions. He refuses to mind her and lacks the most rudimentary training. It was on the advice of a clinic nurse that she sought the agency's help.

Role Incapacity—Drug Addiction

Ruth, eight, and Jimmy, six, frequently have had to beg food from the neighbors. Their parents are drug addicts, and the children are frequently neglected for long periods of time, when the parents are on drugs. The apartment is barren of furniture and the children poorly clothed, since all of the limited family income goes to support the habit. Mr. C. finds it difficult to hold a steady, adequately paying job. Neglect and deprivation are beginning to affect the health of the children adversely.

Role Rejection

Inadequate role implementation sometimes results from role rejection. For many people parenthood is a voluntarily assumed role; for others, however, parenthood is an involuntary burden resulting from a biological accident. There is a conscious or an unconscious rejection of the parental role, on the part of these parents, that results in varying degrees of failure in role performance. These parents are likely to be indifferent, neglectful, or abusive. Some totally abandon the role of parents by deserting their families. The child suffers, or is apt to suffer, as a result of rejection of the parental role, and child welfare services are consequently required to protect the child.

Role Rejection—Neglect and Abandonment

Nancy is almost five. She is headstrong and defiant; she tears her dolls apart and bites other children when she quarrels with them. Her sleep is disturbed by nightmares during which she cries out for her "Mummy."

Nancy's parents, an unstable couple in their twenties, were never happy in their marriage. They quarreled constantly, and frequently separated for long periods. Four months ago they left Nancy with a friend, saying they expected to be out late that night. But next day the friend received a letter saying they were leaving town and could no longer provide for Nancy. They asked that she be taken to the agency.

Role Rejection—Abandonment

Freddy is a brown-haired, chubby little boy almost three years old. At times he is sweet and affectionate; at others, for no apparent reason, he throws himself on the floor of his boarding home kicking and pounding. Often he wakes in the night screaming.

Shortly after Freddy was born, his mother asked the welfare department to place him for adoption. She said that he was illegitimate and that his father had deserted her. Before her story could be checked, she disappeared. Recently a court determination of abandonment was made, and the welfare department turned Freddy over to the agency for adoption.

Role Rejection—Neglect

Mrs. Yvonne E., thirty-one, was sentenced to sixty days in the county jail Wednesday on charges of neglect of children.

The E. case came to the attention of the police department's crime prevention bureau July 22, after a neighbor summoned police. An investigation at about 4 A.M. showed that Mrs. E.'s four children were alone in the apartment. The floors were strewed with decayed food and mildewed clothing; windows were broken and insects infested the bedding; food in the refrigerator was covered with insects, and the children were attempting to fry a spoiled, uncleaned fish. Toilet facilities in the apartment were plugged.

Parental role rejection also includes situations in which parents misuse their power and authority. Physical, emotional, and sexual abuse of children are examples of such misuse.

Role Rejection—Physical Abuse

A little girl with both eyes swollen nearly shut heard a judge describe her mother as "a savage," as he sentenced the mother to one year in the house of correction.

Mrs. Barbara F., twenty-one, admitted pummeling the child, Darlene, three, with her fists and striking her time after time with her shoes and belt. Asked whether she loved the child, Mrs. F., a waitress, replied, "I didn't think much of her from the day she was born." Police were called Tuesday after a baby-sitter, Mrs. Minnie J., noticed that the child's face, legs, back, and stomach were severely bruised.

Intrarole Conflict

Inadequate role implementation sometimes results from problems of conflict in role definition or intrarole conflict. The mother and the father may disagree strongly as to who is supposed to do what for, and with, the child. The mother may expect the father to help her care for the child; the father may define his role more narrowly as primarily that of a provider.

Intrarole conflict may result from the seemingly incongruent demands imposed by the parental role, which requires that one love, yet discipline the child, indulge as well as deprive, free as well as restrict the child. Or conflict may result from differing interpretations of role behavior by the various reference groups with which the person is affiliated; the parents may expect one kind of behavior from their adolescent child whereas the peer group may define expected behavior in quite another, and conflicting, way. Some parents and children may define their reciprocal roles differently. The frequently cited generation gap refers, in essence, to problems of intrarole definition.

Some parents fail to perceive clearly the requirements of the role, or society may have failed to define the role clearly. In periods when the role of parents is changing, it is not clear how parents should behave or what is expected of them. Furthermore, even though parental roles generally might be clearly defined, specific aspects of the role might be ambiguous. For instance, the division of parental energy and time between the child's needs and the parent's own needs may be a matter over which society itself is undecided. The problems deriving from these conflicts impede effective implementation of parental role, and the child may, therefore, suffer.

Intrarole Conflict—Definition of Role

Mr. and Mrs. F. were advised by an elementary-school teacher to apply for help at a child guidance clinic. Paul, their eight-year-old son, was doing poorly in his studies and frequently displayed disruptive behavior in the classroom. He shouted, fought with other children, and was difficult to discipline.

In talking with the caseworker, Mr. and Mrs. F. revealed that the problem of disciplining Paul was a matter of considerable friction between them. Mr. F. had grown up in a home that emphasized strict obedience, respect for elders, and prompt physical punishment for lapses in behavior. He believed that parents should order and children should obey. Mrs. F. felt uncomfortable with this approach. Her tendency was to be more permissive, to allow more latitude, and to permit the children to "express themselves rather than be squelched." As a consequence of this difference, neither parent took responsibility for disciplining Paul. Each would make an attempt at it when emergencies arose, but neither one felt that he or she had full right to try his or her own approach because the marital partner so strongly disagreed with it.

Interrole Conflict

Inadequate role implementation may result when the parental role conflicts with another social role. According to Werble (1960):

When the expectations between the vital social roles occupied by a single actor are inconsistent, contradictory, or mutually exclusive so that compliance with one set of role expectations necessary entails noncompliance with another set of role expectations, we have the problem of role conflict [p. 30].

The occupational role often conflicts with the duties and obligations of the parental role. The father, who is away from the home a great deal because of the demands of his job, faces such a conflict, just as the working mother faces a conflict between her role as a mother and her role as an employee.

Interrole conflict has become a more frequent source of difficulty with the increase of women in the labor force. Male and female parents have to decide on the allocation of child-care responsibilities when both have responsibilites as employees that conflict with parental responsibilities.

Role Conflict—Working Mother

Mrs. W. needed to work and enjoyed her job. Her husband's income as a postal clerk could not meet the needs of a growing family of six children—five girls and a boy. Mrs. W. decided to go to work when it seemed clear that the family was becoming more and more heavily indebted. But two of the children—Mike, two and one-half, and Ruth, three and one-half—were still at home and needed her, and even the school-age children seemed to react negatively to her absence from home. Mrs. W. wasn't sure that being a salesclerk, when she could be a mother, was the best choice to make. Besides, a good deal of her energy was being absorbed in making arrangements with all sorts of people to care for the preschool children during the time she was at work. Concerned about the situation, Mrs. W. came to the agency to discuss her conflicts.

The demands on parents by their own parents may conflict with demands made by their own children. The conflicting demands made by different role requirements stemming from the variety of positions that people occupy simultaneously in a complex society may result in the inadequate implementation of the parental role. In such situations, the child is deprived, and the intervention of child welfare services is appropriate.

Role Conflict—Mother/Daughter

During the last four months Mrs. R. had been more of a stranger than a mother to her three children—Nancy, five; Joan, seven; and William, eleven. Mrs. R.'s father, seventy-six, suffered a heart attack about six months ago. A widower, he was living alone in a six-room house that the family had owned for the last thirty years. He refused to go to an institution, and Mrs. R., an only child, was very worried that he might overextend himself and suffer another sudden heart attack. As a result, she made an effort to visit him daily and care for him. She left in the morning and did not come home until the children were asleep. Mr. R. had been trying to care for the family in his wife's daily absence. Although she recognized that her children were suffering as a result of the family's disorganization occasioned by the care of her father, she felt great guilt if she neglected her duties as a daughter.

Role-Transition Problems

Parental role performance is affected by significant transitions in the lives of parents. A parent whose spouse becomes seriously disabled or dies faces a problem of transition in the necessary readjustment of parental functions to a significant changed situation. Parents whose marriage is being terminated by divorce face problems of parental role transition. A mother who accepts employment after a period exclusively devoted to motherhood faces a problem associated with changing status.

In the normal course of events in the most adequate of families there are problems relating to role transitions. Becoming a parent after years of not being a parent requires an adjustment in social relationship. It requires an adjustment in the relationship between husband and wife, changes in their social life arrangements, and changes in self-perceptions.

As the child grows from infancy through school age through adolescence, parent–child relationships have to undergo readjustment. Previous ways of relating to one another are no longer appropriate. Being a parent to a teenager is a different situation than being a parent to a helpless infant. Making a transition to becoming a stepparent in a reconstituted family is also a difficult transition.

Problems involved in role transition are problems that are the appropriate responsibility of a child welfare agency.

> Bill 29 and Joan 28 were expecting their first child in 3 months. They joined a group sponsored by the local family service agency. The group, composed of young, first-time parents-to-be, was concerned with discussing the childbirth experience, infant development, and the care and handling of infants.

Child Incapacity and/or Handicap

Inadequate role implementation also results from excessive demands made on the role incumbents. The physically handicapped or emotionally disturbed child is incapable of performing the role normally required of a child. Such a child imposes on its parents a burden of care, of specialized knowledge, of patience and control beyond that which any society can normally expect of them, and the possibility of adequately meeting the needs of such a child is reduced. The child's failure to meet the expectations of the parents robs them of the emotional satisfactions that are the rewards of fulfilling their many parental obligations and duties and makes it even more difficult for them to perform the parental role adequately. In such cases, the provision of child welfare services is appropriate.

Excessive Demand—Epilepsy

> Anne is only six, but she knows that she is different, that her parents quarrel constantly over her, and that her older brother and sister are ashamed of her. Anne is an epileptic.
> Anne's father, Jacob L., thirty-eight, a municipal clerk, has never accepted his daugher. He reminds his wife Lillian, thirty-five, that he never wanted a third child. He complains that Anne takes too much of Mrs. L.'s time. Mrs. L., in turn, accuses him of making Anne's condition worse by his refusal to share the parental burden. The L.'s sense of shame has affected the other children: Joseph, thirteen, shies away from the outside world; Dana, ten, is a behavior problem at school.

Excessive Demand—Mental Deficiency

> For years Samuel and Martha W. couldn't understand why their youngest child, Ethel, five, was so different from her four brothers and sisters, ranging in age from seven to fourteen. She could not talk or respond to speech; she had no control over her body functions; yet she was strong and active and kept hurting herself. Ethel is a severely retarded child.
> The care of Ethel, on top of the problem of caring for her four children on the meager income of Mr. W., forty-eight, a peddler, became too much for Mrs. W., forty-three. A social worker, disturbed by signs of neglect the other children showed at a

free summer camp, visited the home and persuaded Mrs. W. to take Ethel to the agency.

Excessive Demand—Emotional Disturbance

During the past two years, Billy, seven, has been unable to sleep more than four or five hours a night. He wakes up during the night screaming and covering his eyes as though he sees something that frightens him. He strikes and bites his brothers and sisters and is destructive of neighbors' property. Billy tends to play by himself, carrying on an intelligible conversation with his toys. He has temper tantrums that last for hours. His behavior is disrupting the entire family and the neighbors are beginning to complain.

Despite their best efforts, Mr. and Mrs. S. seem incapable of dealing with their son's behavior. They are exhausted by their attempts to help him and frustrated and upset because they do not know what to do next. They feel their failure all the more keenly because they have proved themselves to be reasonably adequate parents in dealing with their other children—Kathy, nine; Frank, fourteen; and Sylvia, three. Billy, however, is too much for them to contend with.

Excessive Demand—Brain Injury

Mrs. Janice C., twenty-seven, and his husband Michael, thirty-one, a machinist, face a sorrowful decision. Doctors say their youngest child, three-year-old Susan, must be put in an institution, but they cannot bear to part with her.

Susan is a victim of a progressive brain disease that is expected to take her life within a few years. Mrs. C. is expecting another child, and she finds Susan's care increasingly heavy. Susan cannot sit up by herself or control her movements. She hits her head repeatedly on her crib and high chair, which are carefully padded, and needs constant watching. Moreover, the other two C. children—Lorraine, seven, and Alice, six—resenting the attention given their handicapped sister, are becoming defiant and unruly.

In addition to role inadequacy, the child may generate problems in relationships with parents by rejecting his or her role much as the neglecting father rejects his role. The child who plays truant from school rejects a role as pupil; the child who runs away from home rejects a role as child in the family; the child who isolates himself or herself from contacts with other children rejects a role as member of the peer group.

Child Role Rejection

Jim, twelve, was picked up by the police after having slept all night at the Greyhound bus stop. This is the third time during the past three months that Jim has tried to run away from home. He indicated, when questioned, that he doesn't get along with his family, he doesn't feel as if he belongs in his family, and he wants to be on his own.

There can be problems in the parent–child network that derive from child interrole conflict. The demands of the role of friend in the peer group may conflict with the roles of pupil at school or child in the family.

Child Interrole Conflict

Louis, eleven, and his parents are persistently in conflict about his performance of chores in the home. He is expected to keep his room clean, mow the lawn, cooperate with doing the dishes. More often than not he fails to do these chores. Louis is a very active member of a little-league team and a hockey team. He says that if he is not going to let his team down, he needs to spent a lot of time practicing with them. He forgets to do the things around the house because he has the team on his mind. If he did the things his parents always keep at him for doing, he would have less time for practice.

Deficiency of Community Resources

Inadequate role implementation sometimes results from deficiencies in community resources. For instance, a father will find it difficult to implement the income maintenance aspects of the parental role if there are no jobs available. As Speigel (1960) points out, "Insofar as role activities require technical instruments, equipment, furniture, props, customs, climate and other appropriate physical facilities (including money), a lack or insufficiency of these instrumental prerequisites interferes with role transactions" (p. 369). When adequate employment opportunities, schools, recreational facilities, or health services are lacking, or when social and racial discrimination, overcrowding, and social disorganization are characteristic of the community, parents may find it difficult to implement their roles. The atmosphere of the community needs to be free of the stigma of racial and class discrimination if the parents are to be expected to raise their child with a sense of dignity and self-acceptance. The problems may result not only from the lack of available resources but also from the lack of access to them by particular groups. If discrimination operates to keep some kinds of jobs closed to nonwhites, women, former offenders, former alcoholics, or those who have been mentally ill, the problem for these groups is a deficiency in environmental resources, which adversely affects family role enactment. Efforts to change community conditions that adversely affect social functioning are part of the responsibility of child welfare services.

Community Deficiency—Inadequate Housing

Mr. and Mrs. R. are very much concerned about the threat to their children's healthy development presented by the neighborhood in which they live. Mr. R. has worked steadily for the past fifteen years as an elevator operator in a large office building. They have been living in the same apartment house for the past twenty years. So far they have been able to rear their children—George, sixteen; Alice, twelve; and Susan, seven—without any serious problems. However, the neighborhood in which they live has been rapidly deteriorating. Several women in the apartment house are openly engaged in prostitution. The neighborhood barbershop and candy store are the hangouts for dope pushers, numbers runners, and pornography salesmen. They would like to move out of the neighborhood but cannot find any apartment as large as the one they now occupy at a rental they can afford. Despite their best efforts at being adequate parents, they feel that the counterinfluence of some of the neighborhood elements may negatively affect the behavior of their oldest boy, George, in particular.

Community Deficiency—Unemployment

The men stand around idly on Main Street. There is nothing else to do. Three months ago the local mine, in which most of them have worked for the better part of their employable lives, closed down. The vein was giving out and it was no longer profitable for the mine company to continue operations. Three hundred men were suddenly thrown out of work, and the town industries and services have been able to absorb only a small fraction of this large body of unemployed men. For the rest there remain limited savings, unemployment insurance for a limited period, and then, no one knows exactly what. As miners, as wage earners, these men had been able to support their families. Now there are no jobs available, and they worry about how they might continue to care for their children.

The variety of problems in role enactment described in neatly summarized by Bartlett (1961) when she says that:

the condition with which child welfare services are primarily concerned is the deficiency in these provisions resulting from (1) incapacity of parents, (2) extraordinary needs of certain children, and (3) limitations of opportunities and resources [p. 43].

Recent studies confirm the contention that the social problems outlined in this section are, in fact, the primary concerns of child welfare agencies (Haring, 1975; Shyne & Schroeder, 1977 Packman, 1968.) Such studies attempted a nationwide "census" of the circumstances that resulted in applications for service from child welfare agencies. Findings were that problems in parental role coverage resulting from death, divorce, separation, desertion, imprisonment, and illegitimacy; inadequate parental role performance owing to physical and/or mental illness; parental role rejection manifested in neglect and/or abuse of the child; and inadequate enactment of the child's role owing to emotional or physical disability accounted, in aggregate, for most of the reasons someone, either the family or the community, had called for the help of a child welfare social worker. Environmental circumstances—financial need or inadequate housing—were listed as the most important reasons for service in a very limited percentage of the cases, although they were a contributing reason in a much larger percentage of the cases.

The problems encountered by child welfare agencies change with changes in the society. Earlier in the century, many of the cases that came to these agencies reflected intergenerational and intercultural conflict. The parents, often recent immigrants speaking no English, brought to the parent-child relationship a definition of the parental role that had been shaped in the context of the Old World, whereas the children defined their expectations in terms of the American experience. Currently, however, child welfare agencies encounter problems of intergenerational conflict resulting from the different definitions of parent–child roles caused by a fast-changing culture. The older parent reflects attitudes and convictions very different from those of his or her child, and the conflict is expressed in bitter battles about marijuana, sex, work habits, and so on. A decade ago, parental incapacity arising from alcoholic addiction was a problem frequently encountered by child welfare agencies; today, parental incapacity is often caused by drug addiction, as well.

Whereas fifty years ago child welfare agencies were frequently concerned with children of recently arrived immigrant parents facing difficulties of adjustment to a new and strange world, fifty years from now child welfare agencies may be concerned with families in which the parental role is unfilled because a parent is away on an interplanetary trip that is scheduled to take three to five years to complete.

Problems of role enactment may be the result of social pressures or psychological pressures, or both. In some instances, the most significant component of the problem is a personal pathology; in others, it is the pathology of society. A black man with limited education has difficulty in obtaining and holding an adequate job. Living on a limited income in crowded, substandard housing, he may be led by the pressure of the social situation to desert his family. A middle-class engineer living on a decent regular income in a comfortable suburb may also desert his family because he feels tied down, hemmed in, anxious, and depressed. In both instances, the role of parent has been abandoned, although for very different reasons. As far as the child is concerned, the etiology of the problem matters little. What does matter is that something must be done to fulfill the obligations of the rejected position. Each situation may present a unique combination of psychological and social factors that results in a particular kind of problem.

Some problems are more susceptible to solution through community organization. Others are more susceptible to solution through the involvement of the client in group activity. Still others are most susceptible to solution through work with the individual client. Sometimes it might be helpful to use a combination of approaches.

For instance, the working mother of a preschool child must arrange for child care while she is on the job. If the community lacks day-care services and the problem is of concern to a sufficiently large number of women in the community, social workers would then employ the method of community organization in an effort to establish a day-care center.

Sometimes, however, even if a day-care facility is already available in the community, a mother may be anxious about the effects of temporary role substitution on her relationships with her child. The caseworker might discuss with the mother her feelings about relinquishing her maternal role for some part of each day and her anxieties regarding the child's reaction to day care and might help her make a reasoned decision with which she will be comfortable.

Child welfare social work is not synonymous with casework, although this is admittedly the method of helping most frequently employed. Any and all methods—casework, group work, community organization, social action—are employed, alone and in combination, that can be applied appropriately in effecting some positive change in, and for, the client or the client group. Social system change, social reform, is as much a responsibility of child welfare social work as is client symptom change; prevention is as appropriate as rescue–therapy–rehabilitation. These diverse approaches are complementary in this as well as in other fields of social work practice.

Further, this formulation does not suggest that any one method has to be defined in a particular way. Casework in child welfare can be defined as a method that includes brokerage and advocacy activity on the client's behalf, and its psychotherapeutic interventions may as legitimately employ a behavioral modification as a psychoanalytic or a Rogerian nondirective approach.

Categories of Child Welfare Services

Child welfare services, whether designed to help on the level of community action, group involvement, or individual contact, can be categorized as supportive, supplemental, or substitutive. These categories are not mutually exclusive, and they tend to overlap.

Supportive services include home-based programs and the work of child protective agencies. Supportive services are the first line of defense in dealing with actual or incipient problems in child welfare, when the family and the parent–child relationship system are structurally intact but subject to stress. If the stress is permitted to continue, it might result in a structural break: divorce, separation, desertion, and so on. Supportive services are designed to use the family's own strength to work toward a reduction of strain in the parent–child relationship system.

Casework services offered by home-based agencies on behalf of the child support, reinforce, and strengthen the parents' efforts to discharge their parental responsibilities adequately. And, in dealing with marital friction that would ultimately have deleterious effects on the child, the family agency is offering another supportive service.

Protective services, offered by child welfare agencies for children who have been grossly neglected or abused, are primarily supportive services designed to develop and strength any and all factors in the situation that would enable the parents to enact their roles in a more socially acceptable manner.

Supportive services involve the least amount of environmental modification for the child. As such, they require the least amount of adaptive change. Supportive services, however, require the greatest amount of parental involvement in the process.

Supplementary services are the sound line of defense, called upon when a parent–child relationship is seriously impaired because a significant aspect of the parental role is inadequately covered but the family configuration is such that, with supplementation, the child can continue to live at home without harm. Financial maintenance programs of all kinds—assistance as well as insurance—are, in effect, supplementary services. Financial maintenance programs act *in loco parentis* as far as the income-producing responsibilities of the parents are concerned. Homemaker programs and day-care programs are also supplementary, for both are designed to supplement the parent's enactment of child-care functions.

Substitute services are the third line of defense and are used when the situation is so damaging as to require either a temporary or a permanent dissolution of the parent–child relationship system. A substitute family is offered the child in a foster home, an adoptive home, or an institution. The substitute family may be similar in structure to the normal family, as in the case of the foster family or the adoptive home, or it may be different, as in the case of the institution—the orphan asylum, the residential treatment home, the training school for delinquents, the institution for the physically, emotionally, or mentally handicapped, and so on. The substitution may be temporary (as in the case of a foster home) or permanent (as in the case of an adoptive home). The institution may be employed either as a temporary or as a permanent family substitute. In all substitute family-care arrangements, the natural parent of the child yields almost total responsibility to somebody else for the performance of daily parental obligations in relation to the child.

Although such a categorization of child welfare services has proven useful in systematizing the services, it has been also criticized as retrogressive. The classification scheme tends to give little visibility to services that have primary prevention as their objective. The scheme can be used to justify the maintenance of traditional boundaries between clusters of services that should be integrated with child welfare services, namely family services and mental health services. Classification further suggests distinctions between services that do not actually exist in practice in which mutually exclusive boundaries between services cannot and should not be maintained in effectively serving the client (Magazino, 1983, pp. 217–218).

Some suggest a more parsimonious way of categorizing services into in-home services and out-of-home services. Supportive and supplementary services together are categorized as in-home, the substitute care services as out-of-home.

Figure 1-1 schematically summarizes the services that are the concern of the child welfare services system.

Validation of the fact that these services constitute the essential core concerns of child welfare agencies is substantiated by a detailed review of the activities of public child welfare services in twenty-five states (U.S. Health, Education, and Welfare, Children's Bureau, 1976, pp. 103–104). In all states, substantially all of the following services were found to be among the services offered as child welfare services: social services for children in their own home; protective services; day-care services; homemaker services; foster-family care; social services for unmarried parents; adoption services; shelter care for children in emergency; group home services; institutional care for children.

In their *National Study of Social Services to Children and Their Families,* Shyne and Shroeder (1978) listed the following services as included in their definition of child welfare—counseling, protective services, day care, homemaker service, institutional care, group home care, foster-family care, and adoption service. Services to juvenile delinquents and handicapped children were explicitly excluded from the listing "since these latter (services) are usually provided by other state agencies" rather than by child welfare agencies (p. 14). Responsibility for each of these groups of children is generally assigned to a unit of government other than the State Child Welfare Department. In the case of delinquent children the Division or Department of Corrections is assigned primary concern, whereas handicapped children are the responsibility of the Department or Division of Rehabilitation.

The Child Welfare League of America in its *Directory of Member Agencies* (1985) defines child welfare services as including adoption, day-care service, foster-family care service, group home service, homemaker service, institutional care for children, maternity homes, protective service for neglected children, shelter care for children in emergencies, social services to children in their own homes, social services to families, children and individuals under stress and social services for unmarried parents. These are essentially the services covered in this text as child welfare services. Once again, services to handicapped and delinquent children are not included.

Despite the fact that the income maintenance and social insurance programs impact on the largest number of children in the country needing supplementation, these programs are not generally included in the traditional listing of child welfare services.

We included a chapter on income maintenance and social insurance programs in the three earlier editions of the text. We had included them not only because we regard these programs as deserving of recognition as supplementary child welfare services but also because all child welfare workers need to know about these services since many of their clients might need referral to these programs.

We have deleted this chapter from the current edition not because we have lost conviction in the value and appropriations of this content to child welfare but

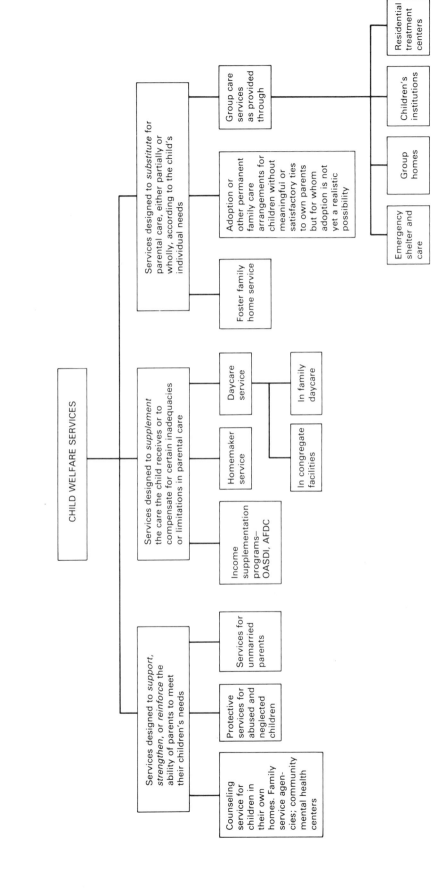

Figure 1-1 The child welfare services system.

because the size of the text was getting out of hand and because we were convinced that most social work educational programs already covered this material in other than child welfare courses. As a consequence the continued inclusion of this content would be redundant.

Exclusion of this material was further suggested on the basis of the fact that very few social workers are involved in these programs. The income maintenance aspects of the AFDC programs are implemented by income maintenance employees not identified as social workers; the OASDI and other social insurance programs operate with almost a total absence of social workers.

An additional reason for deleting the chapter in this edition is the fact the entire welfare system at the both the state and federal level was scheduled for broad reformulation by the end of this decade. The Federal Domestic Policy Council was scheduled to make a report to the President in December 1986 after a full-scale review of the system. Many states had appointed special commissions to make similar studies and were experimenting with substantial substantative changes in their programs, particularly around work requirements. As a consequence, the income maintenance programs in the 1990s are likely to look quite different from the programs as might be described by a text published in 1988. The rapid pace of anticipated changes makes likely the rapid obsolecence of even newly revised content.

Child welfare agencies are further categorized under auspices and source of funding:

1. Public agencies under federal, state, or county auspices are supported by public tax funds.
2. Voluntary nonprofit agencies are generally supported by community-donated funds and further subdivided as under either denominational (Catholic, Protestant, Jewish) or nondenominational auspices. Since voluntary agencies currently receive such a large measure of support from public funds through purchase-of-service agreements, they can legitimately be regarded as quasi-public agencies.
3. Private profit agencies are under proprietary auspices and supported by client fees. These include proprietary day-care centers, homemaker services, group homes, and residential treatment centers.
4. Industrially affiliated agencies, such as factory day-care centers, as part of employee assistance programs.

Although our effort here has been to delineate as clearly as possible the parameter that defines child welfare services as distinguished from other kinds of social services, in practice child welfare services do not operate in isolation. They are offered in conjunction with all of the other services that make up the total social service system, when the utilization of other services is appropriate. Only when the total social welfare system which the child welfare service system is embedded has a sufficiency of diversified resources can the child welfare system operate with optimum effectiveness.

The child welfare service system, then, is a network of public and voluntary agencies in social work practice that specializes in the prevention, amelioration, or remediation of social problems which are related to the functioning of the parent–child relationship network through the development and provision of specific child welfare services: services to children in their own home, protective services, day care, homemaker service, foster-family care, services to the unwed parent, adoption services, and institutional child care.

Plan of the Book

The plan of the book is to present a detailed review of each of these broad categories of supportive, supplementary, and substitute services and to examine the specific programs that fall into one or another of these categories: home-based care, protective service, day-care service, homemaker service, foster care, adoption, institutional care, and services to the unmarried parent.

In the case of each of the services, we present material regarding the following content areas:

1. General historical background.
2. Situations for which the service is appropriate.
3. Scope of the service.
4. Processes in offering the service.
5. Evaluation.
6. Problems regarding the service.
7. Trends in offering the service.

Before presenting a discussion of each of the specific child welfare services, we have included a chapter on the historical and current context of child welfare. This material is designed to provide a frame of reference for the discussion that follows. Following the chapters on each of the services is a chapter on child welfare practices in other countries that provides an international perspective on our problems and the way we meet them.

Bibliography

Antler, Stephen. "The Social Policy Content of Child Welfare," pp. 77–99, in *A Handbook of Child Welfare: Context, Knowledge and Practice.* Ed. Joan Laird and Ann Harttman. New York: The Free Press, 1985.

Atherton, Charles R. et al. "Locating Points for Intervention." *Social Casework,* 52 (March 1971a), 131–141.

Atherton, Charles R. et al. "Using Points for Intervention." *Social Casework,* 52 (April 1971b), 223–233.

Bartlett, Harriett. *Analyzing Social Work Practice by Fields.* New York: National Association of Social Workers, 1961.

Benson, Leonard. *Fatherhood: A Sociological Perspective.* New York: Random House, 1968.

Bernard, Jessie. *Social Problems at Midcentury.* New York: Holt, Rinehart and Winston, 1957.

Blumstein, Phillip, and Pepper Schwartz. *American Couples—Money, Work, Sex.* New York: William Morrow and Co., 1983.

Boehm, Werner. *Objectives of the Social Work Curriculum of the Future.* New York: Council on Social Work Education, 1959.

Boehm, Werner. *The Training of Psychotherapists.* Ed. Nicholas Dellis and Herbert Stone. Baton Rouge: Louisiana State University Press, 1960.

Borstelmann, L. S. "Children before Psychology: Ideas about Children from Antiquity to the Late 1800's," pp. 1–40 in vol. I *Handbook of Child Psychology,* 4th ed. Ed. P. Mussen. New York: John Wiley & Sons, 1983.

Brim, Orville. "The Parent-Child Relation as a Social System's Parent and Child Roles." *Child Development,* 28 (September 1957).

Caplow, Theodore et al. *Middleton Families—Fifty Years of Change and Continuity.* New York: Bantam Books, 1982.

Carstens, C. C. "Child Welfare Services," in *Social Work Yearbook.* New York: Russell Sage Foundation, 1937.

Chescheir, Martha W. "Social Role Discrepancies as Clues to Practice." *Social Work,* 24 (March 1979), 89–94.

Child Welfare League of America. *Child Welfare Directory of Member and Associate Agencies and Supporting Organizations.* New York: C.W.L.A., 1985.

Condie, David C. et al. "How the Public Views Social Work." *Social Work,* 23 (January 1978), 47–54.

Council On Social Work Education. "Child Welfare," in *Description of Practice: Statements in Fields of Social Work Practice.* New York: Council on Social Work Education, 1959, mimeo.

Friedlander, Walter. *Introduction to Social Welfare,* 2d ed. Englewood Cliffs, N.J.: Prentice-Hall, 1961.

Geismer, L. L., and Beverly Ayers. *Patterns of Change in Problem Families.* St. Paul, Minn.: Family-Centered Project, Greater St. Paul Community Chest and Councils, Inc., 1959, Appendix A.

Greenwood, Ernest. "Social Work and Social Science—A Theory of Their Relationship." *Social Service Review,* 29 (March 1955).

Guttenberg, Marcia, Jusan Salasin, and Deborah Belle, *The Mental Health of Women.* New York: Academic Press, 1980.

Haring, Barbara L. *1975 Census of Requests for Children Welfare Services.* New York: Child Welfare League of America, 1975.

Henry, William E. et al. *The Fifth Profession; Becoming a Psychotherapist.* San Francisco: Jossey-Bass, 1971.

Kahn, Alfred S. *Social Services in the United States: Policies and Programs.* Philadelphia: Temple University Press, 1976.

Kahn, Alfred S., and Sheila B. Kamerman. *Not for the Poor Alone.* Philadelphia: Temple University Press, 1975.

Kenniston, Kenneth. *All Our Children—The American Family Under Pressure* (Report of the Carnegie Council on Children). New York: Harcourt Brace Jovanovich, 1977.

Le Masters, Ersel, and John Defrain. *Parents in Contemporary America—A Sympathetic View,* Homewood, Ill.: The Dorsey Press, 1983.

Maas, Henry. "Behavioral Science Basis for Professional Education: The Unifying Conceptual Tool of Cultural Role," in *Proceedings of the Interdisciplinary Conference.* Washington, D.C.: Howard University, School of Social Work, May 1, 1957.

Magazino, Carmine J. "Services to Children and Families at Risk of Separation," pp. 211–254 in *Child Welfare: Current Dilemmas, Future Directions.* Ed. Brenda McGowan and William Meezan. Itasca, Ill.: Peacock Press, 1983.

Meyer, Carol. "Editorial," *Social Work,* 29,6 (November 1984), 499.

Moroney, Robert M. *The Family and the State: Considerations for Social Policy.* New York: Longman, 1976.

Morris, Robert, and Delwin Anderson. "Personal Care Services: An Identity for Social Work." *Social Service Review,* 49 (June 1975), 157–174.

National Academy of Sciences. *Toward a National Policy for Children and Families.* Washington, D.C.: National Academy of Sciences, 1976.

National Association of Social Workers. "Special Issue on Conceptual Frameworks." *Social Work,* 22 (September 1977); 26 (January 1981).

National Association of Social Workers News (May 1970), 7; (May 1986), 1.

National Conference on Social Welfare. *The Future for Social Services in the United States—Final Report of the Task Force*. Columbus, Oh.: National Conference on Social Welfare, 1977.

Neel, Ann F. "Trends and Dilemmas in Child Welfare Research." *Child Welfare,* 50 (January 1971), 25–32.

Nye, F. Ivan. *Role Structure and Analysis of the Family*. Beverly Hills, Cal.: Sage Publications, 1976.

O'Connor, Gerald G., and Mary L. Waring. "Toward Identifying the Domain of Social Work—A Perspective." *Arate,* 6,4 (1981), 1–12.

O'Neill, Onora, and William Reddick. *Having Children: Philosophical and Legal Reflections on Parenthood*. New York: Oxford University Press, 1979.

Ozment, Steven. *When Father Ruled—Family Life in Reformation Europe*. Cambridge, Mass.: Harvard University Press, 1983.

Packman, Jean. *Child Care: Needs and Numbers*. London: George Allen & Unwin, Ltd., 1968.

Parsons, Talcott, and Edward Shils (eds.). *Toward a General Theory of Action*. Cambridge, Mass.: Harvard University Press, 1954.

Perlman, Helen Harris. "Social Components of Casework Practice," in *Social Welfare Forum*. New York: Columbia University Press, 1953.

Pollock, Linda. *Forgotten Children: Parent–Child Relations from 1560 to 1900*. New York: Cambridge University Press, 1983.

Rice, Robert M. *American Family Policy—Content and Context*. New York: Family Service Association of America, 1977.

Richmond, Mary. *What Is Social Casework?* New York: Russell Sage Foundation, 1922.

Rothman, J. *Social Research and Development,* Englewood Cliffs, N.J.: Prentice Hall, 1980.

Sarbin, Theodore. "Role Theory," in *Handbook of Social Psychology*. Ed. Gardner Lindzey. Cambridge, Mass.: Addison-Wesley Publishing Co., 1954.

Schorr, Alvin L. (ed.). *Children and Decent People*. New York: Basic Books, 1974.

Shyne, Ann W., and Anita G. Schroeder. *National Study of Social Services to Children and Their Families*. Rockville, Md.: Westat, August 1978.

Speigel, John. "The Resolution of Role Conflict Within the Family," in *A Modern Introduction to the Family*. Ed. Norman Bell and Ezra Vogel. New York: The Free Press, 1960.

Steiner, Gilbert. *The Children's Cause*. Washington, D.C.: The Brookings Institution, 1976.

Steiner, Gilbert. *The Futility of Family Policy*. Washington, D.C.: The Brookings Institution, 1981.

Turitz, Zitha. Quoted in Helen Hazen, "Distinctive Aspects of Child Welfare." *Child Welfare* (July 1957).

Turitz, Zitha. "Development and Use of National Standards for Child Welfare Services." *Child Welfare,* 46 (May 1967), 245–253.

U.S. Department of Health, Education, and Welfare, Children's Bureau. *Child Welfare Services in 25 States—An Overview*. Washington, D.C.: U.S. Government Printing Office, 1976.

U.S. Department of Health, Education, and Welfare, Children's Bureau. *System of Social Services for Children and Families—Detailed Design*. Washington, D.C.: U.S. Government Printing Office, 1978.

U.S. Department of Labor, Women's Bureau. *The Outlook for Women in Social Work—General Summary*. Social Work Series Bulletin, No. 235-8. Washington, D.C.: U.S. Government Printing Office, 1952.

United Nations, Department of Economics and Social Affairs. *Training for Social Work—An International Survey*. New York, 1950.

United Nations, Department of Economics and Social Affairs. *Parental Rights and Duties Including Guardianship*. New York, 1968.

Werble, Beatrice. "The Implications of Role Theory for Casework Research," in *Social Science Theory and Social Work Research*. Ed. Leonard Kogan. New York: National Association of Social Workers, 1960.

Wilensky, Harold, and Charles Lebeaux. *Industrial Society and Social Welfare*. New York: Russell Sage Foundation, 1958.

2

Perspectives on Child Welfare Services

Factors in the Development of Child Welfare Services

The social problems that are the proper concern of child welfare are as old as mankind. The orphaned, the illegitimate, the abandoned, and the handicapped child have always been with us. In the first section of the first book of the Bible, Genesis, we encounter a problem of sibling rivalry in the conflict between Cain and Abel and concern on the part of the parents, Adam and Eve, about the trouble in their family. Yet professional social work is less than a century old. The question arises, then: How were the problems of child welfare handled before this network of services was developed? Several significant factors help to explain the emergence of the field of child welfare social work:

1. The development of a humanitarian ideology and the growing rejection of previously acceptable solutions.
2. Economic and political changes that reinforced and supported changes in ideology.
3. The increased specialization of social institutions.
4. The "discovery" of childhood.
5. The rise in status of the family and the child.
6. Changes in the "arithmetic of child production."
7. The increase in scientific knowledge.
8. Changes in the legal status of the child.

Ideology and Alternative Solutions

Child welfare services are one part of the total social system. It is to be expected then, that such services reflect the nature of the economy, the family organization, and the position of the child in the particular society. Each society deals differently with the problems of children and families. Children have always been responded to with some ambivalence: wanted and welcomed under certain circumstances, yet an inevitable burden and inconvenience with whom scarce resources had to be shared. Children evoke resentment and hostility as well as love and affection. Potential child welfare problems have been dealt with by contraception, abortion, infanticide, and abandonment.

One general solution to the problems of child welfare is to eliminate them at their source. Dead children present only a very limited problem—that of disposal. And children who are never conceived do not present even this small problem. So the first line of defense against the development of problems in child welfare is contraception. The solution is an ancient one, but one that has always aroused controversy. Judiciously applied, it prevents the problem presented by unwanted children. Indiscriminately applied, however, it threatens the continued existence of the group.

Himes (1936) summarized his detailed historical study of contraception by noting that

> contraception, as only one form of population control, is a social practice of much greater historical antiquity, greater cultural and geographical universality, than commonly supposed, even by medical and social historians. Contraception has existed in some form throughout the entire range of social evolution—that is, for at least several thousand years. The desire for, as distinct from the achievement of, reliable contraception has been characteristic of many societies widely removed in time and space [p. xii].

Egyptian papyri, dating from 1850 B.C., that give contraceptive prescriptions and instructions are part of the elaborate documentary evidence in support of the thesis (Himes, 1936, p. 61). Primitive contraceptive measures were mechanical in nature. A moistened sponge was used as a diaphragm and coitus interruptus— "thresh inside, and winnow outside" was practiced. Prolonged breast feeding, which extended over a two- or three-year period, had contraceptive effects.

If contraception failed, as it often did, people resorted to socially sanctioned abortion or infanticide. Thus, in a study of some three hundred and fifty societies, Devereaux (1976) found abortion practiced in almost all of them. In some forty of these societies, the practice was approved wholly or conditionally, or was regarded with neutral tolerance (pp. 361–371). Lecky (1869) notes, with reference to abortion, that "no law in Greece or in the Roman Republic or during the greater part of the Empire condemned it" (p. 22).

Abortion before "quickening" or before "ensoulment" or before the fetus was "formed," all of which was generally regarded as taking place sometime late in the first trimester, was not seriously questioned in Europe or America until the nineteenth century.

If abortion failed, or if it was not applied in time, infanticide, particularly in selective instances, was then resorted to in dealing with child welfare problems at their source.

Lecky (1869) also points out that "infanticide was almost universally admitted among the Greeks, being sanctioned and in some cases enjoined upon what we should now call the 'greater happiness principle,' by the ideal legislations of Plato and Aristotle and by the actual legislations of Lycurgus and Solon" (p. 27). Reviewing the relevant, and sometimes contradictory, source material, Hands (1968) concludes that "there can be little doubt that the Hellenistic age, with its high incidence of poverty, witnesses infant exposure on a large scale" (p. 69). In the Roman Empire, Lecky (1869) notes, "Pagan and Christian authorities were united in speaking of infanticide as a crying vice of the Empire and Tertullian observed that no laws were more easily, or more constantly evaded, than those which condemned it" (p. 29).

"Gynecology," a text by the Greek Soranus, written in the second century A.D., had a section entitled "How to Recognize a Newborn That Is Worth Rearing," which implies infanticide. The child who was worth rearing was "born in due time" was "perfect in all its parts," and had a "vigorous" cry.

Sumner (1959) indicates that "for the masses, until the late days of the Empire, infanticide was at most a venial crime" (p. 319).

The author of a recent historical survey of infanticide notes that it "has from time immemorial been the accepted procedure for disposing not only of deformed or sickly infants but of all such newborns as might strain the resources of the individual family or the larger community. . . . It was thought altogether natural that proletarians, poverty stricken, and hopeless, should [thus] protect themselves from further responsibility" (Langer, 1974, pp. 354–355). (See also Williamson, 1978.) Stone (1977) suggests that:

> There is a long history of fairly generalized infanticide in western Europe going back to antiquity, when it seems to have beeen extremely common. How far it remained a common deliberate policy for legitimate children in the Early Modern period is still an open question, although it is suggestive that as late as the early eighteenth century in Anjou, priests were instructed to warn their congregations in a sermon every three months of the mortal sin of killing an infant before baptism [pp. 473–74].

Reviews of the more limited literature available from the Far East show the same procedures to have been widely utilized there in maintaining a balance between available resources and mouths to be fed. A Chinese official speaking of Shonsi province in the mid-1860s says:

> I have learned of the prevalence of female infanticide in all parts of Shonsi. . . . The first female birth may sometimes be salvaged with effort but the subsequent births are usually drowned. There are even those who drown every female baby without keeping any. . . . This is because the poor worry about daily sustenance . . . and the rich are concerned over future doweries [Ho, 1967, p. 60].

A British official reporting in 1856 on the situation in one section of India said, "Infanticide is not only occasionally practiced here but uniformly and universally and unblushingly acknowledged" (Panigrahi, 1972, p. 37).

Infanticide often took the form of abandonment. The parents who were unable to care for their child left him to be found and accepted by others who could. If the child was not found or if no one accepted him, nature took its course and neither the family nor the society was further concerned with the child. Parents unable to care for a child, but still concerned over his fate, might choose to abandon him in a well-frequented spot to assure his being found. Thus, in Rome, children were brought to a "column near the Vilabrium, and these taken by speculators who educated them as slaves or very frequently as prostitutes" (Lecky, 1869, p. 30).

The abandonment of infants was resorted to for a long time throughout Europe. Caulfield (1931), analyzing the situation in eighteenth-century England, contends that "dropping [abandoning] of infants was an extremely frequent occurrence during this period and was accepted by all classes without comment" (p. 31). McCloy (1946), in a detailed study of social welfare problems in eighteenth-century France, notes that "one of the saddest features of eighteenth-century French history was the wholesale abandonment of infants by their parents" (p. 238).

"The number of abandoned children is astonishing. As many as one-fourth of all newborn babies and half of all illegitimate newborn babies in Paris were abandoned each year at the state-run and only foundling home in that city" (Fuchs, 1984, p. 1).

The frequently told tale of Hansel and Gretel is, in effect, a story of attempted abandonment; the motivation of the stepmother may be primarily psychological (the rejection of the children of the former wife), but the father accedes to her plan to "lose" them because there is not enough food for both parents and children.

Another historian, reviewing the period between the ninth and thirteenth centuries in Western Europe, indicates that since the poor "were most directly and constantly at the mercy of the demonic cycles of famine, malnutrition, disease and death," their "children were by far the most common victims of parental negligence and despair, of abandonment, exposure and even infanticide, which must be counted among the major threats to young life in this period" (McLaughlin, 1973, p. 119).

The tour—the revolving box built into the front of the church in which the parent placed the child to be received by the church—permitted the anonymous abandonment of children. By 1830 there were some 230 tours throughout France, with 336,297 infants abandoned from 1824 to 1833.

Although abandonment is a private solution that may leave the community with the problem of providing for the unwanted child, it proved to be a public solution as well. The mortality rates for abandoned children were much higher than the already high rates for nonabandoned children. In Elizabethan England many parents were

> too poor to support their children at all and parish records contain numerous entries concerning the desertion of unwanted children who were found dead on the roads from exposure and starvation—a practice which continued among the poorer classes up to the nineteenth century [Pinchbeck & Hewitt, 1969, p. 22].

As late as 1873 the "medical register of New York reported 122 infants found dead in streets, alleys, rivers and elsewhere" (Radbill, 1968, p. 10).

Abandoned children placed in foundling hospitals died at such a rate that although it is likely that the existence of such facilities decreased the number of infanticides, it "may be questioned whether they diminished the number of deaths" (Lecky, 1869, p. 37). The abandoned children dying in the various hospitals in France, notes McCloy (1946), "probably varied at the frightful rate of 50 to 80 percent, by cities" (p. 248). Such resources for abandoned children may be subject to Mead's (1962) accusation that they were "only a prolonged, ritualized method of disposing of the infant for whom nobody wishes to care."

Jonas Hanway, an eighteenth-century English child welfare researcher of parish workhouses that received young children for institutional care, made efforts to follow up the history of each child placed. He found that in many parishes "the mortality of all children received was 80 to 90 percent or, if you please, upon those received under twelve months old, 99 percent" (Caulfield, 1931, p. 140).

From 1781 to 1790, a total of some 20,000 children had been received at the Dublin Foundling Hospital. In 1791, a Parliamentary committee reported that some 17,000 of these had died in the hospital nursery or with their country wet nurses (Robins, 1980, p. 29).

A French doctor, Villerme, suggested that children's foundling homes should bear the inscription "here one kills children at public expense." "Instead of being a protection to the living the institution became, as it were, a charnel house for the dead." (Dunn, 1973, p. 390). (See also Fairchilds, 1976, p. 84.) Another report notes that "in the years 1817–20 the number of foundlings in charge of the Paris Hospital (and interestingly about a third of them children of married couples) was about equal to a third of all babies born in Paris during that period. Of the 4779 infants admitted in 1818, 2370 died in the first three months" (Langer, 1974, p. 359). It was justifiable, then, to call institutionalization of abandoned children "legalized infanticide."

Among the poor, another solution was the selling of children:

> In the days of the Later Roman Empire, the spectacle of children being sold became a sight so common that various regulatory measures against it were passed. The Justinian Code of 534 contained a provision by which a father whose poverty was extreme was allowed to sell his son or daughter at the moment of birth, and repurchase the child at a later date [Boussard & Boll, 1966, p. 493].

Migration was employed throughout earlier period in history in dealing with problems of indigent children. In the classical Greek period, poor families and poor children were transported to colonies on the Italian peninsula.

The seventeenth and eighteenth centuries' need for labor in the new territories such as Australia, North America, and the Caribbean provided the opportunity for wholesale "dumping" and indenture of English orphans, part orphans, abandoned children, and children of poverty-stricken families. Dependent, parentless children were shipped to work on sugar plantations in Barbados and Jamaica.

The motives for these expedients indicate the relationship between these "preventive solutions" and potential problems in child welfare. Devereaux (1976) states, in reviewing the motives for abortion, "Economic factors play a tremendously important role in the motivation for abortion. . . . Anyone familiar with the tremendous economic burden which primitive women carry and with the great poverty of many groups [will understand this]" (p. 13). Miller (1928) notes the relationship of abortion and infanticide in primitive societies to available food supply: "The child must enter the world only when his presence will not crowd or necessitate unwanted economy"; thus infanticide and abortion "are means of restoring the equilibrium between human numbers and natural resources" (p. 30). Sumner (1959) notes that these practices are "primary and violent acts of self-defense by parents against famine, disease, and other calamities of overpopulation which increase with the number which each man and woman has to provide for" (p. 313). Hobhouse (1951) concurs: "To primitive man having a severe struggle for existence, the advent of a new mouth to feed is often a serious matter. Hence infanticide is not an uncommon practice in the uncivilized world and coincides with genuine and even devoted attachment to the child if once allowed to live" (p. 339).

Infanticide and abandonnment resulted more frequently from hardness of life than from hardness of heart. "Urgent want and the sterility of the niggardly earth" were the reasons advanced by the people of Radash Island who allowed each woman only three children, requiring her to kill each succeeding child (Payne, 1916, p. 37). Bossard and Boll (1966) note this same motive for Greek support of infanticide when they repeat the story of the Greek father who, when asked, "Why do you expose your child?," answered, "Because I love the children I have" (p. 614). Hands (1968) points out that "after Emperor Constantine and Theodosius had forbidden the practice of infant exposure, it became necessary to admit the parents' right in extreme cases of poverty to sell a new-born child" (p. 71).

Reviewing the literature on the history of the family, the historian Stone (1981) notes that "evidence is mounting that infanticide by deliberate or semideliberate neglect or direct abandonment to almost certain death in foundling hospitals was perhaps the most important element in family limitation by the poor in early modern Europe" (p. 59).

Child abandonment "was seen by many people in sternly economic terms as one of the few practical expedients which they could reasonably take if the rest of the family were to survive. For desperate parents faced with the unwelcome prospect of an additional mouth to feed, the available alternative was tragically few" (Forrest, 1981, p. 7).

An extraordinary jump (in abandoments) in 1693–94 was a reflection of one of the worst economic crises of the ancien régime (Delasselle, 1978, p. 48). Abandonment rates were correlated with the average nationwide price of wheat in France during the eighteenth century. "Price fluctuations directly influenced the number of abandonments" (p. 71).

Poverty of resources is only one of the motives. If caring for the child is likely to be difficult, abortion, infanticide or abandonment might be employed. If, for instance, the mother dies in childbirth, the child, too, may be killed:

> In Australia the infant is buried alive with its mother or killed and burnt with her corpse. The Semang of the Malay Peninsula wrap mother and child in one shroud, the child being placed on the mother's breast with its face downward. . . . Among the Chiloctin Indians of Canada the death of a mother during delivery leads to burying the child in its cradle with the mother [Miller, 1928, pp. 39–40].

Somewhat similarly, the illegitimate child was aborted or killed not only because of the shame attendant upon the birth of such a child but also because the mother would have found difficulty in caring for and rearing him (Devereaux, 1976, pp. 245–289).

Lacey (1968) notes that in ancient Greece, "The largest number and highest proportion of exposed infants will have been those produced by unions formed out of wedlock. . . . (p. 66). The 1890 edition of the *Encyclopaedia Britannica* notes, "The modern crime of infanticide shows no symptoms of diminution in the leading nations of Europe. In all of them it is closely connected with illegitimacy in the class of farm and domestic servants" (quoted in Bakan, 1971, p. 42).

"Eighteenth-century France was a society where (child abandonment) was taken for granted as a normal event in the lives of the poor, one that was made necessary by grinding poverty—It was tacitly assumed that thousands of illegitimate babies would have to be abandoned each year and unless the child died as a result of exposure it was unlikely that any serious communal charge would be brought against the mother" (Forrest, 1981, p. 118).

A royal edict in 1556 in France "obliged a pregnant unmarried woman to declare her condition to the local magistrate who was in truth to question her as to when, where and by whom she was made pregnant. These *Déclarations de Grossesse* ('Declarations of Pregnancy') were primarily designed to prevent infanticide and shame women out of conception outside of marriage" (Fuchs, 1984, p. 5).

For analogous reasons, deformed or defective children are done away with in some societies. This obviates, once again, a problem in child welfare that is likely to result from the failure of a child to perform adequately expected social roles.

"Among the Indians on the Amazon River, the child was exposed to a test for a right to survival, as all infants immediately after birth were submerged in a stream, but the deformed child was never pulled out again" (Miller, 1928, p. 48). Sumner (1959) quotes Seneca as referring to the "killing of defective children as a wise and unquestioned custom," and Seneca is seconded by Pliny in this (p. 319). Aristotle, too, thought that defective children should be put to death, and the exposure of sickly children among the Spartans is well known. The Roman Twelve Tables clearly stipulated that deformed children were not to be given care (Bennett, 1923).

Abandonment and infanticide of handicapped children were also consequences of the belief that such malformations were the result of witchcraft, God's curse, or mystical influences. Birth of twins was regarded as an ill omen. Twins presented a special problem because such a birth doubled the burden of care and the number of mouths to be fed. Hence, twin births often resulted in infanticide in some societies. For the same reason, children who are born while an older child is still very dependent may be killed because the simultaneous burden of child care is too great. Thus, among the Pima, ". . . if a woman gets pregnant while lactating, she aborts by pressure on the belly. The unborn is sacrificed to the interests of the previous baby 'which the mother loved more because she could see it' " (Devereaux, 1976, p. 310).

Plato's idea was that "men over fifty-five and women over forty should not procreate," and if they did, the child should be aborted or killed, because older parents are not likely to live long enough to see their children become independent. The prevention of childbearing by older parents reduces the problem of dependent orphans.

The child who was difficult to care for because of the death of the father was also a candidate for infanticide as a solution: "In the Hellenistic law of Egypt, after the death of the husband, a marriage-contract is annulled and the widow is empowered to expose her expected child" (Cameron, 1932, p. 108).

Thus the principal candidates for infanticide and abandonment were most likely to be those children who presented the greatest problems in child care: the physically deformed and mentally retarded children and children of illicit, irregular, difficult or impermanent relationships. Such children and such situations are candidates for child welfare services today. Because there were no child welfare services until relatively recently, other alternatives, such as infanticide or abandonment, were employed. A gradually changing ideology regarding the care of dependents, the handicapped, and the deprived, however, made these solutions progressively more unacceptable.

On the other hand, concern for the needs of the less privileged, less capable members of society is not a modern phenomenon. The Code of Hammurabi and the Old Testament provide humanitarian admonitions about caring for people in need.

The Old Testament is filled with repeated exhortations to "open Thine hand wide unto Thy poor brother." The ancient Hebrews were subject to a triennial tithe raised on the property of each family for the benefit of strangers, widows, and orphans. "Greece in the age of Plato provided funds for soldiers' orphans and free medical service for poor children. The famous *pueri alimentarii* in Rome during the period of the Empire was a special semi-governmental service for the charitable maintenance of the children of indigent citizens" (Seligman, 1930, p. 375).

Concern for the dependent and the deprived became one of the central values of Christianity. Christianity preached the sanctity of all human life—even that of the fetus in the womb. This meant that both infanticide and abortion were sinful. Reinforcing and supplementing these theological presuppositions was the humanitarian ideology of the Enlightenment, which provided a secular foundation for the rights of the child.

As a result, some of the previous solutions to child welfare problems—infanticide, for instance—became ideologically inadmissible. But, when society makes such solutions unacceptable, it must provide alternative solutions. At this point, the necessity for child welfare service becomes evident. This relationship is revealed in the history of Western Europe and is noted by Sumner (1959), who says that as a "corollary of the legislation against infanticide, institutions to care for foundlings came into existence" (p. 319). In fact, Constantine, influenced by Christian teaching, in A.D. 315 promulgated a law "to turn parents from using a parricidal hand to their new-born children and to dispose their hearts to the best sentiments. . . ." (Payne, 1916, p. 204). Thus, decreasing the prevalence of abandonment and infanticide by parents who were destitute and desperate was one of the principal objectives of such early provision for public support. The fourth-century Theodosian code included the following directives.

> A law shall be written on bronze or waxed tablets or on linen cloth, and posted throughout all the municipalities of Italy, to restrain the hands of parents from infanticide and turn their hopes to the better. . . . We have learned that provincials suffering from scarcity of food and lack of sustenance are selling or pledging their children. Therefore, if any such person is found who is sustained by no substance of family possessions and is supporting his children with hardship and difficulty, he shall be assisted through our fisc before he becomes a prey to calamity [Quoted in Naphtal & Meyer, 1955, pp. 383–384].

Early in the Christian era, in the second and third centuries, when church revenues were as yet limited, a third of the church revenues were assigned to charitable purposes (Chastel, 1857, p. 95). Orphans, "exposed children," and widows of church members were explicitly mentioned as among those deserving aid as well "as mothers fallen into indigence by the charges of a too large family" (p. 100).

One of the earliest forms of aid to dependent children in nineteenth-century France was termed "Temporary Aid to Unwed Mothers to Prevent Abandonment" (Fuchs, 1984, p. 41).

Hospitals sheltered the sick, the aged, dependent children, and the homeless, and monasteries dispensed relief. Each monastery had an appointed officer, an eleemosynarius, who daily dispersed food and money to those who came for help, in accordance with the rules of the monastic order. Hospitals were both hospitals for the sick and almhouses for the destitute.

As early as A.D. 325, the Council of Nicaea prescribed that xenodochia be established in each Christian village—institutions that had the responsibility of aiding the sick, the poor, and abandoned children (Constantelos, 1968).

Church officials made efforts to find some charitable family to care for exposed and abandoned children. They were in effect engaged in a program of foster home recruitment.

There were some early beginnings of organized child welfare services in medieval Europe. The first asylum for abandoned infants was established in Milan in 787, and in 1160 Guy de Montpellier established the Order of the Holy Spirit for the care of foundlings and orphans. However disastrous the outcomes, as we have noted previously, the foundling homes were an organized attempt to provide an alternative to infanticide and haphazard child abandonment.

The objective that prompted the establishment of the London Foundling Hospital in 1741 accurately reflects the rationale for the establishment of institutions for children everywhere. The objective, as stated in the hospital's charter, was to "prevent the murders of poor miserable children at their birth and to suppress the inhuman custom of exposing new-born infants to perils in the streets and to take in children dropped in churchyards or in the streets or left at night at the doors of church wardens or overseers of the poor."

Trexler (1973) notes that Pope Innocent III "instituted the hospital of the Santo Spirito in Rome because so many women were throwing their children into the Tiber" (p. 99).

In 1712 Peter the Great decreed that Russian monasteries must act as "orphan nourishers" and that "unwed mothers [must] deposit their infants in these asylums through specially built windows which shielded them from the gaze of the receiver instead of 'sweeping these babies into unsuitable places'" (Madison, 1963, p. 84).

Gradually more and more institutions, hospitals, and asylums became available in which to house abandoned and neglected children. A variety of alternative measures arose that predate professional social work: resources such as the workhouse for children, "outdoor relief" (relief outside an institution through a cash grant or the like) for parents who were unable to care for their children, and an elaborate system of "binding out" or apprenticeship training entered into while the child was still very young.

The point, however, is that when a society rejects abortion, infanticide, and abandonment as solutions, it must assume the responsibility to care for the child whose life it has saved. This, then, suggests the need for developing the services and resources that constitute the field of child welfare.

Over time, there were gradual changes in the way the problems of parents vis-à-vis child were met. Changes were made in the ideology that determined the acceptability of certain procedures; from a series of more lethal solutions to more benign solutions, from infanticide, exposure, and abandonment to care and maintenance to ensure survival. Although there were previously sporadic, unsystematic acts of personal benevolence provided for some needy children, there was a gradual assumption by the collectivity of responsibility for care of the child. What was earlier a personal obligation became a religious duty and then a civic duty. Charitable acts were redefined as rights to which needy parents and children were entitled. Such help then became more systematic, more formal, more organized, more institutionalized.

There has been a movement from decisions regarding providing assistance that has large discretionary philanthropic components to statutory regulations that assume more equitable provisions of help in response to legally enforceable rights. Needs become rights and rights become entitlements. There was a shift from thinking about child welfare problems as misfortunes to thinking about these problems as injustices.

Economic and Political Changes

A humanitarian attitude toward the child cannot prevail if the economic situation is unfavorable. Even after the attitude of the Christian church toward children became dominant, instances of child abandonment and child neglect rose during periods of economic distress. Sumner (1959) observes that "in reality nothing put an end to infanticide but the advance in the arts increased economic power by virtue of which parents can provide for their children" (p. 321).

When the great masses of people lived in general wretchedness and a step away from disaster, there was little sympathy generated for the special plight of starving homeless children. Affluence makes affordable the implementation of humanitarian impulses and ideology, and growth in industrial and medical technology made it possible.

The Industrial Revolution, by increasing the productive capacity of all adults, made it possible for them to care for a greater number of dependent children. Society could now afford to support and care for physically handicapped children, mentally defective children, and dependent children whose own parents were unable to care for them.

In analyzing the relationship of the productivity of adults to the needs of the child population, Bossard and Boll (1966) note, "The status of childhood, as reflected in school, work, and child-care standards of all kinds, represents in large measure the relative size of the nonproductive and productive groups and the capacities of the latter to serve the former" (pp. 590–591).

Political factors also increased the need for some community-supported institution to deal with child welfare problems. Social institutions evolve in order to perform a useful function in society, and to permit society to operate more effectively and with less conflict. Child welfare services meet the needs of children, but they also reduce the threat of social disequilibrium. Humanitarian and ethical considerations are often secondary to the need to maintain social stability by providing the necessary social arrangements (in this case, the child welfare services) to deal with problems of social dysfunctioning that did affect a significant number of children (Atherton, 1969). Failure to provide child welfare service entails a possible increase in the number of children who might become delinquent or develop physical and/or mental illness and therefore constitute both a threat to, and a burden on, society.

Finally, the enfranchisement of nonpropertied classes gave political power to a growing number of poor parents who needed the help of the community in implementing their parental role. Ignoring the needs and demands of this growing group of voters would present an internal political threat.

Failure to provide child welfare services poses an external threat that derives from the dependence of modern nation states on a citizen army for national security. In World Wars I and II, very sizable percentages of men in the United States and Britain were found to be physically, mentally, or emotionally unfit for service, partly as a result of childhood deprivation.

Greater technical control over contraception, which led to continued declining birthrates coupled with continued relatively high infant mortality rates, created anxiety about declines in population. The result was an increasing concern about the threat to society associated with a declining population. This gave impetus to the development of infant welfare programs (Dyhouse, 1978).

Support of a network of services for children at even a minimal level of adequacy and consistency could not depend on erratic private, charitable contributions. It required the emergence of a national, secular state, the centralization of power, and the emergence of a national bureaucratic apparatus.

The development of nation-states permitted collecting and distributing revenues that were needed for the allocation of adequate resources for the welfare of dependent children. One impetus for this development is socioemotional, whereas another is administrative.

Until almost the second half of the nineteenth century, most people's identification was geographically very provincial, very circumscribed. People did not think of themselves as part of a French nation-state, but rather as part of Brittany or Languedoc or Gascony; not as part of Spain but as part of Asturias or Andalusia or Catalonia. Perhaps more accurately, people identified with their particular town and its immediate area. Willingness to pay taxes to support the establishment of a network of child welfare services required in some measure a shift of identification from the local area to the nation-state.

Furthermore, a complex network of adequate large-scale child welfare services required the development of a communications and managerial technology and the availability of a bureaucracy to make it work. One cannot imagine effective operation of the current OASDI program in the United States mailing 37 million checks a month or an AFDC program distributing 10 million checks a month without the telephone, rail, truck, and plane network that weaves the county together; without the apparatus to print and sort checks; and without the bureaucracy that is engaged in processing applications and making the countless decisions required for the operation of the system.

Both the nation-state ideology and the technical-managerial apparatus are products of a recent historical period that makes possible the development and support of large-scale child welfare services.

Specialization of Social Institutions

Another factor in the development of child welfare services is the increasing specialization of social institutions and the change, or loss, of functions of some institutions. Among such institutions are the family, religious organizations, and the primary group neighborhood.

Over a long period of history, most people lived in small rural groups in which they grew up together, knew one another intimately, and kept contact with neighboring families over a number of generations. The extended family, including collateral relatives as well as nonrelated but familiar members of the community, assumed some responsibility for maintaining children whose parents were unable to fulfill their role obligations. Problems of child welfare were frequently solved through mutual aid. In underdeveloped countries today, where the organization of communal life resembles that of Europe hundreds of years ago, mutual aid from neighbors and kin is still a frequent source of help. In such societies "there are plenty of orphans but no orphanages." A recent report by the United Nations Children's Fund, describing the effects of urbanization in underdeveloped countries, notes that poverty, hunger, and disease are often a traditional part of the child's life in the rural community, "but there, at least, the child has his natural protection and will seldom be abandoned by the community even if his parents die. In the new environment of the urban slums things are quite different." The impersonal relationships of the city replace the personal relationship of the rural community and require the introduction of child welfare organizations (Sicault, 1963, p. 23).

In an urban society, siblings often live at a distance from each other and from their parents and grandparents. Nor is the obligation of mutual support as firmly sanctioned—the obligations to one's nuclear family take clear precedence over those to one's extended family.

The early parish group, too, was a closely knit primary group—the unifying factor being the sharing of significant beliefs. The parish "was a mutual aid group, the members of which looked out for each other especially during the era of persecution" (Queen, 1922, p. 576). The parish group has lost much of this cohesiveness. Even if it had not, the secularization of modern society would exclude many people from such aid.

The feudal system, with its elaborate structure of rights and obligations, was a more formally contractual kind of mutual aid. As de Schweinitz (1947) says:

> under feudalism there could, at least in theory, be no uncared-for distress. The people who today would be in the greatest economic danger were, in the Middle Ages, presumably protected by their masters from the most acute suffering. . . . Insurance against unemployment, sickness, old age was theirs in the protection of their high lords [p. 2].

Mutual aid was also a feature of another kind of primary group—the occupational family: the guild, which operated as an extended family to protect its members from risks to security. When guilds were small and their members knew one another intimately, they felt a responsibility for one another's welfare and made provisions for the care of the widows and children of deceased fellow members. Queen (1922) points out that, for guild members:

> there was a close community of interest and a sharing of the daily experiences of life. The guild itself was just a primary group with intimate personal relations. . . . This being the case, it was quite natural that we should find the guilds assumed responsibility for the bereaved widows and orphans of their members, educated the latter, and, if they were girls, provided them with dowries [p. 282].

Ultimately all the institutions that had assumed responsibility for dealing with child welfare problems diminished their involvement in such problems or else found that social change made previous solutions untenable. With the growth of an urbanized population, with the growing mobility of the population attendant upon industrialization, the "neighborhood" is less apt to denote a primary group, so that mutual aid through this source becomes less certain. Both the guilds and their modern counterparts—trade unions, professional associations, merchants' and manufacturers' associations—were institutionalized around a primary function other than child welfare. As this primary function—concern with the problems of the occupation—became more complex, the institutions became less concerned with secondary, nonessential functions. The church's religious function took precedence over its eleemosynary concerns, especially after the Reformation, which reduced the resources available to the church generally and, consequently, the resources that it could make available for charitable purposes. Steinbicker (1957) notes that "poor relief was the first ecclesiastical institution to be secularized after the religious revolt."

These changes meant that a new institution had to be developed to deal with child welfare problems. The diminished interest and capacity of institutions such as the neighborhood, the extended family, the guild, and the church in dealing with child welfare problems created a need for child welfare social work, which was designed to fill the gap.

The neighborhood, the extended family, the church, and the occupational group still contribute to helping with child welfare problems. Such resources exist side by side with the more formal professional resources and services, and they are frequently explored by the individual before approaching the professional services. However, only child welfare social work is explicitly concerned with child welfare problems as its primary, specific, institutional responsibility.

At the same time that many social institutions are disencumbering themselves of concern for the child, one institution—the nuclear family—has developed a more specialized concern for the child. As the modern family loses some aspects of its traditional functions—production, protection, recreation, and so on—the problems and satisfactions of childrearing are becoming more central. With such specialization in family function, children become of increasing importance.

The Discovery of Childhood

"Childhood" is a social construct, and there are great variations among societies in how childhood is defined. Only gradually did a recognition develop of childhood as a clearly differentiated life period and children as a distinct demographic group with a special nature, unique needs, and capacities. Along with the gradual idealization and sentimentalization of the child, there was a tendency to revise the priority given children's needs within the family system, and children became people of special concern and care.

The recognition of childhood as a distinct period of life is now so widely accepted that it is difficult to realize that it was not always so. Biological differences, of course, forced a recognition of the child as a being distinct from the adult. But childhood was believed to be a short period "of transition which passed quickly and was just as quickly forgotten" (Ariès, 1962). Throughout most of history, life has been exceedingly short for most people and "maturity" had to be reached early in life. Remember that Romeo was not yet sixteen, and Juliet not yet fourteen, when their fervent, tragic romance was in flower. When the average life span did not exceed thirty years, childhood could not be prolonged. "Conscious of the brevity of life . . . parents were eager to introduce their sons and daughters into the adult world at the earliest possible moment" (Pinchbeck & Hewitt, 1969, p. 198).

The economic position of the family and of society was such that the individual had to become self-supporting as quickly as possible. Children began to earn their living at six or seven years of age. According to a statute enacted in England in 1535, "Children under fourteen years of age, and above five, that live in idleness and be taken begging may be put to service by the government of cities, towns, etc., to husbandry; or other crafts of labor" (quoted in Bremner, 1970, p. 64). William Blake, the poet, began working in a silk mill in 1764, when he was seven years old. An advertisement in *The Baltimore-Federal-Gazette* of January 4, 1808, stated, "This [Baltimore Cotton] manufactory will go into operation this month, where a number of boys and girls from eight to twelve years of age are wanted" (quoted in Trattner, 1970, p. 27).

Stone (1977) notes that in the sixteenth and seventeenth centuries children "lower down the social scale left home at between seven and fourteen to begin work as domestic servants, laborers, or apprentices but in all cases living in their masters' houses rather than at home or in lodging" (p. 107) and "that the period of close parent–child bonding was a relatively short one at all levels of society" (p. 116)—

and, one might add, that the responsibility of parents for the care of dependent children was relatively short in duration. This brevity of childhood would limit the development of child welfare problems (also see Shorter, 1975, p. 26).

Older people in small English villages, recounting their childhood as they lived it in the latter part of the nineteenth century, note how early in life childhood ended for them: "The children helped in their own way. We started field work when we were five or six. . . . I was living in Deplen when I first started ploughing. I was fifteen years old and I had been at work for seven years. . . . I lost my father when I was nine so I had to think about work" (Blythe, 1969).

The English Factory acts of the early nineteenth century, the first legislation concerned with limiting child labor, set age limits for children working at nine years of age. In Tudor England the age of discretion was nine years of age. A person older than nine, like an adult, could be persecuted for a capital crime and could give sworn evidence in court (Hoffer & Hull, 1984, p. XIII). Even though there were many chronologically young people, fewer people were defined as children. Earlier in our history the word *child* referred more often to a kinship relationship rather than an age status.

For a long time, there was no distinctive child dress; it was merely adult dress in miniature, so that there was little symbolic demarcation of childhood and children were very early absorbed into the world of adults. Ariès (1962) says that:

> in medieval society, the idea of childhood did not exist. . . . The idea of childhood is not to be confused with affection for children: it corresponds to an awareness of the particular nature of childhood, that particular nature which distinguishes the child from the adult, even the young adult. In medieval society, this awareness was lacking [p. 128].

Historians of childhood and the family, such as De Mause (1974), Ariès (1962), Shorter (1975), and Stone (1977), provide different explanations for the same phenomenon. All point however to the gradual emergence of childhood and the child within the family as a protected object of affection and sentimental concern during the nineteenth and twentieth centuries. (See also Zelizer, 1985.)

Just as there is a relationship between greater concern for children and the development of a more productive economy, so there is a relation between the development of modern education and the idea of childhood. The view of childhood as an important and significant period evokes a need for a formal, highly developed system of education, which, in turn, reinforces and supports the idea of the distinctiveness of childhood. Age grading becomes part of the way of categorizing people in society.

Defining a person as an adult who is responsible in some measure for self-support at seven or eight years of age and not significantly differentiated at work or play from older people, substantially reduces the number of "children" in the population and the need for child welfare services. Socially expanding the definition of "child" to age eighteen or twenty-one, and regarding such people as dependent and requiring some measure of support, increases the need for child welfare services.

The Status of the Family and the Child

The status of the child is closely related to the status of the family as an institution vis-à-vis other institutions through which people seek the satisfaction of basic needs. The family is, for the child, the only significant social institution to which he or she is related for the first years of his or her life.

The family, although always an institution of importance, came to be overshadowed by other institutions to which adults owed allegiance. The church, the state, the peer group, the army, the guild, the occupation—all have frequently taken priority over the family; and individuals have devoted their primary attention, energy, and concern to these other areas of their lives.

Ariès (1962), in talking about the family in the Middle Ages, indicates that it fulfilled a function—it ensured the transmission of life, property, and names—but it did not penetrate very far into human sensibility (p. 411). According to Ariès (1962), the medieval family "existed in silence: it did not awaken feelings strong enough to inspire poet or artist. We must recognize the importance of this silence—not much value was placed on the family" (p. 364).

More recently, however, the family has become the significant center of our lives. Religion, occupation, the friendship of peers, the state—all are subservient to the family. We invest more of ourselves in the family than in almost any other social institution. The fact that family—and the nuclear family at that—has assumed such central importance in our lives results in an increase in the importance of the child, who is a member of this, but of no other, significant social institution.

Changes in the Arithmetic of Child Production

Another important factor that affects the status of the child is what Bossard and Boll (1966) has aptly termed the *arithmetic of production:* the relationship between birthrate and child mortality rates. For a long time in the history of mankind, many children were born and many died. Parents expected that a high percentage of the children they conceived would be with them only a short period of time:

> In the late 17th and early 18th centuries about half of the recorded children of French peasantry were dead by the age of ten and between half and two-thirds by the age of twenty. In the cities, conditions were worse still, and in London in 1764 forty-nine percent of all recorded children were dead by the age of two and sixty percent by the age of five [Stone, 1977, p. 68].

Spoiled food, polluted water, fire, famine, and infectious disease such as typhoid, dysentery, influenza, smallpox all took their toll on physically vulnerable infants.

Throughout most of European history parent–child relationships were not very intense and were of relatively short duration: "The family was a loose association of transients constantly broken up by the death of parents or children or the early departure of the children from the home" (Stone, 1977, p. 81).

In a society in which a parent's relationship with his or her own children was casual, distant, and brief, with little emotional intensity, it is not very likely that the community will invest very much in providing for the needs of children in general. The segment of society composed of children had low priority in public consciousness and conscience: "The omnipresence of death coloured affective relations at all levels of society by reducing the amount of emotional capital available for prudent investment in any single individual, especially in such ephemeral creatures as infants" (Stone, 1977, p. 65). "Indifference was a direct and inevitable consequence of the demography of the period" (Ariès, 1962, p. 39).

To invest emotionally in children was to invite problems, for people were so often doomed to see children die. If one was to hope to retain psychological stability, one had to maintain an attitude of restrained attachment toward children. Because the child was a transient in the family and because, even if he or she survived, the period of his childhood was short, anything peculiarly identified with childhood was relegated to secondary importance. The family was adult-centered, adult-directed, and adult-oriented. Mitchell (1970), noting these factors, concludes that:

> it is probable that the modern concept of parental love is of comparatively recent origin, and that throughout most of history interest in, and affection for, infants and young children has been at a much more superficial level. . . . If parents were thus unable to develop deep feelings of affection towards their offspring, they would be unlikely to entertain such sentiments toward the children of their neighbors [p. 301]. (In contradiction see Pollock, 1983; Fraser 1984).

Hence it was difficult to get public support for child welfare services to meet the needs of the children of the community.

With advances in sanitation, in public health, and in medicine and with the greater availability of more effective contraceptive measures, fewer children were conceived, but those who were conceived had better chances of surviving. One could allow oneself to develop a deep feeling for the few children one had, with confident hope that such love would not inevitably be followed by sorrow and pain at the child's untimely death. And because children came to be, for many, the results of careful and restricted planning, they were apt to be highly valued when they were born.

The Scientific Revolution

Advances in scientific knowledge have not only increased the productivity of each worker so that fewer productive adults can support a larger number of dependents, but they have also made possible the development of a science of child welfare. Greater scientific concern with the problems of child development and the results of such studies have intensified the importance of childhood. Freud was among the first to call attention to the crucial important of childhood in shaping human destiny, and his work was followed by a host of other studies that examined and clarified the effects of childhood experiences. The years of childhood began to assume greater importance and significance vis-à-vis other periods of life.

The Freudian emphasis on childhood was supported by other scientific advances. The Darwinian point of view that stresses continuity in development, points to the importance of beginnings, and insists that the past is structured in the present became a solidly accepted concept. Childhood assumed an unprecedented importance and became a matter for serious study by child development specialists such as Stanley Hall, E. L. Thorndike, William James, and John Dewey.

But such studies, and the growth in knowledge that resulted from them, did more than heighten the importance of childhood; they also gave rise to a new profession. Professions develop in response to a human need, but the attempt to meet the need can be professionalized only if there is a scientific body of knowledge available to form the basis for professional action. The studies regarding childhood and children became the basis for such journals as *Child Development, Child Welfare; Courrier, The International Journal of Child Welfare, Children Today*—none of which existed one hundred years ago. Ultimately this material is codified and organized so that courses are taught, textbooks are written, and educational programs are developed for the training of professionals in specialties concerned with various aspects of childhood. Thus the expansion and elaboration of special knowledge concerned with welfare services for children made possible a professional field of specialization in child welfare.

The fact that a science of childrearing was developing was the result of a particular interest in childhood and in itself reenforced the idea of childhood.

Legal Status of the Child

The legal status of the child has changed over time, making explicit and re-inforcing the more favorable position of the child in society. At one time, children had the status of chattel: "The child's position in the average family of the masses was for centuries roughly in this order: father, cattle, mother, child" (Despert, 1965, p. 15). Hunt (1969) points out that comparing children to animals was "an image that appears throughout seventeenth-century literature on children. In a total sense the small child was an intermediate being, not really an animal (although he might often be compared to one) but on the other hand not really human either" (p. 125).

Early European legal systems gave little, if any, recognition to the rights of the child. The amphidroma ceremony in ancient Athens, performed on the fifth day after birth, symbolized the actual social birth of the child. Before then, the child, alive but not actually a member of the community, could be disposed of. The Roman concept of *patria potestas* gave the father almost absolute power over his children. In early Germanic law, the child was under the *Munt* of the father, which gave the father authoritative control. Neither the Roman nor the Germanic code made explicit the obligations of the father to maintain and protect the child. Parents in pre-Revolutionary France could obtain a *lettre de cachet* permitting imprisonment of a disobedient child, and the Napoleonic Code clearly defined the subordinate position of the child.

With the gradual acceptance of the rights of the child, parental authority has come to be defined "as a series of rights and obligations on the part of both parents which are to be exercised for the good of the child and which are balanced by a sense of correlative rights and obligations on the part of the child" (United Nations, 1968, p. 11). Parental power, previously exercised in domination over the child in the interests of parents, is now more likely to be regarded as a trust to be employed in the best interests of the child.

From the earlier status of the child as chattel to his or her parents who had absolute right to the child's services, and earnings and control over the child's person and possession, we have come to recognize the child as an independent entity entitled to certain freedoms and rights in response to his or her own needs and interests.

The very real change in attitude toward the status of children is exemplified by the fact that in November 1954 the United Nations General Assembly unani-mously adopted and proclaimed a Declaration of the Rights of the Child, which affirms the rights of the child to have special protection and to enjoy opportunities and facilities that will enable him or her to develop in a healthy and normal manner; to have a name and a nationality from his or her birth; to enjoy the benefit of social security, including adequate nutrition, housing, recreation, and medical services; to grow up in an atmosphere of affection and security, and, wherever possible, in the care and under the responsibility of parents; to receive special treatment, education, and care if one is handicapped; to be among the first to receive protection and relief in times of disaster; to be protected against all forms of neglect, cruelty, and exploitation; and to be protected from practices that may foster any form of discrimination. The 1970 White House Conference on Children affirmed these rights (U.S. White House Conference, 1970).

In the 1970s, stimulated in part by the civil rights and the women's movements, there emerged a "children's rights" movement. A literature became available (Gottlieb, 1973; *Harvard Education Review,* 1973; Wilkerson, 1973; Gross & Gross, 1977; Vardin & Brody, 1979). Laws were codified and specific organizations developed, such as the Children's Defense Fund, concerned with championing children's rights. The American Civil Liberties Union publishes a monthly newsletter concerned with children's rights—the *Children's Rights Report.* And 1979 was designated by the United Nations as the Year of the Child.

The child advocacy movement has accepted the responsibility of speaking for children as a silent, unrepresented, politically disenfranchised minority. A problem arises from the fact that in many respects according rights, entitlements and privileges to children is a sum zero procedure. Increasing the rights of children vis-à-vis the parents necessarily involves a reduction in the parent's prerogatives and degree of control over the child.

Whereas over historical time the balance has moved in the direction of increasing children's rights and diminishing parental rights, the rights of parents are still currently given priority. Unless there is some compelling reason for interference, the state accords the parents the primary control of the parent–child relationship.

The distance we have come, however, is exemplified by the kind of questions that are currently the subject of children's rights controversies. Questions regarding the limits of children's rights currently concern the rights of a "mature" minor to request family planning services, access to abortion, rights of emancipation from parental authority, rights to sue parents, and right to resist commitment for treatment of mental or behavioral disorders.

Legal changes reflect attitudinal changes toward children. During the last five hundred years society has gradually become more child-oriented, there has been an emotional intensification in the relationship between parents and children, and the child has come to be perceived as a person in his or her own right rather than being viewed for his or her instrumental contribution to family functioning:

> While a residual affection between mother and child—the product of a biological link—has always existed, there was a change in the priority which the infant occupied in the mother's rational hierarchy of values. Whereas in traditional society the mother had been prepared to place many considerations—most of them related to the desperate struggle for existence—above the infant's welfare, in modern society, the infant came to be most important [Shorter, 1975, p. 5].

Development of a Child Welfare Services System

All of these factors—ideological changes, changes in productivity, the specialization of institutions, the discovery of childhood, the arithmetic of child production, the changing of status of children—have contributed to the development of a special system, the child welfare services system. This system has developed gradually, and as has been noted some kind of child welfare was practiced long before an identifiable occupational group was assigned this particular responsibility. Community efforts took the form of the *pueri alimentarii* of ancient Rome, almshouses, and the "outdoor" poor relief granted to indigent people living in their own homes. For instance, outdoor poor relief in the late eighteenth century in New York City was offered in response to recurrent problems of child welfare: "husband in prison . . . husband has broke his leg . . . a house full of small children . . . husband at sea . . . husband bad fellow . . . sick and distressed . . . her husband has abandoned her and she has broke her arm" (quoted in Mohl, 1971, p. 25). And side by side with these public efforts to relieve distress and want, we have always had the private acts of goodwill by benevolent individuals and the activities of organized voluntary groups. Thus Hands (1968) notes the distribution of corn and oil and cash in ancient Greece and Rome through the auspices of wealthy benefactors, and in early-nineteenth-century New York City child welfare problems were ameliorated by such private benevolent groups as the Society for the Relief of Poor Widows with Small Children, the Female Assistance Society, the Orphan Asylum Society, the New York Society for the Prevention of Pauperism, and the Humane Society. (The latter, incidentally, dealt with a social situation that no longer presents a problem for child welfare—the imprisonment of a father for debt.)

Professional child-welfare workers were preceded by such gifted and dedicated "amateurs" as Saint Vincent de Paul, who fought during the reign of Louis XIII for the estalishment of institutions for abandoned children; Vives, who in 1525 wrote *On the Relief of the Poor,* the first modern textbook on social work in public welfare; Thomas Carom, who in 1739 energized London into building a hospital for foundlings; Lord Ashley, earl of Shaftesbury, who tirelessly fought for passage of the Factory Acts, limiting the worst abuses of child labor in nineteenth-century England; Florence Kelly, who performed similar yeoman service for American children; and Dr. Bernado and Charles Loring Brace, who nightly collected the abandoned, homeless, parentless children off the streets of nineteenth-century London and New York, respectively.

It would be difficult to measure the influence these individuals had on stimulating a sense of greater community responsibility for services for children. But having noted that the profession of social work and the formal organization of a network of child welfare services was preceded by a variety of preprofessional "social work" efforts to deal with child welfare problems, efforts that existed alongside such responses as contraception, abortion, infanticide, abandonment, child labor, and neighborly mutual aid as procedures for dealing with such problems, it might also be noted that the reverse situation exists today. Alongside the formal system of professional child welfare services, society currently employs many of the classical solutions in dealing with child welfare problems. A rich network of neighborly, volunteer mutual aid exists side by side with the formal agency resources responding to child welfare problems. When a single car accident in Mount Kisco, New York, killed two women and critically injured four others, it left twenty young children permanently or temporarily motherless. Neighbors volunteered to help with baby-sitting and child care and to collect funds for the families (Grehen, 1960). Ethnic, racial, and religious associations exist to offer mutual aid. Self-help groups to which people with common problems are affiliated provide social, psychological, and instrumental support to members.

On a larger scale, the informal network of child care in the black community, existing side by side with the formal agency-care system, is another example of the continuation of earlier historical methods of dealing with child welfare problems before the development of social work. Records of this kind of care go back to the 1860s "in the attention ex-slaves gave to black children orphaned by the sale and death of their parents, by parental desertion and wartime dislocation" (Gutman, 1977, p. 224). Analyzing the 1970 census, Royster (1975) concluded that "informal caring for children is more prevalent in the black community—the overall proportion for categories of children under 19 living with heads of families other than their own parents is much higher for blacks than it is for whites" (p. 3-3).

On the other hand, the ancient procedure of child abandonment as a personal solution to child welfare problems is still frequently employed. An adoption worker in Pakistan, reporting on the work of his agency in 1977, says, "Ours is a voluntary organization which looks after parentless children found abandoned in dustbins, on street corners and at hospitals" (Ispahani, 1977, p. 45). In September 1983, the *New York Times* reported that "every month in Brazil more than 100 infants are left in police stations, hospitals or on downtown streets by mothers apparently hoping that the outside world has more capacity to care for them than they do."

Even infanticide exists as a twentieth-century procedure for dealing with child welfare problems at the source. A government policy of euthanasia in Nazi Germany sanctioned the deliberate killing of defective children; "idiot and malformed children" were killed by "doses of morphine, chloride, and luminol" at the children's institutions to which they had been sent (Meitscherlich, 1949, p. 114). A court trial in 1963 in Liège, Belgium, was concerned with the "mercy killing" of a child born deformed as a result of the mother's having taken Thalidomide (a tranquilizer) during her pregnancy. The family had prevailed upon their doctor to prescribe a lethal dose of a sleeping drug, and the family and the doctor were charged with homicide. During the trial the city of Liège officially sanctioned a referendum of the local population: of those who voted 16,732 approved the infanticide, while only 938 disapproved. The doctor and the family were acquitted (Gallahue, 1963).

A research report published in 1973 noted that of 299 consecutive deaths in a special-care nursery for seriously malformed infants, 43 (14 per cent) were related to the withholding of treatment (Duff & Campbell, 1973). In these instances it had been decided that even if the children could be maintained alive, which was doubtful in many instances, such very defective infants would have "little or no hope of achieving meaningful humanhood" (see also Kohl, 1978).

In a book entitled *Playing God in the Nursery*, Lyon (1985) reviewed the sizable number of "Baby Doe" situations—deformed or defective infants allowed to die despite the medical technology available to prolong their lives. (See also Shelp, 1986.)

The most important of the classical measures currently applied to potential child welfare problems are contraception and abortion. Contraception has widespread community acceptance, and abortion is legal in some countries, illegal but openly tolerated in others, illegal and not tolerated in still others, but common everywhere.

The current widespread support for family-planning facilities is indicated by the fact that whereas public expenditures for such programs were close to zero in 1965, by 1985 such expenditures amounted to 398 million.

Between 1973, when the U.S. Supreme Court legalized abortion, and 1982 some 13 million abortions were performed in the United States. Many of the abortions were financed by public funds through the Medicaid program.

The American Experience

In view of the crucial factors that determine the status of children and the valuation of the child, American child-centeredness becomes explicable. The American ethos is grounded not only in the Judeo-Christian tradition but more particularly in the Humanist tradition of the Enlightenment. A humanitarian concern for the dependent and the underprivileged is congruent with our tradition. A highly industrialized nation, the United States is in an economic position to implement its philosophical attitude. Our pragmatic, secular orientation has resulted in a widespread acceptance of contraceptive measures and the idea of family planning. This attitude, along with our highly developed medical and public health resources, has resulted in the kind of arithmetic of child production associated with high valuation of the child. Our respect for scientific research has led to acceptance, however ambivalent, of the teachings of child-care experts—all of whom have a vested professional interest in heightening the status of childhood.

Some particular aspects of the American experience further help to explain the great emphasis on the child in America. In a nation of immigrants, the experience of parents—related to another time and another place—tends to be discounted. Indeed, parents often had to turn to their children for help in learning the language and customs of their adopted country.

In a tradition-oriented society, the past is revered, and its custodians—parents and grandparents—are respected. In a society oriented toward change, the emphasis is on the future, and hopes, ambitions, and attention are lavished on the child as the future toward which we strive. That orientation of the American culture reinforces the importance of children and childhood, and our positive regard for the individual and for individual development makes the child, not the family, the vehicle for fulfilling the future and reaping its rewards.

The democratic tradition, of necessity, is reflected in family organization. It is difficult for the ethos to sanction autocracy within the family. The tendency toward congruence presses the family in the direction of democratization of internal relationships, suggesting, within the limits of practicability and biological competence, a greater voice for children in the family and less domination of children by parents.

The family that has production as one of its key functions can permit only limited democracy. Somebody has to be "boss" of a productive unit to ensure that the necessary work will be done smoothly, efficiently, effectively. When the family becomes primarily a unit of consumption, family organization can support a greater measure of democracy. This is one of the changes that has taken place in most American families within the last fifty years. With such change has come the possibility of a more democratically organized family and a concomitant enhancement of the status of children.

Childhood has been extended by a perception of the child as a dependent needing protection, by age segregation, and freedom from responsibilities for self-support until he or she was well into adolescence.

During the late nineteenth and early twentieth centuries, American middle-class culture became more child-centered. There gradually emerged a perception of children as precious beings of special importance who needed particular protection and careful prolonged preparation for adulthood. Children represented the future and the embodiment of the American dream. The change involved a decrease in the economic productivity and contribution of the child and an increase in his or her affective and sentimental importance. The change in the validation of the child was aided by an increasing emphasis on the cult of domesticity.

Motherhood and home became increasingly sacred symbols of a well-ordered society and children were the primary objects of attention of the motherhood and home cult (Ashby, 1984, p. 6; Zelizer, 1985).

Affluence of the middle class, which was a growing sector of the population, permitted the removal of many children from the world of work. This, in combination with the concept of the malleability and perfectability of children and conviction in possibility of rational improvement of the young, prolonged the period of education and dependency. This prolongation of a protected childhood was further made possible by industrialization, which required fewer children in the work force and came to require a more educated work force.

These are some of the special factors, unique to the American experience, that have reinforced the growing importance of children and childhood over a period of time. These special considerations give American culture a filiocentric orientation conducive to the development of child welfare services.

A word of caution might be uttered at this point. Whereas families might be child-centered, the society in general, as it formulates public policy, might not be, and is not in the case of the United States. What each family wants for its own children might not be, and is not, what the community is willing to provide for children in general.

Recapitulation

In recapitulation, parent–child problems that today are the concern and responsibility of social work child welfare services have been pervasive and essentially similar throughout history. There is overlap between the past and the present in the ways in which the community deals with such problems. What has changed has been the emphasis, selection, and choice in the utilization of solutions available. Present approaches have been utilized in the past but to a lesser extent; past solutions are utilized in the present to a lesser extent.

The movement has been from the utilization of more lethal to more benign approaches; from private to collective responsibility in dealing with the problems; from personal charity in response to religious motivations to community recognition of rights and entitlements in response to secular sociopolitical motivations; from unstructured informal response to need to more formal structured, scientifically based response to need; from a restrictive definition of need to a broader definition of need. There has been a change from help by self-appointed volunteers who represent institutions that have a principal purpose other than child welfare to the institutionalization of child welfare in an apparatus specifically assigned this responsibility and employing specially designated personnel assigned to implement these services.

The Current Context of Child Welfare Services

Introduction

A historical overview gives us some perspective on the factors that have stimulated changes in child welfare resources and services, but it is also helpful to consider the changes currently taking place in American society that may influence the need for child welfare services.

Historical trends are both more revealing and more relevant than annual statistics, which, because they are ephemeral and soon outdated, are cited here only sparingly, and for illustrative purposes. Throughout, *children* refers to individuals seventeen years of age or younger; *nonwhite* includes Indian, Oriental, as well as black children (black children make up, however, about 95 per cent of this group).

Rather than cite source of statistics at each point we would like to note that most of the statistics cited were derived primarily from government sources such as Bureau of the Census: *Statistical Abstract of the United States, 107th Edition, 1987*. Current Population reports Particularly Series P-20 "Population Characteristics," and series P-23 "Special Reports," and the monthly and annual reports of the National Center for Health Statistics, Division of Vital Statistics.

Additional statistical data come from a number of specialized nongovernmental publications, namely reports from the Population Reference Bureau (Bouvier, 1980; Reid, 1982; O'Hare, 1985), the Family Service Association of America (1984) and the Children's Defense Fund (1984, 1985). Additional specific references are cited where appropriate.

The Child Population

In 1985 there were some 63 million children in the United States—26.5 percent of the total population of 239 million Americans. *The trend is toward a drop in the proportion of children to total population.* In 1960, 36 per cent of the population of the country was composed of children seventeen years of age or younger.

These figures reflect *the trend toward lower birthrates during the 1965–1985 decades*. This was true for both white and nonwhite women. The birthrate among nonwhite women, however, was still somewhat higher than that among whites. As a consequence, the median age of the nonwhite population was younger than that of the white group. A larger proportion of the total population of nonwhites, therefore, was concentrated in the younger age groups. This meant a somewhat disproportionate nonwhite population of risk for child welfare services.

From 1960, when the birthrate—the number of births per 1,000 population—was 23.7 the birthrate dropped to 15.7 in 1985, close to the lowest in our history and below the replacement level for zero population growth.

Through the rest of the twentieth century, we can expect a very gradual increase in the number of children in the population. From some 63,000,000 children under the age of 18 in the United States in 1985 it is anticipated that the number of children will increase to some 68,395,000 by 1995.

The anticipated increase does not result from any increase in the birthrate or the number of children desired or expected by women. It is a result of the increase in the number of fecund women in the population, which reflects the very high number of births between 1947 and 1964, the baby boom period. Given the very large increase in the number of fecund women in the population during the last decades of the twentieth century, the anticipated increase in the number of children is very modest.

In 1960, 36 million women aged 15–44 gave birth to 4.3 million babies. In 1983, 54 million women aged 15–44 gave birth to 3.6 million babies. If the women in 1983 were giving birth at the same rate as their own mothers 23 years earlier there would have been 6.5 million children born in 1983, 80% more than the number actually born. The echo boom that followed the coming to maturity of the baby boomers of the 1947–1964 period was, in effect, only a boomlet.

Although all groups in the population reflect this very long-term trend toward smaller families, black women express a preference for slightly larger families than do white women, and the birthrate is highest among Hispanic women who were not high school graduates. The lowest expected fertility rate occurs among white women with five or more years of college.

The baby boom that occurred between 1947 through 1964, a period of reproductive splurge, has been termed a demographic aberration. During the 1970s and 1980s the country returned to the long march toward lower fertility rates, fewer children, and smaller families that has been the steady trend throughout our history—a trend unbroken except for the baby-boom period. It is a trend that is likely to continue, except for modest, inconsequential yearly perturbations, for the rest of this century.

The trend is also toward the postponement of marriage and childbirth and toward a modest increase in intentional childlessness. Between 1960 and 1986 the proportion of population 25 to 29 years old who had never married increased from about 20.8 per cent to 41.7 per cent among men and from 10.5 to 28.1 among women.

Foregoing childbearing for a career during the time when a woman is in her twenties does not necessarily imply an increase in childlessness, but rather delayed childbearing. Concern about the biological clock and the increasing difficulty of a woman to conceive with increasing age has prompted an increase in childbearing among career women as they approach their thirties. In 1970, 7.3 first births were recorded for every thousand women aged 30–34. By 1982, this had doubled to 14.6 per 1,000 women in that age group. Baldwin and Nord (1984) note that Census Bureau findings indicate that fewer women aged 30–35 said in 1982 that they wanted to have no children as compared with women in that age group in 1976 (p. 9)

Although there have been previous periods of postponed marriage and delayed childbearing in our history, (for instance, during the 1930's depression) the present trend, based on higher educational expectations and women's employment following more prolonged schooling, is likely to be more long-term.

Reflecting the increasing percentage of both men and women in higher education and the postponement of entrance into the work force, there has been an increase in the age at which people first marry. The median age of first marriages for women in 1970 was 20.6 years and 22.5 for men. By 1986 this was 23.3 years for women, 25.5 for men.

Although many of the men and women who are delaying marriage and childbirth are likely ultimately to marry and have children, for some the decision to defer marriage and childbirth may imply a decision not to marry and to remain childless. Further, marrying later in life suggests that this group has less married reproductive time available to have children, so that late marriage is likely to result in lower birthrates.

Intentionally childless marriages are becoming a more acceptable option. The National Organization for Non-Parents is widely disseminating studies that show that some 10 per cent of parents regret having children and that married couples are happier when they are childless. One of the organization's slogans, from the prophet Isaiah, is "Thou hast multiplied the nation but not increased the joy."

Ambivalence toward children is fueled by the increases in the costs of rearing children. A very large percentage of the disposable income of families has to be allocated to children in an intergenerational transfer of funds within the family. A detailed review of such costs led Espenshade (1984) to calculate that the "average American family spends $82,400" per child from birth to age 18 (p. 5). College education costs for the 18–22-year-old-child increase the expenditure substantially to close to $100,000.

Postponement of marriage does not imply a negation of marriage. The marriage rate has been and continues to be consistently very high. As a consequence by age 45 almost 95 per cent of all men and women have experienced marriage. However, with the postponement of marriage it is anticipated that in the near future a larger percentage of the population, possibly 8 or 10 per cent, will remain single.

Between 1970 and 1983, "the number of women under age 45 cohabiting with an unrelated male—shot up more than 700 percent" (Glick, 1984, p. 209). The Census Bureau developed a new category for this group of couples—"persons of the opposite sex sharing living quarters."

Despite the explosive increase, this group constituted only 4.1 per cent of all couple households in 1986. Cohabitation tends to be in the nature of a prolongation of courtship, and many of the cohabiting women manifest traditional attitudes toward marriage.

Although the change in the total population of children represents the total possible pool of potential child welfare social agency clients, changes in particular subsets of children are of greater relevance. These include children living below the poverty level and children living in one-parent families. Such children are generally disproportionately represented in the child welfare social work caseload. Both of these vulnerable subsets of the children's population have been increasing during the 1970s and 1980s despite the fact that the overall population of children had declined from high levels of the 1960's. The percentage of children living below the official poverty level increased from 13.8 per cent in 1969 to 20.1 per cent in 1985. The percentage of children living in one-parent families increased from about 9 per cent in 1960 to 23 per cent in 1985. Concentrations of poverty-stricken children and children in one-parent families were disproportionately higher among minority populations. Consequently, although there will be a smaller total pool of children in the 1990s than in 1970s for which services might be needed, a growing proportion of the smaller pool is likely to require services because of increases in a variety of family factors resulting in family disruption. Therefore there may be a continuing and, speculatively, even a greater need for child welfare services in the 1990s.

The trend is toward a more favorable child-dependency ratio.

With the movement into young adulthood of the baby-boom generation and the decline of the percentage of children in the population, the dependency ratio decreased.

The projected increase in the proportion of the population consisting of productive adults coupled with the decrease in the proportion of the population consisting of young children results in a more favorable child-dependency ratio—proportionately fewer dependent children being cared for by a proportionately larger population of productive adults. When the ratio of dependent children to productive adults is low—when there is a favorable child-dependency ratio—the community is in a more advantageous economic position to provide adequate services for those children who need them.

Some of the decrease in dependent children as a ratio of productive adults was offset by an increase of dependents at the other end of the age continuum. An increase in the number of aged dependents tended to increase the dependency ratio. Overall, however, since 1960, the dependency ratio has been moving in a more favorable direction. In 1960, 100 workers supported 173 children and senior citizens. By 1980, the ratio was 100 producers to 133 dependents and by 1990, it is anticipated that the ratio will be 1:1.

The experience of the 1970–1980 decade graphically illustrates however the fact that the dependency ratio is only one factor in a complex configuration determining the allocation of community resources. A lower dependency ratio means that an increasingly larger productive pie needs to be shared among a smaller ratio of dependent groups. But which of these dependent groups will receive preferential treatment in the allocation of the pie depends on political power and ideology.

The allocation of resources to care for dependent groups in the population is primarily a political decision that follows a country's economic capacity. There is, currently, intensified competition for the increasingly limited tax dollar. In this competition, demographic trends might ultimately have crucial significance. A declining percentage of the population consists of children; a growing percentage of the population consists of the aged. The aged, as contrasted with children, not only have the vote but are organized effectively politically. The actuality is that in allocating the more limited tax funds available, the needs of the dependent aged take precedence over the needs of the population of dependent children and affect adequacy of funding for child welfare services.

The relatively advantaged, more favorable political position of the aged vis-à-vis children is likely to be sustained and even increased during the rest of this century. This is then likely to be translated into public policy that continues to favor the needs of the aged relative to the needs of children.

Whereas the population of the aged will grow modestly but steadily during this period, the political power of this group will be augmented by the bulge of baby-boom adults in their forties and fifties who will be concerned with their needs in their immediate senior citizenship future. At this age few of this group will have dependent children as their focus of concern. They will no longer be part of a constituency for children. They will, however, be concerned not only with their own immediate future needs, as noted previously, but also about the needs of their own dependent aged living parents. Contrawise there has been a reduction in the proportion of adults in the population engaged at any one time in the responsibility of childrearing and consequently a reduction in the proportion of the population who are directly and immediately concerned with the needs of dependent children (Helmick & Zimmerman, 1984). This tends to reduce the size of the constituency that at any one time is in support of public funding to meet children's needs.

Whereas there is an increasing readiness on the part of the community to accept responsibility for meeting the needs of the dependent aged, the family rather than the community is still seen as having the primary responsibility for meeting the needs of children. The aged are elderly through no fault of their own. Nobody "chooses" to be aged. But children are the "fault" of parents, who could have chosen not to have them if they could not support them. Private in-family transfers for the support of children have more sanction than public collective transfers for such support.

Partly as a result of public policy that favored meeting the needs of the dependent aged in preference to meeting the needs of dependent children over the 1965–1984 period, "the well-being of the aged improved greatly whereas that of the young has deteriorated" (Preston, 1984, p. 44). Although the percentage of the aged living in poverty has decreased steadily since 1970, the percentage of children living in poverty has increased since that time. As Gottschalk and Danzinger (1984) note in their review of the poverty trends, "The elderly experienced the largest drop in poverty of any demographic group" (p. 206).

The principal income transfer programs affecting the aged Old Age (OASDI) and Supplemental Security Income (SSI) were cushioned against inflation, and federal programs were uniform throughout the country. In contrast Aid to Families of Dependent Children (AFDC) program, the principal income transfer program affecting dependent children, was not indexed, and the amount of support varies from state to state. The adequacy of income transfer programs affecting the aged was greater than the adequacy of comparable programs affecting children.

Although public programs targeted on low-income children, such as AFDC, have been cut back, programs favoring the aged have expanded. In 1985, governmental per capita expenditures for the aged were some three times greater than they were for the children.

In response to sociopolitical considerations, the dependent aged have been, and are likely to continue to be, given preferred access to public funding when competing with dependent children for available resources.

As noted, the changing components of the dependency ratio move in opposite directions, a smaller number of dependent children and a larger number of dependent aged—so that the ratio of dependents to producers tends, for the immediate future, to be favorable. However, the dependent aged make a greater imposition on public funds and resources than do dependent children, for whose care and support the family takes primary responsibility. Even if the dependency ratio does not become skewed in an unfavorable direction in the immediate future, the fact that a larger component of the dependent population consists of the aged increases the demands on the productive nondependent population.

The Unwanted Child

We owe the child the right to be conceived and born as a wanted child if we are to reduce the need for child welfare services. The deliberate decision to conceive implies readiness to have a child and favorable conditions for his or her reception. An unwanted pregnancy may reflect unfavorable child-care conditions and, hence, increases the probability of need for child welfare services. Family planning involves not only limiting the number of children but also timing their arrival to coincide with the family's readiness to welcome a new member.

There currently appears to be more effective family planning among all groups in the population, although a higher percentage of unwanted pregnancies occurs among nonwhites and the poor.

The illegitimately conceived child, like the deformed child, runs a high risk of being unwanted and constitutes a higher than normal potential need for child welfare services. However, as a consequence of the greater availability of family-planning counseling, genetic counseling, and abortions, the *trend is in the direction of a greater number of children being wanted at birth*. Unwanted marital fertility has continued to decline, so that by 1982 fewer than 7.8 per cent of births to married women were unplanned. This decline reduces the number of children who tax their families' capacity to care for them and who consequently constitute a potential demand for child welfare services.

Between 1973 and 1984, some 13 million pregnancies were aborted. Had these pregnancies continued to term, the population of children in 1983 would have been closer to 75 million rather than 62 million. In general, about 30 per cent of all pregnancies during the 1974–1984 decade were aborted, and about 25 per cent of all abortions involve married women. Abortion supplements family planning in increasing the likelihood that children are born wanted at a time when they are born.

By 1984, there were some 600 genetic counseling centers throughout the United States. This, coupled with the technology of amniocentesis and the availability of abortion, means that fewer children with congenital anomalies might be born.

Voluntary sterilization also decreases the number of possibly unwanted children. Such contraceptive measures have been utilized most frequently among married couples who do not want to have children or who already have as many children as they want. By 1985, nearly half of all couples of childbearing age in the United States had been sterilized (*New York Times*, February 11, 1985).

Infant and Child Mortality

Once he or she is conceived as a wanted child, we owe the child the right to life. *The trend has been toward a steady decrease in infant and child mortality.* Infant mortality rates have declined steadily from 26 per thousand live births in 1960 to 10.6 in 1984. Nevertheless, our infant mortality rate was higher than those of many other industrialized countries.

In 1983, when the U.S. infant mortality rate was 10.9 deaths per 1,000 live births, Finland's infant mortality rate was 6.2, Denmark's was 7.7, and the Netherlands 8.4. Worldwide, the United States ranked sixteenth in infant mortality (*New York Times*, March 16, 1983).

Although the infant mortality rate among nonwhites in the United States is declining, it is still consistently higher than the rate among whites, so that the chances of a nonwhite child's dying in its first year are twice as high as those of a white child's. The high infant mortality rate of nonwhite Americans would have ranked about 31 in a world listing of different countries. In this case, race is a less significant factor than poverty. It reflects the lack of adequate prenatal and postnatal medical care available to the poor, and limited access to contraceptive information and devices that would permit more desireable spacing of pregnancies.

Family Disruption: Death, Divorce, Desertion, Illegitimacy

Once guaranteed the right to life, we owe the child the opportunity to grow up in an intact home under the care of both a father and a mother. The loss of either or both parents increases the risk of the need for child welfare service.*

The trend of family disruption arising from the death of a parent hae been downward. Marrying at the median age of 23.3 in 1985 and bearing few children,

---

*At this point there is some disagreement among the two authors. While recognizing the fact that children can be adequately cared for in a variety of family arrangements—father-mother, single parent, gay and lesbian households, communal care—Kadushin feels that the most desirable, least problematic, arrangement for children is the traditional father-mother pair arrangement. He feels the community should promote the desirability of such a family arrangement in the best interest of children. The first paragraph reflects this prejudice. Martin feels that alternative arrangements are all equally desirable. Martin's phrasing of the first paragraph would be as follows. "Once guaranteed the right to life we owe the child the opportunity to grow up in an intact home under the care of a loving parent or loving parents. The loss of a parent increases the need for child welfare services." Martin also takes exception to some of the explication of single-parent household problems discussed on pp. 65–68.

the modern mother is likely to complete her childbearing phase earlier in life. This, coupled with an increase in life expectancy for both sexes, means that most parents will live through the full period of dependency of their children. Thus there has been a steady decrease in the absolute and relative numbers of orphans—from 6.5 million in 1920 some 16 per cent of the child population to 2.3 million orphans in 1985 some 3.6 per cent of the child population).

Maternal mortality, as one cause of partial orphanhood, has also been decreasing. Although decreasing along with white maternal mortality rates, the rate of maternal mortality among nonwhites was about three times higher than that among whites in 1983. Although life expectancy for both whites and nonwhites has increased, the nonwhite child is more likely than a white to lose a parent as a result of death. By 1985 life expectancy was 71.8 years for white males and 78.7 for white females, but only 67.2 years for nonwhite males and 75.2 years for nonwhite females. These differences, however, are narrowing.

The long-range trend over the course of the last 200 years of our nation's history has been for a gradual increase in the rate of divorce. More recently after an atypical short-term peak in the years immediately after World War II, there was a stabilization of the divorce rate at about 2.2 per 1,000 population between 1950 and 1965, after which the divorce rate rose steadily and rapidly, reaching to rates of 5.2–5.3 in the years between 1979 and 1981. Since then the divorce rate has gradually declined from the 5.3 rate in 1979. Although still considerably higher than the 1965 rate, *the trend for family disruption because of divorce is stabilizing*. The rate during the years 1982–1986 varied between 4.9 and 5.1.

People who get divorced do not reject marriage but merely their marital partner. Many divorced people remarry, "a triumph of hope over experience," as Samuel Johnson once said.

Separations and desertions affect almost as many children as divorce, although statistical data are difficult to compile. Marital disruption is more frequent among urban families, among low-income groups, and among nonwhites.

Income is inversely related to family disruption: as income goes down, family disruption goes up. The higher disruption rate for black families, then, is tied to the fact that a disproportionate percentage of the black population has low incomes.

The recent past has seen a reduction in the disincentives to divorce. No-fault divorce, which is now generally available in most states, made divorce not only easier but less stigmatized. At the same time, there was an increase in publicly supported legal services for the poor, which made dissolving a marriage even more possible. Laws regarding the fairer distribution of property after divorce and the recognition of the homemaker's contribution to family assets increased the possibility of economic independence after divorce. More vigorous enforcement of maintenance and child support payments also helped. Increases in advanced education and job opportunities for women reduced women's anxieties and hesitancies about divorce. More women than ever before now can be economically independent outside of marriage. There is a broader acceptance of divorce as a sanctioned alternative in response to marital dissatisfaction. Delayed childbearing and the presence of a smaller number of children in families further reduce the constraints to divorce.

There is a growing acceptance of the freedom to exercise expanding options in all areas of life. A corollary attitude is a tendency to regard interpersonal commitments as nonbinding if they conflict with an exercise of autonomy.

Although divorce has increased significantly, the total rate of marital dissolutions (the number of marriages ending in divorce or death per 1,000 existing marriages) has not changed very much during the last hundred years. Although many marriages currently are dissolved by divorce, earlier many more marriages were dissolved by death. It was not until the 1970s that more marriages ended in divorce than in death and the total rate of marital dissolution resulting from death and divorce began to actually increase. Death and divorce, however, as a course of marital dissolution have a different impact on children. Divorce is more likely to affect a dependent child than is death of a spouse, which generally occurs later in life. Although total marital dissolution caused by the additions of death and divorce may have remained relatively stable, the consequences for children in the changes in the relative contribution of divorce vis-à-vis death to the total picture have been serious.

The large numbers of children involved in divorce is significant to child welfare concerns. The annual number of divorces granted increased from 479,000 in 1965 to 1,155 million in 1983. Some 1,109 million children were involved in the divorces granted in 1983. Some percentage of these children regain a parent on remarriage of the divorced custodial spouse, but many continue to grow up in single-parent homes.

Another factor of significance for child welfare services is the *trend toward a continued gradual increase in the number of illegitimate births.** In 1984 770,000 out-of-wedlock births were reported. This number constituted 20 per cent of all live births during that year. In contrast, in 1965, there had been 291,200 births out of wedlock, 7.7 per cent of all live births. Because these figures are affected by the total number of unmarried fecund women in the population and the variations in the total number of live births, the number of children per 1,000 unmarried women aged 15 to 44 is perhaps a more accurate measure of change. This rate indicates a gradual change from 23.5 in 1965 to 31 in 1984.

Not only the overall increase in the number of nonmarital births but also the age location of such births is important. An increasing percentage of nonmarital pregnancies has been concentrated in the teenage group. In 1984, women younger than 19 contributed 34 per cent of all nonmarital births. This age group is likely to have limited maturity, experience and financial means to care for children adequately. It has been termed a situation of "children having children."

There is a significant difference in the incidence of illegitimacy among whites and nonwhites, although the difference is narrowing. In 1950 the rate was nearly twelve times higher among nonwhites than among whites. Since 1960 the rate among whites has increased, whereas that among nonwhites has decreased, so that by 1984 the latter was only about four times higher than the former. (The historical, social, and economic reasons for these differences are discussed in Chapter 8.)

The decline in the number of adolescents in the population now that the baby boomers have become older is likely to mean a smaller number of nonmarital births. However, a continuation of the increase in the percentage of teenagers

---

*The Juvenile Rights Project of the American Civil Liberties Union has suggested the terms *marital* and *nonmarital* child to replace *legitimate* and *illegitimate,* which have negative connotations. A marital child is one whose parents were married at the time of the child's birth or whose parents later "legitimized" the child by marriage or court order. Although we are in full sympathy with the point of view expressed, the use of *legitimate* and *illegitimate* in statistics and literature is so standard and the terms are used with such specific meaning that a changeover here would only result in confusion. We have therefore regretfully retained the traditional terms but use the less invidious terms *nonmarital* or *out-of-wedlock* where this can be done without changing the meaning of the statistic or the quotation.

who become sexually active will offset in some measure the decrease in the total number at risk.

An increasing number of single women are sexually active, and there is an increasing acceptance of premarital sex (*New York Times,* May 16, 1985). This, along with the delay of marriage, exposes a larger number of single fecund women to the risk of out-of-wedlock pregnancy for a longer period of time.

The trend is toward an increase in the percentage of children growing up in a one-parent home. However, the great majority of American children grow up in an intact home under the care of two parents.

As a consequence of the continued high divorce rates over a fifteen-year period, and the continued increase in the rate and number of out-of-wedlock births, there was a significantly upward trend in the number and percentage of children living in single-parent homes.

In 1960, some 91 per cent of all American children lived in a two-parent home. In 1985 only 74 per cent of all children under 18 were growing up in a home with both parents, and about one child in every five was living in a single-parent family. The group of children living with both parents included a number of subsets of children, i.e., 63 per cent of children living with both biological parents, 10 per cent of children living with one biological and one stepparent, and 2 per cent of children living with two adoptive parents.

Part of the increase in female-headed families is the result of the increasing tendency of single parents to establish an independent household unit rather than to continue living with parents or other relatives, and the increasing tendency for unmarried mothers to keep their children rather than place them for adoption.

There is a small but growing group of single women, particularly women in their thirties and lesbian women who, deliberately selecting parenthood outside marriage, become single parents by choice. This adds to the number of children living in single-parent female-headed households.

Single-parent female-headed families are formed most frequently as a result of divorce, desertion, or separation (69%); secondly, as a result of an out-of-wedlock pregnancy (25%); and least frequently because of the death of one parent (7%). The increase in single-parent families has been most rapid among young families with young children, among low-income families, and among nonwhite families. White women were more likely to be heads of families as a result of divorce or widowhood; black women were more likely to be in this status because they had never been married.

In talking about those children who did not live with two parents in 1984, we are talking about some 15.6 million children—12.7 million children living in a single-parent family headed by a mother, 1.3 million children living in a single-parent family headed by a father, and some 1.6 million children living in foster homes, in institutions, or with relatives.

Because such statistics are cross-sectional—counting children at some particular time—they underestimate the percentage of children who are likely to be affected by a family disruption at any time during their childhood.

As a consequence of high rates of marital dissolution because of divorce, separation, desertion, and, to a much more limited extent, death, plus the continuing high rates of illegitimacy, it is estimated that in the near future, only a bare majority of all children will grow up in traditional two-parent households in continuous, permanent, undisrupted contact with both of their biological parents.

It is estimated that about 45 per cent of the children born in the mid 1970s will live in a one-parent home for some period before they are eighteen.

The evident importance of these statistics is that a child in a one-parent home, or a child without parents, is a greater than normal risk for the need of child welfare services. The increase in the number of such families increases the likelihood of demand for such services.

The single-parent family is achieving acceptance as a "normal," nonpathological childrearing environment and as a respectable family form. The increase in the percentage and number of children living in single-parent households makes them progressively less atypical and more statistically "normal." There is no inherent pathology in the single-parent family form (Kadushin, 1970; Herzog & Sudia, 1973). However, it is a more difficult arrangement to carry off successfully, if only because the single-parent family is much more likely to be economically deprived.

There is a clear relationship between low family income and the single-parent family structure. If there is some question as to whether single parenthood is a hazard to the emotional and psychological development of children, there is a greater certainty that children in single-parent female-headed families face economic disabilities. Fifty-four per cent of the children in female-headed families lived below the officially defined poverty level in 1985. By contrast, this was true of only 21 per cent of children in husband-wife families.

Another testimonial to the greater need of the single-parent, female-headed family is provided by the information regarding participation in means-tested assistance programs. Whereas about 32 per cent of all children received means-tested benefits of one kind or another, this was true for twice as many or 68 per cent of the children in single-parent, female-headed households. Means tested-programs include AFDC, food stamps, Medicaid, subsidized rental housing, and free and reduced price school meals.

The clearly disproportionate percentage of female-headed families in poverty indicates that "poverty has become a matter not just of economics but also of family structure" (Rodgers, 1986, p. 17).

Lack of adequate support payments by divorced and separated fathers, lower incomes available to mothers if they do work, and inadequate assistance payments that have been further eroded as a result of a long period of inflation have contributed to the increasing poverty rates of female-headed families. Husband-wife families can provide a second adult income, an alternative not available to the single-parent family.

Within the subset of female-headed families with children, the poverty rate is greatest among the nonmarital families and least among the families disrupted by death of the father. This is of significance to the need for child welfare services, since single-parent, female-headed families formed as a result of nonmarital pregnancies are growing at a faster rate than such families resulting from divorce or death.

Because of the higher birthrates of the minority group population as compared with non-Hispanic whites, the decreasing population of children contains an increasing proportion of minority group children. Since single parenthood and associated poverty is disproportionately concentrated among minorities, the changing racial demography of the child population reflects a changing, possibly increasing, demand for services.

In addition to greater income as compared with the single-parent family, the dual-parent family has the advantage of a more assured status in our country; the laws and the mores have been developed largely in support of this kind of family structure; two parents provide the possibility of division of labor that makes the job of parenting less exhausting. The presence of two parents diminishes the possibility of an excessively intense parent-child relationship and provides an extra buffer between one parent and the child in time of crisis. In addition, the dual-parent family provides a greater variety of role models with whom the child can identify in a highly cathected relationship, and it provides a backup parent in the case of the loss or the incapacity of one parent. In our society at the present time, the nuclear, monogamous, heterosexual family, whatever its faults and shortcomings, seems to be the context in which adequate, committed, and continuous long-term care of children, involving frequent, regular, consistent, and positive parent-child interaction, seems most probable and feasible. Other variant (not deviant) arrangements—single-parent families, communal families, sequential monogamous families—are possible but more difficult contexts for providing for the needs of both parents and children.

Recent reviews of the effects of single-parent childrearing tends to highlight the potential and actual difficulties for children of such a family structure. The research tends to show that children growing up in single-parent homes are likely to be educationally and occupationally disadvantaged and have lower earnings as compared with children growing up with both father and mother. They are more likely to have childen out of wedlock, they are more likely to marry earlier, and more likely to divorce and stay divorced than children from two-parent families (Garfinkel & McLanahan, 1986). Although some of this is the result of the fact that single-parent families are the poorest of all demographic groups, there are significant noneconomic variables relating to single-parent family structure that contribute to these outcomes. Such families are not only economically poor, they are poorer than two-parent families in human resources available for care and supervision of children. The female single-parent family head may provide a role model that makes single parenthood a more acceptable option for adolescents thus reducing disincentives to extramarital births.

Eiduson (1983) studied stress on children associated with different family structures (traditional nuclear families, single mother families, unmarried parent families, communal living families). Traditional nuclear families imposed the lowest level of stress. Single mothers report greater stress and strain in their lives than do most other people (Thornton & Freedman, 1982, p. 33).

Whatever the reasons, the fact is that single-parent households are currently represented disproportionately in the caseloads of child welfare agencies, suggesting a heightened need for service on the part of such families. A nationwide study of clients of family service agencies found that "single parent families are disproportionately heavy users of family service" (Beck & Jones, 1973, p. 17).

Of the 1.8 million children estimated to have received social services from public agencies in 1977, 45 per cent were in single-parent homes (Shyne & Schroeder, 1978, p. 9). In 1976 16.4 per cent of all families were single-parent families. The percentage of single-parent families in the child-welfare agency caseloads is then clearly disproportionate to the percentage of such families in the general population. All of this is not to suggest that problems requiring child welfare services are inevitable for the single-parent family, only that they are more likely.

With the leveling off of the divorce rate following 1981, and the smaller in-

creases in the rate and number of out-of-wedlock births in the 1980s, it is anticipated that there will be a slowdown in the increase in the formation of single-
parent families.

By 1990 it is projected that 71 per cent of 64 million children will be living with
both parents, 25 per cent with a single parent, mostly mothers, and 4 per cent will
be living with neither parent. Although the rate of increase in single-parent
(usually mother only) households is expected to increase at a slower pace than
during the 1980s, the more modest rate of increase will still result in about 3
million more children living in such homes by 1990.

Poverty: A Factor in the Need for Child Welfare Services

Poverty is another factor that increases the potential need for child welfare
services. The family living on the edge of poverty faces stresses that increase the
probability of failure in parental role performance and the probability of family
disruption. We owe children the right to be wanted, the right to life, and the right
to grow up in the loving care of both a father and a mother; we owe them, further,
the right to grow up in a family that has sufficient resources to meet their basic
needs. *The trend over the past decade has been toward an increase in the percentage and number of children living in poverty.*

It is difficult to define poverty. However, the federal government uses a poverty
index that is widely accepted and that has been periodically adjusted in response
to rises in the cost of living. By 1986 the poverty index for a nonfarm family of
four was $10,990.

Between 1959 and 1973 the proportion of the U.S. population living below the
poverty level declined from 22.4 per cent to a low of 11.1 per cent. After fluctuat-
ing between 11 and 12 per cent between 1973 and 1979, the rate of poverty
increased steadily to a high of 15.2 per cent in 1983, dropping to 14 per cent in
1985, when 33.1 million Americans were living in poverty.

The picture presented remains essentially the same, except for decreasing numbers and percentages, if one employs a definition of income that includes food
stamps, Medicaid, and housing subsidies as part of income or if one excludes such
income.

The poverty population of the United States is, disproportionately a population
of children and adults in single-parent female-headed family units, and disproportionately nonwhite.

Poverty is related to some of the other contingencies that tend to increase the
likelihood that a family will require child welfare services. Divorce, separation,
widowhood (when there are young children in the family), and unmarried motherhood involve not only a problem in family organization resulting from the loss of a
father figure but also a great probability of a sharply reduced family income, as
noted previously. One of the growing pockets of poverty in the United States is
that of the family headed by a woman. This has been called the feminization of
poverty.

Over time, the single-parent family has become an increasing proportion of all
the families at lower income levels. Not only are such families increasing in
number, but two-parent families move out of poverty more rapidly than one-
parent families, leaving behind a greater concentration of such families and their
children in the lower income group.

Whereas children in families headed by a single woman make up some 20 per cent of the entire population of children, they constitute about 50 per cent of all poor children. In 1983, about seven out of every ten minority children in single-parent female-headed minority group households were poor.

The income problems of single-parent families are intensified in many instances by a failure on the part of separated fathers to make child support payments. In 1981, of the 4 million women due such payments only 47 per cent received them. The average yearly income from such payments was $2,110.

In response to this problem, Congress legislated child support legislation in 1984 that increased the possibility of collecting child support payments. In 1982, a procedure had been instituted that withheld tax refunds of parents in arrears of child support payments.

Some states have agreements that enforce support payments across state lines of parents with payments in arrears who have been located through the computerized Federal Parent Locator system. Some states are considering legislation that would require employers to withhold some percentage of wages due a father who is in arrears of support payments. These efforts to increase support payments are designed to reduce the poverty rate of single-parent female-headed families.

Nonwhite workers are still heavily overrepresented in low-income groups, and the unemployment rate for blacks was, throughout the decade, nearly double that for whites. Because they hold poorer-paying jobs and are subject to higher rates of unemployment, nonwhite families have lagged substantially behind white families in income. Although blacks constituted some 12 per cent of the population, they made up about 31.3 per cent of the total population in poverty in 1985.

Median family income of male-headed black families has lagged consistently behind the median family income of male-headed white families. And median family income for female-headed families lagged significantly behind the median income for male-headed families, white or black. In 1984 the median income of a white family headed by a male was $31,896, of a black family headed by a black male, $24,926. During the same year, the median family income for a family headed by a white female was $12,375; that for a family headed by a black female was $11,168.

The combination of gender and race is the most disadvantageous combination. The poverty rate in 1984 of single-parent black and Hispanic families headed by a woman was five times greater than that of intact white families headed by a man.

Children form a very sizable component of the population of the people in poverty. Poverty has a greater impact on the population of children than it does on the population of women. In 1983, 22.2 per cent of all children lived in poverty whereas 16.8 per cent of all females lived in poverty. The "childrenization of poverty" has accompanied the "feminization of poverty." The poverty rate for children was a full 7 percentage points above the total poverty rate of 15.2 per cent in 1983. In 1983, there were 13.8 million children living in poverty. Children, who represent 26 per cent of the population, make up 40 per cent of all of poor people—an overrepresentation of children in the poverty group.

In 1984 one in five children lived in poverty; "this included 16 per cent of all white children 39 per cent of all children of Spanish origin and over 46 per cent of all black children" (Rodgers, 1986, p. 10).

Not only are children as a group disadvantaged but the younger, more vulnerable children under the age of six have a higher poverty rate than their school-age brothers and sisters, black children under the age of six being the most disadvantaged. When the poverty rate for almost all groups fell in 1984, after rising for the previous five years, the rate for black children under six rose—from 49.4 per cent in 1983 to 51.1 per cent in 1984. Whereas the rate for black children under six increased, the poverty rate for the over-sixty-five age group declined more rapidly than for any other group. Whereas poverty among blacks is three times higher than among whites, and one out of every two black children is in poverty compared to one out of every six white children, the largest number of children in poverty are white. Whereas 4.3 million black children were living in poverty in 1983, 8.5 million white children were living in poverty. Similarly, whereas the poverty rate for female-headed families is four times higher than the poverty rate of male-headed families, most poor people live in male-headed families.

Positive changes in the economic situation do not generally have an impact on much of the poverty population. The situation of children and mothers caring for children, the aged, and the handicapped is not particularly responsive to changes in employment and the wage structure. The "new poor" of the 1980s are often victims of structural changes in the economy, automation, and competition from foreign imports that eliminated high-paying jobs in manufacturing which were replaced by low-paying unstable service jobs (Harrington, 1984). Although it is true that as the tide comes in it raises all boats, it is also true that a rising tide never did much good for a shipwreck.

Working Mothers

Although many mothers work because they want to, most mothers—particularly mothers of pre-school-aged children—work because they have to. The lower the family income, the more likely it is that the mother will be working. *The trend has been toward an increase in working mothers, particularly mothers of preschool children.*

This poses a problem of interrole conflict—the role of mother versus the role of employee—and dictates the need for some temporary substitute child-care service for the dependent child. In 1960 20 per cent of mothers with children under six were working; by 1985, 53.2 per cent of such mothers were employed. This meant that over 8.2 million preschool children shared their mothers with employers. (A more detailed analysis of the working mother is included in Chapter 5.)

The participation of mothers in the labor force has benefits, however. It increases the income level of many families, thus permitting the families to meet the needs of children more adequately; it also moves the child-dependency ratio in a favorable direction because it results in an expansion of the work force and an increase in the country's productivity. Two paychecks provide a higher standard of living, a hedge against periods of unemployment, and a necessity in keeping up with increases in the cost of living.

Labor-force participation rates of Hispanic women were lower than for either whites or blacks. They were more likely to have younger dependent children in the home. There may be less of a tradition of out-of-home employment for this group.

The rapid change of the American family from a single-wage-earner family to a family of both husband and wife as wage earners has implications for the need for child welfare services. As a result of the increase in the number of working mothers, many families have moved out of poverty, have been able to provide more adequately for children, and have built up a cushion of resources enabling the family to deal with transient problems without requiring agency service.

However, increases in the rate and number of working mothers with children under age six increase the need for child day-care services. Increases in the number of mothers in the labor force affect child welfare services in another way as well. Withdrawing from traditional neighboring and volunteering roles in favor of paid employment increases the demands on formal, organized child welfare agencies.

Minority-Group Status: A Factor in the Need for Child Welfare Services

Being nonwhite is a major factor increasing the probability that child welfare services may be needed. Every applicable social indicator reveals the relative disadvantage of the nonwhite American. Among nonwhites, infant and maternal mortality rates, illegitimacy rates, family disruption rates, and unemployment rates are higher. The percentage of nonwhites living in poverty is higher than that of whites, as is the percentage of young children whose mothers are working and the percentage who live in dilapidated, substandard housing. Illiteracy rates are higher among nonwhites, as are high school dropout rates, crime rates, and rates of victimization from crime. The incidence of disabling illnesses is higher among nonwhites; the percentage of children under seventeen who have never seen a dentist is higher. Life expectancy is also lower; median income is lower; lifetime earnings are lower; level of education achievement is lower; frequency of accessibility to adequate medical care is lower; accessibility to higher-status jobs is lower; home ownership is lower; the percentage of the group covered by any kind of health insurance is lower.

As a consequence of their disadvantaged position, the nonwhite population provides a disproportionately large group of recipients of all of the welfare services and a disproportionately large group needing such services.

Table 2-1 recapitulates some of the statistical changes in 1960–1984:1985 that are significant for child welfare services. For purposes of comparison, statistics for whites and blacks are reported separately.

Although there are some differences between the situation of blacks and other racial minority groups such as Orientals and Native Americans, blacks constitute the overwhelming majority of the racial minority groups. Consequently, we have listed for comparison statistics for whites and blacks only. The figures generally show improvement for both whites and blacks, but they also reveal the comparatively more favorable situation of the white population.

There are some special demographic characteristics of the black population that relate to the possible need for child welfare services. Because of higher birthrates and higher death rates among blacks as compared to the white population, the median age of the black population is younger. Children make up a higher proportion of that population. The dependency ratio (the number of dependent black children to black productive adults) is higher than the white population counterpart.

Because of higher death rates, imprisonment rates, and chronic unemployment of young black adults, the ratio of women to marriageable black males is high, reducing the marriage possibilities for black females. Marriage and divorce rates are sensitively attuned to employment opportunities. Blacks are living in an employment context that mirrors the Great Depression of the 1930s. At that time

TABLE 2.1   Trends Relevant to Child Welfare Services

Relevant Factor	Years	White	Black
Number and percent-	1960	55,476,000	8,723,000
age of children in		35.8%	42.0%
population of racial	1970	51,062,000	9,509,000
group		31.1%	42.1%
	1977	53,641,000	9,398,000
		29.1%	38.4%
	1984	51,016,000	9,532,000
		25.3%	33.5%
Birthrate (Per 1,000 population)	1960	22.7	32.1
	1965	18.3	27.6
	1970	15.5	25.2
	1976	13.8	21.1
	1984	14.5	20.8
Infant Mortality (per	1960	22.9	44.3
1,000 live births)	1965	21.5	41.7
	1975	14.2	26.2
	1980	11	21.4
	1984	9.4	18.4
Maternal mortality (per	1960	26	97.9
100,000 live births)	1965	21	83.7
	1970	14.4	55.9
	1975	9.1	29
	1983	5.9	18.3
Life Expectancy at birth	1960	70.6	63.6
(Total: male and fe-	1965	71	64.1
male)	1970	71.7	65.3
	1976	73.5	68.3
	1985	75.3	69.5
Median annual family	1960	$ 5,835	$ 3,233
income	1965	7,251	3,994
	1970	10,236	6,541
	1977	16,740	9,560
	1985	29,152	16,786
Percentage of popula-	1960	18	56
tion below poverty	1965	13	47
level	1970	10	32
	1977	8.9	31.3
	1985	11.4	31.3
Percentage of children	1960	19.2	65.5
in racial group living	1965	14.4	57.3
below poverty level	1970	9.7	39.6
	1976	11.3	40.4
	1984	16.1	46.2
Own children living with	1960	92	75
both parents as a	1965	91	71
percentage of all	1970	87	57
children in the ra-	1977	84.8	46.1
cial group	1984	81	41
Unemployment rates	1960	4.9	10.2
(annual average)	1965	4.1	8.1
	1970	4.5	8.2
	1977	6.2	13.1
	1986	6.6	15

Illegitimacy rate (per	1960	9.2	98.3
1,000 unmarried	1965	11.6	97.6
women 15–	1970	13.8	86.6
44 years of age)	1976	12.7	78.1
	1984	20.1	76.8
Divorced females (per	1960	38	78
1,000 married with	1970	56	104
spouse present)	1975	77	178
	1980	110	258
	1984	134	319
Percentage of mothers	1966	24	40
in labor force (with	1971	29	47
children under 6)	1976	35.5	53.2
	1984	47	55

marriage rates plummeted and people, uncertain of their ability to support a family, delayed marriage.

The divorce rate throughout the 1970s has been consistently higher for blacks than for whites. Many divorced women remarry, but the remarriage rate of white women is higher than that of blacks. If black women do remarry it is after a longer period of time as a single woman.

Blacks are a proportionately smaller percentage of the surburban population and a disproportionately higher percentage of the central area metropolitan population. The black population is concentrated in the central areas of large cities in crowded, less desirable, more dilapidated housing, where rates of crime, vice, and abandoned buildings are high and services are inadequate and in short supply. "Suburbs are overwhelmingly white and central cities are increasingly black" (Reid, 1982, p. 8).

Although infant mortality for both whites and blacks have fallen steadily over the past fifty years, the differential between whites and blacks has remained substantially the same over the last half-century. Black infants have, throughout, died approximately twice as frequently as white infants. Socioeconomic level rather than race is a principal factor here since the infant mortality rates of middle-class surburban blacks approximates more closely the infant mortality rates of whites. Having lower income, and being less educated, younger, and more often unmarried, the black mother often has less access to adequate nutrition and medical care and is more likely to have a baby of low birth weight who is, consequently, more vulnerable.

Nonwhites have a higher birthrate among adolescents, are more likely to give birth prematurely, and have a higher percentage of low-birth-weight children. All of these conditions are associated with increased infant mortality. Nor is it likely that black children can look forward to any inherited wealth. A Census Bureau study on accumulated family wealth found that whereas the median net worth of white households in 1984 was $39,135, the net wealth of black households was $3,397. About 30 per cent of the black households had zero or negative net worth (*New York Times,* July 19, 1986).

For almost every statistic of relevance to child welfare, the minority group child is likely to be disproportionately disadvantaged when compared with the white child. This is particularly true of the statistic with regard to family structure. Although 81 per cent of all white children were living with both parents in 1984, only 41 per cent of all black children were living with both parents. The majority of black children were living in a single-parent home headed by a woman.

Black children are twice as likely as white children to be living in some child care institution, are three times more likely to be in foster care, and are four times more likely to have contact with child welfare services than white children. As compared with white families, families of color received less comprehensive services and the child welfare system was less responsive to such families (Close, 1983).

Statistics suggest the strength and solidarity of the black family. Whereas only 2 per cent of white children who need out-of-home care were cared for by relatives in 1983, some 9 per cent of black children were cared for by grandparents, aunts, uncles, and other relatives.

Hispanics and Native Americans

Starting in the mid-1970s, census data began to include material on people of "Spanish origin" as a separate category. Such data were not available earlier. There were 16,940 million persons of Spanish origin in the population in 1985— 10,209 million persons of Mexican origin; 2,562 million of Puerto Rican origin and additional Hispanics of Cuban and Central or South American origin. In general, children in families of Spanish origin were not as well off as were white children, but they were less disadvantaged than black children. Children under eighteen composed a larger percentage of this group (36 per cent) than the percentage of children in the white or black group.

Persons of Spanish origin, comprising 7.2 per cent of the population of the United States, had some 6 million children under eighteen in 1985. Median family income was slightly higher than that of the black population, but lower than the median income of white families. Some 28 per cent of these families lived below the poverty level. There were more female-headed families among this group than was true for the white population, but fewer such families as compared with the black population. While Hispanic children comprise about 10 percent of the nation's children, about 18 per cent of poor children are of Spanish origin. Within the Hispanic group there are differences in income and family characteristics among those of Mexican, Puerto Rican, or Cuban origin. For instance Puerto Rican families are more likely to be single-parent, female-headed families than other groups of Hispanics. South Americans are likely to be more affluent.

The Hispanic population is growing at a faster pace than either the white or black populations. This results not only from higher birthrates among Hispanics but also from additions to the population as a result of immigration (legal or illegal) from Mexico and other Hispanic countries. Spanish is the non-English language most frequently spoken by social agency clients (Estrada, 1985).

There are about a million and a half Native Americans making up about 0.6 per cent of the population. The Native American population is young and heavily concentrated in the low-income groups. Average life expectancy of Native Americans is lower and infant mortality rates are higher than among non-Native Americans.

The disproportionate numbers of Native American children placed in substitute care, some estimates running to 25–35 per cent of all Native American children, have invoked charges of discrimination and service inadequacy. Recognizing the special relationship between the federal government and the Indian tribes and their members and the sovereignty of the Indian nations, Congress responded by passing the Indian Child Welfare Act in 1978. The act sought to establish guidelines for decisions regarding the removal of Native American children from their homes and to tighten the legal protection given parents and families in child custody matters. Perhaps the most significant aspect of the law, however, was the recognition of tribal courts "as courts of competent jurisdiction in matters concerned with American Indian Child Welfare" (Fischler, 1980, p. 344) (See also Kessel and Robbins, 1984.).

Recapitulation—The Demographic Context of Child Welfare Services

During the near future while birthrates will continue to be low, the larger number of fecund women in the population will result in a modest increase in the child population. Continued high, although stabilized, divorce rates and increases in the number of nonmaritally born children will result in an increase in the number of children growing up in single-parent families most frequently headed by women. Living in this family structure, accompanied by continued relatively high unemployment rates, and inadequate child support both from absent male parents and from public assistance maintenance programs, will result in an increasing percentage of the child population living in poverty. In addition increases in the percentage of mothers with children under six in the labor force will contribute to a growing population of children who might be at risk for child welfare services.

Each of these changes is disproportionately greater for minority group children than it is for white children although the actual number of white children affected is larger. The impact for the Hispanic child population of these changes is less than that experienced by black children but greater than that experienced by white children.

All of the changes of the 1970–1980 period—lower rates of marriage, delayed marriages, increasing cohabitation rates, increasing divorce rates, increases in the number of working women, increases in the single-parent family formation, and decreasing fertility rates—are expected to continue but at a much more moderate pace than was true for the 1960–1980 decades. Most of these changes are likely to stabilize by the end of the century.

Changing Values

Statistical trends regarding the number of children at risk and trends regarding the social contingencies that directly affect the number of children possibly needing child welfare services are very important factors helping us to understand the context in which such services are offered. Of importance, too, is the nature of ideological changes.

We are currently undergoing a change in attitudes toward parenthood that may affect the context in which child welfare services are offered. The concern with zero population growth and the movement for changes in the status of women have diminished the prestige formerly accorded the status of parent. Parenthood is no longer unanimously applauded.

With fewer children and increased life expectancy, women are currently finding that only a relatively small percentage of their productive years is devoted to the full-time maternal role. The average woman may be a full-time mother for about ten years, and as she is capable of being fully productive for a period of some thirty to thirty-five years, the woman who has dedicated herself to motherhood finds herself with either a part-time job or no job at all for a good part of her life. This fact supports and reinforces the orientation of the women's movement toward a de-emphasis on motherhood and a search for alternative life-styles for women. The greater availability and acceptance of contraception, backed up by legalized abortion, help to reinforce these changes in ideology.

There is currently a greater acceptance of a wider variety of childrearing contexts. The definition of the family has been opened for possible reformulation. The traditional definition employed by the Census Bureau is that a "family" is a "group of two or more persons related by blood, marriage, or adoption and residing together in a household." Household includes all people who occupy a housing unit.

The definition suggests a contractual commitment sanctioned by either civil or religious authorities or both and implying the rearing of children.

It is argued that such definitions exclude many variant relationships that might qualify as "family." Definitions including such alternative forms in recognizing the "legitimacy of diversity" have been proposed.

A broader definition of "family" includes "two or more persons who share resources, share responsibility for decisions, share values and goals and have a commitment to each other over time." This would include single-parent "families," extended "families," communal "families," homosexual "families," and consensual cohabiting relationships."

The diversity of family structures was acknowledged when the title of the 1981 National White House Conference on the Family was changed to White House Conference on Families.

There is currently a greater acceptance than previously of the idea of mothers of young children working, and associated with this a reevaluation, if not actualization, of the relative responsibilities of males and females for child care and childrearing. There is a greater acceptance of divorce as a resolution of marital conflict and less stigma associated with nonmarital pregnancies.

There is a growing acceptance, too, of the idea that the responsibility for rearing a child is shared by the parents and the community. The idea of joint responsibility leads to a greater acceptance of day-care centers and other community-centered arrangements for progressively earlier implementation of the partnership.

There is, more frequently now than in the recent past, the recognition of the entitlement of women to individual fulfillment and autonomy within the family system and less tendency to expect women to set aside their own needs and desires in favor of children and the family (Degler, 1980).

Competition between the needs of children and that of other members within the family system is paralleled by a competition for resources between the needs of children and other dependent groups, particularly the growing number of aged within the general social system.

This struggle is played out in a changed political atmosphere that reinforces the traditional American ambivalence and hesitancy about welfare programs. While supporting the general idea of a welfare state, the public endorses programs that are categorical and means tested rather than universal and that provide help at a minimal level on a restrictive eligibility basis for limited periods of time to the "legitimate" and "truly" needy. The general orientation is to view such programs as necessary evils and as measures of social control to prevent civil disorder.

Demographic changes, however, may argue for the possibility of increased support for child welfare programs in the coming decades. The imperatives of demography and dependency argue for the need of Americans generally, and white Americans in particular, to be more concerned with the welfare of children generally, and minority group children particularly, in the immediate future. Between 1990 and 2030, an increasingly larger percentage of the population will consist of older people dependent for their support on a decreasing percentage of younger people. Since whites generally live longer than blacks and Hispanics, a disproportionate percentage of the aged dependent population will be white. Since the birthrate of minorities and Hispanics is higher than that of whites, a disproportionate percentage of the younger population, on which the aged will be dependent, will consist of blacks and Hispanics. A growing awareness of this situation may result in a greater political support of programs that support the health, education, and welfare of the human capital on which the aging population will be dependent, the generation of children generally, and minority group children particularly, over the next three or four decades.

Bibliography

Ariès, Philippe. *Centuries of Childhood*. New York: Alfred A. Knopf, 1962.

Ashby, Leroy. *Saving the Waifs—Reformer and Dependent Children: 1890–1917*. Philadelphia: Temple University Press, 1984.

Atherton, Charles R. "The Social Assignment of Social Work." *Social Service Review*, 43, 4 (December 1969), 421–429.

Bakan, David. *Slaughter of the Innocents—A Study of the Battered Child Phenomenon*. San Francisco: Jossey-Bass, 1971.

Baldwin, Wendy, and Christine Nord. *Delayed Child Bearing in the U.S.: Facts and Fiction*. Washington, D.C.: Population Reference Bureau, 1984.

Beck, Dorothy F., and Mary A Jones. *Progress on Family Problems—A Nationwide Study of Clients' and Counselors' Views of Family Agency Service*. New York: Family Service Association of America, 1973.

Bennett, H. "The Exposure of Infants in Ancient Rome." *Classical Journal*, 13 (1923), 341–351.

Blythe, Ronald. *Akenfield-Portrait of an English Village*. New York: Delta Paperbook, 1969.

Bossard, James H. S., and Eleanor S. Boll. *The Sociology of Childhood*, 4th ed. New York: Harper & Row, 1966.

Bouvier, Leon F. *America's Baby Boom Generation: The Fateful Bulge*. Washington, D.C.: Population Reference Bureau, 1980.

Bradley, Candice. "The Sexual Division of Labor and the Value of Children." *Behavior Science Research*, 14, (1985), 1–4.

Bremner, Robert H. (ed.). *Children and Youth in America—A Documentary History*, Vol. 1, pp. 1600–1865. Cambridge, Mass.: Harvard University Press, 1970.

Cameron, A. "The Exposure of Children and Greek Ethics." *The Classical Review*, 46 (1932), 105–114.

Carter, Hugh, and Pal C. Glick. *Marriage and Divorce—A Social and Economic Study*, rev. ed. Cambridge, Mass.: Harvard University Press, 1976.

Caulfield, Ernest. *The Infant Welfare Movement of the Eighteenth Century*. New York: Paul Locker, 1931.

Chastel, Stephan. *The Charity of the Primitive Churches.* Philadelphia: J. B. Lippincott, 1857.

Children's Defense Fund. *America's Children in Poverty.* Washington, D.C.: C.D.F., 1984.

Children's Defense Fund. *Black and White Children in America—Key Facts.* Washington, D.C.: C.D.F., 1985.

Close, Mary M. "Child Welfare and People of Color: Denial of Equal Access." *Social Work Research and Abstracts,* 19, 4 (Winter 1983), 13–20.

Cohen, Barbara. "Surrogate Mothers: Whose Baby Is It?" *American Journal of Law and Medicine,* 10, 3 (Fall 1984).

Constantelos, Demetrios J. *Byzantine Philanthropy and Social Welfare.* New Brunswick, N.J.: Rutgers University Press, 1968.

Cutright, Phillip. "Components of Change in the Number of Female Family Heads Aged 15–44: United States, 1940–1970." *Journal of Marriage and the Family,* 36 (1974), 714–721.

Degler, Carl N. *At Odds—Women and the Family in America from the Revolution to the Present.* New York: Oxford University Press, 1980, pp. 113–129.

Delasselle, Claude. "Abandoned Children in Eighteenth-Century Paris," pp. 47–82, in *Deviants and the Abandoned in French Society.* Ed. Robert Forster and Orest Ranum. Baltimore, Md.: Johns Hopkins University Press, 1978.

De Mause, Lloyd (ed.). *The History of Childhood,* New York: The Psychohistory Press, 1974.

De Schweinitz, Karl. *England's Road to Social Security.* Philadelphia: University of Pennsylvania Press, 1947.

Despert, J. Louise. *The Emotionally Disturbed Child—Then and Now.* New York: Robert Brunner, 1965.

Devereaux, George. *A Study of Abortion in Primitive Societies,* rev. ed. New York: International Universities Press, 1976.

Duff, Raymond S., and A. G. M. Campbell. "Moral and Ethical Dilemmas in the Special-Care Nursery." *The New England Journal of Medicine,* 289 (Oct. 25, 1973), 890–84.

Dunn, Patrick P. "The Enemy Is the Baby: Childhood in Imperial Russia." *History of Childhood,* ed. Lloyd de Mause. New York: Psychohistory Press, 1973.

Dyhouse, Carol. "Working Class Mothers and Infant Mortality in England 1895–1914." *Journal of Social History,* 12, 2 (Winter 1978), 248–62.

Eiduson, Bernice. "Conflict and Stress in Non-Traditional Families: Impact on Children." *American Journal of Orthopsychiatry,* 53, 3 (July 1983), 426–435.

Espenshade, Thomas J. *Investing in Children—Need Estimates of Parental Expenditures.* Washington, D.C.: The Urban Institute Press, 1984.

Estrada, Leobardo, "The Dynamics of Hispanic Populations: A Description and Comparison." *Social Thought,* 43 (Summer 1985), 23–38.

Eyben, Emiel. "Family Planning in Graeco-Roman Antiquity." *Ancient Society,* 11/12 (1980–81), 5–82.

Fairchilds, Cissie C. *Poverty and Charity in Aix-en-Provence 1640–1789.* Baltimore, Md.: Johns Hopkins University Press, 1976.

Family Service Association of America. *The State of Families, 1984–85.* New York: F.S.A.A., 1984.

Farber, Bernard. *Guardians of Virtue—Salem Families in 1800.* New York: Basic Books, 1972.

Fischler, Ronald S. "Protecting American Indian Children." *Social Work* (September 1980), 341–343.

Forrest, Alan. *The French Revolution and the Poor.* New York: St. Martin's Press, 1981.

Fraser, Antonia. *The Weaker Vessel.* New York: Vintage Books, 1984.

Freed, Doris J., and Henry H. Foster. "Divorce American Style." *Annals of the American Academy,* 38, 3 (May 1969), 71–88.

Fuchs, Rachel G. *Abandoned Children—Foundlings and Child Welfare in Nineteenth-Century France.* Albany: State University of New York Press, 1984.

Gallahue, John. "Tragedy at Liège." *Look* (March 12, 1963), 72–78.

Garfinkel, Irwin, and Sara McLanahan. *A New American Dilemma: The Plight of Single Women and Their Children.* Washington, D.C. Urban Institute, 1986.

Glick, Paul C. "American Household Structure in Transition." *Family Planning Perspectives,* 16, 5 (September–October, 1984), 205–211.

Glick, Paul C. "Living Arrangement of Children and Young Adults." *Journal of Comparative Family Studies,* 7 (Summer 1976), 322–333.

Gold, Rachel B., and Asta M. Kenny. "Paying for Maternity Care." *Family Planning Perspectives,* 17, 3 (May–June 1985), 103–109.

Gold, Rachel B., and Barry Nestor. "Public Funding of Contraception, Sterilization and Abortion Services, 1983." *Family Planning Perspectives,* 17, 1 (January–February 1985), 25–35.

Gottlieb, David (ed.). *Children's Liberation.* Englewood Cliffs, N.J.: Prentice-Hall, 1973.

Gottschalk, Peter, and Sheldon Danzinger. "Macroeconomic Conditions—Income Transfers and the Trend in Poverty," pp. 185–215, in *The Social Contract Revisited.* Ed. D. L. Bawden. Washington, D.C.: The Urban Institute Press, 1984.

Grehen, Farrell. "Mothers, Martyrs of the Speed Age." *Life* (January 18, 1960), 16.

Grier, George. *The Baby Bust: An Agenda for the 70's Special Report.* Washington, D.C.: The Washington Center for Metropolitan Studies, 1971.

Gross, Beatrice, and Ronald Gross. *The Children's Liberation Movement.* Garden City, N.Y.: Doubleday Anchor Books, 1977.

Gutman, Herbert S. *The Black Family in Slavery and Freedom, 1750–1925.* New York: Vintage Books, 1977.

Hands, A. R. *Charities and Social Aid in Greece and Rome.* Ithaca, N.Y.: Cornell University Press, 1968.

Harrington, Michael. *The New American Poverty.* New York: Penguin Books, 1984.

Harvard Education Review, "The Rights of Children" (A Special Issue). Part I, vol. 33 (November 1973); Part II, vol. 34 (February 1974).

Helmick, Sandra A., and Judith D. Zimmerman. "Trends in the Distribution of Children among Households and Families." *Child Welfare,* 58, 5 (September–October 1984), 401–409.

Herzog, Elizabeth, and Cecelia Sudia. "Children in Fatherless Families," pp. 141–232, in *Review of Child Development Research.* Ed. Bettye M. Caldwell and Henry N. Ricciuti. Chicago: University of Chicago Press, 1973.

Himes, Norman E. *Medical History of Contraception.* Baltimore, Md.: The Williams & Wilkins Co., 1936.

Ho, Ping-Ti. *Studies on the Population of China 1368–1953.* Cambridge, Mass.: Harvard University Press, 1967.

Hobhouse, L. T. *Morals in Evolution.* London: Chapman & Hall, Ltd., 1951.

Hoffer, Pertere, and N.E.H. Hull. *Murdering Mothers: Infanticide in England and New England, 1558–1803.* New York: New York University Press, 1984.

Hunt, David. *Parents and Children in Seventeenth-Century France.* New York: Basic Books, 1969.

Ispahani, Begum G. "Pakistan." *Adoption and Fostering, 90,* 4 (1977), 45–46.

Kadushin, Alfred. "The Single Adoptive Parent—An Overview of the Research." *Social Service Review,* 44 (September 1970), 263–271.

Kessel, Frank, and Alexander Siegel. *The Child and Other Cultural Innovations.* New York: Praeger Press, 1983.

Kessel, Jo Ann, and Susan R. Robins. "The Indian Child Welfare Act: Dilemmas and Needs." *Child Welfare,* 68, 3 (May–June 1984) 225–232.

Kohl, Marvin (ed.). *Infanticide and the Value of Life.* Buffalo, N.Y.: Prometheus Books, 1978.

Lacey, W. K. *The Family in Classical Greece.* London: Thames and Houston, 1968.

Langer, William L. "Infanticide: A Historical Survey." *History of Childhood Quarterly,* 1 (1974), 353–365.

Lecky, William E. *History of European Morals,* vol. 2. New York: Appleton-Century-Crofts, 1869.

Lyon, Jeff. *Playing God in the Nursery.* New York: W. W. Norton, 1985.

Madison, Bernice. "Russia's Illegitimate Children Before and after the Revolution." *Slavic Review,* 22 (1963), 82–95.

McCloy, Shelby T. *Government Assistance in Eighteenth-Century France.* Durham, N.C.: Duke University Press, 1946.

McClure, Ruth K. *Coram's Children: The London Foundling Hospital in the Eighteenth Century.* New Haven, Conn.: Yale University Press, 1981.

McLaughlin, Mary Marten. "Survivors and Surrogate Children and Parents from the Ninth to the Thirteenth Century." *The History of Childhood,* ed. Lloyd de Mause. New York: The Psychohistory Press, 1973.

Mead, Margaret. "A Cultural Anthropologist's Approach to Maternal Deprivation," in *Deprivation of Maternal Care.* Geneva: World Health Organization, 1962.

Miller, Nathan. *The Child in Primitive Society.* New York: Brentano, 1928.

Miller, C. Arden. "Infant Mortality in the United States." *Scientific American,* 253, 1 (July 1985).

Minturn, Leigh, and Jerry Stashak. "Infanticide as a Terminal Abortion Procedure." *Behavior Science Research,* 17, 1–2 (Spring–Summer 1982), 70–85.

Mitchell, R. G. "Children in Society," in *Child Life and Health.* Ed. Ross S. Mitchell. London: J. & A. Churchill, Ltd., 1970.

Mitscherlich, Alexander. *Doctors of Infamy.* New York: Abelard-Schuman, Ltd., 1949.

Mohl, Raymond. *Poverty in New York 1783–1825.* New York: Oxford University Press, 1971.

Naphtal, Lewis A., and Reinhold Meyer. *Selected Readings: Roman Civilization, vol. II—The Empire.* New York: Columbia Uiversity Press, 1955.

National Academy of Sciences. *Toward a National Policy for Children and Families.* Washington, D.C.: National Academy of Sciences, 1976.

National Council of Organizations for Children and Youth. *America's Children 1976—A Bicentennial Assessment.* Washington, D.C.: National Council of Organizations for Children and Youth, 1976.

O'Hare, William P. *Poverty in America: New Trends and New Patterns.* Washington, D.C.: Population Reference Bureau, 1985.

Panigrahi, Lolita. *British Social Policy and Female Infanticide in India.* New Delhi: Munshira M. Manoharla 1, 1972.

Payne, George H. *The Child in Human Progress.* New York: G. P. Putnam's Sons, 1916.

Peck, Ellen. *The Baby Trap.* New York: Bernard Geis Associates, 1971.

Pinchbeck, Ivy, and Margaret Hewitt. *Children in English Society,* vol. 1: *From Tudor Times to the Eighteenth Century.* London: Kegan Paul, Trench, Trubner & Co., 1969.

Pollock, Linda A. *Forgotten Children—Parent-Child Relations from 1500 to 1900.* Cambridge, England: Cambridge University Press. 1983.

Preston, Samuel H. "Children and the Elderly in the U.S." *Scientific American,* 251, 6 (December 1984), 44–49.

Queen, Alfred S. *Social Work in the Light of History.* Philadelphia: J. B. Lippincott Co., 1922.

Radbill, Samuel X. "A History of Child Abuse and Infanticide," in *The Battered Child.* Ed. Ray E. Helfer and C. Henry Kempe. Chicago: University of Chicago Press, 1968.

Reid, John. *Black America in the 1980's.* Washington, D.C.: Population Reference Bureau, 1982.

Robins, Joseph. *The Lost Children—A Study of Charity Children in Ireland, 1700–1900.* Dublin: Institute of Public Administration, 1980.

Rodgers, Harrell R. *Poor Women, Poor Families: The Economic Plight of America's Female-Headed Households.* Armonk, N.Y.: M. E. Sharpe, 1986.

Ross, Heather L., and Isabel V. Sawhill. *Time of Transition—The Growth of Families Headed by Women.* Washington, D.C.: The Urban Institute, 1975.

Royster, Eugene C. *Barriers to Foster Care in the Black Community.* Lincoln University, Pa.: Lincoln University, Department of Sociology, June 30, 1975. Mimeo, 235 pp.

Seligman, Edwin R. (ed.). *Encyclopedia of Social Science,* vol. 3. New York: The Macmillan Company, 1930.

Shelp, E. *Born to Die? Deciding the Fate of Critically Ill Newborns.* New York: The Free Press, 1986.

Shorter, Edward. *The Making of the Modern Family.* New York: Basic Books, 1975.

Shyne, Ann W., and Anita G. Schroeder. *National Study of Social Sevices to Children and Their Families.* Rockville, Md.,: Westat, August, 1978.

Sicault, Georges (ed.). *The Needs of Children.* New York: The Free Press, 1963.

Silka, Linda, and Sara Kiesler. "Couples Who Choose to Remain Childless." *Family Planning Perspectives,* 9 (January–February 1977), 16–25.

Snapper, Kurt J., Harriet H. Barriga, Faye H. Baugarner, and Charles S. Wagner, *The Status of Children—1975.* Washington, D.C.: Social Work Research Group, George Washington University, 1975.

Snapper, Kurt, and Joanne S. Ohms. *The Status of Children, 1977.* Washington, D.C.: U.S. Government Printing Office, 1978.

Steinbicker, Carl R. *Poor Relief in the Sixteenth Century.* Washington, D.C.: Catholic University Press, 1957.

Stone, Lawrence. *The Family, Sex and Marriage in England, 1500–1800.* New York: Harper & Row, 1977.

Stone, Lawrence. "Family History in the 1980's—Post Achievement and Future Trends." *Journal of Interdisciplinary History,* 12, 1 (Summer 1981), 51–87.

Sumner, William G. *Folkways.* New York: Dover Publications, 1959.

Thornton, Arland, and Deborah Freedman. "Changing Attitudes Toward Marriage and Single Life." *Family Planning Perspectives,* 14,6 (November–December 1982), 297–303.

Tiffin, Susan. *In Whose Best Interest? Child Welfare Reform in the Progressive Era.* Westport, Conn.: Greenwood Press, 1982.

Trattner, Walter I. *Crusade for the Children.* Chicago: Quadrangle Books, 1970.

Trexler, Richard C. "Infanticide in Florence: New Sources and First Results." *History of Childhood Quarterly,* 1 (Summer 1973), 98–110.

Trost, Jan. "Unmarried Co-habitation in Sweden," pp. 1–6 in *Social Change in Sweden.* Stockholm: Swedish Institute, 1980.

United Nations. *Parental Rights and Duties Including Guardianship.* New York: United Nations, 1968.

U.S. Bureau of the Census. *Marital Status and Living Arrangements,* March, 1977. Washington, D.C.: U.S. Government Printing Office, 1977.

U.S. Department of Commerce. *Census of Population, 1970. General Social and Economic Characteristics—Final Report U.S. Summary.* Washington, D.C.: U.S. Government Printing Office, 1972.

U.S. Department of Commerce. *The Social and Economic Status of the Black Population in the United States, 1974.* Washington, D.C.: U.S. Government Printing Office, July 1975.

U.S. Department of Commerce. *Population Profile of the United States, 1976.* Washington, D.C.: U.S. Government Printing Office, 1977a.

U.S. Department of Commerce. *Social Indicators, 1976.* Washington, D.C.: Government Printing Office, December 1977b.

U.S. Department of Commerce. *Statistical Abstract of the United States, 1978,* 99th ed. Washington, D.C.: U.S. Government Printing Office, 1978.

United States House of Representatives. *Demographic and Social Trends: Implications for Federal Support of Dependent Care Services for Children and the Elderly.* Washington, D.C.: Select Committee on Children, Youth, and Families, April 1984.

United States White House Conference on Children. *Report to the President, 1970,* Washington, D.C.: U.S. Government Printing Office, 1970.

Vardin, Patricia, and Ilene N. Brody (eds.). *Children's Rights: Contemporary Perspectives.* New York: Teachers College Press, 1979.

Wilkerson, Albert E. *The Rights of Children: Emergent Concepts in Law and Society.* Philadelphia: Temple University Press, 1973.

Williamson, Laila. "Infanticide: An Anthropological Analysis," in *Infanticide and the Value of Life.* Ed. Marvin Kohl. Buffalo, N.Y.: Prometheus Books, 1978.

Zelizer, Vivian. *Pricing the Priceless Child—The Changing Social Value of Children.* New York: Basic Books, 1985.

Zelnik, Melvin, and John F. Kantner. "First Pregnancies to Women Aged 15–19: 1976 and 1971." *Family Planning Perspectives,* 10 (January–February 1978), 11–20.

3

Supportive Services:

Home-Based Care

Introduction

The first line of defense in child welfare services is to support, reinforce, and strengthen the ability of parents and children to meet the responsibilities of their respective statuses. Supportive services are designed for children living in their own homes. In these instances a parent or both parents are generally present and show some willingness and capacity to enact their roles effectively. However, there may be difficulties in the parent–child relationship as a result of parent–child conflict or as a reflection of marital conflict.

We start with supportive services because it is, logically, the first service to use when a family needs help with a parent–child problem. We always act on the supposition that until proven otherwise, the best place for the child is in his or her own home. Supportive services are an exemplification of this orientation.

In making use of such services, the family remains structurally intact. The child can remain, and be maintained, at home despite some malfunction in the parent–child relationship system. In offering supportive services, the agency does not take over the responsibility for discharging any of the role functions of either parent or child. The service always remains external to the family's social structure. Supportive service is different from supplementary services, for instance, where some significant aspect of the role is performed by some other parental figure, such as a homemaker, or by some social institution, such as the income maintenance programs.

Two principal agencies offering supportive services are the family service agencies and the child guidance clinics. Since 1975, supportive services have been more broadly defined to encompass a wide variety of agencies indentified as home-based service agencies. The development of these programs grew out of the movement for permanency planning for children. The development of such programs and their principal objectives relate to preventing removal of a child from the home for substitute care. They often tend to focus their service on a particular group of families, namely those exhibiting a high risk for child placement.

The home-based service programs have a special identity, a special sponsorship, and a special objective. The National Clearing House for Home Based Services for Children and their Families is based at the School of Social Work,

University of Iowa. Home based services include not only supportive services but also a wide variety of supplemental services as part of their programs.

Although supportive services have long been an integral and basic part of child welfare, they have received renewed attention in the last decade. Examining the need for "home-based care," numerous authors have described a series of interrelated service components provided to clients with a wide range of family disabilities. Service provision is based on a commitment to involvement of the entire family and support for every individual in the family unit. These services are seen as particularly appropriate and necessary for those families facing imminent loss of their children, should the parents be unable to become minimally effective as caretakers for them.

Efforts to develop intensive services are predicated on a number of assumptions concerning the value of family life to children and society's commitment to strengthening family life. Families are seen as social institutions of central importance for the healthy social and emotional development of children. When parents engage in activities that are harmful to children, their impact on their children is not necessarily "all" or "mostly" bad (Rapoport, Rapoport, & Strelitz, 1977). Even in those cases in which parents have done substantial harm to their children, their removal from home and placement may prove more detrimental. As Wald (1975) suggests, "not only is separation per se damaging, but we lack the ability to insure that a child's placement is superior to his own home" (p. 994). When difficult problems develop in families, our concern for the healthy future of children prompts utilization of intensive home-based treatment efforts to remedy these difficulties. Goffin (1983) reflects these views when she states:

> Current discussions of children's services focus on the recognition of the family as a mediating structure between the child and society, making it the primary unit for the delivery of services to children. Explicit recognition of the family's role in rearing children reflects, in part, a growing understanding of the impact of the environment in which children live and the lack of success of social agencies that have attempted to assume the family's responsibilities. The concept of environment includes the child's immediate setting as well as the encompassing social context. The emerging focus on the family suggests that helping the family may be the most effective way to improve the lives of most children [p. 283].

Yet another argument used to support the need for increased use of home-based services involves the family's right to raise children in our society. As Wald (1975) points out, families are protected from unwarranted interference from social agencies unless they have violated minimal caretaking standards. Even when families violate such standards, home-based care is considered the primary approach for helping these families because it is least intrusive.

Finally, provision of home-based care is predicated on the assumption that there is a social obligation to provide needed supports to families in our society. Families are given ultimate responsibility for the overall health and welfare of their children. However, they are provided with insufficient social resources to carry out that task. While all families find it difficult to fulfill all necessary caretaking obligations, poor and multiproblem families are particularly vulnerable. Families in our society are blamed when children develop problems of any type. It is expected that they will resolve such problems without broader supports, a task that no family can possibly perform. Families burdened with children who have special needs find it particularly difficult to meet this obligation. Home-based services are designed to replace the supports that these families need (Rice, 1977; Bryce, 1979; Jones & Biesecker, 1980a; Knitzer & Olson, 1982).

Home-based services have been conceptualized as a set of comprehensive multi-faceted programs designed to meet the varied needs of child welfare clients. Bryce (1979) includes

> all those supportive and supplemental services to a family in or near the family home. Such services are, or may be, found in that network of established, sanctioned institutions, such as the educational and legal systems, health and welfare systems, political and industrial institutions, and religious and recreational complexes. In addition, the informal services of volunteers and neighbors are included [p. 19].

He goes on to say:

> Services are as complete, comprehensive, and intense as is necessary to effect problem resolution and to strengthen and maintain a family. Staff are available 24 hours a day, 365 days a year, often serving as extended family . . . . The focus may be developmental and/or remedial, and services extended may be under social, health, or educational auspices, yet the needed service components are made available [1981, p. 7].

Effective home-based intervention, according to Clayton-Fechtmann and Seibold (1981), requires that services be "a) comprehensive; b) multifaceted; c) organized; d) persistent; and e) occurring in the natural environment" (p. 274). In a 1982 publication, Bryce reiterates his concern about comprehensiveness by noting "provision of help is available for any problem presented. If the team does not have the expertise or resources needed, it arranges for or creates them in order to stabilize and improve family functioning" (p. 79). (See also Jones & Biesecker, 1980b; Edna McConnell Clark Foundation, 1985.)

A number of specific treatment methods are integral to the home-based treatment model. They include parent treatment, parent education, group work services (Knitzer & Olson, 1982; Magazino, 1983), case management services, advocacy, and family therapy (Meezan, 1983). Magazino (1983) argues that it is particularly important that clients be provided with a mix of both counseling and concrete services. Bryce also considers certain staffing patterns to be fundamental aspects of home-based care. He includes several recommendations:

1. A primary worker or case manager establishes and maintains a nurturing, supportive relationship with the family.
2. Small caseloads, staff availability and the utilization of a wide variety of helping options are available.
3. One or more associates serve as team members or provide backup for the daily worker and may meet regularly with the worker and the family [1982, p. 78].

Research has indicated the long-term positive impact of such programs on children. A review of intervention programs undertaken by the U.S. Department of Health and Human Services (1980) concludes, "the chief implication of the intervention studies of the 1970s is that the result of an intervention appears to be commensurate with the effort that is invested in the intervention. Intensive programs begun in infancy, providing a broad array of services, and involving the entire family have had lasting and measurable benefits for intervention relative to control children long after the programs have ceased" (p. 162). Jones, Magura, and Shyne (1981) highlight the significance of multifaceted programming for clients:

> The finding that a comprehensive program of services is more effective for families than is any single service emerges repeatedly in studies of protective services or work with multiproblem families. Although no single service can be isolated as making a crucial difference, the number of services and perhaps their complementarity are often significant factors. Shapiro's study of protective services found that families who received several services did better than those who received only one or two. They also did better than families who received a great many services, probably again because of the interaction between problem and services—that is, families who need many services are likely to be those with many problems, and therefore be less likely to improve [pp. 72–73].

Historical Background

The development of home-based care has a rich and varied history, one that is inextricably linked to the development of institutional and other substitute care facilities for children. Prior to the late 1800s, no major organization existed that was committed to the preservation of home life for children. Children in families in need of assistance and support might be offered one of several options. The children were sometimes removed from the home and placed in an almshouse or an indentured situation. Some families were offered temporary financial aid in the form of relief, whereas many were simply expected to fend for themselves and find some way to alleviate their financial or personal problems.

In the latter half of the nineteenth century, organizations emerged whose stated purpose included a commitment to serving children in their own homes. The type of family service agency found in many communities today had its origin in the Charity Organization Societies that were established in the United States during the 1880s. Societies were organized to coordinate the activities of the many private charities serving the poor. A statement from the National Conference of Charities and Corrections in 1899 reflects general assumptions about families and the methods of service delivery common in these agencies:

> Your committee is emphatically of the opinion that the "ounce of prevention is better than the pound of cure," and it strongly urges upon all charitable people the absolute necessity for preserving the home wherever possible.
>
> Do not be in a hurry to send the children to an institution until you are convinced of the hopelessness of preserving the home. Remember that, when the home is broken up, even temporarily, it is no easy task to bring it together again, and that a few dollars of private charity, a friendly visit, a kind word, and a helping hand will lift up the courage of the deserving poor; and this is half the battle, because discouragement begets carelessness [Bremner, 1971, p. 352].

Even earlier, the 1881 annual Report of the Massachusetts Society for Prevention of Cruelty to Children, a protective service agency, indicated that "one of our methods of relieving children is to reform the parents—When the home life is not degraded or can be essentially improved it is better not to separate parent and child" (pp. 21–22). These agencies took seriously their moral responsibility to evaluate the extent to which families deserved their help and their obligation to refuse service to "undeserving" families (Gibson & Lewis, 1980).

Another type of organization whose responsibility involved helping poor families evolved during the 1880s and 1890s. Called Settlement Houses, workers in these agencies:

> differed from those in the charity organizations in their approach to the poor; they focused on the neighborhoods and subcommunities near the settlement houses and, more importantly, stressed social problems rather than individual reform. Personal services to families were, however, an integral part of the work [Billingsley & Giovannoni, 1972, p. 37].

A third type of home-based care agency functioned briefly during the latter part of the nineteenth century. Established in March 1865 by an act of Congress, the Freedmen's Bureau was responsible for assessing and alleviating poverty among black families, establishing health and educational services for these families, and dealing with conflicts arising between blacks and their former masters. "In effect, the provision of land, work, and direct relief served Black children within their family, for it was a means of strengthening and keeping those families together. This approach was quite different from that taken by the established child welfare agencies and organizations of the nineteenth century. Short-lasting and inadequate though this endeavor was, it was, in a way, a revolutionary development in child welfare" (Billingsley & Giovannoni, 1972, p. 43). Funding for the Bureau was discontinued in 1871.

The turn of the century saw a slowly growing commitment to provision of services for children who remained with their families. The first White House Conference on Children, held in 1909, describes this investment while continuing to echo earlier concerns for the worthiness of the child's family:

> Home life is the highest and finest product of civilization. It is the great molding force of mind and of character. Children should not be deprived of it except for urgent and compelling reasons. Children of parents of worthy character, suffering from temporary misfortune, and children of reasonably efficient and deserving mothers who are without the support of the normal breadwinner, should as a rule be kept with their parents, such aid being given as may be necessary to maintain suitable homes for the rearing of the children [Bremner, 1971, p. 365].

Despite this commitment, enormous numbers of children were placed in institutions, many of them in large institutions primarily established for care of adults. Proceedings of the 1909 White House Conference on the care of dependent children estimates that some 93,000 children were in residential care and "many additional thousands" were in foster and boarding homes (Bremner, 1971, p. 365).

Until the beginning of the Great Depression in the 1930s, the Charity Organization Societies primarily served an economically deprived clientele, and the problems brought to the agency were those that were closely related to economic need (Cloward & Epstein, 1964). The service revolved around offering, and helping the client to use concrete resources, prominent among which were cash relief grants. At the same time, there was emphasis on helping the poor through the personal influence and interest of the social worker—"not alms alone, but alms and a friend" was thought to be the most desirable method. This philosophy was the historical antecedent of the use of a personal relationship in helping, the principal approach of the family service agency and the guidance clinic of today.

When government agencies assumed primary responsibility for relief grants, both the characteristics of the clientele and the kinds of primary problems brought to the family service agencies began to change. More and more insistently, the agencies defined their function as that of providing help with interpersonal, family adjustment, parent–child, and marital difficulties. By the 1950s, this change in emphasis had been successfully communicated to the community. As a result, the current clientele is more nearly representative of the general composition of the community, since parent–child and marital problems exist at every socioeconomic level.

Early in the twentieth century, the child guidance clinic emerged out of a concern with helping juvenile delinquents. in 1909 Dr. William Healy, working under the aegis of the Juvenile Court of Cook County, Illinois, began a study of juvenile offenders. He attempted to apply some of the newer concepts of psychiatric service derived from Freud's discoveries, and he made explicit efforts to individualize the juvenile offender. In 1917 Dr. Healy's facility, later known as the Institute for Juvenile Research, received state support, and his work was extended to a wider group of emotionally disturbed children, whether delinquent or not. The attempt to individualize each child involved a fourfold approach: "a medical examination to analyze the child's physical assets and abilities, psychological tests to estimate his intellectual capacity, psychiatric interviews to determine his attitudes and the character of his mental life," and a study of the child's developmental history and social situation (Witmer, 1940, p. 47). Thus Healy's approach considered not only the physical and psychological factors in development but the social factors as well, and the dynamic interaction between parents and children as causative factors in the child's disturbed behavior. This fourfold approach characterizes the guidance clinic today.

The pioneer work of Healy was widely disseminated as a result of the sponsorship of demonstration clinics by the National Committee for Mental Hygiene in the early 1920s. The first demonstration clinic was established in 1922 in St. Louis, with a staff consisting of a psychiatrist, a psychologist, and a social worker. Additional clinics were set up in six cities throughout the country: Norfolk, Dallas, Minneapolis, Los Angeles, Cleveland, and Philadelphia. Two traveling clinics were established, operating from three to six months in each city, in an effort to demonstrate the value of such a service and to encourage the community to set up a permanent clinic.

The Commonwealth Fund also set up a program for the training of child guidance workers at the New York School of Social Work. The school established special courses in child guidance and established a psychiatric clinic, the Bureau of Child Guidance, New York City, which was used as a training center for social workers.

Before the demonstration experiment was terminated in 1927, it had established the feasibility and need for such a facility for all children who presented emotional problems. By 1928 a *Directory of Psychiatric Clinics for Children* in the United States, published by the Commonwealth Fund, listed 470 clinics in 31 states offering service to 40,000 children during that year (Harper et al., 1940, p. 332).

Although the central concern of child guidance clinics was the child, it soon became an axiom of clinic practice that "for every problem child, there is a problem parent." Thus the parent, as well as the child, became an object of concern. The delinquent child shared problems of parent–child relationships with other children, many of whom simply manifested the results of such disorders in a way that was less disturbing to others. There was a movement, then, toward helping all children with problems rather than the delinquent child only. A study of the activities of these clinics indicates that many of the supposedly modern innovations in practice, such as the community mental-health orientation, advocacy, and brokerage were integral aspects of this early service (Levine & Levine, 1970).

The Depression of the 1930s brought with it increased use of home-based services, spurred on, in part, by the high cost of institutional care and the magnitude of the need for services. As a consequence, use of both institutional and foster care services declined over a 30-year period following the Depression. Bremner (1974) states that by 1933 approximately 140,000 dependent and neglected children were placed in institutional care. By 1950, this number had dropped to 100,000 and by 1960 to approximately 80,000 (p. 634). Use of foster care faced a similar decrease until the 1960s. During the 1960s, however, use of institutional care stabilized, while use of foster care services increased dramatically. Shyne and Schroeder (1978) estimated that, by the mid-1970s, some 75,000 children were in residential settings whereas the number of children in foster family care had risen to 394,000. Forty percent of the child welfare and AFDC families they surveyed received some type of substitute services (p. 62).

During the 1960s and 1970s, professionals began, once again, to focus attention on serving children at home. Individuals interested in development of these services paid particular attention to programming for the most difficult, demanding, and needy of child welfare clients: multiproblem abusive families who had a long history of agency involvement and a problematic history of disengagement and uncooperativeness with agency personnel. Bryce (1982) considers the St. Paul Family-Centered project, begun in the late 1950s, as the prototype of such services. The project was established to serve multiply impaired families, those facing severe poverty and health problems, and families whose children were considered delinquent, neglected, or in danger of imminent removal. Using many of the principles typifying home-based care programs today, including aggressive outreach and the use of multifaceted services adapted to each particular family situation, the project claimed that it produced some positive change in two-thirds of the families served (Horejsi, 1981).

This reemergent concern for provision of services to improve the home life of children was reflected in activities in the educational and medical arenas as well. During the 1960s, there was rapid growth in preschool educational programs for children from poor families. These included the Head Start, High/Scope, and Home Start programs. In the 1970s, maternal and child health programs received increasing attention (Halpern, 1984). Public child welfare agencies also paid increasing attention to provision of in-home services, particularly to minority children, who were overrepresented among institutional and foster care populations (McGowan, 1983).

Despite attention to preservation of family integrity, child welfare practice has continued to rely on separation of children from their parents as a primary service approach in many cases. Many factors contributed to this overuse. By the early twentieth century, two different types of service organizations existed in the United States. One focused on care of children whose families could no longer care for them; the other dealt with intact families and provided home-based treatment. Child welfare and child advocacy programs tended to perceive placement as their objective, while family service agencies tended to perceive their mission as preservation of family life (Rice, 1978; See also Hartman, 1981). These various service philosophies impacted on agency placement rates.

Families themselves behave in ways that foster professional concern for placing their children. Child welfare families often feel hopeless and helpless about their problems. Because they do not approach agencies with optimism and obvious initiative, agency personnel, believing they are not committed to changing their family life, may ignore service requests unless some major upheaval occurs in the family. However, once the crisis has occurred, it may appear, both to the family and to the agency, that the easiest solution is removal of the child:

> If the negative attitude of a family is accompanied by a great deal of pain, the family may become desperate and seek radical solutions. The sense of hopelessness prevails, but because the pain is so great, something must be done. Under the force of desperation, radical solutions are considered. These may include running away, suicide, divorce, spouse or child abuse, a nervous breakdown, or requesting separations or removal of a "problem child" from the home [Ryan, 1979, p. 273].

A vicious cycle is established, one in which the family fails to seek assistance until problems are of crisis proportions, agencies recommend removal of the child, and neither parents nor agencies sustain motivation to work on the problem in order to reunite the family and child after placement.

Beliefs that children are more important than their parents and require protection from parents contributed to increasing use of foster care and institutional services after the 1960s. The high cost and improper use of such care (Vasaly, 1978), and the realization that large numbers of children remained in care for unnecessarily long periods and suffered because they had no permanent future (Maluccio et al., 1980; Bush & Goldman, 1982) prompted eventual passage of Public Law 96-272, the Adoption Assistance and Child Welfare Act of 1980. Provisions of this act encouraged the use of preventive home-based services, mandated documented use of such services prior to placement, and limited the extent of placement in non-permanent substitute care settings wherever possible. Allen and Knitzer (1983) describe this act as using "a carrot-and-stick" approach to redirect funds away from inappropriate, often costly, out-of-home care and toward alternatives to placement" (p. 120).

The new law placed a ceiling on spending for out-of-home care (Cole, 1982); it mandated a number of tracking and reporting requirements to help prevent the drift of children in foster care and to force agencies to plan more effectively for all children receiving services (Magazino, 1983); it outlined specific protections for parents of children in substitute care, including provision of such care in close proximity to the parents' home and parent participation in their childrens' treatment planning (Allen & Knitzer, 1983).

Federal commitment to the provision of in-home care was also reflected in funding for the National Clearinghouse for Home-Based Service to Children, based at the University of Iowa School of Social Work (Sudia, 1982).

Situations in Which Home-Based Services Are the Appropriate Resource

"The process of taking prompt, decisive action to maintain children in their own homes or place them permanently with other families" (Maluccio & Fine, 1983, p. 195) is called permanency planning. Initially, the concept was developed to support the need for specialized efforts to arrange adoptive placements for children in long-term foster care who could not be returned to their homes. Subsequently, concern for timely restoration of the child to his or her birth family *or* provision of another type of permanent home became the focus of permanency planning efforts. A recent definition developed by Maluccio and Fein (1983) reflects this perspctive: "Permanency planning is the systematic process of carrying out, within the brief time-limited period, a set of goal-directed activities designed to help children live in families that offer continuity of relationships with nurturing parents or caretakers and the opportunity to establish lifetime relationships" [p. 197].

In order to provide a permanent future for children, Public Law 96–272 describes several necessary services (Table 3–1). Three of these services involve treatment of children in the home of their birth parents. whereas two additional services are to be provided for children who must be placed in another setting. In-home services that focus on prevention, remedial assistance to families, and reunification are the focus of this chapter.

Preventive services are designed to assist parents and children to live more effectively together so that current or potential problems do not develop into a major crisis with which the family unit cannot cope. Characteristics of families typically using child welfare services point to the need for preventive efforts on their behalf. Bush and Goldman (1982) state:

> The majority of families who come to the attention of child welfare agencies do not come because parents have suddenly conceived the notion that they no longer wish to care for their children. They come because physical ill health, unemployment, poverty, divorce, poor living conditions, and mental ill health have reduced the parents to circumstances in which they think, or state officials think, that they are no longer capable of looking after their children. Some of these situations could be improved by state intervention such as extra financial aid, temporary in-home care, and help with employment and housing problems [p. 226].

TABLE 3.1   Permanency Planning Services Mandated by Public Law 96-272 (42 USC 625, *Sect. 425 [a](1))*

Home Based Services

1. Preventive Services
   a. Protecting and promoting the welfare of all children, including handicapped, homeless, dependent, or neglected children.
   b. Preventing or remedying, or assisting in the solution of problems which may result in the neglect, abuse, exploitation, or delinquency of children.

2. Remedial Services
   a. Preventing the unnecessary separation of children from their families by identifying family problems, assisting families in resolving their problems, and preventing breakup of the family where the prevention of child removal is desirable and possible.

3. Reunification Services
   a. Restoring to their families children who have been removed, by the provision of services to the child and the families.

Adoption Services

Placing children in suitable adoptive homes, in cases where restoration to the biological family is not possible or appropriate.

Foster Care and Institutional Services

Assuring adequate care of children away from their homes, in cases where the child cannot be returned home or cannot be placed for adoption.

These services are designed to reduce the risk that families will become unable to care for their children and the risk that difficulties with one child will also develop with the child's siblings.

Preventive services have been developed to assist families with four general types of difficulties. Some programs have been designed to overcome broad circumstances (poverty, high family stress, unemployment, and so forth) that make parents potentially unable to carry out their child-caretaking responsibilities and/or create handicapping conditions for children. Programs that assist families in finding safer housing, employment assistance programs, and Head Start are examples. One such program is the High/Scope Parent-to-Parent Model that has been developed in a number of communities. Judith Evans (1979) explains that this is a "low cost community-based educational program" designed to "support and complement parental skills and to assist parents in clarifying their child-rearing goals" (p. 116). The program recruits and trains nonprofessional staff who visit the homes of parents needing assistance in learning about their children's needs and clarifying their own objectives.

Another type of preventive service involves work with adults who find themselves in difficulty that may eventually create problems for their children as well. Knitzer and Olson (1982), in a review of innovative treatment programs, describe two such efforts. The Parent and Child Education Family Center in New York City offers a day treatment program for emotionally disabled adults and a nursery facility for their preschool children. Similarly, the Cambridge and Sommerville Program for Alcohol Rehabilitation in Cambridge, Massachusetts, includes an alcohol education program for the children of participants.

Yet another type of preventive program assists parents whose children are handicapped, disabled, or fact other types of chronic difficulties. Project Home, an early childhood special education program in St. Louis, serves families whose children are severely developmentally disabled. Elardo (1981) describes a sample of the children whose families came to this agency:

1. A six-year-old girl, mental age two years, who did not feed or toilet herself, had a short attention span, and who had regressed since returning home from foster care.
2. A three-year-old girl, mildly retarded with behavior problems—a former child abuse case.
3. A five-year-old boy, learning disabled, with emotional problems, who attended a hearing and speech center during the day and whose mother was mentally retarded.
4. A six-year-old boy, learning disabled with speech and behavior problems and whose mother, a single parent, had a heart condition and severe obesity [p. 42].

The program uses home visitors to help parents with caretaking skills. The Pediatric Home Care Program lodged at the Bronx Municipal Hospital Center was developed in 1970 to help families live more effectively with chronically ill children. Dr. Ruth Stein (1981) states, "in a sense the program aimed to return the care and control of the life of a sick child to the family, based on acquisition of information, normalization of family life, and appropriate self-reliance" (p. 315). The staff of the program include physicians, nursing personnel, and social workers who work as a team with the entire family. Team members also serve as advocates for coordinated services for children who have "multi-system or multidisciplinary problems." (See also Spinelli & Barton, 1980.)

Finally, short-term preventive services may be needed for some families facing common but major crises. These crises may be precipitated by addition of a member to the family or loss of a family member. Kamerman and Kahn (1983) state:

> For families which are not "in trouble" but who are experiencing the normal life milestones and the challenges that they involve and who may have to do so without the support of intimate family and friends and without relevant experience, there is need for a variety of educational, advice, and counselling services. We refer to the periods right before and right after childbirth, the entry of children into child care programs or elementary school, the death of loved ones, the breaking up of families through separation and divorce, and the reconstitution of families—the joining of children of different parents, the development of new parenting responsibilities by step-parents, and so forth [p. 163]. (See also O'Connor, Davis, & Sahlein, 1984.)

The type of home-based care that has received perhaps most widespread attention in recent years involves what we have called remedial help to families facing potential separation from their child (Conte, 1983). There is some indication that public child welfare agencies consider provision of remedial home-based care to be the most basic part of agency services, whereas other preventive efforts are considered less essential, to be provided should time and funds be available. Magazino (1983) includes the following among "at risk" family characteristics:

> Families where there are alleged incidents of neglect or abuse; patterns of severe interpersonal conflicts; parents handicapped by mental illness, retardation, or physical disability; one or more members who are substance abusers; children demonstrating predelinquent or delinquent behavior; parents separated involuntarily from their children because of incarceration or institutionalization; children exhibiting severe emotional or school adjustment problems; parents too young to assume full child-caring responsibilities; and situations in which there is potential physical harm because of the deprivation associated with severe poverty [p. 215].

He notes, however, that no clear, mutually agreed upon definition of "at risk" families now exists.

Families requiring assistance from remedially oriented home-based programs differ from those served by broad-based preventive programs in the acuteness of their current family crisis and in the number and extent of the chronic problems that they face. Haapala and Kinney (1979) describe the situation of one family served by the Home Builders program:

1. The mother was suicidal.
2. Five of their seven children were retarded.
3. The father had had a heart attack last spring and had two strokes since then.
4. Three months before, the mother's rectum had burst. She had been patched together but was unable to have sex and said it felt like firecrackers going off inside her. She also had serious liver problems. She was using many, many drugs—sometimes more than had been prescribed.
5. They still had custody of a 30-year-old son. He had run away two weeks before and was suspected to be in jail in Ohio. They were upset about not knowing how to handle his money without getting into trouble with the state or risking his getting cut off of public assistance.
6. They were trying to get custody of their grandchildren whose 27-year-old mother was committed to a psychiatric hospital, partly for indecent exposure and prostitution. Her husband who was in prison for rape, was trying to get custody of the children. The grandparents did not want this to happen.
7. Their 25-year-old son kept trying to kill his girlfriend and was in and out of jail.

8. Their 21-year-old son was going to have to go to jail in two weeks if he could not pay off fines he had accumulated for shoplifting.
9. Their 18-year-old son had been run over by a school bus when he was four and was unable to talk. They were worried about how he would ever take care of himself.
10. Their 15-year-old daughter drank, smoked, lied, did no chores, sassed everyone, and stayed out late.
11. The 13-year-old daughter was restricted to her room for one year because she lied, stole, sassed, and did no chores [pp. 249–250].

Noting that the family had already been in counseling for twenty years, the authors describe progress members made after participating in intensive treatment at Home Builders for only four to six weeks.

Helping "at risk" families deal with their acute problems requires immediate, intensive efforts to help them understand and deal with current difficulties. "Families in crisis must be offered rescue and must be assisted in assessing the alternatives available to them so they can make decisions regarding their lives" (Hawkins, 1979, p. 106). Helping families deal with more chronic problems requires more wide-ranging service delivery efforts adapted to the needs of each particular family. Many of the services provided to alleviate long-standing difficulties are similar to those provided in other preventive programs. They include financial and housing assistance, and other health and mental health services.

The Comprehensive Emergency Services (CES) Program in Nashville, Tennessee, is an example of an agency providing remedially oriented home-based care. Developed to serve abusive families facing imminent removal of their children, the program was opened after research showed that protective service workers were frequently removing children from the home, placing them in an overcrowded shelter facility, and then returning nearly 80 per cent after their family went to court (Hawkins, 1979, p. 104). The program offers emergency intake on a 24-hour basis, use of emergency caretakers to care for children as temporary guardians when they are left alone and unsupervised, use of emergency homemaker services for parents who need assistance in carrying out routine child care responsibilities, and an emergency shelter for families who have been thrown out of their home or who are passing through the community.

A more structured parent treatment program was developed at the Home and Community Treatment Program (HCT) in Madison, Wisconsin. This program serves clients whose children are in danger of placement in residential care for treatment of their emotional problems (Fahl & Morrissey, 1979). Staff of the program conduct extensive evaluations of family functioning in the home, carry out intensive parent training in the use of behavior modification, and assist parents to continue to use these principles in dealing with their children after case termination. Families stay in the program for approximately nine months and are served by a multiprofessional team. (See also Slater & Harris, 1978; Cautley, 1980; Buckley, 1985.)

A program with a slightly different focus was developed in Iowa City to assist families who have children with developmental disabilities. Called FACT, Family and Child Training, this agency works with families whose children have "a substantial handicap which occurs before age 18, such as mental retardation, cerebral palsy, epilepsy, and autism" (Koch, 1979, p. 157). Describing FACT's philosophical outlook, Koch states, "the program is based on the premise that many parents can and will keep their disabled children at home, if they receive help with the daily care of the child and if some of their emotional needs are met through positive relationships with those who are giving the help. That is, parents need someone to share the load" (pp. 157–158). In addition to offering counseling help with general family problems and assistance to parents in developing appropriate education for their children, the program also provides child care workers who go to the home and help with daily maintenance tasks and a recreational therapist whose job it is to develop appropriate leisure activities for the child as well as the family. The program has provided services to families such as the following (Koch, 1979):

> Billy is a thirteen-year-old boy who attends a special class for the trainable mentally retarded and lives with his parents and younger brother in a small town a few miles from Iowa City. He was referred to the FACT program by his caseworker from the Iowa Department of Social Services.
>
> During the initial home visit, Billy's mother explained that he was becoming more of a problem as he grew older and bigger, that he bullied his younger brother, and was very difficult for her to control. For this reason, she and her husband were considering residential placement for Billy as soon as possible. She also expressed fears that she and her husband were not providing the best possible environment for him and that he might learn more or do better in some other residential setting. Mrs. T was eager to try the FACT Program while keeping the option of residential placement.
>
> After consulting with Billy's teacher and Social Services worker, and after observing him at school, the FACT coordinator prepared an individual service plan. A social worker and a child care worker were assigned to the family by the FACT Program. Primary goals of the plan included implementation of more effective behavior management techniques at home and utilization of recreation activities to help Billy learn to play cooperatively with his brother and other children. Mrs. T also requested we help Billy learn to behave appropriately in stores, restaurants, and other public places.
>
> Billy was enrolled in a special Boy Scouts Troop, accompanied at first by the child care worker. The FACT staff also took Billy on many outings, often including the younger brother and neighboring children. The social worker began meeting with the parents approximately once a week, to discuss a wide variety of problems. She also visited Billy's classroom frequently to learn what behavior management techniques are employed there and to insure that they would also be used at home . . .
>
> There has been considerable improvement in Billy's behavior. Mr. and Mrs. T report that the variety of experiences now available to Billy have helped them feel confident that his needs can be met without placement. They also say that knowing other people are consistently available to be involved with Billy has helped ease the burden of raising him. Although future residential placement may be necessary, it is no longer seen as an immediate need [pp. 159–160].

Two basic methods of service coordination are available to clients needing preventive services. One method involves use of multiple agencies, each providing one or two needed services. Providing services in this way requires special case management effort and can result in a number of difficulties. As Janchill (1983) notes, "for families and children with serious life management difficulties and multiple-level problems, there can be starvation amidst plenty, given the diffuseness and fragmentation of the service system" (p. 354). An alternative approach involves creation of multiservice centers within one agency. A recent federal publication (U.S. Department of Health and Human Services, 1980) calls this "almost a cafeteria style approach," one that allows families to decide for themselves which services and programs they require (p. 162). These programs sometimes allow families to feel more supported and less isolated, and, when located in close proximity to many clients' homes, function much like an "extended family" (Jones, Magura, Shyne, 1981).

Some home-based programs have also been specifically designed to help parents and children live together more effectively after they have been separated because of the child's placement in foster care or residential settings. A recent report from the U.S Children's Bureau (Gershenson, 1983) points out the vast number of families for whom provision of such services may be required. Gershenson found that 49 per cent of all children in substitute care were subsequently returned to the homes of their families or to other relatives (p. 22). The special circumstances under which reunification services are provided and the unique characteristics of the families and of the agencies assisting them are described in greater detail in the chapters on foster and institutional care in this volume.

Scope

Estimates of the extent to which families seeking help from child welfare agencies are served through delivery of home-based services are difficult to obtain, as are estimates of the range and type of services offered. Some data are provided by surveys of public child welfare agencies and in the literature describing voluntary agencies that frequently provide services to child welfare families.

In 1972, Barbara Haring conducted a national census of services requested from child welfare agencies throughout the United States. Information on intake procedures was obtained from 176 child-serving agencies that are members of the Child Welfare League of America. These agencies comprised some two-thirds of all agencies who are League members. All but ten of these agencies operated under voluntary auspices. Participants in the study were asked to provide information about services that families requested during a five-day period.

In addition to request for home-based care, Haring evaluated the extent to which families asked for other support services (day care, financial assistance, homemaker services), protective services and substitute care (adoption and foster care). Requests for home-based care comprised one-third of the more than two thousand requests for service coming to these agencies. Participating agencies varied greatly in the extent to which they were asked to provide substitute services, particularly foster care, in relation to requests for in-home service. The 129 Jewish agencies participating in the study, for example, were more than twice as likely to receive requests for foster care than for services in the home; nonsectarian voluntary agencies considering themselves child and family serving facilities, on the other hand, were four times as likely to receive requests for in-home treatment assistance. The data suggest that clients may perceive public agencies as more likely to provide substitute care, since twice as many requests for adoptive and foster care services were received by those agencies. Voluntary agencies, in contrast, were perceived as providing more in-home services. Whereas 30 per cent of all requests going to those agencies were for adoptive or foster care services, 40 per cent of the requests were for home-based care (pp. 20–22).

Haring also analyzed the relationship between the primary reason clients were contacting the agencies and the types of services they requested. Four different patterns of home-based service provision emerged from this analysis, based on types of client problems. For the first type of problem, services requested were almost exclusively home-based. For example, 70 percent of all clients coming to the agencies because of out-of-wedlock pregnancies requested such services. For a second problem type, most clients requested in-home services, but a substantial minority also requested foster care services. Situations in which clients were experiencing parent–child conflict were of this type. Assessment of a third problem area showed families equally likely to request home-based or substitute care. This occurred when families identified the child's emotional difficulties as particularly troubling. A fourth problem category was associated with very heavy use of substitute care, for a child was born out of wedlock, in situations in which the antisocial behavior of the parent precipitated a request, and where other parental problems (such as imprisonment or physical or mental illness) stood in the way of providing adequate child care (p. 27).

In 1978, Ann Shyne and Anita Schroeder carried out a more extensive survey of requests for services and services offered to public agency clients. This study covered a different pool of agencies than Haring's and made particular attempts to seek a representative sample of public agency requests. Shyne and Schroeder examined services requested by and delivered to both public child welfare clients and those whose families were receiving AFDC benefits. The researchers examined service provision in more than 9,500 cases in 38 states.

Shyne and Schroeder used a different definition of home-based care than that developed by Haring. In addition to supportive services (day treatment, homemaker services, and day care), they included requests for services in the protective service arena and for "counseling." They defined counseling as "the guidance and support by the caseworker of the child and his/her family *provided independently of other services* while the child is residing at home" (p. c–1). Because of this, it is difficult to get an estimate of the total amount of counseling provided since, when it was combined with any other service, only the additional service was enumerated. Shyne and Schroeder also excluded any counseling that was related only to income maintenance or eligibility requirements.

The authors estimated that in 1977 1.8 million children received public social services from child welfare and public assistance workers. In this survey, family difficulties proved to be a much more significant reason for service requests than child difficulties. Almost one-third of all requests occurred because of neglect, abuse, or exploitation on the part of the parent. More than one-quarter of all the cases came to the attention of agencies because of some emotional problem of the parent, and, in almost 20 per cent of the cases, parent-child conflict served as the major reason for needing assistance. Requests for help for children's problems occurred in fewer cases—for the child's emotional difficulties (19% of all reasons), or for problematic behavior at home (17%) or at school (14%).

Shyne and Schroeder examined the role of provision of home-based care in both treatment planning and in treatment provision. Service plans were written for only two-thirds of all the cases they studied. Strengthening the family to lessen the need for placement was a service goal in 23 per cent, but placement of the child in adoptive, institutional, or other forms of substitute care was a major goal in 32 per cent of the cases (p. 60). Workers planned to use "counseling only" in response to only 11 per cent of all the families. Other mental health or educational services were planned for an additional 14 per cent. Although workers planned to use substitute care services in one-third of the cases, 40 per cent actually received such services. "Counseling only" was provided to 19 per cent of the children and 46 per cent of the principle caretakers in this survey. Two-thirds of those children for whom "counseling only" services were recommended received them. Shyne and Schroeder also found that agency workers providing "counseling only" were less likely to have either a social work degree or graduate professional degree than were those providing foster or adoptive services.

The study suggests that a vast number of children continued to be served through provision of out-of-home care. When consideration is given to the fact that the families studied in this survey included a large number of AFDC families, resort to the use of substitute care as a primary treatment modality takes on added significance. The study also suggests that use of counseling is not considered a service requiring as well-trained or professionally qualified staff as is the provision of substitute care services. Nevertheless, "counseling only" services are provided for a significant number of children and families in the United States— some 300,000 children and 700,000 caretakers in 1978.

Community mental health centers also provide counseling services for poor children and their families. There is considerable overlap between these two types of agencies in the type of clientele they serve, and many families receive services in both settings, sequentially or simultaneously. In mental health settings, outpatient family services may be provided through child guidance clinics or through children's service units.

Only 200 of the 2,300 mental health clinics in the United States in 1976 also offered child guidance services. Of the 268,000 children seen in these clinics, only 40 per cent received treatment; 160,800 were only provided a diagnostic assessment (Goldsmith, 1977, p. 892). Some 10 per cent of all clinic clients are children or adolescents (Rothman & Kay, 1977, p. 14). Adolescents age 10 to 14 and boys were more likely to be referred for service to this type of agency.

An increasing number of voluntary agencies are also serving public child welfare clients through purchase of service arrangements. These include both nonsectarian agencies (such as family and children service agencies) and sectarian agencies (operating under Catholic, Jewish, or Protestant auspices). Nationwide studies confirm that parent–child difficulties constitute a high proportion of the problems that bring families to a family service agency. In 1970, 42 per cent of family agency clients presented a problem of "parent–child" relationship at intake, 26 per cent listed a problem of "child rearing or child care," 14 per cent were concerned with the "personality adjustment of a child under thirteen." Clients generally presented more than one problem, but the three major areas were personality problems, marital problems, and parent–child problems (Beck & Jones, 1973). At such agencies, interpersonal adjustment problems are generally given higher priority at intake that are situational problems (employment, housing, and the like). The titles that family service agencies employ for their direct service staff tend to suggest this. Although workers are most frequently called "social worker" or "case worker," a substantial number of agencies identify their direct service workers as "counselor," "family counselor," "therapist," "family therapist," "clinical social worker" (Family Service Association of America, 1983, p. 4).

A report by the Family Service Association of America indicated that in 1982 an estimated 936,000 families were served by family service agencies. About 40 per cent of the clients were involved primarily in family life education programs. The report noted that in addition to the basic casework counseling, there had been shifts over the period between 1962 and 1982 in the kinds of additional special services offered. There had been a progressive increase in family life education, advocacy, day care, and protective services and service to industry programs. Homemaker, adoption, and foster care services had decreased modestly (Family Service Association of America, 1983).

Agencies in 1970 were serving a slightly higher proportion of disadvantaged families than they did in 1960. In 1970 some 51 per cent of agency client families were of lower or upper-lower socioeconomic status. Black clients were served by family agencies in nearly double their proportion to the general population. Despite the efforts of family service agencies to serve more minority families, there was almost no increase in use by members of the black community between 1960 and 1970. Of family agency clientele in 1970, 2.4 per cent were Spanish speaking and 0.3 per cent were of American Indian origin (Beck & Jones, 1973, p. 85).

Stages in the Service Delivery Process

Delivery of home-based services can be conceptualized as a four-stage process. In the data gathering–social study phase, clients develop a basic affiliation with the worker and establish tentative commitment to begin working on their difficulties. In the diagnosis-assessment phase, workers are responsible for evaluating the extent and severity of client problems, for locating the cause of client difficulties within the family and/or its environment, and for devloping a tentative treatment plan with the family. The third stage concerns fulfillment of the treatment contract. During this phase, a wide range of needed services may be made available to child welfare families. Finally, in the termination phase, workers are concerned about the timing and phasing of their decision to end contact with the clients. We consider each of these steps in further detail, focusing in particular on the special needs and requirements of multiproblem families and/or those requiring comprehensive, multifaceted services.

Data Gathering–Social Study

Many parents who are concerned about the behavior of their children do not see the relevance of casework services to the problems they face. Detailed interviews with a stratified sample of eight hundred families drawn from the general population in Westchester County, New York, and supplemented by data provided by the schools was used by reviewing psychiatrists to determine that "a third of the 800 children in the sample were judged to be moderately or severely impaired" (Lurie, 1974, p. 110). Only a very limited number of the parents had actually sought professional help. Many parents interpreted these behavioral difficulties as only a "phase" the child was going through. A small percentage of families come to the child welfare agency, family agency, or clinic after reading or hearing about the work of such agencies through mass communication media—newspapers, radio, television, and so on; these may be regarded as self-referred applicants. More frequently, however, applicants are referred by friends, other social and health agencies. schools, courts, and physicians.

Once the initial contact has been made, the agency and the applicant get acquainted with one another. The agency learns the general nature of the applicant's problems and determines if it is the appropriate agency for helping the applicant. The applicant learns something about how the agency operates and determines if he or she wants the kind of help the agency has to offer, in the way the agency offers it. If both applicant and agency agree that the parents are having a problem with their children, if the parents would like to have the help of the agency in dealing with it, and if the agency feels it can be of help, the applicant becomes a client.

An essential aspect of this intake process concerns the client's initial decision to commit himself or herself to involvement in the service delivery process. In a study of clients who had sought help from a family service agency, Maluccio (1979) outlined several steps clients take to become "engaged" with the worker:

1. The experiencing of inner distress or external pressure by the person.
2. The person's trying to cope by reaching out to significant others.
3. The referral to an agency by self or others.
4. The evoking of expectations in the person, mobilizing him or her to get to the agency.
5. The initial encounter with the worker [p. 178].

During each of these substages, certain conditions must be met in order to propel the individual on to the next substage and into a deepening commitment to obtain agency assistance:

> The person's distress or pressure from an outside source needs to be of sufficient magnitude that it propels him or her to take action (e.g., "I was so upset that I had to do something about it"). The severity of the person's experience with distress or with external pressure leads to a variety of coping efforts, which typically involve reaching out to (or being reached by) formal and/or informal sources of help. When the formal or informal helping agents are perceived by the person as inadequate or inaccessible, a referral to an agency ensues. The referral provokes expectations that, although they are generally unrealistic, stimulate sufficient hope to enable the person to go through the referral process, despite its attendant anxiety, and to get to the agency [p. 178].

Ryan (1979) finds that essential motivators include the client's recognition that something is wrong, a wish that the situation could be different, and a decision to "go public" about the problem by approaching an agency and requesting help (p. 272).

Particular difficulties in developing this commitment may occur with child welfare families. These families may be considered what Maluccio (1979) calls "non-preferred clients." He notes, "the preferred client is someone who is open, responsive, and capable of emotional insight, while the least-liked client was presented as rigid, resistive, and non-verbal" (p. 182). Workers felt competent and fulfilled when working with preferred clients, "while the non-preferred client provoked feelings of self-doubt, inadequacy, and frustration" (p. 182). Some one-third of the individuals in his randomly selected sample of family service agencies' clients were considered nonpreferred. Agencies that serve large numbers of poor, multiproblem families have a disproportionately greater number of these individuals with whom to work.

Horejsi (1981), in a perceptive analysis of this dilemma, notes that many workers are bewildered that families experiencing such pain are also unwilling to accept assistance. He states:

> . . . this paradox is best explained by the concept of learned helplessness. Persons subjected to pain—whether physical or emotional—attempt to escape or fight back. However, if repeated efforts to escape or fight back are unsuccessful, they quit trying and become apathetic. Individuals conclude that they cannot alter their situation, which they come to view as hopeless. Hooker, in describing learned helplessness, notes that "the experimental evidence indicates that learned helplessness develops when one objectively is or believes oneself to be unable to control the outcome of events. This cognitive disturbance gives rise to motivational and emotional aspects of learned helplessness. If a person believes himself to be unable to control the

outcome of life events and fails to see that his actions make a difference, he is less motivated to try" [pp. 14–15].

Individuals who feel hopeless may become angry when approached by potential helpers, as they feel they are, once again, being asked to undertake a fruitless task. Parents may also feel that helpers are too naive and simply do not understand the complexity of the crises they face.

One set of techniques that overcomes client reluctance and despair have been termed "aggressive outreach." More than thirty years ago, staff of the Family-Centered Project in St. Paul, Minnesota, described the use of this approach with families (Horejsi, 1981). Two primary characteristics of this approach include persistence and optimism. Instead of relying on the client to initiate and continue early contacts with the agency, workers assume this responsibility. Workers might, for example, travel to the family's home to initiate contacts and return repeatedly, even when the family refuses to answer the door or expresses hostility. Horejsi (1981) points out, "how a worker responded to initial rejection and hostility proved to be an important factor in forming a working relationship. In subsequent project evaluation interviews, many families explained that they had been pleasantly surprised that the worker kept coming back in spite of how they had treated him/her. To be accepted despite one's behavior was a new experience" (p. 16). Staff of the Family-Centered Project insisted that workers must not give up once they had begun outreach to the family. They considered lack of persistence to be "irresponsible."

Effective outreach requires that workers feel optimistic about the family's potential for resolving its problems (Gourse & Chescheir, 1981). One consequence of feeling pessimistic about a client's ability to change is reflected in use of what Kinney, Haapala, and Gast (1981) call GLOP (Generalized Labeling of People). Typical descriptions of GLOP families include "manipulative," "ineffectual," "passive aggressive" (p. 51), and so forth. Use of these labels produces the following results:

1. GLOP terms are usually vague enough so that people disagree about what they mean and have difficulty specifying what needs to change.
2. Most GLOP is negative, value laden, and blameful. Such terminology can encourage clients to withdraw.
3. Therapists can become discouraged and frightened by a long list of negatives—there may be a tendency to expect the client to live up to the label.
4. Clients are often offended by what they consider to be an oversimplification of their situation.
5. It is poor modeling for clients who frequently already use name-calling with each other and need help in using neutral, specific language.
6. The descriptions are so vague that often it is difficult to present evidence that discounts the label; once they are labeled, it is hard to reverse [pp. 51–52].

The authors give an example of the no-hope approach to working with families: "You're never going to be able to parent your kids because you never received decent parenting yourself" (p. 55).

Haapala and Kinney (1979) argue that workers must assume that family members do not purposefully intend to do poorly or to harm each other. Instead, they make mistakes "because of (1) lack of information—they know of no other way to proceed or (2) wrong information—they think what they are doing will pay off in the long run" (p. 254). To maintain a positive perspective, workers can also reassess their initial expectations of clients. Rather than seeking general acceptance or deep trust early in the casework process, workers can look for tolerance (Horejsi, 1981, p. 18). For families who have had several discouraging contacts with agencies, such a response is more reasonable.

A number of multiservice centers working with resistant clients have pointed out the need for well-organized, brief, and relatively uncomplicated intake procedures conducted as soon as possible after a request for services is made. The Child Adolescent Program, which serves teens and their families in Champaign, Illinois, responds to family crisis situations within 24 hours and less critical family needs within seven days (Clayton-Fechtmann & Seibold. 1981).

Jones, Magura, and Shyne (1981) claim that aggressive outreach is an essential aspect of effective service to clients with special needs. In a study of the need for use of "authority" with resistive clients, Gourse and Chescheir (1981) found that experienced clinicians felt some degree of pressure helped ensure family cooperation and allowed the worker sufficient access to begin to establish a relationship (p. 73). However, there is some disagreement in the literature concerning the degree of "aggressiveness" that is appropriate. Levenstein (1981), for example, feels that use of such methods to encourage clients to join a program that should be voluntary is an "ethical violation of individual rights" (p. 226). Describing a home-based program serving high-risk families in Des Moines, Iowa. Stephens (1979) stresses the voluntary nature of services, "with family and family worker possessing a mutual right to terminate service either when the presenting problems are resolved or when the services seem to be at an impasse" (p. 291). Stephens claims that structuring intake in this way is effective. Within the six-month period between June and December, 1977, twenty-six families were served by this agency, but only three terminated service prior to treatment.

Diagnosis–Assessment

For many years, child welfare practitioners have been concerned about the welfare of children living in families considered "multiproblem," "high risk," or "disengaged" (Tomlinson & Peters, 1981). These families are noted for the range and severity of their difficulties.

> The presenting problems in high risk families may include juvenile delinquency, school truancy, alcoholism, incest, marital strife, physical abuse and neglect, or the institutional placement of children. Emotional ties between family members are excessively strained and sometimes severed, contributing to isolation and mistrust in stressful circumstances. Poverty, unemployment, and low socioeconomic status constitute environmental problems that prevent improved family functioning. As thes families attempt to remedy their problems, they often utilize the services of numerous agencies, yet rarely are able to successfully coordinate these services. Eventually the families become so entrenched in the maze of human service systems that they reinforce the community's image of them as high risk and multiproblem. Often they remain in this scapegoat position, woefully dependent upon systems external to their system [Stephens, 1979, p. 286].

Poverty exacerbates their other difficulties. While undergoing stressful life experiences, these families are unable to purchase the resources or create the types of supports that most families in our society can afford. In working with them, therefore, accurate diagnosis requires understanding of the complex interrelationships among poverty, stress, and resource availability (Dunu, 1979).

Despite similarities in the degree of their dysfunction, these families vary widely in the intensity of their individual difficulties and the impact of these difficulties on their children (Goldstein, 1981).

> Stress can be considered a "pressure," a "burden," or a "chore" that one either "survives" or "cracks under"; it is enduring and has predominantly pathological potential. On the other hand, a crisis is created by a specific event that overwhelms one's usual coping responses because it poses a threat to an individual's or a family's equilibrium. It tends to be time-limited and can have growth potential [Magazino, 1983, p. 240].

Parental mismanagement of child-care responsibilties may also indicate situationally induced or more chronic response patterns:

> A parent's abusive actions may be primarily explainable by personality defects, but this is only demonstrable if the parent's actions are seen across a variety of situations in which the parent is dealing with the child. The more the actions vary across situations, the more necessary it is to look for environmental causes or for person-environment interaction causes. For example, a teenage mother who has abused her infant may also be found to neglect her child's hygiene, leave the child with irresponsible babysitters, and frequently pay little attention to any crying. Her neglect is cross-situational. On the other hand, a teenage mother may show adequate caring, but still neglect the child after a verbal fight with relatives, particularly if the child is extremely cranky. In this case, contextual issues may be highly relevant; they can only be determined, however, by the assessment of variability (Howe, 1983, p. 299).

In order to carry out a comprehensive and meaningful evaluation of the problems and needs of families, one that considers the complexity and variability of their needs, practitioners have begun to use an "ecological" model. This approach is built on four general tenets (Stephens, 1979; Spiegel, 1981; Kraft & DeMaio, 1982).

1. Family relationships and family problems must be analyzed from an interactionist or transactional perspective.
2. A balanced assessment of family functioning requires specific focus on parental strengths, in addition to parental problems.
3. An accurate evaluation of family problems and needs requires sensitivity to cultural and racial diversity in family interaction styles and parenting goals.
4. A complete assessment of family difficulties requires evaluation of the community's failure to provide needed resources and social supports for the family in stress or crisis.

The Transactional Perspective, also called the interactionist or social systems perspective, suggests that the focus for analysis and treatment must be interactions among family members and between the family and its broader social environment. Diagnostic perspectives that are not social-systems oriented tend to locate problems within the individual family member or within the broader environment (Stephens, 1979). An example will help clarify this difference. Mrs. Jones has been raising her children under conditions of extreme poverty. At the present time, she has developed a serious dependence on psychotropic drugs, prescribed by various physicians for her "nerves." Her local child welfare agency became involved with this family after teachers, finding the children often dirty and very hungry, grew concerned about their welfare. Rather than diagnosing the primary difficulty in this case as Mrs. Jones's low sense of self-esteem (the intrapsychic perspective), analysis from a transactional viewpoint requires examination of interaction patterns between Mrs. Jones and her children, evaluation of the support network provided by relatives or neighbors, assessment of availability of broader environmental supports designed to alleviate poverty, and of Mrs. Jones' ability to find and utilize these supports.

Programs utilizing the social systems perspective have tended to pay more detailed attention to the problems and needs of all family members. Janchill (1983), discussing available programming for retarded and physically and learning-disabled children, comments on the need for additional services for parents and siblings. Levine and McDaid (1979), describing family-based treatment services at Youth Service, Inc., an agency focusing on the needs of deprived and delinquent adolescents, discuss the importance of another family figure:

> The staff is intrigued by the role and place of the men in the lives of these mothers. In over 50 percent of the families served, there is an active adult male who plays a role with the family. He may be the husband and father; however, he is often a "paramour", a "step-father," an "uncle" or just a friend. He is usually not listed on any forms, nor is he mentioned at the point of intake. The staff learns of him and relates to him as they work and develop relationships with the family. Since these men seem to play a critical role, it may be necessary to learn more about them, their needs, aspirations, and levels of functioning [p. 268].

Adoption of a social systems perspective has also lead to greater sensitivity to the impact that multiproblem children have on parents. Traditionally, it has been assumed that children's problems are the result of individual parental inadequacy or marital strife. In contrast, today, it is "considered a truism that if parents are to some degree molders of children, children are at least equally molders of parents" (U.S. DHHS, 1980, p. 155). Greater attention has been paid to the impact on families of having a child who is handicapped, emotionally disabled, or otherwise particularly needy.

Finally, assessment of the needs of child welfare families utilizing a transactional point of view led to greater sensitivity to the role of time in the development and maintenance of children's problems. As Werner and Smith (1982) discovered in their research on children who grew into effectively functioning adults despite a great deal of early deprivation, no single traumatic event produces childhood pathology. "Transactions between the constitutional characteristics of the child and the quality of the caregiving environment *across time* determine the quality of the outcome. Breakdown from this point of view is seen as a consequence of some *continuous* malfunction in the organism-environment transactions that prevent the child from organizing his world adaptively" (emphasis in original) (p. 5). Adequate understanding of the source of parent/child difficulties, therefore, involves the search for ongoing, chronic patterns of dysfunctionnal interaction among family members. Howe (1983) suggests that one procedure for discovery of these serious difficulties involves evaluation of "behavioral variability" of family members across a range of contexts. When the behavior of the member is problematic in several different contexts, it becomes a source of potential concern for the worker.

Focusing on the Strengths of Families requires what Howe (1983) describes as a "health/growth orientation," one in which positive adaptation as well as family deficits are dignostic considerations (Tuszynski & Dowd, 1979; Goldstein, 1981). This is a particularly difficult task when client families are hostile and noncooperative or in situations in which the worker fears for the child's emotional or physical well-being. Because of this, the Region III Child Welfare Training Center (1982a) has found that child welfare workers require explicit training in recognition of the adaptive capacities of families and in utilizing family strengths in effective treatment planning. June Lloyd and Daniel Wulff of the National Resource Center on Family Based Services developed the following case example reflecting appropriate worker activity (Region III Child Welfare Training Center, 1982a):

The "C" family was struggling to reunify and reconstruct itself after all three children had returned from spending three months in foster home placements. The family consisted of Mrs. "C," recently divorced, and three children, a fifteen-year-old daughter, a thirteen-year-old son and a ten-year-old son.

The present problem had been escalating conflict among the children. Even when their fighting produced significant physical injuries, Mrs. "C's" responses were ineffective and the children were placed in foster homes. In-home observations confirmed intense patterns of fighting among the children and Mrs. "C's" apparent acceptance of her lack of power to affect their behavior.

School personnel and foster parents expressed strong negative feelings toward Mrs. "C." They observed a general lack of supervision and poor hygiene and described Mrs. "C" as "unloving" and unfit. The family lived on public assistance, grants and food stamps. There were broken windows in the poorly insulated, underfurnished, and flea-infested house.

During a period of in-home observation, it became clear that despite the children's appearance and the condition of their home, there were many real strengths. The family members had immense ability to enjoy one another through family jokes, uninhibited expressions of physical affection and through playing structured and imaginative games. They were able to problem-solve rapidly and specifically and each individual was capable of good self-expression.

The workers learned that Mrs. "C" had left an isolated rural community when she was divorced. In hopes of providing a better life for her children she had chosen to move to the city and now was nearly overwhelmed by the challenge of city life. The children also missed the rural environment they had loved. The children's rough-and-tumble interaction was partially due to its acceptability in their previous community. Now faced with multiple frustrations at school, what appeared to be excessive conflict was their only outlet and coping mechanism.

Circular effects were in motion. Mrs. "C" felt incompetent because she was perceived as incompetent. The more she felt incompetent, the poorer she functioned as a parent. The most helpful service goal was helping Mrs. "C" and her children to gain the confidence to believe that they were "okay." Being known as they were naturally at home, being accepted and having their strengths noticed and validated made this possible. They were then ready to learn matter-of-factly about this community's standards and were able to choose to gain acceptance and approval in some areas . . . .

Had this family not been assessed and served by a family-based approach it is probable that long-term out-of-home care would have resulted for all three children [p. 133–134].

Awareness of cultural and racial diversity among child welfare families is yet another significant aspect of effective diagnostic work. Much of family assessment relies on the use of white middle-class family norms. To the extent that families from other cultural or racial groups differ from this standard, they are considered "deficient" (Region III Child Welfare Training Center, 1982b). Social stereotyping reinforces these negative expectations. The "disorganized Black family myth" (Dodson, 1981), for example, suggests that most black families are matriarchal and that fathers play virtually no role in parenting. Fathers are seen as particularly deficient in fulfilling their financial responsibilities to the family. Mothers, although present, are viewed as highly irresponsible and ineffective as parents. This myth, and others like it, limit the effectiveness of worker interactions with the labeled families.

A quite different perspective is reflected in the concept of "cultural relativity." This viewpoint assumes that the activities and values of any group should not be judged in comparison with one global norm; instead, they should be understood as having integrity and meaning internal to that group (Dodson, 1981; U.S. Department of Health and Human Services, 1980). The social worker who adopts this perspective develops a thorough understanding of the beliefs and preferences of different cultural groups, is aware of the group's right to pass on these values to children, and is committed to adapting treatment goals and strategies so that worker activities blend more effectively with the needs of the family.

Understanding the wide diversity among racial and cultural groups in our society, some researchers have gone on to examine the special strengths and adaptive capacities of disenfranchised families (Hill, 1971). Dodson (1981), for example, points to the evidence that black families, particularly poor black families, utilize the resources and the supports offered by the extended family more frequently than do their middle-class white counterparts. Use of this network lends stability and continuity to children's intimate relationships, and helps families weather periods of special stress (Stack, 1974; National Child Welfare Training Center, 1982). In Mexican-American families, children develop a bicultural identity. As a result, they "exhibit considerable flexibility in their behavior, using problem-solving strategies and perceptual modes of both the field sensitive and field independent cognitive styles, depending on the characteristics of the situation and the task" (Ramirez III & Cox, 1980, p. 57). (See also Gray, 1983, 1984.) Among Native Americans, strong valuation of positive group participation and devaluation of use of intrusive and dominating interpersonal techniques have led parents to rely more on the use of modeling than on power-oriented approaches in childrearing (Hull, 1982; Nybell, 1984).

The need for community services and supports is another critical area of family assessment. The ecological perspective "reconceptualizes the family as a selectively opening and closing system, engaging in exchanges with a wide variety of collateral systems. Many families experience tension because of the inequalities of the asymmetrical relationship with occupational and other more powerful systems" (U.S. DHHS, 1980, p. 220). Without careful assessment of potential areas in which the community has failed to adequately support families, problems are incorrectly perceived as originating within the family. This is particularly likely to occur when client families have faced persistent discrimination (Billingsley & Giovannoni, 1972).

Stephens and Busch (1981) argue that child welfare families, who are often "underorganized," not only need help in rearranging internal relationships but also in learning to function as more effective power brokers with agencies in their environment. Communicating messages to this type of family that confirm its self-image as disabled and inept is particularly damaging, since this serves to entrench the family more deeply in its own misperceptions about itself, while reinforcing worker pessimism about the family's ability to change (Kraft & DeMaio, 1982).

As a result of thorough examination of the family's particular problems and strengths, sources of support and stress, the child welfare worker formulates a treatment plan. The plan must specify specific areas in which both the family and the environment need to be modified. In developing overall objectives, it is particularly important to indicate needs the family considers of greatest priority (Kinney et al, 1981), since treatment activities must meet both the family's felt needs and address major problems as the worker perceives them. The worker and family articulate immediate, short-term objectives that will help the family out of a crisis, as well as long-term goals designed to help prevent the family's involvement in future crisis situations (Butehorn, 1978). Jones and Biesecker (1980a) outline five specific steps toward achieving a usable treatment plan.

1. Actively involve the client from the beginning; Initiate an assessment of the person's strengths and needs.
2. Select a reasonable, achieveable goal.
3. Use the person's strengths and resources to plan the goal.
4. Spell out the steps necessary to reach each goal.
5. Document who will do what and when [pp. 7–8].

Treatment - Intervention

In this section, we consider the overall treatment objectives and discuss treatment considerations of particular relevance for child welfare work with multi-problem families. Specific techniques (family therapy, networking, advocacy, and so forth) are discussed in greater detail in the following section of this chapter.

Treatment efforts with child welfare families assist mothers and fathers in achieving minimally acceptable standards of parenting (Stein & Rzepnicki, 1983). The worker places special emphasis on alleviating specific harm that has been done to the child (Wald, 1975). As Goldstein, Freud, and Solnit (1979) point out, it is only in situations in which parental behavior is a gross violation of minimal standards for acceptable child care that the state has the right to intervene on the child's behalf. These circumstances include the death or disappearance of parents whose children have no alternative parenting resources, commission of a sexual offense against the child, abusive behavior resulting in serious injury to the child, or repeated failure to protect the child against such injury, or the parents' refusal to authorize medical care when such refusal threatens the child's life.

Consideration of minimal parenting standards is now replacing concern about the best interests of the child as a rationale for state intervention in child welfare cases. The best interest doctrine requires that the worker evaluate the best possible living situation for the child and attempt to secure it. Use of this doctrine has come under attack for a number of reasons. "The best interest test permits a degree of discretionary decision-making that is unacceptable in a pluralistic society, since its application often results in the imposition of middle-class standards of child-rearing on poor families. A less pleasant form of this argument is that the best interest test has been used to punish parents for behavior that the community finds distasteful under the guise of acting in the child's best interest" (Stein, 1982, p. 64). Application of the doctrine has also meant that child welfare families are required to achieve standards that are not demanded of the remainder of the community, since all parents need not provide the best possible environment for their children (Stein & Rzepnicki, 1983). The "minimally acceptable parenting" criterion is, then, both fairer and more realistic as a rationale for public agency intervention.

Because highly stressed parents usually have children who themselves have difficulty coping with normal life demands, the child welfare worker provides assistance in allieviating both parental insufficiencies and in managing problematic children. Children's activities with which parents often have trouble coping include:

— Acting out: Screaming, excessive crying, hitting, spitting, biting, destroying property, lying, running away, and general refusal to comply.
— Fearful behaviors: Clinging, sleep problems, and excessive fears of persons, animals, or objects.
— Repetitive behaviors: Head-banging, rocking, unusual gesturing, twirling, nail-biting, thumb-sucking
— Mealtime behaviors: Refusing to eat, overeating, inappropriate manners.
— Withdrawal behaviors.
— Hyperactivity.
— Manipulative behaviors: Tantrums, whining, and the like [Eyde & Willig, 1981, p. 268].

Parents may also need assistance in helping children achieve independent functioning and in learning self-help skills. Parents of adolescents often require guidance in helping their children achieve greater autonomy and in helping teenagers make critical decisions about employment and educational plans (Clayton-Fechtmann, Seibold, 1981).

Whatever the specific problems addressed, child welfare practitioners find that, when dealing with multiply handicapped families, they must develop special sensitivity about the timing element in treatment; give thoughtful consideration to the location of treatment efforts; and be concerned about provision of concrete help to clients while using more traditional "talking" strategies. Timing considerations affect decisions about initial issues to be addressed and about the pacing of client progress over time. When working with multistressed families, it is particularly advantageous to begin treatment with a focus on the problems parents identify (Horejsi, 1981; Clayton-Fechtmann, Seibold, 1981). "The old adage 'start where the client is' is transformed from an ungrammatical aphorism into an absolutely necessary first step" (Koch, 1979, p. 162). Wortman (1981) warns, "the energy resources of the poor, single parent are limited, and her patience already sorely tried. It is important to balance how much you ask of her against how much you give of what she came for" (p. 669).

Home-based service workers must avoid developing unrealistic expectations for rapid client progress. In an assessment of client contacts with the Intensive Services to Families at Risk Project at the University of Nebraska Medical Center in Omaha. Rosenberg, Robinson and McTate (1981) suggest that prevention strategies must seek only limited changes in family functioning and note that workers often must be more directive in the earlier stages of treatment. At the same time, however, clients must experience actual progress during the early stages of treatment. As Wortman (1981) comments, it is "important to structure the contact so that unrealistic expectations do not grow as she waits for some magical result that will not come, early or late. Research has shown that the modal length of contact in family agencies is five to six interviews, so something of importance has to take place in that space or less. Getting to what she wants, what you can realistically give with what expenditure of time and effort, even if the fee is nil, is primary" (p. 669–670) (See also Gwyn & Kilpatrick, 1981).

Clinicians working with multiproblem families find that services are more easily accepted when they are provided on the families own "turf." Services can be made available at outreach locations in the clients' home community, or the worker can meet with the family at its home (Golner, 1980; Gwyn & Kilpatrick, 1981). Chestang (1978) suggests that poor black families perceive the formal professional environment of a social service agency as inhospitable and uncomfortable. When treatment is made available at the client's home, families feel both more comfortable and more in charge. Providing services in the family home has additional benefits. Because members interact in a naturalistic setting, workers obtain more realistic views of family dynamics. The impact of major environmental stresses are also evident in this setting (Bryce, 1982). Workers also have numerous opportunities to model more effective parenting skills and to provide parents with critical opportunities to practice innovative approaches to childrearing under familiar circumstances (Bryce, 1979; Haapala & Kinney, 1979).

Service delivery is also more effective when its aim is to meet the practical needs of family members. Poor clients both want and need assistance with practical problems of daily living (Gwyn & Kilpatrick, 1981). Clients may need assistance in providing a safe and healthy living environment for children, in obtaining needed financial and medical assistance, in arranging appropriate education opportunities for children, in finding safe day-care arrangements, or in carrying out a host of other "daily grind" tasks that are necessary aspects of childrearing (Levine & McDaid, 1979).

Helping families with these activities may seem a relatively unimportant aspect of treatment. Some workers believe that the "real work" with clients occurs only with intensive discussions about feelings and family relationships (Ewalt, 1980; Green & Kolevson, 1982). Clients, on the other hand, are primarily concerned about these more mundane day-to-day issues. In a study of case terminations in a family service agency, Maluccio (1979) verified this disparity between worker and client perceptions of "cure." "It seems that clients were satisfied with having obtained help in relation to specific 'problems in living,' while workers were concerned with overall 'cures' or broad changes in an individual's situation or personality structure" (p. 182). As a result, clients were more satisfied with the outcome of the treatment process. Most clients, having received some concrete assistance, felt that therapy had been of help to them, whereas workers, seeking more deep-seated change, were usually dissatisfied or only partially satisfied with treatment.

Despite the multifaceted, complex, and sometimes life-threatening nature of the disabilities with which child welfare families must grapple, the worker can usually help them make sufficient progress so that removal of the child can be avoided. Adaptation of the content, location, and pacing of intervention to the special needs of this group has helped families progress more rapidly and has left workers better satisfied with client achievements.

Termination

Adopting the standard of minimally effective parenting as a criterion for continued residence of the child in his or her home raises questions concerning the nature of successful treatment outcomes and the conditions under which termination of treatment may be undertaken. Particularly in cases in which the family situation has proved dangerous to the health and safety of the child, closing a case when this standard has been achieved can leave the worker deeply concerned about the continued well-being of the child. Although the worker cannot insist the family accept service, once parents have proven they can provide minimal care, these services can continue to be offered to the family on a voluntary basis.

Multiproblem families differ in the extent to which they need long-term services. Some families come to the attention of agencies because they face acute crises. In these cases, services can be provided on a "prescription basis" (Ryan, 1979). The family and agency identify specific immediate issues that must be addressed. When the family has received assistance in dealing with these issues, services can be terminated. Jones, Magura, and Shyne (1981) found that many abusive parents can receive sufficient assistance from workers on a time-limited basis to help them maintain their families and to manage the crisis.

Other families require service on an "immersion basis." These are families with chronic, long-term problems who are in need of "total overhaul" (Ryan, 1979). Although parenting may be deficient in a number of ways, children benefit from the love and sense of continuity that their caretakers can provide (Magazino, 1983). The Bowen Center Project of the Juvenile Protective Association of Chicago has served a number of clients who need this type of extensive assistance. During its first five years, the project served thirty-five families showing "serious and pervasive family dysfunction and child neglect, extreme pathology, and little evidence of capacity for change" (Jones, Magura & Shyne, 1981, pp. 68–69). Families were in care a relatively long time, from one and one-half to three years. After receiving long-term services, most of the parents showed no more than "intermittent evidence" of growth in their parenting abilities, and most continued to need help. Despite this, the evaluators felt, the children were well served by remaining in their birth family homes.

Describing a program that supports the use of home care for chronically ill children by providing ongoing supports for the children and their parents, Stein (1981) notes that the families varied enormously in their need for ongoing assistance. Families received help for as short a period as a few weeks to one as long as eight years. On the average, families required help from the program for six months (p. 323). Children treated in outpatient mental health settings are also active clients for approximately six months (Knitzer & Olson, 1982).

Specific Treatment Approaches

Family Therapy

Child welfare families, whether poor or not, multiproblem or not, require a range of services that may include treatment of the marital dyad and of the family as a group (Hallowitz, 1980). Consideration of the family context out of which individual problems grow has been a vital component of diagnosis since the earliest years of the social work profession. However, treatment of the family as a group is a relatively recent phenomenon. Family therapy practice emerged after World War II, but it was in the 1960s that it became widely available to clients (Siporin, 1980, p. 14).

Family therapy is based on "dynamically oriented interviews with the whole family," viewed as a behavioral and social system. It focuses on the family as an integrative unit, as a special entity greater than the sum of individual family members. The assumption is that the child is what he or she is because the family is what it is and that if the child is to change, the family must change, too. As the child does not get "sick" alone, he or she will not get well alone. Meeting with the family rather than with individual members permits the worker to obtain a more accurate and more relevant diagnostic understanding of the family. Rather than being told about family interaction, patterns of leadership and control, the allocation of roles, the pattern of intrafamily communication, the nature of conflict, the operation and effectiveness of mutual defenses, the nature of family alliances and rejections, the extent and nature of existing strengths can be directly observed. Intrapersonal problems become visibly manifested in interpersonal encounters.

The field of family therapy currently encompasses a broad range of intervention approaches. The more widely known include structural (Minuchin), communications (Satir & Haley), behavioral (Patterson), and psychodynamic (Ackerman) (Nichols, 1984, p. 104).

Although most family therapists use nonbehavioral techniques, Wells (1981) raises questions concerning their effectiveness. Reviewing research comparing the impact of these approaches to alternative treatment methodologies (individual treatment, group therapy, and "the traditional child guidance model," in which child and parents are each seen in individual treatment), he found only one of eight studies pointed to the clear superiority of the family-oriented approach. Behaviorally oriented family work, on the other hand, has been shown to be effective across a range of studies.

The behavioral approach postulates that disturbed or maladaptive behavior is learned behavior. Treatment therefore consists of "unlearning" the maladaptive response. The focus is on the undesirable behavior itself, the "symptom," rather than on resolving any internal condition that is manifested in the symptom. The behaviorist denies that there is any internal conflict sustaining the behavior that might be perceived by others as a symptom.

Behavioral modification procedures are focused on helping clients to act differently in the expectation that they will then feel differently about their situation. The more traditional kinds of psychotherapies are focused on helping clients feel differently in the anticipation that they then will act differently.

The difference between the two approaches is a difference in seeing the child's behavior as an expression of underlying conflict or as a learned response that must be inhibited or extinguished. There is less concern with "diagnosis" because the "etiology" of the problem is not important. There is more concern with an exact definition of the particular behavior that needs to be changed and with the source and nature of those "reinforcements" that encourage continuation of the undesirable behavior. Laws of learning can then be applied not only to the elimination of undesirable learned behavior but also to the acquisition of new and desirable patterns of behavior.

The behavior was learned and is sustained by the current activities of people in a position to reward and/or punish such behavior, generally the parent. Behavioral modification therapy therefore frequently involves instructing the parents so that they support desirable behavior through prompt and appropriate rewards and/or discourage undesirable behavior by nonreinforcement or by appropriate and prompt punishment.

Various techniques have been developed, such as counterconditioning or reciprocal inhibition, operant conditioning, modeling, and aversion therapy, and these have been applied to a wide variety of children's problems: hyperactivity, temper tantrums, phobias and tics, bed-wetting, retardation, childhood psychosis, delinquency. Some of the techniques have been "translated" for social workers, and their applicability to social work situations has been made explicit (Jehu, 1967; Thomas, 1967; Fisher & Gochros, 1975; Gambrill, 1977; Schwartz & Goldiamond, 1975; Wodarski & Bagarozzi, 1979; Patterson, 1977).

Learning-theory approaches, it is argued, are particularly efficacious with children for the following reasons:

1. The world of "significant others" is more restricted in the case of a child and hence can be more easily controlled.
2. Those closest to the child in a position of authority, the parents, have not only the potential for controlling the child's environment but also the desire to do something about changing the child's behavior. Consequently their cooperation in therapy can be enlisted.
3. Parents, as the most significant figures in the child's life in most frequent contact with the child, are the principal and most potent dispensers of reinforcement and punishment.
4. Maladaptive behaviors for which children are referred often include the specific, well-defined behaviors—temper tantrums, bed-wetting, phobias— most amenable to behavior therapy approaches.
5. In children, learned patterns of behavior have been recently acquired and are not so firmly established as in adults, and behavior more recently learned may be more easily unlearned.
6. There is less ethical objection to controlling and "manipulating" the child's environment than is true for the more independent adult, and there is less objection to establishing behavioral goals for children.

Behavioral modification therapists have actively recruited and trained the parents as co-therapists. The parents are trained to respond to the child's behavior in a manner designed to effect changes in the child's behavior in terms of learning theory (McPherson & Samuels, 1971; Miller, 1975). The following is an account of the way one mother was enlisted as therapist for her child:

> The child in this study was a four-year-old boy, Peter S. He is the third of four children in a middle-class family. Peter had been brought to a clinic because he was extremely difficult to manage and control. His mother stated she was helpless in dealing with his frequent tantrums and disobedience. Peter often kicked objects or people, removed or tore his clothing, called people rude names, annoyed his younger sister, made a variety of threats, hit himself, and became very angry at the slightest frustration. He demanded attention almost constantly, and seldom cooperated with Mrs. S. [Hawkins *et al.*, 1966, p. 100].

Clinic personnel observing the mother–child interaction in the home noted the frequency of manifestations of nine specific objectionable behaviors. Included among these were "throwing objects," "biting his shirt or arm," "pushing his sister," "removing or threatening to remove his clothing," and so on.

> The mother was informed of the nine objectionable behaviors which would be treated. She was shown three gestural signals which indicated how she was to behave toward Peter. Signal "A" meant she was to tell Peter to stop whatever objectionable behavior he was emitting. Signal "B" indicated she was immediately to place Peter in his room and lock the door. When signal "C" was presented she was to give him attention, praise, and affectionate physical contact. Thus, every time Peter emitted an objectionable behavior, Mrs. S. received a signal from the clinician instructing her on her response [p. 102].

On the basis of such programmed learning, the mother developed a changed pattern of interaction with Peter, and the mother, as "therapist," applied the behavioral responses designed to effect changes in Peter's behavior. Use of parents as therapists is called *filial therapy*.

A number of reviews of the clinical experience and research related to filial therapy (Johnson & Katz, 1973; Tavormina 1974; O'Dell, 1974; Reisinger, Ora & Frangía, 1976; Mash, Handy, & Hamerlynck, 1976; McCauley & McCauley, 1977) indicate that although such interventions have achieved successful outcomes, there are also problems, such as initiating parent involvement in such programs and maintaining parental interest and parental persistence in application of the procedures. Such programs require the ability to plan and to persevere with some persistence and consistency in implementing the treatment program and the time and the energy to devote to monitoring the program. All of this requires a well-organized, systematic person with the ability and will to structure his or her life—a tall order for many harassed parents.

Workers might call the parents each week to discuss progress and to encourage continuation in the program. The encouragement and praise of the worker for the parent's efforts when tabulations of behavior frequencies are turned in to the worker and when other evidence of involvement in the program is presented also act to reinforce the parent's continuation of the program.

Additional questions can be raised with regard to the maintenance over time of changed behavior, and the extent to which the parent can generalize behavior learned in one context to contact with the child in other contexts or with regard to other problems.

Critics of the behavioral modification approach raise the question of whether or not the mechanical "rat psychology" conception of behavior and the "manipulative" nature of the procedure are compatible with the humanistic idealogy of social work (Peterson, 1976). The response in the still-continuing debate is the evidence: the parents and children who are living together more satisfactorily as a result of these procedures and the fact that the approach brings to social work a degree of precision and scientific vigor that it previously lacked (Carter & Stuart, 1970; Wells, 1981).

Behavioral approaches may be more effective with clients who are uncomfortable in a nondirective relationship centering on "talk," "self-actualization," and the search for "meaning." Poor, multiproblem families may respond positively to the carefully structured, goal-oriented aspects of this approach. Wells (1981) points out that behavioral therapy offers specific techniques to encourage and reinforce parent participation in the treatment process. Poor families may find monetary rewards for participation especially beneficial, since these funds can compensate them for transportation and child-care costs that they have incurred.

Clark, Zalis, and Sacco (1982) have developed a therapeutic approach specially designed to meet the needs of highly disorganized multiproblem families. Called Outreach Family Therapy, it draws on several widely used family therapy models, but "goes considerably further, including advocacy, intersystems change-oriented strategies and tactics, and the use of surrogate families" (p. 2). (See also Rudestam & Frankel, 1983; Morawetz & Walker, 1984.)

The Family Resources Center Coalition, a grass roots membership organization of programs concerned with strengthening and supporting families, has compiled a directory of some 75 programs (Payne, 1984). These programs represent the most visible and formally structured of hundreds of such organizations scattered throughout the country. Such groups emphasize an ecological approach, parent support, mutual aid and networking groups, a focus on family strengths rather than deficits, reliance on informal sources of helping, collaborative partnership relationships between parents and professionals, and a preventative orientation. These groups are involved in advocacy efforts in favor of families, provide counseling, child-care crises intervention, hotlines and warm-lines providing advice and information, family life education, information and referral, respite services, and toy lending, etc.

Educational and Treatment Groups

Many family service agencies, child guidance clinics, and public child welfare agencies have adopted group approaches to help families with parent–child relationship problems. The group may supplement the individual casework service; often, however, this may be the only form of help offered a family. Supportive service agencies have used two different kinds of group approaches: educational programs and group treatment (or group counseling). The group counseling service is sometimes difficult to distinguish from the ongoing educational program. Both kinds of groups consist of limited numbers of parents who come together with some regularity to discuss parent–child relationship problems with the help of a skilled leader who is provided by the agency. Some distinguishable differences have, however, been identified.

Parent education programs have as their primary objectives the enhancement of both knowledge and skill. They help parents learn more about the developmental needs of their children, the effects of their own behavior as parents, and the impact of their personal feelings of self-worth on their ability to become more effective caretakers. Educational approaches also attempt to teach parents how to interact more effectively, providing them with repeated opportunities to practice new ways to relate to others and to obtain feedback about these efforts (Eyde & Willig, 1981; Magazino, 1983). Parental self-esteem is further enhanced as group participants receive validation and support from other parents, realize their difficulties are shared with others, rather than being unique, and develop caring relationships with others in the group (Cantoni, 1975).

Enhancement of the parents' capacity to cope with childrearing issues more flexibly and creatively is one objective of the High-Scope Program, an educational approach that focuses particularly on parent–infant relationships:

> . . . the focus is not on *eliminating deficits,* but on the challenge of supporting and expanding present skills. Rather than considering parents as an efficient means of getting through to the infant, they are seen as active, autonomous decision makers for the infant and themselves. Rather than teaching parents to use a prescribed set of activities with the child, resources are made available to support and complement parental skills and to assist parents in clarifying their child rearing goals (emphasis in original) [Evans, 1979, p. 116].

The curriculum of education programs is often built around programs of parent training, the most popular of which are Parent Effectiveness Training (Gordon, 1975), Transactional Analysis (James, 1974), and behavior modification (Miller, 1975; Cooper & Edge, 1978). Parent Effectiveness Training helps parents communicate more effectively with their children and, in the process, develop what Gordon considers more functional disciplinary techniques. PET advocates the use of three primary parenting tools. When using "active listening," the parent learns to listen carefully to the child's concern and help the child understand and resolve his or her own problems. Gordon advocates the use of "I" messages when parents find themselves personally affected by a child's behavior. Using such messages, parents encourage children to realize that they have done something that displeases the parent and to remedy the situation. Finally, Gordon advocates the use of negotiation skills in situations in which children refuse to alter behavior of which parents disapprove. He calls this the "no-lose method" of conflict resolution. In order to teach PET, group leaders must complete a training course (Turner, 1980). PET is the most widely taught of the parent education programs currently available (Fine, 1980).

Transactional Analysis was developed by Eric Berne as a technique for use in individual therapy. It was been specifically adapted for use with children and their parents by Muriel James (1974) and others. TA focuses particularly on recognition and expression of feelings and outlines both intra- and inter-personal dynamics that encourage the development of positive or negative feelings. Fine (1980) outlines some of the basic tenets of TA:

1. All persons are born "OK" but may learn to feel "not OK."
2. Each person has three parts to his or her personality: the Parent, the Adult, and Child ego states.
3. Developmental processes that people go through can lead to healthy or unhealthy personality organization.
4. People can become self-aware and actively participate in facilitating their own personality development.
5. Children make decisions about themselves early in life (before age 6) that influence their perceptions, beliefs, and behaviors.
6. The giving and receiving of positive strokes (touching, caring, listening, complimenting, and loving, etc.) is crucial for healthy personality development [p. 10].

Like PET educators, individuals teaching TA must complete training before informing parents about this particular approach.

Educational approaches utilizing behavior modification are structured so that caretakers can learn to identify specific problem behaviors, clarify the circumstances under which the child engages in these behaviors, and develop particular response patterns so that unwanted behavior is discouraged and preferred behavior is encouraged (Cooper & Edge, 1978).

Some educational formats attempt to teach multifaceted parenting skills. The STEP Program is one such example (Dinkmeyer & McKay, 1976). This approach encourages parents to express their feelings more effectively, utilizes some of the communication concepts embodied in PET, and considers disciplinary techniques that were developed by the behaviorists.

Parent education groups can focus on specific issues of childrearing, rather than on overall approaches. In the last few years, the social work literature has described a number of groups of this type. Group workers have assisted parents in coping with grief (Cantoni, 1975), have helped parents who have recently realized that their child is autistic (Samit, Nash, & Meyers, 1980), have worked with families dealing with the ramifications of divorce, and have dealt with stepparent families (Pill, 1981). Stokes and Greenstone (1981) describe a group developed for grandparents who become informal adoptive parents in black families. Key issues of concern in this group included facing "the perennial issue of parental control," raising children already reared in a different generation, tensions that develop between the need to be an "indulgent grandparent" and a "firm parent," and increasing conflict in the marital relationships that result from taking on additional parenting responsibilities (p. 692). Mulvey and Vellenoweth (no date) developed a parent education program especially designed to meet the needs of low-income parents. Group workers have also helped parents understand the needs of their emotionally disturbed or handicapped children (Shearer, 1979; Eyde & Willig, 1981).

In an assessment of the overall effectiveness of parent education, Briar and Conte (1978) point out that there is little evidence that the group process per se helps parents become better caretakers for their children. However, particular training techniques, designed to enhance skills rather than provide general information about parenting, are effective. Behavior modification approaches, in particular, have been shown to be useful in overcoming disciplinary problems (Fine, 1980).

Parent education is based on the assumption that difficulties in parent–child relationships often arise from limited experience and lack of knowledge rather than as a result of any personality difficulty. Group counseling programs assume that the parent has some personality difficulty.

Objectives of therapeutic group programs include assisting parents in remedying some of the most serious effects of these deficits on their children. Parents are also provided with numerous opportunities to enhance their parenting skills, again in an effort to remedy serious deficiencies. Therapeutic groups have, for example, been developed for caretakers who physically abuse children and for those whose very limited knowledge of child development and limited childrearing repertoire have led to neglect.

Troubled parents may be referred to a therapeutic group rather than to individual treatment. The group approach has some unique characteristics that make it the therapeutic technique of choice for some families:

1. The group counseling situation may make acceptance of a treatment relationship easier for some clients. The focus of attention is wider in a group, and the relationship with the social worker is not so embarrassingly intense and threatening as it is in a casework situation.
2. In the group, negative feelings toward the worker, the agency, and the child can often be more easily expressed because of the "safety in numbers."
3. The fear of overdependency on the worker, excited in the one-to-one interview relationship, is less intense in the group.
4. Suggestions for changes in child care may be more easily accepted by some parents in the group situation than in individual interviews. Members of the group identify with one another and tend to help each other find solutions to similar problems. Criticism that would not ordinarily be accepted without resentment may often be accepted from a fellow group member.
5. The parent, in exchanging experiences with others facing similar problems, is stimulated to verbalize negative feelings about the child with less anxiety and comes to view his or her behavior more objectively.
6. Anxiety diminishes as the parent realizes that neither the child nor his or her reactions as a parent are unique. Hearing from other parents that they too have similar difficulties is reassuring.
7. The parent derives value from sharing experiences regarding possible solutions to problem situations. The repertoire of possible solutions available to each group member is increased as those offered by other members are added to those that the group develops in discussing parent–child problems.

Differences in the objectives of educational and counseling groups determine differences in the activity of the worker who serves as group leader. In educational programs the leader is an educator-expert on parent–child relationships and is responsible for presenting to the group what research and experience have determined is the best approach in meeting child-care problems. In therapeutic group sessions, the leader is more likely to be permissive, noncommittal, and neutral. In education groups, it is expected that "authority" might pass at some point from the educator-expert to the "parent-expert" as parents realize the extent of the knowledge and abilities they already possess (Stokes & Greenstone, 1981). In therapeutic groups, authority remains much more centrally invested.

Educational group leaders are more likely to be task-oriented and are concerned with communicating a body of content. Therapeutic group counselors are concerned less with a specific task than with establishing and maintaining an atmosphere conducive to full discussion with a minimum of defensiveness. In therapeutic groups, the focus is on issues of concern to individual members; educational groups, in contrast, spend time discussing predetermined content (Fine, 1980). Parent educational groups are also more likely to be time limited, whereas longevity of therapeutic programs is more variable.

Although educational and therapeutic group development is usually dependent on leadership provided by the child welfare worker, self-help groups look to members themselves for this type of guidance. Typically these groups provide support for participants and stress advocacy and resource development efforts on behalf of children in need. Self-help programming is now available for parents of handicapped, emotionally disturbed, retarded, and chronically or critically ill children. The Sisterhood of Black Single Mothers is an organization founded especially for black women who are raising their children alone (Pizzo, 1983).

Parents have turned to self-help groups when they needed recognition for their strengths as well as for their problems. Some of these groups were devised to combat stereotypic images of parents as incompetent or responsible for their children's problems. These groups encourage a view of parents as "resourceful":

> The Resourceful Parent image conveys the belief that parents are first and foremost doers and decision-makers on behalf of children. Most important for this image is not *what* we are deciding, but *that* we are deciding. The approval or understanding of policy makers or professionals is irrelevant. What matters is that we parents are now thought to be acting on behalf of our children rather than passively waiting for professionals and bureaucrats to do something (emphasis in original) [Pizzo, 1983, p. 71].

This type of self-help group has become increasingly popular in recent years. By 1980 there were one half million of these groups in the United States, providing help to some five million people.

Use of Social Support Networks

A social support network, according to Maguire, "connotes a type of organization based around an individual that provides the love, affection, aid, and protection that the person needs" (1983, p. 64). Networks may consist of "personal" members, those friends or relatives who provide long-term emotional support, and "second-order networks," whose members provide more diverse and less intimate support. Second-order network members may include individuals working for social service or other community organizations (Maguire, 1983). Child welfare personnel help family members more effectively utilize existing supports and develop and mobilize network ties in circumstances in which social supports are insufficient (Conte, 1983).

In child welfare work, evaluation of supports currently or potentially available to clients is critical. Some families requiring help are undergoing major crises. Parents in these situations may tend to isolate themselves from potential sources of support and attempt to handle their problems using only the resources of the nuclear family group. Families facing major difficulties dealing with their emotionally disturbed children or families in the process of discovering and accepting the fact that their children are retarded, autistic, or otherwise seriously impaired may try to cope in this way. Other child welfare families have had very meager support systems for some years. Some sexually and physically abusive parents have experienced this type of deprivation and may no longer recognize the benefits to be derived from social supports.

There are two common misconceptions about client networks, particularly those of poor and minority clients. One assumes that these families have no networks, "that there is no Black community, but only individuals and families who happen to be Black and who are sometimes forced to live together in the same neighborhood because of prejudice and poverty. This view precludes recognition that the community has a meaningful institutional and cultural life of its own" (Billingsley & Giovannoni, 1972, p. 218). In fact, some research indicated that blacks tend to have more extensive personal network ties than have whites (Manns, 1981).

It has also been assumed that, when poor families do have social supports, network members help exacerbate rather than resolve family difficulties. Evaluating treatment outcome in family service settings, Maluccio (1979) comments:

> Clients and workers also identified a number of "external" influences on the outcome and on their satisfaction with it, namely, the client's social networks, the client's life experiences and events, and the agency environment. Clients, more than workers, pointed to the positive influence of friends, relatives, and informal helping agents in the community. Clients tended to view positively their relationship with members of their kinship system, whereas social workers tended to define the same relationships as problems and obstacles in the client's functioning [p. 183].

Studying social relationships in a black inner-city neighborhood, Stack (1974) pointed out the positive influence of stable kin and friendship network relationships on continued survival and emotional health of poor families. Network members served as resources for basic goods (food, clothing, and short-term funds) and provided child care for families who could not afford to pay for babysitting but who do not want to leave their children alone. The black community provides an important buffer between the individual and the larger society, a source of strength and protection for people facing discriminatory practices in their daily lives (Chestang, 1978) (See also Manns, 1981.)

Maguire (1983) describes the impact of community networks (called tiyospayes) on families living on the Sioux reservation:

> If an individual needed help and he or she was a member of one of the larger, more powerful tiyospayes, a job, financial resources, as well as good counsel and advice could be offered. Given the tremendous power of the kin network in that culture, even marital problems could be resolved by the tiyospaye. I was familiar with one case where a married man and father of four was having an affair with a very young

woman. After the wife finally got up the nerve to talk to her grandmother, who headed the tiyospaye, the matter was quickly resolved. Within a week the girl had been moved to the country to live with her rather strict aunt, the husband had been visited by his parents, who informed him that they were "disappointed," and the wife had accepted an offer from her two sisters to relieve her on a regular basis with child care and housecleaning responsibilities. In addition, one of the tribal policemen, who happened to be in the grandmother's tiyospaye, dropped by the husband's place of work to tell him that he would be arrested if he were found any evening without his wife. Finally, his employer at a federal agency told him to change his ways or be fired. The man changed his ways [pp. 21–22].

The process of developing and expanding the social support networks of families is called networking. This therapeutic process has a number of objectives:

—Facilitate rapid connections, familiarity, and readiness to participate, which increases the level of involvement and energy (of the assembled network)
—Develop and encourage the sharing of problems and concerns by members of the immediate family, which allows for increased involvement and exchange of a variety of viewpoints by network members
—Facilitate communications between the family and the extended network system, which emphasizes the need for network activities
—Provide direct intervention and a deeper exploration of the nature of the difficulty during impasse periods, which leads to crisis resolution
—Assist in the development and formulation of temporary support groups, which serve as resource consultants [Conte, 1983, p. 184].

Treatment can be provided on a relatively short-term basis but, because the support network continues to function after professional child welfare efforts have ended, networking "may serve as a means of insuring generalization and maintenance of treatment effects across time" (p. 185). In its work with multiproblem high risk families, the Iowa Chilren's and Family Services found this approach especially useful (Stephens, 1979).

Advocacy and Case Management

Advocacy efforts serve clients for whom required services do not exist, families who do not have adequate access to needed services, and those requiring multiple services that must be coordinated. The Family Service Association of America states:

Family advocacy is a professional service designed to improve life conditions for people by harnessing direct and expert knowledge of family needs with a commitment to action and the application of skills to produce the necessary community change. The purpose of family advocacy services is to ensure that the systems and institutions with direct bearing on families work for those families, rather than against them [cited in Briar & Conte, 1978, p. 17].

Although some child welfare agencies do not consider advocacy a central component of service delivery, the Child Welfare League (1981) argues that this type of client work is essential:

Advocacy assumes an interaction between individuals and the social systems that surround them. The welfare of individuals cannot be isolated from that of the community, so that any attempt to serve one without concern for the other is of little or no avail. It portends a responsibility on the part of the agency (arising from its long and vast experience in serving people) to move from case to case, and to register concern for those external forces and conditions that inhibit people's ability to function [p. 1].

Kamerman and Kahn (1983) claim that this is one of three basic components of programming for families and children, a complement to other preventive and therapeutic efforts.

Because public child welfare agencies cannot provide all needed services for clients, workers frequently must look elsewhere in the community for assistance for them. When needed services are not available, the worker is responsible for helping develop them. Child welfare practitioners may also find that their clients confront barriers in obtaining services, even though they are already available in the community. Problems with accessability may arise when racism, sexism, or other types of discriminatory forces operate to prevent an individual from obtaining needed help. Because child welfare families are already considered inadequate in their inability to carry out essential childrearing functions, failure on their part to participate in needed services may be considered their personal responsibility when, instead, they have been prevented or discouraged from doing so (Hyde et al, 1979). "Blaming the victim" may also occur when agencies fail to coordinate services for troubled families:

> Unless a coordinated treatment plan is implemented among all human service agencies working for the high-risk family, perpetuation is granted to the conflicting pattern of "assistance" from numerous helping systems. Once this conflicting pattern is reinforced, the family's dysfunctionalism becomes chronic. Frequently this chronicity is a by-product of the poor communicative efforts between family and helper systems. The family, however, carries the burden of labeling within the community, partially due to uncoordinated treatment elements [Stephens, 1979, p. 287].

Advocates serve two different types of client groups. Case or client advocacy involves help to individual consumers in obtaining needed services. Class, political, or community advocacy seeks changes in the service delivery system on behalf of groups of current or potential service users (Briar & Conte, 1978; Knitzer & Olson, 1982; Baily & Baily, 1983).

Advocacy may be distinguished from case management activities, although effective advocacy requires utilization of case management skills. Robert Little (1982) describes three distinct components of case management. The first, which he calls "monitoring and recording," includes activities that ensure that client services are documented, that client progress is noted, and that essential forms are completed. This "paperwork" aspect of case management is the most widely known of its functions. In fact, some workers believe these are the only tasks that need to be completed for management to be effective. However, other components are more significant. One, which Little calls "orchestration of services," involves coordination of assistance provided by numerous agencies to the same family. The final component, the accountability function, is one that Little considers most crucial and more difficult to carry out. "The case manager . . . is the person that the organization holds responsible. The responsibility for all planning and delivery of services and payments comes back to a case manager who is the primary accountable figure" (p. 28). It is these latter two aspects of management, the orchestration and accountability dimensions, that overlap with advocacy responsibilities.

Already in the 1950s, the St. Paul's Family Center Project recognized the need to carry out an advocacy, or what was called a "social broker" role (Horejsi, 1981). However, it was during the decade of the 1970s that concern for strengthening advocacy efforts emerged in a number of social service settings. The most notable example of this change in emphasis was the announcement in February 1971 by the Community Service Society of New York that it planned to terminate "123 years of family casework and individual counseling." This oldest and largest family service agency in America explained the policy change by noting that casework and individual counseling "had proved inadequate for the poor who face overwhelming problems in the slums." The general director of the society noted that "If the individual is to be helped, someone has to deal with the complex of social ills that bears on the individual, not just the individual himself. Instead of starting out by saying that 'the individual is the client,' we're going to say the 'community is the client'" (*New York Times,* January 29, 1971). As an alternative, the Society planned to work directly with existing neighborhood groups to deliver services, to exert pressure on government agencies, and to coordinate existing public and private programs.

In the late 1960s, the Family Service Association of America adopted a program of family advocacy (FSAA, 1969). Similarly, on January 4, 1972, the National Conference of Catholic Charities, one of the largest of the nationwide denominational agencies, announced that the "organization planned to supplement its traditional social services [which included supportive family services] with a new focus on political activism" (*New York Times,* January 5, 1972).

By the middle of the 1970s, the pendulum had begun to swing back somewhat. The Community Service Agency, which had signaled its intention to abandon individual casework in favor of community action and development, reversed its orientation a few years later. In 1973 a new director was appointed who supported multifaceted approaches that included individual counseling as one of the principal options. Apparently a community action and community development approach had been more difficult to implement than had been anticipated.

The shift in the early part of the decade toward greater concern with community action and systems change has left a legacy, however, in terms of more explicit interest and activity in advocacy on behalf of children and their families. In response to resolutions adopted by the 1970 White House Conference on Children, a Federal Office of Child Advocacy was established. This office was subsequently closed, but regional and national child welfare resource centers were expected to continue such efforts. Many states have grappled with the development of appropriate organizational structures for advocacy efforts, seeking means to coordinate the work of private and public agencies and of citizens' groups. The publication in 1981 of a *Statement on Child Advocacy* by the Child Welfare League of America reflects this continuing concern.

Conte (1983) describes three key advocacy strategies:

1. Collaborative, in which the advocate attempts to elicit the interest and support of the target system;
2. Mediatory, in which the worker acknowledges differences with the target system and attempts to negotiate an acceptable agreement or compromise;
3. Adversarial, in which the advocate uses actual or implied power to effect needed change (p. 180).

Using an adversarial approach may be uncomfortable for social workers, who have been trained to use "concensus," not conflict, tactics (Sunley, 1980).

Whatever the particular strategies employed, the advocate's ultimate goal includes preparation of the family to assume increasing responsibility for obtaining the services it needs. This has been termed client empowerment. Solomon (1976) describes it as "a process whereby the social worker engages in a set of activities with the client or client system that aim to reduce the powerlessness that has been created by negative valuations based on membership in a stigmatized group" (p. 19). When the worker takes on too much responsibility for meeting client needs, clients tend to view themselves as victims and as incompetent (Billingsley & Giovannoni, 1972; Dunu, 1979; Stephens & Busch, 1981).

Empowerment activities involve more than the worker teaching clients how to interact more effectively with social systems. Clients also must learn the nature of power relationships and differences between powerless and powerful responses to social institutions. As Pinderhughes (1983) explains, individuals who are in powerless positions develop response mechanisms (aggression, passive-aggressive behavior, and so forth) that are reasonable reactions but that also prevent them from obtaining needed services. Family members need to understand the origin of these responses and to have the opportunity to assess their utility in achieving valued family goals.

The following case example depicts the benefits child welfare families obtain from this type of casework assistance:

> Mrs. G. was a single parent who had six children, the four oldest of whom, all male adolescents, were in separate residential placements spanning three states. Mrs. G. herself had spent most of her own childhood and adolescence in various placements. She had a history of ineffective parenting and helplessness. An in-home worker was requested by the Department of Social Services to aid Mrs. G. parent more appropriately, in hopes of preventing the two younger children from being placed.
>
> There were numerous system representatives with whom Mrs. G. had to negotiate. These included a social services field service worker, group home staff, three institutional treatment staffs, school staff, day care staff, a juvenile court officer, and ADC workers. The in-home worker coached and counseled Mrs. G. to assert herself at staffings, as well as to initiate further meetings for monitoring any progress by her children. She gradually moved from a position of passive helplessness with environmental authorities to one of appropriate parenting and assertiveness. The children controlled their acting-out behavior so that three of them eventually returned home. They returned to a changed family life-style with clearer role definitions.
>
> The family worker taught Mrs. G. how to change her behavior with authorities who had previously treated her as an immature, incompetent adult. This behavioral change, taking several months, tipped the homeostatic balance not just in the community environment but also at home. Through individual sessions with the family worker, Mrs. G. began resolving her anger and ambivalence about being a parent. As she explored the potential of being in charge of her own family, the myth of her frailty and helplessness diminished. The family developed a new perspective about itself, which had Mrs. G. making parental decisions rather than her children shouldering that responsibility as before.
>
> Be redefining Mrs. G.'s parenting roles at home and in the community, the in-home family worker drew boundaries that included Mrs. G. as an executive for her family. Heretofore, Mrs. G. had allowed her key parenting operations to be executed by ecological professionals. Once she became active in these operations, the balance of power within changed [Stephens & Busch, 1981, pp. 157–158].

Despite the need, it appears that few agencies have attempted to incorporate advocacy activities among their service delivery efforts. Only two states, New

Jersey and North Carolina, have attempted to develop specialized case management or advocacy services for clients (Knitzer & Olson, 1982). A nationwide census in 1976 of 273 member agencies of the Family Service Association of America indicated that only 28 per cent of the reporting agencies were involved in any advocacy activity, and only 8 per cent had a full-time advocacy staff member (Family Service Association of America, 1977).

In part because they lack the skill, and in part because advocacy engenders a great deal of frustration as workers attempt to deal with unresponsive agencies, "many caseworkers have tended to fall back onto the 'adjustment' solution to environmental problems: the client adjusts, that is, if he or she possesses the 'ego-strengths' to do so" (Sunley, 1980, p. 148). Advocacy can also engender a great deal of opposition from other professionals, who feel that they are being inappropriately challenged (Baily & Baily, 1983). Playing an advocacy role places the worker in a conflictual relation with his or her own agency. Administrators may feel that it is inadvisable for employees to challenge procedures or policies and may put pressure on the worker to terminate such efforts or to leave the agency. Despite these problems, some agencies have incorporated advocacy responsibilities as an ongoing staff function and have dealt effectively with the internal stresses that have ensued.

Evaluation

Research evaluating the efficacy of home-based care for clients has addressed three particular questions:

1. Are these programs generally effective in preventing placement of children who live in high-risk families?
2. In what particular ways do children themselves benefit from the families' participation in home-based care?
3. How do home-based service delivery models combat the types of parenting difficulties that create at-risk situations for children?

Due, in large part, to increased interest in expansion of home-based programs, and to widespread dissemination of information about them by organizations such as the National Clearinghouse for Home-Based Services to Children, and regional Child Welfare Training Centers, a great deal of recent information on program impact has been published. Most of this evaluative material describes the general ability of programs to prevent placement of children who would otherwise have gone into substitute care. Less information is available about specific ways these services affect children or their parents. Program impact in terms of preventing removal is summarized in Table 3–2.

As the table indicates, most programs claim to be highly effective in preventing the removal of children from the home, even in cases in which the family has many chronic and long-standing difficulties. Prevention of placement rates for these agencies range from 50 to 100 per cent. The most extensive of these studies (Yoshikami, 1984) surveyed eighteen public child welfare agencies in five states, collecting information from clients and caseworkers about preplacement prevention services for 272 families. Although in no agency did more than half of these clients make substantial progress toward achieving service objectives, in most agencies almost all clients made some progress toward these goals (pp. 51–52).

TABLE 3.2   Effect of Home-Based Services: Preventing Placement of Children in High-Risk Families

Agency/Service	Program and Client Characteristics	Outcome
Association for Jewish Children Philadelphia (Region III Child Welfare Training Center, 1982a)	For most of families, at least one child judged at high risk for removal; many low-income, single-parent families.	68 families served. Less than 5% of families served over 3 years required placement (pp. 118–119).
Homebuilders Tacoma, Washington (Haapala & Kinney, 1979)	Intensive treatment of families with severe, long-term problems; all at risk. Families experiencing severe crises.	207 families seen over 3 years. 96% stayed together through the crisis and 86% together one year later (p. 248).
Comprehensive Emergency Services Nashville, Tennessee (Burt, 1976)	Services to neglected, dependent, abused children and families; Emergency intake, caretakers, homemakers, family and child shelters.	Evaluation over 4 year project period. 51% decrease in children removed; number of children under 6 decreased from 180 to 0; recidivist cases reduced 88% (p. 663).
Lower East Side Family Union New York (Dunu, 1979)	Services to vulnerable families; case management, networking, advocacy.	193 high-risk families served in 1977. Only 11 had children placed, and 6 of these had children returned within 2 months (p. 223).
ENCOMH Nebraska (Eyde & Willig, 1981)	Respite and family support program for families with severely disturbed and autistic children.	28 families served. None had sought permanent residential care for their children (p. 272).
Child Adolescent Program Champaign County, Illinois (Clayton-Fechtman & Siebold, 1981)	Home-based intervention for violent and severely disturbed adolescents and their families.	150 adolescents served in 1978. 85% of all teens served remained in own homes and 90% in the community (p. 273).
Family-Based Service at Youth Service, Inc. (Levine & McDaid, 1979)	Alternative home-based family education and treatment services for neglecting parents whose children would otherwise enter foster care.	Served 32 at-risk families whose children were in home at referral time. Sixteen (50%) achieved stability and family enrichment (p. 266).
Bowen Center Project Chicago (Jones, Magura, & Shyne, 1981)	Families that traditional agencies cannot reach; families are highly dysfunctional, neglecting.	Only 27 children in 8 families had to be placed (p. 69).
Eighteen public child welfare agencies in five states (Yoshikami, 1984)	Preplacement prevention services for clients at risk of losing their children.	In 1/3 of agencies, 80% of clients making moderate or high degree of progress; in 56%, 60-80% of clients making moderate or strong progress. (p. 51).

However, evidence of success in these studies may be exaggerated:

The low nominal placement rates of several projects evidently were influenced by an inability to identify families who were in imminent danger of having their children placed, or who were "at risk" of having them placed in the near future: by systematic selection of those families willing and able to cooperate with the programs; and by limited community resources even for appropriate placements [Magura, 1981, p. 207].

Overselection of healthier, more resourceful families not only magnifies program impact but also deflects limited service resources from needier families (Giblin & Callard, 1980).

Information about program effects on at-risk children is very limited. Jones, Magura, and Shyne (1981), describing the impact of the Bowen Center Project of the Juvenile Protective Association of Chicago, stated that children who participated "made progress in social and cognitive development" (p. 69). A more extensive study comparing the effect of residential services, foster care, and home-based care was carried out at Rutgers University Social Work Research Center (Geismar, 1979; Wolock et al., 1979). The social functioning of the children was measured at intake and two years later, or at the point at which the family terminated services with the agency. Although children served in their own homes showed more change than those in placement, few of these changes were statistically significant. Geismar believed that these findings were "cause for neither pessimism nor optimism" (p. 327) and calls for more sophisticated examination of program impact on children and families. Wolock et al. (1979) pointed out that children served in their own homes fared no worse than those served through the use of substitute care; however, the "Own Home Programme" children were served at considerably less expense (p. 23).

Perhaps the most extensive and well-replicated studies have been conducted on children receiving early cognitive and social stimulation through Head Start, the Home Start Program, and other infant/toddler visiting programs. Findings from these studies suggest that children may not benefit in all areas of development, although individual programs may help them to progress in specific areas. In an examination of the impact of Home Start conducted by O'Keefe (1979), children made clear gains in school readiness after seven months in the program. However, they made no progress in the social-emotional arena, except on a measure of task orientation. Research suggests that these programs have only modest impact on the children served. Halpern (1984) states, "At the most general level (that is, across outcome domains), it is possible to identify a slight trend favoring treatment over control families in the majority of programs" (p. 36). Without continued support and stimulation, positive program impact also atrophies. O'Keefe used four measures of school readiness in her study of the Home Start Program. After seven months, children had advanced on three of these four measures; however, at the end of one year, they had made significant progress in only one area.

Studies conducted at child guidance clinics on three different occasions by Levitt (1957, 1963, 1972) concluded that the effectiveness of psychotherapy in dealing with emotional illness in children is yet to be proved. He pointed out that a favorable outcome was more likely in cases with identifiable behavioral symptoms, such as enuresis and school phobias, and least likely in cases of delinquency and acting out.

The need for more detailed and sophisticated assessment of the impact of home-based services on children is clearly indicated by these findings. In addition, findings of the limited number of available studies suggest that careful designation of specific areas of expected program effects is necessary. They further indicate a need for thoughtful exploration of the expected degree of program impact on children, particularly when program personnel have only limited opportunities to treat them.

Giblin and Callard (1980) used a variety of measures to evaluate the effect on parents of participating in the PACT (Parents and Children Together) program in Detroit. The service was made available to high-risk families who had or might have children placed in foster care. The researchers assessed the functioning of fifty families who had at least one child at home, and followed their progress over a four-month period. Summarizing their findings, they state:

> Generally a decrease in the number and severity of problems was noted by the counselors. Specifically, the decreases were in the areas of parental lack of independence, parenting problems, adequacy of the home environment, and the availability and use of community resources and social services. At termination, the counselors thought parents were better able to relate to their children and manage them appropriately, to provide a more wholesome and stable environment in which their children might develop and grow, and to manage their own resources and those of their community. The only exception to this trend was the number of problems noted in the area of conjugal discord. Perhaps these problems became increasingly evident to the counselors when the counselors became better acquainted with the families [p. 7].

The study utilized no control group. However, comparisons of family strengths at the beginning of project participation suggested, not unexpectedly, that "PACT was most successful with families that, at the outset, had the fewest problems and the greatest number of resources to meet these problems" (p. 10). Evaluation of the experiences of thirty-two families who volunteered to participate in a placement prevention program that provided education in child management also led Cautley (1980) to conclude that it was the the less disturbed and more resourceful families who benefited most readily.

Bowen Center Project personnel made much more conservative assessments of family progress. They concluded that parents could be helped to sustain a level of minimally effective parenting but could not be expected to continue to function on this level or to progress beyond it without the continued help of social agencies (Jones, Magura, & Shyne, 1981). Parental need for continued long-term help was also noted at the Association for Jewish Children of Philadelphia. In this agency, "long-term service was found to be inevitable. Some families have been active at the agency for six years. The agency becomes the family's 'extended kinship' and is available every day of the year, around the clock" (Region III Child Welfare Training Center, 1982a, p. 118).

Experiences with Home Start services suggest that parents can learn more effective methods of interaction with children. O'Keefe (1979) found that parents taught their children more prereading and prewriting skills, provided them with more books and toys, encouraged them to help with household tasks, and engaged in more positive interactions with them than did parents who had not participated. However, once again, these changes were not consistent across several areas of parent functioning. Even though parents provided better medical care for their children, they did not learn to feed them more nutritionally. In a more extensive analysis of the effect of this type of program, Halpern (1984) questions whether there is sufficient evidence of any clear impact on parents. Looking at qualitative data, such as perceptions of changes in parent functioning, by program personnel, he notes:

> The anecdotal evidence often describes enhanced psychological adjustment to parenting, management of family life, and maternal sense of self-competence; less frequently documents improvement in behavioral dimensions of parent–child interaction, such as managing feeding and enjoyment of the infant, and in a few cases cites enhanced infant health or developmental status [p. 37].

However, there is little validation of these findings using more objective measures.

In addition to examining the effect of service participation on client functioning, studies have explored the importance of various aspects of treatment for client progress. Research conducted by the Family Service Association of America (Beck & Jones, 1973) points out the special significance of the worker/client relationship. The research was based on information obtained from all clients who came to family service agencies during one week in the spring of 1970. Two hundred and sixty-six family service agencies throughout the country reported on some 3,600 cases involving about 13,000 persons who came for service during that week. A high percentage of such cases coming to family service agencies involved parent–child problems.

Of the original group of 3,600 cases, about 1,900 were followed up after case closing, most often through a detailed personal interview. Using a structured interview outline, the interviewer attempted to find out about clients' dissatisfaction and satisfaction with the service and about changes in family functioning that the client attributed to the agency. At the same time, the caseworker responsible for service to the family was interviewed separately by the researchers to determine her or his view of the effects of service. The measures of change were, then, the subjective assessment by clients and workers, independently sharing their perceptions of the results of service.

Focusing on only those cases in which a parent-child relationship problem or a child-rearing problem was presented, the interviewers found that both caseworkers and parents reported improvement in about 63 per cent of the families. Of the children involved in these cases, 35 per cent showed improvement: "There was a marked association of counselor-client relationship with outcomes. With minor exceptions . . . this was found to be twice as powerful a predictor of outcomes as any other client or service characteristic covered by the study, and more *powerful* than all client characteristics combined" [emphasis in original] (Beck & Jones, 1973, p. 8). More recent reviews of psychotherapy outcomes (Reid & Hanrahan, 1982; Thomlinson, 1984) conclude that one of the most clearly identified factors in producing positive change is the basic attitude of the therapist as communicated to the client. It is the caseworker's warmth, empathy, respect, and genuineness rather than professional technique, level or experience, or education that are the sine qua non of success. Yoshikami's (1984) survey of public child welfare clients receiving preplacement prevention services revealed that "according to parents, helpful services were most often characterized by an understanding service provider and by the fact that they produced the desired results" (p. 53), whereas services seemed least helpful when the caseworker appeared judgmental or not understanding.

When we attempt to look beyond the impact of relationship building and assess the effect of various treatment modalities in assisting high-risk parents to enhance their child-management skills, recent program evaluations are less helpful. Because psychotherapy research literature for some time has questioned the effectiveness of individualized treatment strategies, this question is of critical concern. Summarizing the studies of the impact of individual psychotherapy on clients, President Carter's Commission on Mental Health (1978) states:

> the accumulated weight of evidence has shown that psychotherapy, at least in most situations, has a *detectable* positive effect among those treated. While treated patients often improve a great deal during psychotherapy, so do many control patients; relative to these changes, the *added* benefit from psychotherapy, while detectable, is modest. . . . The form of therapy has shown surprisingly little general relationship to effectiveness [emphasis in original] [Vol. 4, pp. 1750–1751].

One of the most comprehensive and sophisticated reviews of therapy outcomes to date, encompassing 475 studies selectively included because they meet certain well-defined research criteria, is that done by Smith, Glass, and Miller (1980). The review concluded that psychotherapy as compared with no treatment was effective, that different types of therapy were equally effective, that how therapy was conducted (group vs. individual length of treatment), experience or professional affiliation of therapist had little significant relationship to outcome. This evidence suggests that some treatment is better than none, that the effect of treatment is modestly positive, and that the specific nature of the treatment may be less significant than are common "nonspecific" effects.

However, other research concludes that programs can demonstrate positive impact when their goals are narrowly defined and when the technology used to achieve these goals is clear-cut (Halpern, 1984). Programs using behavior modification approaches meet these criteria and, as a result, have proven useful. Behavior modification has been used to assist parents in responding more effectively to child problems, to help parents who are facing specific disabilities in their own child-management skills, and to help them meet the needs of exceptional children. (See, for example, Mash, Handy, & Hamerlynck, 1976.) These procedures have been employed with some measure of success with relatively mild problems of deportment, persistent disobedience in the home and in school, fighting with siblings and peers, and food fads, through more serious problems of stealing, firesetting, serious aggression, sexual deviations, enuresis, phobic disorders, shyness and withdrawal, to the most serious problems of autism and childhood schizophrenia (Kazdin & Wilson, 1978, pp. 24–27).

Much of the behavior modification literature does present studies of successful change in children's behavior as a result of such intervention without any evidence of symptom substitution. Even studies contrasting the effects of such intervention with nontreated or differently treated control groups—as reported, for instance, by Christopherson *et al.* (1976) for a child guidance clinic population—show behavior modification as more effective. When additional tests of effectiveness are made, however, such as assessment of outcomes by a variety of procedures and follow-up assessment of maintenance of the change over time, the impact of behavior modification appears to be less potent than anticipated (Patterson, 1975; Kent & O'Leary, 1976).

Efforts have been made to test the comparative effectiveness of psychotherapeutic casework and behavior modification. One of the more rigorously designed of such research efforts was by Sloane *et al.* (1975). The general conclusion was that both procedures are more effective than no treatment at all, and both are almost equally efficacious, the behavior modification approach being modestly more effective with some types of cases. An effort by Luborsky, Singer, and Luborsky (1976) to answer the question of comparative effectiveness by reviewing the results of eighteen different studies with controlled comparisons showed behavior therapy to be superior to other psychotherapies in six comparisons and to be no different in twelve.

Reviewing over seventy studies comparing behavior modification procedurs with alternative nonbehavioral methods, Kazdin and Wilson (1978) conclude that such competitive exercises are not particularly helpful. It is clear, whatever the box score, that behavior modification methods are generally useful in regard to many parent—child relationship problems, that a wide variety of diverse methods of behavior modification have been developed and are being refined so as to increase the probability of their enhanced effectiveness, that they are at least equally effective as alternative nonbehavioral methods and have the clear advantage of being more efficient. Instead of a concern with competitive comparison, the focus should be on defining what procedure is effective with what problem under what circumstances. Such a search should be conducted in a context that is receptive to any answer that is empirically supported by well-defined outcome measures of magnitude of change, desirability of change, consumer satisfaction, and cost effectiveness.

Review of available data describing the impact of home-based services on children and their families and the effectiveness of these programs in preventing placement of children suggests they have helped in maintaining children in their own homes. Beyond this, a program's ability to create a more positive living environment for children and its ability to help children function more effectively in their daily lives have not been clearly demonstrated. As Nuehring, et al. (1983) suggest, a great deal of work must, as yet, be done to clarify overall objectives and to specify treatment methods used in home-based programs before well-designed evaluation can be undertaken. Clarification and specification of program goals and means will, the authors believe, allow the evaluator to develop relevant assessment strategies documenting program usefulness.

Problems

1. The United States is now the only economically advanced country that has no explicit national family policy. Although most governmental decisions affect family life in one way or another, there has been no administrative agency that has as its responsibility ongoing assessment of the impact of such decisions on the family. Kamerman and Kahn (1983) suggest that an adequate social policy agenda for families would embody the following principles:

—a view of the family as a central institution in the society
—a definition of "family" that is sufficiently broad to encompass a variety of types, structures, roles, and relationships while maintaining some discriminatory power
—a definition of "policy" that assumes a diversity and multiplicity of policies rather than a uniform, monolithic, comprehensive legislative act
—a definition of "family policy"— in other words, fami*lies* poli*cies* — that goes beyond the concept of a policy field (specific laws, regulations, activities explicitly designed to affect families, such as Aid to Families with Dependent Children [AFDC], maternal and child health programs, child care services) and/or a policy instrument (labor market or population policies, social control policies) to include all government and, as relevant, nongovernmental policies which seek to affect primary group relationships and structures [p. 151].

Deeply held social values mitigate against development of this type of programmatic focus in the United States. Individualism highlights the effect of personal factors on achievement while deemphasizing the impact of the group. As Rice (1978) comments, "the separation between government and family connects with the very roots of American government. The Constitution avoids mention of the family, and establishes a contract between the individual citizen and his government. Development of individualism was, for years, a cornerstone of assumptions of cultural progress, and the family was often seen as an anomaly" (p. 435).

As a consequence, social agendas have primarily considered the needs of individual children. Advocates have worked on behalf of children, but have failed to address the critical role that families play in children's lives (Rice, 1978). This limited, child-oriented focus has been in turn, responsible for the development of a service delivery system that fails to respond adequately to the need to restore and maintain families (Bush & Goldman, 1982; Magazino, 1983). Goldstein, Freud, and Solnit, in their 1979 publication *Before the Best Interests of the Child,* criticize permanency planning efforts that involve searching for surrogate parents for the child without first demonstrating that the natural parents are, indeed, inadequate.

To redress this imbalance, Morin (1981) calls for the establishment of a national commission for families, that would have responsibility for evaluating the needs of families and for ensuring that adequate services are available to meet these needs.

2. Adequate provision to meet the needs of home-based service recipients can be accomplished if financial incentives are available to encourage service provision and if they are accompanied by financial disincentives to use of out-of-home care (Bryce, 1981). Public Law 96-272 makes available increased funding for preventive and reunification services both by placing a ceiling on the amount of funds available for substitute care and by increasing the federal portion of financial contribution for such services to 75 per cent (Cole, 1982).

Despite these provisions, funding for services to children in the home is insufficient and might be reduced. Providers of home-based programming must compete with foster and institutional programs that are already in place. Methods of referral to and utilization of substitute services are firmly established and familiar to workers; procedures for utilization of home-based services, particularly for use of specialized intensive programs for high-risk families, must be established and workers educated in their use. These services are encouraged by federal legislation, but the amount to be spent on them has not been established. As a result, availability of this type of care is heavily dependent on support provided at the state, county, and community level. Given recent trends toward overall fiscal retrenchment, concern for the financial future of these programs seems realistic (McDaniel, 1981).

Monies available from child welfare sources are not easily augmented through other funding sources. In the MH/MR system, for example, the service most easily provided for seriously disturbed children "remains the most restrictive and costly in-patient hospital care" [Knitzer & Olson, 1982, p. ix]. A number of factors inhibit further development of in-home services to children in that system. Among them are the fact that it has been difficult to arrange MH/MR funding to third-party agencies for such services, or reimbursement for travel costs to the homes of clients, despite the fact that home visits are often a critical aspect of preventive care for at-risk families. MH/MR monies specifically targeted for, programs designed for children and their families have dwindled. It is probable that these will not be reliable collateral resources for child welfare families.

3. Minority children and their families continue to receive less than their fair share of home-based services. Using data collected in the early 1960s by Helen Geder, Billingsley and Giovannoni (1972) argue that black children were less likely to receive services in their own homes than were whites (p. 94). Geder also found that black children were more likely to be placed in foster care than were their white counterparts. A 1970 census of placement of children in substitute care facilities (health, psychiatric and educational) concluded that the placement rate for minority children was 25 per cent greater than that for whites (Knitzer & Olson, 1982, p. 7). (See also Children's Defense Fund, 1986, p. 33). Targeting home-based programming for minority families continues to be an important child welfare concern.

4. Lack of administrative and other agency supports may prevent effective delivery of home-based services. Explicit agency commitment to this type of service delivery is crucial:

> Implementation requires well-trained, confident and highly motivated social workers. They must be able and willing to work many evenings per week, and perhaps for years, with a relatively small group of families. They must be able to cope with intense frustration, rejection, verbal abuse, and sometimes the threat of physical harm. An agency adopting this approach must justify a rather expensive program. Case loads have to be small. Staff turnover must be kept at an absolute minimum. This is a program that must be built upon a long-term commitment, it is not something that you start one year and drop the next because of budget constraints. If you begin with the families, you must be prepared to go the distance. To begin and then drop these families is worse than doing nothing at all [Horejsi, 1981, p. 22].

High case loads interfere with effective service provision for a number of families. Rooney (1982) suggests that prevention workers should provide assistance to no more than twenty-five families at a time. However, in one-third of the public agencies surveyed by Yoshikami (1984), the average work load size was greater than this (p. 54). Some programs providing intensive, sometimes daily, family contact, have found that workers can manage only ten or fifteen families.

Failure to limit the amount and type of case documentation and other paperwork required of child welfare practitioners has also interfered with time available for client contact. Shireman (1983) notes that practitioners currently spend up to 30 per cent of their work time completing required paperwork. Agency policies and procedures may also preclude the use of intensive supervision and team supports that are frequently needed to assist workers in responding to some of the most difficult and demanding clients in the child welfare system. Worker isolation and lack of support in treatment planning and decision making can cause burnout and foster rapid staff turnover (Maluccio, et al., 1980; Conte, 1983; Edna McConnell Clark Foundation, 1985).

5. In large part because of insufficient staff training, workers dealing with at-risk families may have negative attitudes toward abusive parents and may be highly pessimistic about their ability to benefit from even intensive agency assistance. Because parents are expected to be responsible for ensuring that their children grow up to be healthy and happy, practitioners routinely search for parent characteristics that explain children's deficiencies. Stressful life circum-

stances of the family are often ignored (Howe, 1983). Where parents have actively engaged in behavior that does some harm to their children, it is especially difficult to acknowledge the beneficial aspects of the parent–child relationship. To the worker, the parents' faults may seem so enormous that their impact far outweighs that of any strengths.

However, adoption of this attitude makes it extremely difficult for the worker to engage in preventively oriented home-based service provision (Allen & Knitzer, 1983).

Experience alone is of insufficient influence in positively changing child welfare worker attitudes toward parents. According to Meyer (1983), "there are but two ways to prepare staff for practice with families: through careful selection of social work graduates and through intensive staff development. Recent experience has shown that child welfare workers do not pay adequate attention to families unless they have agency supports and training; it is a direction to practice that is not traditional in a field so long characterized as child placement" (p. 487). A recent public agency survey (Yoshikami, 1984) found evidence that, although training needs are increasingly recognized, training participation remains inadequate. In 44 per cent of the programs surveyed, less than three-quarters of the workers had had preparation in placement prevention within the last two years (p. 54).

6. Other stresses inherent in the work of the home-based care practitioners stem from the unique characteristics of multiproblem at-risk families and the worker's obligation to make critical decisions concerning the safety of children and the unity of families. They must make decisions not only about the current welfare of children, but also about the long-term impact on them of remaining in a family environment that is likely to be problematic for some time to come. They must determine at what point the impact of the family becomes more detrimental than placement in another home or an institution. Maluccio et al. (1980) points out:

> . . .In many client situations, it is difficult to evaluate a parent's adequacy or functioning, to assess the quality of parent–child relationships, to estimate the parents' future capacity, and ultimately to determine the bast ways of meeting a child's needs. These difficulties are compounded by the fact that people's needs and qualities change over the course of their development. For example, parents may change in their ability to care for a child as life experiences provide further opportunities for them to enhance their competence and coping capacities. How can workers make these assessments and decisions in light of so much that is uncertain? How can they predict what might happen years from now, especially since they usually meet parents at a point of crisis? [p. 526].

These problems are compounded by the fact that, although workers rely most heavily on parent-related data to predict future outcomes for the child, developmental research has suggested the deficiencies of such an approach. In longitudinal research following normal children over a thirty-year period, attempts to predict the impact of parent behavior on child outcome were wrong in two-thirds of the cases (Wald, 1975). Child welfare practitioners find themselves responsible for making critical decisions concerning the welfare of children with insufficient knowledge to make judgments that are valid.

Workers also experience problems in determining which clients to accept for service, particularly in situations in which service availability is limited. It is difficult to decide if programs should be provided to families who are most likely to benefit extensively from them, or if they should be provided to the most needy families whose movement is likely to be slowest (Levine & McDaid, 1979).

In addition to client access questions, practitioners must grapple with concerns about client rights. Because families have been considered at-risk and are in danger of having their children removed from the home should they fail to participate or cooperate, they are in danger of suffering from "coercive intervention" and "unwarranted state intrusion" (Stein, 1982). Levenstein (1981) argues:

> Such a sensitive setting requires more than ordinary vigilance to safeguard the democratic rights of the individuals and families reached by the program. Among these rights are the right to privacy, the right to retreat to one's home without intrusion by an outsider, and the right to choose between intervention programs that are not legally compulsory. These are the same rights enjoyed by the patrons of center-based programs for pre-schoolers. But parents associated with center-based programs can defend themselves better against violations of those rights. If the violations become too much to deal with, they can take their children, leave the center, and go home. Parents in home-based programs don't have this option. They are already at home; in order to separate themselves from a home-based program, they must evict it. This is hard to do. People are more often polite than not. They do not feel it is courteous to withdraw hospitality once it has been extended (pp. 224–225).

Faced with these varied questions and responsibilities, the prevention worker finds that stress and uncertainty characterize his or her daily functioning on the job. Stress management becomes an essential requirement for continued professional growth. Effective performance as a home-based specialist requires opportunities to consult with other professionals and to seek assistance in decision making concerning clients. Opportunities to obtain supervision and to participate as a member of a treatment team that is, in turn, responsible for making overall client decisions help reduce worker burnout and job turnover.

Trends

1. For a variety of reasons, families utilizing home-based services continue to be those facing the most difficult and complex problems in the community. As children are deinstitutionalized, their families, who were previously considered too disruptive to receive home-based assistance, will become service recipients. Children considered status offenders, who were previously served through the juvenile justice system, may also become service recipients, along with their sometimes neglecting and frequently poverty-stricken families. Child welfare agencies in general, and home-based service providers in particular, will face demands to work with more disturbed, needier families and to do so more effectively than residential institutions or less specialized outpatient treatment programs can do (Janchill, 1983).

2. As state responsibility for decision-making in the delivery of child welfare services increases, there is some danger that federal prevention and reunification goals may be undermined. Schram (1981) summarizes the reasons for this concern:

By decentralizing decision-making for social programs, conflicts over which goals, interests, and groups these programs should serve are kept quietly within the confines of states and localities. The "privatization" of these conflicts diminishes the possibility that they will be resolved in ways consistent with national majorities or sentiments. In addition, the privatization of conflict increases the ability of decision-makers to emphasize goals which are inconsistent with national standards, without attracting national attention. In a time of increasing scarcity of public resources for social services, the privatization of conflict produced by social service block grants is enhancing the ability of established local interests to prod state elected officials to protect the status quo in social service provision. It is within this context, and not in one of reform and innovation, that social services are provided today [p. 90].

As a result of the transfer of decision-making authority from the federal to the state level, there may be more variability from state to state and from locality to locality in the degree to which federal preventive mandates are carried out. Depending on where they live, therefore, families may have available to them a variety of home-based services or no such service opportunities at all.

3. The demand for service delivery programs that can prove they are effective will continue, as will the demand for documentation of efforts on behalf of child welfare families (Stein, 1982). Workers will be required to be more descriptive and factual in the information they provide about cases, in their goal planning, and in their consideration of the balanced rights of all members of the family in making determinations on behalf of children (Stein & Rzepnicki, 1983). Workers will also be expected to continue to document delivery of specific services to clients. "Contracting," "casework by objectives," "task-centered casework," "planned short-term treatment" and similar efforts reflect this emphasis on making explicit the problems that will be worked on, the steps that will be taken to help the family, and the specific time limits within which change is to be accomplished.

4. Consideration of the family as a central diagnostic and treatment unit for effective delivery of child welfare services is reflected in service delivery arenas outside of traditional public child welfare agencies. In the United States military, the need for provision and expansion of in-home services has been recognized in each branch of the service. The Army's Community Service system relies primarily on volunteers to provide "information and referral, relocation services, including the provision of temporary pots and pans and other household items, and help for exceptional children" (Howe, 1983, p. 15). The Air Force has established family support centers at a number of bases and plans to have them available at all major bases before 1989. The Navy has similar plans in developing its Family Support Program. Dissemination of information concerning family based in-home care has been accomplished through the Military Family Resource Center's publication of a newsletter since 1981. The military has also sponsored various conferences and workshops that focus on general services to military families and on specific problem areas, such as child abuse and family violence.

Bibliography

Allen, MaryLee, and Jane Knitzer, "Child Welfare: Examining the Policy Framework," in *Child Welfare: Current Dilemmas, Future Directions.* Ed. Brenda G. McGowan and William Meezan. Itasca, Ill. F. E. Peacock, 1983, 93–141.

Baily, Thelma Falk, and Walter Hampton Baily. *Child Welfare Practice: A Guide to Providing Effective Services for Children and Families.* San Francisco: Jossey-Bass, 1983.

Beck, Dorothy F., and Mary A. Jones. *Progress on Family Problems: Nationwide Study of Clients' and Counselors' Views on Family Agency Services.* New York: Family Service Association of America, 1973.

Beck, Dorothy F., and Mary A. Jones. "Debate with Authors," *Social Service Review,* 3 (June 1976), 312–331.

Billingsley, Andrew, and Jeanne Giovannoni. *Children of the Storm: Black Children and American Child Welfare.* New York: Harcourt, Brace, Jovanovich, 1972.

Bremner, Robert (ed.). *Children and Youth in America: A Documentary History, Volume II, 1866–1932, Parts 1–6.* Cambridge, Mass.: Harvard University Press, 1971.

Bremner, Robert (ed.). *Children and Youth in America: A Documentary History: Volume III, 1933–1973, Parts 1–4.* Cambridge, Mass.: Harvard University Press, 1974.

Briar, Scott, and Jon Conte. "Families," in *Social Service Research: Review of Studies.* ed. Henry Maas. Washington, D.C.: National Association of Social Workers, 1978, 9–38.

Brim, Orville, Jr. *Education for Child Rearing.* New York: Russell Sage Foundation, 1959.

Bryce, Marvin. "Home-Based Care: Development and Rationale," in *Home-Based Services for Children and Families: Policy, Practice, and Research.* Ed. S. Maybanks and M. Bryce. Springfield, Ill.: Charles C. Thomas, 1979, 13–26.

Bryce, Marvin. "Home-Based Family-Centered Care: Problems and Perspectives," in *Treating Families in the Home: An Alternative to Placement.* Ed. M. Bryce and J. C. Lloyd. Springfield, Ill.: Charles C. Thomas, 1981, 5–11.

Bryce, Marvin. "Preplacement Prevention and Family Reunification: Direction for the 80's," in *A Dialogue on the Challenge for Education and Training: Child Welfare Issues in the 80's.* Ed. Ellen S. Saalberg. Ann Arbor, Mich.: National Child Welfare Training Center, 1982, 77–84.

Buckley, Susan. "Parent Aides Provide Support to: High-Risk Families." *Children Today,* 14 (September/October, 1985), 16–19.

Burt, Marvin. "Final results of the Nashville Comprehensive Emergency Services Project," *Child Welfare,* 55, 9 (November 1976), 661–664.

Bush, Malcolm, and Harold Goldman. "The Psychological Parenting and Permanency Principles in Child Welfare: A Reappraisal and Critique." *American Journal of Orthopsychiatry.* 52, 2 (1982), 223–235.

Butehorn, Loretta. "A Plan for Identifying Priorities in Treating Multiproblem Families." *Child Welfare,* 57, 6 (1978), 365–372.

Cantoni, Lucile, "Family Life Education: A Treatment Modality." *Child Welfare,* 54, 9 (November, 1975), 658–665.

Carter, Robert D., and Richard B. Stuart. "Behavior Modification Theory and Practice: A Reply." *Social Work,* 15, 1 (January 1970).

Cautley, Patricia. "Treating Dysfunctional Families at Home." *Social Work,* 25 (September 1980), 380–386.

Chestang, Leon. "The Delivery of Child Welfare Services to Minority Group Children and Their Families," in *Child Welfare Strategy in the Coming Years.* Ed. Alfred Kadushin. Washington, D.C.: DHEW, 1978, 169–194.

Child Welfare League of America, *CWLA Statement on Child Advocacy.* New York: CWLA, 1981.

Children's Defense Fund. *Black and White Children in America—Key Facts.* Washington, D.C.: Children's Defense Fund, 1985.

Christopherson, Edward R. et al. "The Family Training Program: Improving Parent–Child Interaction Patterns", in *Behavior Modification Approaches to Parenting.* Ed. Eric J. Mash, Lee C. Handy, and Leo A. Hamerlynck, New York: Brunner/Mazel, 1976, 36–56.

Clark, Ted, Tracey Zalis, and Frank Sacco. *Outreach Family Therapy.* New York: Jason Aronson, 1982.

Clayton-Fechtmann, Kathryn A., and Janis I. Seibold. "Community and Home-Based Treatment Planning for Adolescents and Their Families," in *Treating Families in the Home: An Alternative to Placement.* Ed. M. Bryce and J. C. Lloyd. Springfield, ILL: Charles C. Thomas, 1981, 273–285.

Cloward, Richard, and Irwin Epstein. *Private Social Welfare's Disengagement from the Poor: The Case of Family Adjustment Agencies.* 1964. Mimeo.

Cole, Elizabeth S. "Implications of the Adoption Assistance and Child Welfare Act of 1980," in *A Dialogue on the Challenge for Education and Training: Child Welfare Issues in the 80's.* Ed. Ellen S. Saalberg. Ann Arbor, Mich.: National Child Welfare Training Center, 1982, 33–42.

Conte, Jon. "Service Provision to Enhance Family Functioning," in *Child Welfare: Current Dilemmas, Future Directions.* Ed. Brenda G. McGowan and William Meezan. Itasca, Il.: F. E. Peacock, 1983, 171–210.

Cooper, John, and Denzil Edge. *Parenting: Strategies and Educational Techniques,* Columbus, Oh.: Charles E. Merrill, 1978.

Dinkmeyer, Don, and Gary McKay. *Systematic Training for Effective Parenting.* Circle Pines, Minn.: American Guidance Service, 1976.

Dodson, Jualynne. "Conceptualizations of Black Families," in *Black Families.* Ed. Harriette Pipes McAdoo. Beverly Hills, Cal.: Sage, 1981, 23–36.

Dunu, Marylee. "The Lower East Side Family Union: Assuring Community Services for Minority Families," in *Home-Based Services for Children and Families: Policy, Practice and Research.* Ed. S. Maybanks and M. Bryce. Springfield, Ill.: Charles C Thomas, 1979, 211–224.

Edna McConnell Clark Foundation. *Keeping Families Together: The Case for Family Preservation.* New York: Author, 1985.

Elardo, Richard. "The Home as a Learning Environment: Rationale, Assessment, and Programming," in *Treating Families in the Home: An Alternative to Placement.* Ed. M. Bryce and J. C. Lloyd. Springfield, Ill.: Charles C Thomas, 1981, 35–49.

Evans, Judith. "The High/Scope Parent-to Parent Model," in *Home-Based Services for Children and Families: Policy, Practice, and Research.* Ed. S. Maybanks and M. Bryce. Springfield, Ill: Charles C Thomas, 1979, 115–124.

Ewalt, Patricia (ed.). *Toward a Definition of Clinical Social Work,* Washington, D.C.: National Association of Social Workers, 1980.

Eyde, Donna R., and Susan Willig. "Home Support for Families with Disturbed Children," in *Treating Families in the Home: An Alternative to Placement.* Ed. M. Bryce and J. C. Lloyd. Springfield, Ill.: Charles C Thomas, 1981, 260–272.

Fahl, Mary Ann, and Donna Morrissey. "The Mendota Model: Home-Community Treatment," in *Home-Based Services for Children and Families: Policy, Practice, and Research.* Ed. S. Maybanks and M. Bryce. Springfield, Ill.: Charles C Thomas, 1979, 225–236.

Family Service Association of America. *Summary of Family Advocacy Program—November 26, 1969.* Mimeo. New York: Family Service Association of America, 1969.

Family Service Association of America. *Agency Program and Funding—1976.* New York: Family Service Association of America, 1977.

Family Service Association of America. *Family Service Profiles—Agency Program and Service—1982.* New York: Family Service Association of America, 1983.

Fine, Marvin. *Handbook on Parent Education.* New York: Academic Press, 1980.

Fisher, Joel, and Harvey L. Gochros. *Planned Behavior Change: Behavior Modification in Social Work.* New York: Free Press, 1975.

Gambrill, Eileen D. *Behavior Modification—Handbook of Assessment, Intervention, and Evaluation.* San Francisco: Jossey-Bass. 1977.

Garvey, William P., and Jack R. Hegrenes. "Desensitization Techniques in the Treatment of a School Phobia", *American Journal of Orthopsychiatry,* 36 (January 1966), 147–152.

Geismar, Ludwig. "Home-Based Care to Children: Harmonizing the Approaches of Research and Practice," in *Home-Based Services for Children and Families: Policy, Practice and Research.* Ed. Sheila Maybanks and Marvin Bryce. Springfield, Ill.: Charles C Thomas, 1979, 325–332.

Gershenson, Charles. *Child Welfare Population Characteristics and Flow Analysis: FY 1982.* Washington, D.C.: Administration for Children, Youth and Families, 1983.

Giblin, Paul, and Esther Callard. "Issues in Evaluation of Action Research: A Social Service Model." *Social Work Research and Abstracts,* 16 (1980), 3–12.

Gibson, Terry, and Mary Lewis. "Sowing the Seeds of Trouble: An Historical Analysis of Compliance Structures in Child Welfare," *Journal of Sociology and Social Welfare,* 7, 5 (1980), 679–707.

Goffin, Stacie. "A Framework for Cenceptualizing Children's Services." *American Journal of Orthopsychiatry,* 53, 2 (1983), 282–290.

Goldsmith, Jerome. "Mental Health Services for Children," in *Encyclopedia of Social Work.* Ed. John B. Turner. New York: National Association of Social Workers. 1977, 891–897.

Goldstein, Harriet. "Home-Based Services and the Worker," in *Treating Families in the Home: An Alternative to Placement.* Ed. M. Bryce and J. C. Lloyd. Springfield, Ill.: Charles C Thomas, 1981, 127–134.

Goldstein, Joseph, Anna Freud, and Albert Solnit. *Before the Best Interests of the Child.* New York: Free Press, 1979.

Golner, Joseph. "Home Family Counseling," in *Social Work with Families: Theory and Practice".* Ed. Carlton Munson. New York: Free Press, 1980, 251–263.

Gordon, Thomas. *Parent Effectiveness Training.* New York: New American Library, 1975.

Gourse, Judith, and Martha Chescheir. "Authority Issues in Treating Resistant Families," *Social Casework,* 62, 2 (2181), 67–73.

Gray, Sylvia Sims (Comp.). *A Sourcebook in Child Welfare: Serving Chicano Families and Children.* Ann Arbor, Mich.: National Child Welfare Training Center, 1983.

Gray, Sylvia Sims (Comp.). *A Sourcebook in Child Welfare: Serving Puerto Rican Families and Children.* Ann Arbor, Mich.: National Child Welfare Training Center, 1984.

Green, Robert and Michael S. Kolevson. "A Survey of Family Therapy Practitioners," *Social Casework,* 63 (February 1982), 95–99.

Gwyn, Felisha, and Allie Kilpatrick. "Family Therapy with Low-Income Blacks: A Tool or Turn-Off?" *Social Casework,* 62, 5 (May 1981), 259–266.

Haapala, David, and Jill Kinney. "Homebuilders' Approach to the Training of In-Home Therapists," in *Home-Based Services for Children and Families: Policy, Practice and Research.* Ed. S. Maybanks and M. Bryce. Springfield, Ill.: Charles C Thomas, 1979, 248–259.

Hallowitz, David. "The Problem-Solving Component in Family Therapy." In *Social Work with Families: Theory and Practice.* Ed. Carlton Munson. New York: Free Press, 1980, 228–239.

Halpern, Robert. "Lack of Effects for Home-Based Early Intervention? Some Possible Explanations." *American Journal of Orthopsychiatry,* 54 (1984), 33–42.

Haring, Barbara. *1972 Census of Requests for Child Welfare Services.* New York: Child Welfare League of America, 1972.

Harper, Amos et al. *American Charities and Social Work,* 4th ed. New York: Thomas Y. Crowell, 1940.

Hartman, Ann. "The Family: A Central Focus for Practice," *Social Work,* 26, 1 (1981), 7–13.

Hawkins, Ray. "Developing Comprehensive Emergency Services," in *Home-Based Services for Children and Families: Policy, Practice and Research.* Ed. S. Maybanks and M. Bryce. Springfield, Ill.: Charles C Thomas, 1979, 103–114.

Hawkins, Robert P. et al. "Behavior Therapy in the Home: Amelioration of Problem Parent-Child Relations with the Parent in a Therapeutic Role." *Journal of Experimental Child Psychology,* 4 (1966), 94–107.

Hill, Robert. *The Strengths of Black Families.* New York: Emerson Hall, 1971.

Horejsi, Charles R. "The St. Paul Family-Centered Project Revisited: Exploring an Old Gold Mine," in *Treating Families in the Home: An Alternative to Placement.* Ed M. Bryce and J. C. Lloyd. Springfield, Ill.: Charles C Thomas, 1981, 12–23.

Howe, George W. "The Ecological Approach to Permanency Planning: An Interactionist Perspective." *Child Welfare,* 62, 4 (July–August 1983), 291–301.

Hull, Grafton. "Child Welfare Services to Native Americans." *Social Casework,* 63, 6 (June 1982), 340–347.

Hyde, James, Jr., et al. "Family Advocacy: Implications for Treatment and Policy," in

Home-Based Services for Children and Families: Policy, Practice and Research. Ed. S. Maybanks and M. Bryce. Springfield, Ill.: Charles C Thomas, 1979, 177–185.

James, Muriel. *Transactional Analysis for Moms and Dads: What Do You Do With Them Now That You've Got Them?* Reading, Mass.: Addison-Wesley, 1974.

Janchill, Sister Mary Paul. "Services for Special Populations of Children," in *Child Welfare: Current Dilemmas, Future Directions.* Ed. Brenda G. McGowan and William Meezan. Itasca, Ill.: F. E. Peacock, 1983, 345–376.

Jehu, Derek. *Learning Theory and Social Work.* London: Kegan, Paul, Trench, Trubner, and Co., 1967.

Johnson, Claudia and Roger C. Katz. "Using Parents as Change Agents for their Children: A Review." *Journal of Child Psychology and Psychiatry,* 14 (1973), 181–200.

Jones, Martha, and John Biesecker. *Child Welfare Training—Goal Planning in Children and Youth Services.* Washington, D.C.: U.S. Dept. of Health and Human Services, 1980a.

Jones, Martha, and John Biesecker. *Child Welfare Training—Permanency Planning Guide for Children and Youth Services.* Washington, D.C.: U.S. Dept. of Health and Human Services, 1980b.

Jones, Martha, and John Biesecker. *Child Welfare Training - Trainer's Manual for Goal Planning and Permanency Planning in Children and Youth Services.* Washington, D.C.: U.S. Dept. of Health and Human Services, 1980c.

Jones, Mary Ann, Stephen Magura, and Ann Shyne. "Effective Practice with Families in Protective and Preventive Services: What Works?" *Child Welfare,* 60, 2 (February 1981), 67–80.

Kamerman, Sheila B., and Alfred J. Kahn. "Child Welfare and the Welfare of Families with Children: A Child and Family Policy Agenda," in *Child Welfare: Current Dilemmas, Future Directions.* Ed. Brenda G. McGowan and William Meezan. Itasca, Ill.: F. E. Peacock, 1983, 147–170.

Kazdin, Alan E. and Terence Wilson. *Evaluation of Behavior Through Therapy: Issues, Evidence and Research Strategies.* Cambridge, Mass.: Ballinger, 1978.

Kent, Ronald N., and K. Daniel O'Leary. "A Controlled Evaluation of Behavior Modification with Conduct Problem Children." *Journal of Clinical and Consulting Psychology,* 44, 4 (1976), 586–596.

Kinney, Jill, David Haapala, and Joan Elizabeth Gast. "Assessment of Families in Crisis," in *Treating Families in the Home: An Alternative to Placement.* Ed. M. Bryce and J. C. Lloyd. Springfield, Ill.: Charles C Thomas, 1981, 50–67.

Knitzer, Jane, and Lynn Olson. *Unclaimed Children: The Failure of Public Responsibility to Children and Adolescents in Need of Mental Health Services.* Washington, D.C.: Children's Defense Fund. 1982.

Koch, Gratia. "Home-Based Support Services: An Alternative to Residential Placement for the Developmentally Disabled," in *Home-Based Services for Children and Families: Policy, Practice, and Research.* Ed. S. Maybanks and M. Bryce. Springfield, Ill.: Charles C Thomas, 1979, 157–164.

Kraft, Sherry, and Thomas DeMaio. "An Ecological Intervention with Adolescents in Low-Income Families." *American Journal of Orthopsychiatry,* 52, 1 (1982), 131–140.

Levenstein, Phyllis. "Ethical Considerations in Home-Based Programs," in *Treating Families in the Home: An Alternative to Placement.* Ed. M. Bryce and J. C. Lloyd. Springfield, Ill.: Charles C Thomas, 1981, 222–237.

Levine, Murray, and Adeline Levine. *A Social History of Helping Services—Clinic, Court, School, and Community.* New York: Appleton-Century-Crofts, 1970.

Levine, Theodore, and Elizabeth McDaid. "Services to Children in their Own Homes: A Family-Based Approach," in *Home-Based Services for Children and Families: Policy, Practice and Research.* Ed. S. Maybanks and M. Bryce. Springfield, Ill.: Charles C Thomas, 1979, 260–271.

Levitt, Eugene. "The Results of Psychotherapy with Children: An Evaluation." *Journal of Consulting Psychology,* 21 (1957).

Levitt, Eugene. "Psychotherapy with Children: A Further Evaluation." *Behavioral Research Therapy,* 1 (1963).

Levitt, Eugene. "Research on Psychotherapy with Children," in *Handbook on Psychotherapy and Behavior Change—An Empirical Analysis*. Ed. Allen E. Bergin and Sol L. Garfield. New York: John Wiley & Sons, 1972.

Little, Robert. "The Public Welfare Connection", in *A Dialogue on the Challenge for Education and Training: Child Welfare Issues in the 80's*. Ed. by Ellen S. Saalberg. Ann Arbor, Mich.: National Child Welfare Training Center, 1982, 25–32.

Luborsky, Lester, Barton Singer, and Lise Luborsky. "Comparative Studies of Psychotherapies: Is It True The 'Everybody Has Won and All Must Have Prizes?'" in *Evaluation of Psychological Therapies*. Ed. Robert L. Spitzer and Donald F. Klein. Baltimore, Md.: Johns Hopkins University Press, 1976, 3–22.

Lurie, Olga. "Parents' Attitudes Toward Children's Problems and Toward Use of Mental Health Services." *American Journal of Orthopsychiatry*, 44 (January 1974), 109–120.

Magazino, Carmine J. "Services to Children and Families at Risk of Separation," in *Child Welfare: Current Dilemmas, Future Directions*. Ed. Brenda G. McGowan and William Meezan. Itasca, Ill: F. E. Peacock, 1983, 211–254.

Maguire, Lambert. *Understanding Social Networks*. Beverly Hills, Cal.: Sage, 1983.

Magura, Stephen. "Are Services to Prevent Foster Care Effective?" *Children and Youth Services Review*, 3 (1981), 193–212.

Maluccio, Anthony. "Selecting Foster Parents for Disturbed Children." *Children*, 13 (March-April 1966), 69–74.

Maluccio, Anthony. *Learning from Clients: Interpersonal Helping as Viewed by Clients and Social Workers*. New York: The Free Press, 1979.

Maluccio, Anthony et al. "Beyond Permanency Planning", *Child Welfare*, 59, 9 (November 1980), 515–530.

Maluccio, Anthony, and Edith Fein. "Permanency Planning: A Redefinition. *Child Welfare*, 62 (May–June 1983), 195–201.

Manns, Wilhelmina. "Support Systems of Significant Others in Black Families," in *Black Families*. Ed. Hariette Pipes McAdoo. Beverly Hills, Cal.: Sage, 1981, 238–251.

Manser, Ellen (ed.) *Family Advocacy—A Manual for Action*. New York: Family Service Association of America, 1973.

Mash, Eric, Lee Handy, and Leo Hamerlynck (eds.). *Behavior Modification Approaches to Parenting*. New York: Brunner/Mazel, 1976.

McCauley, Roger, and Patricia McCauley. *Child Behavior Problems—An Empirical Approach to Management*. New York: Free Press, 1977.

McDaniel, Deborah. "Foster Care in the 1980's." *Children and Youth Services Review*, 3 (1981), 1–5.

McGowan, Brenda G. "Historical Evolution of Child Welfare Services: An Examination of the Sources of Current Problems and Dilemmas", in *Child Welfare: Current Dilemmas, Future Directions*. Ed. Brenda G. McGowan and William Meezan. Itasca, Ill.: F. E. Peacock, 1983, 45–92.

McPherson, Sandra B., and Cyrille R. Sanuels. "Teaching Behavioral Methods to Parents." *Social Casework*, 52, 3 (March 1971), 148–153.

Meezan, William. "Child Welfare: An Overview of the Issues," in *Child Welfare: Current Dilemmas, Future Directions*. Ed. Brenda G. McGowan and William Meezan. Itasca, Ill: F. E. Peacock, 1983, 5–44.

Meyer, Carol H. "Staffing Issues in Child Welfare," in *Child Welfare: Current Dilemmas, Future Directions*. Ed. Brenda G. McGowan and William Meezan. Itasca, Ill.: F. E. Peacock, 1983, 479–502.

Miller, William Hansford, *Systematic Parent Training*. Champaign, Ill.: Research Press, 1975.

Morawetz, Anita, and Gillian Walker. *Brief Therapy with Single-Parent Families*. New York: Brunner-Mazel, 1984.

Morin, Patricia. "The Extended Family Model: Increasing Service Effectiveness," in *Treating Families in the Home: An Alternative to Placement*. Ed. M. Bryce and J. C Lloyd. Springfied, Ill.: Charles C. Thomas, 1981, 135–151.

Mulvey, Laurie and Carole Vellenoweth. *Handbook for Parent Education for Low-Income Families.* Charlottesville, N.C.: Department of Social Services, no date.

National Child Welfare Training Center, *A Sourcebook in Child Welfare: Serving Black Families and Children.* Ann Arbor, Mich.: Author, 1982.

Nichols, Michael. *Family Therapy: Concepts and Methods.* New York: Gardner Press, 1984.

Nuehring, Elaine et al. "Evaluating the Impact of Prevention Programs Aimed at Children," *Social Work Research and Abstracts,* 19, 2 (1983), 11–18.

Nybell, Lynn (Compiler). *A Sourcebook in Child Welfare: Serving American Indian Families and Children.* Ann Arbor, Mich.: National Child Welfare Training Center, 1984.

O'Connor, K. Carol, Susan Glickman Davis, and Nancy H. Sahlein. "Primary Prevention with Mothers and Young Children." *Social Casework,* 65, 9 (November 1984), 559–564.

O'Dell, S. "Training Parents in Behavior Modification: A Review." *Psychological Bulletin,* 81 (1974), 418–423.

O'Keefe, Ann. "Home Start Within Head Start," in *Home-Based Services for Children and Families: Policy, Practice and Research.* Ed. S. Maybanks and M. Bryce. Springfield, Ill.: Charles C Thomas, 1979, 333–342.

Patterson, Gerald. "The Aggressive Child: Victim and Architect of a Coercive System," in *Behavior Modification and Families,* Ed. Eric Mash, Leo Hamerlynck, and Lee Handy. New York: Brunner/Mazel, 1976, 267–316.

Patterson, Gerald. *Families: Applications of Social Learning to Family Life.* Champaign, Ill.: Research Press, 1977.

Payne, Carol (ed.). *Programs to Strengthen Families—A Resource Guide,* Chicago: Family Resource Coalition, 1984.

Peterson, Robert. "Power, Programming and Punishment: Could We Be Overcontrolling Our Children?" in *Behavior Modification and Families.* Ed. Eric Mash, Leo Hamerlynck, and Lee Handy. New York: Brunner/Mazel, 1976, 338–352.

Pill, Cynthia. "A Family Life Education Group for Working with Stepparents." *Social Casework,* 62, 3 (1981), 159–166.

Pinderhughes, Elaine. "Empowerment for Our Clients and for Ourselves." *Social Casework,* 64, 6 (1983), 331–338.

Pizzo, Peggy. *Parent to Parent: Working Together For Ourselves and Our Children.* Boston: Beacon Press, 1983.

President's Commission on Mental Health. *Task Panel Reports,* Vols. 2–4. Washington, D.C.: U.S. Government Printing Office, 1978.

Ramirez, Manuel, III and Barbara Cox. "Parenting for Multiculturism: A Mexican–American Model." In *Parenting in a Multicultural Society.* Ed. Mario Fantini and René Cárdenas. New York: Longman, 1980, 54–62.

Rapoport, Rhona, Robert Rapoport, and Ziona Strelitz. *Fathers, Mothers and Society: Towards New Alliances.* New York: Basic Books, 1977.

Region III Child Welfare Training Center. *Practice Related Home-Based Family Centered Services Course for Master of Social Work Curricula.* Richmond, Va.: Author, 1982a.

Region III Child Welfare Training Center. *Working with Black Families and Children.* Richmond, Va.: Author, 1982b.

Reid, William J. *The Task Centered System.* New York: Columbia University Press, 1978.

Reid, William J. and Laura Epstein. *Task-Centered Casework.* New York: Columbia University Press, 1972.

Reid, William J. and Patricia Hanrahan. "Recent Evaluations of Social Work: Grounds for Optimism," *Social Work,* 27 (July 1982) 328–340.

Reisinger, James J., John P. Ora, and George W. Frangia. "Parents Are Change Agents for Their Children." *Journal of Community Psychology,* 4 (1976), 103–123.

Rice, Robert. *American Family Policy: Content and Context.* New York: Family Service Association of America, 1977.

Rice, Robert. "Reducing Substitute Child Care Through National Family Policy," in *Child Welfare Strategy in the Coming Years.* Ed. A Kadushin. Washington, D.C.: DHEW, 1978, 431–465.

Riley, Patrick V. "Family Advocacy—Case to Cause and Back to Case." *Child Welfare,* 40, 7 (July 1971), 374–383.

Rooney, Ronald. "Permanency Planning: Boon for All Children?" *Social Work,* 27, 2 (1982), 152–158.

Rosenberg, Steven, Cordelia, D. Robinson, and Gay McTate. "Assessment and Planning in In-Home Services." In *Treating Families in the Home: An Alternative to Placements.* Ed. Marvin Bryce and June Lloyd. Springfield, Ill.: Charles C Thomas, 1981, 84–97.

Rothman, Jack, and Terrence Kay. "Community Mental Health Centers and Family Service Agencies." *Social Work Research and Abstracts,* 13, (Winter 1977), 10–16.

Rudestam, Kjell Erik, and Mark Frankel. *Treating the Multiproblem Family: A Casebook.* Monterey, Cal.: Brooks/Cole, 1983.

Ryan, Michael. "Families Program Design: Giving Families Relevance in Treatment," in *Home-Based Services for Children and Families: Policy, Practice and Research.* Ed. S. Maybanks and M. Bryce. Springfield, Ill.: Charles C Thomas, 1979, 272–282.

Samit, Carol, Kathleen Nash, and Janeen Meyers. "The Parents Group: A Therapeutic Tool." *Social Casework,* 61, 4 (1980), 215–222.

Schram, Sanford. "Politics, Professionalism and the Changing Federalism," *Social Service Review,* 55 (1981), 78–92.

Schuerman, John R. "Do Family Services Help? A Critical Review." *Social Service Review,* 49 (September 1975), 363–375.

Schwartz, Arthur, and Israel Goldiamond. *Social Casework: A Behavioral Approach.* New York: Columbia University Press, 1975.

Segal, Lynn. "Focused Problem Resolution (Brief Therapy)". In *Models of Family Treatment.* Ed. Eleanor Tolson and William Reid. New York: Columbia University Press, 1981, 199–223.

Shearer, David. "Parents as Educators: The Portage Project," in *Home-Based Services for Children and Families: Policy, Practice and Research.* Ed. S. Maybanks and M. Bryce. Springfield, Ill.: Charles C Thomas, 1979, 125–135.

Sherman, Edmund A. et al. *Service to Children in Their Own Homes—Its Nature and Outcome.* New York: Child Welfare League of America, 1973.

Shireman, Joan F. "Achieving Permanence After Placement," in *Child Welfare: Current Dilemmas, Future Directions.* Ed. Brenda G. McGowan and William Meezan. Itasca, Ill.: F. E. Peacock, 1983, 377–424.

Shyne, Ann, and Anita Schroeder. *National Study of Social Services to Children and Their Families.* Washington, D.C.: DHEW, 1978.

Siporin, Max. "Marriage and Family Therapy in Social Work." *Social Casework,* 61, 1 (January 1980), 11–21.

Slater, Edward P., and William Harris. "Therapy at Home." *Practice Digest,* 1 (1978), 20–21.

Sloan, Bruce et al. *Psychotherapy Versus Behavior Therapy.* Cambridge, Mass.: Harvard University Press, 1975.

Smith, Mary L, Gene V. Glass, and Thomas Miller, *The Benefits of Psychotherapy,* Baltimore, Md.: Johns Hopkins University Press, 1980.

Solomon, Barbara. *Black Empowerment: Social Work in Oppressed Communities.* New York: Columbia University Press, 1976.

Spiegel, John. "An Ecological Model with an Emphasis on Ethnic Families." In *Models of Family Treatment.* Ed. Eleanor Tolson and William Reid. New York: Columbia University Press, 1981, 121–158.

Spinelli, Lauren, and Karen Barton. "Home Management Services for Families with Emotionally Disturbed Children." *Child Welfare,* 59, 1 (1980), 43–52.

Stack, Carol. *All Our Kin: Strategies for Survival in a Black Community,* New York: Harper & Row, 1974.

Stein, Ruth E.K. "A Special Home Care Unit for Care of Chronically Ill Children," in *Treating Families in the Home: An Alternative to Placement.* Ed. M. Bryce and J.C. Lloyd. Springfield, Ill.: Charles C Thomas, 1981, 313–326.

Stein, Theodore J. "Child Welfare: New Directions in the Field and Their Implications for

Education," in *A Dialogue on the Challenge for Education and Training: Child Welfare Issues in the 80's*. Ed. Ellen S. Saalberg. Ann Arbor, Mich.: National Child Welfare Training Center, 1982, 57–76.

Stein, Theodore J., and Tina Rzepnicki. "Decision-Making in Child Welfare: Current Issues and Future Directions," in *Child Welfare: Current Dilemmas, Future Directions*. Ed. Brenda G. McGowan and William Meezan. Itasca Ill. F. E. Peacock, 1983, 259–294.

Stephens, Douglas. "In-Home Family Support Services: An Ecological Systems Approach," in *Home-Based Services for Children and Families: Policy, Practice and Research*. Ed. S. Maybanks and M. Bryce. Springfield, Ill.: Charles C Thomas, 1979, 283–295.

Stephens, Douglas, and Kay F. Busch. "Strategies of Ecological Change with Families," in *Treating Families in the Home: An Alternative to Placement*. Ed. M. Bryce and J. C. Lloyd. Springfield, Ill.: Charles C Thomas, 1981, 152–164.

Stokes, John, and Joan Greenstone. "Helping Black Grandparents and Older Parents Cope with Child Rearing: A Group Method." *Child Welfare*, 60, 10 (1981), 691–701.

Sudia, Cecelia. "Family Based Services: A Conference Report." *Children Today*, 11, 5 (1982), 12–13.

Sunley, Robert. "Family Advocacy: From Case to Cause," in *Social Work with Families: Theory and Practice*. Ed. Carlton Munson. New York: Free Press, 1980, 145–160.

Tavormina, Joseph B. "Basic Models of Parent Counseling: A Critical Review." *Psychological Bulletin*, 81, 11 (1974), 827–835.

Thomas, Edwin J. (Ed.) *The Socio-Behavioral Approach and Applications to Social Work*. New York: Council on Social Work Education, 1967.

Thomlinson, Ray S. "Something Works: Evidence from Practical Effectiveness Studies," *Social Work*, 29 (January–February 1984), 51–52.

Tomlinson, Rod, and Peg Peters. "An Alternative to Placing Children: Intensive and Extensive Therapy with 'Disengaged' Families." *Child Welfare*, 60, 2 (1981), 95–103.

Turner, Charlene. "Resources for Help in Parenting." *Child Welfare*, 59, 3 (1980), 179–188.

Tuszynski, Ann, and James Dowd. "Home-Based Services to Protective Service Families", in *Home-Based Services for Children and Families: Policy, Practice and Research*. Ed. S. Maybanks and M. Bryce. Springfield, Ill.: Charles C Thomas, 1979, 296–307.

U.S. Department of Health and Human Services. *Status of Children, Youth, and Families*. Washington, D.C.: DHHS, 1980.

Vasaly, Shirley. *Foster Care in Five States: A Synthesis and Analysis of Studies from Arizona, California, Iowa, Massachusetts, and Vermont*. Washington, D.C.: DHEW, 1978.

Wald, Michael. "State Intervention on Behalf of 'Neglected' Children: A Search for Realistic Standards." *Stanford Law Review*, 27 (April 1975), 985–1040.

Wells, Richard. "The Empirical Base of Family Therapy: Practice Implications," in *Models of Family Treatment*. Ed. Eleanor Tolson and William Reid. New York: Columbia University Press, 1981, 248–305.

Werner, Emmy, and Ruth Smith. *Vulnerable but Invincible: A Study of Resilient Children*. New York: McGraw-Hill, 1982.

Witmer, Helen. *Psychiatric Clinics for Children*. London: Commonwealth Fund, 1940.

Wodarski, John, and Dennis Bagarozzi. *Behavioral Social Work*. New York: Human Sciences Press, 1979.

Wolock, Isabel et al. "Three Child Care Programs: A Comparative Study." *Australian Social Work*, 32, 2 (1979), 17–24.

Wortman, Richard. "Depression, Danger, Denial: Work with Poor Black, Single Parents." *American Journal of Orthopsychiatry*, 51 (October 1981), 662–671.

Yoshikami, Rogers. *Assessing the Implementation of Federal Policy to Reduce the Use of Foster Care: Placement Prevention and Reunification in Child Welfare: Volume 1*. Washington, D.C.: Children's Bureau, 1984.

Zischka, Pauline. "The Effect of Burnout on Permanency Planning and the Middle Management Supervisor in Child Welfare Agencies." *Child Welfare*, 60, 9 (1981), 611–616.

4

Supplementary Services:

Homemaker Services

Introduction to Supplementary Services

Home-based agencies, in helping with problems of child welfare, primarily operate to strengthen and reinforce the parents in discharging their parental roles, but they do not in any way attempt to assume the parents' responsibility. The service remains, in effect, outside the family system. Supplementary services, on the other hand, enter into the social system of the family. They are designed to discharge some part, however limited, of the role responsibility of the parent. For the period of time that the supplementary service is offered, the family embodies the biological parent(s) and the supplementary parent in the guise of the agency. Supplementary services include the income maintenance programs, day care, and homemaker service.

Where the parental role is left permanently vacant because of death, illegitimacy, desertion, divorce, or separation, or is temporarily unfilled because of imprisonment, military service, illness, or employment, some dislocation of the parent–child system takes place and necessitates some arrangement for role supplementation.

One of the principal roles of the parent is to provide for the child and ensure his or her healthy development. In our money economy, this means that the family must have a cash income, and the responsibility for implementing the wage-earner role is generally delegated to the father, although the mother may supplement his income. Income maintenance programs are designed to act *in loco parentis*—in place of parents or as supplementary parents—as far as this specific aspect of parental role responsibility is concerned.

Unemployment, disability, or death of the wage earner may result in the loss of family income. Workman's compensation, unemployment insurance, and the Old Age, Survivors', and Disability Insurance (OASDI) are social insurance programs that provide for income maintenance for the family faced with such situations. Public assistance programs—general assistance and the Aid to Families of Dependent Children program—cover some of the contingencies provided for by the social insurances and for others as well. Thus assistance may be granted to families left fatherless through desertion, separation, divorce, imprisonment, or illegitimacy.

The social insurance and public assistance programs are the principal, supplementary programs providing financial help to families with children. They are supplementary programs in that the family benefiting from these programs consists, in effect, of parents, children, and the program itself, which supplements the income producing role of the parents.

As indicated in the preface to this edition we have deleted a chapter on the social insurances and the assistance programs included in earlier editions. We did this, we noted, for the purpose of conserving space and because this content was generally taught in social work social policy courses it had lower priority for courses on child welfare services. We do, however, regard such programs as having inestimable value to families with children, providing the kind of supplementation that many families need. These programs have an impact on lives of more children than any other programs affecting families. We should like to note briefly the extent of such help.

The Old Age Survivors and Disability Insurance Program (OASDI) in 1985 provided 10.7 billion dollars of help to 3.4 million children whose previously employed fathers or mothers had died, were permanently disabled or have retired.

In 1984 Workmen's Compensation Insurance programs provided 19.5 billions of dollars to families of injured workers for medical, hospitalization, and continuing compensation benefits. The Unemployment Insurance programs in 1984 provided 15.4 billions of dollars of help to unemployed workers many of whom had dependent children.

The AFDC program in 1985 provided some $15 billion of assistance to about 11,000,000 recipients of whom some 7 million were children. The average monthly family assistance payment was about $330. The primary reason for the need for such help was that fathers were absent from the home and the children's mother was unable to provide support. In 34 per cent of the cases the child was born out-of-wedlock, 26 per cent of the cases fathers had deserted or were separated and in 21 per cent the parents were divorced. Death, disability, imprisonment, and unemployment accounted for the additional percentages.

In addition to cash benefits, families with children received in-kind supports through means tested assistance programs. These included medical assistance (Medicaid), food stamps, public, or subsidized rental housing, and free or reduced-price school meals.

These billions of dollars of financial grants and in-kind help to families with children are by far the most extensive measures preventing the placement of children in substitute care. Hundreds of thousands of children who might otherwise need out-of-home care are maintained in their own homes with the help provided parents by these programs.

Introduction to Homemaker Services

The social insurance and social assistance programs are designed primarily to meet the needs presented by the fatherless family. Homemaker service is designed primarily to meet the needs of the motherless family, to provide for those crucial aspects of the traditional mother's role—child care and maintenance of the home—when the mother cannot perform these functions adequately.

Both homemaker service and day care are supplementary in-home child-welfare services. Both relate to a problem of interrole conflict. In the case of homemaker service it is generally a conflict between the role of mother and the "sick" role—the behavior associated with a person in medically disabled status. In the case of day care it is generally the conflict between the role of mother and the role of employee.

Unlike most of the other services included in the text, the additional material on homemaker service that has become available since the publication of the third edition is very limited. Although there is a good deal of exhortation about the importance of homemaker service, especially in the literature on permanency planning, very little in the way of explicit research on homemaker service has been done since 1980. Only one book that focused on homemaker service was published between 1980 and this edition of this text (Dexter & Harbert, 1983).

In addition, few periodical articles devoted to homemaker service as relevant to parent–child problems have appeared since 1980 within this time frame. So that this chapter unlike the other chapters in the text includes relatively few, new citations.

Historical Background

These services, under another name, were being offered as early as 1903, when the Family Service Bureau of the Association for the Improvement of the Conditions of the Poor in New York City employed a number of visiting cleaners who supplemented nursing services by "lifting temporarily the simple everyday domestic burdens from sick mothers." These women were later given the title *visiting housewives*. The Association's Annual Report listed their functions: helping in the renovation and restoration of homes; washing, cleaning, and sometimes preparing meals when the condition of the mother prevented her doing so and demonstrating the art of good housekeeping. After 1918, care of the children, which was to be the principal reason for such services during many years of homemaker development, begins to be stated in these reports as the purpose of assignments.

Although Breckinridge and Abbott (1912), in a study of the delinquent child, list "visiting housekeepers" as a service provided to families whose children were in danger of becoming delinquent (p. 173), the first organized homemaker program in the country is generally regarded as that established by the Jewish Family Welfare Society of Philadelphia in 1923. The purpose of the program was to provide housekeeper services to families during the temporary absence of the mother. The Jewish Home-Finding Society of Chicago inaugurated its housekeeper service in November 1924. This agency, on the basis of a standing arrangement with family welfare agencies and other welfare organizations of the community, had previously assumed responsibility for the care of children during the mother's absence from home. Prior to the introduction of housekeeping services, all such children had been placed with foster families. Because many of these children required only temporary care during the hospitalization of the mother for observation, surgery, or childbirth, approximately 40 per cent of the total volume of the work of the agency consisted of short-term foster placements (Kepecs, 1939). This proved to be an unsatisfactory method of meeting the situation because of the continual need to find foster homes and the emotional harm the children suffered by removal from their homes. Homemaker services seemed to be a logical alternative.

Goodwin (1939) describes some of the experiences that prompted the Associated Charities of Cincinnati to institute a visiting housekeeping service in 1933:

As family caseworkers, we had witnessed the turmoil in homes that had to be temporarily broken up because of the mother's illness, and had sensed the anxiety which so frequently resulted from this step for both children and husband. Caseworkers had seen, too, a great many of our mothers postpone much-needed operations or periods of complete rest away from home because they could not face the threat of a broken home. Our experience in attempting to meet these situations on an individual basis, through a neighbor's help, or through employment of another client, had not been satisfactory because we felt that in these situations they had undertaken too great a responsibility without sufficient system of supervision and follow-up [p. 281].

The Housekeeping Aid Program, as it was then called, received considerable impetus during the Great Depression under the auspices of the Works Progress Administration (WPA). Women in need of financial assistance were assigned to families in which the mother's illness or temporary absence required supplementation of the maternal role. Although fewer than a dozen family agencies were sponsoring any form of housekeeper services in 1937, almost five hundred projects were operating under the WPA at that time (Goodwin, 1939, p. 279).

Kepecs (1939) notes (p. 267) that in Chicago alone in 1938 about 150 motherless families were kept together through housekeepers furnished by WPA. The final report on the WPA (1944) notes that housekeeping aide projects

> furnished assistance in housekeeping, care of children, and elementary care of the sick in the homes of needy families in times of illness or other emergency. . . . The services of the housekeeping aides not only provided assistance in emergency situations, but also helped to establish the social principle that services can be extended to needy people in their homes in a more satisfactory and economical manner than through institutional care. . . . Through June 30, 1943, women employed on housekeeping aide projects had made more than 32 million visits into homes where the homemaker was ill or where some other emergency existed [p. 69].

In 1939 a national committee was organized to promote homemaker services. By 1971 this had developed into an independent national organization, the National Council for Homemaker–Home Health Aide Services. It promotes the cause of homemaker service by sponsoring national meetings; developing, collecting, and exchanging information regarding homemaker services; establishing standards and accrediting agencies; publishing a newsletter, as well as books and pamphlets; and providing consultation to communities interested in developing homemaker services.

The National Council for Homemaker–Home Health Aide Service subsequently changed its name to the National Homecaring Council. In 1959, the International Council of Home Help Services was organized.

Reasons that have been advanced explaining the rapid growth of homemaker services in the United States include the following:

1. The continuing trend toward a nuclear family system, which arises from the continuing mobility of our population. As a result, fewer members of the extended family are readily available to substitute for the mother when she is incapacitated or absent.
2. The reduced availability of foster homes, which requires that other resources be developed to meet the children's needs when the mother is not available.
3. The cost of placement for large sibling groups, even if foster homes were available.

4. The growth of hospital insurance programs, which results in increased use of hospital resources—by mothers, among others.
5. Improved techniques for treatment of illness, which permit early return of the mother from the hospital and her rehabilitation at home. Once the mother might have been discharged only when she was ready to resume her functions in the family; now she is encouraged to convalesce at home.
6. The growing appreciation of the value to a child of his or her own home, even one with some limitations, and of the emotional consequences that accompany his or her separation from the family and placement in a foster home. Homemaker service is perceived as a significant component in the configuration of home-based services mobilized to increase the probability of maintaining the child at home.

Definition

The National Council for Homemaker-Home Health Aide Services defines homemaker service as follows:

Homemaker–Home Health Aide Service is an organized community program provided through a public or voluntary nonprofit agency. Qualified persons—homemaker–home health aides—are employed, trained, and assigned by this agency to help maintain, strengthen, and safeguard the care of children and the functioning of dependent, physically or emotionally ill or handicapped children and adults in their own homes where no responsible person is available for this purpose. The appropriate professional staff of the agency establishes with applicants their need for the service, develops a suitable plan to meet it, assigns and supervises the homemaker–home health aides and continually evaluates whether the help given meets the diagnosed need of its recipients [National Council, 1965b, p. 5].

The Child Welfare League of America (1985) defines homemaker service as

a social service in which the community, through its social agencies, helps families by using qualified agency employed homemakers working with a social worker as part of a plan to maintain children in their own homes when circumstances impair or interrupt the ability of their parents to carry out fully their parental responsibilities; and to assure children, in their own families, the love, care, protection, and guidance they need, and to do so by assisting the parents, or other persons caring for children, to fulfill child-rearing responsibilities to the best of their ability. Service elements include: (1) assessing whether the child's needs can best be met through homemaker service, by some other service, or through the family's own resources; (2) placement of a trained homemaker in the home employed as an agency staff member, who works with a social worker in carrying out a case plan to help sustain, restore, or strengthen parental functioning [p. xxv].

Beatt (1957) emphasizes the fact that homemaker service is essentially a casework service:

Homemaker service, as a social service to children, is offered by an agency to give casework help and provide the necessary direct care of children through a supervised homemaker. It makes it possible for parents to keep children in their homes. It is offered where parents, whose ability to provide home care and guidance has been impaired by some crisis, will with this help be able to function effectively and the children will be assured a proper home. Its goal is to strengthen, support, supplement, and/or restore parental capacity to care for children and to prevent the unnecessary and/or precipitous removal of children from their own homes. As in any other tangible social service, casework helps the family and children to use the homemaker's direct care constructively, and to deal better with the problem that has necessitated the service [p. 8].

As the definitions indicate, homemaking service differs from maid service or housekeeping service in at least two important respects:

1. The homemaker goes beyond merely doing the housework and feeding the family. She accepts some responsibility for meeting the emotional needs of the children, minimizing their anxiety and maximizing their feeling of security.
2. The homemaker is, in effect, a member of a team charged with the responsibility of implementing a casework plan "to help restore and strengthen parental functioning or otherwise assure that the child has the care he needs." As a member of the team, the homemaker is supervised by the social agency, to ensure coordination of her activities with the overall treatment plan.

A distinction is made between homemaker service, chore service, and home health aide service. Homemaker service is offered by a trained homemaker and involves child care in addition to routine household care. Chore service is home maintenance activity by an untrained person, and home health aide service is focused on medical care.

Homemaker service is based on the premise that the best place for the child is in his or her own home, that this is the most favorable environment for the development of a healthy personality. Tied to this premise is the conviction that society has the responsibility of assisting the parents to fulfill their role to the best of their ability and that services should be provided by society to enable the parents to care for their children in their own home.

The homemaker's duties are frequently described as "those of the usual feminine head of the household": care and supervision of the children, family laundry, planning and preparation of meals, cleaning and maintenance of the house, shopping, and so on. They may also include the care of a sick member of the family when no actual nursing is involved. Many agencies protect the homemaker by limiting the amount of heavy work that might be required of her (U.S. Department of Health, Education, and Welfare, 1958a, p. 25). An effort has also been made to define the limits of the homemaker's activities as they relate to the nursing of the ill mother at home.

Because homemaker service is offered the family to supplement, rather than substitute for, an inadequately implemented maternal role, the nature of the service varies with the family. In general, the homemaker does not fulfill those duties that the family can perform for itself without undue stress. But, unlike a housekeeper, the homemaker must—if the situation demands it—supplement all components of the parental role: maintenance of the home, socialization of the children, and so on (Child Welfare League of America, 1959, p. 9).

Scope

A national survey of the service indicated that by 1976 there were 3,732 agency units offering homemaker services. As contrasted with the estimated 1,700 homemakers in 1958, the 1976 survey estimated approximately 82,000 homemaker–health aides. It was calculated that service had been growing at the rapid rate of 20 per cent per year during the 1970s (Humphry, 1978; National Council, 1978). A more recent national survey of the number agency units and homemakers offering the service is not available.

Despite the rapid growth of the service in this country, we still lag behind many other countries. The International Council on Home Help Services estimated that the United States had 29 home-helpers per 100,000 population in December 1976. By contrast, Sweden had 923, Norway 840, and the Netherlands 599 per 100,000 population (Little, 1978, p. 284).

The 1976 survey confirmed a longtime trend toward an increasing proportion of the service's being offered by public agencies. Of the units offering homemaker services, 51 per cent were public agencies, as contrasted with 1958, when 75 per cent of all service units were under the auspices of voluntary agencies. The most rapid growth was in the proprietary (for-profit) sector. By 1977, 15 per cent of the homemaker units were under such auspices, and an additional 5 per cent were privately owned "nonprofit" units.

In developing homemaker service as a profit-making enterprise a nationwide group has begun to provide local homemaker services operation under the name Avail-a-Care. They advertise the availability of reference-checked, insured, and bonded personnel for nursing tasks and for homemaking and home management tasks.

Here, as in day care, private-enterprise market factors are beginning to influence developments in the field (Reichert, 1977). It is anticipated that the proprietary sector will continue to grow because governmental funding regulations make payments to such units possible.

Homemaker unit affiliation with the nonprofit public and voluntary agencies was evenly divided in 1976 between social work agencies and health-care agencies. Each represents some 40 per cent of the home-care field. Most homemaker–home health aide service units were relatively small, 50 per cent employing five or fewer aides and only 4 per cent employing one hundred or more aides.

Throughout the 1970s, there was a clear trend in the redistribution of homemaker service efforts away from families with children and nonaged adults to greater concern with the homemaker needs of the aged. The 1976 survey indicated that "relatively little service is given to families with children ... Over three-fourths of all homemaker-home health aide services are now serving the elderly" (Humphry, 1978, p. 3; see also Moore, 1977, p. 31).

In 1984, the Child Welfare League of America in preparation for revising its *Standards for Homemaker Service,* which was formulated originally in 1957 polled member agencies on their homemaker service activities. "Only 15 of the 56 agencies supposedly having homemaker services for children responded to the questionnaire" (*C.W.L.A.,* May 1984, p. 2).

There are no census data available in 1986 that would indicate the number of children receiving this service.

Situations in Which Homemaker Service Is Appropriate

Unlike foster care or institutionalization, which involves temporary substitution of one set of parents for the biological parents, the situations in which homemaker service is thought to be applicable and appropriate are those that are responsive to some degree of role reallocation within the child's own family. The principal aim in providing such service is to enable the family to remain structurally intact during the period when an essential aspect of the role functions performed by the parental pair is being inadequately implemented.

The role that most frequently needs to be supplemented by homemaker service is that of the mother. Homemaker service may be offered when the mother is temporarily absent because of physical or mental illness or convalescence. Generally the father is called upon to cover the role functions of the mother, but sometimes they are allocated to the older child or children. What may also happen is that some less significant, less essential aspect of the mother's role is neglected, while the activities that must be performed if the family is to continue to function successfully are performed with the expenditure of additional energy and time on the part of incumbents of other positions: father, child. Because their own primary roles make heavy demands on their time and energy, and because they may never have learned the skills required for the effective discharge of the maternal role functions, considerable tension may be generated. The presence of a homemaker permits a continuation of the usual pattern of role functions in the family, and helps to maintain family stability:

> Mr. A's wife was committed to a mental hospital and he came to the homemaker agency when he had to cope alone with the problem of caring for his three small children. An elderly relative had tried to take over while he was at work, but the situation became too much for her. Mr. A., a factory worker, could not afford to hire help nor could he bring himself to put the children in foster homes. A homemaker was sent to give day care to the youngsters during the months that Mrs. A. must remain hospitalized. The assignment to the family will continue during Mrs. A.'s subsequent period of adjustment and psychotherapy [U.S. Department of Health, Education, and Welfare, 1958b, p. 43].

Homemaker service may be appropriately offered when the mother is physically present but has lowered capacity to cope with the ordinary demands of her position because of "physical or mental illness, disabilities, convalescence, residuals of illness, [or] complications of pregnancy" (Child Welfare League of America, 1959, p. 5):

> A young mother suffered a postpartum psychosis following delivery of the third child. In this situation, the father was able, by taking his vacation and availing himself of the offers of help made by neighbors, to manage care of the two other children, aged five and two, until his wife was ready for discharge from a psychiatric hospital where she had responded quickly to treatment which relieved the acute phase of her illness. However, the psychiatrist stipulated that she could not assume the responsibility or the pressure of care of her children, and would require further out-patient therapy before she could function adequately as a mother again. Homemaker service made it possible for this mother to return home, where she could oversee her children without assuming full responsibility for their care [New Jersey State Department of Health, 1961, p. 31].

The homemaker service may be offered to help the mother develop more adequate skills in child care and home maintenance. In such cases, role implementation is inadequate because of lack of preparation, training, or knowledge regarding the requirements of the role. The homemaker service has an educational focus in such cases, in areas such as the household organization, meal planning and preparation, maintenance of clothing, childrearing, health care and use of health resources, and money management (Grant & Pancyr, 1970; National Council, 1970).

In other cases, the problem of inadequate role implementation may arise from the mother's ambivalence regarding her role. Here the homemaker, in her behavior toward the children, offers herself as an example of the "good mother," which the client may emulate. The following illustrates the use of a homemaker in a teaching capacity:

> Mrs. Harvey's situation was referred to the agency by the police, who alleged that she was a neglectful mother and recommended that her children "be taken away from her and placed in foster homes at once." The police had been called to her home the previous night, upon complaint of neighbors that Mrs. Harvey's six children, ranging in ages from one to six years, were alone in the apartment and were not being cared for. The landlord claimed that this was a frequent occurrence. The police described Mrs. Harvey's children as dirty and unkempt. The two-year-old twins were unclothed except for undershirts. They had remnants of feces on their bodies, and were sleeping in a bed with a worn-out dirty mattress. The baby was nursing a bottle of curdled milk. All of the children seemed to be underweight and malnourished.

Over a period of months, a caseworker-homemaker team worked closely with Mrs. Harvey and accomplished the following:

> (1) The homemaker, through her close contacts in the home, learned exactly what basic essentials in clothing, bedding, cleaning equipment, and cooking utensils were needed by this family and the caseworker tapped community resources to meet these needs, which required large immediate outlays of money. (2) Mrs. Harvey learned, by the homemaker's example, to give better care to the children, giving attention to their diet, hygiene, rest, and supervised play. The caseworker helped Mrs. Harvey to secure medical care, as needed. Mrs. Harvey also learned to intervene in the children's quarrels calmly, and was able to give up her past screaming, ineffective efforts at discipline. (3) The homemaker helped Mrs. Harvey to learn better to shop and to plan expenditures now that she had a predictable, though still limited, income. They watched the newspapers for bargains, budgeted, and went shopping together [National Council, 1968, p. 47–48].

In some instances, the use of the homemaker fulfills all the purposes previously mentioned:

> Mrs. M. came to the Family Service Agency to request homemaker service because she was expecting to be hospitalized for surgery in the near future.
>
> Homemaker service was provided to the M.'s because it was felt that Marian, sixteen, could not assume major responsibility for caring for her six younger brothers and sisters, which she would have had to do because of Mr. M.'s long hours of work. Because of the emotional problems which two of the children, Dorothy, ten, and Victoria, nine, were displaying in their behavior, it was also felt that a homemaker would be needed to help give the children—and particularly these two—a feeling of security during the time their mother was away. It was expected that the homemaker's observations of the children would give the worker a better understanding of each child and his needs, and would also give the caseworker a clearer picture of inter- and intra-family relationships.
>
> The homemaker was with this family for thirteen weeks. At first it was difficult for the children to accept a stranger in their home, and they directed much of their hostility because of their mother's absence against the homemaker by not speaking

to her. It was not very long, however, before they responded to her warmth and interest. After Mrs. M. returned home, she had to be completely immobilized so that it was still necessary for the homemaker to continue to assume most of the care needed by the children. However, as Mrs. M. gained strength, the homemaker gradually returned this responsibility to her. During Mrs. M.'s hospitalization, the homemaker had been able to feed the family more adequately on less money than the family used to spend. Mrs. M. asked the homemaker to help her with menu planning and shopping lists. By the time the homemaker left, Mrs. M. had learned a great deal in this area. To help keep Mrs. M. occupied during her convalescent period, the homemaker also taught her how to mend and darn [Community Service Society, 1958, pp. 1, 2, Appendix 3].

Homemaker service may be offered to supplement the mother's activities when she is so burdened by the demands of a handicapped or sick child as to neglect the needs of her other children. This is an instance of inadequate role implementation in relation to the care of the normal siblings due to the excessive demands of the sick child: "The homemaker can share in the care of the handicapped child or, by assuming some responsibility for the other children and the home, will free the mother so that she can give more time to the handicapped child" (U.S. Department of Health, Education, and Welfare, 1958, p. 4). The homemaker and the caseworker can also help the family develop a more understanding attitude toward the handicapped or ill child. In some instances, handicapped children themselves have been helped by the supervised homemaker to develop greater facility in feeding, dressing, and toileting (Soyka, 1976).

A middle-aged mother applied [for help] at the suggestion of a friend who knew about homemaker service. The mother said she was physically exhausted and going to pieces from the demands of caring for her three-year-old son. He had been born prematurely and weighed only one and one-half pounds at birth. When he was a year old, it was discovered that he was blind. He had been in and out of hospitals for a respiratory ailment; he whines and wheezes even while he is asleep. Recently there has been a diagnosis of cerebral palsy. . . . He cannot sit up and becomes fretful lying in one position. He shrieks in panic when he cannot hear his mother's voice. The father, an artist, had to travel on his job, but took a job as a laborer to be at home. The father made a device to prop up Eddie, but his balance is poor and he topples over. The mother has to reprop him and reprop him. The mother was told that Eddie would never speak, but she patiently taught him to say a few words. The child has to be taken to the clinic three times a week, and the mother was traveling three hours a day to take him there. The mother was troubled about their neglect of Betty, aged seven. . . . Lately Betty is overeating, stealing money, slashing her dresses, and being openly resentful of her brother. . . . The mother said she had closed out Betty and her husband and concentrated her whole life on the handicapped child.

The homemaker in this family is gradually establishing herself with Eddie, who formerly would not let anyone but his mother touch him. The homemaker persuades the mother to rest. The homemaker admires the mother's courage and is helping her to take short cuts in housework so that she can spend more time with Betty. The aim of the homemaker service is to relieve the pressures on both parents and on Betty, to help Eddie be less fearful, and to achieve better balance in their lives [U.S. Department of Health, Education, and Welfare, 1958a, p. 4].

Homemaker service may be offered when the mother's role is left permanently vacant. In these instances, the mother has died, deserted, or divorced, and custody of the children has been awarded to the father. The aim in such cases is not to effect a permanent reorganization of the family group with the homemaker as a mother substitute but to relieve stress and pressure on the father so as to permit a reasoned discussion of his long-range plans. Stressful situations may precipitate a decision made on the basis of expediency; with the intervention of the homemaker, the stress is mitigated and the situation is stabilized long enough to permit formulation of an acceptable plan.

Such use of homemaker service may also permit more adequate preparation for the placement of children in a more-or-less permanent substitute family arrangement:

> Mr. L., age thirty-nine, his son, age twelve, and his daughter, age five, lived in an adequately furnished apartment in a public housing project. Mrs. L. had died giving birth to a third child which had also died.... Relatives and neighbors had been helping to care for the children since his wife's death, but they could not go on doing so indefinitely.... Mr. L. did not want to give up his children, but he did not know how to care for them properly and manage his home. His daughter, who had been happily attending a nursery school before her mother's death, no longer wanted to go to school. His son missed his mother a great deal and stayed alone in his room much of the time.... The services of the homemaker were provided to the L. family for twenty-three weeks to stabilize the home situation for Mr. L. and his children while the father and the caseworker considered plans for their future welfare and care. It was also hoped that, during the homemaker's stay with the family, the caseworker would be able to get a better understanding of the children and their reaction to their mother's loss. Such information would contribute greatly in deciding the kind of care that would be best for them [Community Service Society, 1958, pp. 32, 33].

Homemaker service may also be offered as a diagnostic aid in determining the best plan for a handicapped child or in evaluating possible neglect in homes in which child care is reputed to be marginal, as well as in testing parents' ability to modify homemaking standards and parent–child relationship patterns.

Less frequently, homemaker service has been offered in the following circumstances:

1. As an alternative to the placement of a child in a detention home or shelter while suitable arrangements for caring are being explored (Johnson, 1956). New York City has been considering "establishment of an auxiliary corps of homemakers who will be available to the police when children are deserted by their parents" (U.S. Department of Health, Education and Welfare, 1960, p. 166; Burt & Balyeat, 1977).
2. As a supplement to day care, when the employed mother cannot remain at home to care for a temporarily ill child, or when day care for the child of a working mother is inappropriate or unacceptable.
3. To supplement the mother's activities "during the summer months for families of migrant farm workers" (U.S. Department of Health, Education and Welfare, 1955, p. 6).
4. To help adoptive parents make the difficult transition to parenthood. This "crisis of parenthood" is a problem of role transition, during which supplementation in adjusting to the new, unfamiliar role is helpful. Similarly homemaker help is offered to parents after the birth of their first child (Brodsky, 1958, p. 11).

5. To permit a mother to attend a clinic on a regular basis or to receive hospital outpatient treatment.

6. To supplement the mother's unfilled role when she must be absent from home because of the illness or death of close relatives, or for educational reasons. For instance, in June 1971 about 500 children under six whose mothers were enrolled in the Aid to Families of Dependent Children (AFDC) Work Incentive Program were cared for by homemakers.

7. Homemakers have been selectively used as a respite service in neglect and abuse situations, giving a harassed mother some rest and rehabilitation time away from the children (Soyka, 1979).

A specialized form of homemaker service, the emergency caretaker or homemaker, has been effectively employed to reduce the danger of precipitous out-of-home placement of children. This service is employed in crisis time-limited situations involving dependent children who are temporarily without a caretaker. Such services are a necessary component in a comprehensive program of services to children designed to reduce the risk of substitute care placement. Brown (1981) has described the operation of such a program in Chicago. Emergency situations in which a parent is suddenly hospitalized, suddenly imprisoned, or missing for a short period can be stabilized for children while keeping them in the home by use of emergency caretakers. The service has helped parents to accept continuing agency services following their return to the home.

More recently there has been a discussion of the use of homemaker service with immigrant families with the aim of ethnically matching the client and homemaker. The homemaker in this situation can help the immigrant family negotiate the unfamiliar environment.

Small nurseries were developed in a few public welfare agencies to care for children while their parents were making application for assistance. An experienced homemaker in charge of the nursery was able to provide help to parents in increasing parental skills, which is illustrated in the following incident:

> An infant, six weeks old, was brought into the nursery by her parents, 19 years old, who were applying for welfare. The baby had cradle cap, was not clean, had poor suck reflex and poor skin turgor. The homemaker changed the nipple on the baby's bottle to a very soft one to make it easier for the child to suck. The parents said that they had not had any training in how to take care of a baby and couldn't understand why she wasn't thriving. They loved her dearly and would gladly accept help. The parents received medical assistance and homemaker service to help them with budgeting and home management as well as with care of the baby. Both mother and father were eager to learn how to be good parents [Soyka, 1979, p. 83].

Spinelli and Barton (1980) describe a variation on the homemaker program using a staff of "Home Management Specialists." The staff was given ten active cases and visited each home for approximately three hours a week. These "specialists" helped the family budget money, write shopping lists, discipline children, and purchase and prepare food, and help the family search for more suitable housing (p. 46).

Intensive home-based service programs that are designed to help maintain children in their own homes and reduce the risk of placement almost always include homemaker service in their package of services.

Although homemaker service, if imaginatively exploited, is a valuable and appropriate resource in a variety of problem situations, statistics reveal that the service is most frequently used in limited kinds of situations. A detailed study of 1,183 cases of families with children indicates that homemaker service was requested in some 88 per cent of these cases because of the illness of the mother or because of her absence from the home because of illness (U.S. Department of Health, Education, and Welfare, 1958a, p. 67). Currently homemaker service is most frequently offered to families with young children to cover emergency situations of limited duration in which the mother is incapacitated or hospitalized.

The child welfare literature emphasizes the utility of homemaker service as having potentialities for maintaining children in their homes and preventing placements. However, available studies of social work activity do not tend to show the widespread use of homemaker service toward this objective. A study involving a carefully selected sample of 18 counties in 5 different states reviewed the cases of 326 families for whom the placement prevention of children was the goal. In only two counties was homemaker service offered to more than 30 per cent of the families. Overall, homemaker service was offered in some 13 per cent of the cases and actually utilized by about 10 per cent of the cases (Yoshikami, 1984, Table B4, p. 162).

The Shyne–Schroeder (1978) national study of social services to children and their families found that only 7 per cent of all cases receiving service received homemaker services (Table 3-5, p. 69). This was generally provided by the local public welfare department.

A recapitulation of the services received by families from protective service agencies between 1976 and 1982 indicated that only 3.9 per cent of the families received homemaker services (Russell & Trainor 1984, Table V6, p. 45). Over time there has been a decrease in the percentage of protective service families offered homemaker service. In 1970, 4.5 per cent of the families were offered such services; by 1982, this had declined to 3.4 per cent (Table V3, p. 41). The 1983 *Annual Report of Child Abuse and Neglect* report noted that overall 3 per cent of the families received homemaker service during the year (p. 23).

A placement prevention demonstration project in New York City involving sixty families whose children were high risk for placement included homemaker services among the services designed to prevent placement (Halper & Jones, 1984).

Although an explicit effort was made to provide homemaker service, it was actually "used in only 15 per cent of the project cases." However "it was a vital service in those cases" (p. 59). The fact that it was not used in a larger percentage of cases was partly a consequence of client resistance. The report notes that "the caseworker's attempts to achieve a quick improvement in child care and/or home management by use of homemaker services or day care were sometimes successful but were frequently either rejected or sabotaged by the client" (p. 26) "In five of the six cases in which workers believed homemaker services was needed although it was not provided the reason given for not arranging it was that the client refused the service" (p. 94).

The research continues, "With homemaker service frequently touted as one of the preeminent preventive services client acceptance and the relatively few cases that are actually affected by the service bear a closer look" (p. 94). It is interesting to note that in a recent extended text devoted to permanency planning (Maluccio, Fein, & Olmstead, 1986) homemaker service is mentioned in passing only occasionally and it is not listed in the index. The eighteenth edition of the *Encyclopedia of Social Work* published in 1987 by the National Association of Social Workers did not include a special article on homemaker service, nor is it indexed as a separate item.

The decline in the percentage of families receiving homemaker services may be a function of the limited availability of the service rather than a decreasing perception of its desirability. Giovannoni and Becerra (1979) reporting on social workers' responses to questions regarding recommended services and their availability, noted that homemaker services were reported as among the least available services. It was "unavailable to 40 per cent of the families who were recommended."

There is a possibility, however, that homemaker service may not be the appropriate treatment option in many child welfare service situations. The problem in the utilization of homemaker service lies in the fact that in addition to the parents whose roles need supplementation because of illness or incapacity, another parent must be available to care for the children in the evening and weekends when the homemaker is off duty. Many of the child welfare agency single-parent families are thus doubtful candidates for the effective utilization of homemaker services.

The Service Delivery Process in Homemaker Service

The most distinctive aspect of homemaker service is that it is generally offered under agency auspices in a casework context, as part of an overall treatment plan, and that the homemaker is under agency supervision to ensure that her activity will contribute to the fulfillment of the treatment plan.

Referrals to the homemaker service unit of an agency often come from caseworkers within the agency aware of a family situation requiring the service. Frequently referrals also come from hospitals and doctors. The largest single referring source consists of family, neighbors, and friends.

Intake and Social Study

Intake in homemaker service achieves the same general purposes as in any agency setting. The social worker must help the client articulate his or her problem and must make clear to the client the kinds of services the agency has available. The social worker also tries to make clear the conditions under which the service can be offered, that is, the conditions of client eligibility. He or she then tries to help the client decide whether or not to use the services available and explores with him or her the alternative solutions to the problem. Because agency resources are limited, the worker has to be sure that the client not only wants the service but can effectively use it.

There might also be discussion of the question of payment for the service. Private agencies require the client to pay something toward the cost of the service, the amount being determined by the client's income and the number of members in the family. At intake, the client must show readiness to "share financial information including verification of income and to pay toward the service in accordance with his ability" (Chambers, 1955, p. 113).

The family's expectation regarding the homemaker is also discussed, as well as the agency's expectation regarding the adjustments that might be required of the family members in assisting the homemaker to fulfill the functions of the missing mother. The structure of service needs to be agreed upon—who does what and when—and an explicit effort is made to help the client understand the distinction between homemaker service and maid service. Also, because in most cases the need for homemaker service is related to the illness of the mother, an attempt is made to obtain a clear picture of the mother's medical condition and the prognosis, her own and the family's attitude toward the illness, and their adjustment to it.

Data Assessment

Not all problem situations that might be helped by homemaker service are regarded as appropriate for homemaker service. Certain additional factors are significant in the agency's decision to offer service. Because the aim of homemaker service is to preserve the family unit, the worker must determine whether the family can and should actually be preserved. Although the general assumption is that the child's own family offers the best environment for healthy development, in some instances the family situation is so damaging that a substitute family would offer the child a better chance for growth.

"The homemaker cannot create a home—but merely sustain what is there." Thus the worker evaluates the family's emotional, structural, and physical resources. The level of family cohesiveness and stability should be such as to make it likely that it will not fall apart. The service must be given with the expectation that the family will again function normally sometime in the future.

An experienced executive director of a homemaker service agency sets the program in realistic perspective:

> Those of us who have worked for some years in homemaker service must sadly admit that it is quite rare that we are asked to come into a family situation in which everything is normal in the relationship, in which the standards of living are somewhat middle-class or approaching middle-class, and in which temporary illness or dislocation threatens an already intact family life which we can protect and preserve with the simple addition of this one very good service. I say we rarely see it, although I admit that it occasionally does happen [National Council, 1968, p. 74].

The agency also must be sure that the client clearly understands and accepts the service. Here the term *client* refers not only to the individual formally representing the family but to all members of the family who have significant power in determining family decisions and whose patterns of life will be significantly affected by the service. Homemaker service may fail if the father accepts the service without consulting the mother or the older siblings, who may be unprepared for the plan or actually opposed to it. The worker also needs to assess the client's willingness and capacity to work with the agency. The agency selects the homemaker to be assigned and determines some of the conditions under which she will work. Thus, through the homemaker, the agency will be in constant contact with the client. In a study of forty-seven unselected clients who were given homemaker service by well-trained and experienced homemakers, the most important single predictive factor relating to successful use of the service was found to be the applicant's attitude toward the part played by the agency in providing and supervising the homemaker: "In 83 per cent of the cases using the service successfully, the family was accepting the agency, whereas 92 per cent of the families using the service unsuccessfully were resistive, or indifferent, to the agency" (Santulli, 1945, p. 345). Many agencies, however, specifically point out that the willingness or ability of parents to accept help with personal problems is not necessarily a condition for providing homemaker service for children.

The worker must also determine whether or not the client has explored other possible resources: a nondamaging reallocation of responsibilities among family members, the help of available relatives, and so on. If resources that might be .exploited do exist, the caseworker has the responsibility of helping the client to plan their effective use.

Unless a twenty-four-hour, seven-day-a-week service is contemplated, the agency must have some assurance that there will be a responsible person available, generally the father, to take over during the time that the homemaker is not on duty.

The interview, or series of interviews, may end with an offer of service or with the refusal of service. The most important single reason for the decision not to offer service is actually a tribute to casework efforts at intake. For instance, in a 1958 nationwide study, 21 per cent of the families not accepted for homemaker service had been helped by the caseworker to use their own resources to move toward a solution of the problem (U.S. Department of Health, Education, and Welfare, 1958a, p. 81). And in another study of homemaker service in New York City in 1959, the Community Council (1961) found that 22 per cent of the requests for service were not accepted because the family had been helped by the caseworker to use other resources (p. 11).

The second most frequently cited reason is the tragic shortage of personnel. In the two studies cited previously, 17 per cent and 20 per cent, respectively, of the requests for service had to be denied because a homemaker was not available.

Treatment

If homemaker service is offered, contact between the client and the caseworker is maintained. One important reason is that introduction of the homemaker into the family creates a unique situation: the temporary introduction into the family system of an adult who has no legal ties to the family, and who substitutes only in clearly defined areas for a key member of the family. The homemaker has a clearly delineated, restricted relationship with the total family system, but one that involves intimate contact and a sharing of parental prerogatives. The caseworker, working with the family and the homemaker, is often helpful in preventing problems and minimizing tensions if they arise.

- The introduction of a stranger into the family's social system poses the problem of her acceptance by family members both as a person in her own right and as a mother substitute. The homemaker, in turn, faces the problem of accepting the members of the family. An additional problem is that the family may have one idea of the way the assigned role of homemaker is to be enacted and the agency and the homemaker may have another. The caseworker operates as a resource person who facilitates the process of mutual accommodation and helps both the family and the homemaker to cope with failures in understanding.

Still another problem is the danger that a competitive situation will develop between homemaker and mother: "The mother may feel her position in the home challenged by the homemaker" (Gordon, 1955, p. 14). Because the homemaker may care for the children and manage the home somewhat more efficiently, the mother might fear "that this may make her husband critical of her management" (Langer, 1945, p. 185). In a study of families receiving extended homemaker service care, it was noticed that:

> Initially, many of the mothers, including the more adequate ones, evidenced great anxiety about their own displacement and fearfulness around the homemaker's role and function in the home. . . . In the more disturbed and deteriorated family situation . . . the adequacy of the homemakers seemed to threaten these mothers. Competition with the homemaker was increased by the positive reports they received from thoughtless, or malicious, relatives or from friends who told them how much calmer and better behaved their children were and how much better organized their households were now that the homemaker was in charge. Not infrequently, these mothers attempted to alienate their children from the homemaker [Children's Aid Society, 1962, p. 103].

Thus the mother may react to the threat to her position by seeking to frustrate the purpose of the service. The mother may press to give up the homemaker before her physical condition warrants it, or overexert herself by assuming functions beyond her physical capacity even while the homemaker is present.

In some cases, problems arise because homemaker and mother have different conceptions of how the mother's role is to be performed:

> The homemaker and Mrs. F. complained of feeling uncomfortable with each other. The homemaker felt that Mrs. F. was a dominating kind of person who had outbursts of anger. The caseworker thought that one of the problems was that, with Mrs. F.'s improvement and the encouragement given her to take over little parts of the household management, the very different orientations toward household management in the homemaker and Mrs. F. came to the fore and caused, or helped support, some tensions between the two. The homemaker tended toward a high degree of organization and efficient economies. Mrs. F.'s tendency in household management was toward haphazard, less organized methods. In respective individual contacts with the homemaker and Mrs. F., these differences in household management were discussed; an attempt was made to remove any emphasis on one way being better than another and to help each of them accept the fact that there were different, equally acceptable ways of managing a household.

The children may find it difficult to accept the homemaker without feeling conflict over their "disloyalty" to their own mother. The situation poses a problem for the children regarding their response to a woman who acts as a mother without at the same time being a mother. The child might feel conflict about accepting discipline from such a person because disciplining is clearly a prerogative of the true parent. As Baldwin (1953) says, "Children feel suspicion and mistrust of the woman who tries to replace, even in part, the mother" (p. 125). In such situations, the caseworker may discuss with the children their anxieties about what is happening to the family, helping them to understand and accept the mother's limited capacity for child care while she is ill.

The situation also poses problems for the father. As Gordon (1955) notes, "The father may feel his position as provider of the family threatened because the agency selects the homemaker, pays her—at least in part—and it is to the agency that she is responsible" (p. 14). The father may also be threatened by the necessity of taking over some of the mother's functions. Acting as a mother, even in a limited way, may create anxiety for the man who is tenuously holding on to his sense of masculinity, as shown in the following case record:

> We discussed, at some length, the duties Mr. F. expected of a homemaker. He was somewhat embarrassed at going over these details such as ironing and so forth.

When I mentioned that, as a man, he might be unaccustomed to some of this "business" but that illness in the family often changed people's roles, he was reassured.

The father may also have difficulty in accepting the assumption of certain aspects of the maternal role by the homemaker:

> Mr. B. had always depended upon his wife to discipline the children, but he resented the homemaker doing it and he would not do it himself [Justiss, 1960, p. 292].

The inability of the father to work cooperatively and effectively with the homemaker may result from feelings and attitudes toward women and mother surrogates stemming from his own developmental experience:

> Mr. Madison, a widower of thirty-five with three children under four years of age, could not get along with homemakers. He was surly, curt, and critical. He was unable to show any appreciation of what was being done for the children. Homemakers tried hard to accept his inability to show any graciousness, but none of them cared to remain long in the home. Gradually, as he and the caseworker discussed the needs in his home and the way he handled these, he was able to talk about some of the experiences that had made him distrustful of women. As he gained some understanding, he found ways to handle more satisfactorily his feelings about women and to find pleasure in friendly, warm relationships with them [Baldwin, 1953, p. 127].

The father and the children may be reluctant to permit any changes in the house, out of "loyalty" to the sick mother. The family may feel that its privacy is being violated by the intrusion of the homemaker into the family and may feel anxious about the possibility that she will disapprove of their ways of rearing the children or managing the home. In the course of one demonstration project, it became clear that some of the more disorganized parents "were fearful that the homemaker would learn too much about some aspect of the family's life that they preferred to keep hidden—such as the whereabouts of the children's father, an illegal source of income, an extramarital affair, or the extent of disturbance in their children" (Children's Aid Society, 1962, p. 103).

Because the request for homemaker service results from some crisis in the family's life, the caseworker may be needed to help with the social and emotional consequences of the crisis situation:

> Mr. K. called the agency for homemaker help in caring for his two children, Mary, eleven, and Raymond, eight and one-half. He was upset about his wife's hospitalization in the middle of the night because of an acute psychotic break. He was overwhelmed with guilt about his wife's hospitalization, thinking that he had contributed to it because he had been unable to face the beginning signs of her disturbance despite his knowledge of a former psychotic break [Community Service Society, 1958, pp. 26, 27].

The father may need help in facing a new, threatening situation occasioned by the change in family structure:

> In the E. family, with four children, twenty-four-hour service was necessitated by the hospitalization of the mother and the long and irregular working hours of the father. Mr. E. was overwhelmed and became agitated when the caseworker or the homemaker tried to enlist his help in planning for the family. He had been overly depen-

dent on his wife and had never participated in the management of the household or the children. With encouragement from the homemaker and the caseworker during the two months his wife remained in the hospital, he gradually assumed a more positive and meaningful place in his family [Children's Aid Society, 1962, p. 103].

The availability of the caseworker is of special importance when the introduction of the homemaker leads to an intensification of the family's difficulties:

> In working with Mr. S., the caseworker learned that he needed to feel totally responsible and to be the only giving person in his family. He had a pathological need to assume both the female and male roles in the family, which made it difficult for him to accept a woman in the home. With his lessened responsibility because of the homemaker's presence, his control weakened so he began drinking, staying out late, and buying for the family in ways which threatened the health and nutrition of the children. The presence of a responsible and efficient woman relieved him of the need to be responsible, while at the same time it threatened his own adequacy [Community Service Society, 1958, p. 45, Appendix].

The caseworker, aware of the underlying problems that may make the service a pathogenic rather than a therapeutic agent, can work toward effecting a more positive use of the homemaker.

Work with the Homemaker

In response to the conflicting reactions to the presence of the homemaker in the home, the caseworker has regularly scheduled conferences with the homemaker as well as with members of the family. This is a service to the family, although an indirect one, for it enables the homeworker to work more effectively with the family.

The social worker is generally responsible for the supervision of eight to ten homemakers. The caseworker sees that the homemaker is assigned to a family and that the assignment is responsibly covered. He sees that each homemaker has an equitable and diversified case load and that assignments coincide with the special competencies and interests of individual homemakers.

The caseworker helps the homemaker move into the family situation as unobtrusively as possible, "to fit into the family as a source of strength with the least possible threat to the status of any member of the family" (U.S. Department of Health, Education, and Welfare, 1961a, p. 9). In order to be able to prepare the homemaker for working with the family, the caseworker has to explore the details of family schedule and routine, the pattern of family activities, the special needs and preferences of the various children, and specific family problems of which the homemaker might need to be aware. The Cook County Department of Public Welfare assigns

> the homemaker prior to the date of expected confinement or hospitalization in order to give the mother and children a better chance to get acquainted with her. . . . This alleviates the fears of the mother as to the care her children will receive during her absence and [helps] the children to adjust to the presence of a stranger [Woldman, 1940, p. 30].

The caseworker also helps the homemaker with her struggle to accept the different ways people may organize their homes and their routines; he or she helps the homemaker accept the difference between these children, who "belong" to other parents, and her own children:

> Mrs. C., the homemaker placed with a family of four school-age children while the mother was in the hospital, felt puzzled and unsure as to how to handle the problem of discipline. She had, in raising her own children, successfully resorted to reasoning with the child and deprivation of privileges as the means of maintaining discipline. This approach did not seem to work with the R. children. They refused to obey her, saying she was not their mother, and no amount of talking to them seemed to be of help. She wondered what to do next and brought this question for discussion to her conference with the caseworker.

Because the homemaker directly encounters many situations that tend to activate strong emotional reactions—mental illness, a neglectful mother, a passive father—she needs to have someone with whom she can talk over her feelings. An opportunity for catharsis may allow the homemaker to return to the family ready to work more comfortably in the situation. The caseworker offers this opportunity as well as an emotioanlly supportive relationship to the homemaker so as to dissipate feelings of discouragement and anxiety regarding her competence. Equally important, the caseworker helps the homemaker to become aware of any "projection of expectations of herself upon the mother or her attitude toward her own husband on the father of the family" (Gordon, 1956, p. 368). The worker also helps her to keep from overidentifying with, or rejecting, any one member of the family (Clough & Wood, 1958, p. 2). He helps the homemaker to counter any tendency to take sides with a child against the parent, or with the family against the agency, to compete with the natural parents for the love and respect of the children, or to compete with the mother for the affection of the father.

The caseworker also helps the homemaker understand and modify some aspect of her behavior that may be having a deleterious effect on family relationships:

> Mrs. Emmons, twenty-eight years old, was hospitalized for a postpartum depression shortly after her second child was born. She left behind a dirty home, a frightened seven-year-old, the three-week-old baby, and a depressed husband. A homemaker about the same age as Mrs. Emmons was placed in the home. This was one of her first assignments and she was eager to make a good impression. She performed many extra chores as well as restoring order, cleanliness, and regularity in the household. Soon glowing reports came to Mrs. Emmons from her husband of the homemaker's skill and many achievements. Mrs. Emmons' depression increased and she showed much apprehension.
>
> Through counseling with her supervisor the homemaker came to understand the effects of her actions on the absent mother. She telephoned Mrs. Emmons at the hospital to ask for advice instead of waiting for Mrs. Emmons to telephone home. The homemaker sent notes and pictures of the children to the mother. When the mother came home six weeks later, the two women were able to work well together, with homemaker's services gradually diminished to two half-days each week until termination some months later [National Council, 1968, p. 125].

Finally, the caseworker helps the homemaker to become aware of any behavior on the part of members of the client family that may be symptomatic of emotional stress: withdrawal, enuresis, thumb sucking, temper tantrums, and so on. Through the homemaker, the caseworker keeps informed of any significant changes in the family situation that might require the help of the caseworker. He or she helps the homemaker to understand and meet the needs of the children.

Although the homemaker and the caseworker ideally cooperatively complement each other, there is potential for friction. The homemaker is concerned with the immediate practical needs of the family; the caseworker is more likely to focus on long-range psychological goals. The homemaker knows the family intimately and has the allegiance of the family, which may cause the caseworker to feel resentment (Cassert, 1970). The caseworker acts as a "consultant" rather than a "doer," as an infrequent visitor rather than a temporary "member" of the family. The homemaker may feel that she has greater familiarity with the situation and may tend to discount much of the caseworker's advice.

Termination

Eventually the homemaker and the caseworker work together to help the family accept termination of the service, with the homemaker gradually doing less and less for the family while the family does more and more for itself. The caseworker helps the family with problems attendant upon the homemaker's leaving:

> Mrs. H., who had trouble with her back so that she could not lift her baby, had been referred for some special orthopedic exercises to strengthen the affected muscles. She resisted working on them and seemed to be slipping into a pattern of letting the homemaker do all the work, while she sat by giving orders and criticizing the homemaker.
>
> Mrs. H. had to be helped to consider whether she wanted to get well and to face the fact that the homemaker was placed to afford her the chance to try to recover [Gordon, 1955, p. 18].

The caseworker helps the homemaker change, as the situation changes, by gradually taking less direct responsibility for the care of the children and the home as the parents are able to assume more of their normal roles.

Evaluation

Homemaker service has a number of advantages over alternative plans for dealing with the problems presented by the motherless family. The most important single advantage is that it permits the child to remain at home during the time that the mother is incapable of fully implementing her role. Homemaker service imposes a far smaller burden of adjustment on the child than foster care, for the child adjusts to the homemaker in the comforting familiarity of his or her own home, family, and neighborhood. The homemaker might be regarded as a "traveling foster mother" who comes to the child.

As the New York City Department of Public Welfare notes:

> [Since the] inception of the program in 1945, Department of Welfare homemakers have cared for over 30,000 children in their own homes, thus avoiding placement and the consequent breakdown of family life that so often results from the separation of children and parents [Snyder, 1962, p. 1].

In 1967 Homemaker Service of the Children's Aid Society of New York served 138 families, enabling "109 children to remain in their own homes during periods when parents were faced with illness or some other crises that would otherwise have propelled the children into placement in foster homes."

More methodologically rigorous studies of family situations that resulted in child placement show that in the worker's judgment, homemaker service might have prevented placement in some of the cases (Jenkins & Sauber, 1966; Shyne, 1969). The studies, however, point to the need for greater flexibility in work schedules for homemaker service, and for the recruitment of "persons whose own background provides them with a familiarity and an understanding not only of the language, but also of the customs and mores of the families they are called upon to assist" (Jenkins & Sauber, 1966, p. 189).

Studies of the prevention of placement of children identified as being at high risk for foster care show that homemaker service is associated with increasing the child's chances of remaining in his or her own home (Sherman et al., 1973, p. 46; Jones, Neuman & Shyne, 1976, p. 58; Burt & Balyeat, 1977, p. 65).

The larger the number of children in the family, the more economical homemaker service is for the community, for "homemaker costs are relatively fixed, regardless of the number of children in the family, while costs for foster care rise in direct proportion to the number of children in the family" (Brooklyn Bureau, 1958, p. 18). Every assessment of comparative costs indicates that homemaker-health aide service is less costly than any of the out-of-the-home alternatives (Robinson et al., 1974, p. 12).

The availability of a homemaker on a twenty-four-hour basis materially reduces the number of children who might previously have been taken to children's shelters when parents were suddenly taken ill at night.

Homemaker service also provides greater assurance that the solidarity of the family will be maintained. The children remain at home and the father continues to carry full, direct responsibility for the discharge of his role vis-à-vis his children.

Homemaker services also contribute to the efficiency and effectiveness of available medical services. Mothers are more likely to accept the necessity for hospitalization if they have assurances regarding the care of their children. Once hospitalized, they are likely to remain as long as is medically necessary, and when they return home, they are likely to follow a prescribed medical regimen rather than attempting to take on too much too soon. Furthermore, because homemaker service permits earlier discharge of many hospital patients, it makes possible a more efficient use of available hospital bed space. According to Justiss (1960):

> Homemaker service provides a type of care which the ill mother can accept more readily and thus it permits her to accept hospitalization. Many mothers have told us that they would rather stay in their own home and die rather than see their children "sent away" to some stranger's home. Offering such service in a rural county in Texas "where, because of inadequate diet, lack of medical care, overwork, and poor health standards, incidence of tuberculosis is extremely high" has resulted in amelioration of a previously dangerous practice. It is reported that "there has not been a single instance of a mother returning home from a hospital against medical advice since the homemaker program has become well established" [pp. 291, 294].

Brodsky (1961) notes that "homemaker service might make it possible for a not too severely mentally ill mother to have hospital day-care treatment service" (p. 15) and a number of unpublished research reports, cited in a review by Sieder and Califf (1976), indicate the successful use of homemakers in maintaining the family unit in cases in which the mother was mentally ill but did not require hospitalization.

Equally important, homemaker service reduces the danger of the damaging effects of role reallocation. Without homemaker service, fathers may miss many days of work in an effort to hold the family together. Even in those instances in which the father remains on the job, his enactment of the wage-earner role may be impaired because of anxiety about what is happening at home. Homemaker service permits the father to devote himself to the demands of his job with less anxiety. Furthermore, if older siblings are forced to assume the responsibility for performing the functions previously allocated the mother, their enactment of their own student role is impaired through reduced attendance and inadequate preparation. Thus homemaker service reduces the tendency for family members to assume a burden of responsibilities that impairs effective enactment of their central roles.

Another advantage of homemaker service lies in the fact that it may make a family more amenable to needed casework help with other problems. As Johnson (1956) notes, "giving families a tangible service of immediate practical value often makes them more receptive toward help with less obvious problems" (p. 10).

Some of the values of homemaker service may be illustrated by the problem situations that develop in its absence. A study by the Almeda Council of Social Agencies of how a sample of families managed in the absence of the mother and the lack of available homemaker service indicates that the older children were kept out of school to care for the younger children; one parent took an unpaid vacation from work; one parent took his younger children to work; children were left with relatives at a distance from home; and children were left at home without supervision of any kind (Federation of Community Services, 1959).

Dexter and Harbert (1983) report on an experiment in eight localities in Finland that attempted to evaluate outcomes of homemaker service. Working under collaborative supervision of a social work project supervisor the homemakers were effective in helping families deal with crisis situations. Early interventions by homemakers prevented the development of more serious problems (pp. 75–77).

Problems

1. A controversy exists as to the most appropriate auspices for homemaker service. Because the need for the service is almost always precipitated by a health problem, there is some argument for tying the service to health, rather than welfare, agencies. In 1976 about 40 per cent of all homemaker services agencies were operating under the auspices of health agencies or visiting-nurse organizations. On the other hand, the service is designed to deal not with the health problem but with the social consequences of illness. It is further argued that tying the service to health agencies might tend to foster a narrow view of the appropriateness of the service and might tend to keep it restricted to situations involving illness. If viewed from the point of view of illness, homemaker service becomes focused on the patient; if viewed from the point of view of social dislocation, the service is more frequently directed in terms of the needs of children and it is more

legitimately classified as a child welfare service. This ambiguity of emphasis may create a problem during the course of offering the service. When a homemaker enters a family because the mother is ill, "Who should be the homemaker's primary concern, the incapacitated adult or the insecure child?"

2. A second controversial question arises: "Is casework an essential part of homemaker service?" If so, it seems logical that homemaker service should be offered primarily, as it is now, by social agencies. Some point out that the selective, appropriate offering of a resource, supported by community funds, requires an intake casework interview; that the effective use of the service requires the kind of coordination and ongoing help provided by the caseworker; and that in all instances, families needing homemaker services are facing some crisis and the caseworker can be helpful in dealing with its consequences (Baldwin, 1953; Brodsky, 1957, 1958). Aldrich (1956) points out that even seemingly uncomplicated situations actually require the caseworker's continuing help. This point receives some empirical support from one nationwide study, which indicates that "about six out of every seven families served in the study were provided casework services as well as homemaker service" (U.S. Department of Health, Education, and Welfare, 1958a, p. 65).

Others, however, suggest that, although casework service is needed to determine if the situation calls for a homemaker as an appropriate resource, "this is quite different from requiring a family to be engaged in a continuing casework relationship. If the public gets the idea that, in order to obtain a homemaker, it is necessary to be involved in a continuing casework relationship, the service either will not be used or will be obtained through auspices other than a social agency." Richman points to the "advisability of accepting families who wish to meet their personal needs through homemaker service but who may not need, or want, help with personal problems" (U.S. Department of Health, Education, and Welfare, 1952). "In many cases the family's only need is for the help of a homemaker in an emergency. They neither require nor want counseling or casework. To add such families to the load of the caseworker is not only burdensome but unrealistic" (U.S. Department of Health, Education, and Welfare, 1960, p.p. 21).

3. Another problem derives from the fact that the essential differences between homemaker and housekeeper services are very often blurred in the minds of the layman and, on occasion, in the minds of professionals. In offering the service, this problem of distinction and definition sometimes arises as the agency strives to keep the service from degenerating into a routine, mechanical housekeeping service. A detailed study of home help services in Great Britain, in which extensive interviews were conducted with homemakers, clients, and the public, made clear that the public and the clients had difficulty in perceiving homemaker services as differentiated from maid service (Hunt, 1970).

4. There is also a question as to the proper allocation of the limited homemaker-service resources. Many of the agencies offer the service to the aged as well as to families with young children. Which group can legitimately claim priority when decisions must be made regarding service limitations?

5. Agencies are "frequently insufficiently flexible" in the number of hours per day and the length of time for which homemaker service is offered (Community Council, 1961, p. 5). Some agencies will not provide service if the homemaker is required for more than eight or ten hours a day; others will refuse service if the homemaker is likely to be required for more than three months. National organizations interested in homemaking service have urged that family need, rather than arbitrary limitations, should determine the way the service is offered.

6. Another problem involves lack of public knowledge and acceptance of home-maker service. A study of homemaker service in New York City in 1959 revealed that approximately two thirds of a group of people identified as needing some kind of a home aide because of illness "had neither contacted an agency nor had been referred to one" (Community Council, 1961, p. 5).

An English study of motherless families indicated that relatives and friends were the principal source of help (George & Wilding, 1972). The relevant social services, such as homemaker service, were a source of help in only a small percentage of cases, mostly to lower-class families and for a limited period. Many of the fathers indicated that they would have preferred homemaker services if these had been more readily available. Accepting the help of friends and relatives incurs an obligation, and one may not be able to reciprocate the favor. A Dutch interview study of some sixty families who received homemaker services indicated that they preferred them to the help of relatives and/or friends and neighbors (Netherlands Institute, 1972, p. 75).

7. Recruitment is a problem. The prestige of the homemaker is not high enough to permit easy recruiting of competent personnel, and the limited availability of professionally trained casework supervisors makes difficult the expansion of service to meet the growing demand. Furthermore the service has limited prestige within the agency. Social workers are oriented to thinking in terms of the better-established resources, such as foster care, for dealing with the kinds of problem situations in which a homemaker might be appropriately employed. This tends to the neglect and derogation of homemaker service (U.S. Department of Health, Education, and Welfare, 1960, pp. 5–6).

8. Funding of homemaker service is an ongoing problem. The service has low visibility and low priority for community support either through community chest funds or tax funds. There are some sources of funding available, but these are far from adequate. Although there is some possibility of federal reimbursement for the expense of providing homemaker service to families receiving public assistance, the service is not specifically identified in federal legislation as an essential, mandated service, as are, for instance, protective services and family planning.

There are a variety of sources of support for homemaker services: Medicare, Medicaid, Title XX of the Social Security Act, and others. Lack of coordination among the variety of sources of support result in a continuing problem for agencies (Moore, 1977).

9. With the growth of service offered by private individuals and proprietary agencies, there is an increasing concern with standards. The National Homcaring Council has established standards and is acting to accredit agencies that meet the standards. This is a difficult task, however, so that by 1978, there were only 124 agencies that were accredited by the council. There is concern that homemaker service, like nursing-home service, may present opportunities for unscrupulous operators. Reports of such substandard services have already been published (*New York Times,* December 13, 1977).

Trends

We have already noted some of the recent trends: the continuing rapid growth of the services the increased proportion of service offered by public agencies; the increasing proprietary-entrepreneurial interest in homemaker service; the decrease in service offered children and families; and the increasing proportion of services offered the aged. There follow some additional trends.

1. One trend in homemaker service is toward an expansion of the service and broader definition of situations in which the service might be used. Families that required extended homemaker service once found it difficult to obtain. As a result of special projects illustrating the value of extended homemaker service and the growing recognition of the clear need for such service, more agencies may make homemakers available either over a longer period of time or for more hours each day. It is likely that the present trend toward an expansion of homemaker service will continue. Growing difficulties in finding foster homes and growing dissatisfaction with the program of foster care will continue to provide an impetus to explore alternative means of meeting the needs of the motherless family.

Developments in other areas are likely to reinforce the need for homemaker service. For instance, the trend toward community-centered psychiatric services, which help to keep more and more of the mentally ill in the community, requires—for its success—supplementary services such as homemaker service.

2. There is also a trend toward a more imaginative use of homemaker service. For instance, California has used funds available through the Children's Bureau Crippled Children's Program to provide homemakers for the mothers of handicapped children so as to relieve them for a few hours a day. Homemakers have also been used with families charged with neglect "in homes in which standards of household management was [sic] so poor as to seriously jeopardize the health and welfare of children in the family" (Shames, 1964 p. 12). The homemaker assisted these mothers in the care of their children and instructed them in better methods of child care. The reports of homemakers have also been found to be of great help in determining actual conditions in families suspected of child abuse (National Council, 1965a, p. 59). And in families with very young retarded children, homemaker service has been used to relieve family pressures and tensions. It has been hoped that as a result, "energies might be released to work out not only appropriate planning for the retarded child, but also to examine and work through family problems created or aggravated by a retarded child" (Retarded Infants Service, 1965, p. 10). Homemakers have also been used effectively with families threatened with eviction from public housing because of poor housekeeping standards, as well as with migrant workers and American Indian families on the reservations (National Council, 1965a, pp. 61–62).

3. Homemakers have been taught the essentials of behavior modification approaches and have been given responsibility for observing, recording, and reporting behavior and implementing techniques for changing maladaptive behavior: "In essence the homemaker serves as the agent through whom the behavior change program is implemented" (Talsma, 1970, p. 4; See also Steeno, Moorehead, & Smits, 1977).

Bibliography

Aldrich, C. Knight. "A Psychiatrist Looks at Homemaker Service." *Child Welfare*, 35 (October 1956).

Baldwin, Ruth M. "Values in Long-Time Homemaker Service." *Social Casework*, 34 (March 1953).

Beatt, Earl J. "Community Organization to Meet Homemaker Service Need." *Child Welfare*, 36 (July 1957).

Breckinridge, Sophonisba, and Edith Abbott. *The Delinquent Child and the Home.* New York: Russell Sage Foundation, 1912.

Brodsky, Rose. *Homemaker Service: Under Whose Auspices and for What Purpose?* Jamaica, N.Y.: Jewish Community Services of Long Island, September 1957.

Brodsky, Rose. "Philosophy and Practices in Homemaker Service." *Child Welfare,* 37 (July 1958).

Brodsky, Rose. *Use of Homemaker Service for Families with Psychiatric Disorders of Adults.* Paper presented at Eastern Regional Conference, New York: Child Welfare League of America, April 20, 1961. Mimeograph.

Brooklyn Bureau of Social Service and Children's Aid Society. *Long-term Homemaker Service-Project Report.* New York, September, 1958.

Brown, H. Frederick. "Effective Use of Caretakers as an Alternative to Placement," pp. 205–221 in *Treating Families in the Home,* Ed. Marvin Bryce; June Lloyd. Springfield, ILL: Charles C. Thomas, 1981.

Burt, Marvin R., and Ralph R. Balyeat. *A Comprehensive Emergency Services System for Neglected and Abused Children.* New York: Vantage Press, 1977.

Cassert, Hilda P. "Homemaker Service as a Component of Casework." *Social Casework,* 51, 9 (November 1970), 533–544.

Chambers, Katherine N. "The Intake Process in Homemaker Service Cases." *Social Casework,* 36 (May 1955).

Children's Aid Society of New York City. "Nine-to Twenty-four-Hour Homemaker Service Project." *Child Welfare,* 41 (March 1962); 41 (April 1962).

Child Welfare League of America. *Standards for Homemaker Service for Children.* New York, 1959.

Child Welfare League of America. *Report to the Standards Committee on the Survey of Membership Regarding CWLA Standards for Homemaker Service to Children.* New York: Child Welfare League of America, May 1984.

Child Welfare League of America. *1984 CWLA Directory of Member and Associate Agencies.* New York: Child Welfare League of America, 1985.

Clough, Tracy C., and Janet C. Wood. "Homemaker Service to Children in a Multiple-Function Agency," *Child Welfare,* 37 (December 1958).

Community Council of Greater New York. *Home Aid Service-Needs of Health Agency Clientele.* New York, June 1961.

Community Service Society of New York. *Report of the Extended Homemaker Service Project,* prepared by Adelaide Werner. New York, June 1958.

Dexter, Margaret, and Wally Harbert. *The Home-Help Service.* New York: Tavistock Publications, 1983.

Federation of Community Services. *Report of the Need for Homemaker Service.* Almeda County, Tex.: Federation of Community Services, January 1959. Mimeo.

George, Victor, and Paul Wilding. *Motherless Families.* London: Kegan Paul, Trench, Trubner & Co., 1972.

Giovannoni, Jeanne M., and Rosina M. Becerra. *Defining Child Abuse.* New York, Free Press, 1979.

Goodwin, Marion Schmakel. "Housekeeper Service in Family Welfare," in *Proceedings of the National Conference of Social Work,* 1938. Chicago: University of Chicago Press, 1939.

Gordon, Henrietta. "Homemaker Service as A Children's Casework Service." *Child Welfare,* 34 (January 1955).

Gordon, Henrietta. *Casework Services for Children—Practices and Principles.* Boston: Houghton Mifflin Company, 1956.

Grant, Jean, and Lucille Pancyr. "The Teaching-Homemaker Service of a Welfare Department." *The Social Worker,* 38, 2 (May 1970).

Halper, Gertrude, and Mary Ann Jones. *Serving Families at Risk of Dissolution: Public Preventive Services in New York City.* New York: Human Resources Administration, February 1984.

Humphry, Gilbert W. (Mrs.). *Shaping the Future of Homemaker-Home Health Aide Services*. Regional Institute Paper. March 1978. Mimeo, 5 pp. New York: National Council for Homemaker-Home Health Aide Services.

Hunt, Audrey. *The Home Help Service in England and Wales*. London: Her Majesty's Stationary Office, 1970.

Jenkins, Shirley, and Mignon Sauber. *Paths to Child Placement*. New York: The Community Council of Greater New York, 1966.

Johnson, Nora Phillips. "Creative uses of Homemaker Service." *Child Welfare,* 35 (January 1956).

Johnson, Nora Phillips. "Homemaker Service for Children With Psychiatric Disorders." *Child Welfare,* 40 (November 1961).

Jones, Mary A., Renée Neuman, and Ann W. Shyne. *A Second Chance For Families: Evaluation of a Program to Reduce Foster Care*. New York: Child Welfare League of America, 1976.

Justiss, Howard. "Hidalgo County Homemaker Program." *Public Health Reports,* 75 (April 1960).

Kepecs, Jacob. "Housekeeper Service for Motherless Families," in *Proceedings of the National Conference of Social Work,* 1938. Chicago: University of Chicago Press, 1939.

Langer, Marian. "A Visiting Homekeeper's Program." *The Family,* 26 (July 1945).

Little, Virginia. "Open Care for the Aged-Swedish Model." *Social Work,* 23 (July 1978), 282–284.

Maluccio, Anthony N, Edith Fein, and Kathleen A. Olmstead, *Permanency Planning for Children—Concepts and Methods*. New York: Tavistock Publications, 1986.

Moore, Florence M. "New Issues for In-Home Service." *Public Welfare* (Spring 1977), 26–37.

National Council For Homemaker-Home Health Aide Services, Inc. *Report of The 1965 National Conference on Homemaker Services*. New York, 1965a.

National Council For Homemaker-Home Health Aide Services, Inc. *Standards for Homemaker-Home Health Aide Services*. New York, 1965b.

National Council For Homemaker-Home Health Aide Services, Inc. *Homemaker-Home Health Aide Services For Families With A Mentally Retarded Member*. New York, 1968.

National Council For Homemaker-Home Health Aide Services, Inc. *Readings In Homemaker Service*. New York, 1969.

National Council For Homemaker-Home Health Aide Services, Inc. *Homemaker Service to Strengthen Individual and Family Life—A Focus on the Teaching Role of the Homemaker*. New York, 1970.

National Council For Homemaker-Home Health Aide Services, Inc. *Growth, Change, Challenge: 15th Annual Report,* 1977. New York: National Council for Homemaker-Home Health Aide Services, 1978.

Netherlands Institute For Social Welfare Research. *Some Selected Studies*. The Hague, June 1972.

New Jersey State Department of Health. *New Jersey Visiting Homemakers—Proceedings of Homemaker Development Seminar*. Princeton, N.J., April 1961. Supplement to *Public Health News* (July 1961).

Reichert, Kurt. "The Drift Toward Entrepreneurialism in Health and Social Welfare: Implications for Social Work Education." *Administration in Social Work,* 1, 2 (Summer 1977), 123–133.

Retarded Infants' Service, and Association for Homemaker Service. *The Value of Homemaker Service in the Family With the Retarded Child Under Five—Final Report*. New York, November 1965.

Robinson, Nancy, Eugene Shinn, Esther Adams, and Florence Moore. *Costs of Homemaker-Home Health Aide and Alternative Forms of Service*. New York: National Council for Homemaker-Home Health Aide Service, 1974.

Russell, Alene B., and Cynthia M. Trainor. *Trends in Child Abuse and Neglect—A National Perspective*. Denver, Colo: American Humane Association, 1984.

Santulli, Mary. "Criteria for Selection of Families for Housekeeper Service." *Smith College Studies in Social Work,* 15 (1944–1945).

Shames, Marian. "Use of Homemaker Service in Families That Neglect Their Children." *Social Work,* 9 (January 1964).

Sherman, Edmund A., Michael H. Phillips, Barara L. Haring, and Ann W. Shyne. *Service to Children in Their Own Homes—Its Nature and Outcome.* New York: Child Welfare League of America, 1973.

Shinn, Eugene, and Nancy Robinson. "Trends in Homemaker-Home Health Aide Services." *Social Work Abstracts,* 10 (1974), 2–9.

Shyne, Ann. *The Need for Foster Care.* New York: Child Welfare League of America, 1969.

Shyne, Ann W., and Anita G. Schroeder. *National Study of Social Services to Children and Their Families.* Rockville, Md.: Westat, 1978.

Sieder, Violet, and Charlotte Califf. *Homemaker Home Health Aide Servcie to the Mentally Ill and Emotionally Disturbed: A Monograph.* New York: National Council for Homemaker Home Health Aide Service, 1976.

Snyder, Ruth. *Homemaker Service—A Supportive and Protective Service for Children and Adults.* New York: New York City Department of Welfare, May 1962. Mimeo.

Soyka, Patricia. "Homemaker-Home Health Aide Services for Handicapped Children." *Child Welfare,* 55, 4 (April 1976), 241–251.

Soyka, Patricia W. *Thursday's Child Has Far to Go—Help at Home For Handicapped Children and Their Families.* New York: National Council for Homemaker Home health Aid Service, 1979.

Spinelli, L. A. and K. S. Barton. "Home Management Services for Families with Emotionally Disturbed Children." *Child Welfare,* 59, 1 (1980), 43–52.

Steeno, T., R. Moorehead, and J. Smits. "Homemakers as Change Agents." *Social Casework,* 58, 5 (May 1977), 286–293.

Talsma, Eugene. "The Homemaker Carries Key Role in Child Behavior Modification." Paper presented at National Council for Homemaker Service, May 1970.

Trager, Brahna. *Homemaker/Home Health Aide Service in the United States.* Washington, D.C.: U.S. Goverment Printing Office, 1973.

U.S. Department of Health, Education, and Welfare. *Homemaker Services: A Preventative to Placement of Children in Foster Care.* Washington, D.C.: U.S. Government Printing Office, 1952. Mimeo.

U.S. Department of Health, Education, and Welfare. *Homemaker Services in the United States: A Directory of Agencies,* 1954. Washington, D.C.: U.S. Government Printing Office, 1955.

U.S. Department of Health, Education and Welfare. *Homemaker Services: A Nationwide Study.* Washington, D.C.: U.S. Government Printing Office, 1958a.

U.S. Department of Health, Education, and Welfare. *Homemaker Services: Twelve Descriptive Statements.* Washington, D.C.: U.S. Government Printing Office, 1958b.

U.S. Department of Health, Education, and Welfare. *Homemaker Services in the United States: Report of the 1959 Conference.* Washington, D.C.: U.S. Government Printing Office, 1960.

U.S. Department of Health, Education, and Welfare. *Children.* Washington, D.C.: U.S. Government Printing Office, March–April 1961a.

U.S. Department of Health, Education, and Welfare. *Homemaker Services in Public Welfare: The North Carolina Experience.* Washington, D.C.: U.S. Government Printing Office, 1961b.

Watkins, Elizabeth G. "So That Children May Remain in Their Own Homes: Homemaker Service Strengthens Aid to Dependent Children Program." *The Child,* 18 (October 1953).

Watkins, Elizabeth G., and Laura Turitt. "Short-term Homemaker Service." *Child Welfare,* 37 (May 1958).

Woldman, Elinore R. "Care of Children in Their Own Homes Through Supervised Homemaker Service." *The Child,* 5 (September 1940).

Works Progress Administration. *Final Report on the W.P.A. Program, 1935–43.* Washington, D.C.: U.S. Government Printing Office, 1944.

Yoshikami, Rogers T. *Assessing the Implication of Federal Policy to Reduce the Use of Foster Care—Placement Prevention and Reunification in Child Welfare.* Portland, Oregon: Regional Research Institute for Human Services, Portland, State University, 1984.

5

Supplementary Services:

Day-Care Service

Introduction

Day care is a child welfare service employed when family care for the child must be supplemented for some part of the day. It is designed to permit the child to be maintained in his or her own home. It also operates to strengthen and support positive parental role enactment. Like homemaker service, day care is primarily concerned with helping the temporarily motherless family—motherless because the mother is working.

Definition: Day Care

According to the Women's Bureau of the U.S. Department of Labor (1953):

> A day nursery or day-care center has as its primary function the provision of good group care and supervision of *supplemental* parental care during the day because . . . parents are unable to care for [their children] due to employment, sickness, or for some other reason [p. 6].

A United Nations (1956) report defines day care as "an organized service for the care of children away from their own homes during some part of the day when circumstances call for normal care in the home to be supplemented." This definition is based on the conception of day care "as a *supplement* to, but not as a substitute for, parental care" (p. 18).

The Child Welfare League of America notes that "Day care is a service for families provided in behalf of children and their parents and designed to *supplement* daily parental care—The purpose of day care is to *supplement* the care and protection children receive from their parents" (Child Welfare League of America, 1984, pp. 9–10).

The Day Care and Child Development Council of America (1970) defines day care as

> a service which provides essential care and protection to children outside their homes for a major part of the day on a regular basis. Good day care assures opportunities for physical, emotional, and intellectual growth to the maximum of the child's

capacity through group programs for preschool and school-age children as well as through family day care.

Two types of programs in addition to day care provide both care and education to children under six. One is the compensatory educational Head Start program initiated in 1965 as part of the "war on poverty." The second is the preschool programs that, in some states, enroll children between three and five in prekindergarten as well as kindergarten programs. Both service a very sizable number of children without reference to their mothers' employment. In 1984 some 5.5 million three- to five-year-old children (52 per cent of all children in this age group) were enrolled in nursery school and prekindergarten.

Congregate and Family Day Care

A desirable aspect of a good program of day care is the availability of diversified facilities. Day care may be given in a group setting (a center), or it may be given in a home. The latter is sometimes called *foster day care* or *family day care*.

In some situations, individual family day care is the more desirable alternative. If, for instance, the child is less than two years old, he or she has not progressed to the point where he or she can effectively operate in a group situation, he or she is less capable of contributing to or profiting from a group experience. In addition, the child is not capable of handling, without assistance, many of the simple routines of self-care—feeding and dressing himself or herself, and so on—so that the child requires more individual attention than is often available in a group situation. Being more vulnerable, both physically and emotionally, the younger child requires the special attention and "mothering" that can be more adequately provided by individual day care (Freud, 1949, p. 69). It is often argued, too, that children two years of age or younger are more likely to encounter increased danger of infection in a group setting.

Earlier editions of the Child Welfare League of America Standards on Day Care recommended that children under the age of three not be placed in day care. In response to changes in thinking regarding this, the 1984 edition of the standards states that "an infant from birth to 2 years of age can benefit from a program designed to meet his or her physical emotional and social needs" (p. 15). Special safeguards and an adult-baby ratio of 3:1 is recommended.

Family day-care licensing generally limits the number of children who can be cared for to six, including the caregiver's own children. Generally no more than two children under two years of age are permitted in a family day-care facility.

Individual care is also desirable for the older child who is emotionally disturbed. The child may be three or four years of age, but he or she may still be exhibiting the emotional needs of a child one or two years old. The child is not, therefore, ready for a group situation and needs the support available through family day care.

In addition, some practical, situational considerations may dictate the desirability of family day care over group day care. A day-care center requires a sizable population of working mothers in a community to make operation feasible. Family day care is a more flexible arrangement; it can be expanded or contracted according to need. It also permits more individualization. However flexible a day-care center may be, it must maintain a schedule of one kind or another. In rural areas, or where the mother's working day begins or ends at some unusual time, family day care may offer the necessary flexibility.

The origin of family day care lay in its greater potential for meeting the individualized needs of particular situations: "Early in 1927 a survey made by the Philadelphia Association of Day Nurseries had shown that care in a day nursery did not meet the requirements of the mothers due to inflexibility of hours, quarantine problems, and exclusion of children suffering from minor illness" (Trout & Bradbury, 1946, p. 3). Individual day care was suggested as a solution and was first used in Philadelphia in late 1927.

Neighborhood based out-of-home family day care has achieved recognition as a desirable alternative option to home-based care and center-based care (Wattenberg, 1980).

The National Day Care Home Study examined family day care over a four-year period between 1976 and 1979 (Fosberg, 1981). Family day care was defined as care provided in a private home other than the child's home. Family day care was identified as the largest, most complex system of care for children of employed mothers in the United States. More children were served by family day care than either the day-care center or care in the child's own home. Family day care is a large-scale cottage industry.

Family day-care homes provided care for many infants and toddlers in contrast to group day-care facilities, which enrolled children in the three–five age group more exclusively. Such homes also provided care for school-age children. "Hence the need for day care for infants and school aged children—which is not being met in centers is being met by the unregulated family day care worker" (Fosberg, 1981, p. 61).

Historical Background

It is difficult to know where the first day-care center was established. Jean Frederick Oberlin, a Swiss minister, opened a *garderie,* or day nursery, in 1767 for children whose mothers worked in the fields. Robert Owen is sometimes given credit for an early nursery established in 1816 in response to a recognition of the need for child care and protection resulting from the employment of mothers (National Society for the Study of Education, 1929, p. 11).

One of the first day-care centers in the United States was established in 1854 at the Nursery and Child's Hospital, New York City. Employed mothers who had been patients at the hospital left their children under the care of the nurses when they returned to work. But the first permanent day nursery in the United States was established in 1863, to care "for the children of women needed to manufacture soldiers' clothing and to clean in hospitals" (National Society, 1929, p. 91). By 1898 the service was so well established that a National Federation of Day Nurseries was founded. By 1900 it was estimated that some 175 such centers had been organized in cities throughout the United States, many of them under the auspices of neighborhood settlement houses.

The 1920s were characterized by important changes. The parallel growth of the nursery school movement during this period accentuated the educational needs of the preschool child and resulted in a growing shift in day-care programs from a purely protective emphasis to one that included a concern for education. Furthermore the increasing acceptance of mental hygiene principles in casework and the professionalization of casework itself resulted in more frequent efforts to include casework services as integral elements in day care.

The Great Depression initially had an adverse effect on the day-care-center movement. Increasing unemployment returned many mothers to full-time home-maker status, and limited funds forced the closing of many centers. Ultimately, however, the Depression, through the Works Progress Administration (WPA), provided a large-scale demonstration of some of the values of day care. Such centers were established by the program throughout the country to provide employment for teachers, nurses, nutritionists, and so on. The service they offered was primarily designed not to meet the child-care needs of the working mother but to provide a healthier environment for children from low-income families. Only children of parents who could not afford the tuition of privately operated nursery schools were eligible for admission to the WPA centers. As the final report on the WPA program notes:

> Many young children from low-income families were cared for in WPA nursery schools. The children were given a daily health inspection and necessary medical services in addition to well-balanced meals, play, and rest in an environment conducive to normal development. . . . These nursery schools everywhere demonstrated their value as an efficient and beneficial mode of child care [Works Progress Administration, 1944, p. 62].

Some idea of the scope of the program established is suggested by the fact that in 1937, forty thousand children were in attendance in the WPA nursery schools during a one-month study period.

This program, established under federal impetus and support, was continued during World War II. With the start of the war and the tremendous increase in the need for manpower, the day-care program became part of a systematic national effort to shift women from homes into factories. More than 3 million married women entered the labor force between 1940 and 1944, many of them mothers of preschool children. The care of the children of working mothers became a problem of concern to many communities. "Increased juvenile delinquency in some communities and high absenteeism in some war manufacturing plants often were attributed to a lack of adequate child-care services" (U.S. Department of Labor, 1953, p. 16).

In further support of this explicit public policy, $6 million, allocated in July 1942 to the WPA, was designated for use in reorganizing its nursery school program in order to meet the needs of employed mothers. When the WPA was abolished by presidential order at the end of 1942, this project was maintained with federal funds made available through the Lanham Act. This Act, concerned primarily with defense housing and public works for defense, was reinterpreted so as to permit the allocation of funds to communities in support of child-care facilities and service. Public programs for day care were supplemented, in some instances, by large industrial firms engaged in war work. The Curtiss-Wright plane factory in Buffalo and the Kaiser shipyards established day-care centers for their employees.

> At its peak, the wartime program of day-care centers for children of working mothers had an enrollment of 129,357 children (July 1944) in 3102 units. By the end of the war, every state, except New Mexico, had submitted request for and received Federal funds under the Lanham act for operation and maintenance of child care programs and some $52 million of Federal funds had been expended for this purpose. . . .
>   It has been estimated that between 550,000 and 600,000 children received care, at one time or another, under the auspices established through the help of the Lanham act. This, despite the serious handicaps which the program faced due to lack of

suitable physical accommodations in many communities and shortages of adequately trained personnel [U.S. Department of Labor, 1953, pp. 9, 19].

Despite urging on the part of the Children's Bureau that local communities establish planning groups to ensure the continuation and development of day-care facilities, and despite the fact that mothers using the centers organized to agitate for a long-range program that—unlike the emergency one, which was based on the needs of industry—was planned to meet the needs of children, the end of the war saw a sharp contraction of facilities. The principal factor was the withdrawal of federal funds through termination of Lanham Act support in February 1946. The shortage of trained personnel, the high costs of operation, and the reduction in the number of working mothers also contributed to this change.

The federal government, in justifying termination of its support, noted that assistance under the Lanham Act for child care had been based on the recruitment and retention of workers for war production and essential supporting services.

For a period of time after World War II, there was little change in the day-care picture. During the 1960s, there was a resurgence of interest in day care. The highwater mark of such concerns was achieved in 1971, when a very extensive child-care development bill was passed by both houses of Congress (but vetoed by President Nixon). Since that time, no similar measure, such as the Child and Family Services Act sponsored by Senators Mondale and Brademus in 1975, has achieved enough support to pass Congress. Despite this failure, however, there has been a steady expansion of both public and private day-care facilities in response to the increased demand. The 1962 and 1967 amendments to the Social Security Act, which provided funding for day care for current, past, and potential welfare recipients on a match of $75 of federal funds for every $25 of state funds, helped to fuel this expansion. Since 1975, Title XX—the Social Services Reorganization Amendment—has provided funding to states for day-care funding. Child care is the largest single category of expenditures in the Title XX social services program. Some states offered limited programs of day-care services to mentally retarded, physically handicapped, and/or emotionally disturbed children. A smaller number of states offered day-care services to migrant children.

In recapitulating the history of day care in the United States, it is significant that widespread support of day-care facilities did not result primarily in response to the needs of children but in response to the needs and demands of adult society: to increase job possibilities during the Great Depression and to increase the availability of women during periods of critical labor shortage in World War II.

Scope

Statistics on the scope of day-care facilities are based on the licensing requirements that allow such facilities to be located and counted. The accuracy of these statistics depends, then, on the adequacy of licensing procedures.

Given variations in licensing procedures from one state to another and differences regarding licensing of day-care centers and family day-care facilities, it is not possible to provide a confident figure on the number of such facilities available in the United States and the numbers of children that can be accommodated.

What we do know is that there has been rapid, steady increase in the number of mothers of children under six years of age in the work force. By 1985, about 53.2 per cent of all mothers with children under six were in the work force. Mothers with children under one year of age were increasing their participation in the work force as well. In 1970, 24 per cent of such mothers were in the work force. By March 1985, 49 per cent of such mothers were in the work force. The rate of labor force participation of mothers of pre–school-age children has increased more rapidly than for the older age groups of children. By 1985, 8.2 million preschool children had a mother in the labor force. It is estimated that by 1990, 60 per cent of all school-age children will have working mothers, 11.5 million preschool-age children and 17.2 school-age children.

Labor force participation rates are highest for divorced women, followed by married women with husband present. Single never-married women have lower labor force participation rates, the lowest rate being among welfare mothers. Black mothers have higher labor force participation rates than white mothers. Hispanic mothers have lowest participation rates.

Because economic necessity is the major reason for women working, labor force participation rates increase with decreases in family income.

Use of day care by families and single parents is in response to the problem of interrole conflict—the conflict between the role of parent and the role of employee. Adequacy of supplementary child care is related to the child care resources available. It is a matter of concern that in 1985 it was estimated that some 7 million children under the age of 13 spent some part of the day without any adult supervision.

Despite all the talk about day care as a "social service," more than half of all such facilities are operated as a business venture. Many of those operating under voluntary auspices are organized by women's clubs, professional women's groups, patriotic organizations, and church organizations. Only a limited percentage of all licensed facilities under voluntary auspices are administered by what might be regarded as social work agencies, such as settlement houses or community centers and child welfare or family welfare agencies.

Effects on the Child

There is considerable research available regarding the effects of mothers' employment on children. Reviews of such research tend to come to very similar conclusions, particularly with regard to the three- to five-year-old child—namely, that if the mother is satisfied with her job and the provision for child care is reasonably good and stable, there is no adverse effect on the child's development. A 1974 review of the research regarding the "consequences for wife, husband and child" of the mother's employment concludes that "the results disprove the theory that maternal employment fosters deprivation of the child" (Hoffman Nye, 1974). A 1977 review notes that "no consistent differences between preschool children of working and nonworking mothers have been found when potentially confounding variables (such as socioeconomic status, mother's age, child's age, mother's attitude toward work, stability of the home, presence of the father and alternative child care arrangements) have been controlled" (Clarke-Stewart, 1977, p. 34). Analogous conclusions are drawn regarding the effects of the mother's employment on older school-aged children; neither school achievement nor general development appears to be adversely affected (Clarke-Stewart, 1977, pp. 47–48).

In an updated review of research first published in 1982, Belsky and Steinberg (1984) found that "with respect to cognitive development there is still no evidence that day care influences the intellectual functioning of children other than those from impoverished homes—with respect to emotional development available evidence generally fails to support the assertion that supplementary child care negatively affects the child" (p. 98).

Other reviews of the research by O'Connell (1983), Watkins and Bradbard (1982), Blum (1983), and Belsky (1984) conclude that the findings do not show consistent adverse effects of out-of-home child day care for 3–5 year old children.

A comprehensive review of early childhood programs by Clarke-Stewart and Fein (1983) concludes that the

> message suggested by the available data is basically reassuring. If children are placed in a decent program after 2 years of age, effects, if any, are likely to be positive—for children less than 1 year of age, there may be some effect on the mother–child relationship; an effect which *may* (emphasis is original) be negative especially if the mother's work responsibilities absorb much of her emotional energies and if the family situation does not alleviate these pressures.

However, the researchers suggest proceeding with caution in translating the research into practice. They note that we need to be reminded that there "are severe limitations in the research—studies were inevitably volunteer subjects attending relatively good programs, effects were assessed with fairly gross measures—The research evaluating preschool programs thus offers no guarantees to a parent about an individual child or a particular setting" (pp. 980–981).

The limitations regarding research on the effects of group center day care on children are even more pronounced regarding family day care. What little is available has failed to confirm any clearly negative consequences of such care (Wattenberg, 1980, pp. 53–54).

Speaking to the specific effects on children of mother's employment as distinguished from the effects of supplementary day care on children, Kamerman gives a more equivocal but analogous answer. Kamerman chaired a special panel on Work, Family and Community of the committee on Child Development Research and Public Policy. In the preface and introduction to a report on the exhaustive studies of the panel, Kamerman and Hayes (1982) state,

> Our conclusion is that the phenomenon itself is far too complex to identify any simple casual nexus between parental employment and effects on children. Work by itself is not a uniform condition experienced in the same way by all adults who are themselves parents. Parents are not the same; nor are their children; nor are the communities in which the parents live, the schools they attend, their neighbors and friends. In effect, if we have any message to communicate after the extensive efforts we have made it would be to tell parents, teachers and professionals 'Don't ask if working parents are good or bad for kids because the answer is it depends' (p. VIII)—'Parental employment in and of itself—mother's employment or father's employment or both parents—is not necessarily good or bad for children' [p. 6].

The general conclusions are further supported by a second report by the National Research Council Panel on Work, Family and Community (Hayes & Kamerman, 1983).

Speaking more directly to the child-care situation rather than mother's employment per se, Lamb (1982), after the reviewing the research, comes to a similar "it depends" answer and identifies some of the factors on which their effects depend.

> Thus, even though enrollment in day care appears not to have adverse effects on socioemotional developments even in infancy, we can only conclude that nonfamilial

care *need not* (emphasis in original) have adverse effects—we do not know whether developmental deviations are more likely to occur when it is employed. Among the factors affecting the influence of extrafamilial care are: the quality of care provided; consistency between the caretaking styles of parents and supplementary caretakers; the opportunity for interaction with other children and the quality of parent/child relationships before and after enrollment in the day care facility [Lamb, 1982, p. 7].

Research tends to show some positive consequences of the mother's employment: relief from financial strain, increased sharing of responsibility in family life by the father and the children, widening of the mother's interests, and increased independence of the children.

There is less unanimity, or perhaps more uneasiness, about the effects of mothers' employment and the need for surrogate care for children younger than two to three years of age. Reports of carefully conducted studies comparing the development of very young children cared for in a day-care center for part of the day over a period of time with that of children cared for at home indicate little difference (Caldwell, 1964; Kagan, Kearsley, & Zelazo, 1977). The children appear to be equally "attached" to their mothers and seem to develop normally. In each instance, however, the experiments were conducted in a carefully designed day-care facility, "well run, nurturant, responsible," guaranteeing high-quality care that is not often available for infants.

Clinicians are somewhat suspicious of the research results and tend to advocate child care by the mother herself during the early years, recognizing the reality that this might not be possible in some families (Fraiberg, 1977). Fraiberg's point of view is supported by an eminent child development researcher, Burton White (1981). They point to the greater possibility of continuity of care when the biological parent assumes the responsibility. Day-care centers, family day care, and baby-sitters have greater turnover over the first 2–3 years of a child's life. They point to the fact that the nonrational, spontaneously affectionate, partisan partiality, limitless concern, and intensity of feeling that characterizes parents' response to their own children is difficult for any nonparent caretaker to replicate. Parental responses give the children a feeling of unique specialness in parental eyes that is not likely to be duplicated in the supplementary caregiving situation.

In response it is noted that few parents have childrearing education or skills—an expertise generally possessed by caregivers in, at least, licensed day-care facilities.

Licensing

"Day care licensing refers to the requirement by law that a license, permit, or certification be secured before a person, agency, or corporation takes on the care of children away from their own home during the day" (U.S. Senate, 1971, p. 27). It may include registration, licensing, and inspection. The licensing procedure rests on a delegation of legislative power to an administrative agency. The required standards for care become, in effect, "little laws." Licensing ensures the maintenance of some minimum standards of day care and reflects the community's concern for the physical and psychosocial safety of its children (Class, 1968; Day Care Child Development Council, 1970; Granato & Lynch, 1972). By 1970 almost all states had made licensing of day-care centers mandatory.

Fewer states, however, had made licensing of day-care homes mandatory. Whereas 90 per cent of the day-care centers are licensed, fewer than 2 per cent of the family-day-care homes are subject to licensing, because most states do not require licensing if such homes offer care to fewer than three children: "Family day-care homes, then, are generally unregulated and unsupervised by any governmental or social agency. Hundreds of thousands of children, including those whose fees are paid by government funds, are cared for in these homes, about which very little is known" (U.S. Senate, 1971, p. 89; see also Keyserling, 1972).

More recent studies tend to be more optimistic about the family day-care situation. Three distinct subsystems of family day care have been identified: (1) unregulated care providers who operate independently and informally of any regulatory system, (2) licensed or registered caregivers who are regulated by some licensing or registering requirement but who operate as autonomous units; and (3) registered homes operating as part of a day-care system or network under the administrative control of some formal agency. By far the largest of the three subsystems responsible for the care of 94 per cent of the children in family day care is the unregulated family day-care subsystem (Fosberg, 1981).

Unlike licensing, registration involves self-regulation by the provider. The provider decides that he or she meets the applicable standards and registers his or her house as a family day-care facility (Washburn & Wasnburn, 1985).

The Child Food Care Program provides important leverage for some control of family day care. In order to qualify for child food care program support, the provider has to meet state standards for family day care. This has encouraged sizable numbers of family day-care providers to come out from unregulated status, where they were beyond any kind of monitoring.

Direct observation of family day-care providers by researchers associated with the National Family Day Care Study found a "high level of involvement with children exhibited by family day care providers" (Fosberg, 1981, p. 76). The activities engaged in by caregivers in involvement with children was generally appropriate to the needs of the children. A good deal of stimulating teaching, play, and helping was manifested and only a limited amount of restrictive behavior was observed. Whereas regulated family day-care homes were more consistently child focused than unregulated homes, "observers and interviewers were consistently impressed by the care they saw regardless of the regulatory status of the home" (Fosberg, 1981, p. 82). "Regulated and unregulated homes—were very similar in their levels of compliance (to licensing requirements). The implications of the similarity of child care groups, from the regulatory perspective, are quite clear: with respect to group size most caregivers are self-monitoring. In general, caregivers—knowingly or unknowingly—conform to the standard applied within each state" (Fosberg, 1981, p. 63).

Licensed and/or registered family day-care providers and those affiliated with a family day-care system under agency auspices were likely to be more committed to family day care, were more likely to engage in this activity for a longer period of time, and were more likely to have some child-care training than the larger group of unregulated–unlicensed family day-care providers.

Licensing regulations are likely to cover such factors as physical facilities, safety standards, health standards, provisions for adequate number and training of personnel, and educational facilities and equipment. They may also indicate the special kinds of provisions to be made for special kinds of children; for instance, a higher ratio of caretakers to children may be required in day-care facilities serving the handicapped.

In the discussion of quality of child care within day care, there are repeated references to adult-child ratios. The ratio itself is no certain measure of the level of warmth, maturity, concern, interest, and so on with which a caretaker may interact with a child. Whereas we find it difficult, if not impossible, to measure such qualities with confidence, we can and do measure adult-child ratios. They do, in a rough way, suggest the necessary, if not the sufficient, condition for quality child care. The ratio has become the objective indicator operationally defining the quality of child care.

Although most licensing statements have emphasized a desirable child–caretaker ratio of one caretaker for six to nine three- to four-year-old children, a national study of the operation of day-care centers showed that the size of the group was an even more crucial variable. If the group is too large, increasing the number of caretakers assigned to the group does not result in a positive outcome. Small numbers of children interacting with small numbers of adults is most effective (Abt Associates, 1978).

There are differences, from state to state, with regard to the specificity of the regulations, the nature of the penalties for violations, the kinds of facilities covered, the regularity and frequency of inspection, and the provisions available for consultation and assistance. There have been some efforts to develop national standards in a model licensing code. Currently, the federal government sets the guidelines for a day-care facility if it is to be eligible to receive federal funds.

The state departments of public welfare are generally given responsibility for implementing licensing legislation; less frequently, such responsibility rests with the state department of health or the state department of education. In any case, the office responsible for licensing may provide supervision and consultation and arrange educational programs, institutes, and workshops to help agencies reach, and maintain, an acceptable level of service.

Social workers who implement the state day-care licensing procedures for the state departments of public welfare thus have two major responsibilities: a supervisory–regulatory function and a consultation function. The supervisory–regulatory function assures the parent and the community that conditions at the day-care center are satisfactory. In discharging the consultation responsibility, the social worker helps the day-care center maintain and, if possible, improve conditions for the children at the center.

Generally licenses, once issued, must be renewed every year. Consequently there is provision for a periodic reevaluation of the day-care center. In many localities, however, the licensing staff is too small to do more than keep up with complaints received and has little power to impose adequate penalties for violations. In addition, licensing laws frequently exclude from the licensing requirement sizable groups of centers, such as those run by religious organizations and public school systems.

Licensing procedure involves considerable administrative discretion on the part of the social-worker licensing agent. Basic standards for the group care of children must be applied sensibly and with some flexibility. The licensing social worker attempts to apply the regulations in a spirit of cooperative mutuality, rather than in a spirit of evaluative assessment. The stance should not be the use of regulations to deny a license, but rather the use of regulations to educate toward the desirability of standards and to motivate their acceptance. Licensing standards should be applied fairly, uniformly, and promptly. A day-care applicant should know what the decision is as soon as possible and should be clearly informed of the reasons for the decision.

Day-care administrators frequently challenge the social worker to justify the standards he or she is attempting to enforce. They question the validity of required child-care ratios and of the credentials demanded of the various day-care-center personnel. They are also keenly aware of inequities in licensing resulting from the application of administrative discretion. Objections frequently come from groups of ghetto residents who have organized a day-care center on their own initiative. The director of one such center comments on licensing requirements:

> The center can help to upgrade the community by giving jobs or on-the-job training to persons among the poor who want to work in day care. They could be people who are qualified and talented with children even though they do not necessarily meet the formal licensing requirements. What does a credential or degree tell you about how good a teacher is? [Lynden, 1970, p. 72].

Despite the questions that are often raised about educational credentials, a nationwide study of day-care centers showed that quality care was associated with "staff specialization in child-related fields" (Abt Associates, 1978; Fosberg 1981).

Different agencies involved in licensing different aspects of a day-care center may fail to coordinate their activities or may even set contradictory standards. One center was criticized by the fire department because the yard-door latch was too high for the children to reach in case of fire. Another department then criticized the center because the yard-door latch was so low that the children could open it and run into the street.

Each of the requirements for a license, designed to protect the children, makes establishment of a center more difficult and more expensive. At what point does the need for adequate care and adequate facilities seriously limit the availability of day care? What specific standards, flexibly enforced, are the minimums that are acceptable to the community? This is still a matter for discussion. Licensing regulations that demand too high a standard substitute a problem of low quantity for a problem of low quality.

Questions have been raised about the jurisdiction and effectiveness of licensing. Operators of commercial centers note that they offer a service to parents of children who pay for the cost of care. They contend that this is a transaction between the parents and the day-care center in which government should not interfere. Licensing suggests that the parents are not fully capable of making a competent decision about what is best for their child and need the state's protection in making a choice.

Effectiveness of licensing is also questioned. Once a facility obtains a license, it can act in defiance of licensing regulations with some impunity. Very rarely is a license revoked, suspended, or not renewed. The burden of proof in obtaining a license rests with the applicant; the burden of proof rests with the state in revoking, suspending, or failing to renew a license. Fairly strong proof of the abuse of licensing regulations is needed if the agency has any hopes that court action will sustain its decision not to renew a license, if challenged by the center.

Because many states have found it difficult to monitor the licensing of family day care, they have been shifting to registration as the procedure of choice. Under registration, inspection of the homes is not required. The caretaker lists the names of the children in the home, and the regulatory agency provides the home with a statement of mandatory standards. Consultation is provided by the regulatory agency to upgrade the skills of the family day caretaker.

Effective implementation by social workers of the licensing responsibility is impeded by the fact that because "licensing is a specialized service and its functions are not included in the curriculum of a master's degree social work program, virtually no one coming into the job is equipped by previous experience to handle its varied responsibilities" (Prescott et al., 1972, p. 70).

An Explanation

During the earlier history of day care, social workers were very much involved in day care—screening applicants for limited day-care resources and counseling with families who wanted to use the service (Steinfels, 1973, pp. 59–64; Greenblatt, 1977). A mother working outside the home was atypical, and in almost every instance, employment was not a matter of choice. Unlike the current situation, the families requesting day care were very likely to be families presenting serious social problems for which social work had been given some responsibility. Because of the nature of the client group to which the service was then directed, day care was closely tied to social work. An unfortunate consequence, however, was that day care, family disorganization, and welfare came to be associated in the mind of the community. The nature of the clientele requesting day care has changed markedly since that period prior to the 1930s, and the day-care field has been making efforts to modify the image.

A major controversy revolves around the question of whether day care is a social utility (like public schools and parks), which every family might need and use at some time, or whether the need and use of day care imply a "problem." Ruderman's (1968) survey of day care in the United States led her to conclude that:

> great numbers of normal, middle class, intact, responsible families with working mothers need day-care services and even greater numbers of such families want it. In fact, as we get away from the problem situations cited in welfare documents [it becomes clear that] day care is primarily a child care program on all levels of society for normal children and normal families [p. 341].

The increase in the number of working women has "normalized" what was previously a deviant status—the working mother. As a consequence, the previous association of day care with social welfare has become progressively more attenuated and less justified.

It is becoming more widely accepted that day care is a "normal" arrangement required by "normal" families. Why, then, the illustrative material here that emphasizes "problem" situations? This follows from the fact that our primary focus in this chapter is really *not* with day care as a recently developed social utility to meet the needs of the contemporary family. The primary focus *is* on the special functions of the child-welfare social worker in day care and the kinds of help he or she can offer to those limited number of families who may have problems in effectively utilizing a social service available to all. One may accept an "institutional" orientation toward day care as such and at the same time hold a "residual" orientation toward the particular functions of the child-welfare social worker in day care.

Consequently our concern in this chapter is not with the greatest majority of families, who effectively utilize day care without requiring the intervention of the social worker. Our concern is with those limited number of families who come to day care as a result of some problem situation and with those parents and children whose use of day care produces, or exacerbates, social problems.

Although day care might become a universal social utility, the personal care services provided by the social worker should be available to the limited number of day-care families who might need and want this option.

Situations in Which Day Care Is an Appropriate Resource

The very largest percentage of children in day care are there because their mothers need to work or both need and want to work. The family is intact, the children present no special problems, and the situation is "normal."

Because our concern in this chapter is sharply focused on the specialized contribution that the child-welfare social worker can make to increase the effectiveness of day care, the illustrative material and citations are highly selective.

The material is intended to represent situations that reflect the contribution that the child welfare social workers might make to day-care clients or those considering the use of day care.

Day care is most frequently used by the working mother. Day care assumes the role functions relinquished by the mother while she is working. This is a problem of supplementary role implementation that results from interrole conflict.

More and more frequently now many mothers work because they want to work. They work because work provides interest and fulfillments of professional aspirations. Occupational careers for women are as acceptable a life-style option as motherhood. In a growing number of instances, fathers provide care for the child while the mother is employed. Statistically however, in the largest percentage of situations where mothers choose to work paternal care is not available. Some kind of child care then needs to be made available when the mother chooses to enter the work force.

In many other instances, working is not entirely a voluntary choice on the part of the mother. Such mothers work because they have to if children are to be adequately supported. Once again fathers, most of whom are also employed, are not available for child care.

Day care may be provided in situations where the child, because of mental, physical, or emotional handicap, presents an unusually heavy burden. Relief to the overburdened mother during part of the day may be sufficient to obviate the necessity for institutionalizing the child. The need for specialized knowledge in dealing with children who are different may be provided by the day-care facility, staffed by people with specialized education. Daily, time-limited group care also provides an opportunity for normal contact with peers for those children who, because of their handicap, might otherwise be isolated from such normal activities.

The Community Welfare Council of the Greater Sacramento area undertook a survey, in 1960, of parents' attitudes toward the possible use of day care for their retarded children; of 199 questionnaires mailed, 66 were returned, 47 of which indicated a positive response to the use of day care. The need for day care was felt by the parents for reasons that related to the needs of the family and the needs of the retarded child (National Association of Retarded Children, n.d.):

> Most parents feel the need for relief from the demands of constant supervision of their handicapped child in order to meet some of their own personal needs, provide

more adequate attention to other children in the family, find employment, and reduce emotional tension within the family.

Parents see the value of day-care services as providing essential social experiences
for their children as well as training, therapy, and education that they, as parents,
are unable to provide.

The two sets of reasons are related. One parent said, in talking about his retarded
daughter:

> The few children in the neighborhood recognize the "difference" and do not want to
> play with her. The lack of companionship and play affects her to such an extent that
> she is becoming extremely irritable. This, with the hyperactive personality, is such a
> burden on my nervous system that I, in turn, cannot always be as objective as I know
> I should be. A service such as this would be a great help and aid to parents like us
> with similar problems. It would afford us the relaxation from these tensions, just as
> I'm certain it would be beneficial to my little girl.

Another parent said:

> The important thing about the program for my child was the opportunity to play
> with other retarded children as the neighborhood children ignore him. We have been
> unable to get a babysitter because of his retardation, and some feel he is catching—
> people just refuse. I need some time away from him so that I can get some of my work
> done.

Some day-care centers have been organized as a special therapeutic facility for
emotionally disturbed children (Lovatt, 1962, Bloch, 1970;). The Virginia Frank
Child Development Center in Chicago, for instance, describes itself as "a specialized therapeutic nursery and kindergarten for children three to five years of age
who are showing signs of emotional and behavioral problems." The center supplements individual therapy by making available a therapeutic environment for
part of the day. Actually, however, very limited day-care facilities are available
to serve the physically, mentally, or emotionally handicapped child.

In some cases, day care may offer temporary relief when the parent–child
relationship is disturbed. The mitigation of constant stress permits reorganization of psychic forces so that the interaction may be turned in a more positive
direction. Day care supports the parents' ability to care for the child and reduces
tension and conflict, increasing the possibility that the child may be maintained
in his or her own home:

> The S. family presented a picture of serious emotional disturbances for which they
> have sought counseling in a family agency for some time. Both parents, threatened
> by their own pathological background, were showing unrealistic fears and anxieties
> over their two-and-a-half-year-old son's "wild" behavior and his refusal to speak. On
> psychiatric exams, the child was found essentially normal and his behavior not
> inappropriate to his age. Both parents genuinely rejected any thought of full-time
> placement but, with help, could accept the partial separation of day placement which
> would lessen the heavy burden of living with their youngster [Gordon, 1957, p. 301].

The following situation illustrates the complexity of interaction in a difficult situation for which day care can be a helpful resource:

> J., five-and-one-half, was referred to the [center] by the Riley Hospital Child Guidance Clinic. She had been blind since birth as the result of oxygen exposure. Although both parents were medical students, the mother was regarded as an emotionally and mentally disturbed person. She resisted enrolling J. in the Nursery and did so only at the insistence of the Clinic. The psychiatrist felt it extremely important for the child to be separated from her mother and to have a normal group experience. She made a fine adjustment in our group and will eventually attend the State Blind School. The mother's attitude also improved [Jackson, n.d., p. 31].

Day care may also be used as an alternative to homemaker service when the mother has died or deserted or when her hospitalization will be prolonged.

> One mother who is suffering from phlebitis is not able to give her active three-year-old son full-time care but, with sufficient rest while he is away from home during the day, she can be relaxed and carry on well for the rest of the time. Her husband brings the child to the center [Yeomans, 1953, p. 7].

The day-care staff, like the homemaker who is assigned to a family to help educate the parents to more adequate child-rearing methods, attempts to communicate knowledge about feeding, discipline, child protection, and so on:

> [When the mother] came to observe the children in the day care center, she noted with some relief that Joe was not the only child who threw things. She has seen that there are other children who "can't cut on the line," as she has tried to force Joe to do. Mrs. B. was most interested to learn from the teacher that Joe is too young to be expected to cut "on the line." Since her anxiety over unrealistic expectations for her children has been relieved, the neighbors report that Mrs. B. doesn't spank her children as much as before [Hansan & Pemberton, 1963]

Day-care facilities have also been used as a remedial measure for a seriously deprived home environment. A United Nations (1956) report points out that, where "shortage or inadequacy of housing leads to overcrowding and to unhealthy living conditions," where "sufficient play space is not available," where there is, "concern about child health and a desire to improve the nutrition of certain categories of children," day-care centers may play a role in child protection, "in combatting child morbidity and mortality . . . in improving the conditioning of underweight children" (p. 23). In such situations the day-care service assures the children "better care than they would receive if they remained at home" (Hansan & Pemberton, 1963, p. 180). Here inadequate parental role implementation results from deficiencies in the environment: lack of adequate living space, play space, toys, food, and the like.

As Merriam (1959) says, "A mother living on the third floor of an apartment building with a four-year-old child and two younger children may be up against a very real problem of being unable to supervise the older child for any outdoor play while also meeting the demands for the care of the young ones" (p. 22).

Of growing importance is the use of day care to prevent the placement of children in substitute care and as a "respite" resource in protective services.

> The oldest of Mrs. B.'s four children was four when this family came to the attention of the Seven Hills Neighborhood House in Cincinnati. Mrs. B. felt that she was going to have to resort to desperate measures to solve her problems, and she told the agency director that she had decided to place her children in foster care. Beset by an inadequate welfare allotment, substandard housing (four children and herself in two rooms), marital difficulties, and full-time care of the children, Mrs. B. was finding life "too much" for her. The day-care center was suggested as a means of relieving some of her child care burdens so that she could re-establish herself [Hansan & Pemberton, 1963, p. 181]. (See also Ceravolo, 1985; Subramanian, 1985).

Some day-care facilities suggest other uses of such resources. Large transatlantic liners provide day-care centers that free the traveling parents of the care of the child during the day. Large department stores and shopping centers provide such resources to permit the parents to shop freely. Similar resources might also be used to permit parents to take part in educational or cultural programs or to take advantage of regular medical or psychiatric treatment programs as outpatients. In each instance, the day-care facilities might, by permitting the parent a greater measure of freedom, contribute to a reduction of parental resentment and parent–child friction and might enhance the parent–child relationship.

Illustrating the use of day care in more normal situations is the following news report:

> The YMCA of Eastern Union County will start a curb service "Mothers Service" on wheels in Linden next month. The YMCA has acquired a thirty-five-foot mobile housetrailer and converted it into a "Jack and Jill" playmobile. The playmobile will set up shop in three different locations in Linden to give mothers two to three hours relief from their youngsters, aged three to five, and time to do some much-needed shopping or other chores [*New York Sunday News,* November 18, 1962].

Such use of day care suggests its appropriateness for keeping tensions within the family at a manageable level by providing periodic relief from the burdens of child care. Of even greater potential importance is the value of such a service to the single parent, who must be mother, father, nurse, teacher, disciplinarian, provider, and housekeeper without possibility of a break.

Evaluation

The material is focused on one component of the program, namely, the social services.

The most important value of day care is that, like other supplementary services, it increases the probability that the child may be maintained in his own home. The mother who must work can do so without finding a substitute home for the child; the handicapped child may not have to be institutionalized; the family facing a crisis may find sufficient relief and support in day care so that it can be held together for the child.

With the use of day-care, millions of children of working mothers who might otherwise need public assistance, are supported independently of the assistance program. The mother's salary, either as a sole wage in a female-headed family or as a supplementary wage in a family headed by her husband, lifts these families out of poverty.

Studies by Shyne (1969) and Jenkins (1966) indicate that the need for foster care might have been prevented in some instances if adequate day care had been available. A study of a demonstration project by a private agency of the value of family day care to forty-two families noted:

> In ten instances—before day-care service was requested—application for full-time care placement had appeared imminent. In nine other situations—though difficult to establish with absolute certainty—from the prevailing evidence of uneasy parent–child relationships and fear of overwhelming responsibilities, it would appear that full-time placement might have eventuated. In fourteen situations an application to public relief was prevented [Foster Family Day Care, 1962, p. 14].

The director of a day nursery details the cooperative action between her agency and a family service agency in holding a family together:

> The mentally ill mother and the four-year-old child were in such a constant state of friction that the father was afraid his wife would do some harm to the child in his absence at work. We were able to arrange for the father to bring the little girl in the morning and call for her on his way home from work in the evening. On week-ends he is able to act as a "buffer" between mother and child. With the continuing work of the Jewish Family Service with the mother, the home was remained together [Goddard, 1957, p. 32].

A review of the clientele of and the problems that prompted their use of a respite center, confirmed the contention "that such facilities do tend to reduce the risk of child abuse" (Subramanian, 1985). However, a national recapitulation of day-care services received by child-maltreating families between 1976 and 1982 shows relatively little change in these services over the six-year period. Throughout this period only a small percentage of families received such service. In 1976, 5.9 per cent of maltreating families with younger children received such services; in 1982, 6.4 per cent of these families received these services (Russell & Trainor, 1984, Table P-V-113, p. 113). The 1983 Annual Report of Child Abuse and Neglect noted that overall 6 per cent of the families received day-care service during a year (p. 23).

A study or preplacement prevention services offered by a carefully selected sample in 18 counties in five different states indicated a modest use of day care in preventing placement. Overall, the service was used in 8.8 per cent of the cases. The results were skewed however by two counties in which day care as placement prevention was used in 42.9 per cent and 35 per cent of the cases, respectively. Five of the 18 counties showed a zero use of day care as a placement prevention service (Yoshikami, 1984, Table B4, p. 162).

In retrospect the limited modest potency of day-care services in affecting placement decisions might have been expected. It is questionable whether the service is a highly appropriate resource for the kinds of families that might be high risk for placement services, at that point in the family history when alternatives to placement are being considered.

The effective use of day care implies the presence of at least one a reasonably well-functioning parent who can regularly bring the child to the day-care facility, pick up the child on schedule, adequately care for the child during at least sixteen hours of the twenty-four-hour day when the child is not in day care and full time over the week-end. It is just the lack of assurance in this measure of care available in the home that might have prompted consideration of placement in the first instance.

Day care is an effective supplementary resource in helping the family become self-sustaining if the parent has sufficient education and work experience so as to be potentially employable. Many of the parents requiring foster care service lack these prerequisites for employment. Additionally, many have physical and mental disabilities that militate against their employability.

Conversely, the lack of day-care services can jeopardize the success of efforts being made to help people who are currently receiving assistance to achieve independence. The federal government reported that in June 1971, four thousand AFDC mothers could not be enrolled in the Work Incentive program "for the sole reason that child care was not available" (U.S. Dept. of H.E.W., 1972).

Day care enables parents to consider the continuation of their schooling, job training or retraining. Day care also is a resource that permits a more natural, more acceptable route to help for families with problems: "Parents who are unlikely to seek professional services on their own initiative often respond to help when it is offered along with day care for their children" (Gilfillan, 1962, p. 416). Some families that might not otherwise have obtained treatment for problems adversely affecting their children are, through day care, more accessible to such help.

Children who might not otherwise have a safe, stimulating place to play are provided such a facility; children who might otherwise be deprived of an experience in group interaction under guided supervision are provided with this kind of enriching experience; and children who might otherwise be left to care for themselves, or left to haphazard, uncertain arrangements for care, are more adequately, more safely cared for as a result of the availability of day-care facilities.

Although the following reported incidents may be atypical, they illustrate the possible dangers to which children might be exposed if the mother has to work and cannot make adequate provisions for child care:

> In a small city in Ohio, an eight-year-old girl was burned to death and her six-year-old brother was severely burned in the roominghouse in which the family lived. Their parents were at work. As a result of the death of a five-year-old girl, burned to death in a Connecticut city while her mother was working, labor leaders made plans for the establishment of additional day nurseries for the care of children of employed mothers.
>
> Too great responsibility is often given to the oldest child in a family. An eight-year-old, left in charge of three younger children until midnight while her mother worked on the swing shift and her father was taking a training course, was unable to give proper aid when one of the younger children was injured.
>
> ... [In one Iowa] city, when a child was hurt in a playground accident, it was discovered that no member of her family was at home all day. The child, too young for school, was just packed off to the playground with a lunch [Fredrickson, 1943, pp. 165–166].

Day care as a supplementary service, then, has great preventive value. It acts to prevent breakup of families, separation of children from their parents, increased dependency on public aid, and dangers and hazards to children. The service provides (1) protection of children, (2) contributes to the child's development, (3) enables some children to remedy deficiencies in their development, and (4) helps prevent family breakdown and placement of the child.

The Social Worker and Day Care

An adequate day-care program requires a team approach, because it involves a partnership of three professions: education, health, and social work. Some families who seek day-care service know very clearly what they want, why they want it, and how to use it. In such instances, the social worker's only responsibility is to see that the community makes the necessary services available and that the potential applicant is aware of their existence. For some families, however, the decision to use day care is reached only after many interrelated questions have been resolved. In such instances, casework services can be of help.

It is not always clear to the applicant that the mother's employment is the most desirable—or, in fact, the only—solution to the family's problems. For the widow, the divorced mother, or the unmarried mother, AFDC may not have been seriously considered as an alternative or, having been considered, may have been rejected without a full knowledge of the program. The opportunity to talk it over with a social worker having detailed knowledge of the program may result in a decision to stay at home and apply for such assistance rather than to seek employment.

If it is decided that some alternative plan is more desirable, the caseworker can help the applicant in implementing such alternative plans—in making application for AFDC, for instance, or in dealing with the problem of role reallocation in the family so that the child can be cared for at home, or with budgeting so that the mother may not have to work. The caseworker acts as the link between the day-care applicant and resources in the community.

On occasion, when a family has an opportunity to explore the additional expenses involved in employment and to estimate the exact additional net income that employment is likely to yield, they may decide that it isn't worth the trouble. Or once they have decided that it is advisable, the discussion has at least prepared them for the reality they encounter.

Even when the mother is convinced that employment is the preferable alternative, she may still be ambivalent and anxious about the step she is about to take. Such a mother welcomes the opportunity, if available, to discuss her doubts and fears with a caseworker. The caseworker helps her to clarify exactly what effects she thinks her employment will have on the children; he or she shares with the mother the knowledge that research has made available regarding the specific effects of mothers' employment on children in different situations and discusses with her what precautions might be taken to mitigate any negative effects. Frequently mothers are less explicitly aware that employment affects not only the younger preschool children but also the older children in the family. Sibling-sibling relations might also be affected. The caseworker helps the mother to become aware of the changes that her working will entail for all her children.

The mother's employment also has effects on the marital-pair subsystem. The change from mother–wife to mother–wife–employee necessitates some reallocation of role responsibilities in the family. Both the father and the mother are involved, by the worker, in exploring the changes that might be made in order to accommodate the mother's plans for employment, the degree of acceptance of such changes on the part of both parents, and the possible dangers and advantages of alternative modes of accommodation to the wife's working. In addition, he or she helps the family to determine whether the mother's employment, with day care, is the most appropriate solution to the problems faced by the family and to explore the availability, feasibility, and acceptability of alternative solutions.

It takes a superwoman to adequately meet the demands of the three different role as employee, homemaker, and parent. There is not only a problem of role conflict but also a danger of role overload. The question of reallocation of function and responsibilities within the family might be discussed with the social worker by the mother, father, and older siblings jointly. The evidence is clear regarding women's shift to the work place; the evidence of a shift of men to household and child-care sharing is more ambiguous. Time budget research suggests that men are not increasing the extent of their participation in homemaking and childrearing to the same degree that women have increased their participation in the labor force.

If the mother's employment is the only feasible plan, she may have doubts about her capacity to meet the test of job demands. For women who have been out of the labor market for some time—and especially for women who have never been in it—self-doubt about adequacy may act as a block to performance. They may use discussions with the social worker to reassure themselves and to test the demands they may have to face. Such discussions take the form of anticipatory socialization to the new role of employee.

These discussions, which attempt to help the family to clarify the decision regarding day care, indirectly have value for the child. They tend to reduce the rate of turnover and assure the child a continuity of experience; they reduce the difficulties the child may have in moving into the day-care situation, because the child's feelings about the program reflect, in some measure, those of his or her parents. "It is only as the parent's anxieties are relieved and she is reassured that her plan to work and use day care is the best interest of herself and child that the mother is able to use day care to the best advantage" (Golten, 1945, p. 58). The family's feelings of comfort with their decision is an important factor in determining the child's capacity to adjust positively to any kind of care.

The application for day care, as is true for similar services, may have been prompted by some problem in family living—low income, divorce, illness, father's loss of job, death, inadequate housing—and the family may need help in dealing with these changes.

For some mothers, the use of day care and the acceptance of employment may be the first step in establishing independence with the anticipation that this will culminate in divorce. The anxiety and the doubts about day care reflect questions regarding the advisability of breaking up the marriage. The mother may use the day-care application to discuss this more significant decision.

> Mrs. M. applied for day care for Harry, four years old, after an argument with her husband. She had threatened divorce and he had taunted her with the statement that she could never support herself. She had been employed as a file clerk before marriage and she wondered if she could find a job now. "Maybe," she said, "if I could really prove to myself that I can get a job, I wouldn't have to take all that stuff from my husband. I would really mean it when I say I am walking out."

The decision to use day-care services results in another series of problems with which families may need help. The child who is being enrolled may experience the first formal, prolonged separation from the family. The caseworker helps the parents prepare the child for the transition by discussing with them how the child might react and how the parents might respnd to the child's ambivalence and resistance and by reassuring them of the "normality" of the child's anxiety.

The child faces the problem of multiple adjustments. She is separated from her parents and expected to accept the care of adults who are strangers to her. She is placed in unfamiliar physical surroundings, generally far from her own neighborhood. Frequently the behavior expected of her may be different from, or in conflict with, what has been demanded of her at home. Therefore the parents must be prepared for some regression on the part of the child, who may temporarily display more infantile behavior. The need for such preparation is confirmed by Thenaud (1945), who, in a study of requests for day-care service, noted that the mothers showed a general lack of understanding of the possible reactions of the children.

The caseworker tries to help the parent understand that children might feel rejected and not altogether certain that the parent will return. It takes repeated experiences of separation and return for confident assurance to develop that the parent will be back. Time sense is so poorly developed in children that for the parent to say he or she will be back "in a few hours" may mean little to the child. This knowledge supposedly helps the parent to accept, without undue embarrassment, the child's crying when she leaves. It also helps to clarify the day-center staff's suggestion that the parent explain repeatedly to the child why she is going, what is going to happen, and that she will be back.

Generally, the family applies for day-care service when the mother and the father are ready. The child's readiness for the experience, a most important factor in assuring the success of the plan, is often not given explicit consideration. The social worker has to make some evaluation of the child's readiness, based on observation of his or her behavior and on information provided by the family. It is suggested that if the child has recently undergone some difficult change (the birth of a sibling, a recent operation, a serious illness in the family), entrance into the day-care situation be delayed. This reduces the imposition on the child of too many difficult adjustments at once.

But the decision to enroll the child also produces a variety of conflicts for the mother. She may have questions about the child's negative reaction to her because she is leaving him or her. She may have questions about her adequacy as a mother for giving up the care of her child to strangers, however temporarily. She may be concerned about the transfer of the child's affection to the "mothers" in the day-care center. She may have some anxieties about the child's adequacy as a reflection of the family's previous care of the child. This anxiety derives from the fact that now, for the first time, the child is performing publicly in a uniform test situation and is being measured by professionals, however informally, vis-à-vis his or her age mates.

Mothers often reflect some of the general ambivalence toward day care and need reassurance that they are not "bad" mothers for leaving the care of their children temporarily to others. They may feel happy at being relieved of some of the burden of child care and feel guilty about this reaction:

> Mrs. M., a friendly, intelligent mother, wanted to place Charles, aged five, and
> Peter, aged two, so that she could go to work. Mr. M. was employed full-time but his

earnings were marginal. . . . The arrangements for her job were practically completed when she applied. The carrying out of the total family plan hinged entirely, however, on the admission of the children to the day-care center. Although working meant a great deal to Mrs. M., she expressed many anxieties about leaving her children. She spoke with emotion as she told the worker, "I want to feel sure that the people taking care of my children are responsible. It's been a hard decision to make, even to consider leaving them for two days a week; but five whole days is even more difficult. . . . Maybe in a year's time I'll be able to take them away from you and go back to being a mother again.

Mrs. M.'s concern about leaving the children was real, and yet she was eager to relieve the financial stress. At the end of the first interview, she was not certain that Charles and Peter were to come to the day-care center. Within a few days she talked to the worker again and at this time she said, "I've thought it over. I am giving them up for a while but I am not really losing them" [Voiland, 1942, p. 101].

Especially for the mother of the very young child, there should be some preparation for the fact that she will be missing much of the gratification of experiencing the early development of the child. One working mother whose friend looked after her eighteen-month-old child said, "After a couple of months I find that my friend can understand what my baby is saying; I cannot. He learns new things from her and I feel I am beginning not to know him" (Yudkin & Holme, 1963, p. 131).

Even if day care is desirable, there must be some discussion of the optimum choice of day care for the particular child. Is group day care the best alternative, or may family day care be better?

The social worker attempts to obtain from the parents a comprehensive picture of the child's level of functioning: likes and dislikes, his or her physical status, aptitudes and limitations, habitual modes of reacting to stress, the most effective ways of motivating the child and of disciplining her or him, the child's reaction to adults outside the family and to care by them. All this information helps the staff to work with the child in the way that is best for him or her and for the peer group into which he or she will be moving. It helps the staff to estimate the difficulty that the child will have in accepting this initial separation.

Some time at intake is devoted to discussing the structure of service and the questions the parent may have about it: fees, family responsibility for bringing and picking up the child on time, care of the child who becomes ill, health examinations, the schedule of periodic conferences with various members of the staff, the nature of day-care routines, and the things the child should and should not bring.

Arrangements are made for preadmission visits to the center and for preliminary acquaintanceships with the people on the staff who will be working with the child. The contacts between the family and the caseworker, the family and the teacher, help to identify day care with the family in the mind of the child and help him or her to see it as an extension of the home situation. For some children, arrangements need to be made for gradual desensitization to and acceptance of separation from the parents. The child may be made to come for only a few hours initially, and gradually the length of stay is increased. It may help to have the parent remain with the child for progressively shorter periods of time after enrollment in the program.

The visit to the center permits the parents to see for themselves what is done there for children and tends to eliminate any fears or illusions they may have regarding the operation of the center. The visit to the center also has diagnostic value for the staff:

> The way the child leaves the mother and takes to the teacher and to the [day care] environment, and the mother's reaction to this, begins to indicate to the worker what value the child has to the mother, the kind of relationship there is between them, and how ready she is to turn him over to another person . . . to use the . . . [day care] for his benefit. Sometimes, if her tie to him is weak, just seeing that he takes to the [day care] . . . and can bear separation from her will make her decide that she is in danger of losing him and that she must not let him go. In a surer relationship, however, this experience may be the very thing to settle her doubts about how he will take day care and separation and reassure her that it is all right to go ahead [Rawley, 1943, p. 20].

Later the caseworker can be helpful to the family in working out any situations that adversely affect the child's adjustment to the center. Paradoxically even the child's positive adjustment to day care may create a problem for the mother:

> Bobby got along unusually well for a child of his age in making the adjustment to the changed surroundings. Mrs. R. was seeing the caseworker at regular intervals and gradually she told us that Bobby liked the nursery so well that he was making a nuisance of himself week-ends because he was constantly asking if this was the day to go to the nursery. She could not understand this attitude on the part of any child. With much concern she said, "It makes me feel that maybe my home is not as good as it should be. Otherwise Bobby would not seem to prefer the nursery" [Voiland, 1942, p. 100].

The necessity of carrying multiple burdensome roles—wife, mother, and employee—may produce cumulative stress that the mother may wish to discuss. The difficulties of doing justice to all of her responsibilities without feeling guilty and/or inadequate may require the opportunity for periodic discussions with a sympathetic, understanding person.

Problems may arise because of differences between the expectations of the parents and the day-care personnel in regard to the child's behavior. If the child has learned to dress and to feed himself or herself more adequately at the center, the parents should be encouraged to expect the same independent behavior at home. This may create a problem for the parent who finds satisfaction in the child's dependency and feels threatened by his or her developing independence. Sometimes the family sets no limitations on the child's behavior and the day-care center institutes some controls. Sometimes the reverse is true and the center will encourage more freedom than the parents are comfortable in accepting. As one parent said, "Children are taught to talk up and talk back to adults in day care. We don't think that's right. Children should show more respect to adults."

Since the day-care facility inevitably impacts on the socialization of the developing child, ethnic and religious group in the community are sensitive to potential conflicts between what is taught in the day-care facility as it might conflict with what is taught the child at home. Blacks and Orthodox Jews have developed day-care centers under their own community sponsorship to ensure continuity of what children are taught at home. This suggests the need for sensitivity on the part of the social worker as well as the whole day-care staff to cultural differences between themselves and the families of the children they serve.

Social workers in day care need to be aware of some of the general disadvantages of congregate day care for children. The sizable number of children dealt with requires some regulation of behavior. Some kinds of behavior must be encouraged by day-care personnel and other kinds of behavior discouraged if they are to retain control and their sanity. Studies by Prescott and Jones (1971) indicate that "programs in day-care centers are marked by an absence of strong feelings and of activities that might evoke them. Many staff members appear to be afraid that open expression of strong desires in the form of anger, dependency, or abandoned exuberance would lead to behavioral contagion and chaos" (p. 55). There is less access to adults, less opportunity to meet highly individual needs in privacy away from the group, less possibility of contact with a wider range of age mates, more scheduling, and more control than is experienced in the home.

Throughout the contact with the family, the caseworker tried to help the parents with problems in childrearing that, in time, would be likely to affect the child's adjustment to day care:

> A mother of a three-year-old had been finding his thumb-sucking a problem. She first taped the child's thumb to the rest of his hand and, when that failed, applied a bitter chemical which had been recommended by the drugstore. When she learned more about the meaning of thumb-sucking to the child, she was able to deal with it with less rigidity, and could feel less guilty and tense about the behavior, which she had thought was an indication of her failure as a mother [Merriam, 1959, p. 25].

Changes in the home situation may be reflected in changes in the child's behavior in day care. Discussing such changes with the parents helps them to understand how changes in the home are affecting the child. A father may have recently lost his job and may be acting more impatiently toward the child at home, resulting in the child's becoming more withdrawn. A grandparent may have died, making the child appear depressed or anxious in the center.

Here, as in other child welfare services, casework acts to help the client learn what is expected behavior in a new and unfamiliar social role: for the mother and father, the role of partial parent; for the child, the role of member of a day-care group. Once having accepted the designated role, the parents and the child are helped to enact it effectively.

Social workers associated with day-care centers lead parent education and discussion groups.

At intervals social workers may evaluate with parents the child's progress at the center and the changes that need to be made to more effectively meet the needs of the child. Evaluation might also include a discussion of where the parents stand with reference to the family's use of the center, of whether use of the facility continues to be the best plan in meeting the family's needs.

Social workers are involved in active efforts to reduce any tendency of parents to abdicate responsibility for childrearing by involving them in participation in center programs. Parents may be helped to participate in day-care program decisions, or they may volunteer to assist in program activity or join parent education and discussion groups. All of this helps to integrate the different environments— home and center—in which the child lives.

Part of the caseworker's responsibility lies in service to the staff in contact with the child, as well as to the family. Rather than being directly involved in service to day-school children or their parents, social workers often act as consultants to the staff in identifying children with emotional disorders, in managing difficult children, and in interacting with resistant parents. As a consultant, one social worker may serve a number of different day-care programs (Radin & Jordan, 1977). The social worker also mediates conflicts between the child-care staff and parents. Mrs. C. felt she was being criticized and abused by the child-care worker if she came late to pick Michael up. While recognizing her strong feelings about this, the social worker explained to Mrs. C. the problems faced by the staff when parents failed to pick up their children.

In liaison between the day-care programs and the community, social workers can make available and activate needed resources, interpret the service and its needs to the community, and help generate and mobilize the support of a pro-day-care constituency.

What seems to be a much needed and desirable service, in line with the responsibility of social work to link people with resources, is an information and referral service, which would provide a family with an overview of the various kinds of day-care resources in the community: location, price range, facilities, size of staff, number of children in the group, and so on. Social workers have helped develop such resources in many communities.

Casework can also contribute to the successful termination of service. Termination may result from situational factors, such as the family's moving, the mother's remarriage, or the mother's return to the home full-time. It may come as a result of the child's growing beyond the age when family day care or group day care is appropriate. It may come because it seems clear that either the child or the family is not able to use the service effectively.

Withdrawal from the service is often relatively easy, especially if the child is leaving, along with other children in his or her group, at the end of a semester. On occasion, however, the reorganization in the life of the child and the family occasioned by termination of service may require some preparation and discussion. If the contact has been satisfactory, the child is likely to have developed relationships of some intensity with the teacher or the family-day-care mother and the peer group of which he or she has been a part. It is not easy to give this up without some sense of loss.

Social workers in day care then use casework, groupwork, and community organization skills to prepare the child and the parents for the effective use of the facility. They work with child, parents, and day-care center personnel in dealing with problems relating to the child in the facility and advocate for the family and for day-care needs with the general community.

Much of what has been said relates both to group day care and to family day care. There are some special features of social work in family day care that must be recognized, however.

Family day care shares many similarities with foster care, generally. It involves, as does foster care, a process of recruitment, evaluation, and selection of day-care parents. The sources of recruitment and the process of selection are similar. Some agencies find that with few exceptions, their "foster family home and family day-care home are really interchangeable" (Jackson, n.d., p. 4).

Some special aspects of family day care, however, evolve because the child returns home every night. Thus contact between the day-care parent and the child's own parent is frequent and regular, so that although the day-care mother is less deeply involved with the child than is the foster mother, she has a tendency to be more deeply involved with the child's mother. And because the child experiences separation every day and lives, in effect, in two homes, he or she might need help in integrating the two major experiences in his life.

Casework with child and mother is similar to that in group day care in that the family is helped to resolve problems that might reduce satisfactory use of the resource:

Johnny, aged twenty-two months, was a relatively easy child to get along with after his mother left him in the day-care home. He ate and slept well and played contentedly with the toys. As soon as his mother appeared on the scene, however, he ran rampant—jumping on furniture, touching things on tables which had been prohibited, and so on. So serious was his behavior when the mother brought and called for him that the day-care mother didn't feel she could continue to care for him unless the mother began taking some responsibility for disciplining him. It was her impression that the mother never said "no" to him, and never corrected him. There was no question but what Johnny was making life difficult for her but she did nothing about it.

Contact with the mother revealed that because she felt so guilty about leaving Johnny (her relatives all disapproved of her plan to work even though father was in service), she tried to make it up to him by keeping the time they were together free of restrictions and discipline. She wanted it to be a happy, carefree period. Of course it was not. Not only was Johnny's behavior at home upsetting, but he was sleeping poorly and was chronically constipated. It had not occurred to the mother that her indulgence was confusing the child.

With the help of the caseworker, she was able to see how important it was that what was expected of the child in each of his two homes be as consistent as possible. She was helped to see, too, for the first time, perhaps, that parenthood carries with it the responsibility for setting the "do's" and "don't's" which are the basis of habit and character formation in children [Golten, 1945, p. 58].

Informal, private arrangements may result in dissatisfaction that might be resolved by an intermediary. Family caregivers may be resentful and disdainful of the mother's decision to work. They may see the working mother as irresponsible: "Delayed payments, inattention to scheduled pickup time" (Wattenberg, 1977, p. 223), and lack of appreciation of the caregiver's function may result in friction.

Social workers have been active in recruiting and training family day-care providers, in providing a support system, and in making the community aware of their availability (Emlen et al., 1971; Sulby & Diodati, 1975; Collins & Watson, 1976; Wattenberg, 1977). Such efforts have been stimulated by the recognition that the family-day-care system is a private entrepreneurial system, largely unlicensed and largely unsupervised, offered by isolated caregivers. Community responsibility toward families would suggest a need for some accountability as to standards and performance.

The fact that specialized social work functions are an important component of day care for the *limited* number of families who *might* need it is recognized in the Federal Interagency Day Care Requirements, suggested but ultimately not adopted, which state that in order to be eligible for support, a day-care center should offer social services. The Department of Health, Education, and Welfare defined social services in day care as "any supportive services apart from actually caring for the child that serve to enhance the functioning of the family as a unit as well as the individuals within it." Although such services are not regarded as a core component of day care, the department argued for their inclusion, since "many child care experts believe no short-term intervention program, regardless of its superiority, can succeed in supporting the age-appropriate cognitive, social, emotional and physical development of a child whose family is overwhelmed by its socioeconomic plight" or other problems. "A comprehensive Social Services component that supports family functioning is necessary to promote the well-being of this child" (p. 82).

In empirical support of its recommendation, the department cited a case study of 450 day-care families conducted in nineteen states in 1977. "Interviews with these clients indicated that approximately one-fourth needed help in (1) getting medical care, (2) getting a better job, (3) getting job training or schooling, (4) getting information on services offered in the community and (5) finding a case-worker or psychiatrist. About three-fourths of these individuals sought help from a social service office" (pp. 82–83).

In recommending a social service component in day-care facilities that receive any federal funds, some specific tasks were assigned to these workers. These included (1) "counseling and guidance to the family in helping it determine the appropriateness of day care, the best facility for a particular child, and the possibility of alternative plans for care"; (2) "coordination and cooperation with other organizations offering these resources which may be required by the child and his family" and providing the information and referral which would enable the the family effectively to use such resources; (3) "continuing assessment with the parents of the child's adjustment in the day care program and of the family situation"; (4) objective determination "of the ability of families to pay for part or all of the cost of day care and for payment" (pp. 241–42).

This information is still a pertinent validation of the need for social work in day care despite the fact that these federal interagency day care requirements have not been adopted for implementation. After repeated postponement of the implementation of the carefully formulated federal interagency day care requirements, they were finally repealed in the Omnibus Budget Reconciliation Act of 1981.

Similarly Head Start guidelines indicate that every Head Start program have a social service program to link the center with the family and the related community services and resources. The social worker in Head Start is charged with the responsibility of being a "strong advocate in obtaining services from local agencies and in referring families to them." Where needed services do not exist, he or she should "work to develop more effective social services" (U.S. Department of Health, Education and, Welfare, 1967).

The social worker in the day-care center thus acts as liaison between the center and the family, the center and the community, and the family and the community. The worker helps inform the families about relevant community programs and refers them to services they may need, as well as counseling parents on family planning, nutrition, health care, and family budgeting, and providing them with information about food stamp programs. Medicaid, employment, housing, and public assistance (Archinard, 1971). (See also Strathy, Heinicke, & Hauer, 1974.)

A study of the interpersonal relationships between parents and caregivers in twelve Detroit area day-care centers indicates the need for social services (Powell, 1978). The study indicated that "much interpersonal exchange between parents and caregivers is superficial in content . . . family-related topics are discussed infrequently . . . with few attempts to coordinate children's" experiences in the home and the center (p. 687). About half of the parents felt that "family problems should be discussed with center staff as a general principle" (p. 685), but some 40 per cent of the parents perceived the caregivers as reluctant to discuss parent-initiated topics.

In a follow-up study of forty-two families involved in a demonstration project in family day care, twenty-nine clients indicated that they were helped by the caseworker in "understanding the child's behavior . . . relieving strain . . . adjusting to [the client's] new life . . . [and] getting . . . [the] child established in nursery school" (Foster Family Day Care, 1962, p. 11). A detailed study of the need for casework services in a California day-care center indicated that of the 197 families using the center, about 70 families acknowledged concern over some family problem, though only 23 families actually asked for help. The parents who sought help were concerned about "children's aggressiveness, hyperactivity, temper, excessive demands, [and] attention-getting behavior" (Rapoport & Cornsweet, 1969, p. 11).

The social work component in day care, as described in *Standards for Day-Care Service,* published by the Child Welfare League of America (1984), and as reviewed in this chapter, exists in only a limited percentage of day-care centers. There is a wide gap between the literature and the actuality. Prescott et al. (1972), who did an intensive study of day-care centers in California, note that the "social work component as described in the Child Welfare League of America Standards for Day Care is virtually nonexistent. . . . The literature on day care has been concerned primarily with day care as it ought to be or as it has been assumed to exist."

Only a limited number of social workers are employed in day care. Ruderman (1968) notes in her study that "only 7 per cent of the day-care centers have the regular services of a social worker" (p. 102). Ruderman's findings are confirmed by a study of ninety-eight hospitals operating child-care facilities for use of their personnel: "Only 7 percent indicated they provided any type of social service for the family" (p. 13).

A national study of 3,100 day-care centers in the United States in the late 1970s indicates that "counseling on child development" was a service available in 86 per cent of the centers. However, other social services such as "counseling on family problems, providing assistance in obtaining food stamps or financial aid, and providing assistance in obtaining community service are least often available in proprietary centers" (Coeler, Craig, Glantz, & Calone, 1979, p. 330). These services were most often available in nonprofit centers enrolling families who were subsidized for day care.

A total of 21 per cent of the centers employed a social worker, but here too there were sharp differences between different kinds of centers. Only 6 per cent of profit proprietary centers employed a social worker, but 39 per cent of nonprofit centers listed such a person (p. 37). In the case of centers in which social workers were not employed, such service might be obtained from other community agencies or on a consulting basis.

Social workers are almost totally absent from direct involvement in the family day-care system. They provide training and attempt to organize day-care providers so that they can be registered for community information and referral services. In a very limited number of instances social workers are part of the family day-care subsystem that consists of the network of homes affiliated with, or under the auspices of, some agency. A budgetary breakdown of the costs of this network subsystem indicated that 6 per cent of the budget is allocated to social services (Fosberg, 1981, p. 117).

The limited number of social services in day-care programs derives from a variety of factors. The programs are operated on limited funds. The first priority is, necessarily, personnel with training and experience in child development and preschool education who work directly with the children. Social work is an adjunctive service, and although day-care programs operate better with it, they can operate without it. The social worker, as a noncaregiver specialist, is regarded as dispensable. Only a limited number of programs have enough funds to permit inclusion of the social services. Teachers often attempt to do social work themselves or seek consultation with a social worker serving a number of programs.

Despite the formal allocation of some responsibilities to social workers, day-care-center teachers do a good deal of informal social work. Because they are in contact with parents when they bring and pick up the child, the teachers establish a relationship that sometimes includes support and counseling (Joffe, 1977, pp. 60–61). Whereas all children in the program need the services of day-care teachers and attendants, only a limited number of children and families need social services. Where a sizable percentage of the families need them, there has been a tendency to see indigenous paraprofessionals—people from the local community employed by the center—as capable of providing them (Radin & Jordan, 1977, p. 168).

Problems

1. Although the percentage of working mothers with young children will continue to increase, there is limited, though growing, public support for the development of day-care resources. An intensive study by the Child Welfare League of America (1962) of leaders in selected communities throughout the United States shows that "most respondents assigned day care moderate rather than high—or low—priority" (p.33).

In part, the priority accorded day care is a reflection of the general lack of knowledge about day-care needs and facilities and the low visibility such problems have, in contrast to the dramatic impact of juvenile delinquency and the problems of emotionally disturbed children or child abuse.

Day care is primarily a preventive program; the children served do not yet have any problems that are disturbing to the parents or the community, although these may develop later as a result of inadequate child care while the mother is working.

The Child Welfare League study (1962) suggests that the reluctance to support day-care services is also related to a negative view of the working mother—the view that she is working because she chooses to do so and/or because she is not primarily concerned with or interested in the care of her children. One respondent said, "Nothing should be done to encourage any further tendency for mothers to find excuses for avoiding the responsibilities of caring for their children." Another said, "I am strongly opposed to any measure aimed at making private or government agencies devices to have mothers unload their responsibility for their children so they can work" (p. 83).

Although there is a gradual erosion of such attitudes as more women work and the ideology of affirmative action and undifferentiated sex roles gain currency, powerful residuals of this attitude still remain. The hesitancy and ambivalence generated by this attitude act as a brake on the expansion of day care.

Conflicting basic values and options come into competition in day care. The work ethic and belief in family responsibility for self-support come into conflict with conviction that the best childrearing requires continual presence of the mother in the home.

There is a lack of a strong national consensus on the legitimacy of governmental support of day-care programs and a lack of commitment to provide the necessary funding. The ambivalence in national consensus was expressed in the listing of recommendation of the 1980 White House Conference on Children. Three of the 60 recommendations related to the support of day care. However, these recommendations were listed as 43, 44, 45—rather low on the list of priorities.

To some extent the debate has been settled by the march of events. Mothers of young children as a part the work force is a fact that won't go away. The question is not whether or not we are going to need and have day care, but rather about the kind and the adequacy of the day care that we are going to inevitably need.

Some people question publicly funded day care because they think public policy should support the mothering needs of preschool children by encouraging mothers to remain at home—the original purpose of the AFDC program. Some question it because it does not make much economic sense in the use of public dollars. Recognizing that good, comprehensive day care may be very expensive,

> it may make more economic sense to pay this to parents to be good child rearers rather than to ask them to surrender the care of their children to others. It would seem that the burden rests on those favoring effective day care to show that children are made better off by being placed in high-quality, high-cost, developmental day care rather than being kept at home with parents to whom are transferred the resources that otherwise would be used in that day care. Parental love is hard to buy [Krashinsky, 1973, p. 168].

Public support of day care involves a number of complicated policy issues. There are questions about what kinds of day-care arrangements should be supported, what groups in the community should get such support, and how such support should be offered. Should public support be given to the informal network of family day care that currently supplies a large percentage of out-of-home care for the children of working mothers? If so, how is it to be regulated? Should subsidies be given to all families with children in day care, to public-assistance families only, or to poverty-level families and the working poor as well? Should the purpose of day care be primarily to reduce the number of AFDC recipients, to provide compensatory education, to further women's rights to determine their life-styles, or a combination of all of these? Should support be in the form of subsidies to day-care operators, of vouchers to parents for use at a day-care facility of their choice, or of tax credits?

There is only limited consensus among the groups supporting day care because they have different motivations (Steiner, 1976), and there is considerable public opposition to government-funded day care (Bruce-Briggs, 1977, Boles, 1980).

2. The Child Welfare League (1962) also found that most respondents preferred some form of in-home individual care by a relative, reducing support for day care:

> Child care has always been a family responsibility and if the child's own mother is unable to care for him the traditional solution has always been an approximation of maternal care . . . in the child's own home, involving other members of the family. This is customary and seems natural. Other arrangements, perhaps, especially organized ones, have been less common and therefore may seem strange or unnatural [p. 49].

Paying for child care makes people uneasy because it contradicts the usual family arrangement of child care out of concern and love. The private family-day-care arrangement, which the mother organizes for herself with some neighboring person, although it has contractual and financial elements, resembles the mutual aid system of an extended family. Hence it is ideologically a more acceptable alternative to group care. Additional reasons for opposition were the lack of personal attention they anticipated for their children, the fact that it was likely to be excessively structured and too much like a school, the danger to a child's health of group care, and the fact that their child was likely to be in contact with children from "less adequate families" (Ruderman, 1968, pp. 315–317).

3. There is a problem in deciding the desirable balance of investment and effort in a day-care center and the informal, but much more extensive, system of the individually operated family day care. Agencies and professionals in the field favor an expansion of day-care centers because they control these facilities and they can implement a program for which their training has prepared them. Family day care is controlled by amateurs and eludes supervision and regulation, but it is and will continue to be used by many families.

Emlen (1971), closely studying family day care over a number of years, found that mothers prefer child care "within three blocks of home," "within five minutes of home," "within easy walking distance of home," "in the immediate neighborhood," "near enough so that my older children can join the little ones after school." He reports that many of the mothers also prefer family day care "not only because it was physically convenient, flexibly accommodating, socially approachable, and consumer controllable, but also because it is perceived, and correctly so, as a comfortable and familiar setting in which the working mother finds a responsible, nurturant caregiver who is capable of providing love and comfort as well as new social learning" (pp. 178–179). Still, many of the mothers would prefer group day care, if it were available, because of its greater continuity and its provision of better learning opportunities (Ruderman, 1968; Willner, 1969; Keyserling, 1972).

Family day care is frequently brought to the family's attention through a newspaper advertisement or a notice tacked up on the local supermarket bulletin board. Although professionals may tend to deplore such informal arrangements, Emlen et al. (1971) found that the majority are not so bad as people suppose, and the sample reported in this study reveals an environment for children the potentialities of which are favorable enough to justify an organized effort to strengthen this type of care as a major resource for day care" (p. 3). The researchers note "that it is fallacious to assume that family day care is inevitably poor if it is not supervised by a social agency" (Collins & Watson, 1969, p. 528). Despite some clearly hazardous examples, many of the family-day-care mothers are personally adequate and capable of meeting the needs of children. (see above p. 181).

Because informal family day care will continue to be used by working mothers, professionals concerned with child care are making efforts to help improve it. The Neighborhood Day Care Exchange Project in Portland, Oregon, locates women interested in providing day care in their homes, offers them training and consultation in child care, and puts them in touch with mothers needing day care for their children (Collins & Watson, 1976).

Recent efforts also include special publications and newsletters developed by state departments of public welfare for distribution to day-care mothers, special training programs developed by community colleges in cooperation with public welfare agencies, and the development of day-care homes as satellites of day-care centers, with training of the day-care mothers by the day-care center.

4. There are still residuals of the association of day care with public welfare. This image of the day-care center is reinforced by the fact that because public day-care resources are in short supply, they are often reserved (through eligibil-

ity requirements) for low-income families, single-parent families, and families on public assistance.

The day-care placement of children of many social agency clients is somewhat different from the general public use of day care. Many social agency clients are provided with day care funded by Title XX or A.F.D.C. allocations for social services. The agency makes payment directly to the day-care provider in many instances. Consequently, a larger percentage of children of social agency clients' working mothers are likely to be found in licensed and regulated day-care centers; fewer are in family day-care facilities, and fewer are cared for in their own homes. Socioeconomic segregation often means racial segregation as well. Thus public day-care programs tend to serve children of low-income nonwhite families, whereas proprietary day-care centers, supported by fees from parents, tend to serve middle-class white families. Whereas middle-income families are "defined" out of publicly supported facilities, low-income families are "priced" out of proprietary facilities. Minority-group children and children of single-parent households are, in fact, heavily overrepresented in nonproprietary day-care centers.

The association between day care and welfare led to a reluctance on the part of some families, noted during World War II, to apply for day care if this had to be done through a social agency (Guyler, 1942). It has been suggested that information about and application for day care should be handled by some agency with more neutral connotations for the public, an agency that is more directly related to the situation that usually prompts the needs for day care, such as the employment services.

5. Another problem is posed by the question of responsibility for day care. Day care meets the definition of a child welfare service. It is an institution organized in response to a social problem, and the social role changes in relation to it. Yet the profession of social work is not certain that it has responsibility for day care. As Host (1963) says, "Too often the recent social work graduate has expressed surprise when day care is described as a child welfare service" (p. 3). And Kuhlmann (1955) notes, "Day care has not yet arrived at the place in the child welfare field where it is viewed as an essential social work program" (p. 23). Although this was written in 1955, it appears to be essentially true today.

Some argue that responsibility for day care should be delegated to the educational institutions rather than to the social service organizations. They note that the school is accepted in all communities as a center for child care; that the school district has an established administrative organization and the housing and the playground space for such centers; that it has available personnel who can assist in the organization, the supervision, and the training of staff; that, in effect, the day-care center merely extends the educational system downward (to include a younger group) and outward (to lengthen the school day of older children).

The problem of responsibility for day care is compounded by other considerations. Although day care meets the criteria for inclusion in any listing of child welfare services, it requires the joint cooperative activity of three professions—health, education, and social work—for effective implementation. Each of these, consequently, has a vested interest in the service. As it stands, however, day care currently belongs more to the commercial-proprietary group than it does to any of the professions. This raises a problem of social policy.

It is argued that the care and the concomitant education of children (because all care involves some education, however informal) should be matters of public concern and support; that permitting day care to develop largely in the hands of proprietary-commercial interests is irresponsible; and that child-care centers ought to represent a community investment in its families rather than a business venture.

The fact that day care has a variety of different possible goals presents a problem of identification. Industry sees day care as desirable in providing a larger and more dependable female labor force; government officials see day care as helpful in moving people off welfare and into employment; educators see day care as early compensatory education that will prepare disadvantaged children more adequately for school; health officials see day care as a case-finding procedure that will bring to light health deficiencies in young children; women's groups see day care as providing women more alternative options in life-styles; social workers see day care as ensuring adequate care and protection for the child whose parents both work. The working mother sees child care as a dependable, stable source of care for her child, giving the child the opportunity of playing with age mates under the supervision of people who are competent to offer some education and training as well. This diversity has resulted in attempts by the different professions involved to incorporate day care within their own particular spheres of influence. As a supplementary parental care facility, it has a social work goal; as a supplementary or compensatory educational program, it belongs to education; as a facility for the physically or mentally handicapped, it can be viewed as a public health resource. Consequently not only are there differences in orientation among health workers, educators, and social workers as to what is important in day care, but there is competitive disagreement concerning who should control the day-care "turf."

6. A problem that has been generally slighted is the need for supervision and care of the school-aged child of working parents (Harris, 1977). Studies show that the mother often has to leave for work before the child has breakfasted and is ready for school, and that she is not available to the child during lunch or between the time school lets out and the end of the work day. School holidays and vacations are a problem, for they do not always coincide with work holidays and vacations. When the child is ill and out of school, most mothers absent themselves from work—at an anxiety-provoking loss of pay for the mother who is the head of a family.

These problems raise the question of public policy with reference to an extended school day. Such measures have been advocated in some communities where there is considerable concern about "latchkey" children: school-aged children who wear a latchkey on a cord, which symbolizes their responsibility for themselves while their parents are at work.

"Children-in-self-care" is replacing the phrase "latchkey children" to identify those school-age children who are left alone to care for themselves after school because their working parents are not available.

Garbarino (1980) noted that the risks associated with self-care by such children are of four types: (1) they will feel badly rejected, alienated, or frightened; (2) they will be treated badly (accidents and sexual victimization); (3) they will develop badly (fail school, not develop full potential, because they are bored and not stimulated); and (4) they will act badly (delinquent or vandal acts).

Some working mothers maintain a sense of their presence with latchkey children by calling home or having the child call them for a short chat at a regular time in the afternoon. "Phone-Friend" hotlines provide information, counsel, and support to children who are alone at home and who want to talk to somebody. Check-in programs enroll a neighbor to keep an eye on a school-age child whose mother works.

A bill was passed in 1984 authorizing the expenditure of $20 million of federal funds for programs for children-in-self-care. However, the administration did not seek funds to finance the program. Local schools are reluctant to use much needed funds to finance programs to meet the needs of latchkey children (*New York Times*, September 16, 1985).

7. Ideally day care should be available to any mother who needs to work, wants to work, or merely wants to share the care of her child.

The most desirable child-care arrangement is physically convenient, flexibly accommodating, socially approachable, consumer controllable, and economically affordable. It provides adequate care and protection of children, and meets the child's physical, cognitive, emotional, and social developmental needs. But the actual situation is far different.

The family that has the greatest difficulty is the one whose income is just high enough to render it ineligible for publicly supported day care but too low to permit proprietary day care. For this family, the working poor, the mother's employment is often a clear economic necessity.

Shortage of trained staff is endemic. Low salaries make difficult the recruitment of adequate numbers of adequately trained people. The low status of day-care providers and pay rates at minimum levels ensure that only a limited number of people with adequate training will be available to do this work. The *Dictionary of Occupational Titles* ranks child-care workers on the same level as parking-lot attendants.

A study of wages and benefits received by child care workers in New York State day care centers found that they were "paid less than zoo keepers, hotel clerks and bartenders" (*New York Times*, November 24, 1986). The job of caring for children in the centers were described as "minimum wage jobs—often below the poverty line," resulting in high turnover. These jobs prove of little interest to college graduates.

Frequently care is not available when the mother needs it. Many women— hospital nurses, waitresses, hotel maids, telephone operators, saleswomen—work weekends or evenings. Yet very few centers are open seven days a week, twenty-four hours a day.

8. There is a bewildering array of sources of government support for day care. Manpower and training legislation make funds available to increase the supply of personnel; educational legislation makes funds available to provide compensatory education; social security legislation provides funds to reduce dependence on welfare; housing and urban development legislation and model cities legislation make funds available to achieve the purpose of urban change. Community groups seeking sources of support need considerable expertise in merely knowing where and how to apply for funds. The multiplicity of sources of funding and aims creates a problem for the day-care services.

There is a problem regarding who should be eligible to apply for federal funds in support of day care. Community-action groups argue that they should be eligible to initiate applications for such funds. Direct access by each community-based group is opposed by others because they regard such a procedure as administratively difficult and inefficient. It could mean that the federal government would have to deal with thousands of different community groups to which it might grant funds directly. Consequently it is argued that only state or city governments should be permitted to act as "prime sponsors" in applications for and distribution of such funds. Community-action groups argue in rebuttal that such a procedure may be administratively more efficient but that it also permits tighter control of funds so that the more miltant social-action groups can be "frozen out."

9. There is a problem in determining the quality of child care provided. Many of the most important elements—concern, empathy, understanding, patience, acceptance, and the like are nebulous. These elements are not easily codified and identified. Assessing the quality of child care accurately requires repeated observations of caretaking behavior with the aid of some standardized instrument. Furthermore, there is no overwhelming consensus on necessary attributes of the quality of care configuration.

10. There is a question of how comprehensive and integrative child-care programs should be. At its most comprehensive, a program can meet the social, educational, mental, and health needs of the child. At its least, comprehensive, child care can provide physical care and protection. Expanding comprehensiveness increases cost and reduces the number of slots available. Decreasing comprehensiveness denies the child services and programs that are necessary for healthy physical, social, and emotional development.

11. There is a perennial problem around adequate funding of publicly supported day-care resources. Day care was the principal social service supported by Title XX funds in 1980. In that year, some $650 million of Title XX funds helped subsidize care for 750,000 low- and moderate-income children in licensed child-care centers and family day-care homes.

Between 1980 and 1983, combined total federal and state spending for Title XX child care dropped 14 per cent. In many states publicly funded day-care resources were reduced. Before, 1982 legislation relating to Title XX funding required that a certain minimum be set aside specifically for day care. When Title XX became a block grant in 1982, this requirement was deleted.

Staff provided by the Comprehensive Employment and Training Act (CETA) at little or no extra cost to the day-care center were lost with the abolishment of the program. Cuts in the U.S. Department of Agriculture child-care food programs meant that day-care centers had to find other sources to fund adequate feeding of day-care center children.

Reduced funding has resulted in tightened eligibility requirement for subsidized day care, more limited training for day-care staff, reduction in staff, relaxation of day-care standards, and the provision of less adequate food for children in day care.

The largest single public expenditure for day care is in the form of dependent care tax credits. Some 6 million families were claiming such a credit in 1984 at the cost to the government of $1.5 billion in lost taxes. Because the credit is related to computing taxes owed the government, low-income families that pay limited taxes are not advantaged by the tax credit.

With a reduction in subsidies, a two-tier system may emerge, one group of centers paid for by those who can afford the best and another for low-income families who cannot support a well-qualified staff and adequate facilities.

12. There is a problem of concern about the possible sexual abuse of children in day care despite the overall limited number of such incidents reported. Day-care personnel and baby-sitters were involved in less than 2 per cent of the reports of sexual abuse collated in the 1982 reports to the American Humane Association.

In response to these concerns legislation has been adopted requiring that checks of arrest records be made of all day care personnel and of those applying for day care positions.

Many different problems are involved in decisions regarding the dismissal of day-care personnel in response to record checks. Decisions need to be made in cases of staff members who have been arrested but not convicted, and those convicted of crimes that have nothing to do with sexual activity. Questions are raised regarding discrimination against former offenders who have since committed no crime, and the violation of privacy rights in day-care agency access to their records.

For the day-care centers such checks are expensive and time consuming. Many cases need to be reviewed to uncover a very small number of possibly injurious staff. Such screening may fail to uncover some potentially harmful staff. For instance, New York conducted screening of 20,000 employees using the child abuse registry and found only 7 employees about whom there might be some concern.

Highly publicized reports about sexual child abuse in day-care centers have resulted in increased costs of running such facilities. Procedures for screening potential abusers make hiring more costly and difficult. In addition, liability insurance premiums paid by day-care centers were substantially increased. In some instances day-care centers were forced to close because of increased insurance costs or because no company was willing to insure them (*N.A.S.W. News*, September 1985, p. 14).

Trends

1. The change in women's employment situation has been revolutionary, but cultural attitudes are changing more slowly. However, there is a growing acceptance of the fact that mothers' employment is "normal," that in most cases it is necessary, that it does not reflect child neglect, and that it is not necessarily harmful to the child. All this suggests a trend toward greater concern with the need for day care and a greater acceptance of day care.

During the 1975–85 decade employment opportunities increased for women faster than they did for men. The gradual continued anticipated increase of mothers working will result in a continuing increase in the number of children needing day care.

The sentiment that determined President Nixon's veto, in 1971, of a bill that would have substantially expanded day-care resources—namely, that it "would commit the vast moral authority of the National Government to the side of communal approaches to a child rearing over against the family centered approach" (*New York Times*, December 10, 1971)—is still prevalent.

In opposition to this feeling that day care might "undermine the American family," there is growing acceptance of the idea that day care might, in fact, help to strengthen the family by facilitating mothers' employment, by intervening to prevent the development of problems in parent–child relationships, and by providing the possibility of maintaining children in the community who might otherwise have to be institutionalized. There is growing recognition that failure to build an adequate number of day-care centers does not result in a reduction of the number of mothers working but merely leads to less adequate arrangements for the care of children.

It is easy, however, to exaggerate the depth of this trend. Public funding of day care for all families who want and can use it would signal a major shift in the relative distribution of responsibility between parents and community for the care and the socialization of America's children. Traditionally, and currently, the principal responsibility for the care and the socialization of the preschool child has rested with the family. Even for the older child, communal responsibility has been narrowly defined as being concerned with his or her education during a limited segment of each day. As a consequence of an extensive public day-care program, the community would begin to share with the parent earlier and more extensive responsibility for the child.

2. There is increasing acceptance of the need for day-care services for expanded age groups. Professionals are increasingly accepting of day care for very young children, and there is a trend toward an expansion of day-care facilities for school-age children. The trend toward out-of-home infant care is stimulated and supported by special projects that have yielded reassuring results. Because care outside the home involves special hazards for the young child, many of the licensing regulations have previously forbidden group care for children younger than two. Preliminary reports now indicate that the needs of infants can be adequately met through group-care arrangements if they include sensible precautions and a high caretaker-child ratio. It is felt that caring for infants and toddlers in a group arrangement is acceptable if the center provides continuity of care by one caretaker for every three children and if the caretakers are warm, consistent, sensitive, and respectful of the child's individuality. Under such conditions, the consequences of "multiple mothering," "separation," and "maternal deprivation" are not likely to be encountered. This prescription is a difficult one to fill, and it is difficult to develop centers that provide, and continue to provide, these desirable conditions.

An increasing number of school districts have established an extended day program that provides care for children between the end of the official school day and the return home of a working parent. As an example of the extension of age groups involved in day care, one might cite the San Francisco's children's center program operated as a special division of the San Francisco Board of Education, which offers a program of day care for children aged two to twelve.

3. There is a trend toward a diversification of the auspices under which day care is offered. Employers have indicated interest in offering day care for the children of their employees because such a service might increase the recruitment of female workers, reduce absenteeism and job turnover, and improve labor relations. For the employee, it means being closer to the child during the day, reducing his or her anxiety and problems about finding day care, and providing continuity of care for the child. The children have contact with the world of work, the opportunity of seeing their parents in the work role, and a greater likelihood of contacts with males. Frequently hospitals operate such facilities for the use of their personnel. The U.S. Departments of Labor, of Agriculture, and of Health, and Human Services have provided similar facilities. The Ford Foundation has provided up to $15 a week as a child-care allowance for their employees with young children. "Children's Place at the Plaza" is a New York State facility for children of state employees in the New York State Capital in Albany. The United States Air Force has child-care centers at many of its bases.

Federal tax regulations enable companies to get a favorable tax break on monies spent in providing day care for children of their employees. By 1985, some two thousand five hundred corporations, triple the number of only three years earlier, underwrote some kind of child-care assistance for their employees. This includes such well-recognized names as IBM, AT&T, Polaroid, Procter & Gamble, and Campbell's Soup.

Employers have used a variety of different approaches in helping to meet the child-care needs of their employees. These include (1) information and referral service to locate child-care facilities for employees; (2) providing vouchers to help defray the cost of child care, (3) subsidizing local day-care centers which reserves space for children of employees; and (4) directly providing a day-care center on the employing premises.

Company expenditures for child care are seen by childless employees as an unequitable fringe benefit in which they do not share. In response, corporations offer a menu of benefits from which employees can choose those that have priority for them.

Reports from employers tend to confirm the fact that the provision of assistance regarding day care tends to improve recruitment efforts, productivity, work morale, and punctuality while reducing absenteeism, job turnover, and worker stress (Perry, 1982; Burud, Collins & Devine-Hawkins, 1983). At the same time there are very few reports of adverse effects of such efforts. The trend is toward a continuing increase in private sector employer-initiated child-care assistance programs.

Industries and services that employ a preponderance of women are most likely to have developed a child-care assistance program. These include textile firms and hospitals. In addition to providing assistance, concerning day care, some employers also assist their employees in reducing the incompatible strains between parental and employees roles by encouraging part-time work, flex-time, job sharing, offering liberal time-off policies regarding care of sick children, allowing phone calls home to latch-key children, and providing maternity and paternity leave following the birth of a child.

Trend, toward employer-sponsored day-care assistance are sufficiently well developed so that there is a book on the subject available (Adolf & Rose, 1985).

Flex-place, the option to work at home, which is increasing with the increased use of computers, is an additional procedure for reconciling the demands of the parenting and work roles.

In 1978, some 40 per cent of all day-care centers were propriatary, operated for profit. Although there is no recent tabulation of profit-making day-care centers, there is reason to believe that the percentage of proprietary day-care centers has increased since 1978.

Most proprietary day-care centers are small, independently owned and operated centers. A smaller number are part of a chain, often franchised.

There was a trend toward making day care a franchise operation. For instance, E. C. K. Chivers and Associates, which handles the franchise for such national operations as Black Angus Steak Houses and Lums, also handles the franchise of what it hoped would become a national network of Kindercare day-care centers. Similarly franchises are available nationwide for Mary Moppet day-care schools, La Petite Academy and Children's World.

By 1984, Kinder-care Learning Centers had established 850 centers nationwide. One franchise system has as its slogan "Laughter, Learning and Lots of Love." The founder of Kinder-Care has been called the "Colonel Sanders of Child Care" in imitation of Colonel Sanders of Kentucky Fried Chicken. The franchise operation and employer-sponsored day care sometimes come together. Ohio Bell Telephone and Western Electric contracted with Singer Learning Centers, a franchise operation, to establish and operate day-care centers for their employees.

Some real estate developers have included day-care centers in new housing areas as an additional incentive to young couples to rent or buy. The day-care center, like the community swimming pool, becomes part of the package of "amenities."

4. There is a trend toward greater explicit diversification of day-care facilities. Previously the literature made distinctions primarily between a day-care center and family day care and between nursery care with a primarily educational purpose and day care oriented more toward care and protection. Currently the literature identifies a "child-development center," a "play-group facility," a "preschool-child-care center," a "school-age-child-care center," a "family-day-care home," a "group-day-care home," a "family school-age-day-care home," and a "group school-age-day-care home." Distinctions revolve around the age and the size of the group offered service and the primary orientation of the facility.

Day-care networks or systems have been developed. They involve a systematic combination of different kinds of day-care facilities under some central administration. Thus a day-care center might develop a series of satellite family-day-care homes as part of its operation by recruiting, training, and offering consultation to the family-day-care mothers.

Diversification involves not only the different kinds of day-care facilities providing care for groups of different ages and sizes, but also timing. Because many women work at night, day-care centers in large cities have developed night-care centers and family-night-care homes.

5. The Head Start program confirmed and intensified the trend toward parental involvement in day-care-center activity. It also tended to enlarge the focus of such involvement. Head Start guidelines require the employment of parents as paraprofessionals and aides in the program whenever possible, and they require parent participation in day-care decision-making and administration. Similarly Federal Interagency Day Care Guidelines had required that whenever an agency provides day care for fifteen or more children, there must be a policy advisory committee or its equivalent at the administrative level where most decisions are made. The committee membership should include not less than 50 per cent parents or parent representatives, selected by the parents in a democratic fashion (Cohen & Zigler, 1977).

There are a number of considerations advanced in support of this emphasis on parent participation. It tends to reduce the separation between home and center for the child. If what is taught in the day-care center is substantially similar to what is taught at home, there is less change and greater continuity for the child in moving from the home to the center every day. This is particularly true if there are, to begin with, cultural and ethnic differences between the home and the day-care center. Through parent participation, involvement, and control, the service potentially strengthens the family rather than separating parent and child. Parent participation reduces the risks of alienating the parents and the center staff. It reduces the danger that parents will feel excluded from an important experience that affects their children, and it reduces the feeling on the part of staff that the children are being dumped. With greater parent participation, it is hoped that day care will strengthen rather than undermine the nuclear family. It might be seen as an extension of the family rather than competition—as another kind of extended-family support system.

Parents can be involved as board members of centers, as members of policy advisory councils, as volunteer workers, as employed paraprofessionals, or through regularly scheduled conferences with the center's staff. They should be encouraged to visit the center and observe its activities when they have an opportunity.

Even if the center staff sincerely desires to get the parents involved, this is often difficult. Parents have to allocate scarce time and energy to this activity.

They have to find baby-sitters and transportation for evening meetings. Zigler and Turner (1982) studied the amount of time parents spend at the child-care center. Most of the time spent occurred at the end of the day when the parents were picking up their children. The average time at the center was 7.4 minutes per day. In most instances (86 %) the mother of the child spent this time.

The level of involvement with child-care provider is likely to be greater in family day care than in day-care centers. The parent in selecting the provider had some recurrent contact and a beginning relationship with the provider.

6. There is a trend from in-home care for children of working mothers to out-of-home care. A study of trends in child-care arrangements of working mothers (Lueck, Orr, & O'Connell, 1982) showed that "there has been a shift away from in-home child care to care outside the home (typically in an unrelated person's home) or in group-care centers. This trend has been especially pronounced for children with well-educated mothers, full-time working mothers, and mothers with relatively high income levels who can afford to pay for child care services" (p. 3).

Whereas in 1958, 4.5 per cent of children under the age of six of ever-married, full-time working women were cared for in group care centers, this figure had increased to 14.6 per cent of such children in 1977. In 1958, 56.6 per cent of children under six of ever-married, full-time working women were cared for in the child's home. By 1977, this figure had dropped to 28.6 per cent (Lueck; Orr & O'Connell, 1982, Table A, p. 6).

As might be expected, out-of-home care is more frequent for children over the age of three than for children under 3 (Lueck, Orr, & O'Connell, 1982, p. 8).

7. There is a growing interest in developing day care for special groups: emotionally disturbed children, mentally handicapped children, and children of migrant workers. The care of such children requires special equipment and personnel with special training who are willing to devote extra time and energy to the children. Such day-care centers also make an explicit effort to involve the parents so that the training and/or the therapy achieved in the center is sustained and supported by the parents in the home. The National Association for Retarded Children has been very active and successful in extending day-care services to such children.

Bibliography

Abt Associates. *National Daycare Study—Preliminary Findings and Their Implications.* Cambridge, Mass.: Abt Associates, January 1978.

Adolf, Barbara and Koral Rose. *The Employers' Guide to Child Care—Developing Programs for Working Parents.* New York: Praeger, 1985.

Archinard, Enolia et al. "Social Work and Supplementary Services," in *Day Care: Resources for Decisions.* Ed. Edith H. Grotberg. Washington, D.C.: Day Care and Child Development Council of America, 1971.

Belsky, Jay. "Two Waves of Day Care Research: Developmental Effects and Conditions of Quality," pp. 1–33 in *The Child and The Day Care Setting,* Ed. R. C. Ainslie. New York: Praeger Publishers, 1984.

Belsky, Jay, Laurence Steinberg, and Ann Walker. "The Ecology of Day Care," pp. 71–116 in *Non Traditional Families: Parenting and Child Development,* Hillsdale, N.J.: Lawrence Erlbaum and Associates, 1982.

Berrueta-Clement, John R., et al. *Changed Lives: The Effects of the Perry Pre-School Program on Youths Through Age 19.* Ypsilanti, Mich.: The High Scope Press, 1984.

Blank, H. *Child Care: The States' Response: A Survey of State Child Care Policies, 1983–84.* Washington, D.C.: Children's Defense Fund, 1984.

Bloch, Judith. "A Preschool Workshop for Emotionally Disturbed Children." *Children,* 17, 1 (January–February 1970), 10–14.

Blum, Marian. *The Day Care Dilemma.* Lexington, Mass.: Lexington Books, 1983.

Boles, Janet K. "The Politics of Child Care." *Social Service Review* (September 1980), 344–361.

Bruce-Briggs, B. "Child Care: The Fiscal Time Bomb." *Public Interest,* 43 (Fall 1977), 88–102.

Burud, Sandra L., Raymond C. Collins, and Patricia Devine-Hawkins. "Employer Supported Child Care: Everybody Benefits." *Children Today* (May–June, 1983).

Caldwell, Bettye. "The Effects of Infant Care," pp. 9–87, in *Review of Child Development Research.* Ed. M. L. Hoffman and L. W. Hoffman. New York: Russell Sage Foundation, 1964.

Caldwell, Bettye. "What Does Research Teach Us About Day Care for Children Under Three?" *Children Today,* 1,1 (January–February 1972), 6–11.

Ceravolo, M. Florence. "The Crises Nursery—A Metropolitan Island of Safety," pp. 475–485 in *A Handbook of Child Welfare—Context Knowledge and Practice.* Ed. S. Laird and A. Hartman. New York: Free Press, 1985.

Child Welfare League of America. *Day Care Report.* New York, September 1962.

Child Welfare League of America. *Standards for Day-Care Services: Revised 1969.* New York, 1969.

Child Welfare League of America. *Standards for Day Care Service—Rev. ed.* New York: Child Welfare League of America, 1984.

Clarke-Stewart, Allison. *Child Care in the Family.* New York: Academic Press, 1977.

Clarke-Stewart, Alison, and Greta G. Fein. "Early Childhood Programs," pp. 917–999, in *Handbook of Child Psychology,* vol. II, 4th ed. Ed. Paul H. Mussen, New York: John Wiley & Sons, 1983.

Class, Norris E. "Licensing of Child Care Facilities by State Welfare Departments." *Children's Bureau Publication, No. 462.* Washington, D.C.: U.S. Government Printing Office, 1968.

Coeler, Craig, Frederic Glantz, and Daniel Calone. *Day Care Centers in the U.S.A. National Profile, 1976–1979.* Cambridge, Mass.: ABT Books, 1979.

Cohen, Donald, and Edward Zigler. "Federal Daycare Standards—Rationale and Recommendations." *American Journal of Orthopsychiatry,* 47, 3 (July 1977), 456–465.

Collins, Alice N., and Eunice L. Watson. "Exploring the Neighborhood Family Day Care System." *Social Casework* 50, 9 (November 1969), 527–533.

Collins, Alice N., and Eunice L. Watson. *Family Day Care.* Boston: Beacon Press, 1976.

Day Care Child Development Council of America. *Basic Facts About Licensing of Day Care.* Washington, D.C.: October 1970.

Emlen, Arthur. "Slogans, Slots and Slanders: The Myth of Daycare Need." *American Journal of Orthopsychiatry,* 43 (January 1973), 23–37.

Emlen, Arthur et al. *Child Care by Kith: A Study of the Family Day Care Relationships of Working Mothers and Neighborhood Caregivers.* Portland, Ore.: DCE Books, 1971.

Fosberg, Steven. *Family Day Care in the United States—vol. I: Summary of Findings.* DHHS Publication (OHDS) 80-30 282 Washington, D.C.: U.S. Government Printing Office, 1981.

Foster Family Day Care Service. *Follow-up Study of Foster Family Day Care.* New York: November 1962. Mimeo.

Fraiberg, Selma. *Every Child's Birth Right: In Defense of Mothering.* New York: Basic Books, 1977.

Fredrickson, H. "The Problem of Taking Care of Children of Employed Mothers." *Social Service Review,* 17 (1943).

Freud, Anna. "Nursery School Education—Its Uses and Dangers." *Child Study,* 26 (Spring 1949).

Garbarino, J. "Latchkey Children," *Vital Issues,* 30, 3 (1980) 1–4.

Gilfillan, Viola. "Day Care as a Therapeutic Service to Preschool Children and Its Potential as a Preventive Service." *Child Welfare,* 41, 9 (November 1962).

Goddard, Gladys. "Potentialities of Day Care." *Child Welfare,* 36, 10 (December 1957).

Golten, Margaret. "Family Day Care: What It Means for the Parent." *The Family,* 26, 4 (April 1945).

Gordon, Bertel. "Criteria for Determining Type of Placement." *Journal of Jewish Communal Service* (Spring 1957).

Granato, Sam J., and E. Dollie Lynch. "Day-Care Licensing." *Children Today* (January–February 1972), 23–24.

Greenblatt, Bernard. *Responsibility for Child Care.* San Francisco: Jossey-Bass, 1977.

Guerney, Louise, and Leila Moore. "Phone Friend: A Prevention-Oriented Service for Latch Key Children," *Children Today* (July, August 1983), 5–10.

Guyler, Cathryn. "Social Responsibility for the Development of Day Care," in *Proceedings of the National Conference of Social Welfare.* New York: Columbia University Press, 1942.

Hansan, J., and K. Pemberton. "Day-Care Services for Families with Mothers Working at Home." *Child Welfare,* 42 (April 1963).

Harris, Oliver C. "Daycare: Have We Forgotten the School Age Child?" *Child Welfare,* 56, 7 (July 1977), 440–448.

Hawkins, Patricia. *Family Day Care in The U.S. Exxecutive Survey National Day Care Home Study: Final Report.* Department of Health, Education and Welfare OHDS 80-30287, 191.

Hays, Cheryl D., and Sheila B. Kamerman. *Children of Working Parents—Experiences and Outcomes.* Washington, D.C.: National Academy Press, 1983.

Hoffman, Lois W. and Ivan F. Nye. *Working Mothers—An Evaluative Review of the Consequences for Wife, Husband and Child.* San Francisco, Jossey-Bass, 1974.

Host, Malcolm, and Patricia Hassett. "Day-Care Services and the Social Work Profession." *Social Work Education,* 11 (April 1963).

Jackson, Theresa. *Day-Care Services as Administered Under Various Auspices.* New York: Child Welfare League of America, n.d.

Jenkins, Shirley, and Mignon Sauber. *Paths to Child Placement.* New York: Community Council of Greater New York, 1966.

Joffe, Carole E. *Friendly Intruders-Child Care Professionals and Family Life.* Berkeley: University of California Press, 1977.

Kagan, Jerome, Richard B. Kearsley, and Philip R. Zelazo. "The Effects of Infant Day Care on Psychological Development." *Evaluation Quarterly,* 1,1 (February 1977), 109–141.

Kamerman, Sheila B., and Alfred J. Kahn. "The Day Care Debate: A Wider View." *The Public Interest,* 54 (Winter 1979), 76–93.

Kamerman, Sheila, and Cheryl D. Hayes. *Families That Work: Children in a Changing World.* Washington, D.C.: National Academy Press, 1982.

Kamerman, Sheila B.; Alfred J. Kahn, and Paul Kingston. *Maternity Policies and Working Women.* New York: Columbia University Press, 1983.

Keyserling, Mary D. *Windows on Day Care.* New York: National Council of Jewish Women, 1972.

Krashinsky, Michael. "Daycare and Welfare," in *Issues in the Coordination of Public Welfare Programs,* Paper No. 7. Subcommittee on Fiscal Policy. U.S. Congress Joint Economic Committee. Washington, D.C.: U.S. Government Printing Office, 1973.

Kuhlmann, Frieda M. "Casework Supervision in the Day Nursery." *Child Welfare.* 34 (March 1955).

Lamb, Michael E. "Parental Behavior and Child Development in Non-Traditional Families: An Introduction," pp. 1–12 in *NonTraditional Families: Parenting and Child Development.* Ed. Michael Lamb, Hillsdale, N.J.: Laurence Erlbaum, 1982.

Lovatt, Margaret. "Autistic Children in a Day Nursery." *Children,* 9 (May–June 1962).

Long, Lynette, and Thomas Long. *The Handbook for Latchkey Children and Their Parents.* New Rochelle, N.Y.: Arbor House, 1983.

Low, Seth. *Licensed Day-Care Facilities for Children: A Report of A National Survey of Departments of State Governments Responsible for Licensing Day Care Facilities.* Washington, D.C.: U.S. Government Printing Office, 1962.

Lueck, Marjorie, Ann C. Orr, and Martin O'Connell. *Trends in Child Care Arrangements of Working Mothers,* Washington, D.C.: Bureau of the Census, June 1982.

Lynden, Patricia. "What Does Day Care Mean to the Children, the Parents, the Teachers, the Community, the President?" *The New York Times Magazine* (February 15, 1970).

Merriam, Alice H. "Day Care of the Young Child: A Community Challenge." *Child Welfare,* 38 (October 1959).

National Association of Retarded Children. Leaflet DR741. New York, n.d.

National Society for the Study of Education. *Preschool and Parental Education, 28th Yearbook.* Bloomington, Ind.: Public School Publishing Co., 1929.

O'Connell, Joanne C. "Children of Working Mothers: What the Research Fills In." *Young Children,* 38, 2 (January 1983), 62–70.

O'Connell, Martin, and Carolyn C. Rogers. *Child Care Arrangements of Working Mothers.* June 1982, Washington, D.C.: Census Bureau, November 1983.

Ogberg, William, and Meyer Nimkoff. *Technology and the Changing Family.* Boston: Houghton Mifflin Company, 1955.

Perry, Kathryn S. *Employers and Child Care: Establishing Services through the Workplace.* Washington, D.C.: Department of Labor, Women's Bureau, August 1982.

Powell, Douglas R. "The Interpersonal Relationship Between Parents and Caregivers in Daycare." *American Journal of Orthopsychiatry,* 48, 4 (October 1978), 680–689.

Prescott, Elizabeth, and Elizabeth Jones. "Day Care for Children—Assets and Liabilities." *Children* 18, 2 (March–April 1971), 54–58.

Prescott, Elizabeth, Cynthia Milich, and Elizabeth James. *The Politics of Daycare.* Washington, D.C.: National Association for the Education of Young Children, 1972.

Radin, Norma, and Bonnie C. Jordan. "Child Welfare: Preschool Programs," pp. 156–169, in *Encyclopedia of Social Work,* 17th issue. Ed. John B. Turner. New York: National Association of Social Workers, 1977.

Rapoport, Lydia, and Donna M. Cornsweet. "Preventive Intervention Potentials in Public Child Care Centers." *Child Welfare,* 48,1 (January 1969), 6–13.

Rawley, Callman. "Casework and Day Care—Beginnings of a Municipal Program." *The Family,* 24 (March 1943).

Ruderman, Florence A. *Child Care and the Working Mother: A Study of Arrangements Made for Daytime Care of Children.* New York: Child Welfare League of America, 1968.

Russell, Alene B. and Cynthia M. Tralnor. *Trends in Child Abuse and Neglect—A National Perspective.* Denver, Colo.: American Humane Association, 1984.

Rutter, Michael. "The Social Emotional Consequences of Day Care for Pre-school Children." *American Journal of Orthopsychiatry,* 51 (January 1981).

Seifert, Kevin. "The Best Men for Child Care Work." *Child Care Quarterly,* 4 (Fall 1975), 188–193.

Shyne, Ann W. *The Need for Foster Care.* New York: Child Welfare League of America, 1969.

Smith, Allen. *Final Report of the National Day Care Center Study: Executive Summary of Children at the Center.* Cambridge, Mass.: ABT Associates, 1979.

Steiner, Gilbert Y. *The Children's Cause.* Washington, D.C.: The Brookings Institution, 1976.

Steinfels, Margaret. *Who's Minding the Children? The History and Politics of Day Care in America.* New York: Simon & Schuster, 1973.

Strathy, Esther, Christopher Heinicke, and Kayla Hauer. "The Role of the Social Worker in a Day Care Center." *Ries Davis Clinic Bulletin,* Spring 1974, pp. 25–37.

Subramanian, Karen. "Reducing Child Abuse Through Respite Center Intervention." *Child Welfare,* 64, 5 (September–October, 1985), 501–509.

Sulby, Arnold, and Anthony Diodati. "Family Day Care: No Longer Day Care's Neglected Child." *Young Children* (May 1975), 239–247.

Thenaud, Agnes. "Survey of Requests for Day Nursery Care with Reference to Postwar Planning." *Smith College Studies in Social Work,* 15 (1945).

Trout, Bessie, and Dorothy E. Bradbury. *Mothers for a Day. The Care of Children in Families Other Than Their Own.* Washington, D.C.: U.S. Government Printing Office, 1946.

United Nations. "Day Care Services for Children." *International Social Service Review,* 1 (January 1956).

U.S. Department of Health, Education, and Welfare. *Guide Specifications for Positions in Day Care Centers.* Washington, D.C.: Social and Rehabilitation Services, 1967.

U.S. Department of Health, Education, and Welfare. *Federal Interagency Day Care Requirements.* Washington, D.C.: U.S. Government Printing Office, September, 1968.

U.S. Department of Health, Education, and Welfare. *Child Care Arrangements of AFDC Recipients Under the Work Incentive Program—Quarter Ended June 30, 1971.* Washington, D.C.: National Center for Social Statistics, February 1972.

U.S. Department of Health, Education, and Welfare. *The Appropriateness of the Federal Interagency Day Care Requirements: Report of Findings and Recommendations.* Washington, D.C.: U.S. Government Printing Office, 1978.

U.S. Department of Labor. *Employed Mothers and Child Care.* Washington, D.C.: U.S. Government Printing Office, 1953.

U.S. Senate, Committee of Finance. *Child Care Data and Materials, June 16, 1971.* Washington, D.C.: U.S. Government Printing Office, 1971.

Voiland, Alice P. "Casework in a Day Nursery." *The Family,* 23 (May 1942).

Washburn, Paul V. and Judith S. Washburn. "The Four Roles of the Family Day Care Providers." *Child Welfare,* 64, 5 (September–October 1985), 547–549.

Watkins, Harriet D., and Bradbard, Marilyn R. "The Social Development of Young Children in Day Care: What Practitioners Should Know." *Child Care Quarterly,* 11, 3 (Fall 1982), 169–87.

Wattenberg, Esther. "Characteristics of Family Day Care Providers: Implications for Training." *Child Welfare,* 56, 4 (April 1977), 211–229.

Wattenberg, Esther. "Family Day Care—Out of the Shadows and into the Spotlight." *Marriage and Family Review.* 3/3–4 (Fall–Winter 1980), 35–62.

Werner, Emmy. *Child Care—Kith, Kin and Hired Hands.* New York: University Park Press, 1985.

White, Benjamin, and Ella Beattie. "Day Care for the Mentally Retarded as Part of Local Health Services in Maryland." *American Journal of Public Health,* 56, 11 (November 1966).

White, Burton. "Should You Stay Home with Your Baby?" *Young Children,* 36 (November 1981), 14–18.

Willner, Milton. "Unsupervised Family Day Care in New York City." *Child Welfare,* 43,6 (June 1969), 342–347.

Willner, Milton. "Family Day Care: An Escape from Poverty." *Social Work,* 52, 4 (April 1971), 30–35.

Wittles, Gloria, and Norma Radin. "Two Approaches to Group Work with Parents in a Compensatory School Program." *Social work,* 16 (January 1971), 42–50.

Works Progress Administration. *Final Report on the WPA,* 1953–43. Washington, D.C.: U.S. Government Printing Office, 1944.

Yeomans, Alfreda. "Day Care—An Alternative to Placement Away from Home." *Child Welfare,* 32 (October 1953).

Yoshikami, Rogers T. *Assisting the Implementation of the Federal Policy to Reduce Foster Care—Placement Prevention and Reunification in Child Welfare.* Portland, Oregon, Regional Research Institute of Human Services, 1984.

Yudkin, Simon, and Althea Holme. *Working Mothers and Their Children.* London: Michael Joseph Ltd., 1963.

Zigler, Edward, and Edmund Gordon (eds.) *Day Care: Scientific and Social Policy.* Boston: Auburn Publishing Co., 1982.

Zigler, Edward, and Pauline Turner. "Parents and Day Care Workers: A Failed Partnership" pp. 174–184, in *Daycare: Scientific and Social Policy*. Eds. E. Zigler and E.Godon, Boston: Auburn Publishing Co., 1982.

6

Supplementary Services:

Protective Services

Introduction

It is difficult to classify protective services neatly as either supportive, supplementary, or substitutive. Protective services are called upon in a variety of situations, characterized by a similar factor: neglect, abuse, or exploitation of a child. The protective service agency is organized around the nature of the problem and uses a wide variety of services—supportive, supplementary, and substitutive—in trying to help the family deal with it. The agency may seek to protect the child by strengthening the home (*supportive*), by supplementing the parent's own efforts to care for the child (*supplementary*), or by removing the child from the home and placing him or her in another home (*substitutive*). Initially, however, activity is directed toward maintaining the neglected or abused child at home. Consequently, protective services may be classified as among the services to children in their own home.

Definition

The Children's Division of the American Humane Association, the national body coordinating the work of protective agencies, defines *protective service* as a specialized child-welfare "service to neglected, abused, exploited, or rejected children. The focus of the service is preventive and nonpunitive and is geared toward rehabilitation through identification and treatment of the motivating factors which underlie" the problem (DeFrancis, 1955, p. 2). Protective service is

> based on law and is supported by community standards. Its purpose is protection of children through strengthening the home or, failing that, making plans for their care and custody through the courts. . . . [It is] a service on behalf of children undertaken by an agency upon receipt of information which indicates that parental responsibility toward those children is not being effectively met [Canadian Welfare Council, 1954, p. 8].

The problems with which the protective agencies are concerned arise from gross parental inadequacy in role performance and from active role rejection.

The parent may be present but incapable of caring for the child, or unwilling to do so. Under the concept of *parens patriae,* that state has an obligation, as a "parent" to all children, to defend the rights of the child. The problem, however, is to avoid "infringing on the rights of the general parent population while simultaneously insuring the rights of a specific child" (Boardman, 1963, p. 8). One might, however, say that parental rights derive from parental obligations. When these obligations and responsibilities are unfulfilled, the corresponding rights may be abrogated. Currently, the right of the parent to the control of his or her child is regarded as an inherent natural right subject to the protection of due process. The natural right is not regarded as absolute; it is in the nature of a trust.

With the concept of *parens patriae,* a third party is introduced into the parent–child relationship, providing the child with some assurance of outside protection and support.

There is a growing acceptance of children as separate entities entitled not only to having their needs met but also to having their rights respected. In recognizing children's rights, society has moved from a perception of children as belonging to their parents to one that sees children as belonging to themselves in the trust of their parents.

With the growing recognition of the separate rights of children, there is less readiness to grant the assumption that parents always have the child's best interest in mind and that parents and children invariably share a community of interest.

The judicial power of the community to intervene on behalf of the child against the parent "has rarely been challenged; only its *extent* has been questioned" (Simpson, 1962, p. 353). The justification of community intervention is based on the need for community self-preservation. The continuity of the group rests with its children. Any danger to the life of the child threatens this continuity. Thus intervention in cases of neglect and abuse is merely an extension of the community's need to intervene against infanticide. More immediately, however, the community's justification for intervention lies in the fact that neglect or abuse of the child is likely to result in an expense to the community: the maltreated child may need care or medical attention at community expense; the maltreated child is less apt to grow up to be a self-sustaining adult.

The humanitarian justification goes beyond these considerations: a child should not be abused, neglected, or exploited; he or she has a right to expect protection and care.

It is often suggested that the privacy of urban living makes imperative a more formal, legalized expression of this concern (Garbarino, 1977). Jules Henry (1963), an anthropologist, notes:

> In a primitive culture, where many relatives are around to take an active interest in one's baby, where life is open, or in large households, where many people can see what a mother is doing and where deviations from traditional practice quickly offend the eye and loosen critical, interested tongues, it is impossible for a parent to do as he or she pleases with his child. In a literal sense, a baby is often not even one's own in such societies, but belongs to a lineage, clan, or household—a community—having a real investment in the baby. It is not private enterprise. The almost total absence of the social regulation of parent—child relations in our private-enterprise culture is a pivotal environmental factor making it necessary to institutionalize community concern in an agency offering protective service [p. 332].

All agencies concerned with child welfare may be said to be protective agencies. In the more specialized use of the term, the *protective agency* is an agency that is given special responsibility in cases of child abuse, exploitation, and neglect. Such agencies are often delegated some specific authority, usually by charter, to act for the community in its collective expression of concern for children.

Some have questioned the distinctiveness and uniqueness of protective service agencies. It is pointed out that all agencies have a responsibility to intervene when a child is abused or neglected, that this authority is inherent in all social work, and that the protective agency, in petitioning for court action, has no greater mandate than any other agency. Nevertheless, the fact is that other agencies in the community tend to attribute to the protective service agency greater responsibility for problems of abuse and neglect.

Kahn (1963) aptly notes that "the protective responsibility is lodged in the whole community" and that all the agencies serving children are, in aggregate, responsible for "protecting" children so as to ensure all their rights. However, the protective service agency does have a special function: "The protection service moves into action only when socially defined minimums are not met or where children are in clear and present danger" (p. 325). And Boehm (1964) indicates that the protective service agency itself "appears to accept the role of 'agency of last resort'" (p. 46).

This may in fact be desirable, because it permits a clear delineation of function, giving one agency the responsibility for court action, freeing the "family agency to continue to concentrate on those families who are motivated to seek service and to refer others elsewhere. . . . The family agency can continue to be perceived as a source of help, not a source of threat" (Rein, 1963, p. 66).

The special responsibility of protective service agencies, or protective service units within a large multifunction agency, is clearly recognized in legislation that would require the reporting of maltreatment of children. The legislation identifies and designates protective service agencies or units as the facility to which such reports should be made.

Historical Background

In earlier periods of history, the child was regarded as a chattel of his or her parents. In its most unrestricted expression, this attitude gave the parents the right to kill the child at birth, to sell the child, to exploit his or her labor, or to offer him or her as a sacrifice to a deity. Although almost every community restricted and regulated such rights to some extent, until recently parental power over the child was subject to relatively few limitations.

Acceptable, sanctioned procedures for disciplining the child differ with the culture and the times. The biblical injunction in Proverbs 23:13–14 might be regarded as sanctioning what might today be termed child abuse: "Withhold not correction from the child for if thou beatest him with the rod he shall not die; thou shalt beat him with the rod and shalt deliver his soul from Hell." Proverbs 22:15 advises us, "Foolishness is bound in the heart of a child; but the rod of correction shall drive it far from him."

In one of the earliest (English) handbooks on the upbringing of the young, parents are advised:

If thy children rebel and will will not bow them low
If any of them misdo, neither curse nor blow
But take a smart rod and beat them in a row
Till they cry mercy and their guilt well know
[Pinchbeck & Hewitt, 1969, p. 157].

Henry IV of France, whom "contemporaries regarded as an especially easy going father" (Hunt, 1970, p. 138), wrote to those caring for his young son:

I have complaint to make: you do not send word that you have whipped my son. I wish and command you to whip him every time that he is obstinate or misbehaves, knowing well that there is nothing in the world which will be better for him than that. I know it from experience, having myself profited, for when I was his age I was often whipped [Hunt, 1970, p. 135].

Given the assumption that the child was born naturally sinful, failure to discipline not only resulted in spoiling the child but further endangering the child's soul.

Children being killed, abandoned, or punished are common themes in the classic literature about children that has long been read to children. Examples of this literature include "Hush-a-bye Baby," "Hansel and Gretel," "The Pied Piper of Hamelin," "Jack and the Beanstalk," "The Little Old Lady Who Lived in a Shoe," "Snow White and the Seven Dwarfs."

In recapitulating the history of childhood, DeMause (1974) says that:

The evidence which I have collected on methods of disciplining children leads me to believe that a very large percentage of the children born prior to the eighteenth century were what would be today termed "battered children." Of over two hundred statements of advice on child rearing prior to the eighteenth century which I have examined, most approved of beating children severely and all allowed beating in varying circumstances except three [p. 40].

Until the early part of the twentieth century, parents were allowed to exploit the labor of their children. A Manchester merchant, testifying in the nineteenth century at a hearing regarding child labor, noted that if a proposed bill safeguarding the health of children in factories were passed, "parents would conceive it a loss of the British birthright, that of control of a parent over his child" (Housden, 1955, p. 47).

The more serious and lethal forms of child abuse have never been condoned in this country, despite the primary concern that has been accorded to the rights of parents. American courts in the nineteenth century did try to protect the child from "grossly unreasonable" or "excessive and brutal" punishment by parents (Mason, 1972).

In a general way, the neglected child has always been an object of concern in America (Folks, 1902, pp. 167–169). The agencies concerned with child protection trace their origin to the dramatic case of Mary Ellen in 1875. The child was cruelly beaten and neglected by a couple with whom she had lived since infancy. There seemed no appropriate legal measure available to protect her. Community leaders, concerned with the situation, appealed to the Society for the Prevention of Cruelty to Animals. This organization brought Mary Ellen to the attention of the court as an "animal" who was being mistreated. Because the law did protect animals from abuse, the complaint was accepted, protection was granted Mary Ellen, and her guardians were sent to prison. As a result of this case, a Society for the Prevention of Cruelty to Children was organized.

The organization of the New York County Society for the Prevention of Cruelty to Children in 1875 was a signal for the development of similar societies in San Francisco, Boston, Rochester, Baltimore, Buffalo, and Philadelphia. Many of the Societies for the Prevention of Cruelty to Children were originally organized as separate voluntary agencies; others were organized as subdivisions of the existing agencies concerned with the protection of animals, because "there was acquiescence in the view of the fundamental similarity of protective work for children and of animals" (McCrea, 1910, p. 138). Over the course of time, some of these agencies have merged with social agencies concerned with child welfare, whereas others have maintained their separate identity. The American Humane Association, originally organized for the protection of animals, established a children's division in 1887 to coordinate the activities of the various voluntary protective service associations that were developing throughout the country. By 1900, 161 such societies had been established throughout the United States (Folks, 1902, p. 173).

The work of these agencies centered on "child rescue." The agency "uncovered" the cases of children who were neglected, abused, or exploited, and worked to remove the children from their homes. The cases that were referred to the societies for prevention of cruelty to children mirror classical situations of abuse and neglect. Illustrative cases that were referred to the Massachusetts Society in 1881 include a "sick girl, 9, beaten and abused by a drunken father and mother"; "Three children 2 and 5 years of age abandoned by father. When found, the mother was lying drunk and miserable"; "Three children, 3–13, dirty, ragged, almost naked. No furniture, no food. Father intemperate and indifferent, mother dead"; "Girl, 9, mother dead. Step-mother had severely whipped the girl"; "Man arrested for incestuous relation with his own daughter, a pretty girl of 12" (quoted in Bremner, 1971).

The emphasis was on legal action, and the agencies agitated for and supported efforts to enact legislation for the protection of children and to enforce these laws. Thus, as Sandusky (1964) notes, "such agencies performed a law enforcement function primarily rather than a social service function" (p. 579).

The New York Society placed agents in all magistrate courts to investigate cases involving child abuse and neglect. Agents of the society were given the power of arrest, and interference with the work of the agent was deemed a misdemeanor. Agents were given considerable police power under legislative authority.

Almost from the start, however, another orientation, less legalistic and more social, was evident. It suggested that the primary rationale for protective services was to help the parents, not to punish them; to keep the family together, rather than to disrupt it. It is a difference between seeing the protective service agency as a law enforcement agency and seeing it as a social agency.

Despite the fact that the current definitions of protective services express a social work rather than a legal emphasis ("protection of the child through strengthening of the home"; "preventive, nonpunitive service geared toward rehabilitation"), the two points of view are inherent in the operations of all agencies. What has been achieved is a greater stress on one, rather than the elimination of either.

The rapid development of protective agencies in the late nineteenth and early twentieth centuries was followed by a period of decline in interest between 1920 and the 1960s. Child maltreatment as a social problem of concern dropped out of the public agenda.

In 1966 a nationwide survey indicated that protective services under public welfare auspices were reported to exist in forty-seven states. However, it was noted "that much of what was reported as child protective services was in reality nonspecific child welfare services or nonspecific family services in the context of a financial assistance setting" (DeFrancis, 1967, p. vii). The survey showed a long-term decline of such services under voluntary agency auspices. The public agency, particularly the local department of public welfare, was more and more frequently given the responsibility for offering such services. However, there was no clearly indentifiable, specially designated protective-service unit in many public welfare agencies.

With the adoption of the new social services title to the Social Security Act—Title XX—protective service was made mandatory. By 1978 protective services were provided universally in all fifty states.

The late 1960s and the 1970s showed an almost explosive growth of interest in the problem of the child requiring protection, with an emphasis on child abuse. This interest resulted from the focus of medical attention on the "battered child."

A national survey reported by Kempe et al. (1962) of children hospitalized because of abuse uncovered some 302 cases. This led to a Children's Bureau conference on the battered child, which was followed within a very short period of time by the adoption of legislation in state after state requiring the reporting of child abuse. As Paulsen (1966) notes, "Few legislative proposals in the history of the United States have been so widely adopted in so little time" (p. 46).

The rediscovery of child abuse in the 1960s came as a result of the activities of pediatric radiologists, pediatricians, and psychiatrists (Pfohl, 1977; Antler, 1978). Consequently the resurgence of interest in child abuse has a more distinctly medical orientation as contrasted with the almost exclusively social work orientation of an earlier period.

A federal Child Abuse Prevention and Treatment Act was passed in January 1974. This act provides for direct assistance to the states to help them develop child abuse and neglect programs.

In order for states to qualify for federal assistance under revisions of the Child Abuse Prevention and Treatment Act, the state statutes on abuse must protect all children under age eighteen; cover mental injury, physical injury, and sexual abuse; include neglect reports and abuse reports; guarantee confidentiality of records; guarantee legal immunity for reporters; and provide for a guardian *ad litem* for children whose cases come to court. Many states have revised their legislation so as to be eligible for federal funds for their protective services programs.

The roller-coaster history of child maltreatment as a social problem deserving public attention requires some explanation. It exemplifies the general finding that programs in favor of children serve a variety of needs only one of which, and not necessarily one of prime importance, is the concern for children.

By 1910, more than 170 organizations devoted, in whole or in part, to child protection had been established in various cities throughout the United States, but, in the following years, interest and concern with the problem peaked and then declined. The *Social Work Yearbook* of 1933 reported that societies for the prevention of cruelty to children were decreasing and it was doubtful whether any new one would be formed." In 1931, there were but 48 "of such societies" (p. 68). This was partly a consequence of public agencies taking over the responsibility for protective services, but it also reflected a decline in the visibility and low priority on the public agenda of child protective services. "By the 1950's public interest in abuse and neglect was practically nonexistent and even social workers did not rate it highly as a professional concern" (Nelson, 1984, p. 12).

In the absence of any sudden dramatic escalation of the number of children abuse, what explains the "rediscovery" of child abuse in the 1960's and 1970's? The "rediscovery" of child abuse was the result of a confluence of a variety of factors. It took place at a time when the baby boom was beginning to decline and pediatricians were in search of additional legitimate functions. During the 1960s, through a series of administrative reorganizations, the Children's Bureau lost many of its functions and tasks that were redistributed elsewhere in the federal government bureaucracy. The Children's Bureau might have ceased to exist in anything other than in name only if Congress had not passed the Child Abuse Prevention and Treatment Act in 1974 (Nelson, 1984, p. 50). The act that gave the bureau the responsibility for a national center for child abuse and neglect also gave it a legitimate *raison d'être*.

The U.S. Senate Subcommittee on Children and Youth was created in 1971 with a broad mandate but no specific charge. Chairman of the subcommittee, Senator Walter Mondale seized on child abuse as an issue of public interest and significance that was within the subcommittee's mandate. The issue thus had support from the medical profession and of professional social workers who were strategically placed in the government apparatus, and had the backing of an influential senator with a congressional committee base.

Strong leadership wedded to professional resources that were available to de-vote time to push the issue was aided by a dramatic label—"The Battered Child," which identified the problem, medicalizing it and gave it visibility for public attention. The fact that this was a "low-cost rectitude" issue, doing good while calling for very limited public funds, helped to obtain placement of child abuse onto the public social issues agenda (Pfohl, 1977; Nelson, 1984; Dingwell, 1979).

Other factors also contributed to the emergence of child abuse as a public concern. The fact that child abuse reporting legislation originally addressed only a very limited issue reduced any potential opposition. In the beginning federal concern with protective services was narrowly focused on physical abuse that was enough to require medical attention. Only gradually was the focus progressively broadened to include other kinds of maltreatment, from physical abuse to neglect, sexual abuse and exploitation, emotional abuse, and, more recently, the protec-tion of infants born with serious congenital anomalies—the "Baby Doe" children. The issue emerged in a manner that had great likelihood of capturing public attention. The focus was on the serious physical abuse of young children. Interest in child maltreatment was intensified by a social and political climate in the 1960s of heightened receptivity to the claims of oppressed subgroups in the popu-lation and readiness to make changes in their favor. Children were perceived as an oppressed group whose rights needed greater recognition.

The development of public concern about child abuse was facilitated by the lack of any organized opposition to the movement, in part, because very few people are willing to be identified as opposing a movement doing something about child abuse. It was also a consequence of the social distance between those who labeled the problem, namely middle-class professionals, and those who were most frequently labeled as child abusers, relatively politically powerless lower-class families.

Having been "discovered" and included on the public agenda, interest in child maltreatment continued to grow and the momentum continued as the topic was given increasing prominence in professional journals and the mass media. Between 1950 and 1980, professional journals published 1,756 articles on the issues of abuse and neglect. Popular magazines published another 124 articles, and the *New York Times* printed 652 stories on the subject. Virtually all of these articles were published after Dr. C. Henry Kempe's famous article the "Battered-Child Syndrome" appeared in the July 7, 1962, edition of the *Journal of the American Medical Association"* (Nelson, 1984, p. 129).

The tremendous expansion of activity regarding the maltreatment of children, with a particular focus on child abuse is exemplified in an annotated bibliography on child abuse published in 1978 listing 2,009 citations of published material, the majority published after 1970 (Kalisch, 1978). An annotated bibliography published in 1984 lists 1,055 items concerned with violence in the family (Kemmer, 1984). Between 1970 and 1985 almost one hundred books have been published devoted in whole or in part to child maltreatment. Given this deluge of material, the content in this chapter is necessarily highly selective.

Distinctive Aspects

The state is, ultimately, a parent to all children. When birth parents neglect, abuse, or exploit the child, the state has the legal right and responsibility to intervene to protect the child. The state delegates this authority to the protective service agency, so that, in effect, the agency functions as an arm of the state and operates with legal sanctions. In such situations, not only does the protective service agency have the right to intervene, it has the duty to intervene. All social agencies have an obligation to concern themselves with any situation of danger or potential danger to children, but the protective service agency has an explicitly delegated responsibility to intervene in such situations.

It follows, therefore, that protective service may be initiated on the basis of a request by someone other than a member of the family. In the case of services discussed earlier, client participation is voluntary; in the case of protective services, client involvement may be involuntary. Protective services deal with those instances of failure in parental role performance in which the parent is unaware of the need for service or is unwilling and/or unable to avail himself or herself of the service that the community has provided.

Once involved, the agency cannot withdraw until the child is clearly no longer in danger. Just as the family is not permitted to decide whether or not it wants the agency's help, the community does not permit the agency to decide whether or not it should offer the service: "The agency cannot leave a client free to accept or reject its services; nor can it withdraw only because the parent has refused or is unable to take help" (Canadian Welfare Council, 1954, p. 8).

The agency's responsibility of staying with the situation as long as danger to the child exists is illustrated in the following case:

> Neighbors complained that a young mother was seriously neglecting her four-month-old daughter, the first and only child. When the child welfare worker visits the home, she found the baby looking very pale and listless and apparently not in good physical condition. She persuaded the mother to take the baby to a clinic, where the child was found to be seriously malnourished and to have a severe diaper rash. On her next visit to the home, the worker found that the mother had apparently done nothing to carry out the doctor's instructions. As the worker talked to the mother

about her lack of care and the seriousness of the baby's condition, the mother ordered her out of the house. The worker agreed to go, but explained that she would have to continue her responsibility for seeing that the baby had more adequate care even to the point of filing petition at court, if necessary [Sandusky, 1960, p. 24].

Because the agency operated on the basis of delegated authority, it may invoke legal sanctions, if necessary, to protect the child and his or her rights. Although all agencies have the right to petition the court for the protection of the children with whom they are concerned, the protective agencies are viewed by themselves, by other agencies, and by the client group as the agency having a special responsibility for invoking such sanctions.

The fact that the court may eventually be involved means that data in providing the service have to be collected with an awareness of what is acceptable and necessary to meet legal requirements.

Protective service is also distinctive in that a time element is significantly involved in service delivery. Investigations have to be made within a short period of time after the report of maltreatment is received. Further, some determination of whether or not this is a substantiated case of maltreatment has to be made within a limited period of time.

Situations in Which Protective Services Are Appropriate

The situations in which protective agencies intervene are those in which the parent is unable and/or unwilling to enact the parental role effectively, and his or her failure constitutes an actual danger to the normal physical, emotional, and social development of the child. The statutory definitions of maltreatment suggests the different kinds of situations. Although these definitions differ from state to state, they generally include most of the following (Katz, Howe, McGrath, 1975):

1. Physical abuse.
2. Malnourishment; poor clothing; lack of proper shelter, sleeping arrangements, attendance, or supervision. Includes "failure to thrive" syndrome, which describes infants who fail to grow and develop at a normal rate.
3. Denial of essential medical care.
4. Failure to insure that the child attends school regularly.
5. Exploitation, overwork.
6. Exposure to unwholesome or demoralizing circumstances.
7. Sexual abuse.
8. Emotional abuse and neglect, involving denial of the normal experiences that permit a child to feel loved, wanted, secure, and worthy.

These general situations, in effect, break down into two major categories: abuse (both physical and sexual), and neglect of one kind or another. Infanticide is the ultimate abuse; abandonment is the ultimate neglect. In this chapter, efforts are made to maintain such distinctions by noting some of the differences in the nature and the etiology of abuse and neglect.

Some regard such distinctions as spurious and false, noting the supposedly frequent overlap of abuse and neglect. Preference is for a unitary term. A more inclusive term might, at times, be appropriate in labeling the behaviors that are of concern. The "mistreated child," the "maltreated child," and the "endangered child" have been among the alternatives suggested. We will use the term *maltreatment* as the more inclusive term covering all forms of abuse and neglect.

The Model Child Welfare Protective Services Act defines a maltreated child as "one whose physical or mental health or welfare is harmed or threatened with harm by the acts or omissions of his parents or other persons responsible for his welfare." In such instances, protective service intervention is sanctioned in defense of the child. The definition includes emotional as well as physical harm, neglect as well as abuse, and potential damage as well as actual harm, and is applicable to institutional personnel as well as to biological parents and parent surrogates. The focus of the definition is on the effects of maltreatment on the child.

Operationalizing a broad definition presents a problem for the social worker in deciding whether a particular situation can be defined as maltreatment. The legislation and literature relating to child maltreatment repetitively describes these situations with words of considerable ambiguity—"proper supervision"; "adequate care"; "unfit place"; "serious harm"; "severe injury"; "mental suffering"; "endangering health"; "suitable environment"; "excessive discipline."

In *People* v. *Schools* (15 Ill. App. 3d, 305 N.E. 2d, 560 at 561 1973), the Illinois court noted that child neglect is "by its very nature incapable of a precise and detailed statement." This echoes a 1974 statement made by Supreme Court Justice Powell in the case of *Smith* v. *Goguen* when he noted that "there are areas of human conduct whereby the nature of the problems presented, legislatures simply cannot establish standards with great precision."

There is controversy as to whether maltreatment occurs if there is intent to harm, but no actual harm occurs (the parent tries to punch the child but misses). Is it maltreatment if there is not evidence of immediate harm but harmful effects are likely to be manifested in the future (for example, derogation of the child leading to low self-esteem in adulthood)? What level of care do we select to determine the threshold of maltreatment—minimal care, adequate care, or optimal care of the child?

The most ambitious attempt, as yet, to define child abuse was made by Giovannoni and Becerra (1979). They presented seventy-eight vignettes describing different kinds and different degrees of abuse to groups of social workers, lawyers, pediatricians, and police officers as well as to members of the general public. They were asked to decide whether each of the incidents described in the vignettes was child abuse. Included in the research form were such incidents as a "parent burned the child on the buttocks and chest with a cigarette"; "parents are constantly screaming at their child, calling him foul names." The study involved some one thousand respondents and included blacks, hispanics, and Native American respondents.

The results indicated that each of the four professional groups involved in dealing with child abuse—social workers, lawyers, pediatricians, police—defined child abuse differently. There was complete agreement among all four groups with regard to only 12 percent of the vignettes. However, social workers and police officers were the ones who were most often in agreement with each other, both groups tending to rate incidents as more serious and requiring intervention than did either the pediatricians or lawyers. Professional experience, functions, and responsibilities and the ideologies related to professional identity appear to shape how abuse is defined. The legal functions of the police are supplemented by social service activities; the social service activities of social workers are supplemented by legal responsibilities. The two groups differ most often in their perception of emotional abuse, to which social workers are more sensitive.

Responses from members of the general community to the same vignettes that were given to these professionals indicated fewer class–ethnic differences than had been anticipated. In general, community respondents rated the vignettes as more serious than the professionals. "Blacks consistently had higher ratings on matters pertaining to nutrition, medical care supervision, cleanliness, education, clothing and housing" (p. 185). A broad range of corporal punishment behavior had been accepted in the lay community. Whereas physical abuse was seen by the lay respondents as serious, they regarded physical abuse as less serious than professionals do. Both groups rated sexual abuse as very serious.

Defining child maltreatment is, in effect, an exercise in deciding the limits of legitimate state intrusion into family life; the reciprocal, relative rights and obligations of parents and children, and the kind of adults a society regards as its valued model (assertively democratic, individualistic, socially conforming and so on). The definition relates to the way parents need to discipline children to achieve the model, the value given to a pluralistic society. The central questions, that relate to a definition of child maltreatment are basic value questions, the answers to which provide a definition of abuse which is then socially defined.

A number of general conclusions might be formulated about the definition of child maltreatment that derive from the currently available research.

1. The definition of child abuse and neglect needs to reflect the fact that these are not unitary phenomena but represent a broad range of diverse events.
2. Any such definition is a social construct that reflects the context in which it is formulated—not only the social-economic-historical context but the professional–occupational context of the definer as well.
3. Different definitions might be needed that are more or less appropriate for different kinds of interventive objectives—social or legal, therapeutic or punitive.
4. Different definitions are appropriate for different age groups. What is physical abuse to the vulnerable infant may be harmless to an adolescent.
5. Despite differences, there is some basic general consensus about the norms that determine the broad limits of minimally adequate care, protection, and maltreatment of children.
6. Operationally and pragmatically for protective service, child mistreatment is defined by the social worker, who, while investigating a report of such an incident, defines the event as child maltreatment.

The problem of arriving at a definition of child maltreatment suggests, some of the problems in determining when intervention by social workers is appropriate and sanctioned in encountering the following situations of child maltreatment.

Physical Abuse

Physical abuse refers to beating a child to the point at which the child sustains some physical damage. The line between physical abuse and harsh parental discipline is difficult to define. As Arnold (1962) says, "forms of punishment considered proper, and even wholesome, in Elizabethan or Victorian days would be considered as abuse today" (p. 3). Silver et al. (1969) raise the question of limits: "For example, if a parent punishes a child with a belt, is it after the fourth slash with the belt that parental rights end and child abuse begins; is it after the belt raises a welt over two millimeters that is becomes abuse versus parental rights?" (p. 804).

The problem is to distinguish discipline that is "legitimate violence" toward children from abuse that is excessive and inappropriate and hence unacceptable violence toward children.

Attempts have been made to distinguish discipline from abuse and excessive punishment from inappropriate punishment. Discipline is more clearly related to the child's behavior; it has a clearly corrective purpose. The discipline is appropriate to, and commensurate with, the child's behavior that the parent is seeking to change. Whereas many parents spank, the abuser "overspanks," with great regularity and great severity. In contrast with abuse, discipline is manifested in a context of loving concern for what is best for the child, without primary emphasis on the needs of the parent.

Some definitions of abuse stress the fact that the behavior is deliberate, with intent to harm the child. Other definitions give intent less consideration on the supposition that what is happening involves a danger to the child, whether it is intentional or not.

The definition of abuse is sometimes determined by the extent of injury to the child. If discipline is so harsh that as a result the child is bruised, abuse has taken place. It is noted, however, that "bruises" come in all shapes, sizes, and forms, some bruises being relatively minor. There would be little doubt, however, that the following examples, reported by local newspapers, would generally be considered physical abuse:

> A five-year-old girl wandered innocently onto a porch after being instructed not to do so. She was kicked back into the house, thrown across the room and hit on the head and face with a skillet.
> The father of a nine-year-old boy blackened his son's eyes, burned his face, hands, and neck, and fractured his skull [Bryant, et al. 1963, p. 126].

A national newspaper survey of published reports of physical abuse conducted by the Children's Divison of the American Humane Association revealed that children were beaten

> with various kinds of implements and instruments. The hairbrush was a common implement used to beat children. However, the same purpose was accomplished with deadlier impact by the use of bare fists, straps, electric cords. T.V. aerials, ropes, rubber hose, fan belts, sticks, wooden spoons, pool cues, bottles, broom handles, baseball bats, chair legs, and, in one case, a sculling oar. Less imaginative, but equally effective, was plain kicking with street shoes or with work shoes.
> Children had their extremities—hands, arms, and feet—burned in open flames as from gas burners or cigarette lighters. Others bore burn wounds inflicted on their bodies with lighted cigarettes, electric irons, or hot pokers. Still others were scalded by hot liquids thrown over them or from being dipped into containers of hot liquids. . . .
> What kinds of injuries were inflicted on them?
> The majority had various shapes, sizes, and forms of bruises and contusions. There was a collection of welts, swollen limbs, split lips, black eyes, and lost teeth. One child lost an eye.
> Broken bones were common. Some were simple fractures; others, compound. There were many broken arms, broken legs, and fractured ribs. Many children had more

than one fracture. One five-month-old child was found to have thirty broken bones in his little body [DeFrancis, 1963, p. 6].

In some instances, child abuse is episodic. Sometimes, however, an abused child has suffered abuse before.

The dramatic material cited, although valid, tends to present a distorted picture of the actualities of child physical abuse. It focuses on the battered child, the child subjected to substantial injury. Whereas the terms *battered child* and *abused child* are often used interchangeably, there is a clear distinction in terms of severity of injury. The term *battered child syndrome* was originally applied to a hospitalized population of children, generally very young, who were so severly injured as to require medical attention. Statistically the more typical *abused child* is a child seven to eight years old who has sustained mostly minor, sometimes moderate, physical injury that has not required medical attention of any kind.

Neglect

The parent who abuses or cruelly mistreats the child is guilty of a crime of commission; neglect is more frequently a problem of omission. The ultimate in neglect, of course, is child abandonment. The abandoned child is, by virtue of his or her abandonment, a client of the protective service agency. In less egregious instances, the child is found to be living in filth, malnourished, without proper clothing, unattended, and unsupervised.

Physical abuse incidents are episodic, discrete, time-limited; neglect is chronic and continual. The affect associated with abuse is sporadic, and is often expressed in impulsive outbursts of anger, aggression, hostility. Feelings of frustration; indifference, inattentiveness, and lack of concern and awareness of the child's condition and basic needs are associated with neglect.

> "Child neglect may be defined as a condition in which a caretaker responsible for the child either deliberately or by extraordinary inattentiveness permits the child to experience avoidable present suffering and/or fails to provide one or more ingredients generally deemed essential for developing a person's physical intellectual and emotional capacities" (Polansky et al. 1981 p. 15).

> "Child neglect is the failure of the child's parent or caretaker, who has the material resources to do so, to provide minimally adequate care in the areas of health, nutrition, shelter, education, supervision, affection or attention" (Wolock, Horowitz, 1984, p. 531).

"Deprivation of necessities" and "inadequate supervision" are the two most frequent forms of neglect. When deprived of necessities, the child is not adequately fed or provided with adequate and appropriate clothing. The child's living conditions are dilapidated, with inadequate heating, insufficient protection from possibility of injury, and lack of proper bed or bedding.

Failure-to-thrive might be listed as a special neglect situation associated with deprivation of necessities. Nonorganic failure-to-thrive results from deprivation of necessities as a consequence of parental–child relationship problems which seriously disturb feeding and eating (Ayoub & Milner, 1985; Oates, 1986).

"Inadequately supervised" children for long periods of time are without access to an adult who is available to meet their dependent needs and protect them from harm.

As Polansky notes, child neglect is secondary to self-neglect in many poverty-level families. The mother fails to adequately meet her own needs even as she fails to meet the basic needs of her children for care, protection, and control. In a sense the parent is a victim rather than a culprit; unfortunate, rather than intentionally neglectful. The neglectful parent may be rejecting the parental role. Frequently, however, such parents inadequately perform the role and/or lack the necessary resources to adequately care for the child.

A woman charged with child neglect described her third-floor cold-water flat to the judge at a hearing:

> It is an awful place to live. The wallpaper is in strips, the floor board is cracked. The baby is always getting splinters in his hands. The bathroom is on the floor above and two other families use it. The kitchen is on the first floor. I share it with another woman. I have no place to keep food. We buy for one meal at a time [Hancock, 1963, p. 5].

The following instances detail the social worker's description of situations encountered in investigating complaints of neglect:

> The family of ten is living in two rooms. The plaster is falling down; window planes were out; the plumbing leaked. The wind howled through cracks and it was bitterly cold. Two young children with frostbitten hands and feet were removed from this home to a hospital [Hancock, 1963, p. 10].
>
> What I saw as I entered the room was utter, stark, disorganization. The room was a combined kitchen—dining room. At the other end of the room two scrawny, owl-eyed frightened children—a girl of about four and a boy of three—stared silently at me. Except for thin cotton undershirts, they were stark naked. They had sore crusts on their legs and arms. They were indescribably dirty, hair matted, body and hands stained and covered with spilled food particles. Sitting on a urine-soaked and soiled mattress in a baby carriage behind them was a younger child—a boy about two.
>
> The floor was ankle deep in torn newspapers. There were feces in about a half-dozen spots on the floor and the air was fetid and saturated with urine odor.
>
> There were flies everywhere. What seemed like giant roaches were crawling over the paper-strewn floor. The kitchen sink and gas stove were piled high with greasy and unwashed dishes, pots, and pans [DeFrancis, 1958, p. 11].

The police are frequently the first to be involved, and police patrol car reports often detail cases of neglect:

> Responded to a complaint concerning three children, ages two to six, left alone in a parked car for several hours. Observation indicated that the children were dirty and unkempt, cold and hungry, poorly clothed, and in need of medical care [Swanson, 1961, p. 44].

Efforts have been made to quantify and objectify the specific elements and circumstances that a worker might watch for in determining neglect. Polansky *et al.* (1978) have developed and revised a Childhood Level of Living Scale, which lists the items associated with possible neglect. The scale is applicable to children between the ages of four and seven years and includes items regarding evidence of the mother's postitive care and concern for the child ("mother uses good judgment about leaving the child alone in the house"; "buttons and snaps of child's clothing are frequently missing and not replaced"); the state of repair of the house ("floor covering prevents tripping hazard"); the quality of household maintenance ("the roof or ceiling leaks"); the quality of health care and grooming ("poisonous or dangerous sprays and cleaning fluid are stored out of children's reach"); emotional care ("mother fails to comfort child when he is upset"); inconsistency of discipline and coldness ("child is often ignored when he tries to tell the mother something"). The scale is applicable to the care of a four to seven year-old-child. There is high correlation between the physical, emotional, and cognitive scale subcategories.

Polansky et al. (1983) used the Childhood Level of Living Scale to test cultural bias related to neglect in populations of white, black, working-class, and middle-class rural and urban women. These varied subculture groups were all substantially in agreement with each other in their perception of what constituted neglectful behavior, the differences were minor and essentially in terms of emphasis. Middle-class respondents were more concerned with psychological care, whereas working-class mothers were more with physical care.

A study of neighbors' reaction to a neglectful family using a social distance scale confirmed, once again, the consensual norms regarding child care that transcend class differences. "Neglectful families are regarded as deviant" so that "ordinary people in their community are inclined to keep their distance from them" (Polansky & Gaudin, 1983, p. 198). Neglectful child care behavior was disapproved by people in similar life circumstances to the neglectful family.

The level of care that the community expects the parent to provide the child varies from one culture to another and within a multicultural community, such as our own, from one subcultural group to another. Yet across all groups there seems to be general agreement on the minimal level of care a parent should provide. An analysis of American Indian law defining child abuse and neglect shows a very considerable similarity of definitions of such situations as used by protective service agencies (Baurley & Street, 1981). There seems little to suggest significant differences in the conceptualization of child abuse and neglect despite, ethnic differences.

In general, the middle-class social worker may not be imposing middle-class standards of care on lower-class clients in substantiating a report of maltreatment.

Medical Neglect

In cases of medical neglect the parents make no effort to see that the child is provided with the medical care the child needs: "One child was covered with sores but not brought to the doctor. In another case, a mother refused the medical advice for follow-up care after a serious illness" (Rein, 1963, p. 44).

Medical neglect is illustrated in the following instance:

> Someone noticed that Sally's (two years old) eye was closed and badly swollen and when nothing seemed to be done about it, he rang up the police, who told the protective agency. When the worker called on her, Sally's mother told him she thought the little girl had run into the end of her brother's toy pistol when they were playing in the garden. She added that she had been bathing the eye to see that it would be all right. The worker asked permission to call a doctor who took one look at Sally and said, "Hospital." There they decided that an immediate operation was necessary. Her father gave his consent and they removed Sally's eye to find that the trouble had not been caused by her running into anything but by an air-gun dart which had entered

the eye and had lain there for twenty days. If the operation had been delayed, the hospital believed that the infection would have spread to her other eye and then probably she would have been blind for life [Allen & Morton, 1961, p. 48].

Perhaps because of their difficulty in obtaining affordable medical care, lower-class families may have developed a greater tendency to ignore signs that would send middle-class families running to a doctor. A persistent cough, chronic backaches, loss of appetite, general fatigue, a low-grade fever, and a continuing infection do not typically result in lower-class parents seeking medical attention for their children.

The question of medical neglect has always been complicated because of the beliefs of certain religious groups, such as the Christian Scientists and Jahovah's Witnesses regarding some medical procedures. Regulations formulated by the U.S. Department of Health and Human Services indicate that failure to provide medical care is not neglect if such failure is in response to a person's religious beliefs, and most states grant exemptions from immunizations that run counter to the parents religious beliefs. However, the federal regulations go on to note that "nothing shall prohibit court intervention to protect the child."

Courts have intervened to set aside objections of Jehovah's Witness parents to blood transfusions that were medically required by an infant suffering from anemia (*New York Times,* April 5, 1984). Courts have also ordered necessary treatment over religious objections even in cases in which the child objected to such treatment as being against his or her religious convictions—as was the case for a twelve-year-old girl suffering from bone cancer (*Time,* April 16, 1984). In cases of medical neglect, courts have generally acted to supersede parental autonomy with regard to decisions concerning medical treatment if there is imminent danger of death to the child or probable serious impairment of the child's health.

In cases of medical neglect, courts and agencies have been sensitive to the subsequent possible negative effects on the parent–child relationship of court-ordered treatment, the possibility of parents using the child as a scapegoat or the child's sabotoging treatment to which there has been some objection (Bross, 1982).

Some states have deleted religious exemption clauses from abuse and neglecting reporting requirements (*Time,* April 16, 1984). This was in response to reports of children who died as a consequence of their parents failure to seek medical help when it was critically necessary.

An even more controversial problem regarding medical neglect gained widespread publicity and debate in 1983–84. This relates to the right of parents to refuse treatment for a child born with serious congenital anomalies. In several cases—known as Baby Doe cases—action was taken by right-to-life activists to petition the court to require the child's parents to consent to medical treatment that they had previously rejected after consultation with their physicians, social workers, and ministers (*New York Times,* October 21, October 22, October 29, November 17, 1984).

The courts generally refused such a petition. The federal government became involved in requesting a review of such a case by the local protective service and in efforts to obtain access to the child's hospital records to determine if the child's civil rights had been violated.

Attempts on the part of the federal government to require hospitals to post notices urging doctors and nurses to report to the local protective services agency any suspicion that the medical needs of a handicapped infant were being neglected, were nullified by the courts. After months of debate, both in and out of Congress, legislation was passed in 1984 defining, as abuse, denial of care to newborn infants who have life-threatening handicaps. Child Abuse Prevention and Treatment Act funds were to be withheld from states that did not set up procedures to investigate and report the withholding of treatment and nutrition from infants "with life-threatening congenital impairments." The legislation, in redefining abuse, again expanded the kinds of cases for which the protective social services have some responsibility.

Educational Neglect

Educational neglect involves failure of a parent to enroll a child in school or parental indifference to chronic truanting of a child who is enrolled. Children might be kept out of school for the purpose of baby-sitting for younger siblings or may be kept home to work. Some school absence may be acceptable, but truancy is defined as absence for five days a month after parents have been notified of the situation. Refusal of parents to enroll a child in special educational programs if a clear need for this has been assessed might also be regarded as educational neglect.

A child may not be enrolled in school, but if carefully planned alternative provisions for the child's education are being implemented this is not regarded as educational neglect.

Emotional Maltreatment

A parent may provide adequate physical care for the child and yet manifest his or her rejection by starving or abusing the child emotionally. Deprivation of affectional support can be as harmful as denial of physical needs.

The Child Abuse Prevention and Treatment Act, adopted in 1974, provides assistance to state child-abuse and neglect programs under certain conditions. One condition is that the states comply with the federal law's definition of child abuse and neglect as a "unified term" that "covers physical or mental injury, sexual abuse, negligent treatment or maltreatment of children under eighteen years of age by a caretaker who is responsible for the child's welfare under circumstances which indicate that the child's health or welfare is harmed or threatened." To be eligible for assistance states are constrained to include mental injury—emotional abuse—as a reportable condition.

Emotional maltreatment is difficult to define in the precise terms required by law, and its consequences are equally difficult to establish conclusively. Despite this, an increasing number of states have included the idea of emotional maltreatment in protective services legislation. Such statutes might refer to the child's "emotional health," "mental well-being," "emotional maladjustment," "emotional impairment," or "mental injury" as requiring intervention without a further definition of the terms used. Some statutes specified the parental behavior associated with emotional maltreatment, such as "denial of parental love or adequate affectional parental association" (Idaho).

Mulford (1958) defined *emotional neglect* as "the deprivation suffered by children when their parents do not provide opportunities for the normal experiences producing feelings of being loved, wanted, secure, and worthy which result in the ability to form healthy object relationships" (p. 21). More recent emotional neglect has been defined as "Acts of ommission or commission by a parent or guardian that are judged by a mixture of community values and professional experience to be inappropriate and damaging " (Garbarino & Garbarino, 1980, p. 8).

Some model statute formulations list some specific behaviors that are indicative of emotional maltreatment. Thus the suggested American Bar Association Juvenile Justice standard notes that emotional maltreatment is "evidenced by severe anxiety, depression or withdrawal or untoward agressive behavior or hostility toward self or others." Given as an additional indication of justification for community intervention is the fact that "the parents are unwilling to provide treatment for such a child" (Wald, 1975, p. 1019).

The National Clearing House on Child Neglect and Abuse defines emotional neglect on its nationwide report form

> as failure to provide the child the emotional nurturing or emotional support necessary for the development of a sound personality, as for example subjecting the child to rejection or to a home climate charged with tension, hostility and anxiety producing occurrences which result in perceivable problems in children.

The Federal Standards on the Prevention and Treatment of Child Abuse and Neglect, published in 1978 by the Children's Bureau, National Center on Child Abuse and Neglect, further define mental injury as

> an injury to the intellectual or psychological capacity of a child as evidenced by an observable and substantial impairment in his/her ability to function with his/her normal range of performance and behavior with due regard to his/her culture [pp. 111–115].

Some states define emotional abuse precisely in terms of specific obervable behavior of children. Thus, Wisconsin defines emotional damage as "harm to a child's psychological or intellectual functioning which is exhibited by severe anxiety depression or outward agressive behavior which is caused by parents or parental surrogates and for which they have failed to obtain treatment necessary to remedy the harm. Emotional damage may be demonstrated by a substantial and observable change in behavior, emotional response or cognition that is not within the normal range for the child's age and stage of development."

The problems of definition and intrusion are somewhat eased by the high correlation between physical abuse and emotional maltreatment.

Although there is general agreement on the difficulty of writing an acceptable legal definition of emotional maltreatment, there is an equally solid consensus that children do suffer from emotional neglect and abuse—even when they are adequately cared for physically. As one court decision noted, "Children are entitled not only to food, clothing and shelter but to guidance, advice, counsel and affection, understanding and sympathy and when they are not accorded them. . . that would constitute serious and severe neglect" (quoted in Gesmonde, 1972, p. 108).

Young (1964) cites various examples of emotional abuse:

> Parents stated bluntly that they hated their children. Some expressed an open wish to kill them or a hope that they would die. Others remarked that they had never liked them, never wanted them. A parent frequently referred to his son as "crazy," the "idiot" or a child was told repeatedly that he was "dumb." In other cases a parent emphasized how physically ugly a child was or called him the "criminal."

"A disheveled woman jerks a toddler down the aisle of a supermarket while she proclaims that he is a stupid bumbling idiot who never should have been born" (Yates, October, 1982, p. 587).

The following is a case of emotional abuse that was called to the attention of a protective service agency:

> Judy's misery was exacerbated by the fact that she was the only child in her family to be treated badly, her two- and four-year-old brothers having a good family life with all the normal treats, outings, and sweets. But not only did she have none of these things, but when her father came home from work she had to leave the room instantly and play either in the kitchen or upstairs in her unheated bedroom. She was never allowed in the same room as her father, even if this meant her being sent to bed as early as five o'clock and never allowed to watch television or sit down to a meal with the rest of the family.
>
> The father made no pretense about his hatred and repudiation of the child, although he admitted that he had no reason to suspect that she wasn't his own. This case came to light because a teacher realized that the child was becoming rude and was bullying the other children to an exceptional degree [Allen & Morton, 1961, p. 113].

Emotional maltreatment includes abusive acts of commission as well as neglectful acts of omission that deny the children the emotional supplies they supposedly need for healthy emotional development. Scapegoating, denigrating, rejecting, ridiculing, humiliating, ostracizing, and undermining the child's self-esteem through perfectionist expectations are all acts of emotional abuse. Parental detachment, emotional indifference, lack of involvement or interest, and affective coldness in relation to the child are all acts of emotional neglect. Emotional neglect involves failure to provide necessary and essential psychological nurturance. Such failure may be the result of ignorance regarding the emotional development of children, personal limitations that make it difficult for the parent to give emotionally to the child, or indifference to the child's emotional needs. Abuse involves direct insults and assaults to the child's ego; overt parental behavior toward the child that impairs healthy emotional development.

Extreme inconsistency in responding to the child as well as inappropriat control are regarded as emotional maltreatment. A child who is dictatorially overcontrolled or whose parents provide no controlling guidelines for behavior is similarly maltreated.

Gabarino, Gettman, and Seeley (1986) define emotional maltreatment as a "pattern of psychically destructive behavior" which takes five forms: 1) rejecting, 2) isolating, 3) terrorizing, 4) ignoring, 5) corrupting-stimulating and reinforcing deviant behavior. (p. 8).

Emotional damage is not thought to be likely if an occasional rejecting, emotionally punitive parental act is manifested in a generally accepting parent–child relationship context. The pattern of emotionally maltreating behavior needs to be persistent, continuous, and cumulative for an injury to the child to be sustained.

The statutes, if interpreted rigorously, would require the intervention of the state with regard to many very wealthy families who fail to provide clear limits to their children. Very permissive disciplinary approaches to the child and easy indulgence of the child's every request and whim because it is convenient for the parent can be interpreted as potentially emotionally damaging to the child. The children of wealthy parents might suffer emotional deprivation. At a conference on the emotional problems of children of the rich and famous, it was noted that "children of the wealthy suffer most from lack of parental contact. Their parents have bought parental surrogates—tennis pros, swimming instructors, governesses and servants" (*New York Times,* May 15, 1985). The children suffer from "affluenza"—lack of continuous, intimate relationship with emotionally nurturing parents. Overprotection, overly permissive discipline, and excessive loving that shield and shelter the child from challenge and hurtful consequences of his or her behavior under expectations that fail to stimulate may also be regarded as emotional maltreatment.

The causal link between parental behavior and the development of emotional–psychological problems in children is very tenuous and ambiguous. The multiplicity of variables to which the child is exposed, the wide differences in children's vulnerability to what might appear to be noxious experiences make the prediction of outcomes very hazardous. Immediate damage is often not manifested; ultimate damage is difficult to definitely attribute to parental behavior.

Reviewing the research on the predictive validity of the effects of parents' behavior on children's mental health, Kavanagh (1982) concludes that "we are left with the problem of legal standards that require the reporting of injury in a situation where observable injury does not always (or in any reliable fashion) follow abuse" (p. 175). (See also Brassard, Germain and Hart, 1987). Whatever behavior is manifested by the child has to be clearly attributable to parental behavior before a charge of emotional maltreatment can be sustained. Until recently parents were "blamed" for developments that are now regarded as resulting largely from factors other than parents behavior. Homosexuality, asthma, autism, and schizophrenia, among others, are currently regarded as the result of variables more important than the input of parents.

Some situations, by their very nature, are supposedly high risk for emotional maltreatment. These include children living with mentally ill or substance-abusing parents, and children living with parents whose marital relationship is characterized by persistent conflict and violence. More controversially, some contend that children living in a homosexual "marriage" context, children living in communes, and children whose mothers returned to work immediately after their birth are higher than normal risk for emotional maltreatment. An emotionally disturbed child does not necessarily imply an emotionally abusing or neglecting parent.

Children manifest emotional disturbance as a consequence of living in poverty, experiencing divorce or the death of a person close to them, and as a result of contact with a punishing teacher or a rejecting peer group. The general social context may also be psychologically injurious. Children experiencing continuous warfare in Beirut or Northern Ireland, children who are constantly exposed to racist or sexist behavior, and children living with the threat of nuclear devastation might be regarded as emotionally abused.

The literature lists other examples of emotional abuse that highlight the question of definition. Thus Walters (1975) says:

If John brings home a report card with five A's and one C, the typical response of middle class parents is not "how well you have done" but "why did you get the C?" This constitutes emotional abuse. Low grades frequently prompt middle class parents to set curfew hours and enforce study time and to limit dating, and their children experience feelings of guilt and worthlessness. This constitutes emotional abuse [p. 37].

As the example illustrates, the greatest concern in including emotional maltreatment as a basis for action is that it may lead to unwarranted intervention in family functioning. There is difficulty in distinguishing between emotional maltreatment and general ineffective parenting that has possible damaging consequences for the child's emotional development. For these reasons, and because the emotional consequences of parental behavior are difficult to predict, some argue (Wald, 1975) that intervention for emotional maltreatment is justified only if clear damage to the child can be demonstrated as a result of repeated, habitual, damaging behaviors toward the child on the part of the caretaker. In the statutes relating to emotional abuse reporting (1) evidence of some persistent manifested observable child behavior indicating emotional difficulties (2) linked, in a probable cause-and-effect relationship to some specific parental behaviors (3) for which the parent(s) fail to take action toward corrective treatment, are generally required.

Emotional abuse may be established when a child who is emotionally disturbed is not provided treatment by the parent or when the parent refuses to accept treatment for himself or herself.

Expert testimony and standardized psychological tests might help objectively establish the extent of the child's emotional and/or psychological impairment. Improvement of the child's emotional adjustment upon removal from the home might experientially establish the validity of parental emotional maltreatment.

Sexual Abuse

Because the material on sexual abuse is so voluminous, we discuss the subject in a special section. At this point it merely needs to be noted that sexual abuse is a reportable event for which protective services have initial responsibility, and that social work intervention is appropriate and sanctioned in such cases (see p. 291–306.)

Exposure to Unwholesome or Demoralizing Conditions

Children living with parents who engage in prostitution or criminal activity, or who experience prolonged, severe alcoholism or drug addiction are also considered in danger. Such behavior on the part of the adult, which is "morally injurious to the child," is illustrated in the following reports:

> Mother had intercourse with several men in the same room in which the three young children slept.
>
> Mother and father were found in a drunken stupor when [the social] worker arrived and neighbors reported that parents frequently engaged in prolonged drinking bouts.

The moral development of a child exposed to frequent contact with deviance is neglected. The child is deprived of the opportunity to develop and internalize socially acceptable standards of conduct. The child needs protection from learning the ways of the gambler, the pimp, the drug dealer, the prostitute, and the thief.

A seven-year-old boy who was checked at customs off a flight from Jamaica was found to be carrying a toy animal stuffed with marijuana. The child was placed by the New York City Department of Social Services (*New York Times*, April 1980).

The *New York Times* reported (April 28, 1981) that four children were removed from their home by protective services after the court decided that their parents were "unsuitable" because the parents had a long arrest record. The children were living in close proximity to grandparents, aunts, uncles, and cousins who, in the aggregate, had been arrested more than four hundred times. The court believed that the children were exposed to role models which increased the probability that they would become criminals in turn.

Exploitation

The child may be forced to work at unreasonable tasks for unreasonably long hours. Often this work is in contravention of child labor laws; sometimes, although technically legal, the child's workload suggests neclectful exploitation. In either instance, the child is denied an opportunity for normal recreational activities and other opportunities for social and intellectual development. Exploitation also involves encouraging the child to beg or steal or to engage in prostitution for the benefit of the parents.

Collective and Institutional Context of Maltreatment

Collective Maltreatment

This presentation of situations that require intervention has been focused on parents or parental surrogates and on the care, or lack of care, of the child in his or her own home. There are, however, other kinds of contexts that present dangers of abuse and neglect of children.

The level of violence in society generally and in mass communication media suggests an acceptance of the use of force in settling interpersonal diputes. The general acceptance of, and acquiescence in, corporal punishment as a disciplinary procedure calls attention to the collective sanction of possible abuse. Although there is some dispute about whether lower-income families are more predisposed to the use of corporal punishment than middle-class families (Ehrlanger, 1974), studies show that the largest majority of parents of all classes see such disciplinary measures as acceptable (Stark & McEvoy, 1970); Blumenthal *et al.*, 1975). Reports from ten thousand middle-class respondents to a national survey conducted in 1977 indicated that 77 per cent thought "children should be disciplined by physical punishment whenever necessary" (Better Homes and Gardens, 1978, p. 66).

Interviews with a random group of one hundred mothers attending a well-baby clinic indicated that one third of the mothers whose children were less than one year of age had physically punished the child. One fourth of the mothers with children under six months of age had already started "spanking" the child (Korsch *et al.*, 1965, p. 1883). Collective consensual norms permit parents to justify the use of corporal punishment, which runs the risk of becoming abuse.

A questionnaire on family violence was mailed to 4,500 practicing psychiatrists in the United States. One of the questions asked was the following, "Do you feel that there are occasions when corporal punishment may serve a useful purpose?" The question was answered "yes" by 72.5 per cent of the respondents (Psychiatric Viewpoint Report, 1985, p. 133).

Racism and sexism harm the child's ability to achieve and maintain a sense of self-esteem. A culture that persistently communicates that blacks are second class or that women are in some ways inferior to men is collectively abusive to black and to female children.

One can similarly point to collective neglect in the failure to provide adequately for all children in the community. *Collective neglect* might be defined as a persistent failure on the part of the community to take action to provide adequate child-care resources despite the clearly established deprivation suffered by a significant group of children in the community. The community is guilty of neglect when it fails to provide adequate housing, adequate levels of public assistance, adequate schooling, adequate health service, or adequate recreational services, or when it allows job discrimination or makes no effort to control an open display of vice, narcotics traffic, and other illegal activity. Malnutrition in children that results from inadequate welfare grant can be regarded as an example of collective neglect.

Early in the history of child protective services, agencies were concerned with community neglect. Carstens, an early child welfare advocate, noted in 1912 that community neglect was manifested by the "city that does not provide adequate playgrounds—sunny and sanitary dwellings, does not enforce laws dealing with school attendance and child labor—that does not remove the corrupting influences within its border."

Over the past half century black infant mortality rates have generally been twice as high as white infant mortality rates. If the black infant mortality rate in 1981 had been as low as the mortality rate, for whites, 5,598 fewer black infants would have died (Children's Defense Fund, 1985, p. 79). These 5,598 preventable deaths that are primarily the result of community neglect, far surpass the 1,000–2,000 annual estimated fatalities caused by child abuse.

A Physicians' Task Force on Hunger in America sponsored by the Harvard School of Public Health found widespread evidence of hunger and malnutrition among children (Physicians' Task Force, 1985). The task force indicated that government policy and "mean-spirited" bureaucratic implementation of assistance programs contribute to the adverse situations that their investigations uncovered.

Neglect on the part of the community in immunizing children against disease may have incapacitating and even fatal consequences for children. In 1977 the U.S. Immunization Survey estimated that 15.5 million children were not fully protected against polio; 9.3 million children were not protected against diphtheria, pertussis, and tetanus; 13.8 million were not protected against measles; and 26.4 million remained susceptible to mumps (*New York Times*, April 7, 1977). The protective service agencies have as great a responsibility to protect children from community neglect as they have to protect them from parental neglect.

Institutional Maltreatment

At yet another level, one can identify abuse and neglect perpetrated by a variety of agencies in society charged with the temporary care of the child. Schools, children's institutions, and day-care centers have been charged with what has been termed *institutional maltreatment* (National Center on Child Abuse and Neglect, 1978b). Institutional maltreatment has been documented in studies such as those by Wooden (1976), and the office of the Comptroller General (1977).

Institutional maltreatment has been defined as abuse or neglect that occurs while the child is under the care, supervision, custody, or control of someone other than the parent. Institutional abuse can therefore occur in childcaring institutions.

Eligibility for state grants under the Child Abuse Prevention Treatment Acts required a system for reporting known or suspected incidents of child abuse in residential facilities. Institutions need and do have explicit policies regarding the use of isolation facilities, locked rooms, physical restraints, and corporal punishment, as well as the use of drugs for medication, and so on to guard against the possible abuse of children. These policies are part of the requirements for institutional licensing.

There is considerable controversy regarding institutional use of physical punishments (aversive therapy) to achieve change in behavior on the part of seriously disturbed children. When positive changes have been achieved as a result of the use of aversive therapy, some institutions feel justified in using such an approach. When the Massachusetts Office for Children and Youth threatened to close the Behavior Research Institute that used such an approach in treating autistic children, the parents of the children making progress, protested the move and obtained a court order preventing closure of the faculty (*New York Times,* December 31, 1985).

A 1979 survey of maltreatment in 1,700 child welfare institutions, as reported by the staff, indicated that some 2,692 complaints were received (Rindfleisch & Rabb, 1983). The maltreatment reported by the staff included unnecessary rough handling, sexual molestation of residents by staff, unjustified restraint and overmedication (Rindfleisch, 1984).

Institutional personnel, in response, note that they are held to a higher standard of care than are parents; activities that are defined as maltreatment of children in institutions are not regarded as maltreatment when these same acts are engaged in by parents. For instance, unlike parents, institutional personnel are forbidden to strike, hit, or spank a child. Secondly, institutional personnel point to the fact that children who require institutionalization present special problems of discipline and control. These children are behaviorally different from the general population of children, and hence different definitions of maltreatment need to be established that are more appropriate to such a population.

Personnel also note that institutional group living in and of itself requires more standardization of behavior, more adherence to group needs than is required in family living. Individualizing client preferences, except in a limited way, creates disruption in the institution, inconvenience, and possible danger to other group members.

Since the institutional context is different from that of the family, the standard definitions of maltreatment that have the family context as the point of reference may need redefinition for the institutional setting (Rindfleisch & Rabb, 1983). The reporting and investigation of institutionalized maltreatment is complicated by a variety of special considerations. Both the protective service agencies and the agency licensing the institution have some responsibility for monitoring institutional programs and procedures that might be regarded as maltreatment. They may differ in their definition of abuse. There have been occasions when a license was granted to an institution whose procedures the protective service agency regarded as abusive.

Institutional maltreatment has low visibility to outsiders. Those in the institution may know about the maltreatment but may feel conflicted about reporting it. Loyalty to the institution may be given priority over reporting requirements. There are further constraints deriving from fear of reprisals by administration as well as negative responses from peers. After all, the report of maltreatment is generally a report to outsiders about actions on the part of peers and colleagues.

Often maltreatment, when observed, is redefined as a staff problem. The action is not perceived as abusive but rather the consequence of ignorance or incompetence on the part of a staff member who needs further training.

For many of the situations that arise in the institution which trigger incidents of apparent maltreatment, there are nagging questions about differences in definition of limits. Children in institutions often need to be restrained from hurting themselves or engaging in aggressive action against other children and against staff. What are the limits of appropriate, acceptable, permissible restraint and discipline in protecting other children, in self-defense on the part of staff, and in acting so that furniture, equipment, appliances are not destroyed?

Procedures that provide opportunities for children to report incidents of abuse, and protect children in using those procedures, may help to reduce institutional maltreatment. Regular, competent supervision of staff members, providing a channel for review of their performance, is a protection to children. An institution that is open to visiting at all times by parents provides additional protection against maltreatment.

In early 1984, the disclosure of sexual molestation of forty-one young children by the staff of a private nursery school in Manhattan Beach, California, sparked a series of reports of such experiences throughout the United States. In 1984 and early 1985, arrests were made of day-care center personnel in New York, New Jersey, Alabama, Tennessee in response to charges of child sexual molestation. The wave of concern triggered screening of all day-care employees, including fingerprinting and checks of criminal records.

Institutions operated under the auspices of religious sects committed to corporal punishment have been cited for abuse. These institutions cite biblical injunctions about such punishment as justification for their activities. In June 1984, Vermont state troopers removed 112 children from such a school and examined the children for signs of abuse. Persistent reports had been received that the school had routinely administered corporal punishment to the children (*New York Times,* June 30, 1984). What is regarded as child abuse by the state licensing agencies is often in conflict with the definition of corporal punishment by such institutions as discipline and not child abuse.

Corporal punishment in the school is a frequently cited example of institutional maltreatment (Maurer, 1974). In 1977, when the U.S. Supreme Court sanctioned corporal punishment in the schools if certain guidelines were observed, only two states had laws that prohibited such disciplinary procedures. Some thirty-three states either allowed or specifically endorsed corporal punishment in the schools (Hyman *et al.,* 1977).

A task force study by the National Education Association (1972) found that 67.5 per cent of the elementary-school teachers questioned supported corporal punishment in the schools.

In the case of *Ingraham* v. *Wright,* the Supreme Court ruled "that spanking by schoolteachers did not violate the Constitution's 8th Amendment ban against cruel and unusual punishment even if the spanking is severe, 'excessive' and medically damaging." The decision was a recognition of the teacher's common-law privilege to inflict reasonable punishment (*New York Times,* April 20, 1977).

In 1985, corporal punishment in schools was allowed in forty-two states. Although most major urban school districts have banned corporal punishment, about 75 per cent of all children are enrolled in school districts that permit it.

Scope and Demographics of Maltreatment

It is very difficult to get accurate statistics on the incidence and prevalence of child maltreatment. There are wide differences between statistics deriving from official reports of maltreatment as compared with the actual frequency of maltreatment, much of which is unreported. This leads to the repeated contention that reported maltreatment is merely the "tip of the iceberg." Statistics of maltreatment vary in terms of the facility which is collecting them, the purpose for which they are collected, and the kinds of events included in the definition of maltreatment. Summarizing a review of the literature on the incidence rates of abuse and neglect, Holmes (1978) found that "they are widely divergent and often questionable in their accuracy" (p. 128)—a statement that continued to have validity through the 1980s.

In 1979–1980, the National Center on Child Abuse and Neglect sponsored a national study of child maltreatment, including both abuse and neglect. A scientifically selected sample of twenty-six counties located in ten states provided the source of the data. In each country, data were collected from the local child protective service agency as well as from other community institutions that were likely to have any contact with maltreated children—schools, hospitals, police, courts. Clear explicit definitions of the different maltreatment conditions (physical abuse; sexual abuse; emotional abuse; physical neglect; educational neglect; emotional neglect) were provided to the respondents and procedures for data collection were standardized. The study was then national is scope, maltreatment was broadly defined, and both reported and unreported events were solicited. The study found that "at least 652,000 children are abused and/or neglected annually in the U.S." (U.S. Department of Health and Human Services, 1981, p. 171). This translates into an annual rate of about one maltreated child for every 100 children under the age of 18 in the United States. It was notable that a sizable percentage of the uncovered maltreated events had not been officially reported.

Despite the comprehensiveness of the data and the care with which they were collected, incidence rates have been criticized as being erroneously low—particularly with regard to the incidence of sexual abuse. The study itself noted that the figures cited in the report were regarded as minimal figures.

There continues to be dispute regarding the actual incidence and prevalence of child maltreatment in the United States. For our purposes, however, the most valid, most comprehensive statistical data available are those provided in the annual reports on child maltreatment that were collected and distributed by the American Association for Protecting Children, a division of the American Humane Association. The American Association for Protecting Children is funded by the National Center on Child Abuse and Neglect of the U.S. Department of Health and Human Services to collect official reports on child maltreatment from all of the states. Such reports have been made annually since 1976 and are continuing. Over time, an increasing number of states have participated in the submission of such data and procedures and definitions have gradually become more uniform. By 1983, ail states, the Virgin Islands, Guam, Puerto Rico, and the

Marianas Islands were submitting reports to the Association. The statistics provided are based on reports to protective service agencies so that unreported maltreatment is not included. Whereas using only reported events as a basis for describing maltreatment variables might misrepresent the actual situation, such statistics are in effect more useful for a social work text. These statistics deal with those cases with which social workers are ultimately actually concerned in doing the work of protective services. Although unreported events are of general concern, reported maltreatment is the particular concern of the social worker. Unless reported, the social agency is not involved.

The reports from the American Association for Protecting Children, then, provide standardized, comprehensive national data over time, of reported maltreatment with which the protective service agency is involved.

Since 1976, the number of cases reported has increased steadily from 416,000 in 1976 to 1,928,000 in 1985. Although the number of reports has increased, the rate of increase from year to year has leveled off somewhat, from 24 per cent between 1976 and 1977 to a 11.6 per cent increase between 1984 and 1985. The reporting rate was estimated at 30.6 children per 1,000 U.S. child population in 1985 (American Humane Association, 1987).

It is questionable whether or not the increased number of reports reflects an actual increase in maltreatment. The number of reports may have increased because the public has been better educated to perceive and report abuse, the number of professional groups mandated to report has increased and professional consciousness regarding the need to report has intensified, the kinds of maltreatment that require reporting has increased, and because reporting procedures generally have become more efficient and sophisticated. The increase may also reflect increases in the factors closely associated with heightened risk of maltreated children,—the number of children living in single-parent families, the number of children living below the poverty level, and increases in the unemployment rate.

The principal type of matreatment reported in 1985 is neglect, constituting some 55.7 percent of all reports received. Physical abuse of varying kinds of severity and including sexual abuse made up some 33 per cent of all children reported. Severe physical abuse requiring medical treatment is a small percentage of the physical abuse reports and is heavily concentrated in the younger, more vulnerable children. In 1985 sexual abuse accounted for 11.7 per cent of all reports. Over time there has been a decrease in the percentage that neglect contributes to the overall statistic and an increase in the percentage of sexual abuse. Agencies are giving lower priority to neglect and higher priority to sexual maltreatment. In response to growing demands for services and decreases in funding, agency neglect reports are more likely to be screened out.

The number of reports received do not give an accurate picture of the nature of the problems facing protective service agencies. There is a considerable difference between reports received and reports finally substantiated. Approximately 45–50 per cent of the reports received prove on investigation not to be valid or substantiated cases of maltreatment. Continuing protective service activity then is concerned with about half of the cases reported.

Substantiation rates are related to the source of reporting. About half of all reports come from nonprofessionals—friends, neighbors, relatives, and anoymous reports. Professional sources of reports of maltreatment include medical, school, law enforcement, and social service personnel. Each of these professional groups provides 10–12 per cent of all reports. Maltreatment of younger children is more likely to be reported by medical and child care personnel; maltreatment of older children is more often reported by school and law enforcement personnel.

Reports from professional sources are more likely to prove to be substantiated than reports from nonprofessional sources. Professionals have a better knowledge of the definition of maltreatment; they have often obtained some preliminary information about the maltreatment before making their reports.

Substantiation of a report depends on a judgement of the seriousness of a reported maltreatment situation. "Seriousness" is a comparative evaluation, one that changes with variations in level of demands made on protective service agencies and variations in resources available. The U.S. Department of Health and Human Services National Incidence Study (1981) noted that, given the fact that child protective resources (staff, service programs, budget) have not kept pace with the dramatic increase in reporting, "substantiation rates have become not so much a question of whether the child and family need help, but rather how badly and urgently help is needed" (p. 14).

The national reports provide descriptive data on the child victim, the child's family, and maltreatment perpetrators. The average age of the maltreated child is slightly over seven years of age. Younger, more vulnerable children are disproportionately represented in the maltreatment statistics; older, adolescent children are disproportionately underrepresented. Boys are more frequently abused than girls, but this was true only for children up to age ten or eleven. Girls are more frequently reported abused from ages eleven to seventeen. The change results from the inclusion of sexual abuse in the statistic—a type of abuse that is reported much more frequently with females as victims and is concentrated in older children.

Activity level, agressivity, risk-taking behavior, destructiveness and temperamental instability of young boys increase their risk for abuse. Sexual risks and the double standard make preadolescent and adolescent girls the objects of stricter parental controls (Wilson, Daly, & Weghorst, 1981). (See also Martin, 1983). The sexually abused child is on the average older than other groups of maltreated children and is much more likely to be a female.

The demographic picture of the maltreating family, according to the National 1983 report of States Statistics collected by the American Humane Association, Children's Division, and a six-year trend report published by that organization (Russell & Trainor, 1984), is that of a low-income family with between two and three children. At a time when about 12 per cent of the U.S. population was receiving public assistance, 47.7 per cent of the maltreating families were receiving such help. The maltreating families were disproportionately single-parent female-headed families. At a time when 20 per cent of children were living in such households, these households accounted for 40.3 per cent of maltreating families. Maltreating families were subject to multiple stress—marital, health, social, and economic. Although maltreatment is found in all socioeconomic groups, it is most frequently reported among the poor.

Selective sources of referral tend to accentuate the skewed class affiliation of reported maltreatment. Public hospitals and clinics, police, and welfare agencies are much more frequently the sources of maltreatment reports than are either private hospitals or family physicians. Low-income people are in contact with the first institutions; middle-class and upper-class people more frequently make use of the private, voluntary sources of help.

Reviewing some of the research on the socioeconomic characteristics of abuse and neglect families, Pelton (1978) concluded that after allowing for justifiable

explanations of discrepancies in reporting, lower socioeconomic groups are disproportionately represented among maltreaters, so that child abuse is not, in fact, a
"classless" phenomenon. Although child maltreatment takes place at all class
levels, proportionately more child maltreatment takes place among lower-class
families. After allowing for the effect of differential reporting, some component of
the disproportionate frequency of maltreatment is a consequence of the greater
situational stress faced by lower-class families and their more limited opportunities for escaping from such stress. However, the fact that many lower-class families living under comparable stress do not maltreat their children suggests that
personality and attitudinal factors account for some percentage of the explanation of maltreatment as well.

Nonwhite families were overrepresented among maltreaters, 18.7 per cent of
the group were black; whereas 9.8 were Hispanic. These are both larger percentages than the relative proportions of these groups in the total population. Since
a very high percentage of black families generally are single-parent female-
headed families receiving public assistance, one might reasonably expect black
families to be disproportionately represented among the maltreatment group. In
summarizing the data of national child maltreatment reports over a six-year
period, Russell and Trainor (1984) noted that "given their disadvantaged socioeconomic status, blacks have always been disproportionately represented among
neglecting families but not necessarily among abusive families" (p. 17). "While
blacks are disproportionately represented among maltreated children this does
not seem to result from a major racial bias in reporting. Instead, it seems to be
related to the basic economic inequality in our society between whites and
blacks" (p. 19).

Breaking down maltreatment statistics to specifics about physical abuse, sexual abuse, and neglect presents a more accurate picture of the situation.
Nonwhites are not more likely than whites to engage in physical or sexual abuse
of children. They are however much more often likely to be reported for neglect,
which is closely related to low income. The heightened reporting for neglect
accounts for the disproportionate statistics relating to nonwhites in the total
maltreatment picture.

The Native American nations have developed their own tribal abuse and neglect legislation, and cases involving abuse and neglect are handled by tribal
courts. A comparison of maltreated Navajo children with their nonabused peers
indicates that abused children more often come from larger single-parent families
supported by welfare assistance programs (White and Cornely, 1981).

Although females (59.6 per cent) are more often listed as perpetrators than
males (40.4 per cent) this reflects an opportunity factor. Many of the reported
families are single, female-headed families, so that females in these families are
the only parent in contact with the child. In general, mothers have more contact
time with their children.

The disproportionate visibility of females in the maltreatment of children is
emphasized further by the relative absence of visibility of males. Martin (1984)
reviewed sixty-six studies of child abuse published during a five-year period and
confirmed the absence of attention given to abusive fathers. Only two of the sixty-
six studies focused on fathers. Apparently, the mother is regarded as the primary
responsible parent even in situations in which the male parent is the abuser.

The nature of the maltreatment differs with the gender of the perpetrator.
Males are associated with more major and minor physical injury and much more
often with sexual abuse and females are disproportionately associated with ne-

glect. The average age of maltreaters was thirty-one–thirty-two years. In the great majority of cases, the perpetrator was the child's biological parent or stepparent, and in a small number of cases, it was the foster or adoptive parent. In cases of sexual abuse, stepparents and other relatives are more frequently the perpetrators; biological-parents, although still the largest group (56 per cent) are less frequently represented in cases of sexual abuse than in cases of physical abuse (85 per cent) or neglect (91 per cent). Sexual abuse perpetrators are likely to be older and more widely distributed along the socioeconomic spectrum than are perpetrators of other forms of maltreatment.

Process in Protective Services

The social work process, the sequential steps taken to achieve the objectives of service, are the same in protective services as they are elsewhere in social work. This process consists of eight basic steps:

1. Primary prevention
2. Report, case-finding, and intake
3. Social study-information gathering
4. Diagnosis-assessment
5. Case planning
6. Treatment-intervention
7. Evaluation
8. Termination

We consider the steps in sequence in discussing the protective service process.

Primary Prevention

Even before client and worker become jointly involved in the social work, process, preliminary activities are directed toward primary prevention. Success at the point of primary prevention would mean that maltreatment is prevented from occurring and the parent never becomes involved with the agency. Rather than being reactive to maltreatment that has occurred, primary prevention expresses a proactive orientation.

Slogans such as "Better to prevent than lament" and "Better to support than report" are proactive statements. Preventive action at the broadest level involves the reorganization of society so as to guarantee jobs and adequate income to all, thus reducing the level of stress contributing toward maltreatment. A change in society values to clearly outlaw violence in interpersonal relationships, particularly with regard to the use of force with children, would contribute to the prevention of maltreatment. A change in attitudes regarding the rights of children in the parent–child relationship would also be helpful.

Family planning support and ready access to abortion would help reduce the number of unwanted children who are high risk for maltreatment. Programs offering prenatal medical and nutritional information may help reduce the number of low-weight and/or premature babies who are also high risk for abuse.

At the general community level, prevention has the entire population of parents and potential parents as its target. The inclusion of knowledge and skills about parenting and child development as part of the high school curriculum would better prepare future parents for raising children with diminished likelihood of abuse and neglect. Parent education programs at the adult level would complement this effort.

Parent education is directed toward increasing knowledge about child development which improves the care givers' child management skills and developing attitudes that will increase positive parent–child interaction. One major objective of such abuse-prevention parent education programs is to reduce age inappropriate expectations regarding child development.

At the child's level, special programs that educate children to recognize signs of parental stress and frustration and educate children to learn appropriate responses to reduce parent–child tension are helpful preventive measures.

One parent education child abuse prevention program includes such topics as "Parenting Styles: Avoid the Extremes"; "The Baby is Here: Now What?"; "Paychecks and Parenting: Coping Tactics for Working Parents"; "Discipline"; "Parent Burnout: I Want My Turn"; "Talking So Kids Will Listen."

In addition to general education about parenting, specific educational programs relating to child maltreatment that are designed to raise the level of public consciousness regarding maltreatment and its onset should be directed toward the general public. Public education of this kind involves dissemination of information about how to deal with stress relating to children. A poster from the National Committee for Prevention of child abuse lists "12 alternatives to whacking your kid" from "stop in your tracks; step back; sit down" to "put on your favorite record."

Primary prevention programs have been developed around the concepts of early bonding. Early firm bonding between mother and child has been explicitly encouraged and supported with the supposition that such bonding reduces the likelihood of abuse. Support groups have been organized that pair an experienced mother with a first-time mother. These groups are designed to help new mothers deal with stresses associated with the transition to parenthood.

A home visitor program as a maltreatment preventive procedure has been proposed but not yet implemented in this country. The program would include periodic visits to the home following childbirth that continue until the child begins school. The visits would be made by a public health nurse or a trained home health aide who would provide the family with information and advice on child care and would do a routine health checkup on the child.

Primary preventive efforts might be directed toward the general public and to the total population of future parents. Since most of this public is not likely to maltreat its children if it does become parents, this is not a very efficient focus for prevention efforts. It is a program designed to innoculate everybody against a disease to which only a limited group might be susceptible. Pregnant women attending a well-baby clinic or women in hospital maternity wards are a more delimited population for such efforts. Since they are about to become parents, they may have a heightened interest in parent education to prevent abuse. An even more efficiently selected target for prevention efforts are those fathers and mothers who can be identified by some procedure as having high potential for child maltreatment.

Successful predictive procedures that can be easily administered would provide a significant advantage for primary prevention. If a group of potential abusers can be clearly identified, efforts can be made to "immunize" them by offering help to reduce their abuse potential. Efforts to sort out this group for special offers of help to prevent maltreatment have engaged a sizable number of researchers.

They have used questionnaires, MMPI subscales, standardized screening instruments, and observations of mother–child interaction to identify high-risk-for-maltreatment parents. The locations for obtaining such data have most frequently been prenatal care clinics and hospital maternity care units.

The procedures are designed to elicit experiences and attitudes and to discern behaviors that are supposedly related to high risk for abuse–developmental experiences as an abused child, stresses in the social environment and available support systems, attitudes toward corporal punishment, expectations regarding child development, and impulse control.

Specifically, observers try to evaluate the mother's attitude toward the child by the way the mother holds the child, maintains eye contact with the child, allows the child to feed at his or her own pace, smiles at the child, and talks to the child. Does the mother address the baby by its name or refer to the child as "it"; was the mother's reaction to learning the baby's sex positive or negative; what is the mother's reaction to the child spitting up or defecating?

Prevention—prediction efforts employ a successive approximation approach in refining predictive instruments so that they are increasingly more sensitive and accurate. Based on variables suggested by the child abuse research literature, one develops a questionnaire, an interview, or an observation schedule, sorts respondents into high-low risk groups, follows respondents to determine whether or not they actually abused their children, checks actual results against prediction, retains those items in the procedure most closely associated with accurate predictions, and revises the procedure based on the results and starts the process again. This is essentially the approach used by Ayoub et al. (1983); Helfer, Schneider, and Hoffmeister (1978); Geddis et al. (1979) and Altemeier, et al. (1984).

Ultimately we may be able to devise a procedure that clearly and accurately identifies high-risk abusers for a program of primary prevention. Although these screening procedures have demonstrated some success in correctly identifying abusive parents, the level of successful prediction is generally modest. Miscalculations, "false positives and false negatives," are unacceptably frequent (Altemeier, et al. 1984). In addition, different procedures tend to come up with different basic factors that distinguish the predicted abusers from the predicted nonabusers. The need for further predictive screening instrumentation is indicated. Furthermore, neglect prediction may require procedures that are different from physical abuse prediction which is in turn different form sexual abuse prediction. Gilbert (1982) has detailed some of the difficulties in developing preventive programs with regard to social problems. McMurtry (1985) has critically analyzed some of the research on child abuse prediction for the purpose of prevention. Giovannoni (1982) outlines the reasons that make development of preventive programs in child maltreatment a dubious undertaking.

An effective prevention program depends on two essential considerations—clear identification of cause(s) of the problem and development of a technology that "eradicates" the cause(s). Preventing child abuse is hampered by the fact that we have identified no clear cause or set of causes and have a very blunt technology to deal with diffuse causal configuration.

In addition to technology, ethics and funding present barriers to large-scale preventive programs. Routine examination of parents to determine their classification as potentially abusive or nonabusive is likely to be regarded as an unwarranted intrusion on personal privacy. Funds for prevention of abuse in the best of all possible world's should not be competitive with funds providing services for children who are actually suffering abuse. But these programs do often compete for funds, and more adequate preventive programs are likely to mean less adequate service programs.

Prevention is the central focus of Children's Trust Fund Programs initiated in Kansas in 1980 and subsequently adopted by other state legislatures. Funds are generated by a surcharge on marriage licenses, birth certificates, and divorce decrees or through specially designated state income tax refunds. Funds for these programs are administered by either a specially organized committee or by the State Division of Children Youth and Families. In either case, funds are provided to support abuse prevention projects and programs (Birch, 1983).

Case Finding and Intake

Crisis intervention programs move us closer to the time of actual imminent risk of a maltreatment event. Even if maltreatment has not yet taken place, there is great danger that it will take place if no one intervenes. Crisis hot lines are offered at this point to avert maltreatment.

An effort has been made to encourage parents who feel that they might maltreat their children, to request agency services voluntarily. Posters and spot radio and TV announcements indicate the availability of parental-stress hot-line services that the parent may call. Such services are accessible in many communities seven days a week, twenty-four hours a day. The service offers supportive listening, advice, and reassurance to a parent who is about to "lose his cool with a kid" or to a parent who has just abused a child and wants to talk about his or her feelings with an interested, accepting person. Hot-line notices posted on bulletin boards in shopping centers and in public toilets, and used in radio and TV spot announcements may read:

Parental Stress Hot-line

Sometimes feel you're going to blow your top? Can't cope any longer? The kids are getting to you? You want help? CALL _____ 24 hours a day, 7 days a week.

Do you know of a child who is being abused? Want to let somebody know about it? CALL _____ 24 hours a day, 7 days a week.

One typical hot-line announcement reads

Are you concerned about angry feelings toward your child? Do you feel you can't cope any longer? Are you yelling or hitting too much or afraid you might, call _____. We care. We'll listen. Talk it over with another concerned parent.

The following is a typical abuse prevention call.

Kenneth, a 39-year-old father of four, called because he's afraid he's going to hurt his oldest son, Michael, aged 17. Last time Michael took the family car without permission and dented a fender. Kenneth was furious and in a blind rage slammed his fist against a wall and made a hole in the plaster. When he realized what he had done he experienced panic at the thought that it might have been his son whom he had hit. It worries him that he was out of control and could have injured Michael (Turner et al., 1981, p. 31).

"Help lines" are crisis intervention hot lines organized to meet the special needs of potentially abusive parents. They provide a stressful parent with a sympathetic, nonjudgmental listener and they offer an information and referral service. Protective service agencies and hospitals often offer a service of this nature with a title such as "Parental Stress Telephone Counseling Service." This service is available statewide on a toll-free basis—twenty-four hours, seven days a week. Callers who request it are guaranteed anonymity.

Respite centers provide a short period of relief or rest from child care for parents who are facing some emergency or crisis. These centers provide full-time shelter care for a limited period when parental stress has built up to a point at which abuse of a child is threatened. The New York Foundling Hospital has a crisis nursery where a child can be left overnight when a parent is fearful of losing control. The average stay is three days. These crises nurseries are open twenty-four hours a day and generally serve children under the age of six.

Temporary relief from child care to "defuse" stress and prevent abuse is also provided by lay volunteers who are available to come to the home for temporary child care.

The abusive or neglectful parent however, does not generally voluntarily apply for agency service. Case finding and the initiation of contact result from the action of other individuals or community agencies.

Initiation of services frequently results from the legal requirement of mandatory reporting. The laws require that professionals who are aware of cases of maltreatment report them to an agency authorized to take action. Originally the laws required the reporting of "nonaccidental physical injury." The conditions that require reporting were subsequently widened to include neglect, sexual molestation, and emotional or mental injury. An effort has been made in the revision of the reporting statutes to give a more specific definition of the conditions that require reporting. The trend has been to increase the maximum age of children protected by the legislation to eighteen years.

The list of professionals required to report is constantly being expanded. It includes, among others, doctors, nurses, social workers, school personnel, day-care-center personnel, legal personnel, and dentists. Although some states require reporting by "any person" having "reasonable cause to believe" that abuse has taken place, additional states encourage, but do not require, such reporting (Education Commission of the States, 1977).

The agencies to which reports are to be made are generally the public welfare agencies or the legal agencies of the community. The laws grant civil and criminal immunity to the professionals required to make such reports, provide penalties for failure to report, and sometimes provide for follow-up. The abuse-reporting laws are essentially a case-finding device that helps the community to identify the abusive family and the abused child.

The National Incidence Study found that mandated professionals tend to report only about 20 per cent of the cases of abuse that they encounter. Studies of mandated reporters indicate that they are frequently not familiar with reporting requirements and procedures, and have difficulty in detecting signs of neglect, emotional abuse, or sexual mistreatment. Ideological barriers to reporting derive from attitudes about the acceptability of corporal punishment by parents and support of parental childrearing autonomy (Levin, 1983; Wilson, Thomas, & Schuette, 1983).

Some mandated reporters feel professionally justified in failing to report a family for child abuse. Their promise of confidentiality to parents who reveal abuse during the course of family therapy conflicts with the legal requirement to report and the obligation to protect the child from possible additional abuse (Butz, 1985).

Professionals have been held liable for failure to report child abuse in relatively few cases, and in even fewer cases, there has been criminal prosecution for failure to report.

Anonymous reports, during which the reporter chooses not to reveal his or her identity, pose a problem. While agencies are obligated to accept such reports, a study of the final disposition of over one thousand anonymous reports by a county protective service agency over a two-year period indicated that a very high percentage of such reports (87%) proved, upon investigation, to be unfounded (Adams, Barone, & Tooman, 1982). Given scarce personnel resources, questions have arisen about the efficiency of accepting anonymous reports.

The person receiving the report needs to make some assessment of the credibility of the report and the person reporting, decide whether or not the nature of the complaint falls within the agency's definition of child abuse and neglect and determine whether or not the child(ren) is (are) in such immediate danger so as to require emergency intervention.

Upon receiving a complaint "made in good faith" of possible maltreatment, the agency is obligated to investigate the situation. In accepting the initial report of alleged maltreatment, the agency makes an effort to obtain as much specific information as possible about the maltreatment, the child, the family, and about the person reporting. What is the nature of the maltreatment; how did the person reporting become aware of it; what are the age and sex of the child; the name, address, and composition of the family; the name and address of the reporter and relationship to the reported family; and how willing is the reporter to have the agency share with the family the fact that he or she initiated the report? How willing is the reporter to testify in court about the maltreatment if the situation eventually results in court action?

When a complaint is initiated by an individual, the agency accepts the responsibility not only for investigating the situation but also for helping the person who makes the complaint. Some people may feel guilty about having made the report or about "interfering" in the affairs of another family; consequently, they need reassurance that their communication will be held in confidence.

The investigation following the receipt of a report and after some initial screening out of reports that have very little credibility or very limited and contradictory information, is a preliminary social study for the purpose of report verification. Regulations require that an investigation be made within a short time after receipt of the complaint so that a child in possible danger may be protected. Investigation must be done expeditiously, before bruises or welts disappear. Such an investigation might start with a check of any previously recorded protective service data on the family.

The first contact by the agency might be made with the person, or the agency, who has initiated the complaint. If the situation seems to warrant further exploration, contact is then initiated with the family against which the complaint has been made. Many agencies suggest that the initial contact with the family be by letter. The letter, it is argued, identifies the agency, gives a general explanation of the service and the community's concern, suggests that help is needed, and gives the parent a chance to react in privacy and to consider what to do. Other agencies prefer to make an unannounced visit. Henry's (1958) study of the effects of such a procedure demonstrates that this approach does not necessarily have the negative consequences usually anticipated by social workers.

Whether the contact is initiated by letter or by an unannounced visit, the approach is direct and frank. It involves a clear statement by the agency that it has learned that the child is in potential danger and that, representing the community, it would like to enlist the aid of the parents in determining what is happening. The focus of the inquiry is not on the investigation of the truth or the falsity of the allegation, which would put the parents on the defensive. The focus is on what should be done—by the agency and parents together—for the optimum benefit of the child. Protective service agencies prefer to "evaluate" rather than "investigate"—and this is an important attitudinal difference: an investigation may be conducted without involving the client; an evaluation implies a joint process, with the parents' active participation. Although in one sense this is an investigation of the situation, in another and more productive sense it is an offer of help to the family.

Child protection, the primary objective, is balanced by respect for family rights and autonomy. The investigatory component ("I am required to see the child to see if she or he is all right") is balanced by the helping component ("What kinds of help do you think you need to make things easier for you"?)

The preliminary investigation is designed to achieve not only assurance of protection of the child, the primary objective, but also the beginning of a possible positive working relationship with the family and a start in the collection of the data necessary for understanding how the family might be helped.

The parents are not given the right to refuse an exploration: "We accept the parent's right to make his own decision, but we question the wisdom of having him base it solely on his impulse to resist help and not include his wish to help his child" (Lane, 1952). The agency does not regard its approach as an intrusion but as a demonstration of concern and an active implementation of its desire to be helpful to both parents and children. As one client noted, "what they do here is protect parents from being cruel to their children" (Bishop, 1964, p. 83). Where resistance is anticipated or previously experienced, and in situations that present some physical danger to the worker, an officer can be assigned to accompany the worker.

The caseworker tries to get an accurate and objective picture of the situation. He or she is concerned with specifics: "the dates and times when the children have been left alone unattended for hours at a time; when they have been absent from school without sufficient reason; when the parents have been intoxicated and unable to function adequately as parents" (Henry, 1958, p. 5). Such details will be required as evidence if and when a petition is made to the court, but even more important, they can be used as a basis for discussing with the parents why the community, as represented by the agency, is concerned about the situation and why the parents themselves should be concerned. Getting evidence of neglect and/or abuse and establishing a relationship with the client are not antithetical procedures. Obtaining such information is, in effect, part of the social-study step in the casework process—a prerequisite for diagnosis and treatment—that is helpful in establishing a relationship.

No intervention by an outsider representing the community can be wholly benign, without some negative consequences, however accepting, understanding, empathic, and benevolent the worker's approach might be. The appearance of the social worker on the doorstep of the family arouses anxiety, discomfort, guilt, shame, defensiveness, as well as anger, resentment, resistance, and opposition.

The social worker, recognizing this, has to act so as to defuse, as much as possible, such responses.

Almost always an effort is made to see the child on behalf of whom the complaint was initiated. In interviewing the child, if the child is old enough to be interviewed, the social worker has to observe some precautions. The social worker has to assure the child that he or she has the parent's permission to talk with the child and that what the child says to the social worker will not be shared with the parents—unless the child explicitly agrees with this. The social worker has to be sensitive to the fact that talking to the child may have consequences for the child's relationship with the parents.

The social worker asks to see the child so as to examine any visible physical injuries. The social worker looks for teeth missing, black and blue marks and other skin discolorations, scabs covering cuts that are healing, rope burns, pinch marks, scratches, and difficulties the child might display in walking or using his or her hands. Where the social worker is uncertain about the extent or nature of injury sustained by the child, a pediatric examination might be required. This may need to be scheduled despite the opposition of the parents. Once again, this requires the use of authority in protecting the child. The worker may supplement the visit by talking to relatives and friends who have knowledge of the situation. This is done only after informing the family that such contacts are planned.

The agency does not disclose to the client the identity of the complainant, because it does not feel this is helpful. However, Varon (1964) suggests that this compounds one of the psychological problems faced by the client: feeling impotent and helpless in the face of social forces that "victimize" him or her and over which he or she has no control, the parent is made to feel more vulnerable and more impotent by an "anonymous" complaint against which he or she cannot contend. The social worker must be aware that the initial contact is apt to arouse the hostility, the guilt, and the defensiveness of parents, for their adequacy as parents is being called into question, their authority over their children is in danger, and the autonomy of the family is being threatened. The parents must be given an opportunity to ventilate their hostility.

Benjamin (1958) has aptly described the prescribed effective professional approach in protective service situations:

> Protective service should reach out to the negligent parents with feeling for them as troubled people, with discernment that life may not have given them sufficient opportunities to develop their capacities for parenthood, and with sympathetic understanding for their inability to cope with their problems alone. Kindness and acceptance should form the basis for every helping relationship. However, understanding is not enough for helping negligent parents. Since they are often disorganized, at times confused or belligerent and destructive in their attitudes, it takes firmness to stop them. . . . Expectations clearly and strongly stated in specific terms give direction to the unorganized client, lift him out of confusion, and help him partialize problems that might otherwise be overwhelming. . . . Implied in the concept of expectation is a concern for the other person and respect for his potential ability to accept his responsibility [pp. 12;–17].

The approach is based on a number of assumptions:

1. The parents are not deliberately or perversely willful in their behavior; neglect, abuse, and exploitation are not the result of happenstance but are

responses to the difficulties, social and/or personal, that the parents face. The behavior toward the child is symptomatic of some serious difficulty in the parents' and/or the family's situation.

2. There is, consequently, a cause for such deviant behavior that, if understood, might be subject to change; people can, and do, change with the help of the agency.

3. The parents themselves are unhappy about the situation. However resistant and defensive they may be to the community's intervention in the family's life, they welcome, in some measure, the opportunity to see if they can effect changes.

4. For the good of the child, the family, and the community, the first efforts should be directed at helping the parents make the changes that would permit the children to remain in their own home without danger.

It may, however, be difficult to communicate these assumptions successfully to the client group. Varon (1964), in interviews with thirteen former clients of a protective service agency and fifty of their nonclient neighbors, discovered that the agency was generally perceived as investigatory and punitive: "Only a fraction of the former clients interviewed appeared able to conceptualize something as complex as authority that is simultaneously coercive and benevolent" (p. 57).

The basis approach—one that combines acceptance and firmness, an attempt to understand rather than to judge, and respect for the parents as people while in no way condoning their behavior—is illustrated in the following case:

The C. family was referred to the child welfare agency by a hospital which treated the six-year-old boy, Wade, for a broken arm suffered in a beating by his mother. Mr. C. began the first interview with the [social] worker by saying, "I want to say directly at the beginning that I approve of all my wife has done." He said the neighbors were prying into his business and they were "neurotic about the whole affair." Mrs. C. agreed with him.

Mr. C. then tried to deflect the conversation from the beating of the child by talking about the neighbors' interference in the past. The worker listened attentively but brought the subject back to the beating by saying that he could see they had had some trouble with their neighbors but the report of serious abuse of the children was the main concern now. Both parents said they whipped the children because they believed in firm discipline and they challenged the worker's right to question this. Mr. C. again attempted to avoid the subject of Wade's beating by describing at length how strict his parents had been with him. Mrs. C. said the children had "evil in them" which had to be controlled.

The worker said he could understand how Mr. and Mrs. C. felt about his being there. He granted that the parents have the right to discipline their children, but pointed out that when a child is injured "the community wants to find out what the problems are and try to help the family. That's why I am here."

Mr. C. maintained that there was not any problem. He began talking about one of the other children's difficulties in school, and with Mrs. C. went into a long tirade about "young teachers" not being firm enough with youngsters.

Again the worker brought the conversation back to the C.'s own disciplinary practices by saying that children had to be dealt with firmly, but the injury of a child was a serious matter. He added, "I can understand that one may be so upset he has trouble controlling himself." Mrs. C. hesitatingly said, "I was so upset and too angry," and broke into tears. The worker replied that, if together they could try to understand why Mrs. C. gets so upset, perhaps the behavior would not continue [Sandusky, 1960, p. 24].

Interviewing parents, children, and other members of the household who might know about the situation is supplemented by relevant information obtained through careful observation.

The social worker often has to make inferences in deciding whether a child's injury is the result of an accident or of willful intentional behavior on the part of the parent. The worker listens to the account of the situation presented by the family. Is the telling complete or vague; consistent or contradictory? Is it reasonable—could those injuries have happened in this way? Is it reliable—is it the same explanation on retelling?

The decision to provide continuing service is based on such factors as the repetitiveness of the parents' harmful behavior, the degree of guilt expressed, the acceptance of "blame," and the nature of the situation that triggered the incident. The following incident indicates a positive evaluation of these factors:

> A hospital reported that a nine-year-old had been brought to the Emergency Room for treatment of a fractured wrist. The mother admitted that the father had caused the injury. The child was treated on an out-patient basis.
>
> An appointment letter was sent to the parents, and both came to the office. Both parents readily admitted what happened. The mother was working, the father was resting after coming home from work. A policeman came to the door with the boy, explaining that he had just caught him on the railroad tracks. The father became upset for various reasons: the shame of having a policeman bring his boy home, knowledge that his son had disobeyed home rules and the law, and anxiety for the injuries that could have occurred if a train had come. The father had a finger missing which made him even more sensitive to the loss of a limb. The father grabbed the boy to discipline him with a belt, they struggled, and somehow in the process the wrist was broken.
>
> The father expressed appropriate guilt for hurting the boy, as he certainly had no intention of breaking his wrist. It was clear that he rarely used a belt, and both parents felt they had pretty good children. There was no expression of any family problems. In this situation, there was no need to protect the child, and the parents were not asking for help with any other problems. Therefore there was no role for continued social work intervention. A letter was sent to the reporting hospital explaining the disposition, with a copy to the parents.

The social worker is involved in a risk assessment evaluation of the child's situation. A configuration of factors have been identified influencing the social worker's decision to substantiate maltreatment and the perception that the child does need the protection of the agency (DiLeonardi, 1980; Craft et al., 1980; Rosen, 1981; Meddin, 1985).

1. Observable evidence of abuse—or an obviously dangerous physical environment, presenting clear hazards to the child's health and safety.
2. The child's level of vulnerability—very young children and handicapped children are not in a position to defend themselves and are more likely to be seriously injured by maltreatment.
3. Child's behavior which is self-injurious—suicidal, erratic, acting out, or self-destructive behavior.

4. Evidence of persistent, repetitive maltreatment of a relatively severe intensity.

5. The maltreatment perpetrator's rejection of the idea that his or her behavior is abusive or neglectful and refusal to accept responsibility for, or show any remorse for, maltreatment of the child.

6. The perpetrator's open rejection of the child, inability to empathize with the child, lack of realistic expectation for the child, and willingness to cast the child in the role of a scapegoat.

7. The parent or parent surrogate's borderline psychosis, obvious emotional disturbance or habitual substance abuse, the parent's inability to control his or her behavior.

8. The parent or parent surrogate's resistive, evasive, uncooperative behavior; the parent is uninterested, and apathetic about making changes in the situation or in participating in using agency services.

9. The family's current or recent subjection to continuing multiple social-psychological stresses.

10. The family's lack of access to an adequate, concerned support system of friends, neighbors, and relatives.

During the investigation of the complaint or report the social worker is faced with making two sequential consequential decisions. The first is to decide whether or not there is sufficient basis for substantiation of the report that this is, in fact, a situation of maltreatment within the definition of the agency's responsibility. The second decision relates to a determination of whether or not the danger to the child is so immediate, substantial, and certain so as to consider taking action to remove the child from the home to a place of greater safety.

Some situations indicate the need for emergency protective removal of the child. These include situations that involve children who have been abandoned, who are living with obviously psychotic parents or with parents who are so "strung out" on drugs or alcohol so that their ability to care for the child is seriously impaired, children in control of parents who clearly express hatred for the child and openly indicate their likelihood of abusing the child again or who have repeatedly inflicted severe and bizarre punishments, and children who have been sexually abused over a period of time.

Social workers employ criteria that consider the consistency, the pervasiveness, and the duration of abuse in deciding whether to press for the child's removal. If the parent is concerned, contrite, and ready to accept help, this circumstance argues against removal. If there is somebody other than the abusive parent in the home who is willing to help restrain the abuser's impulsivity and impatience, or if there is a family-network support system that can be mobilized, this also argues against removal.

The investigation may end in a determination that the child is not being maltreated. However, although the family situation may not be a matter of concern to the protective service, the investigation may have revealed considerable family tension and conflict. In this case, some effort is made to end the investigation with a referral to a family service or mental health agency. The investigation may also end with substantiation of the report and intake of the cases for further protective agency service, or in the emergency removal of the child.

National survey data indicate that upon investigation, some 47 per cent of abuse and neglect reports are "not validated" (American Humane Association, 1986, p. 31). This means that despite the worker's conscientious exploration of the situation, he cannot find sufficient evidence of abuse or neglect. Continued service is more likely if referral has been made by a community agency rather than by a private individual because agencies are not likely to make a referral unless there is some substance to the complaint. Reports of abuse are more likely to be substantiated than reports of the more ambiguously defined neglect. Reports from law enforcement agencies are most likely to be substantiated (Groenveld, Giovannoni, 1977).

The difference between reported and substantiated cases of abuse may be a consequence of the level of evidence required for substantiation that social workers regarded as "too stringent," and a concern about the reaction of the abuser to the determination that abuse had actually occurred. A study of 500 protective service workers in Wisconsin indicated that some workers had changed reports from "found" maltreatment to "unfound" in order to avoid "an adversarial relationship with a client" who has the right to an appeal hearing (Benn, 1981, page 73).

Diagnosis

The voluminous literature on child maltreatment includes findings from surveys, clinical studies, demonstration projects, and analyses of record material and report forms. There have been several efforts to review and summarize this literature (Parke & Colmer, 1975; Holmes, 1977; Polansky, Hally, & Polansky, 1974; Collmer Spinetta & Rigler, 1972; Maden & Wrench, 1977; Allen, 1978; Belsky, 1980; Wolfe, 1985). We attempt to highlight the findings without necessarily citing the specific studies except where the research was particularly noteworthy, generally because a control population of nonabusers was included in the study design.

Some tentative efforts have been made to identify the distinctive attributes of the parents who neglect or abuse their children. However, one of the principal conclusions reached by Young (1964) in her study of the records of 180 families referred for neglect or abuse is that the two groups of parents may have little in common (p. 135) and that neglect and abuse may be different diagnostic groupings.

The picture is further complicated by the fact that within both the abuse and the neglect groups, there are subgroups that have little in common with each other diagnostically, except for the fact that ultimate behaviors toward the child are similar. Merrill (1962) lists four types and Delsordo (1963) describes five types of child abusers, Zalba (1966) defines six types, Gil (1970) suggests seventeen types, and Walters (1975) lists ten types.

Gelles (1973) notes that of nineteen traits listed by various researchers supposedly identifying the personality of the child abuser, there was agreement on only four traits by two or more authors, the other fifteen traits being identified by only one author.

The limited potency of supposedly empirically determined diagnostic indicators in identifying child abusers was noted by Strauss. Studying a national sample of 1,140 families, he identified 10 variables that characterized parents who abused their children in some way or another. When Strauss applied these ten supposedly differentiating variables to the total sample, he found that close to 70 per cent of those families "exhibiting all ten variables did not abuse their children" (Strauss, 1979, p. 223).

Analogous to complex entities such as "juvenile delinquency" and "unwed parenthood," abuse and neglect behavior are a result of a convoluted configuration of psychological, social, and situational factors that result in heterogeneous patterns and make valid generalizations very difficult. Summarizing the results of a review of the available research, Allen (1978) noted that:

> there is no such thing as a "typical example of abuse" which represents the majority of cases, nor is there one factor conclusively present and relevant to all cases. Instead, the research picture suggests that violence is the end product of a complex interaction of individual environmental and interpsychic factors in which the relationship between all these influences varies with the individual [p. 68].

Efforts have been made to compare patterns of parent–child relationship and family communication between maltreating and nonmaltreating matched families on the basis of standard inventories and checklists and observations of the families in the home and in the clinic. Abusive parents and neglectful parents have been carefully separated for study in some of this research. In some studies, samples of family interactions of matched groups of families were audiotaped and/or videotaped for analysis. (Burgess, 1979; Crittenden, 1981; Letourneau, 1981; Starr, 1982; Wasserman, Green, & Allan, 1982; Mash, Johnston, & Kovitz, 1983; Herrenkohl et al., 1984; Oldershaw, Walters, & Hall, 1986; Rohrbeck & Twentyman, 1986).

Although the findings from clinical and empirical research are complex and often contradictory, there is some low-level consistency in the configuration of factors frequently associated with abuse. These include a history of abuse and/or rejection in childhood; low self-esteem; a rigid, domineering, impulsive personality; social isolation; a record of inadequate coping behavior; poor interpersonal relationships; high, unrealistic expectations of children; and lack of ability to empathize with children. Abusers are generally subject to greater than average economic and social stress. They tend to deomonstrate lower rates of positive interaction and higher rates of negative interaction with their children. They tend to employ power-assertive strategies rather than positive incentive strategies in disciplinary efforts; they are less consistent and less flexible and more directive and controlling in their efforts to obtain compliance from children to their demands. Even where abusive parents utilize positive disciplinary procedures, the feeling tone associated with their use is punitive.

Maltreating parents tend to be poor observers of child behavior, to be unsuccessful in child management skills, frequently unsuccessful in disciplinary attempts, and to have generally lower levels of social skills competence.

It is suggested that abusive parents are strict disciplinarians who have rigid expectations regarding child behavior without empathy with a child's needs, feelings, or individuality. The parent is seen as "owning" the child, as being solely responsible for molding the child and as having a sense of righteousness in making autonomous decisions as to what is best for the child. These parents tend to regard the behavior of even small children as willful, deliberate disobedience. Strict discipline is then perceived as justified because the child is consciously disobeying the parent.

Abusive parents may show a tendency to role reversal, in which the parents turn to their children for nurturing and protection (Morris & Gould, 1963). The child is seen as a source of gratification; when the parent is disappointed and frustrated by the failure of the child to meet his or her needs, he or she reacts with hostility toward the child. The failure of the child to meet the parent's needs is seen as willful and deliberate behavior and reactivates the parent's own disappointment in his or her parents when he or she was a child.

Abusive parents are seen as having limited ability to tolerate frustration and delays in gratification. They have a low boiling point and, as a consequence of low self-esteem, react impulsively and intensely to even minor provocations.

Exposing matched abusive and nonabusive parents to videotapes of children crying and smiling resulted in findings that abusive parents were more physiologically aroused than nonabusive parents (Frodi & Lamb, 1980). (See also Friedrich, Tyler and Clarke, 1985). Such parents showed increased heartrate, skin conductance, and diastolic blood pressure in response to their viewing of the videotape. Furthermore, the abusers remain aroused for a longer period of time than do nonabusers. The abusive parents, being more physiologically reactive to aversive stimuli, may have a lower level of tolerance for such child behaviors.

A small percentage of parents is assessed as frankly sadistic, taking positive pleasure in abuse. Another small percentage is psychotic and engages in abuse in response to a distorted perception of reality. An additional small percentage consists of sociopaths who react aggressively to even the most ordinary frustrations. It is estimated that these groups in aggregate make up some 10 per cent of the total group of abusers.

Although it is generally agreed that only a limited percentage of abusive parents are psychotic, a review of studies concerned with the general psychological functioning of abusive parents "sustains the conclusion that abusive parents exhibit considerable psychological dysfunction compared with control groups" (Maden & Wrench, 1977, p. 209).

The fact that a high percentage of reported abusers are young may suggest stress associated with parental immaturity and with youthful marriage and parenthood before being ready for such experiences.

Clinical and research reports persistently point to a poor relationship between the marital pair in the abusive family. Not only are the participants denied support from each other in dealing with their problems, but the conflicted relationship is a source of additional stress and tension predisposing the parents toward aggression displaced onto the child.

Social isolation from relatives, friends, and neighbors and a low rate of affiliation with and participation in community institutions and organizations seem to be problems presented by a high percentage of abusers. As a consequence, they lack an effective social-support network. They have a higher rate of residential mobility than nonabuser controls (Gaudin & Pollane, 1983) and being new neighbors often intensifies their tendency toward isolation (Salzinger, Kaplan & Artemyetf, 1982). Isolated families lack the support systems that might provide information, material resources, and sharing of child-care responsibilities as well as emotional support and succor. Isolated families are further deprived of opportunities for observing, at close range, appropriate childrearing behaviors of others and receiving critical feedback from others that reinforces social norms about childrearing.

Perhaps the most repetitive finding is that abusers have themselves experienced abuse as children. This finding has achieved the status of an axiom. As a consequence of his or her experience, the child learns to employ violence in parent–child interaction. The child takes the abusive parent as a role model and patterns his or her own subsequent parental behavior accordingly. This outcome is consistent with learning theory. This outcome is also consistent with child development theory. Having been abused and rejected as children, having lacked a stable, consistent love relationship in childhood, these parents have experienced inadequate gratification of early affectional and dependency needs. In response to this deprivation, these parents are themselves still children—in their narcissism, their selfishness, their dependency, their impulsiveness—in short, in their immaturity. The idea of intergenerational transmission of maltreatment is thus consistent with theoretical suppositions regarding the effects of emotional deprivation in infancy, which suggests that the deprived child, not having been loved, is incapable in adulthood of loving others.

The idea of intergenerational abuse is theoretically attractive not only because it is consistent with learning, modeling, and socialization concepts but because it permits the social worker to approach the parent with a greater feeling of acceptance. Abusive parents are not to blame. They, too, are victims of their own childhood experiences. As one worker says, "One way I overcome my personal dislike for the way the parent has treated the child—or has allowed a child to be treated—is to view the parent as a child, or as a very childlike adult who was probably abused as a child" (Arvanian, 1975, p. 94).

Although these considerations explain and support the contention that abuse is intergenerationally transmitted, Jayaratne (1977), in reviewing the relevant data, finds little empirical support for the proposition. Following a similar review of the research, Holmes (1977) comes to a similar conclusion. (See also McCord, 1981; Pagelow, 1984, p. 254.)

Some comparisons of abusive parents with a sample of nonabusive parents show that abusive parents generally have had less favorable relationships with their own parents (Melnick & Hurley, 1969; Smith, 1975; Bedger, 1976; Green, 1976; Hunter, Kilstrom, 1979). In all instances, however, sizable percentages of abusive parents had positive developmental experiences, and sizable percentages of nonabusive parents had unfavorable parent–child experiences.

The preponderance of research efforts concerned with trying to formulate a diagnostic understanding of maltreatment has focused on the parent or the parent surrogate. There is a beginning effort to look at the interaction of parent and child rather than at the parent alone in attempts to understand the abuse situation. It is suggested that abuse is the result of interactive behaviors of both the child and the parent. Neither is totally responsible, nor is either totally innocent (Friedrich & Boriskin, 1976; Kadushin & Martin, 1981).

The abuse event is the result of a bidirectional, reciprocal relationship. Some children are more difficult to care for and hence are more likely to evoke aggressive responses. Different children tend to evoke different responses from parents.

It is suggested that from the very start, the child is far from being a passive member of the parent–child dyad, that the child's behavior is both a response to and a stimulus for subsequent parental behavior, that often the child initiates and shapes the nature of the interaction, and that the child conditions parental behavior, selectively rejecting some parental interventions and selectively reinforcing others. Such an orientation suggests that although it is true that parents produce children, there may be much truth in the assertion that children also produce parents.

Studies of temperamental differences in children as evidenced immediately after birth confirm every parent's observation that some children provoke more aggressive reactions than others. Those researchers who have done the most detailed study of infant temperamental differences at birth conclude that:

> the characteristics of the child may foster and reinforce a specific direction of parental attitudes and practices. It is easy to mother a normally active, positively responsive, highly adaptive, routine accepting child whose mood is predominantly cheerful.

> It is quite another matter to maintain the same positive maternal responses to a highly active, poorly responsive, non-adaptive arrhythmic child whose mood is expressed by a preponderance of crying [Thomas, Birch, & Chess, 1963].

As Gelles (1972) notes, the "role of the victim in intrafamily violence is an important and active one. The actions of the victim are vital intervening events between structural stresses that lead to violence and the violent acts themselves" (p. 155). This statement may help explain why some abusive parents are not abusive with all children but only with a selected child.

Studies of abused children by Johnson (1968); Gil (1970); Fergusson, Fleming, and O'Neill (1972); Reidy (1975); Green (1976); George and Main (1979); Wolfe and Mosk (1983); Kinard (1982); Kadushin and Martin (1981); Straker (1981) found abused children to be more difficult, irritating, fussier, negative, unresponsive, hyperactive, and aggressive when compared with their siblings and age mates.

In a study of the circumstances related to 825 physical abuse incidents and some 1,000 physical discipline but nonabusive incidents, Herrenkohl, Herrenkohl, and Egolf (1983) found that "the root of physical abuse is in the parent–child interaction and the child's behavior is a necessary part of that interaction" (p. 430).

The child who is the result of an unwanted pregnancy, illegitimacy, or "forced" marriage is noted as a high risk for abuse in a number of different studies (Nurse, 1964; Elmer, 1977; Fergusson, Fleming, & O'Neill, 1972). Oates, Davis, and Ryan (1983) interviewed fifty-six mothers who had maltreated their children and a matched group of nonmaltreating mothers. Their retrospective recollection of the birth and neonatal experiences indicated that for the maltreating mothers, as compared with controls, pregnancy was unplanned, birth was difficult, the father was unsupportive, and the child was a problem.

Comparing abused children with their nonabused siblings, Lynch (1976) found that the abused child was more likely to have been subjected to an abnormal pregnancy and delivery, neonatal separation, and postnatal illness than his or her sibling controls. Low birth weight is associated with subsequent abuse in a number of studies. Maden and Wrench (1977, p. 202), recapitulating in tabular form the results of twenty studies relating to low birth weight, congenital defects, and birth complications as associated with child abuse, show a statistically significant relationship in at least seven studies.

Two different explanations are presented for the fact that premature babies are apparently at high risk for abuse. First their greater frailty and hence increased need for sensitive care make the mothering of such babies a more taxing yet, perhaps, a less rewarding task because the infant may be less attractive physically and less rewarding psychologically. Second, the frequent placement of such children in special-care units separates mother and child and results in the failure of an early bonding in the relationship.

When asked to identify those factors that, in their experience, are related to child abuse, social workers, child protective workers, psychologists, nurses, and educators highlighted the fact that both parent and child factors are involved (Gillespie, Seaberg, & Berlin, 1977). Items relating the social-situational aspects and individual personality aspects of both abuser and abusee were listed. When rank-ordered in terms of importance, individual personality factors of the abuser and the child were given primary emphasis. These included "Hostile-aggressive low frustration tolerance" of caretaker, "caretaker's inability to cope," "inappropriate performance expectations of child," and for the child, "child defiant of caretakers," "excessive demands of child on caretaker," "hyperactive child," and "child unresponsive to caretakers" (p. 346).

In response to these considerations, it might be suggested that the child's hyperactivity, aggressiveness, apathy, mental deficiency, and so on were the result of abuse rather than an initial contributory element. One might say, along with Bakan (1971), that "the abuse of a child creates a child who invites abuse" (p. 111). In the absence of a longitudinal study that provides detailed data on children before they are abused as compared with postabuse functioning, we are left with some nagging doubts as to the sequence. The research does suggest, however, that certain kinds of child characteristics and behavior, whatever the "cause" of their genesis, are likely to be associated with instigation of abuse.

Some see child abuse not as a parent–child problem but as a family problem. Abuse suggests some dysfunction in the total family configuration, with all family members contributing to the abuse in some measure, and all members affected by it. The total family configuration, it is suggested, then requires treatment (Beezley, Martin, & Alexander, 1976).

Beyond the parent, the child, and the family, the situational stresses resulting from environmental deprivations contribute to maltreatment. Garbarino (1976) compared the child abuse rates of fifty-eight New York State counties and the socioeconomic differences among the counties. Using U.S. Census data, he found that where unemployment was higher, income levels lower, and education levels and opportunities less adequate, the abuse rates were higher. Counties with a disproportionately large number of "economically depressed mothers often alone in the role of parent attempting to cope in isolation without adequate resources and facilities for their children" (p. 183) were more likely to show higher rates of maltreatment. Low family income and working mothers were highly correlated with maltreatment. The conclusion was that environmental stress did have an impact on child maltreatment. Steinberg, Catalano, and Dooley (1981) studied changes in child maltreatment reports over a thirty-month period and related such changes to changes in levels of local unemployment. They found that "declines in the work force are significantly related to reported child abuse" in the two metropolitan communities which were the subject of study. "The variance explaining changes in child abuse by work force change is small," however (p. 982).

Increased unemployment implies increased family stress, but it also entails a shift in child care from those familiar with the role to those, such as the unemployed fathers, who are less familiar with the role.

The impact of a series of negative life changes, events that are likely to induce considerable stress, was associated with child abuse in studies by Justice and Duncan (1976) and Conger, Burgess, and Barrett (1979). When compared with a group of nonabusive peers, child abusers were likely to have higher negative life change scores. Stress resulting from such events has a discouraging effect on the ability to maintain self-control in interacting with children.

Although there is general agreement that a stressful living situation—that is, low-income; inadequate, crowded housing; unemployment or intermittent employment, and discrimination—is associated with maltreatment, it is unclear why most other parents in the same population living with the same stresses do not abuse their children.

In comparing abusive with nonabusive parents, and controlling for social class, Smith (1975) found that there was little difference in the adequacy of housing and financial resources among the two groups. He concluded that "personality disorders . . . are more important than environmental factors in contributing to child abuse" (p. 207) and that "constitutional personality differences are more fundamental than financial factors in the causation of baby battering" (p. 209). In comparing abusers with nonabusers from the same population where both groups were living in a stressful deprived environment, the abusers were more likely to have had a history of disordered chilhood development and subsequent personal difficulties in social functioning than the nonabusive controls (Holmes, 1977, p. 148).

Situational stress is an incremental load imposed on psychological stress, increasing the total stress overload to which the individual is subjected and with which he or she has to cope. A psychosocial explanation that combines both the social stresses, which might act as the "triggering context" for abuse, and the psychological factors, which predispose the caretaker to resort to abuse as a selective response in dealing with child management problems, appears to be a more valid interpretation than either exclusively, psychologically, or sociologically focused explanations.

Maltreatment might then be understood as the end result of interaction among three major sets of variables: (1) a parent who has the potential for abuse, (2) a child who may be somewhat different and/or difficult and who fails to respond in a manner expected by parents, and (3) a crisis situation, which triggers the abusive act. The probability of abuse is increased by social isolation, which reduces the ready availability of help and support from other people; cumulative situational tensions that lower tolerance for stress; and a community context that sanctions interpersonal violence. As Belsky (1980) states, "Psychological disturbances in parents, abuse eliciting characteristics of children, dysfunctional patterns of family interaction, stress inducing social forces, and abuse—promoting social values" (p. 320) provide the ecological framework designed to explain child abuse.

The following case illustrates the complexity of contributing factors:

> Larry, age twenty-seven, is a quiet, shy, unassuming little man who works as a welder's assistant. Since childhood, he has been plagued by a deep sense of inferiority, unworthiness, and unsureness of himself in his work and in all human relations. There is also a deep resentment, usually very restrained, against a world which he feels is unfair. . . . Larry does not recall either mother or father spanking as a routine, but there were constant verbal attacks and criticism. He felt that neither of his parents, particularly his mother, really listened to him or understood his unhappiness and his need for comfort and consideration.
>
> While he was in the army, Larry and Becky planned to marry. She was to come to where he was stationed, and they were to be married at Christmas time. He waited all day at the bus station, but she never appeared. Sad and hopeless, he got drunk. Months later, a buddy told him she had married somebody else the first of January. He saw her again a year later when home on leave. She had been divorced; so they made up and got married. She had a child, Jimmy, by her first marriage. . . . They have had three more children of their own. Mary, age four, is liked very much by both parents. . . . David, age two-and-a-half . . . is "very fine, active, alert, well-mannered little boy." He is quite responsive and both parents like him and are good with him. Maggie, four-and-a-half months old, was thought by both parents to be "a bit different" from birth. She seemed to look bluer and cried less strongly than their other babies and was also rather fussy. . . . Maggie was admitted to the hospital with symptoms and signs of bilateral subdural hematoma. She had been alone with her father when he noticed a sudden limpness, unconsciousness, and lack of breathing.

He gave mouth-to-mouth respiration, and she was brought to hospital by ambulance. There was a history of a similar episode a month before when Maggie was three-and-a-half months old; when alone with her father she had become limp, followed by vomiting. . . . The circumstances of the attack were as follows: Larry's boss told him that his job was over. The construction contract had been suddenly cancelled and there was no more work. Feeling discouraged, hopeless, and ignored, Larry went home, shamefacedly told Becky he had lost his job, and asked her if she wanted to go with the children to her family. Saying nothing, Becky walked out of the house, leaving Larry alone with Maggie. The baby began to cry. Larry tried to comfort her, but she kept on crying so he looked for her bottle. He could not find the bottle anywhere; the persistent crying and his feelings of frustration, helplessness, and ineffectuality became overwhelming. In a semiconfused "blurry" state he shook Maggie severely and then hit her on the head. Suddenly aware of what he had done, he started mouth-to-mouth resuscitation; then Becky came home and Maggie was brought to the hospital [Steel & Pollock, 1968 pp. 119–20]*

In this case, Larry, whose history predisposed him to feelings of insecurity and rejection, enters into a marriage in which his position is uncertain and finds himself the father of a child who is difficult to care for and makes heavy demands on parental patience. These factors provide the potential for abuse, which is then precipitated by a crisis situation during which the child acts in a way that increases the already considerable momentary stress, becoming the immediate target for all past and present frustrations.

It is recognized that thus far, much of the discussion has focused on maltreatment rather than making a clear distinction between abuse and neglect. This approach reflects some of the tendency in the literature to discuss both together as well as the fact that some critical diagnostic factors are common to both kinds of maltreatment. At this point, we distinguish neglect from abuse.

Polansky and his co-workers (1970, 1971, 1972, 1981), identified clusters of behavior typical of some neglectful mothers.

Over the course of decades, Polansky has studied neglectful mothers at close range in diverse settings such as Appalachia and Philadelphia. The studies have identified personality configurations that characteristically identified several different groups of neglectful mothers. The external stress of a deprived environment is, in each instance, joined to inner chaos. Poverty in combination with a character disorder-personality is the most likely equation for neglect.

One group of mothers, characterized by an apathy-futility syndrome, are withdrawn and alienated. Passive resignation to a chronically deprived environment is manifested by a sense of futility—a feeling that nothing can be done to change their situation and that there is no sense in trying. Such mothers show an emotional numbness and little intensity in their personal relationships. They are lethargic and verbally inaccessible.

Another group of mothers are impulse-ridden. Unable to tolerate stress and frustration, they feel a sense of chronic restlessness. They find it difficult to plan their lives, and more often than not they act impulsively. The normal control system for binding impulses appears deficient. They show poor judgment about the probable consequences of the actions they take. The personal relationships of such mothers tends to be shallow and unstable. A third smaller group of mothers shows the symptoms of reactive depression.

*From Henry C. Kempe and Ray E. Helfer, eds. *The Battered Child* 2d ed. Chicago: University of Chicago Press, 1968. By permission of The University of Chicago Press.

Neglectful mothers are generally suspicious and difficult to engage in an effective relationship. Depressed, irresponsible, and generally slovenly, they make it difficult for the social worker to like them.

Such women are more likely to be socially isolated, and are less likely to seek others out or maintain reciprocal relationships with others, or be involved as participants in community groups. Subjective tendencies toward isolation are reinforced by reluctance or unwillingness of others to be close to them (Polansky, Ammons, & Gaudin, 1985).

Comparing the reasons for the social isolation of neglectful families, Polansky, Ammones, and Gaudins (1985) found that such families had the same opportunities for social ties as a similarly situated comparison group of nonneglectful families. However, they were not effectively able to use the opportunities available. Neglectful families were perceived by neighbors as deviant, and others distanced themselves from them. Nor were they able to reach out and involve themselves in informal helping networks as effectively as others.

Polansky and Gaudin (1983) used a social distance scale to test the hypothesis that community isolation of neglectful families was part a result of rejection and shunning by their neighbors. Groups of respondents representing white women, black women, and Hispanic women were offered a vignette picturing the living condition and life-style of a typical neglectful family. In response to questions about their willingness to interact with such a family, all three groups of women indicated a desire to maintain a social distance from such a family. They would be less likely to ask such a mother to baby-sit for them. Nor would they like their children to develop close relationships with children of such a family. They would be less likely to permit their own child to play with the children of neglectful mothers. Isolation of neglectful families may, therefore, result from the community's negative perceptions of them.

Direct observational studies of the interaction of neglectful mothers and their children as compared with the interactional behavior of nonneglectful peers show neglectful mothers to be passive and withdrawn, offering low rates of interaction with their children and showing poorer parent problem-solving skills (Crittenden, 1981; Bousha & Twentyman 1984; Azar, Robinson, Hekimian, & Twentyman 1984). (See also Jones and McNeely, 1980.)

Whereas such studies focused on the characterological problems of neglectful parents, others have emphasized the fact that neglect reports are most heavily concentrated among the most severely economically deprived groups. The relationship between low-income, public assistance as the only source of income, and neglect, is greater than between income and any other type of maltreatment.

Investigating differences between neglectful and nonneglectful mothers among low-income families; both Wolock and Horowitz (1979) and Billingsley and Giovannoni (1970) found that neglectful families were among the poorest of the poor, in the least adequate position to provide adequate care.

Multiple-regression analysis of information from the case records of 489 cases of substantiated maltreatment, including 207 cases of neglect, obtained from county protective service units, indicated that overall there was a "positive relationship between neglect of children and circumstances within the family which indicate a poverty-induced low-living situation" (Martin & Walters 1982, p. 272).

In summary, protective services present a problem for data assessment or diagnosis in that there are no "typical" abusive or neglectful parents. Causation is multiply determined and includes factors relating to the developmental history and personality of the maltreating parent interacting with a particular child, in a stressful situational context in a culture that sanctions violence as a response to interpersonal problems.

Neglect and *abuse* are terms used to describe a wide variety of behaviors that have in common only certain effects on the child. No single cause can explain such behavior. However, abuse may be more often a response to psychological stress, whereas neglect may be more often a response to social stress. Neglect generally results from acts of omission, abuse from acts of commission. Giovannoni (1971) carried the distinction a bit further: "abuse constitutes an exploitation of the rights of parents to control, discipline and punish their children while neglect represents the failure to perform parental duties including those of supervision, nurturance and protection" (p. 649).

Treatment Planning: Evaluation of Family Modifiability

Diagnosis is followed by an effort to evaluate the parents' capacity to change—to determine the degree of modifiability of the child's environment. If it is clear that change will be minimal, one has to assess the relative dangers to the child, of remaining in the home as compared with those involved in separation and placement in substitute care.

The agency must also consider the importance of siblings to the child. One survey of 147 families noted that positive relationships in the sibling–sibling subsystem frequently existed side by side with the overwhelmingly negative relationships in the parent–child subsystem (Canadian Welfare Council, 1954, p. 13). Thus the sibling relationship, as a possible source of strength and support to the child, is an important factor in any decision regarding the child.

One must recognize, too, that no home is wholly bad. The child's parents are the only ones the child has known, and despite neglect and abuse, he or she has developed some ties to them. Protective agencies have often found—to their surprise and, perhaps, chagrin—that they were attempting to "rescue" children who did not want to be rescued."

There is potential for change in the fact that the parents themselves are unhappy and ambivalent about their situation. The degree of ambivalence present in these situations, which the agency can use in helping the parents, is indicated by the fact that one or another of the parents is, on occasion, the source of complaint to the agency. In fact, Kaufman (1957) cites an instance of a mother calling an agency to report herself as a parent maltreating a child. On the other hand, these are difficult clients to work with generally—not only hard to reach but also hard to change. Frequently others have tried before the client was referred to the protective service agency. Thus "60 percent of the cases which eventually come to the Massachusetts Society for the Prevention of Cruelty to Children had been in contact with a casework or guidance agency at some time or other before the protective service contact" (Rein, 1963, p. 133).

The lack of leverage for therapeutic action that characterizes contact with such families is substantiated by Young (1964):

> Neglectful and abusive families show a conspicuous absence of any feelings of guilt about their behavior toward their children; . . . they rarely saw any association between their behavior toward the child and the undesirable behavior in the child, and

they showed little awareness of the unacceptability of their behavior until the community intervened [pp. 175–176].

One of the difficulties in working with such families is that they are not responsive to the informal network of social control, which often acts as an ally to the worker in motivating for change:

> The social pressures which in other groups compel at least minimum outward conformity have little effect upon the families in this study except as they are officially and specifically implemented. . . . Most of the families in this study had little to lose—social status, economic security, community respect, the good opinion of other people were all lacking and, for most of them, always had been. They may have wished they had some or all of these advantages, but if so, their wishing was a wistful longing for the moon, not a force compelling them to effort. They had no incentive to change their behavior or to limit it—they feared no loss and expected no rewards. Social control had lost its major weapons and relinquished its place to official and legal controls [Young, 1964, p. 84].

Although abusive families are likely to be actively resistive to the offer of help, neglectful families are more often accepting of help but unable to use it effectively or productively.

Treatment Aims and Approach

Social agencies carry the major responsibility for helping families after maltreatment is reported and substantiated. Casework counseling was by far the most frequent service offered, provided in about 80 per cent of all cases. Most children who were frequently maltreated remained in their own homes; substitute care was used only in some 20 per cent of the cases, more frequently in cases of sexual abuse than in other kinds of maltreatment. Day care was used in a limited number of cases (5.1%) as was homemaker service (3.9%) (Russell & Trainor, 1984, p. 45). The objective is to reduce the risk and likelihood of further, continuing maltreatment and make the home physically and psychologically safe for the child.

One of the general objectives of the protective service program is to increase parents' willingness to call for agency help when faced with an impending crisis.

The protective service literature is much richer in discussing diagnosis assessment than in discussing treatment intervention. The Child Protection Division of the American Humane Association has developed a comprehensive handbook for caseworkers detailing the steps in the child protective services helping process. After 177 pages of analysis of the preliminary steps, the handbook notes that "Unfortunately treatment in Child Protective Services is the weakest link in the case work process" (American Humane Association, 1981, p. 178). A categorization of 2,700 abstracts of child abuse and neglect research indicate that only 10 per cent of the research was focused on prevention and treatment (Bolton et al., 1981, p. 535).

The core of the agency's work is with the parents, the objective being to prevent further neglect and/or abuse of the child and to alleviate or correct those problems that have led to the situation. The ultimate aim is to preserve the home so that the child's needs can be adequately met within his or her own natural family.

Protective service clients generally resist social work contacts. A study of intensive services offered such families showed that few families initiated a request for an appointment and that families often failed to keep appointments scheduled by the workers (Baher et al., 1976).

Persistence is required, but overvisiting should be avoided, as it may seem like "hounding" to the parent.

In visits to the home, it may be desirable to focus on the needs of the parents, because meeting the parents' needs results in the parents' greater capacity to meet the child's needs. Also, any attention paid to the child during a visit may alienate the parent, who may feel that his or her deficiencies in child care are being emphasized by the worker's satisfactory interaction with the child. Furthermore, as a part child himself, the parent's sense of rivalry with the child for the worker's attention may further excite his or her animosity toward the child. Workers have to maintain a precarious balance between identifying with the children and thus possibly antagonizing the parents or identifying with the parents at the risk of endangering the children.

Parental behavior concerns the protective service agency only in its effects on the child. The parent is not necessarily asked to change his or her personality; it is the situation detrimental to the child that must be changed. As Kahn (1963) says, the obstacles to thoroughgoing change are so great "that more modest attainments are more common—sustaining the child in his own home without damage, correcting specific defects in parental care, correcting and alleviating the effects on the child of prior parental mishandling" (p. 335).

The very presence of the agency may tend to activate latent factors so as to result in a positive change. The demonstration of community power and concern, expressed in the act of intervention, may itself induce change. The parent, impressed by the community's power as represented by the agency, may become less abusive, less neglectful. This change in behavior, "of which the obvious cause is caution lest legal action be taken, is often discounted as an unimportant indication of a client's likelihood of changing his behavior . . . but it *is* constructive behavior though it is reactive to authority. If no more, it shows that the parent recognizes another standard" (Becker, 1972, p. 87). What has been achieved is compliance in response to the worker's authority (Kelman, 1961). The judicious use of authority by the social worker can help effect change (Studt, 1954; Moss, 1963; Foren & Bailey, 1968; Yelaja, 1971).

The client may accept the social worker's efforts out of a concern over the possible social consequences of his or her behavior and a desire to avoid certain specific punishments. The new behavior is not adopted because the client believes it to be good or desirable; the new standards remain external; the client has learned to do or say what is necessary, but there is no inner commitment to the values followed. Continued supervision is necessary because the client has to be kept constantly aware of the possibility of negative consequences for failure to provide adequate care.

The more desirable goal is to change behavior through the internalization of new standards of child care. To support such a change in values and beliefs, the agency must be certain that the living situation—housing, income, and so on— will allow the parents to act in accordance with a changed attitude toward child care.

Agency intervention imposes a penalty: the loss of privacy. The agency claims the right to know what is going on. Out of a sense of shame and discomfort at exposure, the client may be prompted to change in order to get the agency out of his or her life.

Families charged with neglect are likely to be multiproblem families facing severe social and physical deprivation, and because of limited education, they are less likely to make effective use of a psychotherapeutic approach to problem situations. The agencies usually have to prove their value to the client by taking concrete steps to alleviate some of the burdens faced by the family.

The most successful approach seems to be one that directs itself to situational changes rather than psychological changes. Neglectful parents appear to be child-like in their dependency, their disorganization, their impulsiveness, their inability to plan, and their lack of judgment regarding the damaging consequences of foolish decisions. They are helped by a casework approach designed to encourage the development of some kind of routine around which they can organize their lives. Like children, they simultaneously welcome and resent being told, in clear, unequivocal terms, what to do. As Young (1964) says, such parents "want borrowed strength, not freedom of choice—a freedom they lacked the strength to use. The authority of the protective caseworker not only protects the children from parents, it protects the parents from themselves" (pp. 125–126). The caseworker acts as a good parent—direct, frank, firm, but nonpunitive. According to Kaufman (1963), "The worker assumes the role of autonomous ego for these parents. He adopts a kindly but firm supportive parental role" (p. 196).

A study by Kalley (1959) of the factors associated with improvement in clients noted that "the problems with which protective service was most often successful were those where what was not being done for the children and what needed to be done for them was made clear and readily understandable to the parent" (p. 25).

Such clients, in short, require a highly structured definition of unambiguous expectations. In reciprocation, the worker has to show the client that he or she is ready and willing and able to help to effect some improvement, however slight, in the client's living situation. The worker has to prove, as Overton (1959) says, his "utility value to the client" (p. 50). This may involve taking people to clinics and employment agencies, showing the parent how to shop and cook, and giving direct advice where warranted. The agency may have to take the initiative in doing for the clients some of the things they are incapable of doing for themselves—even such simple things as completing an application form for new housing or a new job.

The change in approach is empirically based: some things seem to work. Behind it, however, is the assumption that a therapeutic approach based on a meaningful relationship and dependent for its success on highly developed communication skills between a worker and a client who share some understanding about the psychological causation of problems has not proved to be an effective approach for the kinds of families who make up a considerable segment of the protective service agency's caseload.

A relationship of trust in the worker is hard to establish, and initially the client may be a passive recipient of service rather than an active participant in treatment. The social worker has to be frank in exercising the authority of his or her position. Young (1964) suggests that abusive parents respond primarily to authority used without hesitancy or apology, but at the same time without punitiveness:

> The caseworker who faces abusing parents cannot be afraid of them. They exploit fear and they deride weakness. Neither can the caseworker afford any illusions about them; with intelligence they can be very convincing and remarkably adept at saying what the caseworker wants to hear. . . . Primarily they respect power, and

there is substantial indication that they evaluate any caseworker, or anyone else for that matter, in terms of how much power over them that person has. . . . (p. 95).

By and large, abusing parents were respectful to those they feared, manipulative with those they could use, and indifferent to everyone else. . . .

The greatest asset a caseworker can have in dealing with these families is a deep conviction that no one has the right to abuse the helpless. It is out of such conviction, not anger at the parents, that help is best offered [p. 127].

Furthermore the structure of contact must be informal, more often in the home rather than in the office. One intensive-casework demonstration project with neglectful parents indicated that it is helpful to plan interviews for the same hour of the same day each week to "establish a pattern that our clients could remember and rely on." The procedure was also designed to help the clients develop a greater sense of planning in their lives (Bishop, 1963, p. 15).

The worker needs to accept the expectation of small gains and limited goals, as well as the initial dependency of the client. The expectations set should be realistic; they should be set with some appreciation of class and ethnic differences in the approach toward child care and should, in no instance, be different from those expected from most parents in the community. Drawing on their experiences in helping neglectful mothers in Appalachia, Polansky et al., (1972) note that forming a relationship with such mothers

depends on a worker who has strong convictions about the needs of children and no great need to be popular with every one he meets. . . . The worker can be pretty sure that the mother will be more afraid of him than he is of her. . . . It does not hurt to let the mother save face by expressing her resentment. It is not so necessary to answer an attack as to hear it out. The aim is not to win an argument with her about whether she has a right to be angry, but to win a relationship for the sake of the children. Strength and calmness in the face of attack, even if directed at the worker, usually has [*sic*] a settling effect, and increases [*sic*] her respect for one. If one asks how these characteristics are acquired, we can only reply, "The more you do it, the easier it becomes." For after a time, an experienced child welfare worker handles anger like an electrician deals with current. We respect its force and potential for danger, but we are not all that frightened when we believe we know what we are doing [pp. 56–57].

Bandler (1967) aptly summarizes some of the problems in working with such families and the workers' response to these difficulties:

The nature of the families' processes of communication is extremely complicated and requires special attention in achieving involvement. Language is not a familiar vehicle for communication of feelings, or for identifying and categorizing, or conveying information. These families are action-oriented, concrete in their thinking, and not used to introspection or abstract thinking. They have little or no psychological insight into themselves or their behavior and little or no perception of conflict areas or psychological problems. Their solutions of economic, social, and psychological problems are impulsive and for immediate gain. The future is not taken into account. Consequently planning does not enter into their solutions. Problems in communication are compounded by their failure to trust anyone or any institution. Traditional casework methods, which are based on the assumption of trust and which are developed through ordinary avenues of communication, are not adequate. Consequently certain adaptations of casework concepts and techniques were necessary to achieve the initial goal or involvement. Our families had not initiated help or even recognized that they needed it, so the classic setting of the agency was not possible.

Mutual involvement and the gradual establishment of trust in the worker are achieved through the worker's gratification of dependency needs, which need not lead to insatiable demands. During the period of testing the social worker gradually emerges as a constant object and a figure who establishes some order, and a priority of problems, in their chaotic lives. Through such a relationship there appears to develop some enhancement of self-esteem and some improvement in the management of household and children [p. 291].

The worker's acting as a "good parent" in gratifying client dependency needs is based on the idea that maltreatment results from a deprived childhood, resulting in a lack of trust and an inability to love and nurture. A significant element of the protective-service treatment program, then, is concerned with "reparenting" so as to make restitution for a deprived childhood and to help the client "unlearn mistrust."

The worker's display of concern and interest in the client has positive effects in increasing client self-esteem. The investment of the worker's time and energy is perceived as an objective indication to the client that somebody in the community sees the client as far from worthless and unimportant.

Helping parents to anticipate problems so they can plan to cope with them rather than reacting impulsively when problems arise, helping them to learn alternative procedures for dealing with child management problems so that they can select a more effect option, listening respectfully to but not supporting nonproductive defenses advanced by the parents, building on the parents' abilities to make the smallest changes in their situation, and mobilizing any sources of support in the group of people associated with the client—all are helpful tactics engaged in by the worker.

The social worker needs to communicate predictability if the client is to develop confidence and trust in the worker. This means that the worker shares honestly and fully with the client, in advance, what it is he or she plans to do—even if this includes planning court action.

In implementing treatment plans the worker should actively engage the client to the greatest extent possible and should encourage and accept client suggestions. Protective service clients "usually have very little control over their own lives, and when we intervene we threaten what little control they have—specifically, the control they exercise over their children. If we are to help them change, we need to encourage these parents to take charge whenever possible" (Davoren, 1977–78, p. 113). This might involve encouraging their active participation in implementing any treatment plan and encouraging and accepting client suggestions.

The worker has to be ready to perform a wide variety of roles with these families: adviser, teacher, enabler, intervenor, coordinator of treatment, expediter, supporter, and confidant. There must be a constant effort to identify concrete needs and provide concrete services. Professionals who have worked with such parents have remarked on their emotional inaccessibility, the persistence that one has to display in going out to them physically and emotionally, and the difficulty in liking them while aware of what they did to a child (Davoren, 1968).

The use of contracts is of help but may be difficult to employ successfully with some groups of clients. Protective Service agencies serve involuntary and resistive clients who are often opposed to contracting and do not adhere to them once the contracts are formulated. In fast-changing situations contracts become obsolete quickly. In other instances, contracts are signed by clients who do not fully understand their intent or significance (Jones et al. 1981, p. 77).

Another difficulty encountered by many workers dealing with neglect and child abuse is the acceptance of the "banality of evil." One expects the parent who abuses or neglects his or her child to look and act markedly different from the general run of parents. Instead, such parents are, for the most part, relatively indistinguishable from anyone else.

The worker has also to consider the treatment needs of the children. Because the child's parents are not providing a good parental model, the worker must provide the child with an example of how good parents should act. If the child feels hostile towards the parents, he or she may react with guilt to this feeling of hostility, however justified. He or she may be anxious about what is going to happen and fearful that the family may break up. The child may have been forced to assume responsibility for himself or herself and for younger siblings because of parental default, and, as a result, may resent being denied a true childhood. These are some of the problems with which the caseworker can help the child.

It might seem obvious, but the protective service worker should be aware of the need to turn off the lights and lock the door of any home he or she enters in order to remove a child who has been temporarily abandoned. In transporting a child, the worker must make certain, lest he or she be accused of neglect, to put seat belts on the child and use the safety latch on the car door.

A protective agency, if it is to do its work effectively, needs a wide variety of resources. The agency may make regular payments to emergency foster families who stand ready to accept any child on short notice. The agency also needs baby-sitters or homemakers who are able to go into homes and care for children who are temporarily abandoned. It needs access to foster homes in which children may be placed for longer periods of time. The protective service agency may itself provide such services or it may purchase such services from another agency.

A wide variety of treatment resources have been utilized in attempting to meet the needs of this group of clients. One group of innovations involves "shared parenting" to provide the parent with some relief from the stresses and burdens of unremitting child care, which may lead to maltreatment. Among these arrangements are crisis nurseries, drop-in centers, extended-day-care centers, and parental surrogates.

The following examples of "shared parenting" through day care involves a father who was abusing his four preschool children:

> He explained that he worked at night and tried to sleep and keep his children during the day while his wife worked. He and his wife were having serious marital problems which frequently erupted in verbal and physical attacks upon each other and the children. The father explained that he realized he had whipped the children too hard, but that the problems presented by the conflict between him and his wife, and his inability to get his sleep and watch the children were just too much for his nerves. When the children failed to obey him, he lost his temper and whipped them too hard. Obviously, day care alone is not the answer to this problem but it was one way of reducing the demands made by the children upon their father and of meeting their need for supervision [Medley, 1967, p. 9].

Crisis nurseries operate twenty-four hours a day, seven days a week. They accept children at all hours in order to avoid or relieve a potentially damaging crisis situation by providing short-term relief. As emergency shelters, they do not solve an ongoing problem situation and are most effectively used in conjunction with or as a supplement to other services. A crisis nursery may impose a maximum forty-eight- or seventy-two-hour residential stay for a child and may accept a maximum of five to seven children. The danger of parental misuse of the center as a convenience, rather than as a facility for avoidance of abuse, needs to be monitored. "Drop-in" nurseries permit a mother to place children for a few hours "without much explanation or preparation—in moments of great stress—for no other reason than the mother wants relief" (Kempe & Helfer, 1972, p. 48).

Agencies have experimented with providing relief from child care by organizing a "mom's day out." For one day a week over a six-month period, mothers known to the agency's protective service unit are free of child-care responsibilities, which are taken over by students in a social work program.

In San Francisco, the extended-family center provides a "home away from home" for abused children and their parents. The center cares for children between 9 A.M. and 6 P.M., acting as an extended family to relieve the mother while she receives treatment (Ten Broeck, 1974).

Such programs combine a therapeutic nursery facility for children and group therapy and a family-life education program for parents. While the children are cared for, the parents are involved in group activities. The nursery school and its personnel also role-model desirable parental care (Tuszynski & Dowd, 1978). (See also Gardner, 1975.)

Special live-in treatment facilities have also been developed. The New York Foundling Hospital has established a temporary shelter at the Center for Parent and Child Development in an effort to help parents who have abused their children. The program permits mothers and children to live at the hospital for periods ranging from three to six months. During this time, the children are cared for in the hospital nursery or day-care centers, and the mothers receive intensive individual and group therapy from a multidisciplinary team, which includes social workers. The staff provides a model of good mothering by actual demonstrations of desirable child care. Discharge from residence in the hospital is followed up by a year or more of supervision in their own home by "surrogate mothers," who are paraprofessionals selected from the neighborhood in which the mothers live.

During 1973 and 1974, sixty-two families were provided three to four months of in-patient treatment, followed by a one-year out-patient follow-up. During the period in residence, each mother is assigned to a social worker who acts as a supportive friend, models appropriate parental behavior, and negotiates help in using community resources. Group counseling and psychiatric help are provided (Fontana & Robeson, 1976). A similar program in England is described by Lynch and Ounsted (1976).

Another example of this kind of "engineered community" has been attempted by the District of Columbia Department of Public Welfare: "Women on welfare whose child care seemed substandard were recruited to move into [a specially adapted apartment house] bringing their children with them. In addition to financial help they were offered guidance with housekeeping, health care, child caring . . . even with personal grooming" (Polansky, 1974 p. 128). Parental surrogates or parent aids are paraprofessional "friends" who are available to take over care of the child in the home when some relief is necessary to prevent abuse. In addition, they provide support and friendship, being available to listen to the parent when she wants to talk to some sympathetic mothering person in resolving tension. Parent aids work with the guidance and supervision of the social worker responsible for the family (Lane & Van Dyke, 1978).

Homemakers provide an additional resource for reducing the stress of child care. As supplementary caretakers, homemakers can relieve the frustrated, overburdened mother of some of the load of child care.

Parent-aide services are analogous to, but perhaps one step beyond, homemaker services. Parent aids in "parenting-the-parent" more explicitly than do homemakers, provide social companionship and emotional support.

Case aides provide a human contact for the abusive parent that moderates their behavior (Zimrim, 1984). The very presence of these aids exerts a social-control pressure on the parents to act more acceptingly toward their children. There is a reduction of stress associated with the help in the home that the case aides provide, and an increased self-esteem comes from the attention and concern communicated to the parents by the case aids. Based on a study of thirty-seven closed cases in which parent aids were used, Miller, Fein, et al. (1985) concluded that "improvement was indicated in the vast majority of cases" (p. 42).

As a consequence of the availability of emotional satisfaction and support derived from the relationship with the parent aide, homemaker, and/or supportive day-care personnel, the parent may be able to reduce the demands made on the child for such satisfaction. Such supports tend to diminish the tendency to "role reversal" and the disappointment the parent might feel when the child fails to supply such needs.

Because situations that trigger maltreatment sometimes can be resolved only with money, agencies have experimented with emergency relief funds. Such emergency funds have been disbursed as a cash grant to meet emergency housing costs, including those for rent, for restoration of heat and electricity to a home, or for emergency supplies of food. The funds have had the effect of increasing client confidence in the worker's desire and ability to be of help (Horowitz & Wintermute, 1978).

Efforts have been made through the use of such programs as parent effectiveness training to increase the parents' repertoire of disciplinary procedures. The parent is educated to the use of skills in childrearing that emphasize nonpunitive approaches. The assumption is that abusive parents have not had an opportunity to learn desirable parenting procedures because they lacked effective models in their own parents. Further, such parents know little about child development and need both information and training in good parenting. They need training in expanding their repertoire of procedures for child management beyond the almost exclusive use of punishment.

Behavior modification approaches have been used in some programs to alter the behaviors of both parents and children. Parents have been trained to use behavior modification procedures based on operant-conditioning concepts in changing the behaviors of their children that stimulate abusive responses. Parents have been trained through the use of behavior modification procedures, such as modeling and role playing, to change their behaviors in response to the child. Through modeling rehearsal, practice, and evaluation feedback, parents learn specific behaviors relating to anger management, self-control and impulse delay, child management skills, and stress management. Parents are taught to recognize signs that might lead to abuse, cognitive restructuring of irrational childrearing expectations, and greater tolerance for children's irritating behavior.

The basic presuppositions of these programs is that physically abusive parents suffer from skills deficits—child-management skills, anger-control skills, and problem-solving skills. The parent learns to substitute nonviolent forms of child discipline for violent approaches, and to use time-out, contingency management, and positive reinforcement procedures. Anger control programs involve learning to recognize signs of anger arousal, self-talk, and relaxation procedures. Behavior modification programs have been designed to develop social skills so as to decrease client isolation.

Literature on such approaches most often, details single case studies or small group projects. Treatment takes place in the clinic but more often in the parent's home. A programmed parent education manual and audiotapes provide homework training for clients. Considerable success is claimed for such efforts in reducing abuse.

There has been a sharp increase in use of behavioral modification approaches in treating child abuse and neglect. Articles reviewing these programs have summarized, in one instance, twenty-one studies (Gambrill, 1983), and in another instance nineteen studies are summarized. (Isaacs, 1982).

A number of texts detail a social learning, behavioral modification approach to treating child abusive families. The target of such programs is focused on physical child abuse (Kelly, 1983; Goldstein, Keller, & Erne, 1985).

Programs have been developed to "package" a comprehensive group of services that might be helpful. Here the treatment innovation relates to a change in the service delivery system. A comprehensive system of services to abused and neglected children pioneered in Nashville by the Tennessee Department of Public Welfare materially reduced the number of children who had to be removed from their homes (Burt & Balyeat, 1974). The program included twenty-four-hour emergency intake, emergency caretaker service, emergency homemaker service, emergency foster homes, and emergency shelter care for adolescents and families. The program also coordinated the efforts of local public and private agencies on behalf of abused and neglected children.

The Protective Services Center, established in Chicago by the Juvenile Protective Association but no longer in existence, offered under one roof and under its own administrative control the following services: casework, group work, a daycare center for preschool children, homemaker service, an emergency shelter, temporary foster care, tutoring for children with learning problems, pediatric care, financial aid for special rehabilitative needs, an after-school day-care program, and transportation for children to and from the center. One goal was to help the families establish some predictable routine in their lives. The agency not only had to take children to school but also had to have staff members participate in awakening the children, dressing them, and getting them ready to go. Because of the heavy demands made by the families, only a very limited group could be served by this elaborate program: twenty-six families with a total of 104 children.

Emergency facilities for temporarily "abandoned" children have also been developed. In one California county, a network of "Good Neighbor Homes" was established. These were licensed foster homes that agreed to accept children, at any hour on any day, who needed shelter care. The homes were selected so as to be in the neighborhood of children likely to need such care so that they could remain in familiar surroundings and in the same school while in short-term substitute care (Soman, 1967; Penner, 1968).

A protective service agency in Buffalo, New York, developed a list of "emergency parents" who were available at all times to go into a home and stay with a child who had been left unsupervised and unprotected (Paget, 1967). Each "emergency parent" agrees (for a small fee) to be available for one night of each week. Each is provided with a kit, which includes "blankets, food, cooking equipment, rechargeable flashlight, first-aid kit, light bulbs, disposable diapers, insect spray, and an aluminum folding cot" (p. 128). The work of the emergency parent is as follows:

> The police called the agency saying that they had heard from a neighbor that four children were in a home alone, the oldest nine years of age. A caseworker had to enter the home by a window. He found that an unvented gas stove was filling the home with fumes. All children were asleep, one youngster at the very top of the stairs. There was no doubt that a tragedy had been averted. An emergency parent was placed in the home and the sleeping children were guarded from possible accidents. The emergency parent remained all night and part of the morning, when the single parent returned pp. 130].

Emergency caretakers have been used in Chicago to prevent placement of dependent children reported as being without adult supervision in the home (Brown, 1979). Children whose parents were temporarily and unexpectedly absent because of illness, accident, arrest, or drug abuse were cared for up to sixty hours by such emergency caretakers who remained in the home. If the parents did not return within that time, as they frequently did not, homemaker service or foster placement was provided. Because parents were frequently angry and upset to return home and find a stranger caring for their child, protection needed to be afforded emergency caretakers.

Termination

The agency should plan a target date for termination with the family. But because the agency is responsible for seeing that the child is safe, the agency, rather than the family, has the obligation to make the decision regarding termination. When the parents demonstrate that they can function so that the child is no longer in significant danger, it is time for the agency to consider termination.

Termination of agency contact is justified when safety of the child is assured; parents have convincingly demonstrated a changed, more positive attitude toward the child; parents have developed skills in alternative, more benign forms of child discipline; parents are motivated to involve the agency in the future if there is any likelihood of recurrence of child maltreatment; chronic stresses on the family have been ameliorated; and a social support network is available to which the family can turn for help. Termination should involve a recapitulation of the changes that have taken place, an explicit expression of commendation and support for the changes made, and a review of some of the difficulties that the parents will inevitably face.

Court Action in Protective Services

The process of assuring more adequate care for the child may involve changes in the child's own home or, if this is impossible, removal to a substitute home. If the parents are unwilling or unable to plan the necessary changes, or if the situation involves so clear and present a danger to the child that he or she can be protected only by being removed from the home, the agency may have to obtain court action. In taking such action, the principle followed is that "use of the court should be constructive—as a resource, not as a last resort." The court process needs to be seen as "a means of protecting the child rather than prosecuting the parents" (Thomson and Paget, 1971, p. 44). The caseworker attempts to exercise authority in a positive, supportive manner.

The court has the right and the power to *demand,* as against the social worker's entitlement and power to suggest, to persuade, and to influence. Because the court is a powerful resource, its intervention should be initiated appropriately, cautiously, and selectively toward constructive objectives. In every instance, the rights of the parents to the child must be safeguarded, and the abrogation of such rights—however brief—can be sanctioned only by the court.

If the caseworker feels that the children must be removed from the home, he or she first seeks the parents' voluntary consent. If they refuse, the agency has no alternative but to begin court action. Actually, however, according to the limited statistics available, recourse to legal action is atypical, and most protective service cases are closed without it.

We have already noted that the child continues to remain in his or her own home in some 80 per cent of the cases reported to protective service agencies. Court action is involved in only a limited number of those 20 per cent of the cases in which the child is removed from the home and placed in substitute care. In some instances, the parents voluntarily agree to the plan for placement.

Since 1976 there has been a steady decline in the use of foster care in protective service, from 25.3 per cent in 1976 to 13.4 in 1982 (Russell, & Trainor, 1984, p. 41). Some additional children are placed outside the home with relatives, and a smaller number are placed in institutions.

Because social workers and their supervisors have been sued for inadequately protecting a child, there may be a tendency for some social workers to act defensively in self-protection. A child may be removed because, although there is no clear evidence of immediate danger, the social worker is uncertain about such a possibility (Besharov, 1985).

Court action is required in some 18 per cent of the cases, most frequently in cases of sexual abuse and in those involving younger children, where there is evidence of major physical injuries and the parents deny abuse.

In most jurisdictions, if either a social agency or the police have to remove a child from the home because there is no caretaker available, or because the situation is dangerous, a court hearing must be held within twenty-four hours to determine the appropriateness of the action. Unless the court is satisfied that protection of the child requires his or her removal from the home, the child must be returned to his or her parents.

Invoking legal sanction changes the worker, however temporarily, from helper to adversary. The worker should attempt to help the family understand that the use of legal sanction is an effort to motivate the family to mobilize whatever strengths it has in dealing positively with the problem. Many families may find that this sounds much like the "this hurts me more than it hurts you" gambit, and they find it difficult not to see the worker as pitted against them. However, parental hostility supposedly can be mitigated if the worker clearly explains the action he or she proposes to take and the reasons for it and presents the material in court in such a way as to emphasize the helpfulness of the action to the family. The petition should be presented not as a procedure directed against the parents but as a procedure in behalf of the child.

The very fact that a legal procedure has been initiated may help the parents to mobilize themselves to make the necessary changes. As Hancock (1958) says, "The agency's authority to insist on more responsible care often induces parents to examine their own situation. . . . While they may protest vigorously, they are actually relieved to find strength in an outside factor that requires something of them" (p. 8). The seriousness of the situation exemplified by the agency's recourse to the court may support and reinforce the positive components of a parent's ambivalence—that part of the parent that wants to do right by the child.

In those limited number of instances in which court action appears necessary, the agency files a "formal application to invoke the judicial authority of the court." This is different from a complaint that "reports a condition of neglect which needs exploration" (American Humane Association, 1957, p. 19).

The petition, which is a statement to the court of the fact that the child needs protection, should include "evidence concerning the social and family background, specific conditions and frequency of occurrence of neglect as seen by the worker, parents' attitudes toward the children, whether the family used agency help, and, if so, how they used it" (Moss, 1963, pp. 385–386). The material in the petition should be supported by data from schools, medical facilities, other social agencies, law enforcement agencies, and so on.

The petition that initiates the court process is followed by a preliminary hearing within two or three weeks. At the preliminary hearing, the parents indicate whether or not they will consent to or contest the petition. The hearing is also designed to determine whether the allegations of the petition are true and whether the established facts constitute neglect or abuse.

The preliminary hearing is followed by an adjudicatory hearing to determine whether abuse has taken place as defined by state law. At this point, the social worker has to testify as to the facts of the situation and may be subject to cross-examination. The court needs a "preponderance of evidence"—a balance of the evidence indicating abuse—in order to make a determination that abuse has occurred.

During the adjudicatory hearing the petitioner agency, represented by the social worker, has the responsibility of proving to the court that the child has in fact been subjected to abuse or neglect within the meaning of the statute. Social work data need to be translated into legally admissible evidence that is consistent, reliable, valid, and convincing (Barth & Sullivan, 1985). Records should be factual and unbiased, and should provide the detail that supports the conclusions stated.

In testifying during adjudicatory hearings social workers may be qualified as expert witnesses on child welfare services. If qualified, they can present opinions and make inferences about the likely effects of services on the client situation. If not qualified as expert witnesses, they can merely present the facts as they know them. A social worker may be qualified as an expert on child welfare services but not on child development. In this case the social worker may testify that the mother rarely made any affectionate gesture toward the child but cannot then infer that such action will have various consequences for the child's emotional development.

The adjudicatory hearing is followed by a dispositional hearing, in which a determination is made regarding the placement of the child or on a program of treatment in the child's own home. A date may be set for a future review hearing when progress on the case will be assessed by the court.

At each point in the process, the case may be disposed of. The parents may not contest the proceedings and may agree to some plan that is acceptable to the court and to the agency. Throughout the process, the parents are free to hire a lawyer and, in many jurisdictions, to ask for a jury trial.

The Child Abuse Prevention and Treatment Act of 1974 requires that states provide children with representation in judicial proceedings that affect their welfare. In an increasing number of instances social workers have been appointed as guardian *ad litems* to represent the interests of children in court (Davidson, 1981).

Because the judge is concerned with protecting the rights of the parents as well as those of the children and the community, the material presented by the caseworker in support of the petition should follow the rules of evidence generally deemed admissible by courts of law. The material presented must be relevant, based on actual knowledge rather than hearsay, and supported by sufficient facts. A worker's "certainty" that he "feels" a child is neglected or abused finds little sympathetic response in a court of law; the burden of proof rests with the social worker (Sheridan & Mancini, 1962). "Social workers have a habit of using such words as *seem, appear,* and *wonder* as if they were not sure of what they are saying. . . . The court respects the confidence of a worker who *is* rather than *appears,* who *says* rather than *implies,* and who *tells* rather than *shares*" (Schmidt, 1963, p. 119). In filing a petition, the social worker accepts a responsibility—to the court, the community, the child, and the parents—to prepare the material in a manner that will withstand challenge. The same suggestions apply to the social worker's approach in testifying in court.

The justification for objecting to hearsay evidence is based on four considerations

1. There is no opportunity to cross-examine the person offering the evidence.
2. The statement was not made under oath.
3. The nonverbal communication that accompanied the comment and which may qualify it is not available for observation.
4. The evidence as originally stated may be distorted by the party reporting it.

Social workers need to recognize that courts operate in terms of their own standards and procedures, with a decided orientation to fact and objective evidence. Without clear, well-organized, and specific evidence of maltreatment, social workers are perceived as poor investigators and inadequate witnesses. Lack of precise, objective evidence in support of their recommendations limits court confidence in the worker's planning suggestions.

Social workers are cautioned to avoid casual attire for a court appearance and to prepare in advance by organizing the material for presentation. In testifying, it is suggested that they speak slowly and distinctly, avoid professional jargon and nonverbal responses that cannot be recorded, and refrain from advocacy of a particular outcome, sticking closely to the facts to enhance credibility (Caulfield, 1978, pp. 49–57).

In making a disposition of the case, the judge may decide that there is not sufficient evidence to warrant any action by the court. If, however, he or she decides that there is sufficient evidence, the judge may make one of several decisions. The judge can permit the child to remain at home but place the family under the supervision of the court. Responsibility for supervision may be delegated to the probation department of the court or to a public or private social agency. The designated agency has a continuing responsibility to report to the court regarding the conditions under which the child is living. The parents' refusal to make necessary changes can be brought to the immediate attention of the court. As Beck says, the value of protective supervision is that "the agency's legal responsibility to the court, in reference to the family, is brought into focus and made specific for all concerned" (Beck, 1955, Part II, p. 17).

The judge can also place the child under protective legal custody. The child may be permitted to remain in his or her own home but under the legal custody of a social agency. This is a step beyond protective supervision because the agency given protective legal custody has the "right to care, custody, and control of the child." The agency may remove the child to another home if the parents refuse to make the changes necessary to mitigate the dangers that the child faces.

The court can also terminate parental rights and order the child removed from the home and placed under agency guardianship. Legislation has broadened the options that are available to the agency and the court in seeking to terminate parental rights so that the child can be made available for adoption. Such action can, in some states, be taken (1) if the child has been "abandoned," as evidenced by the fact that the parents have not visited the child on a regular basis without good cause for at least six months; (2) if the child has been "permanently neglected," evidenced by failure for more than a year to "substantially and continuously or repeatedly maintain contact with the child or to plan for his or her future, although physically and financially able to do so"; or (3) if the parent is presently, and for the foreseeable future, unable to provide proper and adequate care for the child by reason of mental illness or mental retardation. A further requirement is that termination cannot be granted if the agency has not demonstrated diligent efforts to help the family speaks to the responsibility of the community as a partner with the parents to make the home fit for the child.

Three levels of proof are generally required in court cases. The most stringent—proof "beyond a reasonable doubt"—is required in criminal cases. The least stringent level—proof by "preponderance of evidence" is generally sufficient in civil cases. A middle level—proof by "clear and convincing" evidence is most frequently required in termination proceedings. This somewhat stringent level of proof is required in response to the gravity of the action being considered and in protection of parental rights. Rejection of the requirement of the most stringent level of proof—"beyond a reasonable doubt" reflects the court's concern about the child's rights and need for protection. In March 1982, in the case of Santosky v. Kramer the U.S. Supreme Court ruled that due process required states to employ the standard of clear and convincing evidence in deciding on termination of parental rights.

All these procedures are designed to prevent hasty or arbitrary action and to make certain that any action taken is in accordance with due process. The court's decision also gives legal sanction to a desirable casework plan and reinforces the authority of the worker or the agency. Legal sanctions can do little to help a child other than to reduce the probability of his or her being injured. The law can dissolve a child's family relationship; it cannot preserve or rebuild it. This is the responsibility and the capability of the social services.

Criminal proceedings are rarely initiated with maltreating parents. Criminal prosecution in case of child abuse is difficult and often ineffective. The child is frequently too young to testify; the parents cannot be made to testify against themselves; and the incident has generally taken place without eyewitnesses. Consequently proof "beyond reasonable doubt" is difficult to obtain.

A number of reasons help to explain the discomfort of social workers with court proceedings.

1. The difference between the helping orientation of the social worker and the adversarial relationships that characterizes court proceedings; between the

informal, conciliatory social work approach and the formal, confrontative legal approach.

2. The difference between the human concerns of the social worker and the more primary legal concerns of the court.
3. The need on the part of the social worker to explain and justify his or her actions to others who do not share his or her approach to the situation, who experience it differently from a different vantage point.
4. The need to share control of the case situation with others and the disappointment, frustration, and anxiety if the social worker's recommendation for the family are not accepted.
5. The concern that the promise of confidentiality to the client may be compromised.
6. The anxiety that comes with being vulnerable to challenge in a critical cross examination; the social workers being open to critical scrutiny and evaluation by opposing counsel.
7. The difficulty in recasting the social worker's perception of the situation in more legal, more objective, more precise terms in accordance with a different kind of standard. The court accepts only objective truth; the social worker in addition credits subjective truth.

As a consequence of these differences, social workers anticipat e court hearing procedures as a personal affront and are intimidated by them. The best antidote to this concern is adequate preparation that assures a sense of self-confidence. In preparing for a court experience, social workers should consult with their agency lawyer. It might help to role-play acting as a witness in response to the lawyer's cross examination.

Use of Group Approach

Contacts with individual families may be supplemented by group meetings of parents to discuss childrearing problems and marital difficulties that affect their handling of children (McFerran, 1957, 1958; Bellucci, 1972; Paulson et al., 1974; Wayne & Avery, 1980). Workers planning such meetings have to consider not only lack of motivation but financial problems, which may make it impossible for prospective participants to hire babysitters and pay for transportation so that they can attend meetings. The agency, therefore, may have to pay for both sitters and transportation.

Parents' attendance at group meetings is interpreted as a demonstration of cooperation with the agency. The agency, however, must be prepared to "require" attendance. Many of the members benefit from the knowledge they acquire and are stimulated "to examine their methods of handling their children and to look at themselves critically." The meetings have, in addition, a "social value for many of the members, especially for some husbands and wives who rarely, if ever, had shared an activity of mutual interest" (McFerran, 1957, p. 33).

Group programs have been developed through the cooperative efforts of the courts, social agencies, and educational institutions. In one instance, the court ordered parents adjudged to be neglectful to attend group sessions devoted to family life education. Failure to attend was regarded as contempt of court. Some of the group meetings were devoted to a didactic presentation of material about children's needs and child development, family finances and budgeting, and health care of children. Other meetings were structured to permit a general nondirective discussion among the parents of problems they were having in rearing their children.

A self-help group of abusive parents has been organized and provides an effective adjunctive group treatment resource. Families Anonymous (FA) was organized in California in 1971 with the help of a social worker. Membership requires that the parent make an open admission of child abuse and express a desire to change.

Families Anonymous was previously called Parents Anonymous and prior to that it was known as Mothers Anonymous. Each change in title signifies a widening of the scope of concern to encompass all members of the family system.

The organization's bulletins indicate that meetings are designed to help members share their feelings about incidents of child abuse and to express their fears of parenthood or their inability to handle the parental role in a constructive and healthy way. As a result of sharing their feelings and attitudes, members begin to understand themselves better and can start suggesting alternatives and answers for themselves and others. A description of the general orientation of group meetings suggests that it "is not a confrontation group, not sensitivity training, not Freudian analysis. I guess you might call it layman's reality therapy. We just don't let people moan about how they were beaten when they were three; we say, 'You're thirty-three now. The problem is to stop doing what you're doing to your children.' "

By sharing "positive behavior alternatives" to abuse, FA educates its members to more acceptable patterns of parenting. As one member said:

> Parents Anonymous gives you something to do besides abusing. It gives you alternatives; instead of hitting, instead of name-calling, it gives you something to do. Instead of throwing a child, you throw a cup or a plate. Instead of responding to a temper tantrum with a temper tantrum of your own, you lock yourself in a bedroom until it's over. Something to do instead of abusing [Collins, 1978, p. 91].

The organization is involved in socializing the abusive parent in terms of parental role behaviors that are socially acceptable. "Support," "caring," and "giving" are repeatedly emphasized in FA meetings and reinforce the ideology of mutual self-help, which is the basic therapeutic factor in the program. The group combines nurturance with an accepting firmness in its unequivocal rejection of child abuse.

Tape-recorded structured interviews with FA members concerning the reasons that prompted them to join indicated that the decisive fact was that the group was perceived as offering the probability of problem-focused help in a context of nonjudgmental acceptance. This was reinforced by the lack of alternative options and a fear of professionals (Powell, 1979). Despite the advantages, many spoke of the threat to personl esteem involved in accepting the label of "Family Anonymous group member."

As is true in other self-help groups, being accountable to the group is an added factor in contributing to self-control. One FA member said that she knew she would be asked at each meeting. "How did your week go?" Just thinking about what her answer would be—and knowing it would be difficult to pretend with other parents—was an important factor in controlling her abusive behavior" (Starkweather & Turner, 1975, p. 156).

FA makes a great point of protecting members' anonymity and confidentiality. This protection permits the members to discuss their experiences without risk of public disclosure. The fact that they are sharing their experiences with other parents who have abused children guarantees their being able to "confess" without danger of rejection, recrimination, or humiliation (Moore, 1983).

Unlike the traditional therapeutic relationship, which sets limits on the extent of personal involvement between the helper and the person being helped, FA deliberately fosters the personal involvement of members with each other. This personalization of interaction is an important component of membership satisfaction in affiliation with the organization, ensuring the availability of an effective social support system. The groups developed through FA meetings act as "surrogate families." Each group member is given the phone numbers of all others in the group and is advised to "reach for the phone instead of the child" when feeling stressed (Holmes, 1978).

In analyzing the dynamics of change experienced by Family Anonymous participants, Collins (1978) concluded that it involves acceptance of the label of child abuser and transformation of the descriptive label into a positive image. Members are gradually transformed into "lay professionals" who perceive themselves as able to help other child abusers because they themselves have, at one time, been child abusers. By 1978 FA was developing a training program for professionals and was involving abusive parents in the education of professionals.

Social workers do not act as group leaders but as "professional sponsors" to local groups. The group leader or chapter chairperson is always a parent who at one time abused a child. Members can identify more readily with such a person than they can with a "professional therapist whose 'experience of abuse' is deemed vicarious at best and voyeuristic at worst' (Collins, 1978, p. 39). The professional sponsor is a resource person rather than a group member or leader. The professional sponsor's responsibility is to offer some specialized expert knowledge, as it may be required; to be a neutral observer; to resolve conflicts, to act as a role model, and to act as a referral liaison with community services that might be required by FA members.

As is true in any group situation, not all abusive parents can be appropriately referred to Families Anonymous. The withdrawn parent, the parent who has difficulty in communicating, the parent who is aggressive, impulsive, and disruptive, or the parent who is defensive, frightened, and anxious about "coming out" as an abusive parent is not likely to be able to use FA as a treatment resource.

In June 1978 Families Anonymous was estimated to have about eight thousand members in some eight hundred chapters. It is defined as a self-help organization providing a "nurturing and therapeutic service" (MacFarlane & Lieber, 1978). By 1986 Families Anonymous had some 1500 groups meeting to discuss child maltreatment.

Families Anonymous membership is primarily white, middle-class, young, and female. In 1977, of some five hundred chapters in the country, only two were identifiably black and three Hispanic. Overall membership was about 4 per cent black (Mohamoud, 1977).

Affiliation with and participation in Families Anonymous is involuntary for some 7 per cent of parents and is mandated by the court. However, beyond the stage of initial resistance, those who come to Families Anonymous through this route are indistinguishable from those who are self-referred (Collins, 1978, p. 8).

The national organization has received grants of support from the federal government, acts as cosponsor to an annual national conference on child abuse, and publishes a semimonthly newsletter, *Parents Anonymous Frontiers*.

A special evaluation of the Families Anonymous program by a research organization, Behavior Associates, found that members of Families Anonymous saw the organization as having contributed to positive changes in their attitudes and behavior toward their children. Positive changes in members' perception of themselves were also achieved (Wheat & Lieber, 1979, pp. 354–367).

The generally positive evaluations of the organization's outcomes needs to be assessed in terms of the fact that membership is voluntary, with the member families having higher education and income than the typical families to which protective agencies offer service. A 20 to 30 per cent dropout rate after the first suggest that those who continue are highly motivated (Wheat & Lieber, 1979, p. 353).

All of the treatment interventions that bring abusive parents together in a group—Families Anonymous, group therapy, parent education programs,—have as one of their goals diminishing the social isolation of abusive parents and providing them with social supports.

Evaluation of Outcome

Early studies that evaluated outcomes of protective service interventions showed that agencies generally achieved some modest level of success (Kelly, 1959; Scherer, 1960; Merrill et al., 1962; Rein, 1963; Bourke, 1963; Varon, 1964; Young, 1964, 1966). However most of the studies were methodologically unsophisticated and without comparison or control groups.

Statements of levels of success were frequently made with the most limited if any, substantiating detail. Typical of such statements is the following, made by Steele and Pollock (1968). It relates to the outcome of treatment of the sixty families included in their study group:

> In the great majority of patients treatment was successful, highly so in some, moderately so in others. Criteria of success were multiple. Of primary importance was a change in the style of parent-child interaction to a degree which eliminated the danger of physical harm to the child and lessened the chance of serious emotional damage [p. 138].

No details are presented of the evaluation procedures employed in arriving at these conclusions. Similarly, Helfer (1975) notes "we should be able to help 70–75 per cent with our present understanding and treatment programs" (p. 41). The basis for such an estimate is not detailed.

Reincidence of subsequent abuse has often been used as a measure of successful intervention. Although reincidence rates assume, with some hazard, that all subsequent incidents have been reported, they are a rough, useful measure of the achievement of the major objective of intervention, namely, that the child not be subsequently maltreated. Reincidence rates vary widely from study to study.

Describing a child abuse treatment program at a hospital-based facility, Holmes (1977) notes that "therapeutic services are intensive and tend to continue for a period of two years or more. The payoff is the reinjury rate of 2.2 per cent which is extremely low" (p. 24). Seventy-two families had been treated at this facility by the time of the report.

Gladston (1975) presents an account of forty-six families with seventy-three children treated at a combined facility: a therapeutic day-care center supplemented by a parents' group, providing a correlated treatment of parents and children. The only explicit evaluation material provided is that "over an average period of seven-plus months of attendance in the project, there have been but two known instances of recurring abuse of children" (p. 380). It might be noted that the parents treated were the most motivated of a much larger number of families originally referred to the project (Gladston, 1975, p. 374).

A report (National Center on Child Abuse and Neglect, 1975) on the work of the Child Protective Services Unit of Hennepin County (Minneapolis), regarded as one of the best in the country, notes that "It is of course difficult to measure effectiveness in the field of child protection. But Child Protective Services (Hennepin County, Minnesota) officials believe that Unit's philosophy has worked. As one indication, the recidivism rate between 1963 and 1973 averaged less than 9 percent in cases of physical abuse and 17 percent in cases of neglect" (p. 20).

Other studies have shown higher recidivism rates, however.

Johnson (1977) provides a detailed study of reincidence based on a careful analysis of the records of all families offered protective services in two cities (Nashville, Tennessee, and Savannah, Georgia) between August 1971 and April 1974. The records were reviewed for the reincidence of maltreatment, the length of time between the repeated events of maltreatment, the severity of subsequent injury as compared with the first injury, and the action taken by the agency. The study concluded that approximately 60 per cent of the reported children had been abused previously; that the more recent incidents had a relatively high probability of being more serious in nature than previous incidents; that reentry into the system occurred in a short period of time in a high percentage of the cases; and that "efforts to rehabilitate parents and prevent further abuse and/or neglect have generally failed" (p. 162).

Rivara (1985) selected for detailed study the records of 74 cases of corporal abuse of children under 2 years of age who were referred to a children's medical center by the Tennessee Department of Human Services. All of the parents were assigned mental health center treatment and parent effectiveness training, but only 33 per cent accepted treatment. Thirty per cent of the children were subsequently abused, but their abuse was unrelated to compliance with counseling treatment. Only some 8 per cent of the total group made "good" progress in counseling.

Studies that evaluate outcomes in terms of changes in parental attitudes and behavior also show variable, but generally modest, positive effects. In a follow-up study of fifty-eight abused children completed by Martin, Beezley, Conway, and Kempe (1974):

> the children were evaluated at a mean of 4.5 years after abuse had first been documented. It was disheartening to note the current behavior of the parents toward the previously abused child. Parents of 21 of the children had had psychotherapy as part of their treatment program; 90 percent of the children of these parents were still in the biologic home. Even though the children were no longer being battered in the technical or legal sense, 68 percent of them at follow-up were still experiencing hostile rejection and/or excessive physical punishment. It should be noted that these

children were faring much better than those whose parents had received no formal treatment [p. 256].

The Comptroller General's office conducted a study (1976) of protective service outcomes. Selecting ten public welfare agencies in six states, they drew a sample of records in each location for each of three periods between June 1972 and June 1973 for a total of 724 cases overall. Case records were examined, and some evaluation was made as to whether the child's circumstances were (1) "critical" (child in imminent personal danger); (2) "serious" (child provided minimal care); (3) "fragile" (potential for danger but not actual danger); or (4) "satisfactory"(suitable parental and social supports being provided to the child). Similar levels of assessment were made from the record material on the child's physical and emotional well-being.

Analysis of the information from the 714 usable records showed that a child was generally in a "serious" or "critical" situation at case opening and that the child's situation generally improved after case opening, the percentage of younger children achieving improvement being significantly greater than that of older children (p. 17). At opening, only 36 per cent of the children were in "fragile" or "satisfactory" situations. At the end of the study, 73 per cent were in a "fragile" or a "satisfactory" situation, indicating improvement in the situation for some 37 per cent of the children served.

Baher *et al.* (1976) reports the effects of an intensive relationship approach to twenty-three families with a history of the abuse of a child under four. The social worker was in contact with the family for at least eighteen months, and during the first three months of the contact, two interviews a week were scheduled with the client. Detailed process recordings were kept of all contacts as well as the results of decision-making conferences regarding clients. The workers had very limited caseloads and were in every instance professionally qualified. The worker evaluated the outcome by comparing the recorded details of first contact with the client's functioning at the end of eighteen months of service. The service was primarily a therapeutic, supportive, and accepting personal counseling intervention designed to meet dependency needs, to offer a positive reparenting experience, and to demonstrate concern in attitude and behavior. Despite the considerable effort expended, the changes in the parents' care of the child were minimal:

> The results . . . relating to the interaction between the mothers and the battered children were disappointing. Only slight positive changes were noted in most aspects of these relationships, leaving many doubts about the effectiveness of our treatment service in improving the quality of mothering. . . . [p. 171). (See also Bedger et al., 1976, pp. 206–207 for similar findings].

The Berkeley Planning Associates (1977) completed the largest most comprehensive child abuse and neglect treatment-outcome study available. It covered 1,724 parents treated in eleven different protective service demonstration projects throughout the nation. Despite the care and detail with which the study was conducted, the study itself notes its principal research deficiencies: there was no control group, the workers provided the data used in the outcome study, the clients were neither observed nor contacted directly, and there was no provision for follow-up.

The workers in the most direct contact with the client in the demonstration project filled out a series of forms developed by the researchers in consultation with practitioners. Data were collected from the time of intake to service termination for 1,724 adult clients during 1975–1976. The forms completed included an intake form, a goals-of-treatment form, and a client follow-up form. A form listing the services provided to the client and a client functioning form were completed at the end of each calendar month. A client impact form provided information on the client at the start of service, and the same form was completed at termination of service.

With reincidence used as an outcome measure, it was found that 30 per cent of the clients served by the demonstration projects abused their children severely or neglected them while in treatment. An evaluation of changes in specific client behaviors, client attitudes, or situational changes showed that in every instance, fewer than 30 per cent of the clients exhibited significant improvement. Less than 40 per cent of the clients improved in at least one third of those areas identified as problems at intake (p. 58).

Treatment interventions that seemed to provide a greater measure of success included lay therapy programs, group parent-education programs, and self-help programs such as Families Anonymous, perhaps partly because such services were more frequently used voluntarily by motivated clients capable of making effective use of the service. Clients who were treated for longer periods of time showed greater positive change, a result that suggests the value of treatment.

Replication of the study between 1979 and 1981 involving 19 demonstration projects treating a total of 986 families came to somewhat similar conclusions. "The findings indicate that despite thoughtful and often very costly interventions over 50 percent of all adult clients were judged likely to mistreat their children in the future and between 40 and 60 percent of the infant children and adolescents receiving services were reabused while their parents were in treatment" (Daro, 1985 p. 2). Greater success was achieved with families involved in sexual maltreatment than was true for those involved in child neglect.

Fitch et al. (1977) studied 140 infants hospitalized in Denver because of child abuse. The children were randomly assigned to a control group and two experimental groups. The first was provided with a limited treatment program; the second group was provided with more extensive treatment programs. Services included marital, educational, and financial counseling; family planning services; individual psychotherapy; anticipatory guidance; role modeling; assertiveness training; socialization group programs; and foster care.

Impact of intervention was measured by comparative changes in child development and by recurrence of abuse over a 30-month period of testing and retesting. The child development scores of the abused nontreated children and those of the treated group were the same (pp. 64–66). However, although 8.7 per cent of the previously abused but untreated group had been reabused, only 2.7 per cent of the abused and treated group had been reabused (p. 169).

Green et al. (1981) studied outcomes of a program that provided outpatient counseling and therapy, parent-group therapy, home visits, and other social services to about 80 parents. As a consequence, 41 per cent of the group improved slightly and 28 per cent improved significantly.

Client reactions to services offered by the protective service agency provide additional evaluation data. Magura (1982) studied thirty-four families who received intensive services at an inner-city office of a public protective service agency. In 70 per cent of the cases clients felt that their situations were "much or somewhat" better at the termination of service as compared with the time of referral. The major improvement cited was "increased self-confidence accompanied by an increased capacity to cope with their feelings and life stress" (p. 523). Clients described the major factor in accounting for their improvement as the individualized personal counseling they received from empathic, flexible, caring workers.

In considering success of such programs, attrition rates need to be taken into account. The Parenting Program for the Prevention of Child Abuse of Cleveland, Ohio, provides a program of intensive intervention with parents in the inner city who are high risk for abuse. Of one hundred families referred to the service in 1979, more than half refused to accept offers of assistance. "The inclusion of those who refused treatment as failures (in our statistic) necessitates a realistic but disheartening revision of our estimates of success rates" (Gabinet, 1983, p. 396). However, the agency achieved some success with 73 per cent of the group who accepted treatment and were seen six or more times. (See also Smith & Rachman, 1984.)

Tracy, Ballard, and Clark (1975) provide evaluation outcome data on families with whom behavior modification approaches to child management procedures were attempted. "The parents' verbal report was used to assess behavioral changes," although this report was further augmented by "direct observation in the home, clinical reports and verbal reports of others." Forty-one treated families provided a pool of 129 kinds of behavior that needed changing. Of these, 84 per cent were rated improved or very improved, whereas 9 per cent were rated worse or the same. Rating of changes was made by the health workers and project coordinator on the basis of some observable indicator. The group studied was composed of families of abused children and families at high risk for abuse. The results are not broken down, so that it is impossible to tell outcomes for the abused families alone.

Additionally, case reports of successful treatment through the use of behavior modification procedures are available in the literature (Polakow & Peabody, 1975; Reavley & Gilbert, 1976; Mastria, Mastria, & Harkins, 1979; Lutzker & Rice, 1984). (See also Isaacs, 1982; Gambrill, 1983).

A limited number of outcome evaluation reports are available on special approaches to maltreating families: group therapy, day care, coordinated services, engineered environments, and team approaches.

Justice and Justice (1976) used goal attainment scaling in determining the outcome of their group therapy programs with abusive parents. Goal attainment scaling involves specifying a series of explicit, behaviorally objectifiable goals and then determining the level at which the goal has been achieved in therapy, for which a change score is computed. The average length of group treatment ran four or five months, one and one-half hours once a week. At the last report (1976), "abuse has not reoccurred among the 15 couples who have completed group therapy since May, 1973. Furthermore, six months follow-ups show that expected levels of outcome . . . are holding up" (p. 119). The change scores were based on self-reports of changed behavior presented by the parents, who had a considerable investment in presenting themselves as improved. All couples in the parents' group were referred by the county child welfare agency. In 75 per cent of the cases, the child had been removed from the home by order of the court. The couples were told that their chances of getting their child back were likely to be greatly enhanced if they accepted therapy. Furthermore the group leader's report back to the county agency was an important determinant of whether the child was to be returned home. There was considerable incentive, then, for the parents to report progress.

Stephanson (1977) describes the results of a preschool enrichment program for abused children and their families, with preschool teachers acting as the primary therapists. There was considerable turnover, and only ten families appear to have remained in the program for more than a year. The children in the program for more than a year "showed a mean IQ increase of 14 compared to a mean gain of 2 for children less than a year and control children. In 55 percent of the one year plus families, a parent had moved from social assistance, usually via educational upgrading, to permanent employment" (p. 133). The researchers note that "like other workers in this field, we have found it difficult to evaluate our project statistically. Many of the tests were invalid. For instance, we administered the Parental Attitude Research Inventory but discovered that several parents could not read and a number complained they could not understand the questions" (p. 314).

Burch and Mohr (1980) compared the effects of an educational program that was offered to abusive parents with a control group that was not provided such treatment. Clients completing the program in *Positive Parenting* showed positive shifts in knowledge and attitudes toward childrearing. The effects of this increased understanding on actual child abuse and neglect-related behavior are inferred.

The Bowen project, conducted between 1965 and 1971 by the Juvenile Protective Association of Chicago, attempted to provide under the auspices of a single agency a comprehensive package of treatment interventions to a limited number of abusive and neglectful families. Over the five-year period, an average of twenty-five workers delivered an average of ten different services to a total of thirty-five disorganized families, which included 162 children. The final report of the project notes that it is possible to describe the treatment but difficult to provide any research evidence on outcomes: "The question of results must of necessity be answered in terms of clinical judgment and case description" (Juvenile Protective Association, 1975, p. 88). A measure of the success is the fact that removal of children by the court had to be initiated for only eight of the Bowen Center's thirty-five families.

The New York City Foundling Hospital is an "engineered environment" providing living quarters for mothers and children. During their residence there, both are involved in an intensive program of rehabilitation. Initiated in October 1972, by January 1974 it had treated thirty-eight families, two of which were subsequently child abuse recidivists. However, in 30–35 per cent of the cases, the child was placed in foster care because the mother did not make sufficient progress (American Academy of Pediatrics, 1974).

Lynch and Ounsted (1976) provide some outcome data on fifty families treated in a similar live-in facility in England. In 20 per cent of the cases, the child was still perceived as in danger after treatment, and the child was placed in foster care. Of the families treated, 80 per cent returned home with their children, and there was no subsequent serious abuse except in two cases (p. 206).

The successful use of foster family care to remove the child from any possibility of danger and the subsequently healthy development of children placed in such substitute care are reported by Kent (1976). He studied the physical and emotional development of 219 abused and neglected children. Obtaining data from the schools and the social workers assigned to the case, he compared the child's functioning at the point of the agency's first contact with the child and a year later. In each agency, intervention had resulted in the placement of the child in substitute care, most frequently in a foster family home. During the year in placement, the child made substantial gains in weight and height and "improved on nearly all the problem behaviors" (p. 28) and in IQ score, academic performance, and school peer relationships (p. 29). Kent concludes that "intervention in the form of removal of the child from the abusive environment had beneficial results" (p. 28).

One of the consequences of the nationwide development of the elaborate infrastructure of child abuse reporting laws, investigation and intervention, has been a reduction in child fatalities resulting from abuse. In New York State there was a 50 per cent reduction in child fatalities, from about two hundred a year to less than one hundred. Ruth and Harry Kempe report that in "Denver the number of hospitalized abused children who die from injuries dropped from 20 a year between 1960 and 1975 to less that one a year" (Besharov, 1983 p. 289).

In summary, the evaluation studies suggest that agencies have achieved some modest measure of success. The amount of change one might reasonably expect the agencies to effect must be assessed against the great social and personal deprivation characteristic of the client families. Even the modest success achieved may have been more than could have been expected initially.

The resources available to treat these families are limited. The technology available to the worker in trying to effect change in such families is blunt and imprecise. The low level of confidence in the technology available to treat problems of child maltreatment is indicated by the fact that 39 per cent of some one thousand seven hundred human services personnel interviewed by Nagi (1977) agreed that "we just don't know enough to deal effectively with problems of child mistreatment" (p. 15).

Scarce resources backed by a weak technology applied to a group of involuntary, disturbed clients resistive to change and living in seriously deprived circumstances would seem to guarantee the likelihood of limited success.

No evaluation of protective service would be complete without some consideration of the contributions made by the very existence of the program. Protective services provide a structured institutionalized procedure for protecting children from actual and potentially damaging abuse and neglect. There is no other organized system in the community to which people can turn in meeting the needs of such children. The existence of the program is a visible statement by the community to parents and other caretakers of children that abuse and neglect of children is clearly unacceptable, socially disapproved behavior. It also communicates the willingness of the community to help such parents with their problems. It is an expression of community concern. Given the contributions made by this agency, the community would have to reinvent such a service if it were to be abolished.

Sexual Abuse

Concern with sexual abuse of children became a major social issue later than the public's awareness of the prevalence of physical abuse. The interest in and concern about the sexual abuse of children markedly intensified in the late 1970s early 1980s decade. Within the five-year period between 1978 and 1983, thirty-five books were published in the United States and in England on child sexual abuse. A flood of newspaper and magazine articles as well as movies and TV shows focused on the subject. By 1985, four national conferences on sexual victimization of children had been held in this country.

Increased attention devoted to sexual child abuse is a result of the general factors that contribute to increased attention to child abuse, but which are intensified by some additional, special considerations. Increased interest in sexual child abuse results from an increased concern with sexual assaults on women of any age. Many of the agencies currently providing service in the area of child sexual abuse began as rape counseling services or battered women's services. Child sexual abuse, rape, and women battering are seen as having a unitary cause by the feminist movement, which is actively involved in all three problems. These problems are perceived as evidence of a patriarchal society that socializes its males to a predatory perception of women as chattels to be exploited in the service of males. Sexual child abuse is regarded as a manifestation of the asymmetrical power relationship between men and women, resulting in male domination and female victimization.

Definition

Some child sexual abuse takes place outside the family circle and is perpetrated by strangers or casual acquaintances. This includes exhibitionism ("flashing"), touching, child pornography, and child prostitution. Of more direct relevance to protective social service agencies is child sexual abuse that takes place inside the child's family circle, in which parents, grandparents, cousins, or uncles are perpetrators.

Official definitions of child sexual abuse are broad and imprecise. The National Center for Child Abuse and Neglect defines sexual abuse as "contacts and interactions between a child and an adult in which the child is being used for the sexual stimulation of the perpetrator or another person." The child is defined as a person under eighteen and an adult is defined as someone five years older than the victim, "in a position of power or control over the victim." This definition focuses on misuse of the child in gratification of the perpetrator's needs and the asymmetrical power relationship between participants in the abuse. Other definitions define sexual abuse in terms of harm to the child.

Thus, Brant (1977) defines sexual child abuse "as exposure of the child to sexual stimulation inappropriate for the child's age, level of psychosexual development and role in the family" (p. 81). Mrazek (1981) define sexual abuse as "activities which are detrimental to the normal development of the sexuality of the child or which control or inhibit his/her sexual self determination" (p. 12).

Other definitions of child sexual abuse focus primarily on the child's dependent status. Sexual abuse is defined by Kempe and Kempe (1984) as "the involvement of dependent, developmentally immature children and adolescents in sexual activities they do not truly comprehend, to which they are unable to give informed consent or that violate the social taboos of the family roles" (p. 9).

Incest is a special kind of sexual maltreatment, defined in terms of the context in which it occurs. The precise traditional and legal definition of incest involves sexual intercourse between those members of a family who are so closely related that they cannot legally marry each other. Anthropologists writing about incest employ a restrictive definition. Thus Bixler (1981) uses the word to mean "heterosexual intercourse between postpubescent consanguineous nuclear family members" (p. 268). The protective service agency definition of incest has been considerably broadened to include a wider variety of activities other than intercourse and a wider group of perpetrators. Incestuous perpetrators include not only biological parents but also stepparents and live-in boy friends, as well as foster and adoptive parents. It includes not only biological siblings but also stepsiblings, uncles, grandparents, and cousins. The list of activities defined as incestuous include, in addition to intercourse, masturbation; oral-genital contact; sexual fondling or touching of breasts, vagina, thighs, or buttocks; exhibitionism and genital exposure, and finger penetration of anus or vagina.

Some agency manuals further include as incestous sexual abuse such activities as "use of pornography," "propositioning for sex acts," "verbal sexual stimulation," and "kissing in a lingering and intimate way" (Kroth, 1979, p. 32; Sgroi, Blick & Porter, 1982, pp. 10–12). One study of incest defines it even more broadly "as a continuum of sexual involvement beginning with intense, inappropriate sexual gazes or gestures and ending with vaginal or anal intercourse" (Lutz & Medway, 1984, p. 319).

The broader definition of incest includes any of these activities that take place between a child and an adult in the child's family system. Incest as currently defined is any intrafamily sexual abuse.

The outer edges of these activities present problems of confusion between normal, nurturant, desirable, affectionate interaction between parents and children and inappropriate exploitative sexual abuse. "The objective distinction between loving support and lustful intrusion—between loving sensuality and abusive sexuality—are disquietingly subtle" (Summit & Kryso, 1978, p. 237). If the traditional legal definition of incest is erroneously restrictive, the broader definition may be intimidatingly overextended.

Sexual Abuse: Scope

Statistics on the extent of sexual abuse are even more confounding and ambiguous than statistics on physical abuse. A variety of different procedures produce the statistics on sexual abuse. These include reports that employ either direct interviews or questionnaire responses from a general population, reports based on information provided by clients of psychiatrists or mental health facilities, and reports received by agencies mandated to receive such information such as social agencies and law enforcement agencies. Statistics both as to numbers and, even more significantly, the nature of the actions included in the definition of sexual abuse vary considerably as one examines each of the various sources of reports.

The percentage of women in the general population who report having been sexually abused as children varies widely. Kinsey (1953) reports 1 out of 4, Finklehor (1979) 1 out of 5, Kercher and McShane (1984) 1 out of 13, Russell (1983) 1 out of 2. A detailed review of 19 studies concerned with the prevalence of sexual abuse shows widespread disparity in results obtained—from a low of 6 per cent of all females to a high of 62 per cent of all females having suffered childhood sexual abuse (Peters, Wyatt, & Finkelhor 1986, Table 1.2, pp. 20–21). The percentage of abuse perpetrated by the father also varies widely from .5 to 1 per cent by Kinsey, to 1.3 per cent in Finklehor, to 4.5 per cent in Russell, to other studies providing other generally lower percentages of fathers' involvement (Goodwin, 1982; Kilpatrick & Amick, 1984; Sedney & Brooks, 1984; Baker & Duncan, 1985).

Wyatt and Peters (1986) have discussed the factors that contribute to the widely different estimates of the prevalence of child sexual abuse. Studies differ in definition of sexual abuse, in victims' age range (younger than 15 to younger than 22), in definitions of childhood, and in procedures for obtaining data (interview; questionnaire) and for recruiting subjects.

Survey data are based on retrospective recall by adult women of events experienced in childhood. They are subject to the usual memory deficits, distortions, and transpositions that are characteristic of retrospective data. Data from mental health clinic patient groups, police, and social agency reports are plagued by errors in extrapolation to the general population because of the selectivity and unrepresentativeness of the groups sampled. As a consequence, the researchers conclude that, "There is not yet any consensus among social scientists about the national scope of sexual abuse" (Peters, Wyatt, & Finkelhor, 1986, p. 16). Another research review of the "Scope of the Problem" concludes that "Methodological problems, coupled with widespread disagreement about definitions of sexual abuse, suggest that any conclusions about the incidence of sexual abuse or demographic factors involved, should be viewed very tentatively" (Waterman & Lusk 1986, p. 11).

Although the "true" prevalence of sexual child abuse is of concern because it enables us to assess the seriousness of the problem with which society has to deal, the statistic is of less importance to the practicing social worker. The population with which the social worker has to deal is not the total population of sexually abused children but rather only those children who come to the attention of the agency through formal reports and referrals. The statistic of primary concern is that of sexual abuse reported to social agencies collected by the facilities authorized to collate such reports nationally.

Survey data generally report the prevalence of sexual abuse—the number of people in the population who have ever been sexually abused over the course of their lifetimes. Report data are concerned with incidence—the number of children who have been sexually abused during the past report year. The agency is concerned with a different kind of incidence i.e. the number of reports that they have had to do something about during a given time period.

Official statistics are based on reports of sexual abuse that come to the attention of the variety of agencies and professionals who are concerned with the problem.

The National Incidence Study conducted in 1979–80, as noted previously, did systematically and comprehensively attempt to determine the incidence of various kinds of abuse. As noted by agencies and related professionals, sexual abuse represented 7 per cent of the total number of cases uncovered, resulting in an estimate of 44,700 cases of sexual abuse known to professionals during the study year. This is clearly lower than the national estimates of sexual child abuse if extrapolated from reports by Kinsey (1953), or Finklehor (1979), or Russell (1983).

The 1985 report of the national statistics on child maltreatment from the American Humane Association (1987) notes that 11.7 per cent of maltreatment reports were of sexual abuse—up from 6.9 per cent of reports in 1982. With 62 million children in the United States, the 113,000 reported as sexually abused represented "an estimated rate of 17.9 sexually abused children per 10,000 U.S. child population" (American Humane Association, 1987 p. 15).

In terms of reporting statistics, sexual abuse continued, in the early 1980s, to be the fastest growing subset of the various kinds of abuse and neglect reports.

The very largest percentage of such protective service sexual abuse reports are of intrafamily abuse. In 58.9 per cent of the cases the natural parent, almost always the father or stepfather, was the perpetrator. As compared with survey data, the official report data show fewer but more serious cases of sexual abuse.

As is true for other kinds of abuse, sexual abuse is underreported. Most retrospective studies show that a high percentage of the respondents did not share their abusive experiences with others. Even when sexual abuse comes to the attention of professionals mandated to report, many do not do so. In one study, only 42 per cent of physicians who treated a child victim of sexual abuse reported the incident, and only 32 per cent indicated that they urged the family to report the incident (James, Womack, & Strauss, 1978, p. 1146).

There is general consensus that the true rate of sexual abuse is probably three or four times higher than the detected rate, that intrafamily abuse constitutes only one segment of a problem which includes extrafamily sexual abuse as well, and that father–daughter incest is a subset of intrafamily sexual abuse of particular significance and concern to the protective social services system. As noted, the perpetrator is most frequently the biological father of the victim, but stepfathers are disproportionately represented in the group.

The perpetrator is generally a white male in his late thirties or early forties, generally older than male physical abusers. The family is generally an intact two-parent family. The marriage has been in existence for some time. The perpetrator group is better educated, more continuously employed, and at a higher income level than in cases of physical abuse. The daughter, victim in 85 percent of the cases, is generally of early pubertal age (10.5 years average). The abuse has been continuing for one half to three years and began when the girl was prepubescent.

Process

The details of the social work process sequence that follow are a composite portrait of the father–daughter sexual child abuse situation derived from a wide variety of reports from different sources by different researchers and practitioners. The sequence attempts to provide a normative statement of the more typical incest situation, recognizing that in every respect there are exceptions in individual instances.

Primary Prevention

At the broadest level, prevention of child sexual abuse, as suggested by feminists, requires a thorough reorientation of male and female relationships. Sexual abuse of females by males will be prevented where true equality between the sexes is achieved and asymmetrical power relationships in favor of the male are eliminated. Feminists see sexual child abuse as a power problem, a gratification of nonsexual needs rather than as a sexual problem. As Herman and Hirschman (1980) note, "The seduction of daughters is an abuse which is inherent in the father-dominated family system; we believe the greater the degree of male supremacy in any culture the greater the likelihood of father–daughter incest" (p. 104).

The child has more often been the target of primary preventive efforts relating to sexual abuse. There has been a proliferation of material designed to sensitize children to the awareness of possible sexual abuse, the right and the need to say "no" to potential sexual abuse approaches, and the desirability of telling someone about these encounters. Dramatic presentations, coloring books, films directed to school-age children, classroom curricula, and so on have been developed to teach children how to distinguish "good touch" from "bad touch" and to encourage an assertive "no" response (Swan, Press, & Briggs, 1985). The didactic instruction is supplemented by role play. Evaluation of such programs shows that children exposed to the programs have more self-protective knowledge than they had at the beginning of the programs or in comparison with a group of children not offered the programs (Wolfe, et al., 1986).

There is some concern about whether children can really distinguish between "good touch" and "bad touch," and whether, as a result, all touch becomes suspect and a cause for concern. Related to this is the concern as to whether such programs inferentially suggests that sexual feelings are reprehensible, to be resisted, and the implications this might have for future inhibitory attitudes toward sex. What does this mean for the majority of children who do engage in solitary genital play and/or play doctor with others (Finkelhor, 1986, pp. 241–242)?

Special sex abuse hot lines are available in some communities. When calling such a number, the child considering reporting sexual abuse hears the following. "Hello. This is a recorded message. If you think you are being sexually abused, please stay on the line—you may feel scared now, but help is available. You don't have to give your name." The caller may elect to remain anonymous, but the hot line provides the child an opportunity to discuss the question of disclosure with a knowledgeable person.

A demonstration "tele-tape" project conducted in Knoxville, Tennessee, focused on sexual abuse. Efforts were made to let the public know that it could call and obtain information on sexual abuse provided by a taped report. The hot line permitted the caller to obtain this information without identifying himself or herself without further involvement. If, however, the caller wanted to report sexual abuse or discuss the problem, a counselor was available. During the first 28 days of operation of the program (February-March, 1978) about 1,400 calls were received although some were duplicate calls, and others were curiosity calls. In 40 instances a further follow-through call was made, particularly by adolescents reporting sexual abuse. In three instances the caller identified himself as the sexual abuser.

Reporting-Referral

In contrast to physical abuse and neglect, friends and neighbors are a more infrequent source of reporting of child sexual abuse. The victim himself or herself is more often the source of the abuse report than in cases of physical abuse. The more frequent source of such referrals is professionals who have had contact with the client and to whom the child has disclosed information about sexual abuse. This includes doctors who have examined the child, school counselors, teachers, and social workers. Mothers and siblings who are aware of abuse are another source of reporting.

The prevalent notion that sexual activity between fathers and daughters is rare, even inconceivable; negative feelings or discomfort generated by such activity; the lack, in most instances, of any tangible evidence of the activity; and doubts about the child's credibility create barriers to reporting. There is no evidence currently available that would support the contention that only a small percentage of incest accusations are false and/or fantasized.

As is the case for other kinds of abuse and neglect, almost all states require reporting sexual abuse for protective service intervention. But unlike other kinds of abuse, sexual abuse more frequently requires explicit notification to the criminal justice system. Sexual abuse is clearly defined as a criminal act in most jurisdictions.

Report Intake

Investigating a report of child sexual abuse presents some special problems. Denial on the part of the parent-perpetrator is likely to be more vehement. Older more verbal children show a greater reluctance to discuss matters that are intimate and socially sensitive. Younger children lack the sexual vocabulary and the knowledge that enable them to describe what happened. The use of anatomically correct dolls with removable parts permits the child to manipulate the vagina, anus, and penis in reconstructing events. Role play and drawings have been productively employed. Even more than in the case of physical abuse, an interview in a neutral setting away from the home, and parents, is required in a case of sexual abuse. The interviewer has to feel comfortable with explicit sexual material, communicate willingness to believe the child, assure him or her of protection against the perpetrator and reduce any sense of guilt and self-blame.

Diagnosis-Assessment

Because of the voluminous material currently available regarding sexual abuse the focus of this presentation needs to be selective. As noted, children are victims of both intrafamily and extrafamily abuse. The latter, most frequently perpetrated by strangers or casual acquaintances, tends to be one-time incidents with which law enforcement personnel and the criminal justice system rather than social workers and the protective social services system have primary concern and responsibility. Intrafamily sexual abuse, perpetrated by persons who are related to the child, tends to be a more repetitive experience and is a primary concern and responsibility of social workers. Any intra-family sexual experience involving children, currently labeled incest, is then the focus of our discussion. But within the number of intrafamily sexual abuses we are being further selective. Mother–son sexual contact is relatively infrequent. Sibling incest, a frequent form of incest, seems to be of limited concern. Although not entirely benign, it is regarded as a less abhorrent, almost expected, aspect of childhood sexuality. This is also true of incest involving cousins in which the age difference between participants is limited.

Father–daughter sexual contact, however, constitutes a high percentage of reported cases of incest and is a matter of considerable concern. Consequently, the principal focus of the presentation relates to intrafamily sexual abuse involving fathers as perpetrators and daughters as victims. In this context, the term *father* is broadly defined and includes biological fathers, stepfathers, unmarried males living in a committed, consensual relationship, and adoptive and foster fathers. Father–daughter incest is the most frequent and most disturbing kind of sexual abuse in the protective service agency caseload.

Culture. The general mores clearly condemn sex between father and daughter. Father–daughter incest runs counter to two strongly communicated taboos, one against intergenerational sex—adult with child—the other against sex between members of certain role sets—parent-child role set, sibling role set, and so on. Set against such inhibitions inculcated by the culture are the disinhibinatory effects of predatory male attitudes toward females that are communicated by a patriarchical culture. This helps the father rationalize his incestuous behavior.

In a study of 930 adult women in San Francisco (Russell, 1984), one of every six women who had a stepfather reported being sexually abused by him. One out of every 40 women in the study was abused by her biological father. Weak as the incest taboo may appear to be, it may nevertheless explain at least partially why proportionately fewer biological fathers compared with stepfathers sexually misuse their daughters (Russell, 1984, p. 20). The incest taboo is weaker in the stepparent situation.

Having a stepfather is one of the strongest risk factors associated with the possibility of intrafamily sexual abuse. It "more than doubles a girl's vulnerability" (Finkelhor, 1984, p. 25). Unlike biological parents, stepparents meet the growing daughter without the opportunity of having developed nonsexual affectional ties over the years in an intimate caring context. This tends to blunt the potency of normally effective incest taboos. As Garbarino and Gillian (1980) note, the "stepfather–stepdaughter relationship seems particularly risky because it combines the authority and opportunities for exploitation that parenthood brings without the natural inhibitions of consanguinity." Sex with a stepdaughter who is a virtual stranger seems less reprehensible than with one's own biological daughter. The increase in the number of reconstituted families following divorce increases the number of families who are at higher risk for incest.

Intimacy of contact during the child's early development may explain the limited incidence of mother–child incest, since such contact is highly likely for most mother–child pairs. The heightened inhibition to incest developed as a consequence of such early intimate contact argues for encouraging greater responsibility for early child care on the part of the father as a procedure for reducing the incidence of incest. Limited involvement of males in early childrearing reduces the potency of the incest taboo for them. The supposition is that active nurturing of the infant female establishes a nonerotic relationship between father and child that makes it more difficult for the father to conceive of the child as a sexual object. Nurturing the dependent child acts to immunize the parent against incest.

In some instances, promiscuous, amoral family attitudes toward sexual activity weaken the strength with which the incest taboo is inculcated.

Some recent social changes increase the risk of father–daughter incest. The increase in the number of reconstituted families and the consequent increase in the number of stepfathers has been mentioned previously. The increase in the number of working mothers leaves the daughter more unprotected in the home, and provides increased privacy for sexual abuse. A home that provides a girl with her own separate bedroom also increases the possibility of private encounters.

Family. The research and clinical material point to the fact that father-daughter incest is a manifestation of a disturbed family equilibrium and occurs in response to an effort to establish an adaptation that is functional. The incestuous relationship is triangular involving father, daughter, and mother.

The family in which incest occurs is likely to be an enmeshed, socially isolated, one in which intergenerational and parent–child role boundaries are vaguely defined and permeable. Because the incest experience requires secrecy, the tendency to isolation is intensified. The family is characterized by father–daughter overinvolvement and mother–daughter underinvolvement, and the reallocation of sexual–affectional roles, with the greatest amount of interrelationship power in the family held by the father (Reposa & Zuelzer, 1983).

The largest percentage of incestuous families are both intact and are reported as having marital problems (Gruber & Jones, 1983). The contradiction may point to incest as an attempt at functional adaptation. A family experiencing marital conflict is maintained intact by the reallocation of sexual-affectional role in incest. The female child is sacrificed to on the altar of family stability.

If the incestuous configuration of changed marital sex roles and generational roles within the family can help preserve family stability, then participants may believe it serves a functional purpose. Participants share the feeling that incest is preferable to family breakdown. When disclosure heightens the risk of family disintegration, all participants have a vested interest in guarding against disclosure.

Incest may maintain family stability by discouraging independence and autonomy of the preadolescent or adolescent girl. The family circle remains tightly knit. Having reorganized the intrafamily relationship between mother–daughter, wife–husband, father–daughter, the family achieves some kind of stability that is maintained, on the average, for a two-and-a-half to three-year period during which the incestuous father–daughter relationship continues.

Father. What has been suggested in attempts to explain the father's behavior? Incest is set in motion in response to the father's sexual–affectional needs. Coming from a conflicted family background and a disturbed relationship with his own father, the father–perpetrator seeks to satisfy sexual–affectional needs in the traditional way by marrying and depending on his wife as a source of such supplies. Ineffectual in social relationships, somewhat shy and diffident outside the family center, the father is home-centered and family-focused. When the marriage starts to come apart or the wife is absent, ill, or emotionally withdrawn, the father's sexual–affectional needs are progressively less adequately met and/or less satisfying. Marital conflict is a pervasive characteristic of the incest family configuration. Unlike many men in similar situations, the father is unwilling or unable to go outside the family circle to find a female replacement or substitutes from his own age group. He may be threatened by the demands of a mature female and anxious about his acceptability. Surprisingly moral in orientation, prostitutes are an unacceptable outlet for him. The father therefore seeks a substitute within the family fortress. A developing oldest daughter is accessible, varied opportunities for contact are plentiful, and relative privacy is assured.

Incest provides a situation in which the father is in control. A child makes fewer demands that a mistress, is less capable of active resistance, has been socialized to compliance, and is already affectionately tied to the father. Incest is easier, more convenient, and less anxiety-provoking than infidelity. The father seeks to continue to meet sexual–affectual needs in a manner that is in line with his general seclusive, introverted enmeshment in the family. Although perhaps diffident and unassertive outside the family, these men are frequently described as domineering and autocratic inside the family circle. Within the socially isolated family, they tend to rule imperiously.

Some small percentage of incestuous fathers are pedophiles. They have a preference for children as sexual partners. The daughter is selected for sexual contact simply because she is a child. Here the key to understanding is a psychological fixation on an immature sexual object rather than a problem in family functioning.

A small subset of fathers engages in incest in response to a promiscuous amoral orientation to sex. Any female, young or old, related or unrelated, is perceived as an acceptable sexual partner. There is no strongly felt inhibition about incestuous sex.

The studies are almost unanimous in finding that only a very small percentage of incestuous fathers are psychotic or seriously emotionally disturbed. Such fathers are not atypically oversexed, although according to Gebhard et al. (1965), they do seem to manifest a higher than normal interest in mouth–genital contact (p. 214).

Alcoholism coexists with incest at higher rates than expected by chance alone. In many instances inebriation was associated with the initiation of the father's engagement to sexual advances to the daughter. Alcohol clearly contributed to the reduction of the father's inhibitions against such behavior.

Very few of these fathers have a record of criminal activity of any kind. Aside from the incestuous activity this is, in general, a law-abiding, socially stable, normal group of citizens.

Using an inventory of stressful life events, Justice and Justice (1976) found that incestuous fathers had experienced significantly more stress preceding the onset of engagement in incest than had been experienced by a group of nonincestuous controls.

Daughter. What helps explain the daughter's behavior in the incest configuration? Whereas some small percentage of children are victims of incest at a very early age, most become involved in late latency—ages 9 to 11. Progressively, the earlier onset of puberty has sexualized many girls at nine and ten years of age. Children are in need of affection particularly from parents who are the most significant figures in their lives and on whom they are totally dependent. It is understandable, then, that a girl would be receptive to affectional attention from her father. At the beginning of the incestuous relationship, activities are only ambiguously eroticized. It might be expected that, uncertain as to what is intended and relatively ignorant about adult sex, the girl might be hesitant about objecting to her father's overtures.

In many cases, the pull toward the father as a source of affectional satisfaction is intensified because the daughter's relationship with her mother is problematic. If the mother–daughter relationship is not providing the necessary affectional support, it is natural that the girl would seek a stronger relationship with her father.

Abuse may begin with sexually stimulating comments, off-color jokes, light touching, exposure, or voyeurism. If the father's first tentative exploratory efforts are passively received or only mildly discouraged, there is a gradual escalation to more advanced forms of sexual activity—i.e., masturbation or fellatio, digital penetration, and as the daughter grows older and more capable of this, actual intercourse.

The parent exploits his position as an adult on whom his daughter is more or less totally dependent for affection and life supplies. Habits of obedience to parental authority, inculcated as a part of a child's socialization, are manipulated. With the younger child, some of the activities are presented as parts of a sanctioned and acceptable game. Older children may be given special preference, treats, and outings by the parent. They may be told that this is the nature of sex education, that it helps keep the family together. Enticement and deception are supplemented by threats of violence, rejection, and abandonment if the child shows a disinclination to continue with the incestuous activity or threatens to disclose what has been happening. Actual violence to the child is used in only a limited percentage of the cases (Finkelhor, 1984, p. 27). The perpetrator seeks to "normalize" the sexual encounter by defining it as a "game," as "sex education," or as a child's duty to a parent.

Gradual, continuing involvement is in response to misrepresentation, threats, participants personality characteristics, and secondary gains. The father's rationalizations about sex education and keeping the family intact may be persuasive. Threats by the father of rejection, abandonment, or physical violence if his daughter refuses exert pressure on her to continue.

Passive acceptance by the daughter may reflect the effects of prior developmental history. The contention is that compliance with the father's requests or demands results from the parent's greater power vis-à-vis the child so that true resistance is not possible. Yet, any parent knows how capable and often successful children are in resisting, frustrating, and denying their parents' requests. Girls who do vigorously object to incestuous parental overtures and resist the parent's initial advances are not ultimately counted in the abuse statistics. The profile of the child who does become involved in incest suggests a child who is more compliant, more passive, and less confident in her capacity to reject the parent.

Whatever predispositions the daughter may have had toward passivity might have been reinforced in interaction with a parent who manifests behaviors associated with incestuous fathers. These fathers tend to be rigid, authoritative, and inflexible in their handling of childhood discipline, suppressing defiance and disobedience and approving compliance. Assertive disobedience would be difficult for children brought up in such a home.

Secondary gains experienced by the daugther reinforce any reluctance to discontinue the relationship. She receives the interest, attention, and affection of her father as a favored child in the family. She may receive special gifts and special privileges. She has a special status in being treated more like an adult-peer than as a child. And, there is the secondary gain in sexual pleasure. Even small children are not asexual as childhood erections and masturbation confirm. The girl approaching puberty or pubertal changes has a heightened sensitivity and responsiveness to any form of sexual excitation.

Noting that many cases of incest are unreported and that the "average duration of incestuous union in reported cases is 3 years," Yates (1982) goes on to say that "one would expect that there had been missed opportunities to blow the whistle and terminate the incest. Reluctance to report the incest is due in part to the child's shame, guilt, and fear of reprisal; however, it is also related to the gratification that the incest provides for the child" (p. 482)—erotic responsiveness being one such gratification.

As Finkelhor (1979) notes "contrary to the stereotype most victims in our study readily acknowledged the positive as well as the negative elements of their experience. They talked about the times the physical sensations felt good or they remembered how their sexual experience with an adult or family member satisfied a longing for affection and closeness that was rarely met at any other time" (p. 65). (See also Sgroi, 1979, p. 8.)

A further secondary gain for the girl is considerable enhancement of her power within the family circle. Threatening exposure either directly or indirectly can be used as a form of blackmail.

Once initiated, the involvement with the father creates its own dynamics that make the daughter hesitant to disclose what is happening. Feeling guilty toward the mother for her betrayal, ashamed of letting others know what has happened, fearful of the criminal consequences for the father if the authorities should find out, and anxious about possible family disruption, the daughter is constrained from disclosing her involvement with her father. Over the two—three year time period that incest interaction is generally pursued, the experience develops some inner dynamics. For the child, repetition decreases anxiety and guilt, and continued joint conspiratorial secrecy increases the disincentives to open disclosure. Positive satisfactions in secondary gains increases the incentives to continue the relationship. Initial passive compliance or tolerant resignation may change to more active participatory acceptance.

The homeostatic balance is precarious, however, it contains inherent elements that inevitably lead to destabilization and termination.

Some terminations are accidental and result from extrafamilial intrusions. In a limited number of cases, a physical examination uncovers the fact that the girl is pregnant, has a venereal disease, or has been physically damaged vaginally or anally, as a result of sexual activity (Rimsza & Niggerman, 1982). A report to authorities comes from a physician, hospital facility, or teacher and incest is disclosed.

On occasion, a mother or a sibling accidentally witnesses father–daughter sexual activities that are so blatant that they cannot be ignored or explained away.

The more potent destabilizing element, however, is the altering relationship that develops with the passage of time and the daughter's growing into maturity. The balance between resistance and acquiescence to a continuation of the incestuous relationship gradually, and in most instances inevitably, shifts in the direction of greater effective resistance on the part of the daughter. Moving into adolescence, the developing woman becomes progressively more interested in establishing a relationship with males of her own age outside the family. In response to such desertion the father acts to attempt to restrict and control any movement by his daughter away from him, which results in growing acrimonious conflict between the pair. With growing maturity the daughter becomes less dependent on her father for support and consequently more capable of asserting and implementing her independence. Establishing a relationship with a boyfriend enables the daughter to meet affectional and, ultimately, sexual needs outside the family and away from the relationship with her father.

Revealing the incestuous relationship may be primarily in response to the desire on the part of the daughter for greater freedom and autonomy and only secondarily in response to a strong motivation to stop the experience. Furthermore, as the girl gets older she is likely to feel somewhat more guilty because she is of age when she is more capable of taking action to stop it or get help, and with advancing age she is more consciously aware of the fact that such activity is atypical and contrary to social norms.

In many instances, with growing effective resistance and opposition to its continuation on the part of the daughter, the incestuous relationship terminates. In effecting such a break, some daughters move out of the home to attend college, to an independent living arrangement, to live with relatives, or to an early marriage. Incest has been initiated, continued over a period of time, and terminated in a sequence that may never come to the attention of the community.

In a study of sixty paternal incest victims, recruited by the researcher over a three-year-period from the general community, DeYoung (1982) notes that the "affair literally runs its course and eventually terminates without any outside interference. In the clinical sample of 60 female victims, the incest eventually terminated of its accord for 47 (78%) of them" (p. 41).

In other cases, the daughter is unable, on her own, to effect the termination she now more actively desires. She may then overtly involve others in supporting and assisting her in opposing the father. The girl overtly and now more openly discloses to a friend, a teacher, or a counselor, or may directly call a protective service agency for help. This is purposeful, voluntary disclosure.

However, the cry for help may be more covert and indirect. The girl may run away or make an attempt at suicide or become openly promiscuous.

As a result of either the overt or covert appeal for help, the protective service agency becomes involved with the family, and incest is terminated.

Mother-Wife. Father–daughter incest takes place within the privacy of the family. Primary preventions require the daughter's protection against the father's advance by other members of the family. Primary prevention requires support by other family members of the daughter's opposition to participation in any sexually related activities with the father. The mother–wife is generally the member of the family who is expected to defend and support the daughter in this context.

It is not known how many incestuous situations are changed by mothers who are aware enough to recognize the situation and strong enough to confront their husbands, and resolve the incest by discussion, challenges, and warnings within the family. Such resolution never comes to the attention of the community.

Some mothers do stop an incestuous family relationship by disclosing and seeking outside help. The mother was the source of the report to authorities in 12 per cent of 660 cases of father–daughter incest analyzed by the staff of the Nationwide Study on Child Abuse and Neglect Reporting (Julian, Mohr, & Lapp, 1980, p. 21).

More often, however, when incest continues, the children have reported that attempts to inform the mother of this have been disappointing. Mothers have reacted to such attempts with disbelief and denial. In some cases the mothers actively punished the daughter for making such suggestions. What explains the mother's failure to protect her daughter? Such women as mothers and wives have their own needs that reduce their effectiveness as protectors and supporters.

Some percentage of mothers, in fact, do not know or suspect that incestuous activities are taking place. Some cannot conceive that it is possible for their husbands to engage in such behavior. Some mothers do not know because they are ill and/or hospitalized; some because, disappointed in their marriage, they are seeking satisfaction in an active social life outside of the home or through full-time employment. The incest between the husbands and daughters often takes place during their absence.

More often, perhaps, the mother does not want to know, cannot afford to know, and defends herself against knowing. The profile of the mother–wife in the incestuous family suggests a diffident, depressed, unassertive, subservient woman. Dependent on her husband for support and affection, at whatever levels of adequacy, she has a lot to risk if she openly challenges him by breaking open his relationship with her daughter. Although the marriage is generally conflicted, the mother, on balance, has more to lose for herself than she has to gain for herself by such disclosure. She may have previously experienced or been threatened by physical violence from her husband, making her hesitant to confront him.

Fearing the disruption of her own marriage, however unsatisfactory it may be, fearing the public humiliation that disclosure would involve, fearing retribution from her husband and the loss of support, and fearing the breakup of the family, the mother remains passively silent.

A 1980 Texas Department of Human Resources study (1981) study of some 1,400 cases of sexual abuse noted that "the non-perpetrator adults, whether employed or unemployed, often left the victim alone with the alleged perpetrator. The majority of nonperpetrator adults were aware of the abuse before the Department of Human Resources involvement and most who knew took no action to prevent further abuse" (p. 10). The nonperpetrator adult in 75 per cent of the cases was the biological mother.

In some limited number of instances, rather than being a passive unknowing member of the incestuous triangle, the mother may overtly or covertly set the daughter up as her substitute in the marital relationship. She may provide opportunities for the daughter to be alone with her husband. She may not openly object when the father engages in some mild sexual play with the daughter within the mother's sight or hearing.

Some of the mothers have gradually reorganized the pattern of mother–daughter interaction in a manner that is conducive to a father–daughter incestuous relationship. With the acquiescence of their husbands they have transferred the responsibility for household management and child care of young siblings onto the oldest daughter. The child has become the "little mother" in the family as a result of such role reversal. Manifesting pseudo-maturity, and enacting the day-to-day activities that are generally the responsibility of the mother–wife in the family makes it easier for the father to misperceive his daughter, not as a daughter, but as a wife substitute.

Several articles decry the accusations of guilt and blame directed at the mothers of sexual abuse victims. Both Wattenberg (1985) and McIntyre (1981) point to the effects of a patriarchal society and childhood socialization to traditional female roles in explaining the mother's behavior. The orientation expressed is that the mothers are being scapegoated when they are accused of collusion in incest. Taught to be passive and unassertive in her relationships with males, the mother has not been empowered by the culture to aggressively act in defense of her daughter.

Treatment

Some of the reactions and behavior manifested during the investigation of sexual abuse may be in response to the "crises of disclosure" rather than a consequence of sexual abuse. The traumas incurred during medical examination, multiple interviews, court testimony, foster care placement, and family breakup, all of which may follow a disclosure of incest, have been termed secondary victimizations.

The actions necessitated by disclosure create problems for all members of the family triangle. The child has to cooperate with the authorities in confirming the accusation. The mother has to decide on either supporting her daughter against her husband or supporting her husband against her daughter. Siblings are also forced into a similar kind of decision of disloyalty to one parent or the other. The father is often forced to leave the home in order to protect his daughter. Alternatively the daughter is placed in foster care. In any case, disclosure results in emotional and often physical disruption of the family.

The series of problems that follow from disclosure described in one research study described these consequences as "devastating" (Tyler & Brassord, 1984). The effects of secondary victimization may need to be a focus of treatment in addition to treatment of the sexual abuse situation per se.

A study of over one thousand social workers having direct experience in handling child sexual abuse cases in public agencies indicated that, although most of them engaged in initial intervention and diagnostic tasks, a smaller percentage actually engaged in treatment. Treatment was generally delegated to more specialized voluntary agencies in the community outside of public child protective services. Furthermore, social workers indicated a reluctance to assume responsibility for treatment tasks even if more training in treatment was provided by the agency (Johnson, 1981).

However, analysis of 205 cases of confirmed sexual abuse reported to protective services found that, whereas some perpetrators and their spouses are willing to participate in counseling, a great number drop out. "Only 40 percent of our sample began treatment with outside agencies and a large number did not continue. The bulk of the responsibility, thus for treatment falls to the protective service worker . . ." (Pierce & Pierce, 1985, p. 43).

As compared with physical abuse cases, sexual abuse cases are more likely to involve both civil and criminal court action and more likely to result in the use of foster care as a treatment procedure. Foster care is used more frequently for the older child who herself initiated the report of abuse.

In 1978, the National Center for Child Abuse and Neglect could identify a scant dozen programs nationwide that are designed to treat the problem of intrafamily sexual abuse. By 1981, the National Center could identify more than three hundred such programs.

The direction that a treatment program takes depends to some extent on the orientation of the treatment facility. A program that focuses on incest as a sexual assault, and see, the perpetrator as a criminal, leans toward a jail sentence for the perpetrator and the daughter as the primary focus of any treatment efforts. Those programs that perceive incest as a family affair see the family unit as the focus of treatment. Such programs work in tandem with the criminal justice system. The legal action does not result in a jail sentence but rather in diversion of the perpetrator to the treatment facility under court supervision. There is the threat of imprisonment for the perpetrator's failure to accept treatment. It is felt that this coercive element is required. (Wachtel & Lawton-Speert, 1983).

A survey of intrafamily sexual abuse treatment centers found that most centers employed a mix of individual therapy, group therapy, family therapy, couples group therapy, and marital therapy. The therapist was more frequently an MSW social worker (Forseth & Brown, 1981). Some treatment programs that are focused on the sexual problem per se provide a relearning, behavioral-conditioning experience. The therapy is designed to redirect the perpetrator's sexual interest to adult nonfamilial females.

The sexual abuse treatment program that has received the most national attention, is most frequently copied, and has produced the greatest amount of explication in the literature is the Santa Clara County Child Sexual Abuse Treatment Program, directed by H. Giarretto. The program operates in close association with the juvenile probation department and the district attorney's office of the county (Giarretto, 1982).

Upon disclosure, a dependency petition and a criminal complaint are filed. The program is convinced that tying the perpetrator to the legal action system increases the probability of his and the family's involvement in treatment. These treatment programs see court action not only as a procedure of ensuring involvement in treatment but also as a means to clearly target the father as explicitly responsible for what happened. Diversion from a jail sentence to the treatment program requires an open admission of guilt by the father.

The treatment program consists of the following sequential steps: (1) individual counseling of father, daughter and mother separately, (2) mother–daughter counseling, (3) marital counseling, (4) father–daughter counseling, (5) family counseling, and (6) group counseling. The treatment orientation is humanistic Rogerian. Through the use of the therapeutic relationship the clients develop a greater understanding of the reasons for their behavior, are helped to change, and are supported in making such changes.

Psychological help is supplemented by emergency financial aid, job and housing assistance, and other kinds of practical help. The professional staff is assisted by volunteers and self-help group organizations. The principal self-help groups are Parents United, which is made up of perpetrators and spouses, and Daughter and Sons United, which is made up of children. There is a special Mother-Daughter group. The objective of the program is to break up the previous incestuous homeostatic family equilibrium and reconstitute the family on the bases that would ensure protection of the child from further abuse. Since alcoholism is frequently a component in the incest configuration, treatment for alcoholism is an additional specific service need.

The average length of treatment of the family is about nine months. Treatment terminates when certain objectives have been achieved. For the father, this involves a clear acceptance of his guilt and a change in his behavior toward his daughter in the direction of a more normal parent–child relationship. For the daughter it means that she understands and believes that she was in no way responsible for what happened, that she forgives her parents, and that she is now more capable of saying "no." For the mother it means empowering her so that she is a more effective protective agent. For the family unit it means better, more open, communication and a reduction in tension among family members. The development of a stronger marital coalition insures that intergenerational boundaries are more clearly defined.

Intake to the treatment program is selective. Perpetrators who are diagnosed as pedophiles, those with criminal records, and drug abusers as well as perpetrators who are resistive to openly acknowledging their responsibility for incest are not accepted.

Sturkie (1983) provides a detailed statement of a structured group treatment program for latency-age, sexually abused children. Meetings are structured around eight themes that include, among others, concern with "body integrity and protection," "secrecy and sharing," "guilt and responsibility," "court attendance."

Evaluation of Sexual Abuse Treatment

The literature provides relatively few systematic evaluations of sexual abuse treatment programs.

The Santa Clara County Sexual Abuse Treatment Program with which Giarretto is identified was started in 1971. An evaluation of the program was conducted in 1978 by Kroth (1979). Three groups of matched clients completed self-report questionnaires—one group beginning therapy, a second group midway in therapy, and a third group near termination of therapy, fourteen months after intake. Research was based on the supposition that if therapy had an effect the terminating group would complete the questionnaires differently than would the beginning group. Fifty-nine per cent of the terminating group indicated that marital interaction had improved during the period in therapy and the likelihood was that some 75 per cent of the spouses would remain together or be reunited. Marital sexual life had improved.

The recidivism rate is cited as a key criterion for the success of the program. Based on a review of other studies, without therapy a recidivism rate of 2 per cent is to be expected for intrafamily sexual abusers. The recidivism rate in the CSATP program was computed at 0.6 per cent, lower than the low, expected rate (p. 125). However, the researchers note that it is difficult to draw a confident conclusion from such small percentages. They go on to say "that the single most important statistic that reflects the efficacy of treatment is not recidivism—but the rate at which victims, offenders and families come forward" (p. 125). Success is indicated by the fact that between 1974 and 1978 the program witnessed an average increase of 40 per cent in the number of referrals.

A systematic evaluation was made of the effects of a coordinated team treatment offered by Connecticut Sexual Trauma Treatment Program to 82 families—54 of which involved intrafamily sexual abuse. According to the therapist's judgment at termination, the child's sexual relationship was resolved or improved in 62 per cent of the cases and unchanged in 37 per cent; intrafamily interpersonal relationships were resolved or improved in 50 per cent of the cases, but adult sexual relationships were unchanged in 60 per cent of the cases.

Therapy was seen to have its greatest effect on the referring problem. The child was judged as being safe from further sexual abuse by the perpetrator or at least protected or in little jeopardy in 62 per cent of the cases. For the majority of families, positive movement was also noted in building social relationships (58%) and resolving interpersonal difficulties (53%).

Change was effected in fewer than half of the families in improving family interaction (49%), handling education-employment-financial trouble (41%), dealing with adult sexual dysfunction (35%), or overcoming alcohol and drug abuse (33%). Overall, the limits to positive change as reported by therapists are sobering (Bander, Fein, & Bishop, 1982, pp. 369–370). It was noted, however, that "maximizing child protection often was attained at the cost of the family's integrity. The perpetrator fathers were often separated from the child and the rest of the family at the conclusion of treatment" (p. 372).

Effects of Sexual Abuse

A question of considerable concern and debate relates to the effects on the daughter of involvement in an incestuous relationship with her father.

Unlike physical abuse and neglect, physical damage is present in only a limited number of these cases (pregnancy, venereal disease, and vaginal or anal tears). Reviewing the results of 7 different studies on medical findings in sexual abuse covering a total 1,200 cases, Schmitt (1983) noted that gonorrhea was diagnosed in about 4–5 per cent of the cases but that syphilis was rarely found (p. 25).

Most often the negative damaging effects are presumed to be psychological and social. The nature of the situation is inherently potentially damaging to the normal development of the child. The parent–child relationship that best meets the child's need is a nonerotic, affectional, protective relationship. There are clear generational boundary differences between the adult and child family members. These are clear boundary differences in expectations and obligation between the significant subsystem role sets in the family structure—the parent–child role set, husband–wife role set, and sibling–sibling role set.

Unlike the typical normative configuration, incest eroticizes the relationship between father and daughter, the mother fails to adequately protect the daughter, and there is blurring of both intergenerational role-set boundaries. The daughter is daughter–wife to her father–husband, and child and adult relate to each other as generational peers in the incest interaction. The difference between what the child experiences in this family and knowledge about how families operate is very likely to be confusing and unsettling to the growing child. As one thirteen-year-old girl said "How can I talk to my friends about their first kiss when I have already had sex with my dad? I am not like they are."

The focus on the sexual component in male–female relationship incest tends to eroticize all such relationships for the child at a too early stage in the child's development. The incestuous relationship interferes with the accomplishment of age-appropriate development. The concern is that the child may learn to seek attention through the exploitation of sex.

Ambivalence about sexual activities, in a nonsanctioned deviant context, presents problems for the development of healthy attitudes toward sex and sexuality. Feeling sexual excitement while feeling ashamed and guilty for such feelings can result in an attempt to deny and supress all such responses. There is a possibility of subsequent displacement of such conflicting feelings onto other, sanctioned contexts such as marital sex. There may be a tendency to negatively associate sex with coercion and aggression. If the child feels exploited and her trust in her father is betrayed, such feeling, through stimulus generalization, may be displaced onto men generally, generating a problem for the child subsequently in relating to men.

An incestuous relationship binds the adolescent more firmly to the family. As a consequence, individuation and independence from the family, necessary developmental tasks of adolescence, become more difficult to achieve.

The absence of protection by the mother that results in resentment and estrangement from the mother by her daughter robs the daughter of an effective female role model.

Aside from any possible physical or psychosocial damage resulting from incest, other, ethically oriented concerns have been voiced that justify community intervention. In discussing what is wrong with sex between adults and children, Finkelhor (1979) states that the most valid answer relates to consent. The child is not free to say "no," and the child is ignorant of the implication of adult sex. For this reason, sex between an adult and a child "cannot be sanctioned under moral standards that requires that consent be present." (p. 403).

Children are a captive population. Incest violates their rights to sexual self-determination, autonomy, and privacy. Clearly and unequivocally for this reason, parents have the responsibility for defining and maintaining appropriate limits of intimacy in the parent–child relationship.

These theoretical effects of incest are difficult to empirically substantiate. At the start, some distinction between immediate, short-term effects and long-term effects needs to be made. The research does establish that many women who as children experienced or witnessed exhibitionism or were intimately touched or propositioned by an adult, retrospectively remembered reacting negatively with surprise, fear, shock, and disgust. More persistent effects, guilt, anxiety, depression, negative self-image, psychosomatic eating and sleep disorders, delinquency—almost every type of problem—have been associated with sexual abuse in one study or another. Studies of prostitutes (Silbert & Pines, 1983) and drug addicts (Gibbons & Prince, 1983) have noted that a high percentage of these groups had been sexually abused as children. Self-destructive behavior has been related to the incest experience (Goodwin, 1982, p. 109; DeYoung, 1982). In working with female clients in therapy for a variety of emotional disorders, clinicians have uncovered childhood sexual abuse experiences as possible contributing factors to difficulties in later adjustment (Herman, 1981; Summit & Kryso, 1978).

Many of the many citations describing long-term negative effects such as prostitution and drug addiction are correlational in nature. Without knowing how the child functioned prior to incest and without knowing the effects of other pathogenic factors in the child's living situation attribution of effects is a hazardous exercise. Silbert and Pines (1983) noted this in concluding their study of 200 street prostitutes in San Fransisco, a high percentage of whom had experienced sexual abuse when they were children. "It is important to remember that because there was no control group in the study (that is, children who may have been abused but did not become prostitutes), the study could not show that sexual abuse *leads* (emphasis in original) to prostitution" (p. 288).

Furthermore, as Meiselman (1978) notes, "It is difficult to separate the effects of incest per se from the family pathology that surrounds it before and after the incest itself occurs. The kinds of disturbed family background that are conducive to the occurrence of overt incest are almost certain to produce developmental difficulties even if incest never occurs" (p. 195). A multivariate analysis conducted with a sizable sample of adults, sexually abused as children, indicates that "the previous mental health status of the victim is the single most important predictor of acute emotional trauma associated with sexual abuse" (Chandler, 1982, p. 55).

A very limited number of studies have attempted to determine long-term effects by use of a control or contrast group. Meiselman (1978) studied the long-range effects of incest and compared clinical data from twenty six father–daughter incest cases in sexually abused psychiatric clients with data from fifty randomly selected controls. The controls were also clinic patients who had no history of sexual abuse. The only statistically significant difference between the two groups of clients related to the frequency of sexual problems. This most frequently included orgasmic dysfunction (frigidity), and much less frequently, promiscuity. Although the difference was not statistically significant, the clients in the incest group seemed "slightly more disturbed" that the nonincest group (p. 201). The researcher concludes that in "my opinion there is no association between father–daughter incest and the development of any kind of personality disorder or serious psychopathology in the daughter as an adult" (p. 203). (See also Burton, 1968.)

Tsai et al. (1979) recruited three groups of women for a contrast study. The groups consisted of thirty clinical patients seeking therapy for problems associated with childhood molestation, thirty women molested as children who had never sought therapy, and a group of thirty women who had never been molested. Groups were matched on the basis of age, marital status, and enthnicity. The Minnesota Multiphasic Personality Inventory (MMPI) and a "sexual experience questionnaire" were used as assessment instruments. The study concluded that women who had been molested but who had never sought therapy "showed no ill effects of the molestation" indicating "that not all sexually molested children will necessarily experience adult maladjustment." Profiles of the molested women in the nonclinical group were "normal" according to well-accepted standards of interpretation (p. 414). Profiles of the thirty molested women who did seek therapy manifested difficulties, among others, in relation to men and to sex.

In addition to the clinical and experimental data a series of personal accounts by incest victims of the deleterious effects of such experiences is available (Armstrong, 1978; Brady, 1979; Allen, 1980; Bass & Thornton, 1983; Gallagher & Dodds, 1985).

On the other hand, it might be noted that there is a body of literature, from what has been termed the pro-incest lobby (Rush, 1980, pp. 186–189), offering testimonials as to the benign or even positive effects of the incest experience from adults who were parties to such a relationship in childhood (Constantine, 1981; Brunoid, 1980).

Mrazek (1981) reviewed twenty-five different studies regarding the long-range effects of sexual abuse. The greatest number of studies were derived from clinical data offered by adult clients who were childhood incest victims. The number of reports citing negative effects were somewhat greater than the number of reports citing no discernible effects (p. 243). However, no one effect was cited by more than any two studies. Thus, if there are long-range effects, it is not clear what they are. This ambiguity as to effects was noted by LaBarbara, Martin, and Dozier (1980). A questionnaire completed by sixty-four child psychiatrists who had some experience in treating incest victims found a consensus among the respondents that incest was pathogenic. However, there was considerable disagreement about the nature of the specific effects suffered.

Reviewing twenty-seven different studies of child sexual abuse, Brown and Finkelhor (1986) separated the studies into those concerned with initial immediate effects and long-range effects. Concluding their review of contradictory reports on initial effects, they note that "the empirical literature on the initial effects of child sexual abuse would have to be considered sketchy" (p. 69). Summarizing long-term effects on victims as adults, the reviewers note that "victims as a group demonstrate impairment when compared with their non-victimized counterparts but under one-fifth evidence serious psychopathology. These findings give reassurance to victims that extreme long-term effects are not inevitable. Nevertheless they also suggest that the risk of initial and long-term mental health impairment for victims of sexual child abuse should be taken very seriously" (p. 72).

Another extensive review of twenty-five studies of effects of sexual abuse, eighteen of which were published after 1985, concludes that a review of the literature "describing the effects of sexual abuse on children leads irrefutably to the ambiguous position that sexual abuse appears to affect some victims and not others" (Conte 1985, p. 117). (See also Lusk & Waterman, 1986.)

Effects of sexual abuse are related to age of onset, use of force, repetition of abuse, nature of the relationship with perpetrator, type of sexual behavior, and age differences between victim and perpetrator. Children who experience repetitive abuse accompanied by threat of or actual use of force, initiated when they are of a younger age, at the hands of a very close relative considerably older than themselves, and where the nature of abuse is oral, genital, or masturbatory activity are likely to be among the more seriously affected.

An additional confounding problem in studying the impact of incest is the fact that it is difficult to separate the effects of incest per se not only from other noxious aspects of the child's life, as noted previously but also from the negative experiences that are frequently encountered following disclosures and exposure. The taking of testimony for legal prosecution of the perpetrator, the anticipation of court experience, the breakup of the family, and negative reactions, including imputation of blame, by the child's mother and siblings all have effects—some of which are likely to be devastating.

Sexual Abuse and the Court

The disclosure of father–daughter incest sets in process a motion that has both criminal prosecution and civil treatment implications. Since incest is a crime, the criminal justice system has an obligation to prosecute the perpetrator. In addition to obtaining information from the child for social study–diagnostic-treatment purposes, information needs to be obtained for the purpose of instituting legal action. The fact that the protective service system and the criminal justice system are both involved incurs the danger of repetitive, redundant interviewing of the child about a matter that is generally difficult for the child to discuss. Legal action may require an unnerving examination for medical evidence, court appearance, and cross-examination.

In recognition of the dangers in such procedures for the child, changes are being made. Protective services and the legal-system have organized team approaches to coordinate their investigations. Specially trained interviewers are recruited, and special interview facilities are made available to reduce the negative impact of the interviews. Interviews are tape-recorded, and the child's testimony on the tape is accepted in court in substitution for a personal appearance of the child.

Videotaping the child's testimony permits a greater measure of privacy, obviates the need for repetitive restatement of the events, and "freezes" the testimony so that the child's recantation of the testimony under family pressure is less likely. Videotaping also permits taking a child's live testimony soon after the abuse is disclosed, when remembrance of details is sharper. In Israel the child's statements are taken by specially trained youth-examiner social workers who act as the child's surrogate in court appearances.

Restricting public access to courtrooms in which incest trials are held and use of one-way screens have also been used to shield the child from the upsetting experiences of testifying in front of a public audience, in open court.

Videotaping testimony supplements changing laws in some states that remove requirements that the testimony of sexually abused children be corroborated by some form of evidence (*New York Times,* April 19, 1984). Some states, such as Kansas and Washington, have statutes that permit admission of some kinds of hearsay evidence in cases of sexual abuse. Such changes have been, and are being, opposed by those who see this as subversion of the rights of the accused. Constitutional questions regarding the defendant's right to confront and cross-examine child witnesses have yet to be definitely decided. Restricting observation of the trial raises constitutional questions regarding access to trial proceedings by the public through the press.

Play talk on the telephone, hand puppet play, and doll play have helped children to testify at child abuse trials. In preparing the child for a court experience, the social worker and the lawyer can role-play-rehearse the child's presentation. A visit to the courtroom might be made to desensitize the child to the formal, oppressive courtroom setting.

Admissability of the child's testimony in court can be challenged in several ways. Can the child differentiate truth from falsehood, facts from fantasy? Can the child understand the meaning of sexual terms and behavior, and be able to withstand suggestions from parents, attorneys, and social workers?

Reviewing the relevant psychological literature regarding the child's susceptibility to influence and ability to differentiate fact from fantasy, Melton (1985) concludes that there is little empirical evidence to question the children's ability to testify without qualification.

Faller (1984) argues that the child is telling the truth in all likelihood because there are few rewards for lying about this and many negative consequences for telling the truth. Children do not make up the stories of abuse because it is not in their interest to do so. Faller also notes that the detail in the child's description of events in doll play, story-telling, and drawing confirms the truthfulness of the reports.

Since professionals are mandated to report sexual abuse and therefore, to violate confidentiality of the relationship with a client who reveals such abuse, the question arises as to whether professionals should give a Miranda Type warning to parents before they disclose information about incest. This is particularly true in the realm of sexual abuse in which parents face the double jeopardy of legal action through protection statutes and criminal persecution through the legal system.

The problem is highlighted in a situation that was reported in the *New York Times,* on January 8, 1984. The stepfather of a 12-year-old girl was charged with molesting her. The stepfather, his wife, and the girl "had voluntarily sought counseling and the alleged molestation was revealed to the counselor." The counselor, as mandated, reported this to the district attorney's office. The girl refused to testify against her stepfather, and as a consequence was remanded to a juvenile detention facility for being in contempt of court. After being held in confinement for eight days, the case was dismissed since the girl continued in her refusal to testify (*New York Times,* January 10, 1984).

Problems

1. The problem of establishing explicit standards in determining maltreatment has not yet been solved by protective agencies. Acceptable minimum levels of parental adequacy vary from community to community and among different groups within the same community. For the agency this means that "since criteria for evaluation of family adequacy have not yet been clearly defined, it is extremely difficult to formulate standards of minimum levels of adequacy in child care below which no child shall be allowed to continue" (Boehm, 1962, p. 12). Actually such standards tend to become established empirically in legal norms as the courts are forced to make definite decisions in particular situations.

State statutes, of course, include a legal definition of neglect, but this definition merely sets broad limits within which each community may define the specifics of neglect. As Meier (1964) notes, "The paradox of neglect laws is that they teem with adjectives and adverbs—*properly, improper, necessary, unfit, insufficient, inadequate*—thus requiring a judgment to be made by the court in each specific instance of alleged neglect to determine whether the child is indeed neglected" (p. 158). The problem of ambiguous definition is frequently expressed as a conflict between the social worker and the community. Not atypical is the case of what appears to be physical neglect ("children are dirty, clothes all torn and ragged; they never have a bath") in a home in which the parent–child relationship is emotionally and socially wholesome; or the case of a loving mother who is somewhat casual in her sexual relations. Although the community may press for action in such cases, the social worker may believe that the situation does not require intervention.

The problem may be expressed as a conflict between the court and the social worker. Situations that appear to the social worker to be clear-cut cases of emotional neglect may be rejected by the court because no evidence of physical damage is available.

If it is difficult to establish a basis for justified intervention in cases of physical neglect and abuse, it is even more difficult in cases of emotional neglect and abuse. A broken arm is a broken arm, but a damaged psyche is more difficult to establish unequivocally. This elusiveness of definition is a problem for the protective service agency because it is not always clear how much, or in what situations, intervention will be supported by the community (Nettler, 1958; Boehm, 1964).

The problem of defining *abuse* and *neglect* is difficult because different norms have to be respected. Involved in every definition is some cultural standard, norm, or expectation of parental behavior, duties, obligations that are not met or that are implemented in a nonsanctioned manner. But *norms, duties,* and *obligations* may be defined differently by different groups in our society.

The need to define *child abuse* in terms of its cultural context is noted by Korbin (1977). Cutting a child's face and rubbing charcoal into the lacerations is regarded as child abuse in the United States, but not among the Yoruba of Africa, who practice scarification and among whom a child without such scars would be rejected by peers. This, for the Yoruba, is the equivalent of painful orthodontia, which we "inflict" upon a child in order to improve his or her appearance, a procedure we do not regard as child abuse. We do not define infant circumcision as child abuse. Initiating rituals such as clitoridectomy, however, would be considered abuse but not among the many African groups who practice this (Abdalla, 1982).

Korbin (1977) points to the fact that people in other cultures think that our custom of putting an infant in a separate bed and often in a separate room is child neglect. Indian children are frequently deliberately left in the care of older siblings; this practice does not constitute neglect. Chicano fathers may demand obedience and overt respect from their children, whereas in white middle-class families, there may be a greater emphasis on democracy.

Kagan (1977) recognizes this dilemma in his observation of

> an uneducated black mother who slaps her 4 year old child across the face when he does not come to the table on time. The intensity of the act tempts our observer to conclude that the mother resents her child. However, during a half-hour conversation, the mother indicates her warm feelings for the boy. She hit him because she does not want him to become a "bad boy" and she believes physical punishment is the most effective socialization procedure. Now her behavior seems to be issued in the service of affection rather than hostility [pp. 40–41].

This example suggests the different norms held by different groups regarding the use of physical punishment in childrearing (Blumenthal *et al.*, 1975, pp. 170–174).

More general norms may be involved as well:

> If parents feel that the natural oils of the baby should be preserved and therefore
> bathe their child only once a week, with the consequence that severe diaper rash
> develops—is that to be defined as neglect, or simply "different" parenting? If parents
> choose not to use their food stamps for vegetables, fruits, milk, etc., and instead feed
> their children nothing but "junk" food, or if they refuse to immunize their children—
> is that considered neglect, or the exercise of parental rights? If a mother insists on
> sending her 10-year-old daughter to school in antiquated lace and organdy instead of
> in a pair of blue jeans, and the daughter is consequently laughed at and isolated by
> the other children—is that emotional abuse, or parental rights? [Holmes, 1977,
> p. 116].

A survey of some five-hundred protective services social workers in Wisconsin
indicated that many of them had encountered problems in defining abuse or
neglect. About 50 per cent of the group noted that sometimes they weren't sure
whether the "bruising was severe enough to qualify as a reportable injury" or
"weren't able to tell if injury was accidental or not." In a more limited number of
instances there were questions about whether or not the incident was a reportable offense because of "differing cultural or religious values" (Benn, 1981, p. 57).

Although there may be consensual agreement on a minimally expected standard of child care, these standards may be applied differently to different groups
in the community. Katz (1968, 1971) points to a double standard: the parental
fitness of the poor is examined, and the parental fitness of the wealthy parent is
assumed. These situational and class differences are also suggested by Walters
(1975) in outlining three different "happenings":

> Mrs. A., a welfare client, enters a tavern at 11 p.m., leaving her three children
> asleep in the car. She is reported to the police, and Mrs. A. is charged with neglect.
> Mrs. A., a welfare client, enters a tavern at 11 p.m., leaving her three children
> asleep in the car. The temperature is -20°, and the police find the children nearly
> frozen. Mrs. A. is charged with abuse.
> Mrs. N., wife of an up-and-coming bank employee, leaves her son in the car in the
> parking lot of a suburban shopping center for "a few minutes." The car windows are
> rolled up, and the inside temperature reaches 120°. On her return, Mrs. N. finds the
> boy unconscious and rushes him to a hospital. The child quickly recovers. Mrs. N. is
> "in shock" and is comforted by her husband and sedated by her physician. No charges
> are filed [p. 25].

The problem of defining minimally acceptable standards of care is related to
the problem of defining the respective rights of parents and children. The balance
between the two differs from community to community, as Maas (1959) found, in
a study of child care in nine different communities throughout the country. Earlier in the nation's history, the law jealously guarded the rights of parents while
according little attention to the rights of children. This attitude is still a strong
influence in our current approach to the problems of abuse, neglect, and exploitation. The protective service agency has to move with considerable circumspection
and with clear evidence of harmful conduct, lest it be accused of unwarranted
meddling: "The rights of parents are protected by tradition and precedent"
(Downs, 1963, p. 133), a tradition and precedent older and more firmly established than any tradition or precedent in favor of the child.

How far may the state intrude into what is an essentially private relationship
between parents and child? However benevolent the intention, such intrusion,
unless clearly limited, may pose a danger to freedom.

The liberalization of abortion and birth control laws is based on the premise that these decisions are private family matters that should be free from community control. The development of a more active role for protective services is a move toward the broadening of community responsibility for intervention in private matters. Consequently, it is argued that clearly deleterious effects on the child of the parents' behavior rather than the parents' behavior itself should be the basis for protective service intervention.

It has been noted, however, that the reluctance to interfere with parental rights also leads to reluctance to report instances of neglect or abuse. Consequently, such cases come to the attention of the protective service agency only when the neglect and abuse have become extreme. The reluctance may ultimately have tragic consequences.

In 1953 a boy of thirteen was referred to a children's court because of chronic truancy. A psychiatric examination established the fact that the boy was "drawn to violence" and represented "a serious danger to himself and to others." Psychiatric treatment was recommended by the psychiatrist and the social workers concerned with the boy's situation. The mother refused to accept the recommendation and refused to bring the boy back for treatment. Should the mother have been forced to accept treatment for the boy? This is the question of limits of protective intervention. Nothing was done. Ten years later the boy, Lee Harvey Oswald, assassinated President Kennedy.

There may be a need for a two-tiered definition of maltreatment—a legal definition at a more restricted, more precise level and a social definition that is broader and more flexible. The justification is that each of the two definitions serves a different purpose and speaks to the responsibilities and functions of two different systems.

The legal definition authorizes community intervention, which may be coercive if necessary, to determine guilt or innocence and to make some determination of punishment. Because the intervention is involuntary, coercive, and has implication for possible punishment, the legal definition has to be worded to protect due process rights. A legal definition requires a clear dichotomous decision—yes it is maltreatment, no it is not maltreatment.

Social agency intervention has no immediate legal implications. It need not be coercive; it can be an intervention that is accepted voluntarily. The social definition suggests an offer of help. There is less danger of violation of civil rights in a social agency intervention than in a legally sanctioned intervention.

Consequently, the social definition can be more inclusive, more general, and more in the nature of a continuum. It permits a more ambiguous decision—"it is not exactly technical maltreatment, but there are many elements in the situation that may be harmful to the child." The nature of the difference between a legal definition of maltreatment and a social definition is manifested in the difference between what is required for a report of maltreatment that may trigger social agency intervention as contrasted with what is required for a petition to the court, which may trigger legal intervention.

The differences between a social definition and a legal definition revolve around the intent to control the behavior of parents as against the intent to help parents in their efforts to change their behavior.

There is a real value in the broader social definition of maltreatment for intervention. Actual maltreatment might not be substantiated, but serious parent–child difficulties are often uncovered. The agency's intervention gives the family access to needed and helpful services.

A two-tiered approach to child maltreatment that involves invocation of social work care in some cases and criminal law in others is further justified on the basis of some of the limiting aspects of criminal law procedures. Legal proceedings are characterized by an accusatory focus, the need for specific objective evidence, and a punitive, retributive objective. It provides a very limited range of interventions for rehabilitation assistance to the offender (Schrier, 1979; Valentine, 1984).

2. When first adopted, federal child maltreatment legislation encountered little opposition. As the kinds of reporting contingencies increased and the programs became more widespread, more opposition has been generated. Each mandated expansion of the explicitly identified concerns of protective service has increased the opposition to the extension of the different reasons for sanctioned intrusion into family life.

The Family Protection Act, which has been introduced in Congress but not as yet passed, reflects this point of view. The act restricts the federal government from interfering with state statutes pertaining to child abuse and explicitly excludes corporal punishment from any definition of child abuse. The Family Protection Act, introduced by conservative congressmen in 1981, revises the federal government's definition of child abuse to exclude "corporal punishment applied by a parent or individual explicitly authorized by a parent to perform such function." Also indicative of a nascent backlash is the birth, in 1984, of an organization called Victims of Child Abuse Laws (VOCAL). The founder of the organization said, "Anyone can misinterpret an action as sexual abuse if it's a carress, physical abuse if it's a spanking, emotional abuse if it's a lecture" (*Phoenix Gazette,* December 18, 1985).

3. Legislation mandating reporting by professionals of cases of child maltreatment and the development of central registries for such reports presents problems for the protective service field (Gibelman & Grant, 1978).

There is a growing disjunction between an increasingly successful reporting system that brings more and more families to the attention of the community and the resources available to help the families identified. The potential for effective service delivery decreases as the size of the clientele grows.

Florida's experience is often cited as a prime example of the potential for an increase in the caseload as a consequence of a well-organized reporting system. Seventeen child abuse cases were reported in Florida in 1970. Following the inauguration of a twenty-four-hour WATS hot line in all parts of the state, backed by a program of education, Florida reported 19,120 cases of child abuse in 1971. Without a commensurate increase in service personnel, however, many reported cases remained uninvestigated, and even fewer were provided treatment (Sussman & Cohen 1975).

There is some complaint that reporting laws are counterproductive. The knowledge that a doctor or a hospital is required to report abuse may make some abusive parents reluctant to bring a child for needed medical treatment. The considerable increase in maltreatment reports that follows the effective implementation of reporting laws imposes a very heavy investigatory burden on protective service agencies. Considerable staff time is involved in checking reports, many of which are not substantiated. This work reduces the staff time available for actually helping those families who need and can use help.

Maltreatment might be regarded as underreported, given the general agreement on the part of researchers that only a limited percentage of actual maltreatment comes to the attention of agencies. On the other hand, maltreatment may be regarded as overreported, given the high percentage of reports that are not substantiated. The problem is to get more complete reporting of those cases in which intervention is justified.

Because many reports are not substantiated (as already noted, nationally some 47 per cent are invalid), a sizable number of families are subjected to an agency intervention that ultimately proves to have been unwarranted. Although it might be better to make some mistakes than to leave any abused children unidentified, the investigation itself is not a benign experience for those families who are unjustifiably reported. A family that is even temporarily labeled as possibly child abusing has to live with the anxieties provoked by the investigation, anxieties that are not easily expunged from the mind. Furthermore, even if the family name is deleted from the central registry, whatever suspicions are aroused in the neighborhood, if a protective service investigation becomes known, may affect the family's relationship with its neighbors.

The fact that reporting and subsequent intervention sometimes do not lead to treatment, even where the report is valid, limits the justification of intervention. The fact that treatment, even when provided, is often not helpful further reduces the justification for intervention.

Professional selectivity in reporting presents a problem. The national data available indicate that school personnel and social workers are the source of a sizable percentage of maltreatment reports. Doctors provide fewer reports, perhaps because only a small percentage of maltreated children may require medical attention. On the other hand, doctors have limited motivation to report. Although the laws generally provide immunity from any prosecution resulting from reporting, many doctors may be reluctant to accuse their patients of abuse or may see reporting as an infringement on the confidentiality of the doctor–patient relationship. More significantly, given the time and effort involved in reporting and the attendant risks, many doctors are not convinced that reporting serves any valid purpose. There is a general complaint that if they do report, they rarely get feedback on what has been done and that very often nothing is done that significantly alters the situation.

Although reporting laws make professionals who are required to report subject to prosecution if they fail to report cases of maltreatment, such prosecutions have been rare. However, successful suits have been filed against physicians, social workers, and police officers who were aware of a case of child abuse and their obligation to report it but failed to do so (Kohlman, 1974; Besharov, 1985).

Most states have made provision for some kind of registry of child abuse and neglect reports. Such registries serve a variety of functions. They provide basic statistical information regarding child abuse and neglect. They provide reports on any given children, often through a source that is accessible twenty-four hours a day, seven days a week, so that doctors, social workers, or school administrators encountering any evidence of maltreatment can have information on previous incidents as a diagnostic aid.

However, the establishment of state registries has also presented a series of problems. The principal one is that a sizable percentage of the maltreatment reports are not subsequently substantiated. This means that the names of many people are initially included in the registry without justification. A procedure, then, needs to be established and, more importantly, consistently implemented for expunging those names from the record. Second, care must be taken to determine who should have access to such records, which contain sensitive, confidential information. Third, some think that knowing the past history of maltreatment may influence the clinician's diagnostic assessment of the situation he or she is currently facing.

4. There is a problem of overlapping concerns in situations calling for protective service not only within the family of social work agencies but also between social work and other professional groups. Law enforcement agencies—the police, the courts—are also involved in protective service situations. Neglect, abuse, and exploitation are not only social problems but legal problems. Many communities have not yet clearly outlined the respective areas of responsibility of the police and the social agencies in protective cases or defined the procedure for effective coordination of the activities of these different agencies in such cases.

The police are also involved in receiving and investigating complaints of neglect and in verifying and evaluating complaints. In some communities, the police become involved in neglect cases because no protective service social agency is available, or none is available around the clock, as are the police.

Attempts have been made to promote cooperation between the police and the existing protective social agencies: the respective appropriate roles and administrative liaison are defined; referral procedures are spelled out; a police officer may be assigned to a social agency; or a police officer and a social worker may jointly investigate a complaint. But because of the lack of clear-cut assignment of responsibility in many communities, there are no "clearly defined channels of communication that enable responsible citizens to know how and where to take action" if they become aware of a situation requiring action (Young, 1964, p. 137).

Maltreatment is often a medical problem as well as a legal and social problem. Consequently there may be possible points of confusion between the responsibilities of doctors and nurses and those of social workers.

Coordination and cooperation are required in situations in which there is possible conflict as to who does what for the client.

5. Although all child welfare agencies face the problem of personnel shortages and high turnover rates, the protective service agencies face particular problems in recruiting staff, especially professionally trained social workers. The problem results partly from the nature of the clientele served and the problem situations for which protective service agencies have responsibility. Because the clients do not initiate the request for service themselves, the social workers may, and do, encounter a great measure of critical hostility and resistance. These require a great deal of patience, strength, and persistence on the part of the social worker.

Also, many of the clients have been referred to the protective service agency before. As one protective service worker notes:

> Most cases which eventually land with the protective agency have been "around the horn" of community services. They display amazing consistency in their "inability to use help" but the protective agency must do something with them! Thus it finds itself with a large and concentrated load of seriously pathological case situations [Philbrick, 1960, p. 7].

Given the same expenditure of effort, the worker is more likely to be rewarded by gratifying client change in contact with the more voluntary client of the family service agency or the child guidance clinic. Noting the great turnover of workers who were assigned to neglectful families, Young (1964) reports that "a good number of the workers said that the apparent futility of their efforts was one of the chief causes of change for them" (p. 114).

In addition to the emotional discomfort involved in working with resistant, seemingly unappreciative clients, there is the physical discomfort and the occasional revulsion experienced by the worker encountering the stink and dirt and disorder characteristic of many neglect cases.

6. Another aspect of the problem lies in the fact that the social workers in a protective service agency face a conflict between their professional image and the demands of the job. In a study of 110 social workers, Billingsley (1964a) concluded that this discrepancy between the realities of practice and the preferences of workers "is significantly more prevalent among social workers in a child protective agency than among their counterparts in the family counseling agency" (p. 477). The worker's professional orientation emphasizes voluntarism and self-determination, but the job frequently requires him or her to seek legal sanctions and to take other action that is in opposition to the parents' wishes.

The job is characterized by a high level of role strain. One aspect of the job requires interventions that are contradicted by other job demands: "Thus, with a given client, the social worker in a child protective agency is required to be a kindly, understanding, nonjudgmental, and accepting therapist; and, at the same time, a firm, resolute, and determined representative of the formal authority of community norms" (Billingsley, 1964b, pp. 17–18). In dealing with this conflict, workers noted that they "often found the mental and emotional gymnastics necessary (in separating the therapeutic and investigatory responsibilities) a source of strain and guilt and at times our position was quite untenable" (Baher, *et al.,* 1976, p. 115). Goldstein et al. (1986) insistently raise the question of the difficulties involved in effectively discharging conflicting roles and responsibilities. Responsibility for treating the parent may contaminate judgments regarding the responsibility for ensuring the child's safety. Concern with conserving family integrity may conflict with a reasoned decision to provide protection for the child by placement.

The characteristics associated with the successful protective-service worker suggest the difficulty of the assignment. Such workers should have a "high tolerance for anger, a relative absence of fear in the face of rage, a willingness to act as a sponge for anger and an ability to use their authority while conveying sympathy and understanding" (Holmes, 1977, p. 160). They should be able to accept hostility from the client without a need to retaliate and to accept rejection without being immobilized. They need to accept client dependence without threatening client independence. They should be able to maintain their morale and convictions in the face of client complaints and ingratitude, frequent failures, and limited success. As a consequence of these difficult demands, "burn-out" is frequently encountered among protective service workers.

Additional anxiety is generated by threats of legal action. Legal actions of civil and criminal liability against social workers in protective service have been related to failure to adequately protect a child. Charges have been that the agencies failed to accept a reports investigation that should have been followed up, failed to make an adequate investigation, and failed to place children, who were subsequently fatally abused, in protective custody.

Civil and criminal liability claims have been initiated against protective service workers for violating parental rights. These claims involved situations in which social workers were alleged to be engaged in slanderous investigations, to be guilty of malicious prosecution of parents, to have violated the confidentiality of parents, or to have deprived parents of their rights by wrongfully removing the child from the home (Besharov, 1985).

The courts have generally sided with the social workers when it was clear that any aggressive and vigorous action they had taken was in "good faith" and in accordance with agency policy and standard practice. Nevertheless, the possibility of such actions has increased the sense of anxiety and harrassment felt by social workers. These, then, are some of the factors that affect recruitment and turnover in protective service agencies.

7. There is a problem in getting the general community to understand and accept the impossibility of avoiding failure in protective services. In some small percentage of cases, the social agency, the family doctor, and the courts will inevitably make a mistake and a child will be fatally injured. Since no system is 100 per cent effective or fail safe, the inevitability of failure in some percentage of cases needs to be frankly shared with the community.

A composite of such a situation is presented based on data from the small, but very highly visible cases given great notoriety by the press:

> A nine-month-old child is physically abused by his young father. The parents are teenagers and the child was conceived out-of-wedlock. Confirmation of the incident of abuse as well as evidence of earlier abuse leads to a recommendation by the social worker, supported by the district attorney, that the child be placed in foster care for protection. It is also recommended, in the interest of preserving the family that the parents attend Families Anonymous meetings and enroll in a Parents Education Program. The court accepts the recommendation.
>
> The social worker arranges for foster care and helps the parents implement the referral to Families Anonymous and a Parent Education Program. During their visits to the child in the foster home, the parents are observed by the social worker to be responding more warmly and acceptingly toward the child and are manifesting changes as a result of the programs in which they are involved. In the interest of providing the child with a continuing relationship and a permanent home, the social worker, after a reasonable period of time, recommends the child's return home—a decision in which both the district attorney and the courts concur. Upon return of the child the social worker keeps contact with the family on follow-up visits.
>
> During one night the child, suffering from temporary indigestion, is fretful and the parents are unable to stop the child from crying. The father had worked overtime that day and was very tired and needed to sleep. At 2 or 3 or 4 o'clock in the morning, the father, in a fit of anger, beats the child and the child dies.

Did the social worker return the child home too early? What signs of changed parental behavior would have been indications of absolute certainty that abuse would never happen again? Should the worker have kept the child in the foster home longer, risking continued discontinuity of the child's relationship with the parents? Were there sufficient grounds for a petition for termination of parental rights in the face of the fact that the parents had accepted treatment and there was a chance of preserving the natural home for the child? Could the social worker have forseen the concatenation of circumstances, which late one night, resulted in a flash of anger during which the father lashed out? As a social worker involved in one such incident said "if we had fifty cases like these and did what we did with this family in 49 cases, it would have worked out—in this case it didn't work out. And, in this case the circumstances were not significantly different than in the other 49."

A review of a series of exhaustive investigative reports conducted after the death of a child from abuse concluded that, "The general picture of practice emerging from the reports is not gross error or failures by individuals on single occasions but of a confluence of succession of errors, minor inefficiencies and misjudgments by a number of agencies together with the adverse effects of circumstantial factors beyond the control of those involved" (Department of Health and Social Security, England, 1983, p. 28).

8. There is a problem associated with the neglect of neglect as a principal source of child maltreatment. Concern with neglect has been deliberately muted. In analyzing the reemergance of child protection as a matter of public concern in 1960, Nelson (1984) notes, "Most professionals agreed that child neglect was more pervasive and harder to remedy than child abuse, yet neglect was downplayed in the agenda-setting process. By design, those who promoted governmental recognition and action for child abuse emphasized that aspect of the cases on which there was *most* concensus and the *strongest* emotions, namely abuse rather than neglect" (pp. 36–37). (Emphasis in original.)

Not only is neglect less dramatic than physical abuse and certainly less titillating than sexual abuse, but it is also more difficult to deal with. Neglect situations are likely to be long-term and chronic, diffuse, and unresponsive. The necessary investment of community finances and agency time and effort is likely to be considerably greater than in cases of physical or sexual abuse. Neglectful parents are more difficult and less rewarding to treat. Progress with such parents has been characterized as "creepy-crawly."

Wolock and Horowitz (1984) note that "child maltreatment as a social problem has come to be defined predominantly as child abuse with child neglect having received relatively little attention and having been dealt with generally as an appendage to child abuse" (p. 531). A computer search in September 1983 using the Social Science Citation Index Data Base revealed 662 citations with 'child abuse' in the title and only 23 articles containing "child neglect" (p. 532).

In contrast to the prolific outpouring of material and widespread concern about sexual abuse, child neglect has been widely overlooked. In the last 20 years, one can cite only two serious book-length studies of neglect, both by Polansky. The number of articles in the popular press and professional journals reflects a similar indifference.

Educational programs that are designed to increase public awareness about child maltreatment and programs raising professional consciousness about reporting responsibilities are almost exclusively focused on physical and sexual abuse. Neglect is rarely identified, described, or given visibility. In deciding how to allocate increasingly scarce protective social resources, neglect is given increasingly lower priority and concern.

The consequence is that, although no one has suggested that the incidence of neglect has been reduced, the proportion of reports concerned with neglect have been gradually diminishing between 1976 and 1985. Fewer neglect reports are accepted for investigation.

Yet from the point of view of every important criteria, child neglect is a much more significant problem than sexual abuse and somewhat more so than physical abuse. Considerably more children are reported for neglect than for either physical or sexual abuse. Child neglect was cited as the "most important reason" explaining the foster care placement of 268,000 of the total of 395,000 children in foster care tabulated by the Shyne, Schroeder (1978) national study. An additional 100,000 children were in care for reasons suggesting neglect—"Child abandonment" 51,000; "unwillingness to care for child" 51,000 (p. 82).

Children referred to foster care because of neglect are likely to stay in care longer than those referred because of abuse. From the point of view of the seriousness of the impact on children, it might be noted that more children die from neglect than from physical abuse or from sexual abuse, which reports zero fatalities.

A nationwide evaluation study of about one thousand clients referred for abuse and neglect found that child neglect results in "more severe damage to a larger percentage of its victims than either physical or sexual abuse. Fifty-five per cent of all cases which resulted in severe harm to children involved child neglect as the primary type of maltreatment" (Quoted in Jackson, 1984, p. 16). National reporting data on fatalities from maltreatment tabulated by the American Humane Association show that fatalities attributable to neglect comprise about half of all the fatalities from child maltreatment (Jackson, 1984, p. 17) (see also Anderson et al. 1983 and Jones, 1987).

Fatalities result not only from medical neglect but from inadequate or indifferent supervision. Children are fatally injured by falling out of windows, ingesting poisons, or being trapped in fires, with no adults available to help. Infants have been abandoned and died before they were found. Children have died from malnutrition as a result of indifference to their needs. Children die as a result of a failure to recognize that they are seriously ill or from indifference about providing medical care for them when illness is recognized.

According to New York City Health Department Statistics, between 25 to 30 children die each year and "scores more are injured" as a result of falling from windows, roofs, and fire-escapes in apartment houses (*New York Times,* May 27, 1979).

9. Funding is a problem in the area of neglect as elsewhere in the social services. Federal funds appropriated explicitly for the implementation of the Child Abuse Prevention and Treatment Act were cut from $22.9 million in fiscal year 1981 to $16.2 million in 1982. In 1983, the American Humane Association's Children's Division conducted a nationwide survey of changes in protective services as perceived by workers, supervisors, and administrators in these services. Over half of the respondents reported decreases in funding and services available to serve an increasing number of clients (American Humane Association, 1983).

Trends

We have already noted some of the recent trends in protective services: the "rediscovery" of child abuse, the greater involvement of the medical profession in this area of concern, federal support for research demonstration projects, the education of personnel, the passage of state reporting laws, the broadening of the focus of concern to include emotional maltreatment, the greater involvement of public agencies in protective services, a relative reduction in private agency effort, and the trend toward increasing the number of professions whose members are mandated to report. We noted the trend toward increased concerns with sexual abuse and a lowered priority to neglect. Some long-term trends and additional short-term trends might also be noted.

1. The most significant long-term trend in protective services has been the move from a punitive approach to a cooperative one. At one time, the tendency was to remove the child from the home; now much more emphasis is being placed on constructive efforts to rehabilitate the family. The maltreating parent is now less frequently viewed as a willful criminal who should be punished and from whom the child needs to be rescued; he or she is seen as a troubled person needing

help. The trend is to view maltreatment as a defect, not a vice. The focus of protective service is not protection of the child from the parent but protection of the child from maltreatment. As Moss (1963) notes, "Children are best protected by adequately functioning parents" (p. 386). Thus the approach now involves identifying and treating the factors that underlie parental maltreatment as against a previous focus on investigation, adjudication, and punishment.

2. There is increasing recognition that child neglect and abuse, despite their legal aspects, are the concern of social work. Legal sanctions can do little beyond restraining the parents from inflicting harm and damage on the child, and the major problem involves providing for the child's adequate continuing care and custody. As the best protection for a child is an adequately functioning family in which parental roles are effectively implemented, this is a problem for child welfare agencies, not for the police and the courts.

3. Because of the complexity of diagnosis and because of the variety of treatment programs and resources that might be needed in treatment, child protection teams have been developed as a service delivery innovation (Schmitt, 1978). This approach permits a more comprehensive and valid diagnostic assessment, with contributions from professionals having expertise in different areas. A team approach also permits a more effective coordination of the many agencies that may be involved in a program of treatment. The team serves a supportive function in that it permits sharing responsibility for difficult decisions, hence limiting the anxiety and guilt of any one member. A team also provides an opportunity for approbation from peers—a gratifying reward in an area of service where the rewards are few and limited.

The basic team includes a social worker, a physician, a psychiatrist or psychologist, and a team coordinator or case manager. Additional team members might include an attorney, a child development specialist, a law enforcement representative, and a public health nurse. Child abuse teams may operate under the auspices of a local child protective services unit or may be based in a hospital with a pediatric service.

Some states have specifically mandated the creation of multidisciplinary child-protection teams in their reporting legislation.

Teams have a variety of names with dramatic acronyms: SCAN (Suspected Child Abuse and Neglect Team); DART (Detection, Admission, Reporting, Treatment Team) (National Center on Child Abuse and Neglect, 1978a).

4. As a result of decreases in funding and in the face of increasing numbers of reports, protective service agencies during the 1980s began to assign priorities in the ages of children who will receive protection and the kinds of situations that will trigger protective services. In general, neglect situations were given lower priority than cases of abuse, sexual abuse was given higher priority than emotional abuse. Children over age thirteen, unless actually physically or sexually abused, were given lower priority because service screening at intake was tightened in response to the more restrictive definition of protective service responsibilities. In an effort to reduce the demands on the agencies, some states began to narrow the scope of their reporting laws (Selinski, 1983).

A 1986 National Survey of agencies by the Child Welfare League of America found that because of lack of resources, many state agencies cannot comply with laws requiring immediate or early investigation of reports. The federal government is one source of state and local funds for protective services. Diminishing federal support and the lack of availability of additional state and local funds to make up the slack, results in reduction of services (Greenan, 1986 p. 7).

5. A survey of pending legislation in forty-six states indicates that the largest number of bills relating to child maltreatment focused on courtroom reform—i.e., videotaping or closed-circuit television presentation of child's testimony, changes in acceptable evidence and appointment of children's attorneys (Greenan, 1986, p. 7).

6. There is a trend toward perceiving child abuse as part of the larger problem of family violence that includes wife battering. Increased employment of police officers, arrest and imprisonment to deal with wife batterers spills over to child abuse. There is greater pressure to take punitive legal action against repeated child abusers. The trend is reinforced by increased concern with sexual abuse that has generally involved criminal persecution of the offender. As a consequence, the trend is toward criminalization of child maltreatment.

The *New York Times* (May 8, 1985) reported that the U.S. Justice Department had endorsed an effort by the National District Attorney's Association to develop a national education and research center on child abuse. In announcing the endorsement the U.S. attorney general stated that "there is no group of people in the country who are in a better position to take action than prosecutors."

A nine-member National Task Force to study family violence appointed by President Reagan and the Attorney General in September 1983 included a disproportionate number of attorneys and police chiefs. Given the composition of the Task Force, there may be reason to be concerned about the future "criminalization" of the family violence problem.

Bibliography

Abdalla, Raqiya H. D. *Sisters in Affliction—Circumcision and Infibulation of Women in Africa*. London: Zed Press, 1982.

Adams—Tucker, Christine. "Proximate Effects of Sexual Abuse on Children, A Report of 28 Children." *American Journal of Psychiatry,* 139, 10 (October 1982), 1252–1256.

Adams, William, Neil Barone, and Patrick Tooman. "The Dilemma of Anonymous Reporting in Child Protective Services." *Child Welfare,* 61, 1 (January 1982). 3–14.

Allen, Anne, and Arthur Morton. *This Is Your Child*. London: Kegan Paul, Trench, Trubner & Co., 1961.

Allen, Charlotte V. *Daddy's Girl*. New York: Berkeley Books, 1980.

Allen, Letitia S. "Child Abuse: A Critical Revue of the Research and Theory," pp. 43–79, in *Violence and the Family*. Ed. J. P. Martin. New York: John Wiley & Sons, 1978.

Altemeier, William, et al. "Prediction of Child Abuse: A Prospective Study of Feasibility." *Child Abuse and Neglect,* 8(1984), 393–400.

American Academy of Pediatrics. *A Descriptive Study of Nine Health-Based Programs in Child Abuse and Neglect*. Evanston, Ill.: American Academy of Pediatrics, April 1974.

American Humane Association. *Report of National Agencies Workshop on Child Protective Services,* Part I. Denver, Colo.: American Humane Association, 1957.

American Humane Association. *Protecting the Battered Child*. Denver, Colo.: American Humane Association, 1963.

American Humane Association. *National Analysis of Official Child Neglect and Abuse Reporting*. Denver, Colo.: American Humane Association, 1978.

American Humane Association. *Highlights of Official Child Neglect and Abuse Reporting— 1982*. Denver, Colo.: American Humane Association, 1984.

American Humane Association, *Highlights of Official Neglect and Abuse Reporting 1983*. Denver, Colo.: American Humane Association, 1985.

American Humane Association. *Highlights of Official Child Neglect and Abuse Reporting 1984*. Denver, Colo.: American Humane Association, 1986.

American Humane Association. *Highlights of Official Child Neglect and Abuse Reporting 1985*. Denver, Colo.: American Humane Association, 1987.

American Humane Association. *Survey of the Status of Child Protective Services Findings and Implications—1983*. Denver, Colo.: American Humane Association, Children's Division, 1983.

American Medical Association. "The Battered Child Syndrome-Editorial." *Journal of the American Medical Association*, 181 (1962).

American Public Welfare Association. *Preventive and Protective Services to Children: A Responsibility of the Public Welfare Agency*. Chicago: American Public Welfare Association, 1958.

Anderson, Luleen S. "Notes on the Linkage Between the Sexually Abused Child and the Suicidal Adolescent," *Journal of Adolescence*, 4 (1981), 157–162.

Anderson, Rosabel et al. "Child Deaths Attributed to Abuse and Neglect: An Empirical Study." *Children and Youth Services Review*, 5 (1983), 75–89.

Anderson, Stephen C., and Michael Lauderdale. "Characteristics of Abusive Parents: A Look at Self-Esteem." *Child Abuse and Neglect*, 6 (1982), 285–293.

Antler, Stephen. "Child Abuse: An Emerging Social Priority." *Social Work*, 23, 1 (January 1978), 58–61.

Araji, Sharon, and D. Finkelhor. "Abusers: A Review of the Research" in *A Sourcebook on Child Sexual Abuse*. D. Finkelhor and Associates Ed. Sage Publications Beverly Hills, Cal., 1986.

Armstrong, L. *Kiss Daddy Goodnight*. New York: Hawthorne, 1978.

Arnold, Mildred. *Termination of Parental Rights*. Denver, Colo.: American Humane Association, 1962.

Arvanian, Ann L. "Treatment of Abusive Parents," pp. 93–101, in *Child Abuse—Intervention and Treatment*. Ed. Nancy B. Ebeling and Deborah A. Hill. Acton, Mass.: Publishing Sciences Group, 1975.

Ayoub, Catherine, N. Jasewitz, R. Gold, and J. Milner. "Assessment of a Program's Effectiveness in Selecting Individuals at Risk for Problems in Parenting." *Journal of Clinical Psychology*, 39, 3 (May 1983), 334–39.

Ayoub, C., and J. S. Milner. "Failure-to-Thrive: Parental Indicators, Types and Outcomes." *Child Abuse and Neglect* 9 (1985), 491–499.

Azar, Robinson, Hekimian, and C. T. Twentyman. "Unrealistic Expectations and Problem-Solving Ability in Maltreating and Comparison Mothers." *Journal of Consulting and Clinical Psychology*, 52, 4 (August 1984), 689–691.

Baher, Edwina et al. *At Risk: An Account of the Work of the Battered Child Research Department*. National Society for Prevention of Cruelty to Children. Boston: Routledge, Kegan Paul, 1976.

Baisden, Major, and Joanna Baisden. "A Profile of Women Who Seek Counseling for Sexual Dysfunction." *American Journal of Family Therapy*, 7,1(1979), 68–76.

Bakan, David. *Slaughter of the Innocents*. San Francisco: Jossey-Bass, 1971.

Baker, Anthony, and Sylvia P. Duncan. "Child Sexual Abuse: A Study of Prevalence in Great Britain." *Child Abuse and Neglect* 9 (1985), 457–467.

Bander, Karen, Edith Fein, and Gerrie Bishop. "Evaluation of Child Sexual Abuse Programs." In *Handbook of Clinical Intervention in Child Sexual Abuse*, Ed. Suzanne Sgroi. Lexington, Mass.: Lexington Books, 1982, pp. 345–375.

Bandler, Louise S. "Casework, a Process of Socialization: Gains, Limitations, and Conclusions," in *The Drifters, Children of Disorganized Lower-Class Families*. Ed. Eleanor Pavenstedt. Boston: Little, Brown and Company, 1967.

Barth, Richard, and Richard Sullivan. "Collecting Competent Evidence in Behalf of Children." *Social Work* (March–April 1985), 130–136.

Bass, E., and Louise Thornton. (ed.), *I Never Told Anyone*, New York: Harper & Row, 1982.

Baurley, Marion, and Matthew H. Street. *American Indian Law: Relationship to Child Abuse and Neglect*. Washington, D.C.: National Center on Child Abuse and Neglect, U.S. Children's Bureau (OHDS) 81–30302, 1981.

Bean, Shirley L. "The Use of Specialized Daycare in Preventing Child Abuse," pp. 137–142, in *Child Abuse: Treatment and Intervention.* Ed. Nancy B. Ebeling and Deborah A. Hill. Acton, Mass.: Publishing Sciences Group, Inc., 1975.

Beck, Bertram. "Protective Services Revitalized." *Child Welfare,* 34 (November–December 1955).

Becker, Thomas T. *Due Process and Child Protective Proceedings—State Intervention in Family Relations on Behalf of Neglected Children.* Denver, Colo.: American Humane Society, 1972.

Bedger, Jean, et al. *Child Abuse and Neglect—An Explanatory Study of Factors Related to the Mistreatment of Children.* Chicago: Council for Community Services, 1976.

Beezley, Patricia, Harold Martin, and Helen Alexander. "Comprehensive Family-Oriented Therapy," pp. 169–194, in *Child Abuse and Neglect—The Family and the Community.* Ed. Ray E. Helfer and C. Henry Kempe. Cambridge, Mass.: Ballinger Publishing Co., 1976.

Bell, Cynthia, and Wallace S. Mylnec. "Preparing for Neglect Proceedings: A Guide for the Social Worke." *Public Welfare,* 32 (Fall 1974), 26–37.

Bellucci, Matilda T. "Group Treatment of Mothers in Child Protection Cases." *Child Welfare, 41,* 2 (February 1972), 110–116.

Belsky, Jay. "Child Maltreatment—An Ecological Integration." *American Psychologist* 35, 4 (April 1980), 320–335.

Benjamin, Liselotte. *Protective Services: A Guide to Its Concepts and Principles.* Pennsylvania Department of Welfare, Bureau of Children's Services, May 1958. Mimeo.

Benn, Donald. *Evaluation of the Implementation of the Child Abuse and Neglect Act.* Madison, Wis.: Division of Policy and Budget, Wisconsin Department of Health and Social Services, 1981.

Berkeley Planning Associates. *Evaluation, National Demonstration Program in Child Abuse and Neglect.* Berkeley, Calif.: Berkeley Planning Associates, 1977.

Besharov, Douglas. "Protecting Abused and Neglected Children—Can Law Help Case Work?" *Child Abuse and Neglect,* 7 (1983), 421–443.

Besharov, Douglas. *The Vulnerable Social Worker.* Silver Springs, Md.: National Association of Social Workers, 1985.

Better Homes and Gardens. *What's Happening to the American Family—Attitudes and Opinions of 302, 602 Respondents.* New York: Meredith Corporation, April 1978.

Billingsley, Andrew. "The Role of the Social Worker in a Child Protective Agency." *Child Welfare 43* (November 1964a).

Billingsley, Andrew. *The Role of the Social Worker in a Child Protective Agency: A Comparative Analysis.* Boston: Massachusetts Society for the Prevention of Cruelty to Children, January 1964b.

Billingsley, Andrew, and Jeanne M. Giovannoni. "Child Neglect among the Poor: A Study of Parental Adequacy in Families of Three Ethnic Groups." *Child Welfare, 49,* 4 (April 1970), 196–203.

Billingsley, Andrew et al. *Studies in Child Protective Service: Final Report to the Children's Bureau,* September 1969. Mimeo.

Birch, Thomas, "The Children's Trust Fund." *Children Today* (July–August, 1983), 25.

Bishop, Julie Ann. An Intensive Casework Project in Child Protective Services. Denver, Colo.: American Humane Association, 1963.

Bishop, Julia Ann. "Helping Neglectful Parents." *Programs and Problems in Child Welfare. Annals of the American Academy of Political and Social Science,* 355 (September 1964).

Bixler, Ray H. "The Incest Controversy." *Psychological Reports,* 49 (1981), 267–283.

Blick, Linda C., and Frances S. Porter. "Group Therapy with Female Adolescent Incest Victims." *Handbook of Clinical Intervention—Child Sexual Abuse.* Ed. Suzann Sgroi, Lexington, Mass. Lexington Books, 1982., pp. 47–75.

Blumenthal, Monica D. et al. *More about Justifying Violence—Methodological Studies of*

Attitudes and Behavior. Ann Arbor: University of Michigan Institute for Social Research, 1975.

Blythe, Betty J. "A Critique of Outcome Evaluation in Child Abuse Treatment." *Child Welfare,* 62 (July–August 1983), 325–334.

Boardman, Helen. "A Project to Rescue Children from Inflicted Injuries." *Social Work,* 7 (January 1962).

Boehm, Bernice. "An Assessment of Family Adequacy in Protective Cases." *Child Welfare,* 41 (January 1962).

Boehm, Bernice. "The Community and the Social Agency Define Neglect." *Child Welfare,* 43 (November 1964).

Boehm, Bernice. "Protective Services for Neglected Children." *Social Work Practice.* New York: Columbia University Press, 1968.

Bolton, F. G. et al. "The 'Study' of Child Maltreatment: When Is Research—Research?" *Journal of Family Issues,* 2, 4 (December 1981), 531–539.

Bourke, William. "The Overview Study-Purpose, Method, and Basic Findings," in *An Intensive Casework Project in Child Protective Services.* Denver, Colo.: American Humane Association, 1963.

Bousha, D., and C. T. Twentyman. "Mother-child Interactional Style in Abuse, Neglect and Control Groups: Naturalistic Observations in the Home." *Journal of Abnormal Psychology,* 93, 1 (February 1984), 106–114.

Brady, Katherine. *Father's Day—A True Story of Incest.* New York: Dell Publishing, 1979.

Brant, S. T. "The Sexually Abused Child." *American Journal of Orthopsychiatry* (January 1977).

Brassard, Marla, Robert Germain and Stuart Hart (Editors). *Psychological Maltreatment of Children and Youth.* New York: Pergamon Press, 1987.

Bremner, Robert H. *Children and Youth in America—A Documentary History, Volume II, 1866–1932.* Cambridge, Mass.: Harvard University Press, 1971.

Bross, Donald. "Medical Care Neglect." *Child Abuse and Neglect* (1982), 375–381.

Brown, Angela, and David Finkelhor. "Impact of Child Sexual Abuse: A Review of the Research." *Psychological Bulletin,* 99, 1 (1986), 66–77.

Brown, H. Frederick. *Treatment Strategies in the Deployment of Emergency Caretakers in Child Abuse and Neglect Cases.* Chicago, Ill.: University of Illinois at Chicago Circle, April 1979.

Brunold, Heinz. "Observations after Sexual Trauma Suffered in Children," in *The Sexual Victimatology of Youth.* Ed. Leroy G. Schultz. Springfield, Ill.: Charles C. Thomas, 1980, pp. 860–866.

Bryant, Harold D. et al. "Physical Abuse of Children: An Agency Study." *Child Welfare,* 42 (March 1963).

Burch, G., and Morh, V. *Positive Parenting: A Solution to Potential Abusing Parents.* Omaha: University of Nebraska Press, 1980.

Burgess, Robert L. "Project Interact: A Study of Patterns of Interaction in Abusive, Neglectful and Control Families." *Child Abuse and Neglect,* 3 (1979), 781–791.

Burt, Marvin, and Ralph Balyeat. "A New System for Improving the Care of Neglected and Abused Children." *Child Welfare,* 53 (March 1974), 167–169.

Burt, Marvin, and Ralph Balyeat. *Comprehensive Emergency Services System for Neglected and Abused Children.* New York: Vantage Press, 1977.

Burton L. *Vulnerable Children: Three Studies of Children in Conflict.* London: Routledge & Kegan Paul, 1968.

Butz, Randall. "Reporting Child Abuse and Confidentiality in Counseling." *Social Casework,* 66 (February 1985), 83–90.

Canadian Welfare Council. *Child Protection in Canada.* Ottawa: Canadian Welfare Council, 1954.

Caulfield, Barbara. *The Legal Aspects of Protective Services for Abused and Neglected Children.* Washington, D.C.: U.S. Government Printing Office, 1978.

Cavara, Marilyn, and Carol Ogren. "Protocol to Investigate Child Abuse in Foster Care." *Child Abuse and Neglect,* 7, 3 (1983), 287–295.

Chandler, Susan M. "Knowns and Unknowns in Sexual Abuse of Children." *Journal of Social Work and Human Sexuality,* 1, 1–2 (Fall–Winter 1982), 51–68.

Children's Defense Fund. *Black and White Children in America: Key Facts.* Washington, D.C.: Children's Defense Fund, 1985.

Collins, Marilyn C. *Child Abuser—A Study of Child Abusers in Self-help Group Therapy.* Littleton, Mass.: PSG Publishing Co., 1978.

Columbia Journal of Law and Social Problems. "Representation in Child Neglect Cases: Are Parents Neglected?" *Columbia Journal of Law and Social Problems,* 4, 2 (July 1968), 230–254.

Conger, R., L. Burgess, and C. Barrett. "Child Abuse Related to Life Change and Perception of Illness." *The Family Coordinator* (January 1979), 73–77.

Constantine, L. L. *Children and Sex: New Funding, New Perspectives.* Boston: Little Brown, 1981.

Conte, Jon. R. "The Effects of Sexual Abuse on Children: A Critique and Suggestions for Future Research," *Victomology, 10, 1–4 (1985), 110–131.*

Craft, John L., Stephen Epley, and Cheryl Clarkson. "Factors Influencing Legal Disposition in Child Abuse Cases." *Journal of Social Service Research,* 4, 1(Fall 1980), 31–45.

Crittenden, Patricia "Abusing, Neglecting Problematic and Adequate Dyads: Differentiating by Patterns of Interaction." *Merrill-Palmer Quarterly* 27, 3 (1981), 201–218.

Crittenden, Patricia. "Maltreated Infants: Vulnerability and Resilience." *Journal of Child Psychology and Psychiatry,* 26 (1985), 85–96.

Daro, Deborah. *Half-full, Half-empty: The Evaluation Results of Nineteen Clinical Research and Demonstration Projects.* Mimeo. 19 pp. Berkeley, Calif.: Berkeley Planning Associates, 1985.

Davidson, Howard. "The Guardian Ad Litem—An Important Approach to the Protection of Children." *Children Today* (March–April 1981), 20–23.

Davoren, Elizabeth. "The Role of the Social Worker," in *The Battered Child.* Ed. Ray E. Helfer and C. Henry Kempe. Chicago: University of Chicago Press, 1968.

Davoren, Elizabeth. "Services to Multi-Problem Families," pp. 111–113, in *Child Abuse and Neglect—3rd National Conference, April 1977.* Washington, D.C.: U.S. Government Printing Office, 1978.

De Mause, Lloyd (ed.). *The History of Childhood.* New York: The Psychohistory Press, 1974.

Dean, Dorothy. "Emotional Abuse of Children." *Children Today* (July–August 1979).

DeFrancis, Vincent. *The Fundamentals of Child Protection.* Denver: American Humane Association, 1955.

DeFrancis, Vincent. *Special Skills in Child Protection Services.* Denver, Colo.: American Humane Association, 1958.

DeFrancis, Vincent. *Child Abuse: Preview of a Nationwide Survey.* Denver, Colo.: American Humane Association, 1963.

DeFrancis, Vincent. *Child Protection Services in the United States: A Nationwide Survey.* Denver, Colo.: American Humane Association, 1967.

Delsordo, James. "Protective Casework for Abused Children." *Children,* 10 (November–December 1963).

Department of Health and Social Security, England. *Child Abuse: A Study of Inquiry Reports, 1973–81.* London: Her Majesty's Stationery Office, 1983.

DeYoung, Mary. "Self-Injurious Behavior in Incest Victims: A Research Note." *Child Welfare,* 61, 8 (November–December 1982a), 577–584.

DeYoung, Mary. *The Sexual Victimization of Children,* London: McFarland and Co., 1982b.

DiLeonardi, Joan W. "Decision Making in Protective Services." *Child Welfare,* 59, 6 (June 1980), 356–364.

Dingwell, Robert. "Social and Legal Implication of Child Neglect: Some Preliminary Considerations." *Child Abuse and Neglect,* 3 (1979), 303–314.

Disbrow, M. A., H. Doerr, and C. Caulfield. "Measuring the Components of Parents' Potential for Child Abuse and Neglect." *Child Abuse and Neglect,* 1 (1977), 279–296.

Downs, William T. "The Meaning of Handling of Child Neglect: A Legal View." *Child Welfare,* 42 (March 1963).

Education Commission of the States. *Trends in Child Abuse and Neglect Reporting Statutes.* Denver, Colo.: Education Commission of the States, Child Abuse Project, January 1977.

Ellis, Robert H., and Joel Skillner. "Child Abuse and Locus of Control." *Psychological Reports,* 48 (1981), 507–510.

Elmer, Elizabeth. "A Follow-up Study of Traumatized Children." *Pediatrics,* 59, 2 (February 1977a), 273–314.

Elmer, Elizabeth. *Fragile Families, Troubled Children—The Aftermath of Infant Trauma.* Pittsburgh: The University of Pittsburgh Press, 1977b.

Erlanger, Howard S. "Social Class Differences in Parents' Use of Physical Punishment," pp. 150–158 in *Violence in the Family.* Ed. Suzanne K. Steimmetz and Murry A. Strauss. New York: Dodd, Mead 197.

Faller, Kathleen C. "Is the Child Victim of Sexual Abuse Telling the Truth?" *Child Abuse and Neglect,* 8 (1984).

Feldman, Ronald. "Damaged Parents and Child Neglect, An Essay Review." *Social Work Research and Abstracts,* 18, 1 (Spring 1982), 3–9.

Fergusson, David M., Joan Fleming, and David P. O'Neill. *Child Abuse in New Zealand.* Wellington, New Zealand: A. R. Shearer, 1972.

Finkelhor, David. "Psychological, Cultural and Family Factors in Incest and Family Sexual Abuses." *Journal of Marriage and Family Counseling* (October 1978), 41–49.

Finkelhor, David. "What's Wrong with Sex Between Adults and Children?" *American Journal of Orthopsychiatry,* 49, 2 (October 1979), 692–697.

Finkelhor, David. *Child Sexual Abuse: New Theory and Research.* New York: Free Press, 1984).

Finkelhor, David. "Prevention—A Review of Programs and Research." in *Source Book on Child Sexual Abuse.* Ed. David Finkelhor and Associates. Beverly Hills, Cal.: Sage Publications, 1986, pp. 199–223.

Fitch, Michael J. et al. *Prospective Study in Child Abuse: The Child Study Program.* Denver, Colo.: Developmental Evaluation Center, 1977.

Folks, Homer. *The Care of Destitute, Neglected, and Delinquent Children.* New York: The Macmillan Company, 1902.

Fontana, Vincent S., *The Maltreated Child,* 2d ed. Springfield, Ill.: Charles C Thomas, 1971.

Fontana, Vincent, and Esther Robeson. "A Multidisciplinary Approach to the Treatment of Child Abuse." *Pediatrics,* 57, 5 (May 1976), 760–764.

Foren, Robert, and Royston Bailey. *Authority in Social Casework.* New York: Pergamon Press, 1968.

Forseth, L. B. and A. Brown. "A Survey of Intrafamilial Sexual Abuse Treatment Centres: Implications for Intervention." *Child Abuse and Neglect,* 5 (1981).

Friedman, R. "Child Abuse: A Review of the Psychosocial Research," in *Four Perspectives on the Status of Child Abuse and Neglect Research.* Washington, D.C.: National Center on Child Abuse and Neglect, 1976.

Friedrich, William N. et al. "Cognitive and Behavioral Characteristics of Physically Abused Children." *Journal of Consulting and Clinical Psychology.* 51, 2 (1983).

Friedrich, William N., and Jerry A. Boriskin. "The Role of the Child in Abuse: A Review of the Literature." *American Journal of Orthopsychiatry,* 46, 4 (October 1976), 580–590.

Friedrich, William N., John D. Tyler and James A. Clark. "Personality and PsychoPhysiological Variables in Abusive, Neglectful and Low-Income Control Mothers." *Journal of Nervous and Mental Disease,* 173, 8 (August 1985), 449–460.

Fritz, Gregory, Kim Stoll, and Nathaniel Wagner. "A Comparison of Males and Females Who Were Sexually Molested as Children." *Journal of Sex and Marital Therapy,* 7, 1 (Spring 1981), 54–59.

Frodi, Ann M., and Michael E. Lamb. "Child Abuser's Responses to Infant Smiles and Cries." *Child Development,* 5, 1 (March 1980), 238–241.

Fromuth, Mary E. "The Relationships of Child Sexual Abuse with Later Psychological and Sexual Adjustments of College Women." *Child Abuse and Neglect,* 10 (1986), 5–15.

Frude, Neil. "The Sexual Nature of Sexual Abuse." *Child Abuse and Neglect,* 6 (1982), 211–223.

Gabinet, L. "Shared Parenting—A New Paradigm of Treatment for the Treatment of Child Abuse." *Child Abuse and Neglect,* 7, 4 (1984), 403–11.

Gagnon, John II, "Female Child Victims of Sex Offenses," *Social Problems,* 13 (1965), 176–192.

Gallagher, Vera, and William F. Dodds. *Speaking Out, Fighting Back: Personal Experiences of Women Who Survived Childhood Sexual Abuse in the Home.* Seattle, Wash.: Madrona Publishing, 1985.

Gambrill, Eileen. "Behavioral Intevention with Child Abuse and Neglect," in *Progress in Behavior Modification, Vol. 15,* New York: Academic Press, 1983.

Garbarino, James. "Some Ecological Correlates of Child Abuse: The Impact of Socio-Economic Stress on Mothers." *Child Development,* 47 (1976), 178–185.

Garbarino, James. "The Price of Privacy in the Social Dynamics of Child Abuse." *Child Welfare,* 56, 9 (November 1977), 565–575.

Garbarino, J., and G. Gillian. *Understanding Abusive Families.* Lexington, Mass.: Lexington Books, 1980.

Garbarino, James and Anne C. Garbarino. *Emotional Maltreatment of Children.* Chicago: National Committee for the Prevention of Child Abuse, 1980.

Garbarino, James, Edna Guttman, and Janis W. Seeley. *The Psychologically Battered Child.* San Francisco: Jossey-Bass, 1986.

Gardner, Leslie. "The Gilday Center: A Method of Intervention for Child Abuse," pp. 143–150, in *Child Abuse Treatment and Intervention.* Ed. Nancy B. Ebeling and Deborah A. Hill. Acton, Mass.: Sciences Publishing Group, 1975.

Gaudin, James, and Leonard Pollane. "Social Networks, Stress and Child Abuse," *Children and Youth Services Review,* 5 (1983), 91–102.

Gebhard, P. H. et al. *Sex Offenders: An Analysis of Types.* New York: Harper & Row, 1965.

Geddis, D.C. et al. "Early Prediction in the Maternity Hospital—The Queen Mary Child Care Unit." *Child Abuse and Neglect,* 3 (1979), 757–766.

Gelles, Richard J. *The Violent Home.* Beverly Hills, Calif.: Sage Publications. 1972.

Gelles, Richard J. "Child Abuse as Psychopathology: A Sociological Critique and Reformulation." *American Journal of Orthopsychiatry,* 43 (July 1973), 611–621.

Gelles, Richard J. "Family Violence: What We Know and Can Do," pp. 1–8 in *Unhappy Families—Clinical and Research Perspectives in Family Violence,* E.H. Newberger and Richard Browne, ed. Littleton, Mass.: Pses Publishing Co., 1985.

George, C., and M. Main. "Social Interaction of Young Abused Children: Approach, Avoidance and Aggression." *Child Development,* 50 (1979), 306–318.

Gesmode, J. "Emotional Neglect in Connecticut." *Connecticut Law Review,* 5 (Summer 1972), 100–116.

Giarretto, Henry. "The Treatment of Father–Daughter Incest—A Psychosocial Approach." *Children Today,* 5 (July–August 1976), 2–5.

Giaretto, Henry. *Integrated Treatment of Child Sexual Abuse.* Palo Alto, Cal.: Science and Behavior Books, 1982.

Gibbons, T. C., and J. Prince. *Child Victims of Sexual Offenses.* London: Institute for the Study and Treatment of Delinquency, 1983.

Gibelman, Margaret, and Stuart Grant. "The Uses and Misuses of Central Registries in Child Protective Services." *Child Welfare,* 57, 7 (July–August 1978), 405–413.

Gil, David G. *Violence Against Children: Physical Child Abuse in the United States.* Cambridge, Mass.: Harvard University Press, 1970.

Gillespie, David F., James R. Seaberg, and Sharon Berlin. "Observed Causes of Child Abuse." *Victimology,* 2, 2 (Summer 1977), 342–349.

Giovannoni, Jeanne M. "Parental Mistreatment: Perpetrators and Victims." *Journal of Marriage and the Family, 33* (November 1971), 649–657.

Giovannoni, Jeanne M. "Prevention of Child Abuse and Neglect: Research and Policy Issues." *Social Work Research and Abstract,* (1982) 23–31.

Giovannoni, Jeanne M., and Rosina M. Becerra. *Defining Child Abuse.* New York: The Free Press, 1979.

Gladston, Richard. "Preventing the Abuse of Little Children—The Parents' Center Project for the Study and Prevention of Child Abuse." *American Journal of Orthopsychiatry,* 45 (1975), 372–380.

Goldstein, Arnold P., Harold Keller, and Diane Erne. *Changing the Abusive Parent.* Champaign, Ill.: Research Press, 1985.

Goldstein, Joseph, Anna Freud, and Albert J. Solnit. *Beyond the Best Interests of the Child.* New York: Free Press, 1973.

Goldstein, Joseph, Anna Freud, and Albert J. Solnit. *Before the Best Interest of the Child.* New York: Free Press, 1979.

Goldstein, Joseph, Anna Freud, Albert J. Solnit, and Sonya Goldstein. *In the Best Interest of the Child.* New York: Free Press, 1986.

Goodwin, Jean. *Sexual Abuse Incest Victims and Their Families.* Boston: Hohn Wright, 1982.

Gordon, Henrietta. "Protective Services for Children." *Child Welfare,* 25 (May 1946).

Gordon, Henrietta. "Emotional Neglect." *Child Welfare,* 38 (February 1959).

Gray, Ellen, and Joan DiLeonardi. *Evaluating Child Abuse Prevention Programs.* Chicago: National Committee for Prevention of Child Abuse, 1982.

Gray, J. D. et al. "Prediction and Prevention of Child Abuse and Neglect." *Child Abuse and Neglect,* 1, 1(1977), 45–58.

Gray, Jane D., Christy A. Cutler, Janet Dean, and C. Henry Kempe. "Perinatal Assessment of Mother-Baby Interaction," pp. 377–388, in *Child Abuse and Neglect: The Family and the Community.* Ed. R. E. Helfer and C. H. Kempe. Cambridge, Mass.: Ballinger Publishing Co., 1976.

Gray, Jane, Christy A. Cutler, Janet G. Dean, and C. Henry Kempe. "Prediction and Prevention of Child Abuse and Neglect," pp. 246–254 in *Proceedings of the 2nd National Conference on Child Abuse and Neglect,* Vol. 2. Washington, D.C.: U.S. Government Printing Office, 1978.

Green, A. H. et al. "Factors Associated with Successful Intervention with Child Abuse Families." *Child Abuse and Neglect,* 5 (1981), 45–52.

Green, Arthur. A Psychodynamic Approach to the Study and Treatment of Child Abusing Parents." *Journal of the American Academy of Child Psychiatry,* 15 (Summer 1976), 414–429.

Green, Arthur, Richard W. Gains, and Alice Sandgrand. "Child Abuse: Pathological Syndrome of Family Interaction." *American Journal of Psychiatry,* 131 (August 1974), 882–886.

Groenveld, Lyle P., and Jeanne M. Giovannoni. "Disposition of Child Abuse and Neglect Cases." *Social Work Research and Abstracts,* 13 (Summer 1977), 24–31.

Greenan, Linda. *Too Young to Run—The Status of Child Abuse in America.* New York: Child Welfare League of America, 1986.

Gruber, Kenneth, and Robert Jones. "Does Sexual Abuse Lead to Delinquent Behavior? A Critical Look at the Evidence.' *Victimology: An International Journal,* 6 (1981).

Gruber, Kenneth, and Robert Jones. "Identifying Determinants of Risk of Sexual Victimization of Youth: A Multivariant Approach." *Child Abuse and Neglect,* 7 (1983), 17–24.

Hancock, Clair. *Digest of a Study of Protective Services and the Problem of Neglect of Children in New Jersey.* Trenton, N.J.: State Board of Child Welfare, 1958.

Hancock, Clair. *Children and Neglect—Hazardous Home Conditions*. Washington, D.C.: U.S. Government Printing Office, 1963.

Helfer, Ray. *Diagnostic Process and Treatment Programs*. Washington, D.C.: U.S. Government Printing Office, 1975.

Helfer, Ray, Carol Schneider, and James Hoffmeister. *Report on Research Using the Michigan Screening Profile of Parenting*. East Lansing: Michigan State University, May 1978.

Henry, Charlotte. *Hard-to-Reach Clients*. Cleveland, Ohio, May 1958. Mimeo.

Henry, Jules. *Culture Against Man*. New York: Random House, 1963.

Herman, Judith L. *Father-Daughter Incest*. Cambridge, Mass.: Harvard University Press, 1981.

Herman, Judith, and Lisa Hirschman. "Father Daughter Incest," in *The Sexual Victimology of Youth*. Ed. Leroy G. Schultz. Springfield, Ill., Charles C Thomas, 1980, pp. 97–104.

Herrenkohl, Roy C., Ellen C. Herrenkohl, and Brenda Egolf. "Circumstances Surrounding the Occurrence of Child Maltreatment." *Journal of Consulting and Clinical Psychology*, 51, 3(1983), 424–431.

Herrenkohl, Ellen C. et al. "Parent Child Interactions in Abusive and Non-Abusive Families." *Journal of the American Academy of Child Psychiatry*, 23, 6(1984), 641–648.

Herskovitz, Lina S., Robert F. Kelly, and Sarah H. Ramsey. "Count, Kin and Children: Determinants of Count Ordered Kin Involvement in Child Protective Proceedings." *Children and Youth Services Review*, 8(1986), 107–132.

Holder, Wayne, and Cynthia Mohr (ed.). *Helping in Child Protective Services: A Casework Handbook*. Englewood, Colo.: American Humane Association, 1981.

Holliday, Kate. "Dial-a-Family." *This Week* (August 4, 1968).

Holmes, Monica. *Child Abuse and Neglect Programs: Practice and Theory*. Rockville, Md.: National Institute of Mental Health, 1977.

Holmes, Sally. "Parents Anonymous: A Treatment Method for Child Abuse." *Social Work*, 23, 2 (May 1978), 245–247.

Holter, Joan C., and Stanford B. Friedman. "Principles of Management in Child Abuse Cases." *American Journal of Orthopsychiatry*, 38, 1 (January 1968), 127–135.

Horowitz, Bernard, and Wendy Wintermute. "Use of an Emergency Fund in Protective Services Casework." *Child Welfare*, 57, 7 (July–August 1978), 432–437.

Housden, L. G. *The Prevention of Cruelty to Children*. London: Jonathan Cape, Ltd., 1955.

Hunt, David. *Parents and Children in History*. New York: Basic Books, 1970.

Hunter, R. S., and N. Kilstrom. "Breaking the Cycle in Abusive Families." *American Journal of Psychiatry*, 136 (1979), 1320–1322.

Hunter, Rosemary, Nancy Kilstrom, Ernest Kraybill, and Frank Loda. "Antecedents of Child Abuse and Neglect in Premature Infants: A Prospective Study in a Newborn Intensive Unit." *Pediatrics*, 61, 4 (April 1978), 629–635.

Hyman, Irwin A., Anthony Bongiovanni, Robert H. Friedman, and Eileen McDomill. "Paddling, Punishing and Force: Where Do We Go from Here." *Children Today* (September–October 1977), 19–23.

Isaacs, Christine D. "Treatment of Child Abuse: A Review of Behavioral Interventions." *Journal of Applied Behavioral Analysis*, 15, 2 (Summer 1982), 273–94.

Jackson, Aeolian. "Child Neglect: An Overview," in *Perspectives on Child Maltreatment in the Mid '80s*. Washington, D.C.: National Center on Child Abuse and Neglect, Children's Bureau, Dept. of HHS, 1984. pp. 15–17.

James, Jennifer, William Womack, and Fred Stauss. "Physician Reporting of Sexual Abuse of Children." *Journal of the American Medical Association*, 240, No. 11 (September 8, 1978), 1145–1146.

Jayaratne, Srinika. "Child Abusers as Parents and Children: A Review." *Social Work*, 22, 1 (January 1977), 5–9.

Johnson, Betty, and Harold Morse. "Injured Children and Their Parents." *Children*, 15, 4 (July–August 1968), 147–152.

Johnson, Clara. "Child Sexual Abuse: Can Handling Through Public Social Agencies in the Southeast of the USA." *Child Abuse and Neglect*, 5 (1981), 123–28.

Johnson, Clara. *Two Community Protective Service Systems: Nature and Effectiveness of Service Intervention*. Athens, Ga.: Regional Institute of Social Welfare Research, 1977.

Jones, Carolyn O. "The Fate of Abused Children," pp. 108–121, in *The Challenge of Child Abuse*. Ed. Alfred W. Franklin. New York: Grune & Stratton, 1978.

Jones, J. M., and R. H. McNeely. Mothers Who Neglect and Those Who Do Not: A Comparative Study." *Social Case Work*, 61 (November 1980), 559–566.

Jones, Mary A., Stephan Magura, and Ann W. Shyne. "Effective Practice with Families in Protective and Preventive Service: What Works?" *Child Welfare*, 60 (February 1981), 67–77.

Jones, Mary A. *Parental Lack of Supervision—Nature and Consequence of a Major Child Neglect Problem*. New York: Child Welfare League of America, 1987.

Julian, Valerie, Cynthia Mohr, and Jane Lapp. "Father Daughter Incest—A Descriptive Analysis," *Sexual Abuse of Children: Implication for Treatment*. Ed. Wayne M. Holder. Englewood, Colo.: American Humane Association, 1980, pp. 17–33.

Justice, Blair, and Rita Justice. *The Abusing Family*. New York: Human Services Press, 1976.

Justice, Blair and David F. Duncan. "Life Crises as a Precursor to Child Abuse." *Public Health Reports*, 91 (March–April 1976), 110–115.

Juvenile Protective Association. *The Bowen Center Project—A Report of a Demonstration in Child Protective Services, 1965–1971*. Chicago: Juvenile Protective Association, 1975.

Kadushin, Alfred, and Judith Martin. *Child Abuse—An Interactional Event*. New York: Columbia University Press, 1981.

Kagan, Jerome. "The Child in the Family." *Daedalus*, 106, 2 (Spring 1977), 33–56.

Kahn, Alfred. *Planning Community Services for Children in Trouble*. New York: Columbia University Press, 1963.

Kalisch, Beatrice J. *Child Abuse and Neglect—An Annotated Bibliography*. Westport, Conn.: Greenwood Press, 1978.

Katz, Sanford. "The Legal Basis for Child Protection," in *Proceedings of Institutes on Protective and Related Community Services*. Richmond, Va.: Richmond School of Social Work, 1968.

Katz, Sanford. *When Parents Fail—The Law's Response to Family Breakdown*. Boston: The Beacon Press, 1971.

Katz, Sanford, Ruth-Arlene W. Howe, and Melba McGrath. "Child Neglect Laws in America." *Family Law Quarterly*, 9, 1 (Spring 1975), entire issue.

Kaufman, Irving. "The Contribution of Protective Services." *Child Welfare*, 36 (February 1957).

Kaufman, Irving. "Psychodynamics of Protective Casework," in *Ego-Oriented Casework*. Ed. Howard Varad and Roger Muller. New York: Family Service Association of America, 1963.

Kavanagh, Charlene. "Emotional Abuse and Mental Injury: A Critique of the Concepts of a Recommendation for Practice." *Journal of the American Academy of Child Psychiatry*, 21, 2 (March 1982), 171–177.

Kelly, Jeffrey A. *Treating Child-Abusive families—Intervention Based on Skills Training Principles*. New York: Plenum Press, 1983.

Kelly, Joseph B. "What Protective Services Can Do." *Child Welfare*, 38 (April 1959).

Kelman, Herbert E. "Processes of Opinion Change." *Public Opinion Quarterly* (Spring 1961).

Kemmer, Elizabeth. *Violence in the Family—An Annotated Bibliography*. New York: Garland Publishing Co., 1984.

Kempe, Ruth S., and C. H. Kempe. *The Common Secret—The Sexual Abuse of Children and Adolescents*. New York, Witt-Freeman and Co., 1984.

Kempe, C. Henry, and Ray E. Helfer (eds.). *Helping the Battered Child and His Family.* Philadelphia: J. B. Lippincott Co., 1972.

Kempe, C. Henry, and Ray E. Helfer (eds.). *The Battered Child.* Chicago: University of Chicago Press, 1968. 2nd ed., 1974.

Kempe, C. Henry et al. "The Battered Child Syndrome." *Journal of the American Medical Association,* 181 (1962).

Kent, J. T. "A Followup Study of Abused Children." *Journal of Pediatric Psychology,* 1 (Spring 1976), 25–31.

Kercher, Glen A., and Marilyn McShane. "The Prevalence of Child Sexual Abuse Victimization in an Adult Sample of Texas Residents," *Child Abuse and Neglect,* 8 (1984), 495–501.

Kilpatrick, D.G., and A.E. Amick. *Intrafamilial and Extrafamilial Sexual Assaults: Results of a Random Community Survey.* Paper presented at 2nd National Conference for Family Violence Researchers, Durham, NH, August 1984.

Kinard, E. M. "Experiencing Child Abuse: Effects on Emotional Adjustment," *American Journal of Orthopsychiatry,* 52,1 (January 1982), 82–91.

Kinsey, Alfred C., et al. *Sexual Behavior in the Human Female,* Philadelphia: W. B. Saunders, 1953.

Knight, Maureen, Mildred Disbrow, and Hans Doerr. "Prediction of Child Abuse and Neglect Measures to Identify Parents' Potential," pp. 259–269, in *Proceedings of 2nd National Conference on Child Abuse and Neglect,* Vol. 2. Washington, D.C.: U.S. Government Printing Office, 1978.

Kohlman, R. "Malpractice Liability for Failing to Report Child Abuse." *Western Journal of Medicine,* 21 (1974), 244–248.

Korbin, Jill. "Anthropological Contributions to the Study of Child Abuse." *International Child Welfare Review,* 35 (December 1977), 23–31.

Korsch, Barbara, Jewell Christian, Ethel K. Gozzi, and Paul V. Carlson. "Infant Care and Punishment: A Pilot Study." *American Journal of Public Health,* 55, 12 (December 1965), 1880–1888.

Kravitz, R. I., and J. M. Driscoll. "Expectation for Childhood Development among Child Abusing and Non-Abusing Parents." *American Journal of Orthopsychiatry,* 53,2 (1983), 336–344.

Kroth, Jerome. *Child Sexual Abuse—Analysis of a Family Therapy Approach.* Springfield, Ill.: Charles C Thomas, 1979.

LaBarbara, Joseph D., James E. Martin, and J. Emmitt Dozier. "Child Psychiatrists' View of Father Daughter Incest." *Child Abuse and Neglect,* 4 (1980), 147–51.

Lamb, Sharon. "Treating Sexually Abused Children: Issues of Blame and Responsibility." *American Journal of Orthopsychiatry,* 56, 2 (April 1986), 303–307.

Landis, Judson T. "Experiences of 500 Children with Adult Sexual Deviation." *Psychiatric Quarterly Supplement,* 30 (1956), 90–109.

Lane, Lionel. "Aggressive Approach in Preventive Work with Children's Problems." *Social Casework,* 33 (February 1952).

Lane, Sylvia, and Vicki Van Dyke. "Lay Therapy: Intimacy as a Form of Treatment for Abusive Parents," pp. 162–167, in *Proceedings of the Second National Conference on Child Abuse and Neglect,* Vol. 2. Washington, D.C.: U.S. Government Printing Office, 1978.

Lapp, Jane. "A Profile of Officially Reported Child Neglect," in *The Dilemma of Child Neglect: Identification and Treatment.* Ed. Cynthia H. Trainor. Denver, Colo.: American Humane Association, 1983, pp. 5–14.

Larrance, D., and C. T. Twentyman. "Maternal Attributions and Child Abuse." *Journal of Abnormal Psychology,* 92, 4 (November 1983), 449–459.

Letourneau, Charlene. "Empathy and Stress—How They Affect Parental Aggression." *Social Work,* 26 (September, 1981), 383–389.

Levin, Patricia G. "Teachers' Perceptions, Attitudes and Reporting of Child Abuse and Neglect." *Child Welfare,* 62, 1 (January–February 1983), 14–20.

Lobb, Michael L., and George M. Strain. "Temporal Patterns of Child Abuse and Neglect: Implications for Personnel Scheduling," *Child Welfare,* 63, 5 (September, October 1984), 453–464.

Lusk, Rob and Jill Waterman. "Effects of Sexual Abuse on Children," pp. 101–118 in *Sexual Abuse of Young Children.* Ed. Kee Mac Farlane et al. New York: Guilford Press, 1986.

Lutz, Susan E., and John P. Medway. "Contextual Family Therapy with the Victims of Incest." *Journal of Adolescence,* 7 (1984), 319–327.

Lutzker, J. R., and J. M. Rice. "Project 12 Ways: Measuring Outcome of a Large in-Home Service for the Treatment and Prevention of Child Abuse and Neglect." *Child Abuse and Neglect,* 8 (1984), 519–524.

Lynch, Margaret. "Risk Factors in the Child: A Study of Abused Children and Their Siblings," pp. 43–56, in *The Abused Child.* Ed. Harold Martin. Cambridge, Mass.: Ballinger Publishing Co., 1976.

Lynch, Margaret, and Christopher Ounsted. "Residential Therapy—A Place of Safety," pp. 195–207, in *Child Abuse and Neglect.* Ed. Ray E. Helfer and C. Henry Kempe. Cambridge, Mass.: Ballinger Publishing Co., 1976.

Lynch, Margaret, and Jacqueline Roberts. "Predicting Child Abuse: Signs of Bonding Failure in the Maternity Hospital." *British Medical Journal* (March 5, 1977), 624–626.

Lystad, Mary H. "Violence at Home: A Review of the Literature." *American Journal of Orthopsychiatry,* 45 (April 1975), 328–344.

Maas, Henry, and Richard Engler. *Children in Need of Parents.* New York: Columbia University Press, 1959.

McFarlane, Kee, and Leonard Lieber. "Parents Anonymous: The Growth of an Idea," in *Child Abuse and Neglect,* June 1978. Washington, D.C.: National Center on Child Abuse and Neglect, 1978.

Maden, Marc F., and David F. Wrench. "Significant Findings on Child Abuse Research." *Victimology,* 2, 2 (Summer 1977), 196–224.

Magura, Stephen. "Clients View Outcomes of Child Protective Services." *Social Casework,* 63 (November 1982), 522–531.

Maisch, Herbert. *Incest,* London: André Deutsch Limited, 1973.

Martin, Harold P. *The Abused Child—A Multidisciplinary Approach to Developmental Issues and Treatment.* Cambridge, Mass.: Ballinger Publishing Co., 1976.

Martin, Harold, Patricia Beezley, Esther F. Conway, et al. "The Development of Abused Children, Part I. A Review of the Literature; Part II, Physical, Neurological and Intellectual Outcomes." *Advances in Pediatrics,* 21 (1974), 25–73.

Martin, Judith. *Gender Related Behaviors of Children in Abusive Situations,* Saratoga, Cal.: Rand E. Publishers, 1983.

Martin, Judith. "Neglected Fathers: Limitations in Diagnostic and Treatment Resources for Violent Men." *Child Abuse and Neglect,* 8 (1984), 387–392.

Martin, M. and S. Walters. "Familial Correlates of Selected Types of Child Abuse and Neglect." *Journal of Marriage and the Family* (May 1982), 267–275.

Martin, Mary P. *1977 Analysis of Child Abuse and Neglect Research.* Washington, D.C.: U.S. Government Printing Office, January 1978.

Mash, Eric, Charlotte, Johnston, and Karen Kovitz. "A Comparison of the Mother–Child Interactions of Physically Abused and Non-Abused Children During Plan and Task Situations," *Journal of Clinical Child Psychology,* 12, 3(1983), 337–346.

Mason. Thomas. "Child Abuse and Neglect: Historical Overview, Legal Matrix, and Social Perspectives." *North Carolina Law Review,* 50 (1972), 293–349.

Mastria, Ernesto, Marie A. Mastria, and Jean C. Harkins. "Treatment of Child Abuse by Behavioral Intervention: A Case Report." *Child Welfare,* 58, (April 1979), 253–261.

Maurer, A. "Corporal Punishment." *American Psychologist,* 29, 8 (August 1974), 614–626.

Mayer, Adele. *Incest: A Treatment Manual for Therapy with Victims, Spouses and Offenders.* Holmes Beach, Fla.: Learning Publications, 1983.

McCord, Joan. "What Can We Learn from the Long-Term View," 5th National Conference, CAN, Milwaukee, Wisconsin, 1981.

McCrea, Roswell. *The Humane Movement.* New York: Columbia University Press, 1910.

McFerran, Jane. "Parents' Discussion Meetings: A Protective Service Agency's Experience." *Child Welfare,* 36, 7 (July 1957), 31–33.

McFerran, Jane. "Parents' Groups in Protective Services." *Children,* 5 (November–December 1958), 223–228.

McHenry, Thomas *et al.* "Unsuspected Trauma with Multiple Skeletal Injuries During Infancy and Childhood." *Pediatrics,* 31 (June 1963), 903–908.

McIntyre, K. "Role of Mothers in Father–Daughter Incest: A Feminist Analysis." *Social Work,* 267 (1981), 26–62 and 462–467.

McMurtry, Steven. "Secondary Prevention of Child Maltreatment: A Review." *Social Work,* 30 (January–February 1985), 42–48.

Meddin, Barbara J. "The Assessment of Risk in Child Abuse and Neglect Investigations." *Child Abuse and Neglect,* 9 (1985), 57–62.

Medley, H. Earl. *A New Approach in Public Welfare in Serving Families with Abused or Neglected Children.* Nashville, Tenn.: Department of Public Welfare, May 25, 1967.

Meier, Elizabeth G. *Former Foster Children as Adult Citizens.* Unpublished Ph.D. Thesis. Columbia University, New York, April 1962.

Meier, Elizabeth G. "Child Neglect," in *Social Work and Social Problems.* Ed. Nathan Cohen. New York: National Association of Social Workers, 1964.

Meiselman, Karin C. *Incest—A Psychological Study of Causes and Effects with Treatment Recommendations.* San Francisco: Jossey-Bass, 1978.

Melnick, Barry, and John R. Hurley. "Distinctive Personality Attributes of Child-Abusing Mothers." *Journal of Consulting and Clinical Psychology,* 33, 3 (March 1969), 746–749.

Melton, Gary B. "Sexually Abused Children and the Legal System: Some Policy Recommendations." *The American Journal of Family Therapy,* 13, 1 (1985), 61–67.

Merrill, Edgar J., et al. *Protecting the Battered Child.* Denver, Colo.: American Humane Association, 1962.

Miller, Katherine, Edith Fein, et al. "A Parent Aide Program: Record Keeping, Outcomes and Costs." *Child Welfare,* 64, 4 (July–August 1985) 407–419.

Milner, J. S. "Predictive Validity of the Child Abuse Potential Inventory." *Journal of Consulting Psychology,* 52.5 (October 1984), 879–884.

Milner, J. S., and Ayoub, B. C. "Evaluation of 'At-Risk' Parents Using the Child Abuse Potential Inventory." *Journal of Clinical Psychology,* 36, 4 (1980), 945–948.

Meier, E. G. "Child Neglect," in N. E. Cohen (ed.). *Social Work and Social Problems.* New York: National Association of Social Workers, 1964, pp. 153–199.

Mohamoud, Joyce. "Parents Anonymous in Minority Communities." *Protective Services Research Institute Report,* 2, 7 (August–September 1977), 5–6.

Moore, Carol W., et al., "A Three-Year Follow-Up Study of Abused and Neglected Children." *American Journal of Diseases of Children,* 120, 5 (November 1970), 439–446.

Moore, Judith B. "The Experience of Sponsoring a Parents Anonymous Group." *Social Casework,* 64 (December 1983), 585–592.

Morris, Marian, and Robert Gould. "Role Reversal: A Concept in Dealing with the Neglected-Battered Child Syndrome." in *The Neglected-Battered Child Syndrome.* New York: Child Welfare League of America, July 1963.

Moss, Sidney. "Authority—An Enabling Factor in Casework with Neglected Parents." *Child Welfare,* 42 (October 1963), 385–391.

Moynihan, D. P. *Family and Nation.* New York: Harcourt Brace Jovanovich, 1986.

Mrazek, P. B. "Definition and Recognition of Sexual Child Abuse: Historical and Cultural Perspectives," in *Sexually Abused Children and Their Families.* Ed. P. B. Mrazek and C. H., Kempe. New York: Pergamon Press, 1981, pp. 5–15.

Mrazek, P. B., and D. A. Mrazek. "The Effects of Child Sexual Abuse—Methodological Considerations," in *Sexually Abused Children and Their Families.* Ed. P. B. Mrazek and C. H. Kempe. New York: Pergamon Press, 1981, pp. 235–245.

Muehleman, Thomas, and Cheryl Kimmons. "Psychologists' View on Child Abuse, Reporting, Confidentiality, Life and the Law: An Exploratory Study."

Muenhow, Ann, and Edward Slater. "Help for Families Coping with Incest: Rebuilding Families after Sexual Abuse of Children." *Social Work Practice Digest,* 1, 2 (September 1978), 19–25.

Mulford, Robert, et al. *Caseworker and Judge in Neglect Cases.* New York: Child Welfare League of America, 1956.

Mulford, Robert. "Emotional Neglect of Children." *Child Welfare,* 37 (January 1958).

Nagi, Saad Z. "Child Abuse and Neglect Programs: A National Overview." *Children Today,* 4, 3 (May 1975), 13–18.

Nagi, S. *Child Maltreatment in the United States: A Challenge to Social Institutions.* New York: Columbia University Press, 1977.

National Center on Child Abuse and Neglect. *Multidisciplinary Teams in Child Abuse and Neglect Programs.* Washington, D.C.: U.S. Government Printing Office, 1978a.

National Center on Child Abuse and Neglect. *Child Abuse and Neglect in Residential Institutions.* Washington, D.C.: U.S. Government Printing Office, 1978b.

National Center on Child Abuse and Neglect. *Study Findings: National Study of the Incidence and Severity of Child Abuse and Neglect.* Washington, D.C.: U.S. Department of Health and Human Service DHHS Publication No. (OHDS) 81-30325, 1981a.

National Center on Child Abuse and Neglect. *American Indian Law: Relationship to Child Abuse and Neglect.* Washington, D.C.: U.S. Department of Health and Human Services Childrens' Bureau (OHDS) 81-30302, 1981b.

National Education Association. *Report of the Task Force on Corporal Punishment.* Washington, D.C.: National Education Association, 1972.

Nelson, Barbara S. *Making an Issue of Child Abuse.* Chicago: University of Chicago Press, 1984.

Nettler, Gwynne. *A Study of Opinions on Child Welfare in Harris County.* Houston, Tex.: Community Council of Houston and Harris County, October 1958.

Nurse, Shirley M. "Familial Patterns of Parents Who Abuse Their Children." *Smith College Studies in Social Work,* 35 (October 1964).

Oates, Kim. *Child Abuse and Neglect: What Happens Eventually.* New York: Brunner/Mazel, 1986.

Oates, R. K., A. A. Davis, and M. G. Ryan. "Predictive Factors in Child Abuse," in *International Perspectives on Family Violence.* Ed. R. Gelles and C. Cornell. Lexington, Mass.: Lexington Books, 1983, pp. 97–104.

Office of Comptroller General of the United States. *More Can Be Learned and Done About the Well-being of Children.* Washington, D.C.: Comptroller General's Office, April 1976.

Office of the Comptroller General of the United States. *Children in Foster Care Institutions—Steps Government Can Take to Improve Their Care.* Washington, D.C.: Comptroller General's Office, 1977.

Oldershaw, Lynn, Gary C. Walters, and Darlene K. Hall. "Control Strategies and Noncompliance in Abusive Mother-Child Dyads: An Observational Study." *Child Development,* 57 (1986), 722–732.

Oliver, Jack. "Some Studies of Families in Which Children Suffer Maltreatment," pp. 16–37, in The Challenge of Child Abuse. Ed. Alfred W. Franklin. New York: Grune and Stratton, 1977.

Overton, Alice, and Katherine Tinker. *Casework Notebook,* 2d ed. St. Paul, Minn.: Family-Centered Project, Greater St. Paul Community Chests and Councils, Inc., March 1959.

Pagelow, Mildred D. *Family Violence.* New York: Praeger, 1984.

Paget, Norman K. "Emergency Parents—A Protective Service to Children in Crises." *Child Welfare,* 46, 7 (July 1967).

Parke, Ross D., and Candace W. Collmer. "Child Abuse: An Interdisciplinary Analysis," pp. 509–90, in *Review of Child Development Research,* vol. V., Chicago: University of Chicago Press, 1975.

Patti, R. *An Analysis of Issues Related to Child Abuse and Neglect as Reflected in Congressional Hearings Prior to Enactment of the Child Abuse and Prevention Treatment Act of 1974.* Seattle: University of Washington, Center for Social Work Research, 1976.

Paulsen, Monrad. "Legal Protection Against Child Abuse." *Children,* 13 (1966), 42–48.

Paulson, Morris et al. "Parents of the Battered Child." *Life Threatening Behavior,* 4, 1 (Spring 1974), 18–32.

Pelton, Leroy. "Child Abuse and Neglect—The Myth of Classlessness." *American Journal of Orthopsychiatry,* 48, 4 (October 1978), 608–616.

Penner, Lewis G. *The Protective Services Center—An Integrated Program to Protect Children.* Denver, Colo.: American Humane Association, 1968.

Perlmutter, Leila, Tamara Engle, and Clifford Sager. "The Incest Taboo; Loosened Sexual Bounderies in Remarried Families." *Journal of Sex and Marital Therapy,* 8,2 (Summer 1982), 83–96.

Peters, Stephanie D, Gail E. Wyatt, and David Finkelhor. "Prevalence," in *A Source Book on Sexual Child Abuse,* ed. David Finkelhor. Beverly Hills, Cal.: Sage Publications, 1986, pp. 15–59.

Pfohl, Stephen. "The 'Discovery' of Child Abuse." *Social Problems,* 24, 3 (February 1977), 310–323.

Philbrick, Elizabeth. *Treating Parental Pathology—Through Child Protective Services.* Denver, Colo.: American Humane Association, 1960.

Physicians' Task Force. *Hunger in America—The Growing Epidemic.* Middletown, Conn.: Wesleyan University Press, 1985.

Pierce, Robert L., and Lois H. Pierce. "Analysis of Sexual Abuse Hotline Reports." *Child Abuse and Neglect,* 9 (1985), 37–45.

Pinchbeck, Ivy, and Margaret Hewitt. Children in English Society, vol. 1: *From Tudor Times to the Enlightenment Century.* London: Kegan Paul, Trench, Trubner & Co., 1969.

Plotkin, Ron C. et al. "A Critical Evaluation of the Research Methodology Employed in the Investigation of the Causative Factors of Child Abuse and Neglect." *Child Abuse and Neglect,* 5 (1981), 449–455.

Polakow, Robert L., and Dixie L. Peabody. "Behavioral Treatment of Child Abuse." *International Journal of Offender Therapy and Comparative Criminology,* 19, 1 (1975), 100–113.

Polansky, Norman, Mary A. Chalmers, Elizabeth Buttenweiser, and David Williams. "Assessing Adequacy of Child Caring in an Urban Scale." *Child Welfare,* 57, 7 (July–August 1978), 439–449.

Polansky, N. A., C. Hally, and N. F. Polansky. *Profile of Neglect—A Survey of the State of Knowledge of Child Neglect.* Washington, D. C.: U.S. Department of Education and Welfare, Community Services Administration, 1974.

Polansky, N., R. D. Borgman, and C. DeSaix. *Roots of Futility.* San Francisco: Jossey Bass, 1972.

Polansky, Norman, and James M. Gaudin. "Social Distancing of the Neglectful Family." *Social Service Review,* 5 (June 1983), 196–208.

Polansky, Norman, and David Williams. "Class Orientations to Child Neglect." *Social Work,* 23 (September 1978), 397–405.

Polansky, Norman, and Leonard Pollane. "Measuring Adequacy of Child Caring: Further Development." *Child Welfare,* 54 (May 1975), 354–359.

Polansky, Norman, Christian DeSaix, and Shlomo Sharlin. *Child Neglect: Understanding and Reaching the Parent.* New York: Child Welfare League of America, 1972.

Polansky, Norman, et al. "Two Modes of Maternal Immaturity and Their Consequences." *Child Welfare,* 49, 6 (June 1970), 312–323.

Polansky, Norman, et al. "Verbal Accessibility in the Treatment of Child Neglect." *Child Welfare,* 50, 6 (June 1971), 349–356.

Polansky, Norman, et al. "Public Opinion and Intervention in Child Neglect." *Social Work Research and Abstracts,* 14 (Fall 1978), 11–15.

Polansky, Norman, M. A. Chalmers, E. Buttenweisser and D. P. Williams, *Damaged Parents—An Anatomy of Child Neglect.* Chicago: University of Chicago Press, 1981.

Polansky, Norman, Paul Ammons, and Barbara Weatherby. "Is There an American Standard of Child Care?" *Social Work,* 28 (September–October, 1983), 341–346.

Polansky, Norman, Paul Ammons, and James Gaudin. "Loneliness and Isolation in Child Neglect." *Social Casework,* 66 (January, 1985), 38–47.

Powell, Thomas J. "Interpreting Parents Anonymous as a Source of Help for Those with Child Abuse Problems." Child Welfare, 58, 2 (February 1979), 105–113.

Presidents Commission for the Study of Ethical Problems—*Deciding to Forgo Life Sustaining Treatment.* Washington, D.C.: U.S. Government Printing Office, 1983, pp. 467–492.

Psychiatric Viewpoint Report. "Violence in the Family: Report of a Survey of Psychiatric Opinion." *Child and Adolescent Psychotherapy,* 2,2 (1985), 128–135.

Reavley, William, and Marie T. Gilbert. "The Behavioral Treatment Approach to Potential Child Abuse: Two Illustrative Case Reports." *Social Work Today,* 7, 6 (1976), 166–168.

Reidy, Thomas J. *The Aggressive Characteristics of Abused and Neglected Children.* Chicago: Rehabilitation Institute of Chicago, 1975. Mimeo, 13 pp.

Rein, Martin. *Child Protective Services in Massachusetts.* Papers in Social Welfare, No. 6. Waltham, Mass.: Florence Heller Graduate School for Advanced Studies in Social Welfare, November 1963.

Reposa, Richard, and Margot B. Zuelzer. "Family Therapy with Incest." *International Journal of Family Therapy,* 5, 2 (Summer 1983), 111–125.

Riede, G. et al. *A Texas Study of Child Sexual Abuse and Child Pornography,* Huntsville, Tex.: Sam Houston State University, 1979.

Rimsza, Mary E., and Elaine H. Niggemann. "Medical Evaluation of Sexually Abused Children: A Review of 311 Cases." *Pediatrics,* 69, 1 (January 1982), 8–14.

Rindfleisch, Nolan. *Identification Management and Prevention of Child Abuse and Neglect in Residential Facilities:* Vol. I. *Summary and Overview.* Columbus, Oh.: The Ohio State University Research Foundation, 1984.

Rindfleisch, Nolan, and Joel Rabb. "The Identification Management and Prevention of Abuse and Neglect in Residential Facilities." *Multiregional Conference on Child Abuse and Neglect.* Ed. C. Washburne, J. Van hull, and N. Rindfleisch, Columbus, Ohio College of Social Work. The Ohio State University, 1983.

Rivara, Frederick P. "Physical Abuse of Children Under Two: A Study of Therapeutic Outcomes." *Child Abuse and Neglect,* 9 (1985), 81–87.

Rohrbeck, Cynthia, and Craig T. Twentyman. "Multimandal Assessment of Impulsiveness in Abusing, Neglecting and Non-maltreating Mothers and Their Preschool Children." *Journal of Consulting and Clinical Psychology,* 52, 2 (1986), 231–236.

Rosen, H. "How Workers Use Cues to Determine Child Abuse." *Social Work Research and Abstracts,* 17 (1981), 27–33.

Rosenfeld, Alvin A. "Incidence of a History of Incest in 18 Female Psychiatric Patients." *American Journal of Psychiatry,* 136, 6 (1979), 791–794.

Rosenfeld, Alvin A. "Incest and the Sexual Abuse of Children." *Journal of the American Academy of Child Psychiatry,* 16 (1977), 334–336.

Rosenfeld, Alvin A. "Sexual Misuse and the Family." *Victimology,* 2, 2 (Summer 1977), 226–235.

Rothchild, A., and S. Wolf. *Children of the Counter Culture.* New York: Doubleday, 1976.

Rush, Florence. *The Best Kept Secret—Sexual Abuse of Children,* Englewood Cliffs, N.J.: Prentice Hall, 1980.

Russell, A. "The Incidence and Prevalence of Intrafamilial Abuse of Female Children." *Child Abuse and Neglect,* 7,2 (1983), 133–146.

Russell, Diana E.H. *The Secret Trauma—Incest in the Lives of Girls and Women.* New York: Basic Books, 1986.

Russell, Diana E.H. "The Prevalence and Seriousness of Incestuous Abuse: Stepfather vs. Biological Fathers." *Child Abuse and Neglect,* 8(1984), 15–22.

Russell, Alene B., and Cynthia M. Trainor. *Trends in Child Abuse and Neglect: A National Perspective.* Denver, Colo.: American Humane Association, Children's Division, 1984.

Salzinger, S., S. Kaplan, and E. Artemyeff. "Mothers' Personal Social Network and Child Maltreatment." *Journal of Abnormal Psychology,* 92, 1 (February 1983). 68–76.

Sandusky, Annie L. *"Protective Services,"* in *Encyclopedia of Social Work.* New York: National Association of Social Workers, 1964.

Sandusky, Annie L. "Services to Neglected Children." *Children,* 7 (January–February 1960).

Sapp. A., and D. Canter. *Child Abuse in Texas,* Huntsville, Tex.: Sam Houston State University, 1978.

Sarafino, Edward. "An Estimate of Nationwide Incidence of Sexual Offenses Against Children." *Child Welfare,* 58, 2 (February 1979), 127–133.

Scherer, Lorena. "Facilities and Services for Neglected Children in Missouri." *Crime and Delinquency,* 6 (January 1960).

Schmidt, Dolores M. "The Protective Service Caseworker: How Does He Survive Job Pressures?" *Child Welfare,* 42 (March 1963).

Schmitt, Barton D. "Medical Evaluation of Sexual Abuse," in *Sexual Abuse—Therapeutic and System Considerations for the Child and Family.* Ed. Claudia Carroll and Bruce Gottlieb. Denver, Colo.: Colorado State Department of Social Services, 1983, pp. 24–26.

Schmitt, Barton D. *The Child Protection Team Handbook—A Multidisciplinary Approach to Managing Child Abuse and Neglect.* New York: Garland STPM Press, 1978.

Schneider, Carol J. "The Michigan Screening Profile of Parenting," in *Child Abuse Prediction Policy Implications.* Ed. Raymond Starr. Cambridge, Mass.: Ballinger Publishing Co., 1982, pp. 157–174.

Schrier, Carol. "Child Abuse—An Illness or a Crime." *Child Welfare,* 58,4 (April 1979), 237–244.

Schultz, Leroy G., and Preston Jones. "Sexual Abuse of Children: Issues for Social Service and Health Professionals." *Child Welfare,* 57 (March–April 1983), 99–108.

Sedney, M. A., and B. B. Brooks. "Factors Associated with a History of Childhood Sexual Experience among a Clinical Female Population." *Journal of the American Academy of Child Psychiatry,* 23,2 (March 1984), 215–218.

Selinski, N. "Protecting CPS Clients and Workers," *Public Welfare,* 41, 3 (1983).

Sgroi, Suzanne. "The Sexual Assault of Children: Dynamics of the Problem and Issues in Program Development," in *Sexual Abuse of Children.* New York: NYC Community Council of Greater New York, April 1979, pp. 3–18.

Sgroi, Suzanne M., Linda C. Blick, and Frances S. Porter. "A Conceptual Framework for Child Sexual Abuse," in *Handbook of Clinical Intervention in Child Sexual Abuse.* Ed. Suzanne Sgroi. Lexington, Mass.: Lexington Books, 1982, pp. 9–37.

Shapiro, Deborah. *Parents and Protection—A Study in Child Abuse and Neglect.* New York: Child Welfare League of America, 1979.

Sheridan, William, and Pat Mancini. *A Social Worker Takes a Case into Court.* Washington, D.C.: U.S. Government Printing Office, 1962.

Shyne, Ann W., and Anita G. Schroeder. *A National Study of Social Services to Children and Their Families.* Rockville, Md.: Westat, 1978.

Silbert, Mimi, and Ayala M. Pines. "Early Sexual Exploitation as an Influence in Prostitution." *Social Work,* 28 (July–August, 1983), 285–289.

Silver, Larry et al. "Does Violence Breed Violence? Contribution from a Study of the Child-Abuse Syndrome." *American Journal of Psychiatry,* 126, 3 (September 1969), 404–407.

Simpson, Helen. "The Unfit Parent." *University of Detroit Law Review,* 39 (February 1962).

Skuse, S. H. "Non-organic Failure-to-Thrive: A Reappraisal." *Archives of Diseases of Childhood,* 60, 2 (February 1985), 173–178.

Smith, David H., and James Sternfield. "The Hippie Communal Movement: Effects of Childbirth and Development." *American Journal of Orthopsychiatry,* 40, 3 (April 1970), 527–530.

Smith, Jane E., and Sid Rachman. "Non-Accidental Injury to Children: A Controlled Evaluation of a Behavioral Management Program." *Behavior Research and Therapy,* 22, 4(1984), 349–366.

Smith, Selwyn H. *The Battered Child Syndrome.* London: Thornton Butterworth, Ltd., 1975.

Soman, Shirley C. "Emergency Parents." *Parade* (January 29, 1967).

Spinetta, John J., and David Rigler. "The Child Abusing Parent—A Psychological Review." *Psychological Bulletin,* 77, 4 (1972), 296–304.

Stark, Rodney, and James McEvoy. "Middleclass Violence." *Psychology Today* (November 1970), pp. 52–54, 111–112.

Starkweather, Cassie L., and S. Michael Turner. "Parents Anonymous: Reflection on the Development of a Self-help Group," pp. 151–157, in *Child Abuse Intervention and Treatment.* Ed. Nancy B. Ebeling and Deborah A. Hill. Acton, Mass.: Publishing Sciences Group, 1975.

Starr, Raymond H. "A Research Based Approach to the Reduction of Child Abuse," in *Child Abuse Prediction Policy Implications.* Ed. Raymond Starr. New York: Ballinger Publishing Co., 1982, pp. 105–134.

Steele, Brandt F. Working with Abusive Parents from a Psychiatric Point of View. National Center on Child Abuse and Neglect. Washington, D.C.: U.S. Government Printing Office, 1975.

Steele, Brandt F., and Carl B. Pollock. "A Psychiatric Study of Parents Who Abuse Infants and Small Children," in *The Battered Child.* Ed. Ray E. Helfer and C. Henry Kempe. Chicago: University of Chicago Press, 1968.

Steinberg, Lawrence D., Ralph Catalano, and David Dooley. "Economic Antecedants of Child Abuse and Neglect." *Child Development,* 52 (1981), 975–985.

Stephanson, P. Susan. "Reaching Child Abusers Through Target Toddlers." *Victmology,* 2 (Summer 1977), 310–316.

Stoetzer, J. B. "The Juvenile Court and Emotional Neglect of Children." *University of Michigan Journal of Law Reform,* 8 (Winter 1975), 351–374.

Straker, G. "Aggression, Emotional Maladjustment and Empathy in the Abused Child." *Developmental Psychology,* 17, 6 (November 1981), 762–765.

Strauss, Murray A. "Family Patterns and Child Abuse in a Nationally Representative American Sample." *Child Abuse and Neglect,* 3 (1979), 213–225.

Studt, Elliot. "An Outline for Study of Social Authority Factors in Casework." *Social Casework,* 35, 6 (June 1954).

Sturkie, K. "Structured Group Treatment for Sexually Abused Children." *Health and Social Work* (1983).

Sudia, Cecelia E. "What Services Do Abusive Families Need?" in *The Social Context of Child Abuse and Neglect.* Ed. Leroy H. Pelton. New York: Human Sciences Press, 1981, pp. 268–290.

Summit, Roland, and JoAnn Kryso. "Sexual Abuse of Children: A Clinical Spectrum." *American Journal of Orthopsychiatry,* 48, 12 (April 1978), 237–251.

Sussman, Alan, and Stephen S. Cohen. *Reporting Child Abuse and Neglect: Guidelines for Legislation.* Cambridge, Mass.: Ballinger Publishing Co., 1975.

Swan, Helen, Allan Press, and Steven Briggs. "Child Sexual Abuse Prevention: Does It Work?" *Child Welfare,* 64, 4 (July–August 1985), 395–405.

Swanson, Lynn D. "Role of the Police in the Protection of Children from Neglect and Abuse." *Federal Probation,* 25 (March 1961).

Ten Broeck, Elsa. "The Extended Family Center: A House Away from Home for Abused Children and Their Parents." *Children Today,* 3 (March–April, 1974), 2–6.

Texas Department of Human Resources. *Intervention in Child Sexual Abuse: A Study of Services Provided by the Texas Department of Human Resources.* Austin, Texas Department of Human Resource, January 12, 1981.

Thomas, A., H. G. Birch, and Stella Chess. *Behavioral Individuality in Early Childhood.* New York: New York University Press, 1963.

Tormes, Yvonne M. *Child Victims of Incest.* Denver, Colo.: American Humane Association. Children's Division, 1963.

Thompson, Ellen M., and Norman Paget. *Child Abuse—A Community Challenge.* Buffalo, N.Y.: Henry Stewart, 1971.

Tracy, James J., Carolyn Ballard, and Elizabeth H. Clark. "Child Abuse Project: A Followup." *Social Work,* 20 (September 1975), 398–399.

Tsai, M. et al. "Childhood Molestation: Variables Related to Differential Impacts on Psychosexual Functioning in Adult Women." *Journal of Abnormal Psychology,* 88, 4 (1979), 407–417.

Turner, Michael. *Parental Stress—Telephone Counseling Service Project Report.* Boston, Mass.: Parents and Children's Services, Children's Mission, 1981.

Tuszynski, Ann, and James Dowd. "An Alternative Approach to the Treatment of Protective Services Families." *Social Casework,* 59, 3 (March 1978), 175–179.

Tyler, Ann H., and Marla R. Brassard. "Abuse in the Investigation and Treatment of Intrafamilial Child Sexual Abuse." *Child Abuse and Neglect,* 8 (1984), 47–53.

Twentyman, C. T., and R. C. Plotkin. "Unrealistic Expectations of Parents Who Maltreat Their Children: An Educational Deficit That Pertains to Child Development." *Journal of Clinical Psychology,* 38 (July 1982), 497–504.

U.S. Department of Health and Human Services, Children's Bureau, National Center on Child Abuse and Neglect. *National Study of the Incidence and Severity of Child Abuse and Neglect,* Washington, D.C.: U.S. Government Printing Office, 1981.

U.S. Department of Health, Education and Welfare. *Child Sexual Abuse-Incest, Assault and Sexual Exploitation.* Washington, D.C.: U.S. Government Printing Office, 1979.

Valentine, Deborah et al. "Defining Child Maltreatment: A Multidisciplinary Overview." *Child Welfare,* 63 (December 1984), 497–509.

Varon, Edith. "Communication: Client, Community and Agency." *Social Work,* 9 (April 1964).

Wachtel, Andrew, and Sarah Lawton-Speert. *Child Sexual Abuse: Descriptions of Nine Program Approaches to Treatment.* Vancouver, B.C.: Social Planning and Research, United Way of the Lower Main Pond, 1983.

Wald, Michael. "State Intervention on Behalf of 'Neglected Children: A Search for Realistic Standards." *Stanford Law Review,* 27 (April 1975), 985–1039.

Walters, David R. *Physical and Sexual Abuse of Children—Causes and Treatment.* Bloomington: Indiana University Press, 1975.

Wasserman, Gail, Arthur Green, and Rhianon Allan. "Going Beyond Abuse: Maladaptive Patterns of Interaction in Abusing Mother–Infant Peers." *Journal of the American Academy of Child Psychiatry,* 22, 3 (1983), 245–252.

Waterman, Jill, and Rob Lusk. "Scope of the Problem," pp. 3–12 in Sexual Abuse of *Young Children.* Ed. Kee McFarlane et al. New York: The Guilford Press, 1986.

Wattenberg, Esther. "In a Different Light—A Feminist Perspective on the Role of Mothers in Father–Daughter Incest." *Child Welfare,* 64, 4 (May–June 1985), 203–211.

Wayne, Julianne, and Nancy Avery. *Child Abuse: Prevention and Treatment Through Social Groupwork.* Boston: Charles River Books, 1980.

Webster-Stratton, Carolyn. "Comparison of Abusive and Non-Abusive Families with Conduct Disordered Children." *American Journal of Orthopsychiatry,* 55, 1 (January 1985), 59–69.

Wheat, Patte, and Leonard L. Lieber. *Hope for the Children.* Minneapolis: Winston Press, 1979.

White, Roger B., and Donald Cornely. "Navajo Child Abuse and Neglect Study: A Comparison Group Examination of Abuse and Neglect of Navajo Children." *Child Abuse and Neglect,* 5 (1981), 9–17.

Wilson, Jean, Dan Thomas, and Linda Schuette. "Survey of Counselors on Identifying and Reporting Cases of Child Abuse." *The School Counselor* (March 1983), 299–305.

Wilson, Margot, Martin Daly, and Suzanne Weghorst. "Differential Maltreatment of Girls and Boys." *Victimology,* 6, 1–4 (1981), 249–261.

Wilson, Thelma Garrett. *Ventura Ventures into Child Protective Service.* Denver, Colo.: American Humane Association, 1960.

Wolfe, David A. "Child Abuse Parents: An Empirical Review and Analysis." *Psychological Bulletin,* 97 (1985) 462–482.

Wolfe, David A., et al. "Evaluation of a Brief Intervention for Educating School Children in Awareness of Physical and Sexual Abuse." *Child Abuse and Neglect,* 10(1986), 85–92.

Wolfe, David, and Mark D. Mosk. "Behavioral Comparisons of Children from Abusive and Distressed Families." *Journal of Consulting and Clinical Psychology,* 5, 5 (1983), 702–708.

Wolock, I., and B. Horowitz. "Child Maltreatment and Material Depression Among AFDC Recipient Families." *social Service Review,* 53 (June 1979), 177–192.

Wolock, Isabel and B. Horowitz. "Child Maltreatment as a Social Problem: The Neglect of Neglect." *American Journal of Orthopsychiatry,* 54,4 (October 1984) 530–543.

Wooden, Kenneth. *Weeping in the Playtime of Others.* New York: McGraw-Hill, 1976.

Wyatt, Gail E. "The Sexual Abuse of Afro-American and White American Women in Childhood." *Child Abuse and Neglect,* 9 (1985), 507–519.

Wyatt, Gail E., and Stephanie D. Peters. "Issues in the Definition of Child Sexual Abuse in Prevalence Research" and "Methodological Considerations in Research on the Prevalence in Child Sexual Abuse." *Child Abuse and Neglect,* 10 (1986), 231–240; 241–251.

Yates, Alayne. "Children Eroticized by Incest." *American Journal of Psychiatry,* 139, 4 (April 1982), 482–485.

Yates, Alyone. "Legal Issues in Psychological Abuse of Children." *Clinical Pediatrics* (October 1982).

Yelaja, Shan Kar. *Authority and Social Work: Concept and Use.* Toronto: University of Toronto Press, 1971.

Young, Leon R. "An Interim Report on an Experimental Program of Protective Service." *Child Welfare,* 45, 7 (July 1966), 373–381.

Young, Leontine. "The Preventive Nature of Protective Services," in *Proceedings of the Institute on Protective and Related Community Services.* Richmond, Va.: Richmond Schol of Social Work, 1968.

Young, Leontine. *Wednesday's Child.* New York: McGraw-Hill, 1964.

Zalba, Serapio R. "The Abused Child—A Survey of the Problem." *Social Work,* 11, 4 (October 1966).

Zimrim, Hanita. "Do Nothing But Do Something: The Effect of Human Contact with the Parent on Abusive Behavior." *British Journal of Social Work,* 14 (1984), 475–485.

7

Substitute Care:

Foster Family Care

Introduction

Foster family care, institutional care, and adoption involve substituting another family for the child's own family, so that someone else takes over all aspects of the parental role on a temporary or permanent basis. Such a change is necessary when the home presents deficiencies so serious that even intensive home-based preventive services cannot assist the family in providing the child with minimally adequate social, emotional, or physical care.

Substitute care involves, for the child, major upheaval in his or her life circumstances. The child experiences not only total separation from the family but also adjustment to a new set of caretakers, a change of location, a change of school, and a change of peer and sibling groups. Because these changes are so drastic, substitute care is regarded as a third line of defense in child welfare. The worker must obtain clear evidence that the child's birth family cannot function with minimal sufficiency so as to maintain the child in the home, despite the availability of extensive services and in-depth family support. To avoid this upheaval in the child's life, every effort has to be made to keep the home intact for the child and to keep the child in the home (Williams, 1972; Goldstein, 1973; Bryce & Lloyd, 1981).

Foster family or institutional care is considered a short-term treatment resource for the child while his or her family struggles to remedy the problems that led to removal and placement. These resources are to be used when the worker believes that there is some possibility that the family can, with sufficient assistance, eventually be reunited (Maluccio & Fein, 1983). When reunification is not possible, the search for a more permanent family for the child is conducted by the adoption worker.

The term *foster care* is often applied to any type of substitute care facility—boarding home, adoptive home, or institution. However, the Child Welfare League of America's (1959) definition is "A child welfare service which provides substitute family care for a planned period for a child when his own family cannot care for him for a temporary or extended period and when adoption is neither desirable nor possible" (p.5).

Note that according to the CWLA, it is care in a *family,* it is noninstitutional substitute care, and it is for a *planned* period—either temporary or extended

(Meyer, 1985). Thus it is unlike adoptive placement, which implies a *permanent* substitution of one home for another, one family for another. To distinguish this use of the term *foster care* from other kinds of foster-care arrangements, we refer to it in this chapter as *foster-family care.*

Changing the child's temporary caretakers frequently involves a change in legal custody of the child. Adoption involves going beyond a change in legal custody to a change in legal guardianship. Legal custody is concerned with the rights and duties of the person having custody to provide for the child's daily needs—to feed and clothe the child, to provide shelter, put the child to bed, send him or her to school, and to see that the child's face is washed and teeth are brushed. Legal custody permits the agency having custody to determine where and with whom the child shall live. Consequently, the agency can move the child from one foster home to another. But the child still legally "belongs" to the parent and the parent retains guardianship. This means that, in some crucial areas of the child's life, the agency cannot act without parent authorization. Only the parent can consent to surgery for the child, consent to the child's marriage, permit the child's enlistment in the armed forces, or represent the child at law. Only with a change of guardianship are the natural parents' ties to child completely severed.

Actually, many long-term foster family placements become de facto adoptions. But the fact that legal guardianship of the child is retained by the birth parents has considerable implications for the nature of the relationship established between foster child and foster family. As long as birth parents retain legal rights to their child, there is a possibility that he or she will eventually return to their home.

When selecting a foster-family home for children, agencies may choose from among the following kinds of noninstitutional twenty-four-hour-a-day arrangements:

1. *Receiving* or shelter homes—specialized boarding homes designed to care for children on short notice for limited periods of time. This service is offered primarily to babies and younger children for whom an institutional arrangement is felt to be undesirable even for a short period of time and in situations requiring emergency removal of a child from a home (Rowe, 1980).
2. *Free work, or wage homes*—the child is placed in a free home, in which the agency pays no board rates, when it is anticipated that the child will be adopted by the family. Work or wage homes may be appropriate for the older child who can make a contribution in recompense for care.
3. *Boarding homes*—the agency and/or the natural parents pay the foster parents a board rate. This is, by far, the most common type of foster-family-care arrangement.
4. *Group homes*—may be viewed as a large foster-family unit or a small institution. It is a living facility within the normal community simulating a family for a small group of unrelated children.

Rowe (1980) describes two common types of boarding foster homes. "Indefinite or medium-length" homes are designed for children who might possibly be returning to their birth home. In these circumstances, it is especially important that parents receive assistance in altering the problems that led to placement of their child, from both the child welfare worker and from the foster family. Ongoing contact between parent and child is crucial since it helps the child maintain a sense of continuity while offering the parent an opportunity to practice more effective child-care skills. "Long-stay or permanent" foster-care facilities, on the other hand, are designed for children whose parents are unable to maintain them in their birth home but who, for one reason or another, are not in a position to break all ties with their birth families and to be adopted. As a child remains in foster care for longer and longer periods of time, contact with the birth family typically diminishes, and the foster parents are increasingly perceived as primary caretakers.

Historical Background

Foster-family care was probably practiced on a limited basis in antiquity. "Under ancient Jewish laws and customs, children lacking parental care became members of the household of other relatives, if such there were, who reared them for adult life" (Slingerland, 1919, p. 27). The early Church boarded destitute children with "worthy widows."

Indenture was an early form of foster-family care that was extensively employed. The Elizabethan Poor Laws provided for the apprenticing of dependent children until their twenty-first year. The master accepted the dependent child into his home, provided him or her with food, clothing, and the necessities of life, and accepted the responsibility for teaching him or her a craft or trade. In addition provision was usually made for some extra payment in the form of clothes and/or money at the termination of the indenture. In return, the child was to work for the master around the house and in the craft or trade as an "employee." Indenture was recognized as a "business deal from which the person accepting a poor child on indenture was expected to receive from the child, a full equivalent in work for the expenses of his support, care and teaching" (Thurston, 1930, p. 10).

The preamble of an eighteenth-century Maryland statute on indenture illustrates the relationship between indenture and the problem of child care:

> Whereas, it has been found by experience that poor children, orphans, and illegitimate, for want of some efficient system, have been left destitute of support and have become useless or depraved members of society, and, Whereas it would greatly conduce to the good of the public in general and of such children in particular that necessary instruction in trades and useful arts should be afforded them, therefore, the justices of the orphans' courts were authorized to bind out orphans, and such children as are suffering through the extreme indigence or poverty of their parents, also the children of beggars, and also illegitimate children, and the children of persons out of this state where a sufficient sustenance is not afforded [Bremner, 1970, p. 266.]

Despite the fact that the indenture permitted all sorts of abuses and exploitation, that "it is morally certain that the experiences of indentured children varied all the way from that of being virtual slaves to that of being real foster sons or daughters" (Thurston, 1930, p. 17), and that there was little guarantee of protection for the child other than public indignation or the foster parents' desire to keep the good opinion of their neighbors, indenture persisted in the United States until the first decade of the twentieth century. It did provide for many children a family life and at least minimal care.

A number of factors accounted for the gradual decline of the indenture as a means of foster-family-care. It was not always profitable for the foster family because children if taken young had to be supported for a period of time before they could make a return on their investment. With growing industrialization and the movement of crafts and trades out of the home, the idea of an apprenticeship located in the family became less feasible. But perhaps of greater importance was the impact on indenture of the abolition of slavery, after which it was hard to justify an indenture that required the apprehension and return to the master of a runaway apprentice and that had some of the characteristics of bondage arrangements. In fact, Folks (1902) notes, "It has been seriously suggested that, with the adoption of the Constitutional Amendment in 1865, forbidding 'involuntary servitude,' the indenture system became unconstitutional" (p. 42).

The real origin of modern foster-family care lies with Charles Loring Brace and The Placing Out System of the New York Children's Aid Society. In the middle of the nineteenth century, New York City faced a problem of dealing with a large number of vagrant children, who existed with minimal adult care, protection, and support In 1849 the New York City Chief of Police called attention to the fact that:

> there was a constantly increasing number of vagrant, idle, and vicious children of both sexes who infest our public thoroughfares, hotels, docks, etc., children who are growing up in ignorance and profligacy, only destined to a life of misery, shame, and crime and ultimately to a felon's doom. . . . Their number[s] are almost incredible and to those whose business and habits do not permit them a searching scrutiny, the degrading and disgusting practices of these almost infants in the school of vice, prostitution, and rowdyism, would certainly be beyond belief [quoted in Langsam, 1964, pp. 1–2].

At about this time the Chief of Police reported ten thousand vagrant children in New York City (Thurston, 1930, p. 97).

Brace, a young minister who became the first secretary of the New York Children's Aid Society upon its organization in 1853, developed a new and distinctive method of dealing with the problem presented by these children. The society would "drain the city of these children by communicating with farmers, manufacturers, or families in the country who may have need of such for employment." The appeal was to Christian charity and to the need for labor on the farms. It involved relocating children from the pernicious influences of urban areas, where there was little for them to do, to rural areas, where there was much for them to do and where the environment was regarded as morally sounder. There evolved a particular program of group emigration and placement that resulted in finding foster-family care in free foster-family homes for about 100,000 children between 1854 and 1929 (Langsam, 1964, p. 27).

The procedure was first to collect a group of children in New York City. Many of the children were known to be orphans; some had been abandoned, so that the status of their parents was unknown. But many of the children were half-orphans or children with both parents living. In the latter cases, an attempt was made to obtain parental consent to the child's relocation. The largest numbers of children were provided by institutions in the city, but the society's agents also had responsibility for locating vagrant, uncared-for children.

After making some effort to eliminate the physically ill, the mentally handicapped and the incorrigible, the children set out for the West or the South in the company of one of the society's workers. The community to which the children were to be sent was encouraged by the society to set up a committee of prominent citizens who had the responsibility of arranging temporary care for the children upon their arrival. Of greater importance was the committee's responsibility to publicize the coming of the children, to encourage families to take them in, and to evaluate the suitability of those families who indicated interest. Upon the arrival in town of the group of children, arrangements were made for their distribution to homes in accordance with the preliminary work done by the local committee.

A report by a pioneer child-welfare worker, Dr. Hastings Hart, to the National Conference of Charities and Corrections in 1884 describes the "placement" procedure:

> I was a witness of the distribution of forty children in ——— County, Minnesota. . . . The children arrived at about half-past three P.M. and were taken directly from the train to the Court House, where a large crowd was gathered. Mr. Matthews set the children, one by one, before the company, and in his stentorian voice gave a brief account of each. Applicants for children were then admitted in order behind the railing and rapidly made their selections. Then, if the child gave assent, the bargain was soon concluded on the spot. It was a pathetic sight, not soon to be forgotten, to see those children, tired young people, weary, travel-stained, confused by the excitement and the unwonted surroundings, peering into those strange faces, and trying to choose wisely for themselves. And it was surprising how many happy selections were made under such circumstances. In a little more than three hours nearly all those forty children were disposed of. Some who had not previously applied selected children. There was little time for consultation, and refusal would be embarrassing, and I know that the Committee consented to some assignments against their better judgment.
>
> The Committee usually consists of a minister, an editor, and a doctor, lawyer, or a businessman. The merchant dislikes to offend a customer, or the doctor a patient, and the minister fears to have it thought that his refusal is because the applicant does not belong to his church. Thus unsuitable applications sometimes succeed. Committee men and officers of the Society complain of this difficulty. The evil is proved by the fact that, while the younger children are taken from motives of benevolence and are uniformly well treated, the older ones are, in the majority of cases, taken from motives of profit, and are expected to earn their way from the start [Hart, 1884].

Although it did not involve a formal contractual arrangement, and the society retained control of the child's custody and could remove the child if it was felt that he or she was being unfairly treated, the free foster-family arrangement was still based on the exchange of child labor for child care. As Thurston (1930) says in summarizing the program, "It is the wolf of the old indenture philosophy of child labor in the sheepskin disguise of a so-called good or Christian home" (p.136).

Opposition of Western states to the "extraditing" and "dumping" of dependent children in their area, the opposition of the Catholic Church to what was regarded as an attempt by a Protestant organization to wean children from their Catholic heritage by their placement in non-Catholic homes, and criticism by the growing number of child welfare professionals contributed to declining use of these placement procedures.

The proceedings of the Annual National Conference of Charities and Corrections frequently included attacks on the dangers involved in the method of selecting free foster homes for children and the looseness and infrequency of supervision following placement.

The first annual report of the Massachusetts State Board of Charities states the core of the problem succinctly:

> As a general rule the persons who now take children into their families from the State institutions do so primarily for their own advantage, and only secondarily, if at all, for the good of the child; but it frequently happens that the child who was taken as a servant secures a place in the affections of the family taking him, and so the connection ceases to be a mercenary one. These cases, however, do not form the rule, it is to be feared.

Although Brace sought to meet these attacks by reports of "research" by agency workers indicating that only a limited number of children were maltreated or turned out poorly, the criticism was never adequately met. The distances over which the society operated and the limited number of workers employed precluded any careful selection or supervision of homes.

The system exacted a price from birth parents as well. "Placing out" at a distance meant a kind of pseudoadoption, and the intent actually was to prevent the return of the child to his or her own home—this, despite the fact that a considerable number of such children did have two living parents. "Mr. S. a widower, worked as a hostler at a New Jersey hotel where he earned ten dollars a month. On such wages he could not afford to supply both his aged parents and his three children, and consequently he relinquished the youngsters to the Home Missionary Society" (Clement, 1979, p. 413). As Thurston (1930) notes, "It does not seem fair to the relatives that they be compelled to surrender a child permanently in order to get whatever care he may need temporarily" (p. 135).

Brace's programs did stimulate the development of similar programs of foster-family placement in free homes by organizations established to do this within particular states. Such State Children's Home Societies as they were called originated with the work of Martin Van Buren Van Arsdale in 1883 in Indiana and Illinois. Van Arsdale, like Brace, was a minister. The purpose of the State Children's Home Societies was

> to seek the homeless, neglected, and destitute children and to become their friend and protector, to find homes for them in well-to-do families and to place them wisely, to look occasionally with discretion into the homes, and thus prevent abuse and neglect, and to replace children, when necessary, to make it possible for persons (without children of their own) to adopt a child, to minister, in comforting assurance to parents in fear of leaving their children penniless and homeless, to protect society by guaranteeing proper home training and education to the unfortunate little ones against its greatest enemies, ignorance and vice, to extend our organization into sister states [quoted in Thurston, 1930, p. 156].

By 1923 there were thirty-four states in which such State Children's Home Societies had been established. The activities of these agencies were, and continue to be, supplemented by sectarian agencies in larger cities, such as the Jewish Child Care Association in New York City and nonsectarian agencies such as the Boston Children's Aid Society.

At the same time the public agencies were pioneering other alternatives. The Michigan State Public School (in reality, an orphanage) opened in 1874; it was created to be a temporary home for all destitute children who had become public charges until the children could be placed in foster family homes. Some nineteen other states soon adopted the same plan. In the late 1860s, Massachusetts pioneered in paying board money to foster families for the maintenance of children who might otherwise have been placed in institutions and who were too young to be profitably indentured. This state also pioneered in more careful supervision of those children who had been indentured by the state.

The Boston Children's Aid Society, under the leadership of Charles Birtwell between 1886 and 1911, carried foster-family care a step further. For each child Birtwell asked, "What does the child really need?" rather than "Where shall we put the child?" The aim Birtwell said, "will be in each instance to suit the action to the real need, heeding the teachings of experience, still to study the conditions with a freedom from assumptions and a directness and freshness of view as complete as though the case in hand stood absolutely alone" (Thurston, 1930, p. 200). This approach required individual study of the child and a variety of different kinds of substitute care—an individualization of need and diversification of services.

Birtwell showed an appreciation for the potentialities of the preventive placement aspects of supportive and supplementary services. For Brace, the long-time placement suggested that the foster parent was, in fact, replacing the natural parent in a pseudoadoptive situation. Given Birtwell's approach, the foster parent-foster child relationship becomes something distinctively different—a means through which the child is ultimately restored to the family.

Birtwell developed a systematic plan for studying foster-home applicant families and a systematic plan of supervision once the child was placed. An effort was made to keep detailed records and to develop principles of action. He was, in effect, attempting to build a science of foster-family care and to professionalize practice.

The history of substitute care in institutions and that of substitute care in foster-family homes are interrelated. The mixed almshouses (see Chapter 10) were at one time a frequently employed resource for the institutional care of children. When, toward the end of the nineteenth century, one state after another began to pass laws prohibiting the use of mixed almshouses for children, they recommended that such children be placed in foster homes instead. Thus the closing of mixed almshouses for children increased the tendency to resort to foster-family care (Folks, 1902, pp. 74–80).

Orphanages frequently used foster-family care as a supplementary resource, both in the early years of the life of the child and then again as the child moved toward greater independence. In taking responsibility for infants, before the advent of pasteurized milk and formula feeding, the institution had to provide nursing care. Consequently orphanages would often place the infant in a foster family for wet-nursing. When the child reached early adolescence, institutions must "dismiss their wards and the usual method when that age arrives is to obtain a place for a child in a private home as an accepted inmate or paid worker before withdrawing institutional care and support" (Slingerland, 1919, p.39).

Throughout the nineteenth century and the early part of the twentieth century, controversy raged between the advocates of institutional care and the supporters of foster-family care over which was the more desirable method. Foster-family care was given official sanction in 1899 by the National Conference of Correction and Charities. At that meeting a report was presented by J. M. Mulrey (1900) in behalf of a special committee of prominent child welfare workers appointed to study the problems of the dependent child and to make recommendations. The report adopted by the conference stated that when a child needed substitute care, consideration should first be given to a foster-family arrangement (p. 167). The

First White House Conference on Children in 1909 stated that "the carefully selected foster home is, for the normal child, the best substitute for the natural home." Thus foster-family care was given a clear preference.

Throughout much of the twentieth century, institutional providers continued to be on the defensive, feeling the need to justify the importance of their programs and explicate the conditions under which they are to be utilized. The child welfare field has come to adopt the perspective that children are to be provided the type of substitute care most like normal home conditions and that it is only when the child cannot function in this type of environment that residential care is to be contemplated.

In the last twenty years, the foster-family care system has, once again, been subject to extensive criticism. Today, as in Brace's time, foster-family care is challenged for its inability to provide some critically important aspects of family life particularly a sense of predictability and continuity (Project Craft, 1980, p. VI–40). The child's birth family or an adoptive family are considered more appropriate permanent resources. However, procedures and policies may stand in the way of the child's eventual move toward one or the other of these more permanent arrangements (Gurak, Smith, & Goldson, 1982). In order to effectively assist in the child's reunification with his or her birth family, intensive services must be offered the parents in order to help them remediate the difficulties that resulted in their child's removal from the home. Agency resources are frequently unavailable for this purpose. Perceptions of some of these families as "unworkable" also prevent successful outreach and assistance to them.

Studies show that the longer a child has been in placement the greater the likelihood that he or she will continue in placement (Maas & Engler, 1959; Jenkins, 1967; Fanshel, 1971, Shapiro, 1972; Fanshel & Shinn, 1978). Families may find it difficult to arrange visitation with agency personnel, may be unable to obtain funds for transportation or child care, and may find agency-based visits with their children highly stressful and unsatisfactory. Without sufficient agency support, parental motivation to see their child diminishes. Many families gradually reorient their lives to the reality that they are no longer actually caring for their children; having reorganized their lives in this way, they may find it increasingly difficult to welcome to idea of the child's return. Over time, the separation between parent and child may become total—except in the legal sense (Musewicz, 1981).

A variety of solutions have been proposed and implemented to deal with barriers to the achievement of permanence. One set of solutions relates to changes in the laws regarding the termination of parental rights so that the foster child who is unlikely to return home can be freed for adoption. The termination of parental rights is more frequently possible now for the child who is "permanently neglected," whose parents fail, despite the diligent efforts of the agency, to maintain any kind of meaningful contact with the child. However, a number of difficulties stand in the way of freeing the child for adoption. Organizational barriers in both the child welfare agency and the court system impede or prevent termination in many instances. "Although the courts have not recognized a limitless parental right to control the destiny of the biological family, it is clear that parental rights are all but absolute, even though they may conflict with the child's need for permanence" (Musewicz, 1981, p. 656). Lack of knowledge of the whereabouts of the parents, active or anticipated opposition by the parents to termination, and the continuing interest of the parents in the child, however vague or intermittent, make action to free the child difficult. Consequently, it has been suggested that changes in values and attitudes need to accompany the development of legal procedures designed to protect the child's right to permanence (Meyer, 1985).

Critics of the foster-family care system have also highlighted the sizable number of foster children "in limbo." Concern with the rights of children has made us sensitive to the entitlement of such children to some regularization of their status (Freud, Goldstein, Solnit, 1973). The decreasing number of white, nonhandicapped infants available for adoption has also prompted reexamination of the status of all children in substitute care in an effort to determine if some of those children could be made available for adoption, thus increasing the supply of adoptable children. The growth and the increasing power of foster-parent organizations has heightened concern with this question, because foster parents are often anxious to obtain some clearer definition of their own status in these ambiguous situations. Increasing public resentment in the 1970s against being taxed to support social programs added concern about program costs and impelled an effort to free more children for adoption.

Nationwide reviews of the performance of the system, by two different child advocacy groups, indicted the system for its failure in meeting children's need for permanence (Children's Defense Fund, 1978, National Commission for Children in Need of Parents, 1979). Violation of the obligation to provide a permanent situation seems most serious in the case of many children who entered the system when very young and were optimally placeable for adoption. (Fanshel, 1979a).

In the face of these concerns, a variety of recent local, state, and federal efforts have concentrated on reducing the foster-family care population. Included among these efforts are the development of monitoring and review procedures and the use of special demonstration and training programs to reunite families and free children for adoption. These efforts culminated in the passage of federal legislation governing the disbursal of child welfare funds that mandates utilization of permanency-planning procedures.

To obtain greater control over the entry and exit of children from the foster-care system, programs have made (1) more explicit intra-agency efforts to monitor plans for the child and to implement more intensive efforts to achieve permanence and (2) arrangements for extra-agency monitoring by courts and citizen review boards, of agency efforts toward permanence. The intent of both internal and external review procedures is to introduce more systematic planning and accountability into the system.

Shireman (1983) suggests that some groups of children are in particular need of periodic assessment. They include children who have begun to "drift toward unplanned long-term care," children who have been in three or more placements, older children, particularly adolescents and those who because of their special needs or minority status may require more intensive caseworker efforts in order to find a permanent home (p. 381). (See also Fellner & Solomon, 1973; Chestang & Heymann, 1973; Atherton, 1974; Rothschild, 1974). Larger agencies have experimented with the administrative review of planning for foster children as a way of preventing "drift" (Claburn & Magura, 1977; Poertner & Rapp, 1980).

Some states have adopted legislation requiring court review of children in foster care at periodic intervals, such as six, twelve, or eighteen months. In 1971 New York was the first state to pass this legislation. Washington, Virginia, and North Carolina now also have such requirements (Musewicz, 1981, p. 684). An alternative approach utilizes volunteers to review cases (Steketee, 1977; 1978; Chappell, 1975). The Children in Placement Project (CIP), sponsored by the National Council of Juvenile and Family Court Judges, is a program of this type. In situations in which volunteers find serious limitations in permanency-planning efforts or in particularly complex cases, this process is augmented by judicial case review.

By 1976, a surprisingly large number of child welfare decisions were subject to internal or external review. Claburn, Magura, and Resnick (1976), obtaining information from state agencies in forty-seven states, the District of Columbia and Puerto Rico, found 24 per cent of the responding jurisdictions required a full court review involving a "statewide statutory requirement for responsible agencies to submit periodic reports to the judiciary justifying the status of children in out of home placement" (p. 397). An additional 29 per cent had developed a "centralized administrative system for regular mandatory reviews of the status of foster children" (p. 397). Thus over half the states had some systematic, mandatory, periodic review that went beyond traditional case supervision.

Administrative and legislative provisions have been accompanied by specific programmatic changes designed to develop a cadre of social workers committed to permanency objectives and skilled in implementing them. The most notable examples are the Alameda Project in California (Stein, 1976; Stein, Gambrill, & Wiltse, 1978) and the Oregon Project (Emlen et al., 1977; Pike et al., 1977). The Alameda Project used three specially assigned workers with a limited caseload (twenty cases "defined as families") who "offered intensive service to the natural parents using behavioral methods of treatment while county child welfare workers provided their usual services to the child in the foster home" (Stein, 1976, p. 39). Case outcomes in the units to which the special workers were assigned ($N = 145$) were compared with cases in a designated control unit in the same agency ($N = 148$). Although the control and the experimental families were well matched in terms of ethnicity, structure, and the reasons that brought the children into care, the two groups were different in terms of the ages of the children—the control group children being significantly older. At the end of two years, a significantly greater percentage (p < .001) of the experimental group children had been returned home or had achieved or were headed for adoption than was true for the control-group children. The researchers attribute experimental group success to early systematic planning by the demonstration workers, facilitating early decision-making on the part of the parents. Contracts provided the specific framework and content for worker-client interaction. They also provided the evidence needed for active steps taken to terminate parental rights in planning for adoption.

The Oregon Project employed a somewhat different set of procedures in dealing with problems of the foster-care system. The project emphasized intensive, systematic casework in achieving permanent planning for children and active, aggressive pursuit of the termination of parental rights. The project design also involved limited caseloads (twenty-five children per worker as opposed to the usual caseload of fifty to sixty children in Oregon) and full-time legal assistance to free children for adoption. The project accepted 509 children for the project from the total (2,283) foster-care caseload. The children selected had been in care one year or more, were twelve years of age or younger, were not likely, in the worker's judgment, to return home, and were considered adoptable. At the end of the three-year period, an impressive 79 per cent of the children were out of foster-family care; 27 per cent had been returned home, and an additional 52 per cent either were in adoptive homes or their adoption was being actively planned (Emlen et al., 1977, p. 5).

Procedures that were found effective in the Alameda and Oregon Projects have subsequently been employed in other established programs, with the help of federal funding. To prevent placement of children in substitute care and to move children out of care more quickly, the state of California (1981) implemented demonstration projects in Shasta and San Mateo counties. Over a two-year period these efforts led to movement out of foster care for over two hundred children, reduction in the average number of days children spent in care, and significant increases in adoptive placements. San Mateo County increased adoptions by 36 per cent, and Shasta County by 67 per cent (pp. 35, 39).

The new Westminster District Office of the Ministry of Human Resources in British Columbia instituted a Permanent Placement Planning Committee that was responsible for tracking children in foster care, ensuring that intensive efforts were made early in their stay in care, and sustaining parental contact with the child. Fifty-nine per cent of the project children achieved permanent placement within a one-year period and planning was in progress for an additional 22 per cent (Levitt, 1981, p. 111). The Children's Aid and Adoption Society of New Jersey developed a training project that enhanced caseworker skill in helping parents deal more effectively with their children and ameliorate personal difficulties. Over the two-year period permanency was achieved for 52 per cent of the 101 children involved in the program. Thirty per cent of these children were returned to their birth family home (Sisto, 1980; p. 109).

The federal government attempted to ensure more effective statewide planning for and monitoring of children by requiring that, in order to receive federal reimbursement for AFDC-FC, states develop individualized child service plans and periodically review these plans. However, until recently many states ignored these requirements or carried them out in a pro forma way (Musewicz, 1981). Although they were expected to do so, no states filed a state plan with the Department of Health and Human Services between 1969 and 1979 (Hubbell, 1981). In 1978, the Administration for Children, Youth and Families began efforts to obtain increased compliance with these federal regulations, but more powerful permanency impetus was created with passage of Public Law 96-272, the Adoption Assistance and Child Welfare Act. This law requires that, in order to receive funding for substitute care from two different sources, AFDC-FC (children who must be removed from their family home because it is detrimental to their well-being) and Title IV-B (general child welfare funds), states are encouraged and, in some instances, mandated to carry out a series of monitoring procedures. On a statewide level an individual agency must be designated to develop a comprehensive state plan. Included in this plan are the state's efforts to extend child welfare services to all areas of the state, to enhance public awareness of the availability of these services, and to ensure linkages between public and private child welfare service providers. The state is also responsible for developing inventories of children who have been in substitute care for more than six months, for disseminating information about basic characteristics of these children, and for monitoring and evaluating utilization of federal funds to maintain them in settings other than their birth family or an adoptive home. States are, furthermore, responsible for developing a tracking system, so that information is readily available about all children in care. This provision is aimed at preventing children from becoming "lost in the system."

Public Law 96-272 also contains a number of requirements that must be met by local child welfare service providers. Each child must have an individualized case plan that includes "(1) a description of the placement setting, (2) an explanation of the appropriateness of the placement, (3) a description and explanation of the appropriateness of the services aimed at achieving permanence to be provided the child, the parents, and the foster parents, and (4) an explanation of the appropriateness of such services with respect to the child's needs while in foster care" (Musewicz, 1981, p. 728). In addition, this legislation outlines procedures for assessing an individual child's progress through the system. After the child has been in care for six months, his or her situation is to be reviewed, using either court or administrative procedures. Within eighteen months after placement, a dispositional hearing is to be held in order to evaluate the agency's achievement of permanency-planning objectives and to clarify the child's future.

These extensive and detailed guidelines indicate the depth of federal commitment to the need for careful, ongoing assessment of the child's circumstances and for efforts to ensure that he or she will experience continuity. Commitment to permanency principles continues to have major impact on provision of this type of substitute care for children.

Scope

The Select Committee On Children, Youth and Families House of Representatives, in a report dated March 1987, noted that there were 276,000 children in foster care during 1984. Turnover was high. About 180,000 children entered and left during the course of the year. Median length of time in care was 17 months.

The rate of children in substitute care of all kinds declined sharply after passage of the Social Security Act in 1935, confirmation of the potency of the Social Insurance and Public Assurance Programs in maintaining children in their own homes. However, after 1960 there was steady growth in substitute care as a result of increases in family disruption from all causes, and this number peaked in the late 1970s. Based on an analysis of a carefully selected sample of 1.8 million children being offered social services, Shyne and Schroeder (1978) estimated that in March 1977, 395,000 children were in foster family homes (p. 112). This represents a rate of six out of every thousand children, the highest rate of foster family care since we have begun collecting national statistics. A 1977 DHEW estimate placed this figure even higher at 485,000 children (Musewicz, 1981). Claburn and Magura (1977) note that between 1972 and 1976 the rate of children in foster family care in New Jersey increased from 4.4 to 5.2 per 1,000 children.

Recent evidence indicates that foster-family placement rates are declining. Analyzing data from Wisconsin, Becker and Austin (1983) reported that placement decreased by 16 per cent between 1981 and 1982. Reporting findings from 1980 and 1982 national surveys, Gershenson (1983) discovered that in 25 states placement rates had decreased. Whereas Kentucky and New Mexico reported 47 per cent fewer children in care, this proportion dropped by 44 per cent in North Dakota, 43 per cent in North Carolina and 41 per cent in Wyoming.

Whereas some attribute this decline to utilization of placement prevention and permanency-planning efforts, Yoshikami (1984) notes that it predated passage of Public Law 96-272 (p. 105). Extent of reliance on this type of care is, in addition, inconsistent from state to state, and utilization has not diminished in all states. Gershenson (1983) describes sixteen states with increased placement rates, the highest being Ohio with 30 per cent more placements and Louisiana with a 24 per cent increase. Different rates result from variations in available placements and in the relative distribution of economic hardship as well as by systemic inhibitors and incentives that place pressure on the caseworker to maintain the child in his or her own home (Hubbell, 1981, p.99).

The number of children in foster care is, in some ways, deceptive. It denotes the number of children living in foster-family homes on a given day as reported by agencies licensing foster homes. It does not, additionally, give consideration to the turnover factor—the flow of children in and out of foster care. In addition, substitute care figures may reflect the number of children who are receiving federal funds for placement, and they are only a minority of all children in care (Musewicz, 1981). The figures fail to indicate children placed in homes privately or informally by families. Rowe (1980) estimates that in England and Wales, some 11,000 children are placed by their parents without public agency assistance (p. 55). In any one year, then, the number of children served by the foster family care system is likely to be much higher than the official figures—how much higher, nobody really knows.

The trend is toward a clear increase in preference for the use of foster-family care as compared with institutional care for those children needing substitute care. In 1933, 47.2 per cent of the dependent, neglected, and emotionally disturbed children needing substitute care were living in foster-family homes, and 52.8 per cent were placed in institutions. In 1982, 76 per cent of children were in foster families or group homes, and only 16 per cent in institutions (Gershenson, 1983, p. 20).

The group home, defined as a residential facility providing twenty-four-hour care in a group setting for six to twelve children or adolescents, is the most rapidly growing foster-care facility. Whereas foster-family care homes reported a 3 per cent decrease in capacity in 1971–1972, group homes reported a 19 per cent increase in combined capacity during the same period. Despite this rapid increase, only about 7 per cent of children in foster care were living in group homes in 1982 (Gershenson, 1983, p. 20).

Black, Native American, and Hispanic children are greatly overrepresented in foster-family care (Hubbell, 1981; Cox & Cox, 1984). In 1982, 34 per cent of all children in care were black and 7 per cent were Hispanic (Gershenson, 1983, p. 16). The number of black children is particularly high among younger age groups. Reanalyzing national data collected by Shyne and Schroeder, Olsen (1982b) found that Hispanic children are more likely to be placed in group care settings, particularly during their teenage years. Whereas 15 per cent of white teenagers were in group homes, 28 percent of Hispanic children were in these settings (p. 576).

The median age of children in foster-family care is higher now than previously, and most of these children are now 10 years of age or older (Bernstein, Snider, Meezan, 1975; Thomas et al., 1977; Shyne & Schroeder, 1978, Vasaly, 1978;). In New York, the average age of children in care rose from 8.3 in 1969 to 11 years in 1973 (Catalano, 1974) and 11.5 years in 1980 (Cox & Cox, 1984, citing Fanshel & Finch); in Maine it is 14 years (Hornby & Collins, 1981). Whereas the number of young children in care is decreasing, the number of adolescents is on the rise (Becker & Austin, 1983). In Maine, the teenage foster care population increased 10 per cent in 20 years. Adolescents now comprise 56 percent of the foster care caseload in that state (Hornby & Collins, 1981). Whereas some of these youngsters have grown up in care, others enter the system as teenagers (pp. 10–11). The median age of children in foster-family homes is, however, younger than that of children in other forms of substitute care, such as group homes and institutions.

Data collected over the past several years consistently indicate that boys and girls are equally likely to be referred for foster-family care services.

Children coming into substitute care currently are perceived as more difficult to care for than their counterparts earlier in the century. Some one in four of these children is impaired in some way. Nine per cent are emotionally disturbed whereas 11 per cent are retarded (Gershenson, 1983, p. 17).

Foster-family services are used primarily for children who come from homes plagued by poverty. Cox and Cox (1984) conclude that 80–85 per cent have been living in families with single parents and they consider this a "conservative estimate" (p. 192). Data collected in 1981–1982 in Wisconsin find that some two-thirds of these children come from homes with only one parent. Black or Hispanic children are more likely than whites to come from these circumstances (Olsen, 1982b). Cox and Cox (1984) report that more than 70 per cent of parents with children in care are earning less than $5,000 a year, and more than half are receiving public assistance; Wisconsin findings indicate that whereas 46 per cent received AFDC, an additional 25 per cent earned less than $10,000 a year (Becker & Austin, 1983, p. 3). Once again, minority families are more likely than their white counterparts to be struggling to survive under severely depriving financial circumstances. Jenkins and Norman (1975) comment that "poverty was typically a 'necessary' but not 'sufficient' condition for foster care" (p. 13).

Predicting trends in the scope of foster care is difficult because opposing social, professional, and organizational forces impact on the system and its clients. Reduction in birthrates has resulted in a smaller population of children and therefore a reduction in the total population at risk for foster-family care. Pressure to reduce the number of children in care, both by avoiding placement of these children and by their more timely removal from the system, may consolidate this downward trend. However, increased marital disruption and economic dislocation may create new populations of children who, because of their own or their family difficulties, are in need of placement. In addition, the trend toward deinstitutionalization in both mental health and corrections has been accompanied by a tendency to provide community-based foster programs for disturbed and handicapped children. Finally, while utilization of reunification and adoptive services may create alternative homes for a number of children in care, there is still a substantial group that has been in foster care for a number of years and who, because of their personal characteristics or their age, are least likely to be returned to their birth families or to be placed for adoption. These children form a core group for whom long-term foster care will probably remain the most widely used option.

Situations in Which Foster-Family Care Is an Appropriate Resource

Permanency-planning principles dictate that foster-family care is to be utilized only after intensive home-based supportive and supplementary service efforts have failed to assist parents in remediating family circumstances that threaten the health and welfare of their children. In some cases, availability and/or opportunity to provide supportive and supplementary preventive care does not exist, and the worker places the child in care on an emergency basis. In situations in which the child has been abandoned or seriously abused, or where the parent becomes emotionally disturbed and cannot carry out minimal child care responsibilities, this type of substitute care arrangement may be sought. However, even in these circumstances availability of crisis-oriented or respite services might provide some families with sufficient opportunity to coordinate their resources or to plan for some other type of short-term child support (Hubbell, 1981). In some instances, foster family care is utilized because the community has failed to provide specialized programming and the family, having no other available options, must relinquish the child to obtain help.

Studies of the reasons that precipitate the need for foster care have tended to group them into three general categories: parent-related problems, child-related problems, and environmental circumstances (Sauber & Jenkins, 1966; Shyne, 1969; Vasaly, 1978; Shyne & Schroeder, 1978; Hubbell, 1981; Gershenson, 1983; Becker & Austin, 1983). Parent-related problems are described as precipitating factors in some 75–80 per cent of all foster-family placement cases. These problems include neglect and abuse of children, abandonment, physical or mental illness, marital conflict, substance abuse, or imprisonment. Jenkins and Norman (1975) distinguish between "socially appropriate reasons for placement," including physical illness, mental illness, and emotional disturbance of the child and "socially unacceptable reasons," which include neglect, "unwillingness, or inability to continue care, abandonment, or family dysfunction" (pp. 14–15). When children are placed for socially unacceptable reasons, parents tend to feel more angry at and less supported by the child welfare agency.

Some typical examples of parent-related placement situations follow.

> I felt very tired and sick, and I went to a hospital in my neighborhood where they told me I need to be hospitalized immediately since I had hepatitis. I told them I had no one to take care of my children, and the doctor took me to Social Service, and the children were placed. I have no friends here in New York, and the only one to take care of my children was my mother-in-law and she was in Puerto Rico [Sauber & Jenkins, 1966, p. 82.]
>
> Dona who is 12, came into foster care after her father was put in prison. Her mother had died six years before, and Dona had been living with first one relative and then another since her mother's death. When Dona's father was convicted of armed robbery, she was living with friends of her father. They were not able to care for her during her father's imprisonment, so they asked the agency to find a foster placement for her [Marr, 1976, p. 49].

Child-related problems provide the primary impetus for placement in 15–20 per cent of the cases. The child may be mentally retarded, delinquent, have physical or emotional handicaps, or display aggressive or other problemmatic behavior in the home, school, or community. Fanshel (1982) notes that "even where children required placement away from their homes because of adjustment difficulties, the inability of the parents to be effective in their efforts to impose discipline was usually an important causal factor in the situation which made placement necessary" (p. 8).

A child-related problem, resulting in the need for foster-family care follows:

> Timmy came into foster care at age five. He was the youngest child in a family of seven children. Timmy's father rarely had a steady job but took odd jobs around the community, which usually lasted for short periods of time. Timmy's mother recognized that Timmy had special needs even when he was a small baby, but she had

little time or resources to spend providing for those special needs. By the time he was five, Timmy was a difficult child to manage because of his hyperactive behavior that kept him constantly moving from one activity to another. He hardly could speak and usually had to be helped to eat and dress. Most of the time the other children ignored or taunted Timmy, for he was often in their way.

The social service agency became aware of the problem when Timmy's father applied for financial assistance. After investigating the home situation, the caseworker suggested that Timmy might need special help and asked that his parents agree to place him in a foster home. As both parents could no longer manage or cope with his behavior, they readily agreed [Marr, 1976, p. 41].

Child welfare workers cite environmental stress and deprivation as primary precipitating factors in a more limited number of instances (3–5 per cent of the cases). Serious financial need, inadequate housing, chronic unemployment, or lack of sufficient social support may prevent a parent from appropriately caring for a child. Fanshel (1982) discovered that environmental conditions also have significant impact on the child's remaining in foster care. In his New York City sample, in 20 per cent of the cases where a mother or father figure was available to the child, inadequate housing prevented the child's return home. Inadequate income contributed as a major or minor factor in one-third of the cases, while unemployment or work-related problems were a major issue in 7 per cent (p. 150). In addition, a significant number of parents, approximately one in three, had difficulty managing the limited amount of funds they did have.

In many cases it is actually a combination of circumstances—involving an adult struggling with severe disability, who has extremely limited financial, personal, and social resources who finds himself or herself unable to care for children whose needs sometimes make them especially demanding and difficult to deal with—that precipitates the need for placement. "Although it is usually a specific crisis that brings children into social agency foster care, during the year prior to placement these families by and large were functioning marginally and had experienced difficulties so severe that it might have been anticipated that further stress could not be tolerated" (Sauber & Jenkins, 1966, p. 111). "The overall picture of the retrospective year prior to placement shows marginal families without sufficient resources to sustain themselves in the community when additional pressures or problems are added to their pre-existing burdens" (p. 61). Whereas workers emphasize the role played by parental disability in these families, the parents themselves stress the importance of the child's behavior or situational stress (Phillips et al., 1971, p. 10; Jones, Neuman, & Shyne, 1976, p. 32).

Referrals come from a variety of sources and are related to the nature of the difficulty. The most frequent initiators of foster care are the parents themselves and/or close relatives in instances of parents' physical or mental illness or inability to care for the child because of social stress, and when the child's behavior makes it difficult to live at home. The police and the courts more frequently initiate placement in cases of neglect and/or abuse.

The nature of foster family care suggests that it is a feasible resource for the child who has some capacity to participate in and contribute to normal family and community living. Such care would be inappropriate when a child presents handicapping conditions of such severity that a family would be taxed beyond its limits trying to care for this child, or when, because the child seriously violates social norms, the community itself will not tolerate his or her behavior. In the past, it was considered preferable to institutionalize children when their parents objected to the use of foster care or when they were part of a sibling group and it was difficult to find a single home for them. These criteria are not considered acceptable reasons for refusing the child a foster family experience today. Even in instances in which children have serious reservations about entering foster care because they feel divided loyalty to parent figures, it is more appropriate to place the child in a foster family setting and to provide casework services to help the child and foster parents make a mutually satisfactory adjustment.

The present feeling is that all children under six requiring substitute care should be offered foster-family care. The need for continuous, close parenting supposedly dictates this. The situation of adolescents is more complex. Some teenagers, struggling to develop independence from adult caretakers, may find the more impersonal atmosphere of a group setting more congenial (Janchill, 1983). However, despite their struggles, most of these youngsters continue to value and need the support and guidance provided by parenting figures, and a foster-family setting is, therefore, preferable for them.

Using assessments of caseworkers and foster parents, in-depth interviews with adolescents, and independent case reviews, Hornby and Collins (1981) found that, compared to their younger counterparts, teenagers were more likely to be in care because of their own personal difficulties—behavior problems, delinquency, emotional illness, or substance abuse. Once in care, they were more likely than younger children to experience multiple moves, to be placed in foster care before or after being in residential treatment and to remain in one foster family home for short periods of time. Whereas foster parents and social workers described 29 per cent of younger children as difficult to place, 49 per cent of the adolescent group was perceived this way (pp. 12–14).

These data indicate the special demands that teenagers make on their foster-care providers. Social workers describe availability of suitable foster families as one of the most significant factors influencing placement decisions for children in this age group (Melotte, 1979, p.56). Nevertheless, evidence suggests that, under appropriate circumstances, foster parents can be highly effective with even the most difficult adolescents. Over a five-year period, some two hundred of these individuals were placed by the Kent Project in foster-family settings in Great Britain. The program stressed provision of adequate pay for foster families, use of ongoing group support for foster parents, and the use of written placement contracts that the adolescent, birth parents, and foster parents participated in developing (Hazel, 1981; Hazel, Schmedes, Korshin, 1983). At the end of the demonstration period, almost three-quarters of this group were functioning very well or in a generally positive fashion and only 15 per cent were considered doing worse or in "disastrous condition." (See also Rosenblum, 1977; Hazel, 1981). Increases in the average age of children coming into and being maintained in substitute care indicate the need for further development of family resources that can meet the special needs of this client group.

Whether or not to provide a child with foster family care is one of the most complex decisions with which the worker is faced (Melotte, 1979), and it is one workers do not easily reach. Requests for foster-care services on the part of clients are generally referred for further study by agencies, and placement requests are more frequently rejected than are requests for other types of services (Haring, 1975, Table 16). Phillips et al. (1971), in a study of 216 cases involving 455 children judged to be in need of service in four agencies, found that, in by far the majority of instances (73% of the cases), home-based care was offered. Placement was made available in only 16 per cent of cases in which families sought help with a parent-child problem (p. 12).

The placement decision requires an assessment of (1) the danger to the child's biological, social, and emotional development of the current living situation, (2) the competence of the parents and their motivation and capacity to make necessary changes, (3) the formal and informal support system that might be mobilized to help in maintaining the child in the home without damage, and (4) the strengths and the vulnerability of the child that determine the level of stress with which he or she can cope without adverse effects.

In their research, Phillips et al. (1971) discovered that client placement families "evidenced greater social and psychological pathology than own home cases" (p. 51), so that "placement children were more likely to receive *grossly* inadequate care in the areas of feeding, supervision, and guidance, warmth and affection, protection from abuse and concern regarding schooling" (p. 44) if care in their own home was continued. The decision to place seems to have been a considered deliberate decision in terms of the best interests of the child, "likely to be taken only if there is evidence of considerable deviance or pathology in the child, his parents, or his living conditions" (p. 87).

Studies comparing the mothers of children in foster care with mothers in comparable circumstances who are caring for their children at home find them to be far more overwhelmed by responsibility for the family, to show emotional disturbance and low-impulse control and to lack the motivation or the desire to keep the family together (Shinn, 1968, p. 119; O'Rourke, 1976). Where fathers are present, they are more frequently seen as inadequate parents (Phillips et al., 1971). Based on research evidence and practitioner impressions, Fanshel (1982) notes that in most of these cases "the parents show massive disability in their functioning and present a considerable challenge as targets of treatment intervention" (p. 8). (See also Cautley, 1980.) There are also likely to be fewer interpersonal resources such as relatives, friends, or neighbors to whom the families could turn for help. Placement is less likely when the mother is concerned about the child and motivated to attempt to change. Studies tend to show that most children who are placed come from families who were provided some type of home-based service prior to the child's removal.

Detailed case-by-case analysis of a sample of 1,000 records of the 1.8 million children offered public social services in March 1977 showed that two thirds of the group were receiving service in their own home. The goal of this service that was most frequently reported was "strengthening of the family to lessen need for placement" (Shyne & Schroeder, 1978, p. 60). Most of these children were also receiving income maintenance and other supportive services under AFDC. Jenkins and Norman (1975) claim, "The much maligned AFDC support probably is the most successful preventive program for keeping children out of foster care" (p. 133).

Jenkins and Norman posed the following question to 125 mothers of children in foster-family care. "Looking back at everything that has happened would you say that placement of your child was absolutely necessary, very necessary, somewhat necessary, or not necessary at all?" Forty-seven per cent considered the placement to be "absolutely necessary," 17 per cent said it was "very necessary," 13 per cent "somewhat necessary," and 23 per cent said placement was "not necessary at all" (p. 111). The negative responses were primarily contributed by those mothers for whom the placement was involuntary (p. 52).

A review by experienced child-welfare workers of the record material in 1,250 cases representing a sample of 29,000 in substitute care in New York City found that in 92.7 per cent, the record reader supported the decision to place the child (Bernstein, Snider, Meezan, 1975). A "large majority of the workers . . . closest to the actual decision" interviewed in a longitudinal study of 624 children entering placement in 1966 "thought the placement absolutely or very necessary" (Shapiro, 1976, p. 58; see also Yoshikami, 1984). When interviewed regarding their perception of the experience, foster children themselves thought the placement was a desirable alternative to their own home situations (Jacobson & Cockerum, 1976).

Sometimes, foster care workers have insufficient and incomplete information about important aspects of family life and agency standards and governmental regulations are too vague to provide helpful decision-making guidelines (Hubbell, 1981). The weightiness of the consequences of their decision exacerbates its difficulty for the worker. "Willingness to gamble upon the parent's restraint can lead to grim tragedy if the judgment is wrong. On the other hand, placing the child in foster care when the home is essentially safe is a costly solution for society and may not really serve the child's welfare" (Fanshel, 1981, p. 685). Faced with this dilemma, many workers choose to be cautious and place the child, preferring the risk of discontinuity in parent-child relations.

The difficulties in making "correct" decisions in alternatives of such complexity are illustrated by the low level of agreement among highly experienced practitioners. Three such judges were offered detailed protocols of families at risk for placement and asked to decide independently on the choice of placing the child or offering in-home service to the family. Although the level of agreement between the three judges was considerably better than chance, there was "far from complete agreement"; complete agreement was achieved on requests in under half the decisions. (Phillips, et al., 1971, p. 83; see also Briar, 1963). Using data from 8,610 confirmed child abuse reports in North Carolina, Runyan et al. (1981) assessed a number of factors that they expected to be correlated with the decision to remove the child from the home. Although some factors such as experiencing a severe injury requiring hospitalization were associated with this outcome as expected, many others such as the presence of severe maltreated children in a family, were not. The authors discovered that highly potent indicators for removal included the type of referral resource and the community in which the abuse occurred. When the courts or police initiated the police report, the child was far more likely to be removed than when the referral came from other sources. This relationship held, even when controlling for seriousness of the abuse. Certain communities were also highly likely to utilize placement services "Individual counties placed from 0–48% of the children reported." (p. 707). Racial and economic factors did not explain these differences.

Rapp (1982) assessed the impact of availability of services on the worker's decision to utilize home-based or substitute care. Using case simulations, he obtained placement decisions from 538 caseworkers. Some were randomly provided with a list of preventive services they were to assume would be available to the families, while others were not given this information. Rapp notes that "virtually no association was found between the decision to place and the experimental condition of optimal availability of services" (p. 23).

It has been contended that a more concerned and focused effort to salvage the home for the child would substantially reduce the rate of placements (Sauber & Jenkins, 1966; Shyne, 1969; Gruber, 1973; Gambril & Wiltse, 1974; Maybanks &

Bryce, 1979; Bryce & Lloyd, 1981). The movement of children into substitute care is sometimes perceived as a political act "to rescue poor children from their parents as opposed to providing money and social services to children in their own homes" (Mandell, 1973, p. 36; Meyer, 1985).

The Child Welfare League of America study, *A Second Chance for Families,* attempted to test this hypothesis (Jones & Neuman, Shyne, 1976). The study compares the typical day-to-day efforts of child welfare workers with those of a special unit of workers given access to special resources, such as day care and homemaker service, and working with a limited caseload. Both the regular workers and the special-unit workers faced the task of serving children, who had been identified as at high risk for foster-care placement. Some 549 families and 992 children were involved in the study. The outcome of interest to us at this point, is whether or not the special efforts and special resources were able to salvage more homes for children. The effort did make a difference, but although statistically significant, the difference was very modest. In 60 per cent of the cases, children were removed from the home by the regular workers; the special intensive unit was forced to place 52 per cent.

There is no question that in some percentage of cases greater commitment to retaining the child in the home or to providing the family with more adequate resources could have prevented placement. There is a residual group of children, however, who would still need placement; even if the best and most adequate of such services were available.

Recruitment, Assessment, and Selection of Foster-Family Homes

One essential resource of this service is, of course, the foster home. Since homes have to be recruited, assessed, and ultimately selected for a particular child, a great deal of agency work is devoted to each of these responsibilities.

Recruitment

Recruitment involves a program of interpretation to the public of the need for foster homes for children and the satisfactions to be derived from fostering a child. All mass communication media have been used by agencies in recruitment efforts: newspaper ads, radio, television, billboards, and placards in buses and subway trains. On occasion, advertisements have been supplemented by presentations before church groups, PTA groups, women's clubs, and so on. Experienced foster parents are asked to participate in these campaigns, since they can convey a realistic conception of foster care.

Such activity is reinforced by the visible enhancement of the symbol of the foster parent. The mayor proclaims a Foster Parent Week, and an award is given to a couple selected as the Foster Parents of the Year. All of this activity develops a "climate of awareness" of the need for foster parents in the community.

Effective recruitment requires an understanding of the forces that stimulate individuals to take a child who is a stranger into their home. Motives for taking on the foster parent role are both altruistic and personal. Foster parents are most likely to point to "love of children, desire to help someone else, and interest in children's well-being" (Hampson & Tavormina, 1980, pp. 109–110).

Children of different ages may appeal to different patterns of motivation. This is confirmed by Fanshel's (1961) interviews with 101 foster couples. "A rather basic dichotomy appeared in the study between those foster parents who cared primarily for infants and those who cared for older children": those who cared for infants were more oriented to private gratifications ("enjoying the presence of a cuddly baby in our home"; "I like the affection I get from children"); those who took older children were oriented toward social gratifications ("knowing I am doing something useful for the community"; "I like helping the unfortunate, downtrodden people") (Fanshel, 1961, p. 18).

This dichotomy was less evident in a more recent study of foster parents of adolescents (Rosenblum, 1977). Although some community-oriented satisfactions are cited as motives for fostering, the principle more frequently emphasized motives related to knowing that one was able to help a particular child, satisfactions in the affection one received from the child, and the opportunity of being able to meet the challenge of a difficult task through the use of homemaker skills.

Wakeford's (1963) study of foster parents in England suggests that motivation is related to class differences. Interviews with 66 foster parents and a group of 148 controls selected at random from among nonfostering married couples showed that the relationship between socioeconomic class and foster parenthood is not related to income but to the higher value and prestige accorded the maternal role in working-class families. The foster mother accepts fostering "as an alternative to maximizing income" by working outside the home. "She is more family-oriented than average. She values the home, there she finds most of her satisfactions and employs most of her skills. There she is in her element." Fanshel (1966) and Babcock (1965) found that many foster mothers came from families with many children, had highly developed homemaking skills, and were positively oriented toward child-care and home-centered activities. Babcock notes that foster mothers "regarded the role of mothering as a main task in life, a task they expect to enjoy" (p. 373). They had little interest in a paid job outside the home. Adamson (1973) also found that foster mothers were home- and child-care-oriented, "house proud," and preferred domestic activities, belonging to few, if any, outside organizations.

Recent data confirm the continued appeal of foster parenting for working-class families. Studying 386 families who were caring for children in the New York City area, Fanshel (1982) found that 44 per cent of the foster mothers and 46 per cent of the fathers had not completed high school. Almost half of the fathers worked as laborers, service workers, or operatives, and only one in four functioned in a white-collar or professional role. Most of these families lived in "modest material circumstances" (P. 227). Data from a Virginia survey (Hampson & Tavormina, 1980), constituting 90 per cent of the active foster parents in a particular region, also point to their limited educational attainment. The average income of the 34 participating families was $794 a month (p. 109).

This traditional picture may be changing to some extent, however. Using Holland's Vocational Preference Inventory, Wiehe (1983) contrasted the personality characteristics of younger foster mothers with those of mothers over forty. Older respondents were "more dependent, less assertive, and adventurous." They were also more traditional than mothers from a control group of nonfoster parents. Wiehe argues that recruitment efforts must be cognizant of the changing attitudes and values of this younger group.

Whereas gratifications obtained through implementing the satisfying role of parent and through in-home employment in a "job" that calls for special child-care skills are the most potent motivational attractions to foster parenting, other, more personal forces also propel individuals to assume this responsibility (Cautley, 1980). Most applicants respond to agency appeals out of some need of their own. "In the wish to serve there is the need to serve." This in no way implies a derogation of foster parents' readiness to accept a child or the capacity to do a good job. Even a desire to find a "replacement" or a companion for one's own child does not necessarily imply failure. A study by Jenkins (1965) of 97 foster homes showed that parents expressing such motives were frequently successful (p. 212). If their needs are complementary to those of the child, the child can be provided the best kind of foster family experience.

Individuals who consider personal motives their primary or exclusive reasons for taking this step may, however, find themselves in more difficulty than those who combine personal needs with more altruistic, child-oriented objectives. Whereas nineteen Virginia foster parents had cared for children on a long-term basis, thirteen had had children for short stays (less than 14 months) or had terminated the child's placement (Hampson & Tavormina, 1980). "Those mothers who had maintained foster placements for two or more years had a significantly higher proportion of 'social motivation', whereas the majority of the others reported more 'private' motives" (p. 110).

Efforts have been made to enlist the cooperation of the black, Hispanic (Delgado, 1978), or American Indian community in recruiting foster homes for minority-group children. Bilingual staff and staff identified with the community enhances recruitment possibilities.

People who have "been there" have greater credibility for the applicant. Friends and relatives who are foster parents develop a social network concerned with interests around fostering and raise the consciousness of others about foster care. Assessing the process whereby 106 foster families from England and Wales eventually had children placed in their homes, Palmer (1981) discovered that 33 per cent had a close friend or relative who was a foster parent, and 37 per cent had close associates who were adopters. One in three foster families had also known substitute parents while they were growing up (p. 42).

Studies of the interest of foster-care recruitment show a high attrition rate among the families that express initial interest. Usually, less than 10 per cent of the original group are licensed and very rarely more than 20 per cent (Ougheltree, 1957; DeCocq, 1962; Glassberg, 1965; Vick, 1967). The largest percentage withdraw voluntarily, a smaller percentage is rejected often for very clear and unambiguous reasons, such as overage or poor health.

Given the shrinking pool of potential foster-care applicants and the large number who express some interest but who fail to complete the application process, agencies find that more intensive recruitment efforts are required. Using sophisticated marketing strategies and multidimensional outreach efforts, agencies have successfully developed a sufficient number of homes for waiting children. For greater effectiveness, multiagency and multistate recruitment efforts have also been organized (Radinsky, 1963; Pasztor, 1985). Evidence suggests that the mass media, particularly television, may be far more effective than printed material in reaching the widest possible audience (Palmer, 1981).

Eight years of recruitment experience led Pasztor (1985) to comment:

> Recruitment themes usually reflected an "open your home and your heart" message, implying that love is all it takes to be a foster parent. Recruitment posters tended to picture a young female waif with blonde hair and sad eyes. The underlying

message was that this obviously uncared for child needed someone to replace her uncaring parents and that the children needing homes were primarily very young, white, and female. The NOVA Recruitment Model requires an agency commitment to upgrading and clarifying the role of foster parents as team members in permanency planning. It uses the approach of "selling the job," not the child. Recruitment posters and accompanying themes show agency foster parents who are Black, White, Hispanic, single, coupled, younger, and older. The message highlights positive role identification and/or family-focused services (p. 195).

She argues that effective recruitment requires active participation of applicants in the decision to take on this responsibility as well as ongoing training and support both before and after a child is placed. This approach has led to higher applicant retention, decreased disruptions, and development of more homes for hard-to-place children (p. 198).

Foster home care is enhanced not only by recruiting more homes but also by reducing the turnover of homes already in the system. "Of all licensed foster homes in San Francisco in 1970, less than one-fifth were still active three years late" (Boyd & Remy, 1978, p. 276). Following the careers of sixty-four families who initially expressed interest in becoming foster parents, Soothill and Derbyshire (1982) found that seven had moved away during the project period. Of the remainder, 21 per cent terminated their foster-care role in the first year, 26 per cent in the second year, 11 per cent in the third year, and 23 per cent in the fourth year (p. 39). Analyzing the reasons why these families withdrew, the researchers discovered that three major factors were operating. Particularly in the first two years families whom the agencies felt were functioning relatively poorly were gradually eased out of their responsibilities. Another group chose to withdraw because personal circumstances (pregnancy, illness, or adoption) interfered with their ability to fully commit time and energy to a foster child.

A third group, which included some of the families who officially withdrew for other reasons, included parents whose experiences with foster children were incongruent with their expectations or who found caring for a particular child very painful. Describing three such families, who had cared for 32 children before abandoning their fostering role, the authors comment:

> . . . they all had a fostering experience in the previous year which had upset them quite significantly. Despite some efforts by social workers to recover the situation, the damage had been done and they were lost to fostering as a result of a bad experience with a placement rather than the stated reasons, which were almost certainly used as an excuse to retire from the fostering scene. It is distressing to record how these . . . (parents) could not cope with rather familiar situations in fostering, namely the notion of rehabilitation to the natural parents in two cases and the possibility of ridicule by neighbors in the other case (p. 40).

In their examination of the differences between short- and long-term fostering, Hampson and Tavormina (1980) found similar stresses operating. "Many complaints centered around childrearing problems such as discipline and the child's behavioral problems, relations with the child's own family, and disruptions within the foster family after the child arrived" (p. 110).

Stressful relationships with the foster care caseworker can also precipitate premature retirement from the fostering role. Hampson and Tavormina (1980) note that in their sample "the most frequent complaint dealt with case management. Eleven mothers indicated that they were unable to communicate well with welfare caseworkers or that the constant changeover in caseworkers was extremely trying. These mothers believed that their jobs could be made easier if their current caseworker were more available and if there was greater continuity of care when a personnel turnover occurred" (p. 110).

The child's relatives comprise one particularly beneficial recruitment resource for a substantial number of children in care (Project Craft, 1980, p. VI–39). Many agencies designate relatives as first choice substitute care resources since placement in the homes of other family members provides the child with much greater sense of continuity than does placement in the home of strangers. Placement with relatives was stimulated by a 1979 Supreme Court ruling that they must be provided with the same federally sponsored foster care benefits as are nonrelative foster families. However, in instances in which the child has resided with relatives prior to agency involvement with the case, foster care payments may still not be provided (Hubbell, 1981).

Social workers have been accused of ignoring the possibility of utilizing kin as a possible placement resource. Lack of sensitivity, particularly to minority group family patterns, and bias in favor of the nuclear family, supposedly accounts for such indifference. However, a study of the utilization by courts in North Carolina shows that in 62 per cent of protective service cases relatives were included in treatment planning (Herskovitz, Kelly, & Ramsey, 1986). Since in most cases the court disposition was based on information provided by social workers assigned to the case, the study indicates a considerable awareness and acceptance of kin resources by social workers. Research has also suggested that in instances in which the child moves to the home of a grandparent, uncle, or other relative, reunification with birth parents is as likely to occur and does so after approximately the same length of time as placement with strangers (Grinnell & Jung, 1981).

Assessment

The agency has the grave responsibility of finding the best possible substitute home for the child needing care. A detailed study of all applicants is necessary, not only because the agency feels an ethical and professional responsibility to children and their natural parents but also because it has a legal responsibility to the community. Foster homes are licensed in most states, and the agency must certify that the home meets licensing requirements.

Some preliminary screening and selection usually proceed on the basis of the objective criteria outlined in state licensing standards (Gross & Bussard, 1970). Single- or two-parent families are usually accepted although married couples are preferred. The state requires that applicants be young enough and healthy enough to provide adequate care and that they have income sufficient to meet their own needs. The state also stipulates that the home provide adequate space for a child, that it meet adequate sanitary and safety standards, and that it be located in a community that offers sufficient academic, health, religious, and recreational facilities.

The more difficult aspects of assessment involve the socioemotional factors that are thought to be desirable in a foster home. These are assessed during a series of interviews with the prospective foster parents, conducted both in the office and in the home. An effort is made to determine the origin of the applicants' interest in foster care, their expectations, and their experience as parents or (if childless) with children generally. Also of interest are the satisfactions and problems they experienced in rearing their own children, the developmental history of both husband and wife, the history of their marriage and their current marital interaction, the changes they anticipate in the organization of the home and in the interpersonal relationships of family members as a result of the introduction of another child and their preferences in foster children. If there are children in the home, some effort is made to obtain their reaction to the parents' plan to accept foster children. When applicants are single, assessment includes evaluation of sources of significant social support and of the applicant's capacity to integrate child-care demands with his or her personal needs for intimacy and for adult companionship.

The social worker also explores with the applicants their attitudes regarding visits by the child's birth parents, their attitudes toward parents who place their children in substitute care, and their probable reaction to the child's eventual departure. Because the agency has a continuing responsibility for the child, some attempt is made to assess the applicants' willingness to work cooperatively with the agency.

Although in the past there were distinct boundaries drawn between foster and adoptive parent roles, today they have become much less distinguishable. Although foster families are expected to care for children only on a short-term basis, many find that their children remain in their homes for several years. These families have difficulty distinguishing their child-care responsibilities from those of other parents (Holman, 1980). In addition, their relationship to the children in their care can, at some point, shift dramatically, since, if these children become available for adoption, foster parents are usually considered primary applicants.

In this situation, applicants must discuss with the caseworker their willingness to raise a child whom, on the one hand they may have to relinquish after developing a close relationship with, or whom, on the other hand they may be asked to care for on a long-term basis. Caseworkers assessing suitability of applicants have an equally problematic time clarifying expectations with regard to the applicant's ability to deal effectively with birth parents. On the one hand preparation of the child for reunification may require that foster parents work in a supportive way with birth families; if, however, the child is made available for adoption, the foster family will not be required to carry out this responsibility (Proch, 1980, 1981; Holman, 1980; Pasztor, 1985).

Attempts have been made to explicate the image of the "good" foster parent, a concept used by workers as a generalized standard against which applicants are assessed (Wolins, 1963). The image incorporates many of the middle-class virtues of "planfulness" and responsibility and tends to reflect attitudes similar to those held by the social worker making the assessment (Dingman et al., 1962).

Another approach to developing valid assessment criteria utilizes factors that distinguish the "successful" foster parent from the less successful one, or that distinguish the accepted from the rejected applicant (Parker, 1966; George, 1970; Napier, 1972; Soothill & Derbyshire, 1982). Neither age nor socioeconomic situation seems to be a sensitive indication of "success," although regular income at a level that permits care of the child without strain is desirable. The developmental history of "successful" foster parents shows wide variation (Cautley et al., 1966).

Studies showed that the more acceptable foster homes tended to be more child-centered and concerned with understanding the child (Colvin, 1962; Kinter & Otto, 1964), were able to maintain a desired balance between permissiveness and control (Paulson, Grossman, & Shapiro, 1974), and were able to maintain better relationships with the natural parents (Shapiro, 1976, p. 55).

Cautley (1980) followed the experience of 145 first-time foster parents over an eighteen-month period after placement. Ratings of foster-parent success were associated with the "ability of foster parents to cope with the common problems of school-age children—prompt and appropriate handling of problems without harshness or excessive discipline and with an understanding of the reasons for such behavior" (Cautley & Aldridge, 1975, p. 53). Familiarity with and competence in child-care and childrearing tasks were associated with success. The foster father's readiness to accept and cooperate with the agency's ongoing participation in the placement, his flexibility, and his concern for the foster child's needs as against his own needs were positively related to the success of the placement, as were the foster mother's ability to individualize the child and her having been the oldest of a number of siblings. High formal religiosity on the part of the parents correlated negatively with success.

A study of sixty families showed that "successful" foster homes, as defined by social workers, were those that were more accepting of the child's behavior and more tolerant of the child's failings (Rowe, 1976). This finding is further confirmed by responses of a sample of one hundred children in foster care (Bush, Gordon & LeBailly, 1977). They depicted the good foster home as one that provided love, care, understanding, and respect for their freedom laced with concerned control.

Foster children describe the good foster parent as "a good-hearted person, one who would let you speak how you feel. Someone who would sit down and find out what you want"; "People who care and would like to help you. There are a lot of times when I goof off bad and they could send me away, but they didn't"; "A good foster parent is someone who shows you the same kind of affection a real parent would"; "someone who is strict enough so you won't get into trouble but lenient so you could have some fun." The standard of material comfort in the foster home, which was generally better than that available in the child's own home, was also a source of satisfaction.

In general, the research supports the sensible suppositions that it is good to select people who have familiarity with children and who have developed parenting skills, who can empathize with, understand, accept, and individualize the child, who have tolerance for child behavior that is different from the behavior the parents are familiar with, and who have a family life with sufficient stability and internal strength to withstand the burden that the foster child imposes, particularly at the beginning of the placement.

The NOVA Model (Pasztor, 1985) is a recruitment device specifically designed to seek out these types of individuals and to encourage them to pursue their desire to become foster parents. Using a group format and experiential content, worker and applicants have opportunities to evaluate how well they can resolve conflicts with children, support the child's ongoing relationship with birth family members, and deal with children and parents who are angry or sad (p. 197).

This research suggests that agencies pay more attention to foster fathers because they play a significant role in determining placement outcome. It also suggests that the applicants' willingness to work collaboratively with agencies is an important criterion for carrying out this role. Ultimately, however, some of foster placement success or failure depends on the particular child—his or her responsiveness, age, ability to adapt, and behavior—and on the nature of the particular interaction child and parents establish with each other. As Anderson (1982) notes, it is only when the child is placed that family assessment moves from the theoretical to the practical level. Fanshel (1966) notes:

Many of the foster parents in this study showed a fairly broad range of behavior with the foster children placed with them. One kind of child could evoke a positive, nurturing kind of response; a child with different characteristics could bring forth almost rejecting behavior from the same foster parent. Although one would expect foster parents who reveal strong ego structures and sound superego values to do uniformly with most children placed with them, their parental capacity must nonetheless be seen as a variable phenomenon. The aim of high-level child welfare practice should be to maximize the parental potential of foster parents through the placement of children who can evoke a positive response in them and the provision of professional casework support to foster parents in order to help them withstand the negative and often seemingly unchangeable behavior of upset foster children [p.162].

Some foster parents reflect the more traditional picture of a home-centered family seeking the temporary care of a child to continue gratification previously experienced in raising their own children, with little need to see foster payments as income supplements. Other parents are interested in "long-term, quasi-adoptive placement." Still others are interested in placements of variable permanence but ones where economic returns for fostering are important complementary considerations to gratification in child care. There are other different configurations of motivations and needs. The group of children needing foster care is also differentiated, with some needing short-term care, some needing long-term care, some requiring greater agency payments to compensate foster parents, and some needing only agency payment covering maintenance. Appeals to different groups may focus on the kinds of children available that most squarely meets their needs.

Efforts have been made to develop systematic procedures for more objective assessment of foster-parent applicants. Touhatos and Lindholm (1977) have developed a Potential for Foster Parenthood Scale distributed by the National Foster Parents' Association. The scale includes a variety of items, some of which require considerable sophisticated interpretation—items such as "gives impression of being a caring person," "is adaptable in expectations of children," "has capacity to undertake the responsibilities entailed in working with a social agency."

Somewhat more attuned to the realities of the assessment procedure as experienced by the worker, Cautley and Lichtenstein (1974) have developed a manual concerned with the selection of foster parents. This manual provides an interview outline for separate interviews with the mother and the father, covering most of the essential items already noted. In addition, however, vignettes of typical foster-parent problems are presented for applicant reaction and discussion. The manual provides a coding outline to help the worker interpret applicant responses to the questions raised in the interviews. This code enables the worker to assess whether a response does indicate, for instance, whether a parent is likely to be child-centered, supportive, and flexible in childrearing and whether the marital interaction indicates a good relationship.

Assessment standards need to be flexibly applied and adapted so that they fit the circumstances of the applicant. Applicants may need the active help of the agency in meeting minimum standards, even to the point of agency support in improving their homes so that more and safer space is available.

Agencies make an effort to be flexible in assessing applicants and in applying licensing requirements. Foster-parent licensing requirements regarding the mother's employment, the age of the foster parents, and the need for religious affiliations are the ones most frequently waived in practice. There is currently a greater willingness to place foster children in a one-parent home and to accept low-income couples as foster parents. In New York City, for example, Fanshel (1982) reports that 18 per cent of foster parents are single, and only one in five earn more than $1,100 a month (pp. 223, 227).

Agencies still, for the most part, prefer to select what is considered a "typical" family—a nuclear, heterosexual couple living in fairly comfortable economic circumstances and espousing middle-class values. The greater the extent to which families deviate from this model—by being homosexual or single for example—the more reluctant and anxious agencies are about selecting them as homes for children (Petersen & Pierce, 1974; Thomas, 1977). In 1984, two children placed with a gay couple after careful agency screening were removed on orders of Massachusetts Governor Dukakis after a story about the placement appeared in the *Boston Globe*. The National Association of Social Workers Massachusetts Chapter joined a class-action suit against the governor for subsequently ordering the State Department of Social Services to refuse foster care applications from gays and lesbians, however well qualified (*N.A.S.W. News,* May, 1985).

The assessment process is structured by the caseworker, and typically involves the applicant's participation in both group meetings and in individual agency-based and home-based interviews with the worker. Group meetings have been used as a screening device. Some agencies, facing the need for a sizable additional number of foster homes, have experimented with self-approval methods (SAM). All foster-parent applicants are automatically approved and licensed after participating in five mandatory training sessions and one home visit. Interviews with foster-care workers and a comparison of foster parents recruited through SAM and more traditional procedures found that the self-approved method recruits were of "high quality" and in some respects more adequately prepared for the role than traditionally recruited parents (Freund, 1976).

In addition to participating in interviews and home visits, applicants are required to provide references who can comment on their character and parenting abilities. Routine checks are conducted to determine that these individuals have no history as physical or sexual abusers. Applicants are also required to complete a medical examination to establish that they are physically capable of caring for a child and have no infectious diseases.

Once these procedures and requirements have been completed, the family is issued a license that certifies their home is authorized to accept children for foster care. In many states, the license indicates the number of children that the home may accept at any one time. Generally, no more than four older children are allowed, with not more than two under the age of two. A license is usually issued for a one-year period. At the end of that time, the agency must review the situation and relicense the home.

Following recruitment, assessment, and approval, an agreement is signed with the agency as part of the licensing procedure. A study (Festinger, 1974) of such agreements used by state departments of social services throughout the United States notes some uniformities. Agreements generally includes a statement of the foster parents' responsibilities for caring for the foster child, helping with the agency's plan for the child, and keeping the agency informed of accidents, illnesses, or changes in the child's location, such as vacations. It restricts the rights of the foster parents to accept other children or to take action for the adoption of the foster child without agency permission. Procedures regarding the biological parents' visits are spelled out. A key aspect of the agreement, appearing in almost all contracts, is the requirement that foster parents agree to the removal of the child at the request of the agency and the relinquishment of contact with the child.

Applicants who are uninterested in foster care or who fail to meet requirements may either withdraw themselves at some point during the application process or may be formally rejected by the worker. Applicant withdrawal accounts for by far the largest proportion of attrition cases (Soothill & Derbyshire, 1981).

Formal rejection situations require that the workers produce a written document stating their reasons for refusing the family a license. Soothill and Derbyshire (1981) found that these cases tended to fall into two categories—those who appeared to meet agency standards but who, upon closer assessment really did not; and those who were poor candidates from the beginning but who insisted that they complete the application process.

Anderson (1982) argues that providing the family with specific reasons for rejection makes this experience easier to tolerate

> For example, a worker's responses to a couple who were quite belligerent reflects this attitude. "We thought you wanted a child, but we weren't sure you wanted an agency. We need people who like working with agencies." (The couple agreed with the agency's assessment). Or to a couple who had a very low score on the Cautley Questionnaire and showed concrete thinking. "You did well in areas where you've had some familiarity with the experience but had more trouble with situations that were new to you. We need people who have an easier time with unfamiliar experiences." The couple expressed sadness but accepted the decision (p. 45).

Selection

The placement of a child involves the selection of a particular home for a particular child. "The focus has shifted from choosing the 'best adjusted parents' to selecting foster parents whose needs meet the needs of the child to be placed" (Kinter & Otto, 1964, p. 361). Selection, then, is on the basis of complementarity of needs. This is not entirely a new idea. In 1867 the Massachusetts Board of State Charities recommended " that a child of passionate temper should not be placed in a family where the master or mistress is of a similar disposition. When such instances do occur there is apt to be trouble pretty soon." Placements of children evacuated from London during the war indicated that "nervous children were best placed in quiet, conventional types of home while the active, aggressive children were best in free and easy homes with companions" (Bowlby, 1951, p. 127). (See also Colvin, 1962). Foster-family care of an emotionally disturbed child may require greater impersonality, less involvement—a relationship that approximates, in some essential ways, the professional relationship. Thus the foster parent who can maintain more emotional reserve may be selected for such a child.

The home that might be good for a child early in life might become unsuitable later (Jenkins, 1965). The age and sex of the foster parents' own children are also significant. Several studies (Bowlby, 1951, p. 129, Trasler, 1960, p. 223) have shown that failures in foster placement, which result in the child's removal from the home, are associated with the fact that the foster parents had a child of the same sex and age as the foster child. The explanation is that such a situation sets up undesirable competition. Cautley (1980) reports that "position of the foster child as the youngest in the family group" was associated with success of the placement (p. 252).

"Matching" involves not only assessment of congruence between needs of the child and the foster family, but also evaluation of the degree to which needs of the birth and foster family mesh. Birth families have a right to insist that a substitute home maintains their racial, cultural, and religious heritage (Hubbell, 1981; Blumenthal, 1983). Typically this involves choosing a foster family whose racial composition and economic circumstances are as similar as possible to those of the birth family. Meyer (1985) is critical of foster care agencies for failing to use these selection criteria:

> For over 100 years, social workers have thought of foster family care as a device to raise the standard of living of poor children; how else can we understand the commonplace practice of seeking foster homes far from the poor neighborhoods the children live in, and offering everything from medical care to Little League baseball and a separate room—all of these things that parents could not afford and that compounded the process of returning children home? [p. 256].

Even more critical for achieving the goals of foster care is the foster parents' ability to work directly with the birth family and/or to encourage the child to consider reunification. This is particularly critical in those instances in which the child's return to the birth home is a placement goal (Holman, 1980). Pragmatically, foster homes must also be located at some navigable distance from the birth home if birth parents are to have any reasonable opportunity to meet regularly with their children (Cox & Cox, 1984).

The selection of a home is not always a conscious, deliberate process. It is often a "search, seek, find" operation, one of expediency rather than an exercise of professional judgment. One of the few attempts to test the frequency with which matching takes place was done by Fanshel and Grundy (1971), who studied some 152 foster homes in New York City. Having available a rating of the Child's Behavioral Characteristics and the workers' responses to a Foster Parent Appraisal Form, they assessed the extent to which "the characteristics of the child were matched with foster parents' special general capabilities." The results tended to "suggest that, for the most part, placements seem to be based upon administrative expediency—children are placed where vacancies exist with little attention on psychological grounds" (p. 28).

Workers are faced with providing the child with "the best plan possible rather than the best possible plan." Inappropriate placements are often the result of the lack of availability of appropriate placement facilities rather than a consequence of a worker's faulty decision.

Process

Intake

There are many different reasons why children come into care. They can be classified in four different categories, depending upon the amount of time the family or caseworker has had to assess the situation prior to placement and the degree to which parents themselves accept the need for placement (See Figure 7-1.) In some situations, the worker has sufficient time to prepare the family, and the parents voluntarily agree to put the child in foster care. This occurs, for

Timing Factor

		Noncrisis Situation	Crisis Situation
Parental Acceptance Factor	Voluntary	Example: Inability or unwillingness of adolescent to care for newborn	Example: Parental need for hospitalization for illness
	Involuntary	Example: Prolonged deterioration in alcoholic parents	Example: Severe abuse or neglect

Figure 7-1: Intake Circumstances

example, when a pregnant adolescent realizes she will not be able to provide appropriate care for her newborn infant. At other times, parents realize they do not have the resources to provide child care and voluntarily seek placement, but planning for substitute care must be done during a family crisis. A parent may suddenly be hospitalized or convicted of a crime and incarcerated. Involuntary placements can also be made after extensive planning or in response to a family crisis. Perhaps the most widely publicized involuntary placement circumstances are those surrounding the removal of children from their home after the worker discovers they have been severely maltreated.

It is difficult to determine the proportion of foster care cases that fall into each of these four categories. Evidence from one state (Hubbell, 1981) indicated that only 8.5 per cent of all placements were voluntary (p. 62).

No matter whether parents cooperate in or resist the placement process, many states require that custody of the child be transferred to the child welfare agency before substitute care can be provided. Describing one state's rationale for this procedure, Hubbell (1981) comments:

> Court participation in voluntary placements is specifically encouraged by the DHR. Its policy manual on foster care acknowledges that "although limitation of parental rights by court ordered custody may tend to weaken family ties, feelings of mutual responsibility and prolong placement, voluntary placements may leave the child in a vulnerable position and jeopardize the most appropriate planning for him." This statement obviously reflects the best interests of the child standard, obstensibly making the child less vulnerable to the whims of his parents. The DHR's policy manual also reflects the best interests of the system. Despite the admitted drawbacks of the court procedure, by adjudicating the case, the state wields greater power and authority over parents and children, assuring that it will have the upper hand (p. 78).

Preparing Birth Parents for Placement

During intake, the caseworker must determine that removal of the child is necessary at this time. Some parents in crisis are unaware of services they might use in lieu of having the child removed:

> Mrs. M., a mother of two preschool children, has recently been deserted by her husband after years of marital conflict. The family had only limited savings since Mr. M. was a semiskilled punch press operator who had earned little more than a marginal income. Mrs. M. had some experience as a beautician before she was married six years ago. She wanted to place the children, go back to school, upgrade her

skills, and then have the children come live with her. She had heard about AFDC but was reluctant to consider it. The worker helped her to feel somewhat more accepting about being "on welfare" particularly because a plan was worked out for part-time day care for the children while Mrs. M enrolled in a beautician course. As a result, she withdrew her request for placement.

Where the behavior of parents poses a clear threat to the life or health of the child, or in situations where extensive use of home-based services has failed to help the family address critical problems, the worker explores the need for foster care services:

> Darlene was seen at a shelter for runaways, where she had told the staff that her father had been sexually abusive and that she would not return home. In repeated contacts with the family, her father vociferously denied that he had been abusive. Her mother, who was physically ill and who did not adopt a leadership role in the family, does not appear to be able to protect or defend her daughter at this time. The caseworker recommended to the court that Darlene be placed in foster care.

> The M. family has had extensive contact with the child welfare agency over a period of many years. This family lives in extreme poverty and the addition of many children to the family over the years has made intolerable demands on the limited income Mr. M has been able to provide. Mr. M is alcoholic and abusive, and Mrs. M is physically disabled and severely depressed. Provision of intensive supportive and supplementary services has helped the family maintain itself, for the most part, although functioning of the parents is minimal and the children continue to have many problems in school and in the community. The parents have been exploring with the worker placement of Jessica, who is now ten. Jessica has been chronically absent from school and appears, at this time, to be school phobic. She has also set two small fires at the home. She is an exceedingly passive and dependent child, who has very strong ties to her mother. Because of their own preoccupations, neither parent appears to be able to marshall the resources to help Jessica remain in school at this time. Mr. and Mrs. M have agreed that foster care may be the best resource for her.

Successful placement needs the continuing active participation of the natural parent and his or her conviction that this decision is the correct one. Bowlby (1951), quoting a study done at the Maryland Children's Aid Society in 1942, notes that where both the child and the natural parent accepted placement, the chances of success for the foster placement were very great. In few cases was the child able to show an accepting attitude toward placement if his or her parents did not themselves hold and sanction such an attitude (p. 119). Families can indicate to their children their acceptance of placement by packing belongings with the child, by including favorite toys, and by providing photos of the family (Jones & Biesecker, 1980a, p. 11). The agency helps parents feel that in helping the child make a comfortable adjustment, they are fulfilling their obligations and demonstrating their concern.

As important as parental acceptance is the caseworker's certainty that placement is a productive option for the family at this time. Workers who feel strongly that child and family should not be separated may make placement more difficult by refusing to consider obvious evidence that the child is not receiving sufficient care or by dealing with family deterioration "by intensifying efforts. As the situation worsens, he finds himself increasingly isolated from the family, and increasingly having to be authoritarian and arbitrary in decisions" (Wilkes, 1980, p. 29).

When the social worker in collaboration with the parents has determined that placement is the most feasible choice the worker then must make clear to the parents that foster care can serve as only a temporary resource. Responsible placement requires that parents be helped to plan and carry out the necessary changes that will ultimately permit the child to return. Ideally, planning for the child's return begins at the same time as planning for the child's placement.

Depending upon their financial situation, the agency may seek to have parents pay some of the board rate for the child, since paying even a limited amount may symbolize to parents their ongoing responsibility for the child. Actually, given the severe financial constraints under which most of these families live, few have the resources to pay any part of the cost of care. Instead payment comes primarily from local, state and federal funds.

The agency may ask parents to indicate their preferences in terms of religion, race, or other characteristics of foster parents. Parents may be asked to visit the foster home and to meet the foster parents prior to the child's placement. Involving the parents in this way, the agency indicates the critical role they play in their child's life and provides them with clear evidence of its desire to work collaboratively with them, rather than "taking over" (Blumenthal & Weinberg, 1984).

The agency stresses the need for ongoing parent/child contact (Jones & Biesecker, 1980a; Blumenthal & Weinberg 1984). Parental visits and other forms of communication, such as letters and phone calls, are encouraged. The agency also asks parents to share as much information as possible about the child so that foster parents can be informed about the background of the child coming into their home.

Despite its value, agencies do not always engage parents in the placement planning process. Interviewing twelve birth families Hubbell (1981) discovered

ten said they had no involvement in a placement decision. "I asked them to please keep them (her two children) together, but they didn't," said Mrs. Sonners. "I never had any say. I didn't know who it was they were living with," commented Mrs. Carey. Two families did have some choice (both were voluntary placements). "We asked for a Catholic home and got it," said Mrs. Richey. "I chose the Jefferson Children's Home," remarked Mrs. Morgan (p. 82). (See also Thoburn, 1980, p. 134).

As the child moves into substitute care, the foster care caseworker helps parents begin to deal with feelings precipitated by the loss of their child. "Separation and loss are seen by the child as potential abandonment and by the parent as anticipatory filial deprivation" (Moss & Moss, 1984, p. 171; see also Jenkins, 1967; Jenkins & Norman, 1972, 1975).

Although all parents fail at one time or another, the failure is usually limited and private—a family affair. Here, however, the extent of failure is almost total, and knowledge of it has to be shared with the agency and ultimately, with the foster parents. This involves a loss of self-esteem, an anticipation of rejection and censure, and an intensification of feelings of inadequacy and shame. This feeling is apt to be intensified with placement and with the pressure to recognize that the foster parents are daily demonstrating more adequacy in the care of the child than the natural parents themselves. As part of a larger study, some 430 parents were asked, "How did you feel the day your child was placed?" (Jenkins & Norman, 1972). Most parents (88%) reported feeling sad, and a significant number (57%) reported feeling empty.

For some parents, the sense of relief they feel in having someone else accept the burden of responsibility for caring for their child engenders strong guilt (Jenkins

& Norman, 1972). Even when parents use placement as a means to punish a child guilt is common (Moss & Moss, 1984).

Placement of the child also usually arouses "considerable anger." "The child's repeated broken promises of improving behavior are met by increasing lack of trust by the parent; the more distrustful the parent becomes, the less lovable the child seems to be. A parent may feel increasingly frustrated and helpless in coping with the child at home. Anger is directed not only against the child but against the self, which may lead to feelings of apathy and depression" (Moss & Moss, 1984, p. 171).

Analyzing the feelings parents had at the time of placement, Jenkins and Norman (1975) discovered that they fell into three distinct categories. Although expressing sadness, nervousness, and worry, Group A, the largest group, was distinguished by feelings of anger and bitterness. This group tended to include parents whose children were placed involuntarily for less socially acceptable reasons (such as abuse or neglect). Angry parents were more likely to come from the most deprived economic circumstances, to be black or Puerto Rican, and to feel alienated. Group B was, in many ways, the antithesis of Group A. These mothers primarily felt relieved and thankful and had children who were placed for more "socially acceptable" reasons, such as uncontrollable behavior of the child or physical illness in the mother. Members of this group tended to have higher incomes, to be white, and to feel less alienated. In contrast to Group A mothers, they also were more likely to accept the need for placement of their child. Group C was a relatively small group, including mothers who were distinguished for their feelings of guilt. Included here were a substantial number who were unable to care for their children due to mental illness. These mothers tended to live in economic circumstances midway between those of Group A and B, and their perspective on the need for placement was more moderate as well (pp. 52–53).

In addition to these feelings, many parents experience fear—fear that once their child has been removed, he or she may never return to the family home (Hubbell, 1981, p.18). Having themselves experienced difficulties in maintaining contact with their children or having heard of difficulties others experienced, parents worry that once the circumstances that led to placement are ameliorated the agency or the court may not recognize this improvement or consider it sufficient and may block parental reunification efforts. They also fear losing the child's affection and respect to the foster parents.

Birth parents may find it very difficult to be honest with the child if this involves an open confession that he or she is not likely to return home in the immediate future. Parents tend to want to tell the child the good news he or she wants to hear rather than the bad news the child has to hear. Feeling their influence with the child weaken, birth parents may demand obedience to themselves rather than the foster parent, even in abstentia. The caseworker, realizing these feelings are normal, helps parents anticipate them, and assists them in finding appropriate means for expressing them.

In order to articulate the goals of foster-care placement, the worker engages in systematic case planning with the family. *Systematic case planning* is defined as the identification of the specific changes the family must make in order for the child to return home, the setting of time limits for achieving these changes, and work that must be done to bring about such changes, including help and support the agency must provide the parents in this process (Wiltse & Gambrill, 1974a, p. 114). Case planning is now required by federal legislation, P.L. 96-272. "The process by which the foster care plan is developed may greatly influence the future relationship between the caseworker and a family; its contents, specificity, and plausibility strongly influence the potential for future family reunification" (Hubbell, 1981, p. 87). Guidelines for planning procedures are carefully spelled out in several manuals (Stein & Gambrill, 1976; Pike et al., 1977; Jones & Biesecker, 1980a).

During a series of meetings with parents, the worker develops a contract that clearly spells out expectations. A *contract* is defined as a working agreement between client and worker concerning the purpose of their interaction and the processes through which that purpose is to be achieved. Written contracts are more desirable than verbal contracts, and the more specific, concrete, and behaviorally oriented the language of the contract, the greater the likelihood that it will be understood, accepted, and achieved. In order to be effective, parent and caseworker must work together to formulate the contract. Once drawn up, it should be open to renegotiation and change (Stein, Gambrill & Wiltse, 1978).

Contracts include expectations for changes in parental behavior or family circumstances that must be made before the child can be returned. In addition, the contract must specify expectations for the maintenance of parental involvement with the child. Contacts specify not only what the client will do, but also what the worker is obligated to do to help the client—agencies that will be contacted, the number of appointments the worker will make with the client, resources the worker will provide, and procedures the client can use in order to arrange for visits. Contracts list objectives in specific measurable terms (mother will visit child in care one hour a week for the next three months; father will contact three rental agencies in a two-day period to find housing with more space; worker will be available every other Tuesday at 2 P.M. for a phone call with father to arrange for visitation with the child).

An example of a short-term contract between a client and a worker follows:

1. (Client), have stated my interest in regaining custody of _____ (Child), and in order to work toward that goal, I agree to the following conditions:

   1. I agree to visit _____ (Child), every Wednesday from 1:00 P.M. to 3:00 P.M. in the (Child Welfare Agency) office.

   2. I agree to meet with _____ (Caseworker), every Wednesday at 3:00 P.M. in the (Child Welfare Agency) office to discuss my visits with my child, to review planning concerning my child, and to discuss changes in my situation as well as any other relevant matters.

   3. I agree to participate in weekly meetings with a counselor from the County Mental Health Clinic.

   4. I agree to keep (Caseworker) of (Child Welfare Agency) informed at all times of my whereabouts and home address.

   1. (Client), understand that failure to meet the terms of this agreement may result in a petition for termination of parental rights to my child, (Child).

                  _____   _____

                    (signed)   (date)

                    (Client)

I, (Caseworker), acting on behalf of (Child Welfare Agency), agree to assist (Client) in her efforts to regain custody of her child, (Child), and, in order to work toward that goal, agree to the following conditions:

   1. I agree to have (Child) at the (Child Welfare Agency) office every Wednesday at 1:00 P.M. for visit with her mother, (Client).

2. I agree to meet with (Client) each Wednesday at 3:00 P.M. in the (Child Welfare Agency) office.

3. I agree to arrange transportation, upon request, for (Client) so that she can attend weekly meetings with the mental health clinic counselor.

4. I agree to maintain (Child) in foster care until a permanent plan can be accomplished for her.

5. I agree to keep (Client) informed of any significant matters relating to her child, (Child), such as illnesses, school progress, etc.

(signed)   (date)
(Caseworker)

It is jointly understood and agreed between (Client) and (Caseworker) that this agreement will continue in effect for a period of ninety days (unless jointly modified) and will be reviewed by (date), to evaluate progress toward meeting the stated goals. [Pike et al., 1977, pp 50–51].

Paying attention to the participatory role that parents must play in contract development is termed a "liaison casework strategy" (Hubbell, 1981). When parents are not considered full partners in case planning they tend to view placement goals as impositions that may be irrelevant to their needs and insensitive to their circumstances. In fact, parents who do not play a significant role in planning may not even be aware of the caseworker's objectives.

It would be to everyone's advantage for agencies to involve parents in developing the foster care plans and to ensure that they fully comprehend the plans. However, most of the natural parents we interviewed were virtually ignorant of the details of their plans or had been so at the beginning of the placement. Nine of the thirteen families said that they either did not know the requirements for unification when their children began foster care or were unclear about them. The remaining four families said that they knew of the requirements. Two of the nine said that the plan had changed. Several flatly stated that there had been no written plan [Hubbell, 1981 p. 88].

In contracting with parents, it is often clearly indicated that failure to work toward change will result in having the agency move toward the termination of parental rights so as to achieve permanence for the child through adoption. Thus one supposedly prime condition of good contracting—that it be honestly entered into without coercion—is at variance with another aspect of contracting with the parents of children in foster care. A widely distributed "Guide for Parents of Children in Foster Care" (New York City Department of Social Services, 1977) notes clearly that, "Your parental rights and responsibilities go together. If you do not carry out your parental responsibilities, you may lose or endanger your parental rights. . . . You can lose your parental rights to your child without your consent if you do not carry out your parental responsibilities while your child is in placement."

As a matter of fact, one value of contracting is that it provides documentation of parental failure to respond to efforts on the part of the agency to help the parent effect changes in those conditions that would make possible the child's return home. The documentation of such service and the lack of response provide the explicit evidence needed to support a petition to the court for the termination of parental rights (Pike et al., 1977, p. 38).

Achieving workable goals is difficult for the worker because of the kinds of families the agency is called upon to help. A random sample of 210 workers' rating of the parental adequacy of parents of children in foster care in Oregon in 1975 rated 73 per cent of the biological mothers and 74 per cent of the biological fathers, when present, as presenting either "major" or "severe" problems in child care. *Major* was defined as follows: "parental problems necessitating the child's placement in foster care are serious and probably chronic." *Severe* is defined thus: "parental problems necessitating the child's placement in foster care are serious, chronic and this parent is unresponsive to efforts to change the situation" (Emlen, 1976, p. 7.3). In a study exploring the circumstances of 145 new foster parents caring for latency-age children, Cautley (1980) concluded, "It was clear that a large majority of the natural families had relatively severe and enduring problems" (p. 47). Some parents who need to place a child have such limited strengths that even the best service may not result in rehabilitation. If, as the relevant studies indicate, lack of motivation to change is one of the factors in the behavior of the biological parents that determine the worker's decision to place the child, we can expect that this same lack of motivation would continue, after placement, to make rehabilitation of the home more difficult. Describing difficulties encountered by a New York City placement prevention project, Halper and Jones (1984) comment, "Although they would verbally contract for services they often did not perform the tasks they had agreed to" (p. 15). They go on to note, "Although written contracts were attempted with a number of clients—and were sometimes a helpful tool, project staff did not find this effective. In most cases most of our clients had poor reading and writing skills and did not relate well to written material" (p. 26).

Here, as in protective services, the worker is faced with implementing a multiple role as helper-facilitator-supporter of the client in planning to change and as evaluator of the outcomes of such efforts. The obligation to the client is to make clear these different responsibilities. "We will work together so that you are no longer alcoholic, or drug addicted, or abusively rejecting of your child, but if within (some specified period of time) the situation has not changed, we will recommend to the court the termination of your parental rights." Service programs involved in such unwelcome dilemmas express confidence that clients can distinguish between a "threat and a clear explanation of realistic alternatives" and that parents respond to such frankness (Pike et al., 1977, p. 43).

Blumenthal and Weinberg (1984) have created a checklist that summarizes the various intake tasks we have been discussing (See Figure 7-2).

Ongoing Work with Foster Care Participants

Figure 7-3 (on page 382) depicts the foster-care worker's responsibility to provide ongoing assistance to the three primary participants in the foster care process—the child, his or her birth family, and the foster parents. This triangle in uneasy equilibrium, is bound together by the agency whose task it is to balance the needs of all three groups. Service delivery is affected by the distinctive attributes of the surrounding community.

Preparation of the Child for Placement and Services to the Child in Placement

After a home has been selected, a child makes brief visits, accompanied by the worker, who acts as a supportive figure during the time the child is separating

Task	Parents	Participants Workers	Children
1. Make decision that child needs to be placed in foster care based on assessment of the family situation, determination of service needs, and evaluation of the alternatives to placement.	X	X	X
2. Discuss foster care service: goals and process.	X	X	X
3. Provide and discuss written material to parents about foster care and their rights, responsibilities, and roles.	X	X	
4. Discuss and clarify: °importance and purpose of parent involvement °importance of regular parent–child contacts °meaning of time to children and why placement needs to be time-limited °parental financial obligations to support	X	X	
5. Inform parents of right to appeal and the mechanism available to them.	X	X	
6. Identify preferred characteristics of foster care placement.	X	X	X
7. Select placement (as close to parents' neighborhood as possible).	X	X	X
8. Preplacement visit.	X	X	X
9. Help prepare child for placement: °explain why child will not stay in own home °explain what the placement will do for the family °reassure about parental love °explain importance of parents' visits and other contacts	X	X	X
10. Share important information about child.	X	X	
11. Determine ability, availability, and willingness of community resources to work with parents.		X	
12. Formulate written service plan, including parent-child visiting plan.	X	X	X
13. Prepare written service agreements or contracts based on service plan.	X	X	

Figure 7-2: Caseworker Tasks at Intake* (*Source: Blumenthal & Weinberg, 1984, pp. 58–60.)

from one home but is not yet incorporated into another. One recommendation has been to remove the child early on Friday afternoon. He or she has time to get acquainted with the home before evening, and the weekend permits contact with the entire family before the child has to face attending a new school on Monday.

Whatever arrangements are made to ease the child's transition, this change is a radical one:

Everything the child has known in the past disappears. Everything he experiences is strange—the bed he sleeps in, the location of the bathroom and the closet for his

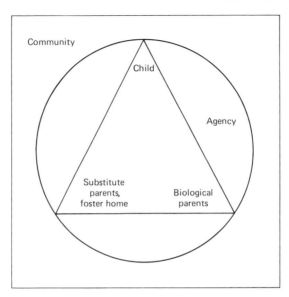

Figure 7-3: Configuration of Relationships in Foster Care

clothes, the food, the family routine, the toys, the yard, the school, the people in close proximity to him. Nothing which happens from day to night is the same and there is no person to look to for a familiar response [Hill, 1957, p. 3].

The movement of the child into the foster home involves processes of separation, transition, and incorporation. Like the parent, separation evokes strong emotions in the child:

1. Feelings of sadness ("I love my family and my home, and I miss my parents");
2. Feelings of loneliness and abandonment ("My parents don't want me." "Will anyone else want me?");
3. Guilt ("I am so bad that my parents had to get rid of me"), which reflects the child's belief that he or she is responsible for breaking up the home.
4. Hostility ("I hope they get hurt for having rejected me." "Nobody else can give me enough so that I feel wanted and important.");
5. Fear for one's survival ("Who will feed me now?" "Can I count on somebody to take care of me now?");
6. Shame ("Why can't my parents be like other parents and take care of me?")

(Littner, 1950; Charnley, 1955; Gordon, 1956; Glickman, 1957; Kahan, 1979; Wittner, 1981; Holleman, 1983; Backhaus, 1984).

Children feel highly ambivalent about their birth families: on the one hand they desperately miss them and want to be with them, and on the other they are ashamed of their parents' inadequacies and angry about their parents' failure to provide them with a stable home. One former foster child comments, "I've got very divided loyalties about my mother . . . When she says something about 'Oh, it's hard for you on your own with two children,' I'll turn round and say 'Yes, well you got rid of me and there was only me' and I say it even now. I feel very bitter about it still" (Kahan, 1979, p. 30). Yet, this young woman "could not bear other people to criticize her mother and as an adult had a continuing sense of responsibility for her."

Individuals undergoing separation experiences typically pass through a series of stages. Children share with grieving adults the need to deny initially the reality of their loss, the task of eventually facing it, and, ultimately, the need to move beyond it and reintegrate their lives. Norton (1981) describes the nature of each of these stages:

> Stage 1: Shock. Some children—in direct contrast to those who react to placement with overt disturbances—present the superficial picture of adaptation to the entire placement experience with a notable absence of any kind of behavior, physical or verbal, that might have made the placement uncomfortable.
>
> Stage 2: Protest. Affectively, children in this stage will experience anxiety, anger, helplessness, and weeping as part of the grieving process brought on by the separation. All these symptoms indicate their rebellion against separation from their natural family and are attempts to regain recognition and acceptance as individuals.
>
> Stage 3: Despair. In the child's apathetic state there are feelings of internal pain and expressions of depression and hopelessness.
>
> Stage 4. Detachment. This is seen as the adjustment stage for the child in foster placement. Affectively there is a sense of mastery—"I've arrived; I've made it." There is a deep sense of pride present as the hope in the future replaces the hoplessness and despair that have been part of the past [pp. 157–158].

Studying the reactions of thirty-five white school-age children through detailed interviews with their foster parents, Thomas (1967) found the children did mourn, although these stages were not always clearly demarcated. Separation and object loss seemed less difficult for children who had some clear idea as to what would happen to them. Surprisingly, there was little difference in the grieving process between children who were visited very rarely and those who received frequent visits from birth parents.

Only minimal attention has been paid to children's attempts to cope with separation from siblings. Meier (1962), in her study of former foster children, found that sibling deprivation was keenly felt and keenly remembered. Ward (1984) describes attempts to maintain siblings in the same foster home as "haphazard." Children in long-term care are particularly vulnerable to multiple losses, since they are more likely to lose contact with birth parents and to be placed apart from siblings:

> Anne and her brother were inseparable when they were young and were boarded out together. Only later did it become clear that the foster parents took Anne because they wanted her brother. Eventually the foster home rejected them both, first Anne and later her brother. Both children had been through experiences of loss and disappointment in the foster home and their own relationship suffered. "In the end we were apart. We are very apart now, my brother and me. There is, a sort of, I don't know, a very wide gap between us . . . It sounds an awful thing to say but I've given him up as a brother. As an acquaintance, well, we keep in touch; as a brother I don't think he'll ever be a brother to me." [Kahan, 1979, pp. 26–27].

Making a successful transition requires that the foster child begin to fit into the foster family, to be socialized in its mores and daily customs. Patterns of eating and dressing, means of problem solving and methods of social control may be at variance with those learned in the birth family home. Major differences between these two home environments can exacerbate the child's fears:

> In general, people find a sense of security in familiarity and sameness. Even in cases of severe child abuse, most children would rather remain with their abusing parents than move to a physically safe, but strange environment. . . . In such cases where involuntary life changes may occur, losing the emotional or psychological security that comes from being in a familiar an predictable environment is more fearsome and stressful than the occasional physical pain [Norton, 1981, p. 157].

Differences in family patterns may be especially noticeable when the child moves from a lower-class to a middle-class family setting, as many children in foster care have to do:

> The children were virtually catapulted to another world upon entering foster care, especially in regard to housing; from ghetto housing to suburbia; from the trailer to a split level in a bedroom community; from a two-bedroom apartment to a ranch-style house with a swimming pool. As the children's physical environment changed drastically, the discontinuity between the homes could be a further wedge that would divide children and parents and deter or complicate their eventual reunification [Hubbell, 1981, p. 82].

Learning the rules of social intercourse in the foster home and becoming comfortable with them is a process that Fanshel has labeled "embedment."

After the move, there is a transitional period during which the child lives physically in the foster home but psychologically, to some extent, in the home he or she left behind. The child lives in one home and loves in another. During this time, children struggle with what, to them, seems an unusual situation—having two families at the same time. Adaptation for them is much the same as it is for children whose parents are undergoing divorce. Eventually, they must arrive at some level of contentment with and acceptance of their dual family status and must learn that they can care about and be cared for by two different sets of parents simultaneously.

Some foster-care literature has implied that the most effective means whereby the child can cope with this situation is by "resolving" or breaking birth-family ties and substituting for them new attachment to the foster family (Meezan & Shireman, 1985). This is analogous to the recommendation that, in divorce situations, children relinquish one parent in order to remain tied to the other:

> Pauline is continuing to make her adjustment, at a quicker rate than expected. At first she was unable to call the foster parents anything—neither *Aunt* and *Uncle* nor *Mother* and *Father,* admitting to her worker a feeling of great strangeness, since they were really not her relatives, and it seemed confusing to her to have two mothers. She thought it might be easier to call them just simply by their first names, something the worker could quite understand. Subsequently, however, there was a change in this and Pauline took the initiative in asking the foster mother whether she could call them *Mother* and *Father.* When assured that anything she would like to call them would be all right, she immediately started calling her foster parents *Mother* and *Father* [Juliusberger, 1961, p. 5].

Given the chronic instability of foster-care placements, however, encouraging this type of family substitution can place the child in a peculiarly vulnerable situation. One former foster resident comments "the only security you have got when you are in care is that that is given to you from the people above. Where you happen to live and the bed you sleep in isn't your bed, because if you move from there somebody else will have it. Nothing is ever completely yours, other than perhaps a few possessions that you have got" (Kahan, 1979, p. 52).

Meyer (1985) challenges the view that foster parents should replace birth parents in the child's affections, and states, "Children never lose their basic conviction that their biological mothers are their real mothers and no one can substitute for them. Foster mothers can complement biological parents' care, they can be better (or worse) parent figures, they can function as parents instead of the biological parents, but they can never be the real parents" (p. 256). She argues that, with the help of the caseworker, children can understand and feel comfortable with the fact that they have lived with their birth family but that they are, for the moment, a part of another family as well. (See also Jenkins, 1981, p.49).

Data from a number of studies indicate that children do, eventually, come to some sense of resolution about their dual family status, although they continue to experience some discomfort and discontinuity. Studying children in the New York foster care system, Fanshel (1982) reports that social workers rated approximately half as at peace with their current family arrangements. A substantial number, however, had some degree of anxiety about their relative standing with their birth and foster family, although few were highly disturbed about this issue. Seven per cent of the six to nine-year-olds and 10 per cent of those ten to thirteen were very concerned (p.258). Assessing the reactions of 121 children in long-term foster care, Thorpe (1980) indicates that an even larger proportion, three quarters, felt comfortable in their foster-family home and wanted to remain there. However, "despite the extent of expected permanence, concern with their security of tenure in the foster home nevertheless coloured the interview responses of several of the children" (p. 91). One of these children says:

> Lynn (14 years old): I don't think you should have to be extra specially obedient but you don't like saying things to foster parents that you might later regret. I argue because I like to stick up for what I believe in, but I think sometimes foster children are frightened to do this. They are afraid of being sent back [p. 91].

Adolescents, who tend to be more aware of their "special" status as foster children, also may be more embarrassed about it and more reluctant to reveal their situation to others (Norton, 1981).

Considering the extensive adjustment that foster children must make when moving into a new home, it is not surprising that a number of them engage in troublesome and obstructive behavior early in their placement (Hampson & Tavormina, 1980, p. 110). Although some go through an initial "honeymoon" period, others begin the struggle to adapt almost immediately. This is a testing period, during which the child probes parental limits and challenges parental control. If separation symbolizes rejection, then rejection is something these children have actually experienced and are fearful of encountering again. Testing is the child's plea for reassurance that she or he is wanted in this home.

Problematic behavior may be indicative of grieving (Jewett, 1982; Garon, Mandell, & Walker, 1984). Difficulties commonly found in each stage of the process are summarized by Norton (1981):

> Stage 1: Shock. Behaviorally, children during this stage seem to exhibit an automatic response without any emotional involvement. Reponse patterns generally include wakefulness, sleep walking, nightmares, night terror, teeth grinding, and upper respiratory infections.

Stage 2: Protest. Anger is expressed in a variety of ways, but is usually directed at the newly emerging self, others, or the person that existed prior to the placement. There are often numerous appeals on the part of the child for help through negative, unacceptable behaviors, but there is also an almost ritualistic rejection of this help by the child throughout the entire protest stage.

Stage 3. Despair. Few demands are made on the new environment. Activities are disorganized and purposeless. There is an apparent lack of goal direction and little motivation to start new activities or form new relationships. . . . There is marked regression as the child withdraws, no longer wanting to relate to individuals that make up the present external world (pp. 157–158).

Although children vary greatly in the amount of time they need to pass through each of these phases, for many, the more extreme responses are short lived. Foster parents can be reassured that, with appropriate caseworker assistance, the child will eventually carry out these separation tasks and begin to function more appropriately.

These separation responses must be distinguished from more maladaptive and chronic disabilities. Because many of the children coming into foster care have lived in depriving family circumstances, some for long periods of time, there are a considerable number whose reactions reflect more deep-seated developmental delay or psychological impairment. Examining fifty children who entered foster care in latency and had been in care for at least five years, Frank (1980) found evidence of serious pathology. He used a 7-point scale, with a score of 1 indicating normal functioning and a score of 7, active psychosis. A score of 4 suggests neurosis and a rating of 5, borderline personality disorder. "Hyperactivity, withdrawal, noncommunicativeness, depression, social isolation, learning problems, impulsivity, manipulativeness, exploitativeness, neurotic symptoms, psychosomatic symptoms, aggressive destructive outbursts, sleeping problems, delinquent behavior, eating problems, grooming problems, habit disturbances, pseudomaturity, and sometimes bizarre behavior or thoughts" (p. 258) typify level 5 children. Level 6 children have the same characteristics accompanied by transient psychotic episodes. Using two independent raters, this study revealed that well over 90 per cent of the children displayed problems at levels 4, 5, or 6.

At the initial measurement point, 18 per cent of the children were functioning at level 5; five years later only 4 to 8 per cent were rated this way. However, the number diminished only because children's symptoms had worsened. While two thirds of the group were rated at level 6 both at the point of initial study and five years later, level-7 disorders, childhood psychoses, were found among 12 to 16 per cent of the group during initial assessment and a disturbing 22–28 per cent five years later.

Casework support for the child, foster family, and the birth family can do a great deal to ameliorate some of the more long-term negative effects of chronic grief and early trauma. In an atmosphere of trust and caring, the social worker assists the child in expressing feelings about removal from the birth family home, about living with the foster family, and about coping with an uncertain future (Norton, 1981). Kahan (1979) graphically depicts the isolation of a child who has no one in whom he can confide:

As a tiny child in in the children's Home (he left when he was 6) he recalled "I used to spend half my time in the toilet actually, standing on the seat looking out of the window at the cars going by to the local. I used to go up there when I had a problem or something. I'd go up looking all gloomy and come down smiling. I used to like being on my own. I still do when I have a problem to sort out. Some people don't need people to talk to. I used to talk to a big elephant once when I had a problem—I used to tell my troubles to that. I used to punch it when I had a few problems, and that was one of my personal toys" [p. 48].

When Derek left this home, the elephant remained behind. Children in Derek's condition are described as in "an emotional deep freeze" or as having "an emotional cutoff." They deny and discount their feelings in an effort to handle them. Unfortunately, denial also prevents them from resolving these feelings.

Because separation is difficult and because the agency is active in implementing separation, the agency often becomes the target of the child's hostility. An older foster child, discussing her memory of separation with her caseworker, said, "You can't help being afraid and you have to hate someone. When I first met you I hated you because you were associated with the break-up of my home" (Kastell, 1962, p. 101).

In addition to providing the child with critical opportunities to ventilate and understand feelings, the social worker serves as an information resource. Both before and after placement, the worker helps the child understand the reasons why placement is necessary, thereby challenging the child's assumption that he or she is solely to blame for it. The worker explains areas in which birth parents are having difficulty and must do some work. The social worker also lets the child know as clearly as possible what is going to happen next, helps the child anticipate this experience and, thereby permits the child to experience change "in small doses" so that he or she can assimilate it emotionally. Throughout, the worker presents the situation as honestly and objectively as possible and tries to do so on a level that the child can understand, on a level that is meaningful to the child.

Particularly in situations in which the child's contact with birth-family members is intermittent and unpredictable, the worker may become the only resource the child can turn to for ongoing information. Children need to be reassured periodically that family members with whom they have not been in contact are still alive; they need information about their whereabouts and their well-being (Colón, 1981).

Some evidence suggests social workers make reasonably explicit efforts to keep children informed. Meier (1962), after lengthy interviews with sixty-one young adults who had spent considerable time in care, notes: "Current perceptions of most of the subjects as to why they could not remain with their own families is based on realistic appraisal of their home situation rather than an unrealistic self-blame" (p. 149). Most of the children in placement came from grossly deprived environments, and many recognized their parents' inability to care for them. Hubbell's (1981) study also indicated that most of the children interviewed understood why they were in placement and what changes their families had to be made in order for them to be returned (p. 110). In her study of ten adults who had grown up in foster care, on the other hand, Kahan (1979) found considerable evidence that children remained uninformed about their families or their future. Examining the situation of 121 children in long-term care, Thorpe (1980) discovered

A disturbing 22 per cent of children had no, or very little, understanding of their background and present situation, the majority had some but inadequate understanding, and only 26 per cent, i.e. a quarter, had what can be called a good understanding. In fact, three children were not even aware that they were fostered. As would be expected, the extent of understanding increased with age, but at all ages a majority of children have limited knowledge and understanding (p. 94).

As is true for any role, clear understanding of the placement situation is an important precondition of the child's adjustment to it. Thorpe (1974) interviewed 122 foster children all over five years of age who had been in the same home for at least a year. Objective measures of the child's adjustment were obtained through completion by both teacher and foster parents of the Rutter Behavior Scale.

Children with a good knowledge of their own background and good understanding of the foster care situation showed better adjustment. Knowledge and understanding were related, as might be expected, to the age at which the child entered foster care, older children being more knowledgeable.

Weinstein (1960), in interviews with sixty-one children in foster care, asked about the reasons that brought them there. Most reasons given were external to the child and centered on the inability of parents to care for him or her. Some of the contingencies requiring placement seem to be easier for the child to accept. Death—clear, unequivocal, and a matter of fate—is perhaps the easiest to accept. Mental illness is more difficult because the parent is apparently physically well, yet is unable to care for the child. (See also Holleman, 1983, p. 154; Festinger, 1983, p. 46.)

By working with both child and birth family, the worker serves as a source of continuity for the child—linking past, present, and future in some kind of meaningful way (Laird, 1981; Colón, 1981). Awareness of this continuity is essential for development of coherent sense of identity:

> Every time somebody went out of my life, a bit of me was there, left behind too. Probably why I look back so much was because I wanted those bits, I wanted to feel a whole person again. Even now I suppose I don't really feel a whole person, I feel as though there's something people have got that I haven't, something indefinable, something I cannot place (Kahan, 1979, p. 46).

Even at very young ages, children struggle to create some kind of coherent picture out of the pieces of their lives:

> A four-year-old girl whose mother was imprisoned played with dolls silently most of the time, but spoke occasionally about her visits to her mother and her wish to return to her. She frequently hugged and snuggled up to the therapist. Her last visit with the therapist occurred soon after her mother had been released from prison and was taking the children home. Upon saying goodbye to the therapist, the child took the therapist's hand and placed it in her biological mother's hand, literally trying to make a connection between important human objects (Kliman, Schaeffer, & Friedman, 1982, p. 216).

The worker establishes continuity by making regular visits to the child in the foster home. Bowlby (1951) suggests that joint interviews with the parents and children "in which the whole situation is exhaustively reviewed and a common plan reached" (p. 120) is another viable means for the worker to introduce continuity themes. By seeing the worker interacting with both the foster and birth family, the child understands that the worker serves as a link to both.

Evidence suggests that, for some children, caseworkers have carried out this task in a meaningful way (Kahan, 1979). Weinstein (1960), on the other hand, cites evidence that social workers do not play a sufficiently meaningful role in the lives of these children. He interviewed sixty-one children who were over five years of age and had been in a secure foster care placement for some time. In Weinstein's study, none of the children perceived the social worker as having a responsibility to facilitate return to parents (p. 44). In only two cases did the answer to such questions as "If you had some trouble or were worried, whom would you like to talk to about it?" or "If you could pick anyone in the world to live with, whom would you pick?" indicate a predominant identification with the social worker (p. 48). Similarly, Gottesfeld (1970) found, "While social workers should be ideal agents for helping the foster child to deal with the conflicts and problems of foster home care, the foster child does not perceive the social worker in this way. Less than half the foster children [in the study group] expressed a need to call their social workers about a problem" (p. 28).

High caseloads and frequent turnover may make it difficult for the worker to play a significant role as a source of continuity. Foster children complain that they see social workers infrequently and that workers change so often it is difficult for the chidren to become comfortable with any one of them. One former client comments that her social workers "all disappeared and somebody new came and it was a new story, from the beginning. I got sick of telling my life story over and over again and not getting anywhere" (Kahan, 1979, p. 126). Workers generally approach foster children with a problem-oriented attitude, so that the child comes to feel that contact is unnecessary unless there is something actually or potentially troublesome he or she has to struggle with (Gottesfeld, 1970, p. 26).

A treatment tool that explicitly focuses the child's attention on issues of identity and continuity is the Life Book. Working together with the child, the caseworker constructs a life history that is both realistic and meaningful to the child (Project Craft, 1980; Thorpe, 1980; Beste & Richardson, 1981; Backhaus, 1984). Using words, pictures, and drawings that are pasted in the pages of a book, the worker helps the child explore the meaning of significant life events and the reasons why changes in his or her living situations had to be made

> An 11-year-old boy started sessions insisting he had never been a baby. The Life Book provided him with pictures of himself as an infant and toddler, and he realized this his initial perception was not true. His caseworker believed that seeing himself well cared for in these pictures helped him to realize that his birth parents did value him, even if he could not stay with them [Backhaus, 1984, p. 554].

Group meetings for foster children also provide a useful mechanism for sharing questions and concerns about being a foster child and the relationship between foster- and birth-family experiences. Groups have proven particularly useful for preadolescents and teenagers, and they have also been successfully used with former foster care clients who are now adults (Kahan, 1979).

Foster Care Services for Birth Parents

Perhaps the most difficult, yet most central responsibility of the foster-care worker is reflected in the work he or she does with birth families. Effective services to parents are of immediate benefit to their children, for the child's ability to effectively adapt to the foster-care experience and to remain undamaged by that experience are most powerfully affected by ongoing relationships with birth-family members (Fanshel & Shinn, 1978). Research also suggests that the ability to keep children out of the foster-care system, once they have been returned home is dependent upon the quality of the work that was done with parents before the child was returned (Block & Libowitz, 1983; Turner, 1984). Professional concern for improvement in reunification services for birth families is reflected in recent Child Welfare League of America publications (Maluccio & Sinanoglu, 1981a; Sinanoglu & Maluccio, 1981; Blumenthal & Weinberg, 1984). Maluccio and Sinanoglu (1981b) recently published a bibliography on casework practice with these clients that contains about four hundred references.

As Figure 7-4 indicates, different parent circumstances call for somewhat different types of family treatment goals. Almost all of the families using foster care services require assistance in ameliorating personal or interpersonal difficulties and in coping with severe life stresses as well as help in developing more effective childrearing capacities. However, families differ in the extent to which they are available to work on these problems. In all cases, one central concern of the worker is to maintain, strengthen, or rebuild parent–child contacts. Even in instances in which children have not met with their birth parents for long periods, reestablishing contact can prove to be highly beneficial (Davidson, 1980, p. 50; Tiddy, 1986).

The various parental circumstances described in this figure suggest somewhat different reasons why children may remain in foster care for long periods of time, even though it has been designed as a means of temporary or short-term care for families. When parents are available, the worker may find that the complexity or chronicity of family problems prevents them from developing even minimally adequate childrearing skills, even with intensive agency assistance. Hubbell (1981) notes that some states mandate that workers may not terminate parental rights so long as parents are making sincere efforts to improve their parenting abilities, even when these efforts are "hopeless" (p. 136). Sometimes agency practitioners feel they cannot cut birth family ties so long as parents are cooperative, even when parental problems will continue to stand in the way of the child's return.

PARENT CIRCUMSTANCES	PARENT SERVICE GOALS
Parent Available: —Parent abusive, neglecting —Parent in stressful circumstances —Child behavior problem	—Enhance parenting skills —Alleviate environmental stress —Teach adaptive childrearing skills —Maintain parent-child contact —Determine ability to regain child custody
Parent Unavailable: Temporary —Parent hospitalized with physical, mental illness —Parent temporarily out of town —Parent seriously abusive of alcohol, drugs	—Assess length of absence —Maintain long-distance parent-child contact —Determine ability, willingness to regain child custody
Parent Unavailable: Long Term —Parent hospitalized for chronic mental illness —Parent seriously ill —Abandonment —Parent incarcerated	—Assess length of absence —Assess ability of parent to maintain or reestablish contact —Evaluate child's need for birth ties and family stability

Figure 7-4. Casework Goals for Parents with Children in Foster Care

Parents who are unavailable to the child, on either a temporary or long-term basis, present a different type of challenge to the worker concerned about "drift". Collecting data from a stratified random sample of children who were served by the child welfare system. Bush and Goldman (1982) discovered that one-third had parents who were deceased or whose whereabouts were unknown. In a study of children who had been in foster care for a year or longer in New York City, Fanshel (1982) finds a similar proportion (30%) had no birth mother or father available to visit them. Reanalyzing data collected from a national sample of cases. Olsen (1982b) discovered 160,000 children in care without a "principal child-caring person." These included one in four of the white children, one in three of the Hispanic children, and 40% of those who were black (p. 576).

Children who are placed because their parents are mentally ill may be especially vulnerable to undergoing inadvertent long-term care. In these families, parent–child ties are maintained, but the mother's disability prevents her from being able to resume care within a reasonable time period. A year and a half after placement, Kliman, Schaeffer, and Friedman (1982) found, childrens' "chances of being discharged seemed to be determined more by availability of fathers or other relatives willing to take them than their mother's condition" (p. 90).

In this section, we concentrate on child welfare practice with parents who are available and accessible. The worker's dual responsibility to remediate family problems and to foster contact with the child will be the subject of concern.

As we have previously mentioned, parents who find they must place children in foster care most frequently do so because they face a variety of economic, medical, psychological, and interpersonal difficulties with which they cannot cope and which community-outpatient programs cannot successfully alleviate. Examining the characteristics of parents referred for services while their children were in care. Kliman, Schaeffer, and Friedman (1982) discovered that only one-third of this group had "no history of mental illness, substance abuse, or abuse and/or neglect of own children" (p. 49). Thoburn (1980) reports caseworkers describe most parents as "trying but unable to cope," "disorganized," or "emotionally neglecting" (p. 46). In addition, in most families, there was indication of severe marital difficulty and, in some cases, of marital violence. While 7 of 51 parents were described as severely socially isolated, few had resources on which they could rely. Only 7 families were perceived as having a warm, supportive, extended family network available to help them through the placement crisis.

These difficulties were interwoven with and contributed to the parents' inability to cope effectively with their children. In general, these parents tended to either be "overindulgent" or "inconsistent." Several families were considered "seriously incapable of meeting the child's needs or were physically harming him" (p. 45). In addition, many of the children were particularly demanding, needy, or disturbed, and required skilled care.

> Social worker about a five-year-old. He was like a little robot. He used to curl himself up like a door mouse. He was depressed and desperately disturbed. And so much at risk because his behavior was so frustrating.

> Mother of a fifteen-year-old. He is a funny boy. It's his nerves. He always has stomach upsets, and every night he still has nightmares all night (Thoburn, 1980, p. 49).

Understanding the degree to which these parents are incapacitated helps explain why many of them appear confused and uncertain about their ability or willingness to continue caring for their sons and daughters (Fanshel, 1982, p. 144).

To help families remediate multi-faceted difficulties requires the use of multidimensional services, "Since these are usually parents who have weak or defective ego structures and who are very needy themselves, they can best be helped through a total therapeutic approach involving ego-building procedures and aid with immediate practical problems as well as with their emotional difficulties" (Maluccio, 1981b, p. 22). Like families served by home-based programs (see Chapter 3), these families may benefit from individual family or group services and may require the worker to serve as an advocate, service coordinator, and resource developer.

The following material describes casework services provided to one birth mother that helped facilitate the return of her children to her home

> Harriett S, 40, was the single-parent mother of 2-year-old twins placed in foster care on a finding of neglect. Mrs. S. had been hospitalized a year earlier, with a diagnosis of schizophrenia, undifferentiated. Since that time, she appeared to maintain herself adequately with psychotropic medication. Workers from the state child welfare agency and an outpatient psychiatric clinic were hesitant to recommend return of the twins, however, as Mrs. S's capacity for caring for them was in question. The practitioner negotiated an agreement on an operational definition of parental competence satisfactory to the child welfare and psychiatric worker. Mrs. S. wanted very much to regain custody of the children, but had not been aware of concrete ways to demonstrate her competence. She also mistrusted the motives of social workers, fearing that they might seek permanent removal of her children. The practitioner explained to Mrs. S. that the judge had to know that her children would be safe with her before he decided that they could return. Specific, concrete tasks in health care, feeding, safety precautions and clothing of the children were mutually developed and carried out. The first tasks were developed and performed with the practitioner and a homemaker present. A few weeks later, weekend visits were arranged, with the practitioner or homemaker dropping in briefly to monitor and give encouragement. Finally Mrs. S. had the children for weekends without practitioner visits. The children were, however, carefully observed when they returned to the foster home.
>
> At the end of eight weeks, all workers involved in the case were satisfied that Mrs. S. had demonstrated competence in caring for her children. She regained custody upon the mutual recommedation of all parties, with the added recommendation that she enter her children into part-time day care as a relief from full-time child care responsibility. The practitioner helped Mrs. S to obtain day care. At a 6-month followup, she continued to provide adequate care and had maintained the children in day care (Rooney, 1981b, p. 142).

Many parents recognize that they must change their behavior or circumstances in order to have their children returned and that they may require some help in accomplishing this. Several studies indicate that they appreciate the contributions made by foster-care caseworkers to this end. Most parents in Hubbell's (1981) survey "spoke positively of their caseworker" (p. 112). Only 1 of the 20 parents Thoburn (1980) interviewed claimed to be dissatisfied with the social worker (p. 112). In their longitudinal study of the reactions of mothers to the placement process, Jenkins and Norman (1975) found that, as a group they rated social worker interest, understanding, and communicative efforts as at least somewhat helpful (p. 64). "Several parents said that agency sessions in which parents met with workers and were helped to understand their problems, or in which workers counsel parents, were extremely useful" (p. 78). Surveying families served by eighteen child-welfare agencies in five states, Yoshikami (1984) also found them generally appreciative of the help they received. Parents considered practical services that got results and were provided by "an understanding service provider" as especially meaningful (p. 89).

Despite an awareness of the need for these services on the part of the social work profession and its clientele, studies show that in actuality little direct rehabilitative programming is offered biological parents (Stone, 1969; George, 1970; Fanshel & Maas, 1962. Hubbell, 1981). Reanalyzing the data from Shyne and Schroeder's (1978) national study of child welfare services, Olsen (1982b) discovered that more than half the families had no social service plans, and that Native American families were least likely to be provided with them. Thoburn (1980) documents a similar situation in Britain. She found that less than half the families in her study had any kind of explicit service contract with the worker (p. 87). However, Yoshikami's (1984) more recent assessment indicates that public child welfare agencies are now complying with P.L. 96-272 case-planning requirements:

> In all five states agency policy required the use of written plans for foster care (including reunification) cases. There were written case plans for 90 percent or more of the cases in 14 of the 18 agencies; this was true of all agencies in three of the five states. In a large majority of the local agencies, supervisors reported that most case plans met agency standards and were developed jointly with parents [p. 71].

In her research on service delivery patterns to families with children in substitute care, Hubbell (1981) found "Nearly half the caseworkers said that their work to reunite the families primarily focused on aiding them in obtaining such services as housing, mental health counseling, day care, or homemaker service. The next most frequent category of work in reuniting families was arranging visits; this was followed by working directly with a child. Only three caseworkers said their reunification efforts included counseling the biological parents" (pp. 112–113).

Conducting an extensive study of efforts to implement Public Law 96-272 covering 18 agencies in 5 states, Yoshikami (1984) found that few families (23%) had "high frequency" contact with caseworkers (3 or more times a month), while 27% did not see their workers every month (p. 92). "In only one-third of the agencies did workers report high availability of services to both prevent placement and reunify families. Worker reports also indicated that services directed towards reunification were less available than those available for placement prevention" (p. 127). (See also Fanshel, 1982, p. 141.)

Families are rarely offered group work services (Thoburn, 1980; Yoshikami, 1984). Because this type of programming can be particularly beneficial to individuals who need to improve their parenting skills, it has been argued that they should be much more widely available (Murphy, 1981; Hess & Williams, 1982; Blumenthal & Weinberg, 1984). "Group work can be an excellent means of countering the problems of isolation, of lack of familial and community supports, and of lack of information about the foster care system and their legal rights" (Carbino, 1983, pp. 16–17).

Client demands, caseworker attitudes, and agency policies and procedures all create barriers to effective service provision for this client group. Kliman, Schaeffer, and Friedman (1982) cite but one example of the casework dilemmas these clients present. Describing the circumstances of parents who have a history of substance abuse or addiction, they comment:

> Despite their initial willingness to cooperate as a group, these mothers faced formidable obstacles in their attempts to establish a secure home for themselves and

their children. Their employment prospects were bleak. Few had the resources or opportunities to avoid the social milieus which helped stimulate their original addictions. For many, enlisting the aid of the biological fathers on behalf of the children, where they were known, carried the danger of increasing the mothers' vulnerability to recurrence of addiction. Their permanent vulnerability to all of the mishaps and frustrations likely to occur in their daily lives made long-range treatment plans for the mothers and placement plans for their children highly precarious (p. 211).

In a study of birth families who had children in care in New York (Fanshel, 1982), more than half were depicted as somewhat or very resistant to seeing the worker, almost half missed appointments, and almost a third were late for them. In addition, among those keeping appointments, "sizeable grooups were rated as being unable to discuss personal problems (52.3%), to be defensive about themselves (59.1%) or to be excessively dependent (51.3%)" (p. 151). Social workers commented:

> Neither mother nor mother's husband is willing to look at the problems which led to child's placement. Child was placed because of a parent–child conflict and because of problems in the marital relationship. Neither parent is willing to accept ongoing therapeutic treatment, which is needed in order for the child to return home. Both parents want the child to remain in care and will not accept responsibility for the situation; neither are they attempting to solve the problem within the family [p. 144].

> Workers make appointments to see mother at her home and arrive to find she is not at home. Unannounced visits also have been in vain. Mother is not home or is suspected to be home but unwilling to receive visit. Contacts by agency are made with children's eldest sister [p. 148].

> Mother is overwhelmed by many personal and concrete problems and is immobilized in terms of seeking relief from her dilemma. Her brief contacts with agency worker caused her much turmoil. Her only meeting with her son was quite a traumatic experience for her, which she dared not repeat [p. 151].

Parental anger and resentment add to the worker's burden, particularly during early family contacts. "A fairly common pattern was for suspicion and dislike before care to turn to resignation and suspicion or goodwill whilst the child was in care, and to goodwill and apprehension on the child's return home, turning to affection and acceptance if all went well" (Thoburn, 1980, p. 84).

The activities and attitudes of social workers themselves have important impact on the outcome of foster care. When the worker believes in the value of parent–child ties and is convinced that the parent has sufficient resources and ability to eventually regain custody of the child, when the worker is sufficiently skilled to implement a service delivery plan for clients with complex needs, and when the worker has sufficient time to provide intensive and, where necessary, long-term services to clients, children are more likely to eventually be returned to their family home. When families receive services from workers who lack this positive outlook or who have insufficient skills or time, their children are more likely to drift into long-term care, and they and their children are more likely to eventually lose contact (Thoburn, 1980).

Large caseloads, a perennial problem in public child welfare, prevent the foster-care worker from providing all families with sufficient attention. The worker tends to respond to crises (Blumenthal, 1983; Blumenthal & Weinberg, 1984) or to invest in more responsive and cooperative parents, since more limited efforts are likely to help them achieve family reintegration (Fanshel, 1982).

Attitudes influence the worker's interpretation of parental reluctance to visit as a sign of the family's inability to cope or as a signal that the family needs help and encouragement in order to build contacts with the child. Likewise, attitudes influence the worker's perception of the meaning of parental pressure to have the child returned. "The way the social workers reacted to this pressure was interesting. In some cases, the pressure was clearly not welcome, and seen as an indication that things would not go too well if children went home, and that the parents would be unlikely to 'cooperate.' In others the social workers seemed to have a greater understanding of the different factors contributing to the parents' need to feel that they could influence the situation" (Thoburn, 1980, p. 128).

Unavailability or lack of access to necessary community services presents another set of barriers to family change (Schimke, 1984). While Thoburn's (1980) study reported three-quarters of the families received assistance from other agencies (p. 74), Turner's (1984) research uncovered a much lower rate of service utilization. He examined the experience of 100 families, 50 of whom had their children returned and the children were maintained at home, and 50 whose children had to be returned to the foster care system. "It is noteworthy that community services were infrequently rendered to parents or children, either while the children were in care or following their return home. During the time the children were in care, 54% ($n = 27$) of the parents of nonrecidivists and 52% ($n = 26$) of the parents of recidivists received no community services" (p. 502). Services to meet the practical needs of these clients—in the financial and housing areas, for example—were unavailable. In his study of foster family care in New York, Fanshel (1982) reports that only 15 percent of the mothers who were available for service were referred by the caseworker to other agencies (p. 154).

Despite understandable tendencies to be protective of children and to feel negative about parents, many of whom have harmed their children, evidence indicates that most foster care caseworkers are fond of the parents with whom they work and that they do believe children can eventually return home (Hubell, 1981, p. 113). These workers feel responsible for providing sufficient outreach services, for making marital and family therapy available to parents needing this type of assistance, and for coordinating programming provided these families by other health, child-care, and social-service agencies.

Maintaining Parent-Child Contact. The extent to which birth parents visit the child and the regularity of these visits not only affect curent functioning of the child but also help determine his or her future life circumstances. Children whose parents visit regularly are better adjusted while in foster care (Fanshel & Shinn, 1978) and are better able to integrate living in two different families. In her research on 121 children in substitute care, Thorpe (1980) found that:

> children often experience the separation from natural parents entailed in coming into care as rejection, and that their feelings of rejection may undermine their sense of personal worth. This was apparent in my research, in that those children who were in contact with their natural parents seemed reassured that they were loved, rather than rejected. They understood that the reasons for their being in care were not because they were bad, unlovable, or 'no-good'; as a result they could tolerate the 'difference' implicit in being a foster child [p. 95].

Note, however, that one study (Festinger, 1983), exploring the impact of long-term care on children, did not find a clear association between well-being and parent visitation (p. 84).

The available research shows that the adjustment of the child in the foster home and the likelihood of returning home are positively related to continuing visits of the biological parents to the child (Weinstein, 1960, Sherman. Neuman & Shyne, 1973; Holman, 1973; Thorpe, 1974; Fanshel, 1975).

Lindsey (1982) reports that encouraging parent–child contact, when accompanied by interventions designed to enhance parent skills, were effective in reunifying a large number of families in the Alameda Project. Whereas one-third of control group children returned to their birth home after placement, almost two-thirds of Project children did so. Whereas more than half of control group children eventually experienced long-term care, only one in five Project children did so (p. 493). Reanalyzing data from Shyne and Schroeder's (1978) national survey of social services to children, Mech (1985) reports that children who had had no visits within a three-month period ultimately remained in care almost one year longer, on the average, than those who received at least some visits during that time. The more often the child was visited, the shorter the stay in care tended to be. While children receiving no visits over a three-month period were in care almost 51 months, children who had had four or more visits remained only 18 months (p. 69).

Gibson, Tracy and DeBord (1984) studied variables affecting length of stay in foster care. An analysis of forty-three children in foster care showed that "intensive and very frequent contacts between agency and family at the very beginning of placement may be necessary to affect the return of the child as quickly as possible" (p. 145). A two-year follow-up study of children in care in New York City (Fanshel, 1982), however, did not uncover a link between visitation and discharge (p. 97).

The worker helps ensure that parent–child contact has continuity by communicating to the parents the importance of visits and the agency's concern about their regularity. Since infrequent or irregular visiting is regarded as the least desirable alternative for the child, because it creates anxiety and frustration and makes planning difficult (Holman, 1973, p. 201; Festinger, 1983), the worker attempts to maintain visiting consistency. Once visits have stopped, for whatever reason, they are very difficult to renew, so the caseworker must remain especially vigilant in monitoring them.

Visiting schedules should be included in contracts formulated between the worker and the birth parents. Regular visiting is reinforced when the caseworker uses praise and approval for parents who fulfill their commitments in this way. When a regular schedule of visits is maintained, the parents might be sent a letter of commendation, whereas failure to visit might prompt a special-delivery letter or a telegram from the agency as a reminder. Parental investment is also reinforced when parents are routinely notified about and included in major events in their children's lives. Parents should be contacted about school reports, medical problems, and the like. Failure to apprise them of these matters provides a chronic source of parental dissatisfaction (Jenkins & Norman, 1975, Thoburn, 1980; Hubbell, 1981).

Because early visiting is predictive of later visiting (Fanshel, 1982; Festinger, 1983; Rowe et al., 1984), it is important for the worker to foster parental involvement early in the placement process. It has sometimes been argued that the primary job of the foster care worker is to monitor visiting. In this view, parents who have or can develop sufficient resources can "prove themselves" by availing themselves by the opportunity to see their children. However, given the nature of the problems these parents face, and the barriers they must sometimes overcome in attaining opportunities to contact their children, it is unwise to use visitation, by itself, as an indicator of parental interest (White, 1981).

Evidence indicates that foster care workers do spend a considerable amount of time on this task. A content analysis of interviews between child–care workers and sixty-five parents of children in foster care showed that 39 per cent of the items identified were concerned with encouragement of visiting. This was the largest single item of discussion, (Holman, 1973, p. 244). Festinger's (1974) study of placement agreements between agencies and foster homes in about forty states shows that child contact plans are routinely included.

Despite these efforts, there are substantial numbers of children in foster care who have little, if any, ongoing contact with their families. Studying children who had been in care for a year or more, Fanshel (1982) discovered that almost half had no contact with adult relatives (p. 26). Children who were not freed for adoption or in the process of being freed were visited more frequently, but 16.8 per cent of this group had no family contacts while in care, 18 per cent had not seen their mothers since they were born, and 12 per cent had not seen them during the past two years (p. 26).

As further indication of the degree of estrangement between children and their families, Fanshel asked workers to assess the intensity of the child's relationship to his or her natural family. "Some 9.6 per cent of the subjects were rated as showing a deep attachment to their families, while 10.1 per cent were seen as having a close attachment. Over a fourth of the children were rated as having some or a minimal attachment to their families. This left over half of the subjects being rated as devoid of a relationship (37.7%) or having families totally out of the picture (13.9%)" (Fanshel, 1982, p. 251).

Evidence suggests that the longer a child remains in care, the more family ties are attenuated. Studying children who were in care three or more years, Rowe et al. (1984) report that only 21 per cent "had even casual contact with a parent during the previous year" (p. 95). Assessing the functioning of individuals who had remained in the foster-care system five years or longer, Festinger (1983) found that more than half (57%) had low or sporadic contact with parents or other relatives, and an additional 15 per cent had had no recent visits. In this study, "sporadic" contact included "few contacts over the span of several years" (p. 74).

Visiting frequency is associated with the reasons for initial placement of the child in care. Like Fanshel, Thorpe (1980) examined the functioning of children in care a year or longer. She found that when children were placed because their mothers were physically incapacitated, they were most likely to be in regular parent contact; children placed because they were disturbed were visited next most frequently; abused or neglected children were least likely to see their parents while in care (p. 67).

To some extent, frequency of visitation is also determined by agency policy. Hubbell (1981), for example, found that in one state parents were not allowed to visit more than once a month. In addition, all visits were arranged at the child welfare office, unless the child's return home was imminent, in which case parents were allowed to visit with their children in their own home (p. 105).

Because some degree of tension, discomfort, and competetiveness are a normal part of birth parent–foster parent relationships, and because visitation itself brings to the fore many of the negative feelings that birth parents and their children have about placement, it is the worker's responsibility to anticipate these problems and to help foster care participants discover means to express their feelings and to constructively meet their needs. Ideally the relationship between foster and biological parent should be one of mutual cooperation toward achieving what is best for the child. Each should recognize and accept the different responsibilities and the different contributions of the other toward making placement the least damaging to the child. Yet there is apt to be considerable deviation from this ideal, As Weinstein (1960) notes:

> The foster mother may define the status of the natural mother as inferior in the relationship. She may be unwilling to entertain suggestions made by the natural mother on the ground that she is inadequate by virtue of the child's being in placement. Any attempts on the part of the natural mother to participate may be resisted as unwelcome interference. The natural mother may see herself as superior in the relationship, according the foster mother a position similar to that of a "hired servant." She may see her position as the child's natural parent as entitling her to the right of unlimited critical review of the foster mother's actions. Such conflicting definitions of the situation may lead to open hostility [p. 13].

Frequently coming from different worlds, foster parents and biological parents often have little in common—except for the child, with whom both may be competitively concerned (Murphy, 1981).

Birth parents exacerbate difficulties in establishing comfortable visiting regimes when they "are disorganized and have standards and schedules for the child who visits at home that are different from those of the foster family; miss appointments without calling, arrive late, and return the child late" (White, 1981, p. 467). Parents may also behave inappropriately during visits, although serious problems with parent behavior are infrequent. Fanshel (1982) found that among children who were not in the process of being freed for adoption, approximately one in ten of the parents had created some type of disturbance while visiting, one in ten had attempted to visit while intoxicated or addicted, and almost 9 per cent had exhibited bizarre or otherwise seriously inappropriate behavior while visiting (p. 51). However, fully half of these mothers had never exhibited any problemmatic behaviors. Some parents had, in addition, specific child-care difficulties. One in ten was described as relating very poorly to his or her children, and an additional one-third were considered marginal. Only one in three appeared to know how to make the visit an enjoyable experience for the child (p. 55). Considering both the frequency of contact and parental effectiveness, Fanshel estimated that one in four was performing as a responsible parent (p. 44).

Birth mothers realize that visits are upsetting experiences, both for them and their children (Jenkins & Norman, 1975). Few parents enjoy visiting, and some find it a painful ordeal. Thoburn (1980) found that it is not difficulties parents encounter with foster families but their own feelings, engendered by the realization they cannot adequately care for their children, that make contact with the child so difficult.

Parents initially may feel intensely competitive with foster parents and fearful of being judged:

> Going on that first visit was very difficult. My first thought was I really didn't want to see Mary Lou. Well, I wanted to see her, but I really didn't. My big thing was I wanted to see what the foster parents looked like, because they're perfect parents. They were the good parents. They were terrific. They were living in a nice home and I wasn't. There was a husband in the foster home. There wasn't in mine.
>
> When I opened the door and saw this blond, thin person. I was just so angry

because she was really attractive and I wasn't. They had everything that I didn't have. So I thought, "Aha, they didn't get me on the dirty housecleaning charges." So I went in with a white glove routine. I didn't care if I saw my daughter at that point. I wanted to check that house out, and if there was anything dirty, I was going to Sally (caseworker) and tell her. But I couldn't find anything wrong. It really bothered me. I was so angry. And then I did find something wrong. My daughter called her "Mommy," and not me. That was the hardest thing. I knew something was taken away because, my God, they took the kids away, they took the money away, they took everything away. Now they took my title away [McFadden, 1980, p. 141].

As placements go on, new sets of difficulties arise:

Parents may find themselves doubting as time drags on whether it will ever be possible to re-establish their family unit, and indeed whether their child will want to return to them. And given these doubts, it becomes increasingly hard for them to maintain contact with him in a positive spirit and face his questions about his future with them, without resorting to unrealistic promises and reassurances which then lead on to further disappointments and increasing lack of trust [Davidson, 1980, p. 48].

If the child is angry at the parent because of the placement, if the child attempts to make the parent feel guilty about the placement, or if the child is unrealistically insistent that he or she be taken home, parents may become acutely uncomfortable and avoid contact (Aldgate, 1976; Davidson, 1980). When the child does not seem to welcome parents and appears unappreciative and difficult to talk with, visits are also likely to drop off.

Foster parents may find it difficult to encourage parent–child contact when they feel competitive with birth parents, when they would prefer to have the child all to themselves, or when they feel that parents do not deserve to be caretakers for their children.

Mrs. G. expressed her very strong disapproval of Mrs. S. as a mother and as a person. She was able to come out and say in no uncertain terms that she disliked Mrs. S. and thought she was a "hateful person." When I tried to discover some of the reasons for the foster mother's feelings, she told me that Mrs. S. had "no respect." I asked her what she meant by this and she said, "She didn't respect me or my home." She told me how she would come into her house smelling of alcohol and how she used to come in and bring men with her and about how she would smoke while she was there, even though Mrs. G. had told her that Theresa was allergic to smoke and that she did not like to have anyone smoke in the same room with Theresa. She said that Mrs. S. would complain about the care she was giving Theresa and told Theresa she was not being well cared for.

The foster mother said she knew Mrs. S. did not like her either and after this last incident, Mrs. S. had never been there again to visit Theresa. Mrs. G. felt that she had tried to be fair about it and had done as much as she could be expected to in allowing Mrs. S. to come into her home, that she felt she had to put up with just too much to let the mother come in and act the way she did. I asked Mrs. G. if she could think of any reason why the mother might act this way, and she said that she could not. She could not understand why people should find fault with someone who had taken care of their children whom they were not able to care for themselves, especially when the care she was giving to Theresa was good and she was feeding and clothing her well. I said these complaints were not surprising to me because we had found that many times parents could come into a foster home and complain about the way the foster mother cared for their children. We have found that the reason the parents did this was mostly because they felt guilty about not being able to care for their children and resented the fact that someone else was able to give them good care. Foster mother said she thought this was true and could see why they would feel that way. The foster mother went on to say she thought if the mother had really wanted to take care of her children, she would find a way to do it, using the old expression "where there's a will, there is a way." I laughingly replied that if all parents could take care of their own children we would be out of business* [Wires, 1954, p. 9].

Interviewing new foster parents, Cautley (1980) found many highly critical—especially of the birth mother. Uninformed foster parents interpreted the child's "early upsets" when visiting as "events to be avoided," rather than part of an adaptation process (p. 263). Approximately one in ten of the parents surveyed by Jenkins and Norman (1975) stated that he or she felt foster parents did things to make visiting particularly difficult (p. 67). Birth parents complain that foster parents intrude on their visits with their children and make significant decisions about the child's life without consulting them. Competition from foster parents may be overt. During a family visit, a foster mother asked the child, "Did you show Mary (the natural mother) what Mommie bought you when we shopped yesterday?" (Murphy, 1981, p. 435). Differences in living standards between foster and biological homes create problems for birth parents, who feel that they may never be able to give their children the material goods easily available in the foster home.

These concerns are reflected in the comments of Mrs. McAdams, a mother of six children who were placed when she became mentally ill.

> The fact that you are visiting your child in a foster home is a reminder that you are, at least for the time being, a failure as a parent. You are very sensitive, especially during the first visits. Sometimes a foster parent, in a well-meaning effort to let you know that your child is doing well in a foster home, will make comments on how well the child is eating, how neat he keeps himself and his room, how happy he is, etc. To me, this type of remark was just an implied criticism of the care I had given my child, and was a verbal slap in the face. . . .
>
> The foster parent who gives you orders and instructions in the presence of your child is another problem. You are told that you should have the child back in the foster home at 5 o'clock, and admonished not to be late, or you are told to be sure little Tommy doesn't go outside without his sweater, as he has just recovered from a cold. These instructions may be necessary, but your kid, no matter how young, is already aware of the fact that you have little authority at this time, and this only increases the child's concern as to how responsible you are. If it is necessary to give the natural parent instructions about taking the child away from the foster home on an outing, it would be better to do so out of the child's presence. . . .
>
> I think it is possible for foster parents and natural parents to have mutual respect for each other, but the very nature of their relationship makes it impossible to avoid elements of jealousy and competition. In the case of my children, finding themselves in the position of having foster parents whom they loved and admired and yet having to cope with me trying to strengthen their love for me and regain their trust was almost too much. This problem took a lot of effort at all levels, before they accepted the fact that love for one set of parents did not imply disloyalty to the other. . . .
>
> I know quite often children return from visits with the natural parents with all

---

* From Emily Wires, "Some Factors in the Worker-Foster Parent Relationship," *Child Welfare* (October 1954). By permission of Child Welfare League of America, Inc.

sorts of plans and promises given them during the visit. It is very difficult to deny a child any hope when the immediate situation seems to be pretty bleak. My kids were able to extract tentative promises of when we would all be reunited, because my pride was killing me and I didn't have the heart to say that I had no home, no money, and no definite time when I would have sufficient emotional and financial resources for getting these things [McAdams, 1972, p. 52].

Like birth parents, foster parents are aware that their own feelings and needs can contribute to visiting tensions. Thoburn (1980) notes, "although foster parents commented about the strains which this sort of role places on them, several of those I spoke to thought it was not impossible to share the care of the children with the parents, and several regularly do so. What they did strongly ask for was recognition for the difficulties by social workers, and particularly for support from the social workers in drawing up clearly understood guidelines about visiting with the parents" (p. 136).

Agency policies and caseworker actions can also interfere with effective promotion of parent-child contact. Analyzing national child welfare data, Olsen (1982b) discovered that one-third of the children in substitute care had no regular contact plan and that workers were least likely to develop these plans for black or Hispanic children (p. 581). (See also Fanshel, 1982; Vernon, 1985.) In some instances, workers actively discouraged parental visits, in others, through "passive inaction," they allow parents to reduce contact (Holman, 1980, p. 81; Thoburn, 1980; Vernon, 1985). Assessing the records of 256 children in care in Illinois, Proch and Howard (1986) conclude:

Most parents who were scheduled to visit did so, and most visited in compliance with the schedule specified in the case plan. Parents who did not have a visiting schedule or who were told to request a visit when they wanted one did not visit. This clearly suggests that a way to increase the frequency of visits is to schedule them to occur more frequently [p. 180].

(See also George, 1970; Gruber, 1973; Thorpe, 1974.)

When children are placed in homes some distance from their birth family home or in inaccessible locations, birth parents, who tend to be very poor, are forced to decrease the frequency of visitation unless they are provided with funds and/or transportation by the agency. In his research on foster-care children in New York City, Fanshel (1982) found that only 1 in 5 parents had been provided with this type of assistance (p. 73). In his five-state survey, Yoshikami (1984) discovered obstacles to visiting (distance, high transportation costs, and so on) in 70 per cent of child welfare agency records. (See also Thoburn, 1980; Jenkins & Norman, 1975.)

On occasions, workers have cancelled visits in an effort to punish birth parents or children for inappropriate behavior or for failing to meet expectations. In addition, agencies have created more restricted visiting policies because some individuals have performed poorly, thereby punishing the many for the mistakes of the few. In many instances, evolution of the requirement that all visits must take place at the agency grows out of one or two particularly troublesome experiences with foster family-based or home-based visiting (Blumenthal & Weinberg, 1984).

In their attempt to maintain a foster home for a child, workers may also attempt to pacify angry foster parents by making increasingly restrictive visitation decisions (Holman, 1980; Rowe, 1980; Cox & Cox, 1984). The pressure to maintain children in a stable situation free from the trauma and damage that visits sometimes create and the pressure to keep foster homes in the system by minimizing impositions on foster parents both act to dampen worker enthusiasm about visiting. Rowe et al. (1984) suggest the situation is even more complex, that the worker, parents, and foster family may collude in creating visitation breakdown:

> We were frequently dismayed and sometimes angered by the way in which social workers so often failed to provide the necessary support and encouragement to maintain visiting. Sometimes they actually seemed to set up "no win" situations for natural parents, first discouraging visits "to let the children settle" and later saying that after such a long gap renewed visiting would be upsetting. But this was by no means the whole story. We found that ambivalence towards visiting seemed to be a prevalent attitude in natural parents and foster children as well as in social workers and foster parents. Everyone seems to draw back from the pain and potential conflict involved (pp. 99–100).

Despite these difficulties, caseworkers and parents do work together to attain reunification in a number of cases. Approximately, one in three of the children in care are returned to their families each year (Becker & Austin, 1983; Yoshikami, 1984). Considering all children who leave care within a year, approximately 40 to 55 per cent are reunited with their birth families (Hubbell, 1981; Gershenson, 1983, Fein, et al., 1983). Moreover, evidence from several sources indicates that parental circumstances and behaviors influence this outcome. Stein, Gambrill, and Wiltse (1978) discovered that, when families had worked to resolve their parent–child difficulties and their personal and marital problems, they were more likely to have their children return (p. 90). Fanshel (1982) created an "Index of Child's Relationship to Natural Family" that measured the extent to which children identified with their families and remained in touch with them. The index was a significant predictor of reunification. While children with high Index scores were more likely to return home, those with low scores were more likely to be adopted (pp. 297–298). Thoburn (1980) argues that it is continued parental pressure to have children returned that powerfully affects workers and influences them to release the child to the family (p. 128). (See also Kliman, Schaeffer, & Friedman, 1982; Yoshikami, 1984, p. 185).

To effectively help children who have been in the foster care system, work must continue with birth families after reunification has occurred. A number of these families continue to grapple with stressful life circumstances that can, once again, prevent them from effectively caring for their children. The limited available evidence indicates that caseworkers take their follow-up responsibility seriously. Within four months of the child's return home, workers in Connecticut were in some type of contact with 79 per cent of the families, by six to ten months after placement, they had contacted 58 per cent of the families, and twelve to sixteen months after reunification, 49 per cent of the families had been contacted (Fein et al., 1983, p. 526).

Social Work Practice with Foster Mothers and Fathers

Although the role of foster parent may appear indistinguishable from that of any other primary caretaker for the child, several specific characteristics make this a unique responsibility. Foster parents do not "own" their foster children. As "parallel" parents, foster parents are family aides. They do not assume parenting responsibility; they *share* it" (Blumenthal & Weinberg, 1984, p. 37). Foster parents cannot encourage the child to develop exclusive emotional investment in themselves. Fanshel and Shinn (1978) documented the strength of these birth family affiliations. When asked to do a sentence completion noting "the person I love best," 51 per cent of the children described a birth parent, but only 9 per cent described a foster parent. When asked to complete the statement "if I could choose anybody to live with, I'd choose," 37 per cent of the children chose the birth family, and only 7 per cent chose the foster family (p. 463). Foster parents must struggle to accept the primary role that birth family members hold in the child's affections.

The fact that the agency is responsible for the basic cost of maintenance of a child indicates an essential difference between foster and birth parenthood. Furthermore, foster parents are responsible for a child for only a limited segment of his or her lifespan. Foster parents cannot plan for the child's future, nor can they legitimately expect to share in the child's future achievements (McCoy, 1962; Hubbell, 1981). Instead, they may play a crucial role in helping a child find a more permanent future in someone else's home.

Foster parents want to provide a child with a home. Yet in getting a child, they found they get an agency as well. The agency sets limits and advances directives as to how the foster parents are to behave toward the child—a situation not normally encountered by birth families. This shared control and responsibility are clearly set forth in instruction pamphlets issued to foster parents. One such pamphlet points out, "Disciplining a child must be done with kindness and understanding. Corporal punishment, which includes striking, whipping, slapping, or any other form of discipline that inflicts the child with physical pain, is prohibited. *Don't forget that prohibited means not allowed.* Disobeying the regulations is cause for cancellation of the foster home license." Avoiding any use of physical means of child control is not an approach that many foster parents would take, if given free choice in the matter. Foster parents typically favor the use of physical disciplinary techniques more frequently and for older-age children than do social workers (Haines, Schumm, & Kennedy, 1981). Effective and permissible means of disciplining have become common discussion topics in foster parents group and agency training sessions (Hampson & Tavormina, 1980; Felker, 1981).

Foster parents are also obligated to discuss the child's behavioral difficulties with the agency, and they are not free to choose and pursue the use of various remedial services for the child without the worker's approval. Frequently, the family must obtain agency approval in order to change sleeping arrangements, or to take the child out of state on a vacation trip.

Although all parents are accountable in a general way to society, there are no formal channels that periodically take a measure of their performance. The foster parents, however, are accountable to an agency, and the yearly relicensing is the procedure by which an accounting is explicitly made. The decision as to whether the child remains or goes rests with the agency. The state license usually includes a clause stipulating that the foster parents must agree to the removal of the child upon the request of the agency. Removal of a child from the biological parents' home can be effected only after due process of law. Removal of the foster child from the foster-family home can be undertaken merely on the basis of the agency's decision. The foster parents' relationship with the child has very limited legal protection. If the foster parents value this relationship, this situation must of necessity make them anxious and desirous of pleasing—and sometimes even of placating—the agency.

Although explicit differences between foster and biological parenthood exist, fostering remains an ambiguously defined role, and its enactment is likely to occasion difficulty. This role includes responsibilities as "caretaker, therapist, compensatory parent, and substitute parent" (Rowe, 1980, p. 58), a potentially confusing set of obligations that may leave the parent frustrated and uncertain, about what is expected:

> To work for (with ? under ?) a child welfare agency, to be paid a pittance, to be asked to parent a child whom no one else is able to parent, to try to love that child and to lose him or her when loving has been achieved, to be supervised by a 22-year-old social worker, to have to deal with school teachers, police, courts, medical appointments, angry biological parents, and the impact of all this upon one's own family—that is the lot and life of a typical foster mother in America [Meyer, 1985, p. 252].

Wolins (1963) attempted to define the role of the foster parent empirically by interviews with nineteen child welfare workers, ninety-three foster parents, and seventy-eight close neighbors of foster parents. The study showed that few of the respondents defined the role in any unique or distinctive way: "More than three-fourths of our foster parents perceived themselves as most like a natural parent. For them, confusion is resolved when they understand others' expectations of them to be no different from those of a natural parent" (Wolins, 1963, p. 30). (See also Ambinder et al. 1962.)

The data suggest that many of the foster parents wish to exclude the case-worker from significant involvement in the life of the foster home—a further manifestation of their desire to act as real parent surrogates, jealously guarding the prerogatives of this role from outside interference. As Weinstein (1960) points out:

> There is little in the way of clean-cut formulations of the limits of responsibility and power to initiate or veto decisions associated with each of the positions in the [placement] system. In consequence, relationships develop in which there are disagreements about the rights and responsibilities of each of the parties. The child may be confronted with three sets of adults, all of whom have some stake in caring for him and planning for his future. In the absence of clearly structured role expectations, both power and responsibility may sometimes be shared, sometimes competed for, and sometimes denied by one or more of the three [p. 15].

Holman (1975, 1980) distinguishes between "exclusive" and "inclusive" foster families. Exclusive foster parents attempt to make the child their own and exclude other relationships. They see foster care as a quasi-adoptive situation. The biological parent is an unwelcome visitor; the social worker is perceived as a "friend" rather than an agency representative with some responsibility for the child. Inclusive foster parents, on the other hand, do not identify themselves as the "real" parents of the child, welcome the biological parents' visits, and see the social worker as a colleague. Holman estimates that two out of every three foster parents are more exclusively oriented, while one in three view their role in more inclusive terms. (See also Adamson, 1973; Me Whinnie, 1978.)

Social worker evaluations agree with these foster parents self-assessments. Using data from New York, Fanshel (1982) found some three-quarters of foster children were rated by workers as "deeply integrated within the foster families to the point of experiencing the foster parents as own family (52.6%) or quite strongly identified with them (25.9%)" (p. 255).

Holman notes that success in fostering is more likely to be achieved with the inclusive concept because, being more closely aligned with the realities of the situation, such an orientation occasions less conflict. Parents providing long-term care, however, find less conflict in adopting an exclusive viewpoint, and more often they tend to perceive their role in exclusive terms.

Playing a role as mediator, with the foster child, birth family, and foster parents, the caseworker provides a variety of services to the foster family. The worker visits the foster home regularly, discussing the child's adjustment and the family's reaction to the child. The worker provides a perspective on the unique role these parents are attempting to play. The worker acts as an adviser-teacher, a counselor, and a source of psychological support, allaying anxiety and providing reassurance when it is needed. The worker also becomes a significant resource for information and guidance when the foster family must seek assistance with medical, educational, or emotional difficulties that arise in the course of living with and helping a particular child. The task of the worker is not to judge the family— removing the child whenever problems arise—but to assist and support the family and to validate its efforts to find effective means of resolving difficulties (Reeves, 1980; Shulman, 1980).

The foster worker prepares the family for the child's arrival by sharing birth family background information, reasons for the placement, the child's developmental history, peculiarities, preferences, special fears, and special pleasures, weaknesses, and strengths. Whatever the foster parent knows or has been told about foster care and about childrearing in general, the worker has to translate at this time into relevant information for this particular placement.

The foster parents' perception of the child tends to shape the way they relate to the child. The worker needs to help the foster parents understand and respond empathetically to the child's actual or anticipated behavior. This should be done descriptively rather than through labeling. Using a diagnostic or psychiatric label tends to brand the child, encouraging misperception of the child's behavior so that it is seen in line with the label, and in general tends to accelerate the development of a self-fulfilling prophecy. This descriptive material becomes fully meaningful only after the foster parents actually see the child behaving in the ways that were anticipated. At these times, discussions with the caseworker are more likely to develop the kind of understanding the child needs from the foster parents.

It is hard for foster parents to understand how a child might still feel some affection for the natural parents, given the nature of the negative treatment he or she has received from them. The fact that the child continues to miss the birth parents and continues to talk about them might be seen by the foster parents as a rejection or as a comment on the adequacy of their care. The worker reassures the foster parent that this is not the case.

Foster parents complain that the agency does not provide them with sufficient background information.

> The Kelley's knew little about why Robert had been placed in foster care, why he had landed in their home, or the requirements for his return home. "He was in some kind of probationary state in another foster home", said Martin Kelley. "No, I can't really say why he was placed here." [Hubbell, 1981, p. 121].

Foster parents also express concern that, when they are provided with material about the child, they are not given it in sufficient detail for it to be helpful (Shulman, 1980). With detailed information, parents have an opportunity to answer the child's questions and to facilitate the child's understanding about birth family circumstances and the reasons why placement has occurred (Kahan, 1979).

In a detailed examination of the placement experiences of 145 new foster parents, Cautley (1980) discovered that "two-thirds of all the families had no more than a total of one or two contacts (joint or individual) with the worker in preparation, and less than a total of three hours was devoted to these" (p. 55). Eight per cent of the families had no preparation whatsoever, "other than a brief telephone call on the same day."

The worker also provides foster parents with an essential perspective on their role and responsibilities, agency expectations, and regulations. The foster parent knows the foster child better than the caseworker ever can, but the caseworker knows foster children and general reactions to foster care situations, and can provide for the foster parent a perspective on this process that is helpful:

> . . . [The caseworker] knows that fostering is largely a matter of trial and error, and that if a fostering fails it may be because he has not selected the right child or the right foster home, or that the child was not yet ready for a fostering experience, or that the interference of the real parents has made the success of the fostering impossible. But the foster parent does not have this experience of fostering as a guide. The foster parent . . . tends to feel that the success or failure of the fostering rests entirely on what the foster home has to offer to the child. To learn that this is not so will relieve the burden on the foster parents [Kastell, 1962, p. 116].

In preparation for placement and in helping the family with the critical adjustment to the child's entrance into the family, contacts with both foster father and foster mother are more likely to lead to the success of the placement than contact with the mother only. Foster fathers tend not to be the passive partners they are generally perceived to be by caseworkers. Their apparent passivity derives from the fact that they see some aspects of child care as the mother's responsibility. Foster fathers, Fanshel (1966) notes, are "quite strong and firm in the areas they perceive to be within their proper area of functioning" (p. 151). (See also Davids, 1968.)

Younger foster fathers demonstrate greater involvement in childrearing and child care. The trend toward greater overlap between maternal and paternal responsibilities suggests a necessity for more detailed inspection of foster fathering (Hampson & Tavormina, 1980). Foster fathers may also be the parents who provide first indications when trouble is developing in the family. The mother may be more reluctant to share incipient problems because, as the principal childcare parent, she may feel they reflect on her adequacy (Weinstein, 1960; Rowe et al., 1984). The foster father is often less hesitant about speaking up. Cautley (1980), for example, found fathers less enthusiastic about and more critical of agency policies and of worker behavior (p. 245).

Another critical task of the foster care worker is to help the family gradually integrate the child into the family unit. The arrival of a foster child means a reworking of the old family configuration. The family's interactional patterns grow more complex with the inclusion of another person and although this may be a source of satisfaction and pleasure, it also may create problems in interpersonal relationships that the worker helps the parents understand and deal with (Shulman, 1980). When their own children are initially enthusiastic about adding a new child to the family group, interested and excited in the child's arrival, parents may be bewildered when enthusiasm rapidly turns to anger as the children compete for parental attention, squabble over space, and learn that they must give to as well as take from each other (Euster, Ward, & Varner, 1982).

Foster parents express concern about the impact of the new child on the integrity of the family unit primarily during the early months of placement (Cautley, 1980). It is during this time that the worker must be readily available and willing to help, to answer questions, and to reassure parents. Patterns of interaction between foster parents and child begin to be established early in the placement. It is easier to establish a good pattern than to reverse a negative interaction. Attitudes toward the worker and the agency likewise begin to be established during this period. The worker needs to make an extra effort at this time in order to establish a cooperative relationship as the basis for further foster family service efforts.

The early period in placement is apt to be a high-risk period. Foster parents feel a sense of frustration and anxiety when they have insufficient information about how to cope effectively with their child, and they see little sign of positive progress. In her meticulous study of the changes that occur in new foster families, Cautley (1980), discovered that, over time, early concerns about potential family disruption gradually give way to an emphasis on child progress and, finally, by eighteen months to a level of foster parent acceptance of their role, with all of its ups and downs (p. 244). The social worker can facilitate the move from one developmental phase to the next. Cautley notes that information must be given to parents when and as they need it, since they cannot fully understand the meaning of this adaptation process and its attendant difficulties until they reach and work through each particular stage.

One of the most important contributions that the caseworker makes to the psychic comfort of the foster parents is assurance that their occasional negative feelings toward the foster child are understandable, acceptable, and entirely normal, that an occasional failure in dealing with the foster child is inevitable, and that negative behavior on the part of the child is not a reflection of any inadequacy on their part as parents. Such reassurance, coming from a representative of the agency that has had experience with many foster placements, is often an effective antidote to the compulsive self-doubt that affects many foster parents as they encounter problems that they had not anticipated in being surrogate parents to troubled children from troubled homes.

Furthermore the caseworker's recognition, in the name of the agency, which represents the community, that they are doing an important job satisfactorily helps to compensate foster parents for the frequent disappointments felt in the slight emotional return they get from the child in response to the considerable emotional energies they invest. Cautley (1980) comments:

> When the families caring for the children perceived as "difficult" were examined, it appeared that the way in which the social worker handled the request for professional help was an important determinant of satisfaction: first, whether the help was provided; and second, the way in which the results were communicated. In addition, it became clear that some sort of return was needed to enable foster parents to continue. The occurrence of the year's anniversary appeared to prompt these new families to review the progress made and consider their investment of time and energy. The return could be an expression of affection from the child; or evidence that the child was improving. But if neither of these occurred, the social worker needed to provide the support, reassurance, and encouragement to the foster parents if they were to be expected to continue [p. 244].

(See also Keane, 1983, p. 162.)

The social worker also carries a central responsibility in assisting foster parents to understand their obligations with regard to the child's birth family, and to learn to interact with and assist that family more effectively (Murphy, 1981; Blumenthal & Weinberg, 1984). Like child-care workers in institutions, foster parents can develop more positive attitudes toward birth families as they have increasing opportunity to interact with them. With caseworker assistance, early mistrust, hostility, and fear can gradually give way to a more facilitative role, and in some instances to the growth of close supportive relationships between birth and foster parents (Lee & Park, 1980; McFadden, 1980; Cautley, 1980; Thoburn, 1980; Ryan, McFadden, & Warren, 1981; Felker, 1981; Davies & Bland, 1981; Meezan & Shireman, 1985). A foster parent's comments on the value of this work with birth families

> I felt very good about this (getting the birth mother to the child's parent–teacher conference) because I had accomplished the goal I wanted to accomplish, and that's to save this family. The day that child came into my home I said, "The kid is going to go home. I know that's going to be the court order. My responsibility is to make sure that he does not return into care." What I know now will happen. She will be able to call me when she needs help when he goes home. And he will have a friend to talk to when he doesn't know what else to do. That is a success story to me, and it works [Hess & Hicks, 1979, pp. 161, 170].

A birth parent describes the critical assistance provided her by a foster mother, who helped her make the decision to eventually relinquish her child for adoption.

> At some point, they could tell the visitations were getting worse and worse. But I was doing it. She (foster mother) finally said to me, "You don't want him, do you? And I said. "No." She got on the phone and told Sally (caseworker) that. She was the first person who had really gotten me to say that. Alot of it's because my mother kept on saying, 'You've got to bring them home'. And I was scared to say anything negative to Sally. So I thought I'd better be good. I had dropped hints in therapy that I didn't want him home, but I'd never really said them directly. It was somehow easier to say it to the foster parent. Because she said it first, she confronted me. It felt good. It was like, 'Thank God, somebody heard me" (McFadden, 1980, p. 148).

Although foster parents can play such a vital role in assisting birth families in this way, data from several sources indicate that they are rarely allowed an opportunity to do so or are provided with sufficient social service assistance in learning to be effective models or sources of support for birth parents (Shulman, 1980; Hubbell, 1981; Fanshel, 1982).

The caseworker provides yet another service to foster families by making available to them and helping them utilize financial and other resources available for care of the child in their home. Children's eligibility for AFDC assistance is carried with them when they are removed from their own family and placed in substitute care. These payments, known as AFDC-FC (FC for "foster care"), are then made to the foster home. In December 1977, about 107,000 children, the majority in foster–family homes, were receiving such assistance, which totaled 32.218 million dollars. For children ineligible for this type of assistance, the child welfare agency can make support payments available out of general child welfare funds. The child welfare agency, in addition to providing these board payments, helps the family utilize resources of the community. It takes care of medical and dental treatment; it provides glasses, orthopedic appliances, and prescription medicine; it makes available psychological testing and psychotherapy for the child.

Although most foster families received some type of monetary assistance, these funds rarely cover the full cost of a child's care. In a four-year study of 596 foster families in Ottawa and Montreal, Shulman (1980) noted that only 65 per cent said they were satisfied with agency payment rates. The author examined the experiences of foster families in eleven different areas and found that this was the one in which least satisfaction was noted (p. 68).

Visits by the caseworker to the home are designed to discharge the supervisory responsibility of the agency. As Kline, Overstreet, and Furbush (1972) say, "The foster parents' primary role is that of surrogate parents to the child within their own family setting under the supervision of an agency that is responsible and accountable for the child's care" (p. 220). The caseworker visits to see how the child is getting along, what more needs to be done, and whether or not the child is adequately cared for. The supervisory components may be threatening to the foster parents and are likely to make them defensive. Some mitigation of the threat comes from the fact that the caseworker attempts to see the foster parents as persons in their own right, rather than as an "environment" for the child. He or she approaches the foster parents with some consideration for their needs and anxieties, assuming that they are not solely interested in justifying themselves and concealing their failings and difficulties but, rather, that they are eager to do a creditable job and to understand the child.

The worker also appreciates that foster parents have a direct and personal stake in the child's behavior and that they face direct and personal consequences when the agency makes decisions on behalf of the child (Edelstein, 1981). The most common complaints that foster parents make are the same as those voiced by birth parents—that they are omitted from the decision-making process and that they are not routinely provided with essential information about the child:

> I did not want the worker to approach my foster son and ask him to participate in the group. I told him this, but he said that he felt "our son" could benefit and was going to do this anyway. So even after bringing up this boy for the last ten years, we did not have the right to be able to say, "No, don't ask him" (Shulman, 1980, p. 70).

Foster parents more frequently ask for support and sanction than for instruction or advice. What they want, and keenly appreciate, is a caseworker who listens with empathy, sympathy, and interest, and who gives them the commendation of the agency for their efforts. Foster parents want and respond warmly to the worker's availability, interest, concern, and willingness to discuss their problems with them in a joint effort to find possible solutions. The worker has greater experience with foster care compared with the foster parents' experience, a wider perspective on foster care, and a structured, problem-solving approach to child-care problems. These are helpful even if the worker may lack a ready, easy answer to questions raised.

One problem, then, for workers involves assuming too powerful a role and in failing to negotiate sufficiently with the foster family. Another involves worker errors in the opposite direction. That is, facing foster family antagonism and fearing the loss of scarce foster homes, workers may make too concerted an effort to avoid criticizing or antagonizing the family, even in situations in which the welfare of the child requires this. Effective foster-care casework service requires the worker achieve a difficult balance juggling at the same time responsibility for the child and the obligation to respect and value the contribution made by the child's day-to-day caretakers.

Although some studies suggest that the worker is seen primarily as performing administrative functions—that is, linking the child and the placement and supervising the placement—other studies indicate that the worker is perceived as a source of understanding and help, a role the worker is more interested in and more prepared to implement.

Interviews with 219 foster parents indicated that "overall the foster parents were highly positive in their view of the agencies" (Rosenblum, 1977, p. 57). Foster parents responded positively to the fact that the worker had a "good understanding of a child or a child's problems," that "the worker treated them with respect and/or like fully capable adults and/or *not* like clients" (p. 57). "Attempting a therapy role with them and their family" is considered disrespectful, an intrusion into private concerns unrelated to fostering. It is perceived as moving the worker's principal concern away from a cooperative arrangement focused on helping the child. Despite considerable ambivalence in their expectations of workers, Rowe et al (1984) report:

> In spite of all the problems we have noted and a good many criticisms, there was a sense of considerable loyalty to the department and the general level of satisfaction seemed remarkably high. Forty-five per cent of foster mothers described the department as "very helpful" and a further 18% said "usually helpful" [p. 167].

In Jenkins and Norman's (1975) study, birth parents rated workers higher on interest and understanding than on helpfulness (p. 64). A more recent survey of Canadian parents (Shulman, 1980) replicates these findings. Sixty per cent of these foster families said that the worker had often discussed the child with them, and 83 per cent of this group felt that the worker was helpful. However, only 30 per cent believed that, as a result of this discussion, their relationship with the child changed for the better. Shockingly only 45 per cent of these experienced foster families had *ever* discussed birth parents with the foster care caseworker, and only 57 per cent had ever discussed their own family's adaptation to the child (p. 71). When these or other issues were discussed, respondents consistently rated the caseworker as very helpful or helpful and claimed, for the most part, that they were satisfied with the worker's input. When criticisms of the worker's role were offered, they centered around "lack of contact and lack of interest" (pp. 69–70).

Use of Group Methods for Foster Parents. Exploration of use of group techniques to educate, support, and assist foster parents has expanded in recent years. This approach can accomplish the following types of objectives.

1. To increase the knowledge and skills of foster parenthood and to improve foster family relationships with the foster child, both through increased tolerance and understanding of the child's behavior and increased skill in dealing with this behavior (Ryan, Warren & McFadden, 1979; Hubbell, 1981).
2. To offer foster parents an opportunity to discuss problems of mutual concern and to build mutual support (Jacobs, 1980). In the safety of numbers, foster parents can express dissatisfaction with agency policy and develop a stronger role in agency decision making with regard to the child (Roberts, 1962).

3. To enhance the status and, hence, the satisfaction of foster parents.

4. To enable the agency to have a better understanding of foster parent experiences and needs.

5. To allow foster parents to gain an appreciation of what the birth family and child need from each other and of the impact of their separation from one another. In the group, foster parents have an opportunity to develop greater tolerance toward the birth family as they learn something about the difficult life situations these parents face (Euster, Ward, & Varner, 1982).

6. To enable foster parents to gain a better appreciation of the agency's difficulties and problems and to help foster parents and agency work toward a consensus about the relative rights and obligations of the agency, birth family, and foster parents vis-à-vis the foster child.

7. To help foster families realize that in some instances, they may fail despite their best efforts and that failure in foster care may result from the child's deficiencies rather from any shortcomings on their part. Foster parents appreciate the truth of this as they listen to other parents discussing some of the problems they have encountered.

8. To serve other agency purposes such as self-screening of potential applicants, expanded opportunities to disseminate information about foster care, sparking and planning recruitment programs, and establishing and evaluating agency foster-care policies [MacDonald & Ferguson, 1964].

Education in foster-parent role enactment provided by agency-sponsored discussion groups (Goldstein & Dall, 1967; Mills et al., 1967) is supplemented by specialized courses offered by schools of social work in cooperation with child-placing agencies. Such a course might meet for ten to fifteen weekly sessions. (Appleberg, 1968; Reistroffer, 1968; Hanwell, et al., 1969. Norgard & Mayhall, 1982). Curricula have also been disseminated by various organizations. The NOVA model used in Florida has since been adopted in several other states (Pasztor, 1985). The Child Welfare League of America publishes a basic curriculum for foster parent education that includes training materials and a variety of audiovisual aids. Using NIMH funding, faculty at Eastern Michigan University developed seventeen course outlines for foster-parent training (Ryan, Warren, & McFadden, 1979). One widely known training curriculum is "Walk a Mile in My Shoes" (Lee & Park, 1980). It helps foster parents to interact more effectively with birth families. (See also Heinritz & Frey, 1975; Marr, 1976; Guerney, 1976). Since 1976, the Foster Parent Education Network, a consortium of individuals interested in training, has been meeting annually at National Foster Parent Association conferences (Pasztor, 1985). Recognition of its utility has led several states—including Arizona, Michigan, Massachusetts, Ohio, and Pennsylvania—to mandate training, either for new foster parents, or for all parents on an annual basis (Pasztor, 1985; Norgard & Mayhall, 1982).

Sometimes group meetings are directed to foster mothers only, but more frequently they are designed for both foster parents. Although the groups often start with didactic instructional material, they usually move to a more informal pattern in which content for discussion is decided upon or influenced by participants. Trainers agree that effective adult learning requires that the concerns and needs of members be specifically addressed.

Training may not be made available to parents as routinely as it should be. A nationwide survey of 173 foster care agencies showed that only 38 per cent offered some type of group service (Weinbach, Edwards, & Levy, 1977). Interviews with thirty-four active foster mothers from a public welfare agency in Virginia indicated that, although twenty-six believed that group training would be of benefit to them, only 10 had participated in any type of educational experience. Only three of these mothers had had more than two hours of training (Hampson & Tavormina, 1980, p. 111).

Where training has been made available, evidence indicates its utility for foster families. Using a behavior modification approach, one program documented positive changes in the behavior of foster children as a consequence of participants' application of techniques learned in the program (Penn, 1978). A two-year follow-up of a behaviorally oriented foster parent training program offered to 105 foster families showed it to be effective in reducing foster parent turnover (Boyd & Remy, 1978). An elaborate evaluation of NOVA educative methods (Simon & Simon, 1982) noted similar results. Compared to control group parents, NOVA group participants were less likely to drop out during intake, were more likely to accept children into care, and agreed more frequently to foster difficult children. Trained families accepted an average of 2.03 children during the study year, while control group families accepted one child. Participating families were also less likely to experience placement disruption or failure. Within a six-month period children were removed from 17 per cent of experimental group and 28 per cent of control group homes. When the reasons for removal were examined, twice the number of control group families disrupted because the parents themselves lacked the ability to deal effectively with the child or agency (pp. 520–523). (See also Noble & Euster, 1981; Lloyd, 1982.)

Group effectiveness is dependent upon the level of preparation and skill that the leader provides and, to some extent, upon the degree of commitment which participants bring with them. Assessing the overall quality of six different eight-week programs, Engel (1983) found that three of the six were of "good quality" (more than half the sessions characterized by good attendance, good participation, and meaningful subject matter), whereas, in the other three, only two of eight meetings could be described this way (p. 205). In some instances, this resulted from variable skills of the group leaders; in others, poor-quality sessions resulted when foster-parent mistrust of the agency's motives or anger at the agency turned meetings into unproductive gripe sessions.

Foster Family Effectiveness. Despite the stresses and strains of their roles, most foster parents are doing an effective job raising the children in their care. Social workers evaluate most foster family homes as very positive living environments for children. In one New York study, some 77 to 84 per cent of foster homes were rated as excellent or good in overall performance (Fanshel & Shinn, 1978). Using more detailed social worker assessments of both the foster mother and father, Fanshel (1982) found most parents rated warm and affectionate. Less than one in ten was described as "objective, cool, or hostile." Most mothers and more than half of the fathers were considered insightful and understanding of the child. More than two out of three foster mothers were rated as having a high or fairly high degree of rapport with the child; however, only one in five fathers received this rating. Very few foster families failed to provide sufficient intellectual stimulation, a harmonious environment, or appropriate discipline (pp. 270–275). Fanshel and Shinn (1978; report that, when foster parents provided the child with a stimulating intellectual climate and utilized democratic childrearing techniques, growth in the child's cognitive abilities was facilitated (pp. 496–497). Using similar measures, Goldston (1982) verified these findings using a sample of fifty-six foster mothers. Most birth parents agree that their children receive adequate care in foster family settings. "On the whole, parents were satisfied with the care given to their children, and apart from the cases . . . where there were divided loyalties which led to considerable unhappiness on all sides, most either thought their children had gained from the experience or come to no harm" (Thoburn, 1980, p.58).

With increasing sensitivity to the child's need for permanency, recent research has focused on additional criteria for effective foster parenthood. These include the family's willingness to consider providing long-term or adoptive care for a child requiring this. In his studies of children in care more than one year in New York, Fanshel (1982) found that four out of five foster parents had been asked to consider potentially adopting the child. When approached, 53 per cent responded in a very positive way, 20 per cent in a somewhat positive way, and one in ten was very much against the idea (p. 242). As expected, foster parents were more likely to be hesitant about adoption when the child had serious medical, emotional, or interpersonal problems, and agencies were less likely to discuss it with families when the child had been in several placements or maintained regular contact with birth parents.

In their research comparing adopting and nonadopting foster families, Meezan and Shireman (1985a) concluded, "It appears that many foster parents can identify themselves as either potential adopters or temporary caretakers at intake, and that agencies should capitalize on this ability. Those who wish to foster should have children placed with them who are likely to return to their biological homes. Those who are interested in adoption should have children placed in their homes for whom this might become the goal of service" (p. 214).

Replacement

The most desirable placement is one that permits the child to remain in the same home during the entire period of time that the child needs care. Removal from one foster home to another imposes on the child emotional burdens associated with separation and change. Every replacement reintroduces separation issues and reinforces previous rejection experiences. Multiple placements increase the child's difficulty in establishing and maintaining a sense of continuity and personal identity, of determining who he or she is and where he or she belongs. Frequent replacement makes it more likely that the child will manifest emotional problems and that subsequent placements will fail (Eisenberg, 1965).

Children experiencing replacement are also usually required to sever all ties to previous caretakers and to the environment with which they had become familiarized. Hubbell (1981) describes the experiences of parents who had cared for seven foster children.

> Once the children left, the relationships ended abruptly. They have not tried to contact any of the children. They admit that they were "kind of afraid to. We'd love to know what's happening but how would the parents feel? If one of our foster kids goes on to another foster home and we contacted him, it might interfere with the new relationship. One of our (former foster) children called once and the (new) foster parents didn't like it" [pp. 122–123].

A survey of families whose foster homes had been closed in Alaska (Baring-Gould, et al., 1983) disclosed that 69 per cent had never been informed of how the child was subsequently adjusting, and 74 per cent had never been encouraged to stay in touch with the child (p. 57). Experiencing this type of abrupt severance, children conclude that relationships are unpredictable and unreliable and that one cannot rely upon people to continue to care or to remain available in the future. These discoveries reinforce the child's tendency to avoid developing close ties and to fear relying on adults.

As Table 7-1 indicates, approximately half the children in care experience a single stable foster home, whereas the remainder must endure replacement experiences. A recapitulation of eleven studies covering the experience of some sixteen thousand children in care an average of two years or longer showed that some 75 per cent of the group had two or fewer placements (Kadushin, 1978, p. 101). Approximately one in five children undergoes three or more placements, while a small minority will be exposed to the trauma of multiple family experiences—in six or

TABLE 7-1. Foster Home Replacement Rates

Source	Data Base	Replacement Rates
Vasaly (1978), p. 56	Reanalysis of data from five states; Various time spans; Foster family care	40%–57% One placement 21%–27% Three + placements
Shyne & Schroeder (1978), p. 118	National data; In care on specific date; Foster family care	53% One placement 22% Three + placements
Fanshel & Shinn (1978), p. 139	Data from New York; In care over five-year period; Foster family care	41% One placement 28% Three + placements
Hubbell (1981), p. 58	Data from three communities; In care over 3 ½ year period; Foster family care	1.8 average placements over 3 ½ years
State of California (1981), p. 101	Data from three counties; Annual rates; Foster family care	46% One placement 31% Three + placements
Kliman, Schaeffer, & Friedman (1982), p. 84	Data from one county; In care over 17-month period; Foster family care	At 6 months: 56% One placement At 12 months: 52% One placement At 17 months: 49% One placement,:wq 27% Three + placements
Fanshel (1982), p. 231	Data from New York; In care at least one year at survey time; Foster family care	64% One placement 13% Three + placements
Gershenson (1983), p. 21	VCIS data from 20 states; Annual rates; Substitute care	53% One placement 27% Three + placements 7% Six + placements
Becker (1983), p. 6	Data from one state; In care on specific date; Substitute care	57% One placement 20% Three + placements
Stone & Stone (1983), p. 13	Data from 3 child welfare units; 64 consecutive cases; Foster family care	48.5% removed from placement prior to completion of agency plan
Festinger (1983), pp. 55–56	Data from New York City; In care at leats 5 years and now aged 18–21; Foster family care	32% of males One-two placements 40% of females One-two placements 68% of males Three + placements 60% of females Three + placements

eight or ten different homes (Gershenson, 1983). (See also Maluccio & Fein, 1985, pp. 126–129).

Some data indicate that breakdown in foster placements are more likely to occur early in the placement process (Kliman, Schaeffer, & Friedman, 1982; Stone & Stone, 1983; Festinger, 1983). However, time in care is also associated with increased disruption.

> As the length of time in care increased, and as the age of the child increased, the number of placements the child experienced grew. For every three years in care between the date of their first placement and the date on which an agency assumed permanent custody, the children studied averaged one more placement [Olsen, 1982a, p. 17]. (See also Hornby & Collins, 1981.)

A child may be moved if the situation in the foster home is not conducive to his or her best interests; if the child's behavior (or that of the child's parents) makes it very difficult for the foster parents to maintain the placement, or if a change has taken place in the foster family situation—a foster parent becomes ill or dies, a foster family must move out of the region, and so on. Sometimes the move is the result of a deliberate plan on the part of the agency—perhaps from a temporary receiving home to a foster-care placement. At other times, moves are precipitous and unplanned (Festinger, 1983, p. 59).

Foster parents derive their principal gratification from their affectionate relationship with the foster child and from evidence the child is responding to their care and effort (Cautley, 1980). Risk of placement termination is associated with a negative relationship between the child and foster parents. In one study, 44 per cent of disruptions reflected changes in the foster home situation, 50 per cent were related to foster child problems (particularly acting-out problems such as stealing, promiscuity, and truancy) and with the foster child's interpersonal difficulties with foster parents (Rosenblum, 1977, p. 87). Children who are more defiant and hostile are more likely to experience multiple placements (Fanshel & Shinn, 1978, p. 143). Analyzing placement patterns in 64 cases, Stone and Stone (1983 described the following foster parent characteristics as significantly associated with placement stability

—Overall rapport between the foster parents and the agency
—Competent foster parents
—Highly motivated foster mother
—Opportunities for intellectual development provided by the foster parents (p. 14)

In addition, the researchers described child characteristics of significance

—Good school conduct— appropriate classroom behavior and response to teacher's discipline, independent of achievement
—Socialization reflected by the child's empathy, sensitivity, maturity, and development of conscience
—The relative absence of aggressive behavior
—Normal attachment as manifest in separation behavior of the child toward his or her natural parents characterized by transient anxiety and depressive signs
—Rapport between foster child and caseworker as manifest in self-disclosure and emotional and verbal spontaneity in meeting (p. 14)

Neither Fanshel and Shinn's nor Stone and Stone's studies found birth family circumstances prior to placement or visitation patterns associated with replacement. (See also Pardeck, 1983; Fein, et al., 1983, p. 538).

Stone and Stone (1983) highlight the importance of the foster-care worker's role in preventing placement breakdown's.

> The results strongly suggest that the degree of contact, active rapport building, and energy expended by the caseworker may be the single most critical variable in determining the outcome of a foster placement. Successful foster placement appeared to depend more on the actions of the protective service worker than on the family problem which precipitated placement, characteristics of the foster child, or characteristics of the foster parents. Moreover, the present findings suggest that the energy expended by the caseworker with the foster parents occurred largely independent of these other potentially related factors [p. 15].

Pardeck (1983) reanalyzing national child welfare data collected in the late 1970s points out that instability of placements is associated with worker turnover, particularly during the child's early years in care (p. 81).

Baring-Gould et al. (1983) contacted former foster families in Alaska in an attempt to understand factors associated with the high rate of foster home closure in that state. They found that lack of social work contact had significant bearing on the family's decision in one-quarter of the cases. For 43 per cent of the eighty-eight families surveyed, the foster-care caseworker had no personal contact within the three months prior to closure. The worker had never visited 37 per cent of the foster children, in the home, had never arranged mutually agreeable visits with 47 per cent of the birth families, and had never offered any type of assistance in dealing with the child's disruptive behavior after a visit to 74 per cent of the foster parents (pp. 56–57).

Foster parents considering having the child removed may decide not to terminate if they can turn to other foster parents for support. In more than half of the closed foster homes in the Baring-Gould et al. (1983) survey, parents had never had informal contact with other foster families; in 70 per cent, they had had no affiliation with foster parent organizations (p. 59).

When replacement must be made, it should be planned and as a result of the participation of the social worker, child, parents, and foster parents. A precipitous removal made in the heat of crisis is to be avoided. If possible, it should have the acceptance of the foster parents, so that they can help the child to move. This is difficult if the move is a result of the failure of the foster parents to cope adequately with the child's behavior, because the move itself is a symbol of their failure. Throughout the replacement procedure, the caseworker must be sensitive to the feelings of the foster parents and must attempt to help them feel less anxious, less guilty, less threatened by the experience. As Herstein (1957) says, the caseworker should "present the reasons for replacement in terms that would be both realistic and within the boundaries of what the foster parents can emotionally and objectively accept" (p. 24).

The caseworker should also encourage the child's expression of feeling regarding the replacement and should help to interpret it in such a way that the child does not perceive the experience as another personal failure.

Exploring the factors that explain why some Indian children experiencing multiple moves dealt with them in a positive way while others experienced emotional difficulties, Long (1983) concluded that "interfamily transfers" were less traumatizing when "the transfer family was emotionally and geographically close to the original parent or parents, and the child did not perceive the transfer as a response to bad or troublesome behavior" (p. 122). On the other hand, children who were suddenly replaced or who were "dumped" on unwilling caretakers experienced more severe trauma and had much more difficulty integrating these alterations in their life circumstances. The social worker's obligation is to help the child perceive the change in a more favorable light through the use of sufficient and well-planned preparation.

Workers may need to pay more attention to these replacement tasks. Baring-Gould et al. (1983) report that, in 45 per cent of closed cases, the foster child was not prepared for his or her move; in an equal number, the foster parents received no assistance in dealing with their personal reactions to the separation. It appears that a great deal more effort could be expended to facilitate the child's move in this way.

Termination

Ideally, activities undertaken on behalf of a child who is in foster care have as their objective movement of the child into one of the following types of more permanent living situations:

1. Planning for the child's return home by working with the birth parents and child toward modification of those conditions that necessitated placement.
2. Planning for termination of parental rights and permanent parental substitution when the child's birth home situation cannot be sufficiently modified.
3. Planning for long-term foster care when the child's ties to the birth family remain strong, the birth family remains intensively involved with the child, but there is little likelihood that the birth family can remediate its problems to the extent of having the child returned. In these situations, permanent or long-term foster care may be the most appropriate solution.
4. Planning for emancipation of the child who is old enough and has sufficient skill to live on his or her own.

The first alternative terminates, of course, in reunification, the second, with adoption of the child, the third and fourth, with the child's achievement of independence.

Many of the key factors in the agency's choice of alternatives are shrouded in ambiguity and subject to change. The modifiability of the child's birth home situation may not be clear when the child is initially placed, and the child's adoptability also varies over time.

Tables 7-2 and 7-3 summarize a available information on the outcome of the foster-care experiences for children. These data suggest that within a year, some one-quarter to one-third of children in foster care are reunified with family members. When children who have already been in care for a period of time are studied, the proportion returning home drops substantially (Fanshel, 1982). Studies that describe the destination of children who are discharged from care (Table 7-3) indicate that approximately one-half of the children who leave the system return to their parents' home or to that of other relatives, whereas only a small minority are placed in adoptive settings. Despite the presence of deep-seated

TABLE 7-2. Outcomes for All Children in Foster Care

Source	Characteristics of Sample	Reunified	Adopted	Emancipated	Still in care; In long-term care	Other
Stein, Gambrill & Wiltse (1978), p. 56	Demonstration Project. Implementation of Alameda Project. Planned outcomes. N = 157 (Control group N = 158).	36% (25%)**	22% (11%)**	—	42% (64%)**	—
State of California (1981), p. 34	Demonstration Project. Permanency Planning Project implemented in two counties. New cases in care during two years, N = 188 (Control group N = 224)	39% (41%)**	—	—	61% (59%)**	—
Lahti, Dvorak (1981), p. 54	Demonstration Project. Oregon Project. Summary of Project Data. N = 509	26% to parents, 3% to relatives	36%	—	36%	—
Lahti, (1982), p. 559	Demonstration Project. Oregon Project. Children under 12 in care 1 + years. N = 259 (Control group N = 233)	26% (24%)**	40% (21%)**	—	34% (55%)**	—
Fanshel (1982), p. 293	Children in foster care in New York 1 + years. N = 372	5%	7%	—	81%	7%
Becker (1983), p. 2	Children in foster care in Wisconsin during two years. N = 10,428	33–40% to parents, 6% to relatives	12–13%	7%	33%	—
Yoshikami, (1984), p. 115	Children in care in 18 sites in 5 states. N = 299	28.8%	—	—	62.9%	8.4% "living elsewhere"
Lawder, Poulin & Andrews (1985), p. 14.	Children in care with Children's Aid Society of Pa. during 1 year. N = 185.	61%	16%	—	18%	5%

**Control group data indicated in parentheses

TABLE 7-3. Outcomes for Children Discharged from Foster Care

Source	Characteristics of Sample	Reunified	Adopted	Emancipated	Permanent Foster Home	Other
Hubbell, (1981), p. 58	Data from one state	56% to parents, 12% to relatives	11.7%	6.8%	—	13%
Gershenson (1983), p.22	VCIS data from 29 states. N = 45,133	42% to parents, 7% to relatives	12%	9%	—	28%
Fein et al. (1983), p. 501	Connecticut children under 14 in care 30 + days. N = 726	73% to parents, 7% to relatives	16%	—	6%	—

family problems that precipitate the need for most placements, reunification remains the primary outcome for these children.

Children who come into care because of physical illness of a parent or because of situational stress are more likely to return home than those who are neglected, abused, abandoned, or have parents who are drug abusers (Fanshel, 1975a, Kliman, Schaeffer, & Friedman, 1982). In Jenkins and Norman's (1975) research, children who were placed because parents were ill or unable to assume care remained for approximately one year; those who were placed because of their own behavior problems or because or severe family dysfunction stayed more than twice as long (pp. 31–32).

The most frequent events related to return home are in line with the intent of foster care: the mother has recovered from a mental illness, the mother has recovered from a physical illness, the parent had received time-limited placement to work out personal plans that are now implemented, the mother has been released from imprisonment, the child has made gains in care that permit return home. In some 73 per cent of the cases in Fanshel and Shinn's (1978) study, what was involved was a change in the family's capacity to care for the child or a change in the child that made it possible for the family to care for him or her (p. 152). In a subsequent study of 1,293 children, Fanshel (1982) verified the relevance of family-related factors in determining whether or not the child was reunified (p. 175).

A child who is most likely to leave care within a reasonably short period of time is one who is visited regularly by parents and whose family is in frequent and regular contact with agency staff (Fanshel, 1975, 1982; Lawder, Poulin & Andrews, 1985; Gibson, Tracy & Debord, 1984, p. 144). Mech (1985), reanalyzing Westat data collected in the late 1970's, concludes that for children who received no visits over a three month period, the average length of stay was more than four years, while for children who received four or more visits during that time, the average stay was only eighteen months (p. 69).

The following case situations are examples of the most frequent discharge disposition, return of the child home:

> Miss R. is an unmarried Black mother supported by public assistance since the birth of her first child. She was 24 years old at the time her three infant children were placed. Miss R. required emergency hospitalization for jaundice and hepatitis, and the Department of Social Services arranged for temporary placement in a foster home. Miss R. was hospitalized for a month. The children were returned to her home several months later when she was able to care for them. She felt that the children had been well cared for and were "healthy and happy." She was grateful for the placement, as it allowed her to regain her health and strength.

> Mrs. R. is a Puerto Rican, Catholic, 24-year-old mother of three who was deserted by the children's father. Her Department of Social Services worker suggested she visit an outpatient clinic at Metropolitan Hospital when she complained of being depressed and nervous. She said she hit the children for the slightest thing. Afraid that she might lose control and hurt her children, she made arrangements to have the children placed. They were still in placement two years later. Mrs. R. continued in treatment, went to work, and began living with a new common-law husband with whom she shortly had a child. By the time of the last study interview, five years after entry, the placed children were discharged home. Mrs. R. said, "I learned I couldn't live without the kids."

> Mrs. T. is a 40-year-old white, Jewish mother, separated from her addicted husband after a stormy marriage, overwhelmed by depression and unable at the time of

placement to care for her four children. She was not able to send them off to school. Previous to the placement there was a homemaker in the home for almost two years. Mrs. T. had been hospitalized and in treatment in the past, although she was not hospitalized at the time of placement and during the five-year study period. She did, however, continue to receive psychiatric care. She said her family thought she was a "bad mother" for placing the children, but she thinks she "did them a favor." Five years after the placement, three of her children were home. One remained in care, and she felt he was doing well, improving in school, and getting advantages like medical care, music lessons, and camp. Mrs. T. is visited weekly by the placement agency social worker and is more optimistic about the future. She has gotten better housing, which had been a severe problem for her.

The children of this 28-year-old Black Catholic mother were placed while she served a short jail sentence for "running numbers." She blames her husband for placing the children. The father's story was different. He said the mother was with another man and he had been paying someone to care for the children and couldn't afford it anymore. The children were discharged to the mother after three years in care. She had gotten out of jail, divorced her husband, remarried, and received "help in getting back" at a mental health clinic. She spoke warmly of the support and interest of the social worker [Jenkins & Norman, 1975, pp. 34–40).

Cross-sectional studies indicate that the average length of time in care is four years or longer (Gruber, 1973; Rowe & Lambert, 1973, p. 37; Bryce & Ehlert, 1974; Catalano, 1974, p. 5; Vasaly, 1978, Fanshel & Grundy, 1975, p. 10; Hargrave, Shireman & Connor, 1975, Fanshel, 1982). Estimates of the proportion of children who remain in care two years or more range from one-third to 76 per cent (Becker & Austin 1983; p. 2; Rowe, 1980, p. 60; Kahan, 1979; State of California, 1981, p. 96). The most comprehensive estimates suggest that almost half the children are in long-term placement (Gershenson, 1983, p. 11). Figures fo individual states vary dramatically; in Oregon, for example, only 5 per cent of children remain in care this long, whereas in New Mexico the rate is 64 per cent (pp. 10–11). Some 10–15 per cent of children are foster-care residents for ten years or longer. The proportion of children in care for lengthy periods has diminished somewhat in recent years. In 1977, 58 per cent stayed two years or more.

An essential difficulty with cross-sectional studies is that they tend to exaggerate the impact of the backlog of all the children who over the years, have been unable to move out of foster care, and underestimate the impact of turnover—the effect of children not in the study because they left the system. Cross-sectional studies do an injustice to the foster-care system because, heavily weighted as they are with an accumulated residual group of children who have remained in care, they picture foster case as less temporary than it is for many children.

A longitudinal study that follows the experiences of the same group of children in care over time gives a different picture of the system. Jenkins (1967) followed 891 New York City children placed over a two-year period. Of this group, 54 per cent had been discharged from care after three months in placement. At the end of two years, 75 per cent of the group had been discharged (p. 451). This longitudinal analysis showed foster care to be a temporary arrangement for most children.

A five-year logitudinal study by Fanshel and Shinn (1978) of over six hundred children in foster care in New York City showed a lower rate of discharge. At the end of five years, 64 per cent of the group had returned home. (See also Tizard & Joseph, 1970, p. 585.)

It is estimated that following the career of a group of children entering foster care would show that 25 per cent are likely to remain in care for long periods of time (Regional Institute Research, 1976). Some of these children have no home to which they might return, are not freed for adoption, or if freed for adoption, are not placeable because they are too old or too handicapped or are older and non-white. Some are in stable, long-term foster-care arrangements. Some are free for adoption and are placeable but are the victims of agency drift and failure to plan effectively.

Black children remain in the foster care system for longer period than do whites (Tizard & Joseph, 1970 Fanshel; & Shinn, 1978; Jenkins et al., 1983, p. 44), and they are less likely to return home upon discharge (Olsen, 1982b; Mech, 1985; Lawder, Poulin, & Andrews, 1985). The older the child, the wider is the disparity. When black children are preschoolers, they tend to stay in care approximately four months longer than their white counterparts; when they are adolescents, they remain in care almost three years longer (Olsen, 1982b). However, parental visiting has more dramatic impact on the length of stay in care for these children than for whites (Mech, 1985, p. 69).

Olsen (1982a) conducted a follow-up study of children in care in four Ohio counties. She compared those who remained in foster homes with the children who were eventually adopted. She found that, as expected, the younger and white children were more likely to be placed in adoptive homes. Whereas agencies moved more quickly toward termination of parental rights for black children (9–½ months earlier, on the average) they moved far more slowly toward subsequent placement of these children in adoptive settings. Black children waited for permanent families approximately two years longer (p. 15).

Frequent, intensive contact by skilled, experienced workers facilitates earlier return for all children (Shapiro, 1976). Aldgate (1980) comments:

> Social work activity, whether in the form of general encouragement, practical support, or more intensive problem-solving help with emotional difficulties had a significant effect on return from care. Perhaps not surprisingly in view of the widespread poverty, practical support in terms of cash or in-kind was seen as the most useful form of intervention by both social workers and parents. A common feature among children in long-term care was the passive attitude of their social workers towards any plans for either rehabilitation or alternatives [p. 23].

Children who leave foster care by becoming emancipated may require special services at termination to replace the ongoing guidance and support that birth families usually provide when children become young adults. To help them bridge the gap between fully supervised family care and complete independence, they may benefit from brief placement in what are called "semi-independent" or "supervised living arrangements" (Hornby & Collins, 1981; Furrh, 1983; Rowe, 1983; Mauzerall, 1983; Pasztor et al., 1986; Barth et al., 1986a, 1986b). These young adults may need employment training, education in financial management, or help with self-care skills. Perhaps of even greater significance are social work efforts to help them maintain a sense of continuity in their lives. Whereas all children leaving care can benefit from maintenance of contact with families with whom they have spent a portion of their lives, those who no longer have links to birth families and those who have undergone multiple placements are particularly in need (Project Craft, 1980, p. VI–101; Zimmerman, 1982, p. 49; Festinger, 1983, p. 299; Maluccio & Fein, 1985). Because an inability to establish or benefit from supportive ties to others is a key characteristic of abusive and neglecting parents, attention to the affiliative needs of children whose primary ties are to foster-care families can serve an important preventive function.

"Termination" is perhaps a misnomer, for many many of the children in care and their families will continue to require assistance after the child returns home. Studying the circumstances of 314 children who left foster family or group care provided by the Jewish Child Care Association of New York, Block and Libowitz (1983) found that approximately three-quarters of the families received aftercare services (p. 63). In their follow-up study of children who had been placed in the family home after foster care, Fein, et al. (1983) reported that twelve to sixteen months after placement, birth families were in need of a wide range of health, mental health, and other services (p. 518). Frequently, then, the family "terminates" contact with one particular program provided by the child welfare agency, but is transferred to or remains in contact with a protective services or general services worker who will be of assistance in meeting ongoing needs.

In addition to assessing long-term service requirements, workers may also need to assist families whose children are undergoing short-term adjustment difficulties associated with changes in their living circumstances and the accompanying loss of foster family ties. The situation here is analogous to that faced by foster families accepting new children into their home. Particularly when birth parents are not skilled at handling stress or managing difficult child behavior, worker assistance in helping them understand the child's reactions and respond effectively can be of critical benefit in preventing escalation of family difficulties at this time (Lahti & Dvorak, 1981, p. 56; Project CRAFT, 1980, p. VI–73).

Inability to get appropriate help can catapult families into replacing their children in foster care. California data from four different counties (State of California, 1981) described from 2 to 22 per cent of children whose cases were reopened within a year. Using data from five states, Yoshikami (1984) found that 15 per cent of the children were moved out of their birth parent home after being placed there. Following the experiences of families who had been reunified with their children utilizing services of the Oregon Project Lahti, (1982) reports that fifteen months after placement 20 per cent of the children had changed homes. She notes that these children still fared better than those in foster care. Sixty per cent of foster children changed homes during this same time period (p. 560). In their follow-up study of children who had been in care with the Jewish Child Care Association of New York, Block and Libowitz (1983) found that after reunification, 28 per cent were again removed. Only one-third of this group returned to foster care, however. Almost half moved into long-term residential facilities, mental hospitals, or penal institutions (p. 18).

Children more vulnerable to replacement are the more difficult children to live with, and they come from families least able to care for them and perhaps least attached to them (Lahti & Dvorak, 1981, p. 56; Block, Libowitz 1983, pp. 70–71). Children who recidivate also tend to have longer exposure to substitute care before their initial family replacement. Although all of the Oregon Project children spent twenty months in care, on the average, those who were subsequently returned to care had spent forty-six months in substitute homes (Lahti & Dvorak, 1981).

By themselves, follow-up services are not sufficient to help some families remain intact. Block and Libowitz (1983) conclude:

> recidivism appeared to be reduced only when the family was either functional
> enough to care for the child with supports to the child, or when the family was

functional enough to know that it needed intervention instead of scapegoating the child. We also know that, regardless of service receipt, recidivism was low among functional families. Dysfunctional families may either choose the wrong services or not be able to benefit from services, and therefore the child will recidivate. If there are conclusions implicit in these assumptions, they are that service delivery must be productive enough when the child is in care to assure that the family is functioning on an adequate level and that aftercare services cannot substitute for intensive services during the in-care period [p. 78].

Evaluation of the Consequences of Foster Family Care

The nineteenth-century controversy over the "placing out" of large numbers of children from metropolitan areas in the East to rural areas in the Midwest and South produced a rash of evaluative reports assessing whether this system was harmful to children. This same concern provides the impetus for recent research efforts. Studies have attempted to answer two general questions:

1. What is the immediate effect of care on children? Are they performing in cognitive, affective, social, and other developmental arenas as well as children who do not experience placement?
2. What is the long-term impact of the foster-care experience? How are these individuals functioning as adults? Have they become productive members of society? Are they performing as well as cohorts who have not been removed from their families?

In addition, research has examined the relationship between performance of the child and various qualities of the child's birth family and foster-care situation. The impact of various service delivery characteristics has also been assessed. Because these findings were discussed in previous sections of this chapter, they are not considered here.

The foster care literature suggests that the placement experience can be destructive to the child. Not only the experience of separation, which poses for the child the loss of established relationships with parental figures, with siblings and with a familiar environment, but also the failure to form attachments in the new environment can prove seriously detrimental to the child's emotional well-being. On the other hand, it has also been argued that children exposed to the more predictable and supportive environment of the foster home, where they are taught more socially acceptable values, may function more adequately than they would if they remained in the more chaotic birth home environment.

It is generally conceded that the physical development of the child in care is good. On the other hand, children in foster care manifest many emotional problems (Vasaly, 1978, pp. 53–63). Assessing the functioning of 121 children between the ages of five and seventeen who had been in their current foster home a year or more, Thrope (1980) found that 39 per cent were seriously disturbed, using the Rutter Behavior Scale (p. 87). When foster parents were asked to describe behavior difficulties of 139 children who had been in care three years or longer, they discussed a number of problems, particularly prevalent in the latency age group (Rowe et al., 1984). Compared to the general child population, ten–eleven-year-olds had more sleeping difficulty and more problems concentrating. They had temper tantrums or lied twice as often, were enuretic four times as often, were six times as destructive, and eleven times as likely to steal as children out of care (p. 79). Recent studies mirror the results of earlier studies (Boehm, 1958), showing a relationship between length of time in care and an increasing percentage of children with emotional problems (Holman, 1973, p. 121; Rowe & Lambert, 1973, p. 154, Canning, 1974, Hargrave, Shireman, & Connor, 1975; Vassaly, 1978, p. 63). On the other hand, some studies show that the physical, intellectual, and emotional adjustment of most children in long-term foster care is satisfactory (Kadushin, 1958; Madison & Schapiro, 1969; Keane, 1983; Zimmerman, 1982).

The essential problem with all of this research, either favoring or damning foster care, is that these are studies of children at one point in time, generally after the child has been in care for some time. Without baseline data the children's functioning at admittance, it is difficult to know whether the problems result from long-term care or if extended care is a consequence of the children's problems. Problem children are more difficult to move out of foster care, so that on might expect a greater proportion of such children to appear in any long-term-stay group. The possibility throughout of confounding concomitance with cause is great. There is no way of knowing whether or not children came into the system maladjusted or whether they developed such behavior while in foster care.

Follow-up interviews with foster parents and children in foster care about a year after placement emphasize the importance of baseline entering data. (Lahti et al., 1978). Data in this study were available on some 490 children over a four-year period before and after fostercare placement. The study showed that children who got along well when they first entered placement were more likely to do well in placement: "The past was a good predictor of the present" (p. 9.4). However, the most powerful of the factors affecting children's well-being in this study was the family's sense of permanency. "Where placements were seen as permanent by the parents, the child's well-being scores tended to be higher" (Lahti, 1982, p. 567). (See also Kliman, Schaeffer, & Friedman, 1982, pp. 151–152).

An additional difficulty, characteristic of many studies evaluating the impact of care, concerns the failure to utilize control groups, More often than not, no comparison is made with the level of behavioral and emotional problems manifested by children living with their own parents. Because all children, as developing organisms, have limited ego strength and are subject to age-specific disorders, normal developmental lags, and heightened responses to transitory stress situations, we need to know if the number and intensity of problems manifested by foster children are atypical, relative to age cohorts. In addition, because the foster-care child population is heavily weighted with those who come from socioeconomically deprived backgrounds, the basis for comparing developmental deficients should not be the population of all children but those from similar circumstances (Cox, 1985).

Avoiding problems with both lack of baseline data and failure to utilize control groups, Fanshel and Shinn (1978) carried out one of the most elaborate and carefully designed and executed foster-care studies now available. Assessments of child functioning were made at intake and at periodic intervals during a five-year period. The authors also used measures that allowed for age-specific normative comparisons.

Various indexes were developed to document carefully the children's bio-psycho-social functioning. These included a Health Status Index, an Emotional Problems Indicator, and a Developmental Problems Index. Information regarding the children's preplacement development, social-emotional adjustment, and behavioral disciplinary problems was obtained from interviews with the biological mother shortly after the child's admission to care.

Depending on the child's age, either the Cattell, the Minnesota Preschool Scale, or the Wechsler Intelligence Scale was used to obtain a measure of the child's intelligence shortly after entrance into care and at stated intervals thereafter. Caseworkers completed a specially devised Child Behavior Characteristics form at the end of the first ninety days in placement, at the end of two and one-half years, and at the end of five years. The information obtained permitted an assignment of scores measuring such items as the child's likability, agreeableness, emotionality-tension, and withdrawal. Other forms completed by the caseworker provided more information regarding emotional maturity, psychosomatic reactions, aggressiveness, and fears. Additional information was obtained from the child's teachers on such forms as the Rating Scale for Pupil Adjustment.

Summarizing the most significant conclusions of the research, Fanshel and Shinn note that "We do not find that the longer a child spends in foster care the more likely he is to show signs of deterioration" (p. 490). "Our findings do not show that children who remained in foster care fared less well with respect to intellectual abilities, school performance, and personal and social adjustment compared to those who returned to their own homes" (p. 479). They go on to say, "however, we feel that our measures of adjustment are not without problems and we are not sure that our procedures have captured the potential feeling of pain and impared self-image that can be created by impermanent status in foster care" (p.479).

Another, less rigorous longitudinal study comparing baseline placement entrance data with data obtained after a period in care was conducted by Palmer (1976). She studied changes in the adjustment of two hundred children who entered foster care after age three and remained in care for at least five years. An assessment was made by two readers who independently read the complete record material. Behavior problems and emotional problems were defined and categorized. Record data at time of placement served as a baseline. The results are as good as the record data and the perceptivity of the record readers. With this caveat in mind, the report showed that behavior problems from point of entry over the five-year period decreased. Over one half of the children who began with serious emotional problems had less serious problems at the end. Although a five-year stay in foster care might not have been helpful, it does not appear to have been harmful for this group of children. This supposition is empirically confirmed in a study by Kent (1976) that in comparing the level of development of abused children at the point of their removal from the home with their functioning after one to two years in foster care, found that they had made improvements physically, cognitively, and emotionally.

Examining the functioning of children who experience long-term care (five or more years) and who, upon reaching adulthood, were emancipated from care, Festinger (1983), like Palmer, found that approximately the same proportion of children displayed social emotional difficulties at the point of placement and at discharge. However, whereas the proportion remained the same, there were changes in the population of troubled foster children over the course of their stay in care. Whereas two thirds of the children who were impaired at the time of placement subsequently improved, a group of equal size who had no initial difficulties subsequently developed them (p. 100). Whereas the number of children experiencing health-related disabilities decreased, the number of foster care residents with learning disabilities increased dramatically over the course of care. "All together 34 per cent of the young adults in the sample were discharged from foster care with a fairly serious health, social and emotional, or educational problem, or a combination of these" (p. 110). Assessments of the functioning of children in these areas were obtained through the evaluation of case records, and the author notes problems with missing information and caseworker bias that must be considered in evaluating validity of these findings.

The relevance of utilizing an appropriate comparison group in order to interpret data correctly is illustrated in a study evaluating the physical and mental health of children in care. Kavaler and Swire (1983) studied a sample of 668 children drawn from eight foster care agencies in New York City serving children in 1973–74. Evaluations were conducted by a team of pediatricians and other professionals associated with Cornell Medical School Hospital. Results of the evaluation showed that a considerable proportion of these children had physical, developmental, and emotional problems that required attention and correction. Forty-five per cent of these children had chronic medical conditions; 20 per cent had multiple disabilities in this area. Their physical growth was "considerably below normal expectancies" (p. 76). Whereas 71 per cent were assessed as normal in terms of their developmental abilities, 19 per cent were considered questionable and 10 per cent abnormal. These developmental assessments examined progress in physical, motor, perceptual, and cognitive skills. Only 4 per cent of these children had no obvious emotional symptoms. Whereas 26 per cent had mild symptoms, for 35 per cent they were moderate, 25 per cent marked, and 10 per cent severe (p. 87).

When the researchers compared results with data available on general populations of children, this group clearly was performing below expected levels. However, when compared to disadvantaged children who lived in similar communities, the levels of physical and psychiatric impairment seemed "roughly comparable" (p. 122). Studying the cognitive and academic performance of 163 children in care with the Children's Aid Society of Pennsylvania, Fox and Arcuri (1980) also concluded that "the general level of functioning was similar to that of low-income and minority children living with their own families" (p. 491). (See also Kliman, Schaeffer, & Friedman, 1982).

The general conclusions that might be drawn from these studies of the immediate outcome of foster family care is that this experience is not clearly injurious to the child's development; at least it is no more injurious than that of other children in similar socioeconomic and environmental circumstances. However, the proportion of children displaying some type of cognitive, social, or emotional difficulty is fairly substantial, suggesting the need for widespread and sometimes intensive services to enhance the child's capacity to perform optimally (Cox & Cox, 1984; Kavaler & Swire, 1983).

Research examining the adult functioning of former foster children has assessed their performance using criteria similar to those employed in short-term impact studies. In the early 1920s the State Charities Aid Association in New York City evaluated all those children who had been under foster-family care through the agency for at least one year and were, at the time of the study, at least eighteen years old (Thies, 1924). This study was, as the agency contends, "the first serious effort to collect, at first hand on a considerable scale, the facts as to the careers of an unselected group of foster children" (p. 6). Information was obtained from interviews by social workers with the foster child or with the foster parents or relatives. The foster children were categorized by "experienced supervisors" as "capable" (subjects who were law-abiding who managed their affairs with good sense, and who were living in accordance with the moral standards of their communities) or "incapable" (subjects who were unable or unwilling to support themselves adequately, who were shiftless, or who defied the accepted standards of morality or order of their communities). Of 562 foster children in the group who were not subsequently adopted and on whom sufficient data for judging were available, 73 per cent were judged "capable" and 27 per cent "incapable" at the time of follow-up. Age at placement was significantly related to outcome, children who were five or younger when placed were more likely to be judged "capable." Outcome was not related to the socioeconomic level of the home but was related to the quality of foster parent-foster child relationships.

Baylor and Monachesi (1939) did a follow-up study of 478 children after discharge from foster care. For most of the children, the research was conducted four to six years after discharge. The Social Service Exchange was used to obtain follow-up information and "visits were made, sometimes several, in the homes of people concerned; employers were visited or sought by correspondence" (p. 414). The material assembled by field-workers was evaluated independently by each of the authors. Of the 478 children for whom a "behavior evaluation" was attempted 67.4 per cent were found to be "behaving favorably" at the time of the follow-up. Children who had been placed for health reasons, because of a "broken home," or because of dependency and neglect showed a much lower percentage of "unfavorable behavior" than children placed because of behavioral difficulties and/or delinquency (p. 417).

The Dutch Child Caring Agency Tot Steun, did a follow-up interview study in 1952–1954 of 160 former foster children born between 1903 and 1920 who had been in the care of the agency at one time for a "considerable length of time" (Van der Waals, 1960). Interviews conducted by social workers ran for two or three hours. The report notes that "the situation of many of these former foster children at the time of the inquiry left much to be desired. Socially, many were rather well established. Only a few were unemployed or antisocial or had lost the parental rights to their own children. However, many felt unsuccessful, dissatisfied, and distressed" (p. 33).

Murphy (1964), selected agency records of mentally normal children who had been in continuous foster-family care for more than five years, whose cases were closed at the time of the study, and who were at least eleven years of age at the time the case was closed. Two senior social workers, who had been with the agency throughout and who had "unusually complete memories," made available their knowledge of the outcome of each of the 316 cases selected for study. The two senior officers divided the 316 former foster children into three categories: Outcome satisfactory ("A") in terms of the child's social milieu; Outcome less satisfactory ("B"), but without signs of pathology; and Outcome unsatisfactory ("C"), usually with signs of pathology. Of the 316 cases 19.3 per cent were given a C rating, about 50 per cent received an A rating (p. 392).

Ferguson (1966) did a follow-up study of some 140 young adults who had been cared for in foster-family homes during childhood in Scotland. At age twenty, 96 per cent of the group were employed or in training and were independently responsible for their own support. The rate of delinquency was high, however, 17 per cent having been convicted of some crime before age twenty. It must be noted that more than 50 per cent of this group had tested IQ scores below 90. Assessing the experiences of young adults in New South Wales some ten to eleven years after their discharge from care at age eighteen, Kraus (1981) also found a substantial number involved in adult criminal activity. This was particularly true for males. Thirty per cent of these men and 7 per cent of the women had been convicted for some type of adult crime. Whereas the child's age at placement or reasons for placement were not associated with adult criminal involvement, the number of placements experienced by the child were correlated. The author hypothesizes that some of the same personality and interpersonal difficulties that caused replacement of the child were also responsible for criminal engagement (p. 113).

Meier (1962) did a follow-up interview study of sixty-one adults between the ages of twenty-eight and thirty-two who had been in foster care in Minnesota for a period of at least five years. The criteria for outcome were based on the interviewers' ratings of the respondents' level of social effectiveness (employment and economic circumstances, care of the home and of the children, social relationships outside the home) and their feeling of well-being (feeling of adequacy, capacity to experience pleasure). Fifteen men and twenty-four women—some 64 per cent of the total sample—had positive ratings in all areas of social functioning, the rest had a negative rating in at least one area, and three respondents have negative ratings in three areas. In summary, Meier notes:

> Current circumstances of these young adults as a group contrast sharply with family circumstances at the time of their placement; with few exceptions they are self-supporting individuals living in conformity with the social standards of their communities. The children of most of them are well cared for. . . . In most areas of adaptation, current functioning compares favorably with that of the general population [p. 2].

Age at first placement and the number of placements were not found to be significantly related to overall social effectiveness and sense of well-being, but they were related to specific aspects of functioning. Meier found that the sex of the foster child was a very important variable in determining response to foster care. The data suggested that being reared away from his own family in itself damaged the male's self-concept whereas for the female the content and quality of the experience were of greater importance. (See also Zimmerman, 1982).

Three recently completed studies have examined the extent of educational attainment, occupational stability, the degree of isolation and availability of social supports among former foster-care residents who are now young adults. Triseliotis (1980) investigated the experiences of forty young adults who had had quite stable, long-term foster-care experiences. Each spent between seven and fifteen years in one foster home. While 60 per cent were coping well and were generally satisfied with their lives, an additional 15 per cent were "coping about half and half" (p. 153). The remainder, 25 per cent, were functioning more poorly:

> Their general characteristic as a group was the absence of a settled way of life, unsteady employment record, economic dependence, no fixed residence, and being in a continued state of transition. They expressed dissatisfaction and disappointment with their present and past circumstances. Some were critical of their foster families, and a minority blamed themselves for "messing" their lives. There was anger, disappointment and in some an element of desolation. They were pessimistic about the future and did not think that their circumstances would change all that much. They generally had a poor self-image, which they attributed to being fostered and to other people's negative perceptions of fostering. Those expressing general dissatisfaction were mostly among those whose foster home relationships were described as "ambivalent," ending up in disruption p. 154].

The functioning of 109 individuals between the ages of eighteen and twenty-eight who had spent at least one year in foster care and who had not been adopted was the subject of a study conducted by Zimmerman (1982). All were placed by the Orleans Parish Department of Public Welfare. The author found that only 39 per cent of this group had completed high school and that, at the time of the study, only 53 per cent of the males and 38 per cent of the females were employed full time. One quarter of the group was receiving public assistance. A substantial minority had potentially serious problems with social isolation as well. Twenty-one per cent were members of a very small and not intense social networks; 28 per cent reported that their most intense relationships were with "no one." Those undergoing unstable long-term placements were least likely to describe supportive relationships with either foster or birth family members (p. 72).

In interviews with sample subjects, Zimmerman asked "How do you feel right now about how your life has turned out?" Thirty-six per cent responded that their life was good and/or that they felt very satisfied; 32 per cent stated that life was "okay." Only 16 per cent expressed clear, persistent dissatisfaction with their current circumstances. The researcher also evaluated "overall social functioning of the former foster children as individuals, based on their performance of certain socially expected behaviors. These minimally expected behaviors are ones that are crucial enough to the society as a whole to require prescribed interventions in any individual's life in instances where the expectations are not being met or are grossly violated. These behaviors are as follows: adherence to the law; self-support, being in the process of preparing for self-support, or being exempt from the expectation because of disability, and caring for one's children, particularly in the case of women" (p. 87). Using these criteria, somewhat more than one quarter of the group was considered functioning well in these areas; an additional 39% was rated functioning adequately. However, almost one quarter exhibited major dysfunction in one area, whereas an additional 10 per cent exhibited serious difficulties in two or three of these areas (p. 88).

Using similar measures to investigate the experiences of former foster care residents who had been in care for more lengthy periods (five years or more), Festinger (1983) gathered material from 277 respondents. She found that this group performing somewhat better educationally than Zimmerman did, with approximately one third failing to complete high school. Associated with this was a somewhat better employment record. Three quarters of the males and 45 per cent of the females were employed full time, whereas one in ten of the young men and one in four women were relying on public assistance (pp. 159, 166).

Festinger concluded that "generally, then, these young adults were managing their lives adequately and feeling quite satisfied with their physical, social, and psychological environments" (p. 133). Their feelings of self-worth and level of life satisfaction were comparable to those found among young adults nationally. Festinger also found that a substantial proportion of this group (82%) agreed with the statement "Generally, I was satisfied with my experience in foster care" and an even larger proportion (95%) agreed that "All in all I was lucky to be placed in foster care" (p. 258). Despite these positive outcomes, however, evidence of social isolation again emerges, as it did for Zimmerman's sample. One in ten agreed that "No one cares much what happens to me" (p. 125), and only two-thirds of these respondents said that their foster family felt like their "own family" (pp. 125, 265).

Data describing the long-term outcome of foster-care experiences are consistent with that reporting more immediate effects of this experience. Although, for the most part, young adults who were exposed to care are functioning effectively in their adult roles, a substantial minority expressed dissatisfaction and live relatively socially isolated lives. Despite their corrective experience in foster family homes, some of these individuals are not performing competently or acceptably as adults, and some 20 per cent to 33 per cent are living seriously troubled lives. These data suggest the need for more intensive intervention to ameliorate or prevent these difficulties while the child is still in care.

Problems

1. Despite some evidence that permanency planning efforts have contributed to stabilization of the foster care population, there is continued concern about the large numbers of children who enter care each year and about the fact that, for many, their stay will be long term. Embodied in Public Law 96-272 are requirements for case planning and monitoring and for intensive efforts to assist parents in remediating problems that led to removal of their children from their home. These requirements have as their objective prevention of inappropriate use of substitute care and, in cases in which it is required, use of care for as short a period of time as possible. Questions have arisen, however, concerning the efficacy of these approaches in ultimately reducing reliance on substitute services to help remediate serious family problems.

Some claim that the requirements contained in Public Law 96-272 merely ask agencies to do what they are already doing, while burdening them with a considerable amount of additional paperwork, which robs time and effort from needed services. Others claim, however, that legal requirements for periodic review and case planning prompt agencies to do what they otherwise would not have done, or would not have done as promptly or conscientiously. Festinger (1975, 1976) finds that review procedures promoted more expeditious, systematic planning in New York. In some instances, court review resulted in the child's being freed for adoption; less often, the child was ordered returned home. Between 1972 and 1974, 46 per cent of the children had been removed from care; by 1975, 71 per cent had left the system. Festinger concludes that court review had a modest catalytic "facilitating impact" on agency decision making in these cases. (See also Wert, Fein, & Haller, 1986).

An alternative approach to case monitoring utilizes a citizen panel to evaluate children's progress. The National Council of Juvenile and Family Court Judges sponsored the Concern for Children in Placement project (CIP), which relied on volunteers for this purpose. It has been claimed that use of these panels fosters substantial reduction in caseloads (Knitzer, Allen, & McGowan, 1978, pp. 161–162). However, a study in Georgia comparing the impact of citizen review boards with that of regular agency review found "no clear indication that the citizen board review alternative to internal case review has lead to more positive outcomes in foster care" (Lindsey & Wodarski, 1986, p. 228).

No matter what particular form it takes, effective case monitoring requires that reviewers have some degree of autonomous decision-making power, competence to make and form decisions in behalf of children, and authority to enforce their recommendations. Without sufficient autonomy and competence, reviews can become a "rubber stamp" process:

> What was entered by the social worker under the heading of "plans" was rubber-stamped by the review, and even where social workers were actively looking to the review to assist in taking a difficult decision, they were rarely satisfied with the

outcome. Typical social worker comments were: "Yes, there was a meeting, but I wouldn't call it a discussion—I just told them what I was planning." "I never have thought of making decisions at reviews—they just give the seal of approval to decisions that have already been made, really" [Vernon, 1985, p. 16]. (See also Musewicz, 1981; Hubbell, 1981; Stein, 1982).

When a child has been in foster care for eighteen months, the Adoption Assistance and Child Welfare Act of 1980 requires a judicial dispositional hearing to determine the child's future status. A national study of such hearings (Westat, 1984) indicates that most often they resulted in a continuation of the child in care. Overall the hearing decision agreed with the agency recommendation in 88 per cent of the cases. Where there were disagreements, the court was more often in favor of continuing foster care than the agency.

Nevertheless, when used appropriately, court or citizen board reviews can "force foster care agencies to sharpen up ambiguous plans for individual children and defend these plans" (Young & Finch, 1977, pp. 68). As a result of explicitly mandated periodic review of cases, fewer children are likely to be without workers assigned to their cases, birth parents may be in more regular contact with the agency, and some additional proportion of children will face less delay in either returning to their birth home or in moving toward adoption.

Perhaps the most serious roadblock to effective use of review procedures is in the failure to institute them in the first place. Hubbell (1981) found that, eighteen months after passage of the federal legislation mandating review, only 52 of 95 counties in one state had met this requirement (p. 93). Undertaking a more extensive compliance assessment in seven states, the U.S. General Accounting Office (1984) discovered:

> ——The extent to which the status of foster children was periodically reviewed as required by the act varied. The act required the state to review the status of children in foster care at least every six months to determine (1) the continuing necessity for an appropriateness of each placement, (2) the extent of compliance with the case plan, and (3) the extent of progress made toward alleviating or mitigating the causes necessitating placement in foster care. Over sixty percent of the cases we examined in three states met the act's requirements, including the frequency of the periodic reviews and participation of natural parents and independent parties when required. In the other four states less than ⅓ of the cases met the act's requirements [pp. 9–10].

In order to prevent long-term use of foster care for children, Public Law 96-272 not only requires assessment of planning for the child but also appropriate, intensive intervention with parents in order to assist them in having their children return home. As we have already indicated, special demonstration projects in a number of states and communities have contributed substantially to our knowledge of the variety and intensity of programming that must be available in order to effectively help families with children in placement. (See, for example, Stein, Gambrill, & Wiltse, 1978; Lindsey, 1982; Lahti, 1982.)

It is claimed that as a consequence of these special efforts a larger percentage of children have achieved permanence either through return home or adoption than would otherwise have been the case. Statistics from states that developed well-organized programs whose explicit objective is permanence show a drop in total foster care caseloads following initiation of such efforts—in South Carolina, from 4,000 to 3,500, in Virginia from 11,876 to 10,369 over a two-year period; in Oregon, from 4,400 in 1972 to 3,600 in 1976; in New York from 44,000 in 1979 to

25,000 in 1984. These efforts also resulted in substantial reductions in the cost of services to children (State of California, 1981, pp. 21). New York foster care maintenance payments dropped from $330 million in 1981 to $254 million in 1984. Some part of this reduction was a result of the reduction in the general population of children, some was a consequence of the growing unavailability of infants for adoption, making possible adoptive placement of a larger number of older foster children. Some percentage of the reduction is, however, a result of permanency planning programs.

Despite their potential benefit, case planning and intensive parent service efforts cannot, by themselves, dissolve the barriers to effective and timely intervention with children in foster care and their families. The limited strengths and deprived circumstances of birth families make their situation highly resistive to change in some instances; characteristics of the child in care and negative attitudes of adoptive applicants toward these children can make finding them permanent alternative families a laborious process; the limited technology available to workers in bringing about intra- and interpersonal changes sometimes makes casework a trial and error effort; and the large caseloads, limited training and education, and high turnover rates of service workers continue to interfere with meaningful provision of foster-care services (Maluccio et al., 1980; Halper & Jones, 1984; Vernon, 1985). Without more concerted efforts to address each of these limitations of the system, inappropriate use of foster care is likely to continue.

2. Even if procedures were developed to more effectively screen children out of foster care and to ensure that their stay there were as short as possible, there would still remain a significant problem with the children already in care who have lived in foster homes for a substantial proportion of their lives. As we have already pointed out, this concern applies to perhaps as many as half the children in care. Removing them from their foster care home may disrupt a stable placement and destroy psychological bonds to the foster family. Returning them to a birth family home in which parents have exhibited chronic childrearing incapacity over a period of years may do them irreparable harm. The question of "permanency" for these children is at once more compelling and more difficult to answer.

Studies suggest that many children perceive long-term foster care as being as permanent as other kinds of arrangements. Based on interviews with parents and children, Lahti et al. (1978) note that their

> single most important finding was that a sense of permanence was one of the best predictors of a child's well-being. However, sense of permanence was not necessarily related to the legal permanence of the placement. Perception of permanence happens without legal sanctions. And it may be absent even when legal sanctions are there— whether the child was in a legally permanent placement, adoption, or returned home or was in a legally temporary foster care made very little difference in his level of adjustment and health at the time of the interview. Perception of permanence was the key [p. 9.3].

The fact that foster care did provide a sense of permanence was evident from the findings: "We have not found foster care to be characterized by unstable placements affording children limited chance for satisfactory adjustment and growth in secure surroundings as we might have expected. While the foster care placements did not equal the adoptive placements in terms of sense of permanence, scores in these areas were surprisingly high" (p. 8.11). "Children in foster care were getting along surprisingly well" (p. 9.6).

More recently, Fanshel (1979) found that for the majority of children who had been in foster homes for an average of 6 years, this had become their "real home." Accepted by the foster parents and attached to, identified with, and integrated into the foster family, most were "at peace with the current arrangements" (p. 63).

Studying children in long-term care, Triseliotis (1980) agrees. "A slow process of psychological bonding seems to develop that gradually cements itself to the point that the foster child becomes indistinguishable from other members of the caretaking family" (pp. 157).

Rowe et al. (1982), also examining the experiences of children in long-term care, report findings that are not quite so positive. Among these 200 children, the researchers found, "When worries over status, fears about leaving and poor integration are put together, no less than 45% of the children and young people were found to be experiencing some painful feelings" (pp. 138). Several feared that, if they behaved badly, they would be sent away, even when their foster parents gave them no cause to believe this would occur. (See also Kahan, 1979.)

The primary difficulty with developing long-term or permanent foster homes for children is the agency's inability to ensure that the child will remain in a stable foster care placement (Maluccio & Fein, 1985; Triseliotis, 1980). One study that followed the careers of children younger than fifteen who had been placed in foster care for at least thirty days (Fein et al., 1983) reported that, sixteen months after the research began, one-third of the children who had been returned to birth families had disrupted; however, 50 per cent of the children placed in permanent foster care had to be replaced in another home (pp. 535).

Children who had experienced disruptions were more likely, as adults, to have violated the law, to be dependent on others or on welfare for financial support, or to be caring for their own children inadequately (Zimmerman, 1982). Placing a child in foster care for long periods without attempting to ensure that the child has a caring family on whom he or she can rely relegates the child to "permanent unpredictable" status that affects subsequent adult productivity and competence. Explicit, planned long-term placements in a quasi-adoptive situation in which foster parents are granted considerable autonomy can be an acceptable alternative for those children who could not return home but who retain deep ties with their birth families. However, the data indicate the need to buttress the stability of such placements. Agencies have experimented with use of contracts. These agreements state that the agency will not remove the child and that the family accepts ongoing responsibility for his or her continued care.

In situations in which the child has lost contact with the birth family or where birth family contact proves destructive, agencies should move toward ensuring permanency through more legally protected channels—by exploring with the foster family or some other family the possibility of adoption. In some instances in which the child has been placed in a permanent substitute home but wishes to remain in some kind of family contact, the possibility of "open adoption" can be explored. In this situation, there is explicit agreement between the birth and adoptive family, outlining the extent to which the birth family can participate in the child's life with his or her new family (Borgman, 1981).

3. There is a continuous problem in finding a sufficient number of adequate foster homes. A 1968 nationwide study of foster-care agencies showed that the most important factor "adversely affecting quality of care" was "lack of facilities—both foster homes and group care resources" (Stone, 1969, p.14). The shortage of homes limits the deliberation with which the social worker can select a home for a particu-

lar child. Despite the practice view that priority should be given to the child's needs, in actuality not need but available resources often determine placements.

The difficulty of finding adequate foster-family homes is likely to become progressively more severe. The competition of the employment market, for which many more women can now qualify, and its substantially higher economic returns will further reduce the number of women likely to be interested in foster care. The large families that once served as the training ground for many foster mothers are a thing of the past, and limited house space makes the addition of another family member difficult. The more open, working-class family, from which foster parents traditionally come, is being replaced by the middle-class family, a compact nuclear group that discourages the entry of newcomers (George, 1970, p. 85). The fact is there are, and probably always have been, relatively few people who are willing to accept the burden and the responsibility of rearing someone else's child.

If foster-family care is in short supply for young children without physical or emotional handicaps, facilities are even more seriously limited for older, delinquent, or handicapped children. Whereas foster families have been found for physically handicapped children (Soeffing, 1975), for severely emotionally impaired children (Goldstein, Gabay, & Switzer, 1981; Davis et al., 1984), for delinquent, drug abusive, or "unmanageable" adolescents (Engel, 1983; Hazel, Schmedes & Korshin, 1983), and for single teenage mothers, many more homes for these children are needed. Children such as the following are in need of temporary family placements:

> The extensive scarring of Sally's body and the resulting psychological trauma has been hard for all. . . .
>
> Child is presently being tested for hyperkinetic reaction in childhood. He is in constant motion, destructive, and has trouble sleeping.
>
> Upon original placement, Claude was a severely disturbed child who exhibited autistic-like tendencies, part of which included unrelatedness to others. . . .
>
> Child was placed in this home after having reported being abused by former foster parents. The present foster parents are trying to get to know this youngster, who has some psychological problems [Fanshel, 1982, pp. 242, 244].

(See also DeVizia, 1974; O'Regan, 1974; Bauer & Heinke, 1976; Moore, 1976; Barker, Buffe & Zeretsky, 1978; Freeman, 1978; Coyne, 1978; Knitzer & Olson, 1982).

The success of special programs in recruiting family care for handicapped children relates to careful selection, adequate education, and sufficient staff support offered the family. (Garner & Jones, 1981; Rosenberg, 1985). Arkava and Mueller (1978) studied forty-three foster homes that cared for handicapped children and compared them with an equal number of homes caring for nonhandicapped children. The handicapped children, most of whom were mentally retarded, were younger, had been in foster care longer, and had experienced more replacements than the other children. Foster parents had to spend more time and energy caring for them, family activities were more restricted because of the children's limitations and because baby-sitters were hard to get, and the care of such children was more expensive because they broke things more frequently. The need for and the willingness to take special training in the care of the handicapped, the need for support services, and the difficulties in recruitment were noted. Having their own children accept the handicapped child and neighborhood prejudice were additional problems they faced. The availability of schools that have the resources for education of the handicapped child needs to be considered as well.

In order to cope with demanding children on a day-to-day basis, foster parents require support and understanding from others as well as opportunities for "time off" or "respite." One agency has offered these services to families using the "Foster Extended Family" model. The agency recruited and trained neighbors, friends, and extended family members who agreed to make themselves available to the foster family when assistance in child-care tasks was needed or when the parents needed temporary relief from child care. Providing this type of support helped the families more successfully care for the young, multiply severely handicapped children who were placed in their homes (Barsh, Moore, & Hamerlynck, 1983). (See also Engel, 1983.) Goldstein, Gabay, and Switzer (1981), describing a successful foster-care program for children who were severely emotionally impaired and had previously been placed in mental hospitals, note that families may also need to have available to them more intensive backup services. Some of these very disturbed children required emergency hospitalization, and plans were made ahead of time with the family for its potential use.

Foster parents are liable, in many jurisdictions, for any damage resulting from the actions of their foster children. Freeman (1978), in reporting on the placement of retarded children, notes that "Two foster homes were set on fire, a neighbor's house was set on fire, two neighbors' houses were broken into" (p. 116). This indicates the need for agencies to provide insurance for families, particularly when they foster emotionally impaired children. In 1973, New Jersey became the first state to finance liability insurance coverage for foster homes and foster parents. Foster parents were insured for up to $300,000 for personal and bodily injury and property damage.

Despite the difficulties, agencies that have developed foster-care programs for such children have noted success in the continued good care and the enhanced development of the children (Bauer & Heinke, 1976).

Innovative efforts have been made to develop programs that are midway between full day care and full foster-family care. Five-day foster care is such a compromise (Loewe & Hanrahan, 1975). The child lives with foster parents during the week but returns home for weekends, holidays, and vacations. Such a facility is appropriate in those instances in which the biological parents are capable of part-time parenting. It maintains the child's relationship with parents, increasing the feasibility and probability of planning for the child's return home. This program is part of a general effort to provide a wider choice of foster-home arrangements to meet the variety of needs presented by different groups of children coming into foster care.

4. The problem of recruitment is related to the problem of finances. Defining the role of the foster parent primarily as the equivalent of biological parents, agencies are uneasy about the question of compensation. There is "an inherent antagonism in our value system, between remuneration and being parents. Families are not marketplaces, and the personal relations offered to foster children are not up for sale" (Rosenblum, 1977, p. 108).

Foster parents most frequently see an acceptable rate as one that adequately meets the cost of maintaining the child in care without requiring any additional contribution from their own pocket. They tend to reject the idea of foster-care payment as an increment to family income or as a payment in recognition of services rendered (McWhinnie, 1978, p.17). As it is, however, foster parents tend to have to use their own funds to pay for a variety of expenses incidental to the activities of the foster child—expenses that are necessary if the child is to be participate as an equal among peers (Thomas et al., 1977, pp. 50–51). These include expenses for clothing above the agency allowance, transportation, recreational activity, parties, toys, games, personal grooming needs, and school expenses. Foster parents, in effect, rather than being adequately supported by the foster-care system, tend, in fact, to subsidize the system.

That compensation is not an academic matter is confirmed by a statistical analysis of the number of foster homes in various states as related to the level of payments in these states. The conclusion indicates that "the effect of the payment level" on the number of homes "is indeed substantial" (Simon, 1975, p. 406).

Payment generally covers food, room, and recreational and personal expenses. There are initial one-time payments in most states for start-up costs, including a wardrobe and some needed furniture. The standard consumer price index or the Bureau of Labor Statistics budget for estimates may be used to determine costs (DeJong & Specht, 1975). At best, however, these methods compute only the direct costs of maintaining a child. Different methods used to compute indirect costs—the cost of parental time and effort in child care—all indicate that indirect costs, which are not reimbursed exceed the costs of direct care (Cully, Settles & VanName, 1975; Cully, Healy, Settles & VanName, 1977).

Increases in maintenance rates have generally lagged behind increases in the cost of living. Consequently, in a time of rapid increases in cost of living, foster parents are asked to accept even less in real income than previously. Board rates are not regarded as taxable income and are not generally regarded as income in determining public assistance grants. But there is no payment for the time and energy devoted to the care of the child.

The Child Welfare League is frank and direct in calling for higher board rates. *Child Welfare,* the organ of the League, calls attention to the fact that "children are 'stacked up' in temporary shelters awaiting more appropriate placement," while boarding rates are far lower than the rates usually received by baby-sitters and in "most cities in the country, a cleaning woman can earn in two days more than foster parents receive in a week" (Glover, 1964, p. 56).

Efforts have been made to study the effects on foster care of the payment of a fee or a salary to foster parents for the time and effort devoted to child care (Jaffee & Kline, 1970). In one experiment, a salary of $200 a month was paid (in addition to the usual basic maintenance allowance), and the foster parents were viewed as agency employees. In a second experiment, a $100 service fee was paid. In general, the effects of such payment were positive:

1. The agencies were less defensive and apologetic in their relationship with the foster parents. The agency felt freer about making task assignments. One agency required that "the foster parents submit a brief monthly report on the child's adjustment." The requirement was met with regularity by most of the foster homes.

2. Agencies were less defensive in presenting the realities of the foster children's difficulties. The workers were less anxious about sharing the details of a child's behavioral difficulties for fear that the foster parents would reject the request for placement.

3. Payment for child care did not adversely affect the quality of care given: "Caseworkers gauged the over-all quality of foster parent functioning to be excellent or good in almost seven of ten cases" (Jaffee & Kline, 1970, p. 82).

4. The payments highlighted and made explicit the value to the agency and the community of the service performed by the foster parents.

5. The foster parents felt a greater sense of identification with the agency and perceived agency staff members as peers and colleagues.

It had been feared that such an arrangement might render foster parents vulnerable to the charge that they were mercenary in accepting a salary for the care of a child and that the children might react negatively to the fact that they were a source of income. Neither effect was confirmed by the study.

It is not certain that such procedures would lead to easier recruitment and longer retention of more foster homes. The limited empirical material available, however, suggests that a modest increment of homes might result. More adequate financial payments do enhance and support foster-family care functioning. And for some, the financial supports make possible the realization of a desire to become foster parents. Compassion and altruism, reinforced by an affective bond between foster parents and foster child and by some psychic recompense to the foster parent in meeting his or her own emotional needs, enable the foster parent to accept with more equanimity the burdens of foster parenthood. However, compassion and altruism, reinforced by psychic return and *adequate* financial reward, may provide a larger pool of foster homes than is currently available.

Providing special payments to compensate foster parents for the additional effort of caring for an emotionally, physically, or mentally handicapped child is a special problem. It requires clear definition of different levels of difficulty and a determination of who sets such special allowances, how they are set, and when they are set, before or after the child is placed (Specht, 1975). The problem of reducing special rates if the child improves in care as a result of the efforts of the foster parents is a difficult decision because discontinuance penalizes parents for their success. Foster parents should be given the right to appeal special rate decisions.

5. In 1959, Maas concluded that "agency relationships with most fathers and mothers of the children in care are such that if parental conditions are to be modified, the process will have to be one of self-healing without any assistance of casework service" (p. 5). Service insufficiency for these clients is as evident today as it was 25 years ago (Maluccio, 1981a, p. 10). Fanshel (1981) comments:

> Biological parents are at the heart of the problem of "drift" and "impermanence" so repeatedly identified in recent years as the dominant feature of a nation-wide system encompassing some 500,000 children in care. Simply put, biological parents of foster children are rarely offered services designed to build upon their strengths so as to enable them to restore their homes as viable abodes for their children. We have a long history in the United States of crassly neglecting biological parents and of treating most of them as if they have no value for their offspring. Once the children enter care, the parents are likely to be treated as discardable [p. 685].

As we have already pointed out, birth parent "neglect" is reflected not only in the failure to provide them with needed services but also in failure to facilitate ongoing parent-child contact. Fanshel (1981), again, comments:

> The loss of large numbers of natural parents to their children is often abetted by the staff members of child welfare agencies. The situation borders on scandal. Even seriously flawed parents continue to have importance for children, for their powerful symbolic significance if not for the full range of childrearing tasks they can be called

upon to perform. This is no more certain way of emotionally injuring children than to give them the message that those who gave life to them have abandoned them entirely, showing no interest in how they are faring [p. 685].

Failure to make available necessary services and supports affects reunification decisions (Finch, Fanshel, & Grundy, 1986). In some agencies, parents who can "help themselves" or who are most vocal in demanding access to their children are ultimately reunified with them (Thoburn, 1980; Yoshikami, 1984). However, parents who demand their child's return without being fully prepared for it are also more vulnerable to recurring childrearing problems. It is not surprising, therefore, that, in a number of these families, further disruptions and separations occur.

Birth parents are the least powerful and least visible members of the foster-care quartet (Hubbell, 1981, p. 47). The vulnerability of the child, the assets of foster parents, and the decision-making power of workers help ensure that their own perspectives are considered. While attempting to insure permanency for children, Public Law 96-272 contains no provisions that birth families must be involved in drafting case plans or in periodic case reviews. This legislation also does not explicate reunification services that must be provided parents or criteria for evaluating agency progress in helping parents confront their disabilities (Musewicz, 1981, pp. 730–736).

Given the complex service requirements of many of these individuals, and the limited amount of time (and sometimes limited skill) of foster-care workers, one can understand some of the reasons why their needs are so often ignored (Thoburn, 1980; Zimmerman, 1982; Hubbell, 1981; Olsen, 1982b; Meyer, 1984). However, as an unfortunate result of this situation, children face major losses in terms of continuity and stability, and society loses as well, both financially and in terms of human potential (Cox & Cox, 1984). A critical problem then, for the foster-care system, lies in the need to provide birth families with more attention and more status. A related difficulty involves the question of how this is to be done without sufficient funds. Without money to create and coordinate needed services, train workers, or to provide them with manageable caseloads, quality programming for these needy clients will never be achieved.

6. Related to the difficulty of providing sufficient assistance to birth families is the problem of having adequately prepared workers available to help them. Hubbell (1981) outlines the pressures and demands of this type of work:

Being a foster care caseworker demands intelligence, fairness, good judgment, empathy, and determination. The job entails being responsible for the safety of foster children, being the target of angry or bewildered biological parents, consoling confused or anxious children, and handling the demands and irritations of foster parents. Among the multitude of duties are removing a child from his family; securing a foster home; developing plans for a child and his family; working with the biological parents for the return of a child; arranging visits, treatment, and medical care; providing transportation; preparing for and attending judicial proceedings; terminating parents' rights; and arranging for adoption. Endless reams of paperwork accompany all of these tasks. It is a job in which there is frequent burnout; many leave it quickly because of the high pressure, low pay, and the lack of rewards for good work [p. 110].

The effective foster care caseworker has extensive knowledge about the functioning of individuals, families, and agencies and skills in direct intervention, case management, and advocacy. Proper preparation for this job requires a strong academic background reinforced by periodic on-the-job training. However, many foster-case caseworkers function without this type of preparation. A California survey (State of California, 1981) found that only one third of the foster care social workers had master's degrees. Examination of the personnel qualifications of a staff of eighteen agencies in five different states (Yoshikami, 1984) revealed that in only eight of these agencies did more than half of the workers have some type of social work degree (p. 90). Availability of training also varies widely from agency to agency and from state to state, although there is some evidence that, in recent years, workers have been exposed to more extensive training opportunities in permanency planning (Maluccio, 1980; State of California, 1981; Fanshel, 1982; Stuart, 1983; Yoshikami, 1984).

In this child-welfare arena, as in others, workers also complain about the amount of time they have to spend fulfilling obligations other than direct client service work. Hubbell (1981) asked fourteen workers to keep a daily log of their activities. She found that, during an eight-hour day, caseworkers spent almost two hours doing paperwork and more than an hour traveling to and from client interviews (pp. 116–117).

The need for intensive family contact, particularly with families who can potentially move toward reunification with their children, and the need to respond to frequent crises suggest that the ideal caseload size for the foster-care worker should be very small. The consequences of carrying excessive client responsibilities are reflected in caseworker comments during a California survey:

> Due to heavy caseload, it is difficult to provide adequate counseling to children and parents to assist in reunification. It is also difficult to meet the State requirement of meeting with the children and parents on a periodic basis. They also find they are not able to provide adequate support to foster children. (Agency with average caseload of thirty-five.)
>
> Caseload much too high. Contact with natural parents suffers since all the time seems to be spent in trying to place the child. (Average caseload of thirty-nine.)
>
> Caseload much too high to handle the work involved. (Average caseload of forty-one.)
>
> If more time could be spent with families, possibly less time would need to be spent in trying to place child in home after home and/or looking for permanent placement. (Average caseload was forty-nine.) [State of California, 1981, p. 99].

Although there is general agreement that small caseloads are necessary, this is clearly "the ideal" and not reality in many agencies. The statewide survey during 1979–80 in California revealed that only 12.8 per cent of the social workers had a caseload of 25 or less; 51.8 per cent had 26 to 50 clients; in more than a third (35.2%) had 51 or more cases (p.98). In his survey, Yoshikami (1984) found conditions slightly better. Two-thirds of the eighteen agencies studied had workers with responsibility for providing reunification services with client loads of 35 or less (p. 90). Problems with caseload size are seriously exacerbated when workers leave their job, since, in many agencies, prolonged periods of time elapse before positions are refilled. The children formerly served by these workers either are unserved or are added temporarily to the already heavy load of the workers who remain (Rooney, 1981; Cox & Cox, 1984). (See also Blumenthal & Weinberg, 1984).

The many stresses and limited rewards of this job contribute to the very high turnover rate and to widespread burnout. A 1973 survey conducted in Great

Britain revealed that one in five social workers had left their jobs during that year. The rate was far higher among direct line staff (28–29%) than among supervisors (9%) (Parker, 1980, p. 31). Thoburn (1980) reports that 40 per cent of the families in her study had had three or more caseworkers while their children were in care.

Under these working conditions, the individual caseworker, no matter how committed, cannot successfully handle job demands unless he or she receives effective supervision and has available the support of colleagues and of the agency. Bertsche (1981) notes, "the teaching supervisor can provide the individualized training in knowledge and skills that are often lacking in the new worker. Especially important in child welfare, supervisors can share decision making with workers in cases that are particularly stressful" (p. 457). The supervisors themselves cannot create a positive work environment without the support of agency management, whom they represent. Administrators of foster care programs must recognize the peculiar demands of this type of work.

7. Providing appropriate services for minority children has proved to be a problem in foster care for a variety of reasons. As we have previously indicated, children of minority heritage whose families face extensive poverty—black, Hispanic, Native American children—are overrepresented in substitute care. A survey of all public welfare and social service agency programs for children in out-of-home care conducted by the Office of Civil Rights found that, among the 301,943 children in care on one day in 1980, 42 per cent were from minority groups, and most of these were black (Jenkins et al., 1983, p. 42).

Evidence indicates that minority children, particularly black children, are less likely than whites to have a clear foster-care plan. In addition, they tend to stay in care far longer, an average of a year or more, and to wait in foster care for more lengthy periods before being adopted (Olsen, 1982b; Jenkins et al., 1983; Mech, 1985). Using a nationwide survey, Jenkins et al. (1983) discovered significant differences in the length of time these children spent in care. (See Table 7-4.) (See also Finch & Fanshel, 1985.)

Foster care poses special problems for some particular groups in the population. The placement rate of American Indian children is considerably higher than that of white children, and almost all such children have been placed in Caucasian homes. Preventive services are in even shorter supply for the American Indian population as compared with the general population, and the extent of poverty is greater. Few American Indian foster homes are available, and many families,

TABLE 7-4. Intergroup Differences in Time in Care[a*]

Time in Care	Ethnicity[b]				
	American Indian	Asian	Hispanic	Black	White
12 months or less		more	less	less	more
12–36 months			more	less	more
36–60 months				more	less
60 months or more		less	more	more	less
Median time in care (in months)	25	14	26	32	20

[a]p < .001 for the designation of "more" than expected or "less" than expected, using a chi-square test.
[b]A blank designates same as expected, "more" designates more than expected, and "less" designates less than expected.

*Source: Reprinted with permission from *Social Work Research & Abstracts*, vol. 19, no. 4, (Winter 1983), pp. 43.

among the limited number of applicants, have difficulty in meeting the licensing requirements. (Center for Social Research and Development, 1976; American Academy of Child Psychiatry, 1977). It is suggested that social agencies do not, as yet, have a clear appreciation of American Indian parenting patterns and the involvement of siblings in the care of younger children. This lack of understanding leads them to perceive the need for intervention and placement where it is not valid (Ishisaka, 1978).

These concerns spurred passage of PL 95-608, the Indian Child Welfare Act of 1978. This legislation emphasizes agency responsibility to insure that families are not needlessly broken up, that every effort is made to maintain the child in his or her tribal community, and that tribal courts retain authority to make decisions on behalf of community children (U.S. Dept. of Health and Human Services, 1982, p. 66).

Recruitment of an adequate supply of foster family homes for black children is equally problematic. One of the barriers to the recruitment of black homes identified by Royster (1975) was the fact that the informal foster-care system was competing with the formal system under agency auspices. Because a larger percentage of black families than white families were already caring for both related and nonrelated children for whom they had accepted responsibility, fewer black families were available for formal foster-care recruitment. In 1970, black families in Pennsylvania, where Royster did his study, "cared for 12.5 per cent of children under 19 who are not members of the nuclear family; whites care for 3.6 per cent" (pp. 3–4). There is a marked difference between black and white informal foster care. (See also Wolf, 1983; Hill, 1977). Differential provision of services to both children and families is explained in part by the need to help these families cope with extreme poverty and, in part, by the tendency to interpret circumstances reflecting the impact of poverty as signs of personal or interpersonal failure. Walker (1981) states, "this has resulted in viewing the Black family as deviant and disorganized and fails to take account that much of the Black family's dysfunction is rooted in poverty" (p. 135). Evidence suggests that poor minority group parents are aware of being devalued in this way (Jenkins & Norman, 1975, p. 80).

Trends

1. The changing nature of the foster care system suggests a trend toward redefinition of the role of foster parents. Foster parents, when adequately trained and supported by agency resources, are in an excellent position to work directly with the child to alter problematic behavior and with the birth family to develop more functional childrearing skills.

Foster parents have begun to organize nationally, and the First National Conference of Foster Parents met in Chicago in 1971. By 1972 some two hundred foster-parent associations had been formed across the country (Rosendorf, 1972). The National Foster Parent Association has played an active advocacy role since the early 1970s, although withdrawal of federal funding has weakened the impact of this group to some extent (Pasztor, 1985, p. 203).

In their local association meetings and at the national convention, foster parents expressed gratification at the support and help they received from social workers. Yet dissatisfactions with social workers' activities are also expressed.

Foster parents want more specific help in dealing with children's problems and often feel that workers are not equipped to offer such help. They tend to feel exploited by workers who visit irregularly and who are not readily available. They think that workers do not always frankly share with them the extent of the children's difficulties or of the biological parents' pathology. They are chagrined that workers often do not sufficiently credit the knowledge they have about the child, and they resent the agency's power to place and remove the child. Foster parents generally want more autonomy and the right to participate in plans and decisions regarding the child (Kennedy, 1970; Close, 1971).

Foster parents recommend that some kind of review procedure be established to handle disagreements between the foster home and the agency, and that, in addition to more adequate compensation fringe benefits (social security, liability insurance, and so on) be provided (Fanshel, 1970; Reistroffer, 1968). There are recurrent suggestions that adequate levels of board rate payments would ensure a larger supply of applicants and resolve the confusion in the agency-foster parent relationship. It is suggested that foster parenthood be clearly established as a job title, that the agency pay adequate compensation, and that the foster parent be clearly recognized as an employee of the agency (Harling, 1981; Stein, 1982).

This approach would further help to differentiate more clearly the foster parent role from the biological parent role. The foster parent would be defined as a person offering full-time physical, social, and emotional care to nonrelated children in a family setting as an employee of a child welfare agency—as a "professional" foster parent (Reeves, 1980). Special training further emphasizes the uniqueness of this role. Foster parent therapists "provide a therapeutic environment" for emotionally disturbed latency-aged children in one New York program (Engel, 1983).

If the foster parent is considered a trusted employee, then much of what is detailed in the literature regarding the contact between the caseworker and the foster family parallels the material on good employer-employee relationships: the need for recognition and appreciation of work well done, the need for support, reassurance, and understanding when the worker is facing some difficulty on the job, and the need for maintaining a high level of morale.

As is true for any job, there are necessary elements of administrative supervision to assure the agency that the job is being competently performed. Caseworker visits to determine how the child is being cared for are also in line with the employer-employee relationship. The agency has to take some responsibility for developing skills, for educating the employee to meet the demands of the job. The educational-advising component in the caseworker's visits coincides with this aspect of the employer-employee relationship.

An alternative viewpoint suggests that foster parents provide most valuable service when they offer a child a "normal" home environment. From this perspective, the parents' status as employees is deemphasized, so that caretaking is not viewed as a business transaction or the child as a source of income. Instead, foster parents are recruited who see parenting as a primary source of psychic satisfaction and who are, therefore, willing to carry out caretaking responsibilities, even when they are accompanied by inadequate pay. Foster parents are, to some extent, ambivalent about their employee status and conflicted about humanitarian vs. monetary motives (Rosendorf, 1972).

With much more extensive emphasis on training, the perspective that foster parents should function as professionals has gained ascendancy in recent years

(Meyer, 1985; Pasztor, 1985). Along with this trend have come increasing demands that financial compensation, recognition, and influence match more closely the type of responsibilities they are given by the agency.

> Foster parents are no longer prepared to be viewed as puppets whose strings are pulled by the social workers at any given time. They are developing and extending their sense of responsibility in this caring process, demanding an input into the decision-making process surrounding the children they care for. They will not be treated simply as a depository for children. Foster parents must be intimately involved in the total caring process for those children to whom they open their hearts, their homes, and often their purses [Reeves, 1980, p. 125].

These parents pose greater challenges to social service staff and to the administration of foster care programs.

2. Professionalization of the foster parent role and increased use of foster families as adoption resources has placed these families in situations of direct competition with birth parents. Unless they prove to be unfit to care for them, the legal claims of birth parents to their children were, in the past, unquestionably preeminent. Now rights based on these blood ties compete with those incurred when bonds of affection develop between foster parent and foster child. Even a fit parent may be denied the return of his or her child if it is decided that the child, who was temporarily given up for foster care, now regards the foster family as a permanent one. Psychological parenthood may take precedence over blood ties, and the child's right to continuity is regarded as having as much significance as the rights of birth parents to the child (Meezan & Shireman, 1985).

There has been a series of court cases that indicate a tendency to shift the emphasis from the requirement that the court establish the biological parents' unfitness in terminating parental rights to an emphasis that requires the parent to prove that termination is not in the child's best interests. The child's entitlement to continuity in the established relationship with the foster parent and the foster parents' investment in that relationship are given some priority over the biological parents' rights to have the child restored to them (Whitten, 1973; McCarty, 1974; Egginton & Hibbs, 1975–1976). This "tug-of-love" conflict is clearly seen in the decision of a federal judge to permit the adoption of a seven-year-old boy by foster parents who had cared for him over a two-year period. The mother had originally accepted foster care for the child because she was handicapped by multiple sclerosis. Subsequently her illness improved to the point where she could care adequately for the child. At the time the mother requested the child's return, she was maintaining a viable, if marginal, home for her two older children. The judge refused the return and sanctioned the adoption on the basis of the foster parents' development of a relationship of psychological parenthood with the child and because of the "severely shortened life expectancy of the mother" (*Washington Star,* July 7, 1974).

As foster parents are specifically recruited to provide more permanent homes for children, this conflict can be expected to escalate. Foster parents already serve as a major adoption resource, providing 60 to 70 per cent of all subsidized adoption placements (Pasztor, 1985, p. 202). When adoption planning is begun with foster families before birth parent rights have been terminated, the interest and desires of the two families are most clearly and powerfully at odds (Gill, 1975).

As foster parents gain in status and prestige, we can expect them to more persistently and effectively advocate for their own position—including their right to serve as an adoptive family for a child in their care. Foster families have pressed for the right to a notice and a hearing before any child is removed by an agency; to petition for the termination of parental rights of parents of a child in their care; to priority in adoption if a child becomes free for adoption; and to be recognized as parties at child custody hearings. A foster-parent organization—Organization of Foster Families for Equality and Reform (OFFER)—scored a significant victory for such rights in the case of *OFFER* v. *Dumpson* when a federal court found that after one year in the foster home, a child could not be removed without the protection of an impartial hearing with the foster child, the foster parents, and the biological parents participating. This decision protected the rights of the child who did want to be returned to biological parents and also provided due process for the foster parent contesting the agency's decision. In July 1977 the U.S. Supreme Court reversed the lower court decision and ruled that the agency could remove a child from a foster home without a hearing. A hearing must be granted only if the foster family requests it and only if the child has been in the foster home for at least eighteen months. However, the very fact that the case came to trial indicated the seriousness with which the foster parents' right to dispute agency decisions is regarded.

Whereas foster parents gain in strength, the danger is that birth parents—the least influential participants in the foster care system—will have their rights abrogated (Conrad, 1985). In many subtle ways, foster parents can discourage visiting on the part of birth families and then point to an erratic visiting pattern as evidence of disinterest in the child, justifying the termination of parental rights. Establishing "psychological parenthood" and alienating a child from the birth family may become, for some, the procedure for increasing the probability of adoption of a child—a "back door" to adoption. The foster care caseworker can contribute to this problem.

> After a placement is made and a child has joined a foster home, that home may become the standard to which the biological family is thereafter compared. Though the biological family satisfies the original criteria for reunification, a caseworker may be reluctant to return a child to his natural parents because of this unavoidable comparison. The foster home may be in a better part of town, better furnished; the foster parents may be more stable and knowledgeable about children; the child may seem happy and healthy. The biological home may have improved, but it is not considered as good as the foster home [Hubbell, 1981, p. 46].

If workers fail to play a mediator role between two families seeking to obtain the right to care for the child on a permanent basis, they can institutionalize systematic inequality of this type.

3. As is true for mental illness and correctional programs, courts are beginning to intervene to order the correction of shortcomings in foster-care service. In the case of *G.L.* v. *Zumwalt,* a federal court mandated improvements of the foster-care system of a major metropolitan area, Kansas City. Shortly after this decision, another federal court decree "was issued placing the operation of the foster care system of an entire state under federal court supervision" (Mushlin, Levit & Anderson, 1986, p. 144). A 1986 district court decision (*Wilder* v. *Bernstein*) required that the city of New York "take over the placement of foster care children from private agencies" (*Civil Liberties,* Summer/Fall, 1986, p. 11) in order to combat racial and religious discrimination.

Since the U.S. government has taken a special caretaking relationship with children placed in foster care, states are obligated to protect the children from harm. Consent decrees seek to enforce the kinds of desirable professional practice incorporated in Child Welfare League of America and America Public Welfare Association Standards for Foster Care.

4. In the near future we may face the difficult problem of finding an increasing number of foster homes for children who are themselves AIDS victims or whose parents are incapacitated by AIDS.

5. Despite professional and governmental attention to reduce the number of children in care, the frequent use of this substitute care resource is likely to continue. After completing their research on placement prevention, Halper and Jones (1984) conclude:

> *The need for foster care will not wither away.* Good, strong, comprehensive foster care services will still be needed despite the growth of preventive services. The studies that have been done on preventive services, including the present one, indicate that the need for foster care is *reduced* but not eliminated through the use of the service. Some families are not capable of providing even minimally adequate care for their children; some families want to relinquish a child and should be permitted to do so; some families will need a brief period of placement; and some families will require a greater service investment to maintain them at an acceptable level of functioning than we will decide to afford. Preventive services will permit us to make some reduction in the incidence and duration of foster care *at the margins;* it will not supplant the need for foster care altogether" [p. 174. Emphasis in original].

Bibliography

Adamson, Gilvary. *The Caretakers*. London, England: Bookstall Publishers, 1973.

Albert, Marilyn. "Preremoval Appeal Procedures in Foster Family Care: A Connecticut Example." *Child Welfare,* 57, 5 (May 1978), 285–297.

Aldgate, Jane. "The Child in Care and His Parents." *Adoption and Fostering,* 84, (1976), 29–39.

Aldgate, Jane. "Identification of Factors Influencing Children's Length of Stay in Care," in *New Developments in Foster Care and Adoption*. Ed. John Triseliotis. London: Routledge and Kegan Paul, 1980, 22–44.

Aldridge, Martha, and Patricia W. Cautley. "The Importance of Worker Availability in the Functioning of New Foster Homes," *Child Welfare,* 54 (June 1975), 444–453.

Allen, MaryLee, and Jane Knitzer. "Child Welfare: Examining the Policy Framework," in *Child Welfare: Current Dilemmas, Future Directions*. Ed. Brenda G. McGowan and William Meezan. Itasca, Ill.: F. E. Peacock, 1983, 93–141.

Ambinder, Walter, *et al.* "Role Phenomena and Foster Care for Disturbed Children." *American Journal of Orthopsychiatry,* 32 (January 1962).

American Academy of Child Psychiatry. *Supportive Care, Custody Placement and Adoption of Indian Children*. Bottle Hollow, Utah: American Academy of Child Psychiatry Conference, April 1977.

Anderson, Lynette M. "A Systems Theory Model for Foster Home Studies." *Child Welfare* 61, 1 (January 1982), 37–47.

Appleberg, Esther. *A Foster Family Workshop Report*. New York: Wurzweiler School of Social Work, Yeshiva University, 1968.

Arkava, Morton L., and David N. Mueller. "Components of Foster Care for Handicapped Children." *Child Welfare,* 57,6 (June 1978), 339–345.

Atherton, Charles F. "Acting Decisively in Foster Care." *Social Work,* 19 (November 1974), 658–659.

Ayres, Martin, "Defining a Child Care Policy." *Adoption and Fostering,* 9, 1 (1985), 17–21.

Babcock, Charlotte. "Some Psychodynamic Factors in Foster Parenthood—Parts I and II." *Child Welfare,* 44, 9, 10 (November–December 1965).

Backhaus, Kristina A. "Life Books: Tool for Working with Children in Placement." *Social Work* 29, 6 (November–December 1984), 551–554.

Baring-Gould, Michael, et al. "Why do Foster Homes Close?" *Arete* 8, 2 (Fall 1983), 49–63.

Barker, Philip, Carole Buffe, and Ruth Zeretsky. "Providing a Family Alternative for the Disturbed Child." *Child Welfare,* 57, 6 (June 1978), 373–378.

Barsh, Elizabeth, Judith Moore, and Leo Hamerlynck. "The Foster Extended Family: A Support Network for Handicapped Foster Children." *Child Welfare,* 62, 4 (July–August 1983), 349–360.

Barth, Richard P. et al. "Contributors to Disruption and Dissolution of Old-Child Adoptions." *Child Welfare,* 65, 4 (July–August 1986), 359–371.

Barth, Richard et al. "Emancipation Services for Adolescents in Foster Care," *Social Work,* 31, 3 (May–June, 1986), 165–171.

Bauer, John E., and Warren Heinke. "Treatment Family Care Homes for Disturbed Foster Children." *Child Welfare,* 45 (July–August 1976), 478–490.

Baylor, Edith, and Elio Monachesi. *The Rehabilitation of Children.* New York: Harper & Row, 1939.

Becker, Michael and Severe Austin. "Alternate Care Case Inventory." Washington D. C.: DHHS, ACYF, July 29, 1983 (Mimeo),

Bernstein, Blanche, Donald A. Snider, and William Meezan. *Foster Care Needs and Alternatives to Placement—A Projection 1975–1985.* New York: New York State Board of Social Welfare, November 1975.

Bertsche, Anne Vandeberg. "Worker Burnout in Child Welfare and Its Effects on Biological Parents." in *Parents of Children in Placement: Perspectives and Programs.* Ed. Paula A. Sinanoglu and Anthony N. Maluccio. New York: Child Welfare League of America, 1981, 445–549.

Beste, Hilary, and Rebecca Richardson. "Developing a Life Story Book Program for Foster Children." *Child Welfare,* 60, 8 (September–October 1981), 529–534.

Block, Norman M., and Arlene Libowitz. *Recidivism in Foster Care.* New York: Child Welfare League of America, 1983.

Blumenthal, Karen. "Making Foster Family Care Responsive," in *Child Welfare: Current Dilemmas, Future Directions.* Ed. Brenda G. McGowan and William Meezan. Itasca, Ill.: F. E. Peacock, 1983, 295–342.

Blumenthal, Karen, and Weinberg, Anita (eds.). *Establishing Parent Involvement in Foster Care Agencies.* New York: Child Welfare League of America, 1984.

Boehm, Bernice. *Deterrents to the Adoption of Children in Foster Care.* New York: Child Welfare League of America, 1958.

Bolton, F. G., Roy Laner, and Dorothy Gai. "For Better or Worse? Foster Parents and Foster Children in an Officially Reported Child Maltreatment Population." *Children and Youth Services Review,* 3 (1981), 37–53.

Borgman, Robert. "Antecedents and Consequences of Parental Rights: Termination for Abused and Neglected Children," *Child Welfare,* 60, 6 (June 1981), 391–404.

Bowlby, John. *Maternal Care and Mental Health.* Geneva: World Health Organization, 1951.

Boyd, Lawrence H., and Linda L. Remy. "Is Foster-Parenting Training Worthwhile?" *Social Service Review* (June 1978), 275–296.

Bremner, Robert H. *Children and Youth in America, A Documentary History,* Vol. 1: *1600–1865.* Cambridge, Mass.: Harvard University Press, 1970.

Briar, Scott. "Clinical Judgment in Foster Care Placement." *Child Welfare,* 42 (April, 1963), 161–169.

Bryce, Martin, and Roger Ehlert. "144 Foster Children." *Child Welfare,* 50, 9 (November 1974), 499–503.

Bryce, Marvin, and June Lloyd. *Treating Families in the Home: An Alternative to Placement.* Springfield, Ill.: Charles C. Thomas, 1981.

Bush, Malcolm, and Harold Goldman. "The Psychological Parenting and Permanency Principles in Child Welfare: A Reappraisal and Critique." *American Journal of Orthopsychiatry,* 52, 2 (1982), 223–235.

Bush, Malcolm, Andrew C. Gordon, and Robert Le Bailly. "Evaluating Child Welfare Services: A Contribution from Clients." *Social Service Review,* 51 (September 1977), 491–501.

California, State of. *Family Protection Act Report* Sacramento, Cal., Author, (January, 1981).

Canning, Rebecca. "School Experiences of Foster Children." *Child Welfare,* 53 (November 1974), 582–587.

Carbino, Rosemarie. "Group Work with Natural Parents in Permanency Planning." in *The Use of Group Services in Permanency Planning for Children.* Ed. Sylvia Morris. New York: Haworth Press, 1983.

Carbino, Rosemarie. *Foster Parenting: An Updated Review of the Literature.* New York: Child Welfare League of America, 1980.

Catalano, Robert. *Research Report on New York State Foster Care.* Albany, N.Y.: State Department of Social Services, October 1974.

Cautley, Patricia W. *New Foster Parents: The First Experience.* New York: Human Sciences Press, 1980.

Cautley, Patricia, *et al., Successful Foster Homes—An Exploratory Study of Their Characteristics.* Madison: Wisconsin Department of Public Welfare, June 1966.

Cautley, Patricia., and Martha Aldridge. "Predicting Success for New Foster Parents." *Social Work,* 20, 1 (January 1975), 48–53.

Cautley, Patricia., and Diane P. Lichtenstein. *Manual for Homefinders—The Selection of Foster Parents.* Madison: University Of Wisconsin Extension, Center for Social Services, 1974.

Cautley, Patricia, and Diane P. Lichtenstein. *The Selection of Foster Parents.* Madison, WI, University of Wisconsin, Extension, 1974.

Center for Social Research and Development. *Indian Child Welfare: A State of the Field Study.* Denver: University of Denver, Center for Social Research and Development, 1976.

Chappell, Barbara. "One Agency's Periodic Review in Foster Care—The South Carolina Story." *Child Welfare,* 54 (July 1975), 477–486.

Charnley, Jean. *The Art of Child Placement.* Minneapolis: University of Minnesota Press, 1955.

Chestang, Leon, and Irmgard Heymann. "Reducing the Length of Foster Care." *Social Work,* 18 (January 1973), 88–92.

Child Welfare League of America, *Standards for Foster Family Care.* New York: 1959.

Children's Defense Fund. *Children Without Homes.* Washington, D.C.: Children's Defense Fund, 1978.

Clayburn, W. Eugene, and Stephen Magura. *Foster Care Case Review in New Jersey: An Evaluation of Its Implementation and Effects.* Trenton, N.J.: State of New Jersey Foster Care Research Project, 1977.

Clayburn, W. Eugene, Stephen Magura, and William Resnick. "Periodic Review of Foster Care: A Brief National Assessment." *Child Welfare,* 55 (June 1976), 395–405.

Clement, Priscilla Ferguson. "Families and Foster Care. Philadelphia in the Late Nineteenth Century." *Social Service Review,* 53 (1979), 406–420.

Close, Kathryn. "An Encounter with Foster Parents." *Children,* 18, 4 (July–August 1971), 138–142.

Colón, Fernando. "Family Ties and Child Placement," in *Parents of Children in Placement: Perspectives and Programs.* Ed. Paula A. Sinanoglu and Anthony N. Maluccio. New York: Child Welfare League of America, 1981, 241–267.

Colvin, R. "Toward the Development of a Foster Parent Attitude Test," in *Quantitative Approaches to Parent Selection.* New York: Child Welfare League of America, January 1962.

Conrad, Kayla. "Promoting Quality of Care: The Role of the Compliance Director." *Child Welfare,* 64, 6 (November–December, 1985), 639–649.

Cox, Martha. *Foster Care: Current Issues, Policies and Practices.* Hawthorne, N.Y.: Aldine Publishing, 1985.

Cox, Martha, and Roger Cox. "Foster Care and Public Policy." *Journal of Family Issues,* 5, 2 (June, 1984), 182–199.

Coyne, Ann. "Techniques for Recruiting Foster Homes for Mentally Retarded Children." *Child Welfare,* 57, 2 (February 1978), 123–131.

Cully, James D., Denis F. Healy, Barbara H. Settles, and Judith Van Name. "Public Payments for Foster Care." *Social Work,* 22 (May 1977), 219–233.

Cully, James D., Barbara H. Settles, and Judith B. Van Name. *Understanding and Measuring the Cost of Foster Care.* Newark: University of Delaware, 1975.

Davids, Leo. *The Foster Father Role.* Unpublished Ph.D. thesis. New York University, New York, 1968.

Davidson, Ralph F. "Restoring Children to Their Families," in *New Developments in Foster Care and Adoption.* Ed. John Triseliotis. London: Routledge and Kegan Paul, 1980, 41–53.

Davies, Linda J. and David C. Bland. "The Use of Foster Parents as Role Models for Parents," in *Parents of Children in Placement: Perspectives and Programs.* Ed. Paula A. Sinanoglu and Anthony N. Maluccio. New York: Child Welfare League of America, 1981, 415–422.

Davis, Diana., et al. "Cluster Homes: An Alternative for Troubled Youths." *Children Today,* 13 (January–February, 1984), 34–36.

De Cocq, Gustave. *The Withdrawal of Foster Parent Applicants.* San Francisco: United Community Fund of San Francisco, June 1962.

De Jong, Gerber, and C. Specht. "Setting Foster Care Rates I: Basic Considerations; II: Special Cases." *Public Welfare,* 33 (Fall 1975), 37–46.

Delgado, Melvin. "A Hispanic Foster Parents Program." *Child Welfare,* 57, 7 (July–August, 1978), 428–431.

DeVizia, Joseph. "Success in a Foster Home Program for Mentally Retarded Children," *Child Welfare,* 53 (February 1974), 121–125.

Dick, Kenneth. "What People Think About Foster Care." *Children* (March–April 1961).

Dingman, Harvey F., *et al.* "Prediction of Child-Rearing Attitude." *Child Welfare,* 41 (1962).

Dubois, Dominic, Betty Mockler and George Mockler. "Foster Parents as Key Workers/ Work with Natural Parents." *Adoption and Fostering.* 8,3 (1984), 30–33.

Edelstein, Susan. "When Foster Children Leave: Helping Foster Parents to Grieve." *Child Welfare,* 60, 7 (July–August, 1981), 467–474.

Egginton, Margaret L., and Richard E. Hibbs. "Termination of Parental Rights in Adoption Cases: Focusing on the Child." *Journal of Family Law,* 14 (1975–1976), 547–580.

Eisenberg, Leon. "Deprivation and Foster Care." *Journal of American Academy of Child Psychiatry,* 4 (1965), 243–248.

Emlen, Arthur. *Barriers to Planning for Children in Foster Care,* Vol. 1, Portland, Oregon. Regional Research Institute for Human Services, Portland State University, 1976.

Emlen, Arthur, et al. *Overcoming Barriers to Planning for Children in Foster Care.* Portland, Ore. Regional Research Institute for Human Services. Portland State University, 1977.

Engel, Joan M. "The Parent Therapist Program: A New Approach to Foster Care of Difficult Adolescents." *Children and Youth Services Review,* 5 (1983), 195–207.

Euster, Sandra D., Vincent P. Ward and Jeanene G. Varner. "Adapting Counseling Techniques to Foster Parent Training." *Child Welfare,* 61, 6 (June, 1982), 375–382.

Fanshel, David. "Parental Failure and Consequences for Children—The Drug Abusing Mother Whose Children are in Foster Care." *American Journal of Public Health,* 65 (June 1975a), 604–612.

Fahlberg, Vera. *Attachment and Separation: Putting the Pieces Together.* Lansing, Mich., Michigan Department of Social Services, 1979.

Fanshel, David. "Specialization Within the Foster Parent Role. 1 Difference Between Foster Parents of Infants and Foster Parents of Older Children." *Child Welfare,* 40 (March 1961).

Fanshel, David. *Foster Parenthood—A Role Analysis.* Minneapolis: University of Minnesota Press, 1966.

Fanshel, David. "Role of Foster Parents in the Future." in *Foster Care in Question.* Ed. Helen D. Stone, New York: Child Welfare League of America, 1970.

Fanshel, David. "The Exit of Children from Foster Care: An Interim Research Report." *Child Welfare,* 50, 2 (February 1971), 65–81.

Fanshel, David. "Parental Failure and Consequences for Children—The Drug Abusing Mother Whose Children Are in Foster Care." *American Journal of Public Health,* 65 (June 1975a), 604–612.

Fanshel, David. "Parental Visiting of Children in Foster Care: Key to Discharge." *Social Service Review,* 49 (December 1975b), 493–514.

Fanshel, David. "Parental Visiting of Foster Children: A Computerized Study." *Social Work Research and Abstracts,* 1 (Fall 1977), 2–10.

Fanshel, David. "Preschoolers Entering Foster Care in New York City: The Need to Stress Plans for Permanency," *Child Welfare,* 58 (February 1979a), 67–87.

Fanshel, David. *Computerized Information for Child Welfare: Foster Children and Their Foster Parents.* New York: Columbia University School of Social Work, March 1979b.

Fanshel, David. "Decision-Making Under Uncertainty: Foster Care for Abused or Neglected Children?" *American Journal of Public Health,* 71, 7 (July,1981), 685–686.

Fanshel, David. *On the Road to Permanency: An Expanded Data Base for Service to Children in Foster Care.* New York: Child Welfare League of America, 1982.

Fanshel, David, and John Grundy. *Computerized Data for Children in Foster Care: First Analysis from a Management Information Service in New York City.* New York: Child Welfare Information Service, November 1975.

Fanshel, David, and H. Maas. "Factorial Dimensions of the Characteristics of Children in Placements and Their Families." *Child Development,* 33 (1962).

Fanshel, David, and Eugene B. Shinn. *Dollars and Sense in the Foster Care of Children: A Look at Cost Factors.* New York: Child Welfare League of America, 1972.

Fanshel, David, and Eugene B. Shinn. *Children in Foster Care: A Longitudinal Investigation.* New York: Columbia University Press, 1978.

Fein, Edith, and Anthony Maluccio. "Children Leaving Foster Care: Outcomes of Permanency Planning." *Child Abuse and Neglect,* 8, (1984), 425–431.

Fein, Edith, et al. "After Foster Care: Outcomes of Permanency Planning for Children." *Child Welfare,* 62, 6 (November–December, 1983), 485–558.

Felker, Evelyn. *Raising Other People's Kids.* Grand Rapids, Mich.: William B. Eerdmans, 1981.

Fellner, Irving, and Charles Solomon. "Achieving Permanent Solutions for Children in Foster Home Care." *Child Welfare,* 42, (March 1973), 178–187.

Ferguson, Thomas. *Children in Care and After.* New York: Oxford University Press, 1966.

Festinger, Trudy B. "Placement Agreements with Boarding Homes: A Survey." *Child Welfare,* 53, 10 (December 1974), 643–652.

Festinger, Trudy. "The Impact of the New York Court Review of Children in Foster Care. A Follow Up Report." *Child Welfare,* 55 (September–October 1976), 516–544.

Festinger, Trudy. "The New York Court Review of Children in Foster Care." *Child Welfare,* 54 (April 1975), 211–245.

Festinger, Trudy B. *No One Ever Asked Us: A Postscript to Foster Care.* New York: Columbia University Press, 1983.

Finch, Stephen, and David Fanshel, "Testing the Equality of Discharge Patterns in Foster Care." *Social Work Research and Abstracts,* 21, 3 (Fall, 1985). 3–10.

Finch, Stephen, David Fanshel, and John Grundy. "Factors Associated with the Discharge of Children from Foster Care." *Social Work Research and Abstracts,* 22, 1 (Spring 1986), 10–18.

Folks, Homer. *The Care of the Destitute, Neglected, and Delinquent Children.* New York: The Macmillan Company, 1902.

Fox, Mary, and Kathleen Arcuri. "Cognitive and Academic Functioning in Foster Children." *Child Welfare,* 59, 8 (September–October, 1980), 491–496.

Frank, George. "Treatment Needs of Children in Foster Care." *American Journal of Orthopsychiatry,* 50, 2 (April, 1980), 256–263.

Freeman, Henry. "Foster Home Care for Mentally Retarded Children: Can It Work?" *Child Welfare,* 57, 2 (February 1978), 113–121.

Freud, Anna, Joseph Goldstein, and Albert Solnit. *Beyond the Best Interests of the Child.* New York: The Free Press, 1973.

Freund, V. W. "Evaluation of a Self-Approved Method for Inducting Foster Parents." *Smith College Studies in Social Work,* 46, 2 (1976), 115–126.

Friedman, Robert, et al. "Length of Time in Foster Care: A Measure in Need of Analysis. *Social Work,* 27, 6 (November, 1982).

Furrh, Paul. "Emancipation: The Supervised Apartment Living Approach." *Child Welfare,* 62, 1 (January–February, 1985), 54–61.

Galaway, B. "Contracting A Means of Clarifying Roles in Foster Family Services." *Children Today,* 5 (1976), 20–23.

Gambrill, Eileen D. "Facilitating Decision Making in Foster Care." *Social Service Review,* 5 (September 1977), 502–513.

Gambrill, Eileen, and Kermit T. Wiltse. "Foster Care: Prescriptions for Change." *Public Welfare,* 32 (Summer 1974), pp. 39–47.

Gambrill, Eileen, and Kermit T Wiltse. "Contracts and Outcome in Foster Care." *Social Work,* 22 (March 1977), 148–149.

Garner, Bruce and Mary Jones. "Specialist Fostering in Essex." *Adoption and Fostering.* 103, 1 (1981), 38–42.

Garon, Risa, Barbara Mandell and Jane Walker. "Helping Children Cope with Separation and Divorce." *Foster Care Journal,* 1, 6 (September, 1984), 5–7.

George, Victor. *Foster Care: Theory and Practice.* London: Kegan Paul, Trench, Trubner & Co., 1970.

Gershenson, Charles. *Child Welfare Population Characteristics and Flow Analysis: FY 1982.* Washington, D. C.: ACYF, 1983.

Gibson, Terry L., George S. Tracy and Mark S. DeBord. "An Analysis of Variables Affecting Length of Stay in Foster Care." *Children and Youth Services Review* 6 (1984), 135–145.

Gil, David. "Developing Routine Follow-up Procedures for Child Welfare Services." *Child Welfare,* 43 (May 1964).

Gil, Eliana. "Foster Parents: Set Up to Fall." *Child Abuse and Neglect,* 8 (1984), 121–123.

Gill, Margaret. "The Foster Care/Adoptive Family: Adoption for Children Not Legally Free." *Child Welfare* 54, 10 (1975), 712–720.

Gingerich, Wallace. "The Wisconsin System for Determining Supplemental Payments in Foster Care: A Reliability Study." *Children and Youth Services Review,* 3, (1981), 69–75.

Glassberg, Eudice. "Are Foster Homes Hard to Find?" *Child Welfare,* 44 (October 1965).

Glickman, Esther. *Child Placement Through Clinically Oriented Casework.* New York: Columbia University Press, 1957.

Glover, E. Elizabeth. "Is Child-Caring important?" *Child Welfare* 42 (February 1964).

Goldstein, Harriet, and Adoline Dall. "Group Learning for Foster Parents. I: In a Voluntary Agency; II: In a Public Agency." *Children,* 14, 5 (September–October 1967).

Goldstein, Harriet, David Gabay, and Robert Switzer. " 'Fail Safe' Foster Family Care: A Mental Hospital-Child Welfare Agency Program". *Child Welfare, 60, 9 (Novermber, 1981), 627–636.*

Goldston, Judith. "The Foster Parents," in *Preventive Mental Health Services for Children Entering Foster Homes Care.* Ed. Gilbert W. Kliman, M. Harris Schaeffer, and Murray J. Friedman. White Plains, N.Y.: Center for Preventive Psychiatry, 1982, 189–200.

Gordon, Henrietta. *Casework Services for Children.* Boston: Houghton Mifflin Company, 1956.

Gottesfeld, Harry. *In Loco Parentis—A Study of Perceived Role Values in Foster Home Care.* New York: Jewish Child Care Association of New York, 1970.

Grinnell, Richard, and Sherri Jung. "Children Placed with Relatives." *Social Work Research and Abstracts,* 17, 3 (Fall, 1981), 31–32.

Gross, Malcolm J. "Custody Conflicts Between Foster and Birth Parents in Pennsylvania." *Social Work,* 29, 6 (November–December 1984), 510–515.

Gross, P., and F. Bussard. "A Group Method for Finding and Developing Foster Homes." *Child Welfare,* 55, 9 (November 1970), 521–524.

Gruber, Alan R. *A Study of Children, Their Biological and Foster Parents.* Springfield, Mass.: Governor's Commission on Adoption & Foster Care, 1973.

Gruber, Alan R. *Children in Foster Care—Destitute, Neglected, Betrayed.* New York: Human Sciences Press, 1978.

Guerney, Louise F. *Foster Parent Training Prospect.* University Park, Penna. 1976.

Gurak, Douglas, David Arrender Smith, and Mary Goldson. *The Minority Foster Child: A Comparative Study of Hispanic, Black and White Children.* Bronx, N.Y.: Fordham University, 1982.

Haines, James, Walter Schumm, and C. E. Kennedy. "Child Guidance as Perceived by Foster Parents and Social Workers: A Research Note." *Child Welfare* 60, 10 (December 1981), 703–708.

Halper, Gertrude, and Mary Ann Jones. *Serving Families at Risk of Dissolution: Public Preventive Services in New York City,* New York: Human Resources Administration, February 1984.

Hampson, Robert B., and Joseph B. Tavormina, "Feedback from the Experts: A Study of Foster Mothers." *Social Work,* 25 (March, 1980), 108–113.

Hanwell, Albert F., et al. *A Guide for Foster Parent Group Education.* Boston: Boston College Graduate School of Social Work, 1969.

Hargrave, Vivian, Joan Shireman, and Peter Connor. *Where Love and Need Are One.* Chicago, Illinois Department of Social Services, 1975.

Haring, Barbara L. *1975 Census of Requests for Child Welfare Services.* New York: Child Welfare League of America, September 1975.

Harling, Delia. "Observation and Assessment by Foster Parents." *Adoption and Fostering* 106, 4 (1981), 39–40.

Hart, Hasting H. "Annual Report." in *Proceedings of the National Conference of Charities and Correction.* Boston: George H. Ellis, 1884.

Hazel, Nancy. "Community Placements for Adolescents in the United Kingdom: Changes in Policy and Practice." *Children and Youth Services Review,* 3 (1981), 85–97.

Hazel, Nancy, Carsten Schmedes, and Pia M. Korshin. " A Case Study in International Cooperation." *British Journal of Social Work,* 13, 6 (12/83), 671–678.

Hegar, Rebecca. "Foster Children's and Parents' Right to a Family." *Social Service Review* 57, 3 (September 1983), 429–447.

Heinritz, Gretchen, and Louise A. Frey. *Foster Care: How to Develop an Educational Program for Staff or Foster Parents.* Boston: Boston University School of Social Work, 1975.

Herskovitz, Linda S., Robert F. Kelly, and Sarah Ramsey. "Courts, Kin and Children: Determinants of Court-Ordered Kin Involvement in Child Protection Proceedings." *Children and Youth Services Review,* 8, 2 (1986), 107–133.

Herstein, Norman. "The Replacement of Children from Foster Homes." *Child Welfare,* 36 (July 1957).

Hess, Peg, and Judy Hicks. "Pulling Together with the Natural family," in Workshop Proceedings of the Tennessee Foster Care Association Annual Conference, March 1979.

Hess, Peg, and Linda Williams. "Group Orientation for Parents of Children in Foster Family Care." *Child Welfare,* 61, 7 (September–October, 1982), 456–466.

Hill, Esther. "Is Foster Care the Answer?" *Public Welfare,* 15 (April 1957).

Hill, Robert. *Informal Adoption Among Black Families.* Washington, D. C.: National Urban League, Reasearch Department, 1977.

Holleman, Barbara A. "Treatment of the Child," in *Child Abuse and Neglect: A Guide with Case Studies for Treating the Child and Family*. Ed. Nancy B. Ebeling and Deborah A. Hill. Boston, Mass.: John Wright, 1983, 145–182.

Holman, Robert. *Trading in Children: A Study of Private Fostering*.London, England. Routledge & Kegan Paul, 1973.

Holman, Robert. "The Place of Fostering in Social Work." *British Journal of Social Work*, 5 (Spring 1975), 3–29.

Holman, Robert. "Exclusive and Inclusive Concepts of Fostering," in *New Developments in Foster Care and Adoption*. Ed. John Triseliotis. London: Routledge and Kegan Paul, 1980, 69–84.

Hornby, Helaine, and Mary Collins. "Teenagers in Foster Care: The Forgotten Majority." *Children and Youth Services Review*, 3 (1981), 7–20.

Hubbell, Ruth. *Foster Care and Families: Conflicting Values and Policies*. Philadelphia: Temple University Press, 1981.

Ishisaka, Hideki. "American Indians and Foster Care: Cultural Factors and Separation." *Child Welfare*, 57, 5 (May 1978), 299–307.

Jacobs, Marc. "Foster Parent Training: An Opportunity for Skills Enrichment and Empowerment." *Child Welfare*, 59, 10 (December 1980), 615–624.

Jacobsen, Elinor, and Joanne Cockerum. "As Foster Children See It." *Children Today*, 5 (November–December 1976), 32–36.

Jaffee, Benson, and Draza Kline. *New Payment Pattern and the Foster Parent Role*. New York: Child Welfare League of America, 1970.

Janchill, Sister Mary Paul. "Services for Special Populations of Children," in *Child Welfare: Current Dilemmas, Future Directions*. Ed. Brenda G. McGowan and William Meezan. Itasca, Ill., F. E. Peacock, 1983, 345–376.

Jenkins, Rachel. "The Needs of Foster Parents." *Case Conference*, 11 (January 1965).

Jenkins, Shirley. "Filial Deprivation in Parents of Children in Foster Care," *Children*, 14, 1 (January–February 1967), 8–12.

Jenkins, Shirley, and Elaine Norman. *Filial Deprivation and Foster Care*. New York: Columbia University Press, 1972.

Jenkins, Shirley. "The Tie That Binds," in *The Challenge of Partnership: Working with Parents of Children in Foster Care*. Ed. Anthony Maluccio and Paula Sinanoglu. New York: CWLA, 1981, 39–51.

Jenkins, Shirley, and Elaine Norman. *Beyond Placement: Mothers' View of Foster Care*. New York: Columbia University Press, 1975.

Jenkins, Shirley et al. "Ethnic Differentials in Foster Care Placements." *Social Work Research and Abstracts*, 19,4 (Winter, 1983), 41–45.

Jewett, Claudia. *Helping Children Cope with Separation and Loss*. Boston: Harvard Common Press, 1982.

Jones, Evan O. "A Study of Those Who Cease to Foster." *British Journal of Social Work*, 5 (Spring 1975), 31–41.

Jones, Martha, and John Biesecker. *Child Welfare Training: Goal Planning in Children and Youth Services*. Washington D. C., U. S. Department of Health and Human Services, 1980a.

Jones, Martha, and John Biesecker. "Training in Permanency Planning: Using What Is Known." *Child Welfare*, 59, 8 (September–October 1980b), 481–489.

Jones, Mary, Renee Neuman, and Anne W. Shyne. *A Second Chance for Families: Evaluation of a Program to Reduce Foster Care*. New York: Child Welfare League of America, 1976.

Juliusberger, Erika. *Phases of Adjustment in a Typical Foster Home Placement*. New York: Jewish Child Care Association of New York, 1961.

Kadushin, Alfred. "The Legally Adoptable, Unadopted Child." *Child Welfare*, 37 (December 1958), 19–25.

Kadushin, Alfred. "Children in Foster Families and Institutions," in *Social Service Research: Review of Studies*. Ed. Henry Maas. New York: National Association of Social Workers, 1978.

Kahan, Barbara. *Growing Up in Care: Ten People Talking.* Oxford: Basil Blackwell, 1979.

Kastell, Jean. *Casework in Child Care.* London: Kegan Paul, Trench, Trubner & Co., 1962.

Kavaler, Florence, and Margaret Swire. *Foster Child Health Care.* Lexington, Mass.: Lexington Books, 1983.

Keane, Anne. "Behaviour Problems Among Long-Term Foster Children." *Adoption and Fostering,* 7, 3 (1983), 53–62.

Kennedy, Ruby. "A Foster Parent Looks at Foster Care," in *Foster Care in Question.* Ed. Helen D. Stone. New York: Child Welfare League of America, 1970.

Kent, James T. "A Follow-up Study of Abused Children." *Journal of Pediatric Psychology,* 1 (Spring 1976), 25–31.

Kinter, Richard H., and Herbert Otto. "The Family Strength Concept and Foster Care Selection." *Child Welfare,* 43 (July 1964).

Kliman, Gilbert W., M. Schaeffer, and Murray J. Friedman. (Eds.) *Preventive Mental Health Services for Children Entering Foster Home Care: An Assessment.* White Plains, N. Y.: Center for Preventive Psychiatry, 1982.

Kline, Draza, Helen Overstreet, and Mary Forbush. *Foster Care of Children—Nurture and Treatment.* New York: Columbia University Press, 1972.

Knitzer, Jane, Mary Lee Allen, and Brenda McGowan. *Children Without Homes.* Washington D. C.: Children's Defense Fund, 1978.

Knitzer, Jane, and Lynn Olson. *Unclaimed Children: The Failure of Public Responsibility to Children and Adolescents in Need of Mental Health Services.* Washington, D. C.: Children's Defense Fund, 1982.

Kraus, J. "Foster Children Grown Up: Parameters of Care and Adult Delinquency." *Children and Youth Services Review,* 3 (1981), 99–114.

Lahti, Janet. "A Follow-Up Study of Foster Children in Permanent Placements." *Social Service Review,* 56 (December 1982), 556–571.

Lahti, Janet, and Jacquelyn Dvorak. "Coming Home from Foster Care," in *The Challenge of Partnership: Working with Parents of Children in Foster Care.* Ed. Anthony N. Maluccio and Paula A. Sinanoglu. New York: Child Welfare League of America, 1981, 52–66.

Lahti, Janet et al. *A Follow-Up Study of the Oregon Project.* Portland, Ore.: Regional Research Institute for Human Services, Portland State University, August 1978.

Laird, Joan. "An Ecological Approach to Child Welfare: Issues of Family Identity and Continuity," in *Parents of Children in Placement: Perspectives and Programs.* Ed. Paula A. Sinanoglu and Anthony N. Maluccio. New York: Child Welfare League of America, 1981, 97–126.

Langsam, Miriam. *Children West:* Logmark ed. Madison: The State Historical Society of Wisconsin, 1964.

Lawder, Elizabeth, John Poulin, and Roberta Andrews. *185 Foster Children: Five Years After Placement.* Philadelphia: Children's Aid Society of Pennsylvania, 1985.

Lee, Judith, and Danielle Park. *Walk a Mile in My Shoes.* West Hartford, Conn. New England Regional Child Welfare Training Center, 1980.

Levitt, Kenneth. "A Canadian Approach to Permanent Planning." *Child Welfare,* 60, 2 (February, 1981), 109–112.

Lindberg, Dwaine, and Anne Wosrek. "The Use of Family Sessions in Foster Home Care." *Social Casework,* 44 (March 1963).

Lindsey, Duncan, "Achievements for Children in Foster Care." *Social Work* 27 (November 1982), 491–496.

Lindsey, Elizabeth, and John S. Wodarski. "Foster Family Care Review by Judicial-Citizen Panels: An Evaluation." *Child Welfare* 65, 3 (May–June 1986), 211–229.

Littner, Ner. *Some Traumatic Effects of Separation and Placement.* New York: Child Welfare League of America. October 1950.

Lloyd, John. "The Foster Child's Impact upon Foster Parents: A Pilot Study." *Journal of Community Psychology,* 10 (1982), 125–127.

Loewe, Bessie, and Thomas E. Hanrahan. "Five-Day Foster Care." *Child Welfare,* 54 (January 1975), 7–18.

Long, Kathleen Ann. "The Experience of Repeated and Traumatic Loss Among Crow Indian Children: Response Patterns and Intervention Strategies." *American Journal of Orthopsychiatry,* 53 (January 1983), 116–126.

Maas, Henry. "Highlights of the Foster Care Project: Introduction." *Child Welfare,* 38 (July 1959).

Maas, Henry, and Richard Engler. *Children in Need of Parents.* New York: Columbia University Press, 1959.

MacDonald, Mary, and Marjorie Ferguson. "Selecting Foster Parents: An Essay Review." *Social Service Review* (September 1964).

Madison, Bernice, and Michael Schapiro. "Long-term Foster Family Care: What Is Its Potential for Minority-Group Children?" *Public Welfare,* 27 (April 1969), 167–194.

Maluccio, Anthony. "The Emerging Focus on Parents of Children in Placement," in *Parents of Children in Placement: Perspectives and Programs.* Ed. Paula A. Sinanoglu and Anthony N. Maluccio. New York: Child Welfare League of America, 1981a, 5–14.

Maluccio, Anthony. "Casework with Parents of Children in Foster Care." in *Parents of Children in Placement: Perspectives and Programs.* Ed. Paula A. Sinanoglu and Anthony N. Maluccio. New York: Child Welfare League of America, 1981b, 15–31.

Maluccio, Anthony et al. "Beyond Permanency Planning." *Child Welfare,* 59, (November 1980), 515–530.

Maluccio, Anthony, and Edith Fein. "Permanency Planning: A Redefinition." *Child Welfare,* 62, 3 (May–June, 1983), 195–201.

Maluccio, Anthony, and Edith Fein. "Growing Up in Foster Care." *Children and Youth Services Review,* 7 (1985), 123–134.

Maluccio, Anthony, and Paula A. Sinanoglu. (Eds.). *The Challenge of Partnership (Working with Parents of Children in Foster Care)* New York: Child Welfare League of America, 1981a.

Maluccio, Anthony, and Paula A. Sinanoglu. "Social Work with Parents of Children in Foster Care: A Bibliography." *Child Welfare,* 60 (May, 1981b), 275–303.

Maluccio, Anthony (Ed.). *Education for Practice with Parents of Children in Foster Care* Hartford, Conn.: University of Connecticut School of Social Work, 1980.

Mandell, Betty. *Where Are the Children.* Lexington, Mass.: Lexington Books, 1973.

Marr, Pam. *Introduction to Foster Parenting.* Vols. 1, 2. Manhattan: Kansas State University, Department of Family and Child Development, 1976.

Mauzerall, Hildegarde. "Emancipation from Foster Care: The Independent Living Project." *Child Welfare,* 62, 1 (January–February, 1983), 46–53.

Maybanks, Sheila, and Marvin Bryce (Eds.). *Home-Based Services for Children and Families: Policy, Practice, and Research.* Springfield, IL: Charles C. Thomas, 1979.

McAdams, Mrs. "The Parent in the Shadows." *Child Welfare,* 51, 1 (January 1972), 51–55.

McCarty, David C. "The Foster Parents' Dilemma: 'Who Can I Turn to When Somebody Needs Me?' " *San Diego Law Review,* 11, 2 (February 1974), 376–414.

McCoy, Jacqueline. "The Application of Role Concept to Foster Parenthood." *Social Casework,* 43 (May 1962).

McFadden, Emily Jean. *Working with Natural Families.* Ypsilanti, Mich.: Eastern Michigan University, 1980.

McWhinnie, Alexina. "Support for Foster Parents" *Adoption and Fostering,* 92, 2 (1978), 15–21.

Mech, Edmund V. "Parental Visiting and Foster Placement." *Child Welfare,* 64, 1 (January–February 1985), 67–72.

Meezan, William. "Toward an Expanded Role for Adoption Services." in *Child Welfare: Current Dilemmas, Future Directions.* Ed. Brenda G. McGowan and William Meezan. Itasca, Ill.: F.E. Peacock, 1983, 425–478.

Meezan, William, and Joan Shireman. *Care and Commitment:Foster Parent Adoption Decisions.* Albany, N.Y.: State University of New York Press, 1985a.

Meezan, William, and Joan Shireman. "Antecedents to Foster Parent Adoption Decisions." *Children and Youth Services Review,* 7 (1985b), 207–224.

Meier, Elizabeth C. *Former Foster Children as Adult Citizens.* Unpublished Ph.D. thesis, Columbia University, New York, April 1962.

Melotte, C. J. "The Placement Decision." *Adoption and Fostering. 95,1* (1979), 56–62.

Meyer, Carol H. "A Feminist Perspective on Foster Family Care: A Redefinition of the Categories." *Child Welfare,* 64, 3 (May–June 1985), 249–258.

Meyer, Carol H. "Can Foster Care be Saved?" *Social Work* 29, 6 (November–December, 1984), 499.

Mills, Robert B., *et al.* "Introducing Foster Mother Training Groups in a Voluntary Child Welfare Agency." *Child Welfare,* 46, 10 (December 1967).

Moore, Paulene M. "Foster Family Care for Visually Impaired Children." *Children Today* (July–August 1976), 11–15.

Moss, Sidney, and Miriam Moss. "Threat to Place A Child." *American Journal of Orthopsychiatry.* 54, 1 (January, 1984), 168–173.

Mulrey, J. M. "The Care of Destitute and Neglected Children—Report of One Committee." *National Conference of Charities and Correction, 1899.* Boston: George Ellis, 1900.

Murphy, Dorothy A. "A Program for Parents of Children in Foster Family Care," in *Parents of Children in Placement: Perspectives and Programs.* Ed. Paula Sinanoglu and Anthony Maluccio. New York: Child Welfare League of America, 1981, 433–439.

Murphy, H. B. M. *Foster Home Variables and Adult Outcome.* Mimeo, 1964.

Musewicz, John. "Failure of Foster Care: Federal Statutory Reform and the Child's Right to Permanence." *Southern California Law Review,* 54 (1981), 633–765.

Mushlin, Michael B; Louis Leavitt, and Lauren Anderson. "Court Ordered Foster Family Care Reform: A Case Study." *Child Welfare,* 65, 2 (March–April 1986), 141–154.

Napier, Harry. "Success and Failure in Foster Care." *British Journal of Social Work,* 2, 2 (Summer, 1972), 187–203.

National Commission for Children in Need of Parents. *Who Knows? Who Cares? Forgotten Children in Foster Care.* New York: National Commission for Children, 1979.

New York City Department of Social Services. *The Parents' Handbook—A Guide for Parents of Children in Foster Care.* New York City: Department of Social Services, January 1977.

Noble, Lynne Stever, and Sandra Euster. "Foster Parent Input: A Crucial Element in Training." *Child Welfare,* 60 (January 1981), 35–42.

Norgard, Katherine Eastlack, and Pamela D. Mayhall, "Everybody Counts: The Foster Family Institute." *Child Welfare,* 61, 4 (April, 1982), 239–246.

Norton, Francis. "Foster Care and the Helping Professions." *Personnel and Guidance Journal* 60, 3 (November 1981), 156–159.

Olsen, Lenore. "Predicting the Permanency Status of Children in Foster Care." *Social Work Research and Abstracts,* 18 (Spring, 1982a), 9–20.

Olsen, Lenore. "Services for Minority Children in Out-of-Home Care." *Social Service Research* 56, 4 (December 1982b), 573–585.

O'Regan, Gerard W. "Foster Family Care for Children with Mental Retardation." *Children Today,* 3 (January–February 1974), 20–22.

O'Rourke, Alice M. "The Psychological Characteristics of Mothers Whose Children Are in Foster Boarding Home Care Compared with Mothers Whose Children Are at Home with Them." Unpublished Ph.D. thesis, National Catholic School of Social Service, Catholic University of America, 1976.

Ougheltree, Cornelia. *Finding Foster Homes.* New York: Child Welfare League of America, 1957.

Owen, Sally T., and Herbert H. Hershfang. "Overview of the Legal System. Protecting Children from Abuse and Neglect," in *Child Abuse and Neglect: A Guide with Case Studies for Treating the Child and Family.* Ed. Nancy B. Ebeling and Deborah A. Hill. Boston: John Wright, 1983, 229–257.

Palmer, David. "Comparing Home-Finding Methods." *Adoption and Fostering,* 106,4. (1981), 41–43.

Palmer, Sally. *Children in Long-term Care: Their Experiences and Progress.* Canada: Family and Children's Services of London & Middlesex, August 1976.

Pardeck, John T. *The Forgotten Children: A Study of the Stability and Continuity of Foster Care.* Lanham, Md. University Press of America, 1983.

Parker, Roy. *Decision in Child Care.* London: George Allen & Unwin Ltd., 1966.

Parker, R. A (Ed.). *Caring for Separated Children: Plans, Procedures, and Priorities.* London: Macmillan, 1980.

Pasztor, Eileen Mayers. "Permanency Planning and Foster Parenting: Implications for Recruitment Selection, Training and Retention." *Children and Youth Services Review* 7 (1985), 191–205.

Pasztor, Eileen Mayers et al. "Stepping out of Foster Care into Independent Living," *Children Today* (March–April 1986), 32–35.

Paul, Sister Mary. *Criteria for Foster Placement and Alternatives to Foster Care.* Albany, New York State Board of Social Welfare, May 1975.

Paulson, Morris J., Sylvia Grossman, and Gary Shapiro. "Child Rearing Attitudes of Foster Home Mothers." *Journal of Community Psychology,* 2 (January 1974), 11–14.

Penn, John V. "A Model for Training Foster Parents in Behavior Modification Techniques." *Child Welfare,* 57, 3 (March 1978), 175–180.

Petersen, James, and A. Dean Pierce. "Socioeconomic Characteristics of Foster Parents." *Child Welfare,* 53 (May 1974), 295–304.

Phillips, Michael H., et al. *Factors Associated with Placement Decisions in Child Welfare.* New York: Child Welfare League of America, 1971.

Phillips, Michael H., et al. *A Model for Intake Decisions in Child Welfare.* New York: Child Welfare League of America, 1972.

Pike, Victor et al. *Permanent Planning for Children in Foster Care: A Handbook for Social Workers.* Portland, Ore.: Regional Research Institute for Human Services, Portland State University, March 1977.

Poertner, John, and Charles A. Rapp. "Information System Design in Foster Care." *Social Work,* 25 (March 1980), 114–119.

Proch, Kathleen. *Adoption by Foster Parents.* Urbana-Champaign: University of Illinois, Ph.D. Thesis, 1980.

Proch, Kathleen. "Foster Parents as Preferred Adoptive Parents: Practice Implications." *Child Welfare* 60,9 (November, 1981), 617–625.

Proch, Kathleen, and Jeanne Howard. "Parental Visiting of Children in Foster Care." *Social Work,* 31, 3 (May–June, 1986), 178–181.

Project CRAFT. *Training in the Adoption of Children with Special Needs.* Ann Arbor: University of Michigan School of Social Work, 1980.

Radinsky, Elizabeth *et al.* "Recruiting and Serving Foster Parents." *Child Welfare,* 42 (January 1963).

Rapp, Charles. "Effect of the Availability of Family Support Services on Decisions about Child Placement." *Social Work Research and Abstracts* 18, 1 (1982), 21–27.

Rapp, Charles, and John Poertner. "Reducing Foster Care: Critical Factors and Administrative Strategies." *Administration in Social Work,* 2 (Fall 1978), 335–346.

Reeves, Christine S. "Foster Care: A Partnership of Skill." in *New Developments in Foster Care and Adoption.* Ed. John Triseliotis. London: Routledge and Kegan Paul, 1980, 118–130.

Region III Resource Center. Children, Youth and Families. *Region III Resource Review for Children, Youth and Family Services.* (Fall 1984).

Regional Institute of Social Welfare Research. *Barriers to Planning for Children in Foster Care.* Portland, Ore.: Portland State University, February 1976.

Reiss, April D. "Family Systems: Training for Assessment," in *Treating Families in the Home: An Alternative to Placement.* Ed. by Marvin Bryce and June C. Lloyd. Springfield, IL: Charles C. Thomas, 1981, 98–108.

Reistroffer, Mary. "A University Extension Course for Foster Parents." *Children,* 15 1 (January–February 1968).

Roberts, V. K. "An Experiment in Group Work with Foster Parents." *Case Conference,* 9 (November 1962).

Rooney, Ronald. "Foster Care: Core Problems and Intervention Strategies." *Children and Youth Services Review* 3 (1981), 143–159.

Rooney, Ronald. "A Task-Centered Reunification Model for Foster Care," in *The Challenge of Partnership: Working with Parents of Children in Foster Care.* Ed. Anthony N. Maluccio and Paula A. Sinanoglu. New York: Child Welfare League of America, 1981b, 135–150.

Rosenberg, Steve. "Treatment of the Emotionally Disturbed, Mildly Retarded Youngster in the Foster Care System." *Child and Adolescent Social Work Journal.* 2, 1 (Spring, 1985), 49–59.

Rosenblum, Barbara. *Foster Homes for Adolescents.* Hamilton, Ont.: Children's Aid Society of Hamilton-Wentworth, 1977.

Rosendorf, Sidney. "Joining Together to Help Foster Children-Foster Parents Form a Natural Association." *Children Today,* 1, 4 (July–August 1972), 2–7.

Rothschild, Ann M. "An Agency Evaluates Its Foster Home Study." *Child Welfare,* 53 (January 1974), 42–50.

Rowe, David C. "Attitudes, Social Class and the Quality of Foster Care." *Social Service Review,* 50 (September 1976), 506–514.

Rowe, Jane. "Fostering in the Seventies." *Adoption and Fostering,* 90, 4 (1977), 15–20.

Rowe, Jane. "Fostering in the 1970s and Beyond," in *New Developments in Foster Care and Adoption.* Ed. John Triseliotis. London: Routledge and Kegan Paul, 1980, 54–68.

Rowe, Jane et al. "Has Long-Term Fostering Changed?" *Adoption and Fostering.* 6, 2 (1982), 10–15.

Rowe, Jane et al. *Long-Term Foster Care.* New York: St. Martin's Press, 1984.

Rowe, Jean, and Lydia Lambert. *Children Who Wait—A Study of Children Needing Substitute Families.* London, England: Association of British Adoption Agencies, 1973.

Rowe, Patricia. "Bridging the Gap: From Foster Care to Independent Living." *Children Today,* 12 (September–October, 1983), 28–29.

Royster, Eugene C. *Barriers to Foster Care in the Black Community.* Lincoln University, Lincoln University, Pa.: Department of Sociology, Lincoln University, 1975.

Runyan, Anita, and Sally Fullerton. "Foster Care Provider Training: A Preventive Program." *Children and Youth Services Review,* 3. (1981), 127–141.

Runyan, Desmond, et al. "Determinants of Foster Care Placement for the Maltreated Child." *American Journal Of Public Health* 71, 7 (July 1981), 706–710.

Ryan, Patricia, Bruce Warren, and Emily McFadden. *Seventeen Course Outlines for Foster Parent Training.* Ypsilanti, Mi. Copyrighted by the Authors, 1979.

Ryan, Patricia, Emily Jean McFadden, and Bruce L. Warren. "Foster Families: A Resource for Helping Parents," in *The Challenge of Partnership: Working with Parents of Children in Foster Care.* Ed. Anthony N. Maluccio and Paula A. Sinanoglu. New York: Child Welfare League of America, 1981, 189–220.

Rzepnicki, Tina, and Theodore Stein. "Permanency Planning for Children in Foster Care: A Review of Projects." *Children and Youth Services Review* 7 (1985), 95–108.

Sauber, Mignon, and Shifley Jenkins. *Paths to Child Placement.* New York: Community Council of Greater New York, 1966.

Schimke, Karen. "Interagency Cooperation and Coordination," in *Establishing Parent Involvement in Foster Care Agencies.* Ed. Karen Blumenthal and Anita Weinberg. New York: Child Welfare League of America, 1984, 97–116.

Shapiro, Deborah. "Agency Investment in Foster Care: A Study." *Social Work,* 17, 3 (July 1972), 20–28.

Shapiro, Deborah. *Agencies and Foster Children.* New York: Columbia University Press, 1975.

Shaw, Martin, and Kathryn Lebans. "Foster Parents Talking." *Adoption and Fostering,* 88, 2 (1977), 11–16.

Sherman, Edward, Renee Neuman, and Ann W. Shyne. *Children Adrift in Foster Care—A Study of Alternative Approaches.* New York: Child Welfare League of America, 1973.

Shinn, Eugene B. *Is Placement Necessary? An Experimental Study of Agreement Among*

Caseworkers in Making Foster Care Decisions. Unpublished doctor of social work thesis. Columbia University. New York, 1968.

Shireman, Joan F. "Achieving Permanence After Placement," in *Child Welfare: Current Dilemmas, Future Directions.* Ed. Brenda G. McGowan and William Meezan. Itasca, Ill.: F. E. Peacock, 1983, 377–424.

Shulman, Lawrence. "Social Work Practice with Foster Parents." *Canadian Journal of Social Work Education.* 6 (1980), 58–71.

Shyne, Ann. *The Need for Foster Care.* New York: Child Welfare League of America, 1969.

Shyne, Ann, and Anita W. Schroeder. *National Study of Social Services to Children and Their Families.* Rockville, Md.: Westat., 1978.

Simon, Julian L. "The Effect of Foster Care Payment Levels on the Number of Foster Children Given Homes." *Social Service Review,* 49 (September 1975), 405–411.

Simon, Ronald, and Denise Simon. "The Effect of Foster Parent Selection and Training on Service Delivery." *Child Welfare,* 61,8 (November–December, 1982), 515–524.

Sinanoglu, Paula A. and Anthony N. Maluccio. (Eds.). *Parents of Children in Placement: Perspectives and Programs.* New York: Child Welfare League of America, 1981.

Sisto, Grace W. "An Agency Design for Permanency Planning in Foster Care." *Child Welfare* 59, 2 (February, 1980), 103–111.

Slingerland, W. H. *Child-Placing in Families.* New York: Russell Sage Foundation, 1919.

Smith, Michael J. "A Question about Parental Visiting and Foster Care." *Social Service Review* (September 1976), 522–523.

Soeffing, Marylane. "Families for Handicapped Children: Foster and Adoptive Placement Programs." *Exceptional Children,* 41, 8 (May 1975), 537–543.

Southill, Keith, and Mike Derbyshire. "Selecting Foster Parents." *Adoption and Fostering* 104, 2 (1981), 47–50.

Soothill, Keith, and Mike Derbyshire. "Retention of Foster Parents." *Adoption and Fostering.* 6, 2 (1982), 38–43.

Specht, Carol. "Selecting Foster Care Rates II: Special Cases." *Public Welfare,* 33 (Fall 1975), 42–46.

Stein, Theodore J. "Early Intervention in Foster Care." *Public Welfare,* 34 (Spring 1976), 39–44.

Stein, Theodore J. "Child Welfare: New Direction in the Field and Their Implications for Education," in *A Dialogue on the Challenge for Education and Training: Child Welfare Issues in the 80s.* Ann Arbor, Michigan: National Child Welfare Training Center, 1982, 57–76.

Stein, Theodore J., and Eileen Gambrill. *Decisionmaking in Foster Care—A Training Manual.* Berkeley, Ca.: University Extension Publications, 1976.

Stein, Theodore, J., Eileen Gambrill, and Kermit T. Wiltse. *Children in Foster Homes: Achieving Continuity of Care.* New York: Praeger, 1978.

Steketee, John P. "The CIP Story." *Juvenile Justice,* 28, 2 (May 1977), 4–11.

Steketee, John P. "Concern for Children in Placement—The CIP Story." *Child Welfare,* 57, 6 (June 1978), 387–393.

Stone, Helen D. *Reflections on Foster Care—A Report of a National Survey of Attitudes and Practices.* New York: Child Welfare League of America, 1969.

Stone, Norman, and Susan Stone. "The Prediction of Successful Foster Placement." *Social Casework,* 64, 1 (January 1983), 11–17.

Stuart, Margaret. *Reunification.* Denver. Region VIII Child Welfare Training Center, 1983.

Thies, S., and Van S. *How Foster Children Turn Out.* New York State Charities Aid Association, 1924.

Thoburn, June. *Captive Clients: Social Work with Families of Children Home on Trial* London: Routledge and Kegan Paul, 1980.

Thomas, George et al. *Supply and Demand for Child Foster Family Care in the Southeast.* Athens, Ga.: Regioal Institute of Social Welfare Research. January 1977.

Thorpe, Rosamund. "Mum and Mrs. So and So." *Social Work Today,* 4 (February 1974), 691–695.

Thorpe, Rosamund. "The Experiences of Children and Parents Living Apart: Implications and Guidelines for Practice," in *New Developments in Foster Care and Adoption* Ed. John Triseliotis. London: Routledge and Kegan Paul, 1980, 85–100.

Thurston, Henry W. *The Dependent Child*. New York: Columbia University Press, 1930.

Tiddy, Suzanne. "Creative Cooperation: Involving Biological Parents in Long-Term Foster Care." *Child Welfare*, 65, 1 (January–February, 1986), 53–62.

Tinker, Katherine. "Do Children in Foster Care Outgrow Behavior Problems?" *Minnesota Welfare*, 8, 4 (October 1952a).

Tinker, Katherine. "Children in Foster Care Who Have Outgrown Problems." *Minnesota Welfare*, 8, 5 (November 1952b).

Tinker, Katherine. "Children in Foster Care Who Remained Disturbed." *Minnesota Welfare*, 8, 6 (December 1952c).

Tinney, Mary Anne. "Role Perceptions in Foster Parent Associations in British Columbia." *Child Welfare*, 64, 1 (January–February, 1985), 73–79.

Tizard, Barbara, and Anne Joseph. "Today's Foundlings." *New Society*, 35, no. 418 (October 1970), 584–585.

Touliatos, John, and Byron W. Lindholm. "Development of a Scale Measuring Potential for Foster Parenthood." *Psychological Reports*, 40 (1977), 1190.

Trasler, Gordon. *In Place of Parents*. New York: Humanities Press, 1960.

Triseliotis, John. "Growing up in Foster Care and After," in *New Developments in Foster Care and Adoption*. Ed. John Triseliotis. London: Routledge and Kegan Paul, 1980, 131–161.

Turner, John. "Reuniting Children in Foster Care with their Biological Parents." *Social Work* 29, 6 (November–December, 1984), 501–505.

U.S. Department of Health and Human Services. *Child Welfare Training: Education for Social Work Practice with American Indian Families*. Washington, D. C.: DHHS, 1982.

U.S. Government, General Accounting Office. *Better Federal Program Administration Can Contribute to Improving State Foster Care Programs* Washington, D. C.: G. A. O., August, 10, 1984.

Van Der Waals, Pauler. "Former Foster Children Reflect on Their Childhood." *Children* 7 (January–February 1960).

Vasaly, Shirley M. *Foster Care in Five States: A Synthesis and Analysis of Studies from Arizona, California, Iowa, Massachusetts, and Vermont*. Washington, D. C.: U.S. Dept. of Health, Education & Welfare, 1978.

Vernon, Jeni. "Planning for Children in Care?" *Adoption and Fostering*, 9, 1 (1985), 13–17.

Vick, J. E. "Recruiting and Retaining Foster Homes." *Public Welfare*. 25, 3 (July 1967), 229–234.

Wakeford, John. "Fostering—A Sociological Perspective." *British Journal of Sociology*, 14 (December 1963).

Walker, Florence. "Cultural and Ethnic Issues in Working with Black Families in the Child Welfare System," in *Parents of Children in Placement: Perspectives and Programs*. Ed. Paula Sinanoglu and Anthony Maluccio. N. Y.:CWLA, 1981. 133–148.

Ward, Margaret. "Sibling Ties in Foster Care and Adoption Planning." *Child Welfare* 63, 4 (July–August 1984), 321–332.

Weinbach, Robert W., Martha Jane Edwards, and Rebecca F. Levy. "Innovations in Group Services to Foster Parents: A Survey of Agencies." *Children Today* (January–February 1977), 18–20.

Weinstein, Eugene. *The Self-Image of the Foster Child*. New York: Russell Sage Foundation, 1960.

Wert, E. Sue, Edith Fein, and Wendy Haller. " 'Children in Placement' (CIP): A Model for Citizen-Judicial Review." *Child Welfare*, 65, 2 (March–April 1986), 199–201.

Westat Inc. *Comparative Study of State Case Review Systems Phase II—Dispositional Hearings*, Rockville, Md.: Westat., 1984.

White, Mary S. "Promoting Parent-Child Visiting in Foster Care: Continuing Involvement Within a Permanency Framework," in *Parents of Children in Placement: Perspectives and Programs.* Ed. Paula A. Sinanoglu and Anthony N. Maluccio. New York: Child Welfare League of America, 1981, 461–475.

Whitten, Patricia. "The Rights of Foster Parents to Children in Their Care." Chicago: Kent Law Review 86 (1973), 86–112.

Wiehe, Vernon. "Foster Mothers: Are They Unique?" *Psychological Reports,* 53 (1983), 1215–1218.

Wilkes, James. "Separation Can Be a Therapeutic Option." *Child Welfare,* 59, 1 (January, 1980), 27–32.

Williams, Carol J. "Helping Parents to Help the Children in Placement." *Child Welfare,* 51 (May 1972), 297–303.

Wiltse, Kermit T., and Eileen D. Gambrill. "Foster Care, 1973: A Reappraisal." *Public Welfare,* 32 (Winter 1974).

Wires, Emily M. "Some Factors in the Worker-Foster Parent Relationship." *Child Welfare,* 33 (October 1954).

Wittner, Judith. "Entering Foster Care: Foster Children's Accounts." *Children and Youth Services Review.* 3 (1981), 21–35.

Wolf, Ann Marie. "A Personal View of Black Inner-City Foster Families." *American Journal of Orthopsychiatry,* 53, 1 (January, 1983), 144–151.

Wolins, Martin. *Selecting Foster Parents.* New York: Columbia University Press, 1963.

Yarrow, Leon, and Robert Klein. "Environmental Discontinuity Associated with Transition from Foster to Adoptive Homes." *International Journal of Behavioral Development* 3 (1980), 311–322.

Yoshikami, Rogers. *Assessing the Implementation of Federal Policy to Reduce the Use of Foster Care: Placement Prevention and Reunification in Child Welfare,* Vol. 1. Washington, D. C.: Children's Bureau, 1984.

Young, Dennis, and Stephen Finch. *Foster Care and the Non-Profit Agencies.* Lexington, Mass.: D. C. Heath & Company, Lexington Press, 1977.

Zimmerman, Rosalie. *Foster Care in Retrospect.* New Orleans, La.: Tulane Studies in Social Welfare, 1982.

8

Unmarried Teenage Parents and Their Children

Introduction

Unanticipated, unwanted pregnancy is a dilemma that is being experienced by increasing numbers of today's teenagers. Adolescent males and females may both find themselves in need of help from the social worker. They rely on the worker to explore the ramification of the pregnancy, the means to prevent its recurrence and choices that must be made about the future of the child. The unmarried mother who has an out-of-wedlock child faces additional dilemmas and often receives assistance in resolving these problems from the child welfare worker. Children who are born out of wedlock account for the major proportion of adoptions by nonrelatives, and a number of young unwed women request help in placing their children in appropriate alternative homes. For teenage parents who choose to keep their children, issues involving self-support, health, and child care become primary. Child welfare agencies are heavily involved with this client population.

Historical Background

Attitudes toward illegitimacy are related to family structure. Negative attitudes toward illegitimacy are designed to protect the monogamous family and associated marital ties. While polygamous societies make little of technical illegitimacy, the Christian attitude toward monogamy and extramarital sexuality resulted in the development of a more punitive attitude toward illegitimacy. Religious sanctions were reinforced by secular motives during the Middle Ages to solidify such attitudes. As Krause (1971) notes:

> It was natural that men, as legislators, would have limited their accidental offsprings' claims against them both economically and in terms of a family relationship, especially since the social status of the illegitimate mother often did not equal their own. Moreover, their legitimate wives had an interest in denying the illegitimate's claim on their husbands, since any such claim could be allowed only at the expense of the legitimate family. Against these forces have stood only the illegitimate mother and the helpless child, and thus it is not surprising that our laws are inconsiderate of the child's interest.

Under English common law, the illegimate child was "son of no one" (*filius nullius*) or "son of the people" (*filius populi*)—without name, without a right to support or inheritance. Yet the illegimate child was not socially stigmatized in pre-Puritan England:

> until the sixteenth century bastardy had not been thought any great shame. Men took care of their bastards, were indeed often proud of them, and in many cases brought them home to their wives or mothers to be brought up. Children born out of wedlock were thus to be found growing up in their father's house with their half-brothers and sisters without a hint of disgrace either to themselves or to their natural parents [Pinchbeck & Hewitt, 1969, p. 201].

The gradual hardening of attitudes arose not only from concern for the sanctity of the family but perhaps, more significantly, from concern for the burden on the community posed by illegimate children. (Brumberg, 1984). Nobody was seriously concerned about the fourteen illegimate children fathered by Charles II, but there was widespread concern about the indigent illegitimate child.

The Poor Law Act of 1576

> made the first legislative provision for illegitimate children so many of whom were abandoned by their parents and left to be maintained from charitable or public sources. The preamble of the Act indicates the spirit in which this problem was approached. "Firste, concerning Bastards begotten and borne out of lawful Matrimony (an Offence againste Gods lawe and Mans Lawe) the said Bastards being now lefte to bee kepte at the chardge of the Parishe where They been borne, to the greate Burden of the same Parishe and in defrauding of the Reliefe of the impotente and aged true Poore of the same Parishe, and to the evill Example and Encouradgement of lewde Lyef: It ys ordeyned and enacted . . ." [Pinchbeck, Hewitt, 1969, pp. 206–220].

The legislation indicated that the mother and the putative father might be punished and both were responsible for support of the child.

> The main concern of Parliament was the relief of public expenditure and the exposure of the moral failure of those who were responsible for bringing the child into the world. . . . Legal sanctions were to be employed against men and women whose bastards become a charge on the community; there were no legal penalties for those who could afford to support the fruits of their own indiscretions [Pinchbeck & Hewitt, 1969, p. 207].

The principal ground of concern then, and one might add, now, "were the economics of maintenance rather than the circumstances of conception" (Pinchbeck & Hewitt, 1969, p. 220).

The English Poor Laws formed the basis for the even more punitive attitudes of Puritan colonists, who punished extramarital fornication and required the parents to support the child who was the result of fornication. Thus Anne Williams, in 1658, petitioned the court for maintenance from Richard Smith "for a child the defendant hath got by her." The court "ordered that the said Richard Smith maintain the child and that the woman for her act committed, be whipped and have thrity lashes well laid on" (Bremner, 1970, p. 52).

Throughout the nineteenth century, the resources available to the out-of-wedlock child for maintenance were the same as those available to any other child who needed help from the community. This included binding out in apprenticeship, indoor or outdoor relief.

Over the last hundred years, there has developed a more compassionate attitude toward the illegimate child, a lessening of the distinctions between the legitimate and the illegitimate child, and a reduction in the discriminations against the illegitimate child. Changing attitudes are reflected in changing terminology—from *bastard* to *illegitimate child* to *child born out of wedlock* or the less frequently employed *extramarital child* and *love child*.

The legal status of the child born out of wedlock differs from state to state, but such a child more frequently now, has a right to inherit from his or her mother and, where paternity is acknowledged, the right to inherit from the father as well. Many states have acknowledged the illegitimate child's rights to benefits under workmen's compensation laws in case the father is injured or killed. Federal legislation has recognized the illegitimate child's rights to veteran's benefits and Old Age and Survivor's Insurance benefits from his or her father's account.

In 1972 the U.S. Supreme Court, granting the entitlement of an out-of-wedlock child to workmen's compensation benefits on the death of the child's father, noted that "No child is responsible for his birth" and that equal protection under the Fourtteenth Amendment should not be denied. But out-of-wedlock children still face substantial legal disadvantages in some states (Krause, 1966, 1971).

The child's status is not indicated on the short-form birth certificate used for such purposes as school registration or job application, which merely lists name and time and place of birth.

Legitimation of the child can now be achieved by marriage of the parents after the child's birth, by petition to the court if the parents are not married, and by the father's acknowledgment of paternity. With legitimization, birth records are changed so as to delete any indication of the child's previous illegitimate status. If the father voluntarily acknowledges paternity, he is obligated to support the child. Bastardy proceedings or paternity proceedings can be instituted to establish the paternity of the child and to force the father to support the child. This is a civil procedure that often, however, resembles a criminal action. If a man is judged to be the father but fails to make support payments, he can be prosecuted. But it is difficult to prove that a particular man is the father of the child. Blood tests merely exclude the possibility; they do not establish certainty. Paternity proceedings are usually instituted by the mother (often required in order to establish eligibility for Aid to Families of Dependent Children [AFDC] assistance) but may be instituted by the state.

The mother is regarded as guardian of her child and as such has the right to custody, care, and control of the child and a right to the child's earnings. Currently there is increasing concern about the rights of the father. In the case of *Stanley* v. *Illinois* in April 1972, the U. S. Supreme Court decided that the unwed fathers "who desire and claim competence to care for their children" have a right to a hearing before adoption plans can be made for the child. What had been previously primarily the mother's prerogative is now extended to the unwed father, and his "entitlement" to the child he fathered is legally recognized. The father's consent to adoption has been required if paternity had been acknowledged or legitimation established. *Stanley* v. *Illinois* required that some effort be made to contact the father even if there had been no acknowledgment of paternity and to provide him the opportunity for some say in the disposition of the child. (The effects of this and related judicial decisions on adoption are discussed in more detail below.) Whether the putative father's consent to abortion must be obtained is an additional, as yet largely unresolved, question. Some states require consent to either abortion or adoption by the parents of the mother-to-be if she is a minor.

In our society, an out-of-wedlock child is one born to a woman who is not legally married to the father at the time of birth. The fact is that a considerable number of pregnancies are conceived prior to marriage, but the subsequent marriage of the couple before the birth of the child legitimizes the conception. This occurrence does not create a serious social problem. Society is less concerned with illicit coition than with illicit births. Less frequently, a child may be legally illegitimate but not socially illegitimate because the father is living in a stable, although not legal, relationship with the mother and accepts responsibility for the care of the child.

In addition to establishing procedures for the legitimation of out-of-wedlock children, societies establish expectations and procedures that both guide and limit the individual's alternatives to bear and raise a child in these circumstances. Since 1800, both contraception and abortion have become increasingly available means to prevent or terminate such pregnancies. By the mid-1800's, abortion was used extensively, particularly by married white women whose families had lived in this country for some period of time (Mohr, 1985). During the latter part of the 1800s, as a result of extensive efforts on the part of the American Medical Association, states passed specific stautes proscribing most abortions; these laws remained virtually unchanged until the 1960s. However, Mohr reports, these statutes were largely unenforced. Instead of beng used as a mechanism to deter the performance of abortions. These laws were primarily used to regulate the provision of these services and to punish those who harmed individuals who received them. Despite the AMA's major role in passage of antiabortion legislation, most abortions were done by doctors, many of whom even advertised their services in local newspapers.

By the turn of the century, increasing numbers of pregnant immigrant women began using abortion opportunities. After 1870, private facilities that were particularly designed to help pregnant young women carry their children to term were opened. Most of these "refuges" were located in urban areas to serve young women who had come to the city to find employment. These homes offered a young woman "the opportunity to regain her composure, to reflect on her situation, to repent, and hopefully to reestablish her dignity, self-worth, and self-esteem by demonstrating her commitment to decency, morality, and Christianity" (Sedlak, 1982, p. 451). The largest network of these homes was operated by the Florence Crittenton Association of America (now part of the Child Welfare League of America) founded in 1890 by a wealthy businessman, Charles Crittenton, in memory of his daughter. The Salvation Army also operated a number of homes. Their mission was to rescue "fallen women" and "betrayed young girls."

These refuges offered women an alternative to infantacide or to the abandonment of their children. They sheltered clients from Victorian intolerance and offered "ruined women" an opportunity to redeem themselves (Brumberg, 1984). The refuges provided intensive religious training, limited education, and extensive practice in domestic work. Women were strongly encouraged to keep their children, since it was believed that learning to carry out mothering responsibilities would help them learn to live as good Christians.

In the 1930's, these programs, termed maternity homes, were taken over by professional social welfare staff. This change in the personnel in these institutions also heralded changes in programming. "The homes were not 'prisons for culprits', argued one social worker, but were 'shelters and schools for the crippled.' Girls were to be admitted to these homes not 'because of their *sin*, but because of their *need*' " (Sedlack, 1982, p. 455). The use of casework services led to much more extensive attention to the client's home life and previous history. At the same time, concern about the client's ability to become economically independent led staff to change their policy with regard to adoption and to advocate its use much more explicitly. These facilities were very popular in the 1950s and 1960s, particularly with teenagers (Aries, 1980). These services were increasingly also made available to black adolescents.

Changes in federal policy beginning in the late 1960s contributed to the ultimate decline in the use of maternity homes as a primary service for pregnant teenagers. A rapid acceleration in the rate of teenage pregnancy fostered increasing federal interest in the problem. Increasing public tolerance for illegitimacy meant that unwed mothers no longer felt pressured to find a safe place to hide and bear their children. Maternity homes, which had previously served this purpose, therefore, became less popular. The rapid increase in the number of pregnant adolescents also suggested the need to focus on the broader social causes of their situation and on the development of more broadly available means to respond to it. Federal support was focused on "community-based, nonresidential, comprehensive-care centers which provided a broad range of health, social work, counseling, nutrition, child care, employment, and educational services in a facility—particularly a public school—that could be conveniently located in inner-city neighborhoods, where demand was increasing" (Sedlak, 1982, p. 458). Congress passed the Adolescent Health Services and Pregnancy Prevention and Care Act in 1978. This legislation created the Office of Adolescent Pregnancy Programs, which was charged with responsibility for stimulating further development of comprehensive programming in the states (Wells, 1982; Dryfoos, 1982).

The federal government also plays a central role in determining the availability of both contraception and abortion services, particularly for teenagers from poor families. In recent years, extensive federal funding has been available for family-planning services, and special funds have been earmarked for expansion of adolescent services within these programs (Dryfoos, 1982). In 1973, the Supreme Court, in two different cases, "stated that the fundamental constitutional right of privacy protects the right of a woman, in consultation with her physician, to decide to terminate her pregnancy" (Paul & Schaap, 1982, p. 5). Particularly in the first trimester of pregnancy, women can, themselves, now determine whether to seek an abortion, so long as they utilize the services of licensed physicians for this purpose. In 1976, in *Planned Parenthood of Central Missouri* v *Danforth*, the Supreme Court determined that minors have a right to obtain abortions. However, in a more recent decision, (*H.L.* v. *Matheson*, 1981), the Supreme Court determined that the states may require that parents be notified before providing abortions to immature and unemancipated minors.

In 1977, Congress passed the Hyde Amendment. This legislation prohibited the use of federal monies to "pay for abortion or to promote or encourage abortions" (Gilchrist & Schinke, 1983a pp. 309–310), except in instances in which the woman's life was in danger or she had been raped (Paul & Schaap, 1982, p. 7). This federal antiabortion stance was reinforcced by the passage of the Adolescent Family Life Act in 1981. Designed to stimulate pregnancy-prevention programming, this legislation "prohibits the distribution of funds to groups that provide any abortion-related services, including counseling or referral, and that subcontract with any agency that provides such services" (Donovan, 1984, p. 222). AFLA funds have also been directed toward projects that promote natural childbirth methods and deemphasize the use of other contraceptive techniques.

By the late 1980's professional social work concerns about teenage pregnancies were twofold—how to prevent these pregnancies from occurring and, in cases in which they do occur, how to ensure that both the teenage parents and their child receive adequate care. Public child welfare agencies are involved with clients who need both types of assistance. A national survey conducted by Shyne and Schroeder (1978) found that approximately 1 per cent of all clients served by these agencies received assistance because they were pregnant teenagers, whereas an additional 1.7 per cent were children of teenage mothers who were in need of help. Although public child welfare personnel are not directly involved in the provision of birth control or abortion services, they make extensive use of referral to agencies which do provide them. Many of the teenage clients they serve are, in addition, in need of comprehensive pregnancy prevention services. When teenagers choose to bear their children, child welfare practitioners have primarily concentrated on serving two particular types of client groups—teenagers wishing to relinquish rights to their children and place them in adoptive homes, and those who are or may be providing inadequate care for their children and are, therefore, potential protective service clients. Child welfare workers may provide both remedial and preventive assistance for these young parents, to help them care for themselves and their children adequately, to ensure that these young mothers have adequate funding to house and feed their infants, and to help them learn to become more skilled as parents for their children.

Scope

National statistics available at the time of this writing indicate that 770,400 babies were born to unmarried women in 1984. This is a substantial rise from 1950, when 141,600 of these babies were born (U.S. National Center for Health Statistics). Out-of-wedlock births thus made up 4 per cent of all births in 1950, but 21 per cent in 1984. Among whites, approximately 13.4 per cent of all babies were born to unmarried women, whereas the rate for blacks was 59.2 per cent. Rates per 1,000 fecund women aged 15–44 are more sensitive indicators of trends. Although the *number* of births occurring out of wedlock have been increasing dramatically and steadily since World War II, the illegitimacy *rate* (live births per 1,000 unmarried women 15–44 years of age) has slowly increased since the 1970's—increasing modestly from 26.4 in 1970 to 31 in 1984.

The illegitimacy rate is particularly high among teenagers. Unwed pregnancies are more frequent among adolescents in the United States than in most other countries (Jones et al., 1985). In 1980–81, almost three-quarters of all births to U.S. teenagers aged 15–19 were conceived outside of marriage (O'Connell & Rogers, 1984).

The trend has been toward a steady increase in the unmarried mother birth rate of teenagers 15–19 years old—from 15.3 per 1000 in 1960 to 30.2 in 1984. By contrast, the out-of-wedlock birth rate of women between the ages of 20 and 34 has dropped during this period.

Whereas the birth rate for white unmarried women increased between 1960 and 1984 from 9.2 per 1000 in 1960 to 20.1 in 1984, the unmarried mother birth rate of black women has decreased from 95.5 in 1970 to 76.8 in 1984. However, whereas the unmarried mother birth rate for white and black women are moving in opposite directions—increasing for whites, decreasing for blacks—the black out-of-wedlock birthrate in 1983 was still some four times higher than the white out-of-wedlock birth rate.

For all age groups, the tendency to marry and legitimate a child has decreased significantly over the years. In 1950, approximately half of the women who conceived children outside of wedlock subsequently married; in 1980 only one in three did so. For teenagers in particular, childbearing between World War II and the early 1960's largely occurred to those who were married; after 1960, childbearing occurred with increasing frequency to adolescents who were not married (Sklar & Berkov, 1981, p. 25). Today, the decision to legitimate a pregnancy by marrying is primarily associated with three factors—race, social class, and intent to get pregnant. White women, the more well-to-do, and those having planned pregnancies are all more likely to subsequently marry (Zelnik, Kantner, & Ford, 1981, p. 163).

Because so many adolescents are now experiencing pregnancy outside of marriage, concern for their welfare and for their children has become acute. Adolescents account for approximately half of all illegitimate birth occurring in the United States and approximately half of all the marital births that are conceived before marriage. Of additional concern is the fact that approximately half of these teenagers go on to get pregnant again within a three-year period after first conceiving (Abel et al., 1982). Tietze (1981) estimates that by age twenty, some one-third to two-fifths of today's fourteen-year-olds will experience at least one pregnancy. One-fifth of these young women will subsequently give birth; 15 per cent will obtain an abortion; and 6 per cent will miscarry or have a stillborn child (p. 153).

Out-of-wedlock births are more prevalent among black teenagers. O'Connell and Rogers (1984) found that, in 1980, some 96 per cent of all first births to black teenagers were out of wedlock; 64 per cent of white adolescent first births occurred to unmarried women. Black teens are also far less likely subsequently to marry than their white adolescent counterparts. Less than 10 per cent of black first-time adolescent parents subsequently married whereas at the same time, 28 per cent of white pregnant teen mothers subsequently married (p. 158).

The data also suggest that "women who begin childbearing early in their reproductive careers—especially if they give birth as teenagers—subsequently have children more rapidly, have more children, and have more unwanted and out-of-wedlock births than women who postpone childbearing" (Trussell & Menken, 1981, p. 234). Teenage pregnant women are, therefore, potentially in need of child welfare services both in their early childbearing years and as they subsequently face the special stresses of large families and multiple births in brief time periods.

A number of factors other than the increase in the population of fecund baby-boom period women have been cited to explain the increase in out-of-wedlock births despite increased family planning and abortion services. Although open to controversy, there does seem to be some basis for the contention that more unmarried women are sexually active than previously and that premarital sexual activity begins at an earlier age, increasing the risk of an out-of-wedlock pregnancy. Thus Zelnick and Kantner (1978) calculate on the basis of interviews with a probability sample of some 4,400 fifteen- to nineteen-year-old women that whereas in 1971 three out of every ten women had experienced premarital sexual intercourse, this number had increased by 1976 to four out of ten (p. 11). In 1971, 47 per cent of unmarried nineteen-year-old women had had sexual intercourse; by 1976 this number had increased to 55 per cent (Zelnick & Kantner, 1977, p. 56). McGee (1982) estimates that, but the time they reach nineteen, some seven out of ten young women will have had intercourse.

Young teens, those below the age of fifteen, are increasingly likely to become sexually active. National surveys of teenagers fifteen to nineteen conducted in 1976 and 1979 (Koenig & Zelnik, 1982) indicate that adolescents who become sexually active at an early age had increased their level of sexual activity substantially between the two survey periods while teenagers who waited to begin sexual activity until later in adolescence had not become more sexually active in the 1979 survey (p. 243). Since the risk of pregnancy is directly correlated with such exposure, the authors conclude, that "this increase in risk among the youngest group of sexually active women resulted from both decreased initial reliance upon the most effective methods of contraception and a sharp increase in the frequency of sexual activity" (p. 246). Zelnik, Kantner, and Ford (1981) come to the same conclusions. "Premarital pregnancy is explained, insofar as we are able to do so, almost entirely by the duration of exposure—the difference between the age at first intercourse and current age. Social variables such as social status, religion and family stability are of negligible importance in accounting for variation in the prevalence of premarital pregnancy once the length of exposure is taken into account" (p. 161).

In part, higher pregnancy rates among black teenagers are explained by the fact that they are sexually active at an earlier age than are white teenagers. White teenagers are, however, catching up. It has been suggested that the increase in sexual activity among white teenagers, particularly middle-class teenagers, may well explain some of the widespread concern that has been generated about teenage pregnancy issues (Goode, 1967, Furstenberg, Lincoln, & Menken, 1981, p. 5; Dryfoos, 1982, p. 35;).

Sexual activity by an increasingly large percentage of the unmarried population has overcome the effects of the increased availability of contraception and abortion.

As a consequence of better health conditions, women are becoming capable of having children at an earlier age than they could previously, thus lowering the age at which they risk a first pregnancy. The mean age at menarche, indicating the onset of fertility, was about 16.5 years in 1870 (Cutright, 1975, p. 18). "With the mean age at menarche currently of 12.5, and a range of 8.5 to 16.5, and an historically typical pattern in which first ovulation occurs two years before menarche, the minimum age for a first pregnancy is 10.5 or even younger" (Crawford & Furstenberg, 1985, p. 535). Better nutrition and health conditions also diminish the number of spontaneous abortions, increasing the likelihood that more of the children conceived will actually be born (Cutright, 1975).

The current increasing tendency to delay marriage also increases the amount of the time during which an out-of-wedlock pregnancy is risked. With sexual maturation taking place earlier and the age of marriage later, the period of nonmarital fecundity is increased, exposing more people to more years at risk of an unwanted, premarital pregnancy.

All of these factors favor a probable increase in the number of children born out of wedlock.

On the other side of the equation, opposing the probability of such an increase, is the greater knowledge about and availability of contraceptive devices and the greater availability of abortion on demand. No matter what numbers of fecund nonmarried women increasingly engage in extramarital intercourse, the combination of contraception and abortion will tend to dampen the increase of children born out of wedlock.

Women are now using contraceptives more frequently and more consistently, even at early ages (Koenig & Zelnik, 1982). "A 1979 profile of use at last intercourse shows about one third (of sexually active adolescents) are using pills and IUD's, 20% were using diaphragms, condoms, or foam, 17% were using the least effective methods (withdrawal, rhythm, douche) and 30% were using no method" (Dryfoos, 1982, p. 38).

The use of contraceptive techniques is directly correlated with pregnancy prevention.

> It is clear that if a sexually active young woman uses a contraceptive regularly, she runs a relatively low risk of becoming pregnant (11%), and if she uses a medical method of contraceptive regularly, she runs an even lower risk (6%). It also is the case that a sexually active young woman who never uses a method is exceedingly likely (58%) to become pregnant [Zelnik & Kantner, 1981, p. 123].

It is estimated that approximately four out of every ten sexually active teenagers are currently using contraceptive techniques of some type.

However, adolescents could make much more effective use of these pregnancy-prevention techniques. Although proportionately, the number of women who have never used any type of contraception has decreased, the number of sexually active women who never used any method of contraception is still substantial (Koenig & Zelnik, 1982, p. 241). Teenagers, in particular, have tended to use the less reliable methods, such as the condom. "If we add together those who never use contraception and those who have never used medical methods, we have around 70% of the sexually active who are not being reached by organized services" (Zelnik, Kantner, & Ford, 1981, pp. 129–130). Medical methods, such as the pill, have a fail rate of approximately 2.4 per cent, whereas condoms have a fail rate four times that amount, 9.6 per cent. The least effective contraceptive methods involve the use of rhythm or natural family planning for which the failure rate is 23.7 per cent (Schirm et al. 1982, p. 68). Women in general, and teenagers in particular, are prone to delay their first use of any method. On the average, teenagers do not seek contraception until nine months after beginning their sexual experiences, a point at which it is already too late for half of them (McGee, 1982, p. 12).

Teenagers are less likely to use contraception consistently than their older age counterparts, and younger teenagers are least likely to use it or to do so regularly. At first intercourse, some 61 per cent of women who are seventeen or older relied on contraceptive methods, whereas only one in three women younger than fifteen did so (Koenig & Zelnik, 1982; see also Presser, 1981b). Black teenagers rely less frequently on contraceptives than do white teenagers. In part, the difference is explained by social class effects, since more well-to-do women of all races are more likely to rely on contraception (Zelnik, Kantner, & Ford, 1981, p. 129).

The removal of impediments to contraceptive use could result in a substantial reduction in the number of unwanted pregnancies:

> In 1976, a little more than one million 15–19-year-olds experienced a pregnancy. About 77% or 780,000, of these pregnancies occurred premaritally. . . . If all the

teenagers who did not intend to give birth had been consistent users of contraception, there would have been about 467,000 premarital pregnancies (half of them intended)—313,000, or 40%, fewer than the 780,000 premarital pregnancies that actually occurred. In other words, the difference between no use of contraception and always-use (by those who did not want to conceive) is about one million pregnancies [Zelnik, & Kantner, 1981, pp. 124–125].

Between 1973, when the U.S. Supreme Court decision made abortion in the first trimester legal, and 1984, 13 million legal abortions were performed in this country. The use of this method of birth control by teenagers almost doubled between 1973 and 1983. In 1973, some 244,000 abortions were performed for girls younger than 20; in 1983, 412,000 abortions were performed for this age group. Teenagers accounted for 27 per cent of all the abortions performed in the United States in 1983. The use of this technique has become a major option for women who seek to terminate unwanted pregnancies. Zelnik, Kantner, and Ford (1981) estimate that the number of unwanted pregnancies was reduced from 82 per cent to 64 per cent between 1971 and 1976 as a result of the availability of this option (p. 162; see also Forrest, Tietze, & Sullivan, 1978; Sklar & Berkov, 1981).

Evidence suggests that the very poor may not have equal access to abortion services, since they are the least likely to use these procedures. The more financially stable the family from which adolescents come, the more likely they are to choose this option for terminating an unwanted pregnancy. Citing data collected in 1978 in Rhode Island, Ezzard, Cates, and Schulz (1985) state, "fifty-six percent of all pregnancies to teenagers living the highest socioeconomic-status areas were terminated by abortions as compared with 22 percent of those among teenagers living in poverty areas" (p. 75; see also Zelnik, Kantner, & Ford, 1981). Black women make disproportionate use of this option; in 1980, they received 30 per cent of all the abortions performed in this country. However, the rate for whites is increasing more rapidly (Kafrissen et al., 1985).

As we have noted, differential patterns of sexual activity, prevention, pregnancy, and parenthood exist among black and white teenagers. Black adolescents engage in sexual intercourse at an earlier age than whites, and this is a primary factor affecting their higher rate of childbirth (Trussell & Menken, 1981, p. 234). Black are also less likely to utilize contraceptives and more likely to turn to abortion as a means of terminating pregnancies.

Although black out-of-wedlock children are more often incorporated into the extended family structure than are such white children, most black unmarried mothers did not intend to get pregnant. Interviews with some 340 single black pregnant adolescents revealed that "two-thirds of the girls were shocked and extremely upset when they first discovered they were pregnant" and that 80 per cent wished they were not pregnant (Furstenberg, 1981). However, although the largest percentage did not intend the pregnancy, a larger percentage of black unmarried mothers in a 1976 national survey intended pregnancy (29 per cent) than did white respondents (19 per cent) (Zelnik & Kantner, 1978, p. 14).

A variety of other factors help to explain the wide, although diminishing differences between white and nonwhite illegitimacy rates. The historical experience of the blacks under a slave system that had little regard for marriage and a high regard for black children, however fathered, is sometimes presented as a component of the cultural "causes" of the problem in the present. Southern law did not recognize slave marriages, so that all slave children were, by law, illegitimate. Children fathered by a white but born of a slave mother inherited her status. It is suggested, then, that the historical experience in slavery is antithetical to the development of a concern that the child be born in wedlock.

Differences in out-of-wedlock birthrates are also the result of differences in access to, and motivation toward, the use of alternative resolutions of out-of-wedlock pregnancies. Contraceptives services are now more available within the black community, and this, in part, accounts for some of the reduction in the black illegitimacy rate. However, substantial differences in service access still remain. Since the passage of the Hyde Amendment, abortion services are also not as accessible to blacks, many of whom are poor and cannot, themselves, afford to pay for this type of care.

The higher unemployment rate among black males and the more limited, lower-paying employment opportunities available to them understandably make many black single pregnant girls reluctant to "solve" a difficult situation by contracting a hazardous marriage. The objective situation perhaps favors the decision that "no marriage is bad; but no marriage is better than a bad marriage." Hasty marriages in response to premarital pregnanccy have low survival rates generally, but this is particularly true in the case of such marriages by young black couples (McCarthy & Menken, 1981).

As Garland (1966) notes, a "middle or upper-class white women who becomes an out-of-wedlock mother biologically has greater opportunities of becoming an in-wedlock mother socially" (p. 85; see also McCarthy & Menken, 1981; Zelnik, Kantner, & Ford, 1981).

Each one of these alternative outcomes of the same out-of-wedlock pregnancy is heavily weighted in favor of the white woman. Consequently, when statistics are collected on the number of out-of-wedlock children in the community, many more black children than white children are counted.

In effect, the number of illegitimate births is related to the number of women of childbearing age in the community, reduced by the number of those not sexually active, reduced by the number who use contraceptive consistently and who don't conceive, reduced by the number who conceive but choose abortion, and further reduced by the number of pregnant, unmarried women who choose marriage before birth.

In all of this discussion, the question of socioeconomic class intrudes as a contaminating factor, so that part of the racial difference in illegitimacy rates is a function of differences in the class distribution of members of the two racial groups.

The Governmental National Center for Health Statistics Study on Illegitimacy notes that "There is considerable evidence that socioeconomic composition is an important factor contributing to the white-nonwhite differential in illegitimacy. It is likely that if it were possible to control for social class, much of the difference between those two groups would disappear" (U.S. Department of Health, Education, and Welfare, 1968, p. 16). Herzog (1964) similarly notes that if "illegitimacy estimates were related to income as well as color, the Negro-white difference would be drastically reduced" (p. 121).

Recent trends suggest that black and white unmarried women are becoming more alike. The percentage of increase of unmarried white women becoming sexually active is greater than for blacks, more blacks are using contraceptives and having abortions than formerly, fewer white women are marrying to legitimize a pregnancy than formerly, and fewer are giving their children up for adoption.

Determinants of Out-of-Wedlock Pregnancy

The social work approach to the single pregnant girl reflects the profession's thinking about the origin of the problem. This has undergone some changes over time. Before the Great Depression, the emphasis on personal and moral inadequacy led to the perception of the unmarried mother as morally promiscuous and/or mentally deficient. During the 1930s, the blame was placed on the socially deficient environment: the broken home and the poverty-stricken home were the factors that "explained" unwed motherhood. Studies of out-of-wedlock births focused on class and color as factors determining attitudes toward extramarital intercourse and contraception.

After World War II, the emphasis shifted to psychological determinism. Out-of-wedlock pregnancy was seen as a symptom of some psychological need—conflict with a dominant mother, lack of response from a passive father, a desire for self-punishment, a search for a dependable love object, an attempt at self-assertion and independence.

Young (1954) noted that "Although a girl would obviously not plan consciously and deliberately to bear an out-of-wedlock child, she does act in such a way that this becomes the almost inevitable result" (p. 22). Out-of-wedlock pregnancy was seen as not only a symptom of individual disturbance but as a symptom of family pathology.

The continuing search for causes has generated a series of studies of personality differences between the single pregnant woman and her single unpregnant sister. Results vary, some demonstrating personality disturbance in the unmarried mothers, some finding them essentially normal (Pauker, 1969, pp. 47–54).

Perhaps one of the most comprehensive and carefully controlled of these studies was that conducted by Vincent (1961). One hundred young unwed mothers were matched in terms of crucial variables with an equal number of single girls who had never been pregnant. In psychological tests, the latter scored consistently at a more positive level of personality functioning, but differences between the two groups were smaller than anticipated and most of the scales showed no difference in the "*direction*" and "*pattern*" (italics in original) of the responses (p. 119). When compared in terms of developmental background, the groups showed an "absence of any statistically significant familial differences" (p. 117). Vincent concluded that "unwed motherhood is not the result of any one personality type, intra-familial relationship, or social situation" (p. 179).

Furthermore, any personality or familial differences that are revealed may emerge in response to the pregnancy rather than causing it (Olson and Worobey, 1984).

Pauker (1969), who asked, "Are they pregnant because they are different or are they different because they are pregnant?," examined the personality profiles obtained *before* conception for a group of unmarried mothers and those of a matched group of nonpregnant peers and found them to be "very similar in shape and elevation" (p. 60). The unwed mothers' group showed no "striking personality difference from other girls," though it included a significantly larger number of girls who came from homes broken by separation or divorce (p. 63).

A careful analysis by Cutright (1971) showed that such factors as level of religiosity, level of secularization of a society, divorce rates, decline of the authoritarian family, and levels of assistance granted the unmarried mother are unrelated to the changes in the illegitimacy rate. In response to Young's contention that illegitimate pregnancy is, consciously or unconsciously, deliberately desired, Cutright (1971), reviewing the relevant research, concluded that "there is substantial evidence that most unwed mothers would prefer to avoid the status" (p. 26). As someone said, "unmarried motherhood is a social status, not a psychiatric diagnosis." (See also Furstenberg; Lincoln, & Menken, 1981, p. 11.)

Currently it is recognized that unmarried motherhood is too complex a phenomenon to yield a particular set of "explanations." There is a growing acceptance of the supposition that, just as there is no juvenile delinquency but rather a series of different kinds of juvenile delinquents, there is no unmarried montherhood but rather a series of different kinds of unmarried mothers who come to the experience through many different routes (Plionis, 1975). Causation may differ with age, with social or racial background, and with personal experience. The determinants are cultural, personal, environmental, and—in some instances—accidental: contraceptives do fail and abortions are not always available. Even with the consistent use of contraceptives, the anticipated failure rate, which varies from 2 per cent for the pill to 18 per cent for spermicides and 24 per cent for rhythm, would result in a sizable number of out-of-wedlock pregnancies (Schrim et al., 1982, p. 73).

Some research and clinical efforts have been directed at the discovery of pathological factors that may affect the teenager's decision to engage in sexual intercourse or to become pregnant. Family dynamics, particularly the nature of the mother/daughter relationship, the extent of family conflict, and the existence of power struggles between teenagers and their parents have been explored (Bolton, 1980). Impulsivity, defective superego development, self-rejection, the desire to punish parents, anxiety about sexuality, loneliness, and passivity are among the individual factors believed to reflect emotional disturbance in adolescents that have been considered to be associated with the tendency to become pregnant. Reviewing this research, Bolton (1980) concludes: the "pregnant adolescent may be much more similar to her nonpregnant peer than previously believed. This summary perspective would lead to the conclusion that the pregnancy was more a chance event than an event mandated through pathological variables in the pregnant adolescent's life" (p. 66).

Mindick and Oskamp (1982) note an

> important relationship between an inadequate contraception and inadequate adjustment. Thus, it is not surprising to find that in instances where severe pathology disrupts effective coping with life's challenges generally, it also disrupts fertility-related behavior as well.
>
> Our question, however, is with the view that sees *all*, or even a very large proportion of excess fertility, especially among teenagers, as the product of severe psychopathology. Considering the nearly one million teenagers who annually become pregnant, and the above-mentioned projection of a 40% pregnancy rate among adolescents before they outgrow their teens, it is hard to see "severe pathology" as the modal cause of the problem. The necessary corollary of such a view would be that nearly half of all American adolescence are markedly disturbed (p. 142).

Bolton also comments that it is particularly difficult to diagnose the existence of pathology in this population, since, at this stage, the individual's personality and sense of identity are "in flux." Moreover, it is difficult to distinguish between "random behavioral testing," which is a normal adolescent activity, and behavior that reflects more disturbed origins (p. 57).

More serious consideration is now given to social factors affecting sexual activity and pregnancy i.e., changing sexual norms, changing attitudes in the relationship between the sexes and toward marriage, the effects of socioeconomic conditions on establishing, and maintaining a viable marriage. As Perlman (1954) points out, psychological explanations are more frequently applied to white, unmarried mothers; cultural explanations to the nonwhite, unmarried mothers. The white unmarried mother is seen as acting out a personal conflict; the nonwhite unmarried mother is seen as responding to a deprived socioeconomic environment (Aries, 1980).

Whereas previously the attempt to understand the unmarried mother focused on differences between those women who were premaritally active and those who refrained from intercourse, more attention is given now to differences among subgroups of the large percentage of unmarried women who are sexually active. What explains the fact that some of the sexually active group consistently and effectively use contraceptive protection, whereas others remain at high risk for pregnancy? What explains the difference between those who, when they find they are pregnant, obtain an abortion and those who do not? What explains the difference between those who, having carried a child to term, keep the child, and those who surrender the child for adoption? Each fork in the road separates one group from another in a highly involved decision-making process.

The Decision to Become Sexually Active

The birth of a child out or wedlock is the consequence of a series of sequential decisions. At each point in the decision-making process, an alternative choice would have prevented this outcome. The first decision is whether to become sexually active or to refrain from premarital sex, and, to a large extent, this decision is determined by the frequency and length of time that teenagers have been dating (Furstenberg, 1981, p. 187).

Boredom, pressure from peers and boyfriends, stimulation from a sexualized environment coupled with the anticipated pleasure from the act itself helps explain why some teens become sexually active. The inhibiting forces of shame and social disapproval are weaker in a society that has experienced the "sexual revolution," one which is more permissive toward premarital sex.

Immaturity and impulsivity are characteristic of many adolescents and help explain the decision to become sexually active despite the risks:

> Teenagers live very much in the here and now. Both immaturity and inexperience affect their thinking processes. One doctor who specializes in adolescent medicine uses the expression "teenage thinking." Teens tend to be less able than adults to assess accurately themselves and their environment, to plan ahead, to anticipate the consequences of their actions, and to develop realistic expectations (McGee 1982, p. 9).

Differences in the level of involvement, and extent of commitment and power balance between the man and the women in a relationship may tip the balance in inducing initiation of sexual activity. Greater desire for independence, higher valuation of achievement, greater of self-esteem, and higher intolerence of deviance are associated with delays in initiating sexual activity.

The Decision to Use Contraceptives

Having decided to become sexually active, unmarried pregnancies can still be prevented if effective contraceptive measures are consistently employed by either the man or the woman or both.

Most adolescents do not begin to use contraceptives until some nine months after they have first become sexually active. Availability, cost, concern about privacy from parents, lack of accurate information, actual misinformation about pregnancy or contraception, and side effects of contraceptives contribute to the delay. Myths about "barriers" to becoming pregnant (if you have sex standing up, or if you jump up and down afterwards, or if this is the first time, etc.) are common among adolescents (Bolton, 1980, Rogel & Zuehlkes 1982).

Lindemann (1975) attempts to define different stages in contraceptive use in a longitudinal analysis. The first stage is an amateurish, inconsistent, hesitant use of contraceptives when sexual activity has just been initiated, intercourse is sporadic, there is confidence that pregnancy cannot happen, and the self-image as a sexually active human being is not yet crystallized. With more frequent, more consistent sexual activity, the woman has a greater willingness to accept her identity as a sexually active woman, a greater openness to sharing this identity with her peers, and a greater deliberateness in seeking information and advice from peers and partners. This "peer perception" stage is followed by the "expert stage," in which the woman becomes more assured in the use of contraceptives and seeks the help of professionals in obtaining the most effective contraceptives. These formulations are based on research interviews with unmarried, sexually active women. Younger women and less experienced women are, therefore, most likely to engage in sexual activity without sufficient preparation.

Sex education and family planning advocates suggest that out-of-wedlock pregnancies result, in part, from a lack of adequate knowledge about human sexuality and contraceptive practices. Data collected during 1972 and 1973 from 1,327 persons participating in planned parenthood rap sessions (Reichelt & Werley, 1981) found these teenagers "were poorly informed in most areas, and lack of information rather than incorrect information was the principal problem" (p. 307). When asked a series of questions about various methods of birth control, many gave incorrect answers or stated that they did not know. More than half of this group gave correct answers on only two out of six questions about the pill, one of four questions about diaphragms, and three of five questions about spermicides (See also Horowitz, 1980; Furstenberg, 1981).

Families and friends remain one of the most widely used sources of information about contraception among teenagers, but many never use these resources either. More than a third of the participants in the Chicago Comprehensive Care Center's pregnancy prevention program stated that they had never discussed contraceptive issues with their families (Burger & Bedger, 1980, p. 131).

Analysis of pregnancy, abortion and contraceptive practices in thirty one countries lead Jones et al. (1985) to conclude that public provision for contraceptive services that are "free, widely available and confidential" has significant impact on preventing teenage pregnancies (p. 61). Morrison (1985) reviewed the findings of 100 different studies published between 1965–1984 concerned with adolescent contraceptive behavior. The review found that many adolescent were deficient in their knowledge about the physiology of contraception, particularly with regard to the period of greatest risk for conception, that females know more about contraception than males, that sex education made only a limited contribution to such knowledge and that greater sexual experience, age, and educational level were associated with increases in accurate knowledge.

Knowledge and accessibility do not however, fully explain failures to use contraceptives. Chilman (1980), reviewing twelve studies relating to this question, indicates little connection between knowledge and behavior. Non-availability ("didn't have it with me," "don't know where to get it," "too expensive") accounts for a limited percentage of reasons for usage failure (Shah, Zelnik & Kantner, 1975).

Only a small minority of sexually active women fail to use contraception because consciously or unconsciously they want to become pregnant. Only 20 to 30% of the women who experience a premarital pregnancy indicate that it had been wanted at the time it occurred (David, 1972, p. 439; see also Presser, 1981b) Nation-wide studies of unwed teenagers conclude that "the overwhelming majority of those who become pregnant indicated that the pregnancy had been unintended" (Shah, Zelnik & Kantner, 1975, p. 34; see also Furstenberg, 1981, p. 188; Zelnik, Kantner & Ford, 1981). Extensive interviews with 226 pregnant teenagers between the ages of thirteen and seventeen who participated in a comprehensive care program in the early 70's suggested that more than one in three of them "simply did not think about the possibility of becoming pregnant" prior to conception of their baby (Burger & Bedger, 1980, p. 117).

Luker (1975), based on her interviews with unmarried, sexually active women, concluded that women who know about contraceptives and have access to them may still fail to use them as a consequence of a personal risk-taking calculus that can be perceived as rational. Pregnancy risk taking is seen as no less rational than the risk taken in "failing to fasten safety belts in cars, cigarette smoking," or engaging in sports activities with a high percentage of injuries such as skiing. What is involved is a cost-benefit analysis balancing the future probable but uncertain risk of becoming pregnant and the consequences of pregnancy against the more immediate and certain costs of contraception. For many, there is still considerable "cost" in contraceptive use, varying somewhat with different kinds of contraceptives. The pill requires a confession to a doctor about nonmarital sex, it has possible side effects, and it requires consistent use, implying a commitment to and anticipation of future sexual involvement and resulting in questions related to self-image. A diaphragm requires the embarrassment of a medical fitting, manual vaginal contact, the patience and cooperation of the male partner, and so on. Each procedure requires some measure of embarrassment, inconvenience, monetary cost, and diminution of maximum pleasure.

Based perhaps on previous experiences with unprotected intercourse that did not result in pregnancy, the risk taker may argue, "I actually have a high chance of not getting pregnant from any one sexual act. If I do get pregnant, I can get an abortion. If I decide against an abortion, becoming a mother may not be so bad and it has some advantages, but I probably won't get pregnant anyhow." It is the certainty of paying present, actual, immediate costs against ambiguous, imagined, possible tolerable costs.

An examination of key characteristics of this decision-making process suggests that individuals who are more conflicted, who are more impulsive and immature, and who are less future-oriented may be more likely to perceive their decision to engage in intercourse as spontaneous. These personality characteristics become mediating variables, affecting the extent to which teenage girls will engage in behavior putting them at risk for pregnancy. A belief that one is in control of one's fate, high self-esteem, and feelings of personal competence are associated with the use of contraceptives. "Fatalism, passivity, a sense of powerlessness, feelings of incompetence and risk-taking" (Chilman, 1980, p. 164) are negatively associated with contraceptive use. (See also Mindick & Oskamp, 1982; Olson & Rollins, 1982.) In a survey of 120 teenagers participating in family planning, pediatric, and prenatal services, Rogel and Zuehke (1982) concluded, "intraphysic and interpersonal factors were most predictive of how soon after first intercourse the girls began contracepting. The most important influence on the timing of first contraceptive use was the girl's own belief that pregnancy depends on luck. Girls who have a feeling of control over pregnancy contracepted sooner after first intercourse" (p. 207).

Mindick and Oskamp (1982) argue that sexually active teens were individuals more likely to be tolerant of deviance in general and more likely to engage in deviant behavior themselves. Research on the relationship between first intercourse and consumption of alcohol (Flanigan & Hitch, 1986) points out that almost half of the subjects of this study had consumed alcohol prior to their first sexual contact. Eighteen percent of these teenage women had had three or more drinks, while one in three of their sexual partners had consumed fairly large quantities of alcohol. "Those who drank and did not plan to engage in sex had been drinking for a longer period of time, in larger amounts, and reported feeling the effects of alcohol" (p. 9) during this first sexual contact. Adolescents in this situation comprised one third of the total group of teenagers who were studied.

Teenagers become pregnant not only because they lack knowledge, make "spur of the moment" decisions, or find themselves unable to decide to delay intercourse. In addition, fear concerning the negative effects of certain contraceptives may induce an adolescent to choose unprotected intercourse rather than take these risks. Burger and Bedger's (1980) survey of participants in a comprehensive pregnancy-prevention and treatment progam found that one third had negative attitudes about birth control. Forty-three per cent expressed concern about the physical harm that might come to them if they used the pill (p. 122). A survey of high school and college students (Olson & Rollins, 1982) found that slightly less than half of the former and only one in four of the latter felt that the pill is "rather safe" or "very safe" (p. 185). Research on eighty-two adolescent females, all of whom had become pregnant for the second time, (Horowitz, 1980) discovered that

> they frequently attribute to various methods risk which are higher than the actual risks. Between a third and half of those in the Miscarriage and Live Birth Groups mentioned these fears, although very few in the Abortion Group did. These fears included the expectation that oral contraceptives would cause uterine cancer, sterility, and deformed children; the IUD was expected to cause infection and hemorrhaging or become stuck inside the uterus. These fears may help explain why so many participants discontinued use of contraceptives after experiencing side effects. If young women perceive these methods as having greater risks than they actually have, minor side effects may be perceived as having serious consequences [p. 173].

A survey of 1,433 individuals aged thirteen to seventeen enrolled in Planned Parenthood programs, examining the reasons why some of them chose to discontinue oral contraceptives use (Ager, Shea, & Agronow, 1982), reports that more than half decided to stop using the pill because of experienced or feared side effects (p. 249).

The failure to use contraceptives or the inconsistent use of contraceptives may result from a variety of additional complex considerations. There may be shame and embarrassment in the overt planning for sex required for effective contraception. For the unmarried women, sex relations are likely to be intermittent, unpredictable, and unplanned. The use of contraception implies the opposite: planned predictability. Planning for, obtaining, and using contraception clearly define the user as a sexually active person. This, rather than actually engaging in inter-course, is the more self-defining action. While engaging in intercourse, one can still deny that one is "that kind of girl." The process of seeking and obtaining contraceptives (coital preparedness) makes such denial more difficult (Raines, 1971; Lindemann, 1975). This presents a woman with a conflict, "for she cannot maintain her self-image as a 'nice girl' through rationally planning possibly 'not to be one' " (Bowerman, 1966, p. 391). (See also Kornfield, 1985.)

The Decision to Abort or Carry to Term

Having become pregnant as a result of the decision to become sexually active, the single pregnant women can still avoid becoming a single pregnant mother by choosing to use abortion services. The decision to obtain an abortion is influenced, in part, by the adolescent's attitudes toward abortion and motherhood. Carrying the baby to term has more overt community sanction. Those who choose to abort have to contend with the residue of negative opinion about abortion which both they and others may espouse. Adolescents who choose to carry their baby to term appear to have stronger ethical reservations about abortion than aborters do. Evans, Selstad, and Welcher (1981) found that both groups were in agreement about the use of abortion in cases in which the woman had been raped, the infant had some serious birth defect, the mother was very young, or the health of the mother was endangered. However, aborters wre more likely to feel that this option was feasible when personal, financial, or family factors suggested its effi-cacy (p. 359). It is of some interest that, in this research, neither the abortion nor birthing group changed these attitudes in any significant way, once having made their own personal decision. (See also Klerman et al., 1982, p. 230.)

There is positive incentive to become a mother, even out of wedlock. Given the approbation accorded motherhood, the lack of strong alternative sources of satis-faction in life for some women, the reduced stigma associated with unmarried motherhood, and the social support available in terms of medical and public assistance, day care, and continuing-education programs, those who feel some desire to have a child or "did not mind" becoming pregnant may tend to see the unmarried mother situation as not seriously disadvantaged.

In comparing unmarried black adolescent women who had their babies with those who chose to have an abortion, Fischman and Palley (1978) found that nearly half of those who delivered their babies had made this decision because they wanted to have a child. "The girls were very happy about the pregnancy" (p. 38). Similarly another study found that the decision not to abort was frequently associated with a desire for a child (Zelnick & Kantner, 1978, p. 14).

Whether the adolescent decides to keep her baby and remain unwed, to marry, or to obtain an abortion, she will tend to be satisfied with this decision. Interview-ing individuals in each of these three situations some six months after they had made their choice. Evans, Selstad, and Welcher (1981) found that 80 per cent of the aborters felt that their decision was the best for them, 80 per cent of the single unwed mothers felt that their solution was best, and 80 per cent of the teenagers who subsequently married felt that this was their best option (p. 361).

Dissatisfied aborters, young women who wished that they had chosen to de-liver, actually resembled the birthing group in most significant respects:

> They were younger, were more often Mexican-American, and tended to have di-vorced parents with significantly poor educational-occupational backgrounds . . . These teenagers had earned poorer grades in school and were less likely to have been earning any money prior to their pregnancies. They were also more conservative in

their opinions about abortion than were those who were satisfied with the decision to obtain an abortin, and they were more likely to have stated at the outset that abortion was not their first choice (p. 361).

Abortion users, like contraceptive users, are more likely to come from advantaged socioeconomic backgrounds. "Whether measured by family income, parental occupation, or parental education, the higher the status the more likely the adolescent is to choose abortion" (Klerman et al., 1982, p. 221; see also Phipps-Yonas, 1980; Evans, Selstad, & Welcher, 1981). Abortion users are also more likely to have significant educational and occupational aspirations that influence them to be concerned about their current academic performance. The decision to abort is also influenced by the adolescents more long-term objectives. In a study of 42 young women who made decisions about terminating or continuing their pregnancies during their teenage years, Lewis (1980) discovered that the most frequently mentioned factors affecting this decision included a consideration of its "effect on own life-goals (education, work)." Whereas teenagers choosing to terminate their pregnancy are more likely to be individuals who "do not want their lives burdened by an unwanted out-of-marriage pregnancy or by a forced marriage" (Chilman, 1980, p. 194), adolescents, choosing to keep their infants may be more concerned with quite different objectives: achieving adult status, getting married, or finding opportunities to establish an independent home of their own. (See also Kane & Lachenbruch, 1973: Bracken, Klerman & Bracken, 1978). Pregnant adolescents who chose to carry their baby to term were more likely to have dropped out of school well before the point at which the baby was born, and they are significantly more likely than aborters to drop out during the six-month period after the baby was born (Evans, Selstad & Welcher, 1981 p. 357).

Fischman and Palley (1978) note that "Young women who carried their pregnancies to term tended to find their schoolwork difficult, and the vast majority of them disliked school. The pregnancy per se did not cause many of them to leave school; rather, they often became pregnant because of their dissatisfaction with school" (p. 37).

> An adolescent girl is told that she should not get pregnant because if she does, she will have to stay home and take care of the baby and be deprived of further education, skilled employment, and high income. That offer can only make sense to a youngster who believes that the job and the money are really options. If the options do not exist, and for many minority youngsters they do not, then who is to say what rational behavior should be [Dryfoos 1982, p. 45].

There are worse things than pregnancy and motherhood, such as failure in school, working in a low-paying, demeaning job, or life as a perennially unemployed young adult. As a consequence of becoming a mother, a woman gains a sanctioned excuse to drop out of a school situation in which she feels defeated and inadequate, to leave a job that is dissatisfying and meaningless, or to give up a living arragement that is a source of tension and conflict. As a consequence of becoming a mother, she finds a meaningful and socially valued focus around which she can organize an identity and her life; a sense of self-worth, self-esteem, and self-fulfillment; and a gratifying interpersonal relationship with another human being.

Often the child is not wanted for his or her own sake but at least partially as a means of achieving another objective: to achieve adult status, to get married, to have "something of my own," or to use as a "passport to freedom and independence."

Motherhood leads to an acceptable and assured means of financial support and medical care that provides the possibility of independent living without parental interference. Motherhood makes one eligigle for AFDC. Given the poverty in which many young teenage mothers may find themselves living, availability of adequate financial and medical assistance may have a powerful impact on both their decision to reject abortion and to become mothers. Surveying individual state policies with regard to AFDC and Medicaid, two of the programs most likely to be utilized by these young parents, Moore and Burt (1982) summarized support opportunities that were available in 1976.

The authors conclude that current AFDC policies favor the adolescent's decision not to marry, since it is far less likely that she and her unemployed husband would be able to obtain benefits than that she, alone, could receive in assistance to support her child.

There is no evidence to suggest, however, that AFDC "causes" out-of-wedlock pregnancies. Analyzing relationship between the levels of grant payments and the access barriers to AFDC as these relate to legitimacy rates to 1965, Cutright (1971) found that AFDC was not an incentive to an out-of-wedlock pregnancy. Janowitz (1976), analyzing somewhat similar factors for a later period, found that for nonwhite younger women, larger welfare payments were associated with higher illegitimacy rates. Moore and Caldwell (1976), analyzing a 1971 national probability sample of fifteen- to nineteen-year-old women, found that "high state AFDC benefit levels and acceptance rates were not found to be associated with greater probability of pregnancy." They concluded that benefits did not "increase the likelihood that an unmarried virgin would have intercourse" and that "there was no evidence that AFDC benefits serve as an evident incentive to child-rearing outside marriage" (pp. 2,3).

Utilizing available data, which suggest that only 36 per cent of unwed teenagers intend to become pregnant, Moore and Burt (1982) attempt to estimate the proportion of these young women who might conceivably choose to give birth in order to obtain AFDC benefits. Acknowledging that teenagers might intentionally conceive for a wide variety of reasons, they suggest that "a maximum of perhaps 90,000 teenagers (36% of the 249,100 unmarried teenage mothers) may have bourne children out-of-wedlock to qualify for AFDC in 1978" (p. 112). Using this figure as an extremely rough estimate, they point out that no more than 8 per cent of all teenage conceptions reflect the desire to have a child in order to receive public assistance.

Singh (1986) also determined on the basis of a state-by-state analysis, that the relevant data "strongly suggest that AFDC Programs with higher benefits and more comprehensive coverage . . . are not associated with high teenage birth rates" (p. 219).

A comprehensive review of the relationship between AFDC benefit levels clearly indicates that there is no relationship between benefit levels and unmarried mother rates. What it does show is that benefit levels are related to a significant decision subsequent to the act of conception itself. When benefit levels are adequate, unmarried mothers are considerably more likely to move out of their parents' home and set up their own households. Benefit levels have a negative influence on their decision to marry and legitimize the pregnancy (Ellwood & Bane, 1985).

The availability of benefits does make it possible for young single mothers to establish homes of their own. Following teenagers who had chosen to abort or to keep their infants some six months after this decision had been made, Evans, Selstad, and Welcher (1981) found that the proportion of aborters who continued to live with their families remained approximately the same (dropping slightly from 79 to 72%), whereas the proportion of out-of-wedlock mothers living with their parents dropped substantially (from 98 to 56%) (p. 358). Benefits also make it possible for mothers to avoid marriages that have a low probability for success because they lack a sound social, emotional, or financial basis. The availability of benefits may influence some women not to have an abortion or not to place the child for adoption because there is a source of support for caring for the child: "The availability of public assistance appears not to *cause* out-of-marriage pregnancy, but it may affect what the young woman does about this pregnancy" (Chilman, 1980, p. 213).

The decision to terminate or not to terminate a pregnancy is also affected by the attitude of significant others in the adolescent's life. More so than their adult counterparts, teenagers are likely to turn to intimates (parents, close friends, or boyfriends), for advice about abortion. They are less likely than adults to rely on the advice of more "disinterested" professionals—doctors, social service professionals, and so forth (Lewis, 1980). A survey of 153 sixteen to eighteen-year-olds (Klerman et al., 1982) concluded that young women who choose to deliver were more likely to perceive their relationship with their boyfriend as permanent. Whereas 7 per cent of the abortion group described their boyfriends as fiancés, 19 per cent of the delivery group did so; 57 per cent of the delivery group and 42 percent of the abortion group had been involved with their boyfriends for over a year. However, both groups tended to describe their relationship to the putative father as very close. In making their decision whether to terminate or maintain the pregnancy, a substantial number of teenagers consider the impact of the child on their relationship with this male (Lewis, 1980).

Evidence concerning the the impact of attitudes of family members, boyfriends, and friends toward abortion and unwed parenthood reveals no clear pattern (Phipps-Yonas, 1980). However, many teenagers, particularly those who choose to deliver their babies, know of other single individuals who are raising children, and a substantial number have single parents within their family network. This may serve to legitimate the teenager's decision to have and raise her baby out of wedlock.

The continued increase in the number of out-of-wedlock births, despite a very large increase in family-planning and abortion services, indicates that this problem is more complex than being merely a question of contraceptive technology, education, assessibility, and availability. "Solving" the "problem" of unmarried motherhood requires attention to ideological, sociological, psychological, and motivational factors as well. Simple, acceptable, widely available, safe, low-cost contraceptive procedures about which all fecund males and females were knowledgeable, backed by readily accessible elective abortion, would undoubtedly help, but it is likely that children would still continue to be conceived and born out of wedlock.

Teenage Unmarried Fathers

For each out-of-wedlock child being carried by a single pregnant girl, there is, of course, a putative father. The putative father was once ignored or regarded only as a source of financial support for the unwed mother and her child. This was followed by a period during which contact was attempted with the putative father because of what he could contribute toward the emotional as well as the financial support of the unwed mother and because knowledge of the putative father was helpful in adoptive planning for the child. Currently contact with the putative father is predicated on the recognition that he might want help in his own right with the problems he faces relating to the out-of-wedlock pregnancy. The movement has been from seeing the putative father solely as a resource of help to the unmarried mother to perceiving him as a person in his own right who might be troubled about a difficult situation in which he is a principal participant.

Studies of the background of the unmarried father indicate that he is generally of the same age, social class, and educational level as the single pregnant girl, and that he has known the girl for some time prior to the onset of the pregnancy (Sauber, 1966; Grow, 1967; Pope, 1967; Pannor et al., 1971; Klermam et al., 1982; Barrett & Robinson, 1982). He is usually not promiscuous: "Relationships between unwed mothers and unwed fathers are much more meaningful than popularly supposed and . . . unwed fathers have more concern for their offspring than is generally realized" (Pannor et al., 1971, p. 85). The relationship of the unmarried father to the mother cannot validly be characterized as either deviant or exploitative. Only a small minority of pregnancies results from short-time contact with casually encountered strangers. In most instances, the unwed father is far from the phantom figure one might expect if the mother were motivated to become pregnant in response to her own private needs and needed a man only for his biological contribution.

It has been claimed that the young single father becomes a father because he is hostile to women, because he wishes to confirm his virility, or because he rejects authority. Having intercourse in order to validate one's self as a male reflects a relatively immature perspective on the nature and meaning of intimacy and of the value of heterosexual relationships. In addition, "impulsivity which characterizes much of the behavioral decision-making style of these men may be indicative of their seizing upon desires of the moment without thought to consequences. This same impulsivity is a measure of the gross absence of self-direction and self-discipline that follows in the wake of their immaturity" (Bolton, 1980, p. 64).

Available data indicate that adolescent males who have children out of wedlock may be somewhat immature, compared to their peers. The responses of a group of unmarried fathers to the California Psychological Inventory substantially mirrors the standard profile. Modest deviations indicated less social maturity and responsibility and more self-centeredness (Pannor et al., 1971, p. 103–106). This lack of clear-cut differentiation between putative fathers and males in general is confirmed by other comparisons of the two groups (Pauker, 1968).

Widely held social expectations reinforce the view that sexual prowess is a measure of masculinity. A 1974 survey, (Finkel & Finkel, 1981) found that seven out of ten male respondents claim that sexual involvement is appropriate, even if one does not have a very meaningful relationship with one's partner. Many young men, as Scales and Beckstein (1982) note, "seem more concerned with the *event* of first intercourse as a right of passage than as the first chance to get to know another person in this intimate way . . . A study of 165 university students, for example, found that both sexes had about the same number of fears and concerns surrounding their first intercourse, but that women were significantly more worried about whether they were doing the 'right thing' and men were significantly more concerned with whether they were doing it right, about their performance as lovers" (p. 270). Since males are socialized to present themselves as virile, it is difficult to determine the extent to which these statements reflect self-presentation to others rather than underlying motivators for sexual behavior.

Perhaps of greatest salience in understanding the role of the putative father is the nature of the communication that occurs between him and his sexual partner with regard to such issues as willingness to become sexually involved and planning for contraception. One common pattern involves the assumption on the part of each partner that contraception is the responsibility of the other partner. However, neither has talked to the other about pregnancy prevention. Both "guess" what the other wants, has done, and will do in this area rather than directly discussing it. In one study (Burger & Bedger, 1980), 49 per cent of the female teenagers interviewed believed that their boyfriends would want them to take responsibility for contraception, 27 per cent thought that he would be willing to use some protection, and the remainder believed that he did not believe in using any kind of contraception. However, 46 per cent of the total realized, "I don't know how he feels about birth control at all" (p. 116). Neither the respondents nor their boyfriends had initiated discussion on this topic in these instances. A 1981 study of 663 black, single, adolescent males attending two inner-city Baltimore schools (Clark, Zabin, & Hardy, 1984) found only 51 per cent who has ever talked about birth control with their girlfriends (p. 81). Previous experience with pregnancy motivates the partners to share these concerns. Prior to their initial pregacy, Horowitz (1980) found that only 38 per cent of a teen-age sample of second time mothers had dicussed the possibility that they would become pregnant; 76% did so after she delivered her first baby. These various studies point to the fact that "ignorance, negative attitudes about contraception, lack of awareness of pregnancy risk, lower moral reasoning level in sexual situations, and a general lack of communication about sex and contraception, thus comprise an important constellation of factors that discourage contraceptive use" (Scales & Beckstein, 1982, p. 276).

In addition to finding themselves in difficulty because they do not know how to talk with their partners about contraceptive practices, young men may also unexpectedly find themselves unwed fathers because they choose relatively ineffective means of contraception. Fifty-five per cent of the adolescent male respondents in a 1974 survey had used the least effective means of pregnancy prevention (withdrawal, douches, or nothing), whereas an additional 28 per cent relied on the use of the condom (Finkel & Finkel, 1981). In contrast a 1981 study of black adolescents found that the proportion relying on withdrawal methods had decreased substantially, to 15 percent, and there had been a concomitant rise in the number using condoms (41%) (Clark, Zabin, & Hardy, 1984).

Unable in many cases to discuss methods for avoiding pregnancy with their partners, adolescent males are equally inhibited in discussing these issues with their families. One study found that only 11 per cent of young men had ever had an opportunity to talk about these concerns with their parents or other family members (Finkel & Finkel, 1981). Because partners and parents comprise two of the primary groups to whom teenagers turn for information and advice, the inability to bring up these issues is a serous drawback for young men who need help in making meaningful decisions about sexual involvement and avoidance of parenthood. Embarrassment can also stand in the way of seeking assistance from professionals about pregnancy prevention (Clark, Zabin, & Hardy, 1984).

Like their female counterparts, young adolescent males may also fear that certain contraceptive practices will have an unexpected long-term negative impact on them. "Some minority group members have reacted to family planning not with indifference but with hostility, seeing it as a form of genocide. Fears that family planning programs aim at reducing the size of the black population appear to be not uncommon throughout the black community. Young black males living in the North appear to hold more strongly to this view" (Moore & Burt, 1982, p. 59).

The circumstances surrounding the decision to become sexually active are as varied for teenage fathers as they are for young women. As Caughlan (1960) noes, the "act which initiates pregnancy" may range from "nothing more than a witless discharge of physiological tension" to the "fullest expression of the most mature relationship. . . . A great variety of psycho-social predisposing and precipitating factors can lead to the onset of this condition" (p. 29).

Social Work Services for Single Pregnant Women

Pregnancy Prevention

Social workers are involved in programs that are designed to protect single women from becoming pregnant. Sex education and contraceptive practice are the two most typical focuses for pregnancy-prevention services. Despite widespread social support for sex education for adolescents, a recent Gallup poll indicates that only 40 per cent of young people ever had a sex education course while in school, and only 30 per cent had course material that explicitly dealt with birth control (Furstenberg, Lincoln, & Menken, 1981, p. 13). Various surveys suggest that as few as 10 per cent and as many as 55 per cent of junior and senior high schools currently offer this type of programming (Moore & Burt, 1982). The widespread variability in the availability of programs is fostered by the failure of individual states to mandate this service. Thirty-one states "encourage" the provision of this training material, although in twenty-one of them the decision with regard to this provision is left to the local school district. In twenty other states, statewide provision for sex education is "extremely limited" or no policy exists with regard to this matter. Even when programming is available in the schools, the amount of time spent on these issues is limited and topics covered include only "reproductive anatomy, menstruation, venereal disease and ethical standards" (Moore & Burt, 1982, p. 64). Sex education is also provided under nonacademic auspices, through social service organizations, religious agencies, and medical or hospital-affiliated programs. Planned Parenthood provides the most extensive service of this type. Whereas nonschool-related programs face difficulties in recruiting and serving teenagers who may be in need of this type of education, they also are more likely to cover far more controversial aspects of sex education.

It is generally agreed that the most useful educational format involves the use of structured discussion groups among teenagers, sometimes with group leadership provided by teenagers themselves, but also relying on the guidancce of an adult adviser (Phipps-Yonas, 1980; Moore & Burt, 1982; Bolton, 1980). Dryfoos (1984) suggests that group discussion of content giving attention to the enhancement of educational and employment opportunities for adolescents helps combat the teenager's belief that she might as well have a baby and move toward adulthood through becoming a parent rather than though a job and self-support.

Gilchrist and Schinke (1983b) developed a social learning theory approach to helping adolescents enhance their skills in dealing with the decisional problems related to becoming sexually active. The program seeks to enhance the adolescents' skills in disclosing positive and negative feelings, making effective refusals and initiating difficult conversations.

Social work services are provided in many family-planning agencies, which are a primary vehicle for helping teenagers choose contraceptive practices that will help them prevent out-of-wedlock pregnancy. In 1976, some 40 per cent of metropolitan family-planning agencies and 20 per cent of nonmetropolitan agencies employed social workers (Torres, 1979, p. 111).

In 1979, 56 per cent of all adolescents at risk for unintended pregnancy were reached by some type of family planning service. One and one half million adolescents received services from family planning clinics, whereas 1.2 million were provided contraceptive services by private physicians (Torres, Forrest, & Eisman, 1981). "There is a great deal of mobility between sources of care; some youngsters prefer the anonymity of the clinic for an initial visit and after that go to their own physician. Others switch from physicians to clinics" (Dryfoos, 1982, p. 40). Organized family-planning services were provided in more than 5,000 sites throughout the country in 1979. More than half of these (58%) were operated by health departments, 14 per cent by Planned Parenthood affiliates, 8 per cent by hospitals, and the remainder by various other types of agencies. Health departments served 40 per cent of all family planning clients, whereas Planned Parenthood agencies served more than 25 per cent (Torres, Forrest, & Eisman, 1981, p. 134). Adolescents comprise one in three family planning clients, and, proportionately, their numbers have been rising steadily in recent years. Many of these agencies offer programs specially designed to reach out to and meet the needs of teenagers.

In large part, the task of the social worker in these agencies involves the provision of essential information about contraceptive options, pregnancy, and childbirth. Usually the worker discusses the range of contraceptives that are available, since one no method meets the needs of most clients (Greydanus, 1982, p. 55). Furthermore, the worker stresses the need for the ongoing use of contraception, since many adolescents rely on their chosen methods only sporadically or begin to use a particular method and then discard it, failing to replace it immediately with another (Zabin & Clark, 1981).

According to Cain (1979), litle discussion of more complex issues, such as the meaning of pregnancy for the adolescent, occurs in these settings. A 1979 evaluation recognized the need for the type of counseling services provided by social workers in these settings, and

> strongly recommended the strengthening of the counseling component in family-planning clinics. . . Additional components recommended included more in-depth counseling to identify problems and assist teens with their concerns about contraception, sexuality, and their lives in general, and to strengthen teen-ager's decision-making skills in resolving their problems [Dryfoos, 1982, p. 39].

Social work services are also provided in agencies providing abortions for adolescents. Most abortions are obtained in "free-standing" clinics rather than hospitals, since the large volume of services in these settings allows for their provision at lower cost to the client (Dryfoos, 1982). In 1978, there were 522 clinics in the United States, most of them in major metropolitan areas.

Social workers assist adolescents in determining whether abortion is the best choice in their circumstances. It is not unusual for individuals to feel ambivalent or to change their mind, a reflection of the fact that this is a difficult decision. As noted previously one study found that some 20 per cent of adolescents who choose abortion subsequently wished they had made another choice (Klerman et al., 1982, p. 227), suggesting the need for social work assistance in making a meaningful decision. Individuals undergoing abortion also can be prepared for the intense feelings of guilt, regret, and loss which some are likely to experience, particularly immediately after undergoing the abortion procedure. For most young women, these feelings are temporary and mitigated to some extent by feelings of relief that an unwanted pregnancy has been terminated.

Although undergoing an abortion may raise issues for the adolescent that may have long-term impact, few teenagers are willing to maintain contact with the social worker, once the abortion has occurred (Cain, 1979). Since pregnancy and abortion can be kept a secret, and since some adolescents, fearing negative reactions from their families or friends, may choose to keep these experiences a secret, they may subsequently find they have few opportunities to evaluate this experience with others. In response the worker highlights client options for seeking further professional help, should they desire it.

Services For the Unmarried Pregnant Woman and Out-of-Wedlock

The decision to reject abortion and carry the child to term presents the unmarried mother with a different set of problems with which the social worker might help her cope.

The single pregnant woman faces not only the practical problems of medical care, finances, housing, and so on, but emotional problems as well. For the married woman, pregnancy is a joyful occasion, and she is applauded and supported by those who are close to her; for the single girl, it is often an occasion for regret, dejection, worry, and social disapproval. Although society is currently more accepting, or at least less openly punitive, in its response to the unmarried mother, she is still considered somewhat atypical and deviant. Very few teens feel unambivalently positive about their situation (Furstenberg, 1981).

Guilt and shame, if manifested at all, are more likely to be evoked by the pregnancy rather than by the sexual activity that caused it (Taylor, 1965), but the general situation in which the single pregnant girl finds herself is apt to evoke strong feelings of anxiety and panic. Denial and distortion of reality are understandable when the reality involves "having to acknowledge that she has been abandoned by the baby's father, that she is in social and economic jeopardy, and that she will either have to relinquish a baby she may love or . . . keep a baby she is not sure she is going to love" (Bernstein, 1971, p. 31). The social worker can help the unmarried mother deal with her feelings about her situation.

For some girls, the pregnancy may precipitate maturity. As a pregnant woman, the girl is perceived as an adult engaging in an adult experience. As a consequence, she may decide to move away from home and establish greater independence, or she may find that she is now emotionally ready for marriage.

Most pressing is the need to discuss and resolve her feelings about the child and to make plans for the child. Innocent though it may be, the child has occasioned considerable difficulty for the mother, which may make the mother feel resentment, and guilt and shame about her resentment.

The social worker can help the mother to distinguish her feelings about plans for the child from those of her family and/or of the child's father. If a woman has a strong emotional need for the child but is persuaded or coerced to give it up, she may incur another illegitimate pregnancy in search of the lost child. The worker can also help the mother to distinguish between what is desirable for the child and what is desirable for herself. As Crockett (1960) says, "Not only is it important that the unmarried mother reach the right decision but also that she reach it in a way that leaves her convinced that she has chosen wisely" (p. 77).

For the unmarried mother who chooses to bear her child, the social worker provides sociotherapy and psychotherapy. Sociotherapy includes income maintenance, housing (in some instances away from the family, in a maternity home or a foster home), prenatal and obstetrical medical care, legal counseling, vocational counseling, and educational counseling. The psychotherapeutic services are intended to help with the emotional disturbance, conflict and tensions occasioned by the out-of-wedlock pregnancy. The services include counseling and emotional support in regard to the woman's changing relationship with her own family, her relationship with the putative father, her changing relationship to peers, her reaction to the pregnancy and the anticipated birth experience, her plans for the child, her changes in self-concept, and the total emotional configuration that might have motivated the girl to become pregnant.

In general, the single pregnant girl is likely to be more interested in sociotherapy than in psychotherapy. Most of the unmarried mothers to whom service is offered are likely to be more concerned with the specific, immediate problems posed by the pregnancy and the birth of the child.

A study of the services offered fifty "young, poor, uneducated" unmarried mothers indicated that although both clients and workers often identified similar problems as needing attention, there was a difference in emphasis (Rubenstein & Bloch, 1978). Both identified problems of housing and financial assistance and of establishing paternity, the relationship with the alleged father, the relationship with the woman's parents, and the decision about the baby as being among those most frequently requiring assistance. However, "workers gave relatively more emphasis to intra and interpersonal factors than to lack of tangible goods and social services . . . clients tended to emphasize their lack of resources and interpersonal rather than intrapersonal problems" (p. 74). However, although the workers had some bias about the intrapersonal nature and sources of the clients' problem, they gave priority to the clients' perception of need rather than to their own preferences. A good deal of the help offered was centered on providing concrete services rather than "therapy." As a consequence, most of the clients were satisfied with the service, felt that they had been helped, and would recommend the service to others, whereas the workers themselves assessed the results as "mildly positive."

Arranging for adequate medical care is an immediate consideration. Pregnant teenagers are more vulnerable than their adult counterparts to a wide range of medical difficulties, including "hypertension, toxemia, cephalopelvic disproportion, caesarean section, abruptio placenta, anemia, and urinary tract infections" (Cooper, 1982, p. 67; see also Sacker & Neuhoff, 1982, pp. 113–114; Stepto, Keith, & Keith, 1975, p. 89). In part because of their own personal physical vulnerability, these young mothers are also more likely to have premature and low birth weight (less than 2,500 grams) infants. Whereas 6 to 8 per cent of adults have premature infants, estimates for teens range from 10 to 31 per cent. One in four low-birth weight babies are born to adolescents (Sacker, & Neuhoff, 1982, p. 122). Prematurity and low birth weight, in turn, predict additional difficulties for the infant. "Low birth weight, the net result of premature labor, premature rupture of the membranes, and prematurity, is the major cause of perinatal morbidity and mortality, in adults as well as in adolescents. It may result in the death (of the child), neurologic defects, seizures, mental retardation, cerebral palsy, learning problems, and stunted growth and development" (Sacker, & Neurhoff, 1982, p. 122). Infants born to adolescent mothers are two to four times more likely to die as those born to adults. The mortality rate is particularly high among black teenage parents who are very young (pp. 126–127).

These unusually high rates of medical difficulty have been attributed to the adolescent's tendency to delay contact with medical services. One study found that, among its participants, almost three-fourths had no medical care or had very late medical care (only in the last trimester) prior to the birth of the baby (Cooper, 1982, p. 67; see also Pakter & Nelson, 1965). Adolescents are also more likely to cancel medical appointments and less likely to follow medical directives than are adult pregnant women. However, the primary determinant of increased medical difficulties is neither the social-emotional nor biologic immaturity of the infant's mother. Instead, it is socioeconomic factors that play a key role. Comparing rates of maternal and infant medical disabilities and deaths cross-culturally, Makinson (1985) concludes that in countries providing quality medical care to all citizens, the gap between adolescent and adult disability rates shrinks significantly. Only in the case of very young mothers (those less than 15 years old) do the data indicate that a combination of socioeconomic and biologic factors are probably operating, since it is particularly in this young age that physiological immaturity contributes to the birth of very small infants.

Socioeconomic factors are particularly powerful in their impact on accessibility to quality medical care and engagement with a responsive medical system. Income also has a powerful impact on diet, which, in turn, can increase or reduce the likelihood of some common difficulties, such as anemia. Preexisting medical difficulties, such as venereal disease, unless effectively treated, can also adversely affect the health of the pregnant young mother and her infant.

When prenatal care is adequate there is clear evidence that this results in a reduction of premature births (Makinson, 1985, p. 135).

Medical care for unmarried mothers with limited resources can be financed through Medicaid. The older unwed mother may obtain financial assistance under the AFDC program, if she is willing to file a complaint against the putative father. If paternity is established, the father will be required to contribute monthly toward the support of the child. If the father is not known, not located, or not able to pay, financial assistance through AFDC is available in some states even before the birth of the child. If employed when she became pregnant, she may be eligible, for medical care through the health insurance policy of her employing organization.

Adequate medical care was provided until recently for many in maternity homes. The maternity home is a specialized institutional facility that was developed to meet the needs of single pregnant women. A nationwide survey showed that there were two hundred such institutions in the United States in 1966, offering services to about 25,000 women (Pappenfort & Kilpatrick, 1970).

In part because so many more single pregnant women are choosing to keep their children, and in part because they no longer want or need the concealment that maternity homes offer, the utilization of these services has declined dramatically. Many of these facilities have closed their inpatient services and are, instead, offering outpatient programs to women. The Crittenton Maternity Home in Detroit is one such example. It reopened as a comprehensive service center in the inner-city named after a black cardiologist, Lulu Belle Stewart.

The unmarried woman who wants to keep her child must be helped to assess her capacity to care for the child as a single parent. If she seriously overestimates her capacity, she may later regret the decision. She may need clarification of the problems that she is likely to face and information about the resources in the community that might be able to help her with those problems.

The social worker provides an opportunity for an exploration of the multiple problematic decisions that the unmarried mother needs to resolve in a context of objective acceptance. Based on her knowledge of probable consequences associated with alternatives and options, the social worker can help the unmarried mother make a decision that has a chance of being individualized and comfortably acceptable.

In helping with these decisions, the social worker is inevitably involved with significant others in the client's life who also influence the decision. The decision to abort or to keep the child often involves the client's parents and sometimes the putative father. The decision to adopt involves the putative father, as does any decision to legitimize the child through marriage. The client's mother is very often an influential factor in these decisions (Young, Beckman, & Rehr, 1975). The worker must often obtain the parents' and the boyfriend's cooperation in implementing these key decisions.

The Unmarried Mother's Family-During and After Pregnancy.   Once the pregnancy has been confirmed, the young woman might need help in deciding whom she wants to tell about it. Perhaps the first question that needs discussion is whether or not to tell her parents and, if so, how to do it. This is frequently a very difficult decision for adolescents. In research conducted in the late 1960s and early 1970s, Furstenberg (1981) discovered that more than half of the 400 teenage mothers in his sample could not bring themselves to reveal their pregnancy to their parents for several months after they discovered it. To assist young women who have decided to make this revelation, the social worker might help her practice this event through role playing. The social worker is available to act as a convenor and mediator in the meeting between teenager and parents about this issue.

Parents frequently hate to be told, yet want to be told. Although learning about the pregnancy may make them feel they have failed as parents, they usually offer emotional support and concrete help. The girl wants to conceal the pregnancy lest she hurt her parents, yet she is relieved and comforted when they rally to her support.

The initial reaction of many parents to this news is negative: shock, disbelief, rejection, disappointment, and guilt. Some three-fourths of the parents in Furstenberg's (1981) study reported that they were astonished, very surprised, that they couldn't believe that the pregnancy was real (p. 191).

However, most families seem to resolve these negative attitudes, if not during the pregnancy, very often after the birth of the baby. Although there is much in the situation that creates conflict between daughter and parents, there is much that moves them toward reconciliation. The parents' guilt and compassion and the daughter's desire to make amends for the pain she may be causing them may move them toward reconciliation. The worker reinforces those tendencies that move parents and child toward mutual forgiveness and attempts to resolve or mitigate the divisive elements in the situation.

For most teenagers and many young adults, the family remains a central resource for meeting both material and emotional needs. Pregnant adolescents, like their nonpregnant counterparts, continue to turn to their families for support;

families remain a significant resource even when they choose to marry. A large-scale study of pregnant adolescents in Baltimore, (Furstenberg & Crawford, 1981, pp. 283–285), conducted during the late 1960s and early 1970s, found that at the time these adolescents discovered they were pregnant, some 88 per cent were living with parents or other relatives. Only 1 per cent were living on their own. One year later, after the birth of the infant, more than three-fourths of these adolescents remained with families or relatives, and only 7 per cent were living alone. Three years after they had became pregnant, two-thirds of the group resided with parents and relatives, and five years after the beginning of the study, almost half of the group did so. Respondents in this survey reported that parents were a significant resource for child care, financial and other forms of material support. This was particularly true for adolescent mothers who continued to live with their families.

Determining how to seek continuing support from families and to what extent and in what ways she would like it provided may be complex questions for the teenager. As Authier and Authier (1982) point out, childbirth is usually accompanied by reestablishment of some dependency ties, particularly between the new parent and her own mother. However, while most new parents have obtained some degree of autonomy from their family before moving toward reestablishing these ties, adolescents find themselves in the difficult position of needing to become somewhat more dependent while not having, as yet, sufficiently established their autonomy.

> Since adolescents are working on the development task of establishing independence, they may have difficulty accepting a dependent role if their mothers increase their nuturing behaviors. However, they may be resentful, without insight regarding the source of their resentment, if their mothers do not supply nurturance. The confusion of the tasks of pregnancy and parenthood with the tasks of adolescence requires special awareness and skill on the part of the professional in helping the adolescent and her family achieve the required delicate adjustments and balances [Authier & Authier, 1982, p. 310].

Satisfactory negotiation around these issues may be complicated in instances where families face longstanding difficulties. Rather than work toward a successful resolution, the family may simply use the issues raised by the adolescent's pregnancy as a new battleground for playing out chronic family conflicts.

The legal status of the teenage unmarried mother complicates this planning situation. If she chooses to live on her own or to seek out resources from outside the family, she may need her parent's legal permission. She may, for example, need to obtain their approval to receive medical care or to enter a maternity home. The teenager may also find it difficult to obtain financial assistance unless her parents can satisfy the agency that they cannot support their daughter and that they are willing to apply for aid in her behalf.

All of these considerations suggest that, for many adolescents, pregnancy must be viewed as a family as well as an individual concern (Abel et al., 1982; Authier & Authier, 1982). Families, themselves, perceive the pregnancy as a matter of concern to all members, not just the adolescent (Bowerman et al., (1966). Although it is important for the worker to contact the family only after obtaining the adolescent's permission to do so, in many instances it becomes highly beneficial for both the teenager and her parents to become involved in a joint planning process.

"The assistance rendered by family members significantly alters the life chances of the young mother" (Furstenberg & Crawford, 1981, p. 298). These advantages, are however, obtained at a price. There may be disagreements about the care of the child and generational conflicts about the nature of the mother's social life and expectations (Barth & Schinke, 1983). The mother may be dissatisfied with her continuing dependent-child status, and she may, in her parents' eyes, become an older sibling to her own child. Her parents may resent the child care they must provide at a time in their lives when they thought they would be free of this task. These stresses push the teenage mother to gradually establish an independent living situation (Hopkinson, 1976; Clapp & Raab, 1978).

Marriage might be seen as a solution to these problems. The decision to marry the putative father is usually a decision to keep the baby. These young families may begin burdened by considerable economic, social, and emotional difficulties. Pregnant adolescents who choose to marry rather than stay single are less likely to complete high school, and therefore, face far fewer sound employment options than do those who complete their academic careers (Howard, 1978). In Furstenberg's (1981) research, the young women who were less "economically ambitious" and who saw themselves as doing poorly in school were more likely to marry (p. 192).

Marriages contracted while women are pregnant are much more likely to end in divorce than marriages in which no pregnancy is involved (McCarthy & Menken, 1981). In Furstenberg's (1981) survey, one-fifth of the pregnant teens who got married separated from their spouses within twelve months; one-third had separated within two years of the date of the marriage, and three out of five of these marriages had dissolved within six years of their inception.

Themes in Social Work Services for the Unwed Father

Unlike young women who find themselves pregnant out of wedlock, young fathers rarely become the target of specialized pregnancy planning and parenting services. A nationwide study of services offered by voluntary agencies to 20,000 unwed mothers in 1966 indicated that only about 7 per cent of the putative fathers were also interviewed (Grow, 1967, p. 46). If the putative father is a teenager, there is a greater likelihood that he will be seen by the agency. When they are provided for these young men, services are typically made available only with the permission of the mothers of their children. Moreover, few of the unwed fathers who come to the attention of social service agencies are provided comprehensive services. (Hendricks, Howard, & Caesar, 1981).

Agencies have not developed programs to serve this client population, in part because the agencies have assumed that these young men do not wish to become involved with the young women, their children, or the agency. Considered "irresponsible," "uncaring," and "selfish" (Scales & Beckstein, 1982, p. 285), these young men have been depicted as being uninterested in a meaningful relationship with the mother and unconcerned about a pregnancy they argue is "her fault" (Chilman, 1985). Even in cases in which they have some sense of commitment, the young men's fear of being held financially responsible for the support of the mother and child presumably leads them to avoid agency involvement and to deny paternity.

However, social workers in agencies that do outreach to these unnamed fathers challenge these assumptions. The agencies that have made a special effort to offer service to the unmarried father have found that he is available, troubled, concerned, and frequently anxious to be of help (Brugess, 1968; Platts, 1968; Pannor et al., 1971; Furstenberg, 1981). Perhaps the agency that has most actively and consistently attempted such a service is the Vista Del Mar Child Care Service in Los Angeles, which serves a predominantly urban, middle-class, white clientele. The agency notes that about 80 per cent of the fathers whom they contact are seen and that the majority of those have four or more interviews with the male caseworker (Pannor et al., 1971, p. 59, Table 17). A public agency that attempted a program of service to unmarried fathers found that in at least 70 per cent of the cases he was "available for interviews and frequently anxious to help in planning for his baby" (Platts, 1968, p. 537). At least one agency requires that the unmarried mother accepted for service be willing to have the agency contact the unmarried father "for cooperation in giving history and consent to adoption" (Burgess, 1968, p. 72). The agency found that 83 per cent of the fathers whom they attempted to reach "made themselves available for an interview" (Burgess, 1968, p. 72).

The failure to make active efforts to include the putative father may be functional. As Barber (1975) notes in a study of unmarried fathers, "The presence of an involved father does complicate the situation. He represents a third opinion which the decision makers have to take into consideration. . . . His exclusion has the advantage of convenience but is fundamentally unrealistic" (p. 20).

Out-of-wedlock fathers could benefit from social work assistance in planning more effective contraceptive use, in working through a variety of issues with regard to their relationship to the out-of-wedlock mother, and in making decisions about the future of their children. For the most part, contraceptive education, like adolescent parenting programs, has focused almost exclusively on services to young women. In 1978, increasing attention was given to male contraceptive needs by the provision of federal funds through the Office of Family Planning. Two hundred and fifty thousand dollars were targeted to develop programming that was specifically aimed at sexual health-care services for males (Scales & Beckstein, 1982). Among the programs sponsored by this grant were a Male Motivation/Education program developed by Chicago Planned Parenthood, a Sexuality Counseling Program sponsored by the Job Corps and Boys' Clubs, and promotion of National Condom Week, which was initiated by a pharmacy group in California.

Although follow-up studies show that most of the unwed mothers who keep their child receive AFDC, the child's biological father is a source of some support for a sizable minority of the group (Clapp & Raab, 1978). At least for the first year or two after the birth of the child, contact is often maintained with the father, although this gradually phases out.

The social worker can be of substantial assistance to the out-of-wedlock father, helping him to determine the extent of financial support he wishes to and can realistically provide for his child. Like the young woman, he must also weigh his short-term and long-term obligations and goals and decide whether to remain in school or to obtain full-time employment.

Contact with the agency can also help the unmarried father clarify his relationship with the mother. Joint sessions with the mother can be helpful in dispelling any romantic, unrealistic fantasies the pair may have about each other. This relationship is frequently sufficiently stable so that the couple will give consideration to marriage, and many of these couples do eventually marry, although their marriages are highly unstable and most eventually dissolve. These young husbands and fathers are particularly burdened, since they must struggle with their own emotional immaturity, extremely limited finances, and the continuing need to rely on their families for support at a time whey they would prefer to be disengaging from them. The social worker can be available to these couples provide them with information about financial and other types of assistance, help them learn to be supportive of each other and to seek important sources of support outside of their relationship, and prepare them for some of the difficult times they may face as they struggle to establish their family.

The young man who chooses to disengage himself from this relationship and from responsibility for caring for his child faces a different set of dilemmas. The norms and values of the core culture require that a man protect and support the female he has impregnated and their child. There are, of course, many different ways in which the unmarried father mitigates any feeling of responsibility, guilt, or remorse. These range from "It may have been somebody else, not me," to "She didn't have to do it if she didn't want to and she should have taken proper precautions." Yet many men do feel remorse and shame if they fail to come to the support and assistance of the mother and child. Unlike the unmarried mother, the unmarried father does not have the physical and social discomfort of nine months of pregnancy and the pain of delivery through which some "atonement" is achieved.

For effective adoptive planning, it is desirable to have detailed information regarding the child's paternal and maternal background. Contact with the putative father can provide more complete information of this nature. (Anglim, 1965). Such knowledge might subsequently be communicated to the adopted child to give the child a more complete sense of identity. The father's involvement is important to the child in other ways as well. Consent to the registration of paternity permits the child to claim and obtain benefits from the Social Security account of the father.

Legally and socially, the position of the unwed father is unenviable. He has been considered responsible for supporting his out-of-wedlock child, yet has been given minimal opportunity to determine his child's future. He has been labeled irresponsible and uncaring; yet his participation has not been considered important enough to seek or to encourage by most agencies that developing programming for pregnant adolescent women and their children. Awareness of the unwed father's lack of status is reflected in the results of two small-scale surveys (Hendricks, 1980; Hendricks, Howard, & Caesar, 1981). Almost all of the young men surveyed were aware that they may need to turn to others for information and support, to help them cope more effectively with their position as out-of-wedlock fathers. Most of these young men recognized the need to discuss with others these types of issues. Although 95 per cent of the unwed fathers said they would be willing to go to a "teenage parenting agency," none of the respondents knew of any particular agency that provided this type of service for them.

The Decision to Keep or Place

There are three possible decisions when one is pregnant: to abort, to carry the child to term and keep it, and to carry the child to term and place it for adoption. Having carried the child to term, the mother has two alternatives: to keep it or to place it for adoption.

Although a very high percentage of nonrelative adopted children are born out-of-wedlock, only a small percentage of children born out-of-wedlock are adopted. Most such children are kept and raised by the unmarried mother and/or her family. Whatever the reasons, the recent trend has been for a greater proportion of unmarried mothers to keep their babies rather than surrendering them for adoption.

Adoption statistics have shown a consistent decline in the proportion of children born out of wedlock who are subsequently placed for adoption. A 1982 study of adoptions by the National Center for Health Statistics showed that before 1973 some 20 per cent of premarital white babies were released for adoption; by 1982 only some 12 per cent of such children were released. Whereas 0.7 per cent of premarital black children were released for adoption in 1973, this figure had fallen to 0.1 per cent by 1982 (Bachrach, 1986, p. 250). (See also Alan Guttmacher Institute, 1981, p. 27.)

In one study of decision making by 500 pregnant, single women, in only 5 per cent of the cases was the adoption decision ever considered: "Professional advice about adoption was almost never sought" (Bracken, Klerman, & Bracken, 1978). Only nine of the 153 study paricipants in one study (Klerman et al., 1982) sought professional advice about adoption. Within the delivery sub-group, only 1.3 per cent decided that they would "probably" relinquish their child, while only 2.6 per cent stated that they "definitely" would place the infant (p. 227). Among 533 adolescent mothers from England and Wales adoptive placement was considered by twenty-six (5%) and completed only by four (Simms and Smith, 1982 p. 43). (See also Miller, 1983.)

In response to a question about why adoption was not considered in their pregnancy decision making, most adolescents indicated they did not wish to go through the entire pregnancy only to 'give up' the infant (Klerman et al., 1982, p. 227).

Whereas many women who previously gave up the baby for adoption did so either because they could not care for it or did not want baby care to interfere with other life plans—education, career, marriage, travel—currently the same women would more likely obtain an abortion rather than give birth to a baby they did not want and were not planning to keep. Consequently a much greater percentage of the women who currently carry their children to term are likely to have decided that they want the child and can care for the child. It is not so much that a higher percentage of women are deciding to keep their children once born, but that fewer children destined to be given up for adoption are being born.

Abortion does everything adoption does for the single pregnant women—and more. It eliminates the risk of having the responsibility for care of a child in a single-parent family, it permits the continuation of education and career, and it eliminates the danger of reduced marriage possibilities and the negative sanctions, however attenuated, associated with unwed parenthood. In addition, abortion eliminates the inconvenience and danger of delivery and the trauma of having to give up a child carried to term. Adoption provides a way out of an unwanted brith; abortion provides a way out both of an unwanted pregnancy and of an unwanted birth.

Among adolescents, adoption is now more frequently perceived as an unfashionable, unacceptable cop-out. If the girl has decided to have the baby rather than having an abortion, there is a sense that she is obligated to care for the child. Adolescent mothers in Simms' and Smith's (1982) study who considered adoption but eventually rejected the idea said, "I just disagree with adoption; I don't believe a woman should have to go through such pain and then have to let her baby go"; "I didn't want to go through all that just to give it away", and "I think he deserved to know his own mother, seeing he'd never know his father" (p. 45).

The tendency to keep rather than to place the child receives additional impetus from the fact that an increasing percentage of children are growing up in single-parent homes. Having experienced this kind of childrearing context, the mother may be more likely to accept it as a viable possibility for her own child in rejecting adoption.

Diminished interest in adoption as an alternative to having the child and caring for it on the part of the mother is reinforced by failures on the part of those responsible for counseling the pregnant teenager in presenting adoption as an option for consideration. Mech (1986) found in a study of pregnancy counselors that "they have difficulty in initiating and discussing adoption with teen clients" (p. 556).

Research efforts have been devoted to determining the distinguishing characteristics differentiating the group of mothers keeping the child from those surrendering the child (Meyer et al., 1956; Jones et al., 1962; Yelloly, 1965, 1966; Gil, 1969; Festinger, 1971; Grow, 1979).

The factor of race is clearly associated with the decision to keep or relinquish the child. More white unmarried mothers give up their children for adoption as compared with black unmarried mothers. There is some controversy as to whether the decision of the black unmarried mother is freely made or a consequence of the more limited adoption opportunities available to black children.

Preference may have been shaped, too, by the historical antecedents of slave culture and subsequent rural living, both of which provide a tradition of extended family care of the black out-of-wedlock child in preference to giving the child up. Whatever the determining factors, research reveals that black unmarried mothers express a stronger preference for keeping their children than do white unmarried mothers. Shapiro (1970) found that one of the strongest and clearest differences in racial attitudes related to the adoption of the out-of-wedlock child: black unmarried women "heavily favored keeping children born out-of-wedlock" (p. 59).

The context in which the decision to keep or surrender the child for adoption is made has been changing rapidly as attitudes toward single parenthood change and as services for single parents change. Consequently, some of the earlier research on this question may not accurately reflect the more recent situation. A study of 210 white unmarried mothers in 1973–74 by Grow (1979) may be more relevant. Comparing those who kept their child with the limited number in the group who surrendered their child for adoption, Grow found, in contrast with earlier research, that there was no difference in the mental health functions of the two groups. The women who kept their children more often came from parental homes broken by divorce or separation, so that they had had some experience with single parenthood. They were more likely to be younger and less well educated than women who surrendered their child, knew the putative father longer and were more likely to maintain continuing contact with him, and lived with parents or relatives during pregnancy. There was, consequently, more assurance of a support system available to provide help in keeping the child. Fewer of the mothers who kept their child were attending school, and motherhood represented less of a change in life-style and career planning than was the case for mothers surrendering the child for adoption.

One of the few adolescent mothers to place her child in Simm and Smith's

(1982) study found herself in the type of circumstances described as typical for relinquishers:

> One young mother lived alone with her parents in a small terrace house with only an outside lavatory. She worked full-time in a textile factory, which she enjoyed, but the pay was low and she found money a problem. She said she had never intended to become pregnant (and) when she did, was very upset when she first thought she might be pregnant, and had considered adoption from that moment on. She had also, briefly, thought about abortion and discussed this with a friend who had informed her that it would "cost alot," so she had dropped the idea. (p. 46).

Timing of the Adoption Decision

The timing and firmness of the mother's decision are important variables. The sooner the mother decides, the sooner the agency can begin to make definite plans for disposition. If she decides upon adoption, the child can be placed in an adoptive home directly from the hospital in which he or she has been delivered. This reduces the possibility of discontinuity of mothering for the child, the problem of adjusting to a number of different mothers, and the trauma of separation after becoming adjusted to some mothering person.

It may be argued that an early decision is in the best interests of the mother as well. If giving up the child is an act of major psychic surgery, it might be less difficult before the mother builds a strong affectional relationship with the child. However, it is also argued that the mother needs some time in contact with the child to resolve whatever decision she has made. A hurried decision entails the risk of subsequent regret and of attempts to reverse the decision, with disruptive consequences for the adoptive parent and the child. Hence the firmness of the decision is as important as its promptness.

Perhaps a two-stage process is desirable: a tentative conclusion before the baby is born and a final ratification afterward.

The agency's principal tenet is to encourage flexibility in decision making, which permits each mother to come to her own decision in her own time. In general, research indicates that most mothers come to a firm, consistent decision either before or shortly after birth of the child. A study of 221 unmarried mothers showed that "four out of every five single mothers reached their decision within a week after confinement" (Triseliotis, 1969, p. 35).

Interviews with 116 mothers in Scotland who carried their out-of-wedlock children to term despite the availability of a publicly subsidized abortion program indicated that most of the mothers decided they wanted to keep the child from the time they realized they were pregnant (Hopkinson, 1976, p. 33). For some, this was a consequence of their continued relationship with the putative father; for some, guilt and a sense of responsibility toward the child were factors. For most of the mothers, however, the decision was based on their emotional involvement with the child and a desire to be a mother to the child. If they had given any consideration to adoption as an alternative outcome, it was not self-initiated but in response to parental pressure. Pannor *et al.* (1971) and Bowerman *et al.* (1966) also found that the women they studied had also made an early decision.

The factors that appear to be related to the decision to place or keep the baby and the findings regarding the timing and the consistency of the decision feed into each other. The decision to place or keep the child is most strongly associated with situational circumstances—age, educational level, socioeconomic position—

which were assessable even before birth of the child and act as principal constraints on the mother, limiting her options. The emotional relationship with the child and attachment to the child are not generally as important a factor in the decision. Realistically recognizing and evaluating her situation even before delivery, the mother generally comes to a decision about what she can do and has to do. Contact with the child only infrequently results in a change of decision. Thus Yelloly (1965, 1966) found that of 160 unmarried mothers, 68 per cent made a decision very early in the pregnancy—a decision to which they held with consistency and upon which they finally acted. In most instances, the decision was based on strong objective considerations, such as the presence of other children of the mother, the married status of the putative father, and the attitude of the mother's parents.

In follow-up interviews with unmarried mothers who kept their children, Reed and Latimer (1962) found that "72 percent of all mothers decided before the birth of the baby to keep the baby." Most were lower-class nonwhites. However, more than "half of the middle-class girls did not decide to keep the baby until after the birth of the baby" (p. 90). Mothers who had few choices made a decision early; mothers with more options made the decision later. The research further notes that mothers with prolonged ambivalence and strong conflicts about the decision are apt to be less emotionally stable and ultimately more likely to keep the child. This finding would suggest that these mothers are less responsible to the constraints of external reality and act more in response to internal emotional needs.

Of interest to social workers is the mother's perception of who helped her make the decision. In the overwhelming percentage of instances, the mothers studied by Bowerman *et al.* (1966) said they turned to their parents for help—most frequently to their own mothers. Female relatives (sisters, aunts, grandmothers) were also frequently consulted: "The alleged father is brought into these considerations relatively rarely . . . [and] it is very clear that the counsel of physicians, social workers, and other professionals (attorneys, clergymen, teachers) is sought by (or 'urged upon') but a small fraction of the respondents, almost all of whom are white" (pp. 197–99). Only about 1 per cent indicated that a social worker had been most important in influencing the decision. It thus appears that in most instances, the caseworker is faced with helping the mother to confirm and implement a decision rather than helping the mother to make it. Raynor (1971) came to the same conclusion in a study of British unwed mothers: 70 per cent of the mothers made their decision before the baby was born. Fewer than two out of five had discussed their decision with a social worker before making it, although the social worker was instrumental in implementing a plan that had already been made.

Stating the data another way, however, accentuates the service need. The studies cited earlier show that 20–30 per cent of the unwed mothers are undecided about their decision, often up to and beyond the birth of the baby. It is this group—a sizable group in terms of numbers—who need and may welcome the help of the social worker in clarifying a difficult, significant decision.

Of interest to social workers is the fact that seeing the child and caring for the child after birth made the decision to give up the child easier for some but more difficult for most of the mothers studied. The preference was to make a firm decision and act on it as early as possible. Most of the mothers indicated that delaying the final implementation of the decision created conflict for them.

Social Service Programs for the Young Unmarried Parent

The mother who keeps her child takes her place in the community along with all other single mothers who are rearing their children without benefit of a husband-father, because of death, desertion, divorce, or separation. The problems encountered by the single parent who comes to single parenthood through an out-of-wedlock birth are not significantly different from those encountered by other single parents. The services required by the unwed mother who keeps her child are, in essence, those required by all single parents: income maintenance, help with housing, day care, vocational education, job referral, help in finding adult companionship, help in making contacts with eligible males, and help in finding satisfying leisure activity. Ultimately these mothers do face a special difficult problem: explaining to the child the whereabouts of the father.

Only occasionally, as in AFDC application or housing project application, is any distinction made between out-of-wedlock single parenthood and other kinds of single parenthood, to the disadvantage of the former. But in general, public policies and socioeconomic conditions helpful to any single-parent family headed by a woman are also helpful to the unmarried mother who keeps her child. Here, as in adoption, the significant factor that differentiates this family from other single-parent families headed by a woman lies in the nature of the genesis of the particular family. Once past genesis, however, the essential points of similarity between all single-parent families headed by a woman are overwhelmingly greater than any differences.

The unmarried mother who receives service from a social agency is the exception rather than the rule. A 1960 nationwide study concluded that "about one out of six mothers who have illegimate children in a year receive service either in public or voluntary agencies near the time of the pregnancy" (Adams, 1962, p. 43). The younger the unmarried mother, the more likely she is to have contact with a social agency. White unmarried mothers are more likely to make contact with voluntary agencies; nonwhite mothers, with a local department of public assistance. A disproportionate amount of the total available social service time and energy has been directed toward white girls above the poverty level who are interested in placing their out-of-wedlock child for adoption (Rashbaum et al., 1963 Shyne & Schroeder, 1978).

Because many unmarried mothers, although needing such service, either may not know of its availability or may be reluctant to use it, some states require hospitals to report all illegitimate births to the local department of public welfare. A social worker then visits the mother, informs her of the services available, and helps her to decide whether or not she wants to use them.

Wisconsin requires that all hospitals "report illegitimate pregnancies" to the State Division of Family Services, "so that social service might be offered the mother." Despite these efforts, the four-year period of 1973 through 1976 showed a decline in unmarried mothers' use of social services—from 67 per cent to 41 per cent. The younger unmarried mothers were more likely to accept service. By far the greatest majority of those accepting service were being aided by a county social-service department; only 15 per cent receiving service from a voluntary agency (Wisconsin Department of Health and Social Services, 1977).

Historically, the unmarried mother who places her child for adoption has received primary attention from child welfare agencies. Only in instances in which young women who keep their children fail to provide sufficiently for them has the agency, primarily through its protective service function, become involved. A nationwide survey of child welfare clients (Shyne & Shroeder, 1978) found that "despite pervasive concern about very early childbearing and its attendant problems, only 11,000 children (less than 1%) were reported as receiving service primarily because their mothers were teenagers" (p. 140). In recent years, however, it has been more widely recognized that young single parents can benefit in a variety of additional ways from the services of the social worker. It has become evident that with sufficient outreach and appropriate provision to meet the highly varied needs of these young clients, many serious parenting problems can be avoided.

For many unmarried mothers who keep their child, the critical period is likely to come at the end of the first year. By then, it is clear that some of the more optimistic plans are not going to be achieved; the romanticism of parenthood has worn off and the confining drudgery of reality has become apparent; the good intentions of support from parents, relatives, friends, and the child's father have worn thin or have been exhausted and possibilities for real change appear more limited.

More adequate financial assistance, child care, and housing are among the most frequently identified unmet needs of this group. Adolescents have available to them a very limited range of options in terms of obtaining financial support. Given their interrupted high school career and the extremely poor job market for them, teenagers find it very difficult to find employment that will allow for self-support and a sufficient income for an infant. Without employment opportunities, adolescents must turn to their families or to public welfare in order to survive. It is estimated that about 60 per cent of all out-of-wedlock children eventually receive public aid at one time or another (Moore & Caldwell, 1976). As of 1975, over half (56%) of women receiving AFDC were teenagers at the time their first child was born. Moore and Wertheimer (1984) predict, "Welfare roles in 1990 will continue to include a disproportionate share of teenage mothers, since 79% of 20–24-year-olds and 52% of 25–29-year-olds projected to be AFDC recipients in 1990 will have become mothers during their teen years" (p. 286). Research carried out by SRI International (cited in Cartoff, 1982), assessing the extent of government spending for teenage families, estimates that the federal expenditures will reach 8.3 billion dollars over the twenty-year period during which young women are raising children born in 1976. For each of the 442,000 out-of-wedlock babies born to adolescent mothers in that year, the federal government will spend an average of $18,710.

Teenage utilization patterns for AFDC are similar to those found among older AFDC recipients. Teenagers try to rely on employment and marital resources and turn to AFDC only intermittently, during crisis periods, particularly when faced with unemployment. Long-term chronic AFDC dependency is not a common pattern for this group (Burden & Klerman, 1984).

In some states, AFDC eligibility is structured so that the teenager receives a higher grant when she moves out of her parental home. In her study, Cartoof (1982) found that some 70 per cent of the forty-five teenagers she talked with moved out of their home within a three-year period, "many in order to become eligible to receive full welfare benefits" (p. 272). However, in doing this, the teenager also cut herself off from personal assistance and child care that family members routinely provided. Regulations mandating that she name the father of her child and procedures for ensuring that he contributes to the infant's upkeep also create greater barriers between her and this source of support. Many of these young fathers are, themselves, in difficult financial straits, and the amount that they are expected to pay for the baby's care may seem excessive to them. Given their erratic job opportunities, limited income, and competing obligations to their own families, these young men who are willing to provide sporadically in small ways for the baby may feel they cannot handle the demands made by public welfare requirements (Burden, Klerman, 1984; Rivera-Casale, Klerman & Manela, 1984).

Analysis of the support networks available to 122 Hispanic and white pregnant teens (deAndra & Becerra, 1984) suggests that mothers are the primary source of caring, guidance, and practical help in the form of child care for these women, particularly when they are unmarried. Husbands and boyfriends provide an additional, highly significant, personal and child-care resource. Among this group, girlfriends are not as central, and their significance to the young mother weakens over time, especially for the Hispanic sample. Wise and Grossman (1980), studying the experiences of thirty young mothers, discovered that two-thirds had a stable relationship with the putative father, one that had lasted more than a year before they became pregnant. For 87 per cent, this relationship was maintained throughout the pregnancy. Having an involved father was associated with less protracted labor and greater involvement of mother and child six weeks after birth. However, young women who were without this type of support did not feel more negatively about the pregnancy or their child, once it was born.

Although many unwed mothers date and continue to be sexually active, loneliness and social isolation are still a problem, particularly for those who live independently and do not work. Employment provides meaningful social contacts as well as income. The desire for counseling and group services is highest among nonworking mothers in independent living situations (Clapp & Raab, 1978).

Multiservice Centers for the Pregnant Adolescent and the Young Unmarried Mother

During the 1960s, there was a rapid development of comprehensive, multiservice, interdisciplinary programs for single, pregnant women. Whereas there were only thirty-five of these centers in 1968, there were 375 in 1975. The staff of these programs initially sought to provide health, educational, and social services for pregnant, school-aged girls living at home. Program coordinators were particularly concerned with preventing school dropout and encouraging those adolescents who had already left school to complete their education. Today, these programs are equally concerned with extending service to young women who have decided to keep and raise their child. In meeting the needs of this group, program objectives also include assistance in completing necessary developmental tasks of adolescence while improving overall parenting abilities (Salguero, 1980). These programs typically draw upon the resources of many community agencies. Frequently, the local Board of Education coordinates its efforts with the local Department of Health, the local Department of Public Welfare, and with private social service providers.

One pioneer program of this nature—the Webster School in the District of Columbia—was organized in 1963 (Howard, 1968c).

Like the anti-poverty programs, comprehensive service programs such as the Webster School were designed to overcome the personal and institutional barriers which confronted pregnant adolescents who, for the most part, were low-income and Black. In practice, this meant that the young women received extended prenatal care to decrease medical risk; continued schooling to achieve economic self-sufficiency; and emotional support to sustain them during a potential period of crisis [Aries, 1980, p. 140].

The program offers educational, health, and welfare services provided by an interdisciplinary team of teachers, psychologists, social workers, doctors, public health nurses, and nutritionists.

Another such program, the Oakland, California, Interagency Cyesis Program, involves the participation of the departments of welfare, health, education, and recreation; the YWCA; community action groups; and voluntary agencies. Through such projects, the girls continue their high school studies with teachers provided by the local board of education. In addition, there are special classes in child care, health care during pregnancy, and home economics. Individual and group counseling is provided by social workers, who also help the girls make use of local social-agency programs. Maternity care is provided by health personnel.

Whereas some of these programs were newly established at the behest of community groups concerned about the plight of pregnant teenagers, others were organized by agencies who had long provided service to this group but had done so primarily through the provision of residential facilities, such as maternity homes. In order to better meet changing client needs, these agencies substituted comprehensive outpatient programs for their residential model (Aries, 1980). Although many of these programs offer educational services in alternative settings, some have attempted to maintain the teenager in her regular academic milieu. Some agencies have offered services to the putative father and the girl's own family. However, few of these programs provide continuing contact with the mother and child. Most girls after they give birth, return to their regular school setting (Wright, 1966; Boykin, 1968; Goodman, 1968; Howard, 1968a; 1968b; Osofsky, 1968; Zober, 1969; McMurray, 1970; McGee, 1982).

The most comprehensive programs provide services in vocational counseling, training, and placement; prenatal, postpartum, and pediatric care; birth control counseling and services; abortion counseling and services; adoption counseling and services; legal counseling and services; casework and group work; psychological testing and psychiatric treatment; child development; parent and consumer education; financial assistance and budget counseling; leisure-time activities; day-care counseling and services; and housing counseling and services (McGee, 1982, pp. 21–22).

Such services were developed in response to a growing sensitivity to the educational consequences of teenage pregnancy. Many school systems had previously required that the pregnant teenager leave school. Separated from her peers if expelled during the pregnancy and having lost a year of school, the girl is understandably reluctant to return to school after the birth of the child. As a result, most of the girls never completed their education and were trapped in a cycle of low-paying jobs and limited income. School systems did attempt to provide continuing education for the pregnant teenager through instruction in the family home or through educational programs in the maternity home, but such resources were available to only a limited number of girls.

Pregnant students now have the option in many school districts either to remain in their regular school program or to transfer to a special school program for pregnant women. Federal government policy withholds federal funds from any school that discriminates against pregnant teenagers by expelling them. The objective of the government is to help such women complete their education so that they can obtain better employment and achieve self-support. A recent survey suggests that academic institutions have made three different types of programs available to students (Zellman, 1982). "Inclusive curriculum programs" offer a full range of academic subjects to pregnant adolescents who do not attend regular classes with their peers. "Supplementary curriculum programs" are offered to adolescents who continue to receive academic credit in their regular junior or senior high school but who also enroll in extracurricular courses on child care and other topics, for which they receive academic credit. Finally, "noncurricular programs" offer counseling, medical care, and referral services to participants outside of the regular academic milieu; no academic credit is offered for participation.

As increasing numbers of adolescents have chosen to keep their babies, social service professionals have devoted more attention to the provision of services for this group following the birth of the child. Because many of these young women drop out of school, either before their infant is born or soon after, programs have paid particular attention to helping these teenagers engage in longer-term educational and financial planning for themselves. In addition, enhancement of parenting skills is a typical service objective. Like pregnant teenagers, adolescent mothers frequently need assistance with health, housing, and other personal and interpersonal difficulties (Cartoof, 1979; Sung & Rothrock, 1980; DeRose, 1982). McGee (1982) describes one exemplary program of this type:

> The program is located in a former elementary school that also houses a family resource center and a preschool, both of which serve the surrounding community. The school provides transportation and attracts about one-third of the school-aged mothers in the district, plus a small number of fathers; in a year, this is about one hundred students, although only half of these students are in attendance at any one time. The program includes academic education, counseling, social services, classes in parenting, in family health, in career development, and in job preparation, health care by cooperating agencies, subsidized work experience for Comprehensive Employment and Training Act (CETA) eligible students, and child care in an infant-toddler center that also serves out-of-school, employed teenagers. Special evening programs for young couples or grandparents are offered each month. The staff is small and does a lot of team teaching and collective program development (p. 36).

The provision of child care for teenagers who are pursuing educational or employment training opportunities is a particularly critical aspect of these services. Some agencies have also developed specialized foster care services or supervised living arrangements for young mothers who have no stable home or who cannot stay with their family, but who are not, as yet, prepared to live on their own (Benas, 1975; Kreech, 1975; Heger, 1977; Palmer, 1981; Sisto, 1985).

In multiple service centers social workers are responsible for the coordination and planning of counseling services, developing working relationships with community health and welfare agencies, and formulating effective referral procedures. They also assist with interpretation of the program to the general public and develop outreach efforts to inform and interest eligible clients in the use of the service. In addition, they formulate social data record forms and maintain appropriate social data records, recruit, train, and supervise volunteers. Social workers are frequently responsible for providing clinical services to the adolescent. These include family therapy, individual and group counseling for the teenager herself, and individual and group counseling for the putative father (Palmer,

1981). Frequently social workers provide group programming as well. The group format is considered to be a particulary relevant one for clients of this age, an especially powerful tool for reaching out to them (Barclay, 1969; Johnson, 1969; Bracken, 1971; Danforth et al., 1971; Kolodny & Reilly, 1972; Bolton, 1980).

Taking responsibility for individual and group sessions with adolescents may prove challenging for the worker. Teenagers may be difficult, evasive clients, who repeatedly miss counseling sessions or sit mute and unresponsive once they arrive. O'Leary, Shore, and Wieder (1984) comment.

> One standardized interview question was, "What do you imagine it will be like being a mother?" The response often was a shrug and "I don't really think about it." In short, workers received little discernible feedback—except the members' continued attendance. In the home visits that were part of the program, workers found that the prospective grandparents would often engage in decisions and planning for the delivery, while the adolescent ostensibly watched television. There were obvious issues about changing family roles, but most of the adolescents did not touch on conflicts with their parents during the pregnancy. They responded differently to individual therapy, most only tolerating sporadic sessions and some more comfortable talking with the worker on the telephone rather than in person [p. 300].

The authors point out that avoidance behaviors reflect the teenager's attempt to monitor and dampen the intensity of the impact of this material. The authors also note that the unwed mother integrates much of what they have heard from the worker only in the final months of pregnancy or after the baby is born.

Follow-up Studies Single Parents and the Out-of-Wedlock Child

A number of consequences supposedly follow from becoming a teenage single parent. Becoming a parent to a child out of wedlock in adolescence reduces the options available to a young woman:

> The girl who has an illegitimate child at the age of 16 suddenly has 90 percent of her life's script written for her. She will probably drop out of school; even if someone else in her family helps to take care of the baby, she will probably not be able to find a steady job that pays enough to provide for herself and her child, she may feel impelled to marry someone she might not otherwise have chosen. Her life chances are few [Campbell, 1968, p. 238].

Adolescence is a time for experimenting with and establishing an identity; early parenthood imposes an identity. Some of the most significant life choices, for which adolescence should be the preparation, are prematurely preempted or foreclosed, choices relating to a career, a mate, and the decision to become a parent. "Unscheduled parenthood" thus has the effect of accelerated "premature status transition, propelling people into positions (parenthood) they are unready or unprepared to assume, and forcing them to relinquish statuses that they currently enjoy (adolescence)" (Furstenberg, 1976, p 4).

The consequence is a higher risk of failure to complete education; premature entrance into the job market, with access only to repetitive, uninteresting jobs that pay marginal wages; early, rapid childbearing; and limitations on the normal opportunities for social development.

The empirical research seems to support the hypothesis. Follow-up studies of adolescent unmarried parents show that they were behind their peers in terms of educational achievement, employment and career opportunities, and income (Furstenberg, 1976; Trussell, 1976; Moore & Waite, 1977; Card & Wise, 1978; Moore & Burt, 1982). Perhaps the most vulnerable of adolescent mothers are those who are sixteen to seventeen years old. When teenagers become pregnant in early adolescence, parents are more likely to encourage and assist them to remain in school and complete their education. When they become pregnant at eighteen or older, these young women can rely on their maturity and better educational attainment to help enhance their earning power. Sixteen-and-seventeen-year-olds, however, are likely to drop out without completing their school degree. Many eventually have additional children, marry, and divorce, and then face the extremely difficult task of raising several children as a single parent (Burden & Klerman, 1984, p. 13).

Two things need to be noted. First, it is not clear that the disadvantaged outcomes are primarily related to out-of-wedlock pregnancies. Many of these adolescents were doing poorly in school prior to the pregnancy and might have dropped out in any case; many came from disadvantaged backgrounds that presented difficulties, even without a pregnancy, for successfully completing the normative sequence of tasks. Second, many adolescent mothers do not conform to the typical "outcome." Furstenberg (1976) says in his analysis of lower-class black unwed mothers, "One of the most impressive findings was the diversity of responses to a common event" (the out-of-wedlock pregnancy); "The outcome of the five-year follow-up was enormously varied" (p.218).

There have been studies that are concerned with what happens to the mother and the out-of-wedlock child who stay together (Reed & Latimer, 1962; Pakter & Nelson, 1965; Sauber, 1965; Wright, 1965; Crumidy & Jacobziner, 1966; Oppel, 1969; Corrigan, 1970; Sauber & Corrigan, 1970; Crellin, Pringle & West, 1971). The results generally are a tribute to the heterogeneity of the unmarried mother group and a confirmation of the fact that no stereotype is applicable to this group as Furstenberg validly noted.

As Sauber and Corrigan (1970) say, "although these women shared the common experience of bearing a child out-of-wedlock and rearing that child, their lives as mothers followed many different paths" (p. 145). Many get married and merge into the two-parent family group; many remain single. Many have additional out-of-wedlock children; some do not. Some are employed full-time and self-supporting; some are employed part-time and receive supplementary help from relatives; some are wholly supported by relatives (including continuing contributions from the putative father); some are supported by public assistance. Some are living with relatives; some with friends; many alone. For most mothers, recreational and social life and involvement in community activity are limited and meager, but most resume their place among an accepting group of friends and relatives. A few have continued their education or have received further vocational training; most, however, have not. A substantial minority face financial difficulty and live in substandard housing. A very high percentage indicated that given the opportunity, they would decide once again to keep the child (Bernstein, 1966, 1971).

In almost all instances, teenage parents appear to be reasonably adequate, concerned mothers who are doing a creditable job rearing their children. Very few of these children are placed in foster homes or with relatives; even fewer are neglected or abused.

One of the earliest follow-up studies of unmarried mothers, which involved interviews with fifty-four women some eight years after their confinement, concluded that "adoption was not necessarily the only desirable solution, as evidenced by the fact that some mothers who kept their children seemed to have done well by both the children and themselves" (Levy, 1955, p. 33).

A study by Reed and Latimer published in 1962 reviewed the situation for 118 mothers, both black and white. Physical and psychological examinations of the children showed the largest majority of them to be "developing normally physically, mentally, and emotionally" (p. 107). Similarly Wright's (1965) interview study of eight unmarried mothers who kept their babies concludes that "contrary to the original hypothesis, a majority of the children were judged to be faring well" (p. 52).

The childrearing practices of unmarried mothers who keep their children are not essentially different from those of comparative samples of low-income black and white mothers, although unmarried mothers are more concerned about restricting aggressive behavior and more likely to stress the importance of doing well in school (Corrigan, 1970).

Oppel (1969) compared the care and development of black illegitimate children with a matched group of legitimate children. The findings did not support the "contentions that mothers of illegitimate children are more likely to give poor care to their children than are mothers of legitimate children" (p. 133). Nor was there any significant difference in development of the two groups of children.

A careful follow-up study of unmarried mothers who kept their babies was conducted by Sauber for the Community Council of New York. The study reported on the adjustment of mother and child one and a half years after birth (Sauber, 1965) and then again six years after birth (Sauber & Corrigan, 1970). Some 90 per cent of the 205 women still in the study when the child was six were black or Puerto Rican. A comparison between these children and legitimate children in the community studied by the Manhattan Survey of Psychiatric Impairment of Urban Children showed that they were essentially similar in emotional functioning (Sauber & Corrigan, 1970, p. 138).

The report echoes the implications of the studies already cited—that "more recognition should be given to the *strengths* of one-parent families rather than too hasty an attribution of pathology to them" (p. 45). The report concludes:

> The study findings clearly challenge many myths about women who have had a child out of wedlock. For the great majority, this experience has not been the beginning of a life of promiscuity, instability, and dependency. Although some have suffered, the majority have coped very well, pursuing their lives in different ways, with the result that, six years after their first child was born, they have, in most respects, blended into the general population of mothers and children and exhibit the wide range of life styles and life situations found among families in the population generally. Perhaps the greatest service that could be rendered to this group is that they no longer be labeled "unwed mothers" but that they be viewed as parents, often single parents, of young children, and that they be provided with the respect and the social and economic supports necessary for them to carry out these roles [p. 157].

Grow (1979) studied the lives of 181 white, unmarried mothers as contrasted with a matched sample of 259 married mothers over a three-year period. At the end of this time, both the health of the unmarried mothers and of the out-of-wedlock child are good and few children had experienced disruption in the continuity of care. Despite negative effects of early nonmarital childbearing on education, employment and income, the children born out of wedlock and cared for by these mothers did not seem to be seriously disadvantaged during the first three years.

A study in Scotland of 116 unwed mothers who kept their child showed the great resourcefulness and determination of these mothers against considerable odds (Hopkinson, 1976). Coming from disadvantaged family backgrounds and having left school at the minimum legal age, they provided good care to their children on limited incomes. They requested social work assistance during crisis periods, and the help provided was in the nature of practical assistance.

Even the younger group of teenage mothers seem to be doing reasonably well. A follow-up study of 144, twelve- to fifteen-year-old mothers found them rearing their children satisfactorily. Most were receiving AFDC, and most continued to receive, and to need, considerable help from their own families (Miller, 1983).

Examination of feelings toward their babies among thirty adolescent mothers (Wise & Grossman, 1980) suggested that these young women had a generally positive attitude toward their pregnancy, and, once the infant was born, they sustained a relatively high level of reciprocity with their babies (p. 460). Those young women who tended to be more emotionally involved with their pregnancy tended to have more realistic perceptions of the baby and to attach more effectively to the infant, once it was born. Infant characteristics also played a role in development of this relationship. It was the larger babies and those with fewer neonatal complications to whom mothers responded more effectively.

Contrary to these generally positive findings, however, are the results of a careful follow-up study in England that compared the development of out-of-wedlock children placed in adoptive homes with the progress made by out-of-wedlock children who remained in a single-parent home with the mother. On the basis of most of the criteria employed in the study, the adoptive child's adjustment and development were in advance of his or her nonadopted out-of-wedlock peer (Crellin, Pringle, & West, 1971).

A five-year follow-up of children of adolescent unmarried mothers showed that they were "less well equipped in terms of cognitive skills than their counterparts in the other samples" (Furstenberg, 1976, p. 214). Results of other studies confirm the "small but significant effects" of maternal age on the child's IQ" (Baldwin & Cain, 1981). However, both social class and availability of other adult caretakers for the child can attenuate the impact of the mother's young age (Simkins, 1984, p. 45; Makinson, 1985, p. 138). Moreover, the age of the mother has no dramatic effect on her child's intellectual capacities. "While statistically significant, the effect on measures of aptitude is small and may be trivial in terms of later achievement" (Baldwin & Cain, 1981, p. 270). Adolescent mothers do appear to be more attuned to developing their infant's and young child's motor abilities and to focus less on stimulation of auditory or visual capacities in their children. As a result, speech delay is common among these children. Teenage mothers can benefit from specific training to enhance their parenting capacities in this respect (Wise & Grossman, 1980; Bierman & Streett, 1982).

In the area of socioemotional development, the impact of adolescent mothering is much less clear-cut. Furstenberg (1976) found "no clear indication that children of adolescent parents are more socially maladjusted" (p. 214). Reviewing a number of studies in this area, Baldwin and Cain (1981) conclude:

> Overall, the effect of the mother's age on her child's social and emotional development is not as clear as it is on her child's cognitive development. It does seem that when an effect of young maternal age was present, it was negative and often was not

evident until the child was nearing school age. Again, evidence suggests that the effect does not result from the mother's age at birth directly, but rather is transmitted through other factors associated with early childbearing, such as educational and economic disadvantage and greater likelihood of marital breakup [p. 271].

Teenagers are less well informed about child development than their more mature counterparts (Vukelich & Kliman, 1985).

Evaluation

Effective assistance to the unwed, pregnant adolescent helps her make an appropriate decision with regard to the future of her infant, helps her learn to avoid becoming pregnant in the future, ensures that she will continue to deal with many other adolescent tasks in a healthy and productive manner, validates her need to become a productive adult through her choice of educational and occupational goals, and, in instances where she chooses to keep her child and to raise it herself, assists her in developing a meaningful relationship with her infant, one that allows her child to grow in a healthy and happy way. As we have indicated, a number of different kinds of programs have been designed to help adolescents achieve these goals. Some programmatic efforts, such as family planning or abortion services, may work with the adolescent in one or two of these areas; other, more comprehensive programs, try to help the teenager deal with any of the particular issues that she may face.

Family-planning services have been especially concerned with evaluating their ability to reduce adolescent pregnancy among the population to whom they make their programs available. Although the evidence from different studies suggests conflicting findings with regard to this issue (Moore & Burt, 1982), a recent, more sophisticated national analysis concludes that these programs can help teens avoid unwanted pregnancy. Forrest, Hermalin, and Henshaw (1981), comparing service delivery patterns with fertility rates between 1970 and 1975, conclude that "for both whites and non-whites, areas with greater increases between 1970 and 1975 in the percentage of adolescents enrolled in family planning clinics had larger decreases in teenage birth rates between 1970 and 1976" (p. 113). The researchers estimate that 1.07 births were avoided for every ten adolescent white participants in the program, whereas 0.9 births were avoided for every ten nonwhite participants. This amounted to 82,000 white infants and 32,000 black infants who could have been born, but who were not, because their teenage mothers took advantage of contraceptive services offered by these clinics. Chamie and Henshaw (1981) estimate that for every federal dollar that has been expended for family-planning services, a savings of two dollars is realized in health and welfare expenditures that would have been provided to the woman and her infant in the following year. The authors state that these savings are even greater for teenage program participants.

One of the better known of the comprehensive counseling programs, the St. Paul Maternal and Infant Care (MIC) Project, has been effective in reducing fertility rates in the school in which it is located by 56 per cent within a four year period. Over a three-year time span, utilization of clinic services rose in the senior high school from one-third to 75 per cent of the student body. The program also claims a very high rate of contraceptive continuation, owing in part to regular follow-up and to "consistency of staff offering personalized services with guaranteed confidentiality; accessibility of free services; and provision of educational and social services prior to the medical encounter, including involvement of the male partner and parents, if the patient so desires" (Edwards et al., 1981, p. 380).

A study of the effectiveness of different approaches to the treatment of unwed mothers in a traditional child-welfare agency concluded that the methods "felt to be most effective are environmental manipulation, both direct and indirect, and sustaining, i.e., offering encouragement and reassurance and fewer instances in which reflective discussion or consideration is involved" (Power & De Chirico, 1969, p. 8). The research included the random assignment of ninety-one single pregnant women to one of three different treatment conditions: tangible environmental supportive service, intensive individual casework services, or intensive group counseling. Differences in functioning at the end of treatment were assessed by a casework research interviewer one month, six months, one year, and two years following delivery and were compared with an assessment of functioning at intake based on interviews and psychological tests. Although environmental manipulation and sustaining were most successful, service generally did not effect any change in most clients: "Relatively few girls have grown through the experience. . . . The large majority resume their previous pattern of functioning as well as previous modes of adaptation" (Power & De Chirico, 1969, p. 8).

Another study conducted in a similar kind of agency obtained its principal data from the unmarried mothers, whose responses to a checklist indicated that they perceived the agency as offering important services:

> They confirmed that their caseworkers had helped them get through the experience as soon as possible, had helped them keep their pregnancies secret, had helped them know how to answer questions about their absence from the community during their pregnancies, had helped them obtain vocational guidance, had helped those clients who wanted to keep their babies to make a suitable plan to do so, had helped those who wanted to place their child for adoption to sign the permanent surrender, had helped school-age girls get back into school and had helped some of the young girls to get back into their own homes [O'Rourke, 1968, p. 473].

Some 32 per cent of the respondents indicated that they had been helped by casework services to develop a greater understanding of themselves and their behavior.

Some recent research on effectiveness of counseling services for pregnant teens has assessed its impact in abortion agencies. One study randomly assigned fifty-three women, aged sixteen to thirty, to either a short-term or more extended therapeutic program. Extended counseling service were more effective helping these women obtain a sense of direction in their lives and enhancing their sense of self-worth (Rutledge, 1985, p. 226). Reviewing a variety of studies of this type, however, Sachdev (1985) notes that there is an "absence of a consensus among investigators on the effectiveness of counseling programs for abortion patients" (pp. 250–251).

A comprehensive program of services (casework, group work, medical and educational services) to a group of 240 teenage unmarried mothers and their families was evaluated by Bedger (1969). Five key areas of functioning—the client's relationship with her family; her relationship with the putative father, the adequacy of her plans for the baby, her plans for her own future, and environmental stress—were rated at intake by the interviewer-caseworker and at closing by the caseworker assigned to the case. The rating at closing showed greatest improvement in the client's relationships with her own parents and in the general family-interaction. Overall, "55 percent of the cases studied were rated [at closing] more positive in functioning on the five areas utilized. In 34.6 percent of the cases change was negative and in 9.6 percent of the cases there was no evidence of change" (p. 43). But as there was no control group, it is not clear that the positive results were ascribable to the comprehensive program offered.

A postpartum intensive group-therapy project involving forty-seven weekly sessions for a limited number of unwed mothers showed participants manifesting a "significant increase in self-esteem," improved impulse control, and increased feminine identification as a result of the experience. Assessment was made on the basis of social work and psychiatric interviews and psychological tests before and after treatment. By contrast, a control group of nonparticipant unwed mothers showed fewer positive changes during this period (Busfield et al., 1969).

There have been a few serious attempts to evaluate multiservice programs. One such evaluation of the Webster School indicated that it was very successful in its principal aim of continuing the girls' education throughout their pregnancy so that they were able to return after childbirth to the regular school at the same level as their nonpregnant peers. It was successful in bringing the girls under prenatal care early in the pregnancy and ensured their receiving such care consistently. As a consequence "the proportion of low-birth-weight infants, the infant mortality rates, and other indices were better for Webster girls than for various Negro populations in the District" (Howard, 1968c, p. 40). However, "repetition of pregnancy among the girls was not reduced as a result of participation in the Webster program. Many girls had second babies within a relatively short period of time" (Howard, 1968c, p. 57; see also McGee, 1982, p. 58).

A six-year study compared the outcomes of school-aged pregnant women who were receiving comprehensive care programs with a control group matched for age and socioeconomic status who received only obstetric clinic service with no continuity of care (Klerman & Jekel, 1975). The children of mothers in the comprehensive care program were more likely to be full-term and healthier newborns. For at least the first two years of service, more of the experimental group completed high school.

At least on a short-term basis, multiservice programs have achieved the greater probability of return to school after childbirth, an improved health outcome for mother and child, and a modest decrease in the likelihood of a second out-of-wedlock pregnancy (U.S. DHHS, 1980; Sung & Rothrock, 1980). Experiences of one program that began operation in Boston in 1973 (Cartoof, 1978, 1979) are typical. As of 1978, the program had been influential in encouraging 80 per cent of pregnant young women who had been served to return to school. However, half of this group subsequently dropped out within the following two years. Some of these young women either eventually completed their education by obtaining a GED; others began employment. The program was highly effective in convincing participants that birth control was important. Of the total group of sixty-seven girls studied, twenty-nine subsequently became pregnant once again, although only fourteen eventually carried their child to term (Cartoof, 1979, pp. 677–679).

An evaluation of the impact of the Educational Services for School-Age Parents Program (ESSP) that is offered to teenagers in New Brunswick, New Jersey (Bennett & Bardon, 1977), compared the experiences of eighty-eight ESSP participants and their ninety-eight children with those of thirty young single mothers and their thirty-four children living in a nearby community. Program clients made greater use of maternity clinic services, tended to remain in school more often, particularly after the baby was born, and had fewer abortions or miscarriages than the control group mothers. However, the research found no evidence that parents in this program were better informed about the developmental needs of their children or that they treated their children differently (approaching toilet training in a different way, or providing their children with such things as immunizations) (pp. 675–676). Assessing the effects of school-aged programs for young mothers in Utah, Bell, Casto, and Daniels (1983) also find that participants were more likely to be employed or in college and less likely to be on AFDC than were their nonprogram counterparts. Participants were also less likely to be referred for child abuse or neglect than were the control group mothers.

Some research assessing the impact of services for adolescent mothers has focused more specifically on the program's ability to improve parent–child relationships and to help parents avoid poor childrearing habits. Roosa (1984) evaluated thirty-one program participants from three school-based programs in Arizona, measuring their knowledge and attitudes at two different points in time. The author found that program involvement helped teenagers learn about the reproductive process and obtain important knowledge about child development. The researcher was more concerned with the program's failure to improve feelings of maternal satisfaction or to help adolescents obtain higher scores on a measure that assessed "encouragement of positive interaction versus hostility towards children" (p. 661). He reasoned that knowledge change that is unaccompanied by changes in attitudes may not produce alterations in behavior toward the child.

Evaluation of the impact of a more intensive program offered to young mothers in their own homes suggests a more positive outcome. These parents were taught more effective ways to stimulate and communicate with their infants and were provided with basic information about their babies' nutritional and health needs (Nuehring et al., 1983). Research on forty-one program participants suggests that they had improved in both their knowledge and in their actual ability to interact more positively with their children.

Numerous researchers have raised questions about whether programs that have impact on a short-term basis continue to affect the lives of young mothers and their children. Most of the research to date thus far has assessed immediate consequences of program participation for clients. Moore and Burt (1982), for example, point out that most studies of the impact of sex education programs fail to look at outcome even three months after the attendees have graduated. Because adolescents may not be consistent in their behavior or their decisions, the lack of available information on this point is a clear drawback. The limited available evidence suggests that program effects probably attenuate over time. (Klerman and Jekel, 1975; Bennett & Bardon, 1977; Cartoof, 1978, 1979).

The current situation with regard to the effectiveness of service in response to the problem of illegitimacy is aptly summarized by researchers who studied 134 black and white unwed mothers receiving agency service and concluded that:

> field observation and the response of the clients in the study raised little question about the capacity of the voluntary social agency to meet the *immediate* needs of the illegitimately pregnant girls who come or are brought for help. Plans are made, medical care is given and babies are placed for adoption when this is desired. . . . There seemed to be ample recognition of the value of agency services. . . . Difficulties in giving help arise in large measure from the fact that social agencies and the professionals they employ impose complex goals on themsevles which usually go far

beyond the goal of meeting a crisis situation. Most agencies aim to give the client an experience of lasting value to bring about long-run changes that are presumed to be constructive [Shapiro, 1970, p. 64].

They are likely to be least successful with regard to these more ambitious long range objectives. Illustratively, one multiple-service agency to adolescent unmarried mothers in Boston found that while program intervention was initially successful, "two years after participation in the program almost half of the mothers have dropped out of school and half have experienced at least one more unintended pregnancy" (Cartoof, 1978, p. 662). As a consequence, the program developed continuing support procedures that included a follow-up visit to each mother on the average of once every three months after the birth of the child. Such continued contact resulted in lowering the rate of school dropouts and reducing the percentage of subsequent unintended pregnancies.

Project Redirection using an innovative approach also reported short-range but not long-range success (Blum, 1984). On entering the program each pregnant teenage girl was assigned to an older volunteer woman in her community who acted as a role model and helped her locate and use social services that are relevant to the problem of premarital pregnancy and its prevention in the future. As a consequence of example, friendship, repetition, simple instruction, support and advocacy provided by the volunteers the teens served by Project Redirection were more likely to have held a job and completed high school than a comparison group of nonserved pregnant teens. The group that received its services also had significantly increased birth control knowledge and had a lower rate of subsequent pregnancies than the nontreated comparison group. However, two years after their involvement in the project, the effects were attenuated and differences between the experimental and control groups were less evident (Kahn and Kamerman, 1985).

Problems

1. There is controversy about how much and what kind of services pregnant teenagers should be provided. Agencies have been criticized for doing "too much" by those who see any help to the unmarried mother as an encouragement of illegitimacy. From this perspective, those who engage in sexual intercourse are "bad girls" and providing help to them is "rewarding sin." Advocates for pregnant adolescents, on the other hand, who perceive their situation as understandable and, to some extent, unavoidable, have criticized agencies for doing "too little." The conflict between those holding these opposing viewpoints has created ongoing difficulties in governmental provision of sufficient help to pregnant teenagers, young single mothers, and their children.

A permissive attitude toward illegitimacy would suggest that it is reflective of pervasive aspects of our culture. Prominent public figures, such as actresses Vanessa Redgrave and Mia Farrow, and a member of the British Parliament, Bernadette Devlin, have proudly, openly, and without apology borne children out of wedlock. Such examples both reflect and encourage a more matter-of-fact attitude toward unwed parenthood. A widely distributed video made popular by Madonna, a teenage idol of the 1980s, "Papa Don't Preach," told of a premarital pregnancy and the decision by the unmarried mother to keep the baby.

Whereas conservatives have claimed that liberal public policies with regard to services and sex education produce increases in out-of-wedlock births, research suggests that they may, on the contrary, encourage the expansion of contraceptive and abortion options that ultimately result in fewer births among unwed young women (Wimperis, 1960, pp. 323–324; Forrest, Hermalin, & Henshaw, 1981). In an article comparing worldwide illegitimacy rates, the 1957 edition of Encyclopedia Britannica comments that "the policies regarding illegitimate children have been especially liberal in the Scandinavian countries, and studies conducted in these countries have produced no evidence that such a liberal policy illegitimacy" (Vol. 12, p. 85). Thirty years later, cross-cultural analysis of pregnancy prevention practice and illegitimacy, conducted by Jones et al. (1985) arrived at the same conclusion:

> Among the most striking of the observations common to the four European countries included in the six country study is the degree to which the governments of those countries, whatever their political persuasion, have demonstrated the clear-cut will to reduce levels of teenage pregnancy. Pregnancy, rather than adolescent sexual activity itself, is identified as the major problem. Through a number of routes, with varying emphasis on types of effort, the governments of those countries have made a concerted, public effort to help sexually active young people to avoid unintended pregnancy and childbearing. In the United States, in contrast, there has been no well-defined expression of political will. Political and religious leaders, particularly, appear divided over what their primary mission should be: the eradication or discouragement of sexual activity among unmarried people, or the reduction of teenage pregnancy through promotion of contraceptive use (p. 61).

Be that as it may, common experience suggests, as Gilbert (1983) notes, that the sanctioning of sexually active behavior that is implicit in programs regarding contraceptive information might influence some adolescents who are not presently sexually active "to give it a try" (p. 53).

Although the provision of services to the pregnant adolescent and young single mother is clearly not a factor motivating her to become pregnant, neither is there any indication that punitive measures, such as voluntary or compulsory sterilization, denial of public assistance, or criminal prosecution, serve to deter teenagers from becoming pregnant. In general, where such measures (particularly restriction of financial assistance) have been implemented, they have not resulted in any reduction of out-of-wedlock birth-rates. These measures have, however, resulted in more deprived living conditions for the children who are ultimately affected by these policies.

It is not our attitudes toward pregnancy, but broad social attitudes about sexuality, that have had a major impact on teenagers. Greater acceptance of extramarital sex, the growing acceptance of the viewpoint that sexual behavior among consenting parties is a matter of personal choice, and the perspective that sex can be recreational as well as relational have allowed adolescents to consider sexual intercourse as a permissible activity. These attitudes, in turn, are tied to changes in behavior, and data indicate that teenagers are experimenting with sexual involvement more frequently and at younger ages, and more often during their adolescent years (Koenig & Zelnik, 1982).

Given this changing behavior, the conflict between more punitive and permissive approaches may be seen as a clash between those who would change our values while ignoring this behavior and those who argue that we must deal with this behavior and its consequences, even if we do not support the attitudes that give rise to it (Granberg, 1985). Advocates for these conflicting positions have been quick to make themselves heard when any legislation dealing with pregnancy prevention or services to young mothers is being considered. The nature of these differences has, in turn, prevented the federal government from developing and implementing a cohesive, adequately funded policy of the type that has proven effective in responding to this issue in other countries. As a result, illegitimacy rates remain higher than they might otherwise have been,

2. Conflict has arisen, not only over whether to provide any services to pregnant adolescents, but also over the type of services that will most effectively meet their needs. Here again, pervasive differences can be found between proponents of conservative and more liberal approaches to this issue. The conservatives' position is embodied in the Adolescent Family Life Act, passed by Congress in 1981. Pregnancy-prevention provisions of this Act focus on the promotion of natural family-planning methods as well as attempts to convince teenagers that abstinence is in their best interest. AFLA is, in fact, "popularly known as the chastity belt" law (Donovan, 1984, p. 222). In addition, this legislation explicitly rules out utilization of some preventive techniques, particularly abortion, by prohibiting "the distribution of funds to groups that provide any abortion-related services, including counseling and referral, or that subcontract with any agency that provides such services" (Donovan, 1984, p. 222). The legislation also promotes programs that encourage adolescents who do become pregnant to consider relinquishing their children for adoption. The antiabortion stance embodied in AFLA is strengthened by the Hyde Amendment. The current version of this amendment states that federal funds may only be used for abortion in extremely limited circumstances, particularly when the life of the mother is threatened or if she is pregnant because she has been raped (Paul & Schaap, 1982, p. 7).

Meanwhile, the proponents of more comprehensive services argue that clients should have the right to consider and to have access to all available contraceptive and pregnancy termination options. Proponents of this position claim that, because significant numbers of unmarried teenagers have not as yet been reached by available family planning services, more aggressive advertising is required. They note that when pregnancy-prevention programs make themselves "inconspicuous" and make only "timid" efforts to reach out to adolescents, they fail to have sufficient impact in helping adolescents avoid becoming pregnant (Furstenberg, 1981, p. 207). Similarly, restricting access to abortion services prevents low-income women, individuals most negatively affected by pregnancy and most likely to become unwed mothers, from having an opportunity to avoid a potential lifelong involvement with poverty.

Some argue that conservative legislation, in addition, tends to advocate the family-planning methods that are among the least effective for adolescents, who can simply not be relied upon to "abstain" from opportunities to engage in sex or to defer their sexual activity until a more appropriate time of the month. These policies can, then, be expected to result in increases in illegitimacy, particularly among the most vulnerable teenagers, those who are younger and less sophisticated, and those who live in poverty.

3. There is a problem with regard to accessibility to contraceptive and abortion services for minors without notification to or consent of parents. All barriers to nonprescriptive contraceptives—vaginal foams, jellies, condoms—have been generally removed, and no state requires parental involvement for teenagers to obtain contraceptive services (Donovan, 1981). However, 20 per cent of family planning agencies, the service organizations most frequently involved in contraceptive counseling with this age group, do require parental notification or consent

(Torres, Forrest, & Eisman, 1980, p. 286). Physicians dispensing contraceptive devices may also refuse to treat minors without parental permission.

Recent Supreme Court decisions on abortions (*Planned Parenthood of Central Missouri* v. *Danforth*, 1976; *H.L.* v. *Matheson*, 1981) have determined that adolescents as a group cannot be refused access to these services. However, for adolescents who are considered immature and unemancipated, states can require parental permission before providing abortions. An unemancipated, immature minor is an adolescent girl younger than eighteen who lives with her family, who is supported by them, and who "does not claim to be mature enough to make the abortion decision on her own and offers no special reasons why her parents should not be told" (Donovan, 1981, p. 243). Whereas states may decide that any abortion program within their jurisdiction must comply with these notification requirements, individual abortion agencies, physicians, or hospitals may also demand these requirements be met (Paul & Schaap, 1982). A nationwide survey of abortion agencies determined that 44 per cent require consent or notification for clients who are fifteen or younger, and 30 per cent require it when clients are younger than eighteen. Whereas 38 per cent of hospitals require parental involvement, only 18 per cent of freestanding clinics did so. Consent requirements are also more typically found in nonmetropolitan areas (Torres, Forrest, & Eisman, 1980, pp. 285–286).

In other areas, minors have won the right to treatment without these restrictions. They can receive pregnancy testing, be treated for venereal disease, and receive drug and alcohol abuse services without parental consent.

One argument in favor of privacy is that the need for parental involvement may deter the adolescent from using pregnancy prevention services. Teenagers are likely to be sexually active, no matter what the service requirements are. They might choose to risk becoming pregnant, obtain an illegal and possibly dangerous abortion, or have an unwanted child rather than deal with their parents' reaction to the knowledge that they have had intercourse and have become pregnant. Parents themselves admit that they are not comfortable providing their children's sex education, and many prefer that schools provide this training for their teenage children (Moore & Burt, 1982, p. 66). Others have argued in opposition to parental notification that teenagers, like adults, should be provided the right to privacy and to control over their own bodies. Some have suggested that the job of the teenager is to learn to deal with her sexuality outside of the family environment and that, therefore, family participation in such decisions may not meet the developmental needs of adolescents (Watkins, 1983).

Of particular concern to these protesting the need for parent notification or consent is the fear that teenagers, confronted by the obligation to involve their parents, will instead evade their responsibility for planning for pregnancy prevention or obtain pregnancy prevention or termination services from illegal sources. Two large-scale surveys (Torres, 1978; Torres, Forrest, & Eisman, 1980) suggest that, for a significant number of young women these may, in fact, be realistic concerns. Contacting 1,170 adolescents who had been abortion patients in 1979–1980, the authors found that 55 per cent of their families already knew that they were planning to obtain an abortion. Among this group, 38 per cent had told their parents themselves that they were pregnant and were planning to terminate the pregnancy, and an additional 13 per cent had parents who actively encouraged them to obtain the abortion. However, 44 per cent of the total group had parents who did not know the adolescent was receiving this service. Twenty-one per cent said that, if they were required to notify their parents, they would do so and continue to come for services. However, 23 per cent said that if parental involvement were mandatory, they would not come to the abortion clinic. Nine per cent of this group said that they would plan to have an illegal abortion if notification was required. A second survey 1,241 adolescent patients of family planning clinics produced similar results. Once again, a significant minority (23%) said they would not come. When asked what they would do instead if notification was required, 15 per cent of respondents in the second survey said that they would use a condom, the rhythm method, or some other procedure that did not require assistance from the clinic; 4 per cent said they would do nothing; and only 2 per cent said that they would stop having intercourse if they had no access to birth control.

Given these findings, the authors estimate that 33,000 teenagers would become pregnant if all family-planning agencies required teenagers to obtain parental notification or consent. Among this group, some 9,000 additional children would be born out-of-wedlock. Some 19,000 teenagers would resort to illegal abortions; 18,000 would ultimately have unwanted births; and 5,000 would run away from home, either to give birth in secret or to obtain an abortion (Torres, Forrest, & Eisman, 1980, p. 291). These studies suggest that the net effect of notification and/or consent laws is likely to be continued sexual activity, not a reduction in sexual activity, but with less effective protection or no protection at all for a substantial percentage of current service users.

The argument in favor of parental notification and/or consent rests on the fact that parents have a "compelling interest" in what is happening to their child, for whom they still have primary responsibility; that providing such options as contraceptives and abortion without parental consent weakens family ties and erodes parental authority; that knowledge about a crucial aspect of their child's life may permit them greater opportunity for counsel and advice; and that the family need to know about the use of a drug such as the pill if they are to deal with the health needs of their children. In addition:

> There is a general presumption in all other areas of the law that parents have the right to control and guide their children's behavior up to the age of majority . . . The Court, in balancing the right of one family member, the minor adolescent, against those of others, the parents, decided that the interests of the adolescent must have priority. Yet, to go one step further and deny parents even the presumptive right to have any influence on the decision or the chance to support and counsel her, is regarded as undermining the concept of parental autonomy too deeply and to be an unnecessary interference with the integrity of families [Ooms, cited in Moore & Burt, 1982, p. 119].

Support for the notion of parental involvement is embodied in legislation governing the distribution of federal funds for pregnancy programming, the Adolescent Family Life Act. AFLA requires both parental notification and consent for all funded services except pregnancy testing, treatment for venereal disease, or in certain problematic family situations—where the child is an incest victim, where the adolescent is likely to be abused if the parent is notified, or where the parent is trying to coerce the adolescent into having an abortion (Donovan, 1984, p. 223). This legislation requires that teenagers desiring abortion counseling must have their parents request it as well.

Some research suggests the value of family involvement in instances in which parents are the main source of their child's sexual education and where their children are closely identified with them. In these families teenagers tend to delay first intercourse and make better use of contraception. Extensive discussion with parents also helps facilitate the teenager's decision to delay sexual involvement. However, this is only true for girls, since few parents appear to think about the necessity for sex education for their sons (Moore & Burt, 1982, p. 66).

In November 1986, a Minnesota law requiring women under eighteen years old either to notify both parents or to obtain judicial approval as a mature adolescent for obtaining an abortion was declared unconstitutional by a federal district judge. At the conclusion of a five-week trial, the judge noted that she could find no factual basis for the argument that the law "furthers in any way the state's interest in protecting pregnant minors or assuring family integrity." On the contrary, implementation of the law had traumatized teenagers and disrupted families. (*New York Times,* Nov. 8, 1986).

Recently, professionals struggling with the relative merits of adolescents' autonomy and parental support have suggested a third option, one midway between these two alternatives. Recognizing the powerful impact of family economic and emotional support for the adolescent and her infant, attempts should be made to involve them. However, recognizing the significance of the fear many teenagers of making their parents aware of the fact that they are sexually active or pregnant, teenagers should also be allowed to decide whether their parents be notified or not. Adolescents who receive a family planning, abortion, or other type of pregnancy-prevention service are to be advised that telling their parents about their situation will be highly beneficial for them. As Moore and Burt (1982) suggest, "counseling oriented to encourage family involvement seems like a reasonable intermediate strategy. Most parents do have resources to share with their children, most parents care about their children, and most parents would be affected by the decision their child makes. Counselors can encourage teenagers to recognize this strong natural interest, without forcing the issue for those who are unwilling (p. 120; see also Furstenberg, Lincoln, & Menken, 1981, p. 385).

Many pregnancy-prevention counselors have utilized this strategy in working with their teenage clients. However, as Watkins (1983) notes, there are complications in implementing this approach. Describing one program that tries to involve parents in the planning process, she note, "The program ran into difficulties in persuading not only the adolescents and their families, but also the clinic professionals that the family's support was worth the trouble" (p. 203). When the need for parental involvement creates too much difficulty for the adolescent or the worker, agencies tend to stop advocating for it and revert to working only with the teenage client.

4. There is a concern that services originally designed to reintegrate the pregnant teenager into the academic mainstream may actually foster segregation and, ultimately, may contribute to the termination of her academic career. For several years, program planners attempted to develop separate educational facilities for adolescents, during the period of their pregnancy. After having the baby, these young women were expected to return to the regular classroom. These programs offered some protection from embarassment and harassment for students who felt that they could not cope with the peer reactions (Zellman, 1982, p. 20). In addition, these specialized programs tended to provide a more comprehensive array of services to program participants and, therefore, were more likely to meet the varied needs of enrollees.

In recent years, separate programs have been criticized for being academically limited and discriminatory. Specialized curricular programs for teenage mothers have tended to suffer from severe limitations in the range of course materials provided to students. They are considered much less demanding than normal classroom work. As Zellman (1982) suggests, these programs largely make "maintenance efforts," attempts to keep the student somewhat academically oriented until she can return to regular schooling.

Instead of providing protection for embarrassed students, inclusive programs have been seen as creating unnecessary segregation from peers (Bolton, 1980; Zellman, 1982; Sedlak, 1982). Critics of inclusive curricular projects advocate programs that help the pregnant teenager by providing supplementary training materials for her, either as regular classroom work for credit or through non-credit courses.

Because teenagers differ—some needing protection and some seeking normative experiences—it would be most helpful if communities could make both of these academic options available (McGee, 1982, p. 34). However, as Zellman (1982) points out, funding limitations make it unlikely that this range of services will be provided in many communities. Instead, one type of program tends to become established and maintained as the primary service for these young women.

5. There is a problem with equitable distribution of services to both pregnant teenagers and to young parents. As we have previously noted, disadvantaged, young, rural, and nonwhite women find it more difficult to obtain abortion services, either because they are not located in an area that is easily accessible or because they charge fees that these clients simply do not have the resources to pay (Forrest, Tietze, & Sullivan, 1978; McGee, 1982, p. 61; Dryfoos, 1982, p. 44). A recent analysis of the availability of abortion services found that "teenagers traveled an average of forty-five highway miles from the city or town in which they live to the clinic site" (Torres, Forrest, & Eisman, 1980, p. 289).

Historically, general programming for pregnant teenagers and younger single parents has been made available more frequently to whites than to blacks. Although this imbalance has been redressed in recent years, some groups continue to be underserved by this type of program. Aries (1980) suggests that it is white working teens who could currently benefit from greater involvement with multi-service centers.

In addition to providing uneven services to different client groups, there are indications that the variety of preventive and remedial programs we have discussed have not been made available to most adolescents who are in need of them, that programming that is made available is frequently segmented and uncoordinated, and that the level of service is insufficient to meet the needs of many clients (Furstenberg, 1981; Moore & Burt, 1982). Since 1972, the Children's Defense Fund, through its Child Watch Project, has been monitoring the delivery of services to child welfare clients. Results suggest that "the lack of support services was particularly noticeable for adolescents, as reported by about one-half of the projects. Most often mentioned were the need for out-of-home living alternatives and programs for pregnant teens" (*Child Watch,* March 1984, p. 3).

Bolton (1980) suggests that it is probably, in part, the publicity attached to issues of pregnancy among adolescents that has led the general public to believe that programs are usually available to meet their needs. However, the data indicate that, for the most part, pregnant teenagers and young single mothers are unserved or underserved. (See also Brown 1982; 1983; U.S. House of Representatives, 1985; Weatherly et al., 1986)

6. The nature of service delivery patterns and the special needs of the client group create unique demands on the social worker serving pregnant teenagers

and young parents. Because these clients frequently require several services, provided by a number of different agencies, the worker must expend considerable effort coordinating the responses of these various programs to her client. However, the nature of social service agency linkages may impede the worker's efforts to carry out this responsibility. "Often this system of referral is rather makeshift and so is dependent on the knowledge, expertise, and commitment of individual staff members. Most communities do not coordinate their services for pregnant and parenting teens" (McGee, 1982, p. 21).

The worker's task is complicated by uncooperative client reactions; many are defensive, evasive, and unresponsive (O'Leary, Shore, & Wieder, 1984). The worker strives to help the adolescent make critical decisions about her future and that of her child, but may fail to see any impact of her efforts or may find, unexpectedly, that her client has been paying attention only after several months have passed. In addition, worker objectives usually are not congruent with client objectives. Whereas the workers wants to help the teenager focus on her future, the adolescent is typically more interested in meeting immediate needs.

Working with clients who place themselves at risk for pregnancy, who jeopardize the health or well-being of their infants or who make decisions that produce deterioration in the quality of their lives, practitioners may become increasingly frustrated. "Staff members speak of their sense of being caught between their natural empathy for young parents and their anger about the preventable nature of the problem" (McGee, 1982, p. 24). Faced with clients who appear uninterested in utilizing their assistance and a service delivery system that appears to create unnecessary obstacles to providing effective services for them, practitioners "often feel overwhelmed. Many service providers thus observe that caring for staff is as important as caring for teen clients" (McGee, 1982, p. 27). As in other areas of child welfare practice, the social work staff dealing with this particular client group requires effective supervision, professional support, and the opportunity to develop new insight and new approaches that comes from interaction with other professionals and with experts in their field.

Trends

We have already noted some of the trends relating to this area of service: an increase in the number of children born out-of-wedlock but a decrease in the out-of-wedlock birthrate for all groups except white teenagers; a decrease in the number of women who, carrying the child to term, surrender the child for adoption; a decrease in maternity home service and an increase in the development of community-based, multi-service agencies targeted on school-aged single pregnant women; and increasing efforts to reduce the legal disadvantages of out-of-wedlock status. Some additional trends follow.

1. There is incongruence between widely publicized public concern about teenage pregnancy and the extent of public commitment to eradication of this problem, particularly through the provision of federal funds. The federal government has not adopted a "leadership role" in program planning for this group, and available federal funds have been diminishing, as have the number and variety of programs targeting services to pregnant adolescents and young mothers (Adler, Bates, & Merdinger, 1985; Ebaugh, Fuchs, & Haney, 1985; Zellman, 1982).

Because broad social policy has not been promulgated to help prevent the development of problems of this type among adolescents, difficulties that they face with regard to pregnancy and parenthood tend to be seen as individualized concerns. Rather than assuming social responsibility for assisting teenagers, attempts have been made to help them meet their needs on a case-by-case basis. Under these circumstances, it becomes the responsibility of the individual adolescent to be concerned enough about her future, to be invested enough in her career, and to be sufficiently caring and nurturant so that she does not desire to have or raise a child until she is more fully prepared to adequately care for it.

Unfortunately, however, teenagers do not have sufficient influence to create the social circumstances that are necessary to meet their needs. This is particularly evident in the areas of employment. Whereas practitioners struggle to convince these young people that they should be concerned about their economic future and that, as a result, they should remain in school and delay childbearing, they do not have the resources to provide the necessary academic training or appropriate job opportunities for these young women and men which would allow them to believe that they can avoid poverty and obtain economic self-sufficiency. Service providers comment, "The mothers we see definitely want to work. If taking a job meant losing only welfare and food stamps, they'd take it, but if it also means losing Medicaid, they just can't do it;" "our young people are desperate to work–but there are no jobs" (McGee, 1982, pp. 42–43).

2. The "problem" of adolescent pregnancy continues to be perceived as primarily a female responsibility. To a large extent, young women are held responsible for becoming pregnant. Young men, on the other hand, although not considered responsible, are also given extremely limited voice in subsequent decision making with regard to termination of the pregnancy or the future of the infant. Professional attitudes and program policy, therefore, reinforce stereotypic gender-linked beliefs that women should be the primary providers of child care, the nurturers of children, while males are mainly important because of the secondary support they provide the mother and the economic resources they bring to the family. Bolton (1980) comments:

> Although pregnancy does appear to have a more significant impact upon the adolescent mother than on the father, the continued design of programs which exclude the father is inappropriate. The isolation of the mother and the provision of secretive "special" services to her in the absence of the young male involved is thoughtless at best and potentially destructive at worst. It is ironic that the female adolescent population, a population in which a much smaller percentage of its members are sexually active than the male population, is considered to be the population *at risk* [p. 218].

Whereas the data suggest the significant role that these young men play in influencing decisions which young women make about the pregnancy and the infant's future, few programs have concentrated on enhancing their involvement. McGee (1982) describes activities undertaken by some innovative agencies:

—Including young fathers or current male partners in counseling sessions, labor and delivery classes, post-pregnancy activities, and social gatherings;
—Involving young fathers in child care and parenting education in an early childhood center;
—Seeking out young fathers on their own turf—the streets, male hangouts—and offering information and counseling and locating a teen-parent program in a center that has an established reputation for attracting young people of both sexes [p. 51].

For the most part, however, programs do not consider the putative father as a primary client and do not make these types of efforts to involve him in programming. It appears that there will continue to be an overemphasis on the responsibility of the female in these situations and underutilization of the resources that the male can provide.

3. Social agencies are beginning to face the effective competition of many other organizations in offering services of prime interest to many unmarried mothers: agencies established by clergy, women's liberation organizations, and grass-roots organizations representing the youth counterculture. Every college newspaper and every underground press publication carries ads or notices about the availability of contraceptive information and abortion counseling. Such groups, which have no official connection with social work, provide access to and sometimes financial aid for abortion and contraception to all women, no matter what their age or marital status.

A testimonial to the growing number of recently developed services is the special listing "Problem Pregnancies" in the Yellow Pages of some phone books.

4. There are some suggestions that the sexual revolution has crested, virginity until marriage is becoming more respectable, and the pleasures of promiscuity have proved illusory. The counterrevolution has received support from the growing concern about AIDS. Widespread education about "safe sex" and the use of condoms as a prophylactic also means the more frequent use of condoms as a contraceptive. Those changes may ultimately affect the out-of-wedlock pregnancy rate.

5. Seeking to increase disincentives to teenage unmarried pregnancies, Wisconsin passed a law in 1985 making grandparents responsible for the support of a child born to their own child less than eighteen years of age. The parents of both the mother and father of the child would be responsible for the infant's support. The law was first implemented in May 1986 when a forty-two-year-old grandparent in Beaver Dam, Wisconsin, was ordered to pay $30 a month to support her grandson until her daughter became eighteen years of age (*New York Times*, May 25, 1986). The law was strenuously opposed by those who felt that it would encourage parents to support abortion of any nonmaritally conceived child and by those who felt the law exaggerated the influence that parents had in regard to adolescent behavior. The law was the first such legislation in the nation and attracted considerable comment and interest.

6. An innovative approach that appeared to be increasingly implemented, despite considerable opposition, is the development of clinics in schools or very near schools which provided family-planning services to the adolescent school population. The clinics, in addition to providing general primary health care, also made available contraceptives as well as information. By 1985 almost 50 communities in 26 states has a clinic either in operation or on the drawing board (Kenney, 1986, p. 44; *American Family*, 1985; Dryfoos, 1985).

One such program, implemented in a junior high school with a black inner-city student body, was evaluated by Zabin et al (1986). The evaluation compared pregnancy rates, contraceptive use, and knowledge of this school's students with the students in a comparable junior high school for which no such service was available. The study found that after $2\frac{1}{2}$ years of clinic operation, pregnancy rates at the school offering such service were reduced while pregnancy rates at the nonserved school had increased. One surprising finding was that boys at the school used the clinic almost as freely as the girls. Accessibility of contraceptive service rather than any change in attitudes was the factor that contributed most significantly to the outcome.

In December 1986, the National Research Council of the American Academy of

Science issued a report based on a two-year study of teenage pregnancies. The report recommended that contraceptives should be distributed free or at low cost to both male and female teenagers in communities in which teenagers congregate and through school-based clinics. It recommended access to abortion with or without parental consent for teenagers who want it and that adoption services should be strengthened. It noted that there was little evidence to suggest that the availability of contraceptives encourages early sexual activity (National Research Council, 1986).

Bibliography

Abel, Rhoda, et al. "Pregnant Adolescents: Cost-Benefit Options." *Social Casework, 63,* 5, (May 1982), 286–290.

Adams, Hannah. *Social Services for Unmarried Mothers and Their Children Provided Through Public and Voluntary Child Welfare Agencies,* Child Welfare Report No. 12. Washington, D.C.: U.S. Government Printing Office, 1962.

Adler, Emily Stier, Mildred Bates, and Joan Merdinger, "Educational Policies and Programs for Teenage Parents and Pregnant Teenagers." *Family Relations, 34,* 2 (April 1985), 183–187.

Ager, Joel W., Fredericka P. Shea, and Samuel J. Agronow. "Method Discontinuance in Teenage Women: Implications for Teen Contraceptive Programs," in *Pregnancy in Adolescence: Needs, Problems and Management.* Ed. Irving R. Stuart, and Carl F. Wells, New York: Van Nostrand Reinhold Company, 1982, 236–259.

Alan Guttmacher Institute. *Teenage Pregnancy—The Problem That Hasn't Gone Away* New York City: Alan Guttmacher Institute, 1981.

American Family. "Preventing Teen-age Pregnancy—Health Experts Turn to a School Based Approach." *American Family,* 8, 11 (December 1985), 1–6.

Anglim, Elizabeth. "The Adopted Child's Heritage—Two Natural Parents." *Child Welfare,* 44, 6 (June 1965).

Aries, Nancy. "Historic Trends in the Delivery of Services to Teenage Parents." *Journal of Sociology and Social Welfare,* 7, 1 (1980), 137–146.

Authier, Karen, and Jerry Authier, "Intervention with Families of Pregnant Adolescents." In *Pregnancy in Adolescence: Needs, Problems and Management.* Ed. Irving R. Stuart, and Carl F. Wells. New York: Van Nostrand Reinhold Company, 1982, 290–313.

Bachrach, Christine. "Adoption Plans, Adopted Children and Adoptive Mothers." *Journal of Marriage and the Family,* 48 (May 1986), 243–253.

Baldwin, Wendy, and Virginia S. Cain. "The Children of Teenage Parents." In *Teenage Sexuality, Pregnancy and Childbearing.* Ed. Frank F. Furstenberg, Jr., Richard Lincoln and Jane Menken, Philadelphia: University of Pennsylvania Press, 1981, 265–274.

Barber, Dulan. *Unmarried Fathers.* London: Hutchinson Co., 1975.

Barclay, Lillian E. "A Group Approach to Young Unwed Mothers." *Social Casework,* 50, 7 (July 1969), 379–384.

Barrett, Robert, and Bryan Robinson. "Teenage Fathers: Neglected Too Long." *Social Work,* 27 (November, 1982), 484–488.

Barth, Richard P., and Steven P. Schinke. "Coping with Daily Strain Among Pregnant and Parenting Adolescents." *Journal of Social Service Research,* 7, 2 (Winter 1983), 51–63.

Barth, Richard P., and Steven P. Schinke. "Enhancing the Social Supports of Teenage Mothers." *Social Casework,* 65, 9 (November, 1984), 523–531.

Bedger, Jean E. *The Crittenton Study—An Assessment of Client Functioning Before and After Services.* Chicago: Crittenton Comprehensive Care Center, April 1969.

Bell, Carolle, Glendon Casto, and Debra Daniels. "Ameliorating the Impact of Teenage Pregnancy on Parent and Child." *Child Welfare,* 62, 2 (March–April 1983), 167–173.

Benas, Evelyn. "Residential Care of the Child Mother and Her Infant—An Extended Family Concept." *Child Welfare,* 54, 4 (April 1975), 291–294.

Bennett, Virginia L., and Jack I. Bardon. "The Effects of a School Program on Teenage Mothers and Their Children." *American Journal of Orthopsychiatry,* 47 (October 1977), 671–678.

Bernstein, Rose. "Unmarried Parents and Their Families." *Child Welfare,* 45, 4 (April 1966), 185–193.

Bernstein, Rose. *Helping Unmarried Mothers.* New York: Association Press, 1971.

Bierman, Babette R., and Rosalie Streett. "Adolescent Girls as Mothers: Problems in Parenting." In *Pregnancy in Adolescence: Needs, Problems and Management.* Ed. Irving R. Stuart and Carl F. Wells. New York: Van Nostrand Reinhold Company, 1982, 407–426.

Blum, Barbara. "Helping Teen-age Mothers: Project Redirection Fosters Long-term Self-Sufficiency." *Public Welfare,* 42 (Winter 1984), 7–21.

Bolton, Frank G., Jr. *The Pregnant Adolescent: Problems of Premature Parenthood.* Beverly Hills, Cal.: Sage Publications, 1980.

Bowerman, Charles E., et al. *Unwed Motherhood: Personal and Social Consequences.* Chapel Hill, N.C.: Institute for Research in Social Science, University of North Carolina, 1966.

Boykin, Nancy M. "A School-Centered Mutlidiscipline Approach to the Problems of Teen-Age Pregnancy." *Child Welfare,* 47, 8 (October 1968), 478–487.

Bracken, March. "Lessons Learned from a Baby Care Club for Unmarried Mothers." *Children,* 18, 4 (July–August 1971), 133–137.

Bracken, Michael, Lorraine Klerman, and Maryann Bracken. "Coping with Pregnancy Resolution Among Never Married Women." *American Journal of Orthopsychiatry,* 48, 2 (April 1978), 320–332.

Bremner, Robert H. *Children and Youth in America—A Documentary History,* vol. 1: *1600–1865.* Cambridge, Mass.: Harvard University Press, 1970.

Brown, Shirley Vining. "Early Childbearing and Poverty. Implications for Social Services." *Adolescence,* 17, 66 (Summer 1982), 397–407.

Brown, Shirley Vining. "How Well Are We Serving the Adolescent Mother: A Look at Public Social Services." *Children and Youth Services Review,* 5 (1983), 135–154.

Brumberg, Joan Jacobs. " 'Ruined' Girls: Changing Community Responses to Illegitimacy in Upstate New York, 1890–1920." *Journal of Social History,* 18 (Winter 1984), 247–272.

Burden, Dianne S., and Lorraine V. Klerman. "Teenage Parenthood: Factors That Lessen Economic Dependence." *Social Work,* 29 (January–February 1984), 11–16.

Burger, Gloria, and Jean Bedger. "Attitudes of Clients Served by the 4Cs," in *Teenage Pregnancy: Research Related to Clients and Services.* Ed. Jean E. Bedger. Springfield, Ill.: Charles C. Thomas, 1980, 107–150.

Burgess, Linda. "The Unmarried Father in Adoption Planning." *Children,* 15, 2 (March–April 1968), 71–74.

Busfield, Bernard L., et al. *Out-of-Wedlock Pregnancy—What Happens Next: An in-depth Survey of Postnatal Unwed Mothers Treated by Long-Term Group Therapy.* Boston: Crittenton Hastings House, 1969.

Cain, Lillian Pike. "Social Worker's Role in Teenage Abortions." *Social Work,* 24 (January, 1979), 52–56.

Campbell, Arthur. "The Role of Family Planning in the Reduction of Poverty." *Journal of Marriage and the Family,* 30, 2 (1968), 236–245.

Card, Josefina J., and Lauren L. Wise. "Teenage Mothers and Teenage Fathers: The Impact of Early Child Bearing on the Parents' Personal and Professional Lives." *Family Planning Perspectives,* 10, 4 (July–August, 1978), 199–207.

Cartoof, Virginia G. "Postpartum Services for Adolescent Mothers." *Child Welfare,* 57, 10 (December 1978), 660–666.

Cartoof, Virginia G. "Postpartum Services for Adolescent Mothers: Part 2." *Child Welfare,* 58, 10 (December, 1979), 673–680.

Cartoof, Virginia G. "The Negative Effects of AFDC Policies on Teenage Mothers." *Child Welfare,* 61, 5 (May 1982), 269–278.

Caughlin, Jeanne. "Psychic Hazards of Unwed Paternity." *Social Work,* 5, 3 (July 1960), 29–35.

Chamie, Mary, and Stanley Henshaw. "The Costs and Benefits of Government Expenditures for Family Planning Programs." *Family Planning Perspectives,* 13, 3 (May–June, 1981), 117–124.

Chilman, Catherine. *Adolescent Sexuality in a Changing American Society.* U. S. Department of Health, Education and Welfare, Public Health Service. National Institute of Health Publication No. 80-1426. January 1980.

Chilman, Catherine. *Adolescent Sexuality in a Changing American Society;* 2d. Ed. New York: John Wiley & Sons, 1983.

Chilman, Catherine S. Review of "Children as Parents" by Shelby H. Miller. *Children and Youth Services Review,* 6, 2 (1984), 148–152.

Chilman, Catherine, S. "Feminist Issues in Teenage Parenting." *Child Welfare,* 64, 3 (May–June, 1985), 225–234.

Clapp, Douglas F., and Rebecca S. Raab. "Followup of Unmarried Adolescent Mothers." *Social Work* (March 1978), 149–153.

Clark, Samuel D., Jr., Laurie S. Zabin, and Janet B. Hardy. "Sex, Contraception and Parenthood: Experience and Attitudes Among Urban Black Young Men." *Family Planning Perspectives,* 16, 2 (March–April 1984), 77–82.

Cooper, Elizabeth. "Prenatal Care for the Pregnant Adolescent," in *Pregnancy in Adolescence: Needs, Problems and Management.* Ed. Irving R. Stuart, and Carl F. Wells. New York: Van Nostrand Reinhold Company, 1982, 66–79.

Corrigan, Eileen M. "The Child at Home: Child-Rearing Practices of Unwed Mothers Compared to Other Mothers," in *Illegitimacy: Changing Services for Changing Times.* New York: National Council on Illegitimacy, 1970.

Crawford, Albert G., and Frank F. Furstenberg, Jr. "Teenage Sexuality, Pregnancy and Childbearing," in *A Handbook of Child Welfare.* Ed. Joan Laird and Ann Hartman. New York: Free Press, 1985, 532–559.

Crellin, Eileen, M. L. Kellmer Pringle, and Patrick West. *Born Illegitimate—Social and Educational Implications.* London: National Children's Bureau, 1971.

Crockett, Mary L. "Examination of Services to the Unmarried Mother in Relation to Age of Adoptive Placement of the Baby," in *Casework Papers.* New York: Family Service Association of America, 1960.

Crumidy, Pearl M., and Harold Jacobziner. "A Study of Young Unmarried Mothers Who Kept Their Babies." *American Journal of Public Health,* 56, 8 (August 1966), 1242–1251.

Cutright, Phillips. "The Rise of Teenage Illegitimacy in the United States, 1940–1971," pp. 3–4, of *The Teenage Pregnant Girl.* Ed. Jack Zackler and Wayne Brandstadt. Springfield, Ill.: Charles C. Thomas, 1975.

Cutright, Phillips. "Illegitimacy: Myths, Causes, and Cures." *Family Planning Perspectives,* 3, 1 (January 1971), 26–48.

Danforth, Joyce, et al. "Group Services for Unmarried Mothers—An Interdisciplinary Approach." *Children,* 18, 2 (March–April 1971), 59–64.

David, H. P. "Unwanted Pregnancies. Costs and Alternatives." *Demographic and Social Aspects of Population Growth.* Ed. C. F. Westoff and R. Parke. Washington, D.C.: Government Printing Office, 1972.

de Andra, Diane, and Rosina M. Becerra. "Support Networks for Adolescent Mothers." *Social Casework,* 65 (March, 1984), 172–181.

DeRose, Ann M. "Identifying Needs, Gaining Support for, and Establishing an Innovative, School-Based Program for Pregnant Adolescents," in *Pregnancy in Adolescence: Needs, Problems and Management.* Ed. Irving R. Stuart, and Carl F. Wells. New York: Van Nostrand Reinhold Company, 1982, 337–362.

Donovan, Patricia. "Parental Notification: Is it Settled?" *Family Planning Perspectives,* 13, 5 (September–October, 1981), 243–246.

Donovan, Patricia. "The Adolescent Family Life Act and the Promotion of Religious Doctrine." *Family Planning Perspectives,* 16, 5 (September–October, 1984), 222–228.

Dryfoos, Joy. "The Epidemiology of Adolescent Pregnancy: Incidence. Outcomes, and Interventions," in *Pregnancy in Adolescence: Needs, Problems and Management*. Ed. Irving R. Stuart, and Carl F. Wells. New York: Van Nostrand Reinhold Company, 1982, 27–47.

Dryfoos, Joy. "A New Strategy for Preventing Unintended Teenage Childbearing." *Family Planning Perspectives*, 16, 4 (July-August, 1984), 193–195.

Dryfoos, Joy. "School-Based Health Clinics: A New Approach to Preventing Adolescent Pregnancy." *Family Planning Perspectives*, 17, 2 (March–April, 1985), 70–75.

Dryfoos, Joy G., and Toni Heisler. "Contraceptive Services for Adolescents: An Overview," in *Teenage Sexuality, Pregnancy and Childbearing*. Ed. Frank F. Furstenberg, Jr., Richard Lincoln, and Jane Menken. Philadelphia: University of Pennsylvania Press, 1981, 394–408.

Ebaugh, Helen, Rose Fuchs, and C. Allen Haney. "Abortion Attitudes in the United States: Continuities and Discontinuities," in *Perspectives on Abortion*. Ed. Paul Sachdev. Metuchen, N. J.: Scarecrow Press, 1985, 163–175.

Edwards, Laura E. et al. "Adolescent Pregnancy Prevention Services in High School Clinics," in *Teenage Sexuality, Pregnancy and Childbearing*. Ed. Frank F. Furstenberg, Jr., Richard Lincoln, and Jane Menken. Philadelphia: University of Pennsylvania Press, 1981, 372–381.

Ellwood, E. T., and M. J. Bane. "The Impact of AFDC on Family Structure and Living Arrangement." *Research in Labor Economics*, 7 (1985).

Evans, Jerome R., Georgiana Selstad, and Wayne H. Welcher. "Teenagers: Fertility Control Behavior and Attitudes Before and After Abortion, Childbearing or Negative Pregnancy Test," in *Teenage Sexuality, Pregnancy and Childbearing*. Ed. Frank F. Furstenberg, Jr., Richard Lincoln, and Jane Menken. Philadelphia: University of Pennsylvania Press, 1981, 355–371.

Ezzard, Nancy V., Willard Cates, Jr., and Kenneth F. Schulz. "The Epidemiology of Adolescent Abortion in the United States," in *Perspectives on Abortion*. Ed. Paul Sachdev. Metuchen, N.J.: Scarecrow Press, 1985, 73–88.

Festinger, Trudy Bradley. "Unwed Mothers and Their Decision to Keep or Surrender Children." *Child Welfare*, 50, 5 (May 1971), 253–263.

Finkel, Madelon Lubin, and David J. Finkel. "Sexual and Contraceptive Knowledge. Attitudes and Behavior of Male Adolescents," in *Teenage Sexuality, Pregnancy and Childbearing*. Ed. Frank F. Furstenberg, Jr., Richard Lincoln, and Jane Menken. Philadelphia: University of Pennsylvania Press, 1981, 327–335.

Fischman, Susan H., and Howard A. Palley. "Adolescent Unwed Motherhood—Implications for a National Family Policy." *Health and Social Work*, 3, 1 (February 1978), 31–46.

Flanigan, Beverly, and Mary Ann Hitch. "Alcohol Use. Sexual Intercourse and Contraception: An Exploratory Study." *Journal of Alcohol and Drug Education*, 1986.

Forrest, Jacqueline Darroch, Albert Hermalin, and Stanley Henshaw. "The Impact of Family Planning Clinic Programs on Adolescent Pregnancy." *Family Planning Perspectives*, 13, 3 (May–June 1981), 109–116.

Forrest, Jacqueline D., Christopher Tietze, and Ellen Sullivan. "Abortion in the U.S., 1976–77." *Family Planning Perspectives*, 10, 5 (September–October 1978), 271–279.

Friedman, Helen L. "Why Are They Keeping Their Babies?" *Social Work* (July 1975), 322–323.

Furstenberg, Frank F., Jr. *Unplanned Parenthood—The Social Consequences of Teenage Childbearing*. New York: The Free Press, 1976.

Furstenberg, Frank F., Jr. "The Social Consequences of Teenage Parenthood," in *Teenage Sexuality, Pregnancy and Childbearing*. Ed. Frank F. Furstenberg, Jr., Richard Lincoln, and Jane Menken. Philadelphia: University of Pennsylvania Press, 1981, 184–210.

Furstenberg, Frank F., Jr., and Albert G. Crawford. "Family Support: Helping Teenage Mothers to Cope," in *Teenage Sexuality, Pregnancy and Childbearing*. Ed. Frank F. Furstenberg, Jr., Richard Lincoln, and Jane Menken. Philadelphia: University of Pennsylvania Press, 1981, 280–300.

Furstenberg, Frank F., Jr., Richard Lincoln, and Jane Menken. *Teenage Sexuality, Pregnancy and Childbearing*, Philadelphia: University of Pennsylvania Press, 1981.

Garland, Patricia, "Illegitimacy—A Special Minority-Group Problem in Urban Areas—New Social Welfare Perspectives." *Child Welfare*, 45, 2 (February 1966), 81–88.

Gil, D. G. "Illegitimacy and Adoption—Its Socioeconomic Correlates: A Preliminary Report." *Child Adoption*, No. 1 (1969), 25–37.

Gilbert, Neil. *Capitalism and the Welfare State*, New Haven, Conn.: Yale University Press, 1983.

Gilchrist, Lewayne, and Steven P. Schinke. "Teenage Pregnancy and Public Policy." *Social Service Review*, 57, 2 (June 1983a), 307–322.

Gilchrist, Lewayne D., and Steven P. Schinke. "Counseling with Adolescents Around Their Sexuality," in *Adolescent Sexuality in Changing American Society—2d Ed.* Ed. Catherine C. Chilman. New York: John Wiley & Sons, 1983b, 230–250.

Goode, William J., "A Policy Paper for Illegitimacy" in *Organizing for Community Welfare.* Ed. Mayer N. Zald. Chicago: Quadrangle Books, 1967.

Goodman, Elizabeth M. "Trends and Goals in Schooling for Pregnant Girls and Teenage Mothers," in *Effective Services for Unmarried Parents and Their Children—Innovative Community Approaches.* New York: National Council on Illegitimacy, 1968.

Granberg, Donald, and Beth Wellman Granberg. "Social Bases of Support and Opposition to Legalized Abortion" in *Perspectives on Abortion.* Ed. by Paul Sachdev. Metuchen, N.J.: Scarecrow Press, 1985, 191–204.

Greydanus, Donald E. "The Health System's Responsibility to the Adolescent at Risk." In *Pregnancy in Adolescence: Needs, Problems and Management.* Ed. Irving R. Stuart and Carl F. Wells. New York: Van Nostrand Reinhold Company, 1982, 48–65.

Grow, Lucille. *Unwed Mothers Served by the Voluntary Agencies.* New York: Data Collection Project for Agencies Serving Unmarried Mothers, 1967.

Grow, Lucille. "Today's Unmarried Mothers: The Choices Have Changed." *Child Welfare*, 58 (June 1979), 363–371.

Hartley, Shirley. "The Decline of Illegitimacy in Japan." *Social Problems* 18, 1 (Summer, 1970), 78–91.

Heger, Donna T. "A Supportive Service to Single Mothers and Their Children." *Children Today*, 6, 5 (September–October 1977), 2–4.

Hendricks, Leo E. "Unwed Adolescent Fathers: Problems They Face and Their Sources of Social Support." *Adolescence*, 15, 60 (Winter 1980), 861–869.

Hendricks, Leo E., Cleopatra S. Howard, and Patricia P. Caesar. "Help-Seeking Behavior Among Select Populations of Black Unmarried Adolescent Fathers: Implications for Human Service Agencies." *American Journal of Public Health*, 71, 7 (July, 1981), 733–735.

Herzog, Elizabeth. "Unwed Motherhood: Personal and Social Consequences." *Welfare in Review*, 2, 8 (August 1964).

Hopkinson, Angela. *Single Mothers: The First Year.* Edinburgh: Scottish Council for Single Parents, 1976.

Horowitz, Nancy. "Contraceptive Practices of Young Women with Two Adolescent Pregnancies," in *Teenage Pregnancy: Research Related to Clients and Services.* Ed. Jean E. Bedger. Sprinfield, Ill.: Charles C Thomas, 1980, 168–178.

Howard, Marion. "Comprehensive Service Programs for School Age Pregnant Girls." *Children*, 15, 5 (September–October 1968a), 193–196.

Howard, Marion. *Multiservice Programs for Pregnant School Girls.* Washington, D.C.: U.S. Department of Health, Education, and Welfare, Social Rehabilitation Service, Children's Bureau, 1968b.

Howard, Marion. *The Webster School—A District of Columbia Program for Pregnant Girls.* Children's Bureau Research Report No. 2. Washington, D.C.: Government Printing Office, 1968c.

Howard, Marion. "Young Parent Families," in *Child Welfare Strategy in the Coming Years.* Ed. Alfred Kadushin. Washington, D. C.: U. S. Government Printing Office, 1978, 195–226.

Janowitz, Barbara. "The Impact of AFDC on Illegitimate Birth Rates." *Journal of Marriage and the Family*, 38, 3 (1976), 485–494.

Johnson, Betty. "The Unwed AFDC Mother and Child Welfare Services," in *The Double Jeopardy: The Triple Crisis—Illegitimacy Today.* New York: National Council on Illegitimacy, 1969.

Jones, Elise F. et al. "Teenage Pregnancy in Developed Countries: Determinants and Policy Implications." *Family Planning Perspectives,* 17, 2 (March–April 1985), 53–63.

Jones, Wyatt C. et al. "Social and Psychological Factors in Status Decisions of Unmarried Mothers." *Journal of Marriage and the Family,* 25, 3 (August 1962), 224–230.

Kahn, Alfred J., and Sheila B. Kamerman. "Personal Social Services and Income Transfer Experiments—The Research and Action Connections," in *Children Youth and Families The Action-Research Relationship,* Ed. R. N. Rapoport. New York: Cambridge University Press, 1985, 101–125.

Kafrissen, Michael E. et al. "Abortion: Incidence, Mortality and Morbidity," in *Perspectives on Abortion.* Ed. Paul Sachdev. Metuchen, N. J.: Scarecrow Press, 1985, 130–140.

Kaltreider, Nancy, and L. Douglas Lenkoski. "Effective Use of Group Techniques in a Maternity Home." *Child Welfare,* 50, 3 (March 1970), 146–152.

Kane, Frances, and Peter Lachenbruch. "Adolescent Pregnancy: A Study of Abortions and Non Abortions." *American Journal of Orthopsychiatry,* 43 (October 1973), 796–803.

Kenney, Asta M., "School Based Clinics: A National Conference." *Family Planning Perspectives* 18, 1 (January–February 1986), 44–45.

Klerman, Lorraine, and James Jekel. "School Age Mothers: Problems, Programs, Policy," in *Studies in Maternal Health.* H.E.W. Public Health Service. Washington, D.C.: U.S. Government Printing Office, 1975.

Klerman, Lorraine V., et al. "The Delivery-Abortion Decision Among Adolescents," in *Pregnancy in Adolescence: Needs, Problems and Management.* Ed. Irving R. Stuart and Carl F. Wells. New York: Van Nostrand Reinhold Company, 1982, 219–234.

Koenig, Michael A., and Melvin Zelnik. "The Risk of Premarital First Pregnancy Among Metropolitan-Area Teenagers: 1976 and 1979." *Family Planning Perspectives,* 14, 5 (September–October, 1982), 239–247.

Kolodny, Ralph, and Willow V. Reilly. "Group Work with Today's Unmarried Mothers." *Social Casework,* 53, 10 (December 1972).

Kornfield, Ruth. "Who's to Blame: Adolescent Sexual Activity." *Journal of Adolescence,* 8 (1985), 17–31.

Krause, Harry D. "Bringing the Bastard into the Great Society—A Proposed Uniform Act on Legitimacy." *Texas Law Review,* 44, 5 (April 1966), 829–859.

Krause, Harry B. *Illegitimacy: Law and Social Policy.* Indianapolis: The Bobbs-Merrill Co., 1971.

Kreech, Florence. "A Residence for Mothers and Their Babies." *Child Welfare,* 54, 8 (September–October 1975), 581–592.

Levy, Dorothy. "A Follow-up Study of Unmarried Mothers." *Social Casework* 36, 1 (January 1955), 27–33.

Lewis, Catherine C. "A Comparison of Minors' and Adults' Pregnancy Decisions." *American Journal of Orthopsychiatry,* 50, 3 (July, 1980), 446–453.

Leynes, Cynthia. "Keep or Adopt: A Study of Factors Influencing Pregnant Adolescents' Plans for Their Babies." *Child Psychiatry and Human Development.* 11, 2 (Winter 1980), 105–112.

Lindemann, Constance. *Birth Control and Unmarried Young Women.* New York: Springer Publishing Co., 1975.

Lightman, Ernie, and Benjamin Schlesinger. "Pregnant Adolescents in Maternity Homes: Some Professional Concerns," in *Pregnancy in Adolescence: Needs, Problems and Management.* Ed. Irving R. Stuart and Carl F. Wells. New York: Van Nostrand Reinhold Company, 1982, 363–385.

Luker, Kristin. *Taking Chances: Abortion and the Decision Not to Contracept.* Berkeley: University of California Press, 1975.

Makinson, Carolyn. "The Health Consequences of Teenage Fertility." *Family Planning Perspectives,* 17, 3 (May–June, 1985), 132–139.

Matějcĕk, Zdenĕk, Zdenĕk Dytrych, and Vratislav Schüller. "Follow-Up Study of Children Born from Unwanted Pregnancies." *International Journal of Behavioral Development,* 3 (1980), 243–251.

McCarthy, James, and Jane Menken. "Marriage, Remarriage, Marital Disruption and Age at First Birth," in *Teenage Sexuality, Pregnancy and Childbearing.* Ed. Frank F. Furstenberg, Jr., Richard Lincoln, and Jane Menken. Philadelphia: University of Pennsylvania Press, 1981, 223–233.

McGee, Elizabeth. *Too Little. Too Late: Services for Teenage Parents.* New York: Ford Foundation, 1982.

McMurray, Georgia L. "Community Action on Behalf of Pregnant School-Age Girls: Educational Policies and Beyond." *Child Welfare,* 49, 6 (June 1970), 342–346.

Mech, Edmund V. "Pregnant Adolescents: Communicating the Adoption Option." *Child Welfare,* 55, 6 (November–December 1986), 555–567.

Meyer, Henry J., et al. "The Decision of Unmarried Mothers to Keep or Surrender Their Babies." *Social Casework,* 39, 4 (April 1956), 106–109.

Meyer, Henry J. et al. "Unwed Mothers' Decisions About Their Babies—An Interim Replication Study." *Child Welfare,* 38, 2 (February 1959), 1–6.

Miller, Shelby. *Children as Parents: Final Report on a Study of Childbearing and Child Rearing Among 12- to 15-Year Olds.* New York: Child Welfare League of America, 1983.

Mindick, Burton, and Stuart Oskamp. "Individual Differences Among Adolescent Contraceptors: Some Implications for Intervention," in *Pregnancy in Adolescence: Needs, Problems and Management.* Ed. Irving R. Stuart and Carl F. Wells. New York: Van Nostrand Reinhold Company, 1982, 140–176.

Mohr, James C. "The Historical Character of Abortion in the United States Through World War II," in *Perspectives on Abortion.* Ed. Paul Sachdev. Metuchen, N. J.: Scarecrow Press, 1985, 3–14.

Moore, Kristen, and Martha Burt. *Private Crisis, Public Cost: Policy Perspectives on Teenage Childbearing.* Washington, D. C.: Urban Institute Press, 1982.

Moore, Kristin A., and Steven B. Caldwell. *Out of Wedlock Pregnancy and Childbearing.* Washington, D. C.: The Urban Institute, 1976.

Moore, Kristen, and Linda J. Waite. "Early Childbearing and Educational Attainment." *Family Planning Perspectives,* 9, 5 (September–October 1977), 220–225.

Moore, Kristen A., and Richard F. Wertheimer. "Teenage Childbearing and Welfare: Preventive and Ameliorative Strategies." *Family Planning Perspectives,* 16, 6 (November–December, 1984), 285–289.

Morrison, Diane M. "Adolescent Contraceptives Behavior: A Review." *Psychological Bulletin,* 98, 3 (1985), 538–568.

National Research Council. *Report on Teenage Pregnancy.* Washington, D. C.: National Academy Press, 1986.

Nuehring, Elane et al. "Evaluating the Impact of Prevention Programs Aimed at Children." *Social Work Research and Abstracts,* 19, 2 (1983), 11–18.

O'Connell, Martin, and Carolyn C. Rogers. "Out of Wedlock Births, Premarital Pregnancies and Their Effect on Family Formation and Dissolution." *Family Planning Perspectives,* 16, 4 (July–August, 1984), 157–162.

O'Leary, Kathleen, Milton Shore, and Serena Wieder. "Contacting Pregnant Adolescents: Are We Missing Cues?" *Social Casework,* 65, 5 (May 1984), 297–306.

Olson, Colleen F., and John Worobey. "Perceived Mother–Daughter Relations in a Pregnant and Non-Pregnant Adolescent Sample." *Adolescence,* 19, 76 (Winter 1984), 782–794.

Olson, Lucy. "Social and Psychological Correlates of Pregnancy Resolution Among Adolescent Women: A Review." *American Journal of Orthopsychiatry,* 50, 3 (July 1980), 432–445.

Olson, Lucy, and Joan Rollins. "Psychological Barriers to Contraceptive Use Among Adolescent Women." In *Pregnancy in Adolescence: Needs, Problems and Management.* Ed. Irving R. Stuart and Carl F. Wells. New York: Van Nostrand Reinhold Company, 1982, 177–193.

Oppel, Wallace C. *Illegitimacy—A Comparative Follow-up Study*. Unpublished Ph.D. thesis. National Catholic School of Social Services, Catholic University, Washington, D.C., 1969.

O'Rourke, Helen A. "The Agency as Seen Through the Eyes of Its Clients." *Child Welfare*, 47, 8 (October 1968), 470–477.

Osofsky, Howard S. *The Pregnant Teenager—A Medical Education and Social Analysis*. Springfield, Ill.: Charles C Thomas, 1968.

Pakter, Jean, and Frieda Nelson. "The Unmarried Mother and Her Child—The Problems and the Challenges," in *Illegitimacy: Data and Findings for Prevention, Treatment, and Policy Formulation*. New York: National Council on Illegitimacy, 1965.

Palmer, Emily. "A Community-Based Comprehensive Approach to Serving Adolescent Parents." *Child Welfare*, 60 (March 1981), 191–197.

Pannor, Reuben et al. *The Unmarried Father—New Approach to Helping Unmarried Young Parents*. New York: Springer-Verlag New York, 1971.

Pappenfort, Donnell M., and Dee M. Kilpatrick. *A Census of Children's Residential Institutions in the U.S., Puerto Rico and the Virgin Islands: 1966*, Vol. 6: *Maternity Homes*. Social Service Monographs, 2d series. Chicago: University of Chicago, School of Social Service Administration, 1970.

Pauker, Jerome. "Girls Pregnant Out of Wedlock," in *The Double Jeopardy: The Triple Crises—Illegitimacy Today*. New York: National Council on Illegitimacy, 1968.

Paul, Eve W., and Paula Schaap. "Legal Rights and Responsibilities of Pregnant Teenagers and Their Children," in *Pregnancy in Adolescence: Needs, Problems and Management*. Ed. Irving R. Stuart and Carl F. Wells. New York: Van Nostrand Reinhold Company, 1982, 3–24.

Perlman, Helen Harris. "Unmarried Mothers," in *Social Work and Social Problems*. Ed. Nathan E. Cohen, New York: National Association of Social Workers, 1954.

Phipps-Yonas, Susan. "Teenage Pregnancy and Motherhood: A Review of the Literature," *American Journal of Orthopsychiatry*, 50, 3 (July 1980), 403–431.

Pinchbeck, Ivey, and Margaret Hewitt. *Children in English Society*, Vol. 1: *From Tudor Times to the Eighteenth Century*. London: Kegan Paul, Trench, Trubner & Co., 1969.

Platts, Hal. "A Public Adoption Agency's Approach to Natural Fathers." *Child Welfare*, 47, 9 (November 1968), 530–537.

Plionis, Betty M. "Adolescent Pregnancy: A Review of the Literature." *Social Work* (July 1975), 302–307.

Pope, Hallowell. "Unwed Mothers and Their Sex Partners." *Journal of Marriage and the Family*, 29, 3 (August 1967), 555–567.

Power, Edward, and Mathew De Chirico. *The Treatment of Unwed Parents—How Determined? How Effective?* Paper presented at Regional Annual Conference, Child Welfare League of America, March 1969, Pittsburgh. Mimeo.

Presser, Harriet B. "Guessing and Misinformation About Pregnancy Risk Among Urban Mothers," In *Teenage Sexuality, Pregnancy and Childbearing*. Ed. Frank F. Furstenberg, Richard Lincoln and Jane Menken. Philadelphia: University of Pennsylvania Press, 1981a, 317–326.

Presser, Harriet, B. "Early Motherhood: Ignorance or Bliss?" In *Teenage Sexuality, Pregnancy and Childbearing*. Ed. Frank F. Furstenberg, Jr., Richard Lincoln, and Jane Menken. Philadelphia: University of Pennsylvania Press, 1981b, 336–349.

Raines, Prudence M. *Becoming an Unwed Mother—A Sociological Account*. New York: Aldine Atherton, 1971.

Rashbaum, M., et al. "Use of Social Services by Unmarried Mothers." *Children*, 10, 1 (January–February 1963), 11–16.

Raynor, Lois. *Giving Up a Baby for Adoption*. London: Association of British Adoption Agencies, November 1971.

Reed, Ellery F., and Ruth Latimer. *A Study of Unmarried Mothers Who Kept Their Babies*. Cincinnati, Ohio: Social Welfare Research, 1962.

Reichelt, Paul A., and Harriet H. Werley. "Contraception, Abortion and Venereal Disease:

Teenagers' Knowledge and the Effect of Education," in *Teenage Sexuality, Pregnancy and Childbearing*. Ed. Frank F. Furstenberg, Jr., Richard Lincoln, and Jane Menken. Philadelphia: University of Pennsylvania Press, 1981, 305–316.

Resnick, Michael D. "Studying Adolescent Mothers' Decision Making About Adoption and Parenting," *Social Work,* 29 (January–February, 1984), 5–10.

Rivera-Casale, Cecilia, Lorraine Klerman, and Roger Manela. "The Relevance of Child-Support Enforcement to School-Age Parents." *Child-Welfare,* 63, 6 (November–December 1984), 521–532.

Rivera, Frederick P., Patrick J. Sweeney, and Brady F. Henderson. "Black Teenage Fathers: What Happens When the Child Is Born?", *Pediatrics,* 78 (July 1986), 151–158.

Rogel, Mary J., and Martha E. Zuehike. "Adolescent Contraceptive Behavior: Influences and Implications," in *Pregnancy in Adolescence: Needs, Problems and Management.* Ed. Irving R. Stuart and Carl F. Wells. New York: Van Nostrand Reinhold Company, 1982, 194–216.

Roosa, Mark A. "Short-Term Effects of Teenage Parenting Programs on Knowledge and Attitudes," *Adolescence,* 19, 75 (Fall 1984), 659–666.

Rosoff, Jeannie. "Blocking Family Planning." *Family Planning Perspectives,* 13, 3 (May–June, 1981), 125–131.

Rubenstein, Hiasaura, and Mary H. Bloch, "Helping Clients Who Are Poor: Worker and Client Perceptions of Problems, Activities and Outcomes." *Social Service Review,* 52, 1 (March 1978), 69–84.

Rutledge, Mark. "Does Counseling Really Help Abortion Patients?" In *Perspectives on Abortion.* Ed. Paul Sachdev. Metuchen, N. J.: Scarecrow Press, 1985, 223–235.

Sachdev, Paul. "Counseling Single Abortion Patients: A Research Overview and Practice Implications," in *Perspectives on Abortion.* Ed. Paul Sachdev. Metuchen, N. J.: Scarecrow Press, 1985, 236–266.

Sacker, Ira M., and Sol D. Neuhoff. "Medical and Psychosocial Risk Factors in the Pregnant Adolescent," in *Pregnancy in Adolescence: Needs, Problems and Management.* Ed. Irving R. Stuart and Carl F. Wells. New York: Van Nostrand Reinhold Company, 1982, 107–139.

Salguero, Carlos. "Adolescent Pregnancy: A Report on ACYF-Funded Research and Demonstration Projects." *Children Today* (November–December, 1980), 10–11, 35.

Sauber, Mignon. *Experiences of the Unwed Mother as Parent.* New York: Community Council of Greater New York, 1965.

Sauber, Mignon. "The Role of the Unmarried Father." *Welfare in Review,* 4, 9 (November 1966), 15–18.

Sauber, Mignon, and Eileen M. Corrigan. *The Six-Year Experience of Unwed Mothers as Parents.* New York: Community Council of Greater New York, 1970.

Scales, Peter, and Douglas Beckstein. "From Macho to Mutuality: Helping Young Men Make Effective Decisions About Sex, Contraception, and Pregnancy," in *Pregnancy in Adolescence: Needs, Problems and Management.* Ed. Irving R. Stuart and Carl F. Wells. New York: Van Nostrand Reinhold Company, 1982, 264–287.

Schirm, Allen L. et al. "Contraceptive Failure in the United States: The Impact of Social, Economic and Demographic Factors." *Family Planning Perspectives,* 14, 2 (March-April, 1982), 68–74.

Sedlak, Michael. "Youth Policy and Young Women, 1870–1972." *Social Services Review,* 56, 3 (1982), 448–464.

Shah, F., Melvin Zelnik, and John Kantner. "Unprotected Intercourse Among Unwed Teenagers." *Family Planning Perspectives,* 7 (1975), 39–43.

Shapiro, Deborah. *Social Distance and Illegitimacy—Report of a Pilot Study.* New York: Research Center, Columbia University, School of Social Work, 1970.

Shouse, Judith. "Psychological and Emotional Problems of Pregnancy in Adolescence," pp. in *The Teenage Pregnant Girl.* Ed. Jack Zackler and Wayne Brandstadt. Springfield, Ill.: Charles C Thomas, 1975, 161–186.

Shyne, Ann, and Anita Schroeder. *National Study of Social Services to Children and Their Families.* Washington, D. C.: DHEW, 1978.

Simkins, Lawrence. "Consequences of Teenage Pregnancy and Motherhood." *Adolescence,* 19, 73 (Spring 1984), 39–54.

Simms, Madeleine, and Christopher Smith. "Teenage Mothers and Adoption." *Adoption and Fostering,* 6, 4 (1982), 43–48.

Singh, Suschecla. "Asolescent Pregnancy in the United States: An Interstate Analysis." *Family Planning Perspectives* 18, 5 (September–October, 1986), 210–220.

Sisto, Grace W. "Therapeutic Foster Homes for Teenage Mothers and Their Babies." *Child Welfare,* 64, 2 (March–April, 1985), 157–163.

Sklar, June, and Beth Berkov. "Teenage Family Formation in Postwar Armerica," in *Teenage Sexuality, Pregnancy and Childbearing.* Ed. Frank F. Furstenberg, Jr., Richard Lincoln, and Jane Menken. Philadelphia: University of Pennsylvania Press, 1981, 23–43.

Steinhoff, Patricia G. "The Effects of Induced Abortion on Future Family Goals of Young Women," in *Perspectives on Abortion.* Ed. Paul Sachdev. Metuchen, N. J.: The Scarecrow Press, 1985, 117–129.

Steinmetz, Martha A. "Role-Playing in a Maternity Home." *Children,* 11, 2 (March–April 1964), 61–64.

Stepto, Robert C., Louis Keith, and Donald Keith. "Obstetrical and Medical Problems of Teen-age Pregnancy," in *The Teenage Pregnant Girl.* Ed. Jack Zackler and Wayne Brandstedt. Springfield, Ill.: Charles C. Thomas, 1975, pp. 83–133.

Sung, Kyu-Taik, and Dorothy Rothrock. "An Alternate School for Pregnant Teen-agers and Teen-age Mothers." *Child Welfare,* 59 (July–August, 1980), 427–436.

Taylor, Lillian E. "Social Attitudes Toward Sexual Behavior and Illegitimacy," in *Illegitimacy: Data and Findings for Prevention, Treatment, and Policy Formation.* New York: National Council on Illegitimacy, October 1965.

Tietze, Christopher. "Teenage Pregnancies: Looking Ahead to 1984." In *Teenage Sexuality, Pregnancy and Childbearing.* Ed. Frank F. Furstenberg, Jr., Richard Lincoln, and Jane Menken. Philadelphia: University of Pennsylvania Press, 1981, 149–154.

Torres, Aida. "Does Your Mother Know . . .?" *Family Planning Perspectives,* 10, 5 (September–October 1978), 280–282.

Torres, Aida. "Rural and Urban Family Planning Services in the United States." *Family Planning Perspective,* 11 (March–April 1979), 109–114.

Torres, Aida, Jacqueline Darroch Forrest, and Susan Eisman. "Telling Parents: Clinic Policies and Adolescents' Use of Family Planning and Abortion Services." *Family Planning Perspectives,* 12, 6 (November–December 1980), 284–292.

Torres, Aida, Jacqueline Darroch Forrest, and Susan Eisman. "Family Planning Services in the United States, 1978–1979." *Family Planning Perspectives,* 13, 3 (May–June 1981), 132–141.

Triseliotis, John. "The Timing of the Single Mother's Decision in Relation to Adoption Agency Practice." *Child Adoption,* no. 3 (1969), 29–35.

Trussell, T. James. "Economic Consequences of Teenage Child Bearing," *Family Planning Perspectives,* 8, 4 (July–August 1976), 184–190.

Trussell, James, and Jane Menken. "Early Childbearing and Subsequent Fertility," in *Teenage Sexuality, Pregnancy and Childbearing.* Ed. Frank F. Furstenberg, Jr., Richard Lincoln, and Jane Menken. Philadelphia: University of Pennsylvania Press, 1981, 234–250.

U.S. Department of Health, Education, and Welfare, Public Health Service. *Trends in Illegitimacy—United States: 1940–1966.* National Center for Health Statistics. Series 21, No. 5. Washington, D.C.: U.S. Government Printing Office, 1968.

U.S. Dept. of Health and Human Services. *Status of Children, Youth and Families.* Washington, D. C.: U.S. Government Printing Office, 1980.

U.S. House of Representatives. *Teen-Age Pregnancy: What is Being Done? A State by State Look.* Washington, D.C.: Select Committee on Children, Youth and Families, 1985.

Vincent, Clark. *Unmarried Mother.* New York: The Free Press, 1961.

Vinovskis, Maris A. "An 'Epidemic' of Adolescent Pregnancy? Some Historical Considerations." *Journal of Family History* (Summer 1981), 205–230.

Vukelich, Carol, and Deborah Kliman. "Mature and Teenage Mothers' Infant Growth

Expectations and Use of Child Development Information Sources." *Family Relations,* 34, 2 (April 1985), 189–196.

Wallace, Helen, et al. "A Study of Services and Needs of Teenage Pregnant Girls in the Large Cities of the United States." *American Journal of Public Health,* 63, 1 (January 1973), 5–16.

Watkins, Susan Cotts. "Book Review of 'The Impact of Teenage Pregnancy on the Family, or Vice Versa?' " *Family Planning Perspectives,* 15, 4 (July–August, 1983), 203–204.

Weatherly, Richard et al. "Comprehensive Programs for Pregnant Teens and Teenage Parents: How Successful Have They Been?" *Family Planning Prospectives,* 18, 2 (March–April 1986), 73–78.

Wells, Carl F. "Introduction." In *Pregnancy in Adolescence: Needs, Problems and Management.* Ed. Irving R. Stuart and Carl F. Wells. New York: Van Nostrand Reinhold Company, 1982, xi–xxvi.

Wimperis, Virginia. *The Unmarried Mother and Her Child.* London: George Allen & Unwin, Ltd., 1960.

Wisconsin Department of Health and Social Services. *Unmarried Mothers in Wisconsin 1976.* Madison: Wisconsin Department of Health and Social Services, 1977.

Wise, Susan, and Frances K. Grossman. "Adolescent Mothers and Their Infants: Psychological Factors in Early Attachment and Interaction." *American Journal of Orthopsychiatry,* 50, 3 (July, 1980), 454–468.

Wright, Helen R. *Eighty Unmarried Mothers Who Kept Their Babies.* Department of Social Welfare, State of California, May 1965.

Wright, Mattie K. "Comprehensive Service for Adolescent Unwed Mothers." *Children,* 13, 5 (September–October 1966), 171–176.

Yelloly, Margaret. "Factors Relating to an Adoption Decision by the Mothers of Illegitimate Infants." *Sociological Review,* 13, 1, New Series (March 1965).

Yelloly, Margaret. "Adoption and the Natural Mother." *Case Conference,* 13 (December 1966), 270–277.

Young, Alma T., Barbara Beckman, and Helen Rehr. "Parental Influence on Pregnant Adolescents," *Social Work* (September 1975), 387–391.

Young, Leontine. *Out of Wedlock.* New York: McGraw-Hill Book Company, 1954.

Zabin, Laurie Schwab, and Samuel D. Clark, Jr. "Why They Delay: A Study of Teenage Family Planning Clinic Patients." *Family Planning Perspectives,* 13, 5 (September–October 1981), 205–217.

Zabin, Laurie et al. "Evaluation of a Pregnancy Prevention Program for Urban Teenagers." *Family Planning Perspective,* 18, 3 (May–June 1986), 119–126.

Zellman, Gail L. "Public School Programs for Adolescent Pregnancy and Parenthood: An Assessment." *Family Planning Perspectives,* 14, 1 (January–February, 1982), 15–21.

Zelnik, Melvin, and John F. Kantner. "The Resolution of Teenage First Pregnancies." *Family Planning Perspective,* 6 (Spring 1974), 74–80.

Zelnik, Melvin, and John F. Kantner. "Sexual and Contraceptive Experience of Young Unmarried Women in the U.S., 1976 and 1971." *Family Planning Perspectives,* 9, 2 (March–April 1977), 55–63.

Zelnik, Melvin, and John F. Kantner. "First Pregnancies to Women 15–19: 1976 and 1971." *Family Planning Perspective,* 10, 1 (January–February 1978), 11–20.

Zelnik, Melvin, and John F. Kantner. "Sexual Activity, Contraceptive Use and Pregnancy Among Metropolitan Area Teenagers, 1971–1979." *Family Planning Perspectives,* 12, 5 (September–October, 1980), 230–237.

Zelnik, Melvin, and John F. Kantner. "Contraceptive Patterns and Premarital Pregnancy Among Women Aged 15–19 in 1976," in *Teenage Sexuality, Pregnancy and Childbearing.* Ed. Frank F. Furstenberg, Jr., Richard Lincoln, and Jane Menken. Philadelphia: University of Pennsylvania Press, 1981, 112–125.

Zelnik, Melvin, John F. Kantner, and Kathleen Ford. *Sex and Pregnancy in Adolescence.* Beverly Hills, Cal.: Sage Publications, 1981.

Zober, Edith. "The Pregnant School Girl." *Child Welfare,* 48, 6 (June 1969), 362–366.

9

Substitute Care:

Adoption

Introduction

Adoption provides permanent substitute care for children whose birth parents are unable or unwilling to provide the necessary support these children need. Adoption involves becoming a parent through a legal and social process rather than through a biological one. A more formal definition depicts adoption as: "a legal process through which a family unit is created by severing the ties between a child and his or her biological parents and legally establishing a new parent/child relationship between persons not related by blood. It thus involves the creation of a family by the state rather than through procreation. Through such state action the adopted child becomes a permanent member of a new family and is entitled to all of the benefits accorded a biological child" (Meezan, 1983a, p. 425).

A number of key principles guide the provision of adoptive services to children, their birth families, and adoptive parents:

1. That the first, best place for the child is with his own family, in his own community, in his own country; that adoption is not appropriate unless all efforts have been made to salvage his family for the child. Adoption is always in substitution of the original, biological home and should not be employed unless it is clear that the child's own family is not likely to be able to provide the care the child needs and is rightfully entitled to.
    This would suggest that family welfare is the best child welfare and that the community is obligated to provide the family with those resources and services that would enable the family to maintain the child at home.
2. If substitute care is needed, the first efforts should be made to find such a home in the child's own racial, national, ethnic, and religious community. Only if it is clear that such resources are not available should the effort be made to find an adoptive home outside the child's community.
3. That the primary purpose of adoption is to provide a permanent family for children who cannot be cared for by their own biological parents. Therefore, the child's welfare, her needs, and her interests are the basic determinants of good adoption practice. Homes should be selected for children, rather than children selected for homes.
4. That adoption is the most desirable form of permanent substitute care where this is the necessary alternative to the child's own family. It is a more securely permanent arrangement than the foster family home. It is more likely to provide the necessary long-term stability and continuity of affectionate, intimate care by the same parent than either the foster family home or an institution. . . .

5. That the welfare of the child requires that a decision regarding the need for permanent substitute care be made as early as possible and implemented with a minimum of delay and uncertainty, and that finality in adoption be achieved as soon as possible, with due regard, however, for other countervailing considerations (Kadushin, 1984, pp.3–4) (See also Cole, 1978).

Historical Background

All of the ancient peoples—the Egyptians, the Babylonians, the Greeks, the Romans—sanctioned adoption. The Bible speaks of it. Pharaoh's daughter adopted Moses and Mordecai adopted Esther. The Code of Hammurabi mentions adoption and the protection that should be given the adoptive parent. Sargon, king of Babylonia, circa 2800 B.C., was adopted. The inscription that tells his story reads:

> Sargon, the mighty king, King of Akkad, am I. My mother was a vestal, my father I knew not. . . . In my city, Azupirani, which is situated onn the bank of the Euphrates, my mother, the vestal, bore me. In a hidden place she brought me forth. She laid me in a vessel made of reeds, closed my door with pitch, and dropped me down into the river, which did not drown me. The river carried me to Akki, the water carrier. Akki the water carrier lifted me up in the kindness of his heart. Akki the water carrier raised me as his own son. Akki the water carrier made of me his gardener. In my work as gardener I was beloved by Istar, I became the king, and for forty-five years I held kingly sway [Quoted in Clothier, 1939, p. 598].

In earlier periods, adoption was not so frequently resorted to in solution to the problem of childlessness, because a simpler solution was socially acceptable. If a wife was infertile, the husband took another woman to bear him children. Thus Sarah, who was childless, urged Abraham to take Hagar, her maid, as a concubine, with whom he then had a child. In ancient Greece and Rome, adoptions were arranged so as to acquire an heir to perpetuate the family or to manage extensive family property. Thus Solon, in Greece, sanctioned adoption as a means of providing continuity for a family line.

In early Rome, one function of adoption was to permit a candidate for office to qualify under the provision "that a candidate who had children, or who had more children, was to be preferred to one who had none or fewer" (Hastings, 1908, p. 113).

In India, adoptions were arranged so as to provide a male heir in order to meet the demands of religious ceremonials. Among the Hindus, the adopting father declared to the adoptive son, "I accept thee for the fulfillment of religion; I take thee for the continuation of lineage" (Hastings, 1908, p. 110). Among the Hindus, as among the Chinese, the need in adoption was specifically for a male child, because "Heaven awaits not one who has no male issue." The childless couple might adopt children so as to be sure of having care in their old age. This is the attitude expressed in a Hawaiian saying, "Feed human beings, for they can be sent on errands" (Carroll, V. 1970, p. 27).

In some cultures, adoptions might be informally arranged between people who knew each other well and who were tied by bonds of mutual obligation. Parents who had too many children gave some to relatives or friends who had none or too few. In such arrangements, there might be continuing and frequent contact between the two families, creating an additional parental relationship rather than a substitute parental relationship (Carroll, V. 1970; Benet 1970).

The focus of earlier adoptions is suggested by the medieval definition of adoption "as a legitimate act imitating nature for the solace and comfort of those who have no children." In earlier periods of history, then, adoption served to meet the needs of adults; today it is supported primarily because it meets the needs of parentless children. There is no body of common law regarding adoption. Consequently there was little precedent for adoption procedures in Colonial America. Abbott (1937) notes that "provision for care of dependent children by means of adoption was probably delayed by the development of the relation between master and apprentice" so that orphans and children of indigent parents could be bound out to obtain care in this way (p. 461).

Orphan asylums continued to use such indentures as one of the principal forms of placing their children until some years after the Civil War. The contract, made between the institution in behalf of the child and the family accepting the child, obligated the family to maintain the child until the age of eighteen "with proper meat drink washing and lodging and all other necessaries fit and convenient for a child of his/her age and condition and to teach the child reading writing and arithmetic as well as some trade; to rear the child in such a way as that he/she may be useful to himself/herself and the community" (McCausland, 1976, p. 23). After the Civil War the words "doth bind" gave way to such phrases as "treated in every way as if the child were the natural child" of the parents.

Prior to the passage of general adoption laws, state legislatures followed the practice of "passing special acts providing for the adoption of particular children by particular adults" (Witmer et al., 1963, p. 29). There is some question about whether Massachusetts or Texas was the first state to pass an adoption law. Nevertheless it is clear that the Massachusetts statute enacted in 1851 became the model for many of the other state adoption laws passed during or shortly after the Civil War. It provided for

1. The written consent of the child's biological parent.
2. Joint petition by both the adoptive mother and father.
3. A decree by the judge, who had to be satisfied that the adoption was "fit and proper."
4. Legal and complete severance of the relationship between child and biological parents.

By 1929 every state had passed some kind of adoption legislation. The adoption laws indicate that "From the outset, most laws [at least as interpreted judicially] have had the welfare of the child as their main purpose" (Witmer et al., 1963, p. 43). Although the laws of the different states varied in effectiveness, the history of adoption has been a movement toward a greater emphasis on the protection of the principals affected by adoption: the biological parents, the adoptive parents, the community, and the child.

The early statutes were intended primarily to "provide evidence of the legal transfer of a child by the biological parents to the adopting parents and provision for a public record of the transfer" (Abbott, 1938, p. 165). The judge's decision that the adoption was "fit and proper" was based only on contact with the parties to the adoption. Recognizing that this was not sufficient to prevent adoption by unsuitable or unscrupulous parents, some states provided for more extensive inquiry regarding the adoptive parents. Thus in 1891 Michigan began to require that the judge make an investigation before finalizing an adoption. This law was later amended to provide for a social investigation by an agency that was, generally, in a better position to conduct such a study. In 1917 Minnesota passed the first law requiring detailed investigation by a local agency or the state department of public welfare and a written recommendation to the court regarding the advisability of permitting the adoption. By 1938, similar laws had been passed in twenty-four states (McGowan, 1983).

Responses to the "application-for-adoption" form used by the Chicago Orphan Asylum in the 1880s and 1890s reflected the adopters' preferences and motivations:

> The blue-eyed, golden-haired little girl was the desire of many; a few wanted a black-eyed brunette; or one "not too homely," definitely "not a redhead." One woman didn't care too much about "looks" but wanted assurance that the child "had not one drop of Irish blood." Disposition and health are defined: "clean, healthy, sensible and good dispositioned"; a "strict Christian, well dispositioned"; "light complexion, well disposed"; "a sunny German girl who can sing." One man requested a boy "possessing some force of character . . . it would be a home where no tobacco or whiskey would be tolerated. Please send five photographs."
>
> Why they wanted a child was often expressed in terms of work; to wash dishes and run errands, to be a companion for an only child or an elderly person living in the family; to "herd cattle, bring in coal, and take care of the cow" (that applicant was turned down immediately); to do light housework; to act as nursemaid. But there were those who loved children and had none, or who wished to extend their love to an orphan. There is only one instance of a woman wanting a child to make a little noise, she couldn't bear the silence when her daughter left home to be married! [McCausland, 1976, p. 64].

Before the introduction of community controls, advertisements such as the following, which appeared in the *Chicago Tribune*, were not uncommon:

PERSONAL—Wanted—Healthy Twins or Baby girl under 6 months, by couple able to give children wonderful home and future. Address KH 385. Tribune. (December 21, 1919)

PERSONAL—Wanted for adoption by wealthy Chicago couple, infant girl or boy. Address KH 386, Tribune. (December 21, 1919)

PERSONAL—Wanted to Adopt Baby month old, by responsible couple; good home. Address B 599, Tribune. (December 21, 1919) [Quoted in Bremner, 1970, p. 139]

Some of the unfortunate situations that might result were reported to a 1925 Commission appointed to study and revise the Pennsylvania statutes relating to children:

CASE VII.
Frances, aged thirteen, recently made a personal application to a social agency stating that her foster father had been having sexual relations with her for the last two years. Upon investigation living conditions were found to be very bad. The foster mother corroborated the child's statements. Frances had been legally adopted in May 1918. She was sold to her foster parents by her mother for a quart of whisky [Quoted in Bremner, 1970, p. 142].

Attempts to provide additional protection for the child included the introduction of a trial period between the time the child was placed in the adoptive home and the time the adoption was legally consummated. Also an increasing number of states required that records of the adoption proceedings, once completed, be closed and sealed and that a new birth certificate for the child be issued at that time. All these changes indicated a shift from emphasis on the purely legal aspects of transfer of the child to a growing appreciation of the human aspects of adoption. These concerns are reflected in the adoption standards promulgated periodically by the Child Welfare League. The League published the first edition of its standards in 1938 (McGowan, 1983).

Even though the legal structure for formalizing adoptions had been established, adoptions had low priority as a substitute-care alternative. The movement began to develop some momentum between 1910 and 1920. Special adoption agencies were established at that time that devoted full time and energy to this particular service. The moving forces behind the establishment of some of the principal private agencies concerned with adoption—Louise Wise, Spence Adoption Agency, and Chapin Adoptions Agency in New York, and The Cradle in Chicago—were women volunteers from prominent and wealthy backgrounds (Romanofsky, 1974).

Adoption as a field of social work practice emerged primarily after World War II. Provision of these services was increasingly recognized as a practice area that required special worker training and preparation, and social work agencies saw these services as their responsibility. As the number of children adopted through agencies grew, there was a concomitant decrease in the number of children who were adopted through other means (Billingsley & Giovannoni, 1972, p. 71). During the 1950s, agencies also participated in the first interracial and international adoptions of children (McGowan, 1983).

During the 1960s a significant shift occurred in the focus of adoption services. As a result of the concern for the growing number of children remaining in long-term foster care, as well as the concern for children who appeared to be "lost" in the foster care system, pressure emerged to find more permanent living arrangements for them (Allen & Knitzer, 1983). The concept of "special needs" embodies a commitment to increase home-based and adoption services for black, older and handicapped children, many of whom have been in long-term care.

> Adoption, unlike other forms of substitute parental care, did not originate as a resource for dependent children, and especially not for poor children. In fact, until the last decade or so, most of the children adopted through agencies were not "poor children"; they were illegitimate babies born to white middle- and upper-income women (Billingsley & Giovannoni, 1972, p. 71).

Recognition that poor children, too, have a right to a home and family led to greater utilization of adoption services for them. This effort, in turn, produced more widespread provision of adoptive homes for black and other minority group children.

Concern for special-needs children led to the passage of Public Law 96-272 on June 17, 1980. This law makes state adoption programs mandatory and, for the first time, establishes federal matching funds so that subsidies can be provided to families who adopt such children if the local child welfare agency determines that a child is not likely to be adopted without the provision of these funds. Subsidy payments may not exceed the amount that foster families receive. The child also remains eligible for Medicaid. The agency and the adoptive family must enter into a written agreement specifying the amount and extent of the subsidy, and families can receive these monies until the child reaches the age of eighteen or twenty-one, should he or she have a mental or physical handicap. By the end of 1981, all the states except Hawaii had passed subsidy legislation (Allen & Knitzer, 1983).

In October 1981, the federal government published a "Model Act for the Adoption of Children with Special Needs," which contains guidelines to the states for developing their own subsidy laws. This model act was designed to

> concentrate on the elimination of barriers to the permanent adoption of special needs children. To encourage and facilitate such adoptions, the final model act provides for financial assistance to families who adopt special needs children, expands the grounds for adjudications freeing such children for adoption, clarifies the roles of adoption agencies and state adoption administrations in arranging and providing support services for adoption, and includes various other provisions to promote and assist the permanent adoptive placement of special needs children [Federal Register, October 8, 1981, p. 50022].

Adoption is now a "two-tier" service system. Some services are made available to individuals who wish to add infants to their families; another set of services focuses on the development of adoptive homes for minority, older, and handicapped children needing permanent homes.

Scope

Adoptions are generally broken down into two principal groups: related and nonrelated. In related adoptions, the child is adopted by a stepfather, a stepmother, a grandparent, an uncle, and so on. Social agencies are not so directly concerned with such adoptions. In nonrelated adoptions, the child is adopted by persons with whom he or she has no family ties. Social agencies are directly concerned in finding the home, evaluating it, and supervising it for a period of time after the child has been placed. Our interest, therefore, is primarily with nonrelated adoptions.

Since 1975 no national, government-conducted study of adoptions has been available. Statistics on adoption since 1975 have been developed as a consequence of special limited studies by the Child Welfare League of America, the American Public Welfare Association, special institutes' studies, and the National Committee for Adoptions. All statistics currently available on adoptions are open to some question regarding comprehensiveness and validity.

The number of children adopted increased from 57,000 in 1957 to 175,000 in 1970—about half of the group in 1970 consisting of nonrelative adoptions. The year 1970 was the highwater mark of adoptions in the United States. Since 1970, there has been a slow, steady decline in adoptions. Selecting twenty representative states for which statistics are available in both years, it is noted that in 1970, 48,744 children were adopted by unrelated petitioners. In 1975, the same twenty states yielded a total of only 29,528 such adoptions (National Center for Social Statistics, 1972, 1977).

Statistics of specific agencies and of particular states exemplify the downward trend. Spence Chapin in New York City, one of the largest voluntary adoption agencies, decreased its placements from 476 in 1967 to 110 in 1973. In 1972 there were 1,785 nonrelated adoptions completed in Wisconsin. In 1984 only 651 such adoptions were completed.

The National Committee for Adoption (1985) conducted a national state-by-state survey of adoptions in 1982. Survey results estimated that there were 50,720 unrelated adoptions in 1982—19,428 arranged by public agencies, 14,549 by private voluntary agencies, and 16,743 independent adoptions arranged by private individuals. Some 14,000 of these were adoptions of special needs children and some 9,600 were adoptions by foster parents. The 50,720 unrelated adoptions in 1982 compares with the peak total of 89,200 such adoptions in 1970.

Adoptions arranged through public agencies and through independent auspices have been increasing, whereas adoptions through private agency auspices have been decreasing (pp. 102–104). Although adoptive placements generally have declined, the percentage of older children placed for adoption has increased. The median age of children placed for adoption in 1983 was between five and six years of age. (See also Gershenson, 1983.)

Young children predominate among those available for adoption through voluntary agencies. "Children under one year of age composed 83% of those accepted for adoption by the voluntary agencies but only 38% of those accepted by the public agencies" (Shyne & Schroeder, 1978, p. 134). Older children, on the other hand, are placed mainly by public agency personnel. They comprise only 6 percent of those accepted for adoption by private social service organizations, but 26 percent of the children accepted for adoption by public agencies.

As a consequence of the reduction in the number of children surrendered for adoption by white unwed mothers (see Chapter 8 p. 495) agencies throughout the country began, in 1975, to stop or to slow down applications for white, nonhandicapped infants. Prospective adoptive parents were explicitly informed that there was likely to be a three- to five-year wait for such a child.

There is some evidence that girls are more readily adopted than boys. Data from Canada suggest that adoptive applicants prefer female children. "The current figure (as of June 30, 1980) of the Adoption Desk indicates that 41% of applicants are requesting girls, 26% are requesting boys, and 33% are requesting either sex" (Lipman, 1984, pp. 33–34).

Black, Hispanic, and Native American children are overrepresented among those available for adoption. Black families are, in fact, adopting black children at the same rate as white families are adopting white children. However, because a larger percentage of the population of black chiildren are in substitute care waiting adoptive placement, as compared with white children, they continue to be in oversupply for adoption. Although black children comprise 14 per cent of the child population, they are 25 per cent of the foster care population, 33 per cent of the children free for adoption, and 37 per cent of the children free for adoption who are not in an adoptive placement (Maza, 1983, p. 2).

Despite the increase in the ability of agencies to place special needs children for adoption, such children continue to present a difficulty for placement. In 1983 some 58 per cent of minority children who were free for adoption and for whom adoption was planned were still waiting to be adopted. The median age of children with a plan for adoption, but who were still unplaced in 1983, was nine years of age. Eighty-three per cent of the black handicapped children available for adoption were waiting to be placed. Statistics from various special national studies of the adoptive situation in 1982–83 reveal that young children are easier to place than older children, white children easier to place than minority group children, and unhandicapped children easier to place than those with handicaps (American Public Welfare Association, 1984).

Minority group children and older and handicapped children thus constitute a disproportionate percentage of the 33,000 children estimated to be free for adoption and waiting nonrelative placement in December 1982 (Maza, 1983, p. 1). Cole (1984) notes that retarded children experience the greatest difficulty in finding permanent families.

Between 1969 and 1976, transracial adoptions comprised between 20 and 35 per cent of all nonrelative adoptions of black children (Feigelman & Silverman, 1983, p. 12). In part because of strong opposition to this type of adoption within the black professional community, the number of transracial adoptions has been decreasing in recent years.

During the period between 1968 and 1975, when the total number of adoptions in the United States first rose and then declined, the adoption of foreign children continued steadily upward—from 1,612 children in 1968 to 5,633 in 1975. This number peaked at 6,500 in 1976. Currently, some 5,000 children from other countries are adopted yearly (Feigelman & Silverman, 1983, p. 11). Since 1958, most of these children have come from Asian countries, primarily from Korea. In 1980, Asian children comprised two-thirds of all intercountry adoptions (Resnick, 1984, p. 276). Almost all of the other children adopted internationally in 1980 came from South or Central American countries, primarily from Colombia (Feigelman & Silverman, 1983, p. 11).

Adoption Clients

Three different groups of individuals make up the clients of adoptive services. They are the children awaiting permanent homes, the birth parents who must relinquish their rights to them, and the adoptive parents seeking to add a child to the family"

Children needing adoption

Children needing adoptive homes come primarily from the following groups:

1. Healthy infants
2. Special needs children
3. Children adopted from foreign countries

Healthy Infants: Healthy infants are still the principal, although diminishing, source of nonrelated children available to adoptive parents. Most of these infants are born out of wedlock. Very few of them are available for adoption because of the death of their parents. These infants are the most sought-after type of adoptable child, although the number of individuals seeking infants far outweighs the number currently available for placement. Infants recently listed on one adoption exchange include the following:

Michael, a one-month-old black infant. Michael is a very healthy, cute little boy. He is alert and observant. His main interests are still eating and sleeping. He has a birth weight of 6 lbs., 6 ozs.

Tara, a six-month old black/Caucasian female infant. Tara is a beautiful baby who is very engaging and expressive. She is sociable and charming and likes to be the center of family activities. She is developmentally on track. Although there are some medical risk factors in her family background, no cause for concern is seen in hers.

Special-Needs Children. Special-needs children include the following groups:

1. Black, Hispanic, Native American or other nonwhite children needing permanent homes.
2. Sibling groups who wish to be placed in adoptive homes together.
3. Children with a variety of handicaps—mental, physical, and emotional.
4. Older children seeking permanent families.

A recent study of the National Adoption Exchange indicates that compared to 1971, current children registered with the exchange are more likely to be older, black, and have physical, emotional, or intellectual impairments. The median age of children registered has risen from 5 to 11; the proportion of black children has risen from two-fifths to more than half; and the proportion of children with physical, intellectual, or emotional impairments has more than doubled in the last ten years (Meezan, 1983a, p. 427).

The following is a short description of children with special needs listed by several adoption exchanges.

D., a charming nine-year-old white boy is healthy and active and enjoys sports. Currently a third grader, D has a learning disability for which extra educational assistance is needed. D. sometimes acts up and can be impulsive.

C., an adorable, white three-year-old girl is a Down's Syndrome child. C., like many young growing children, is wearing corrective shoes for an orthopedic foot problem.

C is an eight-year-old healthy, normal, inquisitive, black child. C. was born with bilateral club feet but a series of corrective operations has straightened this out.

T. is a healthy 12-year-old white boy with light brown hair and blue eyes. He is an appealing boy about to enter the seventh grade, quite creative in arts and active in hockey and baseball.

A brother and sister team need a home together. V., a thirteen-year-old shy boy is close to his sister A., fourteen. These black children are both excellent students and healthy and active in church affairs.

J is a healthy eight-year-old boy who seems very bright for his age. He is aggressive and hyperactive and is having difficulty with peer relationships. He is currently living in a group home.

Children From Abroad. As noted previously, intercountry adoptions have been completed for children coming from a variety of areas of the world. Children placed with American families may come from Korea or southeast Asia. The fathers of these children may be U.S. servicemen. Children have also been placed in the United States from India and from various countries in South and Central America (Colombia, Peru, El Salvador, Mexico, and others). Because professionals believe that these children will have an enriched life in the United States, because these children need special medical services available in this country, or because multinational children will face less discrimination in this country than they would in their homeland, professionals from other areas of the world have allowed these adoptions to occur.

Birth Parents as Adoption Clients

Birth parents who relinquish children for adoption may voluntarily or involuntarily terminate parental rights to their children. Some of the parents who freely relinquish their rights to their children are teenage or older women bearing children out of wedlock. In the past, women in such circumstances have provided most of the infants available for adoption, but in recent years, most have chosen to obtain abortions or to raise their children themselves (See Chapter 8).

Parents may also voluntarily choose to terminate parental rights to their children when they feel that they cannot cope with the child's handicapping condition. The child may be retarded, have severe medical problems, or have cerebral palsy, for example. In their survey of children who had been freed for adoption who were served by public agencies, Shyne and Schroeder (1978) found that, of those children with handicapping conditions, fully two-thirds had been voluntarily relinquished by parents (p. 128).

In contrast to voluntary termination situations, parents may have their rights involuntarily terminated. A growing percentage of older special needs children become available as a consequence of termination of parental rights following serious and repeated abuse and neglect. Termination is often involuntary, at the ruling of the court and the children are then freed for adoption. Almost all the parents who involuntarily relinquished the rights of their children had already had these children removed from their home and placed in foster care settings (Cole, 1978).

Children in foster care are being freed for adoption more frequently and are becoming a growing source of children for adoption. This is particularly true of the large number of children who have been in foster care for some time and have been virtually abandoned by their parents. Concern about permanence for such children has resulted in increasing frequent efforts to terminate parental rights and place the child for adoption.

In their national survey, Shyne and Schroeder (1978) found that 52 per cent of the children awaiting adoption had had their parents' rights voluntarily terminated, while thirty-four per cent had had parents' rights involuntarily terminated. Children from involuntary termination situations tended to be older. Whereas one-half of the waiting children voluntarily terminated were more than seven years old, three-quarters of the children involuntarily terminated were eight or older (p. 127). The survey found that involuntary terminations were related to the abuse and neglect of children by parents who often manifested emotional problems or were mentally ill (p. 128).

As contrasted with the "social orphans" who have been abused, neglected, abandoned by their birth parents, biological orphans whose parents have died and need adoption form only a small percentage of the children available for adoption. Although full orphans constituted 1.9 per cent of the population of children in 1920, only one tenth of 1 per cent of children were full orphans in 1984.

Adoption Clients—Adoptive Parents

Two different types of couples seek to adopt children. Infertile or "traditional" adopters are interested in substituting the adopted child for an infant they cannot have biologically. When asked why they wish to adopt, these individuals tend to provide personal rather than social or humanitarian reasons. These families are not inclined to adopt special needs children (Feigelman & Silverman, 1983, pp. 43–44).

Adoptive applicants who are fertile but elect to add to their family by adoption are known as preferential adopters. They generally express humanitarian rather than personal reasons. Preferential adopters are more likely to join with other adoptive parents and to be more militant about their desire to adopt and about the child they would like to have. They are also more interested in parenting a child of another race, an older child, or a child experiencing difficulties. Possibly because they do not seek to parent an infant, they are also less intimidated by social service agency personnel (Cole, 1984).

Infertile or traditional adopters remain the largest group of adoptive parents. Using multistage area probability sampling techniques, Bachrach (1983) interviewed married women and single mothers from throughout the United States who were 15–44 years old. Based on interviews with 8,611 women, she found that women who were older, childless, and unable to have children were much more likely to adopt than their younger, fertile counterparts. Although 1 to 2 percent of married couples in the United States have adopted children, her study found that 9 per cent of women who were sterile for noncontraceptive reasons adopted, as had more than 5 per cent of those who had never had a child, and 4.4 per cent who were in their mid-thirties to early forties (pp. 862–863). She estimates "that *nearly half* of the estimated 274,000 currently married women who had reached or surpassed age 30 without having had a live birth and were unable to have one *had* adopted a child" (p. 862).

In recent years, fertile or preferential adopters have played an increasing role in providing homes for children in need of them. Between 1955 and 1973, the proportion of childless wives who adopted fell from 6 to 4 per cent, while the proportion of fertile women who adopted rose from 3 to 7 per cent (Bonham cited in Feigelman & Silverman, 1983, p. 13).

Owing, in part, to the rapidly rising demands for adoptive homes, adoption agencies began to allow new groups of parents to make permanent homes for children. Two types of families, in particular—single parents and foster parents—have benefited from more liberalized adoption policies. As recently as ten years ago, each of these groups were actively discouraged from bringing adoptive children into their home.

One of the first published professional studies of single parent adoptions appeared in the social work literature in 1970. In the late 1960's, the Los Angeles County Department of Adoptions placed forty children in single parent homes. Almost all of these parents (39) were women and three-quarters were black or Mexican-American (Branham, 1970). Since that time, the use of single parent homes has spread to other agencies (Costin, 1970; Kadushin, 1970a). Nationwide, some 3,000 to 5,000 such adoptions have been finalized (Feigelman & Silverman, 1983, p. 178).

Almost all of the single adopters are women. In 1975, 2.1 per cent of all unrelated adopters were single females, whereas only .4 per cent were single males (Bachrach, 1983, p. 860).

Although agencies are now willing to accept single individuals as adoptive parent applicants, they still face much more opposition from agencies than do couples. As Meezan (1982a) notes, single individuals remain a second choice for agencies. Single parents report longer delays and more negative agency experience than do couples. To help individuals confront these difficulties, the Committee for Single Adoptive Parents was formed in Washington, D.C., in 1973. The committee acts as an information service to prospective adoptive parents, publishes a periodic newsletter, and encourages the formation of single adoptive parents groups throughout the country.

In general, single adoptive parents have been much more willing to open their homes to special needs children. One survey found single mothers and fathers were twice as likely to say that they would adopt an older child and three times as likely to say they would adopt a black child than couples were (Feigelman & Silverman, 1983, p. 42). Whereas 55 per cent of them had adopted children older than three, only one-quarter of couples had done so. Single adoptive fathers were more willing to consider placement of such children in their home than were single mothers. Such atypical adoptive preferences may develop in response to the fact that agencies are frank in stating that such applicants will be accepted only if they are willing to consider special needs children for adoption.

Single adoptive parents tend to have special knowledge, abilities, and supports that help them deal both with the demands of raising a child on their own and with the special stresses occasioned by raising a handicapped child. A study (Shireman & Johnson, 1976) of thirty-one single adopters showed that they were generally women of moderate income engaged in professional occupations such as teaching and nursing. Although noted as mature with a high capacity for nurturing a child, many were still not completely emancipated from their parents: "They werre strongly tied to and had much interaction with parents and siblings with a corresponding lack of involvement with friends" (p. 107). This may have reflected the agencies' attempts to select single applicants who did have contact with an extended family that could serve as "backup" for care of the child and as a source of male identification. Fifty per cent of these parents had lived in a single-parent home during some time in their childhood, so that they were not strangers to the single-parent family.

Feigelman & Silverman's (1983) survey of 43 single mothers and 15 single fathers also noted that their educational and occupational attainments were higher than those of adoptive couples, and that many had educational and social work professions. In contrast to Shireman and Johnson's findings, however, this survey found that single adopters had less positive support from friends than did adoptive couples. Single adopters, for the most part, adopt a child of their own gender.

Earlier in the history of substitute care, foster family and adoptive services, foster and adoptive parents were clearly separate and distinguishable. There were identifiable differences between the children who received these services, the nature of the problems that occasioned the need for their care, the kinds of parents who were recruited, the criteria employed in their selection, and their subsequent relationship to the agency. Although the 1973 Child Welfare League Revised Adoption Standards notes the acceptability of foster parent adoptions, many agencies actively prohibited these parents from making permanent homes for children. "An experience survey of persons in the field in 1971 revealed that while many of the respondents saw the need for expanding the pool of adoptive parents, only one-third mentioned the idea of foster parent adoption. As late as 1974 almost two-thirds of the states had a cautionary note or a prohibition of adoption in their placement agreements with foster parents" (Meezan, 1983a, p. 446).

Today, foster parents are encouraged to consider taking on permanent adoptive responsibility for foster children with whom they have formed attachments (Proch, 1981). Foster parent adoption policies underwent dramatic change, in part, because of the growing number of children in substitute care needing stable homes. Many families, particularly families who have had no contact with the social welfare system, will not consider adopting such children. Foster parents, in contrast, understand the needs of these youngsters and are experienced in coping with them. In addition, social work practitioners realized that many foster children had formed deep attachments to the families with whom they lived. Interviews with fifty-six adoptive foster parents and twenty-four of their adopted children (Proch, 1980) revealed that many children do not differentiate between foster and adoptive homes. "To them, a home, was a home and a parent was a parent. They always felt that they were wanted and that they would stay with the family" (p. 141). Only children who had experienced multiple moves were aware that adoption provided them with a more permanent living arrangement than did foster care.

Foster parents have also been given adoptive preference because both the courts and the child's birth parents tend to feel more comfortable transferring parental rights when they know the child has already obtained a secure home (Shireman, 1983). During the 1970's and 1980's, foster parents also "disputed agency decisions to remove children from their care as well as the procedures followed when children are removed. Foster parents have sought and been granted by courts the right to adopt despite placement agreements prohibiting this, the right to notice and a hearing before a child is removed from their care, and recognition as parties in child custody proceedings" (Proch, 1981, p. 618).

Currently, the preferential status of these families is determined by the length of time the child has been in their care. The longer the period in which they have lived with the child, the greater the claim it is felt they have for offering a permanent home to that child. Having established themselves as "psychological parents" through long-term care of the child, generally a year or more, such parents are given competitive preference for adoption as against other applicants.

Agencies are also now experimenting with the development of foster homes that, from the point of initial placement of the child, are considered adoptive placements, should the child become legally free for adoption. These are called "legal risk" or "adoptive foster homes" (Gill, 1975; Proch, 1981). In line with this, one agency avoids labeling families seeking to care for a child as either foster care or adoptive applicants. All families are considered as potential temporary or permanent homes for children, all applicants are assessed using the same criteria, and the same standards are used to decide whether to place a child in either a temporary or a permanent home (Hegarty, 1973).

The gradual merging of foster care and adoption means that these previously clearly separate units in an agency have to work more closely together (Dooley & La Franco, 1974; O'Neill, 1972). Because children placed for fostering may end up being adopted, the adoption unit has to be more concerned with all children who come to the agency for service, not only those explicitly referred for adoption. Standards for substitute-home selection methods and the goals of foster care and adoptive services have to be brought more into harmony with each other. The centralization of home finding for foster care and adoptive homes becomes desirable.

By expanding the pool of adoptive applicants to allow single individuals, foster parents, as well as older and even homosexual parents to adopt, agencies are "shifting from seeking 'ideal' adoptive families to recruiting 'real' families with diverse qualities and resources" (Fein & Maluccio, 1984, p. 209).

The Adoption Process

Application Requirements

The purpose of intake in adoption is twofold. The worker attempts to obtain sufficient information about the adoptive applicants, their family and neighborhood circumstances, and their resources and needs, in order to determine whether these individuals have the ability to parent the type of child they are seeking. In addition, intake procedures provide applicants with sufficient information about the needs of adoptive children and the responsibilities of parenting so that the applicants can decide whether they want to provide a home for a child to whom they have not given birth.

In order for applicants to be considered potential adoptive parents, they must meet a series of requirements. Although some of these requirements must be met by any individual seeking to adopt a child, social service agencies have established different expectations for individuals seeking to adopt babies than they do for those seeking to adopt special needs children. Requirements for those seeking to adopt infants are much more stringent and restrictive. Applicants most frequently contact one agency (usually a private one) if they are interested in adopting young children, but a different agency (often a public one) if they are exploring the adoption of older or special needs children. Some private agencies specialize in the adoption of children from a specific foreign country or region of the world. Even in cases in which individuals adopt children from other states or countries, there must be an investigation of their circumstances and motivations by qualified professionals in the state where they reside.

Because the number of individuals seeking to adopt infants far exceeds the number of infants available for adoption, agencies conducting investigations of these individuals frequently utilize criteria they consider indicative of the "best" family functioning. Among the factors assessed are the age of the adoptive applicants, their physical health, their economic stability, their race and religious affiliations, the personality characteristics of each prospective adoptive parent, the stability of their marital situation, and the adopter's ability to parent a child.

In its Revised *Standards for Adoption Services,* the Child Welfare League of America (1978) states that "parents selected for a child should generally be within the age range usual for natural parents of a child that age" (p. 44). Many agencies prefer that individuals adopting infants be no more than forty years old (Martin, 1980; Meezan, 1983a). Out of concern that adoptive parents have sufficient strength and health during the years when their children are growing toward adulthood, agencies also evaluate the overall physical health of applicants, again to insure that their physical condition does not interfere with their ability to parent a child over a period of years. Problems such as overweight can deter couples from adopting.

In evaluating the physical condition of applicants, agencies are also concerned about physical deterrents that prevent the couple from conceiving children. Historically, families were denied access to adoption services unless they could prove infertility. It was assumed that couples that could have children should have them if they wished to raise children. Today, although the exploration of infertility continues to be a major consideration, there is considerably more ambivalence about the need to prove infertility in order to adopt a child. The Child Welfare League's current standards reflect this ambivalence. "An infertility report should not be a requirement for couples who want to adopt a child; a report may be desirable in some cases, however, as an aid in understanding the reason for infertility" (p. 70). The adoption worker also assesses the couple's reaction to their inability to have a child biologically and their comfort in accepting an adoptive child in the place of a biological one.

Financial stability is of some concern to many agencies evaluating adoption applicants. The agency would like some assurance that the family can count on a steady, even if limited, income, and that it will be able to carry the extra burden of child care without imposing a strain on the stability of family relationships (Child Welfare League of America, 1978). Adoption agencies have had mixed reactions to situations in which adoptive mothers are working. Adoption standards state, "A woman who works should not for that reason alone be excluded from consideration as an adoptive applicant, if she is able to remain home with the child for as long as necessary after placement (the length of time will depend upon the child's age and previous experiences), and to provide security for the child by continuity of relationships and of responsible care" (CWLA, 1978, p. 71). Some agencies continue to reject applicants from homes in which women plan to continue their careers (Martin, 1980).

Historically, adoption agencies attempted to match the religious preferences of the child's birth mother with the religious affiliation of the adoptive family. Recent standards suggest that such matching should not be a primary factor in determining an adoptive placement. Although a number of states still require such matching, "recent reforms in these statutes have begun to require religious matching only when expressly requested by the biological mother or only when the child has experienced sufficient religious training to be truly a member of a faith" (Meezan, 1983a, p. 434). Sectarian adoption agencies that have religious affiliations may place more stress on the adoptive couple's religious identification than do other agencies (Martin, 1980; Clayton & Clayton, 1984).

Current adoption standards still state that adoptive applicants should be married and that the marriage must have endured for a sufficient period of time to indicate its stability. Agencies may require that applicants be married from one to three years before they may apply. In situations in which individuals have been previously married, agencies may ask the couple to wait an even longer time before submitting their application (Martin, 1980). Longer marriages give a couple the time to have a sufficient opportunity to test the possibility of a biological pregnancy. Adoptive agencies are also interested in evaluating the quality of the marital relationships. They may consider such factors as the ability of the couple to communicate effectively, to share with each other, and to express their commitment to each other and to their relationship.

Although the agencies are looking for "emotionally healthy" parents, the term itself is open to considerable differences in definition. Even if clearly defined, it would be difficult to measure. Emotional health, as stated in the adoption literature, implies, among other things, a clear understanding of oneself, a relaxed acceptance of all one's weaknesses and strengths, a minimum of unresolved developmental conflicts, adequate enactment of principal social roles, an ability to postpone gratification and to deny self-gratification out of consideration for the needs of others, a flexible conscience that can accept some failure, some occasional sinfulness without crippling guilt, a capacity to form satisfying interpersonal relationships, and the ability to be independent and yet be capable of dependency if it is objectively justified. It is said that in order to be a happy parent, one must first be a happy person.

The adoption worker is also deeply interested in evaluating the overall ability of applicants to be effective parents for children in their care. Since many of the applicants are infertile, they have not had an opportunity to demonstrate to the worker their parenting ability, except through volunteer, short-term child care or other similar experiences. In the absence of direct evidence of parenting abilities, agency workers assess the couple's description of their reasons for adopting, their expectations of children, and their plans for their future family life. Some motives are regarded by the agency as less desirable and more indicative of possible future difficulty. In general, motives that focus on the needs of the adoptive parents are regarded as less acceptable and more suspect than those that center on the needs of the child. However, the same expressed motive can have a positive meaning in the life configuration of one couple and a negative meaning when viewed in terms of another couple's situation. A desire to help a child grow may have positive connotations as expressed by an accepting, understanding couple; but in the case of a rigid, self-centered couple, it may indicate a desire to push the child to fulfill the prospective parents' needs and ambitions.

Couples who wish to adopt a child for the purpose of stabilizing a shaky marriage or as a "replacement" for a recently deceased child are classically suspect, although some may be acceptable.

One important dimension is the extent to which the applicants consciously recognize their motivations. An "undesirable" motivation of which the applicant has some awareness is subject to modification and change; consequently even undesirable motives of which the applicant is aware are likely to be acceptable to the agency.

The records of successful adoptive parents give some idea of the varied motivations for parenthood.

> Mrs. M., who could not conceive a child because of the congenital absence of the uterus, said that both she and her husband had come from large families. "There always had been many nieces and nephews running in and out of the home. She felt that a home was rather lonesome or just too quiet without children. She compares the way the house is when her nieces and nephews are visiting and after they leave. It's so enjoyable having the children around and it's pretty lonesome when the children leave, so that it makes them want to have their own all the worse. It's very lonesome with just the two of them in the house."

> Mrs. W. and her husband, a machinist, could not have children because of an insufficiency of sperm. She said she had always wanted a child. "Playing with a child, dressing it up, teaching it right from wrong, was about the best life that one could imagine. She felt that there are so many little things she loves to do, such as sewing, making lampshades, decorating, collecting things out of doors, that she would like to do with a child. Things don't seem to be quite complete without a child to share it with. Children fill up a home."

> A manufacturer of electrical equipment, whose wife had three miscarriages, said that "raising children would give them a purpose in life. There would be more to life than just having fun and having one's own selfish gratification. If they were able to provide satisfying home experiences to children and could help them grow into healthy normal adulthood, to be good citizens, they would feel that there was some purpose to their lives. Living as a married couple without children was just too selfish a way of life. He felt, too, that what he and his wife had earned and accumulated for themselves should be passed on."

Mr. A., a lawyer, and somewhat older than most adoptive applicants, said that "having a child would keep them from getting in a rut. Both he and his wife had observed this tendency in other couples who are childless. They become selfish, self-centered, and self-satisfied when they get to be fifty. They become smug and sufficient unto themselves. They have a great deal of love that is going to waste and which will be wasted if they wait much longer to try to adopt a child."

Some of the typical responses of would-be parents who were asked to tell why they decided they wanted children included companionship, a significant goal, a purpose in life, pleasure in helping a child to grow and develop. Pleasure in seeing the world fresh again through sharing a child's experience, a bridge into the future, satisfaction in a duty to be performed, the opportunity to share one of life's most significant experiences with friends, and the desire to share affection with a child and receive affection from a child were among the reasons for desiring children.

Paradoxically, even the penalties are sought as pleasures: the noise, the work, the activity, the anxiety that comes with rearing children. These seem to be an antidote to boredom, an insurance against selfish overconcern with one's own narrow desires.

The capacity for parenthood is tied to the factor of emotional health, because the emotionally healthy person supposedly possesses the essential prerequisites for competent parenthood. Yet capacity for parenthood goes beyond emotional health; it includes the capacity to love, accept, and offer emotional security to children; the capacity to permit them to grow in terms of their own individuality; and a readiness to accept, understand, and meet the inevitable behavioral problems of children. The good parent is flexible in his or her expectations and is realistic in accepting the child's limitations; he/she accepts children as an end in themselves rather than as a means toward some parent-defined end; she/he likes children and enjoys them.

Table 9-1 lists some of the less categorical factors that are involved in the agency's decision regarding an applicant's eligibility.

It might be noted that stability is a recurrent criterion—physical stability, emotional stability, financial stability, marital stability. The agency is responsible for acting for the community in behalf of the child too young to choose wisely. The agency needs to guarantee the child a permanent home. Stability presupposes continuity and the likelihood of permanence.

Although these criteria are used by most agencies, particularly when considering families who wish to adopt infants, questions have been raised about their adequacy, particularly when they are applied to all applicants, without consideration of individual circumstances. The 1978 Policy Statement on Adoption written by the New York City Department of Social Services challenges the infertility criterion and states that no proof of fertility can be required (Hartman, 1979). Serious questions have been raised about the economic requirements, particularly when they have been interpreted to indicate that families with moderate or substantial incomes should be given priority over those with limited incomes. Cole asks, "in choosing adoptive parents for a healthy baby with average to above average intellectual potential, how many would opt for the doctor, lawyer, or teacher over the common labourer? Does providing for 'the child's best interest's mean placing her in the highest social class? Or does it mean that once the parents have established their maturity and emotional eligibility and can economically provide that class should not be an important factor?" (Cole, 1984, p. 22). Working class and minority group parents have found it more difficult to

TABLE 9.1.   Rating Sheet for Prospective Parents

Some Criteria in Evaluating Couples Who Wish to Adopt a Child	
Total personality	*Feelings about children*
Family relationships	*Basic love for children*
Work adjustment	*Ability to deal with developmental problems*
Relationship with friends	*Sensitivity to and understanding and tolerance of children's difficulties*
Activity in community	*Ability to individualize child*
Emotional maturity	
Capacity to give and receive love	*Feelings about childlessness and readiness to adopt*
Acceptance of sex roles	
Ability to assume responsibility for care, guidance, and protection of another person	*Absence of guilt regarding infertility*
Reasonable emotional stability	*Mutual decision to adopt*
Flexibility	*Ability to tell child he or she is adopted*
Self-respect	*Attitudes toward biological parents and illegitimacy*
Ability to cope with problems, disappointments, and frustrations	
	Motivation
Quality of marital relationship	*Desire to have more nearly complete life*
Successful continuance of marriage not dependent on children	*Desire to accept parental responsibility*
Respect for each other	*Desire to contribute to development of another human being*
Capacity to accept a child born to other parents	*Desire to love and be loved*

adopt, particularly when they are interested in adopting infants rather than special needs children.

Because many of these criteria are subjective, adoption workers might be tempted to use personal standards in determining which family is best suited for which infant. Bytner et al. (1979) challenge the use of such personal criteria: "concerted effort has been made to discard individual value systems and to look at the prospective parents from the standpoint of what a child would derive from that particular family constellation. Whether or not we would want these same things for ourselvs and our children should not be a consideration" (p. 26).

In the context of a ratio that is favorable to the adoptive applicant, agencies can move, as they have, toward a shift in emphasis in their relationship to the applicant from assessment and evaluation to facilitation and enabling. Where the ratio of applicants to children is such that almost all applicants can be provided with a child, the social worker can be concerned with helping the applicants accept and prepare for adoptive parenthood rather than focusing on determining which applicant is the most acceptable. The tendency, then, is to broaden the definition of the "adoptable" parent and to "screen people in" rather than "screen people out." When the number of infants is limited, however, "requirements" are employed not only, as is usually the case, for the primary purpose of the interests of the child but also to limit the backlog of successful applicants waiting for children.

Agency experience in recruiting homes for children with special needs has resulted in a reassessment of these requirements. In trying to reach out for adoptive applicants for children with special needs, agencies have been willing to accept applicants who do not, in some ways, meet the criteria previously listed. In doing so, workers have begun to question the justification for each of the criteria in terms of its functional utility in the performance of the job of adoptive parenthood.

It has become more and more clear that the essential overriding criteria are the ability of the parents to accept and love and nurture a child, to understand and individualize a child, and to have both the capacity and the competence to deal successfully with the problems of rearing a child. All else is commentary, and some of the criteria listed are now seen as having less importance.

When dealing with applications submitted by foster parents or single parents, adoption workers have a number of special concerns and considerations. When single individuals seek to adopt a child, workers are concerned about their personal motives. Male applicants, in particular, have been scrutinized for possible sexual interest in children. The impact on the child of living with a single prent is also of concern to the worker. Issues that are explored include the adequacy of child-care arrangements during the parent's working hours, the plans the parent has made for continuing child care, should he or she die or become incapacitated, and provisions that have been made for the child to identify with adults of the opposite sex, should they be unavailable on a regular basis in the home. Finally, the adoption worker assesses the single parent's ability to handle the added responsibility of caring for a child with the more limited resources than are available in a two-parent family. The individual's support system may be more closely scrutinized. The worker may be concerned about a single adoptive parent who has few friends or family members available to help with the day-to-day responsibilities of parenting (Kadushin, 1970a; Meezan, 1983a; Schlesinger, 1984).

Widening the pool of adoptive applicants by accepting single parents is part of the effort to increase placement opportunities for special-needs children. As noted previously, agency policy generally states that such applicants will be considered only for the placement of special-needs children. The Child Welfare League of America standards (1978) state, "In exceptional circumstances, when the opportunity for adoption for a specific child might not otherwise be available, a single parent (who may be unmarried, widowed, or divorced) should be given consideration" (p. 68).

In foster family adoptions, workers worry that some children will be adopted "by default" (Proch, 1981). The child may not have been placed in the foster home with any thought of future adoption in mind. However, because the child has remained for a long period in this home, the foster parents eventually may be allowed to adopt.

Workers are also concerned that the converse type of dilemma might arise. That is, foster parents may feel coerced into adopting a child in their care. In one study (Proch, 1980), almost one-third had not intended to adopt a child and would not have adopted the children except for the fact that they feared the children would be removed from their homes if they did not. The research goes on to note, however, "few parents who were interviewed felt that they were overtly pressured by the agency" (p. 139). Forced adoptions turn out less satisfactorily than those in which the parents feel they freely chose to make the child a permanent part of the family (Raynor, 1980).

Shireman (1983) identifies important attributes of those foster parents who are particularly interested in establishing permanent ties to children:

In a study of 60 foster families, about half of whom adopted children in their care, caseworkers identified enjoyment of children (particularly on the part of the mother) and sensitivity to their needs as attributes of foster parents who adopted and identified "a combination of child-centered motives and narcissistic investment in raising children" as reasons for taking children into the home [p 408].

On the other hand, foster parents who are disinclined to adopt cite their concerns about long-term relationships with the child, concerns that their own age or health might interfere with their ability to care for the child on a long-term basis, and the fear of loss of agency supports as disincentives (Meezan, 1983a, p. 447).

Adoption workers have also been concerned about the possible impact on other foster children when one child is singled out and adopted. In addition, questions about protection of the confidentiality for birth parents have been raised, since foster parents may be given more identifying information about birth families than are adoptive families.

Implementing the Criteria in Applicant Assessment

But what empirical confirmation is there that the adoptive agency can make a reliable valid assessment of the various criteria outlined previously relating to establishing the applicant's acceptability? Brieland (1959) designed a study to determine the reliability with which social workers make decisions regarding adoptive applicants. He taped the intake interviews that one caseworker conducted with five different adoptive applicant couples. Brieland then played the tape of these interviews to 184 caseworkers in twenty-eight different agencies in thirteen states. Each worker was given a transcript of the interviews to follow while listening to the tapes. Having heard the tape, each worker was asked to decide whether or not the agency should continue contact with the couple. The percentage of agreement among the 184 workers varied from couple to couple, ranging from 89.1 per cent agreement in the case of one couple to 61.4 per cent agreement in the case of another couple. Overall agreement for the total of the five cases was 73.6 per cent, so that, for the total sample, the percentage of agreement was at a statistically significant level. Although these results suggest some general tendency toward agreement between worker and worker as to how they evaluated each couple, they also indicate considerable disagreement. Brieland (1961) himself has offered a critical analysis of the research problem of such a study and the limitations of the results.

In 1970 Brown replicated Brieland's study, using videotapes of interviews for presentation to eighty-four workers in adoptive agencies. There was 72 per cent agreement regarding decisions on the five couples—but again substantial deviation from the consensus.

The social worker is called upon to assess ambiguously defined entities such as the applicants' maturity, their marital relationship, their reaction to infertility, their attitude toward children, and their capacity for rearing a child. The behavioral criteria by which these factors are measured are nowhere adequately delineated. Furthermore the worker is asked to predict their behavior in the future, in complex interaction with some unknown child. Ripple (1968), in a follow-up study of adoption, found "little evidence that potential for good parenting can be assessed with confidence" (p. 494).

Even applicants who want to be honest and open with the worker may not be able to evaluate accurately how they will react to adoptive parenthood. The following is the case record of an adoptive home from which a school-aged boy was removed:

> Mrs. R. shared with the worker how terribly upset and guilty she was feeling. . . . She commented that she had always thought of herself as having more patience than most people and it was a great surprise to her to learn that she was not patient. . . . She was very critical of herself, feeling that she should have been able to accept John and work with him longer than she did. She continues to be surprised to learn that she does not have the patience she thought she did and that she can get so nervous and upset.

Mrs. R. had presented herself in the application interview as patient and accepting, which she honestly perceived herself to be. In some circumstances, on the other hand, the family's initial strong reluctance is not a good indicator of subsequent success. Parents who had doubts about their ability to care for a child often find that they have skills and strengths that surprise them. This demand of child care actualizes latent potentials.

> Our story starts out like the rest. The tests, the surgery, the heartache. And the wait. The rest is a little different though.
>
> After three years from the initial application, and ten years of marriage, we were offered a "special needs" child. He was born with a cleft lip and cleft palate. He had already been turned down by two other families.
>
> We went through the whole gamut of emotions. Why us? Hadn't we been through enough already? It wasn't fair! How could I possibly care for this child? I don't have the patience. Why are they putting us through this?
>
> Is it possible to have all these negative feelings yet still adopt a "special needs" child and not have regrets? My answer is an emphatic *YES!!*
>
> Eric Ki Moon arrived May 18, 1982. His first operation was three weeks later, his second was four months after that. Now we're awaiting his third operation in April.
>
> After all our doubts and all we've been through, would we do it all again? Yes, and we are! Jilian Soon Yung is scheduled to arrive in April. She was born with a bilateral cleft lip and cleft palate.
>
> Why, with all our initial doubts, do it again? Because in spite of everything, we're basically very selfish. Above all else, we wanted children. We didn't want "perfection." We didn't want "show pieces." We wanted a family. (*Our Magazine,* May/June, 1984, p. 15).

Many applicants, who know what the agency worker is looking for, try to project an image as acceptable adoptive parents (See, for example, Martin, 1980). Isaac (1965) suggests how to produce a favorable impression:

> Use the pronoun *we* not *I;* share the fact that you have problems but that you have "handled" them maturely; while on good terms with own parents indicate that you are not on such good terms so as to seem dependent; if the wife works she should indicate that she is happy on the job—but not too happy so that she is ready to give it up for motherhood; indicate that the marriage is a satisfying one, that there are, however, disagreements and conflicts, but these are satisfactorily resolved [p. 6].

Such efforts on the part of applicants to act the role of acceptable applicants further confounds the worker's attempt to make an accurate assessment.

However, despite these difficulties, which need to be explicitly acknowledged, the fact is that workers in both the Brieland and Brown studies cited agreed with each other on the selection of applicants at a level that was statistically significant. This consistency reflects some consensus on the selection criteria employed and some consensus on the assessment of applicants and confirms the findings of an earlier study (Maas, 1960).

The Intake Process

Recruitment. The first step in the intake process involves facilitating the contact between potential adoptive parents and the agencies seeking to place children in their homes. In the case of infant adoption, agencies frequently must cope with so many applicants that they have devised specific procedures to limit their number. Some agencies, for example, only open their intake for a brief period of time. Others use screening criteria before they undertake any detailed intake process. In the case of special needs children, however, agencies must develop procedures to reach out to potentially interested families and to encourage them to consider possibly adopting children. After all, as Sawbridge (1980) comments, "People do not think of walking into an agency saying, 'I want to be a parent to a deaf, Black ten-year-old'" (p. 172).

General community education and "individual family finding" have been used as recruitment techniques. "Individual family finding" involves efforts to find specific homes for specific children in need (Meezan, 1980). Community education programs may use a wide variety of approaches to publicize the need for more adoptive families, including television and newspaper advertisements and speeches before PTAs, church groups, and other civic and religious organizations. A number of films depicting adoption families, adopted children, and the nature of the adoptive process have aided in recruitment efforts. These films present a realistic picture of the types of children awaiting homes.

Major media campaigns may produce many responses, so agencies using them must be prepared to respond rapidly to inquiries that may pour in after advertising has occurred. Families are confused when they must wait for long periods in order to talk to agency personnel after having been informed that children seeking homes are so desperate (Meezan, 1980, p. 10).

Meezan (1983a) suggests that a more effective type of community campaign is one targeted to a specific portion of the community or a particular type of need. Sawbridge (1980) describes successful efforts to contact the West Indian community in London in 1975–1976. Using the newspaper, radio, personal contacts, speakers at meetings, and other methods, the "Soul Kids" campaign was successful. "The number of enquiries received as a result of the campaign far exceeded the normal number received from West Indians and showed how much interest was potentially present. Linked to that was a clear demonstration of the importance of understanding the expectations and preconceived ideas of the inquirers. In this instance that involved a knowledge of the cultural background from which they had come as well as of their present circumstances and concerns, and a recognition of their likely attitudes to caring for other people's children and to authority" (pp. 171–172).

The mass media have been imaginatively used in recruiting applicants for special-needs children. In 1985, eighty television stations and fifty newspapers ran regular features describing children waiting for adoption. These programs were often called "Wednesday's Child." The Los Angeles County Bureau of Adoption at one time published a quarterly bulletin, *The Top Ten Tots,* about hard-to-place children. In Canada over 130 Ontario newspapers carry a syndicated column called "Today's Child," which presents children needing adoption. The *Detroit Sunday News* has had a special feature entitled "A Child Is Waiting" since 1968. As a consequence of this publicity, homes have been found for a total of 236 children over a six-year period. "Adoption Day in Court" is a procedure used in Los Angeles to publicize adoptions. Media representatives interview and film families waiting in court to finalize their adoptions.

The highly successful Adoption Project for Handicapped Children in Ohio used a monthly newspaper column to describe children awaiting homes. Staff of the project comment, "focusing attention on and directing placement efforts toward a specific child was often the beginning of a series of things happening that eventually lead to placement. It has been our experience that time and effort spent in this way was ultimately productive and seldom wasted effort" (U.S. Department of Health and Human Services, 1980a, p. 19). 58 families initiated adoption inquiries after reading this newspaper material.

The pioneer use of television by the Minnesota Division of Child Welfare as an aid in recruiting homes for hard-to-place children has now become standard procedure (Fricke, 1956). The Los Angeles County Department of Adoption "shows" adoptable children each week as part of a regularly scheduled television program. In almost all cases, these are hard-to-place children. Children under two years of age are personally presented; pictures of older children are shown. There is no indication that the children are hurt by this procedure, although some object to what they call the commercial sale of children.

Some agencies have used closed-circuit television and one-way mirrors to present adoptable children to parents without their being aware that they are being observed for possible placement. Videotape has also been used to "show" a child who lives in one section of the country to prospective parents living elsewhere (Paget, 1969).

Some cities have arranged an Adoption Week to promote adoption (Sarmiento, 1969). An Adoptive Family of the Year is selected, and all the babies available for adoption are brought to a picnic arranged at a local park for all adoptive families in the area. Agencies have experimented with an "adoption party" sponsored by the agency (Edgar, 1975). Fourteen or fifteen children meet an equal number of adoptive couples in an informal get-together where they can mingle freely, play games, talk, and get to know each other.

Applicant—Agency: Mutual Assessment. Once applicants have been recruited and it has been determined that they meet the general requirements for adoptive parents, they may be invited to participate in the intake process. During a series of meetings with prospective parents, the adoption worker seeks to obtain information that will help the family decide whether adoption is appropriate and, if so, the type of child that should be placed in the family's home. Although traditionally the intake period was perceived as an opportunity to judge the family to determine whether they were acceptable and could be approved as adoptive parents, today, workers take on both educational and evaluative responsibilities (Gregory, 1979). The adoption worker's tasks include confronting applicants with the important questions and issues they must think through in order to successfully raise adoptive children, helping parents gain in self-knowledge so that they can make informed decisions about their own needs and values, and challenging unrealistic expectations and perceptions families may bring to the adoption process (Gregory, 1979; Cole, 1978; Hartman, 1979).

In some agencies, contact with the family is primarily through individual interviews, held both at the agency and in the family's home. In addition to formal home interviews, the worker may try to spend other time with the family, sharing in routine family activities or special events in order to get to know family members better (James, 1980).

During the meetings with the family, the worker discusses a number of issues:

1. How the interest in adoption developed.
2. Motivation for adoption.
3. Attitude toward childlessness and infertility.
4. Understanding of children and experiences with children.
5. History of the marriage and current patterns of marital interaction.
6. Developmental history.
7. Educational and employment history.
8. Patterns of social participation.
9. Attitude of the extended family toward adoption.
10. Attitude toward illegitimacy and the out-of-wedlock child.
11. Problems anticipated in adoption and how they must be handled.
12. Attitudes toward working with the agency.

If all goes well, the interviews are followed by a series of home visits, during which the caseworker has an opportunity of seeing the couple react in an informal, familiar setting. The worker is also able to obtain some information about the physical resources of the home and the neighborhood. References, submitted by the applicant, are contacted for whatever additional information they can provide. They not only help the caseworker to see the applicant through the eyes of other people but also indicate the extent to which the applicants are integrated into the community and the attitude of the community toward adoption.

Throughout all of these contacts, the agency, acting for the child, is assuring itself that these applicants will provide an adequate, stable home for the child. It is also helping the adoptive applicants to decide that this is what they really want to do and helping them to adjust to the idea of impending parenthood. The nine months of pregnancy provide the opportunity to biological parents for adjusting to the idea of the significant changes in their lives that will follow the birth of their child. The study period provides an opportunity for thoughtful self-examination, anxious anticipation, and hopeful delay that entails the kind of emotional reorganization that is involved in actual pregnancy. It helps prepare the applicant, emotionally, for parenthood. Some parents go through what has been termed "pre-adoptive pregnancy" at this time (Jewett, 1978).

An adoptive mother, in a retrospective analysis of her experience, said:

> In our thoughts about adoption, my husband and I had raised many questions and hypothetical situations to each other concerning an adopted child. Two of these neither of us could answer satisfactorily. One dealt with the discipline of an adopted child who might remind you that since you are not their real parent they do not have to obey you, and how to cope with an adopted child's curiosity about his natural parents. By answering these questions, the social worker made us feel at this point the interview really began. We began to see the social worker's role as a dual one. The interviews are not only to serve the purpose of finding out about you, but are there to help you and answer any doubts that you may have in regard to an adopted child.

As Campbell (1957) has written, "for successful adoption, children need to be 'taken' by adoptive parents, not merely 'given' by the agency" (p. 184).

Group methods are now frequently used during the intake process. Believing group methods to be particularly effective in recruiting and preparing parents for the adoption of special-needs children, the North American Council on Adoptable Children has helped establish group programming in more than fifty communities (Flynn & Hamm, 1983). Some agencies arrange for a group meeting of applicants to review some general ideas about adoption and agency procedure in processing an application. The content of these meetings tends to be primarily "factual, and the method of presentation instructional," although the aim is partly to reduce applicant anxiety (Stumpf, 1963, p. 88).

As a result of these orientation meetings, couples who are interested in continuing contact with the agency are better informed about what to expect and about what is expected of them (Springer, 1956). Some decide not to submit an application—couples who are very ambivalent about adoption or who clearly cannot meet the eligibility requirements (Vieregge, 1963, p. 102).

Attempts have been made to use group meetings for getting to know the applicants (Dillow, 1968; Wingfield, 1969; Kaplan, 1970; Wiehe, 1972). It has been hypothesized that use of group meetings for the home study "would make it possible to neutralize the study so that fear of the power of the worker would be diminished, defensiveness lessened . . . and preparation for parenthood enhanced" (Kaplan, 1970, p. 128). As Biskind (1966) notes, "Parents in the group situation are freer to acknowledge their perplexities and fears" (p. 145).

In order to help families explore their feelings and needs, prospective parents must actively participate in the group process. Hartman (1979) claims:

> Straight informational meetings are probably less productive than no meeting at all. First, if people have strong misconceptions or anxieties about something, information given to the contrary tends to conceal rather than alter these views. Once people discover their ideas are different or even wrong, they are less likely to discuss them, but that does not mean they are relinquishing them.
>
> A group session, or an individual one, should start with an opportunity for parents to express their confusions, concerns, and questions. Information should be given only after comments are heard and accepted (p. 28).

Group sessions tend to work best when the content includes balanced consideration of both logical decision making and feelings and the needs of both parents and children are discussed.

Groups permit the use of some interpretive material and procedures that would not be feasible in individual interviews with applicants. Group-oriented parent education techniques have been successfully used in these situations. Visual aid material explaining adoption procedures and the current adoptive situation can be profitably used with a group. One agency shows a series of slide programs and relevant movies over its period of contact with a group of adoptive parents. These include slide programs such as "Introduction to Adoption" and "What Are We Waiting for?" produced by the Council on Adoptable Children in Michigan, and "Who Cares About Jamie?" produced by the Massachusetts Adoption Resource Exchange; and movies such as "One of the Family," produced by the Los Angeles Bureau of Adoptions (Goodridge, 1975).

Some agencies schedule group meetings between parents who have completed adoption and new applicants. Adoptive parents act as resource persons, answering questions and sharing their experiences with the group. Group interaction encourages development of a support system, both from within the group, and with other adoptive parents in the community. The Lutheran Social Service of

Kansas and Oklahoma considers adoptive parents an essential part of the helping team. "These adoptive family volunteers participate in the early phases of education and engagement, and they continue to help through the total process including offering post adoptive services" (Hartman, 1979, p. 28).

Because many agencies have long waiting lists, applicants could wait months to obtain initial information when they must be seen on an individual basis for this purpose. Providing initial intake sessions through group means helps expedite this process. Some evidence also suggests that the group format assists in maintenance of adoptive placements, especially among families making homes for special needds children (Flynn & Hamm, 1983; Forsythe & Marshall, 1984).

Parents and adoption workers come to the intake process with differing perceptions and concerns. The worker sees himself or herself in a helping role, whereas parents expect the worker to be judgmental. In order to develop a clear picture of family life, workers require sharing and honesty on the part of the parents. Parents, on the other hand, fearing invasion and rejection, attempt to put their best foot forward rather than to be totally honest (Hartman, 1979, p. 30). Recognizing this, the worker attempts to meet agency requirements while being sensitive to parental concerns. The worker realizes that it is not uncommon for parents to be highly ambivalent during the intake period, feeling, on the one hand, excited anticipation at the thought of adopting a child and, on the other, fear about the changes in the family's life-style this will entail. The worker acknowledges the normalcy of this ambivalence and does not expect parents to be fully enthusiastic. As the worker builds a trusting relationship with the family, misperceptions, disagreements, and misunderstandings can be openly discussed and dealt with (Jewett, 1978).

How does the application and study process actually work out in practice? Bradley (1966) studied the processing of some four hundred applicants in eight agencies.

Bradley checked the social workers' assessments against the decisions actually made in order to determine the factors associated with selection. Those factors having the highest association with acceptance were "positive qualities of couple interaction in their marriage, flexible and outgoing characteristics of both husband's and wife's personalities, the couple's openness, their nonneurotic motivation for adoption, their adequate marital role performance, and their acceptance of infertility" (p. 22). However, applicants were also accepted who "tended to be marginal couples who were considered more suitable for marginal children"—hard-to-place children (p. 188). In other words, there were two alternative but nonsimultaneous routes that led to a positive impression of couples as adoptive prospects, with the "better" couple seen as suitable for the "better" child and the marginal couple seen as more suitable for the marginal child (p. 189). This finding confirms an earlier study, which indicated that applicants who presented qualifications that differed from those generally accepted by the agency sought to improve their chances by indicating a willingness to accept a hard-to-place child (Kadushin, 1962). (See also Triseliotis, 1970.)

From Acceptance to Child Placement

The period between the completion of the study and the actual placement of the child is perceived as a very stressful time. There is the feeling of being in limbo, a fear that the agency may forget or overlook the application, a sense of being unable to control one's destiny, and unnerving uncertainty about when the adoption will be made—if ever. Some repeated brief contacts during this period by the agency might be reassuring.

During this waiting period, the agency is faced with the task of selecting a child for the approved adoptive applicant. One of the most difficult and complex of the adoption worker's many responsibilities is the choice of a particular child for a particular family. Historically, workers have paid attention to physical appearance, attempting to choose an infant whose facial features or hair color or body type is similar to that of the adoptive parents. Workers have also considered the child's intellectual capacity in choosing an adoptive placement. Recent research suggests that these criteria are now given less consideration in placement decisions. In a longitudinal study assessing genetic and environmental influences called the Colorado Adoption Project (CAP) (Singer & Hardy-Brown, 1984), eye, hair, and skin color; weight and height; and occupation and education of the child's birth parents and adoptive parents were compared. Significant correlations were found between the educational level of the birth and adoptive fathers, the education of the birth father and adoptive mother, and the height of the birth and adoptive fathers. Research studies suggest no correlation between characteristics of the adopted infant and of either adoptive parents.

Some adoption agencies refuse to consider these characteristics in making placements. Gregory (1979), for example, describes one agency that decided "parents can identify the sex, the race, and the age . . . they do not consider hair colouring or other features at all in the placement procedure. 'Matching' is out as it does not fit in with their concept of parenting in adoption" (p. 20).

Jewett (1978) suggests three additional considerations that are particularly important when choosing an adoptive family for a child. The worker must consider the kind of child an adoptive family is most eager to have. Considering the parents' preferences and limitations, the worker assesses whether they would enjoy a particular child, whether they would feel satisfaction in raising this type of child, and whether they could tolerate the qualities of this child that are unlikeable or difficult. Second, the worker considers the particular patterns of interaction the child has established, especially destructive patterns which the child is likely to attempt to reestablish in a new adoptive setting. The worker then attempts to choose parents who can resist participating in these destructive interactions (p. 93). Finally, the worker, considering both the type of family the child wants and the type of child the parents want, attempts to find families whose needs mesh with those of the child. Jewett (1978) states

> The meshing of the needs of the child and of the parents can do much to achieve smoother integration, especially at the beginning. Although it can be argued that children need to be exposed to different forms of living to encourage them to expand and cope, it is more important for the child to be accepted from the first for himself as he is. This is more likely to happen naturally when the needs of the child and of the adopting family are compatible. If along with this contentment there is capacity for healthy giving and growth, both child and parents will derive greater benefit from the placement. Such blending helps the child to fit in more readily, to begin to feel secure sooner, and thus to make new ties and to take root earlier after placement [p. 94].

(See also Boyne, 1978).

Rejected Applicants

Not all applicants are successful in becoming adoptive parents. As Michaels (1947) notes, "If it is occasionally necessary to choose between a possible injustice to a family and possible injustice to a child, the agency must, by virtue of its essential responsibility, protect the child" (p. 370).

The agency, however, has a responsibility to deny the applicants in a way that results in minimal damage to their psychic health. The applicants are generally vulnerable: they may have applied because of a condition—the inability to have a child by natural means—that, in itself, is a deep narcissistic wound. However the agency handles the situation, "there is no softness that can remove entirely the sting of being denied parenthood for the second time—first by life, and then by society" (Michaels, 1947, p. 372).

The agency strives to help the applicants come, on their own, to the same conclusion reached by the agency—that they are not ready for adoption and that in pressing their application, they are doing themselves a disservice. If the agency is successful, the applicants withdraw their application as a matter of choice and the agency has performed a helpful service both to the adoptive applicants and to its pool of adoptable children. The following is an example of such a situation:

> Mr. and Mrs. W. came about the adoption of an infant. It had not been absolutely determined that they could not have their own child, although the chances were slim and Mrs. W. felt that she did not want to wait any longer for a child. Mr. W. brought out many questions about the effects of heredity on a child and how adopted children turn out.
>
> The worker pointed out that evidently Mr. W. was not sure he could feel comfortable about being a parent to a child strangers had borne. He enlarged on his own question and fear. The worker told them about the shortage of children, and the need of the agency to limit applications drastically, saying that one of the things the agency needed to know in deciding which families to add to the long waiting list was which were most likely to feel like parents to children placed with them, and that it would be hard for us to know when the W.'s did not know it themselves. The worker suggested that perhaps this was something they needed to settle for themselves first.
>
> Mr. W. seemed very relieved, and Mrs. W. agreed that they should withdraw their request for the present, and explore the possibilities of having their own baby [Michaels, 1947, p. 373].

In the past, it was recommended that agencies purposefully avoid telling rejected applicants why they were being rejected. Michaels (1947), for example, suggests families be told that it is the very large number of applicants that have forced the agency "to turn down even very fine families because of the shortage of children" (p. 375). Others suggest that the worker stress objective factors (age, housing, religion, and so forth) rather than subjective criteria used for eliminating applicants (such as limited capacity for parenthood, or psychosocial deficiencies). Aronson (1960) argues that it would be too cruel and potentially debilitating to be honest with applicants about these more personal reasons for their rejection.

However, avoiding the real reasons for rejection is detrimental to the applicants themselves, since this leaves them in a position to neither challenge nor correct the problems about which they have not been clearly informed. The rejection of an application is easier when the agency shares doubts and misgivings with the applicant as they arise (Kasporwicz, 1964). The final decision is thus something for which the applicant has been partially prepared.

It is difficult to distinguish the applicants rejected by the agency from those who withdraw voluntarily. Agencies responsible for placing children with special needs, who have a smaller applicant pool from which to select, may strive to retain every applicant. However, every agency is responsible for rejecting those applicants who in their best judgment would harm a child placed in their care.

Preparing the Child and Birth Parent for Adoption

In order to adapt successfully in their adoptive home, children may need the assistance of the worker. Particularly in the case of children who are no longer infants at the time of placement, the move to a new home involves separation from the family with whom the child is living, reestablishment of a relationship with an unknown new family, and, for most children, the reworking of old separation issues, particularly those involving the child's biological family. Among children undergoing separation from their birth and foster families, denial, anger, and depression are all common. "One must remember that no matter how much the child likes the prospective family, he also has other feelings—sadness at leaving the family he has learned to love and trust; fear and anxiety about the future; and anger that he has been put in the position of having such confusing emotions" (Project CRAFT, 1980, VI-79; See also Jewett, 1978; Grabe, 1986). A letter written by an eight-year-old child, prior to his placement in an adoptive home, reflects all these aspects of the process.

> Foster care is when a kid goes to another home. A social worker says to the mother and father, "Do you want to take care of this kid?" The parent might say, "Yes, but only for a little while."
> I hate waiting to be adopted. You have to wait until all the paperwork is done to be adopted. You have to go places and see people. Sometimes the social worker or the city loses the papers, or has them in the wrong place. Sometimes they ask stupid questions.
> Sometimes parents split up before you are adopted. Then you have to go to a new home. You feel sad and mad. You want to sit in the corner and kick the wall. You hit people, say curses, say you don't like the food, don't do your homework or silent reading, and you say you don't want to be adopted.
> I hope I'll get adopted soon.

Even at a very young age, separation reactions can be very powerful. Frequently they are reactivated during each new separation experience. Describing her work with Rusty, a young child in foster care whom she was preparing for eventual placement in an adoptive setting, Warfield (1979) notes that, prior to this placement, the child had experienced not only a foster care setting but repeated brief separations from the foster family for medical treatment and for hospitalizations. Warfield describes Rusty's reactions to her attempts to take him away from the foster home for brief trips or for office visits. He would cling to her, stand immobilized, refusing to play with toys, and, after several months, would still avoid physical contact with other staff in the office.

The social worker's objectives include helping the child begin to face what are usually complex and ambivalent feelings about the move. The worker strives to help the child express some willingness to consider moving to a new adoptive home. Kadushin (1970b) outlines the characteristics of children who are ready to begin an adoptive placement:

1. Ability to adjust to loss of old parental ties and to accept new parental relationship. This implies some sense of trust in the adoptive parents' willingness to accept him.
2. Emotional acceptance of the fact that he cannot return to his own parents and that his relationship cannot be revived.
3. Expression of explicit desire for adoption.
4. Behavior which indicates motivation to adjust to the adoptive situation (p. 34).

The social worker also explores the child's understanding of the reasons why parental rights have been terminated. Many children have not been told why they were removed from their birth family home; many have been given only partial information or have been provided with a very vague picture of their birth family's circumstances. As a result, many children harbor powerful beliefs that it was some behavior of their own that led their parents to abandon them. Others hold unrealistic expectations that their birth family will soon return to claim them (Jewitt, 1978, p. 74). "Children must be helped to resolve feelings about their past. In order to do this, they must be given the truth about their parents' situation in a realistic way and at a level that they can understand" (Meezan, 1983a, p. 459). Sawbridge (1980) comments:

> Often a child who has spent some time in care may be very confused as to what originally happened to put him there, and he may still cling to a hope that his parents will come back for him. In one case it was only when a teenager was referred for adoption and efforts made to trace her birth parents that it was discovered her mother had in fact died. Before being able to make new close relationships children need to face, understand, and round off the old, or at least to know how they fit in with the new ones [p. 174].

Another area of exploration concerns the meaning of the child's removal from the foster family. It is particularly helpful if the foster family can participate with the child in a discussion of the reasons why a new home must be found. In addition, the worker explores the child's understanding of family life, expectations concerning the adoptive family, and fears about what will happen in his or her new home.

The worker must not assume that anyone has previously prepared a child for past moves. "In working with the child, you may, in fact, discover that someone very skilled and very sensitive has helped him to understand what has happened. But it is safer to assume that no one has adequately assessed the deep and often confused concerns of the child" (Donley, cited in Jewitt, 1978, p. 67). Because it is so difficult to confront and to encourage expressions of loss, workers may avoid helping the child deal with this experience.

> It is hard not to identify with the pain of a foster parent losing a child and with the child about to be placed. Sometimes workers become quite uneasy about the pain of replacement; they feel guilty for being involved, for carrying the news of the impending separation, for setting the process in motion. It is these feelings, coupled with an unrealistic workload, which accounts for the number of children who are presumed to be prepared for their move into an adoptive home, but who have never really been helped to understand their separation from their original family or the reasons they are being moved again [Jewett, 1978, p. 77; See also Project CRAFT, 1980].

A number of techniques are useful in helping children, particularly less verbal children, get in touch with and learn to express their feelings. Many children may need help labeling the feelings that they do have. "Acting out" feelings may be more helpful to children than talking about them. Jewett (1978) suggests using the "empty chair technique." The child tries to visualize someone sitting in a chair with whom he or she has unfinished business. The child is asked to tell the person about this unfinished business. Another useful approach with children undergoing a move to a new home is the candle ritual. After identifying a number of people who have been important to the child, the worker and child light a candle for each one of them, discussing happy memories and commenting on the meaning of each of those individuals in the child's life. The worker then points out to the child that all the candles are lit, suggesting that people from the past continue to be important, even when one no longer lives with them.

The child cannot work through all feelings regarding separation and attachment to the new family prior to placement but must continue to struggle with these feelings over a prolonged period of time after the move to a new home. Continued ambivalence about the loss of old ties and continued uncertainty about the stability of the new home are normal, as is periodic regression to less adaptive coping levels.

In addition to working with the child, the adoption worker assists the birth family to relinquish the child for adoption. When the birth parents feel that it is in the best interest of the child to be placed in a new home, and when they can share this belief with the child, the child is freed to establish new ties and does so with less guilt and ambivalence (Howe, 1983; Knight, 1985). The preparation of parents, particularly young parents who are relinquishing infants, is more fully discussed in Chapter 8. We focus here on assistance that must be provided parents who are terminating their rights to older children, as well as parents who are undergoing involuntary termination.

Like their children, parents experience powerful, ambivalent feelings about separation. Clarice Freud comments:

> in placement a parent is separated from a part of himself, a part of himself which he may partly love and partly hate. This involves a giving up of some of the satisfying parts of his connection with his child as well as those parts which are not satisfying. His guilt, which is a feeling usually most evident, is based on what he is doing to his child and is also in terms of social disapproval. Perhaps most profound is his sense of inadequacy, which feeling is frequently heightened when he senses a change in the child's attitude toward him and sees the role of the foster parents in the child's life (Project CRAFT, 1980, pp. V-76–V-77).

These feelings are intensified when the parent contemplates permanent separation from the child. The job of the adoption worker includes offering assistance to the parent in making the decision about whether to relinquish the child (Kadushin, 1984), helping the parent to participate in actual separation from the child, and assisting the parent to grieve, once the separation has occurred.

In order to facilitate separation, Knight (1985) recommends that parent and child undergo a termination visit. During this meeting, the parent and child say good-bye to each other, the parent supports the child's move to a new permanent family, and the parent clarifies for the child that this is their last meeting. The worker helps parents prepare for such meetings by offering support and helping the parent anticipate the kind of questions and reactions the child might have. As Knight cautions, workers must anticipate that these visits will be termination experiences for the parents as well as for their children. Parents need to identify their own feelings of loss and plan to take pictures or devise other keepsakes of the occasion, should they desire them. The pain engendered by this occasion may lead some parents to try to avoid keeping this appointment; others might make negative comments about the child or attempt to blame others for the family's problems. Knight recommends that the worker be present during the termination conference in order to confront these negative statements and help the parent and child realistically discuss the reasons why separation must occur.

Results of a survey of 364 birth parents who had relinquished their children for adoption (Deykin, Campbell, & Patti, 1984), suggest that birth parents are in need of further assistance, once separation has been accomplished. The survey found evidence of unresolved grief. "Unlike other permanent losses, for which society has constructed supportive rituals, there is no recognizable support following the loss of the child to adoption" (p. 279). The worker can provide such support. Individuals experiencing unresolved sadness appeared to have problems overprotecting and overindulging children to whom they subsequently gave birth. Although they did not find evidence of subsequent neglect or abuse, the researchers found considerable "generalized anxiety" in interactions between parents and these children.

Placement of the Child in the Adoptive Home

When the agency has determined on a mutually advantageous selection of child and parents, the adoptive parents are called in and given background information on the child. Any questions or doubts they may have are discussed and, if possible, resolved. If all goes well on the verbal presentation, the parents meet the child and a decision is made.

One study of this point in the process notes:

> One factor which increases the anxiety and discomfort of adoptive parents during the placement process is that, unlike natural parents, they can "back out" if they choose. When parents are having their own children, however worried they may feel, they have no choice but to accept it; therefore they have no decision to make [McCormick, 1948, p. 145].

In the past, it has been recommended that prospective adoptive parents and older children be allowed to meet as if by "accident" in a park, supermarket, or elsewhere. Current practice wisdom suggests that this is an inappropriate procedure:

> We are against blind showings. Almost all children beyond the age of four, and some younger, know what is happening. Blind showings imply that the parents are choosing rather than that the decision results from mutual interaction. The rejection the child experiences from a "blind showing" where he is not chosen seems greater than what he feels if the family and child meet and it is decided that they are not the right combination [Project CRAFT, 1980, pp. VI-76].

It has been recommended that in the case where the worker feels the child would be traumatized by this type of contact, videotapes or home movies be taken of the child and shown to prospective parents. Children can effectively deal with the uncertainty of a first meeting when it is made clear to them that the worker is not certain about the outcome (Shireman, 1983). It is helpful if, before the meeting, prospective parents are provided with information about the child's history and characteristics. Before the meeting, the child and prospective parents should also exchange pictures.

Adoptive parents come to this meeting with as much apprehension as the child. One adoptive couple note, "So we drove a great distance on a trip to a mystery. Conversation was unreal and under the thin ice of excitement yawned fears of failure" (Clayton & Clayton, 1984, p. 106).

It is most comforting for both younger and older children to first visit prospective parents in a familiar setting, such as their foster home (Jewett, 1978; Project CRAFT, 1980). Subsequent visits can be arranged at the adoptive home. Typically these visits are arranged for increasing lengths of time. Older children benefit from overnight visits. It is also helpful for the family and child to have opportunities to eat together. On these visits, the child and famly should go through relatively routine activities of daily living, rather than making each interaction a special occasion. It is of help to the children if, particularly during early visits, foster parents pick up the child and return the child to the foster home (Project CRAFT, 1980). Providing opportunities for normative interaction allows the family and child to move beyond the "honeymoon" period and to begin to interact more comfortably. Multiple visits allow the child to experience the move in a positive light.

> In general, it is more dangerous if the child perceives a move as someone coming and "taking" him, than if he perceives it as being "given" to someone else after much preparation and many interactions between the two sets of parents. If a child perceives a move as being taken away by relative strangers, he must live in a perpetual state of anxiety, fearing every knock at the door or every visit by acquaintances. If careful attention is paid to all details of the move, similar circumstances are not likely to recur in the child's life and trigger his extreme anxiety (Project CRAFT, 1980, pp. VI–95; See also Warfield, 1979).

A foster parent describes the outcome of one such gradual placement process:

> The caseworker and I first met the adoptive parents at the Social Service building without Jennifer present. We gave them some pictures of Jennifer and discussed her with them. We reviewed the problems she had in her early placement and how we had helped her through them. We discussed in detail her daily schedule, her eating and sleeping habits, and how we expected her to react in their home. Jennifer's first visit with the adoptive parents was in our home. Since Jennifer was still very wary of strangers, we decided they should gain her trust before making any advances toward her. We just sat around and talked about the weather, the time of day, the trip to my home, anything but Jennifer. For the next week the adoptive parents made daily visits to my home. At first Jennifer would allow them to play with her but nothing else. She still looked to me to wipe her nose, wash her face, take her to potty, or just to give her an occasional hug. As the week progressed, she needed me less and less. We started calling her adoptive parents her "new mommy" and "new daddy" and talked of when she would go to live with them.
>
> The second week the visits moved to the adoptive parents home. We took her there and stayed with her for her first visit in her new home. One day her new parents took her for an all day visit and brought her back. We took her for an overnight visit and they returned her the next morning. Toward the end of the second week Jennifer was happier to go with them than she was to come home to us. When they were around, she looked more to them for her care than she did to me. As if by miracle, she had transferred the love and trust she had in us to her new parents. We were the ones feeling

rejected now. We knew she was ready to make the move. When the day came, both families and Jennifer helped in the packing. This was done in an exaggerated manner so she would know for certain that this was final. She left with a smile and a wave. I was the one crying (Mary Ann Kiefer, cited in Project CRAFT, 1980, p. VI–97).

From Placement to Final Adoption

After the child is placed in the home, there is a trial period, usually six months to a year, during which the child is still under the legal guardianship of the agency. At the end of the trial period, if it is agreeable to both the agency and the adoptive parents, the final adoption takes place through appropriate court action.

The trial period or postplacement service, as it is sometimes more neutrally designated, is based on the recognition that not even the most acute, perceptive study can confidently predict how the adoptive parents will actually feel when confronted with rearing the adopted child. At best, the study "can differentiate between the potentially good prospects and more or less poor risks." This period, then, can be viewed as an extension of the home study. At this point, the parent is actually performing as a parent rather than talking about, imagining, or anticipating parenthood. The period thus serves a protective function, ensuring that the child has, in fact, been placed in a desirable home. This time is, consequently, a threat to the adoptive parents, for the agency might decide to remove the child if problems become serious. Actually, only rarely is a child likely to be removed after placement and before final adoption. Studies indicate that removal occurs in only about 2 per cent of the cases.

The trial period protects the adoptive parents as well. If the child is not developing normally, if a physical or mental handicap becomes manifest, parents can seek assistance from the agency in coping with the child and in seeking appropriate resources. The agency emphasizes that this period is one in which both the parents and the child are helped to develop affiliative feelings. Agency workers are available to help with the inevitable problems that arise as a result of such a radical change in the family's life situation. The agency sees these supportive functions as taking precedence over protective responsibilities (Katz, 1980; Project CRAFT, 1980).

The perception of some adoptive parents is at variance with the intent of the agency. An interview study of fifty-seven adoptive couples in Minnesota indicated "that they felt the 'probation' function reflected the primary purpose of continued contact by the agency," whereas caseworkers unanimously regarded help in successful integration of the adoptive family as the primary purpose. Of these families, 40 per cent felt that postplacement interviews had not been particularly helpful, 19 percent felt that the visits had been of "substantial" help (Gochros, 1962, p. 9). The clients' view of postplacement service as primarily protective is confirmed by another, more limited, study of client reaction (Zober, 1961). Many of these families prefer to turn to family, friends or their pediatricians for help with parent–child problems (Starr et al., 1970, p. 499).

Few of the parents felt that a clear, unambiguous statement of the purpose of the trial period had been communicated by the agency. When it had been, the parents were more likely to feel that the contacts were helpful—especially in two general areas: "reassurance (such as reassurance that they were doing a good job, that their child was developing properly or that the agency would not take the child away) and problem solving (such as provision of child care and developmental information and legal procedural information or help with specific adoption problems such as how to tell their child about adoption)" (Gochros, 1967, p. 322). "The single area of service that the greatest number of adoptive parents considered the most helpful was reassurance that they were doing a good job as parents" (Gochros, 1962, p. 10).

The experience of special needs adoptive parents differ from those of families adopting infants. Adopters of special needs children are much more likely to turn to others for ongoing support over a prolonged period of time after placement. Shireman (1983) cites one study in which 80 per cent of these families remained in agency contact.

Group meetings have been used during the period between placement and adoption and after final adoption. Conklin (1962) found that one of the advantages of the use of groups between placement and final adoption lay in countering the defensiveness of workers in contact with the family during this period. The caseworkers who had made the placement and, for purposes of continuity, were assigned responsibility for contact with the family during this time, tended to defend the correctness of their decision to place the child by failing to recognize incipient problems. The opportunity to observe the adoptive couples in group meetings permitted the agency to get a more objective picture of their circumstances.

Group support may help to overcome the diffidence and anxiety new adoptive parents feel in the period immediately after placement—precisely when they feel least free to share doubts and misgivings and difficulties with the workers (Chappelear, 1967; Schwartz, 1968; Pettigrew, 1969).

Studies indicate that the actual contacts between the agency and the family during this period are infrequent. Gochros (1962) found that visits were made about once every three months, and Triseliotis (1970) found that an average number of 1.6 visits were "paid to each case during the average six months probationary period" (p. 106).

Once the child has lived with the family for at least the amount of time specified as the probationary period, and the agency feels that the family and child are adapting, the family can request that the adoption be finalized. This is a legal procedure, regulated by state law (Brieland & Lemmon, 1977). This procedure is initiated by the filing of a court petition. The court responsible for handling adoption proceedings might be the probate court in one state, the juvenile court in another, and the superior court in still another. The petition, generally filed in the county in which the adoptive parents live, includes the pertinent information regarding the child, the adoptive parents, and the biological parents. Consent to adoption must be obtained from the biological parents. In many instances, the agency has obtained guardianship of the child, and it is the agency that gives consent to adoption. In other instances, it has obtained a signed "surrender" of the child by the biological parents, which authorizes the agency to place the child for adoption. But parental surrender or relinquishment of the child is more ambiguous than the clear termination of parental rights through judicial action. When the child is fourteen years of age—in some states, as young as ten years of age—his or her consent to adoption is also required.

The petition having been filed, a notice of proceeding is given to alert those people affected by the adoption. An official investigation of the circumstances regarding the adoption is then ordered by the court and is usually carried out by the public welfare agency. When the child has been placed by an agency, the agency adoption study is the relevant material offered the court. The investigating agency makes a recommendation to the court based on the information it has obtained.

A hearing is then held, usually in a closed court, at which time the court meets with the adoptive parents, the child, and any witnesses it deems should be heard. The court then makes a decision based on the material made available during the hearing and on the report from the agency authorized to study the adoption. The decision is made in terms of the best interests of the child. The adoption petition may be approved or denied, or a decision may be deferred to some later date.

This order is usually temporary or interlocutory. The final order is not granted until after the passage of some time, six months to a year. During this time, the child lives in the home of the adoptive parents but does not yet legally belong to them. At the end of the trial period, the final order for adoption is approved. Before issuing the final order, the court generally asks for a recommendation from the supervising agency. Once the final decree has been issued, there is the possibility of annulment, but this is rare: the child is the legal child of the adoptive parents.

In many states there is no provision for an interlocutory order, but it is necessary for the child to have lived in the home of the petitioner for some time, usually six months to a year, before a petition for adoption can be initiated. Because in such instances the investigations are made after the child has been living with the adoptive couple for some time, the court is likely to decide adversely only in unequivocally disadvantageous situations. Registration with a public welfare agency *before* taking a child into the home, as is currently required by some states, permits the agency to make an investigation of the desirability of the home before such a relationship is established.

The effect of a final decree is to establish a parent–child relationship between the petitioner and the adopted child and to terminate all relationships between the child and the biological parents. When the final adoption order is granted, the child usually assumes the surname of the adoptive parents. A new birth certificate may be issued in this new name, and the record of the adoptive proceedings is sealed.

For the most part, with the final decree, the legal rights, duties, privileges, and obligations of biological parents and child exist between the adoptive parents and child. But although the child may inherit from the adoptive parents, the child does not, if an alien, gain their citizenship. This has created a special problem in international adoptions, requiring special legislation by Congress to provide for the issuance of nonquota visas to permit "eligible" foreign children to come to the United States for adoption even though the immigration quota of their native country is oversubscribed.

When the child and the adoptive parents are not residents of the same state, the petition for adoption may be initiated in the state where the child lives, but it is more desirable if the action is initiated in the state in which the adoptive parents reside. This procedure expedites the social study of the adoptive applicants, upon which rests the decision of the court to grant or deny the petition. However, bringing the child into the state in which the adoptive parents reside also presents a problem. Most states require the permission of the state department of public welfare before a child is permitted to enter the state for the purpose of adoption. This requirement is meant to protect the state from the necessity of supporting a dependent child if the adoption is not consummated.

Since adoptions are regulated by state laws and since laws differ from state to state, placing children across state lines presents problems. An interstate compact on the placement of children has been developed to expedite such placement. By 1980, forty-three states had enacted uniform interstate compact legislation.

The compact agreement provides protection for children placed across state lines, coordinates the activities of agencies in different states dealing with the same adoptive family, provides for supervision and periodic reports on each interstate placement, and guarantees children financial and legal protection as they are moved from one state to another.

Postadoption Support

Adoptive parents may find themselves in need of periodic or continuing agency support, even though their adoption has been finalized and the child has adapted to living in their home. Many legal adoptions take place before the child is two years of age. Some of the most difficult problems of adoptive parenthood are only theoretical at this point. When parents actually encounter the full impact of the child's questions about adoption, when he or she is five or six, they might want to discuss these issues with the agency and with other adoptive parents.

Bellucci (1975) and Pannor and Nerlove (1977) report the use of groups for the purpose of counseling with parents and older adopted children. In one instance, the children's and parents' groups met separately, and a summary of what had been discussed in the children's group was shared with the parents. The problems that the children were encountering in adjusting to adoption and the expectations of their adoptive parents became clearer to the parents. Sibling rivalry and the confusions associated with being identified with two sets of parents were additional foci of discussion. After separate meetings of parents and children, joint meetings were held. The group meetings had the effect of freeing up communication between adoptive parents and children about questions related to the child's past, which, because they created anxiety, had not been adequately discussed. (See also Campbell, 1957; Collier, 1960; Sandgrund, 1962; McWhinnie, 1968.)

Parents who adopt special needs children may find it especially helpful to obtain ongoing support during their childrearing years (Sawbridge, 1980), as the later years of placement may prove more burdensome than the early years (Macaskill, 1985). "It is generally believed that the more severe the child's handicap, the greater the difficulty of parenting and the greater the stress placed on the family" (Meezan, 1980, p. 35). The general difficulties in the adoptive placement of the older child have been discussed in articles (Hallinan, 1952; Starr, 1955; Schapiro, 1957; Leatherman, 1957; Lawder et al., 1958; Boehm, 1958; Bell, 1959; McCoy, 1961; Epstein & Heymann, 1967; Chema et al., 1970; Sharrar, 1970; Neilson, 1972; Bayley, 1975; Edwards, 1975; Biggert, 1976; Chestang & Heymann, 1976; Belken, 1977; Katz, 1977; Jones 1979a; Holmes, 1979; Brockhaus & Brockhaus, 1982; Mackie, 1982; Nix, 1983; Hapgood, 1984; Jewett, 1984) and in books (Kadushin, 1970b; Carney, 1976; Jewett, 1978).

Postfinalization support services for adoptive families must be "comprehensive, integrated, and characterized by continuity" (Kadushin, 1984, p. 5). Meezan (1980) describes a range of services that are needed:

1. Casework services,
2. The use of volunteer families who have already adopted special needs children,
3. Strong linkages to community resources in order to help the family provide for the individual needs of their special child,
4. Social events,
5. Parent groups (p. 36).

It is difficult to estimate the number of adoptive couples who become involved in postfinalization support services. Some parents resist such contacts, since they serve to differentiate adoptive from other families. The growing number of special needs adoptive placement and the growing availability of adoption support groups suggests that families are making use of these programs in increasing numbers.

Common Problems Faced by Adoptive Families

Once the child is adopted, the family is like all other families—yet different. Consequently it has the same problems all other families face but, in addition, some unique problems that derive from the fact of adoption. Biological parents require no intermediary in achieving parenthood; adoptive parents require the agency. Biological parents pass no test of adequacy; adoptive parents must satisfy the agency of their adequacy. Biological parents can count on the child's arrival within a given period of time; adoptive parents do not know when—or if—the child will come. Adoptive parenthood, unlike biological parenthood, cannot be achieved in private in a moment of impulse; it requires a deliberate process in which motivation must be made explicit and shared with others. Adoptive parents can control the sex of the child, can ensure that the child is without serious defect, and can avoid the discomforts of pregnancy and childbirth; at the same time, they miss the experience of unity with the child in developing life and giving birth.

Once past the point of genesis, the differences between adoptive and biological families grow smaller and the similarities grow larger. Parenthood is primarily a social role, and title to the status *parent* should be reserved for those who actually perform its functions. The Talmud says, "He who raises up the child is called 'father'; not he who begot the child." Krugman (1964) observes, "The differentiation to be made is not between two sets of parents ('natural' and 'adoptive') but between *parents* and those who *give birth* to the child" (p. 357).

As *parents,* then, adoptive parents face all of the problems of adjustment and change in accepting the child into the home that all other parents face with the birth of a child. And they continue to face those problems encountered by all parents in conscientiously trying to raise a biologically, socially, and emotionally healthy child. Like all parents, adoptive parents must learn to accept their responsibilities as caretakers for children, find ways to make changes in the family so that the new member becomes an integral part of that system, and deal with changing relationships with extended family, friends, and the broader community entailed by the alteration in their status from "nonparent" to "parent." However, adoptive parents must complete these tasks while facing a unique set of demands and constraints.

Whereas birth parents must come to terms with the realization that they are about to give birth to a child, adoptive parents confront fears that failure to give birth to a child may not make them "real" parents. Because their parental status is achieved with the consent of the community through selection by a community agency, they may feel they must excel in this role. As one adoptive parent said, "The yardstick by which the adoptive parent, as a parent, is measured is a longer one." They may feel that, because the child has been deprived of bioparents, they have a special obligation. Adoptive mothers and fathers may worry that, since some part of the child belongs irrevocably to the natural parents, the child will reject them if they are firm disciplinarians. If the child develops difficulties, they may assume this indicates that they have failed.

Raleigh (1954), in a study of adoptive families at a child guidance clinic, noted that adoptive mothers "tended to be more overanxious about their children's problems and were more overprotective in their attitudes," which suggests "that the adoptive mothers tended to feel more insecure in their parental role" and had a greater need to appear concerned (p. 70). Adoptive mothers were also more inconsistent in their disciplining than natural mothers and felt less secure in coping with their children's unacceptable behavior (p. 69).

These responses appear to be more common among individuals who choose to adopt because of infertility than they are for families who decide to adopt, even though they have other children or could choose to have birth children instead. One survey suggested that infertile adopters experienced more stress than preferential adopters, even after they had adopted more than one child (Feigelman & Silverman, 1983). The researchers also simultaneously evaluated the effect of characteristics of the child (age, race, age at adoption), responses of others to the adoption, degree of parental stress, and type of adoptive parent (infertile or preferential) on ultimate child adjustment. Findings indicated "that mother's stress was the most significant of all variables" and suggest "that when mothers are overwhelmed with anxiety in assuming their parental roles—experiencing problems from interfering in-laws or limited economic resources, overwhelmed by fatigue—it seems to impair their children's adjustments" (p. 73). Holding parental stress constant, preferential adopters had better-adjusted children than did infertile adopters (p. 74).

In addition to accepting the adoptive child as their own, parents must make room for the child in the family. In any family, the addition of a new member to a family unit precipitates a period of "unbalancing" (Meezan, 1983a) or disorganization (Entwisle & Doering, 1981; LaRossa & LaRossa, 1981).

> What was a couple becomes a three-person system, and that new third person powerfully affects the organization of that system and the relationship between the family and the outside world. The demand for change can overwhelm a couple's adaptive capacities; can cut off sources of nurture, stimulation, and support; and often leaves a young family in a state of crisis. The delicate balance between the family and its world and within the family system is upset. The addition of an adopted child to a family has many of the same effects [Hartman, 1984, p. 12].

Successfully moving through this crisis requires that the family make both behavioral and affective adjustments. Family members work with the new child to establish mutually accommodative routines. Parents of a very active child may find that they can no longer eat supper late in the evening. Their child, who has been used to eating very early meals, will have to learn to wait to eat until a slightly later time. Mutual accommodations of this type result in the development of reciprocity or synchrony, which is essential for the eventual development of attachment (Schaffer, 1977; Stern, 1977). In addition to making changes in behavior, the family also learns to care about the new member and to consider this person an essential part of the family group. Family members learn to "claim" each other (Meezan, 1983a, p. 461), to develop a sense of entitlement. "For the child, issues of entitlement, issues of belonging to a family, raise issues of loyalty. Am I entitled to membership in this family? Does belonging to this family mean that I do not belong to my previous family? Can I be entitled to belong to this family when I haven't been born into it and still have feelings about other adults? . . . The family struggles with the same issues" (Hartman, 1984, p. 9).

The point of first encounter with the adoptive child is generally a very positive, almost overwhelming experience for adoptive mothers. For most of the parents in Smith and Sherwen's (1983) study, a period of suspense and anxiety was followed by relief and feelings of great happiness when they finally had an opportunity to meet the child. Parents engaged in various "claiming" behaviors, such as redressing young children in clothing they had brought with them. (See also Ward, 1981.) Most parents wanted to take the child home as soon as possible; fears that the child might be taken away from them persisted until they left the agency or airport where they and the child first met. The researchers found four different types of feelings that are common for parents at this point.

1. Thrill/Joy/Happiness (64 responses): This category comprises responses of unqualified joy and happiness, such as, "It was love at first sight," "I was flooded with joy," "I just reached out and held her; it seemed so natural."
2. Disappointment (18 responses): The responses in this category were negative and often quite dramatic: "That can't be my child—oh, no!" "I felt trapped," "I felt my life was over!" "I felt my heart sink."
3. Mixture of Joy/Happiness and Fear/Anxiety (39 responses): Responses in this category were ambiguous. They were generally positively-toned but with some fear and insecurity evident: "I was full of fear, but also hopeful, happy, and scared." "I was anxious, but hopeful too." "I was thrilled, but also fearful whether I could handle it."
4. Frightened/Uneasy/Awkward/Inadequate. The mothers responding in this way described their first encounter experiences as feelings of unease, helplessness, inappropriateness, or of not being prepared to cope with the situation. Comments such as: "He looked alien, not mine," or "I couldn't wait to get her out of the agency and home," are typical (pp. 84–85).

After the child comes home, both parents and child begin to assess each other and to seek indications that they are developing feelings of closeness. The early part of the placement period is highly stressful for some families. Jewett (1978) describes a period of postadoptive depression that may occur some six to eight weeks after the child is placed. At this point, parents are beginning to realize the range of difficulties the child has, the amount of time they will need to become attached to this child, and the degree of effort they will need to make in order to succeed at this task. Parents are often fearful that they do not have the capacity to bond successfully. Both they and the child may be exhausted by their struggle to establish new routines and accomplish day-to-day tasks. The first few months are additionally stressful because parents have to make important decisions about children but have insufficient information to use in making them. They find themselves deliberating at length about how to accomplish many child care tasks that will eventually become routine (James, 1980). "Because the child comes with problems, there is the work of trying to figure out what to do about them—a complicated job because a child does not come with directions to guide his new parents in their efforts to help him" (Jewett, 1978, p. 157).

On a short-term basis, parents may have to survive a period of testing, during which the child's behavior appears to get worse no matter what the parent does in response. The child attempts to be as difficult as possible in order to ascertain whether the parents are fully committed to keeping him or her. On a longer-term basis, parents also learn how to deal with more chronic difficulties. Special needs children may find it extremely hard to trust in or rely on any adult; they may have developed habitual behavior patterns that are dysfunctional; they may have other chronic disabilities that interfere with their capacity to respond adaptively and acceptably. We explore these types of problems in greater detail in a later section of this chapter.

James (1980) notes:

> During the beginning stages of any placement, there is a danger of making life too exciting, too stimulating and too extraordinary. New parents are often eager to do the kinds of things they enjoy doing with the child and which no doubt would also be fun for the child. It may be wiser to hold back and try first of all to establish a more ordinary family routine rather than embark upon a series of outings and treats which, while seeming to help the placement along, in reality may be creating unrealistic expectations in not promoting a natural rapport and communication between the child and his parents [p. 189].

While helping the child understand the reality of day-to-day family life, parents, too, struggle with the reality of *this* child with *these* disabilities and strengths. When the disparity between parental expectations of what the child will be like and the real child is too great, adoptive mothers and fathers, like parents whose children are born handicapped, will mourn for the child they hoped to have but did not receive (Schneider & Rimmer, 1984).

Friction between parent and child usually develops over ordinary issues. Parents of older adopted children find themselves dissatisfied with the child's eating habits, for example. They find it intolerable that their son chews food with his mouth open, stuffs food in his mouth, or frequently spills his milk. Parents are often amazed at the extent of their own anger and dissatisfaction, failing to recognize the amount of effort they expend in order to learn to interact more smoothly (James, 1980). During this time, friction between marital partners and among siblings is common. Since some adopted children find it easier to relate to one parent, the "left out" parent may feel jealous and abandoned. Siblings are upset that the new child does not have to meet the same expectations that they do. "An incident which often causes much distress to children is the breaking or damaging of some precious toy or object by the new family member" (Cann, 1980, pp. 215–216).

This process of adaptation and family reorganization may be a relatively lengthy one. Some families begin to feel "settled" only after 18 months to two years (James, 1980). For children who have undergone emotional trauma and multiple placements prior to moving to their permanent home, practice wisdom suggests that it will take one year in a reliable and safe environment to undo the effects of each year of deprivation. One parent describes the adoption of her Korean daughter, who was two years old at the time she came into the family:

> In October of 1981, we drove to Detroit and stayed overnight to meet a 6 A.M. plane. The greeter handed us our child—almost two. She was a very small child, with sweaty, matted hair, huge, frightened eyes, and covered with diarrhea—our bundle of joy . . . we spent the rest of the week trying to make her smile. We held her constantly, and the minute we'd start to put her down, she'd cry. We tried to get her to walk, but she would plop herself down and cry. By the end of the week we were still carrying her around the house, but she would allow us to take her off our laps and seat her right in front of one or the other of us on the floor while she played with blocks. It was sad to see her playing with her hands and feet, as if those were the only "toys" she had.

. . . Where was this instant love, the instant affection and acceptance I was supposed to feel? As I took care of her, all I saw was a stranger. Many months went by before I could look at her and see her, not as someone else's child I was in charge of, but as a member of my family, one of my three children . . .

Over the year we saw gradual improvement not only in speech but in socialization, too. But it was not until her second year here that she really blossomed. She began to talk back to her brothers, ask why, demand and give hugs, smile and laugh easily, as well as cry, be interested in other children, refer to herself by name, and realize who she was in the family unit . . .

Looking back, I wish I'd known some things before we adopted. I'd like to have known that love, acceptance, and adjustment would not necessarily come instantly or even quickly, but that they do come. I was prepared for prejudice against my daughter from the community, but I was not prepared for my own brand of prejudice against the stranger who came into our lives and disrupted them. I was prepared for her adjustment to our way of life, but not prepared to have to make adjustments myself. Now, today, I love my daughter. She belongs in this family and we would be incomplete without her (*Ours Magazine*, January/February, 1984, p. 21).

Unlike the circumstances surrounding the birth of a child, the entry of the adopted child into the home is not marked by any type of public recognition. Adoptive parents must, therefore, create their own special rituals to celebrate this event. To be effective, Hartman (1984) says, these rituals "should be ceremonial, serious and publicly witnessed" (p. 36). She suggests that, at the ceremony, each family member speak about the meaning of the adoption, and that the ritual be followed by some type of party or reception.

Like birth parents, adoptive parents struggle to meet their own personal needs while attempting to reach out to and care for their children. "Children's needs and parents' needs sometimes coincide; sometimes they are irreconcilable and sometimes accommodations are possible which allow for mutual satisfaction. In most families, arrangements have to be worked out to arrive at a tolerable mixture so that neither of the parties concerned will suffer unduly, and these arrangements are subject to change as the individuals develop and the family structure changes" (Rapoport, Rapoport, & Strelitz, 1977, p. 20). When adopting children, particularly special needs children, mothers and fathers may fail to take the time to take care of themselves. "Parents may have to choose when and how they will give to their new child, to avoid becoming so drained that they start to dislike the youngster and see him as a threat" (Jewett, 1978, p. 141; See also Hartman, 1984). One mother describes her feelings as she struggled to cope with her second adopted child, who came into her home at the age of six, as a sense that she was "drowning." She counsels, "Get out of the house, even if he screams when you leave him."

The adoptive family faces yet another task in dealing with the reactions of extended family, neighbors, and others in the community. Society is ambivalent about granting full endorsement to the adoptive parent. The very words "natural mother" or "real mother" suggest that adoptive parenthood is "unnatural" or "unreal." Society's attitude is that biological relationships are more important than social relationships, that "giving birth" is more important than "caring for," and that we are obliged to honor biological relationships for their own sake. Our vocabulary and our legal procedures, which reflect our thinking and our mores, suggest that adoption is a second-best route to parenthood. Adopting a child with special problems or preferring to adopt rather than have a birth child are considered even more unacceptable than adoption of an infant by an infertile couple (Feigelman & Silverman, 1983).

Taking any outsider into a family is rather unusual, and taking an older child, a group of children, or a 'problem' child may be judged by the outside world as quite extraordinary, by some people as altruistic, by others as foolishness verging on madness. Consequently, families may not always find the support and understanding they need to cope with their different family. Comments of 'I told you so' can add to feelings of guilt or failure (James, 1980, pp. 190–191).

In their survey of adoptive mothers, Smith and Sherwen (1983) found that almost three-quarters of these women had friends or extended family members who provided critical support. However, "several mothers said that they received no support from extended family and friends, who, in fact, opposed the adoption. Some families and friends went so far as to sever ties with the adopting mother. 'When you are pregnant, everyone helps you; when you adopt, no one helps you,' is how some adoptive mothers saw it" (p 90).

There are no readily available role models of adoptive parenthood that would help socialize adoptive parents to their status. Whereas the biological parent role almost uniformly elicits from others comments indicating support and approbation, the adoptive parent role frequently elicits comments that contain components of hostility, derision, and rejection.

With adoption, the parent faces the problem of accepting his or her status publicly. Application for adoption may be kept secret, but with the arrival of the child, the extended family and the immediate neighbors become aware of the adoption. The loss of anonymity raises such questions as what to tell friends and relatives about the child's background. But of somewhat greater difficulty is the fact that the adoptive parents now risk public recognition of their infertility. Questions will be raised about why they needed to resort to adoption.

No matter what the age of the child at the point of adoption, all adoptive parents must carry out two additional responsibilities. One involves discussing with the child the fact that he or she has been adopted; the other, talking with the child about his or her past life, particularly about the child's wishes with regard to contact with former caretakers. "Telling" and "search" issues are discussed in greater detail below.

Telling

In the process of "telling," the parent gradually shares with the child the information that he or she has been adopted, helping the child understand why this has occurred, and helping him or her to emotionally accept this fact. The question "How shall I tell my child about adoption?" contains within it a second question, "How do I accept myself as an adoptive parent?" Telling makes explicit the fact of infertility; telling makes explicit the fact that the child has other biological parents; telling introduces the natural parents' image into the family system and threatens the exclusiveness of the relationship between adoptive parents and child. Comfortable telling thus requires not only that adoptive parents resolve their feelings about infertility but also that they be sufficiently confident of the strength of the child's emotional kinship with them. Telling is also anxiety provoking because it raises the whole question of sexuality—how babies are conceived and how they are born. Parents may be diffident about telling because they feel uncomfortable with such questions.

The ability to accept the fact that adoptive children have kinship ties outside of the adoptive family is considered a significant factor related to the ultimate success of the placement (Hartman, 1984). Yet, one study that included both families who had adopted infants and those who had adopted older children found that fewer than one-third of the parents felt they were comfortable discussing their child's background (Raynor, 1980, p. 98).

Telling also raises questions relating to the family's presentation of the fact of adoption to others. What if the child's friends ask about the adoption? Should the school be informed about it? Should neighbors be told when the family moves into a new neighborhood?

Despite the difficulties involved, it is generally agreed that it is desirable for the adoptive parent to tell the child about adoption. Aside from the fact that not telling falsifies the relationship and requires that the adoptive parents live a lie, it is possible that the child might discover, through other sources, that he or she has been adopted. The parents' silence, then, might indicate to the child that they are ashamed or feel there is something bad about the fact of adoption (Smith & Miroff, 1981). Many children who have not been told do subsequently discover that their parents have not given birth to them. When children accidentally learn of their adoptions, or learn of it precipitously in some crisis situation, they react with "panic," feeling "stunned," "profoundly hurt," and "resentment" (Hagen et al., 1968; Paton, 1954; Berger & Hodges, 1982).

Telling is desirable because it requires that adoptive parents and children clarify between themselves the nature of their relationship. Telling is also an ethical matter. Children are entitled to know of their true origins. Rather than threatening the relationship, telling may actually intensify positive feelings between parents and child as they acknowledge their "shared fate." Some research findings suggest that adoptive families who openly accept the idea of adoption, implied in telling, are likely to be better adjusted and have children who are functioning more successfully (Kirk, 1964, pp. 95–99; Feigelman & Silverman, 1983).

There is some controversy, however, over when telling should take place (Berger & Hodges, 1982). Many agencies recommend that telling begin early in a child's life and be reintroduced for discussion at progressively higher levels of complexity. Parents are advised to introduce the word early, to apply the word and the concept in appropriate situations, and to tell the child about adoption simply and directly as one of the facts of life that the child needs to know.

Some psychoanalysts have advised that telling should be delayed until a child is beyond the oedipal stage in development. Telling a younger child supposedly feeds fantasies about and makes more difficult the resolution of the oedipal conflict. It has been suggested that when the child is between six and twelve, he or she can develop a more realistic image of the adoptive situation (Ansfield, 1971; Peller, 1961; Berger & Hodges, 1982). The material in support of this view is very limited, restricted to isolated clinical examples, and contradicted by Witmer et al.'s (1963) study, which showed that a delay in telling was associated with heightened negative reactions on the part of the child (p. 392). Raynor (1980) also concluded that, "telling before five years of age definitely appears to have been the least damaging, even though many did not really understand the significance of the story until much later" (p. 94). In her research, only the children who were five years or older when they were told were shocked or bitter about receiving this revelation.

In an extensive study of adoption perceptions among children between the ages of four and thirteen, both adopted and nonadopted, Brodzinsky, Singer, and Braff (1984) concluded:

Most preschool children are unlikely to understand much about adoption, even though they have been informed of their adoptive status by their parents and spontaneously used the label "adopted" in reference to themselves. The confusion of these young children is particularly evident in their frequent fusing of the birth and adoption concepts. By six years of age, however, most children do differentiate between birth and adoption as alternative paths to parenthood, and they acknowledge the permanence of the adoptive family relationship, although they show no awareness of the reasons for it . . .

Between eight and eleven years, children's conception of adoption broadens. Children now begin to appreciate the uniqueness of this family status, including the many complications that it entails. One outcome of this general increase in adoption knowledge, however, is that for some children the adoptive family relationship suddenly becomes tenuous. Inspection of the interview protocols suggests that much of the child's fantasy life at this time is centered on the biological parent's potential for reclaiming the child and/or the potential disruption of the adoptive family life. Toward the end of this period, however, children typically regain their certainty in the permanence of the adoptive family relationship, although their understanding of the basis of this permanence remains somewhat vague. In fact, it is not until early to middle adolescence that children recognize that adoption involves a legal transfer of parental rights and responsibilities from biological parents to adoptive parents (p. 876).

The authors suggest that telling need not be deferred, although it is clear that children do need to be told and retold about adoption, as their capacity to understand this phenomenon broadens. Adoptive parents need to be educated about this emerging ability to understand so that they do not misinterpret the child's responses or feel that they are remiss if the child does not fully comprehend what adoption means after a single telling. The importance of periodically sharing information about adoption with the child is suggested by Raynor's (1980) findings that most families discuss this issue infrequently. In her study, nearly half had spoken of it only two or three times during all the years the child had lived in the home, and another quarter only as often as once or twice a year (p. 97).

Additional relevant research involves interviews with adult adoptees who shared, retrospectively, their experience in the telling process (McWhinnie, 1967). Another study was based on small group meetings of adult adoptees who met over a period of six months to discuss their experiences in adoption (Hagen, 1968). To a considerable extent the adoptees verify that it is crucial for the parent to share with the child the fact that he or she was adopted, that integration of the meaning of adoption takes place gradually that real understanding is not achieved until adolescence or even early adulthood, and that although it is necessary to reiterate the fact of adoption, it should be referred to only on those occasions when the situation calls attention to adoptive status.

There are also suggestions on how to tell. The general advice is that the parents should share the information confidently, realistically, and positively, without anxiety or apology, suggesting that the parents themselves have to feel very comfortable with the idea of adoption.

Overemphasis is as much an indication of discomfort with the idea as vigorous avoidance. The adoptive parents of the child who said, "I knew. They knew I knew. I even told them I knew. But they still refused to talk about it" are clearly uncomfortable with the fact of adoption. But discomfort is also present in the case of the family of the adopted child who said, "It was good to know that I was adopted, but I wished that they would stop talking about it."

As McWhinnie (1967) notes, in summarizing the reaction of adopted adults whom she interviewed:

> None of these adopted children wanted their adoptive status shrouded in complete secrecy. . . . Equally they did not want constant reference to it. They wanted something in between, where their adopted status was acknowledged without embarrassment and then overtly forgotten so that they were treated exactly as if they were the biological sons and daughters of their adopted parents. . . . Thus they were emphatic that they did not want to be introduced as an "adopted son" or an "adopted daughter." They wanted to feel they belonged in the family and were completely accepted there as a son or daughter [p. 249].

Adoptive parents must communicate to the child that their child belongs to the family just as certainly and securely as a biological child does. Telling, at its best, can be an expression of love and acceptance of the child. Learning how he or she came to be adopted can reinforce the child's feelings of belonging and identity. However, telling can also be used as a weapon. Depending upon the spirit of communication, it may make the child feel obligated for all the adoptive parents have done, or feel threatened that he or she might be "returned" for not giving sufficient satisfaction (Raynor, 1980).

Adoptive parents have to accept responsibility for telling. Earlier studies suggested that adopted children were supposedly indifferent to adoption because they rarely took the initiative in asking questions. More recent research finds, however, that children are eager to know but, despite their curiosity, feel that they cannot initiate discussion about origins out of fear of hurting or upsetting or appearing disloyal to the parents (Jaffee, 1974). Half of the adoptees who participated in Raynor's (1980) study stated that they felt they could not freely refer to the adoption when talking with their parents (p. 98). Although retrospectively adult adoptees may state that they were anxious to know about their past when younger, the child's resistance to hearing may be evident (Tizzard, 1977). The child, as a child, may have difficulty integrating the ideas that another set of parents surrendered him or her for adoption. Reluctance on the part of the child to discuss freely the matter of adoption might be self-protective. Despite this, Berger and Hodges (1982) argue, parents must not collude with the child in an attempt to avoid the issue. "We would argue that some pain is inseparable from comprehending that one is adopted: this does not mean that one must assume it to be so intrinsically painful that one must try to prevent the child from knowing anything about it. Any child, as part of his development, must confront situations with an element of pain. The important thing is that these situations come about at such a time and in such a way that the child has adequate resources to deal with them; and we feel the same applies to knowing about adoption" (p. 70).

Agencies generally recommend that parents introduce the child early and gradually to the idea of adoption through the judicious use of such books as *Why Was I Adopted?* (Livingston, 1978) and *How It Feels to Be Adopted* (Krementz, 1982). Cochran-Smith (1983) has developed an annotated bibliography of children's books that discuss this subject.

A question of pressing concern to the adopted child is "Why did my biological parents give me up?" Frequently the answer is "Because they could not care for you and loved you so much that they wanted the best for you." But the idea that "they loved you so much" is rejected by adopted adults. One woman said:

First of all I don't think it is possible to feel true potential love for a newborn or growing child. This comes from living together. Also if my real parents loved me so much, why did they give me up? I used to think, "Are my adoptive parents going to give me up, too, because I know they love me?" It is more honest to say that there are circumstances which make it necessary to place a child for adoption. It is a question of the ability to be a parent, not a question of love [Hagen, 1968, p. 27].

It is difficult to discuss adoption without implying that the child has been rescued from inadequate parents. Yet to imply this may make it difficult for the child, who has to some extent identified with these parents, to come to terms with his or her history (Berger & Hodges, 1982). The adoptive parents must find means to communicate background information in an accepting, understanding tone, although it may be hard for them to empathize with or understand a birth parent who has given up this child, a child they love and want. One follow-up study showed that there "appeared to be a link between the adoptive parents' attitudes toward the natural parents and the difficulty they found in telling the child he was adopted. Though none considered telling to be easy, those who actually disapproved of the natural parents found it to be more difficult" (Seglow, Pringle, & Wedge, 1972, p. 149).

Children's abilities to grasp reasons for relinquishment change as they become increasingly capable of understanding complex social relations. Brodzinsky, Singer, and Braff (1984) report that more egocentric early school-aged children tended to focus on negative personal characteristics as reasons for placement, although they also realized that financial difficulties and lack of time to care for a child were important. As the children matured, they become even more aware of the impact of financial stresses on the family and begin to mention illegitimacy, immaturity, parental stress, and family conflict as key motivators (p. 876).

When sharing information about their past with adoptive children, parents have been advised to help them construct a "cover story" (Project CRAFT, 1980). The story helps the child provide answers to common questions that strangers ask about why he or she has a different last name than other members of the family, where he or she came from, and other questions about the child's birth family (pp. III-37–III-39). By helping the child practice answering these questions, the parent helps the child create boundaries between public and private family concerns and become more at ease in dealing with what might otherwise prove uncomfortable probing.

Almost all surveys that have been done of adopted individuals suggest that they would like more information about their birth families than they have already received (Berger & Hodges, 1982). Interviewing 105 adoptees, Raynor (1980) discovered that the situation is somewhat more complex. Approximately one-third of her respondents were comfortable with the the amount of material they already had even though some had little background information on their birth families. Another third wished for slightly more information. Thirty-five per cent were rather or very discontented. In general, "those who wished for more usually did not want a great deal of information, but there were just one or two things they longed to know. Most often this was a desire to know the reason behind their being given for adoption or what their birth mother had looked like" (p. 99).

Adoption workers assist parents with the telling process in several key ways. First, they provide parents with sufficient information about the child's back-

ground and about the developmental differences in children's understanding of
the concept of adoption so that parents can realistically discuss the matter with
their children. One study (Nelson, 1985) found that the provision of adequate
information about the child's history was highly correlated with subsequent success of the placement. "We found it among one of the strongest predictors of how
well these adoptions are going. That is, the better the information the better the
adoptions are going" (Community Council of Greater New York, 1984, p. 11).
Workers also help parents with their own emotional response to telling and to
their own status as nonbirth parents of this child. Hartman (1984) finds that
group techniques particularly well-suited for assisting parents with these issues.

The Question of Search

The concern with telling is related to concern with another aspect of adoption,
the search of adoptive children for more detailed knowledge of their roots and for
possible contact with their biological parents. *Search* is defined as the efforts of
either adult adoptee or the birth parent to secure identifying information that
might possibly lead to locating the other party. The need to search derives from
the fact that in many jurisdictions, once a child is legally adopted, the record of
how the child came to be adopted is sealed, and information from the record about
biological parents is not available to the adopted child. It also means that information about the adoptive family in which the child has been placed is not available
to the biological parent.

Sealed records symbolize the dissolution of the relationship between adoptee
and birth parents substituting for it the adoptive parent–adoptive child relationship. Anonymity "helps the adoptive family establish itself as a social unit, free
from outside interference and provide an environment in which the child is encouraged to identify with his adoptive home" without competitive ties and pulls
(Burke, 1975, p. 1200). Sealing the record also protects the out-of-wedlock child
from the stigmatization that might result from a revelation of his or her status
and protects the biological mother from any possibility of subsequent intrusion on
her life by the child she has surrendered.

The question of opening adoptive records does potentially affect the lives of the
biological parents and the adoptive parents as well as the life of the adoptee.
Social and emotional constraints operate to condition the behavior of all parties
in the triangle and to condition their attitude toward the search. The adopted
child might feel this is an "unspoken debt to be paid with acquiescence and
silence: it is a form of emotional indenture even though it is made in the name of
love" (Lifton, 1975, p. 5). To deny the debt is to act as a traitor. (See also Sobol &
Cardiff, 1983.) The birth parent may be restrained by a respect for the privacy of
the adoptive family and the disruption such an intrusion may occasion for them
and the adopted child. The adoptive parents may discourage the search not only
because of the threat to their image as the child's true parents but also out of
concern for the possible hurt to their child that might result from the revelation of
embarrassing background material or a possible negative reception by the birth
parent.

Search is regarded as a potential threat to the integrity of adoption services
because it is considered a violation of the agency's promise of confidentiality and
anonymity to the biological mother and to the adoptive parents (Jones, 1976). Not
being able to provide assurance of confidentiality to unmarried parents may
decrease the advantages of agency placement as compared with black- or gray-

market placements or child abandonment. Anxiety about the possibility of subsequent contact may intensify the biological mother's hesitancy about surrendering her child for adoption, thereby reducing the number of available adoptive infants.

While unsealing records raises a number of concerns, it also has its advantages. There are possible gains for all parties in the relationship as a consequence of the search. Adoptees have the opportunity to learn what they want and need to know about their roots and their heritage. They can feel a sense of continuity with the past, can come to grips more surely with problems of identity, and can, through this experience, correct their fantasies. Birth parents can resolve old guilt feelings and answer nagging questions about what happened to the relinquished child. Adoptive parents can lay to rest the anxieties about the impact of search on their relationship with their child (Triseliotis, 1984). Sealed records suggest secrecy, which is detrimental because it reinforces "the 'as if' concept for the parties involved in the adoption. The adoptive parents, for instance, would like to believe that the child never had any other parents and belongs to them 'as if' she were of their own blood. The birth mother likes to pretend that she never had a child whom she relinquished. The adoptee identifies with the adoptive parents as though they are her 'real' parents" (Sachdev, 1984b, pp. 141–142). Adoptees perceive efforts to protect them from uncomfortable information about their past as dishonest and disabling. Opening these records may mean that the parent–child relationship can be continued with greater honesty and openness.

Lack of access to background information may run counter to the psychological needs of adoptees during their adolescence and young adult years. All adolescents face challenges in defining their uniqueness as human beings and developing coherent, stable self-images. For the adopted teenager, problems of self-image formation are exacerbated by the need to incorporate two sets of parents and by having to do so with only vague, limited knowledge about one set, the birth parents (Sorosky, Baran, & Pannor, 1978).

It is said that adoptees are like amnesia victims who cannot remember some part of their lives; they feel that important aspects of their life story are lost. There may be a sense of psychological amputation, or "genealogical bewilderment" (Sants, 1965; Partridge, 1978; Colón in Project CRAFT, 1980). "It can now be claimed with some confidence from the available evidence that there is a psychosocial need in all people, manifest principally among those who grow up away from their original families, to know about their background, their genealogy, and their personal history if they are to grow up feeling complete and whole" (Triseliotis, 1984, p. 38). Lacking the opportunity to develop a full concept of self, adoptees may develop low self-esteem or various emotional and learning disabilities (Sachdev, 1984b, p. 144).

Genealogical information that would provide the adoptee with a better sense of identity is available from three sources: agency files, records of the court that approved the petition for adoption, and the birth record. Scotland, Finland, and Israel have for some time permitted adoptee access to birth records. This change was legislated in England in 1975 and in several Canadian provinces in the late 1970s. In the United States, intensive lobbying for sealed records during the 1930s and 1940s resulted in passage of sealed adoption laws in all states by 1950. The 1970s and 1980s saw a reversal of this trend.

By 1985 some thirty-five states had adopted laws permitting adult adoptees to obtain identifying information regarding their birth parents (Harrington, 1986). There were differences in the laws regarding the minimum age entitling adoptees to such access and the kinds of information made available, differences regarding the reunion registry systems that provided access, differences in the procedures which enable contact between adoptees and birth parents, and differences in the opportunities provided birth parents to get in touch with adoptees. Some adoption search laws incorporate a "mutual-consent" procedure that allows both adoptive and bioparents to register their willingness to meet if contacted. Other states have a "search and consent" procedure by which third-party intermediaries, generally social agencies, act as liaisons between children and bioparents. Counseling for those seeking access to sealed records is not mandatory in the United States, although it is in Great Britain for persons who were adopted before passage of the 1975 act.

The sealed-record procedure has been viewed as a violation of the Fourteenth Amendment, because it denies adoptees "equal protection of the laws," and of the First Amendment, which can be construed to include not only the right to speak but the right to receive information (Anderson, 1977; Burke, 1975; Prager & Rothstein, 1973). Equal protection of the law is claimed because the sealing of the records causes adoptees psychological pain, suffering, and damage not experienced by nonadopted persons. The contention is that adoptees, as a group, are discriminated against because they are denied information contained in the birth record that is freely available to every other citizen. The agreement made between the agency, the birth parent, and the adoptive parent for anonymity and confidentiality, was, it is said, made without the consent of the adoptee, who is a coequal partner to the information held secret.

Access to adoptive records can currently be obtained in most states on a petition to the courts for "good cause." The problem is that *good cause* has not been clearly defined, and judges, therefore, have considerable discretion in making such decisions. Matters of health, possible genetic defects, and controversial inheritance situations have been among the "good causes" for opening adoption records. A general desire for more knowledge about one's background or the need to resolve problems of identity, a "psychological need to know" has not been as easily accepted as good cause" (Harrington, 1980). In such cases, the judiciary must also determine the agency responsible for seeking birth mother consent, must determine how intensely and for what period of time the search for birth parents should continue, and must decide whether adoptees have the right to information about their past when their birth parents are deceased (Sachdev, 1984b).

Groups of adoptees, and some biological parents whose children were adopted, have organized to press their claim for open records. Orphan Voyage was established in 1954 by an adopted social worker, Jean Paton, to call attention to this problem. More recently, ALMA (Adoptees Liberty Movement Association) was established by Florence Fisher. ALMA publishes a handbook written by a professional genealogist giving advice on procedures to be employed in searching out records. Search committee workshops are conducted to help members with problems relating to search. In 1977 ALMA claimed a membership of ten thousand around the country. In the United States and in other countries, a number of other adoptee organizations with similar goals emerged during the 1970s (Sachdev, 1984b).

Various self-help guides to search procedures are also available. They describe the steps to take to obtain access to birth information, roadblocks to obtaining access, and common feelings and concerns of adoptees who do decide to search. (See, for example, Lifton, 1981; Martin, 1980; Askin & Oskam, 1982).

The Association for the Protection of the Adoptive Triangle (APAP), composed primarily of adoptive parents, supports keeping adoption records sealed. Biological parents have also developed their own group, Concerned United Birth Parents, which now has chapters in twenty-five states. These parents are requesting that adoption records be unsealed after the child reaches a certain age.

Detailed interviews with thirty-eight mothers who earlier in their lives had surrendered a child for adoption indicated that they frequently thought about the adopted child with considerable mixed feelings of guilt, pain, loss, and mourning (Baran, Pannor, & Sorosky, 1976; Sorosky, Baran, & Pannor, 1978). In addition to whatever guilt or shame the birth parent feels about having had a child out of wedlock, there is the additional burden of guilt and shame related to having surrendered the child. Parents are interested in knowing how the child has developed and want to explain to the child what prompted their decision. A desire for expiation and absolution also seems to be common.

The Child Welfare League of America, in its *Standards for Adoption Service* (1978) continues to support the notion of sealed records. "Services to natural parents should preserve confidentiality and keep knowledge of each other's identity from the natural and the adoptive parents" (p. 21). However, this standard-setting organization also realizes that birth and adoptive parents can no longer be ensured confidentiality and has developed disclosure procedures to follow should the agency be ordered to do so by the court or allowed to do so by law. CWLA recommends providing the adoptive family with nonidentifying information about the medical history of the child and the reasons for adoption, if the family requests them.

In an attempt to evaluate agency procedures with regard to sealed records, the League solicited questionnaire responses from 163 member agencies in 1976 (Jones, 1976). Agencies participating in this survey indicated that it was their practice to share a great deal of the information they had concerning birth parents with adoptive families and that they encouraged adoptive parents to share this material, in turn, with the child. Agencies were more reluctant to disclose when the child was relinquished as a result of rape or imprisonment of the birth parent. In 1976, most agencies made assurances of anonymity and confidentiality to birth and adoptive parents. They had conducted occasional searches for birth parents and, in most instances where birth parents were located and contacted, the parents were agreeable to meet with the adult adoptee.

The general feeling of adoption agencies in 1976, as reflected in the Child Welfare League of America questionnaire study, was that the sealed-record controversy had opened a question that would continue to be debated and needed to be resolved. However, agency opinion was that because of the dangers for all parties concerned, identifying information should be made available case by case rather than by legislative revision in favor of blanket accessibility of records. As a corollary, the agencies felt that although anonymity and confidentiality still should be respected, agency information should be more accessible to the adoptee and that agencies should be flexible in sharing what was available.

Recent studies have shed light on the motivations and characteristics of adoptees who choose to search for birth parents, on the differences between searching and nonsearching adoptees, and on the reactions of birth and adoptive parents to search procedures. A survey of 300 adult adoptees (Children's Home Society of California, 1977) revealed that approximately one-third thought about searching for their birth parents "all the time" or "often," whereas 38 per cent rarely or never gave this a thought (p. 20). Most estimates of the proportion of adoptees who will actually engage in a search are lower than this.

Triseliotis (1984) reviewed the statistics and related research regarding the implementation of the British Children Act of 1975 that gave British adoptees access to information regarding their birth records. National statistics over a six-year period indicated that only a limited number of adoptees were sufficiently interested in additional knowledge about origins so as to institute an effort of search. "Those applying for access to their birth records in each of the last three years (1980–1982) represent approximately 0.3 percent of adopted adults in England and Wales and 0.7 percent in Scotland" (p.48). If the percentage applying for access in 1982 were constant over the entire 52 years of the life cycle of an adoptee from age 18 to 70 a total of 21 percent of all adoptees might apply for their birth records. "The fact is that in spite of all the publicity of recent years access to birth records is still a minority response among adoptees" (p.48). More detailed information obtained from counseling sessions with school workers, required of all those who applied for access to birth records, indicated that only about one in five applicants had any interest in actually meeting their birth parents. Most were only interested in receiving information (p.49). In general, counseling showed that adoptees who applied for their birth records to be well adjusted and committed to the adopted parents as their "real" parents.

Weidell (1980) presented a recapitulation of Minnesota's experience with open record legislation over a three-year period. During that period, 332 requests for access to adoption records were filed. Sixty-eight of the applicants were women; the largest number of applicants were in the 26–30 age range. About 12 per cent of the group made contact with their birth parents. A survey of adoptive parents (Feigelman & Silverman, 1983) reported that 15 per cent of their children had asked to see their adoption records and 4 per cent had actually contacted birth families. These parents estimated that 18 per cent of all children would someday seek information or contact. In her interviews with adoptees placed by one agency in Great Britain, Raynor (1980) found that 78 per cent wanted no contact with their birth family, whereas 22 per cent did desire such contact.

Although searchers are not disturbed, they do have a weaker sense of self-identity and self-esteem than nonsearchers (Triseliotis, 1973, 1974; Feigelman & Silverman, 1983; Aumend & Barrett, 1984; Sobol & Cardiff, 1983; Raynor, 1980). Parents describe searchers as having greater adjustment problems, and searching adoptees depict themselves as being more unhappy than nonsearchers. Some evidence suggests that individuals who search were adopted at a later age than were their nonsearching cohorts (Sobol & Cardiff, 1983; Aumend & Barrett, 1984).

The relationship between searchers and their adoptive families may be more problematic. Taking advantage of the fact that Scotland permits access to adoptive records, Triseliotis (1973) interviewed adoptees who had requested such information in 1969 and 1970. Forty-two of the seventy individuals he talked with wanted to actually meet their birth parents, whereas twenty-six only wanted background information. Those who were interested in reunion were generally more dissatisfied with their adoptive families. "There was hope that the natural parents (if found) would make up to them what they missed from other relationships" (p. 159). The group interested in information only were generally more satisfied with current relationships and were primarily interested in obtaining information "that would help them complete themselves and tie up loose ends." In a study of 120 individuals solicited through newspaper advertisements and a self-help adoptive organization, Sobol and Cardiff (1983) reported that searchers remembered more negative childhood episodes with their adoptive families, rated the overall outcome of their adoptions more poorly, and felt more uncomfortable discussing their adoption with their families.

Stein and Hoopes (1985) also found searcher as compared with nonsearcher adoptees to have a more disturbed relationship with their adopted parents. They also note that although the 50 adoptees they studied had curiosity about their origins, only a limited number were actually interested in a search.

Adoptive parent discomfort with the child's adoptive status can contribute to the need to search (Sorosky, Baran, & Pannor, 1974a, b, c; 1975a, b; 1976; 1978). As was true of Triseliotis' group, many of the adoptees in these studies experienced a late, disruptive revelation of adoption. The median age at which the group learned of their status was seven years, much later than is recommended by adoptive agencies, and the fact of adoption was, in 32 per cent of the cases, learned from somebody other than the adoptive parent. Sobol and Cardiff (1983) also found that searchers reported more negative early feelings about their adoptive status and more negative feelings about their status during adolescence. However, search behavior in their study was not related to the atmosphere that surrounded the actual revelation experience (pp. 479, 481). Feigelman and Silverman (1983) did not find that age at revelation was related to the decision to search.

Although these studies appear to suggest that it is the poor atmosphere within the family that, in part, gives impetus to search behavior, one study (Feigelman & Silverman, 1983) found that it was in families in which parents actively supported the child's need for and right to search that children felt most comfortable pursuing information and contact with their birth families. (See also Day [1979] and Simpson, Timm & McCubbin [1981] for more positive views of searcher-adoptive parent relationship.)

While nonsearchers have less information about their birth circumstances, they are also less interested in obtaining this information. Examining the responses of 288 adoptees, Aumend and Barrett (1984) found that one-quarter of the nonsearchers knew nothing about the reasons for their adoptive placement and did not care to know. This was true for only 1.4 per cent of the searchers. Although 47 per cent of the searchers did not know why they were adopted but wondered about the reasons, only 18 per cent of the nonsearchers did so (p. 256). (See also Sobol & Cardiff, 1983.) In general, nonsearchers report themselves as more "satisfied with their lives" and more likely to feel that their adoptive family is their "true" family than do searchers (Children's Home Society of California, 1977). However, nonsearchers also report that these positive family relationships inhibit them from initiating any type of search (Sobol & Cardiff, 1983).

The limited available data suggest that most birth parents do not plan to initiate contact with their children, just as most adoptees do not plan to actually meet with their birth parents. Sachdev (1984b), describing the results of a more recent survey, notes that only one-third of the birth parents who had contacted agencies with regard to their children actually wanted help in either finding or identifying the name of their child (p. 151). (See also Children's Home Society of California, 1977.)

Despite their reluctance to initiate contact, birth parents are usually agreeable to such contact, once their child has requested it. Reviewing such requests over a three-year period subsequent to the opening of adoption records in Minnesota, Weidell (1980) states that only one in three mothers and one in five fathers did not want contact to occur (p. 118). Other studies find an even lower refusal rate (Sachdev, 1984b, p. 152).

In general, adoptive parents are less favorably disposed toward open records than are adult adoptees or birth parents, although most are willing to allow their children access to some information about their past. A study conducted by the Children's Home Society of California (1977), found some 73 per cent were in favor of open records. In a recent survey of 737 adoptive families, Feigelman and Silverman (1983) asked a number of questions about parent attitudes toward access. Sixty-one per cent of the respondents approved of the idea of their children learning about their birth families; only 22 per cent felt their children should not learn about their birth parents; half felt that adoption records should not remain sealed. In fact, 57 per cent agreed that their children, once they reached adulthood, should have unrestricted access to their records, and forty-six per cent were even willing to support minors having limited access to records. However, adoptive parents were more reluctant to support the child's actual meeting with birth parents. Only 19 per cent felt that birth parents should be allowed to contact their adult adopted children; only 25 per cent felt birth parents should have access to current information about their children (p. 199). (See also Feigelman & Silverman, 1986).

Using a nonsystematic sample of 42 adoptive parents, Geissinger (1984) noted, as did Feigelman and Silverman, that most parents in her study (75%) were comfortable with the child's obtaining access to birth records upon reaching adulthood. Geissinger was interested in characteristics of parents who felt most uncomfortable. "The degree of fear about potential losses of adopted children, whether psychological or physical, was found to be influential in determining adoptive parents' position toward the open birth record issue" (p. 584). Mothers and fathers were equally likely to be fearful. When adopted children in the family were older (beyond 10 years of age) and, therefore, more likely to search in the near future, adoptive parents held more negative attitudes about the idea of search.

Although many adoptees feel the greatest sense of curiosity about their origins during adolescence, it is not until they reach adulthood that they generally decide whether or not to act on this desire (Triseliotis, 1973). The formal request for access to records may be triggered by significant experiences related to the human life cycle of accession and abandonment: death of the adoptive parent, an impending marriage, birth of a child, or divorce. Some situational factors may prompt this decision, i.e., the need for a birth certificate for the armed forces, a civil service exam, a life insurance application, or the discovery of an illness that may have a genetic origin (Feigelman & Silverman, 1983; Triseliotis, 1984).

Not all individuals who request access ultimately receive permission to see their records. A long period of time may elapse between the request for birth information and its provision. In the two years since records were reopened in Minnesota, only one-quarter of those who had requested birth certificates actually receive them, whereas half of the individuals who requested contact had actually been in touch with birth families (Weidell, 1980). When adoptees do meet with their biological parents, the meeting proves generally successful and satisfying to the participants in by far the majority of cases. Approximately 80 per cent of these meetings are considered satisfactory (Triseliotis, 1973; Jones, 1976; Stevenson, 1976; Ehrlich, 1977; Lifton, 1981; Sorosky, Baran, & Pannor, 1978). However, research conducted in England (Leeding, cited in Triseliotis, 1984) suggests a somewhat less optimistic outcome with 39 per cent of the contacts described in a positive light and the remainder considered uncertain in outcome (p. 49).

Adoptees who feel positive about their contact with their birth families report a "greater sense of closeness," a feeling of "knowing better where they stood." Information from single case studies of reunions provides support for the view that adoptees personally benefit from face-to-face contact with parents who relinquished them for adoption (Lindemann, 1969; Dalsheimer, 1973; Fisher, 1973; Howard, 1975; Freedman, 1977). In recapitulating her own experiences in finding her bioparents, an experience which involved its share of pain and guilt and ambivalence, Lifton (1975) feels that it is a high-risk venture. The search leads to a very difficult encounter and presents problems in resolving an atypical relationship for which society provides little, if any, preparation. What kind of ongoing relationship should or can one establish with a bioparent late in life? How does one deal with the almost inevitable discrepancy between the fantasy biomother and the reality?

One study conducted by Depp (1982) found that all twelve adoptees who had had birth-parent contact felt that their relationship with their adoptive parents was not negatively impacted. Only one in six of the adoptive parents who were contacted felt that their relationship with their child had deteriorated as a result of the reunion. (See also Sachdev, 1984b.)

In general, female adoptees are more likely to engage in search behavior than are males. Fully two-thirds of searchers are women (Lifton, 1975; Stevenson, 1976; Sorosky, Baran, & Pannor, 1978; Triseliotis, 1984). Frequently, the motivation to search is associated with pregnancy, birth, or adoption of a child. These situations point to a heightened sensitivity to and concern with origins and would impact more potently on female than on male adoptees (Kowall & Schilling 1985). Black children might be more likely than white, Korean, or Colombian children to seek information about their birth families and to ask to see their records. Feigelman and Silverman (1983) report that parents expected 39 per cent of the black children to eventually search; only one in five of the white children, 14 per cent of the Koreans, and none of the Colombian children were expected to seek reunion (p. 220).

As a result of a better understanding of the motives of adoptees seeking information about, or reunification with, their birth parents and of the outcome of these reunions, it is generally agreed that freer access to nonidentifying background information should be granted and that this approach should be augmented by updated information that can be made available to either the biological parent or the adopted child, once he or she has reached adulthood. Here the agency can provide a continuing service. Accepting without equivocation the rights of adoptees to search, the agency can provide help in implementing search procedures and guidelines for conducting a search. The agency can provide preparation for the initial shock of contact based on the experience of others who have searched and found their biological parents. The agency can help resolve the problems of the continuing relationship after contacts (Triseliotis, 1984; Hartman, 1984). Some agencies have already begun to give greater emphasis to the problems that face the adoptive triad—birth parents, adoptive parents, and adopted child—long after adoptive placement.

A word of caution: this discussion of changes with regard to search applies generally to the child surrendered more or less voluntarily by the birth mother. However, change in policy would also apply to those adoptions made as a result of the involuntary termination of parental rights over the clear opposition of the birth parents. In these instances, the birth parents may not feel so friendly toward the adoptive family and may actively seek to disrupt the relationship between adoptee and adoptive parents. Further, in these instances, which are likely to be characterized by severe neglect and abuse and greater pathology in the birth family, the information about origins may be more difficult for the adoptee to handle.

Adoption Disruptions

Once children have been placed in adoptive homes, it is assumed that the child has obtained a permanent family, one that will be his or hers for life. However, in some instances, the child and family fail to develop a mutually satisfactory relationship, and the placement disrupts. Adoption disruptions are defined as permanent removal of the child from the adoptive home at any time before legal finalization of adoption. The fact that many of these children go on to make a success of a subsequent adoptive placement is a justification for calling these removals adoption disruptions rather than adoption failures.

Table 9-2 summarizes a group of studies, most of which were conducted in the 1960s, which evaluated the outcome of infant adoptions. The overwhelming majority of children examined here were white, very young, and without handicap at the time of their placement. Of the 34,499 placements assessed, only 648, or 1.87 per cent, resulted in disruption.

Recent studies have examined the permanency of placements made for older, minority group, or handicapped children, and the disruption rate is clearly higher. (See Table 9-3). The Children's Home Society of North Carolina placed 410 special needs children over an eight-year period from 1967 through 1974. Eight per cent of these children subsequently were removed (U.S. Congress, 1975, p. 401). Spaulding for Children, an agency that has specialized in the placement of special needs adoptees, found homes for 199 of these children between 1968 and 1976. Twenty-one of them had experienced disruptions, although eighteen of them were subsequently re-placed with other adoptive families (Unger, Dwarshuis, & Johnson, 1977, p. 67).

With increases in the number of special needs children placed, an increase occurs in the percentage of adoptions that are disrupted. In 1970, 2.7 per cent of the children placed for adoption in California through public welfare agencies

TABLE 9.2.   Adoption Disruptions: Infant Studies

Study	Agency Auspices	Period Covered by Study	Children Placed	Children Returned to Agency	Disruption Rate
Davis & Douck (1955)	Public	3 years (1951–53)	396	25	6.3%
Calif. Citizens' Adoptions Comm. (1965)	Public-voluntary	1 year (1962)	4,470	85	1.9%
Kornitzer & Rowe (1968)	Voluntary	1 year (1966)	9,614	109	1.1%
Kornitzer (1968)	Public-voluntary	Unclear	664	15	2.2%
Edmonton, Canada (1969)	Public	2 years (1967–68)	3,086	43	1.4%
L.A. County Dept. Adoption (1967)	Public	2 years (1965–66)	4,910	129	2.6%
Lefkowitz (1969)	Voluntary	5 years (1965–69)	8,040	82	1.0%
Kadushin & Seidl (1971)	Public	8 years (1960–68)	2,945	85	2.8%
Goldring & Tutleman (1970)	Public	1 year (1968–69)	2,384	75	3.1%
TOTAL			34,499	648	1.87%

TABLE 9.3.   Adoption Disruptions: Special-Needs Children

Study	Children Placed	Children Returned	Disruption Rate
Children's Home Society of North Carolina (U.S. Congress, 1975)	410	24	8%
Spaulding for Children (Unger, Dwarshuis, & Johnson, 1977)	199	21	10.6%
Ohio Adoption Project (U.S. DHHS, 1980a)	59	8	13.6%
Children in Group Care (Borgman, 1981)	20	9	45%
C.S.R. (1983)	263	20	13%
Wolkend & Kozaruk (1983)	84	5	6%
Spaulding for children (Boyne et al., 1983)	309	66	21%
Tremitiere (1984)	536	72	13%
Coyne and Brown (1985)	1588	138	8.7%
Festinger (1986)	897	116	13%
Kagan & Reid (1986)	78	23	29%
Total	4443	502	11.3%

were returned to the agency. By 1973, this figure had increased 7.6 per cent (Bass, 1975, p. 50). For similar reasons, the province of Ontario experienced an increase in disruptions from 4 to 7 per cent between 1970 and 1978 (Cohen, 1984).

The CSR (1983) report of subsidized adoptions in nine states indicated that "only Kentucky provided data on the disruption rate for special needs placements. Since 1979, Kentucky experienced 20 disruptions out of 263 placements (13.1%); this compares with an overall 5 per cent disruption rate in Kentucky for all adoption placements" (pp. 4–5).

J. Boyne et al. (1983) reviewed the adoptive experience of 273 families who had accepted for adoption a total of 309 children with special needs. Sixty-six of the 309 children experienced adoption disruption, giving a disruption rate of 21 per cent. Elaborate statistical analysis of the detailed data yielded the finding that the age of the child at placement (12–17) was the most important factor contributing to the disruption of the placement. A secondary finding was that success of placement was dependent on the integration of the complex configuration that resulted from the characteristics of the child placed and the adopting family. Interpreting the reasons why age is such a potent factor in explaining disruptions the researchers question the "adequacy of standard psychoanalytic and psychotherapeutic" reasons. Instead they note that as "the child grows older the child also becomes more powerful. The child, whether 'disturbed' or 'not disturbed,' is able to set conditions to which the adult world must respond in one way or another" (p. 31). Age is confounded with other variables likely to contribute to disruption, such as adjustment problems and multiple foster care placements (Proch & Taber, 1985; Festinger, 1986).

Coyne and Brown (1985) found that an overall disruption rate of 8.7 per cent for 1588 developmentally disabled children placed for adoption increased to 17.7 per cent for the subgroup of children placed when over 8 years of age. Age at placement was also implicated in a study that compared 80 cases of adoption disruption with a control group of 80 successful adoptions (Zwimpfer, 1983). This was the case even though the study was confined to children six years or less at the time of placement. But here also the complexity of interaction between the particular adoptive family configuration and the particular child placed tended to help explain the disruption. A child presenting more than usual demands for adoptive family adaptation in contact with parents who were marginally acceptable as adoptive applicants tended to overload the situation and increase the risk for disruption.

The research generally suggests that placing siblings together increases the risk of disruption. The burden on adoptive parents is greater than the single-child placement (Le Pere, 1986). However, Festinger (1986) found that sibling placements were less frequently disrupted in her study. She explains this by suggesting that siblings provide a support group for each other, thereby helping the adjustment to adoption.

Kagan and Reid (1986) studied adoptive experiences of a particularly difficult group of 78 youngsters. The children who were older when placed (mean age 11) were emotionally disturbed and had failed in multiple foster care placements. Most had been institutionalized for a time. Seventy-one per cent of the group achieved legal adoption in the family in which they were placed, for a disruption rate of 29 per cent (p. 67). Success in the adoption was significantly related to the adoptive family's ability to handle the youngster's aggressive-destructive behavior and to the adequacy of the family support systems. Twenty-three per cent of the placements were with single parents, and the rate of success of such placements was not significantly different from that of married couples. However, a small subset of single mothers who adopted male children showed a very high failure rate.

Disruptions are most frequently initiated by adoptive parents, in some cases by the child who wants out, and least frequently by the agency having serious reservations about the home emerging after placement. Borgman (1981) found that children who had not resolved loyalty issues with their birth families had a more difficult time accepting attachment to their adoptive families and, therefore, were more likely to eventually leave their placements. Children in stable adoptive homes were more likely to have parents who had voluntarily agreed to terminate parental rights, whereas those who were in disrupted homes or who had remained in group care without any adoptive placement were more likely to have parents whose rights were involuntarily terminated (p. 397). Unger, Dwarshuis, and Johnson (1977) also note that when adoptive families fail to understand the significance of the child's ties to his or her past, or when the child has undergone experiences that significantly affect his or her ability to trust adults, adoption breakdown is more likely.

The staff at Spaulding for Children identified three general circumstances under which disruptions may occur. The family or child may experience "unrecognized preexisting problems," doubts or expectations that, although initially unrecognized, subsequently interfere with the family's ability to develop satisfactory relationships. "Pre-existing problems that are known but left unexplored" can also interfere with the placement process. Sometimes the worker is aware of these difficulties but chooses to avoid discussing them with the family; sometimes the family chooses to avoid bringing these issues out into the open. Finally, "unpredictable problems," such as financial difficulties, marital stress, or health problems, can tax the family's ability to cope with the normal stresses of adoption and can lead to a disruption in the placement (Unger, Dwarshuis, & Johnson, 1977). (See also DHHS, 1980; Naylor, 1982; Zwimpfer, 1983; Churchill, 1984.)

In a detailed comparison of four disrupted and four nondisrupted families,

Cohen (1984) found that role flexibility and adaptive problem-solving capacities were significant characteristics of families whose children remained in the home. In nondisrupted homes, in addition, husbands played a "pivotal role during the bonding period," providing an essential source of support for both mother and child. In addition, mothers in these families found significant sources of satisfaction outside the family and were not, therefore, primarily reliant on the success of their relationships with the child for feelings of achievement (p. 135). In the same vein, Unger, Dwarshuis, and Johnson found that middle-class families who "need to see measurable positive changes in the children they adopt in order to confirm their expertise for themselves and others" may become overinvested and disappointed with their adoptive experience (US DHHS, 1981a, p. 19).

In a study of disrupted adoptions Festinger (1986) found that where the same worker had continuing responsibility to both the child and the adoptive family, the risk of disruption was reduced (p. 37).

Once disruption occurs, the worker's responsibilities include minimizing the possible damage to the participants, helping both the parents and child deal effectively with separation, and developing alternative placement resources for the child. In most instances, children can be successfully replaced in other adoptive settings.

The worker can review the experience with the child to identify the factors that caused difficulty in this placement and that would need to be explicitly avoided in the next possible placement. The worker should share with the child the fact that the agency is still ready and willing to find another home for him or her. The family, in reacting to failure, may blame the agency for ineptitude in placing the child and for failure to be sufficiently helpful to prevent disruption. The worker has to be ready to accept his or her contribution to the event and, in discussing it with the family, to learn how to handle similar situations more successfully in the future. The worker has to act as a bridge between the child and the family so that both can understand what has happened and divert energy devoted to blaming each other into more productive channels. The worker helps the family to assist the child in the move that must now be made.

In addition, the worker assists the family to eventually consider whether it wishes to attempt to adopt another child. Because a family that has a painful experience with one child may subsequently function very effectively with another, disruption is not necessarily a sign that parents cannot adopt. However, parental perceptions that they are "failures" may make them extremely reluctant to risk accepting another child in care (Jewett, 1978; Churchill, 1984).

Helping families and children work through this type of experience is one of the more difficult tasks that adoption workers face. Because workers feel responsible for helping to choose a good, reliable home for children, confronting the possibility that their selection may not have been an appropriate one generates feelings of panic, self-recrimination, or anger at the adoptive families and/or the children. Rather than confronting the fact that placements for some children do not work out, workers may avoid paying attention to signs of impending difficulties and even ignore the presence of major problems. Zwimpfer (1983) comments, "One adoptive mother asked for the child to be taken away on several occasions before the social worker conceded that problems were severe and unlikely to improve. In fact, of the 80 breakdown cases, only 12 attracted any negative observations at all by the social workers during the supervision period" (pp. 176–177). Once disruption has occurred, workers may tend to avoid the painful feelings that this process engenders by limiting their family contacts and by moving the child as quickly as possible (Unger, Dwarshuis, & Johnson, 1977). The worker may feel anger at the adoptive parents for not having worked harder to make the placement work. If the worker feels strongly that the child was to blame, this may impair motivation to find another adoptive home for the child. Workers can benefit from the support of their colleagues and the insistence of supervisors that they consider and confront these problems.

Ultimately, however, the most powerful disruption prevention incorporates "realistic preparation" with "diligent follow-through" (Katz, 1980). "The experience of the Spaulding staff has shown that it is impossible for workers to be unaware that potentially disruptive problems exist within the family if effective patterns of post-placement communication are developed with families who trust workers and feel they are partners with them in maintaining the placement" (Unger, Dwarshuis, & Johnson in U.S. DHHS, 1981a, p. 34).

The fact that children have been successfully placed following a disrupted adoption indicates the desirability of terminating a difficult placement rather than struggling against heavy odds to salvage it. This fact also suggests the complexity of variables that result in a successful placement and the futility of assigning blame for the disruption. If the worker is to be helpful to the family in this situation, he or she has to recognize, given the background of special-needs children, that some failures are to be expected, that compatibility between family and child cannot always be predicted in advance even with the most perceptive diagnostic skill, and that some problems emerge only in the test of the living situation following placement.

The situation is inherently complex—in effect making a marriage between a parent and a child, both having their own idiosyncratic expectations and hopes, and each facing limits in their abilities to compromise, adjust, and cope with the heavy demands imposed by the arrangement. Some adoptions become a "kind of mismatch—the 'chemistry' appeared to be wrong or soured after a time" (Festinger, 1986, p. 40). (See also Barth et al. 1986.)

Given the difficulties the wonder is not that some 13 per cent of adoptive placements are disrupted, but that better than 80 per cent succeed. Adoptive placement of special needs children involve a calculated risk, but unless agencies are willing to take this risk, many such children would be denied opportunities to succeed in adapting in permanent homes.

Children with Special Needs

One of the most serious problems in the field of adoption concerns the children who are or who might be legally free for adoption, who could benefit from and contribute to normal family living, but who are difficult to place because they belong to a minority group (black, Chicano, American Indian, and so on); because they are older; because they are physically, mentally, or emotionally handicapped; or because they are a part of a group of three or four siblings who should be placed together. This group of children, previously termed hard to place, are now more frequently called children with special needs or children who wait. Each of these situations is discussed further. In addition, as a result of the lack of infants available through traditional adoption channels, adopters have turned to agencies and individuals outside of the formal social service agency network. The field of independent adoptions will also be considered.

Intraracial Adoption of Minority Group Children

As we have previously noted, far more nonwhite than white children are now available for adoption than their proportion in the population would lead us to expect. Systematic exclusion of nonwhite children from adoption programs oriented toward the placement of whites produced a backlog of unattached minority group children in foster care and institutional settings. It is only in recent years and only to a limited extent that the need for specialized placement services for these children has been recognized. Prior to that time, they were considered "unadoptable."

Historically, black families were believed to be uninterested in adopting or were presumed unable to do so due to preoccupation with their own personal problems (Hill, 1977; Day, 1979). Recent reevaluations point out that blacks actually adopt to the same extent that white families do (Herzog & Bernstein, 1965; Bonham, 1977). In fact, "when family structure and income are controlled for, Black couples are somewhat *more* likely than white couples to formally adopt" (Hill, 1977, p. 23). In addition, within the black community, many children have been cared for through more informal adoptive arrangements. Taken in by grandparents, uncles and aunts, or other relatives, informally adopted children live in a household that may or may not include their birth parents. Hill (1977) found that there are ten times more informal than formal adoptive homes in the black community; two-thirds of all the black children who live with relatives are not living with their birth mothers or fathers. Hill suggests that informal adoptive arrangements can be viewed as alternatives to the use of agency adoption procedures and that they may serve as potential resources for formalized adoption as well (p. 24).

Despite these formal and informal adoptive efforts, large numbers of minority group children continue to live in impermanent substitute care settings when they could benefit from placement in permanent homes in the community. Fulfilling the mandate outlined in the Child Abuse Prevention and Treatment and Adoption Reform Act of 1978, the federal government established the Adoption Opportunities program. This program encourages the development of services that will challenge and eliminate significant barriers that prevent more widespread adoptions of special-needs children. In particular, the federal government has emphasized efforts to increase intraracial adoption of minority group children.

Two major roadblocks to adoptive efforts of this type have been identified. The most frequently reported deterrent is economic insecurity. "Again and again it is pointed out that black families have lower incomes, less job security, fewer economic reserves than most white families, and that the incomes, though generally lower, more often represent two wage-earners" (Herzog & Bernstein, 1965, p. 8). This conclusion is supported by those of other studies (Fanshel, 1957; Deasy & Quinn, 1962; Foote & Putnam, 1965; Fowler, 1966). Detailed interviews with 129 middle-class black families in Hartford, Connecticut, revealed that "overwhelmingly our informants attributed the problem [shortage of black adoptive homes] to the prevalence of low income, poor employment, and inadequate housing among blacks" (Foote & Putnam, 1965, p. 48).

Adoption subsidies are designed to help families cope with these economic disabilities. Agencies successfully recruiting minority families have focused on money management and stability of employment as important adoption criteria, rather than absolute income (Gant, 1984). Realizing that, among poor families, women may have to work to augment the family income, agencies have determined that this should not prevent a family from being able to adopt a child. Other criteria that reflect need for substantial income, such as home ownership or provision of a separate bedroom for each adoptive child, have also been deemphasized as necessary requirements in these cases.

Another major deterrent to successful intraracial adoption stems from agency policies and procedures that fail to stimulate interest in adoptions within minority communities and that prevent potential adopters from finding sufficient agency support for their desire to become adoptive parents.

Effective outreach to minority communities requires efforts to involve members of those communities in the development of programs, policies, and procedures, as board members, workers, volunteers, and interpreters of agency need and service (Sandusky et al., 1972; Billingsley & Giovannoni, 1972). Effective recruitment programs have developed strong ties to black churches, black professional organizations, and the black media (Gant, 1984). In addition, these agencies have utilized black parents who have successfully adopted as information resources and recruiters of additional black families. In order to build up a black, Hispanic, or Native American clientele, therefore, agencies that have done few non-white adoptions must take steps to create such an informal referral network (Day, 1979).

Vigorous educational campaigns have helped inform minority communities about the need for additional adoptive homes for children. (Valiente-Barksdale, 1983; Young, no date). Gant (1984) describes other successful educational strategies: "Homes for Black Children—Indianapolis cited promotional ventures with the Indiana Pacers basketball team. The Black adoption program of the Kansas children Service League sponsors gospel musicals with Black churches in Kansas City. Monthly adoption parties inviting potential parents who have been rejected by traditional agencies are sponsored by Spaulding for Children—New York" (p. 28).

To encourage nonwhite applicants, changes have been made in agency procedures to facilitate the processing of inquiries. Successful programs have opened satellite offices in local neighborhoods (Billingsley & Giovannoni, 1972) and have attempted to respond in a timely manner to inquiries. Excessive delay in responding is perceived by applicants as a sign of rejection. In a study of the impact of recruitment efforts for black families in Maryland, Young (no date) found that whereas 83 per cent of the families who eventually adopted children were contacted within a month after the point at which they were referred, only 68 per cent of the nonadopters were contacted this early. Whereas only 4 per cent of the adopters waited two months or longer to be contacted, 18% of the nonadopters heard nothing from the agency before two or three months had passed (p. 26). Making appointments during evenings and weekends, at times when working adults can meet without losing pay, and scheduling appointments at the family home rather than the agency also help convince potential adoptive parents of agency interest in their welfare.

Several public and private agencies have experimented with special outreach programs organized and staffed by black social workers and located in the black community. The Tayari program of the San Diego Office of Public Welfare is an example (Neilson, 1976). Tayari, a Swahili word meaning "family and tribal unity," focused on black homes for black children.

(Day, 1979) reports that agencies vary in their responsiveness to inquiries to black families. One agency made three adoptive placements from sixteen family contacts; a second agency received fifty inquiries but made no such placements.

Research has generally found that blacks complete the adoption process less frequently than whites (Fanshel, 1957; Bradley, 1966; Fowler, 1966).

Day (1979) studied the experiences of 315 individuals in contact with the Division of Adoption Services New York City Department of Social Services. She found that whereas 23 per cent of the black families were eventually approved, 30 per cent of the whites were approved. Black clients were twice as likely as whites to withdraw without providing any particular reason. Day argues that "The category 'failure to maintain contact' implies a failure in communication between social worker and client. If good rapport had been established, the client would have told the worker why he or she was withdrawing" (p. 48). In her study of the results of a recruitment project for nonwhite families in Baltimore, Young came to similar conclusions. Using agency records and in-person interviews with individuals who failed to adopt, she found incongruence between the perceptions of the parents and agency personnel in 62 per cent of the cases. Nonadopters repeatedly complained about lack of agency contact or follow-through and described the workers they did meet as nonfacilitative. For adoptive parents, on the other hand, facilitative workers helped the family survive both the unexpectedly lengthy adoption process and the red tape that stood in the way of their eventually bringing a child into their home.

Effective communication and facilitation require an understanding of the cultural values and background of the families served by the worker, a commitment to helping these families through the complex adoption process, and faith in their ability to effectively raise children who need homes. The literature has suggested that workers should either be of the same culture or racial group as the families or should be educated to understand and deal more effectively with families from other racial groups. Although some research (Festinger, 1972) has found that inability to deal with white workers is not a significant reason for withdrawal, Wachtel (1972) shows a strong correlation between the frequency of agency placement of black children and the proportion of the agency's social workers who are black (p. 6). Day (1979) agrees: "The factor most highly associated with agency placement with Black adopters is the percentage of agency social workers who were Black" (p. 35).

When agencies offer adoption services that are especially adapted to the needs of nonwhite families, there is substantial increase both in the number of families who complete the application process and, ultimately, in the number of children who are placed (Gant, 1984). Evelyn Moore, the director of the National Black Child Development Institute, an organization committed to finding black homes for black children, notes that special outreach and adoptive efforts in Illinois produced a 70 per cent increase in the number of black children placed within a 15-month period. A program in Detroit, Homes for Black Children, placed children with 132 families within one year (*NASW News*, April 1984, p. 9).

Current evidence suggests that black adoptive families are still, for the most part, middle class. Scott (1976), reviewing the results of a special nationwide interagency effort to find black adoptive homes, describes the families of 111 children placed during a one-year period by various programs across the country. Most black applicants were married and had family incomes of over $14,000. About 40 per cent had at least some college education (pp. 28–29). Most of the children placed were under five years of age (p. 47). Only a small percentage of applicants were willing to accept handicapped children, and these were more likely to be single parents. However, analysis of applicants to the Division of Adoption Services in New York City in 1972 (Day, 1979) suggested that blacks had fewer savings, less education, were less likely to be in white-collar jobs, were older, and were more likely to be single than white applicants. Single individuals comprised one quarter of the black families who were seeking to adopt, but only 3 per cent of the whites (p. 45).

Transracial Placement of Minority Group Children

Transracial adoptions—the placement of nonwhite children in white adoptive homes—is one resource that has been developed to meet the needs of these children for permanent homes. In this section, we are particularly concerned with the adoption of children of the same nationality but of a different race than that of the adoptive family. In the United States these are primarily black, Native American, or Hispanic children adopted by whites. Children who are adopted from other countries will be considered in a later section of this chapter.

Transracial adoptions were initiated in the 1950s and continue today. In 1955, New York City set up an Adopt-a-Child Program and San Francisco organized MARCH (Minority Adoption Recruitment of Children's Homes); Minneapolis set up PAMY (Parents to Adopt Minority Youngsters) in 1961; the U.S. Bureau of Indian Affairs and the Child Welfare League of America sponsored a nationwide Indian Adoption Project in 1958. These projects have been reviewed by Billingsley and Giovannoni (1972).

By 1978, only three states cited racial factors as significant eligibility criteria for adoption. Only one state, South Carolina, prevents blacks from adopting white children, although the converse situation, white adoptions of black children, are not illegal in that state (Day, 1979). Despite the lack of explicit legislation preventing transracial adoption, there is a considerable resistance to it, both within adoption agencies and within the legal system (Carroll, 1970; Herzog et al., 1971a, 1971b; Chestang, 1972; Jones, 1972; Chimeze, 1975; Jones & Else, 1979; Simon, 1984). Opponents argue that minority group children benefit most from being reared in families of their own racial heritage:

> Black families build in mechanisms to handle living in a racist society. White families could not provide these for a black child. . . . Identity is all-important and no white family can provide this for a black child. . . . I question the ability of white parents—no matter how deeply imbued with good will—to grasp the totality of the problem of being black in our society—I question their ability to create what I believe is crucial for these youngsters—a black identity [Jones, 1972, pp. 40–41, 157].

It is feared that the child might be perceived "as an alien in the white community and a traitor in the black community" (Madison & Schapiro, 1973, p. 543), lacking security in one and solidarity with the other.

Opponents also claim that support for transracial adoption comes primarily from agencies believing that no black homes are available for black children (Day, 1979). Rather than committing resources and funds to finding these homes, agencies find it more convenient to place black or Native American children with available white families.

Transracial adoptions increased sharply during the latter part of the 1960s, tripling between 1968 (700) and 1971 (2,574) (Opportunity, 1976). However, opposition on the part of nonwhite groups, coupled with the ambivalence of the social work profession regarding its ultimate desirability, has had a decidedly inhibiting effect. There has been a consistent decline in the number of black children placed with white families since the high point, 1972. By 1977, transracial adoption as a program for meeting the adoptive needs of nonwhite children had been sharply curtailed. Even those agencies that had pioneered and held the greatest convictions about the value of such placements were making progressively fewer of them. By 1975, there were only 831 of these placements, accounting for 20 per cent of all black children placed in nonrelative homes in that year (Opportunity, 1976).

Nevertheless, transracial adoption remains the means whereby nonwhite children achieve permanency in a significant number of instances. By 1983, nearly 20,000 black children had been adopted by whites in the United States (Simon, 1984, p. 229). In 1975–1976, fully three-quarters of all the Native Canadian children placed with families were placed with whites (Ryant, 1984). Assessment of the impact of these placements on children and families remains a significant social work concern.

Adoption standards recommended by the Child Welfare League of America reflect shifting professional sentiments with regard to this issue. The 1958 edition of the standards suggested the discouragement of transracial placement: "Physical resemblances should not be a determining factor in the selection of a home, with the possible exception of such racial characteristics as color." The 1968 edition, however, noted that "racial background should not determine the selection of the home for the child. . . . It should not be assumed that difficulties will necessarily arise if adoptive parents and children are of different racial origin." In 1972 this standard was amended: "It is preferable to place children in families of their own racial background." The 1978 edition contains the same language, but adds, "consideration of adoptive parents of other races, however, is one of the means of achieving timely and needed permanence for children. It should be used in a sensitive way. Every opportunity should be used to find a permanent home for a child awaiting adoptive placement" (p. 7).

Legislative sensitivity to the adoptive needs of minority group children is illustrated by the Indian Child Welfare Act giving Indian Tribes control over adoption and by the law passed in Minnesota in 1983 entitled the Minnesota Heritage Child Protection Act. The law requires efforts to place minority group child first with relatives, secondly intraracially and thirdly, transracially and only after prior efforts fail. If placed transracially, the law requires that the family be "knowledgeable and appreciative of the child's racial or ethnic heritage."

Seen as a useful backup resource rather than a solution to the problem of adoptive homes for minority group children, transracial adoptions might still occupy a legitimate useful place in the spectrum of adoptive services.

Researchers have attempted to identify the special characteristics of parents who accept children of another race (Pepper, 1966; Falk, 1969, 1970; Sellers, 1969; St. Dennis, 1969; Raynor, 1970; Priddy & Kirgan, 1971; Zastrow, 1977; Fanshel, 1972; Grow & Shapiro, 1974; Simon & Alstein, 1977; Feigelman & Silverman, 1983; 1984). Such parents are likely to have higher occupational levels and higher educational attainment than adoptive families generally; they are more distant socially and geographically from their relatives; they are more likely to be fertile and to have had children in the family prior to adoption; their motive is more likely to be that of providing a home for a child who might not otherwise tend to be adopted; they tend to be somewhat more individualistic and inner-directed and to have a higher self-concept. As Fanshel (1972) notes, "Repeatedly, the element that has been most noteworthy in the self-descriptions of the [parents] . . . has been a certain independence, often self-referred to as a 'stubborn streak.' . . . It is not that they would not care what their neighbors think; it is rather that they would not allow themselves to be guided in their actions by such considerations" (p. 322).

Some were prompted to accept transracial adoptions in order to ensure that the agency would place a child with them as soon as possible. As is true of the placement of all hard-to-place children, agencies have been ready to relax standards and make concessions in order to increase the number of applicants willing to adopt transracially.

Frequently it appears that the applicant who has accepted a hard-to-place child was initially solely interested in adopting a child; only later, after some discussion of the situation with the agency, did he or she consider a minority-group child, an older child, or a handicapped child. Ladner (1977) notes that of the 136 transracially adoptive couples she interviewed, "There were numerous cases in which the parents would have adopted a white child rather than a black one had a white child been available" (p. 49). However, there are a limited number of people who were initially and specifically interested in adopting transracially, "to help," to be of "some service," to do "some good."

Available research clearly indicates that applicants interested in such adoptions are not meeting some neurotic need or expressing a sense of rebelliousness. It further suggests that the worker's attitude toward the feasibility and desirability of transracial adoptions is an important determinant of the applicants' response. Applicants are sensitive to the worker's attitudes and are more likely to respond positively when transracial adoptions are presented in a flexible, nondefensive manner.

Once the decision has been made to place nonwhite children with white families, the worker needs to be sensitive to the problems associated with such a placement. The family will encounter prejudice, in the extended family and in interaction with the broader community. Prejudice is reflected in parental denial that the child looks "different" and in the wish that "different" features of the child will someday disappear, so that the child will look more like other family members. Some white parents also attempt to deny the impact of racism in the day-to-day lives of their children: they insist their children are treated fairly by others; they can cite no evidence of racial discrimination that their children have been exposed to; they cannot differentiate between the experiences of the nonwhite and white children in their family. However, "the white parents who deny racial discrimination by not discussing it or by pretending that oppression is universal are offering their Black children little help in the present and laying the groundwork for problems in the future" (Day, 1979, p. 107; see also Mullender & Miller, 1985; Grow & Shapiro, 1974).

Most difficult of all are problems these families face relative to the resolution of racial identification. Being Oriental, or American Indian, or black, and living with Caucasian parents in a Caucasian environment, how can the child be helped to develop a stable, secure concept of racial identification? How will the white community react when the child reaches adolescence and begins dating? The child's affectional ties are with the white world of his or her parents, which constitutes his or her reference group for socialization. However, the world outside the family responds to the child in terms of the child's visible racial affiliation. Particularly in instances in which families live in segregated neighborhoods and communities, areas in which these children can find no racially similar reference group, identify confusion or identity devaluation may occur (Mullender & Miller, 1985).

Agencies dealing with these problems have been advised to help parents realize the value of learning about the art, literature, history, and life-style of the child's racial group. Parents must convey the importance of these to the child, who can then develop pride in his or her heritage. Further, it is recommended that the family develop social and professional contacts with people of the child's racial background or that the family move to a racially mixed neighborhood, so that the child may play with children of his or her own race. Parents must also identify and resolve racist feelings that intrude upon their relationship with the child. Simon and Alstein (1977) found that many parents felt they became more racially and socially sensitive as a result of adopting children who came from racial backgrounds different than their own.

If "telling" involves a discussion of sex, "telling" by transracial adoptive parents involves a discussion of race as well. To say, "God made people differently. . . . All people are colored; some people are colored white, some black. . . . Just as people have different color hair and eyes, they have different skin colors" may be sufficient for the young child. Parents and agencies indicate that the seriousness of the problems that will be encountered by these children is a function, in a large measure, of the state of race relations when they reach adolescense.

One social work agency found that these adolescents can benefit from a group experience to help them learn about and understand their racial heritage and to develop pride in their past. The social worker leading this group found it was necessary to work with the white parents of these children, helping them learn more about their child's cultural heritage as well (Mullender & Miller, 1985).

One resource, developed by the parents themselves, may be helpful: associations of transracial adoptive families, which meet to discuss common problems and share solutions. The meetings permit the sharing of a common experience, and members provide social and emotional support for each other. The Open Door Society in Montreal was the earliest of such organizations. There are now Open Door Societies in Indiana, Missouri, Illinois, and Wisconsin. Other organizations include The East-West Society, the Council on Adoptable Children, Families for Interracial Adoption, and the Interracial Family Association. In 1969 such organizations began sponsoring an annual North American Conference on Adoptable Children, devoted in large measure to problems of transracial adoption

International Adoptions

Out of humanitarian concern for the many children who have been displaced, abandoned, or orphaned as a result of postwar upheaval, Americans have adopted foreign children. It has been estimated that there are currently some 10 to 26 million refugees in the world. Approximately half of these individuals are children younger than eighteen, and a significant but unknown proportion of them are parentless (Baker, 1984). Interest in international adoptions has also intensified as a result of the dearth of American infants needing permanent homes. In a study of white families who adopted Colombian children, 87 per cent of parents said that they eventually decided on international adoption because no suitable American child was available (Feigelman & Silverman, 1983, p. 125). Interest in this type of adoption has also been stimulated by the mobility of American families, many of whom have lived abroad for extended periods with the armed forces, or in the employ of foreign branches of American concerns.

International adoptions developed after World War II, when the large number of displaced and parentless children who survived the war led families from other countries within Europe and, eventually, the United States to offer them homes (Resnick, 1984). By 1950, homes had been found for most of these children, and potential adoptive parents began to turn to other sources. Experiencing extensive poverty and prolonged warfare, the countries of eastern and southeastern Asia, particularly Korea and Vietnam, began to provide children for American parents. Korean agencies worked closely with those in the United States to facilitate adoption of children, some of whom were the offspring of American servicemen and Korean women. In part because Korean adoption agencies function much like those in America, collaboration between them and American agencies has a long and congenial history. With greater involvement of American forces in Vietnam, adoptions of children from that country also increased.

Some of the more controversial aspects of international adoptions were more sharply defined as a consequence of Operation Babylift at the end of the war in Vietnam (see Joe, 1978). With the collapse of South Vietnam, the U.S. government sponsored and supported an effort to "rescue" children from South Vietnam for adoptive placement in the United States. As a consequence of Operation Babylift, some two thousand Vietnamese children were flown to the United States for adoption here. Groups that had, over a period of time, been engaged in the placement of children from Korea and South Vietnam—Holt International Children's Fund and Travelers Aid International Social Service of America (TAISSA—were enlisted in the effort.

Since the airlift, there has been continuing agitation about these adoptions because some of the children proved not to have been legally available for adoption. A class-action suit was brought against the government in behalf of the parents of the airlifted children. Bitter custody battles were fought, and in about twenty-five instances, the children were removed from the adoptive homes and returned to the parents. Because of the haste with which the airlift had been organized, the children involved had not been processed through the regular agency procedure, which safeguards adoptive parents from such contingencies.

By 1977 Korea and other Asian countries had taken active steps to reduce the number of their children available for adoption abroad. With the Far East becoming less active as a source of supply of children for adoption, interest is beginning to shift to other areas.

Increasing numbers of children have been adopted from Central and South America, particularly from Colombia. As the war in El Salvador developed, so too did American adoptions of children from that country. Chile, Peru, Ecuador, and Mexico have also sent children to the United States and Canada. On the other hand, very few children have come from Cuba, Argentina, Venezuela, Uruguay, or Paraguay (Pilotti, 1985).

Historically, social service agencies with international affiliates handled these adoptions. One of the principal agencies was Traveler's Aid International Social Service, a voluntary, nonsectarian social welfare agency with headquarters in Geneva, Switzerland, and branches in many countries. Today, local child welfare agencies that have been licensed by the state as approved adoption agencies can facilitate international adoptions for families by completing the family's home study. The home study is then forwarded to an agency licensed to work directly with overseas adoption agencies. HOLT International, S.A.M.E. (South American Missionary Evangelism), WACAP (Washington Association of Christian Adoptive Parents) and the Children's Home Society of Minnesota are among the most widely known of these agencies.

Before a child is moved for adoption from his or her country of origin, a designated agency or agent in that country establishes the fact that the child is "an orphan or deprived of normal family life and that there is no prospect for him to be adopted unless he comes to the United States" (Hochfield, 1963, p. 4). The preadoption requirements of the state of the child's proposed residence must be met and assurance received from an "appropriate social welfare agency that the social investigations have been satisfactorily completed in both countries, that the prospective adoptive home is recommended, and that the child has been found suitable for adoption" before the U.S. Immigration and Naturalization Service will process the child's immigration (Hochfield, 1963, p. 4). The child has to be certified as free for adoption, a passport and exit visa need to be obtained for the child, and an entry visa to the United States has to be cleared.

Currently, no one set of adoption regulation or procedures is used by all countries. Instead, each country has created its own regulations with regard to adoption and emigration practices. Intercountry differences produce a great deal of confusion for families, attempting to understand an individual nation's expectations. For instance

> The adoption of Colombian children by U.S. citizens is subject to the simultaneous supervision of private agencies in Colombia, the national courts of Colombia, the Colombian welfare department, the U.S. and Colombian immigration authorities, and the courts of the states in which the adopting parents live. No single body coordinates these adoptions; at this time, there is no agency that provides information on all of the diverse requirements with which adoptive parents must comply [Feigelman & Silverman, 1983, p. 126].

Lack of standardized procedures has allowed abuses to occur in some instances, especially with regard to removal of children from their homeland without the informed consent of their parents. Particularly in countries where adoptions can be arranged through private attorneys or other individuals who have no agency affiliation, lack of governmental supervision of their activities raises questions concerning proper protection of the rights of child and birth family.

Concern about ambiguities and abuses lay behind several multinational efforts to develop uniform standards. In 1979, the United Nations High Commission for Refugees disseminated draft principles to govern the handling of refugee children who were unaccompanied by their parents. "The principles state unequivocally that no refugee child should be considered for adoption until all avenues have been exhausted and every effort has been made to reunite the child with parents or other members of his family" (Baker, 1984, p. 255). In 1980, the American Public Welfare Association also developed recommended Intercountry Adoption Guidelines. More recently, the Organization of American States, at its Inter-American Inter-Disciplinary Expert Group meeting in Quito, Ecuador, published a series of recommendations that were eventually embodied in a model law for international adoption (Pilotti, 1985). This multinational body endorsed the following principles:

1. Every effort should be made to strengthen family life in the children's own country before any consideration is given to putting the child up for adoption.
2. If adoption is considered, priority should first be given to prospective parents in the child's own country.
3. If this proves to be unsuccessful and intercountry adoption is resorted to, procedures should be developed through private or public licensed agencies with experience in the social welfare international field.

4. The security of the adoptee will depend on national legal norms, as well as on the international private laws that the countries involved in intercountry adoptions decide to follow.
5. Interdisciplinary teams of lawyers, medical doctors, psychologists, and social workers should be involved in the intercountry adoption process so that each individual case may be accurately evaluated from every professional perspective in order to come up with the best possible solution (Resnick, 1984, pp. 284–285).

Laws relating to permitting entrance of children into the United States for adoption were amended in 1975 to permit intercountry adoption by single-parent applicants. Single applicants who are unable to obtain younger children for adoption in the United States have made successful efforts to adopt children from abroad. However, not all foreign countries permit adoption of their children by single applicants.

Proponents of international adoptions point out the ways that children benefit, moving from a society in which their families have very few resources and almost no money to one in which they are exposed to all the amenities of middle-class Western family life. Opponents point to the disadvantages to these children of removing them from their familiar sociocultural surroundings, to the loss of their cultural heritage, and to the problems they are likely to encounter in adjusting to a "racist" society. The Child Welfare League policy on overseas adoptions is that "adoptions outside the child's own country should be considered only when suitable plans cannot be made for him in his own country." The League points out the fact that overseas adoption programs inhibit the development of child welfare services in other countries (Baker, 1984). After the civil war in Nigeria in the 1960s, which left 50,000 children homeless, offers were made by the United States, among several countries, to place many of these children for adoption abroad. The Nigerian government refused the offer and made efforts to meet the needs of its children at home instead, using funds that might otherwise have been expended in an overseas adoption program. As a consequence, some years later, all but a handful of such children are being cared for by their immediate or extended families in their native land.

It has also been suggested that removal of children from their homeland can be interpreted as an indication of that nation's unwillingness or inability to take care of its poor and its children (Resnick, 1984). Removing children from their home country deprives that nation of its most valuable resource, its future citizens. Black organizations have noted, too that the time and energy involved in international adoptions may be misplaced, when so many American black children wait in vain for permanent homes.

Like parents who adopt children interracially, international adopters must examine their own biases about the country and culture from which their child comes. Evidence suggests that some parents do not value their child's culture and attempt to ignore their child's origins. Many Colombian adopters admit that they are uninterested in familiarizing themselves with their child's heritage, that they have little interest in living in a community with other Colombians, and do not encourage their children to value their cultural heritage. Feigelman and Silverman (1983) conclude, "since most of the children appear to be racially 'white,' the most pervasive response among their adoptive parents was to bring up their children as white Americans and to accord minimal positive value to their Hispanic background" (p. 144). Parents of Korean children, whose racial dissimilar-ity cannot be denied, were much less likely to devalue or ignore their child's heritage.

As with children in transracial families, evidence suggests that when parents value their child's racial background and take active steps to encourage the child's pride in his or her culture, children clearly benefit. As one adoptive couple comments, however, "the difficult thing about racism in our particular situations is that when it is directed at Carl, he must deal with it all alone. He does not have the comfort of knowing that the rest of the family shares in his problem. If we were an entire family of minorities, his situation would be much different in this respect. And since neither of us has ever been the victim of racial prejudice, we are ill-prepared to help him develop the skills that are useful in combatting it" (Rue & Rue, 1984, p. 249).

Children coming from other countries often undergo severe culture shock. The pattern of their previous relationships, the scheduling of their daily lives, their language, their food, their basic attitudes and values all change dramatically in coming to the U.S. As a result, the initial period of adaptation may be very difficult for them. Kim (1980) describes the adjustment difficulties of three young children from Korea, all of whom were adopted when they were between fourteen and twenty-eight months of age. Their families subsequently brought the children for psychiatric evaluation, since they were hyperactive, had severe temper tantrums, and had night terrors and what appeared to be visual hallucinations. After extensive evaluation, the author concluded that what seemed at first glance to be severe pathology actually was understandable transitional behavior, as these children struggled with massive changes in their environment. They had, for example, never slept alone before moving into the white middle-class family homes in the United States. Adjustment can also be difficult for refugee children, who have been exposed to brutality, life-threatening conditions, and the loss of their families. In addition, children from very poor countries may come into adoptive families with severe and prolonged medical problems. Feigelman and Silverman (1983) found that fully one-quarter of the Colombian children and 12 percent of the Koreans in their survey required hospitalization or extensive medical treatment after coming to the United States (p. 139).

One mother describes her encounters with her four internationally adopted children:

> After adopting four school-age boys from Korea, I feel that we can now give you the odds: the odds that they will "cherish" an education (0 in 4); the odds that they will hate their new American name (2 in 4); the odds that they will run away (2 in 4, but fortunately not more than 2 blocks); the chance that they will be breathless on Christmas morning (3 in 4); speechless at birthday parties (3 in 4); overwhelmed by their first, and second, and third trips to the supermarket (4 in 4).
>
> The chances of parasites (1 in 4); of lice (0 in 4, but we gave each child a welcoming lice shampoo just for luck); immature behavior (4 in 4); hoarding (3 in 4, but only for the first few days); overeating (4 in 4, but only for the first few years!). The odds that they will be perfect students (1 in 4); get suspended for fighting (1 in 4); need remedial help at home in English, even with the best of school systems (2 in 4). The odds that they will be starved for attention (2 in 4); frightened by attention (1 in 4); or just simply have no idea at all of the possible uses for persons called "mother" and "father" (1 in 4) (Ours Magazine, September/October 1984, pp 11–12).

A considerable body of helpful literature became available to parents who had adopted Asian children. One of the adoptive parents' organizations published a reader concerned with international adoptions (Kramer, 1975). These materials provide Korean and Vietnamese recipes, short vocabulary word lists, a listing of relevant books and films, and so on. A primary vehicle for sharing information and helpful suggestions concerning international adoption is *Ours Magazine*. The content of this journal is comprised, for the most part, of letters, contributed by parents themselves, describing their frustrations with and pleasure in their children, their unexpected and bewildering experiences, and the resources they have found helpful in understanding the needs of these youngsters.

Adoption of the Handicapped Child

That the existence of a physical, emotional, or mental handicap should make a child difficult to place for adoption is almost self-evident (Taft, 1953; Lake, 1954; Beaven, 1956; Colville, 1957; Fowler, 1957; Schapiro, 1957; Fradkin, 1958; Hornecker, 1962; Gallagher, 1968; Franklin & Massarik, 1969; Knight, 1970; Ferman & Warren, 1974; Jewett, 1978.) Children who are physically handicapped or mentally retarded require more than the normal amount of parental time and energy; they require specialized knowledge and facilities; they are likely to impose a greater burden of medical expense as well as medical care; they are less likely than the normal child to enable adoptive parents to derive satisfactions from their achievements; and they are likely to remain dependent for a longer time.

Children with such medical conditions as cleft palate, hernia, asthma, crossed eyes, deafness, blindness, congenital heart defects, or mild cerebral palsy can be, and have been, successfully placed for adoption, as have retarded children.

Franklin and Massarik (1969), who conducted intensive follow-up interviews with 169 families who adopted handicapped children, concluded that "children with medical conditions of all degrees of severity and correctability can be successfully placed and reared in adoptive homes" (p. 399). Most of the children were between five and twelve years of age at the time of the interview. Although the families ultimately proved adaptive and resilient in meeting the handicapped child's special needs, a majority of the parents had expressed some concern at the time the child was presented to them. Only a small minority of the couples had themselves initiated a request for a handicapped child; in most instances, the agency initiated discussion of the possibility of placement for such a child. The agency, in finding homes for such children, tended to be more flexible in applying eligibility criteria and to move more expeditiously in processing applications (Franklin & Massarik, 1969, p. 463). Some of the adoptive parents had originally been foster parents to the handicapped child. An attachment to and a relationship with the child had developed, and adoption resulted. Initial placement for foster care may be a desirable procedure in the case of the hard-to-place child. It permits the parents to develop a commitment to the child without initially feeling an obligation to make the child a full member of the family.

A questionnaire study of administrators and workers of ninety public and private adoption agencies in a six-state area focused on the adoption of physically handicapped children (Ferman & Warren, 1974). The study showed that workers in these agencies had placed 178 children with such disabilities as Down's syndrome, congenital heart disease, cleft palate, epilepsy, muscular dystrophy, and sickle-cell anemia. The adoptive families of such children most frequently fell into three groups: foster parents who had lived with the child for some time, parents who had had personal and/or professional experience with physical and mental disabilities, and parents whose application for the adoption of a white, normal infant was not likely to be accepted because of age, the number of children already in the family, and so on. Experience with a disability as a factor motivating the acceptance of a handicapped child prompted the suggestion that the organizations for parents of handicapped children might be a fruitful source of recruitment.

A national survey of adoptive placements of developmentally disabled children showed considerable willingness on the part of adoptive parents to accept such children (Coyne & Brown, 1985). A questionnaire mailed in 1979 and 1980 revealed that 1,588 developmentally disabled children had been placed in adoptive homes by some 800 agencies. The majority of children placed were mentally retarded or had cerebral palsy, although the group included a scattering of children with muscular dystrophy, epilepsy, cystic fibrosis, and other severe handicaps. Only 26 per cent of the adopted children had lived in the home as foster children. Forty-three per cent had been adopted without subsidy. Although prior contact with a disabled child and the availability of subsidy is important, the figures indicate the encouraging possibilities for placement of handicapped children without these considerations.

Agencies located in rural areas seemed to demonstrate a noticeable ability to make such placements. The life-style of a small town and the greater availability of strong natural helping networks in rural areas were cited as explanations.

Glidden (1985) studied forty-two British families who had adopted or long-term fostered mentally handicapped children. "Most of the families had either work or personal experience and familiarity with handicap" (p. 547). Whereas at the time of the study the results of the placement seemed satisfactory, it was noted that most of the children were preschoolers and the placement was recent. These findings paralleled those by Bowden (1984), who studied the adoptive placement of twenty-three mentally handicapped children.

Emotionally handicapped children are more problematic because their difficulties are multifaceted: impaired academic and cognitive capacities, limited or debilitating means of expressing their emotions, and social disabilities ranging from withdrawal to hyperaggressiveness (Jewett, 1978; Whittaker, 1979). In part, it is the seriousness and atypicality of their behavior problems that make it difficult for adoptive parents to learn to live with these children. In part, their problems are exacerbated by long-term exposure to poverty and highly stressful birth family conditions. Having learned to use maladaptive coping strategies early in their lives, some children spend years solidifying these response patterns, which they then bring to their adoptive homes.

Emotionally impaired children share with many adopted children the need to slowly learn to trust in and grow close to their adoptive families. However, for these children, separation and attachment concerns are especially powerful. For many, their sense of having been betrayed by adults is greater, and rejection experiences have recurred more frequently. For these children, who have been abused in body and spirit, their sense of social isolation is more profound.

Having experienced rejection, these children are likely to anticipate rejection. They are likely to be especially reticent about allowing themselves to feel love for their adoptive parents or to express affection toward them. They are much more likely to test the parents' patience and endurance in order to prove their acceptability. Their adoptive parents, at least initially, may have a harder time and fewer satisfactions. Adoptive parents need to be advised of the need for patience, the slow growth of love and affection, and the slow pace of mutual adjustment. For a few of these children, this attachment may never occur. Having been so damaged in their prior relationships, they may decide not to risk getting close to one more family, or may resist doing so for years (Meezan, 1980, p. 36).

Individual flexibility, facility in developing and using a variety of resources, and a willingness to take risks are all important qualities of parents who learn to successfully care for and love these special needs children. Frequently, parents are called on to change their expectations, their hopes, and their routine ways of dealing with and caring for children (Jewett, 1984; Pizard, 1979; U.S. Dept. of Health and Human Services, 1980, p. 30). To survive the upheaval and stress engendered by these responsibilities, parents must learn to be especially vigilant in finding sufficient support and in meeting other personal needs (Smith, 1980; Frank & Flynn, 1983).

Parents who adopt handicapped children can obtain assistance not only from agency subsidy but through private health insurance or Medicaid and from federal income maintenance programs for disabled children, such as SSI. A greater difficulty is often presented by the lack of special educational and therapeutic services for the handicapped. Adoptive parents of handicapped children need to develop the know-how to find and utilize the resources they need to help them in these tasks (Braden, 1981).

The Older Child

Another sizable group of adoptable but hard-to-place children is composed of older children. The general difficulties in the adoptive placement of the older child have been discussed in articles (Hallman, 1952; Starr, 1955; Schapiro, 1957; Leatherman, 1957; Lawder, 1958; Boehm, 1958; Bell, 1959; McCoy, 1961; Epstein & Heymann, 1967; Chema, 1970; Sharrar, 1970; Neilson, 1972; Bayley, 1975; Edwards, 1975; Biggert, 1976; Chestang & Heymann, 1976; Belken, 1977; Katz, 1977; Jones, 1979) and in books (Kadushin, 1970b; Carney, 1976; Jewett, 1978).

In 1970 it might have been said, with some justification, that a child over two years of age was difficult to place for adoption. With the continuing shortage of adoptable infants, the age at which a child presents difficulty for adoption has increased. By 1980, white, nonhandicapped children up to seven or eight years of age were being placed for adoption with relatively little difficulty. However, a nationwide survey of children being offered adoptive services by public child welfare agencies indicated that, in 1977, adoptive homes could be found for only 36 per cent of children 11–14 years of age and 13 per cent of 15–17-year-olds (Shyne & Schroeder, 1978, p. 131).

Any initial deterrent to placeability ultimately results in additional deterrents. Because the minority-group child or the handicapped child is initially hard to place, delay results in the child's becoming an older child who is now harder to place because of age. Because placeability is greatest at earlier ages, the most effective service to the special-needs child is to make special efforts to place him or her as early as possible.

Adoption of older children presents the agency, the child, and the adoptive parents with some special problems. Because older children placed for adoption have already developed some characteristic ways of reacting to parental figures and to family life, "matching" comes up again as a consideration of significance. Unlike the physical "matching" of the past, which adoption agencies have rejected, this kind of "matching" involves a concern for a good fit between adopter and adoptee in terms of temperamental compatibility: Do they tend to like similar kinds of activities? Are they organized, neat, and punctual? Or are they loosely structured, fast or slow in reacting to events, highly emotional or emotionally bland? (Boyne, 1978; Jewett, 1978).

The selection of an adoptive home for an older child requires the child's active participation, for he or she is consciously and explicitly aware of the experience. Unlike the infant, the older child measures the acceptability of the prospective adoptive couple, and any doubts or hesitancies must be given consideration.

The older child has a vivid memory of a life lived with other people in other places. Adoptive parents have to establish themselves in the child's life either in addition to or in opposition to such memories. Thus parents who adopt an older child can less easily fantasize that the child is truly their own.

An older child is therefore likely to face a problem of competing or conflicting loyalties. Having developed emotional ties of some intensity to either biological parents or foster parents, the child cannot "belong" unconditionally to the adoptive parents without betraying his or her love for the adults to whom he or she previously felt some allegiance.

The older child comes to adoptive parents with an established name and with an established way of dealing with the problems of daily living that may or may not fit into the adoptive family's way of doing things. The adoptive parents must, in some measure, accept the child "as is"; they are deprived of the opportunity of socializing the child, from the start, in terms that are acceptable to them.

The older child is more likely to be a "damaged" child. He or she is more likely to suffer from disabilities as an emotionally disturbed child. However, there are advantages. The older child can participate in family activities, communicate with parents, and be talked to. There is less of the drudgery in training and caring for a totally dependent child, and there is less anxiety about "telling" because the child has experienced the placement and knows that he or she is adopted. Parents who have adopted older children stress these advantages.

> Mother: You have a child that wants to be adopted . . . and that's one thing in your favor . . . and he knows it. . . . I mean he's aware of it . . . that his folks can't keep him. He's already trying to adjust, because he wants to and he's old enough to understand . . . to realize.
>
> Father: We adopted an older child so that we didn't have to go through this diaper wash, two o'clock feeding, walk the floor bit.
>
> Mother: I think that's one advantage . . . of adopting an older child . . . The child knows it's being adopted . . . with an infant you . . . you'd always have to wonder—well, gee—when should I tell her or should I ever tell her . . . and with the older child . . . it's just a fact when she comes. . . .

Independent Adoptions

A number of non-relative placements are achieved each year through a route different from the one we have been discussing. These placements are made independent of social service agencies. In 1971, the last year for which we have national statistics, 79% of the 83,000 children adopted by unrelated persons were placed by social agencies; 17,000 (21%) were placed independently. Litman (1984), evaluating 1978–1979 data from five Canadian provinces, found that independent adoption comprised 12% of the total (p. 32). Despite increased use of adoptive agency services, a significant number of children are still placed in homes through independent means.

The term *independent adoption* applies to a number of different procedures. The natural parents may make their own contact with a person whom they know, through one source or another, wants to adopt a child. Or a doctor or lawyer may know of parents unable or unwilling to care for a child, and a childless couple seeking a child, and he or she may act as the intermediary. This is sometimes termed the *gray market* in adoptions. A third kind of independent placement involves an actual business transaction. In this case, a "black marketeer" undertakes to sell a baby to a couple eager to adopt. No statistics are available that indicate how many of the independent placements are of one type or another.

In some states in which advertising is legal, infertile couples are using the classified sections of newspapers to advertise their need for an adoptable child. Ads placed in 1984 mirror ads placed fifty years ago in newspapers.

> Adoption: very happily married couple would like to adopt white infant. We are well educated and have a comfortable life. Will pay all expenses. Totally confidential. Please call collect any time. (*New York Times,* July 26, 1984).

Whites, with more substantial funds to pay for adoption than non-whites, are more likely to choose this means of adding a child to the family (Gradstein, Gradstein & Glass, 1972; Meezan, Katz & Russo, 1978).

Independent placement involves dangers and disadvantages to the child, to the adoptive parents, to the biological parents, and ultimately to the community. The rights of the child to a good home are not as securely guaranteed in independent placement. The gray market and the black market are oriented to the needs and desires of the adoptive couple rather than to the needs of the child. The agency makes the best effort, however fallible, to find a good set of parents for the child. The couple with whom the child is independently placed has been subject to no assessment process. The only eligibility requirement, in many instances, is ability to pay, which bears little direct relationship to capacity for parenthood and is no guarantee of an emotionally healthy environment for the child.

It might seem from the adoptive parents' point of view that there are obvious advantages in independent adoptions: no "red tape," no elaborate interviews, no need to meet what are perceived as restrictive agency eligibility requirements, and no need to satisfy a social worker about their capacity for parenthood. Yet the seeming advantages may, in fact, be disadvantages. Becoming a parent is not an unmitigated pleasure, nor is the desire for parenthood unequivocal. The agency's interviews with prospective adoptive parents are designed as much to help the applicants clarify for themselves their decision about parenthood as they are to satisfy the agency that the home would be a good one for a child. During exploration of these issues with the agency social worker, the adoptive couple may decide they do not really want to take care of a child.

The independent adoption procedure gives the couple no explicit opportunity to discuss with someone experienced in such matters the problems involved in adoption, the burdens they are undertaking, and the changes adoption will occasion in their lives—problems, burdens, and changes they may choose not to accept once they are made evident.

The supposed advantages of getting a child without agency entanglements is also a disadvantage during the period between placement and final adoption. The adoptive parents are, in some respects, different from biological parents, and there are many unique aspects in the adopted child–adopted parent relationship. The independent adopter's freedom from agency entanglements also means "freedom" from agency help in dealing with the social and emotional consequences of adoption—the problems attendant upon the assumption of this unique role.

Assurance of confidentiality of the adoption may be less firm in independent adoptions than in agency adoptions. Contact between birth parents and adoptive parents, which is deliberately broken in agency adoption, is a greater possibility in the independent adoption. When the natural parents themselves have arranged for placement, they know the identity and, in all likelihood, the whereabouts of the adopters. In one study of 105 private adoptions (Gradstein, Gradstein, & Glass, 1982), half of the biological mothers and adoptive parents had met. Adoptive parents were actually present at the delivery of the child in 19 instances (p. 550). In adoptions carried out through the gray or black market, the identity of the adoptive parents may be kept secret, but the degree to which secrecy is maintained depends upon the intermediary's moral and ethical standards.

Social-agency adoption procedures generally involve the agency's obtaining clear title to the child so that it is in a position to assure the prospective adoptive parents that there will be no difficulty in their legal title to the child. Some independent placements occasion great anxiety for the adoptive couple because they may not be sure that the natural parents will consent to adoption.

Finally, because in some independent placements the sole concern is providing the adoptive parents with a child for a price, any information that is likely to increase the adoptive parents' hesitancy to accept the child may be falsified.

Independent placements involve disadvantages for the unmarried mother as well. Instead of being helped to arrive at her own decision regarding the disposition of the child, she is pressured to make one decision—to surrender the child for adoption. She is also deprived of help with the personal and/or social difficulties that may be related to the out-of-wedlock pregnancy. Nor is there, of course, any effort made either to contact or to help the father (McTaggart, 1980).

Social workers point out that providing families for parentless children is too important to the community to be left unregulated. Social agencies are keenly aware of the dangers cited. Their procedures are designed to protect the child in getting the best possible home and the best possible care while waiting for a home. They are also designed to protect the adoptive parents by freely disclosing any of the child's shortcomings, by assuring confidentiality, by making certain of the legal availability of a child, by helping the parents to make a reasoned decision regarding adoption, and to resolve those problems that might endanger the adoption. They are also designed to protect the unmarried mother by giving her support, care, and protection during her pregnancy, by helping her come to a firm decision regarding disposition of the baby, and by helping her with those problems that may have led to her pregnancy.

A congressional hearing on "baby selling" by the Subcommittee of Children and Youth, Senate Committee on Labor and Public Welfare (U.S. Congress, 1975) indicated that unwed mothers were pressured, misled, and sometimes coerced to surrender the baby for adoption; that birth records were falsified so as to indicate that the adoptive mother, rather than the unmarried mother, gave birth to the child; and that payments of up to $25,000 were made in obtaining a child. There was testimony that some parents, very anxious to adopt, went heavily into debt to pay the price of adoption.

Although the testimony repeated some of the hazards and quasi-legalities uncovered by a previous congressional investigation of black-market practice conducted by Senator Kefauver in the 1950s (U.S. Senate, 1956), there were some differences in the 1970s. Abortion clinics were regularly monitored by black-market operations as an avenue of access to unmarried mothers. There were reports of a file of young men and women who were on call to "make" a baby for a prospective adoptive couple. There were reports of pressures exerted on young unmarried mothers to surrender the child for adoption, of procurers waiting for expectant mothers outside pregnancy clinics and abortion facilities, and of "baby farms" where young women were paid to become pregnant or to carry through their pregnancies if they agreed, in return, to place the child for adoption. It was difficult for those offering testimony at the hearings to estimate the extent of this black market because such transactions are not a matter of record. However, educated guesses resulted in an "unsolid" estimate of some five thousand children involved in such transactions.

A national study of independent adoptions involved questionnaires to 91 social agencies and personal interviews with 131 couples who adopted through independent placement, 115 mothers who relinquished their children for private adoption, and 75 "facilitators," mostly lawyers and doctors, who helped arrange such transactions (Meezan, Katz, & Russo, 1978). The motivation that prompts the applicant to resort to independent adoptive resources is primarily to maximize the possibility of obtaining the kind of child they prefer—a white, healthy infant—with a minimum of delay, inconvenience, and outside control of their decision. A large majority of the group (84 per cent) had had prior contact with a social agency in exploring the possibilities of adoption. Most frequently, they were discouraged because of closed intake or long waiting lists and, additionally, in some cases (15 per cent), because they already had children or because of maximum age and religious matching requirements. Rather than wait the two to three years that seemed to be necessary before receiving a child, they resorted to independent adoption. In 62 per cent of the cases, a white, healthy infant was placed within six months after contact with a child-placing intermediary. Almost 90 per cent of the children were younger than two weeks old at placement, and consequently younger than most agency-placed children.

A more recent but more limited study of independent adoptions, conducted by an infertility counselor in San Francisco, found that, of the 105 infants who had been placed through this means, more than two-thirds were living with their adoptive families within four months of the parents' initiation of efforts to adopt. In all but two cases, adopters had received a child within eleven months of the point at which they began their search (Gradstein, Gradstein & Glass, 1982, p. 549).

Meezan, Katz, and Russo (1978) found that agency procedure and/or worker performance did not make a significant contribution to the applicant's decision to resort to independent adoption, although this was a factor in some instances. Those who had had contact liked the agency for the most part and accepted the need for providing references and participating in assessment interviews.

The parents did recognize some elements of risk in the independent adoption situation. The principal worry was the possibility that the biological mother would change her mind about relinquishment and interfere with the adoption. Anxiety was expressed by 37 per cent of the couples that the child might have a physical problem of which they were unaware. Only a limited number (18 per cent) of adoptive couples were concerned about possible interference by the biological mother who might know of their identity.

The study staff, reviewing all relevant data, judged 13 per cent of the adoptions to be legally questionable. Most adopters were satisfied with the adoption and the children placed with them, whom they reported, in the greatest number of instances, to be developing normally.

The biological mother is drawn to independent adoptive auspices for equally understandable, eminently practical reasons. In many instances (about 50 per cent), she was unaware of an agency service available to meet her problems. But even when the mother is aware of such service, she knows, or soon finds out, that the agency has no option but to provide the needed help under considerations that make it difficult for the mother to accept. Money is available only through application for public assistance; medical help is available only through a clinic; adoption can be pursued only if the father is contacted or, when the mother is a minor, if her parents are informed. If the mother, like most, prefers private medical care and nonstigmatized financial assistance without the involvement of significant others and without administrative red tape, independent adoptive channels provide this kind of care. Mothers see other advantages in independent adoptions, such as greater ability to control the selection of the adopters of their child and the fact that the child will never be placed in foster care, for however limited a period of time. (See also McTaggart, 1980.)

Private-care medical expenses are, in fact, paid by the adopter in most instances, along with housing and maintenance costs in a more limited number of cases. About 30 percent of "the total sample stated that provision of financial aid was influential in their decision to relinquish the child independently" (Meezan, Katz, & Russo, 1978, p. 108). Converging data from the 321 participants in independent adoption—the adopters, the biological mothers, and the intermediary "facilitators"—confirmed the fact that the hypothesized dangers of such adoptions did, in fact, exist, albeit at modest levels of frequency.

Illustrations of some of the risks uncovered by the study follow (Meezan, Katz, & Russo, 1978, pp. 28–35).

1. Unmarried mothers fail to receive the counseling that might be needed:

A disturbed, 16-year-old unmarried mother was referred for counseling after delivery and surrender. She felt she had been forced into the adoption, primarily by her mother. No one had helped her understand her situation, alternatives or consequences. None of her feelings had been dealt with.

2. The adopted child may be placed in a problematic home because there is no obligation in independent adoption to screen applicants in accordance with some criteria which protect the best interests of the child.

Child was placed through a doctor when a family agency refused because of severe medical problems including cancer in one of the spouses. While application was in the process of being turned down, the couple adopted independently.

3. Because the confidentiality and the anonymity of the participants are not as carefully safeguarded in independent adoption, there is a greater possibility of the biological parent's intrusion into the adoptive family's life.

Experience with a biological mother who, during the first year after placement placed pressure on adoptive parents by calling them for "loans" of money when she was in economic difficulties.

4. The legal entitlements of adoptive parents may be in greater jeopardy in independent adoptions.

Biological parents were divorced. Mother had custody of the child. She placed infant with couple who wished to adopt. Biological father filed custody suit, claiming that his rights were not terminated and that he had remarried and could now care for the child. Child was returned to biological father.

5. The adoptive child may be denied information that might significantly influence their decision and/or the child's health situation.

Adoptive parents were not informed that the biological mother and others in her family were severely diabetic. The adoptive parents were under the impression that the biological mother was free of health problems.

Legal reviews confirm that revocation of consent is more frequently attempted in independent than in agency placements because the natural mother is often not psychologically prepared when she signs the consent forms (*Rutgers Law Review*, 1973, p. 712). The likelihood of successful challenge of the placement by the biological mother is greater in independent adoptions than in agency adoptions.

An earlier, large-scale follow-up study of children placed independently showed that the success rates of such placements were generally high, although not as advantageous as agency placements (Witmer *et al.*, 1963). More recently, less extensive follow-up studies tend to suggest the same general conclusion.

Furlough (1974) randomly selected a sample of thirty agency adoptions and thirty independent adoptions made during 1965–1967 and involving children placed before the end of their first year. Studying childrearing practices, the physical, social and emotional environment of the adoptive home, the adoptive child's adjustment, and the process of "telling," Furlough found that there was little difference between the two sets of homes on 322 factors analyzed for levels of significant difference. He concluded that children placed for adoption independently can have the same opportunities for healthy, normal emotional development as those placed by agencies. Despite the essential similarities between the two groups, whatever differences were noted tended to favor the agency placements. Whereas all of the agency homes were intact by the time of the follow-up, only 66 per cent of the children in the independent adoptive homes had a father living with them. In 20 per cent of the cases, the father had died, and in 15 per cent, the father was divorced or separated. Apparently agency homes had been selected with greater care to provide the continuity of a two-parent family for the child. When present, more independent fathers than agency fathers "planned their activities so that they spent all of their time away from the children" (p. 67).

McMahan (1974) studied twenty-three socioeconomic characteristics of all independent and agency adoptions in three counties of Arkansas over a five-year period; 97 agency placements were compared with 131 independent placements. Quantifiable socioeconomic characteristics, such as living accommodations, length of marriage, age, employment, and income did not significantly distingush agency from independent adopters. Independent adopters were more likely to have difficulty in meeting agency requirements regarding the age of the husband and the number of children in the home at the time of application.

Although objectively the child, in each case, is provided with very much the same kind of home, from a subjective point of view agency families were more open and relaxed, had a secure feeling legally, and were unafraid and cooperative. On the other hand, independent families were suspicious, cautious, secretive, and afraid and, in many instances, uncooperative: "This tends to indicate that, for the most part, couples who adopt through a licensed child placing agency feel more secure about the whole process and have a greater peace of mind than do couples who adopt a child from other sources" (p. 84).

The potential hazards in independent adoptions and the advantages of agency adoptions have stimulated pressure to give the agencies exclusive control over adoptive placement. Giving the agency the exclusive right to make adoptions is resisted on a number of grounds, namely, that the superiority of agency adoption as compared with independent adoption is not unequivocally established; that competition with independent adoption has forced agencies to make desirable changes; that people in many sections of the country do not have available an agency that meets licensing standards and has a staff of trained competent workers; that such exclusivity tends to discourage adoptions; that the biological mother would be denied the opportunity of selecting parents for her child; and that legislation giving exclusive control to agencies has not, in fact, resulted in effectively eliminating the gray and black markets. Agency critics recognize, however, that adoptions are of too great a concern to the community to permit haphazard placement. The argument, then, is not between the independent adoptions and the agency but between a social agency monopoly of adoption and some reasonable regulation of independent adoptions (Podolski, 1975; Turano, 1976).

In 1978, Connecticut, Delaware, Minnesota, and Michigan were the only four states that clearly prohibited independent adoptions; there was considerable variability among the other forty-six states in the extent to which they were regulated. Meezan (1980) also suggests that existing laws are structured in ways that prevent or deter adequate enforcement. He notes that many states have no clear regulation of fees and compensation regarding adoptions, whereas some others do not even legally prohibit payment of compensation for placing a child. In some states that do provide more adequate control, penalties for violations are minimal (p. 50).

Attempts to regulate interstate transfers of children have met with limited success, as have attempts to develop state-by-state uniformity in requirements or procedures. There is little likelihood that national adoption legislation embodying these protections will be enacted (Hunt, 1972). Both the gray and black markets are difficult to police because those involved are not likely to claim that any crime has been committed, and the child is too young to initiate such action.

Careful regulation of independent adoptions requires some review of the situation by the Department of Social Services before placement of the child. All fees associated with the birth, placement, and adoption of the child need to be itemized and reported. There also should be provisions for court supervision of each aspect of the process.

Evaluation

Research assessing the "success" of adoptive placements is listed in Table 9-4. Only those studies are included in which definite information is presented regarding sources of data and criteria for outcome and in which some attempt was made at statistical analysis. The studies cited vary in the level of their methodological precision, in the nature and detail of the data obtained, in the criteria for outcome employed, in procedures used to make judgments of outcome, and in the statistical rigor with which the data were analyzed. All of the research cited in the table was primarily, if not exclusively, on white, nonhandicapped, infant adoptive placements.

TABLE 9.4. Adoptive Outcome Studies

Study and Date	Outcome Size of Study Group and Lapse of Time Between Placement and Study	Number and Percentages	Outcome Criteria for Categorization	Data Used for Follow-up Assessment	Auspices
Theis (1924)	235 (adults) 12–18 years after placement	207 (88.1%) 28 (11.9%)	"Capable" "Incapable"	Interviews with adoptive children, adoptive parents, and "other persons" by project interviewer	Agency
Morrison (1950)	24 (children) 10–17 years after placement	18 (75%) 6 (25%)	"Getting along satisfactorily" "Unsatisfactory adjustment"	Interview with adoptive parents by agency workers	Agency
Brenner (1951)	50 (families) median of 4.4 years after placement	26 (52%) 18 (36%) 6 (12%)	"Successful" "Fairly successful" "Unsuccessful"	Observation of children in home, interviews with adoptive mothers by agency workers, psychological tests of children	Agency
Nieden (1951)	138 (adults) 15–20 years after placement	35 (25%) 62 (45%) 29 (21%) 12 (9%)	"Very good" "Good" "Indifferent" "Bad"	Records and interviews with adoptive parents by agency social workers	Agency
Armatruda & Baldwin (1951)	100 (children) at time of placement	76 (76%) 16 (16%) 8 (8%)	"Good" "Questionable" "Poor"	Agency study of adoptive home, study of child by Yale development clinic	Agency
Fairweather (1952)	18 (children) 3–4 years after placement	18 (100%)	"Good"	Interviews with adoptive mothers by agency workers, psychological tests of children	Agency
Edwards (1954)	79 (children) 5 years after placement	69 (87%) 9 (12%) 1 (1%)	"Very happy" "Some problems" "Serious problems"	Information not available	Agency
National Association for Mental Health, England (Estimated 1954)	163 (children) minimum of 2 years after placement	142 (87.1%) 21 (12.9%)	"Satisfactory" "Unsatisfactory"	Agency records	Agency
Davis & Douck (1955)	396 (children) 1 year after placement	371 (93.7%) 25 (6.3%)	Not removed Removed	Agency records	Agency

Study	Sample	Outcome categories	n (%)	Method of data collection	Source
Fradkin & Krugman (1956)	37 (children) during first year after placement	"Good" / "Intermediate" / "Poor"	27 (73%) / 6 (16%) / 4 (11%)	Ongoing contact with parents during first year of supervision, tests of infant	Agency
Witmer et al. (1963)	484 (children) most 9 years after placement	"Excellent to fair" / "Not definitely unsatisfactory" / "Definitely unsatisfactory"	324 (67%) / 39 (8%) / 121 (25%)	Interview with parents and teachers by project interviewers, psychological tests of children	Independent
McWhinnie (1967)	52 (adults) 16–66 years after placement	"Good" and "Fairly good" "Adjustment in all areas" / "Reasonable adjustment in some fundamental areas" / "Adjustment poor in many areas"	21 (40.5%) / 21 (40.5%) / 10 (9%)	Interviews with adoptive children as adults	Independent
Ripple (1968)	160 (children) 9–10 years after placement	"Within the normal range" / "Some problems in adjustment" / "Serious emotional or behavioral problems"	75 (47%) / 47 (29%) / 38 (24%)	Agency records, interviews with father, mother, child	Agency
Kornitzer (1968)	233 children and adults (time lapse varied)	"Success" / "Average" / "Problems" / "Bad"	96 (41.2%) / 85 (36.5%) / 45 (19.3%) / 7 (3.0%)	Interviews with mother by researcher, some fathers interviewed	Agency and independent
Lawder et al. (1969)	200 (families) 8–15 years after placement	"Superior" / "Good" / "Fair" / "Poor"	29 (14%) / 98 (49%) / 53 (27%) / 20 (10%)	Interviews with fathers and mothers together and alone	Agency
Jaffee & Fanshel (1970)	100 (adults) 20–30 years after placement	"Low problems" / "Middle range" / "High problems"	33 (33%) / 34 (34%) / 33 (33%)	Interviews with father and mother separately, questionnaire completed independently by parents	Agency

TABLE 9.4. (Continued)

Study and Date	Outcome Size of Study Group and Lapse of Time Between Placement and Study	Number and Percentages	Outcome Criteria for Categorization	Data Used for Follow-up Assessment	Auspices
Bohman (1970)	122 (children) 10–11 years after placement	34 (28%) 28 (23%) 33 (27%) 25 (20%) 2 (2%)	"No symptoms" "Slight symptoms" "Moderate symptoms" "Problem child" "Requiring institutional care"	Interviews with father and mother together and alone	Agency
Seglow, Pringle & Wedge (1972)	145 (children) 9 years after placement	79 (82%) 23 (16%) 3 (2%)	"Very well" "Not well adjusted" "Disturbed"	Interviews with adoptive mothers, some adoptive fathers	Agency
Klomineck (1976)	100 (children) 5 years after adoption	83 (83%) 17 (17%)	"Average to good social adjustment" "Poor adjustment"	Adoption records; court files; clinical interviews; observation; IQ tests	Agency
Raynor (1977)	105 adoptees, 15–18 years after placement	73 (70%) 26 (25%) 6 (5%)	"Excellent to good" "Barely adequate or marginal adjustment" "Poor adjustment"	Individual taped interviews	Agency
#Lambert & Streather (1980)	115 illegitimate adopted, 294 illegitimate unadopted, 12,076 legitimate unadopted children	No differences in reading ability: adopted boys do more poorly in math; adopted and illegitimate less well socially adjusted in school	Reading comprehension; mathematics tests; Bristol Social Adjustment Guide	Parent and child interviews; mailed questionnaires for teachers	Unclear

Study	Sample	Findings	Measures	Data collection	Subject recruitment
#Hoopes (1982)	260 white children 5–12 years after placement; 68 nonadopted children	Adopted children more dependent at age 5, more acting out in school; behavior not extreme; functioning better as a family unit, more self-worth and comfort with fathers than controls	Child Behavior Characteristics Scale; Bristol Social Adjustment Guides; self-esteem measures	Home interviews with children and parents; teacher ratings; mailed questionnaires to parents	Agency
#Fein et al. (1983)	58 children under 14 discharged from foster care to adoption; 115 returned to birth family from care; 14 in permanent foster care	Children in adoptive homes scored highest in family adjustment; those in foster parent adoptions scored best on Child Behavior measures; no differences in school functioning, emotional, developmental functioning	Further detail not provided	Home interviews with parents or caretakers; agency records	Agency
#Brodzinsky et al. (1984)	130 children 6–11 years after placement; 130 nonadopted children	Significantly more behavior and social problems than nonadopted children, although "still well within the normal range of behavior"	Child Behavior Problems Scale; Hahnemann Elementary School Behavior Scales	Interviews with adoptive mothers; mailed forms completed by teachers	Unclear; recruited from a variety of agency and other sources

#Note: Data depicting proportion of children functioning well are unavailable in these studies

TABLE 9.5.   Recapitulation of Adoptive Outcome Studies

Outcome	Number	Percent
Unequivocally successful	1,739	65.7
"Satisfactory"		
"Very good"		
"Good"		
"Successful"		
"Superior"		
"Low problems"		
"No symptoms or slight symptoms"		
"Excellent to fair"		
"Within normal range"		
"Very well adjusted"		
Intermediate success	482	18.2
"Not definitely unsatisfactory"		
"Fairly successful"		
"Indifferent"		
"Questionable"		
"Some problems"		
"Intermediate"		
"Average"		
"Moderate symptoms"		
"Not well adjusted"		
Unsuccessful	424	16.1
"Unsatisfactory"		
"Poor," "low"		
"Problematic"		
"Unsuccessful"		
"Incapable"		
"High problems"		
"Problem child"		
"Disturbed"		
Total	2,645	100.0

NOTE: Table does not describe research published in the 1980s, since data from these studies are not provided in compatible form.

Table 9-5 summarizes statistics on placement outcome. This recapitulation indicates that approximately two out of three adoptions were judged unequivocally successful; an additional 18 per cent were judged to be of fair, moderate, or average success; only 16 per cent were judged to be failures. It would seem, therefore, that adoptions are, for the most part, quite successful.

Two recent studies reveal information concerning the long-term adjustment of children in permanent adoptive homes. Brodzinsky et al. (1984) asked adoptive mothers and teachers to evaluate the general functioning of 130 of these children, focusing on a series of potential behavioral problems. The adjustment of these youngsters was compared with that of 130 nonadopted children, who were matched for age, sex, race, SES, family structure, and number of siblings. In general, the adopted children "rated higher in psychological and school-related behavior problems, and lower in social competence and school achievement than were non-adopted children" (p. 587). Difficulties were evident both in the home and in the academic setting. These problems were, however, "still well within the normal range of behavior." Research on 260 adopted children (Hoopes, 1982) compared their experiences with those of 68 nonadopted children, and came to quite similar conclusions. Using the Bristol Social Adjustment Guides and the Child Behavior Characteristic Scale, this researcher found adopted children tend to function more independently and to act out more in school than their peers. Again, however, their difficulties cannot be considered extreme. In addition, along some dimensions, adopted children were faring better than their non-adopted cohorts. In particular, the child's family functioned more cohesively as a unit and the children expressed more positive feelings of self-worth and comfort with their adoptive fathers than did the controls. Both of these studies suggest that adoptive families must be more effectively prepared for the development of potential characterological problems in children and for the possibility that these difficulties may persist, albeit at low levels, for several years.

The theoretical child development literature suggests that adoptees will have problems with their sense of identification particularly during adolescence, when developing a stable sense of identity is a major task. The clinical literature suggests a confirmation of this supposition based on case histories of adolescent adoptees referred because of emotional difficulties. However, a study of a nonclinical population of adopted adolescents found no evidence to support the theoretical presupposition. Fifty adopted children fifteen to eighteen years old were matched with forty-one nonadopted peers and evaluated by means of personal interviews and standardized instruments relating to ego-identity and self-image (Stein & Hoopes, 1985). "Adopted subjects showed no deficits in functioning on measures of overall identity when compared with their non-adopted counterparts—There was no significant difference between adopted and nonadopted subjects for self concept—and no indications that the present group of adolescent adoptees suffered from deficit in self-esteem" (p. 34).

Shireman and Johnson (1986) are conducting a longitudinal study of single-parent adoption, that, by 1985, had contacted the families twice, once when the children were four years old and then again when they were eight. Interviews with twenty-two single adoptive parents were supplemented by interviews with children. The lack of continuous contact with a male parent or relative has been thought to present a problem for sexual identification in such adoptions. Apparently this did not prove to be the case in latency (Shireman & Johnson, 1986). At age eight 75 per cent of the adoptees were in "excellent" or "good" adjustment.

But how do agency placements compare with independent placements? And how does the success of adoptive families compare with the success of biofamilies? In the absence of normative data regarding the "success" rate of biofamilies, the latter question is impossible to answer at this time. The material in Table 9-4 however, permits some tentative answers to the first question.

Only Witmer's et al.'s (1963) study is exclusively concerned with nonagency placements, though the studies by Armatruda (1951) and by Kornitzer (1968) offer some additional material. Armatruda's study, although frequently cited to show the superiority of agency placements, is not a true follow-up study because assessment of the home was made at the time of placement. Kornitzer's study shows that only 14.4 per cent of agency placements, but 25.6 per cent of "third-party and direct placements," were categorized as problems or failures (p. 159). Witmer's study shows a failure rate of 25 per cent for nonagency adoptions.

If the data from Witmer's study, and those from the Kornitzer and Armatruda studies concerning children independently placed, are deleted from Table 9-5, the failure rate for agency placements becomes 14.8 per cent—considerably lower than the 25 per cent failure rate of Witmer's study and the 25.6 per cent failure rate of independent placements in Kornitzer's study. Any conclusions must remain tentative because of the differing levels of validity of the data used in the different studies. Justifying the cautionary note is the fact that the information in Table 9-5 indicates that adoptive children who are referred for psychiatric

TABLE 9.6.   Studies of Adopted Children Referred for Psychiatric Treatment

Study	Total Number in Study Group	Number of Adoptees in Study Group	Percentage of Adoptees Referred for Service	Percentage of Referred Adoptees Placed by Agency	Adoption Status—Relative or Nonrelative
Stonesifer (1942)	2,000	48	2.4%	—	Both
Holman (1953)	100	7	7.0%	—	Nonrelative
Pringle (1961)	2,593	210	8.3%	—	Both
National Association for Mental Health, England (1954)	1,152	17	1.5%	—	Both
Schechter (1960)	120	16	13.3%[b]	50%	Nonrelative
Toussieng (1962)	357	39	10.9%	51%	Nonrelative
Humphrey & Ounsted (1963)	2,700	80	2.9%	50%	Nonrelative
Sweeny et al. (1963)	292	21	7.2%	—	Nonrelative
Goodman (1963)	593	14	2.4%	50%	Nonrelative
Ketchum (1964)	196	20	10.7%	"Most often"	Both
Schechter et al. (1964)	—	159 16.6% (41 adults 118 children)	46% (average from three psychiatric facilities)	Nonrelative	
Borgatta & Fanshel (1965)	2,281	123	5.5%	—	Nonrelative

Study	N	Cases	%	%	Relationship
Menlove (1965)	1,314	59	4.6%	—	Nonrelative
Simon & Senturia (1966)	1,371	35 (29 children, 6 adults)	2.6%	—	Nonrelative
Kirk, Jonassohn & Fish (1966)[a]	2,117	132	6.2%	—	Both
Jameson (1967)	390	42	10.8%	55%	Nonrelative
Reece & Levin (1968)	1,017	30	2.95%	56%	Nonrelative
Silver (1970)	80	10	12.5%	90%	Nonrelative
Work & Anderson (1971)	1,282 (outpatients)	56	4.3%	—	—
	363 (inpatients)	34	9.3%	—	—
Harper & Williams (1976)	191	21	11%	100%	Nonrelative
Brinich & Brinich (1982)	12,662	273	2.2% (all patients) 5.0% (children) 1.6% (adults)	—	Both

[a]The table includes only those tabulations from Kirk's study that were presented by the author as having high or medium reliability. [See Kirk, Jonassohn, & Fish, 1966, Table 5, p. 297]

[b]These data were given in the 1964 study.

treatment are just as likely to have been placed through a social agency as to have been independently placed.

Emotional Disturbance in Adopted Children

Another series of studies examines referral of adopted children for inpatient or outpatient psychiatric services. A higher rate of referral for these children might suggest that they are functioning less successfully in their adoptive families than are children who remain in their biofamilies. Table 9-6 describes the relevant research. Some studies evaluate adoptee need for outpatient services, whereas others examine inpatient hospital records. Some of this research focuses on the functioning of children and some focuses on the long-term psychiatric experiences of adults who were adopted as children. Most of the individuals included in this research were adopted as infants or as very young children. Table 9-7 recapitulates the overall findings.

Overall, the data suggest that one in twenty patients at psychiatric and child guidance facilities are nonrelative adoptees. Because it is estimated that only about 1 per cent of children in the population are nonrelative adoptees, it would appear that these individuals are overrepresented among the clinical group. The rate is higher than that for children from biofamilies. This proportion, however, may be lower than that which we have a right to expect, given the insults to psychic health that many adopted children have endured. As Fanshel says, "the controversy revolves around the question of whether adoptive children and natural-born children have the same odds working for them with respect to the opportunity to develop stable personalities and successful life adjustments." The data further show that, in actuality, only a very small proportion of adopted children need psychiatric assistance. Overrepresentation of adopted individuals among this population, although statistically significant, has little social significance (Humphrey & Dunsted, 1963; Loehlin, Willerman & Horn, 1982).

The limited available data suggest that, although younger adopted children may need inpatient or outpatient psychiatric services, once these individuals reach adulthood, they do not use psychiatric facilities with any greater frequency than do their nonadopted cohorts. Examining the use of the facilities at the Langley Porter Psychiatric Institute over a ten-year period, Brinich and Brinich (1982) found that only 5 per cent of child patients and 1.6 per cent of adult patients were adopted. The researchers conclude that whereas adoption may serve as a focus for psychopathology in individual cases, adoption itself cannot be seen as psychogenic. (See also Norvell & Guy, 1977).

TABLE 9.7.   Recapitulation: Emotional Disturbance Among Adoptees

Study	Total Number in Study Group	Number of Adoptees in Study Group	Percentage of Adoptive Children Referred for Service	Percentage of Referred Adoptees Placed by Agency
Total relative and nonrelative adoptions (excluding Schechter, 1964)	32,900	1256	3.8%	—
Total nonrelative *only* Adoptions	10,806	497	4.6%	53%

Several explanations have been offered for whatever over-representation of adopted children does exist in the mental health clinical populations.

Some specific characteristics of the adoptive family may create special stresses for the adoptive child. Most adoptive parents receive their first child in their early thirties, whereas most biological parents have their first child in their early twenties. Patterns of marital interaction and family may have become less flexible with time and may be difficult to change in response to the incorporation of a child in the family system. The adoptive child is more likely to be a first child of older parents and more likely to be an only child. Furthermore adoption is still an atypical procedure for achieving parenthood, an the family may react to the stress of minority-group status.

The child must deal with the "rejection" of biological parents, some "genealogical bewilderment" over his or her origin, and the problem of fusing "good" and "bad" parental images. Adoptive parents must resolve their feelings about infertility and fear of competition from the child's biological parents. Further, however short the period between birth and adoption, every adoptive child faces some experience of early separation and some discontinuity in mothering. All these factors impose possible stresses on the adoptive family.

It has been argued that adoptive families may be more likely to seek professional assistance for solving their problems, thus having children who are over-represented among the clients of social service agencies. Having resorted to an agency for adoption, they are more likely than other families to resort to agencies again. As middle and upper-middle-class families, they may also be more likely to perceive social service agencies as helpful when confronting difficulties with their children (Brinich & Brinich, 1982).

Research suggests that congenital factors may contribute to the problem. Most adopted children are born out of wedlock to young women for whom this is the first pregnancy. Such a pregnancy is likely to be highly stressful, and some of the mother's tension and anxiety might adversely affect the fetus. Furthermore such mothers are likely to get less adequate nutritional and medical care during pregnancy and less emotional support. The higher mortality rate, the higher congenital anomaly rate, and the lower birth weight associated with such pregnancies, cited in Chapter 8, is confirmation of the stressful context of such a pregnancy for the child.

Studies of the genetic background of adopted children tend to show that they have heightened vulnerability to a variety of behavioral disorders. This makes the probability of need for mental health services for this subgroup of the population somewhat greater than the need for such services by the general population. (See Heston, 1966; Rosenthal et al., 1968a, b, c; Rosenthal, 1972; Wender, 1972; Schulsinger, 1972; Goodwin et al., 1973; Morrison & Stewart, 1973; Crowe, 1974; Hutchings & Mednick, 1975; Cunningham et al., 1975a, b; Munsinger, 1975a, b; Rosenthal, 1975; Fisch, 1976; Maurer, Cadoret, & Cain, 1980; Cadoret, Cain, & Grove, 1980).

A series of studies conducted in Scandinavia compared the problems manifested by adoptive children with those of their biological and adoptive parents (Kendler, Gruenberg, & Strauss, 1981; Bohman, 1981; Bohman et al., 1982; Von Knorring, Bohman, & Sigvardsson, 1982; Sigvardsson et al., 1982). Official agencies in both Sweden and Denmark have detailed records of physical and mental illness, alcoholism, criminality, outpatient clinical attendance, school performance, and so on on biological parents of adopted children, the adoptive parents, and the adopted children. The Stockholm Study, for example, has such detailed information on 1,775 men and women born between 1930 and 1949 who were adopted in early childhood. The general overall conclusion is that adoptive adult rates of mental illness, alcoholism, criminality, intelligence, and temperament tend to resemble that of the bioparent more than that of the adoptive parents with whom the children had lived, in many instances, since early infancy. However, generally the rates at which adopted adults manifest problems is lower than the rate manifested by biological parents. Whereas the genetic background of the adoptive child contributes to determining problematic behavior, the influence of the generally more adequate adoptive parents and adoptive home tend to mitigate the potency of these factors.

Other studied in the United States concerning the adoption of identical twins by different families tend to confirm this general conclusion (Scarr-Salapateck & Weinberg, 1975, 1978; Defries, Plomin, Vandenberg & Kuse, 1981; Brown, Plomin, DeFries, 1982; Loehlin, Willerman, & Horn, 1982; Scarr & Weinberg, 1983).

If the conclusion has validity, then one might expect that adopted children born generally to parents who have been problematic would come to adoption in infancy with some, albeit limited, vulnerability and predisposition for developing emotional and/or behavioral problems—predispositions and vulnerabilities which the adoptive environment has to defuse.

Evaluation of Adoptions of Older and Handicapped Children

Few studies have examined overall progress made by adopted older, emotionally or physically handicapped children, or sibling groups. This research is summarized in Table 9-8. In general, parents report that they are satisfied with these adoptions. Approximately 70 per cent of the parents assess their situation as either excellent or good.

Kadushin (1970b) interviewed ninety-one families with children who had been placed for adoption at five years of age or older. The greatest majority of such placements were successful, and the children appeared to be adjusting well. Yet all these children had spent their infancy and early childhood under very deprived circumstances. In almost all instances, the biological parents' rights to the child had been terminated by the courts as a consequence of neglect and/or abuse. The study shows that the older children, despite memories of earlier attachments, do develop strong relationships with their adoptive parents and learn and accept the ways of the new family. In the recuperative environment of a healthy, permanent family, old emotional wounds are healed.

Studying children who had been placed at a young age after being institutionalized, Tizard (1977; 1979) reaches the same conclusion:

> Judged by a number of criteria, then, most of these adoptions must be considered successful. All 30 placements were stable; only three of the 25 couples we visited when the child was eight expressed reservations so serious as to amount to dissatisfaction; only four considered that the child was not attached to them. The only behavior problem reputed (*sic*) frequently was attention-seeking behavior, and this was particularly marked at school. In contrast, the children who remained in institutions or who had been restored to their natural families had more frequent and more severe problems [1979, p. 537].

Nelson (1985) conducted a postfinalization follow-up study of 177 adoptive families who accepted special-needs children. Special-needs children were defined as

TABLE 9.8. Outcome Studies: Adoption of Handicapped, Older Children

	Child Characteristics	Size of Study Group and Lapse of Time Between Placement and Child Study	Number and Percentages	Outcome Criteria for categorization	Date Used for follow up Assessment
Franklin & Massarik (1969)	Moderate to severe handicap	71 children (4–12 years after placement)	26 (37%) 29 (41%) 16 (22%)	"Excellent" "Good" "Doubtful"	Joint interviews with parents; unstructured observation of child
Kadushin (1970b)	Older—age 5–12 at placement	91 children (4–10 years after placement)	67 (73%) 8 (9%) 18 (16%)	"High ratio of parental satisfactions to dissatisfactions" "Balance between satisfactions—dissatisfactions" "Low ratio of satisfactions to dissatisfactions"	Joint interviews with parents; questionnaire responses
Tizard (1977; 1979)	Two years of age or older at placement after institutional care during infancy	30 (2½ years after placement and 6 years after placement)	24 (84%)	"Parents satisfied"; "Mutual attachments strong"	Individual taped interviews; observation of children; teacher reports
Smith & Sherwen (1983)	28 (85%) 3 or older at placement	33 adolescents (9–14 years after placement)	27 (82%) 13 (39%)	Described good things about being adopted; Described no bad things about being adopted	Mailed questionnaires to adolescents
	Second sample: 41% 3 or older at placement	117 mothers of 193 children 2–13 years after placement	(62%) (32%) (6%)	"Positive attitude"; "Positive with problems"; "Negative attitude"	Mailed questionnaires to adoptive mothers
Nelson (1985)	At least 8 years old, handicapped, part of sibling group of 3 or more	177 families (1–4 years after finalization)	73%	"Good or excellent"; "Less than satisfactory"	Individual interviews with parents; agency records

children at least eight years of age, a child emotionally, physically, intellectually handicapped, or a child who was part of a sibling group of three or more children. The study, conducted in Chicago, Detroit, and Houston, involved personal interviews with the families supplemented by case records and mailed questionnaires. Respondents participated voluntarily, so there might be a positive bias in findings. Only 7 per cent of the respondents rated the experience as unsatisfactory, while seventy-three considered it either good or excellent.

During the postplacement prefinalization period, agencies were most helpful in obtaining adoption subsidies for parents. Postfinalization services were less adequately available, although some two-thirds of the respondents indicated that they needed and might have used such services. This was particularly true of help adopters sought in finding special educational programs for children.

The Outcome of Transracial and Foreign Adoptions

Table 9-9 summarizes research on situations in which parents adopted U.S. children transracially or children who are foreign born. Almost all of the transracial studies involved the adoption of black children by white parents. Most of this research based conclusions on interviews with the parents themselves, asking them whether they were satisfied with the adoption and exploring the extent to which their children had developed problems. The studies either utilize no control groups or use white parents adopting white children for comparison. The failure to compare the experiences of these parents to those of black parents adopting black children is a serious drawback of this research.

Transracial adoptions are recent, and the children placed are still quite young. Follow-up research available at this point indicates that sibling acceptance is not much of a problem; young playmates and peers accept such children readily. The negative reaction of neighbors is private, as yet not public; explicitly manifested prejudice is unfashionable and infrequent. Parents frequently encounter stares of curiosity, but rarely overt hostility. As a matter of fact, parents note that it is more embarrassing to have to cope with gushing comments of approbation. Within the more intimate family and peer network, however, support is not as available to these families as it is to those adopting white children (Feigelman & Silverman, 1983, pp. 91–92; Grow & Shapiro, 1974). This is worrisome, since family support has been shown to be related to overall success of adoptive placements. Parents report that transracially adopted children who are old enough to be in school have experienced heckling and teasing, but this has been neither frequent nor persistent; however, children may not consistently share these episodes with adoptive parents.

Fanshel's (1972) study is one of the more rigorous pieces of research exploring the outcome of transracial placements. As a result of a cooperative effort of the U.S. Bureau of Indian Affairs and the Child Welfare League of America, 395 Indian children were placed with white families over a ten-year period. Annual interviews were conducted with the families of ninety-seven of these children for five years after placement. The fathers and the mothers were interviewed jointly and separately, and the adjustment of the child was studied in detail. The overall conclusion "was that the children are doing remarkably well as a group." Health and cognitive development were normal:

> . . . In personality and behavior patterns there are more incipient signs of difficulties than in other areas, [but] this is true of only 30 percent of the children, and most of

these are seen to have moderate rather than serious problems. The children appear to be well-imbedded within their adoptive families and the relationships appear to be as close and devoted as one would find in other kinds of adoptive families or in biological family units [p. 323].

It seems clear that whatever problems might be encountered in the future, the transracial adoptive experience is less problematic than had been anticipated during childhood and latency.

In attempting to answer the question of transracial adoptive outcome, the Child Welfare League in 1971 studied 125 children in transracial adoptive placements (Grow & Shapiro, 1974). At the time of the study, the children were at least six years of age and at the time had been in their adoptive home for three years or longer. On the average, the children were actually nine years of age and had been in their adoptive homes for over seven years. The study was done in seven different cities throughout the United States and Canada. Two in-depth interviews were held with the adoptive parents by experienced social workers not connected with the adoption agencies. The two interviews were held a year apart. In addition, the children were given some standard psychological tests and reports were obtained from their teachers. Grove and Shapiro concluded that the success rate of transracial adoptions (about 77 per cent) compared favorably with the success rate noted in studies of adoption by white families of white, nonhandicapped infants. Relatively little evidence was detected of problems of confusion or denial of racial background in the children studied, most of whom were pre-adolescent (Grow & Shapiro, 1975, p. iii). Most of the children were doing well in the home, in school, and in the community. Their scores on the California Test of Personality compared favorably with those of white adoptive children in white families. (See also Jackson, 1976.)

Zastrow (1977) in a study comparing the responses of white and transracial adoptive parents, found the levels of satisfaction in the adoption, for both groups, to be equally high, although Falk (1970) found transracial adoptive parents to have lower levels of satisfaction and to be somewhat less likely to say that they would repeat the experience. He found that these children were having more problems socially and in school than were white adoptees. In their survey of adoptive parents, Feigelman and Silverman (1983) also discovered that black children were more maladjusted than were whites. However, black children were also older at the time of placement. When the authors controlled for age, these differences in maladjustment rates disappeared (p. 98). As transracially adopted children grew older, an increasing number of them developed adjustment problems, according to their parents.

A highly pertinent question, affecting the future of transracial adoptions, involves the ability of white parents to encourage a sense of positive racial identity and pride in their black children. Equally important is the parents' ability to help the black child to develop sufficient survival skills to maintain a sense of positive self-esteem in a racist society.

The question of racial identity was the direct focus of a study of transracially adopted children conducted by Simon and Alstein (1977). They interviewed and employed projective techniques with 120 black children in white homes. The children ranged from three to eight years of age, the mean age being 4.4 (Table 6.3, p. 40). The procedures employed were a replication of those previously used in a variety of studies by others concerned with the perception of racial identity of black and white children living with their biological parents.

TABLE 9.9. Adoptive Outcome Studies of Transracial and Foreign Adoptions

Study and Date	Nature of Placement Difficulty	Size of Study Group and Lapse of Time Between Placement and Study	Outcome		Data Used for Follow-up Assessment
			Number and Percentages	Outcome Criteria for Categorization	
Graham (1957)	Foreign-born children	50 children (2–10 years after placement)	32 (64%)	"Satisfactory positive adjustment"	Interviews with parents and teachers
			13 (26%)	"Only fair"	
			5 (10%)	"Poor or very poor adjustment"	
Rathbun et al. (1964)	Foreign-born children	33 children (6 years after placement)	5 (15%)	"Superior"	Joint interviews with parents
			16 (49%)	"Adequate"	
			10 (30%)	"Problematic"	
			2 (6%)	"Disturbed"	
Zastrow (1977)	Nonwhite children	44 children (1–6 years after placement)	36 (88%)	"Extremely satisfying"	Interview with parents
			5 (11%)	"More satisfying than dissatisfying"	
			1 (1%)	"Half and half"	
Fanshel (1972)	Nonwhite children (native American)	97 children (starting with 1st year after placement, repeated annual interviews for 5 years)	51 (53%)	"Problem-free"	Joint interviews with parents; interviews with father-mother alone (repeated over 5-year period)
			24 (25%)	"Adequate"	
			10 (10%)	"Adequate but guarded"	
			11 (11%)	"Poor"	
Grow & Shapiro (1974)	Nonwhite children (black)	125 children	69% mothers/ 77% fathers	"Extremely satisfied"	Parent interviews; psychological testing of children; teacher questionnaire
			23% mothers/ 17% fathers	"More satisfied than dissatisfied"	
			5% mothers/ 4% fathers	"Equal mix"	
			3% mothers/ 2% fathers	"Mostly or all dissatisfied"	
			77%	"Child, family coping with some success"	
			23%	"Family in serious trouble"	

Study	Type of child	Sample	Outcome	Categories	Method
Jackson (1976)	Nonwhite children	49 (6 years after placement)	35 (72%) 10 (20%) 4 (8%)	"Highly satisfactory" "Satisfactory" "Problematic"	Group discussions; individual, taped interviews; questionnaires
Kim & Reid (1975)	Foreign-born children	72 (1–4 years after placement)	45 (62.5%) 24 (33%) 3 (4%)	"Adjusting very well" "Good adjustment" "Fair or poor adjustment"	Mailed questionnaire
Feigelman & Silverman (1983)	Nonwhite children (black)	47 families, compared with 65 families adopting white children	30% transracial/ 46% white 47% transracial/ 33% white 23% transracial/ 22% white	"Problem free" "Mostly well adjusted with some problems" "Frequent adjustment problems"	Mailed questionnaires
	Foreign-born children (Korean, Colombian)	46 Colombian, 298 Korean adoptive families	74% Colombian/ 65% Korean 15% Colombian/ 34% Korean	"Child's adjustment fully satisfactory" "Child has emotional adjustment problems sometimes or often"	Mailed questionnaires
Gill & Jackson (1983)	Foreign-born children	36 white parents, 8 black or mixed-race parents	94% fathers/ 92% mothers 3% fathers/ 8% mothers	"Describe relationship as positive but some negative elements" "Serious difficulties; question success of adoption"	Parent and child interviews
Shireman & Johnson (1986); Johnson, Shireman & Watson (1987)	Nonwhite children (black)	26 children 8 years after placement	72%	"Excellent or good Adjustment"	Parent reports; direct observation; standardized tests

The transracially adopted child living in a white family showed little bias in favor of whites. The black child's identification was as accurate as the white child's, which might not have been the case if the back children were rejecting of their blackness and preferred whiteness: "It appears that black children reared in the special setting of multiracial families do not acquire the ambivalence to their own race reported in all other studies involving black children" (p. 158). However, the fact that the mean age of the black children in the study group was 4.4, the age at which the sense of racial identity is just beginning to emerge, raises questions about the stability of the study results.

Grow and Shapiro (1974), examining adopted black children who were at least six years of age, report more disquieting findings. Anywhere from one-quarter to one-third of the children were reported as having some sort of negative feeling about being black. Parents said that one-third were proud of their racial heritage. "For a larger group (44%), the parents said either that they did not know the child's attitude or that he appeared indifferent. Twenty-four percent of the children were described as having attitudes with negative connotations: confusion, embarrassment, or anger" (p. 188). The parents' ability to accept and to encourage racial identification predicted more adequate functioning of the child on a variety of success-related measures.

Results of a mailed survey by Feigelman and Silverman (1983) replicate these results. Not all transracially adopting parents live in environments that encourage or allow the black child to explore his or her racial identity. Although two-thirds of these families lived in areas in which substantial numbers of black families were found, only 39 per cent had a significant number of black friends, and only half of their children had a significant number of black friends. Families who did attempt to live in a an integrated environment and who made explicit efforts to learn about black culture and to communicate about black issues with their children had children who were more likely to identify themselves as black and to express pride in their racial heritage (p. 108). A number of these transracially adopted children also had difficulty in identifying themselves as black. Nine per cent of the children in their samples perceived themselves as exclusively black; 54 per cent perceived themselves as both black and white; but 30 per cent described themselves as white, although they were black (p. 104).

Only three research efforts have compared the racial identity of transracially adopted black children with that of black children raised in black families. The subjects of Womack and Fulton's (1981) study were twenty transracially adopted black children and thirteen nonadopted black children. On the average, these children were five years old at the time of the study. Using the Preschool Racial Attitude Measure, the authors found no significant differences between these two groups. Although they expressed caution about extrapolating from their results, since the children were fairly young, they conclude, "from our research it would certainly appear that transracial adoption is a viable option for Black children who cannot be placed in permanent Black homes" (p. 723).

McRoy et al. (1982) conducted a study comparing the sense of racial identity and self-esteem of thirty black children adopted by white families with thirty black children adopted by black families. Using the Tennessee Self-Concept Scale, the authors found no differences between the children or their parents in these self-evaluation scores. However, like Feigelman and Silverman (1983), they found an association between parental evaluation of black culture and the child's sense of self:

> The data suggested that there was a positive relationship between the child's racial self-perceptions and the parents' perceptions of the child's attitude toward his or her racial background. Parents who viewed their children as being mixed or part white tended to have children who referred to themselves as mixed or part white. Parents who indicated that "human identity" or other characteristics such as intelligence or hobbies were more important than racial identity, and who discouraged the adopted child focusing on racial issues, tended to have children who were reluctant to refer to themselves as belonging to a particular racial group [McRoy et al., 1984, p. 36].

Sixty per cent of the white families attempted to adopt what the authors called a "color-blind" attitude about racial differences. Twenty per cent acknowledged their child's racial identity and attempted to live in an integrated community setting. Another 20 per cent had begun to perceive themselves as interracial families. These were families that were more likely to adopt several black children, and living in this integrated home environment, the children tended to have both black and white friends. In addition, with other black siblings in home, these children "found that they had a subsystem within the family which served as a psychological support network and thus a source of strength in dealing with racial encounters with peers or others" (p. 38). The researchers concluded that it is essential to evaluate the ability of white parents to actively foster and encourage a positive sense of self-worth in the child, one based on full awareness of the importance of racial identity.

In researching racial identification of transracially adopted children at age four and again at age eight, Shireman and Johnson (1986) found an interesting pattern. Whereas the black children in white homes identified themselves as black at both ages, the level of intensification of identity had not changed. This was unlike black children in black homes, whose sense of racial identification strengthened between ages four and eight. At age eight, 72 per cent of the transracially adopted children in the study were making a "excellent" or "good" adjustment. (See also Johnson, Shireman & Watson, 1987.)

Black–white adoptions are transracial but to some extent intracultural, since adoptee and adopter generally share the same langauge and many of the same customs. International adoptions are very often both transracial and more definitely transcultural.

Despite difficulties with prejudice and severely deprived early developmental experiences, follow-up studies of children born in other countries and subsequently adopted by Americans revealed good adjustment (DiViglio, 1956; Colville, 1957; Graham, 1957; Valk, 1957; Welter, 1965; Kim & Reid, 1975; Kim, 1977; Feigelman & Silverman, 1983). Feigelman & Silverman's (1983) research points to the importance of conducting differential assessments of children coming from various cultures, particularly when the racial background of these children evokes varying degrees of tolerance from others. Parents adopting Colombian children experience considerably less social disapproval, both within the immediate family and in less intimate social situations, than do white parents of Korean or black children. As a consequence, these parents seldom feel that their children will face significant social disapprobation or confront racial barriers to achieving their goals. However, parents of Colombian children who can pass for white are also far less likely to emphasize the child's racial heritage or to feel that it is helpful to the child's self-esteem to do so. When examining the adjustment of Korean adolescents, both racial pride, interest, and identification and a factor the authors call "shame," or uneasiness about one's appearance, influenced the overall functioning of these individuals (p. 169).

In general, research on transracial adoptions and on adoption of foreign-born children suggests that these children can develop into well-adjusted individuals who feel good about themselves and their lives. However, the data also repeatedly point out that parents play a particularly important role in helping their children successfully adapt. Not all adoptive parents make the necessary effort to help their children interact with others who are culturally and racially like them, and not all parents attempt to help their children successfully identify with their racial group. In fact, some actively ignore or deemphasize these issues. In these circumstances, their children will also be less likely to acknowledge their differences, and will be less well adjusted than they would be in more supportive family environments.

Problems in Adoption

We have noted some of the problems that are of concern to adoption agencies— the question of declining numbers of children surrendered for adoption, the problem of independent adoption, the problem of insufficient placements for special-needs children, the problem of adoptive disruptions, the problems associated with adoptees' rights and the "search." Some additional problems are discussed.

1. Despite our discussion of the increased possibilities of adoptive placement for children with special needs—the minority-group child, the older child, the handicapped child—finding sufficient adoptive placements for such children continues to present a problem. This is particularly true for the children with multiple deterrents to placement: older minority-group children, minority-group children with handicaps, older children with handicaps, and so on.

With the continuing shortage of white, unhandicapped infants, the definition of *hard-to-place* tends to be revised in the direction of greater difficulty. In 1985 the hard-to-place child was over ten years of age, of minority race, moderately retarded, or physically handicapped.

In 1978 ARENA (Adoption Resource Exchange of North America) had about one thousand children registered with them, 46 per cent of whom were described as slow or retarded; 55 per cent of the children needing homes were school-aged black children, seven years of age or older. It is probably true that no child can or should be identified as "unadoptable," yet it is true that some children are more difficult to place or are less adoptable than other children. The reality is that many more people than are needed come to the agency to offer their homes to white, unhandicapped infants. Very few applicants offer their homes to the mentally retarded or the physically handicapped child needing placement.

Simon and Altstein (1977) substantiate the fact that the willingness to accept one kind of child with special needs does not necessarily suggest willingness to accept another kind of hard-to-place child. Although the parents in their study had all adopted a child of a different race, only 14 per cent indicated a willingness to accept a child as old as five years of age. The mentally retarded child was acceptable to only 1 per cent of the group, and only 8 per cent indicated that they would have been willing to adopt a child with a physical handicap "if they could not have obtained the child they did" (p. 86).

A study of the operations of the New York State adoption exchange indicated the limited interest in the special-needs children available for adoption (Grossman, Epstein, & Nelson, 1976). In January 1975, of the 1,346 families listed, 94 per cent "would accept only a white child under 4 without a handicap. Only 5 percent were interested in adopting a black child" (p. 1).

Although it is true that some applicants have an initial preference for a special-needs child because of ideology, political orientation, a heightened sense of civic responsibility, or some personal experience, this group of adopters is decidedly a minority. It would be unrealistic to expect that the problem of adoption of special-needs children could ever begin to be resolved by the preferences of this small group of applicants. Hence the agency has to educate the community to the availability of such children; actively seek homes through outreach; actively motivate prospective adoptive parents to accept such children; remove disincentives to such adoption by modifying requirements, by prompt home studies, and by immediate placement; and intensify incentives by offering support subsidies for maintenance and medical care.

As the pressure to free those children who have remained in foster care for some time intensifies, the likelihood is that a larger number of older minority-group children will require agency service in finding homes. This presents a problem for the agencies because placement of special-needs children requires considerable time, effort, and skill. It may take two and one half times as long to place older children as it does to place infants.

2. At the same time that children with special needs wait for long periods to find permanent families, agency practices and procedures can place obstacles in the way of individuals who are potentially interested in adopting them. As noted earlier, qualifying requirements that individuals must meet in order to be considered as potential adopters have been developed in an attempt to ensure that families have resources and personnel to easily care for a child. Thus, agencies seek families who have sufficient income, two parents, available extended family, and so forth. Although these characteristics are helpful to families, they are not mandatory for adequate parenting. Evidence shows that some poor, single, divorced adults can raise both birth and adopted children and can do so as well as more traditional families have done (Feigelman & Silverman, 1983; Shireman & Johnson, 1976).

Yet agencies continue to rely on these criteria, even though they screen out potential families for needy children:

> One study surveyed 92 agencies and found the majority continue to have requirements about the length of the current marriage, the presence of other children in the home, and infertility in the couples. A minority had minimum income and minimum space requirements.
>
> In addition, agencies have often barred entire groups of people from becoming prospective adoptive parents. For many years foster parents were not considered suitable adoptive parents and were barred from applying by agency policy and court decision. Single parents have also been barred from consideration by some agencies [Meezan, 1983b, p. 34].

Historically, religious requirements created barriers for potential adoptive families. Parents were required to be of the same religious background as the adopted child or to come from the religious background in which the birth parent wanted the child raised. This created difficulties for individuals from some religious groups, such as Jewish parents, since the number of available Jewish children was relatively low. Inequity was also imposed on the nonreligious applicant.

This individual was penalized for his or her agnosticism and was usually unable to qualify as an applicant for any child. The American Ethical Union, a society of humanists, expressed the perspective of this group:

> Americans, providing that they meet all other standards, deserve equal opportunity to adopt children openly, without having to profess a religion to which they do not honestly subscribe, through legitimate adoption channels. In this area, as in any other, there should be no discrimination on the basis of religious beliefs [*New York Times*, October 11, 1959].

The Child Welfare League of America (1973) suggested that although the religious faith of the natural parent should be respected and, wherever possible, followed in the selection of an adoptive home for the child, "placement of children should not be restricted, in general, to homes with formal church affiliation" (p. 25).

It is somewhat ironic that financial requirements imposed by some agencies may prevent the adopted child from moving into a home in which values and goals are similar to that of the child's birth family. Instead, the child is usually placed in a more middle class family setting, one in which he or she may not be sufficiently achievement-oriented to satisfy the parents. Financial requirements may also stand in the way of development of intra-racial adoptive homes for non-white children. Evelyn Moore, the Executive Director of the National Black Child Development Institute, comments that adoption officials, relying on what she called "white middle-class standards," turn away many lower-income and working-class potential black adopters, encouraging them to become foster parents instead (*NASW News*, October 1984, p. 3).

Single parents are also provided unequal access to the adoption system. Although some agencies are willing to assess their suitability for a particular child, they are usually only considered for severely handicapped children or for those who have disrupted out of two-parent placements (Feigelman & Silverman, 1983; Smith & Sherwen, 1983). Some countries refuse to allow single individuals to adopt, and courts and adoption agencies within the United States offer them little assistance. Other parents have been discouraged from exploring the possibility of adoption because they are fertile or because they already have children in their home. Particularly in cases in which families are seeking to adopt infants, agencies have tended to invoke these criteria.

Single gay or lesbian applicants face a double barrier—singleness and sexual preference. Discouraged from applying and frequently rejected when they do, this group of applicants has rarely achieved adoption. The *New York Times* (June 21, 1979) reported the adoption of a thirteen-year-old boy by a homosexual minister. The report went on to note that "adoptions by homosexual men and women have taken place in several states in recent years" according to the former director of the National Gay Task Force. "A couple of dozen cases were quietly negotiated with full knowledge of local adoption offices." On January 10, 1983, the *New York Times* reported another such atypical, infrequent adoption.

Increased public awareness of the availability of adopted children and expanded public interest in exploring this childrearing option have led to greater pressure on agencies to reexamine these and other adoption requirements. In particular, agencies must differentiate more carefully mandatory from "preferential" criteria. Being able to provide a child with a warm and loving home, to teach a child to live within the law and to care about and respect others are "mandatory" demands that parents must fulfill. Providing the child with a comfortable standard of living, the sole attention of a nonworking mother, or with an exact religious upbringing are "preferential" requirements whose violation will do no essential harm to the ultimate health and welfare of the child. Particularly to meet the needs of the many waiting special needs children, but ultimately to meet the needs of any adopted child, closer scrutiny of these demands is required.

In the absence of such examination, public attitudes toward social service agencies remain skeptical. Adoption workers are accused of being arbitrary, of "playing God," of unnecessarily withholding children from families, and so on. It is partly because of these feelings that the public has not more vigorously supported efforts to legislate against independent placements, and there is still considerable controversy as to whether social workers should be given primary control of adoptions. Adoption concerns social relationships. Adoption "creates" parent–child relationships, and directly affects marriages. Clearly, then, according to our definition of child welfare, it is within the professional responsibility of the social work community. Yet social workers have not succeeded in convincing the public that they should be primarily, if not exclusively, responsible for bringing parentless children and childless "parents" together.

3. The structure of child welfare services and the nature of interagency relationships may also interfere with effective adoption planning. Caseworkers working in foster or institutional care may still consider these children "unadoptable" and may, therefore, find it difficult to facilitate planning for permanent homes for them. Potential parents who have expressed interest in these children have, at times, been actively discouraged, particularly when children are institutionalized (Knitzer & Olson, 1982, p. 68). Meezan (1983a) points out that, because foster and adoptive services are two distinct units within many agencies, workers may find it difficult to coordinate planning and move toward timely adoption preparation. This is problematic, for example, in the case of children whose parents are mentally ill.

4. Interwoven with and further complicating these issues are questions about the relative "rights" of birth parents, adoptive parents, and the adopted child. Under what circumstances do parents have the right to a child's return, even if they have engaged in unacceptable behavior or have had other problems that have interfered with or prevented their ability to carry out child-care responsibilities? On the other hand, at what point does the child's need for permanency outweigh the need to wait for the parent to remediate family problems? Recently, priority has been given to meeting the permanency needs of children (Goldstein, Freud, & Solnit, 1973, 1979; Sachdev, 1984a). This, in turn, has placed increased pressure on birth parents. As Kadushin (1984) notes:

> Rather than an assumption that needs no proof, more frequently now than before, the continued claim of biological parents on their child must be validated by their satisfying specific statutory reqirements. Courts, or community review boards, are charged with periodically reviewing the situation of all children in substitute care to determine whether the biological parents have maintained regular contact, whether the parents are making effective use of agency service so as to make likely the child's return home to a safe situation, and whether the parents are likely to be ultimately capable of providing adequate care for the child. Failure to meet these stipulations provides grounds for termination of parental rights [p. 7].

The reasonableness of these demands has been called into question in situations in which poverty, ill health, or mental problems, which are beyond the control of the parent, seriously interfere with his or her ability to adequately respond to them. In addition, questions arise concerning the disservice done to parents in situations in which they must make major life changes but are given insufficient agency assistance in order to do so, or in situations where they are required to maintain regular contacts with their children but are not provided sufficient access to them. Here, agency programming, personnel or policies may help ensure that parental rights will be terminated, in some instances in which appropriate remedial and preventive parent work would have led to the reunification of the child and parents. Without adequate attention to the rights and needs of the birth family, there is some concern that current adoptive efforts will "redistribute" children from working-class or poverty homes into middle-class families (Pascall, 1984; Kadushin, 1984).

5. For children who have already been placed with adoptive families, serious difficulties have arisen because of the lack of sufficient follow-up services offered by either the adoption agency or other community agencies. Traditionally, social services have been perceived as residual services, available to families who are failing in performance of their social roles. Applying this to adoption situations, it has been assumed that, because children are placed in well-functioning families, no follow-up programming should be needed. Only in unusual circumstances, this view suggests, would special mental health or other supportive services be required. Even when families have adopted disturbed or handicapped children, it has been assumed that good parenting would, for the most part, overcome any trauma the child had undergone—that, in fact, love and a healthy family life would "conquer all." This has proven illusory for many families. "Separated from primary caretakers at whatever age, poorly attached to any one permanent family, exposed to a variety of life-styles, often abused by someone in the process, these children have complex problems that need to be addressed" (Reitnauer & Grabe, 1985, p. 16). Even in instances in which children are functioning fairly effectively in their adoptive homes, they frequently have special issues—questions of loyalty and trust—that prove difficult for parents to respond to efficiently on their own. Follow-up services may be required on a short- or longer-term basis for many families and, as we have pointed out previously, services may be required some years after the child's placement has been finalized.

However, many agencies do not routinely offer follow-up, even in instances in which children have serious behavior problems. "Unfortunately, many agencies and agency workers were playing the same kind of Russian roulette, putting a 'loaded gun' into a famly and hoping the shell would not go off at least not until after finalization" (Reitnauer & Grabe, 1985, p. 6). In addition, mental health and social service workers may not be sufficiently familiar with the needs of these chidren or the special issues involved in adoption to help families adequately cope with difficulties that do arise. Using a questionnaire administered to 141 mental health professionals and 85 adoptive parents in southwestern Pennsylvania, Reitnauer & Grabe (1985) found that professionals were generally less knowledgeable than the adoptive parents about the child welfare system or the current state of the art in child welfare. They were not sufficiently familiar with the children who are typical clients of this system and had misperceptions of the motives of adoptive families. When parents contact social service agencies, attempting to get help, professionals sometimes assumed that they must be trying to get rid of their children.

6. The impact of placing nonwhite children in white homes continues to concern the child welfare profession. In these cases, commitment to racial integra-

tion and assimilation clashes with ideals of cultural pluralism, black autonomy, and black separatism. The idea that a white home is better than no home at all clashes with the contention that "a home and love are not enough to pay for loss of identity" (Ladner, 1977, p. 86).

Transracial adoption suggests white paternalism, a rejection of black values and life-style, and a rejection of racial roots. In addition to the charge that transracial adoption results in a loss of the child's identification with the black community, there is the further accusation that transracial adoption is a procedure designed primarily to meet the needs of white adoptive applicants who lack white children to adopt rather than to meet the needs of nonwhite children, and that a more concerted effort could be made to find nonwhite homes. Transracial adoptions would then be only one approach—and a limited one at that—of a more comprehensive campaign involving a number of different procedures to find homes for nonwhite children.

In April 1972, the National Association of Black Social Workers went on record as being in "vehement opposition" to the placement of black children with white families and called transracial adoptions "a growing threat to the preservation of the black family" (*New York Times,* April 12, 1972). The Association maintains this stance today. Canadian and American Indian groups also complain of similar problems in offering services to Indian children (U.S. Department of Health & Human Services, 1981b; Ryant, 1984). Federal law now mandates that Native American children must be placed with Native American families.

Day (1979) summarizes the issues when she states:

> There are blind spots on both sides in the debate on transracial adoption. Those who advocate transracial adoption tend to ignore the discrimination against would-be Black adopters. Those who oppose whites adopting Black children tend to ignore the thousands of Black children who need permanent homes. With such thousands waiting, it is hard to see how even a spectacular recruitment effort could provide enough Black homes. Since this is so, it is appropriate to consider the question of which whites, among those expressing an interest, ought to be permitted to adopt Black children [p. 112].

The findings of a variety of studies indicate that some transracial adopters are not willing to recognize the child's racial heritage as different from their own. This, in turn, threatens the child's sense of identity and self-esteem (Feigelman & Silverman, 1983; McRoy et al., 1982) and poorly prepares the child to cope with racism that he or she will confront in our society. The dilemma faced by the adoption worker is how to evaluate potential parents to determine which of them can effectively respond to these racial identity related needs of the child and which cannot.

7. With the decrease in the number of children available for adoption, adoptive agencies are beginning to face a question of survival. In the early 1970s, such agencies were beginning to diversify their functions, moving out from adoption to family counseling and family-life education. Such diversification provides the agency with a useful service to occupy staff. A small percentage of agencies have chosen to discontinue their adoption service altogether. Other agencies have reduced staff.

It is likely that the next two decades will see a reduction in the demand for adoptive services. Low birthrates after 1955–1960 in North America and Europe will result in a smaller group of adopters in the near future. The twenty-five to thirty-five age group, which supplies the largest number of adoptive applicants, is likely to be smaller than it has been during the 1970s.

Technological and ideological factors may also decrease the level of adoptive demand. Childlessness has become increasingly accepted as an optional life-style. The decision not to become a parent no longer requires an apology nor occasions as much discomfort as it previously did. The concern regarding population growth and the ideology of the women's movement contribute toward the growing acceptance of childlessness. As a consequence, more infertile couples may choose to adjust to their situation by accepting their childlessness rather than attempting to change their situation through adoption.

At the same time, other factors point to some increasing demand for adoptive children. Because women have been waiting to bear a first child until later in their adult years, more women in their thirties, when they attempt to have a child, discover that they cannot do so and turn to adoption as an alternative. Sterility has also increased. "The proportion of currently married women of child-bearing age who were able to bear children decreased from 73.0% to 61.6% during the period 1965 through 1976" (Bachrach, 1983, pp. 863–864). Although most of these women are sterile for contraceptive purposes, there has also been an increase in the number of childless women who have found it difficult to conceive.

On the supply side there may be a continued long-term reduction in the number of children available for adoption. The single-mother-out-of-wedlock-child family is only one type of single-parent female-headed family. Any policy changes to the advantage of the growing number of single-parent female-headed families generally will be an advantage to the never-married mother as well. Special measures such as housing for single-parent families, increases in day-care facilities, and special maintenance allowances for single-parent families will reduce the difficulties of keeping and caring for the child of the unmarried mother as well as of other single parents. Consequently such mothers are likely to be in a better position in the future to raise their own child rather than surrendering it for adoption. Policy changes are likely to move in the direction of reducing disincentives to surrender the child for adoption.

The general climate of social attitudes has changed in a direction that makes it easier for the unmarried mother to keep and raise her child. Less stigma and social rejection are associated with the status of unmarried mother. An increasingly neutral, less punitive attitude toward the unmarried mother attenuates the incentives toward surrender.

Demographic changes during the next decade will also result in a probable reduction in the number of children available for adoption. The low birthrates of 1975–1985 project a smaller group of adolescents and young adults in the near future. This is the age group for which the rate of illegitimacy is highest and for whom the difficulties in keeping and raising the child are greatest. The pressure of circumstances predisposing to surrender are great for this group, as well as the pressure from significant others, such as parents, on whom the adolescent is likely to be dependent. A decrease in the size of this group will decrease the number of children available for adoption.

It is not likely that with reductions in the number of white, unhandicapped infants available, a continuing high number of nonrelative adoptions will be made. There are currently a sizable number of older, handicapped, minority-group children available for adoption. The number of such children available is likely to increase as foster-care agencies review their case loads and move more actively toward the termination of parental rights of those parents who have manifested little, if any, consistent continuing interest in their child. But if past experience in the shortage of white, unhandicapped infants is suggestive, only a small percentage of potential adopters are likely to move to adopt such newly released children. A larger percentage of potential adopters, moving down the hierarchy of preferences, soon reach a point where the decision not to adopt at all is more acceptable than the decision to adopt the kind of child who is available.

These changes suggest, in general, that reductions in both supply of and demand for adoptable children may result in fewer completed adoptions. On the other hand, increases in the number of infertile women seeking to have children, when combined with reductions in the availability of infants for adoption, suggest increased pressure on both the independent and international adoption markets as sources of these children.

The pattern of supply and demand also suggests that public child welfare agencies can increasingly turn their attention to finding adoptive placements for children in foster care and for other special-needs children. Because fewer infants are available for adoptive homes, increased staff time should be available to provide more concerted and intensive services, both during and after the placement, to families seeking to parent these special children.

Trends

We have previously noted a number of trends in adoption. Perhaps of most pervasive influence has been the decrease in the number of infants available and the resultant heightened attention paid to the adoption of older, handicapped, and other special-needs children; the adoption of children from other countries; and the search for infants through the gray or black markets or through independent adoption procedures. A number of additional trends in the field reflect the concern for widening the pool of parents available to adopt children, greater awareness of the child's need to identify with his or her past, and increased use of adoptive parents organizations and other types of self-help mechanisms to stabilize adoptive families, once children have been placed with them. These and other trends are described as follows:

1. The growing search for adoptive homes for special-needs children has produced a wide range of efforts to reach out and to encourage potential parents to explore the possibility of caring for these children in their homes. Earlier, we discussed the use of various publicity techniques to advertise children who are available in local communities. More widespread efforts have also been made to inform adoption agencies and potential adoptive parents when children are available.

Adoption resource exchange has been defined by the Child Welfare League as "an organized means of exchanging information among agencies about children for whom they have difficulty finding appropriate homes and about adoptive applicants for whom they have no suitable children" (Felton, 1953, p. 26). Ohio was the first to originate a statewide exchange, and now most tend to be an intrastate resource. Exchanges now operate on both regional and national levels as well to promote home-finding for seriously handicapped children.

The adoption exchange has the advantage of increasing the opportunities for placement because it makes available a larger pool of potential adopters for the child and a larger pool of children for the applicant (Jaquith, 1962). Agencies list the children available for placement with a central adoption-resource exchange.

A summary of the essential descriptive data accompanies each name. At the same time, the agencies send summaries of data on adoptive parents who are waiting for children and who have expressed an interest in and a capacity for accepting hard-to-place children.

Adoption exchanges are of the greatest immediate benefit to the hard-to-place child. Schapiro (1957) notes that "state experience with adoption clearance services shows that almost all of the children placed through them are children of minority groups and mixed racial parentage [and] those who are older [or] handicapped" (p. 46). Leatherman (1957) cites the Texas Adoption Exchange as an important factor in the adoptive placement of a sizable number of older children.

In 1967 the Child Welfare League of America established a National Adoption Resource Exchange that included the Canadian agencies and was known as ARENA (Adoption Resource Exchange of North America). The Adoption Reform Act of 1978 provided for a federally sponsored national adoption information exchange using computers and data-processing methods to identify children waiting for homes and parents interested in them. The act provided funding for an organization to supersede ARENA, called NAIES (National Adoption Information Exchange System). Monies were also provided to establish the National Exchange at one central location, the Adoption Center of Delaware Valley in Philadelphia.

Statewide exchange programs continue to function and to coordinate their services with those provided by the National Exchange. As of 1981, twenty-nine states had established exchanges, and an additional ten had information referral services. Ten states published photo listing books that provide pictures and background information about children awaiting homes (Feigelman & Silverman, 1983, p. 32).

Despite these efforts, exchanges have succeeded in placing fairly small numbers of children. Between 1967, when it was organized, and 1976, ARENA placed a total of 1,760 children. This averages somewhat less than 200 children placed each year. More effective use of exchanges has proved problematic for a number of reasons. Meezan (1980) points out that smooth interagency cooperation, which their effective use requires, has been sometimes difficult to achieve. Social service agencies using exchanges for data on children or available families must feel that they can rely on other users to provide valid and comprehensive information. In several instances, they have been disappointed. Other complex issues have arisen concerning the fine line between honest portrayal and attractive presentation of children seeking homes. Deciding that without sufficient opportunity to explain children's difficult characteristics, families will precipitously refuse to consider them, workers have sometimes withheld this information. Without these data, however, adoptive parents have felt that they were deliberately misled.

Recently, both private and federal agencies have attempted to disseminate information about available children through publications. The North American Council on Adoptable Children has published *Adoption in America,* a directory that can be utilized by both agencies and families. Other federal efforts have described specially funded programs to encourage or disseminate information about adoption (U.S. DHHS, 1980a; 1980b).

2. Adoption maintenance subsidy is another incentive designed to increase adoptive placements for special-needs children. Based on their nationwide survey of children receiving public child welfare service, Shyne and Schroeder (1978) estimated that a total of 102,000 children were legally free for adoption but that

one-third of the group required an adoption subsidy if they were to be placed (p. 125). Most of these were children older than nine years of age. The Child Welfare League of America adoption standards recommended consideration of subsidized adoptions as early as 1958. In 1968 New York became the first state to enact such legislation. Within the next ten years, a total of forty-one states and the District of Columbia adopted such a program.

Advocates backed the subsidy concept because, they argued, it offers the child a guarantee of continuity, stability, permanence, and the identity of a family name. In addition, subsidies were perceived as cost effective, more economical for the community than long-term substitute care. These considerations led the United States Children's Bureau to formulate a model state-subsidized adoption act (Katz & Gallagher, 1976). The model act recommended that states adopt the position that the needs of the child for an adoptive home be the central basis for providing subsidy and that the financial condition of the adoptive family not be a major consideration. However, states vary considerably in the extent to which their subsidy laws reflect these provisos.

More uniformity in subsidy legislation was mandated by the Adoption Assistance and Child Welfare Act of 1980, P.L. 96-272. It provided that all states must have in place provisions for subsidy for children having "special needs." When the child is handicapped in some way, part of an adoptive sibling group, an older child, or a member of a minority group, that child is eligible for subsidy when being adopted by foster parents. When placed with adoptive families who had not fostered the child, subsidies can be provided if the agency has attempted to provide an adoptive home without subsidy and has been unable to do so.

The act stipulates that the amount of subsidy should be determined prior to placement of the child in the adoptive home and a written agreement to this effect be given to the adoptive family. The amount of subsidy cannot exceed current foster care payment levels, and subsidies can be continued until the child reaches eighteen or, in the case of severe handicap, until the child is twenty-one. The act also provides that states must continue to offer subsidies, even if the family subsequently moves away from that state. All states except Hawaii now have subsidy legislation, and Hawaii's regulations are covered by an administrative rule (Waldinger, 1982).

Subsidized adoption has, in fact, achieved the objective of increasing the adoption opportunities of children with special needs. A recapitulation of subsidized adoptions in six states—Connecticut, Illinois, Iowa, New Jersey, New York, and Vermont—indicated that "the largest proportion of children adopted were over 6 in every state" (Jones, 1975, p. 738). Many were physically handicapped, mentally retarded, or emotional disturbed, and a disproportionate percentage were black. Almost 90 per cent of the children adopted through the subsidized adoption program were adopted by their foster parents.

Subsidized adoptions provide maintenance payments to help families meet the routine expenses of rearing adoptive children. They are, therefore, of special assistance to foster families, who have relied on that income to help provide child support, and to low-income families who could not otherwise afford to adopt a child. The legislation is designed to make more adoptive homes available for hard-to-place children.

In addition to providing regular maintenance payments, some states have offered special-service subsidies to cover the legal and court costs of adoption, remedial education, speech and hearing therapy, physiotherapy, wheelchairs, braces, and other special expenses. An agency might agree to a time-limited subsidy to permit a family to adjust to the loss of a wife's earnings when she leaves her job upon placement of the child. These are special, time-limited transitional uses of subsidy, used to ensure the success of the placement (Sternau, 1959; Wheeler, 1969).

A special direct-service demonstration project conducted in Chicago in 1972–1974 indicates the value of and the problems associated with subsidized adoption (Hargrave, Shireman, & Connor, 1975). The project established the "adoptability of black children in foster care," and "subsidy was clearly a casework tool of considerable importance" in making this possible (p. 45). A group of physically handicapped children also achieved adoption with the help of subsidies.

Results of subsidy experiences in Cincinnati, Ohio, are similar. Among the 271 children receiving such support as of December, 1980, almost three out of four were black and more than two out of three were placed with foster parents. One third of these children had low IQs, and one in three was severely emotionally impaired. The subsidies were provided to a number of adoptive parents raising children on low or fixed incomes. Forty-five per cent of the adopters had incomes that were less than half of the average for the state of Ohio.

One study (CSR, 1983) has examined the broader impact of passage of 96-272 on subsidy provisions in several states. The varied experiences of program personal and parents in nine different states were evaluated, and the authors conclude:

> First . . . the Federal funds allow more children to move from foster care to perma-
> nent care, thus providing these children with a stable family environment . . . Sec-
> ond, assisted adoption reduces the financial burden on the public. Data suggest that
> adoption assistance represents an average savings of $886 per child per year when
> compared with the cost of foster care. While the net effects are still unclear, the
> return on each public dollar allocated to subsidy is expected to increase [p. x].

Critics of subsidy programs have been concerned that provision of regular payments to adoptive families would make them dependent upon the welfare system, rather than self-sufficient. In addition, they have been concerned that receipt of these payments would segregate and stigmatize adoptive children. But their primary concern has been the overall cost of this program (Shaffer, 1981; Ward, 1984; Freeman, 1984). Proponents of subsidy programs have countered by pointing out that maintenance of special-needs children in foster or institutional settings would be far more financially burdensome than these payments. Cost projections have invariably suggested the economy of adoption subsidies, compared to these alternatives (Jones, 1975, pp. 723, 740, 742; Waldinger, 1982). However, supporters too have expressed concern over costs, particularly if federal support were to be terminated at some future date (CSR, 1983).

A continuing concern about availability of subsidy is that increased pressure might be placed on foster parents to adopt children when they might, otherwise, refuse to do so. Foster parents, fearing the loss of the child, might acquiesce to more permanent arrangements, even when they have serious reservations. Waldinger (1982) found that it was in poorer foster families who had many children and in those families where the foster parents, being older, were concerned about their ability to provide long-term care, that greater reluctance to change from foster to adoptive status was voiced. (See also Proch, 1980; Raynor, 1980). On the other hand, it has been argued that, in cases in which families are reluctant to make permanent commitments to children, it might be better for this fact to be brought out in the open and dealt with by both the family and the child. Potential availability of adoption subsidies might be a catalyst for the family to clarify its commitments (Ward, 1984).

Evidence suggests that subsidy has assisted in placement of adoptive children, particularly those with special needs, and that it has been most helpful to families who have the fewest financial resources for raising children. However, availability of subsidies has not led to major increases in the number of adoptions of this type across the country. As Freeman (1984) says,

> Subsidized adoption is a good idea but it is not a panacea and we must not expect too much of it. It would be surprising if when fully operational through out (*sic*) the country there were over 500 adoption allowances approved in a year . . . Subsidized adoption has enabled some Black families to adopt Black children, has ensured that some handicapped children grow up in the warmth and security of a family environment, and has given some older children the security of knowing that their psychological parents are their legal parents. It will continue to do so [pp. 220–221].

3. Adoptive parent organizations have played an increasingly important role in the adoption process, carrying out advocacy, educative, social support, and recruitment functions. Working on their own, and in extensive collaboration with adoption agencies, they have helped in the tasks of finding adoptive families and maintaining adoption homes, once children have been placed. These groups have proven to be effective advocates for children, helping to disseminate the viewpoint that all children deserve permanent homes and that even multiproblem and severely impaired children can find loving families. Adoptive parent organizations have been instrumental in the passage of federal legislation that has significantly enhanced adoption opportunities.

Adoptive parent groups now exist in every state, and they serve as central sources of information and support for both potential adoptive families and for those who have completed the adoption process. Parent groups typically collect interstate and local information about waiting children and disseminate this information as widely as possible to potential parents. In addition, many of these organizations publish regular newsletters, providing suggestions about adoptive child care, information about resources, and other significant information for adopters. National parent organizations have also published newsletters. One of the most widely known of these is the Organization for United Response (OURS). The OURS Newsletter contains information provided by parents about interracial, international, and other types of adoptive experiences. The Newsletter also includes descriptions of special-needs children awaiting homes. More specialized newsletters are published by the Committee by Single Adoptive Parents and the Latin American Parents Association.

Parents active in adoptive parent organizations have made themselves available to other adoptive families who might need information, respite, support, or other types of assistance. In their survey, Feigelman and Silverman (1983) discovered an

> affinity between the trend to knowingly adopt a disabled child and affiliation with an adoptive parent group. . . . This evidence seems to suggest enormously effective social networks within adoptive parent organizations. Such networks provide knowledge about disabled children available for adoption; they offer social reward and encouragement to families who adopt such children; and they furnish substantial

support, information, and counsel for dealing with the issues that parents of handicapped children inevitably confront [p. 52].

The researchers found that almost one in four of the families in which parents
were active organizational participants had adopted two or more children within
a six-year period. 66 of these families had adopted 120 special-needs children
(p. 54).

Federal recognition of the significance of parent group activity of this type has
been reflected in the provision of limited federal grants to parent organizations to
assist them in carrying out advocacy and educational functions. In addition, some
adoption agencies have worked very closely with parent groups, using them extensively during both informational and follow-up sessions. National leadership for
adoptive parent organizations has been provided by the North American Council
on Adoptable Children, which publishes *Adoptalk,* a newsletter providing information about adoption, resources, and activities throughout the country.

In addition to these more organized efforts, individual publications are also
available to individuals interested in learning more about adoption. Writers have
attempted to guide adopters through the agency process and to provide them with
information about potential problems that may encounter with adopted children
or adoption agencies. Recent publications include Gilman's *Adoption Resource
Book* (1984), Wishard and Wishard's *Adoption: The Grafted Tree* (1979), and
Martin's *Beating the Adoption Game* (1980).

4. Increasing attention has been paid to making timely decisions about the
development of permanent homes for children who are in care. The Model Act to
Free Children for Permanent Placement, published by the federal government as
a guideline for state legislation, recommends that when children have been removed from the family home for a period of one year and the family has not made
sufficient progress toward the child's return, parental rights be terminated and a
permanent adoptive home be found for the child. There have been some recommendations that timing of permanency decisions be based on the age of the child,
with planning done more rapidly in the case of younger children. (See, for example, Ayres, 1985). The longer a child remains in foster care, the more difficult it is
to ensure a successful placement when parental rights are finally terminated
(Borgman, 1981). The trend toward expenditious resolution of the child's status
may make for more adoptions and more successful adoptions.

5. All adoptive families must struggle with the realization that adopted children have a history that differs in significant respects from that of children born
in the family. In our discussion of telling and search issues, it was evident that
current practice wisdom supports the significance of open sharing with the child
about his or her history. Sharing is considered to have positive impact on the
child's sense of self-esteem, since parental communication that the past is worthwhile suggests to the child that he or she need not be ashamed of it. In addition,
sharing has positive repercussions for the adoptive family as a whole, since it
reflects the members' commitment to greater openness and honesty with each
other (Jewett, 1978). Review of the research on search activities also suggests,
however, that both adoptive parents and their children vary in the degree to
which they consider exploration of the past important and the extend to which
they feel comfortable discussing it.

Realizing the significance of the child's past history has led to recommendations that, in some instances, "open adoption" procedures be used. "An open
adoption is one in which the birth parents meet the adoptive parents, participate

in the separation and placement process, relinquish all legal, moral and nurturing rights to the child, but retain the right to continuing contact and to knowledge of the child's whereabouts and welfare" (Baran, Pannor, & Sorosky, 1976, p. 97; see also Borgman, 1982; Amadio & Deutsch, 1983). What Kraft et al. (1985) call "confidential" adoptions now routinely take place. That is, adoptive parents and birth parents are provided with general nonidentifying information. In open adoptions, on the other hand, the birth and adoptive families receive identifying information about each other, and explicit plans may be made for ongoing contact between the two families. Support for the judicious use of open adoption procedures was incorporated in the Model Adoptions Act, legislation that the federal government recommends that individual states adopt as law.

Use of open adoption procedures is explicitly recommended in two circumstances. Concern that their children may not find adoptive homes or may not be treated well in them has prevented some birth parents from relinquishing parental rights. Availability of open adoption may provide them with sufficient security to give up rights to children whom they cannot adequately parent. In particular, some young unwed parents may be less reluctant to terminate rights to their infants if they have some opportunity to obtain information about their subsequent welfare (Baran, Pannor, & Sorosky, 1976). Children who are in their latency or teenage years may also be more comfortable considering adoption if they are not required to relinquish all contact with their birth families or others who have been significant to them. As Borgman (1982) notes, most older children "find it extremely difficult, if not impossible, to suddenly erase ten or more years of relationships, experience, and family history without endangering their basic security and self-identity. For these school-age children, open adoption may be preferable" (p. 219).

The concept of open adoption provides a serious challenge to traditional adoption procedures, requirements, and regulations that have, for the most part, been designed to explicitly protect confidentiality and to sever the child's ties with the birth family. Whereas critics have argued that providing for open adoption flies in the face of tradition (Zeilinger, 1982), proponents claim that open adoptions have been successfully practiced in other places and at others times, and that, this was, in fact, common practice in the United States, particularly prior to World War II (Baran, Pannor, & Sorosky, 1976).

Open adoptions are seen as beneficial for birth parents who can be reassured about their child's well-being and who need not make decisions to never contact their child again, while they are making the difficult decision to relinquish rights to that child. On the other hand, it has been argued that the availability of open adoptions may make decision making too complex and difficult for some birth parents, particularly adolescents (Kraft et al., 1985). Having opportunities to reestablish relationships with their child, they may find it harder to confront the reality of their relinquishment and to mourn the loss of their child in a healthy way. Similarly, critics of open adoption have suggested that the children themselves may not adjust as rapidly in the adoptive home when they continue to have the opportunity to periodically meet with birth parents.

Borgman (1982) offers opposing arguments. Faced with the opportunity to reestablish contact with birth parents, many children may find that they no longer are interested in doing so. Adolescents, especially those who fantasize that their birth parents will rescue them, may find it very helpful to have to meet with those parents and to deal with them as they are. (See also Smith & Sherwen, 1983, p. 132.) Borgman also suggests that there are inconsistencies in our assumptions about children that interfere with our acceptance of the notion that they can tolerate the requirements of this type of adoptive situation:

> Foster care practice encourages continued involvement between the child and biological family, expecially when the plan is directed toward rehabilitating the parents. But when adoptive planning begins, the child is suddenly expected to terminate or reduce involvement with parents and relatives. The author has found this externally imposed expectation to be experienced as arbitrary and bewildering; at worst it stimulates guilt and unworthiness in the child, and often cuts the child off from accustomed sources of emotional support and security when they are needed to face the uncertainties of adoption [p. 223].

Critics have been concerned that adoptive parents, some of whom oppose the notion of open adoption, would not tolerate this practice (Zeilinger, 1982). Proponents have argued that adoptive parents, like stepparents, can learn to overcome their dislike, if they are sufficiently prepared (Borgman, 1982; Sorich & Siebert, 1982). (See also Curtis, 1986.)

Despite the intensity of this debate, there has been no move toward widespread use of open adoption procedures (Kraft et al., 1985). They are considered viable only in cases in which the adoptive and birth families possess sufficient openness, commitment and flexibility so that they can enter into negotiations to develop an agreement with regard to the extent and timing of the child's contact with the birth family and to periodically update and change the contract when it no longer meets the needs of both families (Borgman, 1982). Parents for whom this might be appropriate resemble parents who can successfully develop co-custody agreements in divorce situations.

Sorich and Siebert (1982) describe one agency's experiences with open adoption. The agency began moving toward this practice by developing agreements between birth and adoptive parents with regard to sharing of information. For a period of time varying from one to several years, adoptive parents have agreed to provide annual pictures and other developmental information about the child to birth parents who request it. The authors comment that of the 31 children placed in 1981, "ten birth parents requested sharing for 18 years. Three requested sharing for one year, 14 for two years, and three for three years. Only one birth parent refused sharing" (p. 211). After sufficient preparation and support, almost all the adoptive parents stated that they were willing to share data on the child for at least one year.

The agency then moved to periodic utilization of what was called "semiopen" adoption. Although identifying information about birth or adoptive family are not provided, birth and adoptive parents meet each other prior to placement of the child. The child is not present at these meetings. Semiopen procedures have been used in twenty-four instances in the last five years in this agency (p. 212). The agency subsequently began experimenting with open adoptions, procedures in which contact between birth parent and child would be continued after the adoption was finalized. Only one such adoption had been attempted by the agency as of the publication date.

Agencies have been encouraged to consider utilization of similar procedures to establish routine contact between adoptive children and their siblings, their grandparents, other significant family members or other families with whom they have lived in the past (Sachdev, 1984b).

Despite its infrequent use, the notion of open adoption, like considerations of the child's right to search for birth family, has raised serious questions about confidentiality provisions in adoptive situations. Agencies can no longer promise to keep the identity of birth parents secret, nor can they promise adoptive families that birth families will not eventually discover who they are. In addition, these concerns have revitalized demands that children be perceived in a more complex light, as products of both their past and present. It is the interplay among the child's heritage, his or her past experiences, and current life opportunities that determine the outcome of the adoptive experience. In order to fully understand the nature and impact of these factors, neither the child's past nor the child's need to deal with people and issues from the past can be ignored (Jewett, 1982).

6. Recent changes in the adoption field have produced concomitant changes in the structure of adoption services and the role of the adoption worker providing them. There has been a trend toward increasing specialization and differentiation in adoption programs. Within public child welfare agencies, for example, it is now more common to find special adoption units staffed by workers who are particularly trained to seek out permanent homes for special-needs children. (See, for example, Jones, 1979.) Private agencies also tend to focus on the provision of one particular type of adoption service. Whereas some programs continue to provide homes for infants, others, such as Holt International Children's Service, specialize in meeting the needs of international adopters. Voluntary programs have been organized to offer exclusive services to special-needs children. Spaulding for Children was among the first of these agencies (Gregory, 1979). Starting in Michigan, Spaulding units have been established in several other states. Other agencies, specializing in the placement of "children who wait," joined with Spaulding in 1975 to develop a national network, calling themselves Family Builders Agencies. The network was coordinated by the North American Center on Adoption.

In addition to developing expertise in working with a particular population of adoptable children, workers have also been required, in recent years, to carry out interagency cooperative efforts. It is not unusual for a worker, dealing with a particular case, to have to coordinate with social workers from other communities or states or from other agencies within the same community. Miller et al. (1985) described one prototypical program of this type. In order to facilitate the adoption of wards of the state of Connecticut who were in long-term foster care, collaboration was arranged between the state child welfare agency and a number of voluntary social service agencies. Called the Connecticut Council on Adoption Placement Project, the program allowed the public agency to purchase recruitment, intake, placement, postplacement and treatment services from private providers (p. 238). Agency participants concluded that, despite some confusion and misunderstanding, they were generally very satisfied. Because public child welfare workers had much more extensive experience dealing with special-needs children, they were able to share their expertise with voluntary agency workers, who had much less experience of this type. In return, private agency personnel, having much more time to become deeply involved in individual cases, could give children and parents the attention they needed in order for their adoption to succeed. Workers also commented that joining as members of a team helped boost their morale and gave them new insights and new energy to devote to finding homes for children in care (p. 239).

These changes in agency practice have placed greater demands on child welfare staff. At the same time, development of these new adoption resources has excited and energized these workers. Having increasingly realized the extensive support they must provide to some families dealing with difficult children, they have found they can turn to others performing similar tasks to help them in this effort.

7. New choices are now available as avenues to parenthood. Infertile couples now have opportunities to consider artificial insemination procedures, using either the husband's or donor semen. It has been estimated that some ten thousand births result from use of these procedures annually in the United States (Sachdev, 1984a, p. 290). In vitro fertilization, fertilizing ova with semen outside of the mother's body, has also become an increasingly widespread practice. In cases in which the mother fails to produce usable ova, they may be "taken from another woman (the donor) be fertilized in vitro with the husband's semen and then implanted in the wife (the recipient) so that she will carry the child" (Bromley, 1984, p. 188). More than 120 of these "test tube babies" have been conceived since 1978 (Sachdev, 1984a, p. 291).

In situations in which the woman cannot carry a baby, yet another alternative is surrogate mothering, "renting the womb of a young fertile woman" (Sachdev, 1984a, p. 291). Women accepted for the program are supposedly carefully screened and paid $10,000 to $15,000, ostensibly not for "carrying" the baby, but rather for "time and loss of convenience." The couple select the surrogate from information on file at the surrogate agency. The surrender of the child has to be legalized through the usual adoption procedures. Since the surrogate mother is paid a fee, the question has been debated as to whether or not the procedure violates state laws against baby selling (Keane & Breo, 1981).

Controversies are possible and have in fact arisen on several occasions when the surrogate mother refuses to consent to the previously agreed upon surrender of the child or when the couples refuses to accept the child who is born deformed. As the book went to press, the Child Welfare League of America was planning to recommend elimination of surrogate parenting contracts and payments to surrogate mothers as not being in the best interests of children. At the same time many states were considering legislation to regulate new technological fertility developments such as in vitro fertilization as well as surrogate parenting. (See also Bromley [1984] for ethical and legal aspects of bio-technical conceptions.)

Such biotechnological procedures are not only used by couples who are infertile but also by couples who have been advised regarding the possibility of passing on some genetic defect such as hemophilia, cystic fibrosis, Tay-Sachs disease, sickle cell anemia, and so on. Such couples in earlier times might have been adoptive applicants. Artificial insemination has also been used by lesbians and other single women who are interested in becoming mothers.

Advances in reproductive biotechnology and the increased readiness to utilize these innovations have eroded some percentage of the demand for adoptable infants. Such procedures make possible the birth of children that are at least the biological issue of, and genetically linked to, one member of the infertile couple and the offspring is a member of the family from earliest infancy. Biological technological procedures have been termed collaborative reproductive alternatives to traditional adoption. It has been noted that having achieved the greater acceptance of sex without reproduction, we are now achieving reproduction without sex.

There are impending problems for children conceived as a result of artificial insemination regarding "search." Donors do not want to be identified because they might be charged with support of their child. Identifying information available at the sperm bank, even if the facility was willing to disclose this, is limited.

There are possible problems of unknowing incest committed by two people conceived as a result of insemination by the same donor but unaware of their shared fatherhood.

Each of the biotechnical procedures for conception may be perceived as new adoption alternatives rather than an alternative to adoption. One of the biological parents is a stranger to the child so that such procedures result in a semi-adoption. Since social workers in adoption have had experience with the problems relating to the biological identity of children in adoption and the special relationships among child, bioparents and caretaking parents, social workers are becoming involved in these procedures as well (Bell, 1986).

Availability of these paths to parenthood may well radically alter distinctions usually made between biological and adoptive parenting. In doing so, the status of both birth parent and adoptive parent may be normalized. Rather than perceiving birth parents as incapable of implementing role responsibilities, individuals relinquishing children in these situations are seen as active and responsible. Rather than viewing adopters as unusual people choosing atypical means to parent out of desperation, these adults are depicted as making choices among a number of alternative available means to become parents. Removing negative connotations usually ascribed to participants in this process can only serve to legitimate the status of children who are "chosen by," not born into, families they subseqently call their own.

Bibliography

Abbott, Grace. "Adoptions." *Encyclopedia of Social Science.* Ed. Edwin R. Seligman. New York: The Macmillan Company, 1937.

Abbott, Grace. *The Child and the State,* Vol. I. Chicago: University of Chicago Press, 1938.

Adams, John E., and Hyung Kim. "A Fresh Look at Intercountry Adoptions." *Children,* 18, 6 (November–December 1971), 214–221.

Allen, MaryLee, and Jane Knitzer. "Child Welfare: Examining the Policy Framework." In *Child Welfare: Current Dilemmas, Future Directions.* Ed. Brenda G. McGowan and William Meezan. Itasca, Ill.: F.E. Peacock. 1983, 93–142.

Amadio, Carol, and Stuart L. Deutsch. "Open Adoption: Allowing Adopted Children to 'Stay in Touch' with Blood Relatives." *Journal of Family Law, 22,* 1 (1983–1984), 59–93.

American Public Welfare Association. *The Voluntary Cooperative Information System* (VCIS). Washington, D.C.: A.P.W.A., 1982.

American Public Welfare Association 1982; Indicator Survey 1982. U.S. Department of Health & Human Services, 1984.

Anderson, C. Wilson. "Single Parent Adoption: The Viewpoints of Law and Social Work." Unpublished mimeograph, May 1976.

Anderson, C. Wilson. "The Sealed Record in Adoption Controversy." *Social Service Review,* 51, 2 (March 1977), 141–154.

Andrews, Roberta. "The Transitional Method in the Adoption Placement of Older Infants and Young Toddlers." *Child Welfare,* 40 (May 1961).

Ansfield, Joseph G. *The Adopted Child.* Springfield, Ill.: Charles C Thomas, 1971.

Armatruda, Catherine, and Joseph Baldwin. "Current Adoption Practices." *Journal of Pediatrics;* 38 (February 1951).

Aronson, Howard. "The Problem of Rejection of Adoptive Applicants." *Child Welfare,* 39 (October 1960).

Askin, Jayne, with Bob Oskam. *Search: A Handbook for Adoptees and Birthparents.* New York: Harper & Row, 1982.

Aumend, Sue, A., and Marjie C. Barrett. "Self-Concept and Attitudes Toward Adoption: A Comparison of Searching and Nonsearching Adult Adoptees." *Child Welfare,* 63, 3 (May–June, 1984), 251–258.

Ayres, Martin. "Defining a Child Care Policy." *Adoption and Fostering*, 9, 1 (1985), 17–21.

Bachrach, Christine. "Adoption as a Means of Family Formation: Data from the National Survey of Family Growth." *Journal of Marriage and the Family*. 45, 4 (November, 1983), 859–865.

Bachrach, Christine. "Adoption Plans, Adopted Children and Adoptive Mothers." *Journal of Marriage and the Family, 48* (May 1986), 243–253.

Bagley, Chris, and Loretta Young. "The Long-Term Adjustment and Identity of a Sample of Adopted Children." *International Social Work*, 23, 3 (1980), 16–23.

Baker, Nancy C. *Baby Selling—The Scandal of Black Market Adoptions*. New York: Vanguard Press, 1978.

Baker, Ron. "Parentless Refugee Children: The Question of Adoption." In *Adoption: Essays in Social Policy, Law and Sociology*. Ed. Philip Bean. New York: Tavistock Publications, 1984, 254–272.

Baran, Annette, Reuben Pannor, and Arthur D. Sorosky. "Open Adoption." *Social Work*, 21, 2 (March 1976), 97–100.

Barron, Jerome A. "Notice to the Unwed Father and Termination of Parental Rights: Implementing Stanley vs. Illinois." *Family Law Quarterly*, 9 (1975), 527–546.

Barth, Richard P. et al. "Contributors to Disruption and Dissolution of Older-Child Adoptions." *Child Welfare* 65, 4 (July–August, 1986), 359–371.

Bass, C. "Matchmaker, Match Matter—Older Child Adoption Failures." *Child Welfare*, 54, 7 (July 1975), 505–512.

Bayley, Nessie. "Homefinding for Older Children and the Use of Groups." *Child Adoption*, 81, 3 (1975).

Bean, Philip. (Ed.). *Adoption: Essays in Social Policy, Law and Sociology*. New York: Tavistock Publications, 1984.

Beaven, Paul. "The Adoption of Retarded Children." *Child Welfare*, 35 (April 1956).

Belkin, Alice. "Placing Older Children." *Adoption and Fostering*, 87, 1 (1977), 15–18.

Bell, Cynthia. "Adoptive Pregnancy: Legal and Social Work Issues." *Child Welfare*, 65, 5 (September–October 1986), 421–436.

Bell, Velma. "Special Considerations in the Adoption of the Older Child." *Social Casework* (June 1959).

Bellucci, Matilda T. "Treatment of Latency-Age Adopted Children and Parents." *Social Casework*, 56, 5 (May 1975), 297–301.

Benet, Mary K. *The Politics of Adoption*. New York: The Free Press, 1970.

Berger, Maria, and Jill Hodges. "Some Thoughts on the Question of When to Tell the Child That He Is Adopted." *Journal of Child Psychotherapy*, 8 (1982), 67–88.

Biggert, Linda. "Some Observations on Placement of Older Children." *Adoption and Fostering*, No. 4 (1976), 21–24.

Billingsley, Andrew, and Jeanne Giovannoni, *Children of the Storm: Black Children and American Child Welfare*. New York: Harcourt Brace Jovanovich, 1972.

Biskind, Sylvia. "The Group Method in Services to Adoptive Families." *Child Welfare*, 45, 10 (December 1966), 561–564.

Blotcky, Mark, John Looney, and Keith Grace. "Treatment of the Adopted Adolescent: Involvement of the Biologic Mother." *Journal of the American Academy of Child Psychiatry*, 21, 3 (1982), 281–285.

Bodenheimer, Brigitte M. "New Trends and Requirements in Adoption Law and Proposals for Legislative Changes." *Southern California Law Review*, 49 (1975), 11–109.

Boehm, Bernice. *Deterrents to the Adoption of Children—Foster Care*. New York: Child Welfare League of America, December 1958.

Bohman, Michael. *Adopted Children and Their Families—A Follow-up Study of Adopted Children, Their Background Environment and Adjustment*. Stockholm: Proprius, 1970.

Bohman, Michael. "The Interaction of Heredity and Childhood Environment. Some Adoption Studies." *Journal of Child Psychology and Psychiatry*. 22 (1981), 195–200.

Bohman, Michael et al. "Predisposition to Petty Criminality in Swedish Adoptees." *Archives of General Psychiatry*, 39 (1982), 1233–1253.

Bonham, Gordon S. "Who Adopts: The Relationship of Adoption and Social-Demographic Characteristics of Women." *Journal of Marriage and the Family,* 39 (May 1977), 295–306.

Borgatta, Edgar F., and David Fanshel. *Behavioral Characteristics of Children Known to Psychiatric Outpatient Clinics.* New York: Child Welfare League of America, 1965.

Borgman, Robert. "Antecedents and Consequences of Parental Rights Termination for Abused and Neglected Children." *Child Welfare,* 60, 6 (June 1981), 391–404.

Borgman, Robert. "The Consequences of Open and Closed Adoption for Older Children." *Child Welfare,* 61, 4 (April 1982), 217–226.

Bowden, Liz. "Adpotion of Mentally Handicapped Children." *Adoption and Fostering,* 8, (1984), 38–42.

Bowers, Swithen. "The Child's Heritage—From a Catholic Point of View," in *A Study of Adoption Practice,* Vol. 12. Ed. M. Schapiro. New York: Child Welfare League of America, 1956.

Boyne, John. "A Mental Health Note in Adoption of School-Age and Teen-age Children." *Child Welfare,* 52, 3 (March 1978), 196–199.

Boyne, John, et al. *The Shadow of Success: A Statistical Analysis of the Outcome of Adoptions of Hard-to-Place Children.* Westfield, N.J.: Spaulding for Children, 1983.

Braden, Josephine. "Adopting the Abused Child: Love Is Not Enough." *Social Casework,* 62, 6 (June 1981), 362–367.

Bradley, Trudy. *An Exploration of Case Workers' Perceptions of Adoptive Applicants.* New York: Child Welfare League of America, 1966.

Brantham, Ethel. "One-Parent Adoptions." *Children,* 17, 3 (May–June 1970), 103–106.

Bremner, Robert H. (Ed.). *Children and Youth in America: A Documentary History,* Vol. 2: 1866–1932. Parts 1–6. Cambridge, Mass.: Harvard University Press, 1970.

Brenner, Ruth. "A Follow-up Study of Adoptive Families." *Child Adoption Research Committee* (March 1951).

Brieland, Donald. *An Experimental Study of the Selection of Adoptive Parents at Intake.* New York: Child Welfare League of America, 1959.

Brieland, Donald. "The Selection of Adoptive Parents at Intake." *Casework Papers,* NCSW-1960. New York: Columbia University Press, 1961.

Brieland, Donald. "Selection of Adoptive Parents." In *Adoption: Current Issues and Trends.* Ed. Paul Sachdev. Toronto, Canada: Butterworths, 1984, 65–86.

Brieland, Donald, and John Lemmon. *Social Work and the Law.* St. Paul, Minn.: West Publishing Co., 1977.

Brinich, Paul, and Evelin Brinich. "Adoption and Adaptation." *Journal of Nervous and Mental Disease,* 170, 8 (1982), 489–493.

Brockhaus, Joyce, Patricia Dees, and Robert Herold Brockhaus. "Adopting an Older Child: The Emotional Process." *American Journal of Nursing,* 82, 5 (February 1982), 288–291.

Brodzinsky, David M., Leslie M. Singer, and Anne M. Braff. "Children's Understanding of Adoption." *Child Development,* 55, 3 (June 1984), 869–878.

Brodzinsky, David M., et al. "Psychological and Academic Adjustment in Adopted Children." *Journal of Consulting and Clinical Psychology,* 52, 4 (August 1984), 582–590.

Bromley, Peter M. "Aided Conception: The Alternative to Adoption," in *Adoption: Essays in Social Policy, Law and Sociology,* Ed. Philip Bean. New York: Tavistock Publications, 1984, 174–193.

Brown, Edwin G. *Selection of Adoptive Parents—A Videotape Study.* Unpublished Ph.D. thesis. School of Social Service Administration. University of Chicago, August 1970.

Burke, Carolyn. "Adult Adoptee's Constitutional Right to Know His Origins." *Southern California Law Review,* 48 (May 1975), 1199–1211.

Byrne, Kathleen O., and Matilda T. Bellucci. "Subsidized Adoption: One County's Program." *Child Welfare,* 61, 3 (March 1982), 173–180.

Bytner, Charlotte J. et al. "A Positive Approach in Evaluating Potential Adoptive Families and Children." In *No Child is Unadoptable.* Ed. Sallie R. Churchill, Bonnie Carlson, and Lynn Nybell. Beverly Hills, CA: Sage, 1979, 25–31.

C.S.R. *Study of Adoption Subsidy,* Washington, D.C., C.S.R. Inc., 1983.

Cadoret, Remi, Colleen Cain, and William Grove. "Development of Alcoholism in Adoptees Raised Apart from Alcoholic Biologic Parents," *Archives of General Psychiatry, 37* (May 1980), 561–563.

California Citizens' Adoptions Committee. *Serving Children in Need of Adoption.* Los Angeles. June 1965.

Campbell, Anne. "Principles of Social Work Applied to Adoption Practice, Policy and Procedure," in *Social Work and the Preservation of Human Values.* Ed. William Diton. London: J.M. Dent & Sons, Ltd. 1957.

Cann, Wendy. "Maintaining the Placement." In *New Developments in Foster Care and Adoption.* Ed. John Triseliotis. London: Routledge & Kegan Paul, 1980, 212–223.

Carney, Ann. *No More Here and There—Adopting the Older Child.* Chapel Hill: University of North Carolina Press, 1976.

Carroll, Jerome. "Adoption by Whites of Children of Afro-America Heritage—Some Issues for Consideration." *Adoptalk,* 6 (March–April, May–June 1970).

Carroll, Vern (Ed.). *Adoption in Eastern Oceania.* Honolulu: University of Hawaii Press, 1970.

Chambers, Donald. "Willingness to Adopt Atypical Children." *Child Welfare,* 49, 5 (May 1970), 275–279.

Chappelear, Edith, and Joyce Fried. "Helping Adopting Couples Come to Grips with Their New Parental Roles." *Children,* 14, 6 (November–December 1967), 223–226.

Chema, Regina et al. "Adoptive Placement of the Older Child." *Child Welfare,* 49, 8 (October 1970), 450–458.

Chestang, Leon. "The Dilemma of Biracial Adoption." *Social Work,* 17, 3 (May 1972), 100–105.

Chestang, Leon, and Irmgard Heymann. "Preparing Older Children for Adoption." *Public Welfare,* 34, 1 (Winter 1976), 35–40.

Child Welfare League of America. *Standards for Adoption Service.* New York: CWLA, 1973.

Child Welfare League of America. *Standards for Adoption Service.* New York: CWLA, 1978.

Children's Home Society of California. "Report of a Research Project." *The Changing Face of Adoption,* March 1977.

Chimeze, Amizie. "Transracial Adoption of Black Children." *Social Work,* 20, 4 (July 1975), 296–301.

Churchill, Sallie. "Disruption: A Risk in Adoption." In *Adoption: Current Issues and Trends.* Ed. Paul Sachdev. Toronto: Butterworth, 1984, 115–128.

Churchill, Sallie, Bonnie Carlson, and Lynn Nybell (Eds.). *No Child Is Unadoptable.* Beverly Hills, Cal.: Sage, 1979.

Citizens' Adoption Committee of Los Angeles County. *Natural Parents Who Relinquish Children for Adoption.* Los Angeles. June 1952.

Clark, E.A., and Jeanette Hanisee. "Intellectual and Adoptive Performance of Asian Children in Adoptive American Settings." *Developmental Psychology,* 18, 4 (1982), 595–599.

Clayton, Rob, and Marian Clayton. "An Alternative Family." In *Adoption: Essays in Social Policy, Law, and Sociology.* Ed. Philip Bean. New York: Tavistock Publications, 1984, 100–112.

Clothier, Florence. "Some Aspects of the Problem of Adoption." *American Journal of Orthopsychiatry,* 9 (1939).

Cochran-Smith, Marilyn. *What Is Real? An Adoptive Parents' Guide to Children's Books.* Philadelphia: Mimeo, October 1983.

Cohen, Joyce. "Adoption Breakdown with Older Children." in *Adoption: Current Issues and Trends.* Ed. Paul Sachdev. Toronto: Butterworth, 1984, 129–138.

Cole, Elizabeth S. "Adoption Services Today and Tomorrow." In *Child Welfare Strategy in the Coming Years.* Ed. Alfred Kadushin. Washington, D.C.: US DHEW, 1978, 130–168.

Cole, Elizabeth S. "Societal Influences on Adoption Practice." In *Adoption: Current Issues and Trends.* Ed. Paul Sachdev. Toronto, Canada: Butterworths, 1984, 15–30.

Collier, Catherine. "A Postadoption Discussion Series." *Social Casework,* 41 (April 1960).

Columbia Journal of Law and Social Problems. "Revocation of Parental Consent in Adoption Proceedings, Recent Developments." *Columbia Journal of Law and Social Problems* (1977), 105–109.

Colville, Anita. "Adoption for the Handicapped Child." *Child Welfare,* 36 (October 1957).

Community Council of Greater New York. *Special Needs Adoption: Findings of Recent Research on the Experiences of Families Who Adopt.* New York: Community Council of Greater New York, April 1984.

Conklin, Lloyd, et al. "Use of Groups During the Adoptive Post-Placement Period." *Social Work,* 7 (April 1962).

Cordell, Antoinette, Cicely Nathan, and Virginia Krymow. "Group Counseling for Children Adopted at Older Ages." *Child Welfare,* 64, 2 (March–April 1985), 113–124.

Costin, Lela B. "Adoption of Children by Single Parents." *Child Adoption* (November 1970), 31–33.

Coyne, Ann, and Mary E. Brown. "Developmentally Disabled Children Can Be Adopted." *Child Welfare* 64, 6 (November–December 1985) 607–615.

Crowe, Raymond. "An Adoption Study of Antisocial Personality." *Archives of General Psychiatry,* 31 (1974), 785–791.

Cunningham, Lynn, et al. "Studies of Adoptees from Psychiatrically Disturbed Biological Parents. I: Psychiatric Conditions in Childhood and Adolescence." *British Journal of Psychiatry.* 126 (1975a), 534–549.

Cunningham, Lynn et al. "Studies of Adoptees from Psychiatrically Disturbed Biological Parents. II: Temperamental, Hyperactive, Antisocial and Developmental Variables." *Journal of Pediatrics,* 87 (1975b), 301–306.

Curtis, Patrick A. "The Dialectics of Open Versus Closed Adoption of Infants." *Child Welfare* 65, 5 (September–October 1986), 437–445.

Curtis, Sarah. "The Round Robin Child: Anglia Television Homefinding." *Adoption and Fostering,* 9, 1 (1985), 10–12.

Dall, Adolin. "Subsidized Adoption in New York City," in *Adoption of the Older Foster Child.* New York: New York State Council of Voluntary Child Care Agencies, February 1977.

Dalsheimer, Babette. "Adoption Runs in My Family." *MS* (August 1973), 82–83, 112–113.

Davis, Ruth, and Polly Douck. "Crucial Importance of Adoption Home Study." *Child Welfare,* 34 (March 1955).

Day, Dawn. *The Adoption of Black Children: Counteracting Institutional Discrimination.* Lexington, Mass.: Lexington Books, 1979.

Deasy, Feila C., and Olive W. Quinn. "The Urban Negro and Adoption of Children." *Child Welfare,* 41 (November 1962).

DeFries, J. C. et al. "Parent Offspring Resemblance for Cognitive Abilities in the Colorado Adoption Project: Biological, Adoptive and Control Parents and One-Year-Old Children." *Intelligence,* 5 (1981), 245.

Depp, Carole Hope. "After Reunion: Perceptions of Adult Adoptees, Adoptive Parents, and Birth Parents." *Child Welfare,* 61, 2 (February 1982), 115–119.

Deykin, Eva, Lee Campbell, and Patricia Patti. "The Postadoption Experience of Surrendering Parents." *American Journal of Orthopsychiatry,* 54, 2 (1984), 271–280.

Dillow, Louise. "The Group Process in Adoptive Home Finding." *Children,* 15, 4 (July–August 1968), 153–157.

DiViglio, Letitia. "Adjustment of Foreign Children in Their Adoptive Homes." *Child Welfare,* 35 (November 1956).

Dooley, Dorothy, and Robert La Franco. "Implementing a Plan for Permanence at the New York Foundling Hospital." *Catholic Charities Review,* 58 (October 1974), 5–13.

Dukette, Rita, and Nicholas Stevenson. "The Legal Rights of Unmarried Fathers: The Impact of Recent Court Decisions." *Social Service Review,* 47, 7 (1973), 1–15.

Edgar, Margaret. "The Adoption Party." *Child Adoption,* 79, 1 (1975), 45–50.

Edmonton, Canada. *Report on Adoptions Edmonton, Canada.* Department of Public Welfare, 1969 (mimeo).

Edwards, Margaret. "Adoption for the Older Child." *Child Adoption,* No. 4 (1975), 22–27.

Edwards, M. E. "Failure and Success in the Adoption of Toddlers." *Case Conference,* 1 (November 1954).

Ehrlich, Henry. *A Time to Search.* New York: Paddington Press, 1977.

Entwisle, Doris, and Susan G. Doering. *The First Birth: A Family Turning Point.* Baltimore: Johns Hopkins University Press, 1981.

Epstein, Laura, and Irmgard Heymann. "Some Decisive Process in Adoption Planning for the Older Child." *Child Welfare,* 46, 1 (January 1967), 5–9.

Fairweather, O. E. "Early Placement in Adoption." *Child Welfare,* 31 (1952).

Falk, Lawrence L. "A Comparative Study of Trans-racial and In-racial Adoptions." *Child Welfare,* 49, 2 (February 1970), 82–88.

Falk, Lawrence L. "Identity and the Transracially Adopted Child." *Lutheran Social Welfare,* 9 (Summer 1969), 18–25.

Fanshel, David. *A Study in Negro Adoption.* New York: Child Welfare League of America, January 1957.

Fanshel, David. *Far from the Reservation: The Transracial Adoption of American Indian Children.* Metuchen, N.J.: Scarecrow Press, 1972.

Feigelman, William, and Arnold R. Silverman. *Chosen Children: New Patterns of Adoptive Relationships.* New York: Praeger, 1983.

Feigelman, William and Arnold Silverman. "Adoptive Parents, Adoptees, and The Sealed Record Controversy." *Social Casework* 67 (April 1986), 219–226.

Fein, Edith, and Anthony Maluccio. "Permanency Planning and Adoption:" In *Adoption Current Issues and Trends.* Ed. Paul Sachdev. Toronto, Canada: Butterworths, 1984, 205–214.

Fein, Edith, et al. "After Foster Care: Outcomes of Permancy Planning for Children." *Child Welfare,* 62, 6 (November–December, 1983), 485–558.

Felton, Zelma. "The Use of Adoption Resource Exchange." *Child Welfare,* 31 (June 1958), 26–29.

Ferman, Patricia R., and Bruce L. Warren. *Finding Families for the Children.* Ypsilanti, Mich.: Eastern Michigan University Press, 1974.

Festinger, Trudy Bradley. *Why Some Choose Not to Adopt Through Agencies.* New York: Metropolitan Applied Research Center, 1972.

Festinger, Trudy Bradley. *Necessary Risk—A Study of Adoptions and Disrupted Adoptive Placements.* New York: Child Welfare League of America, 1986.

Fisch, Robert, et al. "Growth Behavior and Psychological Measurements of Adopted Children—The Influence of Genetic and Socio-Economic Factors in a Prospective Study." *Journal of Pediatrics,* 89 (September 1976), 494–500.

Fisher, Florence. *The Search for Anna Fisher.* Greenwich, Conn.: Fawcett Crest, 1973.

Flynn, Laurie, and Wilfred Hamm. "TEAM: Parent-Agency Partnership in Adoption Services." *Children Today,* 12, 2 (March–April 1983), 2–5.

Foote, Gwendolyn, and Rosalind L. Putnam. *Negro Attitudes Toward Adoption in Hartford.* New Haven: The Connecticut Child Welfare Association, September 1965.

Forsythe, Bobbie, and Tommy Marshall. "A Group Model for Adoption Studies for Special-Needs Children." *Child Welfare,* 63, 1 (January–February 1984), 56–61.

Fowler, Irving. "The Urban Middle-Class Negro and Adoption: Two Series of Studies and Their Implications for Action." *Child Welfare,* 45, 9 (November 1966), 522–524.

Fowler, Lowa. "Problem of Adoption Placement in British Columbia." *Social Welfare and the Preservation of Human Values.* Ed. William Diton. London: J. M. Dent & Sons, 1957.

Fradkin, Helen. "Adoptive Parents for Children with Special Needs." Discussion by Ruth Taft. *Child Welfare,* 37 (January 1958).

Fradkin, Helen, and Dorothy Krugman, "A Program of Adoptive Placements for Infants Under 3 Months." *American Journal of Orthopsychiatry* 26 (1956).

Frank, John, and Laurie Flynn. "Group Therapy for Adopted Adolescents and Their Families." *Children Today,* 12, 2 (March–April, 1983), 11–13.

Franklin, David S., and Fred Massarik. "The Adoption of Children with Medical Conditions. Part I: Process and Outcome; Part II: The Families Today; Part III: Discussion and Conclusions." *Child Welfare,* 48, 8, 9, 10 (October–November–December 1969), 459–467, 533–539, 595–601.

Freedman, Joel. "An Adoptee in Search of Identity." *Social Work,* 22, 3 (May 1977), 227–228.

Freeman, Michael D.A. "Subsidized Adoption." In *Adoption: Essays in Social Policy. Law and Sociology.* Ed. Philip Bean. New York: Tavistock Publications, 1984, 203–228.

Fricke, Harriet. "T.V. or Not T.V.—Minnesota Settles the Question." *Child Welfare,* 35 (November 1956).

Friedman, Helen. "Why Are They Keeping Their Babies?" *Social Work,* 20, 4 (July 1975), 322–323.

Fulker, D.W., and J. DeFries. "Genetic and Environmental Transmission in the Colorado Adoption Project: Path Analysis." *British Journal of Mathematical and Statistical Psychology,* 36, 17 (1983), 175–188.

Furlough, Robert. "Agency Adoptions Compared with Independent Adoptions." Unpublished Ph.D. thesis. Florida State University, Tallahassee, 1974.

Gallagher, Ursula M. "The Adoption of Mentally Retarded Children." *Children,* 15, 1 (January–February 1968), 17–21.

Gant, Larry. *Black Adoption Programs: Pacesetters in Practice.* Ann Arbor,: Mich. National Child Welfare Training Center, 1984.

Geissinger, Shirley. "Adoptive Parents' Attitudes Toward Open Birth Records." *Family Relations,* 33, 4 (October, 1984), 57–585.

Gershenson, Charles. *Child Welfare Population Characteristics and Flow Analysis: FY 1982.* Washington, D.C.: ACYF, 1983.

Gershenson, Charles. *Community Responses to Children Free for Adoption,* Washington, D.C.: Children's Bureau. Child Welfare Research Note Number 3, March 1984.

Gill, Margaret H. "The Foster Care/Adoptive Family: Adoption for Children Not Legally Free." *Child Welfare,* 54 (December 1975), 712–20.

Gill, Owen, and Barbara Jackson. *Adoption and Race.* New York: St Martin's Press, 1983.

Gilman, Lois. *The Adoption Resource Book.* New York: Harper & Row, 1984.

Glen, George S. "Adoption: An Added Ingredient." *Ohio Northern Law Review,* 1 (1974), 462–479.

Glidden, Laraine M. "Adopting Mentally Handicapped Children." *Adoption and Fostering,* 9, 3 (1985), 53–56.

Gochros, Harvey. *Not Parents Yet—A Study of the Postplacement Period in Adoption.* Minneapolis, Minn.: Division of Child Welfare. Department of Public Welfare. 1962.

Gochros, Harvey. "A Study of Caseworker-Adoptive Parent Relationship in Postplacement Service." *Child Welfare,* 46, 6 (June 1967), 317–325.

Goldring, Howard, and Janie Tutleman. *Adoption Failures at the Los Angeles County Department of Adoptions.* Unpublished master's thesis. University of Southern California, School of Social Work, June 1970.

Goldstein, J., A. Freud, and Albert Solnit. *Beyond the Best Interests of the Child.* New York: Free Press, 1973.

Goldstein, J., A. Freud, and Albert Solnit. *Before the Best Interests of the Child.* New York: Free Press, 1979.

Goodman, Jerome. "Adopted Children Brought to Child Psychiatric Clinics." *Archives of General Psychiatry,* 9 (November 1963).

Goodridge, Carolyn. "Special Techniques in the Group Adoptive Study for Children with Special Needs." *Child Welfare,* 54, 1 (1975), 35–39.

Goodwin, Donald, et al. "Alcoholic Problems in Adoptees Raised Apart from Alcoholic Biological Parents." *Archives of General Psychiatry,* 28 (1973), 238–243.

Grabe, Pamela (Ed.) *Adoption Resources for Mental Health Professionals.* Mercer, Pa.: Mental Health Adoption Therapy Project, 1986.

Gradstein, Bonnie, Marc Gradstein, and Robert Glass. "Private Adoption." *Fertility and Sterility,* 37, 4 (April 1982), 548–551.

Graham, Lloyd. "Children from Japan in American Adoptive Homes," in *Casework Papers.* New York: Family Service Association of America, 1957.

Gregory, Graeme. "No Child Is Unadoptable." In *No Child is Unadoptable.* Ed. Sallie R. Churchill, Bonnie Carlson, and Lynn Nybell. Beverly Hills, Cal.: Sage, 1979, 12–22.

Grossman, Hanna, Doree Epstein, and Anne Nelson. *An Education of the New York State Adoption Exchange.* Albany, N.Y.: Welfare Research, Inc., 1976.

Grow, Lucille J., and Deborah Shapiro. *Black Children—White Parents—A Study of Transracial Adoption.* New York: Child Welfare League of America, 1974.

Grow, Lucille J., and Deborah Shapiro. *Transracial Adoption Today—Views of Adoptive Parents and Social Workers.* New York: Child Welfare League of America, 1975.

Hagen, Clayton et al. *The Adopted Adult Discusses Adoption as a Life Experience.* Minneapolis: Lutheran Social Service of Minnesota, 1968.

Hallinan, Helen. "Adoption for Older Children." *Social Casework,* 33 (July 1952).

Hapgood, Miles. "Older Child Adoption and the Knowledge Base of Adoption Practice." In *Adoption: Essays in Social Policy, Law, and Sociology.* Ed. Philip Bean. New York: Tavistock Publications, 1984, 54–82.

Hardy-Brown, Karen, Robert Plomin, and John DeFries. "Genetic and Environmental Influences on the Rate of Communicative Development in the First Year of Life." *Developmental Psychology* (1982), 703–716.

Hargrave, Vivian, Joan Shireman, and Peter Connor. *Where Love and Need Are One.* Chicago: Illinois Department of Children and Family Services, 1975.

Haring, Barbara L. "Adoption Trends, 1971–1975." *Child Welfare,* 55, 7 (July–August, 1976), 501–503.

Harper, Juliet, and Sara Williams. "Adopted Children Admitted to Residential Psychiatric Care." *Australian Journal of Social Issues* (1976), 43–52.

Harrington, Joseph D. "The Courts Contend with Sealed Adoption Records." *Public Welfare* 38 (Spring 1980), 29–43.

Harrington, Joseph D. "Adoption and the State Legislatures 1984–1985," *Public Welfare,* 44, (Spring 1986), 18–25.

Hartman, Ann. *Finding Families: An Ecological Approach to Family Assessment in Adoption.* Beverly Hills, CA: Sage, 1979.

Hartman, Ann. *Working with Adoptive Families Beyond Placement.* New York: Child Welfare League of America, 1984.

Hastings, James (Ed.). *Encyclopedia of Religion and Ethics.* New York: Charles Scribner's Sons, 1908.

Hegarty, Cornelius. "The Family Resources Program: One Coin, Two Sides of Adoption and Foster Family Care." *Child Welfare,* 52 (February 1973), 91–99.

Herbert, Martin. "Causes and Treatment of Behavior Problems in Adoptive Children." In *Adoption: Essays in Social Policy, Law, and Sociology.* Ed. Philip Bean. New York: Tavistock Publications, 1984, 83–99.

Herzog, Elizabeth, and Rose Bernstein. "Why So Few Negro Adoptions?" *Children,* 12 (January–February 1965).

Herzog, Elizabeth, et al. *Families for Black Children: The Search for Adoptive Parents. I: An Experience Survey.* Washington, D.C.: U.S. Government Printing Office, 1971a.

Herzog, Elizabeth, et al. "Some Opinion on Finding Families for Black Children." *Children,* 18, 4 (July–August 1971b), 143–148.

Heston, Leonard N. "Psychiatric Disorders in Foster Home Reared Children of Schizophrenic Mothers." *British Journal of Psychiatry,* 112 (1966), 819–825.

Hill, Robert. *Informal Adoption Among Black Families.* Washington, D.C.: National Urban League, Research Department, 1977.

Hochfield, Eugenie. "Across National Boundaries." *Juvenile Court Judge Journal,* 14 (October 1963).

Holman, P. "Some Factors in the Aetiology of Maladjustment in Children." *Journal of Mental Sciences,* 99 (1953), 654–688.

Holmes, Donna. "Adopting Older Children: One Family's Experience." *Children Today* (July–August 1979), 6–9.

Hoopes, Janet L. *Prediction in Child Development: A Longitudinal Study of Adoptive and Nonadoptive Families—The Delaware Family Study.* New York: Child Welfare League of America, 1982.

Hornecker, Alice. "Adoption Opportunities for the Handicapped." *Children,* 9 (July–August 1962).

Howard, Alicia, David D. Royse, and John A. Skerl, "Transracial Adoption: The Black Community Perspective." *Social Work* (May 1977), 184–189.

Howard, Mary. "An Adoptee's Personal Search for Her Natural Parents—I Take After Somebody. I Have Real Relatives. I Possess a Real Name." *Psychology Today* (December 1975), 33–37.

Howe, George. "The Ecological Approach to Permanency Planning: An Interactionist Perspective." *Child Welfare,* 62, 4 (July–August 1983), 291–301.

Humphrey, Michael, and Christopher Ounsted. "Adoptive Families Referred for Psychiatric Advice. I: The Children." *British Journal of Psychiatry,* 109 (1963).

Hunt, Roberta. *Obstacles to Interstate Adoption.* New York: Child Welfare League of America, 1972.

Hutchings, B., and S. Mednick. "Registered Criminality in the Adoptive and Biological Parents of Registered Male Criminal Adoptees," in *Genetic Research in Psychiatry.* Ed. R. R. Fieve, H. Brill, and D. Rosenthal. Baltimore: Johns Hopkins University Press, 1975.

Isaac, Rael J. *Adopting a Child Today.* New York: Harper & Row, 1965.

Jackson, Barbara. *Family Experiences of Inter-racial Adoption.* London: The Association of British Adoption and Fostering Agencies, 1976.

Jaffee, Benson. "Adoption Outcome: A Two Generation View," *Child Welfare,* 53, 4 (April 1974), 211–224.

Jaffee, Benson, and David Fanshel. *How They Fared in Adoption: A Follow-up Study.* New York: Columbia University Press, 1970.

James, Mary. "Home-Finding for Children with Special Needs." In *New Developments in Foster Care and Adoption.* Ed. John Triseliotis. Boston, Mass.: Routledge and Kegan Paul, 1980, 178–195.

Jameson, Grace. "Psychiatric Disorders in Adopted Children in Texas." *Texas Medicine,* 63, 4 (April 1967), 83–88.

Jaquith, Esther. "An Adoptive Resource Exchange Under Private Auspices." *Child Welfare,* 41 (May 1962), 217–219.

Jewett, Claudia. *Adopting The Older Child.* Boston: Harvard Common Press, 1978.

Jewett, Claudia. *Helping Children Cope with Separation and Loss.* Boston: Harvard Common Press, 1982.

Jewett, Claudia. "Placing Adolescents for Adoption." In *Adoption Current Issues and Trends.* Ed. Paul Sachdev. Toronto, Canada: Butterworths, 1984, 101–114.

Joe, Barbara. "In Defense of Intercountry Adoption." *Social Service Review,* 52 (March 1978), 1–20.

Johnson, Penny R., Joan F. Shireman, and Kenneth W. Watson. "Transracial Adoption and the Development of Black Identity at Age Eight." *Child Welfare* 66, 1 (January/February 1987), 45–55.

Jones, Charles E., and John F. Else. "Racial and Cultural Issues in Adoption." *Child Welfare,* 58 (June 1979), 373–382.

Jones, Edmond D. "On Transracial Adoption of Black Children." *Child Welfare.* 5, 3 (March 1972), 156–164.

Jones, Jean Y. "Subsidized Adoption." *United States Congress Adoptions and Foster Care Hearings.* Subcommittee on Children and Youth, Committee on Labor Public Welfare, U.S. Senate. Washington, D.C.: U.S. Government Printing Office, 1975.

Jones, Martha. "Preparing the School Age Child for Adoption." *Child Welfare,* 58 (January 1979a), 27–34.

Jones, Martha. "Aggressive Adoption: A Program's Effect on a Child Welfare Agency." In *No Child is Unadoptable.* Ed. Sallie R. Churchill, Bonnie Carlson and Lynn Nybell. Beverly Hills, Cal: Sage, 1979b, 149–155.

Jones, Mary Ann. *The Sealed Adoption Record Controversy: Report of a Survey of Agency Policy, Practice and Opinions.* New York: Child Welfare League of America, 1976.

Kadushin, Alfred. "The Legally Adoptable, Unadopted Child." Child Welfare, 37 (December 1958).

Kadushin, Alfred. "A Study of Adoptive Parents of Hard-to-Pace Children." *Social Casework,* 43 (May 1962).

Kadushin, Alfred. "Adoptive Parenthood: A Hazardous Adventure." *Social Work,* 11, 3 (July 1966).

Kadushin, Alfred. "Letter to the Editor." *Social Work,* 12, 1 (January 1967), 127–128.

Kadushin, Alfred. "Single-Parent Adopters: An Overview and Relevant Research." *Social Service Review,* 44: 3 (September 1970a).

Kadushin, Alfred. *Adopting Older Children.* New York: Columbia University Press, 1970b.

Kadushin, Alfred. "Adoptive Status—Birth Parents vs. Bread Parents." *Child Care Quarterly Review,* 25, 3 (July 1971), 10–14.

Kadushin, Alfred (Ed.). *Child Welfare Strategy in the Coming Years.* Washington, D.C.: U.S. DHEW, 1978.

Kadushin, Alfred. "Principles, Values and Assumptions Underlying Adoption Practice." In *Adoption: Current Issues and Trends.* Ed. Paul Sachdev. Toronto, Canada: Butterworths, 1984, 3–14.

Kadushin, Alfred, and Frederick Seidl. "Adoption Failure: A Social Work Postmortem." *Social Work,* 16, 3 (July 1971), 32–37.

Kagan, Richard M., and William J. Reid. "Critical Factors in the Adoption of Emotionally Disturbed Youths." *Child Welfare,* 65, 1 (January–February, 1986), 63–72.

Kaplan, Irving H. "A Group Approach to Adoptive Study." *Journal of Jewish Communal Services,* 47, 2 (Winter 1970), 127–135.

Kasporwicz, Alfred. "Interpreting Rejection to Adoptive Applicants." *Social Work,* 9 (January 1964).

Katz, Linda. "Older Child Adoptive Placement: A Time of Family Crisis." *Child Welfare,* 56, 3 (March 1977), 165–171.

Katz, Linda. "Adoption Counseling as a Preventive Mental Health Specialty." *Child Welfare,* 59, 3 (March 1980), 161–168.

Katz, Linda. "Parental Stress and Factors for Success in Older-Child Adoption." *Child Welfare,* 65, 6 (November–December 1986), 569–578.

Katz, Sanford N., and Ursula M. Gallagher. "Subsidized Adoption in America." *Family Law Quarterly,* 10 (Spring 1976), 3–54.

Kaye, Stanley. "Self-Image Formation in Adopted Children: The Environment Within." *Journal of Contemporary Psychotherapy,* 13, 2 (Fall-Winter 1982), 175–181.

Keane, Noel P., and Dennis L. Breo. *The Surrogate Mother.* New York: Everest House, 1981.

Kendler, Kenneth, Alan Gruenberg and John Strauss. An Independent Analysis of the Copenhagen Sample of the Danish Adoption Study of Schizophrenia." *Archives of General Psychiatry,* 38, (September 1981), 973–987.

Kenny, Thomas et al. "Incidence of Minimal Brain Injury in Adopted Children." *Child Welfare,* 46, 1 (January 1967), 24–29.

Ketchum, B. "Reports on Study of Adopted Children." *Child Welfare,* 43 (1964), 249.

Kety, Seymour S. "Studies Designed to Disentangle Genetic and Environmental Variables in Schizophrenia: Some Epistemological Questions and Answers." *American Journal of Psychiatry*, 133, 10 (October 1976), 1134–1136.

Kety, Seymour S., David Rosenthal, Paul Wender, and Fint Schulsinger. "Studies Based on a Total Sample of Adopted Individuals and Their Relatives—Why They Were Necessary, What They Demonstrated and Failed To Demonstrate." *Schizophrenia Bulletin*, 2, 3 (1976), 413–428.

Kim, Dong S. "How They Fared in American Homes—A Follow Up Study of Adopted Korean Children in the U.S." *Children Today* (March–April 1977), 2–6.

Kim, H. T., and Elaine Reid. "After a Long Journey," in *The Unbroken Circle*, Ed. Betty Kramer. Minneapolis: Organization of United Response, 1975, 307–427.

Kim, S. Peter. "Behavior Symptoms in Three Transracially Adopted Asian Children: Diagnosis Dilemma." *Child Welfare*, 59, (April 1980), 213–224.

Kirk, H. D. *Shared Fate*. New York: The Free Press, 1964.

Kirk, H. D., Kurt Jonassohn, and Ann Fish. "Are Adopted Children Especially Vulnerable to Stress?" *Archives of General Psychiatry*, 14 (March 1966).

Klomineck, Wanda. "The Development of Adoptive Children in Their New Family Environment." *International Child Welfare Review*, 28 (March 1976), 43–51.

Knight, Iris. "Placing the Handicapped Child for Adoption." *Child Adoption*, 62, 4 (1970), 27–35.

Knight, Mary. "Termination Visits in Closed Adoptions." *Child Welfare*, 64, 1 (January–February 1985), 37–45.

Knitzer, Jane, and Lynn Olson. *Unclaimed Children: The Failure of Public Responsibility to Children and Adolescents in Need of Mental Health Services*. Washington, D.C.: Children's Defense Fund, 1982.

Kornitzer, Margaret. *Adoption and Family Life,* New York: Humanities Press, Inc., 1968.

Kornitzer, Margaret, and Jane Rowe. *Some Casework Implications in the Study of Children Reclaimed or Returned Before Final Adoption*. Surrey, England: Standing Conference of Societies Registered for Adoption, May 1968. Mimeo.

Kowall, Katherine A., and Karen M. Schilling. "Adoption Through the Eyes of Adult Adoptees." *American Journal of Orthopsychiatry* 55, 3 (July 1985), 354–462.

Kraft, Adrienne D. et al. "Some Theoretical Considerations on Confidential Adoptions, Part I: The Birth Mother." *Child and Adolescent Social Work Journal*. 2, 1 (Spring 1985), 13–21.

Kramer, Betty (Ed.), *The Unbroken Circle*. Minneapolis, Minn.: Organization for a United Response (O.U.R.S.), 1975.

Krementz, Jill. *How It Feels to Be Adopted*. New York: Afred A. Knopf, 1982.

Krisheff, Curtis. "Adoption Agency Services for the Retarded." *Mental Retardation*, 15, 1 (February 1977), 38–39.

Krugman, Dorothy. "Reality in Adoption." *Child Welfare*. 43, 7 (July 1964).

Ladner, Joyce. *Mixed Families—Adopting Across Racial Boundaries*. Garden City, N.Y.: Doubleday & Company, Inc., 1977.

Lahti, Janet et al. *A Follow-Up Study of the Oregon Project*. Portland, Ore.: Regional Research Institute for Human Services, Portland State University, August 1978.

Lake, Alice. "Babies for the Brave." *Saturday Evening Post* (July 31, 1954).

Lambert, Lydia. "Adopted from Care by the Age of Seven." *Adoption and Fostering*. 105 3 (1981), 28–36.

Lambert, Lydia, and Jane Streather. *Children-Changing Families: A Study of Adoption and Illegitimacy*. London: Macmillan, 1980.

Langsam, Miriam Z. *Children West*. Madison: State Historical Society of Wisconsin, 1964.

LaRossa, Ralph, and Maureen Mulligan LaRossa. *Transition to Parenthood: How Infants Change Families*. Beverly Hills, Cal.: Sage, 1981.

Lawder, Elizabeth et al. "A Limited Number of Older Children in Adoption—A Brief Survey." *Child Welfare*, 37 (November 1958).

Lawder, Elizabeth. *A Follow-up Study of Adoptions: Postplacement Functioning of Adoption Families*. New York: Child Welfare League of America, 1969.

Leatherman, Anne. "Placing the Older Child for Adoption." *Children* (May–June 1957).

Lee, Robert, and Ruth Hull. "Legal Casework, and Ethical Issues in 'Risk Adoption'." *Child Welfare,* 62, 5 (September–October 1983), 450–454.

Leeding, Alfred. "Access to Birth Records." *Adoption and Fostering,* 89, 3 (1977), 19–25.

Lefkowitz, Morris. Director of Services. Children's Home Society of California. Personal communication. December 12, 1969.

Le Pere, Dorothy et al. *Large Sibling Groups—Adoption Experiences.* New York: Child Welfare League of America, 1986.

Lifton, Betty Jean. *Twice Born—Memoirs of an Adopted Daughter.* New York: McGraw-Hill Book Company, 1975.

Lifton, Betty Jean. *Lost and Found.* New York: Bantam Books, 1981.

Lindemann, Bard. *The Twins Who Found Each Other.* New York: William Morrow, 1969.

Lipman, Margaret. "Adoption in Canada: Two Decades in Review." In *Adoption Current Issues and Trends.* Ed. Paul Sachdev. Toronto, Canada: Butterworths, 1984, 31–42.

Livingston, Carole. *Why Was I Adopted?* Secaucus, N.J.: Lyle Stuart, 1978.

Loehlin, John, Lee Willerman, and Joseph Horn. "Personality Resemblances Between Unwed Mothers and their Adopted-Away Offspring." *Developmental Psychology* (1982), 1089–1099.

Los Angeles County Department of Adoptions. *Biennial Report 1965–67.* Los Angeles, October 1967.

Losbough, Bilie. "Relationship of E.E.G. Neurological and Psychological Findings in Adopted Children (75 cases)." *A Medical Journal of E.E.G. Technology,* 5, 1 (January 1965), 1–4.

Maas, Henry. "The Successful Adoptive Parent Applicants." *Social Work,* 5 (January 1960).

Macaskill, Catherine. "Post-Adoption Support: Is It Essential?" *Adoption and Fostering,* 9, 1 (1985), 45–49.

Mackie, Alastair. "Families of Adopted Adolescents." *Journal of Adolescence.* 5, (1982), 167–178.

Madison, Bernice, and Michael Schapiro. "Black Adoption—Issues and Policies: Review of the Literature." *Social Service Review,* 47 (December 1973), 531–560.

Maluccio, Anthony et al. "Beyond Permanency Planning." *Child Welfare,* 59 (November, 1980), 515–530.

Martin, Cynthia D. *Beating the Adoption Game.* LaJolla, Cal.: Oak Tree Publications, 1980.

Maurer, Ralph, Remi J. Cadoret, and Colleen Cain. "Cluster Analysis of Childhood Temperament Data on Adoptees." *American Journal of Orthopsychiatry,* 50, 3 (July, 1980), 522–535.

Maza, Penelope. *Child Welfare Research Note 2.* Washington, D.C.: Administration for Children, Youth, and Families, December 1983.

McCausland, Clare L. *Children of Circumstance—A History of the First 125 Years of the Chicago Child Care Society.* Chicago Child Care Society, 1976.

McCormick, Rea. "The Adopting Parents See the Child," in *Studies of Children.* Ed. Gladys Meger. New York: King's Crown Press, 1948.

McCoy, Jacqueline. "Identity as a Factor in the Adoptive Placement of the Older Child." *Child Welfare,* 40 (September 1961).

McGowan, Brenda G. "Historical Evolution of Child Welfare Services: An Examination of the Sources of Current Problems and Dilemmas." In *Child Welfare: Current Dilemmas, Future Directions.* Ed. Brenda G. McGowan and William Meezan. Itasca, Ill.: F. E. Peacock, 1983, 45–92.

McMahan, Ralph S. "An Investigation into the Socio-Economic Characteristics of Child Adopters in Relation to Methods of Distributing Adoptable Children." Unpublished doctoral dissertation, University of Arkansas, Little Rock, 1974.

McRoy, Ruth et al. "Self-Esteem and Racial Identity in Transracial and Inracial Adoptees." *Social Work.* 27, 6 (November 1982), 522–526.

McRoy, Ruth et al. "The Identity of Transracial Adoptees." *Social Casework*. (January 1984), 34–39.

McRoy, Ruth, and Zena Oglesby. "Group Work with Black Adoptive Applicants." *Social Work wtih Groups*, 20 (Spring 1985), 83–95.

McRoy, Ruth, and Louis Zurcher. *Transracial and In-Racial Adoptees—The Adolescent Years*. Springfield, Mass. 1983.

McTaggart, Lynne. *The Baby Brokers: The Marketing of White Babies in America*. New York: Dial Press, 1980.

McWhinnie, Alexina M. *Adopted Children—How They Grow Up*. London: Routledge and Kegan Paul, 1967.

McWhinnie, Alexina M. "Group Counselling with Seventy-Eight Adoptive Families." *Case Conference*. 14, 11–12 (March–April 1968).

Mednick, Sarnoff, William Gabrielli, and Barry Hutchings. "Genetic Influence in Criminal Conviction: Evidence from an Adoption Cohort." *Science*, 224 (May 1984), 891–894.

Meezan, William. *Adoption Services in the States*. Washington, D.C.: DHHS, 1980.

Meezan, William. "Toward an Expanded Role for Adoption Services." In *Child Welfare: Current Dilemmas, Future Directions*. Ed. Brenda G. McGowan and William Meezan. Itasca, Ill.: F.E. Peacock, 1983a, 425–478.

Meezan, William. "Child Welfare: An Overview of the Issues." In *Child Welfare: Current Dilemmas, Future Directions*. Ed. Brenda G. McGowan and William Meezan. Itasca, Ill.: F.E. Peacock, 1983b, 5–44.

Meezan, William, Sanford Katz, and Eva Russo. *Adoptions without Agencies: A Study of Independent Adoptions*. New York: Child Welfare League of America, 1978.

Meezan, William, and John Shireman. "Foster Parent Adoption: A Literature Review." *Child Welfare*. 61, 8 (November–December 1982), 525–535.

Menlove, Frances L. "Aggressive Symptoms in Emotionally Disturbed Adopted Children." *Child Development*, 36 (June 1965).

Michaels, Ruth. "Casework Considerations in Rejecting the Adoption Application." *Social Casework*, 28 (December 1947).

Middlestadt, Evelyn. "Facilitating the Adoption of Older Children." *Children Today*, 6, 3 (May–June 1977), 10–13.

Miller, Katharine et al. "Public-Private Collaboration and Permanency Planning." *Social Casework* 66 (April 1985), 237–241.

Morrison, Hazel. "Research Study in Adoption." *Child Welfare*, 29 (1950).

Morrison, James R., and Mark A. Stewart. "The Psychiatric Status of the Legal Families of Adopted Hyperactive Children." *Archives of General Psychiatry*, 28, 6 (June 1973), 888–891.

Mott, Paul E. *Foster Care and Adoptions: Some Key Policy Issues*. Prepared for the Subcommittee on Children and Youth of the Committee on Labor and Public Welfare. Washington, D.C.: Government Printing Office, 1975.

Mullender, Audrey, and Doreen Miller. "The Ebony Group: Black Children in White Foster Homes." *Adoption and Fostering*, 9, 1 (1985), 33–40.

Mulrey, J. M. "The Care of Destitute and Neglected Children." National Conference of Charities and Correction, 1899. Boston: George Ellis, 1900.

Munsinger, Harry. "The Adopted Child's I.Q.: A Critical Review." *Psychological Bulletin*, 82 (September 1975a), 623–659.

Munsinger, Harry. "Children's Resemblance to Their Biological and Adopting Parents in Two Ethnic Groups." *Behavior Genetics*, 5 (1975b), 239–253.

National Association for Mental Health, England. *A Survey Based on Adoption Case Reviews*. London: National Association for Mental Health, 1954.

National Center for Social Statistics. Office of Information Systems. S.R.S. H.E.W., *Adoptions in 1970*, June 1972.

National Center for Social Statistics. *Adoptions in 1975*. Washington, D.C.: U.S. Government Printing Office, April 1977.

National Committee for Adoption. *Adoption Fact Book: United States Data Issues, Regulations and Resources.* Washington, D.C.: National Committee for Adoption, 1985.

Naylor, Audrey. "Results of a Mismatch." *Zero to Three* (March 1982), 8–11.

Neilson, J. "Placing Older Children In Adoptive Homes." *Children Today,* 1, 6 (November–December 1972), 7–13.

Neilson, J. "Tayari: Black Homes for Black Children." *Child Welfare,* 55, 1 (January 1976), 41–50.

Nelson, Katherine. *On the Frontier of Adoption: A Study of Families Who Adopt Special Needs Children.* New York: Child Welfare League of America, 1985.

Nemovicher, Joseph. *A Comparative Study of Adopted Boys and Nonadopted Boys in Respect to Specific Personality Characteristics.* Unpublished Ph.D. thesis, New York University, 1960.

New York State Commission on Child Welfare. *Barriers to the Freeing of Children for Adoption.* New York: New York State Department of Social Services, March 1976.

Nieden, Margarete Z. "The Influence of Constitution and Environment Upon the Development of Adopted Children." *Journal of Psychology,* 31 (1951).

Nix, Helen. "Sibling Relationship in Older Child Adoptions." *Adoption and Fostering* 7, 2 (1983), 22–28.

Norvell, Melissa, and Rebecca Guy. "A Comparison of Self-Concept in Adopted and Non-Adopted Adolescents." *Adolescence,* 12, 47 (Fall 1977), 443–448.

Ohio District 11. *Adoption Project, Final Report,* Warren, Ohio: Trumbull County Children's Services Board, 1977.

O'Neill, M. M. "Adoption-Identification and Service." *Child Welfare,* 51, 5 (May 1972), 314–317.

Opportunity. *National Survey of Black Children Adopted in 1975.* Portland, Ore.: Boys and Girls Society of Oregon. December 30, 1976.

Paget, Norman. "Use of Video Equipment in a Child Welfare Agency." *Child Welfare,* 48. 5 (May 1969), 296–300.

Pannor, Reuben, et al. *The Unmarried Father—New Approaches in Helping Unmarried Young Parents.* New York. Springer-Verlag, 1971.

Pannor, Reuben, and Evelyn A. Nerlove. "Fostering Understanding Between Adolescents and Adoptive Parents Through Group Experience." *Child Welfare,* 56, 8 (September–October 1977), 537–545.

Partridge, Penny. "On Letting 'Adopted Children' Grow Up: The Psychological Unfinished Business of the Adult Adoptee." Paper presented at the National Symposium on Child Placement, Nashville, Tennessee, October, 1978.

Pascall, Gillian. "Adoption: Perspectives in Social Policy." In *Adoption Essays in Social Policy, Law, and Sociology.* Ed. Philip Bean. New York: Tavistock Publications, 1984, 9–23.

Paton, Jean M. *The Adopted Break Silence.* Philadelphia: Life History Study Center, 1954.

Peller, L. "About 'Telling the Child' of His Adoption." *Bulletin of the Philadelphia Association of Psychoanalysis.* 11 (1961), 145–154.

Pepper, Gerald W. *Interracial Adoptions: Family Profile, Motiviation, and Coping Methods.* Unpublished Ph.D. thesis. University of Southern California, 1966.

Pettigrew, Brenda. "Group Discussions with Adoptive Parents." *Child Adoption,* 1 (1969), 39–42.

Pierce, William L. *Adoption Factbook—United States Data. Issues, Regulations and Resources.* Washington, D.C.: National Committee for Adoption, 1985.

Pilotti, Francisco. "Intercountry Adoption: A View from Latin America." *Child Welfare,* 64, 1 (January–February 1985), 25–35.

Platts, Hal K. "Facts Against Impressions—Mothers Seeking to Relinquish Children for Adoption." *Children,* 17, 1 (January–February 1970), 27–30.

Podolski, Alfred L. "Abolishing Baby Buying: Limiting Independent Adoption Placement." *Family Law Quarterly,* 9 (Fall 1975), 547–554.

Powers, Douglas, and John Powell. "A Role for Residential Treatment in Preparation for Adoption." *Residential Group Care and Treatment,* 1, 2 (Winter 1982), 3–18.

Prager, Barbara, and Stanley A. Rothstein. "The Adoptee's Right to Know His Natural Heritage." *New York Law Forum.* 19 (Summer 1973), 137–156.

Priddy, Drew, and Doris Kirgan. "Characteristics of White Couples Who Adopt Black-White Children." *Social Work,* 16, 3 (July 1971), 105–107.

Pringle, Kellmer M. L. "The Incidence of Some Supposedly Adverse Family Conditions and Left-Handedness in Schools for Mal-adjusted children." *British Journal of Educational Psychology,* 31 (June 1961).

Proch, Kathleen. *Adoption by Foster Parents.* University of Illinois at Urbana-Champaign: P.S.W. Thesis, 1980.

Proch, Kathleen. "Foster Parents as Preferred Adoptive Parents: Practice Implications." *Child Welfare,* 60, 9 (November 1981), 617–626.

Proch, Kathleen. "Differences Between Foster Care and Adoption: Perceptions of Adopted Foster Children and Adoptive Foster Parents." *Child Welfare,* 61, 5 (May 1982), 259–268.

Proch, Kathleen, and Merlin A. Taber. "Placement Disruption—A Review of Research." *Children and Youth Services Review* 7 (1985), 309–320.

Project CRAFT. *Training in the Adoption of Children with Special Needs.* Ann Arbor: University of Michigan School of Social Work, 1980.

Raleigh, Barbara. "Adoption as a Factor in Child Guidance." *Smith College Studies in Social Work,* 25 (October 1954).

Rapoport, Rhona, Robert Rapoport, and Ziona Strelitz. *Fathers, Mothers and Society: Towards New Alliances.* New York: Basic Books, 1977.

Rathbun, Constance, et al. *Later Adjustments of Children Following Radical Separation from Family and Culture.* Paper presented at the Annual Meeting, American Orthopsychiatric Association, Chicago, 1964.

Raynor, Lois. *Adoptions of Nonwhite Children—The Experience of the British Adoption Project.* London: George Allen & Unwin, Ltd., 1970.

Raynor, Lois. "Twenty One Plus and Adopted." *Adoption and Fostering,* 87, 1 (1977), 38–46.

Raynor, Lois. *The Adopted Child Comes of Age.* London: George Allen and Unwin, 1980.

Reece, Shirley, and Barbara Levin. "Psychiatric Disturbances in Adopted Children: A Descriptive Study." *Social Work.* 13, 1 (January 1968), 101–111.

Reitnauer, Paul, and Pamela Grabe. *Focusing Training for Mental Health Professionals on Issues of Foster Care and Adoption.* Mercer, Pa.: Children's Aid Society of Mercer County, 1985.

Resnick, Rosa Peria. "Latin American Children in Intercountry Adoption." In *Adoption: Essays in Social Policy, Law, and Sociology.* Ed. Philip Bean. New York: Tavistock, 1984, 273–287.

Ripple, Lillian. "A Follow-up Study of Adopted Children." *Social Service Review,* 42, 4 (December 1968), 479–497.

Romanofsky, Peter. " 'To Save . . . Their Souls': The Care of Dependent Jewish Children in New York City 1900–1905." *Jewish Social Studies* (1974), 253–261.

Rosenthal, David, et al. "The Types and Prevalence of Mental Illness in the Biological and Adoptive Families of Adopted Schizophrenics," in *The Transmission of Schizophrenia.* Ed. David Rosenthal and Seymour S. Kety. London: Pergamon Press, 1968a, 345–362.

Rosenthal, David. "Schizophrenics Offspring Reared in Adoptive Homes." In *The Transmission of Schizophrenia.* Ed. David Rosenthal and Seymour Kety. London: Pergamon Press, 1968b, 377–391.

Rosenthal, David. "Three Adoption Studies of Heredity in Schizophrenia." *International Journal of Mental Heath,* 1. 1-2 (1972), 63–75.

Rosenthal, David. "Parent Child Relationships and Psychopathological Disorder in the Child." *Archives of General Psychiatry,* 32, 4 (April 1975), 466–476.

Rosenthal, Perihan. "Triple Jeopardy: Family Stresses and Subsequent Divorce Following the Adoption of Racially and Ethnically Mixed Children." *Journal of Divorce,* 4, 4 (Summer 1981), 43–55.

Rowe, Jean, and Lydia Lambert. *Children Who Wait—A Study of Children Needing Substitute Families.* London: Association of British Adoption Agencies, 1973.

Rue, Marilyn, and Loyal Rue. "Reflections on Bicultural Adoption." In *Adoption Essays in Social Policy, Law, and Sociology.* Ed. Philip Bean. New York: Tavistock, 1984, 243–253.

Rutgers Law Review. "Adoption Psychological Parenthood as the Controlling Factor in Determining Best Interests of the Child." *Rutgers Law Review,* 26 (1973), 693–712.

Ryant, Joseph C. "Some Issues in the Adoption of Native Children." In *Adoption Current Issues and Trends.* Ed. Paul Sachdev, Toronto, Canada: Butterworths, 1984, 169–180.

Sachdev, Paul. "Adoption Outlook: Projection for the Future." In *Adoption: Current Issues and Trends.* Ed. Paul Sachdev. Toronto, Canada: Butterworths, 1984a, 287–304.

Sachdev, Paul. "Unlocking the Adoption Files: A Social and Legal Dilemma." In *Adoption: Current Issues and Trends.* Ed. Paul Sachdev. Toronto, Canada: Butterworths, 1984b, 141–168.

St. Dennis, Gerald. *Interracial Adoptions in Minnesota: Self Concept and Child Rearing Attitudes of Caucasian Parents Who Have Adopted Negro Children.* Unpublished Ph.D. thesis. University of Minnesota, 1969.

Sandgrund, Gertrude. "Group Counseling with Adoptive Families After Legal Adoption." *Child Welfare,* 41 (June 1962).

Sandusky, Annie Lee et al. *Families for Black Children—The Search for Adoptive Parents. II: Program and Projects.* Washington, D.C.: U.S. Government Printing Office, 1972.

Sants, H. J. "Genealogical Bewilderment in Children with Substitute Parents." *Child Adoption,* 47 (1965), 32–42.

Sarmiento, J. M. "Adoption Week: A Publicity Project in Adoptive Recruitment." *Child Welfare,* 48, 3 (March 1969), 166–169.

Sawbridge, Phillida. "Seeking New Parents: A Decade of Development." In *New Developments in Foster Care and Adoption.* Ed. John Triseliotis. Boston, Mass.: Routledge and Kegan Paul, 1980, 162–177.

Scarr, Sandra, and Richard A. Weinberg. "IQ Test Performance of Black Children Adopted by White Families." *American Psychologist* (October 1976), 726–739.

Scarr, Sandra, and Richard A. Weinberg. "Attitudes, Interests and I.Q." *Human Nature,* 1, 4 (April 1978), 29–36.

Scarr-Salapateck, Sandra, and Richard A. Weinberg. "When Black Children Grow Up in White Homes." *Psychology Today* (December 1975), 80–82.

Schaffer, Rudolph. *Mothering.* Cambridge, Mass.: Harvard University Press, 1977.

Schapiro, Michael. *A Study of Adoption Practice,* Vol. 3: *Adoption of Children with Special Needs.* New York: Child Welfare League of America, April 1957.

Schechter, Marshall. "Observation on Adopted Children." *AMA Archives of General Psychiatry,* 3 (July 1960).

Schechter, Marshall, et al. "Emotional Problems in the Adoptee." *General Archives of Psychiatry,* 10 (February 1964).

Schlesinger, Benjamin. "Single-Parent Adoption." In *Adoption: Current Issues and Trends.* Ed. Paul Sachdev. Toronto, Canada: Butterworths, 1984, 233–243.

Schneider, Stanley, and Esti Rimmer. "Adoptive Parents' Hostility Toward Their Adopted Children." *Children and Youth Services Review,* 6, (1984), 345–352.

Schulsinger, Fini. "Psychopathy: Heredity and Environment." *International Journal of Mental Health,* 1 (1972), 190–206.

Schwartz, Lita. "Contested Adoption Cases: Grounds for Conflict Between Psychology and the Law." *Professional Psychology: Research and Practice,* 14, 4 (1983), 444–456.

Schwartz, William. "Group Work in Public Welfare." *Public Welfare.* 26 (October 1968), 348–356.

Scott, Della B. *A Report on Characteristics of Registrants for Adoption, Children Placed and Services Rendered by Adoption Agencies.* New York: Travelers Aid International Social Services, 1976.

Seelig, George B. "The Implementation of Subsidized Adoption Programs: A Preliminary Survey." *Journal of Family Law,* 15, 4 (1976–1977), 732–769.

Seglow, Jean, Mia Kellmer Pringle, and Peter Wedge. *Growing Up Adopted—A Long Term National Study of Adopted Children and Their Families.* Windsor, England: National Foundation for Education in England and Wales, 1972.

Seidl, Frederick. "Transracial Adoption: Agency Response to Applicant Calls." *Social Work,* 17, 3 (May 1972), 119–120.

Sellers, Martha. "Transracial Adoption." *Child Welfare,* 48, 6 (June 1969), 355–356.

Shaffer, Gary. "Subsidized Adoption in Illinois." *Children and Youth Services Review,* 3, 1 (1981), 55–68.

Shapiro, Deborah, and Lucille J. Grow. "Not So Bold and Not So Irrelevant. A Reply to Chimezie." *Child Welfare,* 56, 2 (February 1977), 86–91.

Sharrar, Mary L. "Some Helpful Techniques When Placing Older Children for Adoption." *Child Welfare,* 49, 8 (October 1970), 459–463.

Sharrar, Mary L. "Attitude of Black Natural Parents Regarding Adoption." *Child Welfare,* 50, 5 (May 1971), 286–289.

Shaw, Martin, and Kathryn Lebans. "Children Between Families." *Adoption and Fostering,* 84, 2 (1976), 17–27.

Shireman, Joan F. "Adoptive Applicants Who Withdrew." *Social Service Review,* 44, 3 (September 1970), 285–292.

Shireman, Joan F. "Achieving Permanence After Placement." In *Child Welfare: Current Dilemmas, Future Directions.* Ed. Brenda G. McGowan and William Meezan. Itasca, Illinois: F.E. Peacock, 1983, 377–424.

Shireman, Joan F., and Penny R. Johnson. "Single Persons as Adoptive Parents." *Social Service Review,* 50, 1 (March 1976), 103–116.

Shireman, Joan F., and Penny Johnson. "A Longitudinal Study of Black Adoptions: Single-Parent, Transracial and Traditional." *Social Work* 31, 3 (May–June 1986), 172–176.

Shireman, Joan F., and Kenneth Watson. "Adoption of Real Children." *Social Work,* 17, 3 (July 1972), 29–38.

Shyne, Ann, and Anita Schroeder. *National Study of Social Services to Children and Their Families.* Washington, D.C.: DHEW, 1978.

Sigvardsson, S. et al. "Predisposition to Petty Criminality in Swedish Adoptees." *Archives of General Psychiatry,* 39 (November, 1982), 1248–1253.

Silver, Larry. "Frequency of Adoption in Children with Neurological Learning Disability Syndrome." *Journal of Learning Disabilities,* 3, 6 (June 1970), 306–310.

Silverman, Arnold R., and William Feigelman. "Some Factors Affecting the Adoption of Minority Children." *Social Casework,* 58, 9 (November 1977) pp. 554–561.

Simon, Nathan, and Audrey Senturia. "Adoption and Psychiatric Illness." *American Journal of Psychiatry,* 122 (February 1966).

Simon, Rita J. "Adoption of Black Children by White Parents in the U.S.A." in *Adoption: Essays in Social Policy, Law, and Sociology.* Ed. Philip Bean. New York: Tavistock Publications, 1984, 229–242.

Simon, Rita J., and Howard Alstein. *Transracial Adoption.* New York: John Wiley & Sons, 1977.

Simpson, Mark, Heidi Timm, and Hamilton McCubbin. "Adoptees in Search of Their Past: Policy Induced Strain on Adoptive Families and Birth Parents." *Family Relations* 30, 3 (July 1981), 427–434.

Singer, Leslie M., David M. Brodzinsky, and Anne M. Braff. "Children's Beliefs About Adoption: A Developmental Study." *Journal of Applied Developmental Psychology,* 3, 4 (October–December, 1982), 285–294.

Singer, Leslie et al. "Mother-Infant Attachment in Adoptive Families." *Child Development,* 56 (1985), 1541–1544.

Singer, Sandra M., and Karen Hardy-Brown. "Selective Placement in Infant Adoptions." In *Adoption: Current Issues and Trends.* Ed. Paul Sachdev. Toronto, Canada: Butterworths, 1984, 87–100.

Sklar, June, and Beth Berkov. "Teenage Family Formation in Post War America." *Family Planning Perspective*, 6 (Spring 1974), 80–90.

Smith, Carol Lindsay. "The New Families Project." In *New Developments in Foster Care and Adoption*. Ed. John Triseliotis. Boston, Mass.: Routledge and Kegan Paul, 1980, 196–211.

Smith, Carole R. "Adoption Advice: A New Service." *British Journal of Social Work*, 6, 2 (1976), 158–175.

Smith, Dorothy, and Laurie Sherwen. *Mothers and Their Adopted Children:—The Bonding Process*. New York: Tiresias Press, 1983.

Smith, Jerome, and Franklin I. Miroff. *You're Our Child: A Social-Psychological Approach to Adoption*. Lanham, Md: University Press of America, 1981.

Smith, Rebecca. "The Sealed Adoption Record Controversy and Agency Response." *Child Welfare*, 55, 2 (February 1976), 73–74.

Sobol, Michael, and Jeanette Cardiff. "A Sociopsychological Investigation of Adult Adoptees' Search for Birth Parents." *Family Relations*, 32, (October 1983), 477–483.

Sorich, Carol J., and Roberta Siebert. "Toward Humanizing Adoption." *Child Welfare* 61, 4 (April 1982), 207–216.

Sorosky, Arthur D., Annette Baran, and Reuben Pannor. "Adoptive Parents and the Sealed Record Controversy." *Social Casework*, 55, 9 (November 1974a), 531–536.

Sorosky, Arthur D., Annette Baran, and Reuben Pannor. "Opening the Sealed Record in Adoption." *Journal of Jewish Communal Services* (1974b), 188–196.

Sorosky, Arthur D., Annette Baran, and Reuben Pannor. "The Reunion of Adoptees and Birth Relatives." *Journal of Youth and Adolescence*, 3 (1974c), 195–206.

Sorosky, Arthur D., Annette Baran, and Reuben Pannor. *The Effects of Sealed Records in Adoption*. Paper presented at American Psychiatric Association meeting, May 6, 1975a, in Anaheim, California. Mimeo, 7pp.

Sorosky, Arthur D., Annette Baran, and Reuben Pannor. "Identity Conflicts in Adoptees." *American Journal of Orthopsychiatry*, 45, 1 (January 1975b), 18–27.

Sorosky, Arthur D., Annette Baran, and Reuben Pannor. "The Effects of the Sealed Record in Adoption." *American Journal of Psychiatry*, 133, 8 (August 1976), 900–904.

Sorosky, Arthur D., Annette Baran, and Reuben Pannor. *The Adoption Triangle—The Effects of the Sealed Record on Adoptees, Birth Parents and Adoptive Parents*. Garden City. N.Y.: Anchor/Doubleday, 1978.

Spaulding for Children. *Older and Handicapped Children Are Adoptable: The Spaulding Approach*. Chelsea, Mich., 1975.

Springer, Helen. "Sharing Responsibility with Applicants to Adopt." *Child Welfare*, 35 (March 1956).

Starr, J. "Adoptive Placement of the Older Child." *Casework Papers*. New York: Columbia University Press, 1955.

Starr, Philip et al. "Early Life Experiences and Adoptive Parenting." *Social Casework*, 51 (October 1970), 491–500.

Stein, Leslie M., and Janet L. Hoopes. *Identity Formation in the Adopted Adolescent—The Delaware Family Study*. New York: The Child Welfare League of America, 1985.

Stern, Daniel. *The First Relationship: Infant and Mother*. Cambridge, Mass.: Harvard University Press, 1977.

Sternau, Amelia. "Short-Term Financial Aid for Adoptive Parents." *Child Welfare*, 38 (October 1959).

Stevenson, P. S. "The Evaluation of Adoption Reunions in British Columbia." *The Social Worker*, 44, 1 (Spring 1976), 9–12.

Stonesifer, Elsie. "The Behavior Difficulties of Adopted and Own Children." *Smith College Studies in Social Work*, 13 (1942).

Stumpf, Margaret. "Group Meetings for Prospective Adoptive Applicants." In *Group Methods in the Public Welfare Program*. Ed. Norman Fenton and Kermit Wiltse. Palo Alto, Cal.: Pacific Books, Publishhers, 1963.

Sweeny, Dolores et al. "A Descriptive Study of Adoptive Children Seen in a Child Guidance Clinic." *Child Welfare*, 42 (November 1963).

Taft, Ruth. "Adoptive Families for 'Unadoptable' Children." *Child Welfare,* 32 (June 1953).

Theis, Sophie Van Senden. *How Foster Children Turn Out.* New York: State Charities And Association, 1924.

Tizard, Barbara. *Adoption—A Second Chance.* New York: The Free Press, 1977.

Tizard, Barbara. "Adopting Older Children from Institutions." *Child Abuse and Neglect,* 3 (1979), 535–538.

Toussieng, Povl. "Thoughts Regarding the Etiology of Psychological Differences in Adopted Children." *Child Welfare,* 41 (February 1962).

Tremitiere, Barbara T. *Disruption: A Break in Commitment.* York, Pa.: Tressler-Lutheran Service Associates, July 1984.

Triseliotis, John P. *Evaluation of Adoption Policy and Practice.* Edinburgh University, Department of Social Administration, 1970.

Triseliotis, John P. *In Search of Origins.* London: Routledge and Kegan Paul, 1973.

Triseliotis, John P. "Identity and Adoption." *Child Adoption,* No. 4 (1974), 27.

Triseliotis, John P. "Obtaining Birth Certificates." In *Adoption: Essays in Social Policy, Law, and Sociology.* Ed. Philip Bean. New York: Tavistock, 1984, 38–53.

Turano, Margaret. "Black Market Adoptions." *Catholic Lawyer* (Winter 1976), 48–69.

Unger, Christopher, Gladys Dwarshuis, and Elizabeth Johnson. *Chaos, Madness and Unpredictability.* Chelsea, Mich.: Spaulding for Children, 1977.

U.S. Congress. *Adoption and Foster Care 1975. Hearings Before the Subcommittee on Children and Youth of the Committee on Labor and Public Welfare.* U.S. Senate. April, July 1975. Washington, D.C.: Government Printing Office, 1975.

U.S. Deparment of Health and Human Services. *Adoption Project for Handicapped Children: Ohio District II.* Washington, D.C.: DHHS, 1980a.

U.S. Department of Health and Human Services. *Broadening Adoption Opportunities.* Washington, D.C.: DHHS, 1980b.

U.S. Department of Health and Human Services. *Adoption Disruptions.* Washington, D.C.: DHHS, 1981a.

U.S. Department of Health and Human Services. *Child Welfare Training: Education for Social Work Practice with American Indian Families.* Washington, D.C.: DHHS, 1981b.

U.S. Senate. *Hearing Before the Subcommittee to Investigate Juvenile Delinquency of the Committee on the Judiciary.* Washington, D.C.: U.S. Government Printing Office, 1956.

Vaitenas, Raminta. "Children with Special Needs: Perinatal Education for Adoption Workers." *Child Welfare,* 60, 6 (June 1981), 405–412.

Valiente-Barksdale, Clara. "Recruiting Hispanic Families." *Children Today,* 12, 2 (March–April 1983), 26–28.

Valk, Margaret. *Korean-American Children in American Adoptive Homes.* New York: Child Welfare League of America. September 1957.

Vieregge, Elizabeth. "Experience with Applicants in a Single Preadoption Group Meeting," in *Group Methods in the Public Welfare Program.* Ed. Norman Fenton and Kermit Wiltse. Palo Alto, Calif.: Pacific Books, Publishers, 1963.

von Knorring, A., M. Bohman, and S. Sigvardsson. "Early Life Experiences and Psychiatric Disorders: An Adoptee Study." *ACTA Psychiatric Scandinavian,* 65, (1982), 283–291.

Wachtel, Dawn D. *Adoption Agencies and the Adoption of Black Children.* Washington, D.C.: Adoptions Research Project, 1972.

Waldinger, Gloria. "Subsidized Adoption: How Paid Parents View It." *Social Work* 27, 6 (November 1982), 516–521.

Walton, Sarah. "A Federal Perspective of Child Welfare: There is No Hitching Post in the Universe." In *Treating Families in the Home: An Alternative to Placement.* Ed. Marvin Bryce and June Lloyd. Springfield, Ill.: Charles C Thomas. 1981, 24–34.

Ward, Margaret. "Culture Shock in the Adoption of Older Children." *The Social Worker.* 48, 1 (Spring 1980), 8–11.

Ward, Margaret. "Parental Bonding in Older-Child Adoptions." *Child Welfare,* 60, 1 (January 1981), 24–34.

Ward, Margaret. "Subsidized Adoption: New Hope for Waiting Children." In *Adoption:*

Current Issues and Trends. Ed. Paul Sachdev. Toronto, Canada: Butterworths, 1984, 253–266.

Warfield, Martha J. "Treatment of a Two-Year-Old in Preparation for Adoption." In *No Child is Unadoptable.* Ed. Sallie R. Churchill, Bonnie Carlson, and Lynn Nybell. Beverly Hills, Cal.: Sage, 1979, 110–119.

Weidell, Ruth. "Unsealing Sealed Birth Certificates in Minnesota." *Child Welfare,* 59, 2 (February 1980), 113–119.

Weingarten, Victor. "Breaking the Barrier of Confidentiality." *Child Welfare,* 37 (April 1958).

Weiss, Andrea. "Symptomatology of Adopted and Non-adopted Adolescents in Psychiatric Hospital." *Adolescence* 10, 80 (Winter 1985), 763–774.

Welter, Marianne. *Composition of Adopted Older Foreign Born and American Children.* New York: International Social Service, 1965.

Wender, Paul H. "Adopted Children and Their Families in the Evaluation of Nature-Nurture Interaction in the Schizophrenic Disorders." *Annals Review of Medicine,* 23 (1972), 355–372.

Wheeler, Katherine B. "The Use of Adoptive Subsidies." *Child Welfare,* 48, 9 (November 1969), 557–559.

Whittaker, James K. *Caring for Troubled Children.* San Francisco: Jossey-Bass, 1979.

Wiehe, Vernon. "The Group Adoptive Study." *Child Welfare,* 51, 10 (December 1972), 645–649.

Wingfield, F. "Prospecive Adopters Groups: An Experiment." *Social Work,* 26, 4 (October 1969), 14–16.

Wisconsin Department of Health and Social Services. *Unmarried Mothers in Wisconsin—1974.* Madison, Wis.: Division of Family Services, 1977.

Wishard, Laurie, and William R. Wishard. *Adoption: The Grafted Tree.* San Francisco: Cragmont, 1979.

Witmer, Helen et al. *Independent Adoptions.* New York: Russell Sage Foundation, 1963.

Wolkend, Stephan, and Anne Kozaruk. "The Adoption of Children with Medical Handicap." *Adoption and Fostering,* 7, 1, (1983), 32–35.

Womack, William, and Wayne Fulton. "Transracial adoption and the Black Preschool Child." *Journal of the American Academy of Child Psychiatry,* 20, (1981), 712–724.

Work, Henry H., and Hans Anderson. "Studies in Adoption: Requests for Psychiatric Treatment." *American Journal of Psychiatry,* 127, 7 (January 1971), 948–950.

Young, Ruth. *Adoption of Black Children: An Assessment of the ABCD Project in Maryland.* College Park, Md: University of Maryland School of Social Work, n.d.

Zastrow, Charles. *Outcome of Black Children-White Parents Transracial Adoptions.* San Francisco: R & E Research Associates, 1977.

Zeilinger, Richard. "Readers Forum." *Child Welfare,* 61, 7 (September–October, 1982), 478–479.

Zober, Edith. "Postplacement Service for Adoptive Families." *Child Welfare,* 40 (April 1961).

Zwimpfer, Diane. "Indicators of Adoption Breakdown." *Social Casework,* 64, 3 (March 1983), 169–177.

10

Substitute Care:

The Child-Caring Institution

Introduction

The *child-caring institution* is the third type of facility that offers total substitute care for children who cannot remain in their parents' home but who need specialized services other homes cannot provide. The foster home is a temporary facility; the adoptive home is a permanent one. Both provide the child with family care. The child-caring institution, like the foster home, provides temporary substitute care; however, it does so in a group setting. A *children's institution* is defined as a twenty-four-hour residential facility in which a group of unrelated children live together in the care of a group of unrelated adults. Calling such facilities residential centers, the Child Welfare League of America (1982) notes that their services should be provided on a time-limited basis and should provide treatment assistance for both the child and the child's family:

> The residential center assumes a degree of responsibility for providing conditions favorable to the growth and development of children who are not being reared for a time by their families, and for helping children and their parents with difficulties preventing the children from growing up in a family and enjoying the opportunities that, in our society, the family is primarily expected to provide [p. 3]

Recent federal legislation sets an upper limit on the number of children that can served in institutions for dependent (but not delinquent) children. To receive federal reimbursement, no more than twenty-five children must be in residence (Public Law 96-272, 94 Stat. 504).

Many different kinds of institutions serve different kinds of children. Among them are the following:

1. Institutions that perceive their role as providing homes for dependent and neglected children. They are a modern analogy to the old orphan asylum.
2. Institutions that provide specialized services for physically handicapped children. There are separate institutions for children who are blind, deaf, crippled, asthmatic, and so on. These organizations provide educational, medical, and social services. Children in these settings may also be emotionally handicapped.

3. Institutions for retarded children, most of whom are severely retarded, and many of whom are multiply handicapped.
4. Institutions for the confinement and rehabilitation of juvenile delinquents. They are often called training schools.
5. Institutions that provide treatment for emotionally disturbed children and their families. They are known as residential treatment centers.

Two types of transitory care facilities are particularly commonplace. Emergency facilities accept children on a short-term basis while a study is made of their family and personal situations in order to determine the best plan for their care. Diagnostic or observation centers also serve children for a limited period of time. Staff in these agencies are trained to carry out more detailed psychological, physical, and social studies of residents and their family circumstances.

Residential treatment programs have experimented with innovative variations on the seven-day-a-week type of residence. Day treatment programs have become increasingly popular. Children reside at the center during the school day, but return to their homes each evening and during the weekend. Tovey (1983) describes these programs as particularly helpful to families, enabling them to enhance their ability to live with their disturbed children and to find needed resources in the local community. (See also Ross & Schreiber, 1975.) Another residential treatment variation provides services only on weekends (Astrachan & Harris, 1983). This is appropriate for families who live some distance from the center, for families who have supportive educational services available in their home community but need additional treatment services for their children, and for those who, because of special parent problems or the extreme demands made by their children, need some regular respite care (Weisfeld & Laser, 1976).

Although institutions deal with the child who faces some problem in the parent–child relationship, many institutions are not under social-work child-welfare auspices, perhaps because the central problem is perceived as a medical problem in the case of the physically handicapped child; as a problem of law enforcement in the case of the juvenile delinquent; or as a medical, educational, or vocational problem in the case of the mentally deficient child. Hence institutions operate under the auspices of many different professions.

Residential treatment services, which are primarily paid for through public child welfare funds, may be provided directly by the agency itself, or purchased from other public or private providers. A national survey of agencies (Shyne & Schroeder 1978) found that the public child welfare agencies themselves most often provided emergency care services, serving 69 per cent of the children needing such assistance. Residential treatment services, on the other hand, were more frequently purchased from other agencies (71%) (p. 68).

Group Homes

The group homes may be viewed as large foster-family unit or a small institution. It is a living facility within the normal community simulating a family for a small group of unrelated children. The group home requires more extended discussion, not because it offers service currently to any significant number of the children in substitute care, but because it has become an increasingly commonplace alternative to in-patient residential care.

The group home may be that of a private family whose members have been recruited because of their understanding of and willingness to work with a large group of children. More frequently, it is a single home or apartment owned or rented by the agency and staffed by "foster parents" who are employed by the agency (Greenberg, 1963). It is established in a residential community and is indistinguishable from neighboring units. A married couple may be employed on a free-rent-and-board basis, plus a board rate for each child, or on the basis of a straight monthly salary. The "group home parents" work around the clock, much as they would if these were their own children.

The Child Welfare League of America Group Home Standards Statement (1978) suggests that group homes "should not be used for fewer than five children or more than twelve. A group of six to eight children is optimum because it is small enough to allow for individualization and large enough to remain a group even if a member is (temporarily) absent" (p. 27). It is further recommended that both boys and girls under twelve be included together in a group home. For older children, careful planning is necessary in relation to facilities and supervision. The children should participate with staff in the development and implementation of house rules.

Children selected for group homes must be able to live with the group without endangering themselves and others. The children need to be well enough to attent school regularly. An attempt is made to preserve some balance in the group, so that some aggressive youngsters are tempered by some quieter ones and some relatively normal adolescents. Gula (1964) estimates that group homes, "accepting referrals from a wide range of referral agencies, admit less than half" (p. 13).

The group home is an intermediary facility. It offers some of the personalization of family living typical of family care, yet permits some of the distance from adults possible in an institution. Consequently the group home is selected for "emotionally detached youngsters who are either too fearful to risk exposure of their feelings in close relationships or simply do not know how to find their way in close relationships" but who can operate without difficulty in the normal community (Schwartz & Kaplan, 1961, p. 10). It is also selected for adolescents because their principal developmental tasks revolve around establishing independence from parents and parental surrogates, and it is desirable to offer the kind of diluted, attenuated parental relationships characteristic of the family group home.

The group home has greater therapeutic potential than the foster-family home, particularly for the adolescent. Therapeutic changes in the child's behavior in the foster-family home depend on what the foster parents can make available in terms of relationships with the child and models of acceptable behavior. The group home makes these available, but it also provides a peer group interaction which helps to control and modify undesirable behavior.

The group home owned and staffed by the agency offers additional advantages to emotionally disturbed children. The pay may be high enough to permit the employment of staff with some professional training; the fact that it is operated by the agency may allow heavier demands on the staff in meeting the special needs of emotionally disturbed children and in providing the scheduling necessary for special classes, appointments with psychotherapists, and so on. The group home owned and operated by the agency has the additional advantage of permitting staff to be somewhat more relaxed, tolerant, and accepting of the inevitable minor destructiveness of emotionally disturbed children.

The group home may serve as a "halfway house" for children who are ready to be discharged from an institution but who are not yet ready to return to their own families. It permits the orderly, progressive reintroduction of the child back into the community.

The different institutions serving different groups of children are, of course, apt to differ in many essential details. All have in common the fact that they are group-care facilities that provide total substitution for the biological parents' care of the child. This implies, then, that many significant elements are common to all institutions. Our concern in this chapter is with those general factors that are characteristic of all institutions. However, whenever we do encounter the more particular practice of institutions, we will focus on institutions for the dependent and neglected and on residential treatment centers for emotionally disturbed children. These institutions employ the bulk of social workers working in residential child care.

Historical Background

The institution has a long history. The *xenodocheion* established by the Council of Nicaea in 325 to give shelter to the sick and the poor became asylums for abandoned children as well. In 787 Datheus, Archbishop of Milan, established an institution to care for children. Concerned about abandonment of children, he noted: "These horrors would not take place if there existed an asylum where the adulterer could hide her shame but now they throw the infants in the sewers or the rivers and many are the murders committed on the new-born children" (Payne, 1916, p. 294). Similarly the pitiful condition of the many abandoned children in fifteenth-century France attracted the sympathy of St. Vincent de Paul, who established homes for *enfants trouvés* in 1633.

But although there existed a limited number of institutions exclusively concerned with caring for children, the more typical pattern was to have the children share an institution with other deprived groups in the population. Admission records of the New York City Almshouse note that some 15 per cent of the admissions between 1736 and 1746 involved "young and parentless children—the orphaned and the deserted—who would remain until the beginning of their apprenticeship" (Rothman, 1971, p. 39).

Placement in an almshouse was one of four available options for poor dependent children in the seventeenth and eighteenth centuries. In the form of outdoor relief, families had very limited access to home-based financial assistance. Some children were also farmed out, "a system whereby individuals or groups of paupers were auctioned off to citizens who agreed to maintain the paupers in their homes for a contracted fee" (McGowan, 1983, p.48). Children could be indentured, a system in which they served as apprentices and were taught a trade, working until the cost of their care had been paid. Typically, children were placed in almshouses and then were identured.

Only a few institutions exclusively for dependent children had been established by the end of the eighteenth century. One was opened in New Orleans as a result of the need to care for a large number of children orphaned by an Indian massacre at Natchez. Another was established as a result of a yellow fever epidemic in Philadelphia. More frequently, however, children requiring institutional care were consigned to mixed almshouses "to live with the aged, the insane, the feeble-minded, and the diseased. They were usually cared for by the ignorant employees;

their physical needs were negelected. . . . Those who survived knew only the life and routine of a pauper institution" (Abbott, 1938, p. 4). Some almshouses did make an effort to see that children's needs were met, however. The Rules and Orders for the Management of the Work House in Boston, dated 1739, noted:

> That when any children shall be received into the House, there shall be some suitable women appointed to attend them; Who are to take care that they be wash'd, com'b and dress'd every morning, and be taught to Read and be instructed in the Holy Scriptures . . . and that the rest of their time be employ'd in such work as shall be assigned them [quoted in Whittaker & Trieschman, 1972, p. 397].

In general, however, arrangements to provide institutional care for children were made for the convenience of the community, not out of concern for the individual child. Provision of minimal care in the cheapest way was considered adequate care for both the young and adults who were poor and unable to care for themselves (McGowan, 1983).

Although additional institutions for children were built early in the nineteenth century, the number of children in mixed almshouses continued to grow. As investigation after investigation confirmed the undesirable conditions under which the children lived, growing dissatisfaction led to increasingly insistent demands that this method of caring for children be prohibited. Thus the Board of Public Charities for the State of Ohio, in its report for 1869, declared:

> Nearly one thousand children in the poor-houses of Ohio! What is to be done with them? Think of their surroundings. The raving of the maniac, the frightful contortions of the epileptic, the driveling and senseless sputtering of the idiot, the garrulous temper of the decrepit, neglected old age, the peevishness of the infirm, the accumulated filth of all these; then add the moral degeneracy of such as, for idleness or dissipation, seek a refuge from honest toil in the tithed industry of the county, and you have a faint outline of the surroundings of these little boys and girls, all more or less intelligent, many of them bright and beautiful, in such homes as these. How deeply must every human sympathy be touched with the reflection, that to these little children the poor-house is "all the world" [Abbott, 1938, p. 52].

There were some attempts at compromise by making separate institutional facilities available to children on almshouse grounds, but these attempts were few and unsatisfactory. Because funds had already been invested to build poorhouses and alternative care situations for children were unavailable and costly, children remained in almshouses throughout the first half of the nineteenth century (McGowan, 1983).

During the latter part of the nineteenth century, many states prohibited almshouse care for children. Thus New York State, in 1875, declared that children should "be removed from almshouses and provided for in families, asylums or other appropriate institutions." This meant that alternative forms of care had to be provided for the literally tens of thousands of children who had to be removed from almshouse care in one state after another. By this time, both foster care and institutions exclusively concerned with children, such as orphanages, had been developed. And, as Thurston (1930) notes, "as children were withdrawn or refused admission to almshouses, the tendency to build orphan asylums—already strong—was stimulated" (p. 90).

The number of children in orphanages rose from 200 in 1790 to 123,000 in 1910 (Downs & Sherraden, 1983). Moreover, both the number of children residing in all types of institutions and the length of time they remained in them increased throughout the nineteenth century. In 1790, the number of institutionalized children per 1,000 children under the age of 21 was 0.62; by 1910 this rate had risen to 3.13 (p. 273). Downs and Sherraden believe that labor market changes that produced decreases in the need for child labor, coupled with the large influx of immigrant children to the United States, led to the increased use of this type of care.

Most children in institutions prior to the latter half of the nineteenth century were white children. Most institutions that were built specifically for children also had specific policies excluding blacks (Billingsley & Giovannoni, 1972).

The asylum was seen as shelter, sanctuary, and training school for the child. Moralism dictated the routine, and a premium was placed on order, obedience, and character development through work. As Keith-Lucas and Sanford (1977) point out

> The orphanage had as one of its primary purposes the saving of children from both physical and moral degradation. Since it could not possibly serve all those who were subject to these threats—and family life at home in extreme poverty, with little schooling and almost no religious instruction, were seen as degrading—the Home tended to select "worthy" or promising children and to dismiss them if they proved to be idle, ill-behaved, or ungrateful. The threat of dismissal was a powerful one, in view of the alternatives. The philosophy of saving the child from degradation also accounted for the almost universal practice of cutting the child off irrevocably from any family that he had, particularly if the family were judged to be immoral, ignorant, or irresponsible [p. 6–7].

Institutions were developed under the auspices of benevolent organizations, charitable individuals, and religious groups. An early history of social work notes:

> Institutions are in favor with the benevolent because the work done is so manifest. . . . Buildings are obvious and the money that goes into them takes a concrete form gratifying to contributors. The churches prefer such life for the children dependent on them because the children can be so easily isolated from teachings other than their own and there is opportunity for catechetical instruction [Warner, 1942, p. 134].

Public institutions were also developed under municipal, county, and state auspices. The first state institution was established by Massachusetts in 1866, and many states followed the pattern of housing dependent children in one central institution and placing them in families as soon as possible. The nineteenth century also witnessed the development of special institutions for the care of the physically handicapped, the deaf, the blind, the mentally retarded, and the delinquent. Thus, by 1923 the U.S. Census on Children Under Institutional Care listed 1,558 "orphan asylums" (Thurston, 1930, p. 39).

But even while the special institution for children was superseding the almshouse, serious questions were being raised about the advisability of any kind of institutional care for children. The late nineteenth and early twentieth centuries witnessed a continuous, prolonged, and often acrimonious debate in child welfare circles between the proponents of institutional care and advocates of family foster care (Wolins & Piliavin, 1964).

Increased recognition of the importance of the family to the child's healthy psychosocial development resulted in a growing preference for family foster care. The prevailing negative attitude toward the institution was strongly reinforced, by a United Nations report, *Maternal Care and Mental Health,* by John Bowlby (1951), which provided a detailed review of a considerable body of research showing the deleterious effects of institutional care on child development.

Erving Goffman, in his well-known 1961 publication, *Asylums,* also raised serious questions about the impact of institutional life on inmates. He argued that they developed survival skills that were mandatory for continued functioning in the institution, but that these skills inhibited them in their ability to adapt successfully, once they were released from care (Dore & Kennedy, 1981). Concern was also growing about instances of abuse or severe neglect in substitute care.

The deinstitutionalization movement grew out of these concerns. Child welfare workers developed a hierarchy of preferences. The child's own home, even if it were inadequate, was felt to be better than the best foster home; a foster home, even if inadequate, was felt to be better than the best institution. As a result of these professional and political shifts, increased use was made of foster care, and institutions were used less often, particularly for dependent children.

Today, the institution is retained as an option, one component of the continuum of services available, to be used when it best meets the needs of the child and the family and after less restrictive alternatives have been either unsuccessfully attempted or considered but found to be inappropriate. As an option, the institution is linked with other components in the continuum of services. There is reluctant acceptance of the idea that institutional care may be an exceptional but nevertheless necessary and potentially helpful form of placement (Small, 1984).

The resolution of the controversy resulted not only from the redefinition of the problem but also from a more ciritical attitude toward Bowlby's major thesis—that institutional care was likely to be harmful to the child. More recent research has softened the negative attitude toward the institution and contributed to the growing readiness to use it when it meets the needs of the child (Casler, 1961; World Health Organization, 1962; Witmer & Gershenson, 1968; Wolins, 1969a, b, 1974; Moyles & Wolins, 1971; Child Welfare League of America, 1972; Rutter, 1974; Langmeier & Matejcek, 1975; Tizard & Rees, 1975; Thomas, 1975a).

Professionals recently, have felt a need to clarify the nature of institutional policies and procedures that produce the least restrictive environment for children in this type of setting. A number of factors are seen as contributing to a positive institutional experience. Institutions should be small in size, and the living units within which children reside should also be small. The size of living units has actually decreased over the past several years from twenty to twenty-five children in the 1950s to eight to ten children by the late 1960s (Keith-Lucas & Sanford, 1977, p. 9). Children should also reside in institutions that are situated as close as possible to their home community (Skarnulis, 1979). Decreased distance between the institution and home helps promote continued parent contact and facilitiates the child's ability to return to that community. Finally, institutions should be oriented to and integrated with the surrounding community (Seidl, 1974). Such agencies utilize as many community resources as possible for the children in group care, including recreational, education and social resources. Using these resources allows the institution to provide as normalized an experience as possible for children (Whittaker, 1979; Dore & Kennedy, 1981). The impact of these provisions on the structure of treatment for children is considered in a later section of this chapter.

The "Uniqueness" of the Institution

The fact that institutional care is provided on a twenty-four-hour basis in a facility in which the children reside and in a location that is physically demarcated in some way from the rest of the community creates some unique advantages that can be exploited for the special needs of some children. These same factors also create potential disadvantages. Both the positive and potentially problematic aspects of this type of service must be evaluated in order to determine whether it is appropriate for a particular child.

1. Staffing patterns in the institution offer opportunities for a diluted emotional relationship and provide the child with a greater variety of potential parenting figures. Because the child has to share houseparents with many other children, his or her relationship with these adults is likely to be attenuated. This permits the child to maintain a certain "safe" psychological distance from parenting figures and allows him or her to modulate contact in accordance with emotional needs. At the same time, staff are in a position to make fewer demands on the child than birth or foster parents would. Because the staff have primary relationships outside the institution, they are better able to control their demands that the child be giving or caring when he or she cannot do so. Staff are also specifically trained to reduce their personal needs as they relate to the children, just as they are trained to deal with the child's negative behavior without also rejecting him or her (Child Welfare League of America, 1982). The child also has available a number of adult staff members with whom he or she may form attachments. The child may also choose to develop intensive relationships with teachers, social service staff, or other employees. There is a greater chance that, in the institution, the child will find some kind of person with whom he or she wants to identify.

The number and variety of available caretakers also create a potential difficulty for the child. He or she may fail to develop a primary relationship with any staff member, and this fact may go unnoticed by the various individuals responsible for day-to-day care. Staffing patterns and high turnover among caretakers also create problems of continuity of care for children who do form attachments. One's primary identification figure may only be available for brief periods during the week or for only a few months before being replaced. A survey of institutions conducted for the Child Welfare League of America by Russo and Shyne (1980) found that 20 per cent of these facilities had an annual child care turnover rate of 50 per cent or more; an additional 20 per cent had a turnover rate between 30–49 per cent, and 30 per cent of the facilities had a turnover rate between 20–29 per cent. Only 1/3 of the 125 agencies contacted had low staff turnover (p. 15).

2. Unique programmatic and structural elements of the institution help create a treatment environment that is particularly powerful in its impact on children. The fact that institutional living rquires rules, regulations, and a certain routine may be an advantage to many children who need this type of structure in order to reinforce their own efforts at self-control.

The institution is also aligned with those components of the child's ambivalence that strive to maintain control and to manifest acceptable behavior. The child recognizes that staff will support efforts to refrain from impulsive, unacceptable behavior.

Some of these children have come from chaotic and unpredictable home situations. The explicit and predictable structure of the institution relieves the child of responsibility from making decisions regarding his or her behavior—decisions that may occasion anxiety. Routine simplfies the child's life and permits him or her to know, with some assurance, what to expect. For children experiencing very limited control, the institutional environment also provides a set of comprehensive services (educational, social, physical, and recreational) that the child is not, as yet, able to fully utilize in the community (Janchill, 1983).

Of special importance is the fact that residential group care involves planning the child's daily living experience so tht it will be optimally therapeutic. Institutional staff can deliberately select children for a cottage group in accordance with some explicit considerations, such as the kind of friends each of the children needs. A child who is having difficulty with peers in one cottage can be moved to another living unit with a different peer group. The institution can regulate the demands it enforces on the child in line with the child's inadequacies. It can particularize the details of the living situation and, within limits, structure the child's reality to meet his or her clinical needs.

> [It can provide] a flexible low-pressure environment for the deeply disturbed sensitive child, a clearly defined, more rigidly organized environment for the acting-out aggressive child who needs help in controlling his impulses. The environment for the young impulse-driven schizophrenic child with little personality structure must give greater weight to such considerations as the use of space, the allotment and scheduling of time. It might provide for greater emphasis on order and regularity and movement in personal routine [Alt, 1960, p. 131].

Also, because many institutions control the child's educational program, they can provide a more individualized curriculum, permitting a slower pace with more intensive personal tutoring.

Programmatic and structural elements of institutional care also allow for greater responsiveness to the special needs of children and provide a greater tolerance for their unacceptable behavior. "The greater symptom tolerance in an institution applies not only to acting-out behavior, but to withdrawn or bizarre behavior—for example, a child who sits by himself and will not talk or one who refuses to bathe for weeks" (Lerner, 1952, p. 107). A child can also be permitted a greater range of destructive behavior in an institution than in a normal home. None of the staff "owns" the institution, so that destructive behavior, although deplored, does not arouse the intense reaction it might evoke from foster parents whose furniture was being ruined. The institution is in a better position than a private home to "absorb" such losses. By the same token, "the diffusion of the child's hostility among many adults makes it easier for any one staff member to take" (Child Welfare League of America, 1964, p. 7).

These same structural characteristics can, however, create difficulties for children in care. Of particular concern is the fact that the presence of regular routines and institution-wide rules may not allow staff to sufficiently individualize a child's treatment program.

As a congregate-care facility dealing with a sizable group of children, the institution needs regulations and rules. "One of the characteristics of total institutions is described by Goffman as follows: 'Each phase of the member's daily activity is carried on in the immediate company of a large batch of others, all of whom are treated alike and rquired to do the same thing' " (Gregory, 1980, p. 261). In less rigid therapeutic settings, a conflict arises between the need for some regimentation and the therapeutic need to individualize treatment for each child.

Adapting rules to the needs of particular children results, in turn, in conflict. Children are confused and upset when they see their peers treated differently for an infraction of the same rules. The problem is how to reconcile these contradictory needs and expectations in a situation in which the procedure is open to the scrutiny of the client group.

The institution is currently faced with a dilemma that arises from greater sensitivity to children's rights. The child has the right to treatment in the least restrictive setting and without coercion. As a consequence of attempting to adhere to granting such rights, institutions need to resolve difficult conflicts between children's rights and children's needs, and the rights of the individual child versus the rights of the group of children in the institution. The dilemma is that in satisfying children's rights, we may be denying children's needs (Mayer & Pearson, 1975). What if, in order to help the adolescent, the most desirable prescription is a controlled environment, and the adolescent, in claiming his or her rights, rejects this alternative? Respecting his or her rights denies him or her access to what he needs in order to have a more satisfying life.

Living with children inevitably involves problems of discipline, setting limits, and establishing controls. This is especially true in a group context composed of chldren who are there in the first place because they have difficulties in behavior control. Institutional child-care workers employ all of the procedures traditionally utilized by parents in attempting to get the child to act in a socially acceptable manner: appeals to reason, use of the power of the relationship and the risk the child runs of alienating the workers, the withholding of privileges or the providing of extra privileges, and so on. In addition, group living provides an opportunity for appealing to the need of the group and the group's judgment of the child's behavior as a leverage for control.

However, all of these procedures may fail. Even in the most accepting of settings, restraints may occasionally be necessary (Linnihan, 1977, p. 686), in apparent contradiction to the rights of the child. Protection of the child, the child-care worker, institutional property, and the rights of the other children may ultimately dictate the exercise of authority and the use of physical restraint, "time-out" facilities, "control rooms," or "quiet rooms" (Endres & Goke, 1973; Drisko, 1981).

The use of punishment or physical restraint places very difficult demands on staff. The appropriate use of punishment requires that staff act out of consideration for the needs of the child, and not in anger or out of a desire to hurt (Drisko, 1981). The use of such restraint also involves the use of the least amount of force needed to accomplish control objectives. This is always considered a procedure of last resort. However, it is particuarly difficult for staff to remain calm, competent, and child-oriented in a situation of this type, which is highly emotionally charged and potentially physically dangerous (Beker, et al 1972).

Professional ambivalence about the use of time-out and physical restraints is reflected in the results of Russo and Shyne's (1980) study of 144 residential facilities. Only one fifth of these agencies had used secure confinement in the last five years, and only thirteen out of the thirty-two facilities using it had done so fairly often or very often in the last year. The authors note, "of the 26 agencies reporting the number of residents requiring secure confinement in the last year, the range was from none to more than 75% of the resident population" (pp. 51, 53).

The use of physical restraint or secure confinement creates two particular problems. First, although such efforts may be effective in stopping behavior that is out of control, such techniques do not help children understand the causes of their behavior, clarify staff expectatons concerning behavior, or learn to internalize these expectations (Buckholdt, & Gubrium, 1979). Second, the possibility that staff may inappropriately use these techiques is always present and must be closely monitored. Russo and Shyne (1980) found some residential facilities that acknowledged leaving children in secure confinement for long periods of time. Twelve institutions in their survey stated that children could be placed in such confinement for up to twenty-four hours (p. 53). In a participant observation study of residential care, Buckholdt and Gubrium (1979) found:

> Children are very sensitive to the way that staff members use their discretion in determining the length of time-outs. Any dispute can easily become the basis for a conflict in which the child's outrage and the staff member's desire for control intensify each other and eventually lead to a blow-up. On numerous occasions we observed children who were assigned two or five minutes of time-out actually serving 10 or 15 minutes or even longer, because the staff member "forgot". On one occasion, for example, a boy in cottage three served 60 minutes of what was to have been a 5 minute time-out because he was sent to an area in which he was out of sight and forgotten until the staff member noticed that he was missing from dinner [p. 107].

Even with careful supervision and monitoring, institutional procedures can prove abusive for children (National Center on Child Abuse and Neglect, 1978).

A final drawback of institutional care, connected with the carefully controlled and developed structure of such agencies, is that children may be trained to function effectively within this setting but not to function well in their home or the local community (Gregory, 1980). Some residential programs focus a great deal of attention on what Janchill (1983) describes as boundry maintenance:

> Such programs attempt to hold to their distinctiveness by controlling client selection, delineating special treatment methods and techniques, restricting the movement of clients in and out of the program, as well as staffing pattern exclusiveness. Specialized programs often claim that the very handicaps of the clients require these special measures. However, excessive boundary maintenance can diminish the constructive effects that other relationships and interactions can have on the specialized program and its clients [p. 350].

To counteract this tendency, Whittaker (1979) states that program planning must focus on the client skills that have what he calls "maximum portability" (p. 10; see also Maier, 1981). Children should be taught a range of skills that will ultimately help them function more effectively in the general community and in their own home. Furthermore, assessment of a child's progress must be based on development of community-based abilities. A child who is moving toward this goal may not necessarily be functioning more effectively inside the institution.

This discussion of the structural components of institutional care suggests that the residential center's ability to control the child's environment proves to be a major advantage of such care, but can also present serious difficulties for the child and prevent his or her ultimate readaptation to the community, if the structuring is not carefully monitored and specifically designed to enhance normative life skills.

3. The fact that the child lives his or her daily life as a member of a peer group means that the group has power to control behavior. Group pressure can be applied

to motivate the child to become more conforming and less deviant (Eiskovits, 1980). Intimate daily living with a peer group provides the possibility of exploitation of group interactions as a catalyst for change. Through identification with the peer group, the child is able to accept and want what the group accepts and wants. For instance, one boy at first resented contact with the institutional social worker. The worker, consequently, delayed scheduling an appointment.

> All of H.'s group went to their regular appointments with their workers and H. became increasingly annoyed by this "neglect" when he received no appointments. After two months, he finally asked, "What the hell is the matter with that jerk of a social worker? Can't that guy write? Why doesn't he send me a pass for an appointment?" The worker, at this point, finally sent H. his appointment. The boy immediately was involved in an intensive treatment relationship [Schulman, 1954, p. 322].

However, all facets of peer group interaction are not under staff control. The children themselves informally assign social roles to group members as leaders and followers, exploiters and exploited. The group also develops its own code of behavior, to which it expects members to conform if they want to be accepted by and included in the group.

It is to be remembered that many of the children served by the institution are teenagers. Distrust of and hostility toward adults are at their height at this time, even among teenagers who have not experienced difficulty—and these children have known little except hurt and pain from the adults they have encountered. Furthermore the need for acceptance by the peer group and dependence on the peer group are very great during adolescence. The peer group can, therefore, exercise considerable control over those who refuse to conform to its code by threatening to reject them.

Problems arise when this informally developed social subsystem operates to encourage and support behavior that is in opposition to that officially sanctioned by the institution. In this situation, group living—the distinctive feature of the institution—creates a serious problem of competition between the formal, official system and the often incompatible, informal subsystem (Polsky, 1962).

The group code generally discourages the kind of intimate, psychologically open relationship with institutional staff that is necessary to the achievement of the therapeutic aims of the agency. According to Ohlin and Lawrence (1959), "Under existing circumstances, the inmate as a client must run the risk of social rejection by his peers to gain full advantage of the treatment experience" (p. 9). Furthermore the social structure of the group is built along autocratic lines, leaders and followers having markedly unequal status and interpersonal relationships being characterized by the exploitation of the weak by the strong. This, too, is in contravention to what the institution is trying to teach about democratic group living characterized by understanding and acceptance.

Fisher (1979) provides an example of the effect on children of an institutional setting in which staff are not sufficiently in control of the peer social system. In the detention center she describes, "one's fate is sealed on arrival day. Each new boy is physically challenged. If he doesn't defend himself, he will be beaten up or threatened sexually.... Group homosexual assaults are common among the older boys. Younger boys are simply taken sexually; sometimes they offer themselves" (p. 202).

A problem inherent in group homes as well as in institutions is the contagious effect that children have on each other. Whatever differences there are from child to child, they share the stigmatized fate of referral to the facility, most frequently because of some behavioral and emotional problems. The peer group, which supposedly is a principal agent of therapeutic change, is often made up of a heavy concentration of disturbed children. Healthy, well-adjusted children coming from a stable, wholesome background are a missing ingredient in group composition. The peer culture established by such a one-sided mix of children can work to impede rather than to accelerate desirable changes in the children. Inherent in the nature of the group is the risk of the development of what has been termed *secondary deviance* in response to stigmatized labeling and peer-group contagion.

The powerful but potentially problemmatic nature of residential care demands that it be used judiciously only after careful consideration of the needs of children that mandate such treatment. The nature of the residential experience also requires that a child's stay in this type of setting be regularly monitored. Each of these requirements is discussed in detail in the sections that follow.

Situations in Which Institutional Care Is the Appropriate Resource

The utilization of institutional care is based on the worker's decision that the child cannot be treated effectively in his or her own home and that neither foster home care nor adoption are appropriate alternatives. Children who are removed from the home because of parental inadequacy are more likely to be placed in a foster family or made available for adoption. Those children referred for institutional care are more likely to have been removed from their home as a result of their own inadequacy in implementing their roles, primarily because of emotional, physical, or mental handicaps. The children usually experience multiple disabilities in their emotional development, social relationships, and cognitive and academic functioning. They have difficult relationships with adults, including their parents and teachers. The longstanding nature or seriousness of their problems has heightened parental and community intolerance. Some children placed in institutional care have also experienced multiple foster placements that have ended in failure. All of these factors, taken together, form the basis for the decision that the child needs a more structured and protected environment that residential facilities can offer.

James Whittaker (1979) describes the multifaceted problems that children in residential care tend to exhibit. Included are intrapersonal difficulties, such as problems with impulse control and expression of feelings, and low self-esteem; interpersonal problems, including disabilities in relating to family members, peers, and other adults; and external difficulties, which typically involve learning problems and deficits in a child's ability to play. One common social-emotional difficulty involves deficits in basic trust of others. For some children, this deficit arises out of long-standing problems in parent–child relationships. The child's inability to reach out to and depend upon adults is the result of his or her conflicting feelings about birth parents. On the one hand, the child yearns for reestablishment of the relationship with the birth parent; on the other hand, the child is deeply angry and hurt by the parent's failure to care sufficiently (Taylor et al., 1976). For some children, conflicts around the need for attachment and independence surface in adolescence and are reflected in a number of ways. The teenager becomes excessively withdrawn, engages in passive-aggressive behavior, or develops repeated conflicts with authority figures. Another typical characteristic of these children is a tendency to externalize their problems.

> For example, a girl would say that she performed poorly in school because her teacher was inadequate or because she had no private place to study; or she had few friends because everyone else had more money and didn't want to bother with her. Girls would say they slept poorly, ate too much, bit their nails, because other people wanted to hurt them, put them away, or ridicule them. Rarely did a girl come in saying she did poorly in school because she didn't work, had no friends because she was unpleasant, had neurotic traits because of personal conflict [Taylor, et al., 1976, p. 10].

Because institutionalized children also may exhibit problems with impulse control and appropriate expression of emotions, excessive aggression, running away, and sexual acting out are common. Whittaker (1979) suggests that because these children have difficulty integrating their ideas, their feelings, and their behavior, "lashing out at other persons, at objects, or at self becomes the characteristic way of dealing with frustration, strain, or anxiety" (p. 22). These characteristics, in turn, produce learning deficits, problems in the child's ability to assess behavior, consider its consequences, and learn from experience. Mayer, Richman, and Balcerzak (1977) point out that decisions regarding institutionalization depend on the child's ability to control impulses. If the child tends to distort reality and live in the world of fantasy and cannot postpone gratification, then the protection and control provided by the institution may be necessary and appropriate.

Children requiring residential services may exhibit behaviors that the community finds clearly atypical, perhaps bizarre, and sometimes dangerous. More than one-third of the children admitted to one residential treatment center "were aggressive, violent and giving to attacking others"; "hyperactive"; "prone to stealing, lying and setting fires" (Oxley, 1977b, p. 494). The child who sets fires or engages in repeated acts of vandalism, the child who masturbates openly, who soils himself or herself, or who exhibits unrelieved apathy is not likely to be acceptable in a foster home. This type of child may, in fact, have been repeatedly rejected by a succession of foster parents and may, therefore, need to experience the greater tolerance of deviation that the institution can provide. Children referred to one residential treatment facility were characterized by:

> "Screaming fits and unmanageable at home"; "timid, fearful and withdrawn, screaming and fear of adults"; "found to be carrying out 'an under-cover reign of terror' in the school"; "picks fingers raw, frightful temper"; "mother at wits' end—boy has violent temper, antagonistic to everyone"; "soiling, enuresis, destructive behaviors"; "unaccountable bursts of sobbing; preoccupied with fire; a considerable danger in the home"; "sleeps badly, screams at night, night terrors"; "never spoke in the house; 'used to cry if you looked at him,' no life, no spontaneity, no interests"; "destructive, unruly, disobedient, spiteful, and uncontrollable"; "restless, completely uninhibited, acting on strong instinctive impulses, very difficult, and has terrible rages in which he kicks and bites and nothing is safe from him"; "truancy and unwillingness to go to school, suffers from sudden and extreme panics and anxieties" [Balbernie, 1966, pp. 137–167].

Not all children admitted to residential institutions exhibit extreme atypical behavior. In a survey of 144 residential settings, Russo and Shyne (1980) found that whereas 38 per cent of children residing in such settings were severely disturbed, an equal proportion were only mildly disturbed (p. 29).

Children in need of residential care frequently have a range of interpersonal disabilities, reflected in their interaction with peers, parents, and other adults (Whittaker, 1979). They may be excessively manipulative, expending a great deal of energy working to develope conflicts between themselves and others or encouraging others to engage in conflict situations. Some children are excessively dependent and clinging, reaching out indiscriminately to others for caring and support. Frequently, when these children have opportunities to develop close relationships with others, they become fearful and withdraw. Others cope with their fears about forming relationships by remaining highly isolated. They develop particular behavior patterns that "turn-off" others and, therefore, reinforce their seclusion. Children may also develop powerful roles as scapegoats.

Accompanying these social-emotional deficits are a range of cognitive disabilities. These include: "hyperactivity, emotional lability, impulsivity, distractability, perseveration, and perceptual difficulties" (Whittaker, 1979, p. 32).

Children are placed in institutional care when their parents, because of their own personal circumstances or problems, are unable to provide the type of support that is needed, or when parents, overwhelmed by the child's special needs and disabilities, can no longer cope. In a study examining the family characteristics of institutionalized and noninstitutionalized retarded boys. Wolf and Whitehead (1975) found that the former group had families in which parent–child and marital relationships were significantly poorer, families in which both mothers and fathers had severe difficulty relating to the child, and homes in which they had undergone many more disruptive experiences. In a study of parents and their adolescent children placed in a large residential facility in Los Angeles, Malin (1981) found two distinctly different sets of family dynamics. In those families taking what she described as the "long pathway" to placement (approximately half the families in the sample), "although there seemed to be brief and intermittent periods of what appeared to be relative 'calm' and 'normalcy,' the parents reported that the problems became progressively worse as both child and family relationships deteriorated through the years" (p. 484). These children had experienced early life trauma and, for many, early medical problems as well. The children were hyperactive, and early and long-standing learning disabilities (frequently dating from the preschool years), and engaged in intensive competition with their siblings. Parents felt that there had been and continued to be an inadequate emotional fit between themselves and their children.

Baily and Baily (1983) describe one such family:

> Both parents admitted that they were absolutely exhausted from caring for Linda. They had lost many of their adult friends because few could tolerate her provocative behavior and because she required the full attention of the parents. Linda's irritability, restlessness, and short sleep requirements had worn out the parents as well as the two younger siblings. The father had been so preoccupied by her behavior and his inability to help her that he could not give full attention to their small business. As a result, sales had fallen off. The mother begged for Linda's placement, "not because we don't love her, but because we're no good to her the way we are" [p. 127].

Other families took what Malin described as the "short pathway" to placement. In these homes, there was little indication of early severe trauma or prolonged difficulties with the child. Parents felt that they had adequately raised the child through the early and latency years. However, recent family stress (divorce, remarriages, or death), coupled with the child's emerging sexuality and adolescent bids for independence, created major stress in the family and led the parents to feel that the child was out of control.

The decision to offer institutional care may be based not on what the child brings or fails to bring to the situation but on the parents' responses. The natural parent who is greatly threatened by the loss of a child's affection to foster parents may be better able to accept his or her child's placement in an institution. The fact that the child has to share the institutional parent figures with a group of children reduces the natural parent's anxiety. Furthermore the institution is perceived as being sufficiently different from family living so that the parent may feel less guilty if the institution succeeds where he or she has failed with the child. The parent can attribute such success to the special facilities and the professional staff of the institution.

The agency is under pressure to institutionalize some children, not in response to the needs of the child but in response to the community's demand for protection from deviant behavior.

Mayer, Richman, and Balcerzak (1977) further note that referral for residential treatment is often made because other facilities have been eliminated. A child who is too disturbed to live in the family and in the community is also too disturbed to live in a foster-family home or a group home, so that by the process of elimination only the residential treatment center is left.

As in the case of foster-family care, institutional child care is rarely offered without some prior preventive efforts (Hylton, 1964, p. 126). In an examination of forty-five referrals to a residential treatment program, randomly chosen over a four-week period, Martin, Pozdnjakoff, and Wilding (1976) found that in 85 per cent of the cases a variety of services had been offered in an attempt to retain the child in the community. Institutional "placement was not sought lightly or offered as a reflex" (p. 271).

In studying the placement history of 215 children placed in residential treatment care, Maluccio's and Marlow's (1974) findings were similar. Institutional care was not the first choice but followed an attempt to deal with the problem in the community, "nearly all of the children and their parents having been active with at least one community agency." The decision to refer the child for institutional care was made "after a prolonged period of services to the child in his own home" (p. 230, see also Bloch & Behrens, 1955; Oxley, 1977b, p. 495).

In a study of 267 children placed in seven institutions in Texas, Schwab, Bruce, and McRoy (1984) found that five of the twenty factors predicting acceptance of the children into care involved the previous utilization of evaluative and treatment services in the community or some other residential settings.

For some children, institutional care may not be the least restrictive setting, but it may be the least detrimental alternative, better than continued living in a family or foster family homes that cannot cope with a child's disruptive behavior.

There are also contraindications for the use of residential care. Institutional placement is generally contraindicated for infants and very young children. These children are too young to profit from group living and require the intensive relationship and parenting that are more likely to be available in a family setting. Examining the types of services offered to child welfare clients nationwide, Shyne and Schroeder (1978) found that the only type of institutional service offering a significant number of infants was emergency care (p. 71). Bryce (1979) also suggests that when children experience disabilities in only one area of their life, community-based treatment resources should be available to help them (pp. 16–17). Children requiring help in developing more adequate peer group relationships, for example, may benefit from more normative experiences within the local community. Children requiring special education have a right to receive it in their home community. Bryce also suggests that when parents request residential services because they are uncomfortable with receiving home-based services or placing the child in foster care, this provides an insufficient reason for removing the child from the community and placing him or her in such a highly structured therapeutic environment.

Some children, on the other hand, may be too seriously disabled to function in the relatively open environment of the residential setting. Children who are clearly suicidal, highly assaultive, or so severely distrubed that they cannot function in an open setting may require placement on a locked ward of a hospital (Taylor et al., 1976).

Ideally, then, institutional placement is offered the child and the family after some considered assessment of the situation. Ideally the child should not end up in an institution simply because more desirable alternatives are not available. Institutional care should be "treatment by choice rather than treatment by default" (Schulman, 1954, p. 319). It appears, however, that here, as elsewhere, there is a gap between the ideal and reality. Studies of chidren in care reveal wide variations from community to community in the relative proportions of children placed in foster care and in institutions (Maas & Engler, 1959, p. 15; Wolins & Piliavin, 1964).

A national census of children and youth in substitute care, sponsored by the Office of Civil Rights in 1980, found that the overall placement rate per 1,000 children ranged from a high of 14.71 in the District of Columbia to 5.25 in Alaska and lows of 1.17 in Hawaii and 1.11 in New Jersey. Variations in per capita income, per capita taxes, unemployment rates, and the racial composition of the state population did not account for a significant amount of the variation in rates of placement according to an analysis of an earlier study conducted by the Urban Institute, Washington, D.C. (Koshel, 1973, p. 36). Differences in the frequency with which the institution is used can be attributed to community attitudes toward different types of substitute care, to expediency, and to a lack of availability of alternative resources (Wolins & Piliavin, 1964, p. 43).

A national survey of two thousand children's institutions indicated that 36,000 children had been accepted or retained because this was the only expedient and feasible plan, though not the best (Pappenfort & Kilpatrick, 1969, p. 457). At the same time, the institutions did not have room for some 54,000 children that they felt needed and should have gained admittance. In summary, over a "one-year period, directors of children's institutions reported that they made 126,829 decisions about children in need that they personally considered contrary to the best interests of the child in question, simply because of administrative problems or because the appropriate resource was not available" (Pappenfort & Kilpatrick, 1969, p. 458). A more recent survey (Russo & Shyne, 1980) states:

> Nearly two-thirds of the facilities reported that they occasionally find it necessary to admit or to keep children or youths who do not "belong" in the program, but only 3 per cent are faced often with this situation. The reason cited is the lack of any other suitable resource for the residents in question (p. 19).

Maluccio and Marlow (1972), after reviewing the relevant literature, concluded:

> The decision to place a child in residential treatment is presently a highly individual-
> ized matter based on a complex set of idiosyncratic factors defying categorization.
> The literature does not indicate agreement on consistent criteria or universal guide-
> lines and it is not certain whether institutions diverse in origin, philosophy, policy,
> and clientele can agree on a basic set of premises [Maluccio & Marlow, 1972, p. 239;
> see also Hill, 1976, p. 31].

There are indications that black and Native American children receive differential treatment in the substitute care system. Whereas the overall placement rate
for whites is 3.1 per thousand, the placement rate for black children is 9.5 and for
Native-American children is 8.8 (Mech, 1983, p. 660). Some states (the District of
Columbia, Maryland, Virginia, Indiana, and Ohio) are particularly prone to place
black children outside the home. Black children are also much more likely to
remain in placement for prolonged periods. Nearly 35 per cent of black children
were in substitute care settings for five years or longer (p. 667). Institutional
placement is also much more likely to be provided for boys than for girls (Russo &
Shyne, 1980, p. 21).

It is repeatedly noted in social work journals that referral to the institution
should be based on diagnostic study of the child. Nevertheless a study of the
records of five hundred children admitted into residential treatment showed that
less than 10 per cent had a "complete psychiatric evaluation" and that about 60
per cent were referred on the basis of psychological testing alone (Bedford &
Hybertson, 1975).

Like some decisions in foster care, the decision to refer a child to a residential
treatment center may be often "more a decision of desperation than of deliberation," of chance rather than choice.

Rather than placement's being a haphazard phenomenon, there is a general
consensus regarding which kind of child belongs in what kind of facility, but
reality keeps the worker from making placement decisions based exclusively on
defensible criteria. For instance, the most pressing need identified in a study of a
two thousand-case sample of some twenty-nine thousand children in substitute
care in New York City was in the area of institutional care and group homes.
Children were inappropriately placed in other facilities because there was no
space available in residential treatment centers and in group homes and residences (Bernstein, Snider & Meezan, 1975).

Briar (1963) attempted an experimental study of how social workers go about
making the decision to offer the child an institution or foster care. Study findings
indicated that social workers do take into consideration the extent of the child's
emotional disturbance and the preferences of the biological parents. Greater emotional disturbance in the child and opposition by the biological parents to foster
care were associated with choice of the institution rather than a foster home. This
finding is clearly in line with a decision based on diagnostic assessment. However, the study also showed that social workers in an agency that stressed foster
care tended to recommend such care, whereas workers in agencies committed to
institutional care tended to recommend this kind of care. This, then, is another
factor influencing the decision process that violates the principle that decisions
regarding the use of the institution should be based on diagnostic considerations.

A recent survey of child welfare professionals conducted in Ontario (Goldberg
& Dooner, 1981) found that social service agency staff who used residential care
for their clients based their referral decision primarily on their previous experi-

ences with a particular center (p. 357). Keith-Lucas and Sanford (1977) also suggest that familiarity and agency policy may dictate the choice of substitute care:

> It is a sad commentary that even today a child whose parents turn to the church for placement has perhaps four chances out of five of being cared for in a group, while one entrusted to fate because of neglect or dependency will almost inevitably be tried in one or more foster-family homes. This is not so much a matter of differing beliefs in the values of the two kinds of care—most social workers at least recognize that some children need one kind of care and some another—as it is that each group has only one type of care readily available to it [p. 89].

Taylor (1973) suggests a number of additional factors that affect worker decisionmaking, factors that may lead workers to make incorrect decisions regarding placement or to rely on criteria other than the needs of the child, the family, and the community. Social workers in the community faced with the problem of making referrals to institutions are often not familiar with changing intake policies of institutions and not familiar with details of institutional living at facilities they have never had the opportunity of visiting.

In an attempt to deal with the complexity of decision making in situations in which children might require residential care, some agencies have developed specially designed evaluation units where team members, who have expertise in both child assessment and knowledge of community resources, have an opportunity to conduct an intensive assessment and to develop a proposed treatment plan. One such program was developed by Children's Garden (Kirgan, 1983). The agency opened a special group home where children stay for approximately three months, during which time they are evaluated medically, psychiatrically, and educationally. The child's family is also assessed. Staff recommend a particular type of placement designed to achieve specially designated short- and long-term goals for the child. A follow-up evaluation of the effectiveness of this diagnostic process found that in 87 per cent of the cases in which the staff recommendations were implemented, service delivery has been functioning effectively since the children were discharged from the evaluation unit (p. 163).

In summary, the child admitted to an institution is a school-aged or older child who is sufficiently emotionally disturbed so that he or she cannot be maintained in the community even when community-based treatment is available, but is not so disturbed as a homicidal or suicidal patient, who might be a danger to himself or herself and others. The typical child in this kind of center is difficult to control at home, his or her behavior is not tolerated well by the parents, and the child's relationship with the parents is unsatisfactory. The school finds it difficult to handle the child and the community is rejecting.

The agency sees both parents and children as capable of making some change. This is the configuration presented by the institutional staff when outlining their admissions criteria.

Scope

Overall about 232,000 children were living in institutions in 1980. The largest number of these institutionalized children were in correctional facilities and homes for the physically or mentally impaired. Such institutions are generally not regarded as falling within the concerns of traditional child welfare agencies. Homes for dependent and neglected children and residential treatment centers for emotionally disturbed children are more directly the concern of traditional child welfare services. Institutions for the dependent and neglected have been defined by the Census Bureau as follows: "This class of homes covers orphanages and other institutions which provide long-term care of children; it also covers institutions generally known as receiving homes or shelters, which provide temporary care primarily to children whose homes have been broken by illness, desertion, death, and social crises."

The residential treatment center is defined by the Department of Health and Human Services as "a somewhat heterogeneous group of mental health facilities which have one characteristic in common—that is, the provision of round-the-clock treatment in care to persons primarily under 18 years of age who are diagnosed as having an emotional or mental disorder" (Redick & Witkin, 1983, p. 1). The term is generally applied to facilities that provide a total therapeutic program for children whose emotional problems are sufficiently serious so that outpatient treatment is not regarded as a suitable alternative. The structure, staffing, and programs are designed to provide a planned and controlled therapeutic living environment for the child.

In 1980, 35,000 children 18 years of age or younger were living in homes for dependent and neglected children. There were more boys than girls and a slightly disproportionate percentage of blacks (20% of the total) in the population of such facilities. There were 2,306 homes for dependent and neglected children, most of them small and the largest majority under private auspices (U.S. Department of Commerce, 1984, p. 5; p. 26; p. 65.).

There were about 21–22,000 children 18 years of age or younger in residential treatment centers in 1980. As of January 1980, there were 368 residential treatment centers in the United States, providing a total of slightly more than 20,000 beds for children. These facilities were used by 18,276 residents at the end of 1979. Many of these facilities were small; the overall average bed size was 54 to 55 beds. Some two-thirds of all the residential treatment centers open in 1979–80 had fewer than 50 beds, and only 9 to 10 per cent had 100 beds or more. However, these larger institutions accounted for some one-third of all available beds. Some 95 per cent of these facilities operated under private auspices (Redick & Witkin, 1983, p. 3).

Statistics suggest that institutional placements for dependent and disturbed children are not made on a long-term basis. A survey conducted for the Child Welfare League of America (Russo & Shyne, 1980) found that the average length of stay in general child care institutions is nine months and in residential treatment facilities, only fifteen months (p. 11). A census of residential treatment centers conducted in 1979–1980 (Redick & Witkin, 1983) found that the average length of stay for children in all such facilities was 196 days (p. 16).

The changing composition of the population of children's institutions is reflected in the fact that 75 per cent of the children in "children's homes" in 1923 were full orphans; in 1957 only 8 per cent of these children were full orphans (Keith-Lucas & Sanford, 1977, p. 8). During the fifteen-year period between 1961 and 1977, greater use was made of residential treatment centers. Whereas in 1961, less than 1 per cent of all child welfare clients were in such facilities, in 1977, 2 per cent received residential treatment services (Shyne & Schroeder, 1978, p. 35).

There were wide variations in the relative availability of residential facilities to children in different states. In 1980, the state of Maine made available some 145 beds per 100,000 children, whereas the state of Tenneses made available only two beds per 100,000 (Redick & Witkin, 1983, p. 13).

Treatment in the institution is largely a responsibility of the casework staff. A study of over 600 residential treatment centers notes that they employed over 1,600 full-time social workers, the greatest majority of whom had a master's degree: "Social workers along with school teachers were employed more universally in residential treatment centers than other types of professional personnel. . . . and were utilized to a greater extent than [members of] any other professional discipline" (U.S. Dept. H.E.W., 1971, pp. 11–12). A 1966 nationwide study of children's institutions in general revealed that psychiatrists were seeing 10,000 children for treatment or counseling, and social workers were offering service to 65,000 children (Pappenfort & Kilpatrick, 1969, p. 453).

The Redick and Witkin (1983) survey of residential treatment centers confirmed the importance of social work in implementing the professional function of the institution. There were 2,419 social workers employed in such facilities as compared with 654 psychiatrists. In addition, whereas almost all of the social workers were employed full time, only 7 per cent of the psychiatrists were employed full time (Table 8, p. 18).

The Social Worker's Role in Institutional Care

The social work staff of residential institutions plays a central role in planning for and delivering therapeutic services to children and to their families. The job of the social worker begins when a child is referred for possible placement at the center; continues as the worker helps structure the daily living environment of the child, plans home visits, and devises other treatment strategies in ongoing work with the parents and child; and ends only after the child has left the institutions and is receiving other ongoing support services in the community. Each of these arenas of social work responsibility is considered in the following sections.

Preparation for Placement

The social worker's effectiveness in initiating contact with the child and his or her family is an important first step in the development of an ongoing treatment relationship. In preparing the child and family for placement, the worker must carry out five essential tasks. First, the workers play a central role in determining whether the child should be placed in residential care or may appropriately be served through some other form of therapeutic intervention. In early discussions with the family and the referring worker, the institutional social worker explores the seriousness of the child's difficulty, the inability of the parents to continue caring for the child, and the type and extent of community-based efforts that have already been made to resolve these problems. It is only when other alternative forms of treatment are clearly inappropriate or when they have failed to effectively help the family that residential services should be considered (Davies, 1980, p. 51).

The important role of the social worker in screening potential clients for residential care was confirmed in an experiment conducted in Israel in which "two local public welfare offices were operated for a period of 18 months by a university-guided team of social workers to test the effects of innovative work on rate of institutional placement for dependent children" (Jaffe, 1970, p. 7). The two experimental offices emphasized exploration of solutions other than institutional care. Two control offices that had received the client's initial request for institutional care showed a significantly larger proportion of institutional placements than the two experimental offices.

Drawing on information provided by the parents, the child, the referring worker, and other agencies in contact with the family, the institutional social worker then conducts a social study of the family. This is the worker's second major intake task. The Child Welfare League of America (1982) describes the type of material that must be obtained. The following information about the child is necessary:

> Characteristics of the child: age, ethnicity, current developmental level (physical, social, intellectual, and emotional) and deviations from what is considered normal at that age; functioning at home, with peers, and in other significant life situations; ability to cope with life tasks expected of children of that age; nature of the child's reltionship to the parents and other family members; capacity to form close relationships with adults and peers; degree of health and pathology in the personality structure. Education: grade-level functioning, existence of learning difficulties. Social work, psychological, or psychiatric services the child has received for help with his or her emotional problems (pp. 25–26).

The following information about the parents is necessary:

> Family circumstances: constellation of family group; current situation (social, financial, emotional, health factors) as it affects the parents' ability to care for the child; problems that may have affected the child's development and may influence the outcome of the plan for placement (e.g., return to family, extended foster care, termination of parental rights); relationship of each parent to the child, to one another, and to other children in the family; potential of the parents or other significant family members for meeting the child's needs and their accessibility for help.
>
> Parents' expectations of placement: help requested for the child and themselves; other solutions attempted; degree to which the parents can be involved, the role they see for themselves and significant family members while the child is receiving care; their plan for, and understanding of, length of stay and termination; the way in which they are preparing the child for placement, [p. 26].

The worker's third task is to provide parents and child with necessary information about general rules, expectations, and agency procedures. Children must learn about the structure of their daily life in the residential facility (how they will eat, bedtime, television privileges, etc.); they need information about expected behavior and consequences for violations of these expectations; children also need to know about the nature and extent of contact they will have with their family, other individuals, and agencies outside of the institutions; finally, they must be told about expectations concerning their participation in individual, group, and other types of therapy, the reasons why they need to participate, and consequences for failing to do so (Hall, 1980, p. 66; Interstate Consortium on Residential Child Care, 1980).

Parents, too, are in need of information concerning the structure and consequences of placement. The worker discusses with them their relative responsibility for making essential and day-to-day decisions concerning the welfare and activities of the child (who will determine where the child goes to school, whether the child participates in activities in the community, and whether the child receives medical treatment, for example); parents are also interested in information concerning their access to the child (when and how often they are allowed to visit and when the child is allowed to visit home); finally, parents, like their children, must be given information about the extent they are required to participate in therapy while the child is in care. The Interstate Consortium on Residential Child Care (1980), a group of treatment experts from fourteen states, recommends that the following areas be explicitly negotiated with parents:

1. Arrangements regarding family visits, vacation, mail, gifts and telephone calls;
2. Arrangements as to the nature and frequency of reports to, and meetings involving, the parent(s) or guardian and referral agency;
3. Provision for notification of parent(s) or guardian and/or the placing agency in the event of unauthorized absences, medical or dental problems and any significant events regarding the child [p. 93].

Providing these types of data helps the family and child in a number of ways. As the family obtains a clearer picture of what is expected, the institutional environment appears less forbidding and strange. Institutional placement involves very radical changes in the life of the family. As Beedell (1970) says, "the variety of new contacts with adults and other children which face a child joining a residential unit are almost comparable to those an adult would face who moved to a new town, changed her job, broke an engagement to marry, and contemplated another all in the same day" (p. 34). More difficult yet is the fact that the child is asked to live with peers whom he or she has no say in choosing. "Each child had to adjust in some way to children he had never seen before, who may or may not like him, and whom he may or may not like, and with whom he will be constantly thrown" (Konopka, 1968, p. 34).

Telling the family about the nature of the child's life in the institution and the type of responsibilities parents are expected to assume also enhances the family's realization that parents' needs are important and that parents' views are valued by the worker. Sharing this information helps enhance client self-esteem and encourages more active participation in treatment. "If the client is consulted and kept informed, even where little choice exists, he at least has time to make preparations. The more realistic his perception of the kind of institution he is entering, the better he is likely to cope with the demands of group living" (Ward, 1980, p. 29). Explaining expectations also helps ease the child's transition from home to institution. When parents accept the need for placement and take responsibility for preparing the child for the move, the child is also more accepting of placement and more comfortable in making the transition.

The worker uses initial contacts with child and family to begin to work on yet another placement task, building rapport. Establishing a positive relationship with a client is an essential aspect of any effective treatment process. Early contact with family members offers an opportunity for the worker to demonstrate caring, interest and concern for the welfare and needs of all family members as they struggle to cope with the placement process. "This is a delicate time, as in all initial contacts, because it is here that true engagement takes place. Although the need for the skill of initial engagement is recognized from the first point of referral to the agency, a non-empathetic telephone response at referral can often take a long time to overcome" (Hall, 1980, pp. 65–66).

Finally, at intake, the worker helps both child and parents cope with typical worries and fears. Two types of concerns are particularly common. One involves a deep-seated anxiety that, should the child separate from the family, he or she will never return. The child fears being abandoned by parents; the parents fear the child will reject them or find other "better" parents. Although this concern can never be fully addressed until both child and family realize that contact can be maintained during the placement process, the worker lays the groundwork for challenging it during in the initial placement process. The worker explains that the institution, rather than isolating the child from his or her life prior to placement, tries to provide services that are part of a total system of support to the family. The worker also stresses the fact that institutional care is only temporary. It is not intended to supplant the family. Services are designed to help the family make needed changes that will enable it to once again assume major care for the child (Whittaker, 1979).

Both parents and child also fear that the need for institutional care indicates that the family's problems are severe and irremediable. The child perceives himself or herself as especially crazy or bad, so bad that being locked up is necessary. Parents also perceive themselves as terribly inadequate, so poor at carrying out their tasks that someone else must take on their role and do a better job in order to help their child.

Parents expect institutional staff to blame them for the child's problems (Critchley & Berlin, 1981). Once again, the worker lays the groundwork for confronting this fear by communicating acceptance of and respect for the parents. By suggesting that treatment will be time-limited and by helping family members pinpoint particular problems to work on, the worker suggests that family difficulties can be resolved. By encouraging family members to express both positive and negative feelings about the placement process, the institutional setting, and each other, the worker helps members develop a more realistic evaluation of both the strengths and problems of the family and of the particular areas in which the institution can be helpful in resolving difficulties (Child Welfare League of America, 1982).

Once sufficient information has been gathered, the worker schedules a case-planning conference to help synthesize the data, make a final determination that the child requires residential care, and to develop beginning treatment goals. The referring worker, the child's parents, and other extrainstitutional professionals who will continue to work with the family should attend this planning conference. A final step in placement involves the development of a treatment contract with both the child and his or her parents. This contract spells out the specific problem areas to be addressed, the types of treatment strategies that will be used, and expectations that the family and child will participate actively in the treatment process throughout the child's stay in care (Keith-Lucas & Sanford, 1977; Ward, 1980).

The institutional staff should be prepared for the child's arrival, and they, in turn, should have prepared the group with which the child is to live. The social worker and the institutional staff should discuss how the child is likely to affect the group and how the members of the group are likely to affect him or her. This implies that the group has been selected with some thought as to how its composition will further the treatment plans for this child. Also, "some institutions have a 'Welcome Committee' of two or three children in each cottage or section to introduce the new child and help him to feel at home" (United Nations, 1956, p. 38; see also Eisikouits, 1980).

Work with the Child in Care

Caseworkers have a continuing responsibility to work with the child once he or she is moved to the institution. The child must undergo separation from parents and significant others in his or her past life, must learn to care about and become attached to significant individuals in the institutional environment and, at the end of placement, must reexperience separation from institutional staff and readjustment in the broader community. Helping the child effectively carry out this work is a central responsibility of the social worker. Equally as significant is helping the child confront and alter the cognitive, social, and behavioral disabilities that prevented his or her continued residence in the community. The worker also helps the child learn to more effectively interact with both staff and peers with whom he or she is in daily contact inside the institution.

In leaving their homes and experiencing placement in a residential setting, children react in ways similar to those of children who experience the death of a parent or some other significant loss. Children grieve for their loss and move through a series of stages in resolving their grief (Jewett, 1982). The caseworker also assists the child in working on a range of behavioral problems. The worker's principal long-range objective is to help the child so that he or she can, once again, function in the general community. As Whittaker (1979) suggests, institutional staff "should not merely help children gain insight, or manage their behavior, but should help them build competence (and confidence) in a wide range of areas" (p. 81). In order to develop or reestablish these abilities, Maier (1981) stresses the importance of the opportunity to practice repeatedly the kind of effective coping skills that the child will need to utilize upon discharge. For some children, developing competence can include learning very basic daily living skills, such as preparing food, shopping, and physically caring for oneself (Epstein, 1982).

In order to maintain an adequate living environment for children, especially for emotionally and sociall disabled children living in groups, the institutional staff must also be concerned with managing problematic behavior on a day-to-day basis. In their survey of residential centers conducted for the Child Welfare League, Russo and Shyne (1980) found that coping with daily behavior of children was considered a moderate problem for 59 per cent of the responding institutions and a severe problem for an additional 12 per cent (p. 45). Common difficulties that staff confront include serious aggressive episodes; incidents in which a child steals, lies, or takes drugs; problems with sexual involvement between children in the institution; and children running away (Beker et al., 1972). The social worker is responsible for helping staff develop effective techniques for identifying problematic behavior and responding to it. Staff help the child learn to substitute more acceptable means of coping and interaction. In assisting staff with this task, the worker keeps in mind potential differences in goal planning based upon objectives involving the child's return to the community and objectives involving the child's effective adaptation to the institution. The first objective must be the primary one and must be given priority, even when it conflicts with the staff's immediate need to manage the child's institutional performance (Maier, 1981).

Treatment Approaches in Working with the Child in Care

In order for the child to achieve program goals, the social worker relies on a range of treatment skills. In particular, the ability to provide individual treatment for the child, to work with child-care staff to develop an effective treatment milieu, and the ability to structure a range of group experiences for the child are significant.

On the basis of a significant relationship with the caseworker, the child is helped to explore the dynamic basis of behavior, and to change this behavior. Psychotherapy in the institution is more likely to center on the dynamics of present behavior rather than on material out of the child's past. This, as a matter of fact, is an advantage to the caseworker because he or she can reach the child at a time of emotional stress to discuss conflicts through which the child is living. Treatment moves out of the office into the child's immediate reality for on-the-spot therapy:

> When S., a thirteen-year-old youngster, was adamant in refusing to return to her group and marched up and down the institution's "campus," it was her [case] worker who joined her in the march. The material handled during this time was not all dissimilar to the content of their interviews: the child's feeling that she was too sick to be helped, that her rejection by the family was devastating and motivated these overwhelming feelings of hopelessness. When she marched past the gate, she said she could not control herself and not even the worker could control her. On the ensuring three-mile hike through neighboring towns and the final return to the grounds of the institution, the child received not only the demonstration of the worker's ability to control her, which diminished her feelings of anxiety, but also some insight into her current concern about her mother's illness and its relationship to the incident [Schulman, 1954, p. 322].

Although the structure and objectives of individualized child treatment within a residential setting grew out of the experiences gleaned from outpatient care (Whittaker, 1979), this work differs from outpatient child treatment in significant ways. Brodie (1972) notes that the institutionalized child, cut off from his or her family, tends to express feelings of rejection and ambivalence much more strongly. Expresson of these feelings, in turn, "places a considerable amount of stress on the therapist's energy and on his capacity to manage anxiety and anger without interfering with the therapeutic process. It also provides him with more therapeutic leverage than is possible in outpatient treatment" (p. 123). The worker's ability to deal effectively with issues of confidentiality is also complicated by the need to share some therapeutic materials with staff.

Treatment in the children's institution generally consists of individual casework or psychotherapy supplemented by the change-producing effects of the therapeutic milieu.

> We conceive of the residential treatment settings as a psychodynamically determined environment in which the total living experiences of the child are contrived and integrated with individual treatment compromising a unified therapeutic plan. The total life of the child, including his group living experiences, relationships with adults and children, school classes, work assignments, and recreational activities, becomes part of the therapeutic experiences of the child. . . . The experimental aspects of the child's life are consistent, parallel, and intermesh with the process of individual treatment [Schulman, 1954, p. 319].

"Residential treatment differs significantly from outpatient and other treatment methods by taking responsibility for total management of the child's current experience-in-living. It attempts to monitor and modify, for therapeutic gain, all facets of the child's life" (Child Welfare League of America, 1972, p. 37). Treatment efforts in this context are purposefully focused on several facets of the child's problems; at the same time, the child's various abilities to cope more effectively are supported:

> A therapeutic milieu is a specially-designed environment in which the events of daily living are used as formats for teaching competence in basic life skills. The living environment becomes both a means and a context for growth and change, informed by a culture that stresses learning through living [Whittaker, 1979, p. 36].

In work with the child, the worker cannot play a purely supportive role, since he or she must integrate individual treatment objectives with other milieu-based therapeutic plans. In fact, the difficulties workers face in coordinating individual and milieu programs has led Whittaker (1979) to suggest that milieu treatment be considered the central treatment modality for children, whereas individual sessions should be conducted only with some children as an adjunct to this program (p. 123).

The composition of the peer group with whom the child primarily interacts is an important consideration in designing an effective milieu. Keith-Lucas and Sanford (1977) describe two particular types of peer group arrangements. The "traditional peer group" consists of children who are all of generally the same age and all the same sex. The authors feel it is particularly helpful for work with disturbed children, many of whom are facing similar types of difficulties. The authors believe that a "mixed-sibling group," which consists of children of different ages and both genders, may be more effective when the primary concern of the agency is family problems. They do note that the mixed-sibling type group is more difficult for staff to manage, and this should be considered in determining the most effective type of group composition in any particuarly agency (pp. 29–30).

The size of the cottage group varies, but it is rarely under eight and rarely more than fifteen. This is the primary group, the family of peers with whom the child lives. In the area or cottage assigned to the group, the child is alloted a private place, a bed, furniture for clothes. He or she eats with the group in the dining area in the cottage. The child may attend the regular community schools or be assigned to the school on the institutional grounds organized in accordance with a curriculum approved by the local board of education and staffed by licensed teachers. The institution provides recreational facilities—television in the cottage, playing fields, scheduled movies—and, in addition, the child might be involved in the recreational programs of community agencies, such as the YM- and YWCA, the Boy and Girl Scouts, and the Little League. The children are also given an allowance and are expected to perform the kinds of chores normally demanded of a child in the family: making their beds, helping with the dishes, and so on. Older children may be paid for the performance of institutional maintenance tasks: working in the yard, cutting wood, assisting in the library and in the canteen, and so on (Child Welfare League of America, 1982).

Here, as elsewhere in the child-care services, there has been a gradual shift in the basic orientation of the rationale of treatment programs. Those based on psychoanalytical psychology have less acceptance currently, whereas behavior modification approaches are gaining ascendancy.

More and more frequently, the literature reports experiences with behavioral modification. There is a clear delineation of the privileges and rewards that follow from behavior changed in a positive and desirable direction and loss of privileges and withholding of rewards for failures to comply (Browning & Stover,

1971; Meyer, Odom, & Wax, 1973; Crenshaw, 1976; McInnis & Marbolin, 1977; Whittaker, 1979). Rather than attempting an explanation of the intrapsychic conflicts that result in the child's emotional difficulties, and then providing the opportunity for reexperiencing and resolving these conflicts in the therapeutic interaction, an institution that is oriented toward reeducation and behavior modification adopts an alternative hypothesis as to what needs to be done: "We assume that the child is not diseased, but that he has acquired bad habits" (Hobbs, cited in Whittaker, 1979, p. 72).

Currently, many residential institutions have instituted some type of point system, token economy, or "incentive system." Using this system, children obtain points in order to earn privileges and lose points when they engage in unacceptable behavior or violate program rules. Whittaker (1979) argues that the use of such systems should be limited to certain areas of the child's life. Attempting to construct programs to cover all aspects of a child's functioning creates a cumbersome system that is extremely difficult to implement consistently. Because incentive systems are commonly used for all children in the residential unit, Whittaker also believes that they should be accompanied by individualized programs for each child; because children can learn through exposure to a variety of teaching techniques, Whittaker believes that the system should never be used by itself. Rather he believes it should be accompanied by other group-oriented individual approaches, including the use of modeling and role-playing (p. 95).

Recently, there has been increasing recognition of the need to integrate training in the sociobehavioral area with programs that enhance cognitive and communication skills. One such effort was implemented at the Walker Home and School in Needham, Massachusetts (Small & Schinke, 1983). The authors assigned forty-five children in the program to one of four experiential conditions. One group experienced training in both the cognitive and problem-solving arenas; a second received only cognitive training; a third group was structured simply for discussion; whereas the last group received no group training whatsoever. The groups that received cognitive and problem-solving training did significantly better in a test designed to measure the child's ability to generate alternative solutions to problems and in several dimensions of the Devereaux Behavior Scale. (See also Rosen, Peterson, & Walsh, 1980.)

Another current concern of clinicians utilizing behavioral techniques in residential settings involves strategies for helping the child make the transition from being externally controlled by staff to learning internal control. This is particularly important for children who are emotionally deprived, many of whom have a tendency to exhibit little self-control, and most of whom have had extensive experience with others' attempts to control their behavior. The development of self-control is important for children moving toward maturity, and it is tied to the ability to make more mature moral judgments (Larsen, 1981). One effort to bridge the gap between externally and internally controlled incentive systems was devised by staff at Achievement Place:

> When a youth first enters the program, his points are exchanged for privileges each day. After the youth learns the connection between earning points and earning privileges, this daily point system is extended to a weekly point system, where he exchanges points for privileges only once each week. Eventually, the point system is faded out to a merit system, where no points are given or taken away and all privileges are free (Wolf, Phillips, & Fixsen, cited in Whittaker, 1979, p. 90).

Neilans, Israel, and Pravder (1981) found that children could learn to monitor and assess the appropriateness of their own behavior and could do so without increasing their general disruptive behavior in the institution. (See also Dimock, 1977.)

Group Work With the Child in Care. Group workers have been assigned special functions in the child-caring institutions (Schulze, 1951; Konopka, 1970). Most frequently, they are concerned with the supervision and coordination of special recreational services. In the more advanced institutions, they might be asked to develop programs of group psythotherapy or to organize meetings of cottage groups offering guided group interaction. Groups have been used as a therapeutic corrective device to aid in the child's normal development. Groups have also been used as an aid in dealing with the day-to-day functioning of the institution. Some children's groups meet regularly to discuss daily plans and activities; others meet to discuss common problems that arise in living together (Whittaker, 1979). Groups have also assisted in the management of the institution itself (Baxter, 1963).

The peer group experience tends to be a particularly meaningful one for children in residential care, as Taylor et al. (1976) discovered in their follow-up survey of girls who had been discharged from a group home. Years after their residential experience, these individuals remembered the positive aspects of peer group interaction, even when they had had significant problems with peers while in residence.

Implementing effective group activities in a residential setting makes special demands on the group worker. Because all children require interactional experiences, and all children should have opportunities to participate in the development of rules and programs in the living unit, those who are particularly poor group members must be accommodated. Workers must also plan group programs for children who have limited cognitive abilities, short attention spans, and poor control over their impulses. As Raubolt (1983) points out, workers usually find themselves dealing intensively and extensively with power-control issues with these children.

Children who have a variety of opportunities to experience helping, in one-to-one contacts with professional and child care staff, in day-to-day interactions with their peers and adults in their living milieu, and in specially designed group experiences, have a greater opportunity of finding the kinds of assistance they need to enhance their coping capacities and to deal effectively with their problematic behavior. Different children require different types of assistance from the institution. Whittaker has suggested some techniques of special help for particular problems that are commonly encountered in residential treatment settings (Figure 10-1).

Working with the Child's Parents

Because children have the right to a permanent home, a significant aspect of the social worker's job is to help the family maintain or develop such a home while the child is in care. It is the worker's first obligation to explore with the child's birthparents the feasibility of returning the child to that setting. Although institutionalized children may have experienced long-term family stress and may have undergone abusive experiences with their parents, their family ties frequently remain strong, and their desire to maintain these ties is powerful (Laird,

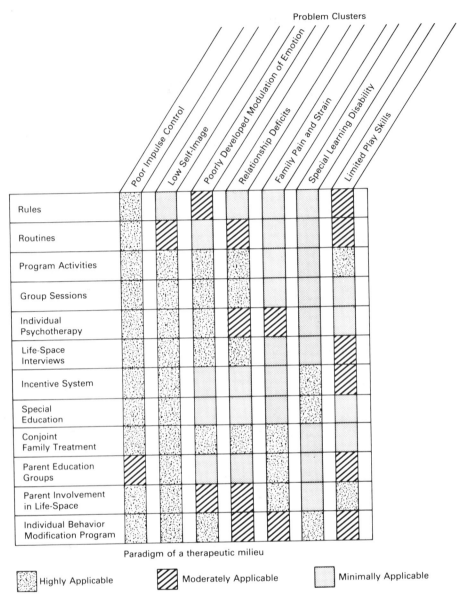

Figure 10-1. Paradigm of a Therapeutic Milieu (Source: Whittaker 1979, p. 40.)

1981). In a study of children's feelings about family members Jaffe (1977) compared the degree of emotional involvement and the extent the child expressed negative and positive feelings toward various family members. Few differences emerged among 60 institutionalized children, 108 children waiting to be placed in institutions, and 86 children who remained at home. Children in each group expressed approximately the same number of feelings and approximately the same proportion of positive feelings. Children awaiting placement did express more negative feelings, but only toward their fathers.

The worker is also obligated to examine the child's continued involvement with the family, since family participation in treatment enhances the benefit of the residential experience for the child (Mora, et al., 1969; Criss & Goodwin, 1970;

Fahl & Morrissey, 1979; Krona, 1980). After extensive experience working with emotionally handicapped children and their families in both inpatient and outpatient settings, Critchley and Berlin (1981) conclude:

> We have come to the conviction that parental participation in the milieu and educational aspects of our program and in family, couple, or individual psychotherapy, depending on the severity of the parental disability, is critical to the improvement or recovery of the disturbed child. That conviction stems from many years of previous work with the child alone and parents alone, which usually has not altered the parents' capacity to deal with the child in the home setting. Nor has such separate treatment been effective in overcoming circular conflicts that have an early origin and now often seem to have a life of their own despite the enhanced capacities and different needs of both child and parents [p. 153].

When children are treated but parents do not participate in the residential experience, the child frequently returns to the hospital and "quickly regresses, often never again to attempt such integrated behavior and relationships" (p. 154).

Whether parents receive the treatment they need or not, many children do return to their birth family after having been placed in institutions. Data from Colorado and St. Louis suggest that approximately half the children in group care return to their homes (Wolins, 1978). However, a study conducted by Bush and Goldman (1982) of children in various types of substitute care at least one year found only 18 per cent could realistically return home (p. 231). Because parents may play a significant role in maintaining a child's problem, and because they may benefit from professional advice in learning to deal more effectively with their difficult children, the residential worker is obligated to attempt to provide needed services to them.

One of the most substantial changes in professional perspectives on residential care in recent years is the insistence that service be made available to these families. Whittaker (1979) discusses the need to consider parents as full partners in the treatment process. Keith-Lucas and Sanford (1977) state that institutions are now in a "family oriented or coplanning phase". In their view, parents must not be seen simply as clients; instead, their expertise with regard to their child, their strengths as caretakers, and their personal needs must be addressed. Residential institutions must provide opportunities for parents to interact with institutional staff, to engage their children, and to serve the institution itself. Parents are to be included in the daily activities of the agency; their participation is not to be limited to occasional visiting. A range of treatment and educational experiences should be made available to them (U.S. Department of Health and Human Services, 1981).

Although the need to encourage increased parental participation is acknowledged by a number of experts on institutional care, many institutions continue to restrict severely the parents' role and to closely control the amount of contact they have with their children (Buckholdt & Gubrium, 1979; Small & Whittaker, 1979). As Finkelstein (1980) notes, "much lip service is paid to the concept of 'working with the family', but most funding patterns provide 24-hour-a-day residential care only for the youngster and, at best, an hour or so a week for the family. Group care is child rescue and care-oriented; it is not family-focused" (p. 34).

In those instances in which the child's family is unavailable and will remain so in the future, institutional staff are obligated to pursue alternative permanency opportunities for the child. These may include foster or adoptive care. Some residential agencies are also exploring the use of temporary homes for the child, "resource families," "volunteer families," or Big Brother-Big Sister programs. These programs provide a community-based adult friendship network for the child who is unavailable for foster or adoptive care, but whose parents cannot provide the types of support and involvement the child needs (Moran, Niedz & Simpson, 1975; Interstate Consortium on Residential Child Care, 1980; Williams, 1983).

Parents are encouraged to participate in their child's residential experience in two primary ways. First, the social worker seeks to establish regular contacts between family members and between parents and staff through such mechanisms as visitation planning, observation on the living unit, parent participation in special activities, and involvement in case-planning conferences. Secondly, parents are encouraged to participate in more traditional treatment-oriented activities, including individual and family therapy, parent support groups, and educationally oriented parent programs.

Parental Visiting and Participation. The social worker frequently begins planning parental involvement in the child's care by discussing and arranging for visits to the child. Although historically, some institutions have sought to limit or prevent parent–child contact during the initial months of the child's placement, this policy has proved detrimental to the well-being of the child and integrity of the family unit.

> In this first few weeks the child needs more than at any other time to know that he has not been abandoned, that his parents are still there, that co-planning is followed by co-working. A plan should call for close communication in the earliest stage of placement. A telephone call on the night of placement is often a real source of assurance [Keith-Lucas, Sanford, 1977, p. 51].

Visiting is to be encouraged and facilitated even in those situations in which the parents refuse to participate in other forms of treatment offered by the agency (Child Welfare League of America, 1982, p. 34). Visitation should also not be denied simply because a child is not performing well in the institution; neither should it be used as reward for good behavior. (Finkelstein, 1980; Bush, 1980; Child Welfare League of America, 1982).

The agency must make active efforts to encourage this type of interaction through the establishment of a flexible visitation schedule, one particularly designed to meet the needs of parents who must travel long distances to see their children. Agencies who accept children whose family live some distance away must consider offering transportation in order to facilitate parent–child contact (Interstate Consortium on Residential Child Care, 1980). Without overt attempts to engage the family, the child may lose contact with them.

> In looking at the distance of the facility from the family home, it is important to remember the saying "Out of sight, out of mind." It is not uncommon to see close family groups slowly deteriorate when a handicapped member is placed. At first the visits to the facility are frequent and warm, but interests change and loyalties wither. Economics and logistics intervene. When parents and brothers and sisters have to spend many hours traveling to distant residential facilities and must absorb the expense of such trips, it is no wonder that ties get broken. The decreasing frequency of visits becomes a source of guilt for family members who begin to devise rationalizations, such as the staff are better trained, the handicapped person is happier, or the placement will only be short-term [Skarnulis 1979, pp. 73–74].

Home visits can be beneficial to both the parent and child, since they provide excellent opportunities for parents to practice more effective means of caring for and controlling the child. Home visits also provide the social worker with opportunities to develop a more detailed understanding of parental strengths and disabilities, as well as opportunities to assess the effectiveness of recommendations that he or she has made to parents.

Initial parental visits to the institution may be marked by strained relationships with both the child and the staff. Parents, who feel guilty about placing their child away from home and worried about their inadequacy as parents, may express these concerns by being critical of institutional policy and staff activities (Mayer & Marsushima, 1958). They may be highly sensitive about situations in which their child appears to be abandoning them or incidents during which they fear that staff can observe their inability to control their child. The child, in turn, fearing parental rejection, may be unusually distant, hyperaggressive, or exceptionally disobedient. In this situation, the parents' desire to impress the staff conflicts with the child's need to express anger and fear. By the end of these early visits, all family members may feel frsutrated and angry. However, in order to move through this early adjustment phase, the parents' visits must continue.

Despite this initial discomfort, institutional staff do recognize the positive value of parental visiting. In a study of children in different substitute care situations, Aldgate (1978) showed that children in residential care were actually more frequently and more consistently visited than children in foster family homes. Although one component of the difference might be those children with stronger family ties may originally have been selected for institutional rather than foster care, the data show other factors operating. Parents feel more encouragement to visit children in institutions, there are fewer constraints and greater flexibility in when and how they may visit without fear of disrupting the child's living situation, they feel less competition from the institutional staff for the affection and loyalty of their children, and the institution provides greater opportunity to be alone with the child when parents visit.

Institutional structure offers an excellent opportunity for a variety of other types of parental involvement on a day-to-day basis. Parents have been invited to observe the child-care staff and its use of various childrearing techniques. The staff in these situations can also assist parents in practicing the use of more effective techniques.

> Joe whips off his new baseball cap and begins tearing it as if on cue. His father starts yelling and cursing. Joe escalates his destructive behavior; mother joins in, screaming; and a scene unfolds that has been repeated at home countless times.
>
> "Just ignore him, Mr. A. Joe wants you to be angry. He wants control of the situation. Let's play cards," a calm voice directs. The three sit down to a game of cards while Joe sits quietly in a corner. He seems relieved. A 12-year-old, he is too young to be controlling his parents [Littauer, 1980, p. 225].

Structuring parental participation in various decision-making situations can be a means of demonstrating staff willingness to work with parents. Krona (1980) describes one agency in which staff routinely discuss all major disciplinary decisions with parents. Simmons, Gumpert, and Rothman (1981) used family conferences, during which the social service and child care staff met with parents, for a similar purpose.

Institutions have used a range of family treatment techniques, including conjoint family therapy and sociobehavioral training (Krona, 1980; Heiting, 1971, U.S. Department of Health and Human Services, 1981, and parent support groups. Parent support groups prove a very powerful intervention tool, a mechanism for alleviating the isolation of parents, for helping them draw on the expertise and ideas of other parents, and for encouraging them to attempt to try new approaches with their children.

Simmons, Gumpert, and Rothman (1981) note that parent group workers are usually confronted by problems stemming from poor attendance during the early phases of group formation. In part, this reflects the crisis-oriented nature of the parents' life-style. Once the child has been removed and the pressure to cope with him or her has been assuaged, this type of parent has a tendency to become preoccupied with other matters and therefore, to feel little need for group support. The authors note that aggressive outreach on the part of staff, accompanied by insistence that parents have an invaluable role to play in the child's care, helped them reestablish regular attendance (p. 381). Parent education and group psychotherapy approaches have also been proven effective (Winder et al., 1965; Small & Whittaker, 1979).

Institutional programs for parents must be multifaceted. No one specific type of program or intervention will meet the needs of all parents, just as no one treatment approach is helpful for most children. Corder et al. (1981) suggest that programming be established on a variety of levels, depending upon the motivations and abilities of individual parents. Level One programming is designed for parents who initially seek only respite care for their child. The focus of assistance for these individuals is educational and support-oriented. Level Two programming is designed for more involved parents. The authors suggest that might benefit from more therapeutically oriented group approaches and from the use of behavioral training. Level Three involvement is offered to parents who seek more intensive involvement on a daily basis. For these individuals, staff provide opportunities to participate in the activities of the living unit (pp. 258–259). Oxley's (1977a) survey of parent need points out that parents themselves request a range of involvement options.

Problems in Working with Parents

A major deterrent to effective involvement of parents in residential programs is staff attitudes (U.S. Department of Health and Human Services, 1981). Because staff may feel that the parents have harmed the child to such an extent that they can no longer be trusted to provide essential child care, they may conclude that the harm parents can do it outweighs any possible benefit their contact with the child might bring (VanderVen, 1981). Staff may also believe that parents, beset by a host of complex and longstanding problems, are essentially untreatable (Corder et al., 1981). These beliefs are buttressed by a folklore, a collection of stories about parents that describe why they are not to be trusted:

> Stories about parents get passed on and added to until staff members come to know some of the parents very well, so well that their character is taken for granted. Certain mothers come to be known as hysterial, certain fathers as totally irresponsible and uncaring, some mothers as completely cold and without emotion, other mothers as bizarre and really strange, certain parents as impulsive, others as self-destructive, some as explosive, and so on (Buckholdt & Gubrium, 1979, p. 53).

The desire to rescue children from their problematic family situation is reflected in staff response to social worker efforts to engage parents in the treatment process. As a consequence of their desire to protect children from a difficult home situation, staff may begin to actively compete with parents. They may conclude that children can best be helped to "forget" their birth families by learning that others can love and care for them better. However, as Mayer and Marsushima (1958) point out, "child care workers must always remember the adage that one can take children away from parents, but one cannot take parents away from children" (p. 145).

When staff complement their belief that children must be protected from untrustworthy parents with a conviction that, no matter how much outreach or therapeutic work is done, parents are essentially untreatable, their negative attitudes become fully solidified. Because many children in institutions for the dependent and neglected come from broken, multiproblem homes, fewer of these parents are seen by the agencies as being amenable to treatment, and 47 per cent of the institutions for the dependent and neglected have not provided caseworker therapy for families (Pappenfort et al., 1970a, p. 267). However, of the residential treatment centers, 83.7 per cent provided caseworkers for parents (Pappenfort, et al., 1970b, Table 250, p. 267). Some parents whose children are in care are, indeed, particularly resistant to social service intervention. Tittler et al. (1982) found that the extensiveness of parental problems, including such factors as mother–child distance and the amount of environmental stress, were more predictive of treatment outcome than actual progress in counseling. Corder et al. (1981) note that some parents seem to have "given up" on their child. They were mainly interested in using residential care to obtain respite from the stresses of child management, and their interest in participating in therapy was much more limited than was that of other parents. Some of the parents who are willing to accept the services offered by the agency have characteristics that make them especially irritating and frustrating to work with. Critchley and Berlin (1981) state:

> A small group of parents, whose severe depression coupled with helplessness as a coping mechanism, proved particularly anxiety-provoking for the staff. At first, the staff attributed the interactional problems entirely to the parents' pathology. As a result of individual supervision and numerous case conferences, staff members were able to look at their own intense feelings about the parent. It became clear that when staff members' feelings of anger, despair and hopelessness about helping the parent were not talked about openly, they contributed to intensive interactions that often culminated in angry criticism or studious avoidance [p. 152].

Techniques are available to help staff begin to resolve this dilemma. Administration of the residential center must adopt a proactive parent stance. "First, the home needs to have the conviction that it exists, not to take charge of neglected, dependent, or troubled children, but to help a family find the best possible solution to its difficulties" (Keith-Lucas & Sanford, 1977, pp. 39–40). In addition, staff and parents must be forced to interact with each other on an extended basis. Critchley and Berlin (1981) point out the process that occurs here. Initially, both staff and parents voiced very negative attitudes toward each other. "Parental behavior was interpreted by milieu staff as indicating indifference or anger towards their child or the staff. This, in turn, generated feelings of anger in the staff, which found covert expression in workers' interaction with the parents. Parents sensed this covert anger, which only reinforced their perception of the staff as rigid, dogmatic, and anti-parent" (pp. 151–152). Continued regular interaction, coupled with continued pressure on staff and parents to work collabora-tively, eventually led to increased staff understanding of the needs of the parents. Staff members were then able to identify with the parents' sense of frustration and inadequacy in dealing with their difficult children. Staff also began to allow parents to make mistakes as they, themselves, erred in attempting to effectively deal with the child. "A difficult lesson learned by both staff and parents was that often a sensitive use of trial and error under controlled conditions was the only way to determine the most positive and helpful ways to respond to a child" (p. 152). Over time, staff criticism was replaced by staff support. (See also Littauer, 1980.) To make this transition effectively, staff risk giving up their "superperson" status (U.S. Department of Health and Human Services, 1981), whereas parents risk confronting their fears that staff will blame them and that they will find themselves truly ineffective parents. Van Hagen (1983) comments that this atti-tude change will only occur over an extended period of time. It is also very helpful for staff to realize some successes with parents, to have some visible sign that their efforts have had an impact on families (Simmons, Gumpert, & Rothman, 1981; Van Hagen, 1983).

Termination.

Intake, life in the institution, and discharge from institutional care are all different steps in a single process. Preparation for and help with the return to the community are an important unit in the process. As Kahn (1960) says: "Rehabili-tation must ultimately take place in the community. Institutionalization is, at best, a successful period of removal from the community in order to help the individual equip, and prepare himself for his return" (p. 14).

Planning for discharge must begin at the intake conference (Interstate Consor-tium on Residential Child Care, 1980, p. 102). Periodic reviews of the child's progress are scheduled throughout the child's stay. In addition to assessing changes in the child's behavior, long-term goals and tentative discharge dates are discussed at these meetings. Termination should occur when the child has re-ceived maximum benefit from institutional care. To hold the child beyond this point is to deny him or her some measure of a more normal life.

The social worker is responsible for helping the child and family make the transition from the institution into the community. Working with the child at the time of discharge provides yet another opportunity to help work through feelings about separation (Child Welfare League of America, 1982, p. 86). Both anger and withdrawal are common responses; both mask strong feelings of ambivalence and sadness. The child looks forward to returning home but will miss the individuals with whom he or she has formed a close and caring relationship in the residential center (Bale, 1979). Regressive behavior is also common among children making this transition. Bale suggests that children need separation rituals, events that mark their leavetaking and provide other children opportunities to express their regret that the child is leaving. These rituals can also be of value to staff who, like the child, have mixed feelings.

Discharge planning may involve vocational counseling and job placement train-ing for adolescents being prepared for a return to their home communities. This type of life skills preparation has been combined with a program for locating entry-level jobs for these individuals (Barchi, 1977). Academic planning is an-other aspect of the social worker's task during the discharge period.

A family conference should precede the actual discharge of the child from the institution. The purpose of this meeting is to evaluate the child's and family's needs and to determine the types of services and other supports that must be available so that the child can effectively reintegrate with the family or function effectively in some other type of living arrangement. A nationwide survey indicates that about half of the institutions were providing some kind of aftercare service to former residents (Pappenfort & Kilpatrick, 1969, p. 455). Institutions for emotionally disturbed children were among those that were most likely to have established some specific provisions for this type of service. If the child is returning home, gradually extended visits prior to discharge help parents and child begin to work through the various issues they will face together. Returning the child to the parents' home precipitates a normative crisis, as the family works to reintegrate the child into the family group, struggles to reestablish mutually agreed-upon rules and expectations, and learns to readapt to the special needs of the child who was in care.

Termination may involve an intermediate stage between the institution and the return home. In some cases, foster-family care is indicated for the child as further preparation for living in the normal family setting. Some children cannot go home because they have no home to go to or because their parents are still not ready to accept them. They, too, might need foster care. However, foster care is not always available for these children or, if available, may not be desirable because the child is in late adolescence.

For such children, transitional residence clubs have been established. These are extensions of the institution, located in the city. The child lives in the residence club, as he or she might live in a large hotel. The resident has greater freedom, more autonomy, and more responsibility for organizing life than in the institution. In addition, the residence club staff stands ready to assist the child with personal, vocational, and educational guidance. Staff members are assigned to every floor of the residence and are readily available for interviews. Bellefaire, a residential treatment center in Cleveland, operates a number of group homes accommodating four or five children (Greenberge & Mayer, 1972). The homes are "one-family dwellings in a middle-class suburban area and are indistinguishable from other homes on the street" (p. 423).

It has been suggested that institutions coordinate the need of institutional children for contact with some interested adult with the need for aftercare. Thus foster parents could be selected a year in advance of the child's planned discharge. They might visit the child at the institution and have the child visit with them on weekends and holidays. They would be paid on a standby basis even before the child is placed in their home.

Residential treatment centers are developing a postdischarge foster-care program of their own. For instance, the Astor Home for Children in New York has licensed foster homes that the institution has recruited for care of its children.

The institution, or the parent agency administering the institution, takes responsibility for aftercare follow-up of children who are moving to other settings. Usually, fewer and fewer contacts with the child are scheduled over time, and ultimately institutionally initiated contact is terminated. However, children should be encouraged to revisit the agency since this allows them to maintain a sense of connectedness with their past. The emphasis should be on a continuum of care from services to the child and family before institutionalization, through the institutional experiences, and during the period following discharge.

The Social Work/Child Care Team.

If social workers and psychiatrists share responsibility for individual psychotherapy, the entire staff shares responsibility for creating and maintaining the therapeutic environment. Although all share in this task, it is the particular responsibility of the child-care worker. These workers go under different names in different institutions: *cottage parent, houseparent, group parent, counselor, group counselor, residential worker, group living staff.* Whatever the title, the principal task is the same: the day-to-day care of the child. He or she is the nearest thing to a full-time parent assigned to the child. The staff member lives with a small group of children in a cottage or in a circumscribed section of a building, sees to the children's feeding and eats with them, gets them to bed on time and wakes them up, is concerned with their personal hygiene and their clothing needs, settles fights and disputes among them and disciplines those needing discipline, cares for and comforts them when they are sick, gets them off to school and is there to greet them when they come home, makes sure they do their homework and often helps with it. He or she is responsible for the daily living arrangements for the individual child, for the needs of the group as a group, and for the maintenance of the living quarters (Child Welfare League of America, 1982, pp. 65–76).

The Child Welfare League of America (1964) indicates that "the childcare staff is the heart of the program in an institiution for children" (p. 61). The disorganization resulting from a strike of childcare staff in Canada indicates the stabilizing effect these individual have on the lives of children in care (McConnell, 1982).

The professional clinical staff—the social worker, the psychiatrist, the psychologist—have ultimate responsibility for diagnosing the child's problem and planning his or her treatment. But the child-care worker—in direct, intimate, continuous contact with the child—has the primary responsibility for implementing the treatment plan. It is this staff member who, in disciplining the child and arranging for his or her daily needs and activities, organizes the child's life in accordance with the treatment plan and provides the content of the therapeutic living experience (Child Welfare League of America, 1982).

A rich literature is being developed directed toward the education of houseparents. Manuals and detailed accounts of institutional child care point to particularly sensitive times in the day's routine (wake-up time, meals, going to bed) and to recurrent types of problems (stealing, wetting and soiling, running away, sexual activity, disruptive and destructive behavior on the grounds and in the cottage) (Mayer and Mutsushima, 1965, 1969; Trieschman, Whittaker & Brendtro, 1969; Beker et al., 1972; Klein, 1975; Adler, 1976; Lambert, 1977; Maier, 1981). These books further offer suggestions on how to deal with such events and such problems in a therapeutic manner.

Because child-care staff play a central role in the life of children, the need for collaboration between their goals and those of the social worker is particularly important. The social worker consults with the child-care worker, explaining what the child needs, obtaining feedback about how the child is reacting to the treatment plan, and soliciting the help of the worker in reformulating the treatment plan.

However, child-care workers and social workers, having different responsibilities, necessarily have different perspectives on what they regard as important. In studying the residential treatment center, Polsky and Claster (1968) found that child-care workers emphasized activities concerned with meeting institutional demands: cottage housekeeping, maintaining the institutional standards regarding language or dress, and regulating the child's relationship to subsystems in the institution, such as school, work, and appointments with therapists (Polsky Claster, 1968). Social workers concerned with therapy emphasize individualization and flexible interpretation of institution regulations in terms of the need of the particular child.

The child-care worker is likely to be oriented to the cottage group as the unit of treatment and concern; the social worker, to the individual child. Both are concerned with seeing that the children adhere to institutional norms, and both discourage behavior that is disruptive of the social system of the institution, but social workers are more likely to give precedence, where there is a conflict, to those activities that presumably facilitate the child's therapy, change, and psychological development (Dick, 1971; Reichertz, 1978).

In a study of nine Canadian institutions, Reichertz (1978) found that staff expressed generally humane and supportive attitudes toward children in care. However, they were also "more oriented towards control than the promotion of learning" (p. 245), tended to emphasize the highly structured use of discipline, and deemphasized the child's role in decision making (p. 247). Differences in perceptions and expectations can, in turn, lead social work and child-care staff to develop negative views of each other. Studies of the relationship between social workers and cottage parents indicate a relationship often characterized by resentment, differences of opinion, and lack of mutual respect (Piliavin, 1963). The caseworkers resented the cottage parents' emphasis on control, their intrusions into the caseworker's counseling responsibilties, and their failure to carry out treatment plans developed by clinic workers and agreed upon in case conferences. The cottage parents, on the other hand, felt that the caseworkers were either unrealistic in their treatment of the children or in the appraisal of the possibilities of program implementation within the cottages.

Differing expectations lead to conflict. The child-care worker may expect that the social worker will provide clear and explicit "solutions" for coping with behaviors that disrupt cottage life. The social worker finds it difficult to communicate the fact that there are often no ready-made "solutions."

On the other hand, the social worker expects the child-care worker to implement a treatment program in the cottage, and the child-care worker may find it difficult to communicate the disruptive consequences of the social worker's recommendations. Confidence and respect between the two groups are eroded. As one houseparent said, "I can't get through to the social worker what the kid is like in the cottage."

The conception of social work and child-care staff as forming a treatment team can help to decrease stress between these two groups and can offer them a mechanism for resolving conflicts that do develop. The team concept emphasizes shared responsibility for decision making among various individuals who are responsible for the child's progress and encourages the use of collaborative rather than authoritarian decision-making procedures (Fulcher, 1981). When problems arise with the child, the team is responsible for resolving the difficulty. No individual member of the team is seen as responsible for the child's lack of progress (Child Welfare League of America, 1982, pp. 20–21).

Evaluation

Studies evaluating the impact of residential services on children have considered four different questions:

1. Did the children progress during their stay and care? These "outcome studies" (Durkin & Durkin cited in Whittaker, 1979, p. 189) usually assess global progress of children during their stay in care. A few studies have examined the impact of residential services on specific aspects of child behavior or disability.
2. Do children maintain their positive progress for some time after leaving residential care? These are "follow-up" studies.
3. What are the particular components of treatment that have positive impact on children? This research measures program "effectiveness".
4. How do the clients themselves assess their experiences? What do they consider to be the most positive and problematic aspects of residential care? These are "consumer" studies. Because there has been almost no evaluation of the impact of residential care on parents, this assessment will focus only on the impact of care on child clients.

Johnson and Reid (1947) studied the outcome of the treatment of 339 children accepted for treatment at the Ryther Child Center in Seattle, Washington, during the period 1936–1945. Treatment was categorized as "successful" if the child was subsequently able to adjust at home or in a foster home, in school or at work, and if he or she was living in accordance with community legal standards. Seventy-five percent of the group were rated "satisfactory" by these criteria. There was limited information available for assessment in some cases, but in general, children who were younger at the time of admission to care were more likely to have been successfully treated.

Silver (1961) reports on a study of fifty-four children placed by the Jewish Family and Children's Service of Detroit in two different residential treatment centers. He notes that 60 per cent evidenced some positive change in behavior as a result of their stay at the residental treatment center, 20 per cent showed no change, and an additional 20 per cent showed a negative change. There is no indication in the report as to how the judgment was made. Success in treatment was related to the diagnosis. Silver states that, "in the neurotic group, there was a preponderance of positive outcome; on the other hand, in the combined category of character disorder and psychotic," (p. 201) there were fewer children who had positive outcome. Success in treatment was related to time in treatment, but not to whether the children and/or the parents had an awareness of their need for treatment.

Maluccio and Marlow (1974) studied the outcome of 215 children placed in residential treatment programs by the state of Rhode Island. The case records were used as the basic source of data, supplemented by mail questionnaires completed by the treatment institutions. The records varied in completeness of detail.

Because of the limited residential-treatment facilities in Rhode Island, many of the children had to be placed out-of-state, which adversely affected continuing contact between the child and family and the efforts made by agencies to offer treatment services to the family.

Although discharge from residential care after an average of two years resulted from "successful treatment" in two thirds of the cases, in one third of the cases the treatment center confessed its "inability to help the child." The institution's own ratings of the change achieved by the child, which were obtained through the mail questionnaire without any substantiation, indicated "substantial" or "moderate" improvement in 48 per cent of the 76 children for whom such data were obtained.

The Children's Reeducation Center in Greenville, South Carolina, treating mildly or moderately disturbed children from six to twelve years old, had a 90 per cent success rate in returning children to public school. The program is based on reality therapy and behavioral modification and involves frequent parental visiting and a program of postrelease support (Hobbs, 1970, p. 202). (See also Weinstein, 1974.)

Results of these outcome studies are similar to those noted by Fineberg, Kettlewell, and Sowards (1982) who reviewed improvement rates on adolescents in residential care. The research they assessed showed an overall rate of progress that varied between 66 per cent and 87 per cent (p. 344). More descriptive studies that present clinical accounts of success of residential treatment are those by Redl and Wineman (1951, 1953) and by Bettleheim (1951, 1955).

More detailed evaluations of specific components of change in children's behavior were conducted by Rausch et al. (1959) and Millman and Schaefer (1975). Rausch (1959) conducted a detailed observational study of a small group of six emotionally disturbed children in residential treatment. The behavior of each of these children "was characterized by such overwhelming aggressiveness that they could not be tolerated by community, schools, foster parents, or parents" (p. 10). Trained observers taped details of a particular child's behavior in six different kinds of interactional situations. The observational protocols were coded by at least two coders working together to categorize the nature of the behavior that had been observed. Observations were repeated after the child had been in residential treatment for eighteen months:

> Over a year and a half, the interpersonal behavior of the children shifted considerably. The major changes were in the relations of the children with adults. Here there was primarily a decrease in hostile, dominant behavior and an increase in passive, friendly behavior. The appropriateness of the behavior increased both in relations with children and adults. The patterns of change were consistent with treatmment aims, and they seemed, at least in part, a function of the treatment program [p. 25].

Millman and Schaefer (1975) report on the use of the Devereux Child Behavior Rating Scale by child-care counselors and the Devereux Elementary School Behavior Rating Scale by teachers and teachers' aides at Children's Village, a residential treatment center for emotionally disturbed boys. The counselor who knew the boys in the cottage and the teachers who knew the boys in the classroom periodically completed the forms, which assessed observable behavior. Ratings for over one hundred boys over the period of a year showed most significant changes in "socal isolation," "coordination," "need for adult contact," "impulsivity," and "emotional detachment." There was less change in "social aggression" and "unethical behavior" (p. 696). "According to staff ratings, the deviant behavior of a group of preadolescent boys in residental treatment tended to show a slow, steady and often significant improvement over a 12 month period" (Schaefer & Millman, 1973, p. 160). "Behavioral competence" scores (personal hygiene, social functioning) improved more readily than "behavior control" factors (impulse control, acting out).

In summary, outcome studies focusing on particular aspects of the child's behavior point out that children appear to learn to express anger more appropriately. In addition, they appear to become attached to staff and, therefore, to express these feelings through greater cooperativeness, greater friendliness, and decreased amounts of isolation and detachment.

Another group of studies examines the post-institutional adjustment of children who have been released from residential care. These studies assess the extent to which children who have benefited from such care maintained their positive level of adaptation once they returned to their home and community environment.

Black and Glick (1952) used the Glueck Prediction Scale to evaluate the success of the treatment program at Hawthorne Center. Applying the scale to one hundred delinquent boys,they determined "that the relative chances of the Hawthorne boys for making a good community adjustment," if they had not received treatment, "were slight." In only eight of the one hundrd cases "was there an even chance of not recidivating." Follow-up study of the group five years after discharge revealed that 74 per cent of the boys had not committed any offense for which they might have been arrested (p. 39). The difference between the high prediction and the actual rate is attributed to treatment received at Hawthorne. The validity of the results depends, of course, on the validity of the Glueck Prediction Scale.

A follow-up mail survey of parents of children served at this residential treatment center asked about the child's adjustment after discharge and the parents' assessment of the help offered by the center (Schaefer, 1976). Responses from thirty-five parents indicated marked or slight improvements in functioning in about two thirds of the cases.

A follow-study was done on seventy boys who had been admitted to a residential treatment center at an average age of eight-and-a-half years and who remained in the institution about three years (Oxyley, 1977a, 1977b). The follow-up, four years after discharge, showed that some 83 per cent of the group had made positive changes from admission to follow-up. Improvement was associated with greater parental involvement in the treatment program and was attributed to the agency's explicit requirement of such parental involvement.

Assessing the impact of a short-term (nine-week) treatment program on 105 teenage boys and girls who participated in it. Fineberg, Kettlewell, and Sowards (1982) rated the children at admission, discharge, and at six weeks and six months after discharge. Using a Target Symptom Scale in interviews with both the child and with his or her mother or father, changes in symptoms, such as conduct disorders, problems with feelings, and problems with thinking, were evaluated. Results indicated the children made significant gains during this short-term program and maintained those gains throughout the follow-up period (p. 340).

Taylor et al. (1976) contacted twenty-four women graduates of group homes in which they lived for approximately two years during their adolescence. The women were contacted an average of five years after their discharge from the home. The researchers examined their current performance in the academic and employment arenas, the stability of their current living situation, and their relationships with peers. The researchers found that the women made an overall positive shift in their adjustment level between intake and follow-up points. However, total adjustment levels rose from only 4.9 (on an 11 point scale) to 5.5 at the time of follow-up. These women were performing satisfactorily in their general living situation and in their peer relationships; however, they were not functioning as well as could be expected in work or school settings.

Lewis et al. (1980), conducting a follow-up investigation of the adaptation of forty-three adolescents who had been residents of a treatment institution for approximately two years, report findings that contradict this generally positive picture. Both male and female and black and white children participated in the program. Criteria used as evidence of negative postdischarge adaptation included indication that the child had three or more placements, evidence of severe psychiatric problems or problems with the law, and any subsequent placement in a psychiatric hospital or treatment facility. Using these criteria, the authors found that more than two-thirds of these children experienced problematic postdischarge adaptation. Children who were doing more poorly had entered the residential institution at a later age than those who were doing well. They were also more likely to exhibit psychotic symptoms during their stay in treatment.

One of the factors that may help explain the inconsistencies between the findings of the Lewis et al. (1980) study and that of other follow-up research we have cited has to do with the level and quality of supports that are available in the child's post-discharge environment.

Allerhand et al. (1966) conducted a follow-up study of fifty boys discharged from Bellefaire, a residential treatment institution in Cleveland. Data for the study included a two-hour taped interview with each boy, interviews with his parents, and psychometric examinations of the boys. Included among the eleven different areas of social functioning assessed by the researchers were participation in family life, dating patterns, stability of school or work situation, and presence or absence of disciplinary actions in the community with regard to the boy. On the basis of the assessment, 64 per cent of the fifty children were manifesting successful social performance at the time of the follow-up study. One of the more significant findings is confirmation of the fact that adaptation at point of discharge is not in itself indicative of adaptation at follow-up. The incongruence between expectations at discharge and actual performance at follow-up was related to the level of stress or support provided by the living situation to which the boy returned: "It is the supportive or stressful nature of the post-institutional milieu that appears to be the critical factor in success, without regard to the within-institution career pattern" (p. 142). Only at the extreme end of the continuum were the boys' adaptations at discharge impervious to the effects of the postdischarge environment. For some, the capacity for adaptation had been so strengthened by the institutional experience that they could successfully cope with postdischarge stress; for others, who had been unable to respond even to the benign environment of the institution, no amount of postdischarge support seemed sufficient to enable them to adapt with adequacy. Postdischarge levels of adaptation were also a function of the extent to which the recommendations of the Bellefaire staff for aftercare living had been implemented. The researcher points out that institutional living prepares the child for institutional living but because the child ultimately needs to take his place in the community, the institution needs to provide the opportunity for more direct exposure to community demands.

The results of this study receive support from a follow-up of children who had been treated at Children's Village, a residential treatment center in Connecticut. The researchers found that "continuity and support following residential treatment was essential to postdischarge adaptation" and that "the greater the degree of support in the postdischarge environment the greater the degree of the child's adaptation to the environment" (Taylor & Alpert, 1973, pp. 50–51). Work with the child's family is clearly indicated. Of the seventy-five children studied, 31 per cent were judged to have achieved signficant change in both self-esteem and behavioral functioning, 47 per cent were throught to have achieved significant change in behavioral functioning, and 22 percent were felt to. have made no change or to have regressed during their stay in treatment.

A very limited number of studies have turned from examination of the characteristics of children in care to the study of the impact of particular program elements on these children. Two research projects have been undertaken in recent years. Each uses essentially the same methodology, developed by George Thomas (1975a) in his study of the effect of various types of institutional programs for dependent and neglected children in Georgia.

Thomas (1975a) developed criteria that evaluated the degree to which residential institutions are community-oriented. These institutions, he hypothesized, would be both responsive to the needs of the broader community and committed to preparing children for effective functioning in that community. They would, therefore, not be highly restricted in their intake criteria; they would not keep children in care for long periods of time; and they would attempt to adapt their program to changing service needs. This type of program would also attempt to replicate within the institution, as closely as possible, the types of child-care experiences usually found in family settings (p. 11). Thomas assessed the impact of institutional life on the verbal, cognitive, and social functioning of children. Approximately 1,750 children in 36 institutions throughout the state were evaluated, and their responses were compared to those of approximately 1,200 public school children. Results indicated that institutional care cannot be considered "bad" for children, in that it does not appear to affect adversely their overall performance. However, different types of institutions did have differential impact on children. The organizations that are most likely to positively affect cognitive competencies were those with a relatively stable and highly controlled environment, organizations in which the child could establish predictable long-term ties to both other children and to staff. Community-oriented and child participatory types of programs, which were not as control oriented or as long term, did not have as positive an impact in this area.

However, community-oriented agencies were effective in enhancing the child's social and affective abilities. Thomas states, "social competencies are enhanced through a positive ongoing relationship with at least one staff member within a relatively open institutional environment marked by high child exposure to community experiences and services and high participation in institutional decision-making processes" (p. 130). Likewise, staff continuity and programmatically induced participation served to enhance the child's emotional capacities (p. 131). Thomas did note that a number of other factors, including selective admissions and increasing maturation of the children, had a major impact on these emerging abilities. He concluded that community-oriented institutions do provide positive living environments for children and that they should be encouraged; however, the institutional program itself is not the only factor affecting children. A good residential environment will not serve all developmental needs of the child.

In her research on the impact of institutionalized children in Canada, Reichertz (1978) reached similar conclusions. She studied programs offered by eight Anglophone centers in the Montreal area and utilized the measurement techniques and tools that Thomas developed. She found:

> Although the institutional sample size was small, certain community-oriented characteristics emerged repeatedly in a pattern which differentiated institutions according to their community-orientedness and the observed levels of change in child competencies. The differentiating characteristics included: staff/child ratio and deployment, staff turnover, staff interaction with the community. . . , discipline-reward and daily life decision-making. . . . In addition, staff attitudes towards children and

the community and their commitment to a treatment philosophy appeared to play an influential role in the improvement of children over the one year period [p. 291].

Two recently published consumer-oriented studies have examined the reactions of former clients of institutional care. In their research with graduates of a group home for adolescent girls, Taylor et al. (1976) asked the women to assess their relationships with various staff and peers of the home and to discuss the overall effect of the program on their lives. These women primarily remembered their peer experiences as positive and felt that their caseworker played a relatively unimportant role in their experiences while in residence. They were most negative about their relationships with the child care staff. "Particularly lacking was a sense that the girls viewed the child care staff as providing a nurturing environment and as gratifying the more basic or dependent needs. The memories convey an impression that the childcare staff did not supply the kind of day-to-day psychological nurturing that the girls hoped for" (p. 86).

These views are echoed in a larger-scale study conducted by Bush (1980). He contacted a randomly selected group of 370 dependent and neglected chilren living in a major metropolitan area. Two-hundred-sixty-nine of these children had lived in institutions at some point during their childhood, and 90 were living in residential institutions or group homes at the time of the interview.

These children, too, described unsupportive staff relationships and lack of nurturing as major concerns. "Children do not consider institutions supportive places to reside. The children who were living in institutions at the time they were interviewed felt less comfortable, loved, looked after, trusted, cared about, and wanted than children in any other form of surrogate care or than children who had been returned to their original families. They were less likely to want to remain in their placement than any other set of children; they even rated institutions poorly on a dimension of loneliness, a problem that institutional care is supposed to mitigate" (p. 244). Children were more negative about institutions than they were about group homes, although they raised questions about staff relationships in the group setting as well.

Not all children rated institutional life in a negative light. Adolescents tended to view it more favorably than did their younger counterparts. A small group of children enjoyed their residential experiences. They liked the greater freedom, the regularity and predictability, and lack of competition in these settings (p. 246).

Admittedly there is limited information currently available regarding the effects of institutional care and of particular programmatic and process components specifically (Walton, 1980; Payne, 1981). At the same time there is a need to recognize and address the real problems associated with institutional care as revealed by the research.

Problems

1. The nature of residential life places special performance demands on staff of these institutions. In agencies serving children, the need to provide high-quality care and to make important decisions that may have long-term consequences for children serve to increase the amount of stress experienced by both child-care and social-service workers.

Child-care workers have the greatest direct responsibility for caring for troubled children and for implementing their treatment programs. Yet, they are the individuals in the residential organization with the least power and status:

> The lack of required training, status and pay for the child care worker is remarkable in view of the breadth of her responsibility. She is not only the primary caring and educative person, outside the confines of formal education, she is also the primary group leader and the second most active (behind the child's peers) counselor for children. She is an evaluator of the child's progress and as such takes an active part in planning for him. She may be involved in therapeutic plans for him. She is his advocate (Keith-Lucas & Sanford, 1977, p. 70). (See also Simon, 1956; Mayer & Marsushima, 1965.)

Child-care staff carry out these responsibilities under highly demanding working conditions. Keith-Lucas and Sanford (1977) describe the worker as functioning "in the midst of a swirl of constantly shifting activity" (p. 70). Mattingly (1981) describes the worker's job environment as a "pressure cooker" (p. 155). Yet, despite their responsibility to choose therapeutically effective responses in an atmosphere that is highly charged and frequently chaotic, child-care workers must function under the direction of others and must defer to professional clinical staff of social workers, psychiatrists, and psychologists.

Their low status in the organization is reflected in their low pay. Although one-third of direct care staff have college degrees (Russo & Shyne, 1980, p. 13), more than half of them make less than $8,000 per year (Myer, 1980). In a survey of almost 500 individuals working in child care and residential treatment institutions in 24 states, Myer found that four out of five of these individuals were dissatisfied with the pay they received. Low-organizational status suggests to these workers that they have little influence on decision making and this, in turn, affects their morale (Mattingly, 1981).

As a result of this situation, workers who remain in their job experience frustration and burnout. Workers experiencing burnout typically feel "emotional exhaustion, depersonalization, and lack of personal accomplishment" (Mattingly, 1981, p. 157). These feelings induce a variety of job-related problems. Some staff find it difficult to draw clear distinctions between their personal and work lives, others become increasingly rigid in their attitudes and decisions; still others lose their sense of critical judgment or express feelings of stress through physical symptoms. Limited job satisfaction also causes many child-care staff to leave this position within relatively short periods of time. As we have noted, Russo and Shyne (1980) found a very high turnover rate in residential facilities. Surveys of job retention among houseparents in community living arrangements (group homes or apartments for retarded children and adults) found the average length of stay for these individuals was only 6.8 months (Leonard, Margolis, & Keating, 1981, p. 330). Myer (1980) found that most respondents (72%) in his interstate survey of child-care staff had been in the field less than five years. Those who had decided to leave their positions cited a concern about financial factors (19%) and job frustrations (15%) or a desire to further their education or move on to another profession (37%). When directors of child-care institutions were asked in a nationwide study to list their recommendations for change, the one most frequently listed was for "raising the quality of the child care staff through recruitment and higher salaries and/or increasing in-service training" (Pappenfort & Kilpatrick, 1969, p. 458).

Social workers, too, face job stress that makes their work inherently difficult.

Although they have higher status and receive a higher salary than do child-care workers, they are also expected to play a more central and responsible role in planning and coordinating services for the child (Pecora & Gingerich, 1981). The social worker has to be knowledgeable about all aspects of the child's functioning in the living unit, the school, and the community. He or she must understand the child's family and peer relationships. The worker carries central responsibility for developing an appropriate treatment plan and ensuring that the plan is carried out by staff at the institution. Powers (1981) states that residential social workers must engage in planned "risk taking." This may include deciding to accept an especially difficult child for treatment, confronting staff who may be placing blame on the child when it is the program that is at fault, and "pushing and prodding" the treatment group into new and varied challenges (p. 176). Powers states that the worker who takes risks must also be prepared to experience failure and must protect himself or herself from being unduly discouraged when it occurs.

Although social workers have central responsibility for planning for the child, they do not hold centralized authority for making decisions with regard to the child. This increases the amount of stress which they experience. The social workers must share authority for decision making with the child-care staff, the child's teachers, and the institutional administration. In hospital settings, they must also share authority with medical and nursing personnel. In community-oriented institutions, the boundaries between the organization and the community are more permeable. Thus, outside individuals and agencies have greater influence on decision making with regard to children in care. It is "a maxim in organizational theory that the degree to which an organization is open to environmental influences is inversely related to the degree to which it can maintain control over its ongoing functioning. Uncertainty is thus introduced into institution functioning, placing increased stress on the organization and requiring additional program adaptations such as changes in staffing patterns and treatment approaches" (Dore & Kennedy, 1981, p. 379). The social worker plays a central role in engineering these adaptations.

To assist both the child-care and social work staff in dealing effectively with this situation requires that the administration of the institution be sensitive and reponsive to staff needs. To some extent, administrative decisions can help dissipate the impact of job stress through such mechanisms as adjusting work schedules, arranging vacations and sabbaticals, maintaining low case loads, and instituting other procedures that reinforce the view that all staff are important individuals in determining the well-being of children in care. In addition, adequate training and supervision of child-care and social-service staff help provide these workers with needed ongoing supports and with resources and assistance in making difficult decisions with regard to the lives of the children who are being served.

2. A significant aspect of evaluation is concerned with the deficiencies inherent in institutional care. The earlier concern that institutionalization traumatizes the child because it imposes maternal deprivation and stimulus deprivation seems to have given way to a more critical analysis of the problem, as already noted. It is currently conceded that a reasonably well-organized institution with a decent child–staff ratio can provide the child with the affectionate care and stimulation he or she needs for adequate growth (Witmer & Gershenson, 1968, p. 81). The research on infant deprivation, which was the basis of so much of the concern, is not applicable to most institutional populations, which are composed largely of

children between ten and twelve years of age—well beyond the critical period for maternal deprivation.

It is difficult, however, even for those institutions with a low child–staff ratio and adequate resources, to provide continuity of care, which requires a relationship with a nurturing adult who has primary responsibility for care of the child over a significantly long period in the child's development. Discontinuity in care in the institution results from the fact that a twenty-four-hour caretaking day is likely to require three sets of different parents, that caretakers need days off and vacations, and that all institutions have a very high staff turnover. A constant problem for institutional management is the shortage of trained staff and the associated problem of high staff turnover. Many, particularly younger, workers view the position as a temporary one.

The institution's failure to provide consistent staff coverage is particularly problematic for children whose lives have had so little continuity and predictability.

3. Questions have been raised concerning whether children are appropriately placed in residential institutions. Two complementary difficulties have been noted. Children who can no longer function in the community and who need the specialized services offered by residential institutions may be denied care because sufficient space is not available. On the other hand, children may be accepted or maintained in care who should be served, instead, in the community. These are, typically, the children who are functioning at a higher level, whose problems are more minimal, and who are easier for staff to relate to and to control.

Residential facilities are unevenly distributed throughout the country. Some states have no residential treatment institutions, whereas others do not have temporary shelters or detention homes. There are major variations among the states in the relative availability of the various types of substitute care. Wolins (1974) comments, "For example, in 1974, Illinois had capacity for about 20,000 in foster family care, 5,500 in institutions and 348 in group homes—a ratio of about 57:16:1. At the same time, neighboring Kentucky reportedly had . . . a ratio of about 3.5:20:1" (p. 97). As a result of these discrepancies, some children receive no services, whereas others are placed in inappropriate settings. Children who clearly do not belong there may be committed to adult wards in psychiatric hopsitals or held in prison. In addition, appropriately used institutions may be overcrowded, as they attempt to serve the large number of children requiring care. As a result, these institutions may find that custody is the only service they can offer.

Some states that do not have sufficient placement for emotionally disturbed children have been sending them to facilities outside of the state or even outside of the country. For instance, Illinois has sent children needing institutional care to Canada (*Chicago Tribune*, July 27, 1975). (See Children's Defense Fund, 1978, pp. 57–74.)

The shortage of residential treatment center facilities is chronic and growing. In a national survey of AFDC and child welfare clients, Shyne and Schroeder (1978) found that only 62 per cent of the children for whom institutional services were recommended actually received them (p. 64). A more recent study of residential mental health services for children (Knitzer & Olson, 1982) found that 18 of the 44 states examined in the research were working to increase the number of children served in residential care. However, most of these new programs were very small. Only five states were intending to serve more than 50 children through these expanded efforts (p. 45). As a result, increasing numbers of children who could benefit from a residential experience may never receive this type of care.

On the other hand, institutions may accept children for care who would be better served through outpatient resources. Knitzer and Olson (1982) estimate that 40 per cent of all children placed in hospital settings do not belong there. They describe a 1979 audit of District of Columbia children in psychiatric hospitals that found 44 per cent could have been served as outpatients; a New York 1977 survey found that 25 per cent could have been served outside the institution; a 1979 New Jersey survey found that 40 per cent of the children were admitted inappropriately or stayed in care too long (p. 46). More careful management of the flow of children into and out of residential care could result in the freeing of space for those most in need of such services and in the development of more adaptive options for children who do not need such a restrictive environment.

4. Another of the current problems of the institution is one we tend to associate with a past period in our history. In 1950 Albert Deutsch published a detailed, and shocking, nationwide report of child-caring institutions that were guilty of neglect and exploitation of the children living in them. He described training schools in which the housing was dilapidated and overcrowded; the food scanty, monotonous, and inedible; the educational and recreational resources primitive or nonexistent; and the care of the children, at best, indifferent, and at worst, clearly irresponsible. A report published in 1970 of conditions in children's institutions around the country mirrored the 1950 findings (James, 1970). A report in 1976 (Wooden, 1976) repeated the 1970 findings.

A survey of a sample of eighteen institutions in five states caring for children receiving Aid to Families of Dependent Children (AFDC) support payments was conducted in 1976 by the Office of the Comptroller General (U.S. Office of Comptroller General, 1977). Deficiencies in seven of the eighteen institutions were noted, primarily with regard to physical facilities: "children sleeping on mattresses on the floor in cramped and dingy rooms"; "broken and dirty bathroom facilities which were cited by two health agencies as inadequate" (p. 25). Licensing did not guarantee "that institutions maintained their facilities at acceptable levels" (p. 27). Although defects were found in the facilities, there were no findings regarding neglect and abuse of the children in the institutions surveyed.

Ensuring adequate physical care, let alone healthy social and emotional care, for children in institutions appears to be a recurrent problem. It might be noted, however, that for the most part, the horrendous examples cited by Deutsch, James, and Wooden concern facilities for delinquents. The residential treatment center and institutions for the dependent and neglected are not as frequently indicated, although there are deficiencies.

In its *Standards for Residential Centers for Children,* the Child Welfare League of America (1982) notes that

> Corporal punishment, including slapping, spanking, paddling, belting, marching, standing or kneeling rigidly in one spot, or any kind of physical discomfort should not be used. Generally, this is viewed by the child as a manifestation of the adult's aggression rather than punishment and reinforces any feelings he or she may already have that the world is a hostile, angry, fearful place. For many children, it is a repetition of earlier experiences that have contributed to their problems [p. 53]. [See also Interstate Consortium on Residential Child Care, 1980, p. 99].

By 1977, most states had procedures for reporting abuse and neglect in institutions and provisions for an independent investigation of any reports of maltreatment. The Interstate Consortium on Residential Child care (1980) includes this reporting requirement in its guidelines (p. 86).

5. Despite increased commitment to working with the parents of children who are in care, many families receive little or no assistance from the staff of residential institutions. A survey conducted in Colorado found that between 47 per cent and 71 per cent of parents were involved in treatment, depending upon the particular type of institution surveyed (Reported in Wolins, 1978, p. 113). Conducting his own survey of participants in the 1976 CWLA Working Conference on Group Care in North America, Wolins (1978) found only 30 per cent felt they were successful or very successful in achieving parent involvement to the extent they wished (p. 112). Although parents, themselves, contribute to this problem by resisting staff efforts to help them, staff themselves are also resistant, as we have previously noted. More intensive efforts to develop effective outreach and treatment strategies for these families and to overcome staff ambivalence must be undertaken to provide maximum benefit to children in care. However, many institutions are not fully committed to this effort.

6. Institutions and group homes face a problem of public acceptance when they attempt to locate in a community. At best, these agencies are tolerated rather than fully accepted. A survey of households in Cleveland, conducted by the Federation for Community Planning, discovered that only 15 per cent were in favor of allowing a group facility for troubled adolescents in their neighborhood; 51 per cent of the respondents were actively opposed to such an effort (Solomon, 1983, p. 364). When institutions attempt to relocate in community-based settings, there is often organized opposition through the use of petitions, testimony at zoning- or planning-board meetings, picketing, and court action. Destruction of group home property and facilities and harassment and scapegoating of residents have also occurred.

Community members are fearful about possible deviant behavior of group home children and feel that nonwhite and troubled children belong somewhere else "with their own kind" (Solomon, 1983). In addition, deinstitutionalization has resulted in an influx into some neighborhoods of group homes for the mentally ill and mentally disabled, drug users and ex-offenders. Until a more equitable distribution of group homes is achieved, some neighborhoods find themselves "saturated" with such facilities.

The tolerance quotient of the community and the community schools for deviance varies, but it is rarey very high. Whatever the level of acceptance of deviant behavior within the group home itself, the fact that it is located in the community and that the children live "in" the community a good part of the time sets limits on the kinds of children the group home can include (Mayer, Richman, & Balcerzak, 1977).

Faced with the problem of community opposition to group homes, one group of agencies attempted an interorganizational effort (Stickney & Capaiuolo, 1976). The Community Resident Information Services Program assists in locating sites for group homes, provides consultation on zoning and community relations, works with citizens' groups, and serves as an information exchange and a resource bank for relevant studies and reports. Based on their experience, they suggest a thorough study of the community and its residential pattern, a slow low-profile approach, and the involvement of community leaders in planning for the institution or group home. Selecting an appropriate neighborhood that is likely to be receptive, or at least not strongly opposed; preparing the neighborhood for the opening of the group home; gradually bringing the home up to a full complement of children; and sharing group-home facilities with the neighborhood whenever possible—these have been among the tactics that make it easier for the neighborhood to accept the group home. (See also Janchill, 1983.)

Weber (1978) has identified the different neighborhood variables that the group-home developer needs to be aware of in deciding on a strategy for entry into the community. He suggests, among other things, educating neighbors through one-to-one contacts by the house parents of the projected group home, being frank about possible problems but indicating procedures for keeping them to a minimum, and being clear about the legal basis that gives the group home the right to open. Pierce and Hauck (1981) describe one agency's efforts to use these factors in successfully opening a community-based facility.

Making the decision to attempt to locate a residential facility in a particular neighborhood can be problematic. On the one hand, locating in an inner-city or transient area may invoke less opposition. Davidson (1981) identifies three types of neighborhoods in which resistance is likely to be low, "those in which deviant behavior is tolerated, those whose residents do not regard the neighborhood as sufficiently important to warrant defending it against intrusions, and those which lack the resources necessary for effective political mobilization" (p. 222).

On the other hand, attempting to develop community-based institutions in suburban areas raises a great deal of resistance unless the children are from more "acceptable" client groups (dependent, retarded, or handicapped). However, even in these settings, there is a tendency to locate the facility in areas that are physically or visually isolated from the rest of the neighborhood (Davidson, 1981, p. 237).

Trends

1. A principal trend in institutional care is the change in the nature of the population served. The development of supportive and supplementary services has reduced the number of children requiring substitute care. Now the children who require it are more frequently those who are so disturbed or who come from a situation so disorganized that even supportive and supplementary care would not permit them to be kept in their own homes or in foster homes.

The institution tends to serve the most difficult of the most difficult cases. The change is noted by Jonsson (1972), who says:

> The nice children that we used to get . . . pale, with sorrowful faces and shy, quiet manners . . . [have been replaced by] unhappy children who express their longing for understanding and tenderness in a language which is natural to them; swearing, and pestering and using foul language, kicking and punching and stealing, playing truant, bad table manners, sex talk, smoking, and boasting [p. 42].

In a survey of sixty-five residential facilities affiliated with the Child Welfare League of America, Russo and Shyne (1980) found 46 per cent had made changes in their intake policies in the last five years that reflected a commitment to accept more difficult youngsters into care. Twenty-nine facilities now accept more disturbed children; nine now accept delinquents; an equal number accept status offenders; and nine are admitting youngsters with lower IQs. Few programs had recently excluded difficult youngsters from their facilities. The authors conclude, "the responses described here in respect to changes in admission criteria support, in a general sense, the population figures that show some increase in the proportion of residents who might be expected to engage in disruptive behavior"(p. 32). These institutions did report increased problems with client use of marijuana (56%) or other drugs (49%), and increased evidence of both physical (45%) and verbal aggression (43%) among the children (p. 45).

Close examination of admission data at the Youth Residence Center, a treatment facility operated by the Jewish Child Care Association in New York City, led Weintrob (1974) to the realization that the agency had undergone a major shift in population. Owing, in part, to the closing of the state hospital facilities for adolescents and decreased funding for psychiatric hospitalization, this program found itself facing major increases in clients referred by psychiatric sources, increases in the number considered schizophrenic or depressed, a marked rise in the number who had previously been hostpialized or needed short psychiatric hospitalization during their placement, and changes in the proportion of children who required major tranquilizers and antidepressants during their stay.

Facilities undergoing these types of change must, frequently, make major alterations in their programming in order to effectively respond to client needs. Administrators must also more adequately prepare staff to deal with highly aggressive or withdrawn children and with severely psychiatrically disturbed youngsters. Failure to implement these changes can threaten the continued existence of the institution. St. Joseph's Home for Children in Minneapolis faced a major influx of delinquent children as a result of child welfare agency referrals. Because the home was not sufficiently prepared, the staff lost control over the children, neighborhood residents were intimidated, and the police were called upon to act as control agents for the institutions. "What happened, Director Lenarz repeats, is that St. Joseph's got into trouble because it did not know what it was getting when it took so many seriously troubled youths" (Murphy, 1983, p. 106).

Some residential institutions have responded to the need for services for increasingly disturbed children by establishing intensive treatment units, special facilities for individuals who might otherwise need or who are graduating from state mental hospitals. Zaslaw, Krenk, and Slaughter (1983) described a typical client of such a facility:

> Jane is a 13-year-old half Caucasian and half American Indian female who has experienced 14 moves in residence over the past 7 years. Over the same period, she has attended 12 different schools. She and her family have been involved with the state social service agency since Jane was 5. Open residential treatment programs would not accept Jane because of her extremely aggressive behavior toward peers, chronic truancy and running away, and extremely poor impulse control. Jane grew up in a physically abusive environment and experienced a parenting style of alternating rejection and acceptance. Jane has a history of somatic ills and recurring respiratory, ear, and eye infections. She has an average IQ and functions approximately 2 years behind academic grade level. The professionals who have evaluated her consistently see her as very immature and undersocialized [pp. 41–42].

2. Changes in the conception of the service delivery system and in the nature of the particular population served by institutions have led to alterations in both the nature and purpose of the institutional program itself. From general placement settings for children needing substitute care, these agencies have evolved into "specialized residential settings with staffing and facilities to meet the needs of groups of children with common problems and needs" (Child Welfare League of

America, 1982, p. 1). The modern institution is said to be a "filling station, not a parking lot." Yesterday's "inmate" is today's "patient".

Growing commitment to the concept of community-based care and attention to the child's need for continuity of care have led to the blurring of boundaries between institutional and noninstitutional services (Dore & Kennedy, 1981, p. 380). Many organizations have developed ancillary services for chldren, including group homes, foster care homes, home-based treatment services, and special programming for adoptive parents. Within this system, the transfer of children from one type of service to another has been facilitated. A child may move from an inpatient residential unit to a group home and, eventually, to a foster home sponsored by the same agency. Developing these multifaceted services within one organization may assist children in moving out of residential care in a timely fashion; however, children may also remain in this social service delivery system for a longer period of time. It remains to be seen whether this expansion in services will help facilitate the development of permanent living arrangements for children who are in need of them.

3. Although the general trend is clearly in the direction of a reduction in institutional care and an increase in community-based care, this is still a matter of some controversy. Some of the anticipated advantages of deinstitutionalization to community-based care are found to be more difficult to achieve, and some of the disadvantages are becoming more apparent.

The promise of large savings in the difference between institutional costs and group-home costs is proving to be somewhat illusory. Group-home costs creep up to within stalking distance of institutional costs. Part of the costs are shifted to the general community. Because the group homes use many of the services in the community that the institution provides for out of its budget, group homes appear to be more economical. An audit report of the New York City Comptroller's Office (1977), which provides the funds for most of the children in substitute care in New York City, noted that the cost of care of the child in a foster-family home in June 1977 was $4,904 on an annual basis, of institutional care $13,408, and of group-home care only slightly less, at $13,140 (pp.3–4).

Although group homes are located in the community and are thus closer to the child's family, they have not been any more successful than the institutions in sustaining continued contact between parents and children (Citizens Committee for Children of New York, 1976, pp. 33–34).

Community group-home living offers temptations that a more sheltered institutional environment can control: "Any 'action' these youngsters want is available to them in the streets. The pull of street culture and the promise of hustles are strong. [The community group home] has to deal with gangs, with pushers, with bars," with pimps, and so on (Levine, 1977, p. 147).

Concluding a review of available evidence, Thomas (1975b) says that "There is very little in the way of research findings demonstrating clearly the advantage of either half-way houses or group treatment homes—we simply do not know whether the group treatment home is superior to institutionalization or not" (p. 21).

The ideological gains in terms of the normalization and the least-restrictive environment of community-based facilities are, however, clear advantages for the child.

4. The increasing complexity of the demands made on child care staff, fostered by the transfer from a custodial to a treatment focus, increased attention to the broader context in which children's problems develop, insistence on the need for

greater contact with parents, and demands that the worker be skilled in contacts with a variety of members of the community, has generated concern about the need to more adequately prepare and educate these individuals to take on these complex responsibilities (Beker, 1975; Whittaker, 1979; VanderVen, 1981; Beker & Maier, 1981). Awareness of the demands made on the child-care worker has led to widespread interest in professionalization of this role in the institution. Advocates for professionalization insist on adequate training, more congenial working conditions (including a shorter work week and better pay), and the establishment of some type of career ladder, which does not now exist for child-care staff (Beker, 1975; Whittaker, 1979). Whittaker (1979) suggests that career advancement should include opportunities to work with children in increasingly sophisticated ways. At the present time, child-care staff are limited to the attainment of some type of administrative position within the organization. The need to establish better working conditions and more adequate training mechanisms are recognized by the Child Welfare League of America (1982), the Interstate Consortium on Residential Child Care (1980) and other organizations concerned with the quality of care provided children in institutions. Child-care workers themselves have begun to organize in order to facilitate their job performance. Some twenty regional, state and local child-care worker associations are now in existence (Whittaker, 1979, p. 217). These organizations have been concerned with the development of standards for adequate performance and for the development of certification and training mechanisms for child-care staff. In 1975, the National Task Force on Child Care Associations was convened, and in 1977 the National Organization of Child Care Worker Associations was born. These groups had worked closely with both the American Orthopsychiatric Association and the Child Welfare League of America in their efforts to develop this profession. A journal devoted to residential child-care practice, *Child Care Quarterly*, began publication in 1971 (Whittaker, 1979).

Although there has been increased attention to the need for training, most child-care staff have available to them only a few courses, offered at their agency or through some local college or other organization in the community. Some community colleges have organized one- or two-year nondegree programs for the child-care staff. The first and most widely known degree program was developed by the Department of Child Development and Child Care at the University of Pittsburgh in 1970. Other degree programs are now available in New York, San Antonio, Seattle, and Vermont (Whittaker, 1979).

There is disagreement in this field concerning the type of professional status that child-care should attempt to achieve. Should it seek to be a profession, developing influence based on its own achievements; should it opt to be a semiprofession, dependent for its status on the profession with which it affiliates; or should child-care staff perceive themselves as having an occupation and turn to unions to help achieve the working conditions they desire (Beker, 1975; Whittaker, 1979; Toigo, 1981; VanderVen, 1981)? Consideration of political and social factors has led various experts to reach different conclusions with regard to this question.

5. Attention continues to be focused on the need for greater access to institutional care for black, Hispanic, and other minority children needing this service. Historically, very few institutional programs have been available for these children, either in organizations exclusively serving a minority group or in integrated institutional settings (Billingsly & Giovannoni, 1972). Therefore, providing help for them requires desegregation of white institutions. The fact that

segregated institutions can be denied public funds has stimulated more equitable service delivery policies. Desegregation has meant changing not only intake procedures but staffing patterns as well, opening employement at all levels in the institution to minority group applicants.

Despite these difficulties, many institutions have successfully integrated both staff and children. Today minority group children are still denied equal access to the more expensive and treatment-oriented forms of care in group homes and residential treatment centers (Shyne & Schroeder, 1978, p. 153). Minority children are also more likely to get improper care when they are placed in institutions (Wolins, 1978). Minority group children continue to be diverted from treatment settings by being labeled delinquent or status offenders, whereas their white counterparts are considered emotionally disturbed or dependent children.

6. Including families in the treatment-planning and service-provision aspects of residential care is a concern that will continue to be addressed by the residential care field. Whether family work receives the funding and attention it deserves from residential care providers is a question that remains to be answered.

Bibliography

Abbott, Grace. *The Child and the State*, Vol. 2. Chicago: University of Chicago Press, 1938.

Adler, Jack. *The Child Care Worker 1975*. New York: Brunner/Mazel, 1976.

Aldgate, Jane. "Advantages of Residential Care" *Adoption and Fostering*, 92, 2 (1978) 29–33.

Allerhand, Melvin E. et al. *Adaptation and Adaptability: The Bellefaire Follow-up Study*. New York: Child Welfare League of America, 1966.

Alt, Herschel. *Residential Treatment of the Disturbed Child*. New York: International Universities Press, 1960.

Astrachan, Myrtle, and Don Harris. "Weekend Only: An Alternate Model in Residential Treatment Centers." *Child Welfare*, 62, 5–6, (May–June 1983), 253–261.

Baily, Thelma Falk, and Walter Hampton Baily. *Child Welfare Practice: A Guide to Providing Effective Services for Children and Families*. San Francisco: Jossey-Bass, 1983.

Balbernie, Richard. *Residential Work with Children*. Elmsford, N.Y. Pergamon Press, 1966.

Bale, Tom. "Saying Good-bye in Residential Treatment." *Child Welfare*, 58, 9 (November 1979), 586–596.

Barchi, Carl F. "A Community Reentry Model." *Child Welfare*, 56, 9 (November 1977), 593–600.

Baxter, Mary Jane. "House Council—An Integral Part of Residental Treatment for Disturbed Children." *Catholic Charities Review* (May 1963), 46–47.

Bedford, Linda, and Larry D. Hybertson. "Emotionally Disturbed Children: A Program of Alternatives to Residential Treatment." *Child Welfare*, 54 (February 1975), 109–115.

Beedell, Christopher. *Residential Life with Children*. New York: Humanities Press, 1970.

Beker, Jerome. "Development of a Professional Identity for the Child Care Worker." *Child Welfare*, 54, 6 (June 1975), 421–431.

Beker, Jerome et al. *Critical Incidents in Child Care*. New York: Behavioral Publications, 1972.

Beker, Jerome, and Henry W. Maier. 'Emerging Issues in Child and Youth Care Education: A Platform for Planning." *Child Care Quarterly*, 10, 3 (Fall, 1981), 200–209.

Bernstein, Blanche, Donald A. Snider, and William Meezan. *Foster Care Needs and Alternatives to Placement*. New York: New York State Board of Social Welfare, November, 1975.

Bettelheim, Bruno. *Love Is Not Enough*. New York: Free Press, 1951.

Bettelheim, Bruno. *Truants from Life*. New York: Free Press, 1955.

Billingsley, Andrew, and Jeanne Giovannoni. *Children of the Storm: Black Children and American Child Welfare.* New York: Harcourt Brace Jovanovich, 1972.

Black, Bertram, and Selma Glick. *Recidivism at the Hawthorne-Cedar Knolls Schools.* New York: Jewish Board of Guardians, 1952.

Bloch, Donald, and Marjorie Behrens. *A Study of Children Referred for Residential Treatment in New York State.* New York: New York State Interdepartmental Health Resources Board, 1955. Mimeo.

Bowlby, John. *Maternal Care and Mental Health.* Geneva: World Health Organization, 1951.

Briar, Scott. "Clinical Judgment in Foster Care Placement." *Child Welfare,* 42 (April 1963), 161–169.

Brodie, Richard D. "Some Aspects of Psychotherapy in a Residential Treatment Center," in *Children Away from Home: A Sourcebook of Residential Treatment.* Ed. James K. Whittaker and Albert E. Trieschman. Chicago: Aldine-Atherton, 1972, 121–131.

Browning, Robert M., and Donald O. Stover. *Behavior Modification in Child Treatment.* New York: Aldine Publishing, 1971.

Bryce, Marvin. "Home-Based Care: Development and Rationale," in *Home-Based Services for Children and Families: Policy, Practice and Research.* Ed Sheila Maybanks and Marvin Bryce. Springfield, Ill.: Charles C Thomas, 1979, 13–28.

Buckholdt, David, and Jaber Gubrium. *Caretakers: Treating Emotionally Disturbed Children.* Beverly Hills, Cal.: Sage, 1979.

Bureau of the Census, U.S. Department of Commerce. *1976 Survey of Institutionalized Persons—Current Population Reports,* p. 23, No. 69. Washington, D.C.: U.S. Government Printing Office, 1978.

Bush, Malcolm. "Institutions for Dependent and Neglected Children: Therapeutic Option of Choice or Last Resort?" *American Journal of Orthopsychiatry,* 50, 2, (April, 1980), 239–255.

Bush, Malcolm, and Harold Goldman. "The Psychological Parenting and Permanency Principles in Child Welfare: A Reappraisal and Critique." *American Journal of Orthopsychiatry,* 52, 2, (April, 1982), 223–235.

Casler, Lawrence. "Maternal Deprivation—A Critical Review of the Literature," *Monograph of the Society for Research in Child Development,* 26 (1961).

Child Welfare League of America. *Standards for Services of Child Welfare Institutions.* New York, 1964.

Child Welfare League of America. *From Chaos to Order: A Collective View of the Residential Treatment of Children.* New York: 1972.

Child Welfare League of America. *Standards for Group Home Service for Children.* New York: Child Welfare League of America, 1978.

Child Welfare League of America. *CWLA Standards for Residential Centers for Children.* New York: Child Welfare League of America, 1982.

Children's Defense Fund. *Children Without Homes.* Washington, D.C.: Children's Defense Fund, 1978.

Citizen's Committee for Children of New York. *Group Home for New York City Children.* New York Citizens Committee for Children, December 1976.

Corder, Billie et al. "What Does the Parent–Consumer Want from the Houseparent? A Survey and Recommendations." *Child Welfare,* 60, 4 (April 1981), 255–262.

Crenshaw, David J. "Teaching Adaptive Interpersonal Behavior: Group Techniques in Residential Treatment." *Child Care Quarterly,* 5, 3 (Fall 1976), 6–16.

Criss, Florence L., and Ray C. Goodwin. "Short-Term Group Counseling for Parents of Children in Residential Treatment." *Child Welfare,* 49, 1 (January 1970), 45–48.

Critchley, Deane, and Irving Berlin. "Parent Participation in Milieu Treatment of Young Psychotic Children." *American Journal of Orthopsychiatry,* 51 (1981), 149–155.

Crone, J. Edwin. *Getting Started as a Residential Child Care Worker? A Guide for Beginners.* New York: Child Welfare League of America, 1983.

Davidson, Jeffrey. "Location of Community-Based Treatment Centers," *Social Service Review* 55, 2 (June, 1981), 221–241.

Davies, Gareth. "Assessment, Labelling or Expedience?", in *Residential Care: A Reader in Current Theory and Practice.* Ed. Ronald G. Walton and Doreen Elliott. Oxford: Pergamon, 1980, 43–53.

Deutsch, Albert. *Our Rejected Children.* Boston: Little, Brown, 1950.

Dick, Harry. "Nature and Significance of Changes in the Houseparents' Role in Institutions for Children." *Journal of Health and Human Behavior,* 12, 4 (December 1971).

Dimock, Edmund T. "Youth Crises Service: Short-Term Community-Based Residential Treatment." *Child Welfare,* 56 (March 1977), 187–195.

Dore, Martha, and Karen G. Kennedy. "Two Decades of Turmoil: Child Welfare Services 1960–1980." *Child Welfare,* 60, 6 (June, 1981), 371–382.

Downs, Susan Whitelaw, and Michael Sherraden. "The Orphan Asylum in the Nineteenth Century." *Social Service Review,* 57, 2 (June 1983), 272–290.

Drisko, James. "Therapeutic Use of Physical Restraint." *Child Care Quarterly,* 10, 4 (Winter 1981), 318–328.

Eisikovits, Rivka. "The Cultural Scene of a Juvenile Treatment Center for Girls: Another Look." *Child Care Quarterly,* 9, 3 (Fall 1980), 158–174.

Endres, V. Joseph, and Douglas H. Goke. "Time Out in Residential Treatment Centers." *Child Welfare,* 52, 6 (June 1973), 559–563.

Epstein, Norman. "A Residence for Autistic and Schizophrenic Adolescents." *Social Casework,* 63, 4 (April 1982), 209–214.

Fahl, Mary Ann, and Donna Morrissey. "The Mendota Model: Home-Community Treatment," in *Home-Based Services for Children and Families: Policy, Practice and Research.* Ed. Sheila Maybanks and Marvin Bryce. Springfield, Ill.: Charles C Thomas, 1979, 225–236.

Fineberg, Beth, Paul Kettlewell, and Stephen Sowards. "An Evaluation of Adolescent Inpatient Services." *American Journal of Orthopsychiatry,* 52, 2 (April 1982), 337–345.

Finkelstein, Nadia Ehrlich. "Family-Centered Group Care." *Child Welfare,* 59, 1 (January 1980), 33–42.

Fisher, Susan. "Life in a Children's Detection Center," *Child Abuse and Violence.* Ed. David Gil. New York: AMS Press, 1979, 200–208.

Fox, Murray. "Maternal Involvement in Residential Day Treatment." *Social Casework,* 66, 6 (June 1985), 350–357.

Fulcher, Leon C. "Team Functioning in Group Care," in *Group Care for Children: Concepts and Issues.* Ed. Frank Ainsworth and Leon C. Fulcher. London: Tavistock, 1981, 170–197.

Garrison, William T. "Inpatient Psychiatric Treatment of the Difficult Child: Common Practices and their Ethical Implications." *Children and Youth Services Review,* 6, 4 (1984), 353–365.

Goldberg, Kenneth, and Mark Dooner. "Rethinking Residential Treatment." *Child Welfare,* 60, 5 (May 1981), 355–358.

Grant, Dannie, C. Edwin Knight, and Donald K. Granvold. "Institutionalized Youth's Perceptions of Resident-Staff Relationships." *Child Care Quarterly,* 13, 1 (Spring 1984), 62–67.

Greenberg, Arthur. "Agency Owned and Operated Group Foster Homes for Adolescents." *Child Welfare,* 42 (April 1963).

Greenberg, Arthur, and Morris F. Mayer. "Group Home Care as an Adjunct to Residential Treatment." *Child Welfare,* 51, 7 (July-August 1972), 423–435.

Gregory, William. "Secure Provision for Children and Young People," in *Residential Care: A Reader in Current Theory and Practice.* Ed. Ronald Walton and Doreen Elliott. Oxford: Pergamon Press, 1980, 253–262.

Grollman, Earl (Ed.). *Explaining Death to Children.* Boston: Beacon Press, 1967.

Gula, Martin. *Child-Caring Institutions.* Washington, D.C.: U.S. Government Printing Office, 1958.

Gula, Martin. *Agency Operated Group Homes.* Washington D.C.: U.S. Government Printing Office, 1964.

Hall, E. Stephanie. "Collecting and Using Data for Assessment," in *Residential Care: A Reader in Current Theory and Practice.* Ed. Ronald Walton and Doreen Elliott. Oxford: Pergamon, 1980, 63–75.

Harsch, Barbara. "Power Struggles between Child Care Worker and Youth." *Child Care Quarterly,* 12, 4 (Winter 1983–1984), 263–270.

Heiting, Kenneth H. "Involving Parents in Residential Treatment of Children." *Children,* 18, 5 (September–October 1971), 163–167.

Hill, Alice. *Toward and Evaluation of the Use of Residential Group Facilities by Local Child Welfare Agencies.* Washington, D.C.: The Urban Institute, September 1976.

Hobbs, Nicholas. "Project Re-Ed New Ways of Helping Emotionally Disturbed Children," in *Crisis in Child Mental Health: Challenge for the Seventies.* Joint Commission on Mental Health of Children. New York: Harper & Row, 1970.

Holleman, Barbara. "Treatment of the Child," in *Child Abuse and Neglect: A Guide with Case Studies for Treating the Child and Family.* Ed. Nancy Ebeling and Deborah Hill. Boston: John Wright, 1983, 145–182.

Hylton, Lydia. *Residential Treatment Center, Children Program Costs.* New York: Child Welfare League of America, 1964.

Interstate Consortium on Residential Child Care. *Residential Child Care Guidebook.* Trenton, NJ: Interstate Consortium, 1980.

Jaffe, E.D. "The Impact of Experimental Services on Dependent Children Referred for Institutional Care." *Social Work Today,* 1, 2 (May 1970), 5–8.

Jaffe, Eliezer. "Perceptions of Family Relationships by Institutionalized and Noninstitutionalized Dependent Children." *Child Psychiatry and Human Development,* 8, 2 (Winter, 1977), 81–93.

James, Howard. *Children in Trouble—A National Scandal.* New York: David McKay Co., 1970.

Janchill, Sister Mary Paul. "Services for Special Populations of Children," in *Child Welfare: Current Dilemmas, Future Directions.* Ed. Brenda McGowan and William Meezan. Itasca, Ill: F. E. Peacock (1983), 345–376.

Jewett, Claudia. *Helping Children Cope with Separation and Loss.* Boston: Harvard Common Press, 1982.

Johnson, Lillian, and Joseph Reid. *An Evaluation of Ten Years Work with Emotionally Disturbed Children.* Seattle: Ryther Child Center, 1947.

Jonsson, Gustav. "Introduction to New Staff," in *Children Away from Home—A Sourcebook of Residential Treatment.* Ed. James K. Whittaker and Albert E. Trieschman. New York: Aldine, 1972.

Kagan, Richard. "Using Redefinition and Paradox with Children in Placement who Provoke Rejection." *Child Welfare,* 59, 9 (November 1980), 551–559.

Kahn, Alfred. *When Children Must Be Committed.* New York: Citizens' Committee for Children of New York, June 1960.

Keith-Lucas, Alan, and Clifford Sanford. *Group Child Care as a Family Service.* Chapel Hill: University of North Carolina Press, 1977.

Kirgan, Doris A. "Meeting Children's Needs Through Placement: The Placement Evaluation Program." *Child Welfare,* 62, 2 (March-April, 1983), 157–165.

Klein, Alan F. *The Professional Child Care Worker—A Guide to Skills, Knowledge, Techniques and Attitudes.* New York: Association Press, 1975.

Knitzer, Jane, and Lynn Olson. *Unclaimed Children: The Failure of Public Responsibility to Children and Adolescents in Need of Mental Health Services.* Washington, D.C.: Children's Defense Fund, 1982.

Konopka, Gisela. "What Houseparents Should Know," in *Children in Care.* Ed. J. N. Tod. Essex, England: Longman Group Ltd., 1968.

Konopka, Gisela. *Group Work in the Institution,* revised. New York: Association Press, 1970.

Koshel, Jeffrey. *Deinstitutionalization—Dependent and Neglected Children.* Washington, D.C.: The Urban Institute, December 1973.

Krona, David. "Parents as Treatment Partners in Residential Care." *Child Welfare,* 59, 2 (February 1980), 91–96.

Laird, Joan. "An Ecological Approach to Child Welfare: Issues of Family Identity and Continuity," in *Parents of Children in Placement: Perspectives and Programs.* Ed. Paula Sinanoglu and Anthony Maluccio. New York: Child Welfare League of America, 1981, 97–126.

Lambert, Paul. *The ABC's of Child Care Work in a Residential Setting.* New York: Child Welfare League of America, 1977.

Langmeier, Josef, and Z. Matejcek. *Psychological Deprivation in Childhood,* 3d ed., Ed. G. L. Mangan. New York: John Wiley & Sons, 1975.

Larsen, John. "Applying Kohlberg's Theory of Moral Development in Group Care Settings." *Child Welfare,* 60, 10 (December 1981), 659–668.

LeCroy, Craig Winston. "Residential Treatment Services: A Review of Some Current Trends." *Child Care Quarterly,* 13, 2 (Summer 1984), 83–97.

Leonard H. Skipton, Howard Margolis, and Daniel Keating. "Salient Factors Influencing Resident Advisor Turnover: An Exploratory Study." *Child Care Quarterly,* 10, 4 (Winter 1981), 329–333.

Lerner, Samuel. "The Diagnostic Basis of Institutional Care for Children." *Social Casework,* 33 (March 1952).

Levine, Theodore. "Community-Based Treatment for Adolescents: Myths and Realities." *Social Work,* 22 (March 1977), 144–147.

Lewis, Melvin et al. "The Undoing of Residential Treatment: A Follow-Up Study of 51 Adolescents." *Journal of Child Psychiatry* (Winter 1980), 160–171.

Lewis, W. W. "Ecological Change: A Necessary Condition for Residential Treatment." *Child Care Quarterly,* 13, 1 (Spring 1984), 21–29.

Linnihan, Patricia. "Adolescent Day Treatment A Community Alternative to Institutionalization of the Emotionally Disturbed Adolescent." *American Journal of Orthopsychiatry,* 47, 4 (October 1977), 679–688.

Littauer, Celia. "Working with Families of Children in Residential Treatment." *Child Welfare,* 59, 4 (April 1980), 225–234.

Long, Kathleen Ann. "The Experience of Repeated and Traumatic Loss Among Crow Indian Children: Response Patterns and Intervention Strategies." *American Journal of Orthopsychiatry,* 53, 1 (January, 1983), 116–126.

Maas, Henry, and Richard Engler. *Children in Need of Care.* New York: Columbia University Press, 1959.

Maier, Henry W. (Ed.). *Group Work as Part of Residential Treatment.* New York: National Association of Social Workers, 1965.

Maier, Henry W. "Essential Components in Care and Treatment Environments for Children," in *Group Care for Children: Concept and Issues.* Ed. Frank Ainsworth and Leon Fulcher. London: Tavistock, 1981, 19–70.

Malin, Naomi Rawitch. "Pathways to Placement of Adolescent Children." *Social Work* 26, 6 (November 1981), 482–487.

Maluccio, Anthony N, and Wilma D. Marlow. "Residential Treatment of Emotionally Disturbed Children: A Review of the Literature." *Social Service Review,* 46, 2 (June 1972), 230–250.

Maluccio, Anthony N., and Wilma D. Marlow. "Residential Treatment of Disturbed Children." *Child Welfare,* 43, 4 (April 1974), 225–235.

Mandelbaum, Arthur. "Parent-Child Separation: Its Significance to Parents," in *Parents of Children in Placement: Perspectives and Programs.* Ed. Paula Sinanoglu and Anthony Maluccio. New York: Child Welfare League of America, 1981, 313–326.

Martin, Lawrence, Ija Pozdnjakoff, and Joyce Wilding. "The Use of Residential Care." *Child Welfare,* 55, 4 (April 1976), 269–278.

Mattingly, Martha. "Occupational Stress for Group Care Personnel," in *Group Care for*

Children: Concept and Issues. Ed. Frank Ainsworth and Leon Fulcher. London: Tavistock, 1981, 151–169.

Mayer, Goetz, and James Pearson. "Social Control in the Treatment of Adolescents in Residential Care: A Dilemma." *Child Welfare,* 54, 4 (April 1975), 246–256.

Mayer, Morris F. "The Group in Residential Treatment of Adolescents." *Child Welfare,* 51, 8 (October 1972), 482–493.

Mayer, Morris F., and John Marsushima. *A Guide for Child Care Workers*. New York: Child Welfare League of America, 1958.

Mayer, Morris F., and John Marsushima. *Supervision of Houseparents*. New York: Child Welfare League of America, 1965.

Mayer, Morris F, and John Marsushima. "Training for Child Care Work: A Report on a National Conference." *Child Welfare,* 48, 9 (November 1969), 525–532.

Mayer, Morris F., Leon H. Richman, and Edwin A. Balcerzak. *Group Care in North America*. New York: Child Welfare League of America, 1977.

McConnell, Wendy. "A Labor Strike Illuminates Social Dynamics in a Children's Residential Center." *Child Welfare,* 61, 8 (November–December 1982), 505–514.

McGowan, Brenda. "Historical Evolution of Child Welfare Services: An Examination of the Sources of Current Problems and Dilemmas," in *Child Welfare: Current Dilemmas, Future Directions*. Itasca, Ill.: F. E. Peacock, 1983, 45–92.

McInnis, Elizabeth T., and David Marholin. "Individualizing Behavior Therapy for Children in Group Settings." *Child Welfare,* 56, 7 (July 1977).

Mech, Edmund. "Out-if-Home Placement Rates." *Social Service Review,* 57, 4 (December 1983), 659–667.

Meyer, Margit, E., E. Odom, and Bernice S. Wax. "Birth and Life of an Incentive System in a Residential Institution for Adolescents." *Child Welfare,* 52, 8 (October 1973), 503–509.

Millman, Howard L., and Charles E. Schaefer. "Behavioral Change: Program Evaluation and Staff Feedback." *Child Welfare,* 54, 10 (December 1975), 692–702.

Mora, George et al. "A Residential Treatment Center Moves Toward the Community Mental Health Model." *Child Welfare,* 48, 10 (December 1969), 585–590.

Moran, Michael S., Barbara Niedz, and Gregory Simpson. "The Resource Family: Helping Emotionally Disturbed Children in Residential Treatment." *Children Today,* (November–December 1975), 26–29.

Mordock, John. "Evaluation in Residential Treatment: The Conceptual Dilemmas." *Child Welfare,* 58, 5 (May 1979), 293–302.

Moyles, William E., and Martin Wolins. "Group Care and Intellectual Development." *Developmental Psychology,* 4, 3 (1971), 370–380.

Munson, Robert F., and Martina M. Blincoe. "Evaluation of a Residential Treatment Center for Emotionally Disturbed Adolescents." *Adolescence,* 19, 74 (Summer 1984), 253–261.

Murphy, Terry. "A Troubled Home for Troubled Kids." *Minneapolis, St. Paul,* (December 1983), 103–106, 168–169.

Myer, John. "An Exploratory Nationwide Survey of Child Care Workers." *Child Care Quarterly,* 9, 1 (Spring 1980), 17–25.

National Center on Child Abuse and Neglect. *Child Abuse and Neglect in Residential Institutions: Selected Readings on Prevention, Investigation, and Correction*. Washington, D.C.: DHEW, 1978.

Neilans, Thomas, Allen Israel, and Marsha Pravder. "The Effectiveness of Transition to a Self-Control Program in Maintaining Changes in Children's Behavior." *Child Care Quarterly,* 10, 4 (Winter 1981), 297–306.

New York City Comptroller's Office. *Audit Report on Foster Care Agencies' Achievement of Permanent Homes for Children in Their Care*. New York: City Comptroller's Office, June 1977. Mimeographed, 81 pp.

Ohlin, Lloyd, and William Lawrence. "Social Interaction Among Clients as a Treatment Problem." *Social Work,* 4 (April 1959).

Oxley, Genevieve B. "Involuntary Clients' Responses to a Treatment Experience" *Social Casework,* 58, 10 (December 1977a), 607–614.

Oxley, Genevieve B. "A Modified Form of Residential Treatment and Its Impact on Behavioral Adjustment." *Social Work,* 22 (November 1977b), 493–498.

Pappenfort, Donnell et al. *A Census of Children's Residential Institutions in the U.S., Puerto Rico and the Virgin Islands: 1966, Vol. 2: Institutions for Dependent and Neglected Children.* Chicago: University of Chicago, School of Social Service Administration, 1970a.

Pappenfort, Donnell et al. *A Census of Children's Residential Institutions in the U.S., Puerto Rico and the Virgin Islands: 1966, Vol. 4: Institutions for the Emtoinally Disturbed Children.* Chicago: University of Chicago School of Social Service Administration, 1970b.

Pappenfort, Donnell, and Dee Morgan Kilpatrick. "Child Caring Institutions 1966: Selected Findings from the First National Survey of Children's Residential Institutions." *Social Service Review,* 43, 4 (December 1969), 448–459.

Payne, Chris. "Research and Evaluation in Group Care," in *Group Care for Children: Concept and Issues.* Ed. Frank Ainsworth and Leon Fulcher. London: Tavistock, 1981, 247–270.

Payne, George H. *The Child in Human Progress.* New York: G. P. Putnam's Sons, 1916.

Pecora, Peter, and Wallace Gingerich. "Worker Tasks and Knowledge Utilization in Group Child Care: First Findings." *Child Welfare,* 60, 4 (April 1981), 221–231.

Phillips, Michael, Barbara Haring, and Ann Shyne. *A Model for Intake Decisions in Child Welfare.* New York: Child Welfare League of America, 1972.

Pierce, Lois, and Victor Hauck. "A Model for Establishing a Community-Based Foster Group Home." *Child Welfare* 60, 7, (July—August, 1981), 475–482.

Piliavin, Irving. "Conflict Between Cottage Parents and Caseworkers." *Social Science Review,* 37 (March 1963).

Polsky, Howard. *Cottage Six—The Social System of Delinquent Boys in Residential Treatment.* New York: Russell Sage Foundation, 1962.

Polsky, Howard, and Daniel S. Claster. *The Dynamics of Residential Treatment—A Social Systems Analysis.* Chapel Hill: University of North Carolina Press, 1968.

Polsky, Howard and Carl Goldberg (Eds.). *Social Systems Perspectives in Residential Institutions.* East Lansing: Michigan State University Press, 1970.

Powers, William. "Risk-Taking in the Residential Treatment of Emotionally Disturbed Children." *Child Care Quarterly,* 10, 2 (Summer 1981), 173–178.

Raubolt, Richard. "Treating Children in Residential Group Psychotherapy." *Child Welfare,* 62, 2, (March–April 1983), 147–155.

Rausch, Harold et al. "The Interpersonal Behavior of Children in Residential Treatment." *Journal of Abnormal and Social Psychology,* 59, 1 (January 1959), 9–26.

Redick, Richard, and Michael Witkin. "Residential Treatment Centers for Emotionally Disturbed Children, United States, 1977–1978 and 1979–1980." *Mental Health Statistical Note No. 162.* Washington, D.C.: DHHS, 1983.

Redl, Fritz, and David Wineman. *Children Who Hate.* New York: Free Press, 1951.

Redl, Fritz, and David Wineman. *Controls from Within.* New York: Free Press, 1953.

Reichertz, Diane. *Residential Care: The Impact of Institutional Policies, Structures, and Staff on Residential Children.* Montreal: McGill University Press, 1978.

Rosen, Paul, Lawrence Peterson, and Barry Walsh. "A Community Residence for Severely Disturbed Adolescents: A Cognitive-Behavioral Approach." *Child Welfare,* 59, 1 (Janaury 1980), 15–25.

Ross, Andrew L. "A Study of Child Care Staff Turnover." *Child Care Quarterly,* 13, 3 (Fall 1984), 209–224.

Ross, Andrew L., and Lawrence S. Schreiber. "Bellefaire's Day Treatment Program: An Interdisciplinary Approach to Emotionally Disturbed Children." *Child Welfare,* 54, 3 (March 1975), 183–194.

Rothman, David J. *The Discovery of the Asylum.* Boston: Little, Brown, 1971.

Russo, Eva, and Ann Shyne. *Coping with Disruptive Behavior in Group Care.* New York: Child Welfare League of America, 1980.

Rutter, Michael. *Maternal Deprivation Reassessed.* Baltimore, Md: Penguin, 1974.

Schaefer, Charels. "Follow Up Survey by Mail." *Social Work,* 21, 4 (July 1976), 327–328.

Schaefer, Charles, and Howard E. Millman. "The Use of Behavior Ratings in Assessing the Effect of Residential Treatment with Latency-Age Boys." *Child Psychiatry and Human Development,* 3 (1973).

Schulman, Rena. "Treatment of the Disturbed Child in Placement." *Jewish Social Service Quarter,* 30 (Spring 1954).

Schulman, Rena. "Examples of Adolescent Group Homes in Alliance with Larger Institutions." *Child Welfare,* 54 (May 1975), 341–349.

Schulze, Susanne. *Creative Group Living in Children's Institutions.* New York: Association Press, 1951.

Schwab, A. James, Jr., Michael E. Bruce and Ruth G. McRoy. "Matching Children with Placements." *Children and Youth Services Review,* 6, (1984), 125–133.

Schwartz, Miriam, and Isadore Kaplan. "Small Homes—Placement Choice for Adolescents." *Child Welfare,* 40 (November 1961).

Seidl, Frederick. "Community-Oriented Residential Care: The State of the Art." *Child Care Quarterly,* 3 (Fall 1974), 150–163.

Shostak, Albert L. "Staffing Patterns in Group Homes for Teenagers," *Child Welfare,* 57, 5 (May 1978), 309–319.

Shyne, Ann, and Anita Schroeder. *National Study of Social Services to Children and Their Families.* Washington, D.C.: DHEW, 1978.

Silver, Harold. "Residential Treatment of Emotionally Disturbed Children: An Evaluation of Fifteen Years' Experience." *Journal of Jewish Communal Service,* 38 (1961).

Simmons, Gladys, Joanne Gumpert, and Beulah Rothman. "Natural Parents as Partner in Child Care Placement," in *Parents of Children in Placement: Perspectives and Programs.* Ed. Paula Sinanoglu and Anthony Maluccio. New York: Child Welfare League of America, 1981, 375–388.

Simon, Abraham. "Residential Treatment of Children." *Social Service Review,* 30 (September 1956).

Skarnulis, Edward. "Support, Not Supplant, the Natural Home: Serving Handicapped Children and Adults," in *Home-Based Services for Children and Families: Policy, Practice and Research.* Ed. Sheila Maybanks and Marvin Bryce. Springfield, Ill.: Charles C Thomas, 1979, 64–76.

Small, Richard. "Prevention, Permanence, and Reunification: Family-Centered Helping in the Changing Field of Group Child Care." *Preventoin Report* 1, 6 (Spring–Summer 1984).

Small, Richard, and Steven Schinke. "Teaching Competence in Residential Group Care: Cognitive Problem Solving and Interpersonal Skills Training with Emotionally Disturbed Preadolescents." *Journal of Social Service Research,* 7, 1, (Fall 1983), 1–16.

Small, Richard, and James Whittaker. "Residential Group Care and Home-Based Care: Toward a Continuity of Family Services," in *Home-Based Services for Children and Families: Policy, Practice and Research.* Ed. Sheila Maybanks and Marvin Bryce. Springfield, Ill.: Charles C Thomas, 1979, 77–88.

Solomon, Phyllis. "Analyzing Opposition to Community Residential Facilities for Troubled Adolescents." *Child Welfare,* 62 4, (July–August 1983), 361–366.

Stein, Theodore, and Tina Rzepnicki. *Decision-Making at Child Welfare Intake: A Handbook for Practitioners.* New York: Child Welfare League of America, 1983.

Stickney, Patricia, and Anthony Capaiuolo. "From CRISP: Strategy for Community Residences." *Child Welfare,* 55 (January 1976), 54–58.

Taylor, Delores A., and Stuart W. Alpert. *Continuity and Support Following Residential Treatment.* New York: Child Welfare League of America, 1973.

Taylor, Joseph L. et al. *A Group Home for Adolescent Girls—Practice and Research.* New York: Child Welfare League of America, 1976.

Taylor, Samuel. "Institutions with Therapeutic Residential Programs for Children," in *Child Caring: Social Policy and the Institution.* Ed. Donnell M. Pappenfort, Dee M. Kilpatrick, and Robert Roberts. Chicago: Aldine, 1973, 200–225.

Thomas, Geoge. *A Community-Oriented Evaluation of the Effectiveness of Child Caring Institutions.* Final Report to the office of Child Development, HEW, Project No. OCD-CB 106. Athens, Ga.: Regional Institute of Social Welfare Research, 1975a.

Thomas, George. *Is Statewide Deinstitutionalization of Children's Services a Forward or Backward Social Movement?* Urbana-Champaign: School of Social Work, University of Illinois, 1975b.

Tizard, Barbara, and J. Rees. "The Effect of Early Institutional Rearing on the Behavioral Problems and Affectional Relationships of 4 Year Old Children" *Journal of Child Psychology and Psychiatry,* 16 (1975), 61–73.

Thurston, Henry. *The Dependent Child.* New York: Columbia University Press, 1930.

Tittler, Bennett et al. "The Influence of Family Variables on an Ecologically Based Treatment Program for Emotionally Disturbed Children." *American Journal of Orthopsychiatry,* 52 (January, 1982), 123–130.

Toigo, Romolo. "Child Care—Occupation or Profession: Searching for Clarity." *Child Care Quarterly,* 10, 3 (Fall 1981), 242–249.

Tovey, Robert. "The Family Living Model: Five-Day Treatment in a Rural Environment." *Child Welfare,* 62, 5, (September–October 1983), 445–448.

Trieschman, Albert, and Bernard Levine. "Helping Children Learn to Deal with Sadness," in *Children Away from Home: A Sourcebook of Residential Treatment.* Ed. James Whittaker and Albert Trieschman. Chicago: Aldine-Atherton, 1972, 107–113.

Treischman, Albert, James Whittaker, and Lawrence Brendtro. *The Other Twenty-three Hours.* Chicago: Aldine, 1969.

United Nations. *The Institutional Care of Children.* New York, 1956.

United States Department of Commerce, Bureau of the Census. *1976 Survey of Institutionalized Persons.* Current Population Reports, No. 69, Washington, D.C.: U.S. Government Printing Office, 1978.

U.S. Department of Commerce. *Persons in Institutions and Other Group Quarters.* Washington, D.C.: Bureau of the Census, 1984.

U.S. Department of Health, Education and Welfare, National Institute of Mental Health. *Residential Treatment Centers for Emotionally Disturbed Children, 1969–1970.* National Health Statistics Series A, No. 6. Washington, D.C.: U.S. Government Printing Office, 1971.

U.S. Department of Health and Human Services. *Family Involvement in Residential Treatment: A Support System for Parents.* Washington, D.C.: DHHS, 1981.

United States Office of Comptroller General. *Children in Foster Care Institutions-Steps Government Can Take to Improve Their Care.* Washington, D.C.: U.S. Government Printing Office, February 1977.

Van Hagen, John. "One Residential Center's Model for Working with Families." *Child Welfare,* 62, 3, (May–June 1983), 233–241.

VanderVen, Karen. "Patterns of Career Development in Group Care," in *Group Care for Children: Concept and Issues.* Ed. Frank Ainsworth and Leon Fulcher. London: Tavistock, 1981, 201–224.

Walton, Ron. "Evaluating Residential Care as a Method of Social Work Intervention," in *Residential Care: A Reader in Current Theory and Practice.* Ed. Ronald Walton and Doreen Elliott. Oxford: Pergamon Press, 1980, 223–230.

Ward, Liz. "The Social Work Task in Residential Care," in *Residential Care: A Reader in Current Theory and Practice.* Ed. Ronald Walton and Doreen Elliott. Oxford: Pergamon Press, 1980, 25–36.

Warner, Amos G. et al. *American Charities and Social Work,* 4th ed., New York: Thomas Y. Crowell, 1942.

Weber, Donald E. "Neighborhood Entry in Group Home Development." *Child Welfare,* 58 (December 1978), 627–642.

Weinstein, L. *Evaluation of a Program for Re-Educating Disturbed Children: A Follow-up Comparison with Untreated Chidlren.* Washington, D.C.: U.S. Government Printing Office, 1974.

Weintrob, Alex. "Changing Population in Adolescent Residential Treatment: New Problems for Program and Staff." *American Journal of Orthopsychiatry,* 44, 4, (July 1974), 604–611.

Weisfeld, David, and Martin S. Laser. "Residential Treatment and Weekend Visits Home." *Social Work,* 21, 5 (September 1976), 398–400.

Wenger, Carmela. "The Suitcase Story: A Therapeutic Technique for Children in Out-of-Home Placement." *American Journal of Orthopsychiatry,* 52, 2 (April 1982), 353–355.

Whittaker, James K. "The Changing Character of Residential Child Care: An Ecological Perspective." *Social Service Review,* (March 1978), 22–36.

Whittaker, James. *Caring for Troubled Children: Residential Treatment in a Community Context.* San Francisco: Jossey-Bass, 1979.

Whittaker, James K. and P. Pecora. "Outcome Evaluation in Residential Child Care: A Selective North American Perspective." *Community Care* 1984, 71–87.

Whittaker, James K., and Albert E. Trieschman (Eds.). *Children Away from Home—A Sourcebook of Residential Treatment.* Chicago: Aldine, 1972.

Williams, Elizabeth. "Host Family, Big Brother/Big Sister Volunteer Program." Pittsburgh: Holy Family Institute, 1983. Mimeo.

Winder, Alvin et al. "Group Therapy with Parents of Children in a Residential Treatment Center." *Child Welfare,* 44 (May 1965).

Witmer, Helen, and Charles P. Gershenson. *On Rearing Infants and Young Children in Institutions.* Children's Bureau Research Reports No. 1. Washington, D.C.: U.S. Government Printing Office, 1968.

Wolf, Lucille, and Paul Whitehead. "The Decision to Institutionalize Retarded Children: Comparison of Individually Matched Groups." *Mental Retardation,* 13, 5 (October 1975), 3–7.

Wolins, Martin. "Group Care: Friend or Foe." *Social Work,* 14, 1 (January 1969a), 35–53.

Wolins, Martin. "Young Children in Institutions—Some Additional Evidence." *Developmental Psychology,* 2, 1 (1969b), 99–109.

Wolins, Martin (Ed.). *Successful Group Care: Explorations in the Powerful Environment.* Chicago: Aldine, 1974.

Wolins, Martin. "Observations on the Future of Institutional Care of Children in the United States," in *Child Welfare Strategy in the Coming Years.* Ed. Alfred Kadushin, Washington, D.C.: DHEW, 1978, 90–129.

Wolins, Martin, and Irving Piliavin. *Institution or Foster Family—A Century of Debate.* New York: Child Welfare League of America, September 1964.

Wooden, Kenneth, *Weeping in the Playtime of Others.* New York: McGraw-Hill, 1976.

World Health Organization. *Deprivation of Maternal Care—A Reassessment of Its Effects.* Geneva: World Health Organization, 1962.

Zaslaw, Gerald, Christopher Krenk, and James B. Slaughter. "Developing a Secure Treatment Unit in a Private Agency." *Child Welfare,* 62, 1 (January–February 1983), 38–44.

11

Child Welfare Services in Other Countries

Introduction

All countries have child welfare problems that are similar to those encountered in this country. All of the world's children are dependent for a long time and are cared for, primarily, in families. And all over the world parents fall ill, die, desert, have children out of wedlock, struggle with limited resources, and so on. Children who suffer from neglect, abuse, and physical, mental and emotional handicaps are encountered everywhere in the world.

Madison (1968), after a comprehensive review of family and child welfare services in the Soviet Union, concludes that "the Soviet definition of child welfare services would not differ essentially from the definition currently used in the United States" (p. 175). Although child welfare services in all countries are not identical, there are similarities that suggest common problems and analogous solutions. Everywhere "common societal needs seem to generate somewhat similar institutional responses" (Kahn & Kamerman, 1976, pp. 362–363), so that everywhere the same kinds of child welfare services have been developed: supportive, supplementary, and substitute services. And everywhere, the service delivery systems seem to face similar kinds of problems: inadequate financial support, shortages of trained personnel, problems of service integration and coordination, overlap and ambiguous spheres of program responsibility.

The following three case studies from three widely separated countries— Poland, Zambia, and Japan—are a testimonial to the universality of child welfare problems.

Poland

A social inspectress learned, during her supervision of the guardianship of little Mania, that the latter loved her "guardian" so much that she wanted to become her real daughter. Mrs. N. shared the same desire. She had taken in the child when a baby from the hands of her mother, a girl in great despair, who had subsequently disappeared. The guardian had taken preliminary steps with a view of adopting the little girl, but the formalities had seemed too complicated. Mania bore, in fact, the name of her mother, and it was first of all necessary to initiate a long procedure in order to clear up the situation. With the help of the guardianship court and the police, our inspectress had a search carried out in several provinces, and ended up by finding the mother. The latter was married, had three children, and her husband knew nothing of the fourth. The mother at once consented to the adoption of her first illegitimate child, and everyone was happy [Veillard-Cybulska, 1966, pp. 24–25].

Zambia

Joan Mulonga, aged twelve, came to the office and complained she had no school uniform and was not getting enough to eat—all because her father is sick with asthma and out of work; her mother works as a nursemaid but does not earn enough to keep them. Asked her to ask one of her parents or both to come and see me as soon as possible.

Mr. Mulonga came as requested. He knew his daughter had been to see me; he had in fact sent her himself. He had had an attack of asthma and had not been able to come himself. Said he has had asthma for twelve years or so. He is a chef by profession and is married to a Coloured woman from South Africa. Because of his asthma he cannot keep a job—he is always getting attacks and employers say they cannot afford to keep sick men. He has been to many doctors who have failed to cure him. Is now undergoing treatment at . . . Clinic. His wife is working as a nursemaid but does not earn enough for the family. He has considered taking a light job as an office orderly so that his asthma will not bother him but he has not been able to find one yet. Has also thought of returning to his village in the Fort Janeson area but with his Coloured wife who is not accustomed to village life he cannot do this. They are presently short of food and his daughter requires school uniforms. He thought we might help. I said we were prepared to help but would have to look into the situation more fully. Issued him with a voucher for rations pending inquiry [Clifford, 1966, pp. 19–20].

Japan

Mrs. F., age thirty, a graduate of junior high school, has a husband, a university graduate, age thirty-three, a son, five, and a daughter, two. Because Mr. F. is an only son, the couple live with Mr. F.'s mother and are partially dependent on her. Mrs. F. came to our agency saying she could not tolerate the home situation longer because of the over-close relationship between Mr. F. and his mother and the fact that his mother was trying to dominate her. The couple had married for love immediately following Mr. F.'s graduation from university and after he had secured his first job. From the beginning his earnings were insufficient and mother helped financially. Mrs. F. complained that they had no privacy even in the bedroom and that the grandmother not only gave "blind love" to the two grandchildren but also that she insisted on controlling everything in the family, doling out money to Mrs. F., and making her account for what she spent. Mrs. F. felt that her mother-in-law treated her like a maid and when she complained about this Mrs. F., Sr., scolded her for acting superior. We worked with Mr. F. and tried to help him play a more dominant role in the family. But the two women could not get along so the young couple decided to live separately from Mrs. F., Sr., and we closed our case [Dessau, 1968, p. 121].

The Caseworker (1974) was written by a Hungarian novelist, George Konrad, who had been a child welfare worker in Budapest. Originally published in Hungary some twenty-five years after the Communists came to power, the novel details his experiences with child welfare problems in that country. The problems would be familiar and recognizable to any American child welfare worker. They involve the same lugubrious litany of abandoned children, neglected children, parents overwhelmed by the burdens of caring for children on limited resources, the loss of a father or a mother and subsequent parent–child difficulties, and disturbed and handicapped children. The fact tht the setting is Hungary and the context is a Communist society does not alter the essentially human problems that the worker needs to resolve.

The growing industrialization and urbanization of more and more of the world results in changes with which we are familiar and which directly and indirectly affect the need for child welfare services: the gradual decline in the family's ability to meet the needs of child care traditionally met through mutual aid from the tribe or members of the immediately available extended family, for example.

Many recent trends affecting children, which might be regarded as unique to the United States have, in fact, been experienced in many other countries. The United Nations 1982 report on *The World Social Situation* points to the fact that a "general weakening of various forms of authority and accepted values which bound individuals together, having gradually generated both a greater individual freedom and a more fragile society" (p. 1),

> The growing economic independence of women and the equal rights movement are changing relations within the nuclear family towards more individual autonomy. . . .
> In many societies participation in social and political life has been increasing through organized groups voicing interests and concerns. This has meant both a stronger democratic process and a greater difficulty in reaching consensus on basic values as well as on the distribution of efforts and benefits [p. 2].

Like the United States, most countries experienced a trend toward reduced funding for social services generally and for child welfare in the 1980s. Analyzing the changing situation in a number of different countries Cornia (1984) concluded that the "share of social expenditure out of total" in government expenditures "is shrinking. The deterioration in child welfare appears widespread and unambiguous" (p. 215).

An increasingly large population of aged who are living longer, a prolonged period of high percentage unemployment, accompanied by persistent high inflation, falling or plateauing of rates of income growth, and a steady rise in health care costs began in the late 1970s and early 1980s to impose an increasing burden on available government revenues. The United Nations, 1982 *Report on the World Social Situation* noted that

> since the late 1970's the heterogeneous social landscape has become clouded . . . the industrial countries have experienced a distinct slowing down in economic growth. The main concern regarding equity has shifted from a fair share in growth to a fair distribution of the cost of retrenchment. . . . Expectations for a betterment of living standards in the immediate future have been dampened. [p. 1]

As a consequence of the need to slow the pace of the growth of the welfare state, if not actually retrenching on growth previously achieved, most highly industrialized countries began in the 1980s to reconsider the limits of welfare state obligations. The trend tended to be the same in all countries despite differences in ideological commitments and rhetoric. In 1983–84, countries such as Portugal, Spain, Italy, France, Sweden, and Greece, under Socialist party control, were implementing policies similar to those being advanced by the conservative Reagan administration in the United States and the Thatcher government in England.

A 1982 review of Social Security in eight highly industrialized countries pointed to similar problems in each of the countries. The title of the review, *The World Crisis in Social Security* (Rosa, 1982) summarizes the conclusion.

In response to increasing difficulties in financing welfare state programs at the levels legislated, "austerity budgets have been adopted in France, Belgium, the

United Kingdom, Italy, the Netherlands, Denmark and still other countries" (Spivey, 1985, p. 15).

Whereas changes are being made, the basics of the Social Security System and the ideology of the Welfare State continues to be supported. The programs are being pruned rather than dismantled.

Everywhere there are more women in the labor force, including mothers of young children; this has resulted in a reexamination of relative child rearing responsibilities of men and women. Rates of divorce and out-of-wedlock pregnancies have increased in the Communist world and the social democratic countries as they have in the United States.

By the 1980s, the divorce rate in the Soviet Union was almost as high as the divorce rate in the United States (Moskoff, 1983). (See also Imbrogno & Imbrogno, 1986.)

Women's increased participation in the labor force, whether in response to a need on the part of the economy for additional workers, a need on the part of the family for additional income, or as a consequence of personal desire on the part of women for a career is shaping the direction of child welfare service. All of the many countries in which this change has taken place have struggled with resolving the conflict between women's traditional roles as child bearer and child rearer and employee. A variety of child-care alternatives are being implemented including some that have not been considered in this country.

Everywhere there is an increase in single-parent families, and everywhere these families are apt to be economically disadvantaged. For instance, although only 1 per cent of Japanese families are receiving welfare, 23 per cent of female-headed families are receiving such assistance (Nakamura, 1976, p. 205). Everywhere there is an inequitable distribution of wealth and everywhere there is a problem of poverty. In September 1974, the Soviet Union announced a new program offering a public assistance subsidy to 12.5 million children in low-income families (*New York Times,* September 28, 1974). Every country has its minority groups, and everywhere minorities face some disadvantaging discrimination.

Despite changes and problems, the family is universally regarded as the most desirable context for childrearing. The Soviet Union has not been able to develop a wide-scale program of boarding schools as originally planned, and the communal kibbutz is "home" for only a very small percentage of Israeli children. In neither the Soviet Union nor Israel nor anywhere else has the concept of a nonfamily context for child rearing gained widespread acceptance. There is general consensus that good family welfare is the best child welfare.

In all countries, despite ideological differences, there is acceptance of governmental responsibility for the care of dependent children. The trend is to broaden the contingencies that are defined as requiring community intervention to attempt to provide more adequately for the children involved in these situations, and the community is accepting greater partnership with parents in the responsibility for the rearing of the preschool child.

Despite these impressive similarities, there are differences in the frequency with which different kinds of problems are encountered and in the nature and pattern of services that have been developed to deal with them. Among the factors that determine differences in the programs are the following:

1. Attitudes toward "preventative" solutions: contraception, abortion, abandonment and child labor.
2. Child dependency ratios.

3. Level of economic wealth of the community.
4. Political and administrative development.
5. Prevalent attitude toard women and children.
6. Position of the nuclear family vis-à-vis other social institutions in the community.
7. Historical antecedents in coping with child welfare problems.

Preventative Solutions. The classical preventive solutions to potential child welfare problems are acceptable and continue to be practiced in most countries. Contraception is, of course, widespread and has gained great acceptance. Sterilization continues to be a most popular form of birth control worldwide. More often it is the woman who is sterilized through tubal ligation rather than the man through vasectomy (Johnson, 1983, p. 45).

Free sterilization is available to Danes who have reached the age of twenty-five. Application, however, must be made through a doctor (Marcussen, 1980, p. 61).

As in Denmark, contraceptives are widely used in the United States but other countries are freer about advertising and distributing contraceptives. This is in contrast to our restrictions, for instance, with regard to advertising contraceptives on television.

In 1981, the French government sponsored a series of family-planning advertisements on television. The commercial offers no technical advice. It consists of brief scenes. In one, a mother surrounded by four children says, "I like children around, but frankly another one would be too much." In another, a young mother is shown with a baby in a stroller. "I'm going to have another," she says, "but I think I'll wait a while." A voice over says that "there are 1,413 information planning and family centers in France. The means to plan your life exist. Learn about them. You have a right to this information. Contraception is a public right" (*New York Times,* November 29, 1981). Family-planning services are readily available to teenagers in the Netherlands, where vending machines dispensing condoms are as accessible and almost as numerous as vending machines dispensing cigarettes. "Some family planning and social maternity programs have promoted condoms through special events such as the distribution of free samples of condoms and slogan writing contests. In Egypt, condoms have been handed out at festival and sporting events. Thailand promoted a 'cops and rubbers' program which provides all policemen in Bangkok with condoms" for distribution on request. (Population Information Program, 1982).

A detailed review by Tietze (1983) of the abortion legislation worldwide indicated that 28 per cent of the world's 4.5 billion people lived in countries in which abortion was prohibited without exception or where the exceptions were very limited, principally to save the life of the mother. On the other hand, 39 per cent of the world's population lived in countries which allowed abortion on request without specifying reasons. The additional 37 per cent lived in countries in which abortion was permitted with the requirement that certain medical or social circumstances were met. (See also Tietze & Henshaw, 1986; Henshaw, 1986). In January 1984, Greece legalized abortion "though the practice has long been common and even officially tolerated" (*New York Times,* January 27, 1984). The law requires the husband's consent to the abortion if the woman is married. In 1982, Turkey was one of the first of the Islamic countries to legalize abortion (*New York Times,* February 8, 1982). However, in the predominantly Muslim Arab countries, abortion remained strictly illegal, as in some Central and South American countries. However, in South America, the law does not reflect reality, and millions of illegal abortions are performed in these countries each year (*New York Times,* March 23, 1975; May 26, 1977).

Access to abortion is universal in those countries in which abortion is permitted and where a public health program is in operation. Abortion, available to all, is one of the public health services. This is in contrast to our own system, where access to a public supported abortion requires meeting a means test. In Poland "women are entitled to temporary disability benefits after an abortion" (Kahn, & Kamerman, 1976, p. 198). However, in some countries, France and Yugoslavia being examples, the availability of an abortion requires the acceptance of some counseling about family planning.

India, which began to permit abortions on demand in 1971, found subsequently that more drastic measures were necessary to prevent the birth of unwanted children. In 1976 India attempted the first large-scale governmental program of coercive if not actually compulsory population control through enforced sterilization (Landman, 1977). It was proposed that civil service positions, free medical facilities, low-interest government loans, and government-subsidized housing be available to men with more than two children only after they agreed to a vasectomy. Men with two children who agreed to be sterilized were paid 150 rupees, roughly the equivalent of half a month's salary of an urban unskilled worker. As a result of a determined campaign using such incentives and disincentives, it was reported that between April and December in 1976, 7 million sterilizations were performed in India. However, the fall of the government of Premier Indira Gandhi was attributed to the backlash against such rigorous population control measures.

Perhaps the most notably successful effort to prevent excess births has been achieved by the People's Republic of China. This success is attributed to systematic, comprehensive programs making modern contraceptives, sterilization, and abortion widely accessible with the unequivocal support of government units at all levels. In addition, the active participation of all communal and neighborhood citizen groups was directly enlisted in the effort. The present Chinese constitution makes it a national duty for husbands and wives to practice family planning (*New York Times,* December 5, 1982). Population control "is in response to an effort to regulate human reproduction so as to achieve a balance between population, income and growth in the production of material means" (Muhua, 1979, p. 350). (See also Bell, 1983).

The need for limiting the birthrate if there is some danger that the demand for supplies will run ahead of production is illustrated by China's "One Child, One Family" policy. Even if the goal is achieved through the end of the twentieth century, the population in China will peak at 1.2 billion people, an increase of 192 million from 1984. China has legislated a variety of incentives and penalties in an effort to control population growth. In support of the one-child-per-family limit, one-child families get extra cash allowances and priorities for housing, medical care, and schooling. Families who have another child are required to pay an extra tax to share the state's cost of bringing up the child. Maternity benefits are withheld and medical care related to the pregnancy must be paid for by the family. Second and third pregnancies are aborted, sometimes in response to coercion by community family-planning committees. Rates of seventy to eighty abortions for every 100 live births have been reported (*New York Times,* May 18, 1984).

In addition to paid maternity leave, China provides the working woman with a paid abortion leave of 14 days (Dixon, 1981, p. 297). Since boys are preferred it is reported that families who have one child and it is a girl, resort to infanticide (*New York Times,* July 4, 1985). This practice persists in China despite active government attempts to prevent such actions. Propaganda posters extolling the virtues of the one-child family usually show a girl as the one child.

Abandonment of children as a solution for the parents, if not for the community, is still prevalent. The Brazilian government estimates that 7 million children under the age of eighteen "have lost all or most links with their families and are 'abandoned or marginalized' " (*New York Times,* October 23, 1985).

> In many large cities in newly industrialized countries a ragged army of abandoned children lives on the streets. By night they sleep wrapped in newspapers, stretched out in doorways, littered alleys and discarded construction tubing. During the day, some shine shoes in public squares, sell gum, peanuts and candy on street corners or beg from stalled drivers at crowded intersections. Others shoplift clothing and food or filch wallets, watches and jewelry from passersby. Every month in Brazil more than 100 infants are left in police stations, hospitals or on downtown streets by mothers apparently hoping that the outside world has more capacity to care for them than they do (*New York Times,* November 11, 1983; see also DeDuran 1983.)

Child labor as a solution to child welfare problems is still widespread.

In 1979 the International Labor Organization compiled a report on child labor which it submitted to a United Nations working group on slavery. It noted that more than 55 million children under 15 were then engaged in the labor force. The International Labor Organization estimated that the use of child labor had increased by 20 per cent in 1979 and was expected to rise in the future.

A U.S. Department of Labor Study published in 1980 reported that child labor was still a source of support for millions of families throughout the world and a resource in meeting the needs of children. In Morocco, children eight, nine, and ten years of age were a significant percentage of the carpet industry labor force. In Thailand, children from the age of 11 worked in glass factories. In India, 16.5 million children aged 5 to 14 are working (U.S. Department of Labor, 1980).

In a review of children's work in the Third World Bradley (1985) notes that "Children begin to work at five or six and by age seven to nine they bathe cattle, herd poultry, supervise gardens and care for younger siblings" (p. 165). They fetch water, cut fodder and gather firewood.

And early death from infanticide or the lack of resources "prevents" many high-risk children from becoming child-welfare-service clients.

The hunger-famine belt above the equator, including such countries as the Sudan, Ethiopia, Guatemala, and Bangladesh, experienced severe food shortages in 1974 and again in 1984. As a result, death and malnutrition affected millions of the children in those areas of the world. It is estimated that in Africa alone 5 million children died from hunger-related causes in 1984. The millions of children who are literally starving to death in countries experiencing famine have been termed "nutritionally battered children."

The children's fragility and vulnerability and their total dependency on adults make them the likely first victims of natural and man made disasters—earthquakes, floods, famine, war, and revolution. In many countries the death of millions of children in early childhood is still, as in the past, a "preventive solution" to child welfare problems.

Dependency Ratios and Levels of Industrialization

Dependency ratios—the ratios of productive adults to dependent children in the country—vary widely, affecting child welfare needs and resources.

In 1985 there were, in the developed countries, approximately sixty-three adults caring for twenty-six dependent children; in the developing countries, fifty-six adults were faced with the care of forty dependent children.

The dependency ratio is significant because it reflects the burden imposed by the unproductive group on the productive group. Where the relative number of producers is small, production is limited and has to be thinly distributed. The special programs required by the dependent must be funded from these already scarce resources.

The differences for children in the two sectors of the world, resulting fom the contrasting dependency ratios, are further exacerbated by a growing maldistribution of wealth between the two sectors. During the 1960s, the world total gross national product increased by some $1,100 billion. About 80 per cent of this increase went to the developed sectors, which contain only one quarter of the world's population; "only 6 percent of the increase went to countries where per capita incomes average $2000 or less, but which contain 60 percent of the world's population" (Titmuss, 1972, p. 3).

The United Nations (1963) notes, "No country can afford to move into programs of social entitlement until its economic resources have reached a point where a substantial amount can be made available for social expenditure" (p. 109).

> The proportion of total governmental expenditure on social services varies direclty with per capita gross domestic product. As gross domestic product rise public expenditure on social services also rise. The richest countries spend more than half their budget or nearly 15 percent of their domestic product on social services. In marked contrast the low income developing countries were able to devote only a little more than one quarter of their governmental budget or less than 5 per cent of their domestic product to such services [United Nations, 1979, p. 37].

Not only are developing countries characterized by high-dependency ratios and limited resources, but they also face a heavy need for investment capital for economic development. Investment of capital in industry may, in the long run, result in more adequate child-welfare resources and services. In the short run, however, the needs for such resources and services compete with the needs for child welfare services.

The problem is not only one of allocating limited financial resources but also one of allocating limited human resources. When there are few people in the country who have an opportunity for professional training of any kind, social work cannot easily compete with such professions as medicine, teaching, or engineering. As a United Nations (1963) report indicates, the limitations on the social service programs in the underdeveloped countries are dictated by their absolute poverty of resources in money, personnel, and institutional structure (p. 106).

In the last analysis, the wealth of the community is the essential basis for any system of social welfare. And the degree of industrialization is decisive in determining the level of wealth. However, even if sufficient wealth were available, it might be deployed for child welfare services only if there is a favorable attitude toward the needs of the child. Thus, in some developing countries, the emphasis on investment in industry is sometimes balanced by the recognition not only that children are the beneficiaries of economic development programs but that they are themselves an investment. Adequate provisions for children then become part of the national economic strategy. It is as necessary to improve the quality of human resources as it is to increase the supply of capital resources.

Dependency ratios and the level of industrialization of the economy dictate not only the amount that might be made available for social welfare but also the kinds of social problems to which social welfare gives priority. It is not likely that a highly developed program of child welfare services will be given priority in countries where most people live in villages, "where there is little transportation, no telephone, no school, no doctor, only the most primitive housing and few, if any, literate people" (United Nations, 1965, p. 41). Priority in these countries must be given to the most basic needs: keeping the child alive, keeping him or her fed, and providing him or her with the beginnings of an education.

In many parts of the world, children suffer from chronic semistarvation (Sicault, 1963). Undernourishment resulting from lack of food is compounded by malnourishment arising from lack of the all-important proteins required by the growing child. Milk is still a luxury food in many underdeveloped countries. *Kwashiorkor,* a widespread diet-deficiency disease of children in such countries, comes from an African word that, literally translated, means "first-second." It connotes "the disease the first child gets when the second is expected" and is associated with weaning and denial of the mother's milk.

Many childhood diseases are widespread in underdeveloped countries, sapping the energy and vitality of the children and reducing their capacity and motivation for learning. Malaria, trachoma, bilharziasis, diarrhea, parasitic infestations, yaws, and chronic hunger make these children dull and apathetic. Despite improvements in health conditions and the resulting reduction in infant mortality rates in the developing countries in recent years, these rates are still, in some instances, four and five times higher than they are in more economically advanced countries. And those countries that are still confronted with the most elementary problems of food needs, health needs, and educational needs for all children can hardly be expected to develop great concern about the services needed by groups of specially deprived children. Where all are deprived, those who are specially deprived lose any claim to special treatment.

Three quarters of the world's children, nearly a billion of them, live in developing countries. Of the hundred children born every half-minute in these areas, twenty will die in their first year; two thirds of the remainder are likely never to see adolescence; and only one in four reaches "old age"—which, in terms of the average length of life in some of these countries, is about thirty-eight years. Only a little more than half of those who survive to age five in the developing countries will ever set foot in a classroom. Fewer than 40 per cent of that half will complete the elementary grades. Large numbers of children live on the pavements in Bombay and Calcutta or grow up under the most deprived environmental circumstances in the *favelas* or *ranchos* of Latin America or the *bustees* or *shuggies* of India. Makeshift housing in one shantytown or another is "home" for a sizable percentage of the world's population of children—a "home" without water, heat, electricity, sewerage, or a garbage disposal system.

Illegitimacy rates are ten times greater in some countries than in the United States. In some countries the illegitimacy rate is as high as 60 to 70 percent of all births; in these circumstances what is needed is a policy to organize the family rather than one to strengthen it.

Table 11-1 shows some of the differences between the developed countries and

TABLE 11-1. International Comparison of Selective Factors

Economically Advanced Nations		Developing Nations	

Per Capital Gross National Product in U.S. Dollars—1982

West Germany	12,280	Laos	90
United States	13,160	Bangladesh	140
Norway	14,300	Burma	190
Switzerland	16,840	Haiti	290

Ruth Sivard, *World Military and Social Expenditures* (Washington, D.C.: World Priorities, 1985 pp. 41–43.

Calories Available as Percentage of Daily Requirements—1982

France	141	Cambodia	87
Belgium	139	Mozambique	80
United States	138	Mali	74
USSR	133	Ghana	72

Ruth Sivard, *World Military and Social Expenditures* (Washington, D.C.: World Priorities, 1985), pp. 42–43.

Infant Mortality Rates (Number of Deaths of Infants Under 1 Year of Age per 1,000 Live Births)—1983.

Finland	6.2	Iran	101
Switzerland	7	Kenya	121.6
United States	10.9	Ethiopia	143
USSR	25.3	Somalia	200

United Nations Demographic Yearbook—1984. New York: United Nations, 1986, pp. 337–341; for USSR, *New York Times,* Oct. 28, 1986.

Female Life Expectancy at Birth—1983

Japan	79.8	Bolivia	53
Sweden	79.6	Chad	44.6
Netherlands	79.4	Afghanistan	37
United States	78.3	Gambia	36.5

United Nations Demographic Yearbook—1984. New York: United Nations, 1986, pp. 450–478.

Percentage of School-Age Population in School—1984

Canada	98	Thailand	64
United States	99	Saudi Arabia	55
Japan	97	Chad	24
Australia	89	Niger	17

The World Bank Atlas—1987. Washington D.C. The World Bank, pp. 6–9.

Percentage of Children Fully Immunized Against Polio—1984

France	97	Uganda	8
Czechoslovakia	98	Syria	22
United States (1982)	98	Peru	28
Sweden	99	Pakistan	44

Population Reports Series L, No.5 Baltimore, Md.: Johns Hopkins University Population Information Progam, March–April 1986 p. L-156.

the underdeveloped countries in regard to some essential factors affecting the welfare of the child.

The limited development of general community services for health, education, and welfare in the underdeveloped countries means that a great deal of child welfare is concerned with the problem of inadequate role enactment resulting from deficiencies in community resources. These difficulties lie outside the parent–child relationship network but affect it adversely.

Thus, although child welfare services in the more advanced countries may have to be provided on an individual basis for those children who lack the normal arrangement for care—the child of the broken family, the emotionally disturbed child who cannot make good use of the family that is available—child welfare in the underdeveloped countries is more concerned with providing for all children, on a mass basis, those essential primary conditions necessary for normal, healthy development. Whereas child welfare is concerned in the United States with the handicapped child who cannot use the available schools, the problem for child welfare in the underdeveloped countries is to make schools available in the first place.

In contrast to our concern with children's psychological well-being and our focus on emotional parent–child interaction, marital conflict, substance abuse, and nonmarital pregnancies, the underdeveloped countries are concerned with hazards to children of malnutrition, inadequate sanitation, high-density housing, dirty water, poor quality and quantity of medical care. Quantity of life, sheer survival rather than quality of life is the keynote of concern. For such children, child welfare services, of necessity, have a different orientation and a different set of concerns.

Political and Administrative Development

The concept of childhood as a clearly differentiated period in development having special needs and special rights is associated with the development of nation-states. A review of constitutional provisions relating to childhood of 139 nations showed that formal claims for responsibility for children was not associated with differences in level of economic or social development. It is part of a worldwide expansion of state authority over children as a consequence of the needs of nation-states for developing a citizenry committed to the nation. Although the institutional claims are worldwide, the ability to implement responsibility for, and control over, lives of children varies (Boli-Bennett & Meyer, 1978).

The development of child welfare services and associated Social-Security programs is dependent on the ability of the country to develop a sophisticated administrative and fiscal apparatus. It requires birth registration procedures to determine how many children there are and where they are located, which permits the certification of age for social security.

The provision of services requires the opening of local offices, the establishment of forms and procedures for record keeping, accounting, and a communications system so that people can be reached, checks sent, and appointments made. A workmen's compensation program requires associated medical services; an unemployment insurance program requires associated job-finding and vocational retraining services. A network of social services requires the recruitment, training, and deployment of many workers who possess the necessary skills. An efficient social-insurance program requires the acceptance of a strong central authority so that a uniform program can be administered in a standardized manner throughout a country.

A well-developed social-insurance and income-maintenance program requires a population that can read and write so that forms can be completed; a postal service that efficiently covers the country; an address system so that people can be located for postal deliveries; birth, marriage, and death registry to provide documents related to eligibility; and a banking service if payments are made by check. These programs then require a well-developed network of related institutions and a sophisticated administrative infrastructure, which may be lacking in some countries, particularly in rural areas (Mouton, 1975, pp. 64–67).

The Relationship of the Nuclear Family to the Community

Child welfare services are also affected by the other institutional arrangements available to meet the needs of children. In a relatively simple, localized, self-sufficient society, which until recently characterized Africa, "The family and tribal pattern of relationship and responsibility function to meet the recognized social needs of its members. Not only the parents but the larger family group assumed responsibility for the rearing of children" (United Nations, 1963, p. 105). Family and tribal organizations furnished protection against some of the same risks and difficulties for which social services are organized in the more highly industrialized countries. A United Nations (1966) report on child welfare services in Africa notes:

> The concept of adoption is new in Africa as is also the concept of illegitimacy. By virtue of the extended nature of the family system, adoption has not been necessary in the past and has been looked down upon. Children have been valued in and of themselves and relatives have considered it their obligation to look after orphans and neglected children. For example the response from Sierra Leone comments, "There are no adoption laws, but the family system is such that as a rule there are hardly unwanted children. Children are cared for even by nonrelatives" [p. 26].

In more traditional societies, kinship fostering, child lending, and other informal transactions in sharing the responsibilities of parenthood provide substitute care for children. Substitute care takes place not only because parents have died or are ill or working but because one family has too many children to care for and another family has too few. There is a redistribution of children from those who have too many to those who have none.

Such solutions to child welfare problems, however, become progressively less feasible as a society becomes more industrialized. With the movement to urban areas, the extended family disperses and traditional solutions no longer apply. Hasan (1969), discussing social security in India, points out that "the joint family is disintegrating with increasing urbanization" and that the "family is losing both the capacity and the willingness to act as the sole agent responsible for providing social security" (pp. 193–194). A process of "detribalization" takes place. The movement to the city brings a dependence on wage employment, on a money economy. The authority of the father is diminished, for he no longer is head of a family production unit. With this decline in paternal authority comes a painful reallocation of role responsibilities and privileges between the different generations within the family group and between husband and wife. In the new industrialized, urbanized society, the family may have no tie to any group which feels a direct responsibility for its welfare. At the same time, the instability of the urban family results in increasing numbers of deserted mothers and abandoned children. Urbanization, then, increases the likelihood of child welfare problems while it simultaneously denies the structure through which such problems were previously resolved. The network of tribal mutual aid and support weakens and there arises a need for the institutionalization of child welfare services: "In developing societies, social welfare services emerge to meet human needs that can no longer be satisfied exclusively through the traditional institutions of a more static period" (United Nations, 1965, p. 10).

Although adoption was once unknown in Africa and the word did not appear in the language, by the 1970s changing social conditions in Africa dictated the need for such a service. The tribal clan or extended family is no longer available to provide child care. In 1974 in Kenya, 300 people were approved for adoption and 60 children were locally adopted through the work of the Kenyan Child Welfare Society (Miller, 1978, p. 19). Such changes come slowly, however. The United Nations (1974) sent a questionnaire to member nations regarding programs for children in need of substitute care and reported that such programs as foster care and adoption were given low priority in most of the developing countries: "The highest priority indicated is for basic health, nutrition and day care services, especially for the young child . . . very few countries give any priority to services for children in need of substitute care" (p. 4).

Attitude Toward Women and Children

Industrialization and urbanization change the position of women in the family. A changing attitude toward the child is tied to a changing attitude toward the mother. More adequate care of the child requires more adequate education of the mother and a greater concern for her needs. The mother suffering from "maternal depletion syndrome"—resulting from early marriage, frequent pregnancies, inadequate diet, and overwork—can hardly be expected to meet the needs of the child. An important aspect of child welfare in the developing countries, then, is concerned with the child indirectly through concern with the mother. A changing, more positive attitude toward the needs of women is expressed in the establishment of women's clubs and social centers, set up side by side with children's clinics, devoted to the teaching of mothercraft and homemaking and to helping women with the problems they face.

Poverty of resources alone does not always explain the difficulties encountered in providing adequate care for the child. Sometimes cheap, healthy foods, such as peanuts, are available, but it may not be traditional to offer these to children. Up to a point, the improvement of children's health may be more directly affected by educating the parents than by increasing the supply of doctors or medicine. But this often requires programs directed toward the reduction of illiteracy, particularly that of women.

There is a clear association between women's literacy rates and infant mortality rates. Where women are better educated, fewer children are likely to die in infancy (Sivard, 1985, p. 29).

The Influence of Historical Precedent and Ideology

The pattern of child welfare services is determined by the nature of earlier institutionalized approaches to similar problems (United Nations, 1964). Countries previously under British control, in accordance with the British pattern, rely heavily on voluntary agencies; former French colonies associate social service with health and nursing activity and stress family allowances; Latin American countries stress social service offered under the auspices of the Catholic Church.

Countries that, like the United States, value independence, autonomy, individualism, self-reliance, and self-fulfillment are likely to be more resistant to welfare legislation than are countries that value the idea of community responsibility for the welfare of all of their citizens. Different countries also give priority to different groups in the population in allocating welfare resources. France is strongly child-oriented; Denmark is more strongly oriented to its old people.

Ideological differences regarding the respective roles of father and mother, the relative responsibility of the community and the family regarding child care and child rearing, and the extent of legitimate and appropriate interference by the state in family matters, determine, in some measure, differences in child welfare services and policies.

Religious ideology is a factor determining the nature of services developed. Adoption is less acceptable to Islamic law, although it does occur in Islamic countries.

Differences in child welfare services result from differences in the availability of alternative institutions that have sanctioned responsibility for child welfare problems. The kinship group, the extended family, or the tribal organization may perform such services, as is the case in sections of Africa. Trade union organizations in East European countries act to provide child welfare services to families. Where primary group relationships—the family, the neighborhood group, the trade union in the shop, and so on—are strong and effective, there is less need for formal agency assistance in responding to parent–child problems.

Some Selective Comparisons: Child Welfare Service Here and Abroad

Having discussed some of the factors that affect the development of child welfare programs generally, we now review the different categories and services—supportive, supplemental, and substitutive—and point to variations and modifications found in other countries. Because of the possible appropriateness of these variations and modifications to our own child-welfare problems, most of the countries cited are similar to the United States in levels of industrialization and standards of living.

It would be an impossibly lengthy task to review in detail the child welfare programs of even a representative group of countries, so we must be quite selective. Our purpose is to call attention to those aspects of these programs that we might consider in strengthening our own child-welfare programs. Consequently the result is not likely to be a fair comparison. To do justice to our own program, we would have to cite the weakness of the foreign programs to which we call attention. If we were to present a balanced picture, for instance, of the Soviet welfare system as it affects children, we would have to note that the social insurance system does not cover agricultural workers as adequately as it does industrial workers, that there is no unemployment insurance system in the Soviet Union, that political "undesirables" can lose their rights to social security, that there are limited statistics available on social problems and no published evaluations of Soviet services, that mothers of young children may be denied financial assistance if they refuse to accept work or work training, that income maintenance programs for divorced or deserted mothers are inadequate, and that the low level of social insurance payments and a very limited program of public assistance payments leave large groups of recipients in poverty (Simanis, 1972; Minkoff & Turgeon, 1976; Madison, 1977a,b; *New York Times,* November 19, 1978; McCauley, 1979).

Infant mortality rates are considerably higher and life expectancy is lower in the Soviet Union as compared with the United States. However, given the aim of stimulating thinking toward a broader, less ethnocentrically based perspective on child-welfare services, a selective presentation of alternative approaches appears justified.

Because of the different mix as to what is included in the education, health, and social welfare package, the differences in the history of the welfare state in various countries, the differences in levels of living, it is difficult to compare the U.S. efforts at meeting welfare needs, broadly defined, with that of other countries. During the 1960s and 1970s, there was a marked increase in the portion of the gross national product devoted to social welfare in all of the industrialized countries.

The Organization for Economic Cooperation and Development reports "that between 1960 and 1981, social expenditures in the principal western European economies leaped from 14.5 to 26.3 percent of their total output of goods and services. Over the same period, the rise in the United States was from 11 to 21 percent" (*New York Times,* February 19, 1984).

In 1981, the United States ranked fourteenth among nineteen industrialized nations in the percentage of the gross national product devoted to social expenditures. It was behind not only the Scandinavian countries, Belgium and the Netherlands, France, and West Germany, as expected, but it also ranked lower than Italy and Canada (Rosen, Fanshel, & Lutz, 1987, p. 116).

Whereas expenditures for social welfare increased substantially in the United States in the 1960s and 1970s, a question might be raised as to whether our efforts are commensurate with our resources. Despite our subjective feeling about being overtaxed, we are generally undertaxed as compared with other nations having more adequate and more generous welfare programs.

"In 1980, the U.S. ranked fourteenth among twenty four industrialized countries in terms of total taxes paid as a proportion of gross domestic product" (Palmer & Sawhill 1982, p. 3). A review of comparative distribution of wealth in seven highly industrialized nations found that although the United States ranked third in per capita gross national product in 1982, it ranked seventh in the share of the gross national product going to the poorest fifth of the population (Townsend, 1986).

Kahn and Kamerman (1983a; b; c) attempted to make comparisons around more specific programs of particular concern to social work. They compared the level of generosity and adequacy of income transfers to different kinds of families across eight different industrialized countries. Income transfers in the United States were compared with those of Sweden, Germany, France, Canada, Australia, England, and Israel. Because income transfer programs differ in the grant levels from state to state, Kahn and Kamerman selected two states to represent the United States, New York and Pennsylvania—New York because it is one of the states with the highest assistance grant levels and Pennsylvania because it is closer to the grant level median. The year-end 1979 net income for each family was computed considering all earnings and income transfers available in the

particular countries—child allowance, housing allowance, public assistance, unemployment insurance, food stamps, refundable tax credits, and maternity benefits. To standardize a basis for comparison, the family year-end net income was
then expressed as a percentage of the countries' net average production wage.
Whereas the level of adequacy of help to families provided in the United States as
compared with that of other countries differed for different kinds of families, in
general some other countries such as Sweden, France, and West Germany tended
to be consistently more generous in benefits and supports provided. Of fifteen
different types of families studied, Pennsylvania ranked 8 or 9 in comparison of
the level of generosity of nine different country comparisons (1983b, Table 4, p.
26; 1983c). Kahn and Kamerman attribute the difference to the fact that France,
Sweden, and West Germany have an explicit family-oriented social policy program designed to promote the well-being of children and families. Willingness to
accept a higher burden of taxes is also associated with different levels of generosity of help.

Supportive and Protective Services

A. Supportive Services. Great Britain is one of the relatively few countries
to have developed a highly professionalized program of supportive services. It has
a network of family service agencies, many of which are affiliated with the national council of family casework agencies. Operating under the auspices of some
family service agencies are the Family Discussion Bureaus, which offer marital
counseling. The government provides grants-in-aid to such organizations.

The work of the Family Service Units in Great Britain started during World
War I, when conscientious objectors founded the Pacifist Service Units to care for
disorganized, bombed-out families in large English cities. As a result of their
contact with the families, and the realization that many of the difficulties presented by the families were not the result of the war, the units began to work
toward helping the families resolve some of their basic problems. Although casework is the principal method of aid, the units operate in a distinctive way. The
staff lives together in a house in the district they serve, and its members are
available to families in the district on a twenty-four-hour basis. The staff attempts to demonstrate, in this home, that standards can be maintained even
though the housing is poor. In establishing a relationship with families who he
cannot be reached through "talk" alone, the caseworker may go into the home and
assist the family directly by scrubbing floors, washing clothes, caring for the
children, cooking a meal, and so on (McKie, 1963; Philip, 1963).

Holland has attempted to help the multiproblem family in an even more comprehensive way. It has set up special villages, known as *reeducation centers,* to
which the family is moved. Employment for the father is obtained in the neighborhood, and the children go to the village school. Through demonstrations, teaching, and counseling by social workers who visit daily, the families learn how to
manage the home, how to budget, and how to live together with less friction.

In 1973 Japan had 149 child guidance centers handling some 244,000 cases:
"Each child guidance center has shelter facilities for children who are brought into
the center because they have been deserted, their families have broken up or they
have run away" (Nakamura, 1977b, p. 201). A table of the problems that bring
children to the child guidance centers indicates that problems manifested by children in Japan are similar to those encountered in the United States (p. 200).

For many parents seeking help, the complexity of social services is baffling. They need help not only in determining where to go but also in understanding the eligibility requirements and the procedures. The British have established a network of Citizens' Advice Bureaus to help people find their way around the complex world of social services. Simple explanations are offered, information about what is available is given, and referrals are made to the proper agency (Zucker, 1965; Leissner, 1967).

Another supportive service of interest is the subsidized vacation. The Norwegian government provides subsidies to families in order to enable housewives to have an annual two-week vacation, preference being given to housewives with small children. France and Germany maintain family holiday homes—nonprofit establishments designed to permit the family to vacation together. The Swedish government supports, through grants-in-aid, holiday homes for housewives. During their absence, vacationing mothers may arrange for homemakers from the local social-welfare bureau to prepare meals for their husbands and children and to do housecleaning. Such homemaker service is given at community expense if the family of the vacationing mother cannot afford to pay (Uhr 1966, p. 17)

For whatever it's worth in the supportive effect it might have, we note that whereas the United States celebrates Father's Day and Mother's Day, East Europeans celebrate International Children's Day: in Bulgaria, it is regarded "as a big public event in which it is the duty of all to participate" (Veillard-Cybulska, 1969, p. 13); in Poland, the motto for the day is "The upbringing and the education of children is the responsibility of all" (Veillard-Cybulska, 1966, p. 51). May 5 is officially designated "Children's Day" in Japan.

The Dutch post office issues a special set of children's stamps every year. A portion of the income derived from the sale of stamps goes to support the Dutch Foundation for the Child, an organization concerned with children's rights.

In 1981, Norway instituted the office of a special ombudsman for children. "His function is to see that children's interests are being taken care of in all sectors of society" (Bratholm & Matheson, 1983, p. 588). Anybody who thinks that a child is getting a raw deal may complain to the ombudsman. Sweden also has a children's Ombudsman. However, such a function in Sweden is not a government-supported institution but was developed by the *Swedish Save the Child Federation*. The Ombudsman staff are children's advocates who exert pressure on the authorities, the legislature, and the social services to correct situations that affect children adversely. They see themselves as the representatives of children watching over the rights and needs of the population of children.

B. Protective Services

If protective services are included as supportive services, we might note that most countries provide sanctions in the case of neglect by parents of their duties toward their children or in case of child abuse. Although all countries have legislated services protecting the child from neglect and abuse, most do not identify child abuse as an explicit concern. A detailed review of protective services in different countries concludes that except for Canada and England "no other country studied has found it necessary to develop the kinds of specialized programs we have in the United States for identifying such children. The major debate relates to whether or not child abuse represents a phenomenon distinct from maltreatment of children generally and whether it warrants special policies and programs" (Kamerman, 1975, pp. 36–37). Many countries, however, have some national organization concerned with child protection. In West Germany, the German Child Protection Federation which had, when established in 1898, been called the Association for the Protection of Children from Exploitation and Abuse, operates crisis lines and shelters for abused children. In Israel there is an Israeli Association for Child Protection. In Germany, a medical specialty, Social Pediatrics, has led to the development of local children's centers employing an interdisciplinary team serving a population that includes children who are high risk for abuse because of family conduct or family living situation (McGhee, 1981).

An international questionnaire study conducted under the auspices of the International Union of Children's Welfare in 1977 elicited responses from twenty-five different countries, nine outside Europe. The responses indicated that throughout this wide range of countries, corporal punishment against children was very widely used at schools and in the homes (Edfeldt, 1979). (See also Nwako 1974; Loening, 1981).

In 1979, the Swedish Parenthood and Guardianship code, which regulates questions concerning the care of children, was revised by legislative act to prohibit the use by parents of any physical punishment against children. The pertinent clause said that "the child may not be subject to physical punishment or other humiliating treatment."

It was recognized that such a blanket outlawing of any form of physical discipline by parents would be difficult to enforce (Solheim, 1982). What was intended, however, was a clear official message to parents that corporal punishment was unacceptable. The objective was to foster a community-wide attitudinal change toward the use of corporal punishment in the home. In reinforcing the intent of the legislation a large-scale program of public information was mounted explaining the law and its rationale. A parent education program designed primarily for new parents was developed and implemented. Parents were granted time off for work to attend, and financial compensation was provided for any loss of wages. Among the education pamphlets developed and distributed as part of these educational programs was one entitled "Can You Bring Up Children Successfully Without Smacking or Spanking?" The law, when passed, was regarded as a consciousness-raising pedagogic law and included no specific penalties for its violation. Since the passage of the law there have been a few reported instances of children requesting action against their parents. In August, 1984, the father of an eleven-year-old boy was fined $12 for having "birched his son." The boy "who had used his father's bicycle without his permission and who had fought with a friend" had complained to the police about his father's use of corporal punishment (*New York Times,* August 16, 1984).

Norway also has laws banning physical punishment, and such a law has been proposed in Finland. Public opinion polls in Sweden and Finland indicate a greater public opposition to corporal punishment as contrasted with similar polls in the United States (Peltoniemi, 1983). In 1986 the British Parliament banned corporal punishment in any school "run or supported by the government." "Caning" was still permitted in privately financed schools (*New York Times,* July 24, 1986).

The "confidential doctor" system was developed in the Netherlands to deal with the question of child abuse reporting. Identified, designated "confidential doctors" are perceived as the person to whom neighbors, teachers, and family doctors report suspicion of child abuse. Reporting to a friendly, interested medical professional is seen as being easier than making a report to an official body. "Confidential doctors" provide service without reference to the official Child Protection Board or the legal authorities. "Confidential doctors" enjoy not only a great deal of authority but a great deal of public confidence as is evidenced by the greatly increased rate of their use (Christopherson, 1981, p. 371).

Children under fourteen who are victims of sexual abuse in Israel can only be "interrogated by a 'youth interrogator' specially appointed for the purpose by the Minister of Justice." If the "youth interrogator" is of the opinion that it would be harmful for the child to testify in court, then no such testimony will be taken. "In such cases (by way of exception to the 'rule against hearsay evidence') the youth interrogator himself may present a report of his interrogation to the court which will be admissable as evidence. However, corroboration of this evidence is required in order for the defendent to be convicted" (Goldstein, 1983, p. 481).

As a preventive measure associated with the higher risk for the abuse of congenitally handicapped children, women in Israel "who are at least 37 years old at the beginning of their pregnancy, and younger women under certain circumstances, have a right to a free amniotic fluid examination in order to discover genetic problems, diseases and malformations of the fetus which may be diagnosed prior to birth" (Goldstein, 1983, p. 442).

Countries that provide for periodic examinations of young children may regard child-abuse identification programs as superfluous. The community becomes aware of child abuse as a consequence of such regularly scheduled reexaminations.

The detection of potential child-welfare problems and efforts at prevention are assisted by programs of periodic visits to the families by health and social work personnel during the child's infancy. France, for instance, has a program of compulsory medical, psychological and social examination of children at definite intervals between the ages of three months and thirty months. Since 1970 these examinations have been made a prerequisite to the payment of family allowances. They supplement the four prenatal obstetrical examinations required of the mother in order to qualify for maternity benefits. A social worker also makes a prenatal visit to the home to become acquainted with the family, to discuss possible problems, and to inform the family of social welfare benefits and services.

In Hungary, the district nurse, who performs social work functions in addition to traditional nursing functions, regularly visits all families with children from birth until six years of age. Visits are made every ten days during the first two months after birth, then once a month until the child is a year old. The child is then visited every two months between the ages of one and three and every four months between three and six years of age (Hermann & Komlosi, 1972, p. 371).

In Sweden, child welfare centers throughout the country check the child's health during the first two years of life through a series of home visits. Recently a special control examination at age four was introduced for all children. The aim was to detect the behavioral and social problems as well as the medical problems of children at this age.

Periodic review of the child's situation by community representatives provides regularly scheduled protection for the child in China also:

> When a mother returns home from a maternity hospital with her new-born infant, health workers from her lane station, accompanied by the doctor working there, call to see how she feels and advise her on child feeding. They visit the baby two or three times during the first month after birth. Whenever it is ill, a doctor can be summoned at any time, providing treatment free of charge. The infant continues to receive check-ups every three months until it is 18 months old. Check-ups are than

scheduled at six-month intervals until it reaches the age of three, after which it is examined once a year [Wen, 1977, p. 116].

Supplementary Services: Social Insurance, Homemaker Service, Day Care

A. Social Insurances and Maternity Options. The most recent review of social security programs throughout the world (U.S. Department of Health, Education, and Welfare, Research Report 59, 1984) summarizing the programs in 128 countries from Afghanistan to Zambia, indicated that all countries provide some protection to the wage earner and his or her children and family. Workmen's compensation was the program most frequently listed; unemployment insurance was least frequently listed. The countries with the most comprehensive programs of protection, which include many of the industrialized countries, cover old age, disability, work injury, unemployment, and health insurance, including temporary illness, maternity benefits and family allowances. The United States is somewhat exceptional among the highly industrialized nations because it has no national health insurance program, no temporary sickness or maternity assistance program, and no family allowance program.

The Soviet Union does not have a program of unemployment insurance. Because the state takes responsibility for ensuring that all who can and want to work have employment, the lack of such a program is not regarded as a deprivation. It suggests that unemployment insurance is a public policy option made necessary by a system that consistently operates with some percentage of its potential work force unemployed. A job guarantee program might be considered a more desirable alternative approach to providing family income.

The most widespread kind of social insurance of direct interest to children is the family allowance. Originally adopted in France to encourage a higher birth rate, its spread to more than sixty countries was based on the idea that the existence of dependent children should not give rise to undue inequalities in family levels of living. The program provides for the payment of a regular allowance to every family for the support of each child and corrects the imbalance between family income and family need.

Family allowances are sometimes called a social or a moral wage because they make family support needs, as well as the value of labor, a determinant of family income. Family allowances and maternity benefits are based on the rationale that the community generally, as well as the family specifically, benefits from the birth of a child. Children are the future producers of the country's wealth. Since the community benefits from the birth of the child, the community then should help parents to support and rear the child.

Family allowances have a redistribution effect from those who are childless to those who have children and must incur the cost of raising them. In most countries, they are not regarded as taxable income.

It is a particularly important source of regular supplementary income to a single-parent-employed, female-headed household. Such a family would not be generally eligible for any kind of support in the United States.

According to Norwegian child allowance regulations, a single parent is entitled to an allowance for one child more than the actual number of children in the family. This helps increase the amount of support available to the single-parent family (Bratholm & Matheson, 1983, p. 568).

The allowance is designed for adopted and foster children as well as for natural children. In most countries, allowances are paid to all families with dependent children regardless of employment status or family income. In some countries, they are paid only to families with limited income, only to people in certain occupations, or only upon the birth of the second or a third child.

Family allowances are usually financed by a tax on employers or out of general governmental revenue. Generally there is a cutoff point for eligible children, which ranges between fourteen and eighteen years; however, this cutoff point may be extended for children who are in school or who are sick or handicapped.

"About 67 countries have family allowance programs, including all the industrial countries except the U. S." (U.S. Dept. H.H.S 1984, p.xxv). Currently the United States is the only highly industrialized nation without such a program.

One might point to our own income tax reductions for each dependent child as an indirect family allowance program; however, most of the countries that provide family allowances do so in addition to allowing income tax reductions.

Eligibility requirements may restrict access to such allowances. Thus family allowances become available to families in the Soviet Union only after the birth of the fourth child. With an increasing percentage of Soviet families being limited to one or two children, an increasing percentage of families remain ineligible (Madison, 1975, p. 253).

The support provided by the programs usually amounts to 5 to 10 per cent of median wages in the country. Child allowances for three children were equal to 40 per cent of the average wages in 1980 in Czechoslovakia (Havelka & Radvanova, 1983, p. 293). In the Congo, family allowances during the first year of the child's life are "conditional on the child's receiving a periodic medical check-up which is free of charge" (Tcnibinda & Mayetela, 1983, p. 200). Israel has special allowances for large families of four or more children under the age of eighteen (Jaffe, 1982, p. 120).

In special instances, family allowance grants are increased. For instance, in Czechoslovakia, families taking care of a disabled child who has not been placed in an institution become entitled to double the family allowance for that child (International Social Security Association, 1974, p. 28).

In addition to the actual additional income provided to the family, family allowances provide a sense of security. Guaranteed by the government, they provide a dependable regular income.

Unlike the United States, most European countries have government-operated health insurance programs. The particular significance for child welfare, aside from the increments to family income that result because the insurance pays the family's medical bills, is that it provides prenatal, delivery, and postnatal medical care for every mother and child and guarantees the possibility of adequate medical attention for every child. This may help account for the fact that in 1982 the United States ranked 16th in the world in infant mortality rates.

Medical care for the pregnant woman, and indirectly health care for the fetus, is provided for almost all European women through nationalized health care systems. By contrast, it is estimated that more than 25 per cent of American women in the primary childbearing age range of eighteen to twenty-four, who account for 40 per cent of all births in the country, have no health-care coverage, and as a result are unlikely to receive adequate medical attention. State Medicaid eligibility limits and other restrictions leave many poor, fecund women without such help (Gold & Kenny, 1985).

Health insurance plans provide medical care, sickness insurance, and substitute income when the wage earner is ill. Although most of the industrialized nations make sickness insurance available as part of the social insurance system, the United States does not. Those countries having social-insurance sickness benefits increase the insurance or provide supplementation when the wage earner has dependent children. In West Germany, full wages are provided for the first six weeks of illness and 75 per cent thereafter. Both East Germany and West Germany provide extra sickness benefits for wage earners with children. A two- to seven-day waiting period is imposed in most programs before sick benefits are available, and cash benefits are most frequently set at 50–75 per cent of average earnings.

Although labor force participation is required in most countries as a qualification for receiving sickness benefits, in Sweden housewives who are incapacitated by illness are eligible for such help.

Sickness insurance also covers wages for limited periods during the time a parent has to stay home to care for a sick child. For instance, in Bulgaria, should a child under the age of three fall ill, the working mother can obtain paid leave to care for the child (Veillard-Cybulska, 1969, p. 6). Most frequently such coverage is limited to a period of five to fifteen days and is often restricted so that only the mother is eligible. In Sweden, Norway, and Austria, in an effort to encourage sharing of child-rearing responsibilities, both the father and mother are eligible for such paid leave in caring for a dependent child.

In addition to health insurance, which provides free medical care, many countries protect the working mother and her child by offering maternity benefits. As early as 1919, the Maternity Protection Convention formulated by the International Labor Organization called for twelve weeks paid maternity leave—six weeks before and six weeks after the birth of the child. Maternity benefits compensate the family for the loss of the mother's wages during pregnancy, enable her to stop work earlier in the pregnancy, and permit her to remain home with the baby for at least a minimum period after birth. Such benefits assure the possibility of mother–child postnatal bonding.

France increased maternity leave from fourteen to sixteen weeks in 1980 and made adoptive parents eligible for such leave. The working Soviet mother receives maternity benefits at the rate of 100 per cent of pay for a sixteen-week period—eight weeks before and eight weeks after confinement. Italy's social insurance system provides 80 per cent of earnings up to thirteen weeks before and eight weeks after confinement. In Yugoslavia, "working women are entitled to 133 days of paid maternity leave and subsequently their working day is reduced by four hours until the child reaches three years of age" (Scaberne, 1969, p. 23). Israel grants working women a three-month leave at 75 per cent of salary at the time of confinement. The women may return to work and "be permitted an hour less work per day until the end of the year at the expense of the employer" (Neipris, 1971, p. 298).

Special additional consideration is given in atypical situations. Thus, in Czechoslovakia, maternity leave is extended from twenty-six weeks to thirty-five weeks at 90 per cent of gross average earnings if the mother gives birth to twins or if she is unmarried.

As a protection to both mother and child, maternity benefits are frequently made on condition that the mother use the free medical care provided during the pregnancy. For instance, France pays a prenatal allowance with the onset of pregnancy; the nine monthly payments due for the period of pregnancy are divided into three, each being paid after the medical examination and provided that the examination has taken place at the proper time. With this kind of induce-ment, 95 per cent of all French expectant mothers, for instance, are under medical care (Central Union, 1968, p. 22).

A modification of the maternity leave plan in Sweden permits the family to decide whether the father or the mother will stay home to care for the child during a period after birth. If the wife works, the two are free to split the total time available to suit their own needs. Whereas the paternity leave option had limited takers when it was first introduced, it gradually became more popular and acceptable, and by 1984 around 20 per cent of fathers were taking some paternity leave.

Norway has a similar, but more limited and more ambivalent, eighteen-week maternity leave policy. Only the mother is eligible for the first six weeks after the birth of the baby, but the additional twelve weeks can be split between the father and mother. However, the father can elect to take unpaid paternity leave for up to one year with full job protection (Henriksen, Halter, 1978, p. 62).

France gives some formal recognition of the father's involvement in the birth of the child in a special provision—*congés de naissance*—which provide a three-day holiday with pay for the father within fifteen days before or after the birth. If a woman who was eligible for maternity allowance died in childbirth or within a year of birth, her husband in Israel is "eligible for a special allowance of 75% of wages for a period of 12 weeks if he stopped work in order to take care of a child" (Jaffe, 1982, p. 132).

Unlike some one hundred and seventeen other countries, the United States has no formal statutory maternity leave requirements or benefits protecting the preg-nant mother and infant child. Such benefits include paid leave for some time before and after the birth of the child, continuation of employee entitlement to building job seniority, and guarantee of security of the job from which leave has been taken for childbirth and early childrearing (Kamerman & Kahn, 1981; Hewlett 1986).

The Pregnancy Discrimination Act of 1978 does prohibit treating pregnant employees differently "for any employment-related purpose." The same sickness-disability benefits and protection accorded other employees in "their ability or validity to work needs to be granted the pregnant employee." But because there is no statutory requirement that employers provide disability coverage, many work-ing women are not covered by the Pregnancy Discrimination Act. Short-term disability insurance coverage is an option of employers in most states. When the employer chooses not to provide disability insurance, women employees are not covered for pregnancy.

Some corporations have provided benefits as a matter of company policy, not because it is a statutory requirement. "Although accurate statistics are elusive, it is believed by experts that only about 40 percent of working parents have access to maternity benefits" in the United States "and those who do rarely get more than six weeks off and are usually not paid" (*New York Times,* November 28, 1985). State laws enacted in Montana, Connecticut, California, and Massachu-setts that give pregnant employees special entitlement to job leaves and job return guarantees were challenged by the American Civil Liberties Union as well as by the National Organization for Women (NOW) and The National Association of Manufacturers. The opposition to such legislation was based on the fear that preferential legislation in favor of women would threaten the advocacy of equal rights for women and that employers would be more reluctant to hire women if they were to be burdened with the expense of special treatment.

At the time this book went to press, legislation introduced by Representative Patricia Schroeder of Colorado was being discussed in congressional committee that would provide men and women a minimum of 18 weeks of unpaid leave to care for newly born, newly adopted, or seriously ill children. Gender neutral, the bill would also provide 26 weeks of job protection following these events. Most American women, however, would still lack the paid maternity leave available in most other countries. The United States is far behind many other countries then in providing protected maternity-childbirth leave and wage replacement benefits to female workers.

Many countries pay a birth grant—a lump sum to help the family with the temporary increases in expenses associated with the birth. In 1977 the birth grant in East Germany was $420, in France about $365, in Hungary $125, and in Finland $65. In Argentina, a birth grant, which in 1977 amounted to about $300, was also paid upon the adoption of a child (U.S. Department of Health, Education, and Welfare, Research Report 50, 1978, p. 9).

The People's Republic of China provides maternity benefits of 100 per cent of earnings for up to fifty-six days before confinement and fifty-six days after delivery. In addition, there is a birth-grant lump sum "equal to current value of 5 feet of cloth" (Sidel, 1976, p. 190).

As an alternative to providing day-care services for the very young child so as to permit adequate care of the child while the mother works some countries provide extended support benefits to the mother in lieu of working. Postpartum maternity benefits are a step in this direction. In replacing wage-earned income, maternity benefits permit the mother to remain at home for a period of time and care for the child without income loss. Extending this concept, some countries provide maternity benefits for the first two or three years of the child's life.

In response to a concern about declining population, East Germany gives mothers a half-year off at full pay after the birth of a child and makes it possible for working mothers to extend their leave of absence up to a year while keeping their jobs and getting monthly stipends (*New York Times,* April 28, 1978). Hungarian women are entitled to a maternity leave from employment of twenty to twenty-five weeks at full salary. If employed for a year prior to the child's birth they can subsequently elect to stay home and care for the child until the child is three years old. During this period they receive a grant that is almost half of the average salary for women (Ferge, 1978, p. 175). Austria has a more modest program; it permits the mother to receive financial support through unemployment insurance for the first year after the birth of the child (Krebs & Schwartz, 1978, p. 206).

Women employees who opt to stay at home to care for a child for the first two or three years of the child's life are given credit, in these programs, for those years in the computation of pension time. Maternity leave allowances, subsequent support payments, and the continued counting of this period of child care toward pension coverage reduce the pressures on mothers to return to work after childbirth.

In 1981, the Soviet Union announced a new program of paid maternity allowances. Starting in 1982, women in the Soviet Union would be entitled to allowances up to the equivalent of $66 a month for one year following the birth of a child. The program was part of an effort to reverse the country's falling birthrate (*Reuters Newsdispatch,* November 6, 1981, Moscow).

The extension of maternity leave is viewed with some ambivalence on the part of some women in other countries where similar measures have been proposed. There is a feeling that such measures may be implemented at the expense of a greater commitment to day care and jobs for women and that the pressure to stay at home to care for the young child will erode options for women (Scott, 1977). Knowing that a woman can leave work with support for two or three years following the birth of the child may make employers more hesitant to hire women. Further, an absence of two or three years from employment may adversely affect a woman's career. The policy comes close to being a "mother's wage," since it involves paying the mother for remaining in the home to care for the child in preference to returning to employment. The fear is that, in strengthening the woman's position as mother, it weakens her position as a woman, reinforcing the traditional stereotyping of female roles.

Since more women are entering the labor force in all industrialized countries, efforts are being made to seek a new balance between the demands of work and family. Family-sensitive employment policies and practices have been adopted abroad. In addition to maternity–paternity benefits, up to sixty days of paid leave to care for a sick child, and an extra leave of two weeks when a child enters school or a day-care center, Sweden has pioneered in reorganizing the workplace to accommodate to the women's interrole conflict between employee and parent.

Sweden makes an explicit effort to provide opportunities for flexible time (flex-time) employment, joint job sharing, and part-time employment for mothers. Swedish parents have a right to a six-hour working day with a cut in pay until a child is eight years old. A majority of Swedish women work part time when their children are very young and then assume full-time work when their children enter school. (*New York Times,* May 25, 1984).

Soviet legislation explicitly recognizes the problems of the working mother in making special provisions "to create the most favorable condition for women to combine a job in social production with bringing up children" (Progress Publishers, 1982, p. 69). These include transfer to easier jobs during pregnancy, paid maternity leave, job and seniority protection, birth grants of money, special additional paid holidays, preferential rights to vacations, and sick care child leave.

The Soviet Code of Labor Legislation requires that "enterprises and organizations employing a high proportion of female laborer shall organize creches and kindergartens, nursing rooms, and also rooms for the women's personal hygiene—women with children under one year of age shall be granted nursing breaks for not less than thirty minutes every three hours" (Tulkanova & Azarova, 1982).

In the USSR adoptive mothers are granted paid leave of about two months following adoption and an unpaid job-protected leave of one year.

B. Public Assistance Despite extensive Social Security programs, all countries find the need for a public assistance program. Almost everywhere social insurance is backed up and supplemented by a means-tested public assistance program. In England, these are called *supplementary benefits;* in France, *allocation supplementaire or l'aide sociale;* in Sweden, *social hjälp.*

Some countries do far more than we do in advertising the availability of such programs and encouraging people to implement their eligibility. For instance, there is little, if any, advertising of the Aid to Families of Dependent Children (AFDC) program in the United States. On the other hand, there is great concern in Great Britain with what they call *take-up*—the percentage of eligible people who actually apply for the benefits to which they are entitled. To implement this concern and to give the programs visibility, the British post offices and many other public buildings have posters informing people of allowances—including those affecting children—for which they might apply. Government-supported Citizen Advice Bureaus located at the neighborhood level distribute leaflets and offer advice regarding application procedures.

Indirect procedures have also been adopted to help maintain family income at a level that would permit adequate care of the child. Hot school lunches at little or no cost and free distribution of food to low-income families supplement the family budget. Rent allowances go further than subsidies of low-cost housing. Denmark, for example, has a system of differential rents for families with three or more children living in flats built especially for such families. Rent reductions of up to 70 per cent are given according to the number of children. In France, housing allowances can range up to 85 per cent of the rent for families with four or more children.

In Denmark, low-income families may also receive textile discount coupons of specified value to be used toward the purchase of children's clothing. In Belgium, Greece, France, and Scandinavia, large families are given special reductions of 50–75 per cent on train and bus fares. Sweden provides free holiday travel, once a year, to a place of rest and recreation for members of low-income families.

As a commentary on the relationship between ideology and policy it might be noted that in Communist China self-help, self-reliance, and neighborhood mutual aid rather than reliance on state-supported services characterize the approach to family and child welfare. In some essential respects the Chinese orientation mirrors the traditionally family-oriented approach of American conservatives. The social assistance system reflects an analogous conservative point of view that "where possible, individuals have been encouraged if not required to support themselves and their families by undertaking additional work rather than of seeking welfare support. Preoccupation with possible work disincentive efforts of welfare support—has always dominated the focus of welfare administration" (Dixon, 1981, p. 2). Glorifying the work ethic, the Chinese welfare system provides "only minimal relief to its recipients but only after it has been ensured that they have exhibited the essential characteristics of diligence, frugality and thrift in their daily lives" (Dixon 1981, p. 3).

C. Homemaker Services. Homemaker service is more highly developed in some countries than it is in the United States. In Great Britain, homemaker service is one of the programs offered as part of the National Health Service Act—Britain's socialized-medicine plan. In Finland, legislation requires that there be homemakers available in every public health district to work closely with midwives and public health nurses. As a result, the number of homemakers per capita is much higher than in the United States.

In 1972 the Netherlands had 1 homemaker per 380 population. At that time, the United States had 1 homemaker per 7,000 population (Kahn & Kamerman, 1975b, p. 105). Both Sweden and Norway provide temporary "child-care attendant service," a homemaker being available to care for the employed mother's child who, being ill, cannot be cared for in the usual day-care center group. In addition, Germany has a special organization that offers homemaker service to large families, on the theory that giving the mother of a large family an opportunity for a break from unremitting child care is sensible preventive therapy.

Although there is no formally established program of training for homemakers in the United States, several European countries have such a program. Holland has an eighteen-month curriculum; France, which classifies homemaker service as a social profession, offers a seven-month program; Finland has schools offering a two-year course in homemaker training; Sweden offers a fifteen-month homemaker training course in fourteen schools scattered throughout the country (Nordstrom, 1969). In every instance, the courses offer a combination of theoretical material and practical fieldwork in a hospital, a child-care institution, or supervised placement in a family.

The National Health Service Act of 1946 establishing a comprehensive national health service in England included homemaker service in its provisions. Section 29 of the act empowered local health authorities to provide "domestic help for households where such help was required owing to the presence of any person who is ill, lying in, an expectant mother, mentally defective, aged or a child not over compulsory school age."

Like the emergency caretaker in the United States some local authorities in Britain have developed "night sitting services" to care for children left alone. Such mobile night watchers are equipped with radio communication (Dexter & Harbert, 1983, p. 42).

D. Day Care. Expansion in the employment of married women gives rise everywhere to the problem of the need for day care. Many European countries apparently do not share our reluctance to have a day-care facility associated with the mother's place of work or our reluctance to offer group care to children under three years of age. Consequently, especially in the East European countries, the factory *crèche,* or infant nursery, is quite common (United Nations, 1956, pp. 18–44). Part of the greater need for and, hence, the acceptability of group care is predicated on the fact that a significantly larger percentage of women in East Europe work outside the home than is true in the United States. In addition, the housing shortage there makes home care less feasible.

All new Soviet apartment buildings are required to reserve a minimum of 5 per cent of their space for a *crèche,* and "all enterprises employing more than 500 workers must provide nursery and *crèche* facilities" (Radin, 1970, p. 31). Every effort is made to provide adequate care. A "patronage nurse," implementing the role of a social worker, visits the homes of children whose families are applying for day care to help integrate the child's experience in the day-care center and the home (Orlova, 1969). The nurseries that enroll children at three months of age have one "upbringer" for every four children at the younger age levels.

China, too, provides widespread day-care facilities for children and infants. Such services are necessary because almost 90 per cent of all Chinese women are in the work force (Sidel, 1972). Nursery rooms are available in most factories and other work places. There are some full-time nurseries open day and night, and some parents take their children home only on weekends. Approximately 50 per cent of the children between one-and-a-half and three years of age are cared for in communal nurseries; grandparents care for an additional large group of children.

In Japan, the Sony Corporation operates a day-care center for its many women employees. Twice a year, the children are given complete medical checkups. The children study English from the age of two-and-a-half years through Sony tape recorders (Bayh, 1970).

Other countries, such as France, Belgium, and Israel, provide some kind of day care, at least half-time, for a larger percentage of their three- to five-year-old children than does the United States. An effort is being made to extend kindergarten education downward and universalize such a program for all three- to five-year-olds.

In Scandinavia day-care centers are part of the architecture of large apartment complexes, keeping the facility close to home. In Czechoslovakia the effort is made to locate a creche for a young child no further than 800 meters from the home.

Denmark stipulates that at least a fifth of any day-care center staff, which the government subsidizes, must be male to give children early contact with both genders.

As is true for the Head Start program in the United States, other countries have supported day care as a compensatory resource for disadvantaged groups in the community. Thus day care in Israel is directed toward the Sephardic-Oriental population with the objective of more adequately socializing children from that group to a school setting and preparing them for elementary school. Public welfare offices in Israel have "outposted" social workers to day-care settings "seeking to locate problematic child-care and family problems before they reach the welfare office or other social agencies" (Jaffe, 1982, p. 116). Child-care facilities in China as in the Soviet Union perform a political-indoctrination function as well as child-protection and child-development functions. In the 1970s kindergarten children were taught "The five loves—Chairman Mao, the Communits Party, the Motherland, Collective Life, and Physical Labor. Thse are continually reinforced by patriotic songs and dramatic mime" (Dixon, 1981, p. 309).

An essential aspect of a more subtle political indoctrination involves teaching the child the priority of the group over self, the priority of collective needs over individual needs.

The Nurseries and Child Minders Regulation Act passed in Britain in 1948 ensures a more careful overview of information child care arrangements than is possible in the United States. As in the United States, a large percentage of young children of British working mothers are cared for in nonrelative family homes. Local officials in England are required to register all such homes. A person who fails to register can be fined or imprisoned. "In exchange for registration a child minder is given safety equipment, strollers, highchairs, training courses, free milk for the children and access to toy libraries and drop in centers" (*New York Times,* September 4, 1984).

In addition to day-care centers and the infant's nursery or *crèche,* Norway has a large number of "park aunts," who look after children of preschool age in parks and playgrounds. The mother who needs to shop or visit a clinic, or who merely wants to catch her psychic breath, may leave the young child with the park aunt for part of the day. In Sweden, " 'afternoon homes' and 'walking tours' are provided in many neighborhoods. Under this arrangement one of the women in the neighborhood takes care of the children of employed mothers and, when the weather will permit, takes them on tours" (Rosenthal, 1967, p. 82).

"Baby parking" in *Haltes-garderies* is provided in France:

> In this institution, during the day, for a limited time, and on an occasional basis, care is given to children ranging from 3 months to 5 years, or 18 months to 5 years. A maximum of 20 children is permitted in such centers. The service is available both to working and to nonworking mothers and provides some freedom for the nonworking mother who may otherwise be completely tied down to home and child care. These centers are usually related either to full-day day care programs or to nursery schools [Kahn & Kamerman, 1976, p. 157].

Substitute Care: Foster Care, Adoptions, Institutions

All industrialized countries find that they are required to provide substitute care for some percentage of their children in foster-family homes, adoptive homes, or institutions.

Hazel (1976), a member of the Council of Europe's Coordinated Research Group, which examined the use of substitute care in seventeen different European countries, summarized her experiences by noting that "In all the industrialized European countries there are children who can no longer remain in their own home with their parents because society is no longer willing to tolerate their conduct or because their parents are ill, separated, have disappeared or have neglected or ill-treated their children" (p. 310).

Given the limited availability of comparable statistics, it is hard to know whether or not the United States tends to employ substitute care more frequently than other similarly industrialized countries. The chronic problems that plague the foster-care system in the United States are not unique to us. Britain, with a supposedly more adequate social welfare problem, faces the same problems. In 1983, the British Association of Adoption and Foster Care Agencies presented evidence on this to the House of Commons Social Services Committee. The material showed that "too many children may come into care unnecessarily; too many children once in care stay in care too long; too many children in care are cared for in ways which are inappropriate to their needs" (British Association for Adoption and Fostering, 1983, pp. 12–13).'

The lack of adequate services for ethnic minority children and the disproportionate use of substitute care services for minority children is as much an English problem as it is an American problem (Roys, 1984).

Early in the century, adoption was of little importance as a child welfare service in Europe. However, as a result of the large number of children orphaned by two world wars, European countries became more interested in adoption. Legislation legalizing adoption was passed in countries where no such legislation had previously existed: in Denmark in 1923, in Britain in 1926, and in Portugal in 1967. Existing adoption laws were revised to give greater protection to the child and the adoptive parent. Current legislation in most European countries is, for the most part, similar to that in the United States (United Nations, 1953, 1956; 1963; Moore, 1968; Hoksbergan and Gokhale, 1986).

Unlike procedures in the United States, however, a foreign child adopted by a British citizen is automatically granted British citizenship. This ensures for the child a greater feeling of identification with the adoptive family and suggests that he or she has the same status as a natural child.

British child welfare legislation attempts to provide maximum protection to all parties in the adoptive relationship. "Since 1982 it has been illegal for anyone other than a local authority or an approved adoption society to make arrangements for the adoption of a child. The only exception to this rule is where a mother places her child for adoption with a close relative." (Hall, 1986, p. 58). Denmark stipulates that before an adoption order is granted, information shall be elicited as to whether a fee has been paid or is to be paid any of the interested parties. All adoptions are channeled through social agencies in Australia and Israel, and independent adoptions are legally outlawed.

The attitude toward religious preference in adoption tends to be permissive. In Denmark, there is no legal provision in the adoption law concerning the child's religion and no legal bar to placing a child of one religious affiliation with adoptive parents of another. In England, the mother may express a religious prefer-ence, which then determines the religious affiliation of the adoptive couple with whom the child is placed, but when unmarried mothers do not indicate a prefer-ence, the agency is permitted to place the child with a family of any religious affiliation. An Agnostics Adoption Society is available to offer service to those adoptive couples who are reluctant to declare a religious affiliation or who have none.

In England, as in the United States, the number of nonrelative adoptions has decreased. In 1968, 16,184 such adoptions were made in England. By 1984, the number had decreased to 3,683 (Hall, 1986, Appendix I, p. 74).

There is a general adoption imbalance throughout the world. There are too few children available for adoption in the developed countries and too many children needing parents in the underdeveloped countries. This has established a pressure and a rationale for intercountry adoptions and, at the same time, fuels opposition to such adoptions by nationals in the underdeveloped countries.

The shortage of children available for adoption is even greater in some Euro-pean countries than in the United States. Sweden and the Netherlands, having very few of their own children available for adoption, have been actively recruit-ing children for adoption from abroad. Sweden has established a special organiza-tion, the Council for Intercountry Adoption, to facilitate such adoptions. There were 2,888 petitions for adoption in Sweden in 1975. In 1,380 instances (48 per cent), the child was of Asian descent. In 4 per cent of the cases, the adopter was a single parent (Sveriges Officiella Statistik, 1976, p. 72). In addition to Sweden and The Netherlands other countries such as Denmark and West Germany have had more extensive experience with international adoption than does the U.S.A. Larger percentage of their adoptees come from abroad. Follow-up research in each of these countries comes to a consensual conclusion that such adoptions are, for the most part, successful, the children growing up well adjusted and the adoptive parents satisfied with these adoptions (Hoksbergan and Gokhale, 1986).

Part of the problem of children available for adoption in these countries results from the lower out-of-wedlock birth rates in these countries as compared with the United States. A two-year project conducted by the Alan Guttmacher Institute compared teenage sexual practices, pregnancy, and abortion rates along with public policy in the United States and five other developed countries—Sweden, Great Britain, France, the Netherlands, and Canada (Jones et al. 1985). White adolescent pregnancy rates in the United States were double that of their French and British peers and six times the rate of their Dutch peers. Adolescent abortion rates in the United States were also higher than for the other countries studied. The sexual activity level of teens was roughly the same in each of the countries studied, so that this factor did not explain the higher pregnancy and abortion rates in the United States. Maternity and welfare benefits provided the pregnant mother were even more generous for the most part in the other countries. The research accounted for the difference in teen pregnancy rates between the United States and other countries on the basis of the fact that sex edcuation and contra-ceptive services were more widespread and comprehensive in the other countries and that contraception was more consistently utilized by sexually active teens in the comparison countries (*New York Times* March 13, 1985). (See also Boethius, 1985).

In contrast with a pattern of premarital sexual activity among adolescents in the United States, Japanese, Chinese, and Korean adolescents manifested a pat-tern of premarital abstinence (Senderowitz & Pakman, 1985, p. 8).

In response to the universal problem of finding adoptive homes for special-needs children, other countries have developed specialized organizations.

And, as in the United States, special efforts have been made to recruit minority-group adoptive homes for racial minority children awaiting adoption. In 1975 nine London boroughs conducted a special project known as "Operation Soul Kids." An agency specializing in the adoptive placement of children with special needs, known as Parents for Children, has also been funded.

Parent to Parent Information on Adoption Services (PPIAS) is a group that was formed in Britain in 1971 by parents who had adopted hard-to-place children. As a self-help and mutual-support group, they act as a resource to prospective adoptive parents considering the adoption of a child with special needs. For instance, one of their members who has adopted an older child or a racial minority-group child might meet and discuss her experience with an applicant considering the adoption of such a child.

Some countries have been in advance of our own in dealing explicitly with the problem of disclosure of background information to adoptees. We previously noted (p. 581) that Finland, Scotland, and Israel permit adoptees to examine their birth records. The British Children Act of 1975 provided that children adopted after 1975 are entitled, on request, to a certified copy of the original birth record at eighteen years of age. A person adopted before 1975 can likewise obtain a copy of the birth document, but only after an interview with a counselor. An English organization called Jig-Saw is the counterpart of the American organization ALMA—concerned with the rights of adopted children and their search. Although adoptees in England over the "age of eighteen have the right to information about their birth records, fewer than expected have taken advantage of this" (Freeman, 1983, p. 643).

After a period when the adoptee in Israel had unqualified rights to inspect his or her adoption record on reaching age thirteen, the more recent legislation qualified such access. Currently, a "welfare officer is authorized but not required to allow the adoptee to inspect the adoption record" (Goldstein, 1983, p. 438). In describing the open record procedure in Israel, Jaffe (1982) points to comes interesting aspects. The procedure required that

> 45 days elapse between the date on which the adoptee formally requests to see his record and the date on which his request is granted . . . The waiting period is used by the Adoption Services to enable the chief adoption officer to read the case record in advance and to invite the adoptee for a conference to establish a relationship to understand his needs and to prepare him for any surprises he might find in his record. To discover that one was "found in a suitcase" or "abandoned by a prostitute" is not an easy thing to learn about one's past and the Adoption Service provides whatever support it can to soften the impact [pp. 90–91].

Research regarding the extent to which Israeli adoptees seek access to their files, which are available to them under the Adoption Statutes, indicates that only 6.6 per cent of the eligible adoptees actually exercised this option (Jaffe, 1982, p. 209).

Sweden has recognized the problem of "Search" for children conceived as a result of artificial insemination. The 1985 Act on Articifical Insemination by Donor recognizes the child's "right, when mature enough, to learn about the name and biodata of the biological father, i.e. the sperm donor does not have the right to lifelong anonymity." (Andersson 1986, p. 29).

Although the worldwide trend is toward the increasing use of foster-family care in preference to institutional care when substitute care is needed, there are wide differences in the proportion in which different substitute-care facilities are used. In 1973 there were 14,300 children in institutions in Indonesia and 2,000 in foster-family homes, and there were 10,000 children in institutions and 2,000 children in foster-family homes in Israel. In the Netherlands in the same year, there were 10,000 children in institutions and 9,500 in foster-family homes (United Nations, 1974, pp. 12–13).

Sweden, having made a definite effort to reduce the use of institutions for children, has 80 per cent of its children in substitute care, either in the homes of relatives or in foster-family care. The effort is made to place even seriously disturbed children and delinquents in foster-family care rather than in institutions. The orientation is toward minimum use of substitute care whenever possible (Hazel, 1974, p. 310).

And, as is true in this country, greater efforts are being made to provide adoptive homes for children in institutions. In Germany, the "popular magazine Brigette runs a series with large colour photographs captioned Holt Die Kinder aus den Heimen—get the children out of the institution"—the children featured being older or handicapped (Benet, 1976, p. 92).

Efforts have been made to use the institution as the locus for treating the whole family rather than the child only. Thus Ska, a "children's village" located not far from Stockholm, reorganized its program in 1972 so as to accommodate whole families rather than individual children. Some of the families in the treatment program include "a mother, father and seven children ages 3–15 years. The family has had extended contact with social welfare and child welfare authorities. A couple of the older children are drug users and the father has an alcohol problem." "Family composed of mother, father and three children ages 10–16 years: crises connected with the children's school truancy, vagabonding, glue sniffing. Father ill." The families, living in their own apartments in the institution, have continuing responsibility for the care of their children. The therapeutic work is with the family as a treatment unit (Borjeson, 1974).

Developing a stronger link between the institution and the community to which the child is being returned has gone further in some European countries than here. In Sweden, the institutional worker "may accompany the child when he returns home and may remain there all day or even overnight until he has settled down" (Hazel, 1975, p. 772). In France the institutional worker may continue to work with the child in the community after his or her return. In West Germany, the institution is used in deliberate integration with foster-family care:

> Disturbed children in care may first be admitted to a therapeutic institution where the staff seeks to understand and help them. At the same time, the institution acts as a center for the training and support of qualified foster families to whose care the children are gradually transferred. The whole process is carefully planned, the residential staff, the social worker and the foster parents working together as a team of which the child's parents may also be part . . . residential establishments acting like the hub of a wheel from which the [foster family] placements radiate like a series of outposts [Hazel, 1976, p. 324].

Some attempts have been made in Europe to develop distinctive types of institutions for dependent and neglected children. The most notable example is the "children's village," established originally in Austria by Hermann Gmeiner. The village consists of a series of ten to sixteen cottages, each with a "mother" and, ideally, nine children, both boys and girls, of various ages from babyhood to adolescence. Only those children who are healthy enough emotionally and physically to live in a family without receiving special attention are accepted. The "mother" is given a budget for each child and cares for the children as though they were her own. The children attend the local school and are a part of the local community. The mother buys food at the village store and the "family" may supplement the budget by planting and tending a kitchen garden. The mothers are carefully selected, undergo a four-month training period, and either are unmarried or are childless widows. The *Dorfleiter,* or village manager, provides the only "fathering" that is officially available. Familiar with each child in the village, he has the responsibility for advising the mothers and serving as a combination judge, mediator, and father confessor. Every village has a corps of "family helpers," often cottage mothers in training, who assist the mothers or substitute for them during time off or vacation or when they are ill. There is some evidence that a sense of family develops among the children in a particular cottage and that the movement is successful in achieving its aim of healthy child-rearing for many of the children it accepts.

The SOS Children's Federation, which sponsors the children's villages, has built about 222 such villages throughout the world and by 1985 had facilities in more than fifty-five countries on five continents.

Institutions for children in Europe include, as a key staff member, a professional known as an *educateur,* who has no counterpart in American institutions. The *educateur* has the responsibility of resocializing the child assigned to the institution, organizing the child's activity in such a way as to ensure changes in the child's behavior (*International Child Welfare Review,* 1971; Linton, 1969). The distinctive difference in the approach of the *educateur,* sometimes called an *orthopedagogue,* lies in the techniques he used for resocializing the child:

> [This may include use of] ceramics, painting, weaving, woodwork, metal craft, puppets and marionettes, home economics, interior design, music, dance, body movement and expression, hobbies, and physical and vocational re-education. In addition the *educateurs* are trained to use radio, television, and films, cultural events, holidays, birthdays, and sporting events as techniques for activating and re-educating the maladjusted child [Linton, 1969, p. 322].

The idea is to reach the child through meaningful activity that involves interaction between the child and the *educateur.*

Unlike the houseparent in this country, the *educateur* is not responsible for the maintenance of the child's living facilities. In France, some of the *educateurs* work with gangs in the slum areas and are employed in youth centers.

The European *educateur* function, with its emphasis on resocialization, has influenced the development of programs in this country. The Re-Ed (reeducational) experimental programs for disturbed children here are patterned on the *educateur* model.

The Unmarried Mother—The Out-of-Wedlock Child

Some of the legislation regarding the unmarried mother–out-of-wedlock child pair is more humane in the Scandinavian countries than in the United States. In Norway, for instance, the state, rather than the mother herself, takes the responsibility for establishing paternity. In Denmark, once the question of paternity is established and the father's contribution to the care of the child is determined, the mother is entitled to advance payments of the father's contribution from public funds; the authorities then undertake to recover the amount from the father. Such advance payments are also made to the divorced mother when the father defaults in making support payments. In these countries, once paternity has been established, the child's right to inherit from the father is also granted (Morrisey, 1968).

In Sweden a mandatory paternity action is instituted in nearly all cases of illegitimate births in which the father does not voluntarily acknowledge the child, and fathers are determined for 95 per cent of all children born out of wedlock. Once paternity is established, support obligations are rigidly enforced as an essential supplement to comprehensive social services.

Private agencies in France have been experimenting with housing for the unmarried mother and the illegitimate child. These are known as *hôtels maternelles*. While the mothers are working, infant nurses, and later kindergarten teachers, care for the child. The mothers pay for the child's upkeep and, in general, finance the maintenance of the home.

Britain has developed a somewhat similar arrangement: working mothers' hotels. The mother and the child live at the hotel for a period of a year or two after the birth of the baby. The hotel staff cares for the child while the mother goes out to work. The hotels are open to widowed mothers and deserted wives as well as unmarried mothers. Similar housing is available in Denmark (Wynn, 1964, p. 145).

New Zealand has a statutory provision that a child welfare worker must be notified, in confidence, in every case of illegitimate birth. This gives the social worker the opportunity of making an offer of help to every unmarried mother (Anderson, 1963, p. 4).

Recognizing that from its start in life, the out-of-wedlock child is handicapped by virtue of its lack of a father's protecton, European countries provide for the appointment of a public guardian to the child (Wimperes, 1960, pp. 333–340). In Germany, the Local Youth Board provides a guardian at the birth of the child to assist the mother and protect the child through the development of a personal relationship with the family. In Sweden, the child welfare guardian "sees that the child receives the financial benefits to which he is entitled and can start executive proceedings against a father who neglects to pay maintenance" (Wester, 1970, p. 5). As a consequence of the advocacy activities of such guardians, paternity has been established for an estimated 90 per cent of out-of-wedlock children in Sweden. In Finland, a "communal godfather" is appointed for each illegitimate child. Sometimes the appointed guardian is a professional social worker; sometimes he or she is a lay volunteer selected by the child welfare board. The trend has been toward reducing the guardian's control over the family and making this appointment voluntary rather than automatic. Unmarried parenthood is sharply stigmatized in China. No income support is available to the unmarried mother. "Such mothers were under considerable pressure to marry or have the child adopted or fostered" (Dixon, 1981, p. 317) (see also Dixon and Kim, 1985).

The social disorganization resulting from rapid urbanization of some African cities that do not have the resources necessary to deal with such internal migration makes for increases in the out-of-wedlock births. This results "in the abandonment of many babies in such places as public toilets, dustbins and street corners" (Okeahialam, 1984, p. 71).

Organization of Child Welfare Services

One of the most persistent problems faced by American child welfare is the coordination of the work of the many different agencies dealing with various aspects of the child's situation. The social agencies in Paris have been experimenting with a plan to meet this problem. The city is divided into districts. All the public and private agencies in the district offering family service coordinate their efforts under a combined staff. The combined staff, in effect, forms a new agency that represents all of the agencies. The workers in the coordinating group remain staff members of the agencies that employ them, but they form a unified social-work department offering the family services in the district. The workers of the united agency elect a director—usually an outstanding, experienced worker—to coordinate the work of the members of the combined family-service unit (Schorr, 1965).

In France, some 25 per cent of all social workers are general, all-purpose workers, similar, perhaps, to our rural social workers. Called *polyvalent social workers,* and sometimes called *family social workers,* they cover all geographic areas: "These social workers, mostly female, are trained in a system which combines basic social work with some elements of public health nursing. The relevant law requires coverage by one polyvalent worker of each sector, a geographic area with a population group of some 5,000" (Kahn & Kamerman, 1976, p. 333).

A comprehensive review of social welfare programs in Britain by the Seebohm Committee (1969) made radical suggestions for total reorganization of the pattern of service. The proposal, adopted by Parliament in 1970, was to unite all government-supported social workers in a community in one department under their own administrative control and supervision. Service would be offered by a team of ten to twelve social workers through area offices serving populations of 50,000–100,000 people. Separate child-welfare services would merge with other personal services to individuals and families to form a comprehensive, community-based, family-oriented agency offering a wide variety of services. The objective of the reorganization of British social services was to meet the total requirements of the individual or family, rather than a limited set of symptoms, by providing community-based and family-oriented services that are available to all. The objective was to provide "a single door on which anyone might knock for help with confidence of getting it" (Gandy, 1977, p. 47).

In the Soviet Union, social services are more closely tied to social insurance than they are in the United States. This permits a much wider access to family problems than is true for social insurance agencies in the United States. Similarly, Australia has organized a special casework service within its general social security administration, and French social security agencies employ social workers to perform *polyvalent* social duties, which include family casework and the handling of problems with which families may be faced. France, too, combines social services and the social insurances:

> One of the characteristic features of the French social security system is that it links a program of health and social services to the agencies that administer benefit payments. That means that these organizations are not merely administrative and financial agencies, but that they use part of their resources to activate a true program of services for the benefit of their members [Laroque, 1969, p. 182].

The French family-allowance system, for instance, makes available such services as homemaker service, day care, and family holidays to family allowance recipients (Rodgers, 1968, p. 317).

The Soviet Union and other European countries organize their child welfare services in a pattern different from ours. In these countries, all social service functions are considered ancillary to some other primary concern. Thus family counseling and service for young children are provided by health agencies; those for older children and young people, by educational agencies.

Although no particular, explicitly designated professional social-work group exists in the Soviet Union, the functions that the social worker performs for the child are just as necessary there as elsewhere. In the absence of a profession of social work, these functions are performed principally by the school-teacher, the nurse, and the trade union (Madison, 1960, 1963, 1964b, 1968). The teachers have the responsibility for being aware not only of the educational progress of the child but of psychosocial development as well. In discharging this responsibility, the Soviet teacher is aided by the fact that he or she moves with the child through the first four years of schooling. The teacher visits with the parents regularly in the home and in the school to discuss problems and to give advice regarding the upbringing of the child. The schools may recommend to the local district soviet government the removal of children from the care of their parents (in cases of neglect) and may be asked by the local government to consider adoptive homes for children who are available for adoption. The work of the teacher is supplemented by the children's inspector, who is also an employee of the educational system. He or she is responsible for dealing with truancy and behavior problems, investigating complaints of child neglect, and supervising the placement of children on the very few occasions when foster care is employed.

Child welfare functions are performed by the "patronage" or "social" nurses, operating out of district clinics, each clinic composed of a team of one pediatrician and two patronage nurses responsible for service to 1,000 children: "Since the team serves the same children throughout their childhood and adolescence both in their home and in the clinics, it becomes thoroughly acquainted with them, their families, and their total life situation" (Madison, 1963, p. 322). The nurses are primarily concerned with the health problems of the children, but they also have the responsibility of helping the family with the social and emotional problems encountered by the child as well as with problems of housing, financial assistance, guardianship, and so on: "It is compulsory for a nurse and a doctor attached to the local infant welfare clinic to visit the child in his home on the day he leaves the hospital or on the following day. They examine the state of health and living conditions of the newborn baby and give advice to the mother" (U.S. Department of Health, Education, and Welfare, 1969, p. 103). The district clinic is the central organization to which the family relates in meeting the physical and health needs of the child throughout childhood. This system provides not only integrated care but also continuity of care.

The work of the teacher and the patronage nurse is supplemented by the trade unions, which have been given the responsibility for discharging some of the "helping" functions in connection with social problems faced by families of union members. The trade unions have developed child welfare programs and attempt to involve their members as "patrons" for children who need help:

> The "good" trade union committee concern themselves not only with providing summer camps for the children of the employees but also with giving emotional supportive help to the widow who is losing control over her adolescent son or to the unmarried mother who is rearing her youngster single-handedly [Madison, 1964, p. 200].

More emphasis is placed on the use of volunteers in direct work with parents around parent–child problems. A teacher concerned about a child might request that members of the union committee in the plant where the father works talk to the father. The local soviet may ask a "good" mother to make a visit to give advice to the family.

Comradeship courts in factories, housing blocks, or collective farms, with "judges" elected by their peers, use "measures of social pressure" to "help" neglectful or ineffective parents become more competent. The comradeship courts stand behind parents' committees made up of neighbors who take the initial responsibility for seeing that parents adequately care for their children. Parents' committees "are composed of parents who have been successful in raising their own children" (Veillard-Cybulska, 1965, p. 133). They help the parent to relate to the child and offer practical assistance, such as seeing that the children attend school and helping an overburdened mother with child care.

All the child-care manuals emphasize the fact that all citizens have a concern for all children. What might be regarded as meddling in someone else's affairs in the United States is an act of good citizenship in the Soviet Union. It is, in effect, an implementation of the principle of child advocacy.

Many European countries demonstrate a greater willingness to involve local lay leadership and volunteers in the responsibility for child care. For instance, in Sweden, the child welfare boards take the responsibility for major services in the local community. Members of local child-welfare boards are judges, teachers, physicians, and nurses, who serve as citizens rather than in their professional capacity. The board has the right to employ professional social workers to implement its decisions, but it has the ultimate responsibility for seeing that child welfare services are provided to any child in the community who needs them. In Sweden, the social welfare boards have an advocacy-social action function: "They must try first of all to influence children's living conditions in general. They are to see to it that there are playgrounds, day nurseries, leisure time activities and so on" (Elmer, 1975, p. 121).

Other countries make greater use of lay helpers and volunteers than we do in our child welfare programs. Associated with this approach is a greater emphasis on decentralization and consumer participation in service delivery. In Yugoslavia, great emphasis is placed on the principle of "solidarity and mutuality" in social policy making and service delivery in the work place and the neighborhood (Smolik & Krikovic, 1977).

Nakamura (1977) reports that there are some 160,000 "volunteer workers in child welfare" in Japan. Commissioned by the Minister of Health and Welfare, they are selected from "among those people who are considered mature, with relevant life experiences" and are expected to serve a term of three years. During the 1972 fiscal year, such "volunteer workers in child welfare" dealt with 243, 403, family problem situations (p. 199).

As in the Soviet Union, many of the child welfare functions are implemented in China by members of workers' committees at the place of employment or by residents' committees in the neighborhood. *Peking Review* (November 3, 1978) notes that residents' committees elected by neighborhood residents "promote family planning and are smooth hands at mediating in petty squabbles and settling family bickerings." For example:

> An old man was anxious to have a grandson. He was disappointed because his daughter-in-law gave birth to two granddaughters for him. He often found himself

locked in one altercation after another with her. Pien Ai-hua, member of the residents' committee in charge of women's affairs, patiently persuaded the old man to do away with the decrepit idea of looking up to men and down on women. Meanwhile she asked the daughter-in-law to respect the old man and take good care of him. Her mediation paid off: Quarrels between the two began to simmer down.

Intrusions by co-workers and neighbors into parent-child relationships are sanctioned and there is clear rejection of the idea that any special training is required in providing such "help" (see also Sidel, 1977; Dixon 1981; Mok, 1983).

In Holland, many dependent and/or delinquent children are placed under the supervision of a family guardian, a private person of good conduct who volunteers to devote his time to helping the child and the family without pay. Organizations of family guardians serve as a link between the volunteer and the juvenile judge and also recruit, train, and supervise family guardians. The family guardian is generally assigned one or two children and their families. Although there is some difficulty in recruiting family guardians, most of the child welfare experts note with surprise that many people still volunteer for such work and are very consistent in discharging their responsibility. As a matter of fact, there is less turnover among family guardians than among professional social workers; families assigned a family guardian have greater continuity of care. A report from the Dutch Ministry of Justice points out that the activity of the volunteer family guardian is "not typical casework. It is rather a matter of pedagogic influencing through a confidential relationship. The family guardian represents a bit of healthy society within the family." The help offered may vary "from practical advice connected with the choice of school or a profession to serious, penetrating talks" (Rood-DeBoer, 1966, p. 22).

In Denmark, volunteers are used as supervising guardians to assist the family with advice and guidance in matters relating to children. And in Poland, "social guardians" are appointed to offer assistance to families in trouble in an effort to "improve the financial, social, and educative condition, cooperate in the fight against alcoholism, hooliganism, prostitution, ill treatment of children, and against all social scourges" (Veillard-Cybulska, 1966). The People's Councils in Rumania, composed by lay volunteers, perform similar functions, offering "legal and social assistance services taking the form of surveillance, primarily of a preventative nature, which intervene effectively only if and when the physical development, education, upbringing, vocational training of the child are endangered by the improper behavior of the parents or their negligence manifested in its upbringing" (United Nations, 1967, pp. 51–52).

Supranational Child Welfare

There are organizations that offer child welfare services across national boundaries. International Social Service (ISS) conducts an intercountry adoption program: the International Union for Child Welfare, publishers of the *International Child Welfare Review,* conducts international child-welfare seminars and conferences and stimulates child welfare research; the United Nations International Children's Emergency Fund, better known as UNICEF, is active in combating disease and hunger, has equipped maternal and child health centers throughout the world, has inoculated millions of children against a variety of infectious diseases, has distributed billions of pounds of food to hungry children, and has trained thousands of midwives. The United Nations Bureau of Social Affairs collects and disseminates information regarding child welfare problems throughout the world; various agencies of the United Nations offer technical assistance to nations in developing their child welfare services in a demonstration of international mutual aid.

In 1959 the United Nations adopted a Declaration of the Rights of the Child, which explicitly recognizes the right of the child to grow up with affection and acceptance with parents in a home that provides adequately for his or her physical, social, emotional, and spiritual needs. It stipulates, furthermore, that the child should be given special protection by the community against all forms of neglect, abuse, and exploitation. The Declaration of the Rights of the Child stands as an explicit statement of what the people of the world hope they can achieve for their children.

A PERSONAL COMMENT

Throughout the text, the writers have consciously and deliberately refrained from intruding themselves into the material. At this point, they are taking the liberty of editorializing. The impulse to make a personal comment stems from a firm commitment to child-welfare social work, the values for which it speaks, and the task it is asked to do. It stems from a conviction that child welfare workers are engaged in one important sector of the most significant task of any community: the task of rearing the next generation. Nothing—not all our building, not all our production, not all our scientific advances—can equal in importance the work of helping, in whatever way, to ensure that our children, who constitute our eternity, grow to adulthood healthy in mind, body, and spirit. Socrates, at his wisest, noted this:

> If I could get to the highest place in Athens, I would life my voice and say, "What mean ye, fellow citizens, that ye turn every stone to scrape wealth together and take so little care of your children to whom ye must one day relinquish all?"

The most meritorious of societies is the one that welcomes the question, "Is it well with the child?" and answers, truthfully, "All is indeed well."

We recognize that given our present knowledge and technology and limited resources we often cannot do as much as we seek to do. But the task given to child welfare social work is eminently important and eminently worth doing. "If it is not given to us to complete the task, neither can we abandon it."

The Talmud, emphasizing the importance of each individual life, says, "If, during the course of your own life, you have saved one life, it is as if you have saved all mankind." Few occupations give us the opportunity of participating in the saving of a life. The everyday work of the child welfare worker is concerned with just that—reclaiming a child for life. It is to be expected that such a task would be very difficult. It is also to be expected that there are few, if any, tasks that offer the same degree of satisfaction and the same sense of accomplishment.

The task is large and difficult. The aims and hopes have to be commensurately modest. The medieval medical dictum is applicable and appropriate here: "To cure some time, to relieve often, to comfort always."

The red wine of life, the passion in the encounter with children denied a childhood, needs to be included here as an addition to the factual data regarding child welfare services. It is included in the child welfare worker's job.

A. K.
J. A. M.

Bibliography

Anderson, Lewis G. "Child Welfare in New Zealand." *Indian Journal of Social Work,* 24, 1 (April 1963).

Andersson, Gunilla. "The Adopting and Adopted Swedes and Their Contemporary Society", pp. 23–34 in *Adoption in Worldwide Perspective.* R.A.C. Hoksbergen and S. D. Gokhale (Eds). Berwyn: Swets North America, 1986.

Bayh, Marvella. "Russians and Japanese Ahead in Day Care." *Voice,* 3, 2 (February 1970), 3–4.

Bell, Cynthia. "Family Law: Notes form China." *Social Work,* 28 (May–June 1983), 239–240.

Benet, Mary K. *The Politics of Adoption.* New York: The Free Press, 1976.

Boethius, Carl G. "Sex Education in Swedish Schools: The Facts and the Fiction." *Family Planning Perspectives,* 17, 6 (November–December 1985), 267–279.

Boli-Bennett, John, and John Meyer. "The Ideology of Childhood and the State: Rules Distinguishing Children in National Constitutions." *American Sociological Review,* 13 (December 1978), 797–812.

Borjeson, Bergt. *Reestablishing an Identity: Family Treatment at Ska Children's Village.* Stockholm: Child Welfare Board, 1974.

Bradley, Candice. "The Sexual Division of Labor and the Value of Children." *Behavior Science Research,* 19, 1–4, (1984–1985).

Bradshaw, Jonathon and David Piachaud. *Child Support in the European Community.* London: Redford Square Press, 1980.

Brathholm, Anders, and Wilhelm Matheson. "The Rights of the Child of Norway," pp. 537–600, in *Law and the Status of the Child,* Vol. 4. Ed. Anna M. Pappas. New York: United Nations Institute for Training and Research, 1983.

British Association for Adoption and Fostering. "BAAF Evidence to Select Committee." *Adoption and Fostering,* 7, 1 (1983), 11–17.

Central Union for Child Welfare in Finland. *Child Welfare in Finland.* Helsinki: Central Union for Child Welfare, 1968.

Christopherson, R. J. "Two Approaches to the Handling of Child Abuse: A Comparison of the English and Dutch Systems," *Child Abuse and Neglect,* 54, (1981) 369–73.

Clifford, W. A. *Primer of Social Casework in Africa.* New York: Oxford University Press, 1966.

Cornia, Giovanni A. "A Summary and Interpretation of Evidence" p. 211–212 in *The Impact of the World Recession on Children.* R. Jolly, and G. Cornia (Eds.). New York: Pergamon Press, 1984.

David, Henry P., and Robert McIntyre. *Reproductive Behavior: Central and Eastern European Experience.* New York: Springer, 1981.

DeDuran, Sonia. "Child Legislation in Columbia," pp. 101–181, in *Law and the Status of the Child.* Ed. Anna M. Pappas. New York: United Nations Institute for Training and Research, 1983.

Dessau, Dorothy. *Glimpses of Social Work in Japan—Revisited.* Kyoto: Social Workers' International Club of Japan, 1968.

Dexter, Margaret, and Wally Harbert. *The Home Help Services.* New York: Tavistock, 1983.

Dixon, John, and Hyung S. Kim (Eds.). *Social Welfare in Asia.* London: Croom Helm, 1985.

Dixon, John H. *The Chinese Welfare System: 1949–1979.* New York: Praeger, 1987.

Dixon, John H. "The Chinese Workers' Social Assistance System, 1949–79.," *International Social Work,* 24, 1 (1981), 1–13.

Edfeldt, Ake W. *Violence Toward Children—An International Formulative Study.* Stockholm: Radda Barnen, 1979.

Elmer, Ake. "Sweden's Model System of Social Service Administration," pp. 196–218, in *Meeting Human Needs,* Vol. 1. Ed. Daniel Thurz and Joseph Vigilante. Beverly Hills, Cal.: Sage, 1975.

Ferge, Zsuzsa. "Hungary," in *Family Policy.* Ed. Sheila B. Kamerman and Alfred J. Kahn. New York: Columbia University Press, 1978.

Freeman, Michael. "The Rights of the Child in England," pp. 601–674, in *Law and the Status of the Child,* Vol. II. Ed. Anna M. Pappas. New York: United Nations Institute for Training and Research, 1983.

Gandy, John M. "Scottish Governmental Reorganization and Human Service Delivery by Teams," pp. 33–54, in *Meeting Human Needs,* Vol. 2. Ed. Daniel Thurz and Joseph Vigilante, Beverly Hills, Cal.: Sage, 1977.

Garmezy, Edith. "Meeting the Problems of Illegitimacy—The Danish Way," in *Effective Services for Unmarried Parents and Their Innovative Community Approaches.* New York: National Council on Illegitimacy, 1968.

Gold, Rachel B., and Asta M. Kenny, *Paying for Maternity Care,* New York: Alan Guttmacher Institute, 1985.

Goldstein, Stephen. "The Rights of the Children in Israel," pp. 411–93 in *Law and the Status of the Child, Vol. II,* Ed. Anna M. Pappas. New York: United Nations Institute for Training and Research, 1983.

Hall, Tony. "The Adoption Revolution in Britan," pp. 57–78 in *Adoption in Worldwide Perspective.* R.A.C. Hoksbergen and S. D. Gokhale (Eds.). Berwyn: Swets North America Inc., 1986.

Hansan, Saiyid Z. "Social Security in India: Limited Resources—Unlimited Need," in *Social Security in International Perspective.* Ed. Shirley Jenkins.

Havelka, J., and S. Radvanova. "Czechoslovak Law and the Status of the Child," pp. 203–314. *Law and the Status of the Child.* Ed., Anna M. Pappas. New York: United Nations Institute for Training and Research, 1983.

Hazel, Nancy. "Child Placement Policies in England, Belgium and Sweden." *Social Work Today,* 5 (August 1974), 309–311.

Hazel, Nancy. "Residential Care as the Key to Fostering—The German Experience." *Social Work Today,* 5 (March 1975), 771–772.

Hazel, Nancy. "Child Placement Policies: Some European Comparisons." *British Journal of Social Work,* 6, 3 (1976), 315–326.

Henshaw, Stanley K. "Induced Abortion: A Worldwide Perspective," *Family Planning Perspectives,* 18.6 (November–December, 1986), 250–254.

Henriksen, Hildur V., and Hariet Holter. "Norway," in *Family Policy.* Ed. Sheila B. Kamerman and Alfred J. Kahn. New York: Columbia University Press, 1978.

Hermann, Alice, and Sandor Komlosi. "Early Child Care in Hungary." *Early Child Development and Care,* 1 (November 1972), whole issue.

Hewlett, Sylvia A. *A Lesser Life: They Myth of Women's Liberation in America,* New York: William Morrow, 1986.

Hoksbergen, R. A. C. and S. D. Gokhale. *Adoption in Worldwide Perspective.* Berwyn: Swets North America Inc., 1986.

Imbrogno, Salvatore, and Nadia Imbrogno. "Marriage and Family in the USSR: Changes are Emerging." *Social Casework* (February 1986), 90–100.

International Child Welfare Review. Special Issue—"The *Educateur*" (February 1971).

International Child Welfare Review. "Born in a Foreign Country; Adopted in Denmark." *International Child Welfare Review* (March 1978).

International Social Security Association. *The Role of Social Services in Social Security: Trends and Perspectives.* Geneva, 1974.

Jaffe, Elezer, D. *Child Welfare in Israel.* New York: Praeger, 1982.

Johnson, Jeanette. "Vasectomy—An International Appraisal." *Family Planning Perspectives,* 15, 1 (January–February 1983), 45–48.

Jones, Elise F. et al. "Teenage Pregnancies in Developed Countries; Determinants and Policy Duplication." *Family Planning Perspectives,* 17, 2 (March–April 1985), 53–63.

Kahn, Alfred et al. *Neighborhood Information Centers—A Study and Some Proposals.* New York: Columbia University School of Social Work, 1966.

Kahn, Alfred, and Sheila B. Kamerman. *Child Care Programs in Nine Countries.* Washington, D.C.: U.S. Department of Health, Education, and Welfare, Publication No. OUD 30080, 1975a.

Kahn, Alfred, and Sheila B. Kamerman. *Not for the Poor Alone—European Social Services.* Philadelphia: Temple University Press, 1975b.

Kahn, Alfred, and Sheila B. Kamerman. *Social Services in International Perspectives—The Emergence of the Sixth System.* Washington, D.C.: U.S. Government Printing Office, 1976.

Kahn, Alfred, and Sheila B. Kamerman. *Income Transfers for Families with Children—An Eight Country Study.* Philadelphia: Temple University Press, 1983a.

Kahn, Alfred J., and Sheila Kamerman. "Income Maintenance Wages and Family Income—Some Lessons for the United States from Other Countries." *Public Welfare* 40 (Fall 1983b), 23–48.

Kahn, Alfred J. and Sheila B. Kamerman, "Income Transfers and The Mother-Only Families in Eight Countries." *Social Service Review,* 57, 3 (September 1983c), 448–464.

Kalvesten, Arina-Lisa. "Changes in Sweden." *Adoption and Fostering,* 95, 1 (1979), 41–43.

Kamerman, Sheila B. "Eight Countries: Cross National Perspectives on Child Abuse and Neglect." *Children Today,* 4 (May–June 1975), 34–40.

Kamerman, Sheila B., and Alfred J. Kahn. "Who's Taking Care of Our Children?" New York: Columbia University School of Social Work, October 1978, mimeo, eight pp.

Kamerman, Sheila B. "Work and Family in Industrialized Societies." *Signs: Journal of Women in Culture and Society* (Summer 1979).

Kamerman, Sheila B., and Alfred J. Kahn. "Comparative Analysis in Family Policy: A Case Study." *Social Work* 24 (November 1979), 506–512.

Kamerman, Sheila, and Alfred Kahn. *Child Care, Family Benefits and Working Parents—a Study in Comparative Policy.* New York: Columbia University Press, 1981.

Konrad, George. *The Caseworker.* Harcourt Brace Jovanovich, 1974.

Krebs, Edith, and Margarete Schwartz. "Austria," in *Family Policy.* Ed. Sheila B. Kamerman and Alfred J. Kahn. New York: Columbia University Press, 1978.

Landman, Lynn C. "Birth Control in India: The Carrot and the Rod." *Family Planning Perspectives,* 9, 3 (May–June 1977), 101–110.

Laroque, Pierre. "Social Security in France," in *Social Security in International Perspective.* Ed. Shirley Jenkins. New York: Columbia University Press, 1969.

Leissner, Aryeh. *Family Advice Services.* Essex, England: Longman Group Ltd., 1967.

Lindstrom, Marita V. "Finland: Communal Control of Social Services," pp. 129–150, in *Meeting Human Needs,* Vol. 2. Ed. Daniel Thurz and Joseph Vigilante. Beverly Hills, Cal.: Sage, 1977.

Linton, Thomas. "The European Educateur Model—An Alternative-Effective Approach to the Mental Health of Children." *Journal of Special Education,* 3, 4 (Winter 1969), 319–327.

Loening, W.E.K. "Child abuse among the Zulus: A People in Cultural Transition." *Child Abuse and Neglect,* 5 (1981), 3–7.

Macussen, Ernst. *Social Welfare in Denmark.* Copenhagen: Det Danske Selskab, 1980.

Madison, Bernice. "Contributions and Problems of Soviet Welfare Institutions." *Social Problems,* 7, 4 (Spring 1960).

Madison, Bernice. "Welfare Services for Children in the Soviet Union, 1945–1963." *Child Welfare,* 42, 7 (July 1963).

Madison, Bernice. "Canadian Family Allowances and Their Major Social Implications." *Journal of Marriage and Family Living,* 26, 2 (May 1964a).

Madison, Bernice. "Social Welfare: Soviet Model." *Social Service Review,* 38, 2 (June 1964b).

Madison, Bernice. *Social Welfare in the Soviet Union.* Stanford, Cal.: Stanford University Press, 1968.

Madison, Bernice. "Soviet Income Maintenance Policy for the 1970's." *Journal of Social Policy,* 2, 2 (April 1973), 97–117.

Madison, Bernice. "Social Services for Families and Children in the Soviet Union Since 1967." *Child Welfare*, 53, 7 (July 1974), 423–434.

Madison, Bernice. "Social Services Administration in the U.S.S.R.," pp. 241–280, in *Meeting Human Needs*, Vol. 1. Ed. Daniel Thurz and Joseph Vigilante, Beverly Hills, Cal.: Sage, 1975.

Madison, Bernice. "Social Services for Women: Problems and Priorities," pp. 307–332, in *Women in Russia*. Ed. Dorothy Atkinson, Alexander Dallin, and Gail W. Lapidus. Stanford, Cal.: Stanford University Press, 1977a.

Madison, Bernice. *Soviet Income Maintenance Programs in the Struggle Against Poverty*. Washington, D.C.: Kennan Institute for Advanced Russian Studies, 1977b. Mimeo, 92 pp.

McAuley, Alastair. *Economic Welfare in the Soviet Union—Poverty, Living Standards and Inequality*. Madison: University of Wisconsin Press, 1979.

McGhee, Charles L. "Child Abuse in the Federal Republic of Germany." *Victimology: An Educational Journal*, 6 (1981), 1–4.

McGhee, Charles L. "Responses to Child Abuse in World Perspective." *Victimology: An International Journal*, 10, 1–4 (1985), 140–162.

McKie, Eric. *Venture in Faith*. Liverpool: Liverpool and District Family Service Unit, 1963.

Miller, Bette S. "Background document Prepared for International Union of Child Welfare." Geneva, Switzerland. August 1978. Mimeo unpublished, 39 pp.

Minkoff, Jack, and Lynn Turgeon. "Income Maintenance in Eastern Europe." *Social Policy* (March–April 1976), 33–45.

Mok, Bong-Ho. "In the Service of Socialism: Social Welfare in China." *Social Work*, 28 (July–August 1983), 269–272.

Moore, Joyce. "Adoption in Denmark." *Child Adoption*, 54 (1968).

Morisey, Patricia Garland. "From Scandinavia to the Urban Ghetto—Implication of Scandinavian Welfare Programs for Services to Unwed Mothers," in *Effective Services for Unmarried Parents and Their Children—Innovative Community Approaches*. New York: National Council on Illegitimacy, 1968.

Moskoff, William. "Divorce in the U.S.S.R." *Journal of Marriage and the Family* (May 1983), 419–425.

Mouton, Pierre. *Social Security in Africa—Trends, Problems and Prospects*. Geneva: International Labor Office, 1975.

Muhua, Chen. "Birth Planning in China." *Family Planning Perspectives*, 11, 6 (November–December 1979), 348–353.

Nakamura, Sumiko. "Japan: National Perfectural and Local Social Services," pp. 197–219, in *Meeting Human Needs*, Vol 2. Ed. Daniel Thurz and Joseph Vigilante. Beverly Hills, Cal.: Sage, 1976.

Neipris, Joseph. "Social Service in Israel—A Review of Programmes and Policies." *Journal of Jewish Communal Services*, 47, 4 (Summer 1971), 289–315.

Nordstrom, Margarita. "Social Home Help Services in Sweden," in *Readings in Homemaker Services*. New York: National Council for Homemaker Services, 1969.

Nwako, Festus. "Child Abuse Syndrom in Nigeria." *International Surgery*, 59 (November–December, 1974), 613–615.

Okeahialam, Theodore C. "Child Abuse in Nigeria." *Child Abuse and Neglect*, 8 (1984), 69–73.

Organization for Economic Cooperation and Development. *Social Expenditures 1960–1990u*, Paris: O.E.C.D., 1985.

Orlova, Nina V. "The Protection of Children's Rights and Interests in the U.S.S.R." *International Child Welfare Review*, 23, 4 (October 1969), 15–21.

Palmer, John L., and Isabel V. Sawhill (Eds.). *The Reagan Experiment*. Washington, D.C.: The Urban Institute Press, 1982.

Peltoniemi, Teuvo. "Child Abuse and Physical Punishment of Children in Finland." *Child Abuse and Neglect*, 7 (1983), 33–36.

Philip, A. F. *Family Failure*. London: Faber & Faber, Ltd., 1963.

Population Information Program. *Barrier Method*. Population Reports Series HNO6 Baltimore, Md. Population Information Program, Johns Hopkins University, 1982.

Progress Publishers. *Soviet Legislation on Children's Rights*. Moscow: Progress Publishers, 1982.

Radin, Norma. "Preschool Programs of the U.S.S.R." *Child Welfare*, 49, 1 (January 1970), 29–36.

Reifen, D. "Legal Protection of Children in Sexual Assult Cases," pp. 141–152 in *Child Abuse*. Ed. A. Carmi and H. Zimrin. Berlin: Springer Verlag, 1984.

Rodgers, Barbara N. et al. *Comparative Social Administration*. New York: Atherton Press, 1968.

Rood-DeBoer, M. *Child Care in the Netherlands*. The Hague: National Foundation for Child Welfare, 1966.

Rosa, Jean-Jacques (Ed.). *The World Crises in Social Security*. San Francisco: Institute for Contemporary Studies, 1982.

Rosen, Sumner M., David Fanshel, and Mary E. Lutz (Eds). *Pace of the Nation—1987—Statistical Supplement to the 18th Edition of the Encyclopedia of Social Work*. Silver Springs, Md.: National Association of Social Workers, 1987.

Rosenthal, Albert H. *The Social Programs of Sweden—A Search for Security in a Free Society*. Minneapolis: University of Minnesota Press, 1967.

Roys, Phillip. "Ethnic Minorities and the Child Welfare System." *International Journal of Social Psychiatry*, 30, 1–2 (Spring 1984), 102–118.

Scaberne, Bronislav. "Child and Youth Welfare in Yugoslavia." *International Child Welfare Review*, 23, 1 (October 1969), 22–35.

Schaefer, Dieter. "Federal Republic of Germany, Report III" in *Cross National Studies of Social Service Systems*. A. Kahn, Editor. New York: Columbia University School of Social Work, 1976.

Schorr, Alvin. *Social Security and Social Services in France*. U.S. Department of Health, Education, and Welfare, Social Security Administration Research Report No. 7. Washington, D.C.: U.S. Government Printing Office, 1965.

Scott, Hilda. "Women's Place in Socialist Society: The Case of Eastern Europe." *Social Policy*, 7 (March–April 1977), 32–85.

Seebohm, Frederic, Chairman. *Report of the Committee on Local Authority and Allied Personal Social Service*. London: Her Majesty's Stationery Office, 1969.

Senderowitz, Judith, and John M. Pakman. *Adolescent Fertility: Worldwide Concerns*. Washington, D.C.: Population Reference Bureau, 1985.

Sicault, George. *The Needs of Children*. New York: The Free Press, 1963.

Sidel, Ruth. *Women and Child Care in China*. New York: Hill and Wang, 1972.

Sidel, Ruth. "People Serving People: Human Services in the People's Rupublic of China," pp. 163–196, in *Meeting Human Needs*, Vol. 2. Ed. Daniel Thurz and Joseph Vigilante. Beverly Hills, Cal.: Sage, 1976.

Sidel, Ruth, and Victor Sidel. "The Human Services in China." *Social Policy*, 2, 6 (March–April 1972), 25–34.

Simanis, Joseph. "Recent Changes in Russian Social Security." *Social Security Bulletin*, 35, 12 (October 1972).

Sivard, Ruth. *World Military and Social Expenditures—1985*, Washington, D.C.: World Priorities, 1985.

Smolik-Krikovic, Nada. "Yugoslavian Self-managing Communities," pp. 151–161, in *Meeting Human Needs*, Vol. 2. Ed. Daniel Thurz and Joseph Vigilante. Beverly Hills, Cal.: Sage, 1977.

Solheim, Joan S. "A Cross-Cultural Examination of the Use of Corporal Punishment on Children: A Focus on Sweden and the United States," *Child Abuse and Neglect*, 6 (1982), 147–154.

Spivey, W. Allen. "Problems and Paradoxes in Economic and Social Policies in Modern Welfare States." *The Annals of the American Academy of Political and Social Science*, 479 (May 1985), 14–30.

Sveriges Officiella Statistik. *Social Varden 1975*. Stockholm: Statistiska Centralbyran, 1976.

Tchibinda, Jean, and Narcisse Mayetela. "The Rights of the Child in the People's Republic of the Congo," pp. 183–220, in *Law and the Status of the Child, Vol. 1*, Ed. Anna M. Pappas. New York: United Nations Institute for Training and Research, 1983.

Thursz, Daniel, and Joseph Vigilante. *Meeting Human Needs, Vol. 1: An Overview of Nine Countries*. Beverly Hills, Cal.: Sage, 1975.

Thursz, Daniel, and Joseph Vigilante. *Meeting Human Needs, Vol. 2: Additional Perspectives from Thirteen Countries*. Beverly Hills, Cal.: Sage, 1977.

Tietze, Christopher. *Induced Abortion—A World Wild Review*. New York:: The Population Council of New York, 1983.

Tietze, Christopher, and Stanley Henshaw. *Induced Abortion—A World Review—1986*. New York: Alan Guttmacher Institute, 1986.

Titmuss, Richard. *Developing Social Policy in Conditions of Rapid Change—The Role of Social Work*. 16th International Conference on Social Welfare. The Hague, August 1972, Mimeo.

Townsend, Peter. "Why Are the Many Poor." *International Journal of Health Services*, 16, 1(1986), 1–32.

Tulkanova, V. N. and E. Azarova. *Soviet Legislation on Children's Rights*. Moscow: Progress Publisher, 1982.

Uhr, Carl G. *Sweden's Social Security System*. U.S. Department of Health, Education, and Welfare, Social Security Administration Research Report No. 14. Washington, D.C.: U.S. Government Printing Office, 1966.

United Nations. *Study on Adoption of Children*. New York, 1953.

United Nations. *Processes and Problems of Industrialization in Underprivileged Countries*. New York, 1955.

United Nations. *Comparative Analysis of Adoption Laws*. New York, 1956.

United Nations. "Objectives in Social Policy for Improving Family Levels of Living." *International Social Service Review*, 5 (September 1959a).

United Nations. "Social Insurance and the Family." *International Social Service Review*, 5 (September 1959b).

United Nations. "Social Security and the Social Services." *International Social Service Review*, 5 (September 1959c).

United Nations. 1963. *Report on the World Social Situation*. New York: 1963.

United Nations. *Patterns of Social Welfare Organization and Administration in Africa*. New York: 1964.

United Nations. *Family, Child and Youth Welfare Services*. New York, 1965.

United Nations. *Family, Child and Youth Welfare Services in Africa*. New York, 1966.

United Nations. *Organization and Administration of Social Welfare Programmes—A Series of Country Studies: The Union of Soviet Socialist Republics*. New York, 1967.

United Nations. *Report on the World Social Situation*. New York: Department of International Economic and Social Affairs, United Nations, 1982.

United Nations Department of Economic and Social Affairs. *Organization and Administration of Social Welfare Programmes—A Series of Country Studies: Romania*. New York, 1967.

United Nations Department of Economic and Social Affairs. Economic and Social Council. *Children and Adolescents in Slums and Shanty-Towns in Developing Countries*. New York, March 1971.

United Nations Department of Economic and Social Affairs, Economic and Social Council, Commission for Social Development. *Protecton and Welfare of Children—Report of the Secretary General*. New York: United Nations, November 25, 1974.

United Nations Department of Economic and Social Affairs, 1978 *Report on the World Social Situation*. New York: United Nations, 1979.

United Nations Children's Fund. *Children and Youth in National Development in Latin America—Report of a Conference*. New York, 1966.

United Nations Children's Fund. *Strategy for Children*. New York, 1968.

United States Department of Health, Education, and Welfare, Public Health Service. *Special Report: The First U.S. Mission on Mental Health to the U.S.S.R.* Public Health Service Publication No. 1893. Washington, D.C.: Government Printing Office, 1969.

United States Department of Health, Education and Welfare, Office of Research and Statistics. *Social Security Programs Throughout the World—1977.* Research Report No. 50. Washington, D.C.: Government Printing Office, 1978.

United States Department of Health and Human Service. *Social Security Programs Throughout the World—1983.* Washington, D.C., Social Security Administration Research Report No. 59, May 1984.

United States Department of Labor, Bureau of International Affairs. *The World's Exploited Children: Growing Up Sadly.* Washington, D.C.: U.S. Government Printing Office, 1980.

Veillard-Cybulska, Henryka. "Aspects of Child Welfare in the People's Democracies. I: U.S.S.R." *International Child Welfare Review,* 19, 3 (1965), 101–132.

Veillard-Cybulska, Henryka. "Aspects of Child Welfare in the People's Democracies. II: Poland." *International Child Welfare Review,* 20, 1(1966), 5–61.

Veillard-Cybulska, Henryka. "The Welfare and Protection of Children and Adolescents in Bulgaria." *International Child Welfare Review,* 23, 4 (October 1969), 3–13.

Wen, Wei. "Child Care in New China." *Assignment Children,* 39 (July–September, 1977), 115–119.

Wester, Astrid. *The Swedish Child.* Stockholm: The Swedish Institute, 1970.

Wimperes, Virginia. *The Unmarried Mother and Her Child.* London: George Allen & Unwin, Ltd., 1960.

Woschiechowski, Sophie. "Poland's New Priority: Human Welfare," pp. 169–195, in *Meeting Human Needs,* Vol. 1. Ed. Daniel Thurz and Joseph Vigilante. Beverly Hills, Cal.: Sage, 1975.

Wynn, Margaret. *Fatherless Families.* London: Michael Joseph Ltd., 1964.

Yu, Shen, Wang Deyi, and Wu Changzen. "Chinese Law and Status of Children," pp. 71–91, in *Law and Status of the Child.* Ed. Anna M. Pappas. New York: United Nations Institute for Training and Research, 1983.

Zucker, Mildred. "Citizen's Advice Bureaus—The British Way." *Social Work,* 10, 4 (October 1965), 85–91.

Index